THE HOLOCAUST

NORA LEVIN

The Holocaust

THE DESTRUCTION
OF EUROPEAN JEWRY
1933–1945

SCHOCKEN BOOKS • NEW YORK

To R.

Then can I drown an eye...
For precious friends hid in death's endless night.

Library of Congress Catalog Card Number 67-23676
ISBN 0-8052-0376-1

Manufactured in the United States of America

First Schocken edition published in 1973

B 9 8 7 6 5 4 3 2 1 0

ACKNOWLEDGMENTS

LIKE TEACHING, the process of writing uses up everything emotionally and intellectually significant to the individual, both past and present. Acknowledging the huge indebtedness involved in such an accounting is impossible, not only because the shaping influences are so subtle and numerous, but because one is not consciously aware of many of them. There are several debts, however, that I am fully conscious of and wish to gratefully acknowledge: to Robert L. Crowell, who, in a spirit of bold and generous faith in an amateur writer, originally suggested that I undertake the writing of *The Holocaust*; to my sister and brother-in-law, Dorothy and Charles Fogel; to my old friends Pearl and Joseph Yenish for their interest and moral support during a three-year abstinence from living while the manuscript was being written, and to Joseph particularly for his help in securing several sources and in translating passages from Hebrew; to a little boy Danny Eskin for keeping open the life-line to youth; to Judi Fogel, Marlene Spector and Jean Fogel for their typing assistance; to Maurice Frankenhuis for his unusual generosity in sharing his experiences of the Nazi occupation of Holland; to my friend Edith Finch for reading several chapters of the manuscript and making helpful suggestions.

I am deeply grateful to three teachers, Margaret H. Peele, Helen Twaddell and Elizabeth A. Fewsmith, who first opened my mind's eye and ear to literature and history; to my mother and father for having conveyed in the subterranean ways of all inherited traditions a vision of their now vanished Mogilev and Bialystok; to my old friends in the "Federative Committee" who many years ago, at resounding meetings, shared the humor, warmth, eloquence and cutting edge of their marvelous Yiddish with a novice; and to women, like Alisa Shidlovsky and Mina Ben-Zvi of Israel, for radiating the moral earnestness still alive in an almost-destroyed people. I owe an incalculable debt, which I can only record, to my late friend Rose Lavin, who made of friendship a gift and of living an art. Her perceptive criticism would have made *The Holocaust* a much better book than it now is. For what it is, I must and do bear full responsibility.

For the right to reprint copyrighted selections in this book,
the writer and publisher are indebted to:

THE AMERICAN JEWISH COMMITTEE for *Harvest of Hate* by Leon Poliakov, copyright 1954 by the American Jewish Committee, and for their permission to include selections from the following issues of *Commentary*: "The Last Days of the Warsaw Ghetto," by Zivia Lubetkin, May 1947; "On the Agenda: Death," August 1949; "The Spy of God," by Leon Poliakov, August 1965; copyright © 1947, 1949 and 1965, respectively, by the American Jewish Committee.

THE LEO BAECK INSTITUTE for "A Jewish Theatre Under the Swastika," *Yearbook I*, Leo Baeck Institute.

E. P. DUTTON AND CO., INC., for *Kaputt*, by Curzio Malaparte, copyright 1946 by E. P. Dutton and Co., Inc.

FARRAR, STRAUS & GIROUX, INC., for five lines of "Chorus of the Rescued," by Nelly Sachs, translated by Michael Roloff, from *O The Chimneys*, by Nelly Sachs, copyright © 1967 by Farrar, Straus & Giroux, Inc.

HOUGHTON MIFFLIN COMPANY, for *Their Finest Hour* and *Triumph and Tragedy*, by Winston Churchill, copyright 1949 and 1953, respectively, by Houghton Mifflin Company; and for *Story of a Secret State*, by Jan Karski, copyright 1944 by Jan Karski.

THE JEWISH PUBLICATION SOCIETY OF AMERICA for *Blessed is the Match*, by Marie Syrkin, and *A Century of Jewish Life*, by Ismar Ellbogen, copyright 1947 and 1944, respectively, by The Jewish Publication Society of America.

ALFRED A. KNOPF, INC., for *Berlin Diary*, by William Shirer, and *Pius XII and the Third Reich*, by Saul Friedländer, copyright © 1941 and 1966, respectively, by Alfred A. Knopf, Inc.

The Editors of *Life* for "Eichmann Tells his Own Damning Story," *Life*, November 28, 1960, and December 5, 1960.

J. B. LIPPINCOTT AND COMPANY for *Fighting Ghettos*, edited by Meyer Barkai, copyright © 1962 by Meyer Barkai.

THE MACMILLAN COMPANY, for *And the Crooked Shall Be Made Straight*, by Jacob Robinson, © 1964 by Jacob Robinson.

MC GRAW-HILL BOOK COMPANY, for *Notes on the Warsaw Ghetto*, by Emmanuel Ringelblum, edited by Jacob Sloan, copyright © 1958 by Jacob Sloan.

S. G. PHILLIPS, INC., for *Desperate Mission*, by Alex Weissberg, copyright © 1958 by Alex Weissberg.

FREDERICK A. PRAEGER, INC., for *Martyrs and Fighters: Epic of the Warsaw Ghetto*, edited by Philip Friedman; published in 1954 by Frederick A. Praeger, Inc., Publishers, New York; copyright 1954 by Club of Polish Jews, Inc., New York.

SIMON AND SCHUSTER, INC., for *Rescue in Denmark*, by Harold Flender, copyright © 1963 by Harold Flender, and *The Capture and Trial of Adolf Eichmann*, by Moshe Pearlman, copyright © 1963 by Moshe Pearlman.

VIKING PRESS INC., for *Minister of Death: The Adolf Eichmann Story*, by Quentin Reynolds, Ephraim Katz, and Zwy Aldouby, copyright © 1960 by the authors.

THE WORLD PUBLISHING COMPANY, for *The House of Ashes* by Oscar Pinkus, copyright © 1964 by Oscar Pinkus.

Grateful acknowledgment is also made to Marie Syrkin for her kind permission to use her translation of the poem "Babi Yar" by Yevgeny Yevtushenko; to Robert M. Morgenthau for permission to quote passages from "The Morgenthau Diaries VI—The Refugee Run-Around," which appeared in *Collier's*, November 1, 1947; and to Eric Boehm for permission to use excerpts from his book *We Survived*, published by Yale University Press, 1949, reprinted 1966 by Clio Press.

CONTENTS

PHOTOGRAPHS

Photograph Credits / Key to Abbreviations

Baeck = Leo Baeck Institute, New York
Centre = Centre de Documentation Juive Contemporaine, Paris
Frankenhuis = The Frankenhuis Collection
Ghetto = Ghetto Fighters House, Haifa, Israel
Netherlands = Netherlands State Institute for War Documentation
Seminary = Jewish Theological Seminary of America
State = State Jewish Museum in Prague
Yad Vashem = Yad Vashem Archives, Jerusalem
YIVO = YIVO Institute for Jewish Research
Wide World = Wide World Photos

MAPS

CHARTS

FOREWORD

THE DESTRUCTION of European Jewry during World War II has by now become part of history. It is a finished chapter, a catastrophe from which Jews can scarcely hope to recover. The physical and spiritual heartland of a two-thousand-year-old civilization has perished forever. Yet the further we move away from Planet Auschwitz in time, the closer we move toward making it part of the modern Western consciousness. The Holocaust refuses to go the way of most history, not only because of the magnitude of the destruction—the murder of six million Jews—but because the events surrounding it are still in a very real sense humanly incomprehensible. No one altogether understands how mass murder on such a scale could have happened or could have been allowed to happen. The accumulation of more facts does not yield this understanding; indeed, comprehensibility may never be possible. Nevertheless, the accumulation continues. Currently, there is an eruption of interest in diaries, survivors' accounts, poetry and fiction based on the Holocaust. To remember what happened and to know more about what happened assuage somewhat the acknowledged failure to comprehend what happened. Only now, a full generation's distance from the Nazi gas chambers, do we seem ready to make the fate of Europe's Jews part of the Western historical experience, part of what the twentieth century has meant. It was this century, as André Malraux has said, which killed man.

In spite of the vast accumulating literature, however, an abyss still lies between those who endured the unimaginable and those who did not. The survivors themselves remain pendant between the living and the dead, searching, like the poet Nelly Sachs, to pierce the realms of each:

> We, the rescued,
> From whose hollow bones death had begun to whittle his flutes,
> And on whose sinews he had already stroked his bow—
> Our bodies continue to lament
> With their mutilated music . . .

The struggle to overcome this abyss is not only an attempt to comprehend the terrifying magnitude of human suffering, but to understand how a regime of twelve short years could so totally unhinge a whole structure of traditional Western values. For the Nazis did no less. They forced their victims to undergo a wholly new order of human experience and, inevitably, had to undergo vast changes themselves during this transformation. For the first time in history, human beings were processed into matter, and the processing began while they were still alive.

This unthinkable historical reality happened in twentieth-century Europe, in a civilization shaped by Western religious, moral and intellectual traditions. In creating a state in which senseless mass murder and the exploitation of human corpses became a civic duty, Nazism destroyed these traditions. The persecutor, no longer considering his victim human, himself ceased to be recognizably human.

In Hitler-Germany, a highly developed people devised the rationale and methodology for exterminating six million human beings—over a million of them children—and for converting them into fat for soap, hair for mattresses and bone for fertilizer. For the Nazis, Jews became part of the non-human universe—the objects of functional exploitation, undifferentiated from other non-human matter in nature, and requiring the same detachment. This new formulation enabled mass murderers to think of themselves as technicians following orders and to call mass murder "special treatment." The accompanying obliteration of all customary human feelings—remorse, guilt, or pity—created a new phenomenon in history which defied the judges at Nuremburg and made the trials an exasperating, if well-meant effort to lift international law to a new level, while the Nazi transvaluation of meaning in language left judges, prosecutors and spectators stupefied, as the victims themselves had been.

The victims, too, during the Nazi regime had been deprived of so much of their humanity that many of them existed from hour to hour in the concentration camps and ghettos, spectral figures, unable to remember who they were, or to feel the ties of kinship or experience pain, hunger or even hatred. Their persecutors—good family men—dined, played with their children, fed rabbits and joked at parties after mass killings in the pits or gas chambers. Clearly, the Nazis had devised a new technological objectivity in dealing with human suffering and death. Jews were their objects, the first men of the twentieth century to be denatured into matter.

Ordinary human beings simply cannot rethink themselves into such a world and ordinary ways to achieve empathy fail, for all of the recognizable attributes of human reaction are balked at the Nazi divide. The world of Auschwitz was, in truth, a new planet.

A nation in the middle of Europe dedicated not only to mass annihilation but to the complete depersonalization of millions of human beings represents a sharp rupture in the continuum of a Western moral order which, despite its many deviations, held to a certain conception of the life of man in the universe. Even during its most barbarous onslaughts, some margin of human response remained, both for the victim and persecutor. In the Nazified world, the narrowest of them were destroyed.

Yet the Nazi disruption of Western traditions did not sweep over Europe out of a vacuum; its antecedents lay in German history, and its portents were signaled in the post-World War I literature which described

Europe as being on the verge of disintegration, and earlier, in the brilliant and frightening insights of Friedrich Nietzsche. "There will be wars," Nietzsche had written, "such as have never been waged on earth. I foresee something terrible. Chaos everywhere. Nothing left which is of any value, nothing which commands: 'Thou shalt!' " Nietzsche and others prefigured and predicted the moral nihilism of the twentieth century, the revolt against reason and the limitless pursuit of the irrational. Nazi Germany materialized the progression toward this chaos.

In the following account, I have tried to write a history of this progression by emphasizing the following, major elements: the rise of Hitler to power, the creation of a terror-state, the step-by-step Nazi program of the destruction of Europe's Jews, the Jewish struggle to understand its fate, the military and political context of this period, the specific relationships between Germany and the areas it occupied or controlled, and the varied forms of Jewish resistance. I have tried to keep the first part of the book in chronological order, although this was not always possible. The section on deportations, however, deals in separate chapters with each nation from which Jews were deported to the death camps.

Source materials on the Holocaust are multiplying faster than they can be used, and the problem of selectivity has become extremely difficult. Nuremberg documents and the pathfinding works of Poliakov, Reitlinger and Hilberg are indispensable, but as the late Dr. Philip Friedman, the distinguished scholar urged, there must also be some effort to write an account of the Holocaust from the inside, that is, to see events through the eyes and minds of the victims. With very limited credentials, I have tried to penetrate their inferno and to record, with very limited resources, not only the scope of their suffering but their mental and physical ordeal in trying to fathom and then resist the Nazi design. In this attempt to broaden the dimensions of historical accounts of the Holocaust, I have drawn heavily on English sources from *Yad Vashem* (the official Holocaust archival authority in Jerusalem), frequently letting the documents speak for themselves. The narrative, of course, also contains other aspects of the destruction. I have not attempted to strike a single perspective, but rather, to show the unfolding tragedy by shifting from one focus to another. Moreover, I have devoted considerable space to what is greatly condensed in other works. For example, I have devoted an entire chapter to the Brand rescue mission. I have also described at some length the tragically slow awakening of German Jewry and the death-tinged blossoming of its *Kulturbund*, the dilemmas of the Jewish councils, the rescue efforts of the young Palestinian parachutists and the *Mossad* (Immigration Committee) and the slow evolution of the Jewish fighting organizations in the ghettos. These episodes and others may seem disproportionately extensive to the professional historian, but in my view, they are important not only because they describe representative responses of Jews to their fate, but also because they reveal the diminishing—not to say non-existent—margins of choice to which Jews were reduced before the end. Through these episodes, I have tried to convey the struggle of human beings to deal rationally with the irrational, to first disbelieve, then dimly and finally starkly understand that they were face to face with a completely new dimension of anti-Semitic persecution.

The Jewish reaction and inner life are one set of lenses in this complex history. The rise of Hitler to power and his acceptance by Germany is also developed in some detail, for without coming to grips with this phenomenon, we find a nation's capability for genocide to be totally incomprehensible. Moreover, the rootedness of anti-Semitism in Europe conditioned the host countries to consider their Jewish nationals disposable and made it relatively easy for Hitler to count on their cooperation. There were some obstructions, of course—in Denmark, Bulgaria, Belgium and France and in those areas controlled by Italy—but with few exceptions, the Nazis could count on a fairly deep growth of native anti-Jewish feeling. In the section on deportations, beginning with Chapter 19, I have tried to analyze the depth of this feeling and the historical background of each nation's "Jewish problem." Moreover, unappeased territorial ambitions and vehement nationalisms were often intermixed with anti-Semitic trends and affected the fate of Jews. The extent of German military control over the nations of Europe was also a controlling factor in achieving the "Final Solution."

The specific anti-Jewish Nazi measures—political, economic and "legal" —are examined chronologically. Jews became victims of a cunning strategy, designed to destroy them but disguised as a plan for "resettlement in the East." Elaborate, paralyzing deceptions were employed to confuse, shock, starve the victims—to render them helpless. The process was piecemeal but progressively destructive, with each step planned to reduce resistance and to further weaken the victims and prepare them for the last processing. After the "legal" phase of persecution, the Nazis turned over control of Jewish emigration to the Gestapo, a step which gave Reinhard Heydrich full control of all Jews in occupied Europe. This was followed by forced ghettoization and deportations to the death camps.

The Nazi political and military absorption of Europe is described in some detail because each case of Nazi aggression diminished the possibilities of either Jewish escape or resistance. Strange legalisms occasionally saved Jews. Certain interventions and pressures also staved off deportations. Sometimes a small area of sovereignty left to an occupied country was utilized to stop the transports.

Diplomatic maneuvers and the progress of the war were also crucial. In my view, Hitler's decision to invade Russia, the subsequent staggering German losses and Hitler's intoxication with war (the army, it was said, was his only home), destruction and mass death, released the nihilism of the Hitler state—and its chief architect. Hitler burned all his bridges as the war eroded Germany's confidence, its treasures and huge armies. Hitler's decision to invade Russia was made sometime during the winter of 1940–41. At the same time he decided to annihilate the Jews of Europe.

The changing tide of war greatly affected Jewish lives, but not in a predictable way. Allied advances did not necessarily save Jewish lives. More often, the reverse was true. The most intensified deportations in Europe took place in Hungary in the last phases of the war when the Allied victory was imminent.

The military resistance of Jews during the Hitler period is a complicated chapter in itself. In many countries—France, the Soviet Union, Holland, Belgium, Greece—a million or more Jews fought in the nation's army or resistance forces and their identity melted into the general national forces. Their participation, as Jews, is often glossed over, especially in those accounts which accept the idea that Jews were "led like lambs to the Nazi slaughter"—a phrase which is misleading because it assumes an unjustified omniscience. Jews resisted in many different ways, not least of which was their tenacity in staying alive in the doomed ghettos much longer than the Nazis expected. They also resisted physically much more than is generally known and under conditions that are scarcely credible. I have alluded to some of these instances without, I trust, exaggerating their importance or imbuing them with a disproportionate value.

Collective resistance was never possible; by the time Jews grasped the reality that they were doomed to be killed no matter what they did, they were isolated, weakened and abandoned. But they struggled to endure and to create communities of a kind in the Nazi ghettos. I have described the resistance in the Warsaw Ghetto rather fully, not only because it was the apotheosis of Jewish resistance during the Holocaust but because the factual data for this resistance are fullest. The inner life in the ghetto can also be glimpsed—the struggle against hunger, disease and isolation, as well as the struggle to pierce the fog of Nazi intentions and to retain human attributes of a community.

The extermination of two-thirds of Europe's Jews was not inevitable. It has become fashionable in modern literature and psychology to speak of a "landscape of violence" in which victims are co-guilty with their persecutors. A complicity, it is said, exists between assassin and victim. Such a view may provide interesting tours de force for armchair psychologists or new modes of expression for the spent forms of the traditional novel, but it is a dangerous and irresponsible plaything for the writer of history. The Jews of Europe were victims—in the old-fashioned sense—of a criminal regime in an overwhelmingly unequal contest. They were also victims of an indifferent, not to say, hostile world. Before the West was caught in the flames of war, there were countless opportunities to save them. None were used. After the war spread, the opportunities were fewer, but hundreds of thousands could have been saved. Nevertheless, with few exceptions, which I have described, the will to rescue them was non-existent. This moral failure, if we may still use such an old-fashioned phrase, still haunts the West.

The German-Jewish symbiosis has often been analyzed in the search to understand how near-total annihilation of one people by another could have been the culmination of a thousand-year relationship. In the grip of the utterly irrational belief that Jews formed a conspiracy plotting to destroy the nation, the German people repudiated ordinary appeals to facts, reason, common sense and even national self-interest. In the past, German thought scorned these humdrum principles as superficial, hypocritical and unin-spired. In their philosophy and literature, Germans have longed to tran-scend the shallow pockets of experience by plunging into great spiritual depths, by carrying ideas to their ultimate, by daring to plunge where man has not yet been. Faust, Wotan, Tristan and Isolde, and Nietzsche's Übermensch are significantly German figures. Subjectively, it seems, the German is not afraid of chaos despite his passion for external order, meticu-lous organization and obedience to authority. By contrast, the Jew, sub-jectively, dreads chaos. His world view, from the dimmest beginnings of his history, requires an orderly universe and the image of man balanced against extremes and subject to law. Traditionally, the Jew does not ask unanswerable questions, or, if he does, does not insist on answers to baffling paradoxes. The tribe of Job continues to wrestle with God; it does not dare to say, as Nietzsche did, that God is dead. Was it, one wonders, the ancient Jewish habit of submitting to the limitedness of all human knowl-edge and experience that the Nazis found most execrable in their enemy? The German plunge into "world without limit" made it possible to process human beings into matter, to create unpersons, to reach a new pitch of meaninglessness in history. I have tried to write a history of this descent and the Jewish struggle to wrest meaning out of it.

Nora Levin
October, 1967
Philadelphia

Part I The Preparation

1 The Past Is Prologue

EARLY IN JUNE 1941, an American newspaper correspondent in Berlin[1] noticed that a little book of Russian short stories was missing from the window of a bookshop across from his apartment on Wittenberg Platz. The bookshop was next to a restaurant he often patronized, a place called Alois, operated by the half brother of Adolf Hitler. It seemed odd, and perhaps significant, for the book had been displayed for more than a year. The book was *Schlaf schneller, Genosse* (Sleep Faster, Comrade), a collection of short stories by the Soviet writer Mikhail Zoshchenko. The title-story described a rickety Russian hotel in which a sign appeared above each bed: "Sleep faster, comrade, for another comrade needs your bed." *Schlaf schneller, Genosse* had been one of the few Russian books published in Germany after the signing of the German-Soviet pact in August 1939. The stories were all satires on life in Soviet Russia—frank, bold, and extremely funny. Even so, Nazi officials believed that publication of the book showed that Germany was not afraid of Soviet literature. The book had been sold out in three days and several more editions had to be printed. Now it was gone from the bookstores.

It was a small episode, and yet the correspondent kept turning it around in his mind for possible meanings. He decided to go into the bookshop and ask the salesgirl if she had anything at all on Russia. Inside, he was taken to a shelf filled with political books carrying strident titles: *My Life in the Russian Hell, The Truth about the Soviet Paradise, The Betrayal of Socialism.* The books portended something ominous. The newsman cast about for more clues. The Russian language newspaper *Novoye Slovo*, which the Nazis published in Berlin for Russian emigrés, had taken a sudden unfriendly turn. There were rumors that Germany would soon demand the Ukraine. A member of Hitler Youth who practiced his English on the American was ordered to be at local party headquarters, but he was not required to be in uniform. This meeting could mean a change in propaganda line. From Moscow came a report that German panzer units had arrived in southern Finland. Americans who lived in the Adlon Hotel in Berlin noticed that several suites of rooms on the top floor had been rented by the German Foreign Office. A team of typists and civil servants had been seen entering with mounds of paper. The doors to their rooms were being guarded by armed German soldiers in steel helmets. It was obvious that documents were being prepared.

At 3 A.M. on Sunday, June 22, 1941, newsmen were roused out of their beds and called to a special press conference. In the small council room of the Foreign Office where Bismarck had once debated, sleepy reporters sat blinking at a battery of microphones on a center table flooded by klieg lights. The small corps of men, many of them sons of wealthy Prussian families, who served on the staff of the Foreign Minister, Joachim von Ribbentrop, stood behind the table in the handsome blue-black uniforms and gold sashes of the Foreign Office. Ribbentrop, looking trim in a double-breasted brown jacket and black trousers, saluted his staff stiffly, stuffed his right fist in his pocket and, with his left, picked up a sheaf of papers on the table. His voice was deep and hoarse: while Germany had loyally abided by the Nazi-Soviet Pact, he said, the Soviet Union had repeatedly broken it. She was practicing sabotage, terrorism and espionage against Germany and was conspiring with Britain for an attack on German troops in Romania and Bulgaria. By concentrating all available Russian forces on a long front from the Baltic to the Black Sea, she was menacing the Reich. Ribbentrop's voice rose dramatically: "The Soviet Union is about to attack Germany from the rear in its struggle for life. The Führer has therefore ordered the German Armed Forces to oppose this threat with all the means at their disposal."

It had come. The opening to the East, on which Hitler had brooded for fifteen years, had suddenly materialized. A passage from *Mein Kampf* was prophetic:

> And so [Hitler had written], we National Socialists take up where we broke off 600 years ago. We stop the endless German movement toward the south and west of Europe and turn our gaze toward the lands of the East. . . . When we speak of new territory in Europe today, we must think principally of Russia and her border vassal states. Destiny itself seems to wish to point out the way to us here. . . . This colossal empire in the East is ripe for dissolution, and the end of the Jewish domination in Russia will also be the end of Russia as a state. . . .[2]

Hours before the sun rose over the long frontier, more than three million German troops began to move east into the unending space of Russia. German guns roared over hundreds of miles. The Nazi-Soviet Pact was blasted, and overnight the German people had a new mortal enemy.

The plan to smash Russia began ripening in Hitler's mind soon after the conquest of western Europe in the early summer of 1940. He was sure that Britain could not hold out alone and that Russia could be crushed in six weeks—two months at the most. But Britain did not buckle and the war against Russia drained life and treasure out of the Third Reich for almost four long years. The two-front war which had haunted German generals for a century became a nightmare reality. It became the most murderous war in history, destroying thirty million lives. It brought down in ruin the western liberal bourgeois order ushered in with great hope by the French Revolution. It also, almost literally, extinguished the Jews of Europe. Hitler's decision to invade Russia and Germany's inability to win a quick victory sealed their doom.

At first victims of Nazi propaganda, the Jews of Europe ultimately became victims of the most appalling murder machine in history. A relentless process of persecution, segregation and deportation to death camps claimed almost six million Jews, a million and a half of whom were children. With them perished a unique religious and intellectual civilization as well as immense contributions to general European life. In Germany, the descent from persecution to death took several years. In the western countries overrun by Germany the process was much swifter. But in eastern Europe, where the largest masses of Jews were concentrated, the process was swiftest of all and was made possible by the stepped-up tempo of war.

Between 1933 and 1938, Hitler was still mindful of the force of world opinion; he moved cautiously in dealing with the "Jewish question." During this period, the mass murder of Jews would have aroused outrage at home and abroad. But with the outbreak of war against Poland, he was able to start his deadly action. Wartime controls and systematic terror paralyzed opposition. Germans were exhorted to make new sacrifices for the New Order. Not only the Germans, but the western Allies, too, became preoccupied with fighting the war. Hitler exploited the general involvement in the war as cover for killing Jews. The protracted war against Russia then engulfed mass murder. New pressures subsequently arose from staggering German losses and Hitler's hysterical demand for victory. These pressures required ever greater national exertions and a final titanic effort. The image of the Jew as despoiler of victory did not fail Germany as the tide of victory ran out. In 1942 and 1943, as the Jews became more and more helpless, and as their numbers shriveled, they were nevertheless described by the Nazis as a powerful and hostile nation plotting to destroy Germany and acquire world dominion. Extermination of starved and terrorized Jews became the desperate self-deception of a nation losing a war which it could not admit it was losing.

The mass exterminations actually began with the invasion of Russia in June 1941 and continued with mounting excesses for the next three years. The impact of military activity on the fate of Europe's Jews can be charted. By the time Russia was invaded, all of the large Polish ghettos had been enclosed. Deportations to the German-controlled Government-General in

Poland were intensified. The *Einsatzgruppen* (mobile killing squads) had been instructed to murder Jews at will. On July 31, six weeks after the invasion, Göring ordered Reinhard Heydrich to bring about a "complete solution of the Jewish question in the German sphere of influence in Europe." This order meant extermination. Its execution was made possible by the intensification of the war.

In August 1944, Adolf Eichmann reported to Heinrich Himmler that six million Jews had been killed.

By the middle of April 1945, the Nazi empire which had once stretched from the Caucasus to the Atlantic had shrunk to a small corridor in the heart of Germany. The Russians were storming the gates of Berlin. Fifty feet below the city in a concrete bunker, Hitler raged against the Nazi hierarchs and generals. As the end drew near, he shouted accusations interspersed with wild hopes and half-crazed mutterings. In the end as in the beginning, he expressed maniacal hatred of the Jew. There was also a charge to the German people to uphold the "laws of race," but not a word of grief or remorse for the ruin he had made of Europe. A vindictive destructiveness was Hitler's only legacy. He ordered all military and industrial installations destroyed so that nothing would be left with which the German people could start their reconstruction. "If the war is lost," he told Albert Speer, the War Production Minister, "the nation will also perish." The early summer sun fell upon scenes of terrible wretchedness as lost human beings began their animal scavenge for food and shelter. Hitler had materialized Nietzsche's dark prophecy: "Where we live, soon nobody will be able to exist."

Systematic genocide as it was practiced by Germany has no precedent in modern history and nothing of such magnitude in recorded history. It is sometimes said that if the Germans could lend themselves to near-extermination of a whole people, other nations are similarly capable. Possibly so. But these speculations beg the question. Mass murder of a people on the scale reached in Europe under Hitler has never before occurred.

No one can know with certainty the explanation for such unparalleled destruction. It is obvious, however, that Nazi Germany had to overturn all traditional values in the process of converting mass murder into a civic virtue. Partially, at least, this was made possible by the force of national myths and habits of thought and by the impact of certain historic forces, some unique to Germany, some shared by the rest of western Europe.

Germany's past was shaped by the great movements that have affected all of western Europe: the struggle for unification, the commercial revolution of the sixteenth century, the Protestant Reformation, the revolution of 1848, the process of industrialization, World War I and the postwar maladjustments rooted in the vast upheavals created by the war. The nations responded in various ways. Likewise, all of Europe has had its "Jewish problem"; every country has exhibited its inability to "solve" this problem by varying evidences of anti-Semitism. The interaction of these complex forces, and the peculiar German response to them, created a nation in the very center of Europe which, in the twentieth century, was ready and willing to exterminate other human beings like vermin.

Many questions are asked in trying to come to grips with this terrifying fact. Did Germany take a fateful wrong turn somewhere in her history? Had she never really absorbed the so-called Western liberal tradition? Did the German traditions of militarism, unquestioning obedience to authority and exaltation of the power-state unfit the nation for the responsibilities of parliamentary democracy? Why has there been such a desperate "schism of the soul" possessing the most enlightened Germans—the sense of not fully sharing Western civilization, of having ambivalent feelings about Teutonic barbarism, nature worship and the exhilaration of the spirit through war? Did belated unification create so many unresolved conflicts— and World War I many more—that Germans grasped National Socialism frantically for a philosophy of living that would give meaning to their lives? What in German culture created the need to fuse so much hatred and contempt in the image of the Jew? Only tentative answers can be suggested and these, in turn, generally raise new questions.

All nations develop myths out of their history. Often these are not only more potent than the facts of history but express a nation's way of interacting with the facts. In Germany, the myth-forming process has tended to repress national responsibility for wrong turns and errors. The mistakes have been converted into projections of another's guilt. The myths of the "stab in the back," the "encirclement" of Germany, the "contamination" of cosmopolitanism have displaced German responsibility and created external scapegoats. In the process leading to the exterminations, the myth of the Jew as "race poisoner" and "enemy of the nation," and its inverse—the myth of Aryan race supremacy—have had a fatal power in German thought.

The German propensity for general theories, for a world view (*Weltanschauung*), has also had a profound effect on the way the nation has assimilated experience and applied knowledge. Darwinian theories of the selection and survival of the fittest in the struggle for existence led to fantasies of national superiority on the part of many thinkers in the late nineteenth century, but Germans expressed them more sweepingly, and, most important, took them more seriously than others.

Moreover, a deep-rooted German need for transcendence and mission, combined with the daring to carry out ideas to their ultimate, also contributed to the appeal of an ideology with genocide as its center. Faust with his overreaching will, Wotan willing his own destruction, and Tristan and

Isolde, dying in an ecstasy of love, are significantly German. This piercing of the ultimate has been described by Thomas Mann: "If Faust is to be the representative of the German soul, he would have to be musical, for the relation of the German to the world is abstract and mystical, that is, musical—the relation of a professor with a touch of demonism, awkward and at the same time filled with arrogant knowledge that he surpasses the world in 'depth'."[3] This "depth" has frequently resulted in a complete divorce of the ideological from social and political realities, a divorce which achieved its extreme expression in the extermination of almost six million Jews, a national deed which achieved no meaningful purpose, but was the expression of an "ideal."

The life of a nation is infinitely complex and historians can select out of vast sources only certain forces and events that suggest a pattern. Much can never be plumbed. The case of Germany is fraught with riddles but certain trends are clear. Retarded unification under Bismarck in 1871 created among Germans a feeling of being behind the rest of western Europe and apart from it. By way of compensation, an attitude of German superiority developed. Moreover, under Bismarck, Germany was still basically a loose confederation of states within a feudal social order. Bismarck had also raised up the specter of France, the "problem" of the Catholics and the Social Democrats, all issues which continued to be unassimilated after the heady imperialism of the 1890's.

The religious split in the nation, instigated by Luther, also further sundered the nation. Whereas elsewhere in Europe, religious changes had consolidated national power, in Germany, Lutheranism fostered disunity. Germany is part Catholic, part Lutheran. Luther also crushed the spirit of popular revolt and conditioned Germans to look upon revolt as evil or doomed to failure. The failure of the revolution of 1848 reinforced this view and robbed the rising middle class of faith in their own political capacities.

While apparently yearning for the organic national unity achieved in western Europe, German writers and historians expressed and also aroused popular contempt for Western thought and principles: Individualism, pacifism and democracy were scorned. Perhaps nothing is more revealing of this temper of mind than the ideas of Thomas Mann in the period prior to World War I. Mann was later to disavow them, after having experienced the Nazi assault on civilization, but in his early work he contrasted the bourgeois, superficial civilization of the West with the "profound and instinctive forces of life," culminating in German militarism. He welcomed the war of 1914 as the best safeguard against the democratization of Germany, "as purification, liberation, an enormous hope. . . . The German soul is opposed to the pacifist ideal of civilization, for is not peace an element of civil corruption?" In his *Reflections of a Non-political Man*, written in

1917, Mann has a long and bitter attack on the Western intellectual who concentrates his efforts primarily on social and political matters. Western optimism and belief in progress are contrasted with the conservative, nonpolitical German romantic who is in touch with a deeper reality. The prevalence of so many nonpolitical "romantics" in Germany who regarded politics as hypocrisy and deceit hastened the rise of National Socialism. Mann later deplored this unrealistic view of political life and the apparent German incapacity to pursue politics as an art of compromise and common sense.

Many German writers, including Mann, have also commented on a deep-seated sense of inferiority that gnawed at the German spirit. To the outside world, however, nineteenth-century Germany—industrialized, energetic, powerful—was factually impressive. The facts should have created a sense of security and unity; instead, many Germans felt melancholy and insecure about the reality of their nation. They did not *feel* that they were part of a welded nation. Hatred of another is often the other side of self-contempt. If, indeed, Germans lacked what they so ardently envied in others, the image of the Jewish people as a people united by a national religion might assume exaggerated importance. Unacknowledged envy of France and England were also translated into self-deprecation and arrogant expressions of superiority.

A nation so conscious of inner divisions is highly vulnerable to real and fancied "non-German" forces. Many Germans preached the necessity of purging German culture of all foreign influences and destroying all movements toward an open society. "Foreign" ideas were suspect. The study of foreign languages was considered dangerous. Western ideals of personal liberty and tolerance were attacked. A myth of encirclement developed, a fear of contamination by outside influences, partly strengthened by Germany's lack of natural frontiers. The German plain is intersected by great rivers that divide but do not enclose or protect the country. Historically, this situation has made Germany the stamping ground of invaders —a condition which Germany shares with other European nations—but which served to aggravate the fear of encirclement among Germans. Situated in the very center of Europe, open to influences and incursions from all sides and deprived of national unity until a very late date, Germans developed a turned-in passion for *Deutschtum*, Germanness, and fear of the non-German. The image of the Jew became enmeshed with the "foreign" and "cosmopolitan." One emotion based on hate was to fan the other based on love. Under Hitler, all-consuming hatred of the Jew became the counterpart of fiery devotion to the fatherland.

It is generally agreed that the Nazi movement was spearheaded by pathological personalities, but the acceptance of Nazism by masses of Germans cannot be explained without conceding that the situation inside Germany fostered the influence of such individuals and made their leadership possible. The German extermination of Jews can be interpreted broadly as a logical extension of a two-thousand-year anti-Jewish tradition initiated and nourished by the Christian Church, or as a drastic new departure from centuries of familiar persecution, pogroms and forcible expulsions. In either case, the Christian view of the Jew throughout European history formed the basis of the anti-Jewish propaganda worked up by Nazi minds and accepted as a program of action by large numbers of Germans. The minds may have been sick and the German people too susceptible to old myths about Jews because of their extreme fears, hatreds and envies, but the key formulation had had a long history. The destruction of European Jewry could not have happened without this historic preparation.

The conditioning of Germany toward Jews was similar to that of all Christian Europe, but was exacerbated by nineteenth-century theories of race and the peculiar twistings of German history. The rejection of the Jew by Christian Europe prevailed until the French Revolution and hung just below the surface of Europe's life thereafter. The segregation of the Jew and his isolation from the general community—necessary steps in Hitler's plans for extermination—had already had a long history.

The Nazis wanted to protect German racial purity from "contamination"; the Christian Church and State wanted to "protect" the Christian community from Jewish teachings and the allegedly harmful consequences of contact with Jews. Historic Christianity would not tolerate the Jew in his midst—the Jew who stubbornly refused to accept Christian truth and who would not convert. In a rabid convulsion of rejection, Jews were expelled from one Christian country after another, often after whole communities were murdered. Between the thirteenth and sixteenth centuries, Jews were expelled from England, France, Italy, Bohemia and the Germanic states. The unconverted Jew polluted Christian society; the "racial" Jew polluted German society.

In page after page of *Mein Kampf*, Hitler depicts the Jew as defiler of German purity. The language is crude and the ideas are abhorrent to the modern liberal spirit, but the words are merely latter-day racist versions of age-old views of Christian leaders. For Martin Luther, for example, the Jews were "like a plague, a pestilence, pure misfortune in our country." Where Hitler depicts the Jew as the mortal enemy, blocking the road "to salvation for a struggling Aryan mankind," Luther charged that Jews "hold us captive in our own country." In most of his imagery about the Jew, Hitler is simply reechoing the medieval Christian stereotype of the Jew as criminal, parasite, evil incarnate, aiming at world conquest—an image powerfully reinforced by Luther, Fichte, Father Jahn, generations of German historians and nineteenth-century ideologists of racism, all of whom fatally influenced German thinking about Jews.

The German response to Hitler's anti-Semitism is sometimes discussed as if Hitler invented particularly satanic notions of the Jews, grotesque and monstrous ideas to which the Germans succumbed with pathological fervor. In fact, however, he detonated hatreds, taboos and superstitions that had lain for centuries in the deep consciousness of a continent that had not solved its "Jewish problem." The French Revolution emancipated the Jew from the medieval ghetto but it did not emancipate Europe from its anti-Semitism. Hitler's own fanatical anti-Semitism fed the destruction and Hitler carried out the anti-Jewish war as a coldly premeditated political action, having learned from an earlier period in German history that exploitation of anti-Semitism yielded huge political and economic profits. He freely admitted that anti-Semitism was "the most important weapon in our propaganda arsenal." However, in stocking his arsenal, Hitler borrowed freely from old Christian teachings and utilized most of the practices associated with the traditional subjugation of the Jew. He revived book burnings, ghettoization, blood accusations, the ban on intermarriage, exclusion of Jews from normal economic, social and cultural life of society, from schools and public office. He also borrowed the medieval use of the Jewish badge to mark the Jew with visible identification. The Hitler era added new intensities of degradation, new scales of horror and stripped away all earlier limits, but the main precedents had already been established. Upon these Hitler superimposed the language of racism and applied the psychology and techniques of mass propaganda.

The Nazis saturated the German mind with hate and horror of the Jew, a prerequisite to extermination. The stronger the horror, the more absolute was adoration of the fatherland. If only a small number of Germans gassed and tortured Jews to death, a very large number could stand by because of the shame, contempt and evil which were felt to attach to Jews. Without this conditioning during a period of profound national maladjustments, the segregation, deportation and systematic extermination of Jews could not have happened.

Although the physical destruction of Jews was carried out by Hitler, the idea was seriously proposed seventy years before Hitler came to power. As far back as 1862, a German-Jewish philosopher, Moses Hess, perceived the struggle to come and wrote prophetically: "The race war must first be fought out and definitely settled before humane and social ideas become part and parcel of the German people." Hess was not taken seriously. His Marxist readers believed that a race war could never arrest or submerge the class struggle; his liberal readers mocked his prediction that liberty, tolerance and ideals of human brotherhood could be jeopardized; Jewish readers, too, dismissed him as an "alienated Jew"! And yet, a few years later, during the life of the Second Reich, the Empire of 1871, there developed in Germany a new religion, a cult of race based on the apparatus of anthropology and the elevation of theories of blood and soil to final "truths."

Germany had just won a decisive victory over the French. Bismarck's "blood-and-iron" policies had created a powerful, even dominant nation. A strident economic and political nationalism erupted. In this new age, it was argued, the national state must be the power-state whose highest duty was to increase its power and safeguard itself against individualism, party strife, parliamentary inefficiency and every trace of national weakness. In the atmosphere of this period, called by one historian "the seed-time of totalitarian nationalism,"[4] many Germans succumbed to the cult of race. The myth of a "master race" destined to conquer the world and subdue lesser "races" gripped many Germans. Influential scholars and writers were carried away by a rampant social Darwinism. Possibly masking deep uncertainties and insecurities, the devotees of this movement exalting the state also exalted physical fitness and strength. In the competitive national militarism and imperialism of the time, it seemed obvious that the Germans must belong to a superior race. It then followed that anyone who displayed "German" qualities of boldness, bravery and energy must belong to that race. Since the prevalent physical type of German was tall, blue-eyed, longheaded and blond, anyone having these characteristics must also possess superior qualities of courage and intellect. Contributors to this racial "science" were legion throughout Europe, but they took themselves —and were taken—most seriously in Germany. German nationalism and imperialism thus became impregnated with ideas of German racial superiority.

The "Aryan" myth, which Hitler used with great cunning, was an off-shoot of this obsession with race. The use of "Aryan" resulted from a confused meaning of the word. Philologists had used it earlier to denote a family of related languages including German, Greek, Latin, Celtic, Slavic and Sanskrit. They also theorized that there must once have been an original, single, primitive Aryan people. But now the racialists identified this people with the tall, blond, longheaded Germans and concluded that the Germans must be the Aryans par excellence—the purest, strongest and noblest of all peoples, the greatest of culture-bearers.

Into the service of German Aryanism was pressed an old French aristocrat, Count Joseph Arthur de Gobineau who claimed descent from a ninth-century Norman pirate. In his Essay on the Inequality of the Human Races, written in 1853–54, Gobineau had taken the view that he and his fellow French aristocrats were superior to the French masses by virtue of their purer Aryan stock. This hardly made him popular in France, but in Germany his ideas, under modification, were applauded. The decisive events of history are determined by the iron law of race; human destiny is decreed by nature and expressed in race, according to Gobineau. Furthermore, "history shows that all civilization flows from the white race." The jewel of the white race was the Aryan, which survived as a superior race. "The Aryan German," Gobineau wrote, "is a powerful creature. . . . Everything he thinks, says and does is thus of major importance."

The Germans modified Gobineau to include *all* Germans, whereas he had marked for distinction only western Germans. This notwithstanding, Gobineau's influence began to spread in Germany and Gobineau societies were organized. He was particularly popular with the Bayreuth circle of the composer Richard Wagner, who had himself also written in a vehemently racist, anti-Jewish strain. But it was an Englishman, Houston Stewart Chamberlain, who settled in Bayreuth and married Wagner's daughter, who became the idolized prophet of the Nazi Party. Chamberlain was the son of a British admiral, drawn during a very precocious youth to the glories of German philosophy and militarism. He became a German citizen while still a young man. Like Gobineau, Chamberlain found the key to civilization in race. He claimed that the Nordic peoples (Nordic, Aryan and German were used interchangeably), especially the Germans, were the master race of the world, the creators of everything great and good. By pursuing what he called "racial anthropology," he concluded that anyone who thought or acted like a German, and anyone who looked like one must belong to this superior race. Within such a definition, great men such as Columbus, Dante and St. Paul were seen as proof of German cultural supremacy. And the Jews? Chamberlain devoted the longest chapter of his book, *The Foundations of the Nineteenth Century*, to them. In the first section he condemned "stupid and revolting anti-Semitism," but soon slipped into the very vulgar anti-Semitism he attacked. The Jews are described as a "negative" race, a "bastardy," fully justifying the Aryan denial of them. The way of salvation for the world, according to Chamberlain, lay in the assertion of Aryan mastery, with every German giving his utmost for the holy cause. His book, written in a dazzling style by a scientific dilettante, sent Wilhelm II into ecstasies and provided the Nazis with the text for their racial myth.

Chamberlain was one of the first of the intellectuals in Germany to see a great future for Hitler at a time when his rowdy manners, violent extremism and demagoguery were still considered ludicrous by most Germans. The hypnotic magnetism that was later to enthrall millions of people captivated Chamberlain in the early 1920's. The two men met at Bayreuth, and although ill, half-paralyzed and disillusioned by Germany's defeat in World War I, Chamberlain was thrilled by the young Hitler. "You have mighty things to do," he wrote him later. "My faith in Germanism had not wavered an instant, though my hope—I confess—was at a low ebb. With one stroke you have transformed the state of my soul. That in the hour of her deepest need Germany gives birth to a Hitler proves her vitality.... May God protect you!"[5] Chamberlain's book not only had an enormous influence on Hitler but had an astounding sales success in Germany.

The feverish outpouring of racist literature in the late nineteenth century gave traditional religious anti-Semitism a new vehemence and modernity. Political parties were formed using anti-Semitism as a weapon for purely political ends. This development occurred first in Germany. Superimposed on the medieval image of the Jew as the anti-Christ, devil, moneylender, poisoner of wells, murderer of God and eternal wanderer was the new image of the Jew as competitor, parvenu, skeptic, liberal, capitalist, Marxist, world-poisoner, corrupter of national purity—everything that represented frightening forces in the modern world. Such diverse categories of evil united strange partners in a fused attack on Jews as the diabolical enemy, unalterably "foreign" and conspiratorial.

Hatred of the Jew as a poisoning influence in every part of Germany's national life was first exploited politically by Adolf Stöcker, a spellbinding court preacher in Berlin who founded the Christian Social Workers Party in 1878 and used the party's mass meetings to attack Jews. In this year of economic depression, Stöcker blamed Jews for business failures, profiteering and domination of liberal political movements. He went much further: "The Jews are a nation within a nation, a state within a state, a race in the midst of another race." German blood contains the German soul and "modern Judaism is a foreign drop of blood in the German body—one with destructive power." It was Stöcker who first coined the slogan *Deutschland, erwache!* ("Germany, awake!") later to be revived by the Nazis. The Germany Stöcker awakened, however, was not the Germany of the workers, but of the same groups that responded to Hitler with greatest enthusiasm—the lower middle classes of restricted income and limited property who yearned for social status and a special place in a world that was fast passing them by. Artisans, petty officials, shopkeepers and clerks flocked to Stöcker's call. Discouraged, displaced by the social unrest of the period and unaccustomed to rely on themselves for leadership, they found direction under Stöcker. He embodied their desire for authority and a strong state, their aversion to an open society and their search for status. Stöcker also played on the same fears that Hitler was to use: fears of Marxist socialism and capitalism with which the Jew was identified.

In 1879, Stöcker joined with William Marr, a sensation-mongering journalist who had founded the League of Anti-Semites to "save the German fatherland from complete Judaization" and together they submitted a petition of nearly 300,000 signatures to the government. "The blending of the Semitic with the German element of our population," the document read, "has proved a failure. We are now faced with the loss of our national superiority through the ascendancy of Judaism, the steadily increasing influence of which springs from racial characteristics which the German nation cannot and must not tolerate unless it wishes to destroy itself." The petition demanded various curbs on Jewish life in Germany—rather mild in the light of what was to come—but they nevertheless are symptomatic of a strong tendency among Germans to blame others for problems or crises they cannot manage themselves. Jews became the perfect whipping boy. In Stöcker's time they constituted 1.2 percent of the population of Germany.

Additional anti-Semitic parties arose, culminating in a substantially united German Social Party which reached its greatest strength in 1893. In that year, a quarter of a million voters sent 16 deputies (out of 397) to the Reichstag. The party lingered on to rival and then succumb to the Nazis. Political representation alone, however, did not reflect popular feeling. Small-scale pogroms, boycotts and demonstrations accompanied a flood of books, pamphlets and newspapers devoted to Jew-baiting. Influential historians who made a religion of German nationalism also ranted against Judaism as *unser Unglück*, "our misfortune." That single cry, *Die Juden sind unser Unglück*, was to reverberate on Nazi billboards, banners, handbills and out of the throats of millions of Nazi zealots. Violent and abusive language which provided Hitler with more of his slogans and metaphors was also furnished by Eugen Dühring, a German philosopher of this period who expressed contempt for the "inferior and depraved" Jews. "The duty of the Nordic peoples," he wrote, "is to exterminate such parasitic races as we exterminate snakes and beasts of prey." The impulse to physically destroy the Jew was thus recorded. Anti-Semitism had calibrated a new scale.

There were few political leaders of the late nineteenth century who refused to make political capital out of this anti-Semitic agitation. Furthermore, a tradition of criminality and lawlessness, which became commonplace under Hitler, infiltrated the anti-Semitic agitation. Germans resorted to perjury, forgery, embezzlement, and assault in order to make anti-Jewish accusations stick. Publishing houses thrived on the dissemination of periodicals, books, and broadsides that created or fed stereotypes about Jews. Outright falsification of facts and superheated exaggerations created monstrous images of Jews that ate away at the nation's soul.

From the value judgments of a democratic tradition, Germany developed traditions that are radically antagonistic to those from which British, French and American democracy have grown. The values of the Enlightenment were rejected during the Second Reich and failed to have any meaning for most Germans during the Weimar Republic after World War I. Such a divergence from the West was bound to create many unsolved problems and ambivalent attitudes, a few of which have been suggested. For the Jews of Europe, this divergence was to be catastrophic, for the nationalism the Germans responded to was hostile to all of the values of the bourgeois revolution with which Jews have been linked: democratic progress, liberalism and capitalism. In fact, Jewish emancipation was channeled through these movements. In German eyes, these ties made Jews the enemies of German national interest.

In analyzing this syndrome, the popular German attitude toward capitalism is significant. Because German industrialization was a comparatively late growth, a German working class developed that was much less bourgeois in its outlook than the working class in either France or England. Few small-scale enterprises so characteristic of France and England appeared in Germany. Thus, German workers who were employed in large-scale businesses had little hope of ever becoming capitalists and distrusted capitalism itself. Living by competition exposed them to sudden decisions, unsettling movements, accidents of success and failure, risks and mobility —all disruptive of a well-ordered, hierarchical society in which they felt safe. Capitalism also exposed them to economic forces which made them feel helpless and unrooted. For a people needing the bonds of order and custom, these apprehensions were felt acutely.

The Jew became identified in the popular mind with the frightening powers of the new economic system, as he had been identified with the inefficiencies and uncertainties of democracy and with the chaos and boundlessness of liberalism. The intellectual capstone to the popular uneasiness about capitalism was Werner Sombart's massive work, *The Jews and Modern Capitalism*, written as the Second Reich drew to an end. As has so often happened in German history, the prestige of scholarship was pressed into the service of anti-Semitic beliefs and gave them the stamp of scientific truth. Sombart theorized about the impact of the Jewish religious ethic upon capitalism. He not only exaggerated the role of Jews in the rise of modern capitalism but formulated a hypothesis about certain "Jewish" traits which fitted them to become capitalists. Succumbing to the racist ideology of the time, Sombart also stressed the "racially" determined predisposition of Jews to "materialistic commercialism."

The anti-Semitic literature of the 1880's in Germany is frequently reminiscent of the older religious tradition which attributed sinister, secret and uncanny powers to the Jew. However, under the old Christian view of the curse upon the Jew, he could be restored to grace by embracing Christianity. Nineteenth-century racial anti-Semitism, however, put an end to this alternative, for race was seen as an eternal law, a force for good or evil, a force engrained in the blood. The Jew became a physical entity, a definite human type whose characteristics could be defined and measured. From Gobineau on, the claim of race became total for the writers who took up "racial science." The unchangeable facts of nature were biological laws. "Jewishness," Dühring had said, "can only be ended by putting an end to the Jews themselves." Baptism no longer mattered. Still, alongside this racist outpouring, revivals of medieval religious practices also persisted. The most potent of these was the ritual murder accusation.

The ritual murder charge was fabricated in the Middle Ages and alleged that Jewish religious practice required Jews to slay Christian boys and use their blood in baking mazzot for Passover. This myth could be changed according to need. At times it was said that the slaughter of a pure Christian virgin was required, or sometimes the slaying of a grown youth. In culturally backward regions, Jews lived in terror each Easter season, fearing the charge of child murder. In more forward areas, anti-Semitic agitators exploited the popular superstitions that had found expression for centuries in religious drama, ballads and in the shrines of the purported infant martyrs. In the nineteenth century, these superstitions could still be fanned and the subsequent agitation made to serve the political ends of anti-Semitic political parties. In the period 1880–1900, several ritual murder charges were made in Germany and Austria-Hungary. The most notorious was the Tisza-Eszlar trial.[6] During the course of the trial, detailed reports were sent to Germany and strengthened German anti-Semitic parties. Later, an imaginary portrait of the supposedly murdered girl was publicly exhibited at the first anti-Semitic congress in Dresden in 1892.

In Tisza-Eszlar, a small town in Hungary, a fourteen-year-old girl, Esther Solymosi, disappeared on April 1, 1882, four days before Passover. It was reported that she had last been seen in the vicinity of the synagogue and the rumor spread that the sexton of the synagogue murdered her, drained her blood and dismembered her body. Local police and court officers conducted an investigation but could not find the slightest basis for establishing guilt. On May 19, the county court nearby sent a notary to act as examining judge, a man named Bary, who placed Jewish suspects under police surveillance and began his inquiry by examining the sexton's five-year-old son. It later developed that criminal officials had crammed a story of the father's guilt into the boy's mind by threats and then sweets and money. The babble of the child dominated the investigation but he could not maintain any consistency. The boy's older brother was also bullied into testifying against his father. Meanwhile, no trace of the girl's body was found. Several months after her disappearance, however, a corpse was washed up along the shore of the Theiss River. The remnants of clothing were identified as that of the girl and the body, although in an advanced state of decay, showed no signs of having been mutilated. But public opinion was now so poisoned that medical experts on the spot declared that the body was that of an older girl who had died very recently. It was now insinuated that the body was smuggled in by Jews and clothed in Esther's clothing to conceal the crime. Jewish rivermen were accused of body snatching. Confessions were wrung under brutality and torture. Eighty Jews were imprisoned, most of them for fifteen months, until the trial was concluded. The trial was held in the summer of 1883, and for six weeks the terror of anti-Semitic agitators vied with the efforts of the defense attorney, a member of the Hungarian House of Deputies, to bring sanity into the courtroom. At the end, the court declared that the charges could not be proven—no confession could be forced from the sexton by any means—and an unqualified acquittal was rendered.

The grossness of the Tisza-Eszlar affair discredited the ritual murder lie in Hungary, but it continued to be revived in Austria and was used by the Nazis in Germany. Himmler, for example, in May 1943, wrote to Ernst Kaltenbrunner, head of the Reich Main Security Office, urging the staging of ritual murders in Romania, Hungary and Bulgaria and their "proper exploitation" in the foreign press, especially in England and the United States.

Powerful as the ritual murder charge was in gripping the popular imagination, a more deadly fantasy developed in the twentieth century, one that combined both medieval and modern forms. This was the myth of the Jewish world conspiracy, the existence of a secret Jewish government aiming at world domination. This myth, like the earlier ones that Jews poison wells, kill Christian children for their blood and profane the consecrated wafer, lacked a shred of reality, but this fact did not diminish its force. Quite the reverse. Based on the principle of mass psychology that Hitler seized—the big lie—the myth of a Jewish world conspiracy was a lie big enough to gain credence and grow by its very bigness.

Taking its demonology from the medieval belief that Jews were a conspiracy of the devil working for the destruction of Christendom, the modern myth was vastly more elaborated. All of the most characteristic features of the modern world—capitalism, labor movements, revolution, wars, depressions and booms—were seen as secret maneuvers of a Jewish plot aimed at world domination. The Jew thus imagined is not only mysterious and sinister, as in the Middle Ages, but also symbolic of everything that is felt as frightening in the modern world.[7] The principal instrument for this myth was the notorious forgery known as the *Protocols of the Elders of Zion.*

The *Protocols* were fabricated by Russian émigrés in France in 1895 during a period of revolutionary unrest and smuggled into the Czar's court. The work described an alleged scheme for a Jewish world conspiracy, planned and recorded in an assembly of Jewish leaders. It implicated liberals, Freemasons, radicals, bankers, even the underground railways—everything which a reactionary Czar might want to suppress, but the *Protocols* made little impression in czarist Russia. They became important, however, during the Bolshevik revolution and the civil war in Russia in 1919–20, when Russian monarchists fleeing to the west carried copies in their bags and had them distributed to the troops in the "White" armies. Their version made the Russian Revolution a Jewish plot.

Despite conclusive proof that the *Protocols* were a gross forgery, they had sensational popularity and large sales in the 1920's and 1930's. They were translated into every language of Europe and sold widely in Arab lands, the United States, and England. But it was in Germany after World War I that they had their greatest success. There they were used to explain all of the disasters that had befallen the country: the defeat in the war, the hunger, the destructive inflation. At first the deposed Hohenzollerns financed the campaign; later it became the very center of Nazi ideology. Hitler used the *Protocols* as a manual in his war to exterminate Jews.

Germans before Hitler had preached the necessity of destroying Jews, and small-scale exterminations had actually taken place in Europe, but only Hitler dared to go beyond older limits and push the idea of extermination to actuality. In the Nazi scale of "values," mass murder became a duty as well as a mission and the murderers exulted in their acts. Unarmed and helpless people, including babies and old women, were portrayed as part of a vast, terrifying enemy that had to be cleansed from the earth, while the mission was seen not as a "decadent" humanitarian problem of conscience but as a brave and difficult undertaking.

There is a tragic irony not only in the fact that, collectively, the Jews of Europe were the weakest possible enemy the Germans could have chosen—without a land, a government, allies or a central authority—but that the Nazi delusion of their plot for world domination reached a deadly fanaticism at a time when Jews were, in fact, more divided than ever. The Jews of the twentieth century were as diversified as the nations of the world where they had lived and as idiosyncratic as the intricate forces that had shaped their history. They were, to use crude classifications, committed Jews and assimilationists, nonobservant and Orthodox, Zionists and internationalists, radicals and capitalists, Socialists and Communists, freethinkers and mystics. In the gamut of their occupations, they ranged as widely as their host countries would permit, and in their economic levels, they were, as are all other peoples, rich, poor and intermediate. Had they been more uniform and more united, more of them would have been saved. Of political power, they had none, and the largest, single, safest Jewry, American Jewry, achieved very little in their pleas to the Allies to save fellow Jews in Europe from wholesale massacre.

One Nazi leader, Erich von dem Bach-Zelewsky, who was an anti-partisan chief on the Russian front, recognized these facts and was forced to acknowledge the untruth of the conspiracy myth in testimony given after the war:

> I am the only living witness but I must say the truth. Contrary to the opinion of the National Socialists that the Jews were a highly organized group, the appalling fact was that they had no organization whatsoever. The mass of the Jewish people were taken completely by surprise. They did not know at all what to do; they had no directives or slogans as to how they should act. This is the greatest lie of anti-Semitism because it gives the lie to the old slogan that the Jews are conspiring to dominate the world and that they are so highly organized. In reality, they had no organization of their own at all, not even an information service. If they had had some sort of organization, these people could have been saved by the millions; but instead, they were taken completely by surprise. Never before has a people gone as unsuspectingly to its disaster. Nothing was prepared. Absolutely nothing.[8]

But the lie was lived and acted upon. It not only developed an autonomy completely divorced from reality in Germany where Jewish families lived with their neighbors amicably—German Jews were among the most assimilated in the world—but it rubbed off on much of the world in a vague, half-repressed form during the Hitler period and after the war. Today it is being used in places to work up the passions of people who have virtually no Jewish neighbors left. The facts of the recent decimations are no match for the fantasy of the Jew summoned as the source of all evil.

Obviously, not all Germans during the Hitler period were delusional. Many were paralyzed by the shocking violence of the regime and terrorized into silence. There were also pure sadists, looters and opportunists who used the Nazi ideology to justify their crimes. But the "bearers" of this ideology were seized by the need to purge the earth of Jews, and it was these bearers who led Germany to destroy 72 percent of Europe's Jews. German acceptance of such a regime was at first grudging. The Nazi bid for power failed several times, but when it succeeded, Germany had taken a fatally wrong step, much more disastrous than any taken in her entire history.

National Socialism was not an inevitable outcome of German history, but neither was it accidental. The catastrophe of the war, and more particularly the German interpretation of the defeat, the disorientation of the postwar period and the failure of Germany's experiment with democracy in 1918 made Hitler's appeal possible. Whereas most of the nations in World War I suffered most acutely from the shattering war—the first total war in history—Germans could not accept defeat. They endured the war, accepted progressive mobilization and bore the hardships stoically. But they could not grasp the reality of defeat. More specifically, they could understand it only as the work of criminal conspirators. Hitler defined the internal enemy—the Jews—already made vulnerable by earlier propaganda. The elimination of this "enemy" became the core of Hitler's mission. German Army leaders also nurtured the legend of the "stab in the back," although in the last month of the war they themselves appealed for an armistice, fully acknowledging at the time that the war had been lost to superior military forces. Within a year, these leaders had denied their own responsibility for defeat.

The subsequent German skirmish with revolution in 1918—the "Jewish" revolution that Hitler made into a monstrous evil—was almost stillborn. In November, some soldiers' and workers' councils were established on the Russian model, but the Social Democrats did not want fundamental changes in Germany. Aside from some isolated bloody incidents, the regime of the Kaiser was replaced quietly; there was no revolution. The nobles kept their estates, the civil servants kept their positions and the industrialists kept their factories. On November 9, a Social Democratic deputy in the Reichstag proclaimed the creation of the German Republic from the balcony of the Reichstag building and a new constitution was drafted in the tranquil atmosphere of Weimar.

The Weimar Constitution of 1919 was a paper-perfect framework for a parliamentary democracy, but it did not register any of the strong traditions of the German people. It stood outside their history like an artificial graft. Indeed, the proclamation of the Republic on the eve of the armistice was a fluke of the moment, something that popped into the heads of the Social Democrats who were pushed to the political stage after the Kaiser abdicated. The Social Democrats were primarily trade-unionists, many of whom had no genuine convictions about democracy and no understanding of the dynamics of political power. Primarily, they wanted a larger share in a parliamentary government which they rather vaguely hoped would achieve Socialism without upsetting the social order. The petty bourgeoisie, meanwhile, were shattered by the failure of the monarchy. If the Kaiser could be publicly ridiculed, if military officers could be attacked and a saddle maker installed as President, what could the little man put his trust in?

The Kaiser had gone, but the generals remained. Not only the generals, but the spirit and substance of the Old Reich clung tenaciously. Most Germans regarded the Weimar Republic as an interim state, an importation from the West. They refused, in fact, to give up the word "Reich" and, significantly, Field Marshal Paul von Hindenburg, who became first President of the Republic, remained attached to the old Empire until he died and was called President of the Reich.

Der Kaiser ging . . . die Generäle blieben. The Kaiser goes . . . the generals remain. A few hours after the Republic was proclaimed, Provisional President Friedrich Ebert concluded a fateful pact with the generals. Ebert

agreed to maintain the Army in its old tradition and to put down revolution, while General Wilhelm Gröner, speaking for the Army, pledged the
support of the armed forces in maintaining the new government. Gröner
honored his pledge, but none of the other military officers did. At no
time did they serve the new government loyally and, in the end, they betrayed it to Hitler. Other elements as well—the Junker landlords, the rulers
of the vast industrial cartels and the ranking officials of the civil service
—not only strengthened the right-wing forces in Germany, but abandoned
the Social Democrats when collective responsibility was imperative. They
were biding their time, waiting to burden the democratic republic with
the responsibility for the military disaster of their own making.

Ebert's mistake was to agree to let the generals raise corps of volunteers
to fight off any Communist revolutionary risings. These "free corps" were
originally meant to uphold the government's authority, but they soon
became the recruiting ground of the Reichswehr (Army) and eventually
the nucleus of Hitler's Storm Troops. The members of the free corps also
formed themselves into fellowships and secret organizations, one of which
was the German Workers' (later the Nazi) Party which Adolf Hitler
joined in 1919. At first, secretly equipped by the Reichswehr, these roving
freebooters were used mainly to fight the Poles and Balts on the disputed
eastern frontiers, but soon they were backing plots for the overthrow of
the Republic. The volunteers came from the ranks of the demobilized
soldiers who could not find jobs or a way back to the Germany of 1918
after the war. In 1920, a brigade of these men occupied Berlin in a putsch
against the Republic. This was the Brigade Ehrhardt, flaunting swastikas
on their helmets. There was an ominous note in their marching song:

> *Wir sind keine Judenknechte,*
> *In Deutschland soll immer nur ganz allein*
> *Ein Deutscher unser Führer sein.*

> (We are no slaves of the Jews,
> Forever and ever in Germany
> Shall only a German our leader be.)

The putsch failed, but the treatment of the traitors is very significant:
705 persons were charged with high treason, but only one, the police
president of Berlin, received a sentence—five years of "honorary confinement." When Prussia withdrew his pension, the Supreme Court ordered
it restored. In 1926, a German court awarded the military leader of the
putsch back payment of his pension to cover the period during which he
rebelled against the government. The traitors to Weimar became honorable fellows.

As democracy had been held in contempt as a decadent, Western
notion, the Germans of the Weimar period developed no taste for citi-

zen participation in political life and consequently, gained no experience. Politics generally was dismissed as hypocritical and compromising and few men wanted to be sullied by it. Decisions were left to authorities while the people of the nation looked on passively. Yet, no authority comparable to the church and throne of imperial Germany could inspire respect or obedience. The Weimar Government had no heroes or heroics; it was not very efficient and was incapable of arousing strong national devotion. Moreover, noticeable brutalization of German political life took place after 1918, a foreboding of the lawlessness of the Hitler years.

There were also many political assassinations, 350 committed by organizations of the Right. Of these, 326 went unpunished; only one was punished by a death sentence. In contrast to the tender treatment given the traitors and assassins, hundreds of German liberals were sentenced to long prison terms on charges of treason for revealing the Army's constant violations of the Versailles Treaty. The laws of treason were ruthlessly applied to the supporters of the Republic, whereas those who tried to overthrow it (as Hitler was to learn after his abortive putsch in 1923) got off with the lightest sentences or none at all.

The Versailles Treaty, one of Hitler's prime targets, was attacked in Germany from the moment its terms were published on May 7, 1919. The Treaty, which had been imposed on Germany by the victorious and vindictive Allies, had many serious defects. The accusation of sole German war guilt was a gross historical error and needless blunder. Some areas such as the Saar and Upper Silesia were German in character and their transfer from Germany violated the principle of self-determination. Germany's colonies were also taken away and an indeterminate reparations was imposed. The Army was restricted to 100,000 long-term volunteers and prohibited from having tanks or planes. The General Staff was outlawed and the Navy reduced to little more than a token force. These terms were intolerable to a people that talked itself into believing that it had not really lost the war—the war was referred to as a *Zusammenbruch*, a collapse, never as a defeat. The myth of German invincibility lived on, making the Treaty unacceptable even after many of the objectionable provisions were modified. Forgotten were the vast annexations and indemnities that Germany herself had demanded during the war as a condition for peace, and the punitive Treaty of Brest-Litovsk imposed on Russia in March 1918. Forgotten also, or repressed, was Germany's share in starting the war.

Stubbornly, Germans refused to admit that they had had anything to do with the outbreak of the war. The nation's historians poured out a voluminous literature aimed at vindicating Germany's past. There was no serious examination of the foundations of the power-state or of German militarism. The historians wrote in a surge of self-pity and self-justification. Defeat in the war was ascribed to the deceit of the enemy and treason at home at the hands of the Jews and Communists. A superior people had lost. History had wronged them. The country had been dealt a stab in the back.

The hatred of the Treaty pervaded the nation and extended to every class. This feeling proved to be one of the most serious blocks to organizing an effective opposition against Hitler both before and after he came to power. The feeling persisted after Allied concessions blunted some of the offending terms of the Treaty and after the Germans themselves ignored others. In 1933, as in 1919, Germans still refused to bear any responsibility for the outbreak of World War I or the consequences of defeat. Stung by the cunning demagoguery of Hitler, they still believed that they had been maltreated. They refused to acknowledge facts: the bulk of the reparations had never been paid; the United States had made massive loans; Locarno peace pacts and admission of Germany to the League of Nations demonstrated Western goodwill toward a former enemy. In July 1932, German reparations were liquidated by a conference at Lausanne. For several years Hitler had been using the burden of the reparations as the butt of his propaganda campaign. When reparations were abandoned because of the depression, few Germans were aware of it. Even today, many Germans feel that Hitler deserves credit for having ended reparations.[9]

A year before Hitler became Chancellor, the great German writer Hermann Hesse wrote of this national habit of evading responsibility under a veil of self-pity:

> Germany has completely neglected to appreciate her appalling share of responsibility for the World War and the present situation in Europe. She should have acknowledged it—without thereby denying that her enemies, too, bore a heavy share of responsibility—and undertaken a moral purification (as France, for instance, did during the Dreyfus Affair). Instead, Germany has used the harsh and unjust peace treaty as a pretext to lie to the world and to herself about her own guilt. Instead of understanding her own errors and sins and correcting them, Germany talks big again, as she did in 1914, of her undeserved pariah position and reproaches others, sometimes the French, sometimes the Communists, and sometimes the Jews, with responsibility for every evil.

The Army began to circumvent the military restrictions of the Treaty from the beginning and the officers' corps not only maintained the Reichswehr in the old Prussian tradition, but allowed it to become the real center of power in the Republic. It did not support the Republic as the Army leaders had promised, but small as it was, it exerted increasing political influence. At every critical juncture, political leaders had to ask: "Will the Reichswehr back us up?" instead of assuming its loyalty. Under the Weimar Constitution, it could easily have been subordinated to the Cabinet and Parliament, as in other democracies; in Germany, it was not. It remained a state within a state, independent of the national government. Political leaders succumbed. Many of the Socialist ministers frankly wanted to revive the proud soldier memories of an older military tradition.[10]

The feeble democracy of Weimar came under increasing attack and abuse. Conservative economic interests undermined the new government by subsidizing political parties and a political press that were clearly aimed at destroying the Republic. In Bavaria, which in the early 1920's had a right-wing government largely because of the influence of the Reichswehr, Adolf Hitler had already found a place in the antirepublican tide. He was an educational officer in a Munich regiment combating pacifism and democracy and lashing out at the "invisible foes"—the Jews and Marxists. He had made anti-Semitic harangues at an Army lecture course and made a good impression on his superiors.

The Republic held on for a short time following the disastrous inflation of 1923 but then collapsed under the widening depression of the early 1930's. Ironically, in the late twenties, Germany enjoyed an interval of astonishing prosperity, and was, indeed, the most prosperous country in western Europe. New homes, schools, parks, public buildings and hospitals were built and provided employment. Industrial machinery was revamped. Trade flourished. The Dawes Plan and generous loans from the Allies checked the chaos of inflation. Although much of the borrowed money went out as reparations payments, at least one third was used to finance an internal boom. The Treaty was being liquidated, but its detractors did not give up.

This was a lean period for Hitler and the Nazi movement. But patiently Hitler dreamed and schemed. He found his opportunity during the Great Depression. The main support of German prosperity—foreign loans and world trade—collapsed in 1930 and caused unemployment and dire want for millions. The Nazis, who were now holding sixty meetings a day throughout Germany, were becoming a serious political force. Hitler shrewdly began to convince Germans that only he could rescue the nation from disaster and from the "shackles" of the Peace Treaty. The masses of people were unwilling or unable to accept revolution; democracy had failed. Hitler's call for a *Volksgemeinschaft* (people's community) made a strong appeal. The ranting demagogue with a comical moustache now became savior and prophet. Had he not always predicted that the German people would be destroyed by Germany's defeat, by the Versailles Treaty, for which the Jews were responsible?

Hitler's National Socialist German Workers' Party, which had polled less than a million votes in 1928, polled over six million by 1930, giving the party 107 seats in the Reichstag, making it the second largest party in the country. Hitler skillfully bid for Army support by playing on its fears of Bolshevism. Nazis began to infiltrate the ranks of the Army. In 1930, a famous trial in Leipzig foreshadowed the future.

Three young officers, admitting that they would not fire on Nazi rebels in case of an armed Nazi revolt, were arraigned on charges of treason. Hitler appeared as a witness. Using his spellbinding talents he fooled the president of the court and Army officers into believing that the idea of an armed revolt was madness, that the Nazis would come to power only by constitutional means. He also predicted that out of the puny Reichswehr a great army of the German people would arise. Dramatically, he spoke of the coming "German National Revolution," the rescue of the enslaved nation. The generals began to feel better disposed toward a movement they had formerly regarded as a threat to the Army. They began to ponder whether National Socialism might not be just what was needed to unify the people, to make the Army great once more, and restore the old Germany. Typically, the sentences of the three young officers were mild: they were found guilty of conspiracy to commit high treason but were sentenced to only eighteen months of fortress detention.

By 1931, politics as well as military activity was taking to the streets and clubs of Germany. The Nazis had the *Sturm Abteilungen*, their Storm Troops; the right-wing veterans, their private army, the *Stahlhelm* (Steel Helmets); and the workers' sports clubs and trade unions, their Iron Front, the *Reichsbanner*. These fronts became outposts of security for insecure men. They wore distinctive uniforms, called demonstrations and did regular tours of "duty" in their respective meeting halls. They all paraded dramatically; some plotted to overthrow the Republic. The Weimar democracy was further battered and shamed by these paramilitary organizations.

A further symptom of the inner feebleness of the regime was the strange combination of support given to von Hindenburg in 1932. The old hero of Tannenberg, a dyed-in-the-wool monarchist, was backed for the presidency not only by the Right, which had supported him before, but by the more liberal parties which had opposed him, but which now saw him as the savior of the Republic. Hitler, who was not even a German citizen, decided to run against him. In the bitter and confusing campaign that followed, all of the traditional loyalties of class and party cracked. To Hindenburg—a Protestant, a Prussian and a monarchist—went the support of the Socialists, the trade unions, the Catholics and the remnants of the democratic middle-class parties. To Hitler—a Catholic, an Austrian, a man from nowhere—was rallied the support of upper-class Protestants of the north, conservative Junkers and monarchists. Hitler solved the problem of citizenship by a comic-opera maneuver: the Nazi Minister of the Interior in the state of Brunswick named him an attaché of the Brunswick legation in Berlin.

A propaganda campaign was then launched such as Germany had never seen. Cities and town were plastered with shrieking colored posters and flooded with Nazi pamphlets and party newspapers. Loudspeakers mounted on trucks roared through quiet medieval streets. Hitler himself crisscrossed the country whipping crowds into frenzied enthusiasm. Three thousand party meetings a day jabbed at real and fancied grievances. *Sturm Abteilungen* (S.A.) terror squads roamed the country. Anti-Semitic appeals drew cheers and applause.

Hindenburg won in a close election, but the master demagogue and "great simplifier" was on the stage of history at last. When he finally possessed it, the Jews of Europe were marked for destruction.

2 Hitler

A LITTLE OVER A YEAR after the aging German President von Hinden-burg had interviewed Adolf Hitler and decided that, at most, the "Bo-hemian corporal" might one day become a Postmaster General, Hitler was sworn in as Chancellor of the Reich.[1] On January 30, 1933, the aim-less Austrian who had lived in doss holes as a youth and had queued up for soup at nunnery gates, had come to the threshold of power through sheer will, a cunning political touch, and a fantastic faith in his mission to regenerate Germany. For long, seemingly hopeless years he had kept his ragtag party from disintegrating by skill, luck, and hypnotic oratory and had finally made himself an acceptable and familiar figure. Cleverly, he made common cause with the industrial magnate and head of the German Nationalist Party, Alfred Hugenberg, against the Weimar Re-public in the battle against the Young reparations plan, and later drew conservatives and nationalists to his side by leading them to believe that only he could give them the kind of Germany they wanted. Moreover, the rapid decline of the Weimar government in the early thirties played into his fierce ambitions. Hindenburg was virtually senile; the strength of the moderate parties was thinning out; the Social Democrats had ex-hausted themselves in intraparty strife and the struggle with Communists, who themselves were obsessed with only one objective: the political end of the Social Democrats. Political leaders intrigued, plotted, double-crossed each other in the scramble for power and showed less and less concern about the fate of the fragile democracy which had never really struck root in Germany. In fact, most of them looked for expedient alli-ances which would bring about its quick end.

Hitler had shrewdly gauged the pent-up fantasies of the officers' corps, and as early as 1929 deliberately cultivated their sympathy. They, in turn, had some misgiving about the low thuggery and undisciplined street violence of the Nazi storm troops and for a time feared that the private, paramilitary S.A. threatened the Reichswehr itself. But Hitler showed remarkable canniness in timing his moves, at first toward and ultimately against the tradition-bound generals, until they were eventually swallowed up in the Nazi absorption of the state. The swelling ranks of the S.A. and Hitler youth organizations made a deep impression on the officers' corps: a dazzled if blinded youth offered limitless possibilities for a great, renewed German army instead of the cramped 100,000-man force dictated by the Versailles Treaty. Nazi Party influence within the Reichswehr became perceptibly stronger, particularly among the younger officers and new recruits. Conversely, the leadership of the S.A. included many former Army officers. Unable to resist the allure of Nazism from the very first, the generals were to watch with numbed stupefaction, disbelief or ineffectual mutterings as their contained caste-bound world was chopped away bit by bit and replaced by an underworld state.

One of the master intriguers during the last days of the Republic was General Kurt von Schleicher, a close friend of Hindenburg's son. Schleicher was a key figure after World War I in the confidential negotiations with Moscow which led to the camouflaged training of German officers in the Soviet Union. He was also a power in the officers' corps as well as in politics. In the Army he could make or break officers, and in politics he created and unraveled webs of intrigue to which the feeble Republic succumbed in the years just before Hitler's accession to power. The most serious of his manipulations was his conniving to get Army support for his choice of Chancellor, a move which undermined the non-political tradition of the Army and cracked its strength in the nation. It was Schleicher who made the first serious contact with the Nazi leaders, Ernst Röhm and Gregor Strasser in 1930, a move which paved the way for Hitler's chancellorship two years later and, ironically, for Schleicher's own murder subsequently. Schleicher openly urged the addition of Nazi members to the cabinet and persuaded Hindenburg to interview the "Bohemian corporal." Hitler delivered one of his endless monologues at the time, and the talk was superficially a failure, but the fact that it had taken place had momentous consequences. Henceforth, Hitler would have to be taken seriously as a political factor.

In 1932, the last year of the Weimar Republic, there were five elections, which all but exhausted the financial reserves of the Nazi Party. The last one, on November 6, cost Hitler 34 seats in the Reichstag. But in the war of nerves that followed, Hitler had the greater staying power and Schleicher's machinations further strengthened his leverage. Certain that the new Chancellor, von Papen, would become his tool, Schleicher made the following bargain with Hitler: in return for his acceptance of von Papen, he promised to have the ban on the S.A. lifted. Hitler, seeing the fast crumbling of the Republic—by this time the Chancellor was ruling by presidential decree without the consent of the Reichstag—agreed, and the summer of 1932 saw a wave of wild and bloody street fighting and murder by S.A. gangs. Hindenburg himself sternly lectured Hitler on these excesses, but Hitler had sniffed the elixir of power and determined to settle for nothing less than the chancellorship.

A confused whirl of schemes, shifts and maneuvers at the top resulted in von Papen's fall, Schleicher's succession and then his own sudden fall. Meanwhile, Hitler was closing in. Von Papen, thirsting for revenge against Schleicher (who had turned against him) met Hitler on January 4, 1933, in Cologne, at the home of the banker Baron Kurt von Schröder, a man who had already contributed funds to the National Socialist Party. There, the three men discussed the possibility of a Nazi-Nationalist coalition cabinet. By one of those chance twists of history, the meeting took place when Nazi Party prospects were at their darkest. Gregor Strasser, Hitler's political lieutenant, had resigned, depressing the whole movement and Hitler particularly; funds had dried up and morale was extremely low. Joseph Goebbels himself wrote at this time: "All prospects and hopes have quite disappeared."

But in their common adversity, Hitler and von Papen came to terms and set the terrible Nazi juggernaut on its way. The details of their meeting are still in dispute, but several things are clear: out of the meeting came an understanding that German business interests would take over the debts of the Nazi Party. The parties also agreed to a Hitler-von Papen cabinet. Von Papen, meanwhile, had been reassuring Hindenburg that such a cabinet would have a Reichstag majority and Hindenburg promised von Papen (who became the new Vice-Chancellor) that he would always accompany the new Chancellor, Adolf Hitler, in talks with the President. Superficially, von Papen appeared to have guarded against a Hitler-dominated cabinet; only three Nazis, Hitler, Wilhelm Frick, and Hermann Göring, were admitted, but once the door to power was opened to Hitler, there would be no way to shut it again. The conservatives were complaisant: the National Socialists were "framed in"—to use Hugenberg's famous expression—by reliable German Nationalists and Hindenburg's men. They did not hear Hitler vow at his Reich Chancellery window: "No power on earth shall bring me out of here alive."

Hitler had cleverly cultivated the idea that he would always uphold the principle of legality in his struggle for power—a device which fooled conservatives and the Army and deluded them into thinking that they need never worry about reining him in or becoming anything more than their chariot driver. Hitler himself, in promising to achieve his goals by constitutional means, remembered not only the historic German revulsion against revolution but the dismal failure of his Munich putsch in 1923. In prison, he had firmly decided to make his next political thrust by legal means, to do nothing which would alienate the Army and industrial leaders whose support he needed. This decision was an expedient; it had nothing to do with principles—Hitler had none—just as the dropping of the radical socialist wing of his party and, later, his ruthless purge of Röhm and other S.A. leaders who wanted a "second revolution" were expedients in his relentless drive to power.

In the January 30 ceremony, Hitler swore to uphold the Weimar Constitution. In fact, he never formally abrogated this Constitution, although he drew support from Germans who were contemptuous of the weak Weimar regime. Rather, he overcame the Constitution with constitutional means and set to work, as he himself said, "to pour the State into the mould which corresponds to our ideas."

His opportunity came on February 28, the day after the Reichstag went up in flames. This fire was a Nazi-instigated act of destruction,[2] one of many to follow, which would serve to justify harsh counterblows. Hitler convinced the confused, deteriorating Hindenburg that the fire was the signal for a Communist revolt and the Reich President signed an emergency decree prepared for him by Hitler under Article 48 of the Constitution. This decree, euphemistically called "For the Protection of People and State," abolished the constitutional guarantees of freedom of speech, assembly, protection of property, and freedom from illegal search. It also imposed the death sentence for a number of crimes, including serious disturbances of the peace. As soon became evident, this was also the death sentence for the Republic. This decree marked the leap to the Hitler dictatorship.

Hitler exploited the constitutional framework in one further maneuver. The Papen-Hitler coalition actually did not command a majority in the Reichstag, as von Papen had promised. Hitler made it appear that the Center Party had made impossible demands for inclusion in the government, thus giving him an excuse to hold new elections. Solemnly he promised Hindenburg and von Papen that however the elections turned out, the cabinet would remain unchanged. With the Prussian Ministry of Interior (including the police organization) under Göring, with the Brown Shirts on the streets and his own demagogic genius just beginning to find its range, Hitler was confident of the outcome. When, on February 20, industrial giants, including men from the Krupp and Farben combines, pledged three million reichsmarks for the Nazi-Nationalist cause, Hitler had reason to be jubilant.

Between February 28 and March 5, the date of the elections, the Brown Terror broke loose.

By making the trumped-up Communist threat "official," Hitler threw millions of peasants and middle-class Germans into panic; they feared that unless they voted for the Nazis at the coming elections, the Bolsheviks would take over. Several thousand Communists, Social Democrats and liberals were arrested, including members of the Reichstag who were legally immune from arrest. This was Germany's first experience with Nazi terror supported by the government. Truckloads of storm troopers roared through the streets breaking into homes, rounding up victims and taking them to S.A. barracks where they were tortured and beaten. Meetings of the democratic parties were banned or broken up; only the Nazis and their Nationalist allies were able to campaign unmolested.

Freely using the resources of the national and Prussian governments and the wealth contributed by business and industry, the Nazis carried on an election campaign unprecedented in Germany. The state radio carried speeches of Hitler, Göring and Goebbels all over the country. Jack-booted storm troopers marched through the streets draped everywhere with swastikas. At night there were mass rallies, torchlight parades and bonfires.

The Nazi cry *Juda Verrecke* (Let the Jews croak) had accompanied the tramp of storm troop boots from the first days of S.A. demonstrations and marches. During the week of March 6, 1933, the words took on new meaning. Germany witnessed the first wave of official Nazi terror and stood by. Mobs of S.A. troops swaggered up and down the streets beating, looting and killing Jews at will. The police had been instructed not to interfere and stood by passively. Army officials and members of the *Stahlhelm* and *Reichsbanner* were present. They also stood by.

But despite the frenzy of propaganda and terror, German voters still withheld the two-thirds majority needed by the Nazis to establish arbitrary government by parliamentary consent—another legalism that Hitler was planning. The Nazis obtained 288 seats in the Reichstag, only 44 percent of the popular vote. Together with their allies, they were able to scrape together a bare majority. But a two-thirds majority was needed to alter the constitution. Once having this, Hitler could rest his dictatorship on the constitutional foundation of a single law. He achieved this by a deceptively simple device, again cloaking the seizure of power—this time, absolute power—with legality.

In a shrewdly conceived dramatic gesture, he decided to open the new Reichstag in the Garrison Church at Potsdam, the great Prussian shrine where the Hohenzollerns had worshiped and where Frederick the Great lay buried. The church was a hallowed place to which Hindenburg himself had made pilgrimages. Thus Hitler linked his rowdy, rag-tag movement with the past impressive glories and traditions of imperial Germany, and once again, the Junkers and barons, the generals and businessmen— the old order—could appease their apprehensions about the Austrian upstart. How could they hesitate to grant him their entire confidence, the full powers that he claimed? The answer came on March 24.

The Reichstag was assembled in the Kroll Opera House. Outside, blackshirted S.S.* men encircled the building. Inside, S.A. patrols filled the cor-

---

* *Schutzstaffeln*—Elite Guard.

ridors menacingly. Most of the Social Democratic and Communist deputies had already been arrested; other "undesirable" deputies were prevented from coming because their "postal addresses were unknown." The Center Party had received lavish promises from Hitler and assurances from Hindenburg that Hitler would not govern under the Enabling Act without consulting him. Their support gave Hitler the two-thirds majority he needed. Thus, quite legally, by a vote of 441 to 84, was parliamentary democracy interred in Germany. The Reichstag quite literally committed suicide.

The Enabling Act, which became the fundamental law of the Hitler regime, gave Hitler the arbitrary power he craved. He was now not only independent of the Reichstag but also independent of the President. The government now had the power to enact laws for four years without approval by the Reichstag; these laws were drafted by Hitler himself and put into effect immediately.

The Enabling Act contributed the second constitutional pillar to Hitler's rule. Every four years thereafter, the Reich cabinet under Hitler was dutifully prolonged by a rubber-stamp Reichstag which met only a dozen times up to the war. It held no debates or votes and never heard any speeches except those of Hitler.

Now, one by one, Germany's most powerful institutions began to surrender to Hitler and to pass quietly, unprotestingly out of existence. All rival parties were destroyed or dissolved themselves. It became a criminal offense to maintain or form any political organization other than the National Socialist German Workers' Party. Similarly, all possible competition to the Nazi Brownshirts such as the *Stahlhelm* and *Reichsbanner* were abolished or absorbed. The regular Army, the Reichswehr, took longer to absorb, but when Hitler added the presidency to the chancellorship in August 1934, he likewise became Supreme Commander of the Armed Forces. The free trade unions were destroyed, partly by Nazi trickery, partly by union naïveté—the Nazis insisted on joining in the celebration of May Day and stole the show—and partly by repression. Union headquarters were occupied, funds were confiscated and labor leaders were arrested.

The power of the federal states had now passed to Hitler. For the first time in German history, Germany became a completely centralized state. By abolishing the separate powers of the individual states and making them subject to the authority of the national government, Hitler succeeded where even Bismarck had failed. The diets of all states were dissolved and Reich governors were appointed, each a Nazi, to carry out the policy of the Chancellor. Göring's key position as Minister of Interior in Prussia, which constituted two thirds of Germany, enabled him to remove hundreds of republican officials, replacing them with Nazis, mostly S.A. and

S.S. officials. Trickery, brutality, lightning speed, mock show of deference, and terror all played their role, but as Hitler never ceased to boast, he and National Socialism had come to power "legally."

Hitler was completely dependent upon the Reichswehr's acquiescence in these revolutionary actions. Closely linked with the Junker aristocracy and enjoying enormous prestige with the business and industrial leaders, were the Army generals and professionals. To keep their support and make sure he would have their assistance for his rearmament plans, Hitler crushed the radical demands of his own S.A. troops. The S.A. not only wanted a "second revolution" but absorption into the Reichswehr so that they could then absorb it. This meant a showdown with Ernst Röhm, chief of staff of the S.A., and, allegedly, Hitler's closest friend.

In the spring of 1934, at the beginning of Hindenburg's last illness, Hitler's determination to succeed the President led him to make a deal with the Reichswehr. The Army promised to support his candidacy if he eliminated Röhm and the power of the S.A. Hitler was willing to make the barter. For his survival and the fulfillment of his far-flung dreams, the Army must be his. The mingled boldness and discretion with which he approached the generals reflected his political touch at its surest; the ruthless liquidation of his erstwhile comrade and S.A. leaders showed that he would stop at nothing to keep his leash on power.

An internal power struggle within the Nazi Party clinched Röhm's fate. In the summer of 1933, Göring, tired of his commonplace S.A. uniform, aspiring to a glorious career in the Luftwaffe (the Air Ministry was established under him in May 1933) and lured by the trumpery of power elsewhere, made a fateful appointment in his police organization at a time when he needed an ally against Röhm. His self-created Prussian Gestapo clashed frequently with Röhm's S.A. street police. Heinrich Himmler, nursing his small band of S.S. Blackshirts, was also chafing under the supervision of Röhm. When, on April 1, 1934, Göring appointed Himmler as chief of the Prussian Gestapo, the two were reinforced in an anti-S.A. alliance. The bloody purge of Röhm and other S.A. leaders on June 30, 1934, was engineered by Himmler's S.S. The triumphant days of the S.A. were over. The Reichswehr, seeing only that a potential rival had been eliminated, felt nothing but relief. Despite the murder of two of its generals—Schleicher was one—during the purge, and the brutal executions by Himmler's S.S. of erstwhile comrades, it was blind to the danger of the S.S., which would soon become far more dangerous than the S.A. had ever been, and which would ultimately strangle not only the Army but the state itself.

The Army, industrialists and bankers were main props for the Nazi regime, but these were hardly enough to escalate Hitler into power. Much force, deception, sly playing off one group against another and a compelling persuasiveness added to his effectiveness. But these qualities would be insignificant without his power to win over the German masses. The Nazi Party polled only 44 percent of the popular vote in the 1933 electoral test, but this happened before Germans saw Hitler in action. By the time he hit his stride, he satisfied the deepest cravings of most Germans who saw in him a mirror of themselves, "the seismograph of the people's soul."³ He knew how to play on the most melting harpstrings of German history and frustration. Skillfully, he won over those who had suffered from unemployment and inflation, and those who blamed the "Bolshevik-Jewish" conspiracy for Germany's defeat in World War I. The numerous lower-middle classes, unorganized and badly hit by the depression, the youth looking for a cause in the postwar void, the "front-line comrades" who, like Hitler himself, failed to find their way after the war—these were the groups that felt great, unexpressed needs, hatreds and jealousies, and found themselves readily following a man who had come from nothing. Avid for recognition and prestige, they were captivated by titles, uniforms, thrilling slogans and the new sense of solidarity that Hitler inspired. They identified themselves with his shabby beginnings. Early impressive achievements ensnared the people further—they even deceived such realists as Lloyd George and Winston Churchill—and enabled a credulous nation to accept great sacrifices. Who could believe that the "Winter Help" drive with its powerful slogan, "No one shall go hungry and cold," would be used ultimately to finance armament projects? Hitler shamelessly exploited the all too ready and naïve idealism of Germans, for whom he had only contempt, in order to create first a compliant, then a frantically enthusiastic and finally a terrorized mass which would serve his insatiable appetite for power.

In the early years, the conquest of unemployment and the lifting of the Versailles restrictions were the palpable successes that made him enormously popular. The Saar was brought "home"; the demilitarized Rhineland was boldly and bloodlessly occupied; the whole frustrating past was being rapidly liquidated. The spectacular 1936 Olympic games in Berlin, which particularly impressed English and American visitors, also created much admiration. If their personal freedoms were being taken away, if their culture was being destroyed and their life and work regimented as never before, the Germans did not seem to mind. Foreign visitors flocked to the Third Reich and enjoyed its hospitality. Everything was available to them except the military installations, the concentration camps and the underground forces of violence which became a daily living reality in Germany after 1933. Foreign visitors did not see the men who were arrested, beaten and murdered to satisfy a personal grudge or taste for sadism; nor did they see the cellars to which S.A. gangs carried off anyone they disliked or wanted to blackmail or torture. Nor did the Germans themselves seem to be troubled by these inner signs of social decay; the exterior was more wonderful than they had dared to hope.

The German language also served the Nazis. Their slogans were cunningly designed to appeal to vague longings of a people who were bold in speculative thinking and philosophy but submissive under authority, who felt superior to other peoples but had to live under a peace dictated by their "inferiors." Emotion-loaded words swept the Germans into a delirium of enthusiasm and imbued them with a sense of mission: *Sturm, Rasse, Kampf, Glaube, Volk, Opfer, Schicksal* (assault, race, struggle, faith, people, sacrifice, destiny) resounded throughout the Nazi era. Perhaps most important to Hitler's success was his skill in winning the support of influential and respectable circles to National Socialism, thus giving it the technical competence, which the early Nazis lacked, to carry out his purposes. Although the moral and political character of the Nazi program and of its leaders stood quite clearly revealed to all Germans during the process of Hitler's rise to power, not only nationalists and industrialists, but intellectuals, religious leaders, scientists, artists, writers and musicians— some of them Nobel prize winners—came to the support of the movement. All were willing to be led to a glorious, regenerated future. Like the masses, they, too, became mesmerized. At first, some may have been squeamish about the methods used by Hitler, but they soon welcomed "real" authority and German *Volkstum* instead of the "weak" and "cosmopolitan" parliamentary democracy. At one of the last meetings of the *Verein für Sozial-politik*, Werner Sombart proclaimed the end of free discussion as a prerequisite for scholarly work: "This art of discussion is gone," he said. "Not discussion but decision now dominates the scene. The creation of a political will comes about today by quite another way. It is no longer the indirect way of influencing public opinion but the direct way by the Führer principle.... I, for my part, say, 'Thank God that this is so!'"

The dean of German literature and former idol of the radical left, Gerhart Hauptmann, led millions of non-Nazis to vote "yes" in Hitler's first plebiscite. Hauptmann looked forward to his first meeting with Hitler as though it were like Goethe's meeting with Napoleon. After the meeting, which consisted only of a handshake, the great imaginative creator of *The Weavers* and *The Sunken Bell* told his friends that "it was the greatest moment in my life."

And yet the so-called ideology of National Socialism was vague, elusive, and full of sudden improvisations despite the facade of a much vaunted program. The future lay resplendent, though only vaguely sketched. Reflecting the Munich coffeehouse drifter who had become "sick with yawning" at the thought of "sitting one day in an office," the Party program was a plaything of Hitler's moods and intuition and so full of generalities that any and every group—farmers, small shopkeepers, workers, business-men, and professionals—could read into it whatever they wanted. Hitler fished in the reservoirs of all sections of the population, ready to name a scapegoat for every group, and glibly promising to gratify the needs of every class. One of the most penetrating analysts of the Nazi period, Her-mann Rauschning, an early member who soon left the Party, has said that the leaders of the movement hadn't the slightest idea what they were going to do after they achieved power. The program was mainly the "graft-ing of all sorts of different fruits on the stem of the common crab-apple planted at the time of . . . meetings in the beer-house in Munich": pan-Germanism, anti-Semitism, racialism, militant nationalism and socialism. The generalities were bent to the needs of power, and the needs were limitless. Every material promise was couched in spiritual, mystical terms that aroused deep emotions among many Germans. New converts imag-ined themselves making sacrifices instead of joining a destructive move-ment. Contradictions were resolved by resorting to the mystique of racism or national redemption. In the planks that are specific, there can be traced a zigzag course of disregard, compromise and contradiction of the original program.

For example, the doctrine of racialism, a core idea of Nazism, was modi-fied almost from the very beginning of the movement. The original "pure" concept held that only the "uncontaminated" population between the Elbe and Weser rivers were "pure Nordic Germans"; these were to consti-tute the elite leadership and eventually provide the sole population of Ger-many. But as the Nazi Party grew into a mass party, it became impossible to tell millions of followers that they were racial inferiors. "Aryan" and "Nordic" were then applied to all Germans as the superior race and the definition was later stretched to include Mediterranean Italians and Orien-tal Japanese. Power always outraced principle. Despite repeated declara-tions that he wanted Germany only for Germans, Hitler even ignored pan-Germanism. Thus, in March 1939, he marched into Prague and made Bohemia and Moravia, with their Czech population, not a puppet state like Slovakia, but part of the Greater Reich. Moreover, when the long, pro-tracted war created serious labor shortages, the racial doctrine was thrown over and thousands of Ukrainian and Russian women were brought into Germany to be mated with German men in order to replenish the German labor supply. Such "descendants of Germans" were to be "re-Germanized" in Hitler's improvised racial formula.

Ideology ebbed and flowed, but the prime scapegoat for Germany's troubles, the Jew, constituted an unchanging motif. The Jew objectified and embodied all of the specific, intense hatreds of the Nazi era: he was the "November criminal" and traitor who gave Germany "the stab in the back" in World War I; he was both Marxist and international capitalist;

he was both pacifist and instigator of World War II; he was the devil as well as the ally of the clericals. Above all, he was the debaser of the German race. Anti-Semitism, an old and deeply rooted phenomenon of Europe, and most especially of Germany, proved to be the single most important instrument used by the Nazis to consolidate their power at home and abroad. Vague and diffused anti-Semitism, always close to the surface of European life, was cleverly exploited by Hitler; again and again, Jew-baiting excited masses of people and raised them to frenzied, barbaric acts of destruction. In the end, millions were involved in the extermination of Jews in one way or another.

After 1933, hatred of the Jew was raised to the level of "law." *Rassenkunde*—racial science—was taken with deadly seriousness by Germans, most notoriously by German scientists who taught what was called *German* physics, *German* chemistry and *German* mathematics. As early as 1937, there appeared a journal called *Deutsche Mathematik*. Its first editorial soberly proclaimed that any idea that mathematics could be judged nonracially carried "within itself the germs of destruction of German science." Some of the most esteemed scientists in Germany fervently believed that "science, like every other human product, is racial and conditioned by blood." It then followed that modern physics "is an instrument of world Jewry for the destruction of Nordic science" and Jewish participation in science, a worldwide plot to pollute science and thereby to destroy civilization. These ideas may sound like the hallucinations of paranoia—some writers have suggested that Germany *was* paranoid during the Hitler regime—but they cannot be dismissed simply as wild, aberrant rantings of a few men. These ideas dominated Germany's intellectual climate during the Hitler era.

As Germans like things to be both orderly and solid—*gründlich*—Nazi propaganda was systematically infiltrated into every department of national life. Religion, science, history, philosophy and law had to recast their old premises and substance to make room for the danger of the "Jewish poison." Not only were S.S. thugs and criminals and street gangs infected by this race virus; all of the conventional professions were similarly diseased, the ultimate perversion manifesting itself in the horrible so-called medical experiments.

The essential emptiness of Nazi "ideology" was revealed after Hitler consolidated his power and made war. After their fantastic conquests, the Nazis had no social, economic or political program for the occupied territories. Naked power and exploitation of conquered peoples were the only motive power both at the beginning and end of the conquests. Europe was not remade; it was destroyed. Nor was there any remaking of the social order in Germany by the Nazis. Policies, programs, administrative reorganization were improvised on the basis of Hitler's whims, intuitions or orders.

Where he was vague, others improvised. Himmler, possibly, was the only Nazi who constructed his S.S. empire logically, from small beginnings with specific goals in mind. But this empire, like everything else in Nazism, was destructive. In the end, Himmler's empire devoured the state itself. The Nazi mission was, in fact, a devouring one. The promised regeneration of Germany never came.

At the center of this nihilism was the war against Jewry. There was no Nazi ideology aside from anti-Jewish ideology. All of the pseudoscientific, historical and sociological books of the Nazi schools and institutes had no other point of reference. Without this destructive, demonic core, there is nothing at all to the much-proclaimed Nazi *Weltanschauung*. And at the center of the war against Jewry was Hitler. The longer we stare at Nazism, the more our eyes focus on Hitler. He was its creator, its law, its being. His death would have been a deathblow to the regime. His death would have been a deathblow to the death camps.

In the autobiographical sections of *Mein Kampf*, Hitler himself established the time and place of his earliest hatred of Jews. It was during his life in Vienna, from 1909 to 1913, that Hitler became a conscious and violent anti-Semite. The Vienna of this period was dominated by the Christian Social Party, whose leader was the mayor of Vienna, Karl Lueger. Lueger was a rabble-rousing anti-Semite and demagogue whom Hitler grew to admire almost idolatrously. Later he was to use with uncanny skill the tricks of manipulating masses of people that Lueger had perfected on a small scale. In Vienna, Hitler also became a voracious reader of the Christian Social Party's anti-Semitic literature. The writings of Gobineau, Chamberlain, and translations of the *Protocols of the Elders of Zion* were common fare. Among this voluminous propaganda was an irregularly published magazine called *Ostara* (named for the Teuton goddess of beauty), put out by a deranged racial mythologist named Adolf Lanz, and undoubtedly read by Hitler.[4] Lanz' central idea of a blond master race called the *Heldlinge* (heroes) enthralled the twenty-year-old Hitler who already had been smitten by early Nordic legends of gods and heroes. Lanz lived and studied in a monastery in Vienna for six years and then left to establish an order of his own, "The Order of the New Temple," whose principal aim was to foster "pure" racial foundations based on the "Aryan" type. He called the "pure" group by various names such as *Assinge* (German gods) and *Heldlinge* and the rest of mankind *Chandalas* (the name used in India for the Untouchables), or "monkey people" (*Afflinge*) and hobgoblins (*Schrättlinge*). There was no possibility, he believed, of improving the Aryan race while the *Chandalas* continued to exist. Between these two extreme groups there is continual war; thus, the biological necessity of destroying inferior peoples, the "brood of mixed blood." Lanz also deplored the "racial shame" of blond women living with the *Afflinge* and urged polygamy in the master race and "marriage helpers" for breeding colonies of racially pure children. The destruction of human beasts (*Ausrottung des Tiermenschen*) was Lanz' primary goal. The worst among these, he said, were the Jews, a mixture of the most debased elements of ancient peoples who had long since disappeared. Detailed programs were worked out for stage-by-stage as well as sudden annihilation: enslavement, sterilization by X ray, starvation, forced labor, expulsion and physical destruction—all of which the Nazis carried out.

It is impossible to know with certainty what poisonous brew of influences or experiences were responsible for Hitler's subsequent boundless hatred—the only "genuine" conviction he had, it is said, without any opportunistic motive—but Lanz' brochures must surely have been potent. At twenty, he was living his most ragged, tramplike existence, finding it impossible to establish real contact with any other human being and jealously guarding his artistic vanity from the "frauds" of the world. It was a vulnerable time for an idler, full of wild dreams, sore at a world that hadn't recognized him and morbidly concocting utopias of pure Germans. Besides the anti-Semitic literature, the sight of Jews—particularly East European Jews—filled Hitler with hatred and disgust.

> While walking through the Inner City of Vienna [he wrote], I suddenly encountered an apparition in a black caftan and black sidelocks. Is this a Jew? was my first thought. For, to be sure, they had not looked like that in Linz. I observed the man furtively and cautiously, but the longer I stared at this foreign face, scrutinizing feature for feature, the more my first question assumed a new form: Is this a German? . . . Wherever I went, I began to see Jews and the more I saw, the more sharply they became distinguished in my eyes from the rest of humanity. . . . Was there any form of filth or profligacy, particularly in cultural life, without at least one Jew involved in it? If you cut even cautiously into such an abscess, you found, like a maggot in a rotting body, often dazzled by the sudden light—a kike! [There follow lurid allusions to uncouth Jews seducing innocent Christian girls and adulterating their blood, a theme frequently found in later Nazi literature.] Gradually [he continues], I began to hate them. . . . For me, this was the time of the greatest spiritual upheaval I have ever had to go through. I had ceased to be a weak-kneed cosmopolitan and became an anti-semite.[5]

The cosmopolitan atmosphere of Vienna, which once captivated so many, also sickened him.

> My inner revulsion toward the Hapsburg State steadily grew. . . . I was repelled by the conglomeration of races which the capital showed me, repelled by this whole mixture of Czechs, Poles, Hungarians, Ruthenians, Serbs and Croats, and everywhere the eternal mushroom of humanity— Jews and more Jews. To me, the giant city seemed the embodiment of racial desecration. . . . The longer I lived in this city, the more my hatred

grew for the foreign mixture of peoples which had begun to corrode this old site of German culture.[6]

Hitler distinguished peoples into racially pure and racially impure ones. Interbreeding of races he regarded as "a sin against the will of the Eternal Creator. . . . Whoever," he wrote, "ignores or despises the laws of race . . . places an obstacle in the victorious path of the superior race and, by so doing, he interferes with a prerequisite condition of all human progress." Hitler's racial theory had its origin in his anti-Semitism. The Jew was no longer a human being, but the embodiment of all evil, into which Hitler projected all that he hated, feared and envied: capitalism, socialism, modernism in the arts, pacifism, humanitarianism, democracy, Bolshevism and befouling of racial purity. He soon convinced himself that a Jewish world conspiracy lay waiting to destroy the Aryan peoples.

It is not necessary to dwell on the psychoanalytical aspects of Hitler's anti-Semitism, but attention has been drawn to one factor that may have had lasting significance: Hitler's first contact with a Jew was probably with the physician Dr. Eduard Bloch, who in 1908 treated Hitler's mother during her last illness, cancer of the breast. The intimacy between the doctor and Frau Hitler was permeated with overtones of brutal assault and mutilation, represented by the ablation of her breast. "Poisoning" by injection was represented, during the last months of her illness, by the doctor's almost daily hypodermics of morphine to alleviate the suffering woman's pain. Significance is also attached to the fact that Hitler was aware of the blood relationship between his parents, and that this accounted for the death of three of the five children born of this marriage.[7]

The sexual origin of Hitler's anti-Semitism is now generally accepted, although analysts can only unravel the windings of Hitler's fantasies conjecturally. The blood relationship between the mother and father was "so restricted as to border on incest," in the phrase of one biographer.[8] Since Hitler's father had been an illegitimate child (and had used his mother's maiden name of Schicklgruber until late in life), his paternity is dubious. It is thus uncertain whether Klara Hitler, twenty-three years her husband's junior, was his second cousin or his niece. The boy Adolf knew about the blood relationship between his parents. Undoubtedly he also heard that there was something improper in such relationships, particularly in a Catholic country. He may have even heard that there were "dangers" in marriages between close relatives.

Hitler himself had a strange, passionate love affair with his own niece, Geli Raubal, twenty years younger than he. Their relationship deteriorated steadily, however, and the girl died under mysterious circumstances. Geli's mother, Hitler's half-sister, Angela, kept house for him for many years thereafter and again Hitler lived in the intimacy of a blood relationship. It has been suggested that these relationships—in addition to the abnormally close one he had with his mother until her death—engendered conflict, guilt and fear of both the physical and psychic dangers of incest. In a massive projection, he threw these unconscious feelings—actually his own self-hatred—upon the Jew. The Jew then became the incestuous, blood-poisoning criminal and murderer.

In Vienna, the mixture of races, and particularly the presence of "Jews and more Jews" appeared as the personification of "racial desecration." In one of the most pondered passages of *Mein Kampf*, Hitler releases his pathological envy and hatred: "For hours, the black-haired Jew boy, diabolic joy in his face, waits in ambush for the unsuspecting girl whom he defiles with his blood. . . ." No Jewish "crimes" of which the Jew is guilty —in politics, economics or art—compare with the Jewish sin of poisoning Aryan blood. To Hitler, *Rassenschande*, racial sin, is equal to venereal disease. He is filled with horror at sexual relations between Jews and Germans. These are a subtle and diabolical plan of "world Jewry" to undermine the racial vigor of Germans. In this unconscious process, the demons in Adolf Hitler had to be exorcised by destroying the Jew.

The Jew was cast as a defiler of German purity in the earliest formulations of the Nazi program, at one of the first meetings of the German Workers' Party on February 24, 1920. The meeting was held in the Festsaal of the Munich Hofbräuhaus at a time when the party membership numbered several hundred. In the course of a brawling, disorderly meeting, Hitler announced the twenty-five points of the party program which he and several others had hastily drawn up—a hodgepodge of appeals to the workers, lower middle class and peasants. Although for tactical reasons Hitler declared the planks "unalterable" in 1926, by the time the party came to power, most of them were ignored, except those which concerned Jews. Of the twenty-five points, eight dealt directly or indirectly with Jews. For example, Point Four served ominous notice to the future: "Only a member of the race can be a citizen. A member of the race can only be one who is of German blood, without consideration of creed. Consequently, no Jew can be a member of the race." Point Seven proposed expulsion of noncitizens when the German economy required it. Point Eight demanded that no Jews be permitted to enter the country and that Jews who had immigrated to Germany since the start of World War I be compelled to leave.

During the years of preparation, the Nazis were relentless in their anti-Jewish attacks in press, speech, and action. In 1925–27, when the Republic enjoyed its greatest stability, Jewish cemeteries were desecrated in increasing numbers and rioting against Jews grew. Anti-Semitic bills were regularly introduced into state and national legislatures; at least 700 racist and anti-Semitic newspapers flourished.[9] After Rosh Hashanah services in

1931, as Jewish worshipers left the synagogues of Berlin, truckloads of Blackshirts fell upon their victims with cries of *"Heil Hitler! Juden raus! Schlagt die Juden tot!"* ("Hail Hitler! Out with the Jews! Beat them dead!") By 1932, when Hitler polled over 13 million votes—37 percent of the total —Röhm's 400,000 S.A. troops in terror squads roamed the streets of Germany and threatened to take the nation by force. Nazi Party instructions to local officials were: "The natural hostility of the peasants against the Jews must be worked up to a frenzy."

The first official act of the Nazi government directed against Jews was the boycott of Jewish enterprises on April 1, 1933. This was in retaliation against a boycott movement against German goods started by Jews and non-Jews alike soon after Hitler became Chancellor. Goebbels called the unfavorable foreign reports of the new regime "atrocity tales" spread by Jews, and Julius Streicher organized a retaliatory boycott. The mere announcement of the boycott produced such panic in non-Jewish industrial circles that Hitler was urged to abandon it. He refused to cancel it, but limited it to one day, Saturday, April 1. Several days before, Nazi rowdies had driven Jewish lawyers and judges from the courts, and Jewish physicians from hospitals.

In calling on the German people, Streicher wrote in the March 31, 1933, issue of *Völkischer Beobachter:*

> The same Jew who plunged the German people into the blood-letting of the World War, and who committed on it the crime of the November Revolution [Weimar] is now engaged in stabbing Germany, recovering from its shame and misery, in the back. . . . The Jew is again engaged in poisoning public opinion. World Jewry is engaged again in slandering the German people. . . . Millions of Germans longed to see the day on which the German people would be shaken up in its entirety to recognize at last the world enemy in the Jew. . . . At 10 A.M. Sat., 1 April, the defensive action of the German people against the Jewish world criminal will begin. A defensive fight begins, such as never has been dared before throughout the centuries. . . . National Socialists! Strike the world enemy![10]

On April 1, pickets were posted in front of all stores, factories and shops belonging to Jews, and in front of Jewish professional offices to prevent anyone from entering. The campaign was carried out flawlessly, although the material damage to the Jews was less than to the German economy, which was then virtually bankrupt, although very few Germans knew it.[11] However, the boycott revealed the completeness and efficiency of Nazi espionage. Nazis already possessed lists of Jews and Christians married to Jews and their financial interests. A follow-up check on these lists was made on June 7, 1933, to make sure that they were complete. Orders were sent by *Propagandaleiter* Bang to all district directorates. The subject was "List M 18, Jew Baiting": "You will receive in the next few days a list of the communities of your districts in which you will find the Jewish firms and businesses of your district. You will immediately check in your whole district whether the addresses given are correct or whether some have been forgotten. The highest importance is to be placed on accuracy since the list is to be printed." The order then goes on to discuss ways of shaming "miscreant" Germans who buy from Jews, including the placing of anonymous newspaper articles to expose such purchases. The order also instructs district committees to "secure female clerks from Jewish stores, who can then very easily name those who purchase in Jewish shops."

Not only were the Nazis perfecting their methods of outlawing Jews. As a consequence of the boycott, the conviction spread that it was permissible and even desirable to destroy the economic life of Jews. Later measures were based on this presumption.

Several days after the boycott, a decree of April 4 barred Jews from civil service and public employment at all government levels. About five thousand Jews lost their jobs as a result. Many of these decided to leave Germany and try to build their lives elsewhere. Others left because they were endangered by their political activities. Jewish intellectuals also left in large numbers in 1933. Among the early emigrants there were also some people of wealth who took a pessimistic view of the future and preferred to accept some immediate loss to a possibly greater risk later. Events were to prove them right, although in 1933 no one could know what lay ahead. Those who fled in 1933 had no backlog of immigrant experience to draw on and they left without adequately preparing themselves for a new life. Many had vocations that were useless elsewhere, or, more correctly, were unused. The exodus in 1933—37,000 Jews—proved to be the largest from Germany in any single year thereafter.

For the Nazis, 1933 was only the beginning. They were not yet in full control of Germany. The old ministries still acted as restraints. All political opposition had yet to be extinguished, the voice of the churches silenced, internal warfare among clashing Nazi forces abolished, law traduced, and the Jew made into a public enemy. For these ends, an apparatus of terror was needed.

3 The Apparatus of Terror

AFTER THE MID-THIRTIES, every seam and corner of German life was pervaded by the Nazi presence. An elaborate network of systems formed the principal instruments of terror—the Leadership Corps, the Gestapo, the *Schutzstaffeln* (Protective or Elite Guard) or S.S., and the *Sicherheitsdienst* (Security Service) or S.D. These were the organizations that carried out propaganda missions, administered the concentration camps and carried out mass murder in the extermination camps. They also conducted interrogations under torture, impressed foreign workers for slave labor and supervised "medical" experiments.

The Leadership Corps of the Nazi Party was the chain of command by which Hitler's plan of conspiracy, conquest and killing was channeled. Every member of the corps was sworn in annually and took the following oath: "I pledge eternal allegiance to Adolf Hitler. I pledge unconditional obedience to him and to the Führer appointed by him." Immediately below Hitler were the Reich leaders: Alfred Rosenberg, Baldur von Schirach, Wilhelm Frick, Martin Bormann, Hans Frank, Robert Ley, Joseph Goebbels, and Heinrich Himmler. Each was directly responsible to Hitler for a specific facet of Nazi policy and carried out his directives through administrators. Germany was divided into many large administrative regions, each called a *Gau*, and each administered by a political leader, the *Gauleiter*. The *Gau* was further subdivided into counties, urban and rural districts, cells and blocks, each with its own level of leader.[1] Thus German life was saturated with Nazi officials or agents. The *Blockleiter*, who was responsible for fifty households, kept a dossier on each citizen and generally had a collaborator in each family to keep every member in line. There were half a million *Blockleiters* in Germany preaching and extolling National Socialism and making sure their individual charges did the same.

Terror, as such, is of course not new in history. Both in the French and Russian Revolutions terror was used as a revolutionary act to wipe out opposition and whip up the fury of the people. No distinctions were made as to individual guilt; whole classes were declared guilty and were liquidated. But the terror was directed against actual or potential enemies; it was not used, as it was in Germany, as a deliberate weapon to disrupt human personality. With the Nazis, terror acquired a new meaning and purpose. Hitler

> wanted to use terror not merely against opponents, and not merely as a deterrent, or momentary stimulant, but as a permanent educational instrument aimed at the German people as a whole—followers as well as enemies —for the purpose of extirpating inconvenient values. The concentration camps were intended not only to break the prisoners as individuals and to spread terror among the rest of the population by using the prisoners as hostages for good behavior, but also to provide the Gestapo members with a training ground in which they are so educated that they lose all human emotions and attitudes.[2]

In his talks with Hermann Rauschning, even before he became Chancellor, Hitler had said:

> We must be ruthless. We must regain our clear conscience as to ruthlessness. Only thus shall we purge our people of their softness and sentimental philistinism, of their Gemütlichkeit [easygoing, genial nature] and their degenerate delight in beer-swilling. We have no time any more for fine sentiments. . . . I don't want the concentration camps transformed into penitentiary institutions. Terror is the most effective political instrument. I shall not permit myself to be robbed of it simply because a lot of stupid, bourgeois mollycoddlers choose to be offended by it. It is my duty to make use of every means of training the German people to cruelty, and to prepare them for war. . . . A violently active, dominating, intrepid, brutal youth—that is what I am after. Youth must be all this. It must be indifferent to pain. There must be no weakness or tenderness in it. I want to see once more in its eyes the gleam of pride and independence of the beast of prey. . . . Anybody who is such a poltroon that he can't bear the thought of someone nearby having to suffer pain had better join a sewing circle, but not my party.[3]

The defenselessness of the individual in a totalitarian society has sometimes been described as slavery, a condition in which the individual has no independent existence but must obey blindly and do the tasks set for him to perform. Within certain limits, the *Blockleiter* might determine certain tasks or standards in Nazi Germany, but there was no individual bondage to him or any other Nazi. The individual German was free to make many decisions without grave risk, but he had to be careful of a supreme, if remote and invisible, power. This was much worse than an immediate master, because the power which a citizen in a totalitarian Germany had to obey and propitiate was inscrutable. A man could never be sure if he was obeying.

However, once declared a public enemy, he was treated as such by everyone and was outlawed from the human community. There was no appeal to ordinary justice, reason or decency or any hope of being restored to civil existence once outlawed. This was the Kafkalike world in which opponents of the Hitler regime found themselves. Liberals, Socialists, Communists, militant Catholics, protesting Protestants and anti-Nazi intellectuals were declared public enemies. Above all others, Jews were outlawed and labeled as people who had no right to exist, no matter how they behaved. The force of the inscrutable power in Nazi Germany was felt through systems of authority which overlapped each other. The function of one often vaguely merged into the function of another, resulting in a deliberately contrived confusion and evasion of responsibility. The power of the state became faceless.

The first system of terror was the Gestapo, organized by Hermann Göring. Göring was one of the three Nazis in the coalition cabinet formed when Hitler became Chancellor. But no specific office could be found for him and he was named Minister Without Portfolio, with the understanding that he would become Minister of Aviation as soon as Germany had an air force. Little notice was paid when he was appointed Minister of the Interior of Prussia, an office that controlled the Prussian police.[4] Göring at this time was a man full of energy and drive, admired by Hitler and his closest adviser. Technically, he was responsible to von Papen; actually, all of his dealings were with Hitler. By the curious system of dual government which existed in Germany, the Prussian Ministry of the Interior carried out the work of administering two thirds of Germany. In the crucial years 1933–34, Göring was second only to Hitler in assuring the Nazis of success. His energy and ruthlessness together with his control of Prussia were indispensable in securing Hitler's ultimate victory.

Göring began manipulating the personnel of the Prussian police almost at once. Mirroring the general acceptance of Hitler throughout the nation, the regular police had stood by as the S.A. Brownshirts bullied their way to power and brawled in the streets at will. Göring purged the police, replacing many of the career officials with Nazis, and within a month of his appointment, he added 50,000 Auxiliary Police to the regular force by the simple expedient of issuing white arm bands to S.A. and S.S. men. They were then armed and given full police powers. The new business of the police was not only to "abet any form of national propaganda" but to substitute arbitrary violence for law. "Every bullet," Göring said, "which leaves the barrel of a police pistol now is my bullet. If one calls this murder, then I have murdered. I ordered all this.' I back it up. I assume the responsibility, and I am not afraid to do so."

Even so, Göring wanted a small police apparatus of his own, a personal terror squad to be used not only against his political opponents but against his rivals in the Party. This he created in April 1933—without any official authorization—by detaching Department IA of the old Prussian Political

Police from its place in the Prussian Ministry of the Interior and setting up a separate headquarters in a commandeered art school in Prinz Albrecht Strasse of Berlin. He did this so that Department IA could be more easily kept apart from the Prussian state apparatus which still included many anti-Nazis and lukewarm officials. This was the beginning of the *Geheime Staatspolizei* (Secret State Police), the Gestapo.

A state organization, the Gestapo became the accomplice of the S.A. and S.S. and Göring forbade any action against these Nazi Party forces. Unlike the ordinary police, the Gestapo was not concerned with the prevention and detection of crime, but with the suppression of all independent political thought and the elimination of all opposition to the Hitler regime. At first it was Göring's instrument of terror—itself a world of double cross, blackmail and murder. Members of the Gestapo arrested each other and intrigued in a welter of violent power struggles. A year later, when Göring became Minister of Aviation, the Gestapo began to expand as an arm of the S.S., the second system of terror in the Third Reich. This expansion was accomplished by a mild-mannered chicken farmer and racial fanatic, Heinrich Himmler.

Himmler[5] was a colorless, puffy-cheeked, dreary man who would never have attracted notice without the black and silver uniform from which he was seldom parted. During the war, propaganda chief Goebbels forbade photographing him in a shooting outfit because he looked so absurd. But he was patient and cautious and shrewd. He also had "ideals" and was quite ready to sacrifice millions of human beings to an abstract idea, the myth of Aryan supremacy. Before the end of the war, Himmler directed the murder of millions of Jews, Slavs and Gypsies, but none were on his conscience. He believed that he had participated in a holy mission to purge the earth of racial inferiors. His early life, however, hardly prepared him for his lifework.

Himmler was the son of a Bavarian schoolmaster. He was brought up as a devout Catholic, had a quite ordinary education and served as an officer cadet toward the end of World War I. After the war, he bought a small chicken farm and worked as a fertilizer salesman. It was from a fertilizer factory not far from Munich that he joined the march during Hitler's attempted putsch in 1923. Persistently, he tried to get the Nazi leader and one of Hitler's bitterest enemies, Gregor Strasser, interested in him. Strasser had set up a Party headquarters office in a single room in Himmler's native town of Landshut. He finally yielded and took Himmler on as an office assistant. In this job Himmler began to collect confidential reports made by S.S. spies on Party members, thus building up secret files later used by Heydrich in the Security Service.

Himmler was a plodder. As Strasser became more and more involved in national Party affairs, Himmler was often in charge of the office in

Landshut. He began to see that the differences between his boss and Hitler offered opportunities for him. Quietly he began to betray Strasser and pass confidential information on Party members to Hitler. He also became a friend of Walter Darre, a Nazi "blood-and-soil" crank who wanted to breed a future race of blond Nordic leaders as world overlords. Himmler was an easy convert. He transferred his interest in breeding chickens to breeding a Nazi elite and master race.

This elite would be created out of the *Schutzstaffeln*, the S.S. Black Guard which in the 1920's was simply a special guard for Hitler and other Nazis, made up of a few dozen fanatical Party members. Himmler envisioned the Black Guard as supermen of the future. He admitted to Hitler: "If I had power to rule this superb handful of men, I could help perpetuate the Nordic race forever. They would become the bulwark against that wave of Jewish influence which threatens to drown our beloved German people." This struck a responsive chord in Hitler and, to everyone's astonishment, Hitler appointed the colorless Himmler Reichsführer S.S. in 1929.

In that year the S.S. was still subordinate to the S.A., the Storm Troops, and numbered only 280 members, but Himmler proceeded to build this force into a combined private army and police force, enlisting only the most ardent followers of Hitler. By the time Hitler became Chancellor, the S.S. had reached a strength of 52,000. But in addition to open membership, a shadow corps of S.S. officers was recruited. They kept their affiliations secret until the Nazis controlled the state. Thus, in key positions all over Germany, including government offices in which membership in any political party was forbidden, there were S.S. officers waiting to put on their black cloaks and boots.

The mission of these Blackshirts was to protect Hitler and the internal security of the Reich, but until the purge of June 30, 1934, Himmler was little known, even in Party circles, outside his native Bavaria, and worked under the shadow of Röhm. After the purge, however, Himmler rapidly increased his power and on July 26, 1934, the S.S. was made independent of the S.A. Soon this highly disciplined and loyal force became much more powerful than the S.A. had ever been and eventually succeeded as a rival to the Army, whereas Röhm's 2,500,000 Brownshirts had failed. Earlier, in April 1934, another block of power was carved out for Himmler: Göring named him chief deputy of the Prussian Gestapo and Himmler immediately began to build up a police empire of his own.

Himmler's interest in a police apparatus had been rewarded a year before when he became Chief of Police in Bavaria. Himmler (and Heydrich) had represented the strength of the Nazi movement in Bavaria and played a major role in carrying out a Nazi coup d'etat there after the March 5, 1933, national elections. This secured Bavaria for Hitler. After the Bavarian government was overthrown, Himmler contented himself with asking for and getting the post of Chief of Police in Bavaria. He thereupon was determined to capture the entire police machine within his S.S. net. He could not hope to crush Göring, but could, and did, use him as an ally in their common desire to smash the power of Röhm's S.A. forces. When Himmler came to Berlin in April 1934 to take over the Prussian Gestapo—not as S.S. leader but deputy police chief under Göring —the terrible machine of terror within Germany was created. Later it was to become the scourge of a continent.

In July 1934, as a reward for carrying out the executions in the Röhm purge, Himmler became completely independent of the S.A. and was henceforth responsible only to Hitler. The S.S. became an independent branch of the Party, and as the Gestapo became absorbed by the S.S., it became more and more its creature. After the Röhm purge, all opposition to the Nazis was silenced. The anti-Nazis had been crushed in the streets, the rigged law courts, the torture barracks of the S.S. and the cellars of Prinz Albrecht Strasse.

A cloak of legality was given to the arbitrary arrests and imprisonment of victims in concentration camps. The legal-sounding term was *Schutzhaft*, or "protective custody," based on the Law of February 28, 1933, which suspended the clauses of the constitution guaranteeing civil liberties. However, "protective custody" did not protect a German from possible harm, as elsewhere, but punished him by putting him behind barbed wire and exposing him to inhuman treatment.

The first concentration camps sprang up quickly during the first year of Hitler's rise to power. By the end of 1933, there were fifty of them, mainly set up by the S.A. to beat up victims and blackmail their relatives into paying large ransoms. Sometimes the victims were murdered out of pure sadism. After the Röhm purge, many Germans hopefully thought that, as all opposition to the Nazis was now wiped out, confinement in the concentration camps would end. On Christmas Eve, 1933, Hitler had announced an amnesty for 27,000 prisoners, but Göring and Himmler evaded the order and few were actually released. Himmler clearly saw the value of the camps as a means of terrorizing the people as well as eliminating opposition to the regime.

After the Röhm purge, the concentration camps were turned over to S.S. control. Guard duty was given to the Death's-Head units (*Totenkopfverbaende*), whose members were recruited from the toughest, most ruthless Nazi elements and who wore the sinister skull-and-bones insignia on their black tunics. The more infamous camps before the war were Dachau near Munich, Buchenwald near Weimar, Sachsenhausen near Berlin, and Ravensbrück in Mecklenburg. Millions of human beings were done to death in the concentration camps and subjected to torture and debasement unimagined. But even worse horrors were to come after the war began when extermination centers, slave labor-into-death camps and camps for so-called Nazi medical research were devised.

Unlike Göring, the unspectacular but patient Himmler did not want or need the outer mantles of power; he pursued the center at white heat. Shrewdly cautious and cold-eyed, he watched Göring dissipate his immense energies and edged him out of the police and security fields. These Himmler planned to remake into a super S.S. state. He had a literal, awful directness that enabled him to set up machinery to execute the racist orders and exterminations which Hitler mouthed. For Himmler, these orders were the noble mission of the S.S., "a page of glory in our history." There was nothing violent or volcanic in this bloodless man. Nor was he cruel or sadistic. He was a Nazi "idealist." Throughout the triumphant period of Nazism when other leaders shamelessly used their power to acquire fantastic wealth, Himmler remained the pedantic petty bourgeois. He surrounded himself with ignorant astrologers, masseurs, butchers and racial "anthropologists" that fed his grandiose fantasies. Until the end, he believed that the mass murder of millions of human beings and the forced breeding of others would indeed create an Aryan elite of supermen. He had, moreover, no deficiency of power lust. After Röhm was eliminated and Göring elevated, Himmler concentrated on destroying the officers' corps and swallowing the Reichswehr into the S.S. maw.[6] First, however, other things demanded attention.

The absorption of the Gestapo into the S.S. did not receive "legal" sanction until 1936. For several years it had developed and ramified under Himmler without official authority. It was given this sanction on February 10, 1936. At the same time the Gestapo was raised above the law. After this date, no one could appeal from a decision of the Gestapo, and the courts were forbidden to reexamine its decisions. Thus it was that many persons acquitted by the courts or released from prison could immediately be rearrested by the Gestapo and taken into "protective custody," that is, sent to a concentration camp. After this absorption, Himmler netted the entire police apparatus. In June 1936, he was appointed Chief of the German Police, which included not only the political police (Gestapo), but the uniformed or Order Police. The total force was divided into Security Police, composed of Gestapo and Criminal Police, numbering about 65,000 men, and Order Police of several hundred thousand. Air-raid wardens, fire-brigademen and foreign auxiliary policemen from occupied territories brought the total strength of the Order Police to 2,800,000 by the end of 1942.[7]

For the first time in German history a unified police was established for the whole of the Reich, with Himmler in control. This was tantamount to putting the police in the hands of the S.S. Himmler had already conquered a vital organization of the state and pushed it into the framework of the Nazi Party. Now virtually a state within a state,* a supreme command of the S.S. was set up consisting of twelve departments which duplicated practically every department of the government, so that there was no sphere of official life, not even the armed forces, which was immune to the black-cloaked S.S. The main body, for example, the *Allgemeine*, was itself organized on military lines and divided into districts, subdistricts, regiments and other lower formations down to platoons. At the outbreak of the war, it numbered almost a quarter of a million men. When the Third Reich ended, it numbered five million. The *Waffen S.S.*, the military arm of Himmler's octopus, contained nearly thirty divisions. Because of the crippling manpower shortage, it was obliged to lower its original standards of "purity," designed to make it the elite of the German armed forces. From 1942 on, it established Flemish, Dutch and other "Germanic" units. Step by step, regulations were loosened until, at the end of the war, the S.S. had on its roster Latvian, Ukrainian, Cossack, Uzbek, Estonian, Belorussian, Polish, Bosnian, Arab and Indian units. The snobbery of purity yielded to a need for manpower arising from competition with the weakening Wehrmacht.[8]

Himmler also presided over massive population upheavals. After the invasion of Poland in September 1939, he was appointed head of a new organization: the Reich Commissariat for the Strengthening of German Folkdom (*Reichskommissar für die Festigung des deutschen Volkstums* —R.K.F.D.V.), which involved him in fantastic schemes, many of which were applied, to expel Jews and Slavs from eastern Europe and repopulate the areas with ethnic Germans or persons considered "Germanizable."

Another substructure in the S.S. state was an echelon called the "Higher S.S. and Police Leaders." In Germany, they were the S.S. counterpart of the *Gauleiters* of the provinces. As the war spread, they were appointed to Crakow, Warsaw, Lublin, Oslo, Paris, The Hague, Belgrade and Athens. In Russia, there was an S.S. and Police Leader for each of the three Army Groups and one for "special duties." These twelve leaders, supreme in police matters, served under the direct command of Himmler and Heydrich. Technically, they were Himmler's own representatives with military commanders and civil governors in their respective areas. They were a hard core of tough Nazi "old fighters" and represented a victory of the S.S. over the civil administration. Their exact role was never defined, however. This vagueness was deliberate and characterized the fog that enveloped the whole German police organization. Himmler may have created the office simply to prevent Heydrich from dominating the police, just as he prevented him from controlling the concentration camps.

* Chart of S.S. structure, p. 53.

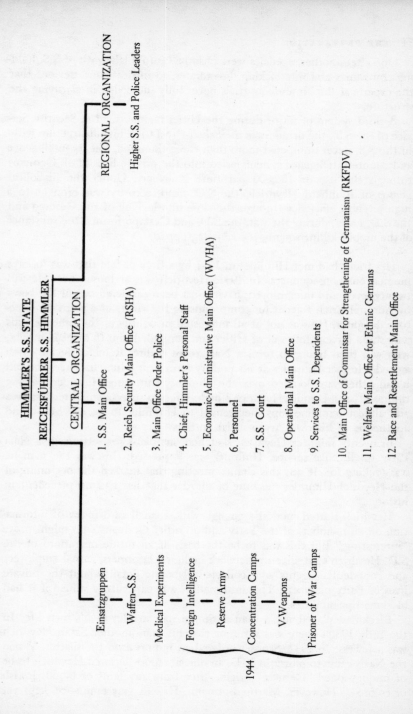

HIMMLER'S S.S. STATE

REICHSFÜHRER S.S. HIMMLER

CENTRAL ORGANIZATION

REGIONAL ORGANIZATION

Higher S.S. and Police Leaders

1. S.S. Main Office
2. Reich Security Main Office (RSHA)
3. Main Office Order Police
4. Chief, Himmler's Personal Staff
5. Economic-Administrative Main Office (WVHA)
6. Personnel
7. S.S. Court
8. Operational Main Office
9. Services to S.S. Dependents
10. Main Office of Commissar for Strengthening of Germanism (RKFDV)
11. Welfare Main Office for Ethnic Germans
12. Race and Resettlement Main Office

Einsatzgruppen
Waffen-S.S.
Medical Experiments
Foreign Intelligence
Reserve Army
Concentration Camps
V-Weapons
Prisoner of War Camps

1944

One after another, agencies were absorbed into a labyrinth of S.S. holding companies and interlocking directorates, so intricate and devious that the experts at the Nuremberg trials never fully succeeded in clarifying the structure.

A third system of terror during the Hitler regime was the Security Service of the S.S., the dread *Sicherheitsdienst* (S.D.). This substructure within the S.S. never numbered more than three thousand, but its intelligence and counterintelligence systems pried into the private lives of all Germans through the use of 100,000 part-time informers. Under the diabolical genius of Reinhard Heydrich, the S.D. head, security was brought to a high pitch of efficiency through the close interlocking of the Gestapo and the S.D. Later, during the war, the S.D. and Gestapo formed the substance of the mobile killing squads, the *Einsatzgruppen*.

Heydrich[9] had met Himmler in 1931 by a trick of fate that was to have momentous consequences. In 1931, Heydrich was at loose ends. He was twenty-seven and unemployed, having just been cashiered out of the Navy by Admiral Erich Raeder for compromising the virtue of a shipyard director's daughter. He was not at all interested in politics at the time, but his wife was a fervent follower of Hitler and persuaded him to meet Himmler, who was then trying to form a Nazi corps d'elite. Reluctantly Heydrich agreed. He met Himmler at his poultry farm near Munich. There the tall blond lithe giant loomed over the blinking, stuttering Himmler wearing rimless glasses. Despite Heydrich's high, staccato speech, small restless eyes and almost feminine hips, he seemed to Himmler to be the blue-blond apotheosis of his own Aryan racial fantasy.

In twenty minutes Heydrich sketched out plans for setting up a Nazi Party intelligence service. Himmler was impressed; this was the man he was looking for. It was this chance meeting that marked the beginning of the Heydrich-Himmler machine of murder that has had no precedent in history.

Heydrich started modestly enough with a small card index of information on all members of the Party and on other Germans who might prove "interesting." But this was to be the basis of all future operations of the S.D. Heydrich's intelligence network included informers, casual employees and confidential agents who collected elaborate details about the private lives of Party members. This information was particularly valued if it had blackmail possibilities.

Blackmail played more than a simple role in Heydrich's own life. In the early 1930's there was a rumor that his grandmother Sarah Heydrich was a Jewess. In 1932, Strasser ordered an inquiry into the matter. When the Nazis came to power in 1933, an official report declared Heydrich to be of unquestioned "German" origin, "free from any taint of blood, Jewish or colored." However, Martin Bormann, Hitler's gray eminence, kept yet another set of files containing evidence alleging that Heydrich's maternal grandmother was indeed Jewish. When Himmler heard of this, he immediately went to Hitler, who then ordered Heydrich to be sent to him. Hitler later told Himmler that Heydrich was a "highly gifted but highly dangerous man, whose gifts must be reserved for the Nazi movement." Heydrich's alleged non-Aryan background was ideal blackmail in the Nazi world. Presumably fearing Party exposure of the story, he would obey any order blindly and carry out assignments that other men might shrink from. What Himmler did not know was that Heydrich had built up a dossier on Hitler himself so that someday he, too, could be blackmailed.[10]

As Heydrich watched Himmler recruit for the S.S., he was struck by the low mental quality and mediocre caliber of the average S.S. man. He also knew that good policemen are often poor intelligence officers. He was therefore determined to recruit brighter candidates for his own S.D. Many were secured from the ranks of displaced university graduates who were unable to find jobs. Some of them dabbled in history, philosophy or Teutonic archaeology, but these genteel pursuits were no bar to later assignments carrying out orders in the murderous *Einsatzgruppen*, or enforcing the sinister Night and Fog Decrees. The purpose of these orders was to seize persons "endangering German security" in the conquered countries of the West. These victims were not immediately executed but were made to vanish without a trace into the night and fog of the unknown. No information as to their whereabouts—not even their places of burial—was permitted. The number of Europeans who disappeared into the night and fog was never established at Nuremberg.[11]

Heydrich was inordinately ambitious, but he did not crave publicity and preferred to wield power in the background. He had an acute perception of the moral, professional and political weaknesses of all of the Nazi leaders and played one against the other like a sinister puppet-master. The terror and suffering that he inflicted on his fellow-Germans was only a prelude to later unparalleled crimes against the Jews of Europe. His absorption in espionage, dating back to his experience in the Navy, combined with enormous nervous energy, a brilliant ice-cold intellect and skill in manipulating the weaknesses and ambitions of others, gave the Third Reich its master spy. Were it not for his chance meeting with Himmler, he would probably have been a concert violinist of great distinction.

Heydrich was recognized as chief of the S.D. officially in 1932. At the beginning, the S.D. was simply to watch over members of the Party and report any suspicious activity. Röhm and his storm troopers were among the first victims of the S.D.'s spying. By April 1934, Heydrich had become head of the Berlin Gestapo under Himmler and played a bloody role in the Röhm purge of June 1934. By 1936, Himmler turned over the administration of the Gestapo to Heydrich and the line between the Gestapo and the S.D. thereafter became extremely blurred. On November 11, 1937, the peculiar affinities of the two agencies were recognized by "law," under the Nazi compulsion to legalize the illegal. The S.D. was required to assist the Gestapo and vice versa. The distinctive functions which these agencies once had all but disappeared and in the period when Jews were deported and murdered "Gestapo" and "S.D." were used interchangeably. After the war started, outside the Reich, the Gestapo and S.D. were completely centralized down to the local or unit level.

Meanwhile, the engulfment of the state by the S.S. advanced rapidly. By 1937, Himmler as Reichsführer S.S. had achieved another of his major objectives: all rulings issued by his office were validated as ministerial decisions. By 1938, all members of the Gestapo and Criminal Police (*Kriminalpolizei*, or Kripo) were required to join the S.S. And in 1939, there came one further structural shift that laid the basis for yet another substructure: The Gestapo and Criminal Police together were joined into the Main Office Security Police—technically an agency of the state. Parallel with this "state" security system was the Nazi Party Security Service, the S.D., all of which Himmler had turned over to Heydrich. These contained about 70,000 men. In control of these, Heydrich set in motion the destructive forces of *Kristallnacht*, the Night of the Crystal Glass, November 9, 1938. In September 1939, after the war had started, the state and Party services under Heydrich were merged into a massive administrative unit, the RSHA (*Reichssicherheitshauptamt*—Main Office for the Security of the Reich). The RSHA was a creation of Heydrich. It fused party members with civil servants and its seven bureaus could send men into the field to carry out the most drastic Nazi decisions.

The swamping of state administrative agencies by the S.S. was now virtually complete. The RSHA was a vast network not only in the Reich, but after the war began, in the occupied territories and invaded countries. It served as the main division of the twelve comprising the S.S., but obscured the importance of its own seven branches by referring to them by the prosaic German word for "office" or "bureau"—Amt. Amt IV was better known as the Gestapo, which numbered about 30,000 men. Among its sections, the Gestapo had a Jewish Affairs Section—Section 4 of Amt IVB, called "IVB-4" for short. The head of this section was Adolf Eichmann. Section IVB-4, an unheralded merger of the Central Emigration Office and the Jewish Affairs Section of the Gestapo in the spring of 1940, was to become in the years 1941-44 the center of the Nazi machinery of deportation and death for the Jews of Europe. From the Arctic to the Spanish border, branches of IVB-4 were set up with an area chief and staff working directly under Eichmann's office in Berlin.

By 1940, the old civil service melted into the S.S. machine. Heydrich's position was now publicly recognized. For the first time, he emerged before the German public as a major figure. Officially subordinate to Himm-

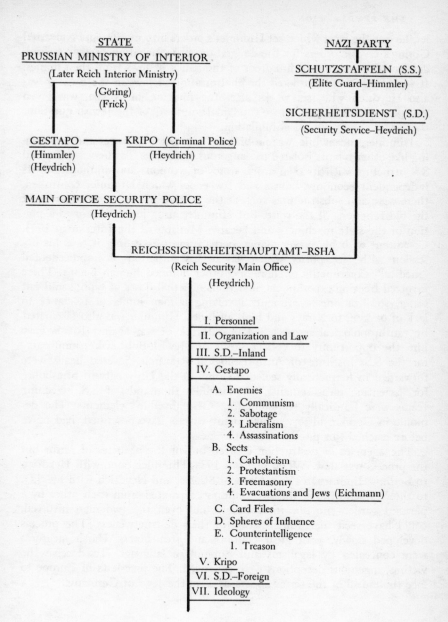

STATE
PRUSSIAN MINISTRY OF INTERIOR
(Later Reich Interior Ministry)
(Göring)
(Frick)

NAZI PARTY
SCHUTZSTAFFELN (S.S.)
(Elite Guard–Himmler)

SICHERHEITSDIENST (S.D.)
(Security Service–Heydrich)

GESTAPO — KRIPO (Criminal Police)
(Himmler)   (Heydrich)
(Heydrich)

MAIN OFFICE SECURITY POLICE
(Heydrich)

REICHSSICHERHEITSHAUPTAMT–RSHA
(Reich Security Main Office)
(Heydrich)

I. Personnel

II. Organization and Law

III. S.D.–Inland

IV. Gestapo

    A. Enemies
       1. Communism
       2. Sabotage
       3. Liberalism
       4. Assassinations
    B. Sects
       1. Catholicism
       2. Protestantism
       3. Freemasonry
       4. Evacuations and Jews (Eichmann)

    C. Card Files
    D. Spheres of Influence
    E. Counterintelligence
       1. Treason

V. Kripo

VI. S.D.–Foreign

VII. Ideology

ABSORPTION OF STATE POLICE AND SECURITY FUNCTIONS BY RSHA

ler, he was the lever which set Himmler's orders into motion and converted Göring's cryptic orders for the emigration and evacuation of Jews to sudden brutal expulsions of hundreds of thousands of Jews from their homes. It was Heydrich who ordered the ghettoization of Jews in the East. It was also Heydrich who, six weeks after the invasion of Russia, was given sweeping authority to organize the "final solution" of the Jewish question, the Nazi euphemism for annihilation.

Himmler, meanwhile, was probing for new fields of power and functioning like other tyrants isolated in dangerous eminence. To the vastly layered S.S. structure with its own army, stores of weapons and ammunition, its independent economy, courts and law code, which Himmler controlled, there were also substructures such as the RSHA, which absorbed many of the old functions of the state. But Himmler also "legally" claimed a portion of the state machinery and became Minister of the Interior in 1943. Coexistent with his power mania, perhaps even exceeding it, was his obsession with race purity which led to his initiation of unprecedented "medical" experiments on Jews and other doomed human beings. These involved freezing experiments, injections of lethal doses of typhus and salt water, sterilization, experiments involving human limits of tolerance to lack of oxygen, to X rays and high altitudes. Himmler was also fascinated by "anthropological research." The outbreak of war against Russia gave him the opportunity to collect skulls of "Jewish-Bolshevik commissars" for the S.S. Institute of Anthropological Research. Severed heads were forwarded in hermetically sealed tin cans to the University of Strasbourg for "scientific measurements." Meanwhile, thousands of S.S. screening teams were frantically searching for "Germanizable" elements. The demonic in German history, which many writers have described, had never before reached this pitch of destructiveness.

The agencies of destruction evolved out of the agencies of terror but the process was slow. When in April 1934, Himmler came with Heydrich to Berlin—Himmler to Prinz Albrecht Strasse, and Heydrich with his S.D. to the Wilhelmstrasse, the two buildings separated from each other by a pleasant garden—no one in Germany, not even the two men involved, could have seen the ultimate scale of their destructiveness. The process developed slowly, with great cunning and stealthiness. Harsh measures were concealed by legalisms and camouflage language. To deceive the victims, ingenious deceptions were contrived. The first Jews of Europe to face the ordeal of the terror apparatus were the Jews of Germany.

4 The Jews of Germany: 1933-1938

GERMANY IS REGARDED as the birthplace of modern Judaism. In the wake of emancipation, German Jews were the first to assimilate the secular culture of their environment and to jettison most of the traditional religious civilization of East European Jewry. Assimilation was pursued enthusiastically, not only because of its practical advantages but because of the accompanying sense of cultural and social progress and spiritual liberation. The walls of the ghetto had fallen. Life's possibilities now lay open for Europe's Jews. In this revolutionary process, German Jewry led the way and influenced many other patterns of Jewish life, including even those of Eastern Jewry which resisted the process forcibly. Nourished on the liberal values of the Enlightenment, German Jews had a much greater breadth of outlook and experience than Eastern European Jews, but when the Nazi storm broke, they were much less prepared for the task of survival.[1]

Assimilation and emancipation notwithstanding, the Jewish Question remained very much in evidence in Germany in the nineteenth and early twentieth centuries, though German Jews tended to ignore it or call it a passing residue of the past. Deeply influenced by German thought, they had developed extremely passionate ties to their country and uncritical adherence to German national interests which often led to a blind loyalty to the state. A peculiarly intense attachment to Germany led some Jews to anguish over German-Jewish "duality" and to probe the meaning of Jewish identity. This fundamental emotional and cultural conflict contributed to a Jewish complex, an inner Jewish split that was not resolved in time to strengthen German Jews for the Nazi assault. Of all the Jews in Europe, the dazed and bewildered Jews of Germany were most unprepared for the fate that was to engulf them. Abruptly, the state prohibited them from describing themselves as members of the German *Volk*. This shock deprived them of the moral and cultural essence of their life. The strange German-Jewish symbiosis became a dead fact of history.

The harsh reality of early anti-Jewish Nazi measures dawned slowly. At first it was hoped that the Nazi program could somehow be reconciled with the integrity of German Jewish life, but early pitiful attempts along these lines misfired. The Nazis were not interested. Then followed a phase in which German Jews believed National Socialism to be a transitory affair, a situation that would pass but that must not be aggravated by anti-Nazi actions. This attitude was shared by most of the Western world in the early 1930's. In April 1933, during the boycott of German goods, the Jewish community of Berlin cabled the Chief Rabbi of Great Britain urging that all "acts of propaganda and boycott" be stopped. "Spreading false news . . . will create difficulties and tarnish the reputation of our homeland," they wrote.

In the same period, an organization of Jewish war veterans attacked emigrants as people who had "deserted" their fellow Jews and who were now "shooting arrows from secure hiding places" to the detriment of Germany and the German Jews. "Nobody can rob us of our German fatherland," they continued. ". . . In that we fight this battle, we carry out a German, not a selfish Jewish fight." They had faith that so long as the situation was defined, so long as there were "laws," they could live under them on the assumption that one can live under any law.

Even the Zionists, as late as June 1933, appealed to the Nazis not to snap the long historical relationship between the two peoples: "The National Socialists, in their demonstrations, designate the Jews as 'enemies of the state.' That designation is incorrect. The Jews are not enemies of the state. The German Jews desire and wish for the rise of Germany, for which they have always given, to the best of their knowledge, their resources, and that is what they wish to continue to do." This statement was issued a month after the massive book burnings.

Hopes were also pinned on non-Nazi members of the new government, and Vice-Chancellor von Papen tried to foster such hopes. It was also recognized that the Nazi Party itself was not unified—the followers of Röhm were calling for a radical revolution—and Nazi leaders made contradictory statements regarding the Jews and their fate. There were lulls in their attacks. Even Boycott Day, April 1, 1933, did not destroy these hopes. Moreover, the very violence and extremism of Nazi anti-Jewish propaganda appeared to Jews—as to others—to be too barbarous for belief. These illusions were soon destroyed.

On April 4, 1933, Jews were barred from civil service and public employment at all government levels—the first law specifically dealing with Jews. Three days later, administrative regulations followed based on a definition of "non-Aryan" descent. A person of "non-Aryan descent" was defined as someone who had one Jewish parent or Jewish grandparent. This definition was the "Aryan paragraph" which was soon applied by many private individuals and organizations as well as government agencies. This definition put a premium on proving descent and affected "Aryans" as well as "non-Aryans." Anyone who wished to be employed by the Reich or the Party had to search for the records of his ancestors. Often he needed as many as seven documents: his own birth certificate, the certificates of his two parents and of all four grandparents. It became a point of honor to put "Aryan" clauses into effect and bar Jews from certain fields of activity. Nazi propaganda leveled at the State Enemy began to stick, and Jews soon began to feel the stigmata of isolation. The German people were told that world anti-German reaction to the April boycott on Jewish business was entirely due to *Greuel-propaganda* (atrocity propaganda); criticism of Nazi actions was described as the Jewish conspiracy at work, the collusion of Jews in Germany with Jews elsewhere.

The aspersion on their loyalty pierced German Jews where they were most vulnerable. Disbelievingly, they reeled under a succession of charges and actions. The orderly state to which they were so extravagantly attached was snapping apart. To make matters worse, they were without authoritative representation. They lacked a central body to act as their spokesman. Every joint action of Jews required laborious coordination among the hundreds of legally recognized religious communities into which German Jews were organized, called *Kehillot*, or among the *Landesverbände*, the State Associations of *Kehillot*. Under the impact of the Nazi assault, a united agency was urgently needed to speak for the 525,000 Jews of Germany.

One man, Dr. Leo Baeck, the Rabbi of Berlin, an unusually gifted spiritual leader, was able to command the respect of all factions and local groups. In September 1933, Dr. Baeck was elected president of the new body called the *Reichsvertretung der Deutschen Juden* (Representative Council of Jews in Germany). This was much more than a national committee of State Associations. It was a broad representation of Jewish organizations and movements in Germany: Zionist, Orthodox religious, relief and welfare agencies, veterans and youth groups, but it confined itself to the task of political representation.[2] German Jewry had at its disposal an impressive group of agencies and institutions to carry on specific functions of welfare, emigration, education and fund raising. What was needed was a body representing German Jews vis-a-vis the government. The *Reichsvertretung* tried to be this voice. It also negotiated with Jews abroad for political assistance and funds. It tried to fight the obscene hate propaganda, the increasing incidents of desecration of Jewish property, mob violence and imprisonment, and it tried to handle the maze of legal and human problems that grew out of the Nazi restrictions. Its policy was to hold on, to gain time, to utilize the narrowing area as a basis for a viable life.

The main forces in the newly established *Reichsvertretung* were two polar movements—the Central Union of German Citizens of Jewish Faith

(*Centralverein Deutscher Staatsbürger Jüdischen Glaubens*) and the Zionist Federation of Germany. Their cooperation, in view of the diverse personalities and convictions of the organizations, was quite remarkable. Through their publications, the *Centralverein Zeitung* and especially the *Jüdische Rundschau*, which expressed Jewish defiance and pride, they were able to speak to the Jews of Germany during fearful days. One of the most important decisions of these groups was to concentrate urgently on giving Jewish youth a future by preparing them to emigrate. The Zionist Federation already had the necessary machinery—Youth Aliyah.

Adults, too, left Germany but the panic emigration in 1933, involving a total of 37,000 German Jews, had left a train of disappointments and failures which slowed down the process for the next few years. Moreover, other strong pulls among German Jews slackened the exodus. Many believed, particularly in the early years of the regime, that it would be possible to work for a renaissance of Jewish culture in Hitlerized Germany. They believed that they had time for a reconstruction, that reasonable discussions could still be had with government officials, as in the past. Like a sick man fighting death, unaware of the nature of his struggle, German Jews experienced a new strength before the end, magnificent bursts of spiritual renewal on the eve of extinction. At the same time, this retrieval of old buried Jewish springs delayed recognition of the doom facing them. For some, it meant stoically meeting the fate they only dimly comprehended.

On the edge of disaster, the Jews of Germany had to discover that emancipation had not only unshackled them but had deprived them of valuable ties. The *Reichsvertretung* itself had to travel the long and difficult road of return.[3] But under the guidance of Leo Baeck and Martin Buber, the Jewish philosopher and educator, Jews in Germany learned that a Jewish world existed rich enough to be sustaining. In 1933, Buber suggested to the *Reichsvertretung* that a cultural institute (*Bildungs-Amt*) be established for German Jews, not an emergency structure, but a "house able to withstand all weathers." The image and goal of this education were, in a way, existentialist: education for the most exposed man of all, the Jew, who would draw on his own inner strength to overcome the dangers of his position, which he could not, and did not wish to evade.[4]

The *Bildungs-Amt* did not take shape, but adult Jewish education in Hitler Germany tried to guide itself along the lines of spiritual resistance expressed by Buber. For the individual—torn out of his career, his leisure, the whole framework of his life shattered—new sources of strength had to be found in the Bible, Jewish history, Hebrew, and Jewish religious practices, without giving up the values of the European humanist inheritance. Lectures, seminars, classes and studies were set up for Jewish teachers who were forced to give up their careers in general schools, for youth leaders, rabbis, Jewish women and teachers in newly established Jewish institutions. The impact of the changes wrought in these groups then radiated out to the general community.

It would distort the truth, however, to magnify the sustaining power of these efforts. In the first two years of the Nazi regime, before the passage of the Nuremberg Laws in 1935, the power of spiritual resistance grew stronger; after 1935, as external pressures became harsher, the power of average men and women to cope with them diminished. The leaders of the *Reichsvertretung* and adult education movements at first shared the general belief that the Nazi regime would be short-lived. Rabbi Baeck, however, after the 1933 boycott, saw it as the beginning of the end. "The thousand-year-old history of German-Jewry is at an end," he prophesied. But others seemed to feel that a more or less extended period would allow the Jewish community a provisional life. In forecasting the terms of that life, up to 1935, opinions differed, but the inner resistance of individuals was strengthened by the hope of an early collapse of the Nazi regime. After 1935, the terror and destructiveness escalated, and German Jews, day by day, had to face the reality of their dissolution. In this mood, second only to the urgency of evacuating Jewish children, they faced the problem of educating them.

Many problems had to be surmounted. There was, for example, the shift in school-age population, brought about by internal migration (the gravitation to the large cities), emigration, constantly changing state orders, a shortage of teachers, and, above all, Nazi propaganda which asphyxiated the child's world. Buber has caught this atmosphere:

> The children see what is happening and are silent, but at night they moan in their dreams, awaken, stare into the darkness. The world has become unsafe . . . the soul no longer finds its way into the world. It becomes hardened and callous. . . . That is how men become bad. . . . Parents, teachers . . . what is to be done against resentment? I know nothing else but this: to bring something unshakable into the world of the child. . . . That does not mean opposing one racialist image by another . . . we are not one other example of the species-nation; we are the only example of our species. We are Israel.[5]

Children who had grown up in a land they loved now had to learn to bear rejection and hatred. City after city raced to set up Jews' benches in their schools; "racial science" was made compulsory; teachers and classmates became silent or hostile. Suddenly, the Jewish child's world became not only uncertain but untrustworthy. He suffered for a past he only dimly understood, if at all. The shrunken world of the family offered little support. Often Jewish children were forced to look on as their fathers were whipped in public or taken to concentration camps.[6]

At the opening of the school term in April 1933, after the Easter recess, many Jewish parents refused to send their children back to German public schools, although at the moment the Nazis had taken only the first step in eliminating Jewish pupils from the schools: a fixed quota of Jewish children for secondary schools. In the following months, the existing Jewish schools were enlarged and new ones founded. In the first six months of its existence, the *Reichsvertretung* allocated one fifth of its budget to education.

Great adjustments had to be made for teachers as well as pupils. The exclusively Jewish environment, the task to make Judaism the center of education, the restlessness and turmoil of the first months, the individual reorientation to a wholly different intellectual and social world—these adjustments had to be made in an atmosphere that lacked the orderliness of German schools. The children reacted to the shock of events and the perplexities at home with noise, nervous activity and exaggerated liveliness. The absolute identification with the new school, which soon became their life, was to compensate for the sudden loss of the old and the depressed atmosphere at home.[7] By 1937, 61 percent of all Jewish children attended Jewish schools. Externally, the policy of the government was baffling.

The Nazi attitude toward the Jewish schools was full of contradictions, making it impossible for the Jewish community to gauge the intentions of the government. While gradually expelling Jewish children from state schools, they gave subsidies to Jewish elementary schools and paid Jewish teachers pensions until 1939. They also, in the early years, allowed Jewish educators great latitude in setting up courses of study in direct antithesis to the Nazified school system. Often Jewish schools were not inspected for months or years. Even when they were, there was seldom interference with the way they were run. Thus, while destroying the whole fabric of Jewish life in Germany, the Nazis maintained their financial obligations to a small piece and allowed it autonomy. This same bizarre, inconsistent policy is to be found again and again throughout the Holocaust: a crevice of legal rectitude or unmutilated life in a welter of inhumanity.

The Jewish school was a world in itself where the Jewish child could be fortified to bear his Jewishness with pride. The Nazis were indifferent to the curricula; as a result, the child was given not only work in the Bible, Jewish history, Hebrew and Palestine, but lessons involving the "other Germany"—the heritage of humanist Germany. While the exclusion of Jews from German culture was being proclaimed, Jewish children in their Jewish schools were reading Schiller, Goethe, Hölderlin, the poetry of the romantics and other great works from the great German literary heritage. This paradox becomes even more striking when it is realized that this literature was interpreted in a way diametrically opposed to the Nazi oppression of individual and political freedom.[8] Moreover,

Jewish students read the works of authors who were banned in Nazi Germany. The stories of Thomas Mann and poems by Hofmannsthal, the books of Jakob Wassermann and Stefan Zweig were popular with adolescents. Contrary to what might be expected, the students did not reject everything in German culture, but responded to works that had been treasured in the past and were now being destroyed.

Jews in artistic fields also sought to find meaning in the "closed society" which Germany's Jews had been so happy to push into past history after emancipation. Solace and purposeful work had to be found for Jewish actors barred from the stage, for musicians expelled from orchestras and artists barred from galleries and museums. In the mood of this search, the *Jüdischer Kulturbund*[9] was organized.

The moving spirit behind the *Kulturbund* was Dr. Kurt Singer, a man of great warmth, energy and ability. A nerve specialist by profession, Dr. Singer was also a gifted musician. He had founded the Doctors' Choir in Berlin in the 1920's and became its conductor. Early in 1933, he called together Jewish representatives in various artistic fields to work out the framework of a Jewish cultural organization. He then took his proposals to the German authorities and argued persuasively for them. By June, he had obtained official permission to create a *Jüdischer Kulturbund* and immediate preparations were made to obtain subscribers as well as actors, musicians, stagehands and electricians—all of whom had to be Jewish. Against a monthly payment of 2.50 marks, members were offered two presentations a month from the full repertoire of opera, drama and music. Immediately 19,000 persons joined and 200 Jewish artists were given steady employment.

Many observers have commented on the brilliance and originality of German cultural life in the 1920's. Jewish actors, musicians and producers had contributed a great deal to this reputation, but they were generally the most assimilated Jews, least versed in Jewish culture. As no mere act of will or external compulsion can quickly synthesize a new identity for the most sincere of searchers, these artists had to struggle to find a new identity. Having seen their old life canceled out, as Jews they had to find new artistic selves and new forms of expression. "Without a constructive idea of Jewish art," Dr. Singer was to write later, "did we wake up from our depression and isolation, and grope our way like blind men toward Jewish spiritual values." Significantly, the first production was Lessing's *Nathan the Wise*, a play in the humanist tradition, in which the Jew Nathan, whose wife and children have been murdered, proclaims the message of tolerance and humanity. As in the schools, the Jews in the *Kulturbund* tried to balance Jewish themes in the repertoire with those from general European culture, but the audiences at first clung to the works they were familiar with: Aeschylus, Shakespeare, Schiller and Shaw.

Later they were more responsive to Eastern Jewish masterpieces and translations from the Hebrew.

The attitude of the Nazi officials toward this enterprise, as toward the Jewish schools, was unexpectedly neutral. At the beginning, Dr. Singer contacted several government offices and the Gestapo. Finally Hans Hinkel in the Prussian Ministry of Education was appointed to represent the government in its dealings with the *Kulturbund*. Hinkel developed a genuine regard for Dr. Singer and permitted the organization complete autonomy for a time, often against the objections of party co-workers. This personal relationship also made it possible for a cultural organization for the whole Reich to be set up, with a membership of over fifty thousand, involving all of the large cities and many small towns. As late as April 1935, Hinkel deplored the problems that were created because local officials and Party men did not follow a consistent policy in handling Jewish cultural activity. "This gave Dr. Singer and myself," he said, "the idea to unite within one association the many large and small societies. Such an association would be in your and our interest and have also the advantage of my giving central directives to the Gestapo centers and other authorities in the provinces as to how to handle the affairs of the *Kulturbund*."

But soon the cultural autonomy of the *Kulturbund* became a farce. Every sentence and every note of the repertoire had to be submitted to censors well in advance. First, Communist and revolutionary references were banned; then genuinely "German" art was banned, including Schiller and the German romantics, but not Goethe, who had a bad reputation as a cosmopolitan. He was blacklisted later together with all German classics. Even in the plays of Molière and Shakespeare, the censor's red pencil was used freely. Beethoven was prohibited. Mozart, an Austrian, could be played until the *Anschluss* in 1938. The only German composer whose works were permitted until the very last was Handel, although even he was compromised in the eyes of the Nazis by his love for England and his use of biblical themes.

Policy changes were sudden and followed no pattern but made life increasingly difficult for the *Kulturbund*. Subscribers fell away because of emigration or financial stress. By 1938, German Jewish life was weakened by economic blows, physical threats and physical depletion. Resignation and defeatism hung about those who could not emigrate. The *Kulturbund* faced serious financial problems and seemed ready to dissolve when the November pogroms of 1938 swept the country. Jewish homes, shops and synagogues were plundered and destroyed; thousands of Jews were dragged to concentration camps. Then, three days later, the *Kulturbund* was ordered to renew its work!

More ostracized than ever, more destitute and isolated, the dazed Jews in Berlin were ordered to open the theater in the Kommandantenstrasse. *Kulturbund* musicians, actors, electricians and others in concentration camps were released. In such a mad, incoherent world of sudden terror and lunacy, German Jews had to learn to live and then to die.

The dilemma of the victim was how to cope with a fitful, inconsistent persecutor who dangled his victim in all possible ways before the end, and who occasionally let his victim slip away through a fluke, a bribe, a legalism, an intervention. Above all, the Nazis cultivated the illusion that there would be a way out. Among German Jews, with their traditional regard for official processes and promises, their illusions lasted long and their preparations for escape were slow. The Nazis, of course, contributed to the belief that there would be time.

The policies of the government between 1933 and 1935 fostered a false optimism during the period when German Jews might have saved themselves. Hitler was busy elaborating his dictatorship and the totalitarian state after the bloody purge of June 1934. He fought the churches. For a while, Jews were let alone. Their community and organizational work, in fact, would not have been possible without official toleration. Goebbels himself boasted that the Nazis had made it possible for Jews to pursue their own cultural work. Moreover, there was no financial crackdown on the organized community agencies. This seeming protection contrasted sharply with the measures directed against individual Jews (the boycott action and the effects of the "Aryan paragraph") and further enhanced the illusion that the community would not be sacrificed. Contributing to this mirage was the helpfulness of certain leftover Weimar officials.

In 1934, the government officially revoked the tax-exemption status of major Jewish organizations. By 1936, this repeal was extended to charities. If these measures had been carried out, Jewish community life would have been virtually paralyzed, and synagogues, welfare institutions, schools, hospitals and the Jewish press would have had to stop their activities. But for several years no one bothered to observe these regulations and the lower-level tax authorities continued to apply the principle of nondiscrimination among taxpayers in the Weimar tradition. From 1936 on, the Nazi director of the German Finance Ministry, Fritz Reinhardt, pressed for compliance, but his pressure was not effective until the radical Nazis dominated all levels of government. This came only after the Munich Pact.

The first blow to the *Reichsvertretung* and its associated agencies came on March 28, 1938: Jewish communities and associations were deprived of their position as public bodies. On the following day they were deprived of their tax-exemption status. These laws hampered the activity of the *Reichsvertretung*; it now had to depend more and more on outside help.

The once rich Jewish community—in 1933, Jewish communal assets were estimated at 300 million reichsmarks—could meet only one third of its budget; the rest had to be made up by the American Joint Distribution Committee.

The first frontal attack on all individual Jews in Germany came in September 1935, with the passage of the Nuremberg Laws. Up to this time, some Jews were persecuted, hounded and beaten up. These excesses were officially deprecated, but they were also excused as the "irrepressible" reaction of Germans to years of alien—that is, Jewish—domination. In the new Germany, the Nazis said, there would be no excuse for illegality. The natural feelings of the people would be given "legal" expression. The boycott of April 1 and the book burnings were thus "legal." For two years the Nazis cultivated this policy, with careful attention to outside reactions. By 1935, the Nazis became bolder and felt convinced that no international action threatened them. The Nuremberg Laws were the result. These measures reduced the entire Jewish population of Germany to twentieth-century helots.

The Nazi bureaucrats in the Interior Ministry had brooded over these laws for some time. The stumbling block was the problem of how to define a Jew. This was exactly the problem that had blocked the anti-Semitic members of the Reichstag in the 1890's from proposing an anti-Semitic law. Who is a Jew? In the Nuremberg Laws, the Jew was defined negatively as someone ineligible to German citizenship. The law provided that only persons of "German or related blood" could be citizens, and that citizenship was acquired by a grant of a certificate of citizenship. This was called the "Law Respecting Reich Citizenship of September 15, 1935." Jews were thus robbed of their citizenship and became Staatsangehörige, subjects belonging to the state. The second law, the "Law for the Protection of German Blood and German Honor" of the same date forbade marriage and sexual relations between Jews and Germans and imposed heavy penalties for transgressions. Jews were also forbidden to employ German female servants under forty-five years of age and were forbidden to display the German flag. Thirteen supplementary decrees which followed delineate the whole course of Hitler's anti-Jewish war down to the last decree, which was published July 1, 1943, when the Reich was theoretically purged of Jews.

The pretext for the Nuremberg Laws was Hitler's anger at an organized Jewish protest against a film being shown in Berlin. After the laws were passed, Hitler said that now the Jews could lead their own lives as they could in no other country. In a conversation on September 23, 1935, between Dr. Hjalmar Schacht, Acting Minister of Economics, and a representative of President Roosevelt, S. R. Fuller, at the American Embassy in Berlin, Schacht interpreted the Nuremberg Laws for the American representative. He first pointed out the "international character" of Jews and Roman Catholics which constituted a domestic problem in many countries insufficiently understood elsewhere. When Fuller questioned him closely about the poor treatment of the Jews under the Nuremberg Laws, Schacht said: "I never was in favor of our treatment of the Jews, but the new laws announced at Nürnberg give protection to the Jews. They are now guaranteed the same rights as any other minority within Germany, such as Poland, for instance." He further explained that they could engage in their businesses with government protection.[10] This was a typical Nazi rationalization.

The Nuremberg Laws were a triumph for the extremists among the Nazis and marked a sharp progression toward an irreversible anti-Jewish policy. No Jew could thereafter escape the sweeping dragnet of intensified persecution. As the definition of Jew was elaborated, the victim became a helpless target for whatever seized the Nazi mind. The Jews of Germany withered under these new blows but did not dream that they were a mere prelude to destruction.

The administrative regulations which followed the Nuremberg Laws were based on the definition of "non-Aryan descent" first described in the decree of April 7, 1933. A person of "non-Aryan descent" was someone who had a Jewish parent or grandparent. But the Nazis were not satisfied. Were half or quarter-Jews as dangerous an influence as three-quarter or full Jews? Serious, casuistic discussions took place. Dr. Kurt Blome, secretary of the Medical Association, and later Deputy Director of the Reich Health Office, proposed that half-Jews be considered Jews because "among half-Jews the Jewish genes are notoriously dominant." This view later became party policy, but the decrees and regulations were written in the Interior Ministry, where the civil service attitude was somewhat different. The Party wanted to combat the part-Jew who was considered a carrier of "Jewish influence," whereas the civil service wanted to protect that part which was German in the part-Jew.

The authors of the final definition were Dr. Wilhelm Stuckart and Dr. Bernhard Lösener. They had to work quickly, inasmuch as the terms "Jew" and "German" had been used in the laws of September 15 and carried criminal sanctions but had not been defined. Lösener rejected the Party's proposal to equate half-Jews with full-Jews. "In principle," he wrote, "the half-Jew should be regarded as a less serious enemy than the full Jew, because in addition to Jewish characteristics, he possesses so many Germanic ones which the full Jew lacks."[11] Lösener also believed that a boycott against half-Jews would be opposed by the German people. There was the further problem of the armed forces, which would be deprived of a potential 45,000 men, and the problem of marriages between

Germans and half-Jews. In view of these difficulties, Lösener proposed that half-Jews be sorted into two groups: one, those who had a Jewish religious affiliation or those married to Jews; and two, those who were not affiliated or were married to non-Jews.

These proposals were incorporated into the First Regulation to the Reich Citizenship Law, issued on November 14, 1935. In this regulation, the Jew is defined as someone descended from at least three Jewish grandparents or from two if: (a) he belonged to the Jewish religious community on September 15, 1935, or later; (b) he was married to a Jew as of that date or later; (c) he was the offspring of a marriage contracted with a three-quarter or full-Jew after September 15, 1935.

Despite their racist slogans, in the last analysis the Nazis had to resort to religious criteria in defining a Jew. But they now had their definition, a solution to a problem that had defied an earlier generation of anti-Semites. This definition appears to be a relatively harmless measure in the light of what was to come. No Jew was physically harmed by it. But it had a much greater built-in danger than any act of Nazi violence, or even the riots of 1938. For the definition was the first of a chain of measures, one leading to another, escalating in severity and leading ultimately to the annihilation of western European Jewry. The Nazi bureaucrats in 1935 did not blueprint the destruction, but the beginning definition was crucial. Once a Jew was defined and described, he could be expropriated, isolated, ghettoized and exterminated.

The Nazis built on the old foundations of European anti-Semitism, but did much more than carry on terrible pogroms on a vaster scale. They set in motion an inexorable process of ever-accelerating destructiveness and did nothing to stop it. Earlier pogroms had been stopped short of total destruction. Under the compulsion of their own inner destructiveness and the temptation to carry their racist ideology to the literal limit, the Nazis moved from one measure to another, daring each time to plumb new depths of their will to enact their dogma. The Nuremberg Laws were the beginning. Hundreds of edicts followed, each leading to more drastic exclusion of Jews from the general community, economic misery and helplessness. Each successive blow was believed by the Jews to be the last, particularly since lulls almost always followed drastic measures. The victims did not remain in one position for long, and the changes were always for the worse, but no Jew in 1935 could foresee the end of this disintegrating process, as indeed no Nazi could.

The visible effects of the Nuremberg Laws were in themselves devastating. Jews became pariahs in German life by government decree. The ban on intermarriage and sexual relations between Aryans and Jews led to poisoned social relations. "Race defilement is worse than murder" became the new commandment for many Germans. The depraved Streicher's

Der Stürmer suffused the minds of millions of readers with horror and fear of Jews and gave rise to easy blackmail schemes. Many Jews were brazenly accused—with no evidence—of having sexual relations with Aryan women. A casual public encounter between a Jew and Aryan could lead to the arrest of the Jew and confiscation of his business. The rantings about blood and honor were often only a front for brutal robbery of Jewish property. Furthermore, as the orders and actions of the Gestapo were no longer subject to judicial review, Jews were now at the mercy of the police, their racial lusts and their greed. The rubric of race defilement did not end with the physical being of the Jew; his animals were also a source of evil. Village councils forbade Jews the use of the community bull for their cows; veterinarians refused to clip dogs owned by Jews. German children were also pulled into the Nazi subworld. Years of indoctrination and exposure to brutality had desensitized them. As the Jew was now officially the State Enemy, they plunged eagerly into barbarous cruelties against Jewish children. If their better instincts shrank at these excesses, they blamed themselves and were ashamed of their weakness.

The Nuremberg Laws also deprived Jews of political rights and economic normalcy. They could not vote or hold public office. Jewish editors, musicians, artists and writers had already been excluded from the guilds. Dismissals of Jewish workers from business and industry soon followed. Most of the five thousand Jewish civil servants in Germany had been dismissed under the law of April 7, 1933. The rest, with the exception of teachers in Jewish schools, were chiefly Jews who had served in the government since August 1, 1914, or Jews who had fought in World War I. Under a decree issued on May 21, 1935, only those of Aryan descent could serve in the armed forces. The subsequent definition of Jew enabled the War Ministry to conscript *Mischlinge* Jews (half-Jews who were not affiliated with the Jewish religion or who were not married to Jews). Jews, as defined in the November 14 regulation, however, could not serve. Any remaining Jewish civil servants still employed in 1935 were removed by the end of the year.

The Jews of Germany had only spiritual armament with which to fight the Nuremberg Laws. Dr. Baeck composed a special prayer for the somber Yom Kippur service in 1935 which followed their passage. "We stand before our God," the prayer read. "With the same courage with which we confess our sins, individual and collective, we shall declare with deep aversion that the lies against us, and the defamation of our religion and its teachings, are far beneath our dignity. We stand by our faith and our fate. . . . We stand before our God. . . . Before Him we bow, but we stand upright before men. . . ."

Dr. Otto Hirsch, director of the *Reichsvertretung*, distributed copies of the prayer to all synagogues in Germany to be read. As a result, both he and Dr. Baeck were arrested and confined in the S.S. prison in Columbia House. Both men suffered frequent arrest and Dr. Hirsch, intermittent tortures. In 1941, he was sent to Mauthausen concentration camp and murdered.

There was no official decree at this time directing firms to dismiss their Jewish personnel, but Party pressure and propaganda were strongly persuasive. Each company made its own decision about its Jews. Long-term contracts at first created legal difficulties, but the courts generally upheld dismissals through the usual route of rationalization. Characteristic is a case decided by the highest court in Germany, the *Reichsgericht*, in 1936. A German movie company claimed that it had the right to fire a Jewish stage manager with whom it had a long-term contract because of a clause terminating employment in case of "sickness, death, or similar causes rendering the stage manager's work impossible." The court held that the clause was applicable without qualification on the ground that the "racial characteristics" of the plaintiff amounted to sickness and death. In the thinking of Germany's highest judges, the Jews had already ceased to be living organisms.

Some firms transferred their Jewish personnel abroad, but invariably transfers were gradually reduced. As dismissals gained momentum, the conditions under which Jews were fired became harsher. Severance pay settlements and pensions were progressively reduced. Later, a decree of June 14, 1938, precipitated the firing of Jewish directors and managers. Under this decree, the Interior Ministry defined "Jewish enterprise" as any business owned by a Jew or having a Jewish legal representative or board member. By the end of the year, these dismissals were compulsory.

However, none of these measures touched what the Nazis considered the citadels of "Jewish domination," the independent Jewish stores and businesses. (In fact, the percentage of Jews in commerce in Germany was 3.3 percent of the total population.) The taking over of Jewish business establishments by German owners was called "Aryanization" (*Arisierung*). It was this process more than any other which destroyed the capacity of Jews in Germany to survive economically, for over 60 percent of the Jewish population earned a living as independent owners of stores and businesses. The first phase of Aryanization, from January 1933 to November 1938, was a period of so-called voluntary Aryanization; transfers of ownership were supposedly based on voluntary agreements. The second phase, following the November pogroms, was a period of compulsory Aryanization. However, no sale of Jewish property under the Nazi regime was based on a freely negotiated contract. Jews were under pressure to sell. The longer they chose to wait, the greater the pressure and the smaller the compensation. The Nazis also aimed at cutting off Jewish-owned companies from their customers by anti-Jewish boycotts, and from their suppliers through allocation measures.[12] The boycott of April 1, 1933, planned to fan "popular" hostility against the Jews, was later widened to include boycott action by civil servants, government agencies, suppliers and "loyal" Germans. Under such pressures, many Jewish-owned businesses sold out.

Early in 1938 there was some difficulty in finding enough German buyers for the remaining Jewish-owned businesses. The German Economy Ministry stepped in to force price levels down by requiring official approval of all contracts for the transfer of a business from a Jew to a German. In this process, the value of trademarks, goodwill, pending contracts, and any other factors enhancing the value of the enterprise were eliminated. On April 26, 1938, the Interior Ministry ordered all Jews to register all property in excess of 5,000 reichsmarks (about $2,000). There followed a decree defining "Jewish enterprise." With these preliminary measures, compulsory Aryanization began.

By the end of 1937, the Jew in Germany had no civil rights. He was not a citizen. He could not vote or attend a political meeting. He had no liberty of speech and could not defend himself in print. He could not be employed as a civil servant, or work as a writer, artist, musician or actor before the Aryan public. He could not teach or work in a public hospital or belong to any professional organization. If he were starving, he could receive no aid from the *Winterhilfe* organization. If he owned a business, his livelihood had either vanished or was in danger of evaporating. He was denied food and drugs in certain stores. He had to face the day-by-day ostracism of his neighbors and friends. Emigration was his only answer.

During 1937, 23,000 Jews left Germany, bringing the total number who had left since 1933 to 129,000. This represented a little over one fourth of the Jewish population of Germany in 1933. In the following year, 1938, conditions worsened and the urgency to leave Germany became sharper. But the opportunities diminished.

5 The Year 1938

THE EVENTS OF 1938, which mark the great divide between emigration and annihilation of European Jewry, must be understood in the context of the Nazi consolidation of power in Germany and Hitler's foreign policy aims. By this time the Gestapo had become part of the S.S. and the S.S. was in control of important levers of power. Convinced that his regime was now firmly established, Hitler decided that the time had come to reveal his secret intentions to trusted military and political leaders.[1] This he did at a meeting on November 5, 1937, which has become known as the "Hossbach-Protokol," from the name of the man who kept minutes, Hitler's military adjutant Friedrich Hossbach. At this meeting Hitler announced that he aimed at war, first against Austria, then Czechoslovakia. A few months later, in February 1938, he eliminated two top-ranking generals who opposed his war plans and swept Konstantin von Neurath out of the Foreign Ministry, replacing him with a Party man, the shallow and compliant Joachim von Ribbentrop. Hitler's decision to go to war, the subsequent Nazi occupation of Europe and the long ordeal of war made helpless victims of Europe's Jews. Each Nazi oppression thereafter diminished the possibilities of either escape or resistance.

The two generals who were eliminated were Werner von Blomberg, Minister of War, and Werner von Fritsch, Commander in Chief of the Army. The fall of these men and the subsequent reorganization of the High Command of the Wehrmacht broke the power of the officers' corps and reduced it to a leaderless, divided and impotent condition. Hitler then took over direct personal command of the entire Wehrmacht, and the Wehrmacht thereafter became a victim of Hitler's uncanny triumphs in 1938—the Anschluss and Munich.

In the background of this development was the vaulting ambition of Himmler and the jealousy of Göring. Himmler sought Fritsch's downfall because Fritsch stood in the way of expansion of the armed S.S. units, the Waffen S.S. In Fritsch's view, these units threatened the status and power of the Wehrmacht as the "sole arms bearer of the Reich." Himmler also saw compulsory military service as a dangerous and unwelcome break in the Nazi Party's relentless drive to capture the allegiance of German youth. Hitler, who fundamentally hated the officers' elite anyhow, backed Himmler. Blomberg was Göring's quarry: he was jealous of Blomberg's promotion to *Generalfeldmarschall*. Once again, the Himmler-Göring combination proved to be too mighty for the opposition.

Either Himmler or Göring gave Hitler a dossier on Fritsch faking a sordid accusation of homosexuality against him. Blomberg had recently married a woman with a dubious past. Rumors of this mésalliance were fanned into a scandal. Both men withdrew from active army activity although both reputations were later rehabilitated—but not until after Hitler's annexation of Austria. The Fritsch-Blomberg affair paved the way for the annexation of Austria and the subjugation of Czechoslovakia.

Subsequently, Hitler made no pretense of his contempt for the Wehrmacht, for he no longer had to cultivate its allegiance as in the early years. Certain Army leaders were to make further efforts to stop his reckless military gambles—the opportunities as well as the attempts were many— but they never succeeded.

This period coincides with a sharpening Nazi policy toward the Jews of Germany. Their situation became progressively more exposed as the year wore on. A storm of decrees fell upon them. Early in January they were required to change their names. So-called "Jewish" names and the addition of "Israel" and "Sarah" became compulsory by August. In March, the legal recognition of Jewish community bodies was abolished. This meant they not only lost their tax-exemption status but also lost their legal right to impose taxes on members. There followed the property registration order in April and the drawing up of lists of well-to-do Jews in police precincts and revenue offices. A clause in the registration regulation was soon to be exploited for large-scale confiscation of Jewish property. The clause read: "The authority in charge of the Four-Year Plan [Göring] may take the necessary steps to ensure the utilization of the property which has to be registered for the needs of the German economy." The supervision of Jewish religious communities, the *Kehillot*, was tranferred from the central Gestapo office to the local Gestapo (Stapo) commands.

Some measures remained concealed from the Jews. In June, four different lists were prepared for sweeping mass arrests, one at the tax offices, one at the local police stations, one at the criminal department of the police, and one at the Gestapo commands. The "June Action" (*Juniaktion*) quickly followed in Germany. First, on June 9, the Great Synagogue of Munich was destroyed on the personal order of Hitler. Then followed the destruction of the synagogues in Nuremberg and Dortmund. On June 15, the lists of Jewish names were put to use. Fifteen hundred Jews were arrested throughout Germany. These were termed "asocials" by the Nazis. Their "crimes" were mostly minor infractions of the law such as parking violations. The victims were sent to concentration camps and were released only on condition that they emigrate at once. On June 28, in Berlin a journalist, Bella Fromm, witnessed these events:

> The entire Kurfuerstendamm was plastered with scrawls and cartoons. "Jew" was smeared all over the doors, windows and walls in waterproof colors. It grew worse as we came to the part of the town where poor little Jewish retail shops were to be found. The S.A. had created havoc. Everywhere were revolting and bloodthirsty pictures of Jews beheaded, hanged, tortured and maimed, accompanied by obscene inscriptions. Windows were smashed, and loot from the miserable little shops was strewn over the sidewalk.[2]

Meanwhile, the German absorption of Austria in March 1938 was yielding handsome profits. Toward the end of May, mass arrests of Jews to facilitate spoliation and hasten emigration were being reported by the American chargé d'affaires in Vienna and Adolf Eichmann was perfecting his "Center for the Emigration of Jews"—a device which plundered and expelled Jews simultaneously.

During the summer of 1938, an international failure further strengthened Hitler's hand. As their life became increasingly unbearable, German Jews strained to leave the country. Many were now stripped of their resources, and had to depend on Jewish welfare agencies. The plight of the Jews, while considered an internal affair of Germany, could not be completely ignored. A High Commission for Refugees from Germany had been created by the League of Nations but had proved ineffectual. (James MacDonald, the Commissioner, had resigned in protest against the Nuremberg Laws and the subsequent inaction of international diplomacy.) A large, worldwide forum representing thirty-two nations was called at Evian, France, in July 1938. The Jews of the world had great hopes for the conference, particularly as it had been called at the initiative of President Roosevelt. American leadership in an international effort to find new homes for refugees was looked upon as a promising omen of a change in American immigration policy. On this question, the past years had been extremely bleak. Very few Jews had been admitted to the United States between January 1933 and June 1938—a total of only 27,000 in six years, although the annual German immigration quota was 25,957.[3] Under American law, unused quotas of previous years could not be utilized in subsequent years. The restrictions imposed by American consuls were also severe. A new policy was hoped for. But the warmth of the President's call was soon punctured by a curious nullifier issued by the American State Department: "No country," the State Department declared, "would be expected to make any change in its immigration legislation."

No nation did. The United States, however, promised to admit the full quota of German immigrants. Areas of questionable settlement possibilities such as British Guiana, Madagascar, Kenya and Alaska were suggested, but no concrete plans were put forward. A sixty-five-year-old Viennese Jew, Dr. Heinrich Neumann, was released from a concentration camp and sent by the Reich Governor in Vienna to the conference with a secret proposal.[4] He was to inform the delegates that the Nazis were prepared to allow the emigration of Jews at $250 per head, or a flat rate of $1,000 per family. The mission was odious to the man, but he went to Evian, hoping to rescue at least some German and Austrian Jews.

However, the delegates were not sufficiently interested in any concrete plans, nor did they have the necessary indignation to overcome existing difficulties. Many, nevertheless, passed moral judgment on the Germans as blackmailers. Some from Latin America admitted that their governments would be unwilling to accept Jews because of possible retaliatory economic sanctions by Germany. There was a great flow of oratory and bustling committee meetings amid the numerous squabbles, but a very plain fact soon unfolded: no country was willing to open its doors to Jews. The words of the Zionist leader, Chaim Weizmann, addressed to the Palestine Royal Commission in 1936, were prophetic: "Today almost six million Jews are doomed to be pent up in places where they are not wanted, and for whom the world is divided into places where they cannot live, and places into which they cannot enter."

A Jewish delegate has described the atmosphere of dejection:

When the old trees of Evian cast their evening shadows over Lake Geneva and the bright lights of the Casino shone across the serene waters, I was overcome with grief and despair over the situation. . . . All our work would soon be ended by a policy of *sauve-qui peut.* The course which the Evian Conference was taking, the undue haste in which the representatives of the Jewish organizations had to present their remarks on their memoranda before the President of the Conference—because about thirty delegates could, obviously, not be heard in detail—was a tragedy whose certain end was destruction. The gates had been closed before us.[5]

The conference was over in a week.

One particularly ominous chord was struck at Evian by the Swiss representative, Dr. Heinrich Rothmund, a former chief of the Swiss Federal Police. Rothmund spoke about the threatening refugee "inundation" of Switzerland after the German occupation of Austria. Three or four thousand refugees had already crossed the frontier, Rothmund reported. In their flight, these Jews had taken advantage of a German-Swiss agreement abolishing visa requirements for either side. Later, there was another wave of immigrants, and Swiss authorities interned some at Dupulsau; others were shunted back to the Reich. Rothmund threatened that unless the flow stopped, "Switzerland, which has as little use for these Jews as has Germany, will herself take measures to protect Switzerland from being swamped by the Jews with the connivance of the Viennese police." The "inundation" continued; on a single day, forty-seven Jews arrived in Basel. The Swiss quickly increased their police guards and patrols at the Austrian frontier, on the mountain passes, and at Basel.

The Swiss then set a new machinery in motion. They insisted that visa controls be resumed or that special passports be issued to German Jews showing that their bearers were Jews. The Germans carried this suggestion to its full limit. On September 29, Germany decided to mark all passports of its Jews, regardless of their destination. The negotiations with the Swiss had disastrous consequences. A Reich decree of October 5 followed, requiring all German passports of Jews to be stamped with a large red "J." Passports of Jews residing abroad were to be similarly stamped. Officials began to compile lists of Jews who did not present their passports for marking. These regulations formed part of an elaborate system of document-stamping and identification of Jews which later made them easy prey for Nazi officials. German Jews living outside the Reich were not immune. The identification system was extended to thousands of Jews who had emigrated to countries that were later occupied by the Germans. As a further Nazi control, by the end of 1938, every Jew in the Reich had to have an identification card available to officials at all times.

Public opinion, meanwhile, had to be prepared for these harsh measures and more to come. The whirlwind was self-feeding. The outrages in June were only a beginning. Hitler needed more riots, and Göring and Goebbels needed them too. All were preparing for war, each in his own sphere. Yet the German people were not ready. In Berlin, for example, in the hours before the September conference in Munich, gloom pervaded the city. The marching columns of the Wehrmacht left the people coldly indifferent. "With such a people," Hitler had observed, "one cannot go to war." In truth, the German people had acclaimed Chamberlain an emissary of peace. When the news of the Munich settlement first came in, a wave of relief swept the city. Few Germans were thinking of "Sudeten Germany." They would have to be stirred up in time, but for a while their attention had to be diverted from the idea of war. The November riots of Kristallnacht, The Night of the Broken Glass, served both purposes.

A pretext for the riots was found in the slaying of a German official by a Jewish youth, Herschel Grynszpan. Grynszpan killed the man in a desperate act to avenge his parents' suffering during their deportation from Germany to Poland. The youth's father, Zindel, had come to Germany from Poland in 1911. He opened a grocery store in Hanover and remained there, but did not apply for naturalization. In the fall of 1938, when the

German government ordered the expulsion of former Polish nationals to Poland, Zindel Grynszpan was probably unaware of such an order. At the Eichmann trial in Jerusalem, he recalled the expulsion:

> On the twenty-seventh of October, 1938—it was a Thursday night—at eight o'clock, a policeman came and told us to come to Region Eleven [Police headquarters]. He said: "You are going to come back immediately; don't take anything with you, only your passports."

The Grynszpans went, husband and wife, a son and a daughter. When they arrived at the police station, they saw a large number of people, some sitting, some standing and many crying. The police were shouting,

> "Sign, sign, sign!" . . . I had to sign; all of them did. One of us did not. His name, I believe was Gershon Silber, and he had to stand in a corner for twenty-four hours. They took us to the concert hall, and . . . there were people from all over town, about six hundred people. There we stayed until Friday night, about twenty-four hours, yes, until Friday night. . . . Then they took us in police trucks, in prisoners' lorries, about twenty men in each truck, and they took us to the railroad station. The streets were black with people shouting: "*Juden raus* to Palestine!" . . . They took us by train to Neubenschen, on the German-Polish border. It was Shabbat morning when we arrived there, six o'clock in the morning. There came trains from all sorts of places, from Leipzig, Cologne, Düsseldorf, Essen, Biederfeld, Bremen. Together we were about twelve thousand people. . . . It was the Shabbat, the twenty-ninth of October. . . . When we reached the border we were searched to see if anybody had any money, and anybody who had more than ten marks—the balance was taken away. This was the German law, no more than ten marks could be taken out of Germany. The Germans said, "You didn't bring any more with you when you came; you can't take out any more!"

They walked a little over a mile to the Polish border where the Germans planned to smuggle them into Polish territory.

> The S.S. men were whipping us, those who lingered they hit, and blood was flowing on the road. They tore away our suitcases from us. They treated us in a most brutal way. This was the first time that I had seen the wild brutality of the Germans. They shouted at us, "Run! Run!" I was hit and fell into the ditch. My son helped me, and he said: "Run, Father, run, or you'll die!"
>
> When we got to the open border . . . the women went in first. The Poles knew nothing. They called a Polish general and some officers who examined our papers, and they saw that we were Polish citizens, that we had special passports. It was decided to let us enter. They took us to a village of about six thousand people and we were twelve thousand. The rain was driving hard, people were fainting—on all sides one saw old men and women. Our suffering was great. There was no food; since Thursday we had not eaten.[6]

They were now in Zbonszyn where they were taken to a military camp and put in stables.

This forced expulsion was Heydrich's first deportation.

From Zbonszyn, Grynszpan wrote to his son Herschel, who had gone to live with an uncle in Paris. The boy, pained by the news of his parents' deportation and hoping to shock the world into action in behalf of Jews, determined to shoot the German ambassador in Paris. He went to the embassy, but was sidetracked to the counselor, Ernst vom Rath. When vom Rath asked him what he wanted, he fired at him and two days later, vom Rath died.

There followed the pogroms of *Kristallnacht*, an orgy of arson, property destruction and murder of Jews on a scale not yet experienced in Hitler Germany. The German press called these actions a "spontaneous demonstration of the German people" reacting to the news of the murder of vom Rath, but they were actually planned and guided by Heydrich.

On the evening of November 9, Goebbels had notified Party chiefs who had gathered in Munich to celebrate the Beerhall putsch that anti-Jewish demonstrations, including destruction of shops and synagogues, were to be organized and carried out by the Party. However, the Party must not appear to have instigated the actions. These instructions were immediately telephoned to the provinces by the Party chiefs. The key figure, however, was Heydrich, who now controlled the S.D., the Gestapo and the Criminal Police. At 1:20 A.M. on November 10, he flashed an urgent teletype message to all headquarters and stations of the Police and S.D., instructing them to get together with Party and S.S. leaders "to discuss the organization of the demonstrations." In his instructions, Heydrich ordered the burning down of synagogues so long as German life and property were not endangered. Business and private apartments of Jews were to be destroyed and police were not to hinder the demonstrators. Further, he ordered "in all districts, as many Jews, especially rich ones . . . to be arrested as can be accommodated in existing prisons. For the time being, only healthy men, not too old, are to be arrested. Upon their arrest, the appropriate concentration camps should be contacted immediately in order to confine them in these camps as fast as possible."[7] The "folk instinct" had been carefully plotted and directed, but in many places it was released before vom Rath died.

The teletyped instructions were carried out thoroughly throughout Germany and Austria. In summarizing the results of the action to Göring, Heydrich reported that 815 shops, 171 homes and 76 synagogues were destroyed; 36 Jews were killed, and 36 seriously injured; 191 synagogues were set on fire. However, according to Heydrich, these "figures given must have been exceeded considerably" as the reports were made urgently. Some 20,000 Jews were arrested and sent to concentration camps, Buchenwald chiefly.

Reports of the observed violence were filed by foreign representatives.

The American Consul General in Berlin reported that early in the morning of November 10, synagogues in Württemberg, Baden and Hohenzollern were set on fire by well-disciplined and apparently well-equipped young men in civilian clothes. He had also received reports that synagogues in Stuttgart, Karlsruhe, Freiburg, Heidelberg and Heilbronn had also been put to flame.[8] Doors had been forced open and the furniture drenched with petrol. The American consul in the Leipzig district learned that the plan of "spontaneous indignation" leaked out in Leipzig several hours before news of vom Rath's death was broadcast. Gestapo contacts in Leipzig spent most of that night drawing up lists of fated victims. Knowing in advance what was to happen, many stayed up to witness the actions.

Local crowds looked on the destruction benumbed and aghast. An American witness has described the scene in Leipzig:

> Jewish dwellings were smashed into and the contents demolished or looted. In one of the Jewish sections, an eighteen-year-old boy was hurled from a three-story window to land with both legs broken on a street littered with burning beds and other household furniture. . . . Jewish shop windows by the hundreds were systematically and wantonly smashed throughout the city at a loss estimated at several millions of marks. . . . The main streets of the city were a positive litter of shattered plate glass. . . . The debacle was executed by SS men and Storm Troopers, not in uniform, each group having been provided with hammers, axes, crowbars and incendiary bombs.[9]

There was no attempt to quench the fire except where non-Jewish property was involved. Many Jews were thrown into a stream that flows through the city zoo. S.S. men commanded horrified spectators to spit, jeer and defile them with mud.

The timing of the Crystal Night pogroms is significant. Pretexts for anti-Jewish actions were never in short supply in Nazi Germany. There had even been an earlier assassination of a Nazi by a Jew. In February 1936, David Frankfurter, a Jewish youth, had killed the Nazi Gauleiter in Switzerland, Wilhelm Gustloff, but there were no serious repercussions at the time. The destructiveness of November 1938 could be dared and carried off because now Hitler had nothing to fear—from Germans, from Jews, or from the world. His successes were dazzling enough to give triumphant assurance to any intuition or excess. In the spring of 1936 he had carried out the military occupation of the demilitarized Rhineland without opposition. In the summer of the same year, Berlin was host to the Olympic games and visitors from the Western world marveled at the prosperity and well-being of the Germans. In 1937, the Rome-Berlin axis was forged while both partners were expanding their military power. The world watched. In 1938, Germany absorbed Austria without hindrance and bullied the Western powers into sacrificing Czechoslovakia at Munich. The Evian Conference in July had failed dismally to provide refuge for the harassed Jews of Germany. Hitler could dare to go on to ever more radical pitches of destruction. There was nothing to stop him. The Jewish leadership in Germany tried gallantly to grasp the whirlwind.

The *Reichsvertretung* was shut down on November 11 and occupied by the Gestapo, but officials made efforts to contact government offices. Dr. Baeck, the president, and Dr. Otto Hirsch, the director, tried to see Dr. Meissner, the State Secretary in the Reich Chancellery, but the attempt was futile. Another effort was made to speak to contacts in the Ministry of the Interior. This also failed. Himmler's S.S. had cut these last lines. One final link remained with the Foreign Ministry. Ernst Marcus, the director of Paltreu Company, attempted an indirect approach.[10] He called Werner Otto von Hentig, the head of the Oriental Department, by public phone and was granted an interview immediately. At the Foreign Ministry building, in the small waiting room, an old servant greeted Marcus and expressed open revulsion at events. S.S. men, meanwhile, paraded up and down the corridors. Hentig, too, expressed his shame, and willingly used his influence, at great personal risk, to protest a fresh action from starting. Marcus had heard that Goebbels planned to organize a procession of Jewish men through Berlin under S.A. escort and that other degrading individual Party actions were being planned. Hentig interceded with Under-Secretary of State Ernst von Weizsäcker, pointing out the detrimental effects of the riots on German foreign policy. Goebbels' plans (he was Gauleiter of Berlin as well as propaganda chief) were not destined to come off, but not because of von Hentig's well-intentioned efforts. Hentig, however, did secure the release of the arrested members of the *Reichsvertretung* and other Jewish functionaries from concentration camps.

The Jewish leaders were able to use only one additional lever—the "pipe transaction"[11]—in their attempt to moderate the havoc of November 9–10. This involved a large-scale transfer of steel pipe to Palestine by *Stahl Union*, the German Steel Combine—a transaction made possible by the *Ha'avara* agreement, a modified clearing agreement between the German government and the Jewish Agency for Palestine.* About £120,000 were at stake. The Steel Combine were very anxious to sell their pipes which had been produced to specification. The pipe transfer had been approved, but Palestine refused to make payment because of Nazi persecutions. Gregor Segall, an assistant to Marcus, approached the Foreign Currency Department in the Ministry for Economics and explained that the work of the transfer agency, Paltreu, was being hampered. Jewish employees of the agency were being detained in camps, and there was no money with which to operate because Jewish bank accounts had been blocked. If the govern-

* Representative Jewish body officially recognized to deal with Great Britain on matters affecting Jews in Palestine during the British Mandate.

ment wished the agency to continue, funds and workers would have to be released. The director of the Combine also spoke to the ministry and the transfer was cleared. Employees from Paltreu, including Marcus, were released from camps.

The Paltreu office was one of the few Jewish offices left intact after the November actions. It was actually able to complete several dozen transfers to Palestine and to process a number of emigration certificates before it was closed down.

The immunity of Paltreu to the November wave of destruction is a typical instance of the mechanical Nazi adherence to orders. Legally, Paltreu was an "Aryan" company, although its personnel was as completely Jewish as was its business. Its capital, however, was split in such a way that in the eyes of the law, it was considered an Aryan enterprise. Paltreu shares belonged to the banking houses of Wassermann and Warburg, which had already been Aryanized, and to the Anglo-Palestine Bank which, inasmuch as it was a foreign firm, was considered neutral. In the registers of Jewish firms drawn up in the summer of 1938, Paltreu was not among them. Jewish shops had been quite methodically wrecked on the basis of these lists. Paltreu was immune.[12]

All Jewish political organizations were disbanded after November 10, but the *Reichsvertretung* was allowed to resume work. The emigration department of the Palestine Office (a division of the Jewish Agency) and the *Hilfsverein der deutschen Juden* (German Jewish Relief Association), as parts of the *Reichsvertretung*, were also allowed to continue. However, in typically irrational fashion, the Nazis arrested the very Jews they needed—those employed by the *Hilfsverein*, the primary emigration agency. As a consequence, no Jew was inclined to take a position with the *Hilfsverein* after the November pogroms and Jewish emigration suffered. Then, less than a month later, Jewish emigration officials were told that they themselves were forbidden to emigrate because mass emigration of Jews would be slowed down if they left. The experiences of some who were arrested also suggest that the Gestapo was not yet altogether clear about its objectives. One survivor has described this inside confusion:

The officers who had come to arrest me had no instructions on exceptional cases; they only had to deliver a certain number of Jews. When they failed to find someone, or were unable to take him along, another had to be arrested in his stead. . . . After many hours of waiting in the Police Presidium Charlottenburg, Am Kaiserdamm, we reached the Police Prison Alexanderplatz at about 8 o'clock. It was quite clear that neither the officers who had made the arrests nor the officials in the Police Presidium had the slightest idea of what they should do with us. They were confused and telephoned in our presence for further instructions.[13]

The *Hilfsverein* and *Reichsvertretung* employees were not alone in bewilderment at their world gone berserk. The *Kulturbund* was ordered to reopen on November 20.

Benno Cohn, a survivor, has recalled the summons to see Hinkel on Saturday, November 12. Cohn was summoned in his capacity as chairman of the *Kulturbund*. Dr. Singer and several other active members were also called. "Herr Hinkel received us standing, with his entire staff," Cohn recalled.

> After a deliberate pause, he told us: "In the name of the Reich Minister for Propaganda, I have to inform you of the following:
>
> 1. Jews are forbidden henceforth to attend German theatres and concerts;
> 2. The Cultural Organization must resume its activities as from the 20th of the month and present a repeat performance of its latest play."
>
> Our surprise left us speechless. Then Singer said quietly: "Herr Reichskulturwalter, the Jews of Germany at present have quite other desires than going to the theatre. Tens of thousands are detained in concentration camps. The producer is under arrest. Do you believe that Jews will go to the theatre at the risk of being jailed?"
>
> Hinkel consulted his Nazi assistants. Then he gave his answer: "I will immediately issue all instructions to enable you to start on time. You must give the performance. Submit a list of the actors who will take part."
>
> Cohn asked if he would please discuss the situation created by the riots, but Hinkel expressed his regrets. "I am sorry; my mission is confined to the field of culture."[14]

On Monday, November 14, four days after the pogrom, the *Jüdischer Kulturbund* staff was called to a meeting. A survivor has recalled that morning:

> The meeting on that Monday morning was ghostlike. The smoke was still rising from the burnt synagogues and the debris of the pogrom lay in the streets. Ring up the curtain! The Jews must go on play-acting! A wave of indignation went through the small gathering. But it would have been suicidal to resist the order and, what is more, there was the opportunity to free imprisoned colleagues. . . . Only the choice of the opening play was left for them to decide.
>
> Julius Bab, in a recalcitrant mood, suggested *Charley's Aunt*—what would better reflect the senselessness of their situation. But such a provocation would not have passed unnoticed and would have defeated its own purpose. Somebody proposed a piece fitting the solemnity of the hour—yet no play could even remotely do justice to the tragic farce they were called upon to perform. In the end, it was agreed to resume the rehearsals so abruptly stopped on November 9, of a Scottish students' play, *The Wind and the Rain*.
>
> The Jewish theater embarked on its last, most unreal epoch. On the first night of *The Wind and the Rain*, the wide sweep of stalls and circles was once more illuminated. Candelabra glowed brightly from the domed ceiling and usherettes in their neat black costumes were posted on the red carpets in the gangways. In innumerable homes, women were waiting for some news

of their arrested husbands and sons; elsewhere, people were sitting among the ruins of their existence. And, in the Jewish theater, the lights went up again. Dressers and wardrobe mistresses scuttled around as usual. Players in dressing rooms hastily put on finishing touches to make-up. No one laughed, talked or even quarrelled.

At 7:25 the first bell rang. Few people had come, mostly women and old folk, and, of course, three men in bowler hats carrying brief cases, the inevitable delegation of the Gestapo. At last the curtain rose and the footlights flooded the stage. There was the parlor in a Scottish boarding house with a fire flickering in the grate. At first, the voices of the players trembled uncertainly as the spotlights fell on their faces, but soon the magic of the stage engulfed them and they played magnificently. They were supposed to be a little tipsy after much champagne at a ball. The gramophone blared a rumba and they laughed and danced, in their world of pretense and make-believe, one week after the pogrom.[15]

This decision of Hinkel cannot altogether be explained today. There are several possibilities. The Nazis may have been surprised by the shock of the civilized world to the November pogroms and may have needed a gesture of "tolerance" as a stratagem. Hinkel had been a civil servant but was in the Ministry of Propaganda by November 1938. His health was already undermined by alcohol; he did not want another assignment. He may have thought that excluding Jews from general theaters and cinemas would add to his own importance as Reich Culture Administrator. The order to reopen the theater may have been made simply to give Nazis a chance to sadistically watch Jews suffer the bitter irony of performing a play in the midst of the shambles. This was done throughout the Holocaust, even outside the gas chambers, when Jews were called on to sing or play the violin before their death. A comparison with the strategy of camouflage used later by the Nazis in the Polish ghettos comes to mind, but does not seem valid. In 1938, the Germans wanted the Jews to leave Germany; they went to great lengths to get rid of them. In 1942, they clearly planned to exterminate them. Deluding the masses in the ghettos facilitated their physical annihilation. During the period following the November rioting, there were still apparently contending views within the Nazi hierarchy. Goebbels, as Propaganda Minister, was still trying to be a decisive voice in making policy on the Jewish question—he had actually called the riots into being. According to one historian, the November action was a bid for power by Goebbels and the Brownshirts (S.A.) who had been overshadowed by the S.S. since the Röhm purge.[16] During the pogroms, the S.S. was not notified until after S.A. forces had been at work for several hours.

There were also forces represented by men like Schacht who wanted slow, orderly measures taken against the Jews, those that would yield maximum economic gain for the state. In the very early period, it is known that a small group within the Nazi Party even looked favorably upon the creation of a Jewish state in Palestine, although wanting the removal of Jews from all positions in German cultural and economic life. Doubtless there were other views which existed briefly until the Gestapo crushed all but its own and assumed control of the Jewish fate in January 1939.

In Berlin, some of the *Reichsvertretung* leaders had seen police and firemen standing idly by while synagogues were burning. No help was offered Jews fleeing their burning stores. It quickly became apparent that the Gestapo was in control. The dazed Jews also learned that some of their colleagues had been taken to the concentration camp at Sachsenhausen. Those who remained at large avoided going home. They met together in attics, clandestine apartments, and in the semidarkness of subways. Dr. Baeck was ordered by the Gestapo to remain at home. Ironically, a few men believed that as soon as Göring returned from Munich, he would intervene to blunt the horror of the night. Göring was thought to be less brutal, more easygoing and jovial than the rest. He liked soft living and even had a certain individual charm. His loyalty and generosity to friends were well known. This illusion was quickly blasted. On the night of November 10, Göring spoke on the radio. "Everything is quite official," he said. "The Jews have to pay a collective fine of one billion marks, twenty percent of their property." Significantly, the Finance Ministry, not the Party was designated as the recipient of the fine.

The fine that Göring referred to was *Sühneleistung*, the "Atonement Payment," imposed on German Jews after vom Rath's assassination as punishment "for their abominable crimes." All Jews who had registered their property under an earlier decree were liable. Two billion reichsmarks of Jewish wealth had already been taken. Five billion remained,* 20 percent of which gave Göring the one billion he demanded. The Finance Ministry collected this money in four installments ending August 15, 1939. As the cash, art objects, foreign exchange and securities began coming in, the Ministry had second thoughts about the 20 percent levy. Another 5 percent was added, payable on November 15, 1939. The final total went over Göring's mark by 126 million marks. This money was fed immediately into the gigantic German rearmament program.

The year 1938 was a year of mobilization for Germany, but there was a critical shortage of funds in the Reich treasury. In a top secret memorandum[17] of a meeting of the Reich Defense Council on November 18, this shortage was revealed. At the meeting, which consisted solely of a three-hour lecture by Göring, he spoke at great length about the "very critical situation of the Reich Exchequer," relieved initially through the

---

* The official rate of exchange was 2.40 reichsmarks for $1.00 but the value of the mark was generally lower.

billion-reichsmark fine imposed on Jews and "through profits accruing to the Reich in the Aryanization of Jewish enterprises."

A full assessment of the results and implications of the events of November 9–10 was made by the Nazis. For this purpose, Göring called a meeting[18] of the Council of Ministers on November 12 in the sumptuous new building of the Ministry of Aviation. Significantly, although Heydrich was not a minister, he was also present. Göring's opening words indicated the comprehensive nature of the meeting. "Today's meeting," he said, "is of decisive importance. I have received a letter which Bormann sent me by order of the Führer, asking that the Jewish question be now, once and for all, treated in its entirety and settled in some way. Yesterday the Führer telephoned me to point out again that decisive measures must be undertaken in a coordinated manner."

Göring concentrated on economic measures: Jews would have to be eliminated completely from the German economy and existing measures would have to be intensified. But he was also concerned about the wasteful destruction of the riots to the economy. "I have had enough of these demonstrations," he said. "They don't harm the Jew, but me, who is the last authority for coordinating the German economy. If today, a Jewish shop is destroyed, if goods are thrown into the street, the insurance company will pay for the damages. . . . It's insane to clean out and burn a Jewish warehouse, then have a German insurance company make good the loss. And the goods which I need desperately, whole bales of clothing and whatnot, are being burned; and I miss them everywhere. I may as well burn the raw materials before they arrive."

An insurance expert was called in and a long technical discussion followed involving the problem of insured damage. Hilgard, the insurance expert, stunned the meeting with the announcement that $6,000,000 worth of plate glass had been shattered, belonging not to Jewish shopkeepers, but to their non-Jewish landlords. The panes were made in Belgium and the amount of damage equaled a half-year's production of the Belgian glass industry. At least $3,000,000 in foreign exchange would have to be produced to import replacements. The total property damage was estimated at 25,000,000 reichsmarks. Heydrich added that the loss in consumer goods, lost taxes and other indirect losses would run into the hundreds of millions. Göring was furious. He told Heydrich that 200 Jews should have been destroyed instead of so much valuable property. Heydrich, however, could report only 36 killed.

The final decisions on these matters dealt more blows on the Jews. All Jewish insurance claims were paid by the insurance companies and then were confiscated by the government. Jewish property owners were then ordered to repair the damage to their property. Uninsured losses, including looted jewelry, furs, and other valuables, remained total losses. Nothing was returned. The Jewish communities were later saddled with clearing the rubble of the streets. Göring gave Hilgard a broad hint that the insurance companies could expect a secret refund from the government on claims paid to insured German property owners.

Heydrich, however, had other things on his mind. Economic details were not the fundamental issue for him. "In spite of the elimination of the Jew from economic life," he said, "the main problem, namely, to kick the Jew out of Germany, remains." He then boasted that the "Center for the Emigration of Jews" in Vienna had already removed 50,000 Jews from Austria, at least 45,000 of them "legally." When Göring asked how this was done, Heydrich explained: "Through the *Kultusgemeinde* [Religious Community Organization], we extracted a certain amount of money from the rich Jews who wanted to emigrate. By paying this amount, and an additional sum in foreign currency, they made it possible for a number of poor Jews to leave. The problem was not to make the rich Jew leave but to get rid of the Jewish mob."

Heydrich then suggested that a similar procedure be set up in the rest of the Reich. This was the mainspring that later set Eichmann's deportation apparatus in motion. Heydrich also had other ideas: he wanted the Jews isolated more and suggested an identifying insignia. "Because of the Aryanizing and other restrictions, Jewry will become unemployed," he predicted. "The remaining Jews will gradually become proletarians. Therefore I shall have to isolate the Jew so that he won't enter into the German normal routine of life." Heydrich then spoke fragmentarily about matters that would soon have life-and-death significance for Jews once he organized his hazy thoughts more carefully. He idly mentioned ghettos and movement controls. When Göring suggested that Jews might have to buy some things from Aryans, Heydrich answered readily, "No, I'd say that for the necessities in daily life, the German won't serve the Jew any more." Göring remonstrated, "One moment, you cannot let them starve. . . . The Jew will have to buy food and stockings." To this Heydrich replied, "We'll have to decide whether we want that or not."

Schwerin von Krosigk, Minister of Finance, and former Rhodes scholar, admitted that ghettos were "not very agreeable," but drew certain conclusions from the tossed remarks of Heydrich: "We'll have to try everything possible, by way of additional exports, to shove the Jews into foreign countries. The decisive factor is that we don't want to keep their proletariat here. That would be a terrible burden. (Frick: "And a danger!") . . . The goal must be, as Heydrich said, 'Clear out what we can.' "

Göring commented that he would not like to be a Jew in Germany. He then ended the meeting on an ominous note: "If in the near future, the German Reich should come into conflict with foreign powers, it goes without saying that we in Germany should first come to a showdown with the Jews. Besides that, the Führer shall now make an attempt with those foreign powers which have brought the Jewish question up to arrive at a solution of the Madagascar question. He explained it to me November 9. He wants to say to the other countries: 'Why are you always talking about the Jews? Take them!' "

Thus was the fate of Jews in the Third Reich bandied about in a free-floating gush of words that lasted for four hours. The consequences were soon to come in massive hammer blows against the despairing and debilitated victims.

After the November riots, economic spoliation was intensified by compulsory Aryanization of Jewish-owned enterprises. A substantial factor in this process was the impatience of the two big ministries—the Finance Ministry and the Economy Ministry—and Göring, who was in charge of the Four-Year Plan, for a bigger share of the spoils.[19] "Voluntary" Aryanization was too slow. Local Nazis were also impatient. In Franconia, Streicher's district, Party officials decided upon their own solution, which Göring later investigated and found highly irregular. After the November pogroms, the deputy Gauleiter in Franconia apparently thought that it was "unthinkable that after the Jews had had their property smashed they should be able to own houses and land." He therefore suggested that such property be Aryanized and a large share of the proceeds accrue to the Gau (the district). He believed that this transaction was not only a service to the Party, but was justified as a "National Socialist action." The Aryanization was accomplished by the alienation of properties, the surrender of claims, especially mortgage claims, and a drastic reduction in buying prices. The payments allowed Jews were about 10 percent of the nominal value.[20] One Jew after another was called in and made to sign a paper transferring his real estate to the Gau, the city of Furth, or some other worthy purchaser. For example, from the Jewish community organization, the city of Furth acquired 100,000 reichsmarks' worth of property for 100 reichsmarks. From a private Jew, the city took 20,000 reichsmarks' worth of real estate for 180. There were some difficulties in the courts, but they were soon overcome. Instead of entering the purchaser as the Gau, which had no "legal personality," Gauleiter Streicher's name was suggested. The Party officials, however, thought that Streicher's name should be left out. All then agreed to insert the name of the Deputy Gauleiter instead.

For Göring, however, these irregularities were distasteful, and the pushiness of little Party men, more so. "It is easily understood," he said, after he decided that "trustees" would handle the Aryanization of the larger establishments, "that strong attempts will be made to get all these stores to party members and to let them have some kind of compensation. I have witnessed terrible things in the past; little chauffeurs of Gauleiters have profited so much by these transactions they have now about a million. You, gentlemen, know it. . . . Of course, things like that are impossible. I shall not hesitate to act ruthlessly in any case where such a trick is played. If the individual involved is prominent, I shall see the Führer within two hours and report to him. . . . We shall insist upon it that the Aryan taking over the establishment is experienced in the business and knows his job. Generally speaking, he will have to pay for the store with his own money."[21] Such skirmishes with Party hacks, however, did not keep Göring from the main business.

From July to December 1938, the ministries wiped out the remaining structure of Jewish business and self-employment. Commercial services, such as real estate and credit agencies were liquidated. Licenses were withdrawn from Jewish physicians (they could treat Jewish patients by special permission) and lawyers. Retail shops, department stores, and mail-order houses were liquidated. Industrial enterprises and real estate were sold or liquidated with the assistance of "trustees," appointed by the Economy Ministry. Stocks, bonds, and other securities were to be deposited with the Finance Ministry and marked "Jewish." The state was supposed to benefit from the use of the "trustee." In arranging for sales, he was to set the price for the Jewish owner as low as possible and then collect the highest possible price—the actual value of the asset. But German buyers were not disposed to pay more under forced Aryanization than under "voluntary." The state then turned to taxing the new purchasers.

In this economic upheaval the Jews suffered severely. Göring's plan for their complete elimination from the German economy was well advanced by the end of 1938. In a speech made in Berlin on November 15, 1938,[22] Walter Funk, Minister of Economics, joyfully reported that out of seven billion marks of registered Jewish assets, Germans had already come into possession of two billion marks' worth of Jewish property. The Reich itself received another two billion marks in Reich Flight Tax (this tax, amounting to one-quarter of the emigrant's assets at the time of leaving the country, was first levied in 1931 to deter emigration; it eventually yielded a total of 900,000,000 RM) and "Jewish Atonement Payment" sums before the end of the year. These were ruinous levies upon an already stricken community.

Paradoxically, however, the November pogroms were the last occasions for violence against Jews in the streets of Germany for the rest of the Nazi regime. Thereafter individual Jews were not molested, nor were selected groups. The subsequent lull in physical violence deceived many Jews into thinking that the worst was over. What more could the Nazis do? The Nazis, for their part, had to give up "excesses" as a method for very compelling reasons. Things had happened November 9–10 that they had not bargained for. In addition to the heavy damage to non-Jewish property, there were repercussions abroad. The foreign press reacted strongly against the riots, the boycott against German goods spread and the German Foreign Office was flooded with cancellations of contracts. Jews in Germany bearing foreign passports had recourse to diplomatic intervention and pressed for indemnification. In England, the barbarities were compared to the sinking of the *Lusitania* and the shooting of Nurse Edith Cavell during World War I. The American ambassador to Germany left in protest. The Nazis thus had to develop a new technique in their war against the Jews.

Göring opposed what were euphemistically called *Einzelaktionen*, single actions, because losses to the German economy were great and Germany's financial situation was still critical even after the Jewish fine moneys began coming in. But he was not alone. The Foreign Office was disturbed by repercussions abroad. Actions which yielded to "baser instincts" were not productive. When the mob was turned loose, things got out of hand. In the end, pogroms did not accomplish anything lasting. In the future, Nazi actions against the Jews were to be taken systematically, without amateurish street fighting—that is, in an "orderly" way that would allow for proper and thorough planning of each measure through memoranda, correspondence and conferences. Henceforth the advisability of each measure would be weighed carefully to avoid hasty, wasteful action.[23] This change ruled out Goebbels' plan to march Jewish men through the streets of Berlin.

This decision marks a revolutionary change in the history of anti-Semitism. Bureaucrats, with the air of confident specialists, would now deplore "crude" anti-Jewish prejudice and "old-fashioned" excesses and put into motion drastic murderous actions by muffled language. Anti-Semitism became professionalized and mass murder became an administrative process. Later, a whole language camouflaging murder created a distance-machinery between the murderous specialist-policy maker and the murderers. Professionals like Eichmann and Höss would frequently condemn the crude and vulgar actions of individual Germans who could not control their anti-Semitic rages while they themselves perfected the assembly-line techniques of mass murder. To the end, Eichmann denied that he was anti-Semitic.

Late in September 1938, when the Fifth Supplementary Decree had expelled Jews from the last of the liberal professions, Wilhelm Stuckart, who had drafted the Nuremberg Laws, made an ominous observation. The aim of racial legislation, Stuckart said, had now been achieved, but many of the decisions reached through the Nuremberg Laws would "lose their importance as the Final Solution of the Jewish Problem is approached." The dread words "Final Solution" did not yet mean what they were later to mean—total annihilation—but it is obvious that the Nuremberg Laws were merely a way station to more drastic feasures. After Munich, Jews were not only hostages for any future demands that Hitler might make on other countries, but a rich exploitable prize over which rival forces in the Nazi state battled. One such force was Heydrich.

To Heydrich, the failure of the Western powers to support Czechoslovakia at Munich suggested the possibility of using small nations as dumping grounds for German Jews. Sensing the drift of events, Poland took quick action. The Polish Government invalidated passports of all Polish nationals living outside Poland. Exceptions were made of those Poles who had their passports specially stamped by the consulates by October 29, 1938. However, Polish consulates had been instructed not to renew the passports of Jews who had been abroad for more than five years. On October 28, one day before the deadline, 15,000 Jews in Germany holding Polish passports, were served deportation notices and became stateless overnight. A few days later, 10,000 or more were bundled into trucks and shipped to the frontier station, Sbonszyn. Poland refused to let them enter. This expulsion—Heydrich's first mass deportation—drove thousands of Jews to the freezing no-man's land near Sbonszyn. The grim postlude of Kristallnacht followed.

Heydrich, now head of the Gestapo, clearly wanted a forced, total expulsion of Jews, using fast, rough tactics to get them over the "green frontier" after plundering them thoroughly. He achieved his first success along these lines in Austria and wanted the same quick results in Germany. More conservative forces, however, like Schacht, had another approach.

Dr. Hjalmar Schacht, in 1938, was head of the Reichsbank as he had been under the Weimar Republic until 1930. Although he tried to portray himself as an opponent of the Nazi regime after the war, Schacht actually contributed much to bring about its rise. He performed the indispensable task of breaking down big business distrust of Nazi "radicalism" and winning its support for Hitler. Whereas, under the Republic, he haggled bitterly about every small Reichsbank advance to the government and demanded many policy concessions each time he made one, he unhesitatingly made twelve billion marks available to the Nazis through a scheme of credit inflation. Through his financial legerdemain, Schacht diverted productive capacity, which should have been used to pay commercial debts and reparations, into arms manufacture and the purchase of foreign raw materials to stoke rearmament.[24]

In his approach to the Jewish question, Schacht wanted to squeeze the most he could out of Jewish assets and ease the drain of foreign exchange. He also wanted to exploit Jewish emigration for the purpose of increasing German exports. In this, he not only tangled with Heydrich, who had no time for orderly emigration processes, but also with Göring. Like so many other Nazi satraps, Göring craved power—especially the trappings of power—in many fields. By 1936, he was not only Air Minister but also head of the Four-Year Plan, which already threatened Schacht's position at that time as Minister of Economics. Schacht, on his side, was openly contemptuous of Göring; he considered him an amateur in economic matters. Göring geared his Four-Year Plan to German self-sufficiency and pushed for a vast program of production of *Ersatzstoffe* and increased public borrowing. He seemed to think he could impress Schacht by telling him that in financial matters Frederick the Great, too, was an inflationist. Schacht, however, opposed the high cost of producing synthetics and substitutes when it seemed so much easier to capture markets for German exports and have solid foreign exchange. He also opposed the Party's huge purchases of foreign exchange for foreign propaganda programs and stepped up rearmament expenditures. But Schacht was not fast enough for either Göring or Hitler. His ingenious barter schemes, uphill cultivation of Germany's export trade with Latin America and crafty utilization of blocked accounts lacked the impulsiveness and heedless daring of Hitler. Ultimately, Hitler clinched the struggle in Göring's favor, but Schacht remained a considerable influence even after he was stripped of his power as Minister of Economics in 1937. In December 1938, while still head of the Reichsbank, he went to London—with Hitler's blessing—bearing an emigration scheme. Temporarily, Heydrich was pushed to the sidelines and Göring's steaming pressure was lifted.

Briefly, Schacht's plan was to freeze the remaining assets of German Jews and use them as security for a long-term loan to Germany, raised by Jews abroad or by an international committee. He estimated that a billion and a half marks in foreign currency would be raised, enough to finance an orderly emigration of Jews within three to five years. Interest and amortization, meanwhile, would be used to buy German goods. Schacht also insisted that the boycott against Germany be lifted.

This plan was discussed with George Rublee, director of an intergovernmental committee which had emerged out of the Evian Conference. A number of problems soon developed. The American Government had serious doubts that such a large sum could be raised under the terms outlined. Undersecretary of State Sumner Welles wired Rublee that "the plan is generally considered as asking the world to pay a ransom for the release of hostages in Germany and to barter human misery for increased exports." Jewish leaders, fearful of adding strength to the already spreading myth of "world Jewish rule," opposed setting up a private all-Jewish committee. Instead, they believed the matter should be handled exclusively by governments. On December 20, a meeting of financial experts in Paris reported that there was no possibility for individual financiers to raise the sums proposed by Schacht. The amount was now up to two billion marks —a half billion had been added for servicing charges. These experts also objected to making confiscated Jewish property the basis for an increase in German exports.

Meanwhile, Schacht spoke to Hitler on January 2, 1939, and over the violent protest of Foreign Minister von Ribbentrop, who felt pushed out of his domain, was told to continue negotiations. Rublee was invited to Berlin and the Foreign Office was instructed to withdraw its opposition to his visit. Hitler was apparently sufficiently impressed with Schacht's proposals to appoint him special delegate for the promotion of Jewish emigration on January 5. But this recognition was short-lived. On January 7, Schacht became alarmed at the financial consequences of Göring's rearmament program—Germany's debts had tripled, foreign currency reserves were exhausted and armament expenditures were to shoot up 300 percent; he protested the reckless spending. Hitler sent for him; they quarreled violently and on January 20, Schacht was dismissed as head of the Reichsbank. Within the scant six weeks that Hitler had toyed with Schacht's proposals, his mind had hardened against "giving up" Jewish assets.

The purpose of rearmament, of course, was to strengthen Hitler's hand in foreign policy. A relaxation of the rearmament drive would have had considerable economic benefits for Germany. It would have also slowed up Hitler's war timetable and saved many Jews. But success had weakened the caution which Hitler had shown in the first years of his regime. He was intoxicated by his victory at Munich. His military and political gambles were paying off handsomely. By the end of 1938, he dared to risk new ones. Existing military directives for the "protection of German frontiers," the liquidation of the remainder of Czechoslovakia and the occupation of Memel were supplemented by one for the occupation of Danzig. Poland would then follow. Göring's rearmament program had to go forward.

Four days after Schacht's dismissal, on January 24, the omnipotence of the Gestapo in emigration matters received the status of a decree. On that day, Göring wrote to Frick, Minister of the Interior, ordering him to put Heydrich at the head of a Central Emigration Office for Jews within his ministry. Heydrich was empowered to "solve the Jewish question by emigration and evacuation in the way that is most favorable under the conditions prevailing at present."

Heydrich had won after all. The Gestapo now had complete control over all Jews in Germany and German-conquered lands and Adolf Eichmann's "Emigration Center" in Austria was to become the hub of Jewish fate.

6 Eichmann in Austria

THE ACQUISITION OF AUSTRIA was one of Hitler's most cherished ambitions. "German Austria must return to the great German Motherland," he wrote on the first page of *Mein Kampf*. From 1933 on, German pressure was applied to Austria, first cautiously, then brazenly. In the end, Austria succumbed, unable to resist Hitler's threats, weakened by unresolved political struggles and abandoned by the powers that had pledged to guarantee her independence. By 1936, Hitler had already armed and occupied the Rhineland without being challenged. When he annexed Austria without the slightest interference, he knew he could carry out other aggressions with impunity.

World War I had torn up the polyglot Austro-Hungarian Empire which for centuries had held together many diverse peoples. Out of the numerous ill-formed states that emerged and received the official blessing of the Treaty of Versailles, Austria was among the saddest. A territorial amputation had taken place and Austria was reduced to a small, mainly agricultural state that somehow had to support the great city of Vienna with almost one third of the whole nation's population. The country staggered under the enormous burden of an army and administrative machinery suitable for a great power and communications and trade facilities for a huge hinterland that no longer existed. A republic had been established in 1919 but its stability was shaken by economic and political crises and by Hitler's pressures after he took power. Unceasing demands were made on the Austrian Government to force members of the satellite Austrian Nazi Party into the Cabinet and key posts in the administration. Austrian Nazis were trained in an Austrian legion organized in Bavaria. Nazi bomb outrages were committed on the railways and at tourist centers. Inflammatory leaflets were showered over Salzburg and Innsbruck, disturbing the daily life of the cities. Meanwhile the Socialist masses in Vienna and the conservative Catholic parties warred against each other with words and rival armies—both illegally armed. In 1934, the republic was abolished and a clerical-conservative dictatorship was established under Chancellor Engelbert Dollfuss, who tried to fight down the Nazis and the

Socialist workers at the same time. In Austria as in Germany, this Catholic-Socialist struggle only served to help the Nazis. Within a few months, Dollfuss was murdered in an attempted Nazi putsch.

Franz von Papen was then appointed German Minister to Vienna for the explicit purpose of organizing the overthrow of the Austrian regime. He was assigned to encourage the underground Austrian Nazi Party, then receiving a German subsidy of two hundred thousand marks a month, and to win over leading political figures.

The new Chancellor, Kurt von Schuschnigg, was a cultivated man with impeccable Old World manners, deeply devoted to his country and brave in nineteenth-century terms, but unable to cope with Nazi blitz *politik*. Fear of a German invasion led him ultimately to yield to Hitler. After Dollfuss' murder, Schuschnigg determined to make concessions to Hitler, believing that, in this way, he could save Austrian independence. The first concession came in 1936 after Hitler marched into the Rhineland. A new German-Austrian treaty followed in which Hitler reaffirmed Austria's sovereignty, while Austria acknowledged herself to be a "German state." These were the published provisions. In secret clauses, however, Schuschnigg agreed to amnesty certain Nazi political prisoners and to appoint representatives of the "National Opposition"—a euphemism for Nazis—to positions in the government.

Throughout 1937, the Nazis stepped up their campaign of terror and infiltrated the police. Goebbels hatched stories describing "Red" disorders, shootings, pillaging, and oppression of Austrian "Germans," that is, Nazis. Meanwhile, the German General Staff was instructed to draw up military plans for the occupation of Austria.

On February 11, 1938, a week after Hitler had removed the old-guard generals who had opposed his plans for an early war against Austria and Czechoslovakia, he began the last phase of the campaign to wear down Schuschnigg. The Austrian Chancellor was invited to Berchtesgaden. Several important German generals had also been pointedly invited to the *Berghof*. Hitler ranted hysterically about Schuschnigg's obstinacy and demanded that the Austrian Nazi Party be incorporated into the Government-sponsored Fatherland Front. He also demanded that Artur von Seyss-Inquart, a favored Nazi candidate, be made Minister of the Interior with authority over the police and security. Schuschnigg knew that this ultimatum meant the end of Austrian independence. The alternative was a German invasion.

Schuschnigg capitulated, but told Hitler that only the President of the Republic could constitutionally agree to his terms. The President balked for a few days until Hitler began shamming military actions. On February 16, the Austrian Government yielded. Seyss-Inquart was named Minister of Security and a general amnesty was proclaimed for all Nazis, including those involved in the murder of Dollfuss. Massive Nazi demonstrations throughout Austria was then set off, and with Seyss-Inquart in command of the police, no effort was made to curb them. Early in March, Schuschnigg decided to make one more desperate effort to hold off the Germans: he decided to hold a plebiscite and ask the people whether they wanted a "free, independent, social, Christian, and united Austria"—yes or no.

Schuschnigg announced that the plebiscite would be held on Sunday, March 13. The news threw Hitler into a fury. There was as yet no official plan for military action against Austria. The general staff had only a theoretical plan drafted for a Hapsburg restoration, but Hitler ordered an immediate military occupation of the country. Fearing a bloody war between two German states, Schuschnigg called the plebiscite off and resigned. Meanwhile, Austrian Nazis had gained control of the streets as well as the Chancellery. A Nazi-drafted telegram was sent by Seyss-Inquart requesting urgent German help "to establish peace and order in Austria." On March 11, Seyss-Inquart became Chancellor of Austria.[1]

The following day, Hitler set off for Austria and received a tumultuous welcome in Linz, the city of his youth. A triumphal entry into Vienna was planned for that night—a vindictive dream of the obscure postcard painter who had once starved in the streets of the city—but the German Army was not quite ready. Panzer units came to a standstill near Linz in spite of perfect weather and good road conditions. German tanks driven by green troops broke down and defective motorized heavy artillery jammed the road to Vienna. Petrol had to be rushed in and many of the crippled vehicles had to be loaded onto railway trucks. A remnant straggled into Vienna early the following morning.

Hitler seethed with anger over the breakdown of his military machine, but appearances were preserved and an official parade was mounted. The crowds massed for Hitler's entry cheered wildly, but many Austrians were frightened. Hitler's car was closely hemmed in by police cars bristling with S.S. troops in black uniforms and caps bearing the sinister skull and crossbones. Although some Austrians had longed for this day, more dreaded it. Had Schuschnigg's plebiscite been carried out, the people would have unquestionably voted against Anschluss.[2]

But the day after Hitler's entry into Vienna, Anschluss was decreed. "Austria," the document began, "is a province of the German Reich." The once great empire was now Ostmark, a province, and Vienna, the once great imperial center, became a provincial administrative seat. Without firing a shot and without the slightest interference from the other powers, Hitler had added seven million subjects to the Reich and gained a strategic position of immense value. He now possessed not only the gateway to southeast Europe but the certainty that neither France nor Great Britain would stop his next aggression. Chamberlain still shrank from the possibility of war; France had no government at all during the Austrian crisis, and all signs pointed to continued political instability and social unrest there. Mussolini, who had sent troops to the Brenner Pass in 1934 when the Nazis attempted to seize the Austrian government, now said that Austria was "immaterial" to him. For Germany, this was the beginning of the "flower war," the *Blumenkriege*. "Not bullets, but flowers greet our soldiers," said Goebbels as the Germans moved into Vienna, and later into Prague.

For many Austrians, including those who had welcomed the Anschluss, the German Nazi invasion proved to be a shocking experience. The conquerors came with their characteristic mixture of arrogance, ignorance, terrorism and corruption. For the Jews of Austria, the invasion was a compound of horrors, not only those perpetrated by the Germans, but also those of the native Austrian Nazis. Observers have written that some of the worst anti-Semitic excesses in Europe took place in Vienna. An American newspaper correspondent witnessed the first days following the Anschluss:

> For the first few weeks, the behavior of the Vienna Nazis was worse than anything I had seen in Germany. There was an orgy of sadism. Day after day, large numbers of Jewish men and women could be seen scrubbing Schuschnigg signs off the sidewalk and cleaning the gutters. While they worked on their hands and knees with jeering storm troopers standing over them, crowds gathered to taunt them. Hundreds of Jews, men and women, were picked off the streets and put to work cleaning public latrines and the toilets of the barracks where the S.A. and S.S. were quartered. Tens of thousands more were jailed. Their worldly possessions were confiscated or stolen. . . . Perhaps half of the city's 180,000 Jews managed, by the time the war started, to purchase their freedom to emigrate by handing over what they owned to the Nazis.[3]

Economic spoliation of Jews in Austria proceeded at once. There were no preparatory measures. Jewish businesses were confiscated directly or placed under an "Aryan" commissar. Anyone who held out against the pressure was arrested or forced to leave the country. Private plundering both in Vienna and in the provinces began the night of March 11. Austrian Nazis in every district had ready proscription lists of those who would best repay house searches. The plundering was done with great brutality, or, in some cases, with cynical courtesy. The press handled these activities deceptively.[4] Newspapers published communiqués issued by the police warning the public that "Communists" in storm troopers' uniforms were making "illegal requisitions" and urging prompt reporting of such cases to the police. When Jews who took these accounts seriously telephoned the police, they were told that all the police were out and that only a caretaker was on the line. When they went in person to complain, they were frequently arrested or abused physically.

The building of the *Kultusgemeinde*, the Jewish community organization, was occupied by S.S. guards who closed the soup kitchen and stole the food supplies.[5] Special passes were doled out to poor Jews. When they were admitted to the *Kultusgemeinde* building, they were forced to do tormenting exercises and to scrub the floors with their praying bands.

Overnight, from playing a large role in the cultural and economic life of the city, Viennese Jews lost their means of livelihood, their property and, in many cases, their sanity. Women whose husbands had been arrested at random received small parcels from the postman with a curt note attached: "To pay, 150 marks for the cremation of your husband. Ashes enclosed from Dachau." In many homes, suicide was discussed matter-of-factly as the only way out.

Private looting was generally accompanied by physical violence. The subjugation of Austria brought coarse and bestial elements to the surface. The Austrian legionnaires who had been waiting to cross into Austria since 1934 were finally unleashed. They hungered for jobs, plunder and revenge. Lueger's demagogic anti-Semitism that played on the discontents of the petty bourgeoisie and Church-inspired ritual murder fabrications that flourished in Austria also discharged barbarous cruelties.

After the Anschluss, Germans by the thousands flocked to Austria where they could buy sumptuous meals which had been unavailable in Germany for years. German businessmen and bankers also poured in to buy up concerns of dispossessed Jews at a fraction of their value. Meanwhile, trucks laden with private plunder streamed back toward Germany. The Reich treasury also benefited. Four hundred million schillings' worth of gold left the coffers of the Austrian National Bank for the impoverished Reichsbank in Berlin.[6] Berlin then dismissed Austrians from postal and telephone services in Vienna and replaced them with a highly trained army of spies and censors. The Nazi system of terror by informers was soon set in motion.

On July 21, 1938, the Vienna *Völkischer Beobachter* published a statement on the results of the government's confiscation of Jewish wealth:

> The property reported by the Jews is being dealt with according to the Hollerith system. When this process is finished, it will be possible to give an exact figure for the value of Jewish property in Austria. At present, estimates vary from three to eight thousand million schillings. Within six weeks we shall have laid hands on all Jewish fortunes above 5,000 marks; within three years, every single Jewish concern will have been Aryanized.[7]

Jews, in a frenzy, rushed to leave the country after the German occupation. All roads to the frontier were jammed with fleeing taxicabs and motorcars. The last train to Czechoslovakia was packed with fugitives, but hundreds were dog-whipped and robbed and dragged off to camps before the train pulled out. The rest rode on in prayerful thanksgiving for a time, but were turned back at the Czech border. The frontiers of all other surrounding countries were immediately closed.

Jewish families who had lived for generations in Burgenland villages were vilely beaten and driven out of their homes by storm troops. They were taken to an island breakwater on the Danube and loaded onto a dilapidated boat. Neither Hungary nor Czechoslovakia permitted them to disembark. Some sought refuge in desolate Alpine huts and in the dank fields of Bohemia outside the new German frontiers. Linz and Graz raced to be first to rid themselves of Jews. The pressure to drive Jews out was maintained by terror and intimidation. Foreign and stateless Jews were ordered out of the country within twenty-four hours after the Anschluss. Many Jews from the provinces were brought to the capital destitute, and Viennese Jews were ordered to house and look after them until they emigrated. Jewish hospitals, schools and convalescent homes were taken over for this purpose. Moshe Auerbach, an emissary of the Jewish Agency* Immigration Department, has described in somber colors the situation prevailing in Vienna at the end of October 1938:

> Some of the members of the town-kibbutz were injured, one youth-center was destroyed and the boys were beaten up. What most characterizes the situation of the Jewish masses here is their bewilderment, despair prompted by the feeling of their inability to find a way out, and above all—fear. Any day may bring new persecutions. Hundreds, maybe thousands of Jews have been ordered to leave the country within a short period. The Jewish Community and the Palestine Office are packed with people. The Jewish Community is endeavoring to send people off to various countries, but, . . . the openings for emigration are very limited. One has to admire the skill of the masses to find their way to various countries such as Trinidad, Haiti, San Domingo, etc. Indeed, the situation here is such that the only solution is to leave as soon as possible; here one has nothing to live on, no where to live. . . . Despair is so great that people are ready to live in detention centers abroad. Leading personalities of public institutions have become reconciled to the idea that the days of the Vienna Jewish Community are numbered, at most one year or two.[8]

The November pogroms which struck German Jewry like a thunderbolt were for Austrian Jews a continuation of persecution which had begun seven months earlier. Heydrich's orders had been issued at 1:20 A.M. on November 10, and covered Austria as well as Germany. In Vienna, by then, it was already known that riots were to be instigated thanks to

---

* The Jewish Agency was officially set up under the Palestine Mandate to direct the absorption of Jews into Palestine. It represented Jews in Palestine and abroad in all negotiations with the British.

Gauleiter Hofer who had been in Munich the previous day to celebrate the Beerhall putsch and had directly flown to Vienna. Austrian Jews suffered the same destruction hailed upon German Jews. S.S. detachments destroyed the synagogues; S.D. units confiscated Jewish archives and libraries; the S.A. and Gestapo closed and sealed any Jewish enterprises still standing. Fifteen thousand Jews were taken off to concentration camps.

An official report of a Vienna S.D. unit, dated November 10, stated that operations were completed "thoroughly and rapidly." Jewish merchants were arrested, their shops emptied, and their goods centralized in one warehouse. All participants in the rioting wore civilian clothes, as directed. The Nazi official then commented on the attitude of the "Aryan" population: "The vast majority of the Aryan population not connected with the National-Socialist Party has a negative attitude toward today's events. The steps taken against the Jews are considered by the sensitive Viennese to be too harsh," resulting from the illegality of the pogroms. Had the operations been carried out on the basis of some law or in accordance with an earlier regulation, the official observed, the population would have undoubtedly cooperated. "It is natural that the operation made a deep impression on the Jews. The events paralyzed the Jews to such an extent that they could not even exhibit the customary outbursts of despair. It may be stated with certainty that after today's events the Jews have lost every vestige of desire to carry on."[9] Jews were indeed despairing. On November 10, 680 men and women committed suicide.

On the Nazi side, as in Germany during the pogroms, there were crosscurrents of action; a single policy had not yet evolved. Party members dervished in a swirl of anarchy. A then-obscure official in charge of the Vienna Central Emigration Office, *Obersturmführer* Adolf Eichmann, was powerless to prevent the destruction of the important central emigration card index in the Jewish Community office by rampaging S.S. men. Of the Jews arrested on November 10, 1,226 held emigration papers. Why had they been arrested? In Graz, the authorities wanted their city to have the honor of being the first urban center in Austria to be *Judenrein*, but they had planned, they said, for the "orderly" emigration of their Jews. Eichmann had agreed to a transfer of five million marks to Palestine, making possible the emigration of 600 Jews. But the November zealots torpedoed the plan. The S.D. commander of Styria-Graz was openly critical of the damaging results of the November pogroms:

These actions are not particularly effective in ridding the district of the Jews. It must be placed on record that as a result a number of conditions basic to the emigration of the Jews have been destroyed and their reconstruction will require much effort. The instructions of *Obersturmführer* promised that up to December 31, 1938, not a single Jew would remain within the borders of Styria. Now the achievement of this objective is very doubtful, and even more so the concentrated resettlement of 600 Jews in Palestine has been postponed. . . . On behalf of the local office, it must be stated that it might have been better if the actions had not taken place in the province of Styria. At any rate the legal measures were far more favorably received than the acts of destruction.[10]

The Nazis were still divided as to ends and means. Auerbach reported that all of the boys in three *hachshara* centers (training farms for Jewish youth planning to go to Palestine) were arrested. One kibbutz was liquidated. Then, on November 10, a special emissary was dispatched from Berlin to Vienna with instructions to go from jail to jail to release all Jews who had any connection with the Palestine Office. Eichmann himself visited the Palestine Office and ordered an accelerated emigration in order "to put an end to the Jewish question in Vienna" by March 1939.

In spite of these conflicting policies, however, one thing was clear: Austria was far ahead of Germany in getting rid of its Jews. As Heydrich had boasted, between April and November 1938, Austria had eliminated 50,000 Jews. Germany had eliminated only 19,000 in the same period. Eichmann's strategy was to force the *Kultusgemeinde* to collect foreign exchange holdings from wealthy Jews in order to finance the emigration of the poor. The faster pace in Austria was also the result of an assembly-belt technique which Eichmann was perfecting. In November it still had some flaws. Soon thereafter it would be a model for other centers to follow. After the invasion of Russia, his far-flung organization would transport millions of Jews to death camps.

The Jewish Emigration Center in Vienna was set up in April 1938. Heydrich had gone there to arrange for Hitler's reception after the Anschluss and to organize the Gestapo command. Both he and Himmler also took advantage of their stay in Austria during the first weeks of the Anschluss to set up a huge concentration camp at Mauthausen on the Danube near Enns, thus avoiding the expense and trouble of transporting thousands of Austrians to the concentration camps of Germany.

Among the civil servants who accompanied them was Adolf Eichmann. Eichmann already knew a great deal about the lot of German Jews. He also knew that many German bureaucratic obstacles had impeded their emigration. In Germany, every prospective emigrant had to acquire more than a dozen official papers certifying his health, good conduct, property holdings or disposition, tax payments, emigration opportunities and other details. Many offices were involved in this processing and slowed down the exodus of Jews. Eichmann suggested the idea of uniting the numerous administrative offices in a single Gestapo department[11] to speed up emigration. Heydrich accepted the suggestion and put Eichmann in charge of the new Central Bureau for Emigration in Vienna.

The background of this unprepossessing and colorless bureaucrat who would soon develop an insatiable appetite for dispatching Jews to their deaths hardly prepared him for his lifework. It was quite ordinary, as was the background of most of the Nazi mass murderers.

Eichmann was born in Solingen, Germany, in 1904. His mother died when he was four and the surviving family went to Linz, Austria, where (as had Hitler) he spent his youth. He is described as a lonely, melancholy boy, shabbily dressed, seldom playing with other boys. He was dark-complexioned and, suspected at times of being Jewish, was taunted with the cry "*Der kleine Jude.*" Teachers recall that he disliked school and refused to study, that he was touchy, moody and withdrawn. When he was thirteen, enrolled in a public school in Thuringia, his name was mentioned in a local newspaper as one of the leaders of a gang of schoolboys who had cruelly tormented a Jewish classmate. As if prefiguring his later career, he was made to keep a precise account of each boy's turn to beat up the Jewish boy. (Twenty years later, this same child, Ulrich Cohn, died in a concentration camp.)

As an adult, Eichmann gave the impression that he had a burning ambition to study electrical engineering but was thwarted when the postwar inflation pauperized his father and forced him to leave school. It is more likely that he was forced to leave high school as well as the Linz Higher Institute for Electro-Technical Studies after two years because he was a poor student. For a while he walked the streets unemployed. Finally, in 1925, he secured work as a salesman for the Austrian Elektrobau Company. After two and a half years, he took a job as traveling salesman for the Vacuum Oil Company of Vienna. (The professional label of "construction engineer" which appears on official Party documents is an exaggeration.) During this period, apparently, he came out of his shell and began to emerge as a talkative, gregarious, hard-drinking man with a dashing red motorcycle, who made frequent trips along the Vienna-Linz road.

For a time, according to several accounts, Eichmann was intrigued by some Vienna Jews whose homes he visited and whose company he enjoyed. He even picked up a smattering of Hebrew and Yiddish. But it is likely that these strangers with their voluble talk and lighthearted warmth also made him ill at ease. The Jews of the old inner city, moreover, repelled him and the Austrian anti-Semitic press inflamed a growing antipathy. Hitler's speeches were also casting a hypnotic spell. He admitted:

After hearing the F. speak I felt a loathing of myself that I had mixed with those Jews who were the enemies of the German people and who defiled our blood. I felt a certain change in my outlook coming over me. I began to think these foreign-looking people were, indeed, the enemy of us all.

They all seemed to be traders and financiers, people willing to take very little part in the real work of the community, people who insisted our ways had nothing to do with them. It seemed wrong that they should try to cut themselves off, to keep together when they should be sharing our fate with us. I wondered about my friendship with Jews and I felt that they had always treated me as someone rather inferior. I felt that no country, unassisted by others, could have beaten the German army during the war. I believed that Hitler was right when he said that one people had intrigued to link as many nations as possible against our country and bring about the terrible times we were then going through.[12]

Eichmann began going to Nazi Party meetings and in 1927 joined the youth section of the Austro-German Veterans Organization. On April 1, 1932, he joined the Austrian Nationalist Socialist Party. He also joined the S.S., which was already working toward Anschluss. When he was sworn in by Himmler, he met Ernst Kaltenbrunner, who was later to become head of the Reich's Security Office, and whose protégé Eichmann became. Eichmann's increased Nazi activity brought him to the attention of the Austrian police, who were then completely loyal to the government, but he slipped their surveillance by making his way to the German border and eventually to Berlin. On a Gauleiter's recommendation, in the summer of 1933, he was sent to Lechfeld on the German-Austrian border for military training and for a few months he worked in the S.S. Austrian Liaison Office in Passau. He was then sent to the Bavarian S.S. camps in Lechfeld and Dachau where the "Austrian Legion in Exile" received its training. According to his own account, these fourteen months of training were as boring as selling: "The humdrum of military service—that was something I couldn't stand, day after day, always the same, over and over again the same." But he had advanced to the rank of *Scharführer* (corporal) and new possibilities loomed in Heydrich's S.D., the Security Service, as jobs were opening up. By this time, the S.D. was not only spying on Party members but it was becoming the information center for the Gestapo. Eichmann seems to have known nothing of its real nature, but thought that it guarded important Party leaders. "I thought this was what I had read about in the *Münchener Illustrierte Zeitung*—when the high Party officials drove along, there were commando guards with them, men standing on the running boards of the cars. . . . In short, I had mistaken the Security Service of the Reichsführer S.S. for the Reich Security Service . . . and nobody set me right and no one told me anything." His first job in this "disappointing" unit (if we are to accept Eichmann's words) was once again dull; he was no more than a file clerk typing out data on Freemasons who were under Nazi surveillance. Eichmann, however, apparently did this chore well and learned a great deal meanwhile about S.S. organizational procedures. Within a few months, Himmler established the

Scientific Museum for Jewish Affairs in the S.D., and Eichmann received the job of heading the project. With his marked penchant for systematic and pedantic work, he thrived on his new job.

Eichmann admitted his interest and zeal in the interview with Wilhelm Sassen, the Dutch journalist, before his capture in Argentina:

> I must confess that I did not greet this assignment with the apathy of an ox being led to his stall. On the contrary, I was fascinated with it. My chief, General Reinhard Heydrich, encouraged me to study and acquaint myself even with its theological aspects. In the end, I learned to speak Hebrew, although badly. Some of my early work was with the Nuremberg Laws, in force since 1935. Under the formula adopted at that time for "Final Solution of the Jewish Question," the laws were intended to drive Jews out of all phases of German life. My experience in this field was often of a confidential and rather embarrassing nature—as when I established that the Führer's diet cook, who was at one time his mistress, was 1/32 Jewish. My immediate superior, Lieutenant General Heinrich Müller, quickly classified my report as Top Secret.[13]

His real career had begun. This assignment took Eichmann into the field which gave him the power and recognition he craved. Soon he was moved to a more active position in the Jewish Section of the S.D., where he worked closely with the Jewish Section of the Gestapo. Eichmann shrewdly calculated that this was an office to stick to; it had a future for a man with a driving ambition but no outstanding abilities and without the glamour of some of the blond giants around Heydrich. In a movement that pivoted on an axis of rage against the Jew, very few knew very much about the hated enemy; it was enough to hate. Eichmann cleverly saw an opportunity to become unique in Party circles; he would become an expert on Jewish affairs. He made himself familiar with standard anti-Semitic literature and learned what he could about Jewish religious beliefs and customs and Jewish national and communal movements. He concentrated on the organization of the Jewish community in Germany, the religious bodies and the branches of the Zionist movement and studied their literature. In 1938, within three years, he was appointed head of a separate unit in the S.D. called "Jewry" and was promoted to *Untersturm-führer*, the equivalent of a second lieutenant.

Here, surely, is a man with his eye on the main chance, not the expressionless, painstaking bureaucrat obscured behind records and filing cabinets. Besides, Eichmann had become an astute manipulator and knew which men to flatter and which to ignore. He made himself known to Leopold von Mildenstein, the head of a special Palestinian and Middle East intelligence section of the S.D., and obtained an assignment to Palestine in 1937. A very interesting aspect of the arrangements for the trip concerns Eichmann's request for an enlarged wardrobe allowance. His appetite for good living had increased; he was often seen at the Adlon Hotel bar and the expensive restaurant, Horcher's, frequently in the company of a comely blond girl. The text of the request has survived:

> To: The Director of the Central Department II-1
> Subject: Trip Abroad
>
> For the purpose of the trip abroad that has already been certified, there is an urgent need to add to my wardrobe. Since I'll have to come in contact with Arab princes and the like, I will need a light suit, a dark suit and a trench coat.
>
> Therefore I ask for an allowance, the amount of which is to be computed when I arrive there. Whatever is left, if anything, I ask you to regard as a loan which I will pay back in installments.
>
> [Signed] Adolf Eichmann
S.S. Hauptscharführer

The request was turned down "for reasons of principle."[14]

The association of Eichmann with Palestine has another bizarre aspect. For a time, in order to impress his S.S. acquaintances and Jewish community officials with his specialized knowledge, he cultivated the legend that he was born in Palestine. Some Nazi Party bosses in Vienna actually suspected him of being a Jewish spy and questioned him closely about his origins. To them, too, he told the story that he was born in the German colony of Sarona.

Eichmann's stay in Palestine was very brief. British authorities ordered him out of the country after a few days. On his return trip to Germany, he stopped at Cairo and met either the Grand Mufti himself or several of his agents. These contacts with Arab leaders continued during the war and gave the Germans a handy excuse for blocking the efforts of Jews to reach Palestine when their situation was desperate.

Eichmann's co-worker Dieter Wisliceny, who during the war worked under Eichmann as a subordinate in transporting Jews to death camps, gave the following picture of him during the early phase of his career: "Anyone who, like myself, first met Eichmann in 1934, could only get the impression of a most colorless creature. At that time, he was the typical subordinate, pedantic, punctilious—also, in his personal relations—devoid of any thorough knowledge but possessing a certain general education. I myself, even as late as 1940, could not have predicted the subsequent evolution of his character and would not have considered it possible."[15]

Eichmann's own account of his work in the Austrian Emigration Center was recorded during the police examination prior to his trial in Jerusalem. According to this version of his story, he had read Herzl's *Der Judenstaat*, the famous Zionist classic and had become a "convert" to Zionism. From then on, as he repeated again and again, he hardly thought of anything but a "political solution"—how to "get some firm ground under the feet of the Jews." He also had read Böhm's *The Zionist Movement* and, he explained, became fascinated by the "Jewish question" because the idealism of the Zionists was so similar to his—an idealist being not only a man who believes in an idea but who lives for it and is prepared to sacrifice everything and everybody for the sake of it. Soon after his "Zionist" phase, Eichmann willingly, even zealously, sacrificed millions of Jews for the sake of his "ideal." After 1941 he did everything in his power to stop Jews from fleeing the continent for Palestine so that he could fill up his transports for the death camps. He did not reveal in court or to Sassen that he together with a co-worker, Herbert Hagen, had prepared a vicious anti-Zionist report in 1937 which stated that the plan for emigration of Jews to Palestine "was out of the question." In the course of his apprenticeship in the Nazi world, Eichmann became, like the others, a self-righteous liar and an expert in double-talk.

The documents and witnesses surrounding the Austrian phase of Eichmann's work deny his fabrication that a "harmonious" relationship developed between him and the Jewish community leaders. To Sassen in Argentina, he spoke of his work as "forced evacuation." To Hagen, in Berlin, he wrote a letter dated May 1, 1938:

> I sure made these guys shake a leg, believe me. That's why they are already hard at work. I have asked the Jewish Community Organization and the National Zionist Union to supply 20,000 destitute Jews for the period from May 1, 1938 to May 1, 1939. . . . Tomorrow, I'll check up again on those outfits—the Jewish Community and the Zionists. I do that at least once a week. I have them completely in my power; they don't dare to make a single step without asking me first. That's the way it ought to be; they can be better controlled this way.[16]

Between 1938 and the outbreak of the war, the Central Emigration Office, under Eichmann's control, forced the departure of 100,000 Jews from Austria. "Heydrich," according to Wisliceny, Eichmann's co-worker for eleven years, "was much impressed with the purely organizational scope of Eichmann's achievements . . . and promoted him rapidly. In November 1937 Eichmann had become S.S. Assistant Storm Troop Leader; by April 1938 he was Leader, and in the fall of 1938 he was Chief Storm Troop Leader. In the circumstances then prevailing, this was an unusual career." Later, when Eichmann assumed power over an empire of murder transports, his personality was far from that of a colorless, pedantic bureaucrat.

In his reign over the fate of Austrian Jewry, Eichmann seemed to be trying on one posture of authority after another as if testing out his new role. Several witnesses at his trial described his unpredictable states, ranging from extreme politeness to vicious savagery and obscene cursing. Other survivors have recorded his early cooperation in getting Austrian Jewish youth to Palestine. A Zionist leader, Dr. Franz Mayer, had first met Eich-mann in 1936 or 1937. During that time, Mayer was actively engaged in trying to get Austrian Jews to Palestine and in connection with this work was called to the Gestapo headquarters several times. On some occasions, Mayer testified, Eichmann asked him questions about Jewish affairs. "He seemed like an official who comes to you and says, 'I want to learn. Please explain.' At the time, I found him cold but correct and quietly behaved. He would address me as 'Herr' and ask me to sit down."

It was a very different Eichmann whom Mayer met in February 1939 at the Gestapo headquarters in Vienna, in the Rothschild Palace, to which he and leaders of the German Jewish community had been summoned. The witness was shocked by the change in Eichmann. "I had always thought him a lowly bureaucrat, a clerk doing a job, filing reports. And here I found a man of coarse and brutal behavior, master of our life and death. He would not let us come near his desk. We had to remain stand-ing." When one member of the delegation put his hand in his pocket, Eichmann shouted some obscenities and called him a "sack of dung."[17]

As Eichmann intended to apply his processing techniques to Berlin, the delegation was invited to tour the building and see how Austrian Jews were dealt with. Dr. Mayer likened the building to a flour mill linked to a bakery or conveyor-belt factory: "You put in a Jew at one end, with prop-erty, a shop, a bank account and legal rights. He passed through the building and came out at the other end without property, without privi-leges, without rights, with nothing except a passport and order to leave the country within a fortnight; otherwise he would find himself inside a concentration camp."

A bizarre episode,[18] described by Gerson Friedman, a witness at Eich-mann's trial, shows the Nazi mind in its early tease-and-terror seesaw, a process brought to diabolical perfection in later years when starving hu-man beings could be seduced to their deaths by marmalade and bread. Friedman and two others in the Central Office were ordered to pick up Gestapo helmets, put them on, and then swear their loyalty to the Ge-stapo on a Bible. The three men, in a reflex of fear, obeyed; the S.S. officer shook hands with each man and then handed them documents giving them free access to all Gestapo offices and scribbling his signature on each. The signature read "Adolf Eichmann." Friedman said, "The inci-dent made no sense at all, but during those first few months of the Anschluss many things happened which made no sense."

At another time, Friedman tried to protect a Jewish woman from an attack by an S.S. man. He was arrested and expected the worst, but to his amazement the man to whom he was brought at Gestapo headquarters asked him to "help establish law and order in Vienna." He gave Fried-man a special document authorizing him to do this.

This document and the one given to him by Eichmann were put to good use. The Gestapo clerks stamped the applications of those Jews who were denied exit visas with a large "D"; these Jews were destined to go to Dachau. The approved applications were stamped "PD." Friedman discovered that the poorly paid Gestapo men could be bribed. By judicious bribery he managed to obtain one of the PD stamps and saved a number of Jews from Dachau. Then he took a bigger gamble. He made an appointment with Eichmann, handed him a bulky envelope, and said gravely, "I plead with you to facilitate the approval of emigration applications. I know that to do this you will have to hire extra clerks. I would be very happy to pay their salaries."

Eichmann opened the envelope, blinked, smiled with satisfaction and said, "Thank you, Herr Friedman. This will help a great deal."

Somewhat later, Moshe Auerbach, the Jewish Agency emissary, arrived in Vienna with orders to supplement what was known as *Umschlag*, the change from useless occupations among Jews to productive ones. Eichmann was known to want Jewish youth in this plan to increase agricultural and industrial production. Auerbach came to Eichmann's office, stopped a few feet from his desk, came to attention and saluted him smartly.

"Come closer," Eichmann snapped.

Young Auerbach took a step forward and stopped.

"I said come closer!" Eichmann shouted.

"I am a Jew," Auerbach said coldly.

Later he would be known to Nazi officers as *der Wilde von der syrischen Grenze*—the wild man from the Syrian border.

Eichmann pointed to a chair and ordered him to sit down. Then Eichmann showered him with questions. How long had he lived in Palestine? Where had he been born? What sort of work did he do in Palestine? He listened attentively as Auerbach explained that the pioneering youth movement in Palestine (*Hechalutz*) was interested in training a thousand Jewish youths of Austria in agricultural and other useful work needed to build Palestine.

Eichmann nodded approvingly. "While they're here they could be producing, and then if they could be sent to Palestine it would mean another thousand Jews out of Austria." Then he raised a question. "How will you transport these people to Palestine? How will you get ships and get them through the British blockade?"

"If you approve of our plan," Auerbach replied, "I guarantee the transportation will be arranged. We have friends in Italy and Greece who will take us there."

Eichmann agreed and allowed a thousand Jewish boys and girls to train on farms and in factories.[19] Other similar projects involved the Gestapo and young emissaries from Palestine in parodies of agreement, enabling some Jews to leave Hitler Europe. The Palestinians learned sooner than others that at certain times the Gestapo could be reached—if the price was high enough.

Eichmann's assignment to Vienna in 1938 was not only a significant phase in his career. It changed the nature of the Nazi war against Europe's Jews. The Eichmann operation in Austria marked the beginning of forced emigration of Jews, carefully organized on a large scale and deliberately using physical violence, blackmail and the threat of concentration camps to drive Jews out. The confusion of the days of the November pogroms was soon overcome as Eichmann found his stride. In one year he succeeded in expelling 100,000 Jews. When the May 1939 census was taken, there were only 113,824 Jews left in Austria, almost all of them concentrated in Vienna.[20]

As he became more professional, Eichmann sloughed off any residue of former restraint and courtesy. Totally absorbed in his work, he became a zealous technician, bent on carrying out orders. He, too, made the leap from "crude" anti-Semitism to an "objective" solution of the Jewish problem. "Through all this period," he told Sassen, "I saw the Jewish problem as a question to be solved politically. So did Himmler and the entire Gestapo. It was not a matter of emotion. My S.S. comrades and I rejected the crude devices of burning temples, robbing Jewish stores and maltreating Jews on the streets. We wanted no violence. One of my former officers was expelled from the S.S. for beating up four or five Jews in the cellar of our offices. . . . Each of us, as an individual had no wish to harm the Jew individually."[21]

Eichmann's efficient work came to the notice of Nazi officials. Toward the end of 1938, in recommending him for promotion to the rank of captain, the Inspector of Security Police and Security Service in Vienna wrote: "His work is good, energetic and shows initiative. He has a great capacity for independent action, particularly in organization. He is known as a specialist in his field. He is currently responsible for Jewish emigration in general."[22] Not only was his model processing system in Vienna giving him a reputation as an "expert on the Jewish question," but he also became an authority on evacuating Jews. His power increased swiftly.

On January 24, 1939, when Göring instructed Heydrich to take charge of the emigration of Jews, he ordered the creation of a Reich Central Office for Jewish Emigration. Using Eichmann's operation in Vienna as a model, suboffices were also established in Berlin and Prague. These were in the hands of the local Gestapo chiefs, who were in turn responsible to Eichmann. On January 30, his recommendation for promotion to captain read, "Eichmann directs the entire operation."

From the beginning, Eichmann's branch offices gave their orders to the organized Jewish community. Many of the financial transactions which led to the emigration of poor Jews were the product of this coercion. When the war broke out, the Gestapo offices did not disband, but assumed complete control of the Jewish community organizations. They dictated measures on emigration, taxation, housing, registration of property, forced labor and movement restrictions. Under duress, the Jewish agencies were converted from autonomous organizations serving the Jewish community to instruments for carrying out Gestapo orders dealing with Jews.

In Vienna, the traditional name of the community organization, the *Israelitische Kultusgemeinde*, was retained until December 1942 when it was dissolved. Soon after the Nazis entered Vienna, the leading Zionist in the *Kultusgemeinde*, Dr. Desider Friedman, and other Jewish leaders were sent to Dachau allegedly because the council failed to collect the 800,000 schillings demanded by the Nazis. The men were released in February 1940, but were transported to Theresienstadt in 1942.

Eichmann's system came at an opportune time for Nazi Germany. Jews were not leaving the old Reich quickly enough. Besides, the acquisition of more Jews in Austria was a mixed blessing—their wealth could be plundered but their existence in Reich territory (Austria was now part of the "Greater Reich") was an affront as well as a challenge to the Nazis. The failure of international diplomacy to create emigration outlets for Jews also aggravated the problem. By the end of 1938, the Nazis knew that a "radical" solution to the Jewish problem could not be solved by emigration alone. An official document surveys the year's progress on this problem, runs over a gamut of possibilities for solutions only to extinguish them. Every route becomes a cul-de-sac. The document was a Foreign Office Circular entitled "The Jewish Question as a Factor in German Foreign Policy in the year 1938" distributed to all German diplomatic representatives abroad one week after Heydrich became head of the Reich Emigration Office. It had ominous overtones: "The fateful year 1938 has brought nearer the solution of the Jewish question simultaneously with the realization of the 'idea of Greater Germany,' since the Jewish policy was both the basis and consequence of the events of the year 1938." However, the paper continues, many new problems are developing. First, the Jews of Germany are not leaving fast enough. Their elimination from politics and culture, and most recently from economic life, has been accomplished, but there are still too many Jews. "The final goal of German Jewish policy is the emigration of all Jews living in Reich territory." Romania, Poland, Italy, and Hungary are praised for writing laws "in the fight against Jewry" but international diplomacy is castigated for not finding places where Jews can go. Yet, the Nazis refuse to release Jewish wealth to facilitate emigration. Jewish property is really German national property taken away from the German people. "The transfer of even a fraction of this property would be impossible from the point of view of foreign exchange. The financing of mass emigration of German Jews is therefore still obscure."[23]

The Foreign Office then broadly suggests that emigration schemes are futile anyhow because "almost every State in the world has in the meantime hermetically sealed its borders against these parasitical Jewish intruders. . . . Many States have already become so cautious that they demand a permit made out by German authorities for Jews travelling with German passports stating that they may return to Germany." The influx of Jews into other countries has created resistance to new waves. Great Britain opposes free immigration of Jews to Palestine. Besides, Germany regards the formation of a Jewish State as dangerous. What is the answer? the circular asks with mock concern. There is nothing left to do; "Germany will therefore take the initiative herself, in order to find ways, means and destination for Jewish emigration from Germany."[24]

The Third Reich thus self-righteously sees no way out. The Jewish question cannot be solved in ordinary ways.

For Jews, the vise was closing. They were being locked in from the outside and squeezed out from the inside. Reinhard Heydrich, the man who had a taste for brutal measures, had been given control over their emigration. Adolf Eichmann had set up a very efficient machine in Vienna, but dumping ground for his expelled Jews was nowhere to be found. The Third Reich was narrowing its alternatives for Jews. Meanwhile, Hitler's war demon was again set loose. On May 28, 1938, he had served warning: "It is my unshakable will that Czechoslovakia shall be wiped off the map."

The easy absorption of Czechoslovakia in 1939 created 120,000 more Jews for the Heydrich-Eichmann combine while the drift to war in Europe made escape from the Continent increasingly difficult. Inexorably, the Jews were being robbed of free choices.

7 Munich

On APRIL 21, 1938, just eleven days after the Nazis held their own "plebiscite" on Anschluss, Hitler called in General Wilhelm Keitel, new Chief of the High Command of the Armed Forces, to discuss "Case Green." Keitel had come completely over to Hitler's side after the Blomberg-Fritsch denouement, and had no independent prerogatives of command whatsoever; he was Hitler's executive agent and issued orders only in Hitler's name.[1] "Case Green" was the code name for a surprise attack on Czechoslovakia, first drawn up in June 1937, and later elaborated by Hitler in a lecture to the generals in the famous meeting on November 5. In his talk with Keitel, Hitler ruled out a surprise attack because of hostile world opinion, but recommended either military action following a diplomatic crisis, or, preferably, "lightning-swift action as a result of an incident," such as the assassination of the German Ambassador linked with an anti-German demonstration. Otherwise, Hitler warned, prolonged military action would lead to a European crisis, intervention, and a division of the spoils. Victory had to be achieved within four days.

Rumors of German plans leaked out and the Czechs dispatched troops to the Sudeten region bordering Germany. This partial mobilization enraged Hitler and furnished the stimulus and pretext for a decision to crush the Czechs at the earliest opportunity. On May 30, the directive on "Case Green" was signed by Hitler and distributed to the three service chiefs. The preamble read: "It is my unalterable decision to smash Czechoslovakia by military action in the near future. . . . Accordingly, the preparations are to be made at once."[2] Keitel's covering memorandum declared that the execution of plans must be assured by October 1, 1938, at the latest.

The Republic of Czechoslovakia, which Hitler was determined to destroy, was the creation of the peace treaties, so hateful to the Germans, following World War I. Except for the problem of minority groups which wanted more autonomy, Czechoslovakia was considered the most democratic and progressive state in central Europe. One of the aggrieved groups was the Sudeten Germans, who actually fared better than the others. Hitler had contrived grievances for them and, since 1935, had subsidized the Sudeten German Party by fifteen thousand marks monthly. Fifth-column activities within Czechoslovakia led by Konrad Henlein were supplemented by efforts to disrupt the ties between the Czechs and their allies, England and France. In May, the Wilhelmstrasse dispatched Henlein to London to create the impression that the Czechoslovakian state was gradually "decomposing" and that it was impractical to uphold its structure. By the latter part of August, German preparations were well advanced and the "Sudeten crisis" approached fever pitch. Inflammatory speeches were made at the annual Nuremberg rally to whip up a war spirit. On September 15, Neville Chamberlain, British Prime Minister, flew to Berchtesgaden.

Within the higher Wehrmacht circles, another conflict with Hitler was brewing. This time the leading protagonist of the opposition to Hitler was General Ludwig Beck, Chief of the General Staff. Beck had originally welcomed Hitler's seizure of power and his restoration of Germany's military prestige, but he was uneasy about the infiltration of Nazi ideas among the junior members of the officers' corps. More important, he was thoroughly alarmed over Hitler's hurtling foreign policy and the evidence, after the Fritsch affair, that Hitler was bent on destroying all semblance of independent leadership in the Wehrmacht. He strongly opposed a war for which Germany was not ready and one which would surely involve England and France.

Beck's position, however, was far from strong. His support of Fritsch had aroused Hitler's distrust and there was no common ground between him and Keitel. After the triumphant Anschluss, Hitler's prestige was greater than ever. Furthermore, Beck had no direct access to Hitler; another man, General Walther von Brauchitsch, Commander in Chief of the Army, stood above him in the chain of command. But he had, at least, the weapon of the pen, and he took to writing vigorous staff memoranda recording his views. He conceded Germany's need for more territory, but he pointed to the dangers of Anglo-French intervention and Germany's unreadiness for a general war. None of these papers produced the slightest effect. Von Brauchitsch was obviously not relaying Beck's views in his conferences with Hitler.

Beck then decided that stronger measures were needed. All of the senior generals must take responsibility for preventing the inevitable disaster that would strike Germany in a general war. He told von Brauchitsch that, as Chief of the General Staff, he was unable to carry out Case Green, that it was militarily unsound and that all of the commanding generals in the three services must present a united front against Hitler and resign in a body if he proved adamant. At long last, it had begun to dawn on Beck that he was confronting a problem much deeper than how to put an end to Case Green. He realized that the menace of war was not simply a momentary, mad idea of Hitler's, but an intrinsic part of an evil system. Beck was face to face with the Third Reich itself.[3]

Accordingly, his proposals in July went far beyond anything he had yet written. The Army generals must seek allies among the surviving "better" elements in Germany and there must be reforms: peace with the church, restoration of justice, an end to S.S. control, no war at this time. But interestingly, at this stage in his thinking, Beck was not in favor of a putsch. Hitler was to remain.

Beck delivered these views at a meeting of all the commanding generals on August 4 and made a deep impression. None expressed views opposing his analysis of the military situation, but they did not act. No decisions were taken during or after the meeting. Apprehensive the generals might be, but they were too fearful, or too ambitious, or too dazzled by Hitler's past triumphs to oppose him.

Hitler soon learned that Beck had read his most radical memorandum to the commanding generals. Now confirmed in his distrust of Beck, he ignored him and conferred with von Brauchitsch. Von Brauchitsch in turn began to deal directly with Beck's subordinate, General Franz Halder. In the middle of August, Beck resigned, and then summoned the section chiefs of the OKH (Army High Command) General Staff. He delivered a short lecture to the officers on the historic "independence" of the General Staff and then quietly departed. Hitler cannily refused to release the news of his resignation to the press. Had the news of an open break on so high a level been publicized, Chamberlain might have thought twice about trying to reach "peace in our time" with Hitler. The name of Beck's successor was not announced for several weeks, by which time the crisis had passed.

However, around the retired Beck, a cluster of army men, including Halder, began to gather and make plans to head off Hitler or remove him from power. These contacts led to the first organized "resistance" within the officers' corps, feeble and diffused though it was. Vague plans were made to seize governmental power by a military putsch centered in Berlin. Troops would seize government buildings and a temporary military regime would be established. Hitler's presence in Berlin was considered essential to the success of the plan. There he could be sequestered and brought into one of his own People's Courts on the charge that he had recklessly tried to plunge Germany into a European war and was therefore no longer competent to govern. But the circle of conspirators was small and their plans had not been worked out in any detail. By the time the conspirators were ready to act, Hitler's bluff and bluster had given Germany another stunning triumph.

Throughout the summer of 1938 there was considerable evidence to strengthen Hitler's intuition that the Allies were anything but willing to go to war for Czechoslovakia. Early in June, the London *Times* had urged the Czechs to hold a plebiscite in the Sudetenland, and to allow such areas as desired to join the Reich. On August 3, von Ribbentrop informed the major German diplomatic missions that there was little fear that Britain, France or Russia would intervene over Czechoslovakia. On the same day, Chamberlain had packed off Lord Runciman to Czechoslovakia on a curious mission[4] to act as a "mediator" in the Sudeten crisis. But everyone, including Chamberlain, knew that Runciman's mission to "mediate" between the Czech government and the Sudeten leaders was impossible as well as absurd. Henlein was not a free agent, but merely Hitler's puppet. The Czechs knew perfectly well that Runciman had been sent to pave the way for the handing over of the Sudetenland to Hitler. According to a German Foreign Office memorandum of August 6, Sir Nevile Henderson, the British Ambassador to Germany, had remarked at a private party that "Great Britain would not think of risking even one sailor or airman for Czechoslovakia, and that any reasonable solution would be agreed to so long as it were not attempted by force." This same man had written to Lord Halifax, the British Foreign Secretary, a scant month earlier: "I honestly believe the moment has come for Prague to get a real twist of the screw. . . . If Beneš cannot satisfy Henlein, he can satisfy no Sudeten leader. . . . We have got to be disagreeable to the Czechs." Hitler's intuition was proving much more accurate than his Army's carefully drawn arguments against war.

Meanwhile, the conspirators who were planning to act as soon—and if —Czechoslovakia was attacked, sent agents to London to sound out Britain's true intentions and to try to influence its decision. The first, Ewald von Kleist, saw the chief diplomatic adviser to the Foreign Secretary and Winston Churchill, still in the political wilderness. With both men, Kleist stressed that Hitler had set a date for attacking Czechoslovakia, that German generals would act to stop Hitler if Britain and France would declare publicly that they would not stand by idly. Churchill sent a ringing letter back to bolster the conspirators, but Chamberlain discounted much of what Kleist reported. However, he instructed Henderson to convey a sober warning to Hitler and to prepare a personal contact between himself and Hitler. According to Henderson's own story, he persuaded Chamberlain to drop the first request, but gladly went to work on the second. This was the first step toward Munich.[5]

The conspirators continued their efforts to warn the British government. Henderson described these warnings as "largely propaganda and clearly biased." On September 7, the London *Times*, reflecting official thinking, was pursuing another, quite different tack: "It might be worth while," the *Times* leader ran, "for the Czechoslovak Government to consider whether they should exclude altogether the project, which has found favor in some quarters, of making Czechoslovakia a more homogeneous State by the secession of that fringe of alien populations who are contiguous to the nation with which they are united by race. . . ."

Hitler, meanwhile, went off to the Nuremberg rally where the spectacle of massed power and pageantry had the usual self-intoxicating effect. At the rally Göring made a bellicose speech: "A petty segment of Europe is harassing the human race. . . . This miserable pygmy race is oppressing a cultured people, and behind it is Moscow and the eternal mask of the Jew devil." Simultaneously, the Czechs gave the Sudeten leaders every demand they asked for. But this was the last thing the Sudeten politicians and their directors in Berlin wanted. On instructions from Germany, Henlein suddenly broke off all negotiations with the Czech government, giving some shabby excuse about alleged Czech police excesses.

The threatened victims began making their preparations. The airport and all railroad stations in Prague were full of Jews desperately trying to find transportation to safer parts of Europe. Gas masks were distributed to the Czech population. The word from Paris was that the French government was beginning to panic at the prospect of war and that Chamberlain would meet Hitler's demands at the expense of the Czechs. The Czechs were not consulted at any point. Russia, they learned to their sorrow, was under no obligation to come to their aid unless France did. Czechoslovakia was being abandoned.

Chamberlain was ready to give Hitler what he had wanted—Sudetenland —"after peaceful negotiations." But, as in all of his past international dealings, as soon as the first concession was made, Hitler immediately raised his demands. Chamberlain's reasonableness was spoiling Hitler's real desire to destroy the Czech state, to humiliate President Beneš and expose the feebleness of the Western powers. Hitler wanted, above all, to act unilaterally. Meanwhile, the Hungarians and the Poles came forward with claims on Czech territory, adding fire to Hitler's blackmail. New demands were presented to the Czechs; they responded with a general mobilization.

The capitulation at Munich followed on September 29. Hitler was permitted to march into Czechoslovakia, to occupy the Sudetenland and control the vast Czech fortifications there. Later he installed a pro-German fascist government. Poland and Hungary received the spoils they wanted. Within a month after Munich, the Czech nation existed at the mercy of Hitler. The Beck-Halder "plot" crumbled quickly after Hitler's stunning, bloodless victory.

The Western powers had lost a golden opportunity to put an end to the menace of Hitler's Third Reich. Never again, after Munich, was Germany so unprepared for war. Never again were Hitler's threats so hollow or his bluff so vulnerable. For the Jews of Europe, the disintegration of

Czechoslovakia brought to full tide the German *Drang nach dem Osten* —the pull to the East—eventual war, and their destruction. In a long, rambling speech to the Reichstag on January 30, 1939, Hitler publicly proclaimed what he had undoubtedly had in mind for some time: "Today I will once more be a prophet. If the international Jewish financiers inside and outside Europe should again succeed in plunging the nations into a world war, the result will be . . . the annihilation of the Jewish race throughout Europe." In the years to come, Hitler would often remind listeners of this prophecy and, on at least five occasions, he repeated the words verbatim in public. In the final phase of his aggression, the invasion of Russia, he carried out his threats.

After Munich, the conservative wing of the officers' corps was crushed and the Army stood poised to destroy the rest of Czechoslovakia at the first opportunity. The German Foreign Office now planned to drive a diplomatic wedge between the Czech provinces of Bohemia and Moravia and the eastern province of Slovakia, so that the Czech Government would collapse. Independence for Slovakia became the new line. "An independent Slovakia," wrote a German Foreign Office official immediately after Munich, "would be a weak political organism and hence would lend the best assistance to the German need for pushing forward and obtaining space in the east." Agents were sent in to agitate the Slovakian separatist movement. The Slovakian leader, Monsignor Josef Tiso, was summoned to Berlin and on March 14, 1939, the Slovakian diet in Bratislava declared its independence. Hungarian troops by a prearranged plan occupied Ruthenia, the eastern tip of Czechoslovakia. The aged and ailing President Emil Hácha was brought to Berlin and "confidently placed the fate of the Czech people in the hands of the Führer." On March 16, Hitler formally incorporated Bohemia and Moravia into the Third Reich as a "protectorate." German diplomats abroad were instructed to say that action had been taken "with the full agreement of the Czechoslovakian government."

With this proclamation, more than 120,000 Jews in Czechoslovakia were delivered over to the Gestapo. The number may have been as high as 130,000 as a result of the refugee exodus from Austria. Within the next six months, the Gestapo expelled 35,000—a pace exceeding that of Austria. On July 26, 1939, Eichmann set up another emigration center in Prague modeled on the one in Vienna and demanded the emigration of 70,000 within a year. It fell to the Jewish Community Council to provide a daily quota of Jews. If the emigrants were not produced and their capitation fees not paid, Eichmann threatened concentration camps. Thus, the poorest members of the community suffered first. Those who had property negotiated with the Gestapo on their own. The "quota" Jews demanded by Eichmann were dumped with their exit permits at ports and frontiers. Thousands were put aboard German ships with bogus Latin-American visas or with precious British permits for Palestine (now reduced to 1,500 a month). When Dr. Kafka, the president of the Prague Jewish Council expressed doubts about the ability of the Council to raise the necessary funds, Eichmann replied: "If you do not get these Jews out of the country, I will order the arrest of three hundred men per day and I will send them to Dachau and Merkelgrün, where I am sure they will become very enthusiastic about emigration."

As in Vienna, Eichmann carried out his duties with unremitting zeal. In Prague, he mastered the individual psychological blitzkrieg which left the victim confused and helpless by sudden menacing changes. A ruthless use of power would be followed by a sudden and inexplicable release of what appeared to be almost human sympathy. An example was the case of Naftali Palatin, a medical student at the University of Prague, who had secured 350 visas for Palestine. Eichmann ordered all of the people involved to be out of the country within two weeks. There was a desperate and finally successful effort to get a ship, when, suddenly, Palatin was ordered to leave Czechoslovakia with his wife but without their six-month-old daughter. Palatin saw Eichmann and asked permission for his wife to take the baby to her grandparents in Latvia for the time being.

Eichmann burst out laughing and asked, "What kind of solution is it to send a child to Latvia? How long do you think it will be before we arrive there? Now I want to show you something." From the table he picked up a Hebrew-language newspaper *Davar*, shouted that it contained a bitter attack on the Nazis and threatened a worldwide Jewish boycott of German goods. "You Jews hate us!" he shrieked. "If you had arms you would fight us. We in the Gestapo have rifles, machine guns and bullets. We will line you up before the transport you use and start shooting. Where will you stand? At the beginning of the line or at the end? You are the leader. You could choose. You will be able to stand at the end of the line and live a few more minutes!"

Then, suddenly, Eichmann sat down and said wearily, "All right. You can have an exit permit and a reentry permit for your wife."

Amazingly enough, he kept his word. Palatin's wife took their baby to Latvia and returned alone. Eichmann again summoned Palatin. His manner was affable. When Palatin pointed out that the departure date fell on Yom Kippur, he said understandingly, "Oh, certainly, you cannot be expected to leave on such a holiday." They settled on October 13 for the departure.

Palatin was giddy with relief and as he moved to the door, Eichmann asked if he would do him a favor. Palatin, bewildered, nodded dumbly.

"Tomorrow morning you will bring me the passports of your father and mother." The voice was steel-like. "They are not leaving with the transports. They remain as hostages. I will kill them like dogs if any of the passengers on the transport ever return here. I will kill them if when you arrive in Palestine you say one bad word about Germany. I will kill them if you say that I handled you cruelly or that you suffered under the rule of the Third Reich."

A few days later, Palatin and his wife left on the transport to Palestine. Long afterward he heard that his father had been shot, that his mother had been sent to the gas chambers, and that his small child and her grandparents in Latvia had all been killed.[6]

Encounters of this kind in which great cruelties were fitfully punctuated by recognizably human gestures—including the dangle of hope—occurred throughout the Holocaust and created victims robbed of all natural powers of resistance. The senselessness of the Nazi world conformed to nothing known in previous Jewish experience.

Meanwhile, in Czechoslovakia, the destruction of their economic life caused general destitution among Jews.

On the very day the Protectorate was proclaimed, Zionist leaders considered dissolving their organization. They debated the wisdom of continuing to function under the whiplash of the Gestapo. But the idea was rejected. Had they or any of the other Jewish organizations closed down, valuable services would have suddenly stopped, making the situation facing the Jews much worse. As it was, three main organizations—the Supreme Council of the Union of Jewish Communities, the Prague Jewish Community and the Joint Social Commission (made up of sixteen organizations) —were taking care of thousands of refugees from Germany, Austria and the Sudetenland, helping them find shelter and work. They also played an important role in the emigration of the indigenous Jewish population of Bohemia-Moravia.[7]

There was an agreement, for example, between the Jewish organizations and the British Government under which certain funds from a British loan to Czechoslovakia, granted after Munich, could be used—and by these organizations alone—to finance Jewish emigration. These agencies also served as an address for Jews in other countries. The closing down of Jewish communal organizations in Czechoslovakia, as elsewhere, would have exposed countless thousands of Jews to chaos and untold misery. They would have been utterly abandoned to their fate. The noose around the agencies grew tighter as the war was intensified, but for several years they channeled emigration, provided for the education, welfare and religious needs of the community and took care of the destitute. No other agencies in the state would have done this. In 1942 and 1943 the Jewish Council drew up lists for deportation to the ghetto of Theresienstadt. No Jew in Prague knew that Theresienstadt was a transit camp whose inmates were destined to go to Auschwitz. Nor did Jewish officials know this. The argument is sometimes made that had the organizations liquidated themselves, the Nazis would have been deprived of organized information about Jews. But in Czechoslovakia, as elsewhere, the Nazis had access to this information anyhow. In the Protectorate, for example, such records were originally under Czech control: the central government record offices contained personal data on every inhabitant in the country, including his religion, and the local offices of vital statistics contained records which included the religious affiliation of parents of every resident.[8]

In Germany, the Nazis had at their disposal the addresses of all Jews owning property valued at more than 5,000 reichsmarks, the addresses of Jewish businesses, identification cards marked with a "J" and ration card lists. The census of May 17, 1939, covering Germany, Austria and the Sudeten region supplied the German Government with a complete file of special cards on origins and education of the population. The main item on these cards was the question: "Was (or is) one of the grandparents a full Jew by race?"

In the Netherlands, the Jews were doubly registered, first under ordinary cards kept in each population register, and second, in a special registration of Jews made early in 1941.[9]

The campaign against Jews in the Protectorate falls into two distinct stages. In the months following the German seizure of power, it took the form of economic liquidation—the confiscation of Jewish property and the ousting of Jews from economic life. The second stage began when the Nazis reached an agreement with Russia in the summer of 1939 to repatriate German minorities in the Baltic countries and then decided, instead, to resettle them in the newly acquired Czech territory. In order to make room for them, Jews had to be expelled. This expulsion coincided with the spread of the myth that Jews would be allowed to form a permanent colony in the "Lublin reservation" in Poland. A foretaste of future hardships came in July.

On July 2, groups of Jewish children were stopped by Nazis at the park gates in Moravska-Ostrava and Brno and were systematically beaten up. A few days later, Czech children were taken to an anti-Jewish exhibition organized in an arcade at Prague under the auspices of Streicher's *Stürmer*. Later that month anti-Jewish riots were staged in Brno, Moravska-Ostrava and Budiejowice during the course of Nazi victory parades. On July 26, Eichmann's office was set up to coerce Jews to emigrate. Jewish property, whose estimated value was $120,000,000, was ordered registered. Six Jewish communities and fifty synagogues were dissolved in Sudetenland.[10]

The Nazis profited from the forced emigration. Jewish emigrants had been leaving Czechoslovakia under a transfer agreement with the British government whereby they deposited 450,000 kronen per £3,240. On August 7, the Germans dropped this ratio to 450,000 kronen per £1,000. Capitalist emigrants to Palestine, for their part, were obliged to deposit 300,000 kronen with the National Bank in addition to 150,000 kronen "flight tax."[11] Curiously, in the Nazi pressure on Jews to leave, an exception was made of physicians. They were actually forbidden to leave, because they would be needed for the expanded war that Hitler was planning.

On August 11, the mass expulsion of Jews began in earnest. All Jews were ordered to leave the provinces and concentrate in Prague within a year. Once in Prague, the Gestapo ordered 200 to leave the country daily. But, quite literally, they had no place to go. The broad hint in the January 1939 Foreign Office circular, that if emigration outlets could not be found, Germany herself would have to find her own solution, materialized quickly after Germany's attack on Poland in September. The dumping ground, inevitably, would be Poland. Before the end of 1939, some 45,000 Jews had been shoved into Lublin.[12]

The dismemberment of Czechoslovakia not only hastened the war and accelerated drastic actions against the Jews of Europe. It also opened up opportunities for vast population upheavals that sprang from Himmler's grandiose racial fantasies. Himmler was in Hitler's entourage when he rode into Prague and was dazzled by the new opportunities for power and resettlement projects. The new realm could become an "experimental garden" for S.S. schemes, creating a new aristocracy of Aryan blood. Himmler was in an ecstasy over these new vistas and toyed with the idea of deporting six million Czechs "to the East" after the conquest of Poland to make room for "pure" Germans in Czechoslovakia. These resettlement projects, which, during the war were to become expressions of mad obsessions, reveal, as does the war to annihilate Jews, the inner destructiveness of Nazi ideology. The core was death.

Until Munich, German minorities were merely protected by the mother country. They were let alone as hostages for German good intentions. In 1938, the Liaison Office for Ethnic Germans (*Volksdeutsche Mittelstelle* —VoMi for short) took charge of all ethnic German activities throughout the world. Himmler immediately infiltrated it with S.S. personnel. After the conquest of Poland, he created his own agency for strengthening Germandom—the RKFDV—and began methodically to move back to the Reich all Germans and "Germanizable" elements living under foreign governments and to cleanse the Reich of all alien elements. Himmler's wild dreams included the revival of the Carolingian kingdom of Burgundy, the transplanting of the English to the Baltic states, the elimination of dark-haired Germans and official encouragement of bigamy among a blond warrior caste. In the Protectorate, persons claiming any German blood were to be classified according to "documentary" evidence; lacking this, they would be subject to "racial examination." If the results were positive, they would be "re-Germanized." About 45 percent of the Czechs were deemed "Germanizable." The rest were disposable.

With the German occupation of Moravia and the military domination of Slovakia, the borders of German power crept ominously around Poland. Now all of western Poland lay between the upper thrust of Prussia and Pomerania and the lower pincer of Silesia, Moravia and Slovakia. The Jews of Europe had very little time to flee a continent fast succumbing to Hitler.

8 The Struggle to Leave Europe

WITH THE EXCEPTION of the panic exodus of 1933, Jewish emigration from Germany up to the end of 1937 had been fairly well organized. Jewish agencies were able to retrain emigrants for the vocational specifications of receiving countries and to give financial assistance to needy Jews. Within ten or twelve years, it was believed, at a steady rate of 25,000 emigrants a year, Hitler could have his Germany cleansed of Jews. By the end of 1937, 129,000—25 percent of the Jewish population—had already left Germany.

But in March 1938, the Nazi take-over in Austria created a new crisis: there were now 185,000 more Jews for whom refuge had to be found. Moreover, the appointment in February 1938 of von Ribbentrop, an avowed Nazi, as Foreign Minister, was a bad omen for the relief agencies. After the "June Action," and particularly after the November pogroms, Jews frantically wanted to leave Germany. But the Nazis made planned emigration impossible. In abandoning the cautious work of the old-line ministries, the new extremists no longer recognized that Jews waiting for visas and certificates had to be left a narrow basis of existence in order to go on living until they could emigrate. The Nazis were not interested in their problems; Jews would simply have to go. Ten years was too long to wait. The Reich had to be purged of Jews swiftly.

The shock of the sudden change in emigration policy was felt not only by Jews but by German officials who had worked coöperatively with Jewish relief agencies in the early years of the Hitler regime. The Reich Office of Migration in the Ministry of the Interior, which handled Jewish emigration, had been staffed by men who were accommodating and sympathetic.[1] They showed full understanding of the view of the *Hilfsverein der deutschen Juden* (German Jewish Relief Association) that Jewish emigration to all countries (except Palestine, where the situation was different) had to be channeled so that Jews could make a contribution to their host countries. They not only believed that emigrants must be prepared for a new life through skills, language, and proper orientation, but that the entire procedure be legal. Moreover, they realized that some Jews were unfit for emigration and ought not to be encouraged to leave. In 1936 and 1937, these officials still felt safe enough to declare that if emigration had to be forced upon Jews, it should be carried out "in a manner befitting a civilized nation." This produced a very benevolent attitude in questions regarding the transfer of Jewish property. The *Reichswanderungsamt* (Office of Migration) had no desire to chase penniless Jews across the frontier. As a consequence of this constructive policy, most of the German Jews who emigrated between 1935 and 1938 were able to take root and build new lives outside Germany.

In 1938 the situation changed radically. A complete shift in the political center of gravity unsettled the base of the old ministerial staffs to such a degree that they frequently consulted with Jewish community leaders for advice. For example, in December 1938, officers of the *Hilfsverein* called at the Office of Migration to intercede for the thousands of Jews who were in concentration camps after the November roundups. The Gestapo ordered these Jews to emigrate within a few weeks or remain in prison. The German officials were plainly shocked by the news. Likewise stunned, Jewish leaders prepared a detailed memorandum urging an extension of the Gestapo deadline. They asked the emigration officials to pass their request on to the Gestapo. This was done willingly. However, when the fate of the memorandum was questioned, the German officials, fearful and uncertain, telephoned the Jewish leaders to ask what they knew and whether *they* thought the ministry officials could make inquiries of the Gestapo. The old executive authority on Jewish emigration had become helpless.[2]

The emigration question was also discussed by diplomats. Immediately after the Munich conference, British Prime Minister Chamberlain had prepared a special mission to Germany to discuss economic matters, loans, and the possible return of German colonies. But the November pogroms put these issues on the shelf. However, the inflamed Jewish question offered the possibility of new negotiations. At the behest of Chamberlain, the South African Minister of Defense, Oswald Pirow, visited Hitler and suggested that German Jews be resettled in former German African colonies. The project would be financed by an Anglo-American loan and Germany would not lose a penny in foreign exchange. Hitler indignantly rejected Pirow's suggestion. How could he offer the lands where "the blood of so many German heroes had been shed?" How could the "bitterest enemies of the Germans" be resettled there? Hitler thumped away at one of his favorite themes: the Jewish problem, raising its head everywhere —in Poland, in Czechoslovakia, in France, in England. It was not only a German but also a European problem. "The British ooze humanitarian sentiments," he told Pirow, "and do nothing to help. . . . What do you think would happen in Germany, Mr. Pirow, if I withdrew my protecting hand from the Jews? The world could not imagine it." Nothing came of Pirow's overture.

Pirow's visit had taken place on November 24. Just three days earlier, in a discussion of possible places in the British Empire where Jews might be settled, Chamberlain had warned the members of the House of Commons that "the interests of native populations must not be prejudiced" in considering the British Empire for Jewish resettlement purposes. The British Colonial Secretary agreed that twenty-five settlers and their families could go to Kenya.

That same week, on November 17, the British Ambassador in Washington called on Sumner Welles, American Undersecretary of State, and offered him half the British immigration quota (65,000 per year) for the coming year for the benefit of German Jews. Welles rebuked him, saying that the quota was not his to offer. He also reminded the Ambassador that the President had officially stated a few days before at a press conference that the United States had no intention of increasing the annual quota already established for German nationals (25,000). Between 1933 and July 1, 1938, the United States had admitted 27,000 German Jews.

On November 24, the same day of Pirow's visit to Hitler, the problem of the Jewish refugee was once more the topic of official conversation—this time in Paris. Chamberlain and Edouard Daladier, the French Premier, and their Foreign Secretaries, Viscount Halifax and Georges Bonnet, conferred in preparation for a forthcoming meeting with von Ribbentrop to discuss closer French-German relations. Bonnet said that France already had 40,000 Jewish refugees and could not permit a new immigration on a large scale. Chamberlain expressed sympathy for the plight of the refugees but pointed to "the serious danger of arousing anti-Semitic feeling in Great Britain." He reported that 500 Jewish immigrants were currently being admitted to Britain each week. Tanganyika was willing to admit some, but the Germans later opposed this offer on the ground that Tanganyika was "by right a German colony and will in time return to Germany." Chamberlain thought that the most "hopeful" territory was British Guiana, but that the Jews would have to find the money for the development of a settlement. He expressed the hope that the French Government could exercise some beneficial influence over von Ribbentrop and bring about a relaxation of German policy.

Von Ribbentrop, however, refused to have anything at all to do with international committees concerned with the Jewish question, and he vehemently refused to yield up Jewish wealth for financing any resettlement projects. On his side, Bonnet urged Germany to take steps to keep Jews from coming into France. His government was actually thinking of sending 10,000 of them elsewhere, possibly to Madagascar. Von Ribbentrop commented that "we all want to get rid of our Jews. The difficulty is that no country wishes to receive them."[3]

Early in January 1939, Ambassador William Phillips presented a note to Count Galeazzo Ciano, Italian Minister for Foreign Affairs. The note was from President Roosevelt and directed to Mussolini. Roosevelt had given advice to Europeans on resettlement schemes and the convening international conferences devoted to refugee problems, but had not asked for the slightest modification in American immigration policy. In the note to Mussolini, Roosevelt suggested opening Ethiopia to Jews. Mussolini countered by suggesting the Soviet Union, Brazil and the United States. "If that country [United States]," he wrote, "were to increase its density of population from the present 41 per mile to the Italian level of 345, it could accommodate about a billion more people."

While diplomats bandied the immigration problem back and forth, the very lives of Jews were becoming increasingly precarious. Eichmann was stepping up his quotas in Austria. The Poles had barred thousands of Polish Jews expelled from Germany in October 1938. In Germany, the November pogroms and economic depredations had plunged the Jewish community into despair. Countries were sealing their borders. Two ominous questions were forming: How could the Reich free itself of Jews faster than it was acquiring them? And how could Jews leave the Reich if there was no place to go?

In Hitler's threatening speech to the Reichstag on January 30, 1939, he made sarcastic accusations against the West: "It is a shameful example to observe today how the entire democratic world dissolves in tears of pity but then, in spite of its obvious duty to help, closes its heart to the poor, tortured people." With Hitler's compulsive need to carry out threats and "prophecies," the threat to annihilate Jewry—which was made in this speech—may have helped propel the action. The questions—whether he exhausted emigration policies, or became impatient with their slow results, or merely waited until the West talked itself out of real solutions and became impotent in the face of the problem, thus permitting him to go ahead with his extermination plans—these are impossible to answer with certainty. It is likely that he wanted to implicate the Western nations as passive onlookers. His emigration "plans," the chief one of which was to ship Jews to Madagascar, were never very realistic, while his war timetable consumed any serious proposals that may have existed in the Third Reich. The Gestapo, meanwhile, not yet in complete control of emigration, supported schemes involving settlement in such uninhabited and unexplored parts of the globe as the Oriente region of Ecuador and the Mato Grosso of Brazil and berated Jewish officials for not taking up these cynical proposals. At the same time, the Gestapo drew support from the large pro-Nazi German colonies in South America for stringent immigration laws.

While pressuring Jewish officials and complaining that Jews were not leaving Germany fast enough, the Gestapo also spread propaganda which described Jews everywhere as parasites and Bolshevik agents. It also planted newspaper stories aimed at making prospective emigrants obnoxious to host countries. "No One Wants to Have Them" or "People Seek Protection Against Jewish Immigrants" were typical headlines. Jews themselves became panicky. As the coercion increased, they resorted to doctored papers. Relief agencies lost their steadiness and the countries that were sought as refuge stiffened in their opposition to new admissions. Some emigrants indicated spurious destinations: they secured visas for Paraguay in order to obtain transit visas for Argentina, with the intention of staying in Argentina. There were also many emigrants who obtained papers by falsifying occupations. For example, South American countries offered special terms for farmers. So as to qualify, Jewish emigrants bribed German peasants into giving them the necessary certificates. A new class of Jewish "landowners" suddenly arose. Brazil had very easy terms for emigrants who owned real estate there. This news led to a flourishing trade in landowner title deeds for land in unexplored Brazil.[4] It was also possible for wealthy emigrants to buy foreign passports or residence passports. Lucrative profits were made by travel agents and consuls, some of whom were themselves German citizens and Nazis. They had Jews to sell and could manipulate the market at will. The Gestapo, which encouraged this illicit traffic, is known to have received as much as 250,000 marks for official passports.[5]

After the "June action," Jewish emigration authorities no longer enjoyed the luxury of legal procedures. Desperation forced illegalities upon them. The circumventions resorted to in 1938 under mounting pressure and Nazi propaganda led certain South American countries to restrict immigration. This, in turn, created greater pressure on other countries. By this time, Jews wanted to leave Germany at any price and any self-humiliation. The purposes of the Gestapo and the Ministry of Propaganda were further served by such illegalities. The cycle churned on.

The American Joint Distribution Committee (JDC), the worldwide Jewish welfare agency, tried to break this cycle. In the early years of the Hitler regime, the big question before the JDC was how to help the Jews of Germany without helping the Reich. The agency maintained many of the German Jewish refugees who had fled to France, but something tangible had to be devised for the Jews who were left in Germany. A formula was finally found. The agency promised repayment in dollars for marks deposited in Germany either with the local Jewish communities or with the Central Committee for Jewish Relief (*Zentral Ausschuss der deutschen Juden für Hilfe und Aufbau*). If children could be smuggled out, JDC would pay in dollars for their education. If adults could acquire visas, the organization would care for them in transit and pay their passage in dollars. (The shipping lines would accept nothing else.) Meanwhile, the marks they left behind would be a contribution from JDC for the work of the Central Committee.[6] If the donors did in fact escape, they would get their money back in the currency of any country not dominated by Germany.

This plan had modest beginnings, but grew in importance during the war. In lands conquered by the Germans, Jews gave all they had to local organizations which had been approved by JDC against the promise of the agency to repay later. About $13 million was raised for such projects behind enemy lines. The local Jewish organizations were sometimes raided and their books confiscated, but generally, this subterfuge was well concealed.[7] As late as 1959, claims were still being made and honored on behalf of participants in these arrangements. Had the local Jewish organizations dissolved, thousands of Jews who escaped in time would have found emigration impossible. As it was, almost $4 million of the $5.5 million deposited in New York by friends and relatives of would-be emigrants had to be refunded by the JDC. These refunds represented Jews who never got out.

The major agency for the rescue of Jews, however, was the *Mossad le Aliyah Bet* (Committee for Illegal Immigration), organized by Palestinian Jews in 1937. It was this movement that was the lifeline to abandoned Jewish islands perishing in the abattoir the Nazis were to make of Europe. It was also *Mossad le Aliyah Bet* that eventually broke Britain's grip on Palestine. Around the *Mossad*, the remnant of European Jewry rallied after the war to force the creation of the State of Israel.

The *Mossad* was organized in 1937 to cope with the increasingly exposed position of Europe's Jews. Not only was there danger in Germany but also in Poland where there was talk of disposing of a million "surplus" Jews, and in Romania, where Jews were subject to increasing economic and political disabilities. The *Mossad* sent emissaries to Paris, which was to serve as headquarters, to eastern Europe, and, most risky of all, to Berlin and Vienna, where, for a time, the Gestapo was willing to allow *Mossad* agents to organize convoys of Jews bound for Palestine. Moshe Auerbach, the *Mossad* emissary to Vienna, for example, dealt directly with Eichmann.

Despite the Arab terrorism of the 1930's and the progressively tighter immigration restrictions of the British mandatory regime, Jews naturally gravitated toward Palestine as a refuge. Their fellow Jews welcomed them and the risks experienced there seemed less hazardous than elsewhere. The importance of Palestine as a solution for Jews is apparent from the following statistics: During the three-year period, 1933–35, out of 200,000 Jewish migrants from Europe, 123,786 entered Palestine, nearly half of them—61,000—in the year 1935.[8] By 1936, however, the British, reacting to Arab terrorism, signaled their intention to cut off the escape route. The Palestine Royal Commission, anxious to preserve Britain's interests in a stable Middle East, showed little sympathy for Jewish refugees when it began its deliberations. One member, Sir Horace Rumbold, observed that "the Jews were an alien race in Palestine." And the commission, although silent on the question of illegal Arab immigration, criticized the Jewish Agency for not smoking out illegal Jewish immigrants. In July 1937, the commission, headed by Lord Peel, declared that the Mandate to establish a Jewish National Home in Palestine was "unworkable." Stricter immigration restrictions followed and the number of Jews entering Palestine rapidly declined from 61,000 in 1935 to less than 30,000 in 1936 and to under 11,000 in 1937.

For the German Jews, who were particularly exposed, Palestine was crucial. Up to the middle of 1938, Palestine had received one third of all the Jews who had emigrated from Germany since 1933—50,000 out of a total of 150,000.[9] Many German Jews still felt attached to Europe and from 37,000 to 40,000 Jews went to other European countries during this period—to their sorrow. But the pull of Palestine was both emotional and practical. After having been cast out of a country which they had loved, many German Jews recovered their self-respect by associating themselves with the cause of Zionism. Young people especially were attracted by the Zionist ideal. There were also practical advantages made possible by the Ha'avara (transfer) agreement which had been worked out between the Reich Ministry of Economics and the Jewish authorities of Palestine in 1933. This was a modified clearing agreement that benefited both sides: A Jew emigrating to Palestine made a contract with a German exporter for the transfer of certain goods to Palestine. The exporter, in turn, was paid with funds from the blocked account of the emigrant. On his arrival in Palestine, the emigrant received what was due him in Palestine currency from the Jewish Agency. This arrangement made it possible for 50,000 German Jews to emigrate to Palestine without losing their assets. Later it was supplemented by a barter agreement involving the exchange of Palestine oranges for German timber, wrapping paper, pumps, and farm machinery. Jewish emigrants could also purchase orange groves in Palestine by depositing marks in Germany. The accounts accruing were then transferred through a supply of German exports.

This agreement coincided with German economic interests and was for that reason severely criticized by many Jews in Palestine, but it was of decisive importance in the promotion of orderly Jewish emigration. It also deprived the Nazi extremists of the opportunity, in at least one field, to lead Jewish emigration into utterly chaotic channels at the end of 1938.[10]

Hitler's own attitude toward Palestine was, of course, decisive in any of these negotiations. A brief sketch shows much fluctuation in his views but official approval of Jewish emigration to Palestine finally emerged a short time before the British issued a new set of immigration restrictions in May 1939. Up to 1936, Hitler's policy was characterized by great reserve: he was still cultivating the illusion that National Socialism would not break the continuity of German foreign policy of the pre-Weimar past. In the case of Palestine, this was a cautiously benevolent attitude toward Jewish plans for establishing a homeland and neutrality regarding the British Mandate. The *Ha'avara* agreements were carried out with only occasional eruptions from radical Nazis who ranted against "unfair" treatment of Germans in Palestine at the hands of Jews. Official statements from various ministries during the early Nazi regime showed that Palestine was preferred over other countries in Nazi emigration schemes, but in 1937 a new line seemed to be forming. The first signs came after the publication of the British Royal Commission Report (Peel Plan) in the summer of 1937. Suddenly transfer negotiations in progress were held up and German immigration officials were under constraint. It was very puzzling. At first, no explanation could be found. Then rumors began circulating that Hitler had made some unfavorable remarks about Palestine after the British issued the Peel Report. It appeared that the *Ha'avara* might be merely a temporary expedient and that the export of German goods no longer mattered in the new international strategy Hitler was plotting.

A note from the Ministry of Foreign Affairs, dated March 10, 1938— a few weeks before the annexation of Austria—seemed to foreshadow a policy change. It said:

> The influx into Palestine of German capital in Jewish hands will facilitate the building up of a Jewish state, which runs counter to German interests; for this state, instead of absorbing world Jewry, will someday bring about a considerable increase in world Jewry's political power. Germany is not interested in facilitating the emigration of rich Jews who take their capital with them. Germany is far more interested in a *mass* Jewish emigration.[11]

The Peel Report had recommended the partition of Palestine and the establishment of a Jewish state in a tiny part of the country. Hitler compared such a state to the Vatican and saw in it a spiritual center for "the international Jewish conspiracy." In this light, German Jewish manpower and money were strengthening a nascent Jewish state and would have to be stopped. Although the Peel Plan was not implemented, the subject caused Hitler considerable anxiety, for when Lord Halifax came to Berlin on a special mission during this period, Hitler surprised him by beginning their conversation with a question about the "Jewish state" in Palestine.

The Palestine Desk in the Wilhelmstrasse at this time was held by Werner Otto von Hentig, a critic of the Nazi regime, but a man whose foreign service experience could not be ignored or wasted. Hentig had already dealt with the Palestine problem in Constantinople, where he served with the Germany Embassy. In Berlin, he had often seen and heard Weizmann and had been deeply impressed by him. He was also attracted to the daring of the Zionist experiment. Hentig advised Ernst Marcus, who was employed by the Paltreu Company, a subsidiary of the *Ha'avara* Company, to prepare material proving that the contribution of German Jews to the upbuilding of Palestine was small as compared with the share of Polish Jews and the financial contribution of American Jews. Marcus prepared such a memorandum, which served as a basis for a "Report to Hitler by the Foreign Office."[12] Hentig himself prepared a brief, arguing that there were certain advantages to Germany in the establishment of a Jewish state. Other divisions within the Foreign Ministry, however, submitted negative recommendations. Several months passed. Since Foreign Secretary von Neurath could not make a decision himself, it was decided to bring the question to Hitler directly, at a moment when he was psychologically accessible.

A short time before the *Mossad* emissary, Auerbach, arrived in Vienna, von Hentig phoned Marcus to tell him that Hitler at last had made a favorable decision and that all obstacles in the way of emigration to Palestine were now removed.

The Palestinian emissaries had come at the right moment, but they had very little time. On October 21, 1937, a British ordinance had given the High Commissioner in Palestine the power to set *political* limits on immigration, which in no case was to exceed one thousand a month, regardless of economic absorptability, and to establish a Jewish proportion of this maximum. Several weeks later, the schedule was announced for the ensuing eight months: 800 per month for Jews. When the schedule for the subsequent six-month period came up, the Jewish quota was further reduced to 3,000 (6,000 a year). The actual numbers of Jews entering Palestine during this period were: 10,536 for 1937 and 12,868 for 1938. "Illegal" immigration had already started. By the end of 1938, hundreds of "illegals" were entering Palestine monthly. Hardly a week passed without a secret night landing somewhere along the coast.[13] Some of these boatloads had been organized by Auerbach in Vienna and by Pino Ginsberg in Berlin with the connivance of the Gestapo.

The only exception to the chaos the Gestapo deliberately provoked in Jewish emigration was emigration to Palestine—at least in the early years of the war. Later, when the almost insuperable obstacles of British inflexibility were overcome—and this happened only very occasionally—Eichmann's organization stopped at nothing to prevent the convoys from leaving for Palestine. In 1938 and later, whenever possible, young Palestinian Jews made deals with the devil to save lives.

To Austrian Zionists, it seemed a cruel joke to have Moshe Auerbach, a farmer from Galil, match wits with Eichmann, but Eichmann seems to have been impressed by the self-assurance and blunt speech of this new type of Jew. He had already agreed to let a thousand Jewish youths train in preparation for Palestine. In discussing the transportation of these boys and girls, Eichmann had insisted that it be left to "private enterprise," that is, the Gestapo. But Auerbach could not wait. He found his way around the city looking for anyone who could help him—honest and dubious characters alike—as long as they could get boats. He met a Signor Metossiani, who in turn introduced him to an engineer named Karthaus, who had connections in Yugoslavia. At that time Yugoslavia was an important embarkation country, and at a cost of twenty marks per person, Karthaus obtained 20,000 transit visas which enabled Jews to cross Yugoslav territory. The Yugoslav government also insisted that the emigrants leave for a specific destination; whereupon Karthaus obtained Mexican visas for them. Now, all that was needed was a seaworthy vessel.

Another young Palestinian, Zvi Yehieli, had been wandering around the bays of Athens and the port of Piraeus for weeks looking for one. He finally came to an agreement with the owner of an old Greek passenger ship, the *Colorado*. The ship was not only old, but slow and cumbersome and had a defective propeller. Makeshift repairs were made and plans were set for the *Colorado* to pick up passengers in the Yugoslavian port of Susa, take them out to sea in the vicinity of Corfu, and then transfer them to the faster and safer *Otrato*.

Meanwhile, Ginsberg had received permission from the Gestapo in Berlin to remain in Germany. He moved about freely and began to revitalize the Zionist Organization's headquarters at 10 Maineckestrasse and to mobilize Jewish youth. Funds for training farms were provided by the *Reichsvertretung*. By giving the Nazi officials a guarantee that he could arrange their immediate emigration, Ginsberg was able to save hundreds of young Jewish boys and girls from concentration camps. A certificate signed by him became a highly prized document. The Gestapo demanded that four hundred sail every week, but fantastic sums of money were demanded for ships that were little more than battered tubs. Ginsberg replied that he was not in Berlin to receive orders from the Gestapo but to work together with them on a project of mutual benefit. It was finally settled that the first transport of German Jews would join the group in Vienna.

Four hundred Jewish youths from this project ultimately landed on the shores of Palestine and secretly slipped into the *kibbutzim*, but not before they had experienced hair-raising mishaps and near-misses that were to become routine for *Mossad* projects. The train carrying the young pioneers was stopped at the Austrian-Yugoslav border because their ship had not yet arrived. When the ship finally pulled into port, hours late, Yugoslav officials insisted that it be thoroughly inspected—a not too subtle hint that they expected a substantial "gift." Two days after the ship sailed, presumably bound for Mexico, stories appeared in the Yugoslav press describing a mystery ship carrying four hundred Jews to Mexico and returning to port empty after only two days! There were demands for a government investigation and Auerbach's special access to Yugoslavia was temporarily withdrawn.

The transport, however, arrived safely in Palestine. The news spread. Auerbach now became open prey for speculators and agents. He no longer had to seek out contacts; they pursued him in hotels in Vienna. It soon became evident that certain Nazis backing emigration to Palestine had reached agreements with shipowners to get rebates on fees. Gestapo agents reaped large profits from the extracurricular transport business. The rates skyrocketed. Eichmann himself was involved in the competition and was so annoyed at Auerbach's independence that he ordered him to leave Austria.

With Auerbach out of the way, Eichmann next turned on the Revisionist Zionists. The Revisionists wanted mass Jewish immigration into Palestine and immediate recognition of a Jewish state in the original area of the Mandate. They had been organizing small boatloads of twelve or fifteen refugees; Eichmann ordered them to stop. The Gestapo allowed Jews to go to Palestine only as long as they could control the shipping arrangements. A whole wave of agents now made their deals with the Gestapo for dubious vessels at fantastically high rates. Left in Vienna to carry on Auerbach's work was Echud Avriel. Both men later went to Istanbul, which became the primary center of Jewish activities after the war started.

Meanwhile, some of the shipowners that had made deals with the *Mossad* agreed to be paid in German money or in German goods destined for Greece. This meant that large convoys could now leave directly from Germany. *Mossad* representatives occasionally collaborated with shipping agents but preferred to work alone, buying or leasing ships directly from the owners. With great nimbleness, they were establishing themselves not only in Germany and Austria but in the Balkans, in Poland and Czechoslovakia, where they organized convoys of Jewish youths and got them through the ports of the Black Sea, Yugoslavia and Greece. Their work was often wrecked by freak accidents, missed contacts, or moody owners. They had to keep the morale of the convoy high while waiting for papers, clearance, proper equipment and supplies. The actual crossings were often nerve-racking. Yet they went doggedly ahead, methodically expanding their work on the Continent and perfecting their organization in Palestine to facilitate "illegal" landings. This was the only Jewish "international" in World War II. A fatal blow to their work in Europe came from the British.

After a long history of whittling down Jewish claims in Palestine—from 60,000 square miles of territory originally to 2,000 square miles recommended by the Peel Commission—the British abandoned their Mandate completely in 1939 and issued a White Paper on May 17 to a stunned Jewry. As of April 1939, only 75,000 immigrants would be allowed to enter over the next five years: 10,000 per year and, an additional 25,000 "as a contribution towards the solution of the Jewish refugee problem." After the five-year period, there would be no further Jewish immigration unless the Arabs acquiesced. Jewish hopes for this refuge were shattered. A torrent of criticism rained down from non-Jews as well as Jews, from members of Parliament, the British press and public, and from the League of Nations. But the British Government was not to be shaken from its position either in the spring of 1939 or later in the midst of the decimations when certificates to Palestine were literally tickets to life.

The key to Britain's intentions was exposed even before ratification of the Mandate by the League. Britain took charge of Palestine after World War I and put the administration of the country in the hands of the Colonial Office rather than the Foreign Office, as France had done in the case of Syria. This move indicated that the approach to the untried mandatory question would not differ from the approach to any crown colony: the development of Palestine was to be made subservient to British imperial considerations.[14] For the British, Palestine was an overland bridge to India, an indispensable link in the chain of the empire's defenses.

Haifa was the terminus of the pipeline from the Arab oil fields and an important fueling station for ships, planes and armies. Palestine as a whole was an important base for an air, naval and land defense of the Suez Canal. The promises made both in the Balfour Declaration and in the terms of the Mandate from the League to secure a Jewish national home in Palestine were to become minor irritants in such an imperial accounting.

Arab terrorism in the thirties flared with tacit British consent. Terrorist gangs recruited by the Mufti of Jerusalem, a political adventurer whom the British themselves had once imprisoned, shot down Jewish workers in the fields, burned crops and looted with impunity. Twenty thousand British troops stood by. The Jewish settlements were disarmed.

American senators who visited Palestine in 1936 observed that the prolonged terror was "due to a manifest sympathy for the vandals and assassins displayed by many officers." The antipathy of the Palestine civil servants toward Jews has been noted by many observers. Thus, on top of imperial design not to relinquish Palestine despite its obligations under the Mandate, the British in Palestine had no sympathy for the duties they had been entrusted to carry out because of their own undisguised anti-Jewish feelings.

By the middle thirties, British officials had convinced themselves that 400,000 Jews in Palestine constituted a threat to 950,000 Arabs, surrounded though they were by forty million additional Arabs. "The National Home is already too big," the Peel Report stated. "Four hundred thousand is a formidable fraction in a total population of 1,300,000." Having done nothing to quench Arab terrorism when it began, the British stood by impotently when it flared under the demagogic cleverness of the Mufti. The Arabs had declared a general strike in 1936, but the British neither declared martial law nor illegalized the strike—two actions justified by law, and the neglect of which, as the League of Nations Mandates Commission noted, had caused Jewish immigration to suffer.

The British were castigated by the League for having violated their obligations under the Mandate and by the United States for neglecting to consult with the American Government before changing policy. But the British were undeterred.

In its last dying moments, the League, speaking for the nations that still accepted the fundamental principles of international law, taxed Britain with a flagrant breach of the Mandate. Soon even this feeble voice was extinguished in the moral anarchy that surrounded Munich. To mounting Arab blackmail and terrorism in 1938, the British answer was the punitive White Paper of 1939.

The British finally took action against the man they had nurtured. They arrested the members of the Arab Higher Committee and deposed the Grand Mufti from his post as president of the Supreme Moslem Council. The Mufti sought asylum in the Mosque of Omar, then escaped to Beirut where he directed new waves of terror and anti-British actions. Eventually he linked his destiny with that of Hitler and served as Hitler's mouthpiece to the Arab peoples.

The British were to reap only bitter fruit during the war as a consequence of their Palestine policy. The Arabs, far from defending British interests in the Middle East, undermined it. Subsidized heavily by the Nazis, they allied with Hitler during the war. In Directive No. 30 to the Middle East, dated May 23, 1941, Hitler wrote: "The Arab Freedom Movement is, in the Middle East, our natural ally against England." Palestine Jews, having no other choice, fought with the British where they could as if there were no White Paper, and fought the White Paper as if there were no war.

To enforce their policies, the British were required to station troops in Palestine that were needed desperately elsewhere. Commenting on the intransigence of colonial policy, Churchill wrote to Lord Lloyd, the Secretary of State for the Colonies, on June 28, 1940:

The failure of the policy which you favour is proved by the very large numbers of sorely needed troops you have to keep in Palestine . . . the whole probably more than twenty thousand men. This is the price we have to pay for the anti-Jewish policy which has been persisted in for some years. Should the war go heavily into Egypt, all these troops will have to be withdrawn, and the position of the Jewish colonists will be one of the greatest danger. Indeed I am sure that we shall be told we cannot withdraw these troops, though they include some of our best, and are vitally needed elsewhere. If the Jews were properly armed, our forces would become available, and there would be no danger of the Jews attacking the Arabs, because they are entirely dependent upon us and upon our command of the seas. I think it is little less than a scandal that at a time when we are fighting for our lives these very large forces should be immobilised in support of a policy which commends itself only to a section of the Conservative Party.[15]

Churchill wrote again on August 10, 1940 to General Ismay, and again on September 24, to Eden, then Secretary of State for War, about the continued waste of troops in Palestine. The colonial mentality could not be dislodged. The key, in this situation, was the arming of Jews in Palestine. This had been requested for a long time but the Colonial Office and then the War Office had balked. As early as August 29, 1939, Dr. Weizmann, the Zionist leader, asked to have the Jewish people represented in its own identity among the armed forces that would be mobilized for Hitler's defeat. The appeals went through the bureaucratic mills for four years. Not until the autumn of 1944 was a Jewish Brigade finally authorized.

Paradoxically, some British were helping Jews while Royal Commissions were destroying the Mandate. The British people repudiated the official policy of the Colonial Office and—at the time when British naval patrols were already seizing ships carrying "illegal" Jews—were generously admitting thousands of Jewish refugees from Germany, Austria and Czechoslovakia. In the nine months following the November 1938 outbreaks 80,000 Jews found refuge in England. They came through private as well as organizational efforts, non-Jewish as well as Jewish. The Central British Fund for German Jewry, which had been founded in 1933, was particularly active. One of the most heart-warming efforts was the Children's Movement, under the chairmanship of Lord Gorell. Between the spring and fall of 1939, 9,350 children, mostly Jews, were brought to England. According to British law, children could not be scattered all over England among private families unless each of them had a guardian. So, obligingly, Parliament passed a Guardianship Act, and Lord Gorell found himself custodian of an enormous family. The quiet, generous kindness of British families made the Children's Movement a triumph of rescue and rehabilitation. Adults were first accepted on a restricted basis, as transmigrants, then as internees and ultimately as persons eligible for British citizenship.

On quite another level, however, the British had declared war on all Jews coming into Palestine outside the official quotas. The British policy was implemented in the early summer of 1939. The borders of Palestine were now closely guarded. Patrol boats roamed up and down the coast and new police stations were established. On June 1, the Romanian ship *Lizel* was caught off the coast of Jaffa and 900 Jews from Czechoslovakia and Austria were captured. On June 7, a ship was spotted near Acre and its passengers were taken to a prison in Haifa. On June 30, the ship *Astir* was apprehended near Migdal Gad with 724 passengers aboard, most of them from Danzig. It was turned back to sea, but set out again for Palestine and transferred its passengers to a sailing vessel. This time both British and Arab police captured the passengers.

In July 1939, in the harbor of Flushing, Holland, 500 bedraggled men, women, and children crowded against the rusty rails of the Danish steamer *Dora*, condemned as unseaworthy by the Dutch. They were German-Jewish refugees bound for a "far-off country," supposedly Siam. On the same day, three other small ships limped into Beirut, Syria. Disease, starvation and a wave of suicides had swept through the 1,400 Jewish passengers. But as stretcher-bearers carried the dead and sick ashore, Syrian officials forced the third vessel to put to sea again. It was declared free of disease. For two weeks, these ships had been cruising along the shores of Palestine. Whenever they entered Palestine territorial waters, British destroyers and patrol boats turned them away. From London had come an order banning all immigration to Palestine for six months.

The British war against Mossad was on. R.A.F. planes joined the naval patrols; British agents were sent to Europe to try to discover the ports from which the ships sailed. Pressure was applied to Turkey to close the Bosporus to refugee ships coming from the Danube by way of the Black Sea. On July 26, when Malcolm MacDonald, the Colonial Secretary, was asked the size and number of British ships engaged in preventing Jewish refugees from landing, he replied that one division of destroyers and five launches were engaged in this task. In two months, British patrol forces had captured 3,507 immigrants. During this period, MacDonald refused Weizmann's petition for the rescue of 20,000 children from Poland, with the chilling observation that "he fully realized the tragic consequences of his refusal for those involved."

The British were sealing up escape hatches at the very moment that Nazi officials were loosening them. In the late summer of 1939, Pino Ginsberg, the *Mossad* emissary in Berlin, had just concluded the biggest deal he had yet made with the Nazis. Under this agreement, 10,000 Jews were to be evacuated from Emden and Hamburg, thus avoiding the problem of transit visas. The first four ships had already been negotiated, and the *Reichsvertretung* had made the first payment. The ships were scheduled to arrive in Palestine early in October.

On August 23, the German-Soviet nonaggression pact was signed. Ginsberg made a lightning tour of all of the training farms in Germany, distributing money and giving last-minute instructions. On September 1, the day that Germany invaded Poland, he was ordered by the *Mossad* headquarters in Paris to leave Germany immediately. Before he left, he returned to the Gestapo office and received assurance that he could continue his work if war was not declared. On Sunday, September 3, Ginsberg crossed into Holland; two hours after his arrival, Britain declared war on Germany.

On September 2, the day after the invasion, a convoy of Jewish youths was taken off the ship *Tiger Hill* by the British in Tel Aviv and imprisoned at the army camp in Sarafand. There were 1,400 on board, the largest ship yet organized by the *Mossad*. The ship's arrival in Palestine represented months of preparation and skillful diplomatic maneuvering by young Ruth Kleiger, a *Mossad* agent in Bucharest. The convoy had gathered in Warsaw early in August and had reached Constanza, Romania, in a chartered train. The *Tiger Hill* was in port ready to sail, but the emigrants were not permitted to leave the train. Britain, at that time, was negotiating a loan with the Romanian Government, and one of the conditions was that no more refugee ships be allowed to pass through Constanza. Ruth Kleiger succeeded in winning over several Romanian officials and was even granted an interview with the sympathetic King Carol. After several days, the order was rescinded and the convoy was taken in locked cars under armed guard to the ship. A plague of troubles then descended: the food supply ran out; a young girl died of scarlet fever; water rations were almost exhausted, and new stores were denied the refugees by the authorities in Turkey and Rhodes. Sickness spread through the ship; fighting broke out among the stokers; the tender which was to take some of the immigrants ashore sprang a leak and had to be discarded. British patrols opened fire when the ship approached Nebi Yunis in southern Palestine and killed two men—the first of many killings to come. The debarkation experts then decided to run the *Tiger Hill* openly onto a sandbank off Tel Aviv. Hagana (Palestine Jewish self-defense) patrols were set up along the beach and Jewish sailors stood by with ropes and small boats. A few hundred succeeded in getting ashore, but most of the boatload were immobilized by armed British police and interned. Thereafter, *Mossad* ships bearing "illegals" met one disaster after another. The British treated them as enemy targets. At a somewhat later date, on October 16, 1940, the spirit of the British pursuit was revealed in a message sent by

British Central Intelligence Division headquarters in Jerusalem to the Port and Marine Police and intercepted by SHAI, the intelligence division of Hagana: "The illegal immigrants now at sea and whose arrival is expected at any moment are to be detained upon arrival on the shore in their ship or in small boats. This is of special importance as among these illegal immigrants are enemy agents. . . ."[16]

There were strange, often difficult routes of escape from the Continent for the lucky few. Until Italy's entry into the war in June 1940, Italian ports were free. Black Sea ports were also open for those who could reach them. When Russia absorbed Lithuania in 1940, she gave safe conduct to Lithuanian Jews and refugees from Poland who were willing to try the bitter hazards of trans-Siberia. It is estimated that 4,000 crossed to Japan this way. Thousands tried to cross the Spanish frontier, but only those with visas for countries beyond Spain were permitted to enter.

In almost all cases of Jews using water routes, steamship fares had to be paid in dollars. Those who had visas had to be backed by the Jewish Agency if they were going to Palestine, and by the JDC if they were going elsewhere. JDC devised a Transmigration Bureau to meet the problem of dollar fares. The bureau provided dollars in return for local funds deposited with approved local agencies. The fare amounted to about $500 per person. The bureau also welcomed deposits in New York and elsewhere from friends and relatives of would-be emigrants.

Lisbon, the gateway to the Atlantic, also offered hopes to those refugees who left Nazi-occupied Europe before the war broke out. Even as late as June 1940, trains ran regularly to Lisbon from Berlin, Vienna and Prague, supervised by German guards as far as the Spanish border. German tourist agencies planned the schedules of these trains and met them at Lisbon. But at Lisbon, the agonizing visa ordeal took place. For some refugees, the visas for Portugal were not in order. For others, the long wait for ship space often invalidated American visas. A case of this kind involved the Navemar, a ship privately chartered to sail from Spain to the United States. The ship was an old freighter with no facilities for passengers, not even toilets. Tiers of bunks had been fitted into the airless holds. Passengers took turns on the deck for a breath of air, surrounded by live oxen. The captain had vacated his cabin in return for $2,000 per person for everyone who could squeeze into it. By the time the Navemar sailed, the American visas of the passengers had expired. The JDC Director Joseph Schwartz in Lisbon cabled the Department of State and asked that the visas be extended. He then induced a reluctant Portuguese government to allow the passengers on shore where they would be supported by the JDC. The ship was considered impossible to live on, but everyone was afraid to leave. Would there be another one? Meanwhile, the State

Department had sent the requested extension. There followed a grotesque absurdity so common during the war. The American consulate was unable to process hundreds of new visas because of a typewriter shortage. Typists were helpless before this sort of bureaucratic breakdown. JDC in Lisbon sent two Jews out into the city to acquire typewriters at any cost. In the end, the Navemar did sail and made it to the United States.[17]

Lisbon was also the destination of highly paid smugglers who brought refugees through France, over the Pyrenees into Spain and then Portugal. This dangerous escape route was used most successfully for children until Vichy abruptly closed the border. Lisbon remained available as a corner of relative safety through 1941, although the Jews waiting there feared a German occupation any day and any hour. Money was available, ships could be bought, smugglers could be bought, police and S.S. men could be bought—but there was no place for the refugees to go.

It was inevitable that a documents racket develop, feeding on the desperation of Jewish refugees. There are countless stories of unscrupulous travel agents and consuls who sold worthless documents at exorbitant prices. The case of the German liner *St. Louis* is one of the many episodes of hopes dashed by worthless pieces of paper. The *St. Louis* left Hamburg on May 14, 1939, bound for Havana, Cuba. There were 937 Jewish passengers aboard, all of whom had American quota permits and special permits to stay temporarily in Cuba until American visas were processed. On May 30, thirty passengers were allowed to disembark at Havana; the others were told that their landing permits were worthless—they had ignored the new immigration restrictions decreed by Cuban President Frederico Laredo Bru on May 5. On June 2, President Bru ordered the *St. Louis* to leave Havana. Several passengers attempted to commit suicide, but the Cuban President refused to relax restrictions. An escort of 26 Cuban police boats accompanied the ship as far as Morro Castle to pick up any passengers who might jump overboard. Vigilance committees on board tried to maintain discipline. Soothing but false reports were spread that if no other haven could be found, the United States would admit the refugees right away. Instead of heading back to Hamburg and certain imprisonment for the passengers, the *St. Louis* cruised slowly off the American coast for three days, waiting hopefully for an offer of a temporary haven. On June 5, President Bru announced that he would grant temporary refuge if relief organizations would be willing to provide $500 for each passenger. The Joint Distribution Committee began to make arrangements, but before they could be completed, the offer was rescinded.

The German Government, meanwhile, refused to allow the ship to go on to Shanghai. The ship continued its aimless cruising. After thirty-five days, England, France, Holland and Belgium finally agreed to divide the human cargo. When this plan was announced, a spokesman for the League of Nations High Commissioner warned: "One thing we must state is that if these [passengers] are taken care of by certain governments, it is not to constitute a precedent for other shiploads." There was no place to go but the refugees kept pressing against closed doors. The *St. Louis* was one of a small fleet of refugee ships roaming American waters at the time in search of a port. Three ships with 200 Jews aboard were ordered back to Germany after Paraguay and Argentina refused to accept them. Mexico turned away 104 who arrived on the French steamer *Flandre*. The British liner *Orduna* with its 72 Jewish passengers was forced to turn away from Cuba.

Possibly as many as 13,000 Jews from the Old Reich left during the first two years of the war. In the Greater Reich, which included Austria and the Protectorate of Bohemia and Moravia, the majority of the 375,000 Jews left were almost completely destitute and unable to buy their way out. By midsummer of 1939, the *Reichsvereinigung*, which succeeded the *Reichsvertretung*, was a virtual prisoner of the S.S. state, and German Jews, the most assimilated Jewry in the world, now turned in upon itself and the spiritual solace of Judaism for whatever comfort and strength it could find. On October 1, 1941, when extermination in the East had already been practiced for several months, all emigration from the Reich was forbidden; on that date, the official *Reichsvereinigung* statistics show 163,000 Jews still living in the Reich. By this time, the high death rate had eroded the life of the community perhaps as much as deportations; Himmler's statistician, Dr. Richard Korherr, put it as high as 85 per thousand.

The fate of Polish Jews who migrated in 1939–40 to the newly established Russian borders is a matter of controversy. According to a postwar Polish commission, they numbered about 300,000. After June 1941, 400,000 more fled east.[18] Over a million Jews from prewar Poland passed under Russian rule after the Nazi-Russian pact. Many of these were undoubtedly killed in the German invasion of Russia. Those who refused to accept Russian citizenship were sent, for the most part, to Siberia and Central Asia, where they took their chances under primitive conditions and a harsh climate. About 150,000 Jewish exiles in Russia returned to Poland after the war. In the fall and winter of 1939, the Germans deported hundreds of Jews across the Russian frontier and then shot them when they attempted to return because the Russians refused to have them. An order from the Supreme Command of the Army, dated September 20, 1939, ordered unit commanders to prevent the recrossing of the San and Bug rivers by fugitive Jews. A few days later, hundreds of Jews, who were trying to return home, were turned out of the town of Jaroslaw at half an hour's notice and pushed across the San River on rafts, where they were fired on by German Security Police or left to drown.[19] By January 1940, the Foreign Office intervened after several Russian complaints, and the dumping at the border ceased.

Meanwhile, home-grown and German-financed Nazis in the United States, England and countries of western Europe and Latin America injected anti-Semitism into native politics and, as Hitler had predicted, were not only raising the specter of a Jewish "world conspiracy" but spreading fear that the refugees would infect native populations and insidiously rise to power and wealth. That a great deal of this propaganda rubbed off to inflame already existing "moderate" anti-Semitism must be admitted as a powerful factor in the general world indifference that prevailed through the agony of Europe's Jews. After the November pogroms, Goebbels had said: "Drive out the Jews with one suit and a handbag and throw them on the charity of the democratic world." The Foreign Ministry then picked up the theme:

> The poorer and therefore the more burdensome the immigrant is to the country absorbing him, the stronger that country will react and the more desirable is this effect in the interests of German propaganda. The object of this German action is to be the future international solution of the Jewish question, dictated not by false compassion for the religious Jewish minority, but by the consciousness of all peoples of the danger which it represents to the racial composition of the nations.[20]

Hitler himself had said: "Anti-Semitism is a useful revolutionary expedient. Anti-Semitic propaganda in all countries is an indispensable medium for the extension of our political campaign. You will see how little time we shall need in order to upset the ideas and criteria of the whole world, simply and purely by attacking Judaism." Anti-Semitism was, indeed, Germany's chief *Exportartikel*. Institutes in Germany, amply provided with funds, were continuously churning out stock Nazi material on Jews in all languages and brought out new editions of the *Protocols of the Elders of Zion*. It is not possible to know to what extent parties abroad were financed, but in 1934, after only one year in power, the Nazis were spending 286 million marks on general propaganda abroad. By 1936, this figure had risen to nearly 500 million. Arab leaders in Palestine who followed the pro-Nazi Grand Mufti of Jerusalem received over 60 million of this.

After the outbreak of war, token gestures in behalf of refugees continued. In an address delivered on October 17, 1939, to the members of the Intergovernmental Committee on Political Refugees, President Roosevelt urged his audience to study the problem of resettling several million people rendered homeless by the war. The President's remarks, while arousing hope among the uprooted, created a stir in diplomatic circles. The British and French governments expressed concern over the implications of preparing for large-scale refugee work. They contended that one of the objectives of their war against Germany was to eliminate doctrines of racial and religious bigotry, and that victory for the Allies would eliminate the need for any large emigration program. The Committee agreed that there should be no open admission of such a problem and then proceeded to discuss the immediate problem of refugees from Greater Germany.

The most important colonization plan was the Dominican Republic project for the settlement of 100,000 Jews. The Agro-Joint Board, an affiliate of the JDC, subscribed $200,000 immediately. A 26,000-acre tract was chosen for the first settlement, with the initial colony to consist of 500 people. Fifty Jews had already arrived in the spring of 1940 but by June, Italy's entry into the war drastically cut the means of transport from Europe.[21] All Italian major ports of embarkation were closed. At this time, it was estimated that 175,000 Jews from Germany, 120,000 from Austria, and 20,000 from Czechoslovakia were temporarily in other parts of Europe. About 40,000 were in France. After France declared war on Germany, these refugees were under double jeopardy. They were not only homeless; they were enemy aliens.

Many thousands could not meet the immigration requirements of the United States or Latin America, but chose to wander without legal status rather than remain in German-held territory. During 1939, there were many ships, not only in the Atlantic, but also in the Mediterranean, the Danube and Black Sea, unable to land their passengers. Most of them sought to reach Palestine from such scattered places as Salina, Romania, Kladova in Yugoslavia, the Greek islands, and Beirut, Syria. Some attempted to make the trip to Palestine overland through the Balkans. Several others sailed around Africa and reached Palestine after forty-five days.[22]

War-torn and turbulent, Shanghai was the only place on earth where Jews could flee without restriction or even the requirement of a visa. Only four thousand Jews, however, made their way to this refuge in 1939. The war imprisoned Europe's Jews but almost 1,600 from central Europe left the Continent a full year after the war broke out. They were part of a large convoy of 4,000 refugees that left Bratislava, Slovakia, on September 4, 1940. Most of them perished on the seas, but almost 1,600 survived as "illegal" immigrants on the island of Mauritius under British custody.

The original convoy consisted of four Danube steamers. This large transport had been arranged by Bertold Storfer, a Viennese Jew with the consent of, and probably the cooperation of, German authorities. Among the passengers were about 300 belonging to various Zionist youth groups from Czechoslovakia who had been detained in Bratislava for almost a year; Storfer finally extricated them. Another group of several hundred from Vienna were interned in an abandoned munitions factory on the outskirts of Bratislava called "Patronka" where they were guarded by the Slovak Hlinka Guard. A third group of about 500 Danzig Jews had been organized by the *Kultusgemeinde* of the city and joined the convoy in Bratislava. These three groups sailed on the *Helios*. The *Schoenbrunn* sailed with about 600 passengers from Vienna; many of them had been imprisoned in concentration camps and were released on the understanding that they would leave the Reich at once. These two ships reached Mauritius; the passengers on the *Pacific* and the *Milos* were transferred to the ill-fated *Patria*.

The refugees had been provided with visas for Peru and Paraguay, but it was perfectly clear to everyone that they were bound for Palestine. The Germans undoubtedly permitted this convoy to leave a whole year after the outbreak of the war, counting on the influx of "illegal immigrants" to incite Arab anti-British riots. Moreover, the Germans were, at the time, repatriating *Volksdeutsche* from Bessarabia and transporting them to the Reich on the Danube steamers. The exorbitant fares paid by the Jews covered the passage of the German repatriates.

The convoy passed Budapest, Belgrade, the Iron Gate and Turnu Severin without incident, but near Ruse on the Bulgarian side of the Danube, the refugees saw a shocking sight. The *Pencho*, a decrepit paddle steamer with several hundred "illegal immigrants" on board, was anchored offshore. The ship was unseaworthy and was not permitted to call at a port or continue her voyage. The Bratislava convoy gave the *Pencho* some of their food rations and moved on to Tulcea, Romania. There the passengers of the *Helios* and the *Schoenbrunn* were transferred to the *Atlantic* on September 14. The *Atlantic* was an old Greek freighter of about 1,400 tons improvised for human cargo. Every square foot of space in the gangways and on deck was jammed. Food and medical supplies were scanty. The vessel sailed from Tulcea on October 7 and reached Crete on the sixteenth. There the refugees were caught by the outbreak of the Greek-Italian war and held up. When they finally were able to sail, a new difficulty arose. The crew refused to leave Crete and began to throw a large part of the precious coal into the sea. Members of Hagana aboard, under the leadership of Erwin Kovacs, an engineer, took over operations and set sail on November 8. The coal supply soon ran out and the ship was stripped of every piece of wood that was not vital: masts, chairs, walls, planks and beds. On November 12, the *Atlantic*, now virtually a floating metal skeleton, was met by British tugs and dragged into the harbor of Limassol, on the island of Cyprus. The refugees were filled with joy; they were now under the protection of the British, they believed.

The British agreed to escort them to Haifa upon payment of £480 for provisions and a supply of coal. With a British man-of-war escort, the *Atlantic* arrived in Haifa on November 25. British officials there said the passengers would be kept for a time in quarantine on board the *Patria* in Haifa Harbor. Passengers of the other two ships in the Bratislava convoy had already been transferred to the *Patria*. The transshipment began almost immediately. After a few dozen people had left the *Atlantic* the horrified refugees witnessed a terrifying spectacle. A loud explosion was heard, the *Patria* capsized and sank within minutes. An act of sabotage to prevent the deportation of the immigrants had tragically misfired. Over two hundred Jews were drowned.

The remainder on the *Atlantic* were transferred to the reception camp at Atlit, where the refugees lived in huts separated by barbed wire. On the evening of December 8, they were ordered to pack their luggage and prepare for their departure. They were not, however, told of their destination. The interned Jews worked out a plan of passive resistance: they were to sleep naked, refuse to dress in the morning and then refuse to leave. During the night the camp was surrounded by large enforcements of the British Palestine police and by British soldiers. The first forcible detention of Jewish refugees by the British was underway.

The following morning the Jews were ordered to dress for departure. They refused. The police began to clear the huts by force. Heavy truncheons were used indiscriminately and many were wounded. All were dragged from their huts, thrown into trucks and covered with blankets. Shocked and dejected, the refugees were taken aboard two large Dutch liners. The voyage to Mauritius took seventeen days.[23] At the beginning of the voyage, constables of the Palestine police behaved brutally and struck some of the refugees. Other indignities were practiced. The police commander refused to let the deportees celebrate the festival of Hanukkah. Later in the voyage, the Dutch crew gave them clothing and candles.

On December 28, two days after the ships dropped anchor in the harbor of Port Louis, the capital of Mauritius, the iron gates of the Central Prison at Beau Bassin closed behind the last of the 1,580 refugees. The gates did not open for fifty-five months. Thousands of certificates under the White Paper of 1939 remained unused during this period.

The British battle against Jewish refugees bound for Palestine intensified during the war and continued unabated when the half-human remnant were liberated from concentration camps after the war. The *Mossad* did not stop its work in this struggle but was forced to develop new strategies as British seizures on the seas became more punitive. In the end, the *Mossad* was transformed from a small, modest rescue action into a revolutionary movement that swept the Jewish community in Palestine and the survivors of Hitler Europe into a nascent state.

Meanwhile, in 1939, while Jews were being shunted from port to port, the Nazis carved out a great reserve in Poland, the Government-General, as the first of their dumping grounds for unwanted Jews. As a preliminary, some excuse had to be found to go to war against Poland.

9 The Invasion of Poland

IN THE SUMMER OF 1938, before Germany occupied the Sudetenland, the German Ambassador to Poland reassured Hitler that Poland would not allow the Soviet Union to send troops or planes through or over her territory in order to help Czechoslovakia. The Poles also had their eyes on coal-rich Teschen in Czech Silesia and the Germans capitalized on their interest. On September 21, 1938, nudged by Germany, the Polish Government demanded that Czechoslovakia hold a plebiscite in Teschen, a region which contained a large Polish minority. Polish troops were then moved to the frontier. On September 30, Czechoslovakia gave way to the decision made at Munich and the Polish Government sent a 24-hour ultimatum to the Czechs demanding Teschen. In joining in the pillage of Czechoslovakia, Poland momentarily enjoyed the spoils of Munich, but Poland's turn under the Nazi heel was soon to come.

When it did, it was obvious that Poland had not learned anything from the experience of Austria and Czechoslovakia. Of all the countries that lay on the borders of Germany, Poland had most to fear. Yet she was most blind to the German danger. Aside from the arms restrictions clauses, possibly no other provision of the Versailles Treaty was so much resented by Germans as the one establishing the Corridor, by which the "inferior" Poles cut off East Prussia from the rest of Germany and gained access to the sea. Yet, in the face of this recognized German antagonism, Poland's policy became increasingly pro-German, while her relations with Russia deteriorated. During the Munich crisis, the British and French ambassadors were denied access to the Polish Foreign Secretary. Hitler shrewdly played at wooing Poland until he could absorb Austria and Czechoslovakia. Meanwhile, he was eroding the traditional friendship between Poland and France and threatening Russia by demanding that Poland join the anti-Comintern Pact.

Too late, Poland realized her vulnerability. On March 15, 1939, Hitler occupied Bohemia and Moravia and sent troops to protect "independent" Slovakia on Poland's southern border. At this time, Maxim Litvinov, the Russian Foreign Minister, was making proposals for collective security, but

Chamberlain, still distrustful of Russia, found them "premature." The British Prime Minister, however, finally gave Poland guarantees that Britain would support her if she were attacked by Germany. Hitler, meanwhile, began to seek a rapprochement with the Soviet Union. Russia's exclusion from Munich had aggravated the Soviet distrust of the West. Litvinov was abruptly dismissed, an indication of a new Soviet policy orientation. Italy was then formally drawn into Hitler's plans by concluding a military alliance with Germany—the Pact of Steel—which deceived Mussolini into thinking that he could bask in a long interlude of peace. On May 23, the day after this pact was signed, Hitler told his Army, Navy and Air Force chiefs that Poland was now Germany's logical target. Not Danzig or a railroad line through the Corridor, but living space and food supplies in the East. "There is, therefore, no question of sparing Poland," he said, "and we are left with the decision: To attack Poland at the first opportunity." But this would not be a repetition of the Czech affair, he warned. "There will be war." Poland would be attacked and England and France would undoubtedly have to be taken on in a life-and-death struggle. "The idea that we can get off cheaply is dangerous; there is no such possibility. . . . We must burn our boats. It is no longer a question of right or wrong, but of life or death for eighty million beings."

As his plans developed, however, there was considerable uncertainty in Hitler's thinking, a groping around for sure ground and deep anxiety about England. He often belittled the English and scoffed at them as sons of the idle rich, but feared their resourcefulness and staying power in a long war. Nevertheless, he had a personal appetite for speedy, uninterrupted triumphs and he felt a lingering resentment of Western interference—such as it was—at Munich. In his mind, Chamberlain had spoiled his entry into Prague.

The Wehrmacht was easily persuaded to go ahead, although less than a year before many of their leaders had opposed the possibility of war over Czechoslovakia. So far as the record shows, not a single military chief questioned the wisdom of Hitler's course as it was outlined on May 23.[1] Not only the elimination of the Corridor, but the destruction of Poland as a nation had been a basic aim of the officers' corps through the postwar years. At the very least they were bent on recovering the Pomeranian and Silesian lands transferred to Poland under the treaty. At Nuremberg, two of the generals expressed this strongly felt urge: "A war to wipe out the desecration involved in the creation of the Polish Corridor and to lessen the threat to separated East Prussia surrounded by Poland and Lithuania was regarded as a sacred duty though a sad necessity."

This war, thus started by Hitler's willfulness and the Wehrmacht's sullen need to avenge a historic territorial wrong, would be the war, the start of which Hitler would blame on the Jews, and the spread of which would destroy millions of their number, as Hitler had predicted in his speech of January 30. The German pact with the Soviet Union in August 1939 clinched Hitler's decision.

The immediate problem of neutralizing the Soviet Union was now solved, at least for the time. Stalin's inveterate distrust of the West and need to buy time at the expense of Poland disposed him favorably to a separate deal with Germany. Hitler gladly agreed to his taking large chunks of eastern Europe. The Nazi-Soviet Non-Aggression Pact, which stunned the partners almost as much as it stunned the world, was signed on August 23, 1939. It permitted Hitler to hold to his September 1 timetable.

"Operation Himmler," another crude device to cloak Germany's aggression—this time against Poland—was next contrived. Using condemned concentration camp inmates dressed in Polish army uniforms, the Gestapo staged a fake attack on the German radio station at Gleiwitz, near the Polish border. Poland was to be blamed for attacking Germany. At daybreak on September 1, German warplanes roared toward their targets and within minutes were giving Poles, soldiers and civilians alike, sudden death and destruction that were soon to become a dread daily experience for millions in Europe. Poland was about to suffer her fourth partition; this time, only two nations, Germany and the Soviet Union, picked up the spoils.

From the first moment of their invasion of Polish territory, the German armies committed a succession of atrocities on the Polish civilian population.[2] Unarmed inhabitants were fired upon indiscriminately, on streets and in homes. There was no local resistance of any kind in many areas barbarized, and Polish troops were either in retreat or nonexistent. Nevertheless, the slaughter continued. German troops of Army Group South shot down hundreds of civilians in Sosnowiec, Kajetanowice, Pinczow and Kilejoweic. Thousands of Poles were killed by troops and S.S. police. Reports of Nazi massacres in Poland began to fill the world press. No technicalities, legal considerations, or preparatory steps evolved in Poland under Nazi occupation.[3] The aim here, Hitler had bluntly said, "was the elimination of living forces, not the arrival at a certain line. . . . The destruction of Poland shall be the primary objective."

In such a welter of barbarity, Jews were easy prey. Indiscriminate shooting of Jews became a popular pastime and Jewish communities were massacred on a wholesale scale. During the first three months of occupation, massacres occurred in Chelmnik, Konskie, Kutno, Lowicz, Lukow, Zdunska-Wola, and Przemsyl. In Ostrowe, all male Jews were shot after being forced to dig their own graves. Pogroms broke out in Lask, Sieradz, Czestochowa, Nowe Miasto, and Lodz. In Prztyk, the anti-Semitic right-wing party, the Naras helped Nazi guards assault Jews. Hundreds of synagogues were destroyed. The Nazi press announced the formation of fire brigades devoted to burning synagogues and books.[4]

Jewish community leaders were singled out in some areas. Bund leaders and officials of the Jewish community in Krakow were killed in October 1939. In the following month, Jewish leaders were killed in Lodz, Tarnow, Kielce, Busk, Chielnik and Stopnik. Mass arrests occurred simultaneously. At first Jews were charged with resisting, or concealing arms, or violating currency regulations. Then, no explanations were given and Jews were rounded up for transfer to Lublin, forced labor in Germany, or for internment. By the end of December 1939, it is estimated that 250,000 Jews had died in Nazi-occupied Poland through shootings, starvation, or disease.[5]

When the invasion began, German forces poured into Poland from the north, the west and southwest. In the west and southwest lay cities and small towns with large Jewish populations. Following the German armored columns and lorries and motorcycles were the *Einsatzgruppen*, the "action groups" of the Security Police and the S.D. These were semi-military formations following in the wake of Hitler's armies to annihilate civilians, particularly Jews. Many of the men in these units had organized the pogroms of November 10, 1938. The S.S. quickly understood that they could do anything they wanted to with Jews. Sometimes it was more diverting to torture than to kill them.

The very sight of a Polish Jew in his traditional dress was a warrant for any abuse. Every barbarity was a good Nazi deed, an exploit to be celebrated by the press and glorified in the movies. Photographs were sent home of Germans cutting off beards and earlocks of Jews and forcing Jews to pull them about in carts. S.S. men broke into Jewish homes and apartments, forced young and old to undress and dance in their nakedness, arm in arm as phonographs played. Rape was optional, if one wanted to risk being tried for race defilement. Jewish girls were haphazardly arrested, made to wash the feet of their jailers and then drink the dirty water.

On September 3, the Germans occupied the industrial town of Bielsko in Silesia. Many Jews had fled at the beginning of the invasion, but 2,000 remained. These were all rounded up and herded into the courtyard of a local Jewish school and cruelly beaten. Some were hung up by their hands and covered with boiling water. The nozzles of rubber pipes were put into the mouths of others and water pumped into them until their stomachs swelled and burst. All Jewish synagogues and schools were burned, and stores and homes were plundered.

On September 4, the Germans took Kalisz, a city with a Jewish population of 30,000. There the great synagogue was transformed into a prison camp. The Holy Scrolls were ripped and made into a huge bonfire which

Baltic Sea

LITHUANIA

• Vilna

• Kovno

REICHSKOMMISSARIAT

EAST PRUSSIA

OSTLAND

BIALYSTOK
DISTRICT

INCORPORATED TERRITORY

✳ Treblinka

Chelmno ✳

• Warsaw

REICHSKOMMISSARIAT

POLESIA

Lodz •

LUBLIN
"RESERVE"

✳ Sobibor

UKRAINE

Maidanek

VOLHYNIA

GOVERNMENT-GENERAL (1939)

• Krakow

✳ Belzec

Lvov •

✳ Auschwitz

GOVERNMENT
-GENERAL (1941)

SLOVAKIA

GALICIA

• Bratislava

HUNGARY

• Budapest

ROMANIA

POLAND UNDER GERMAN RULE

Prewar Poland

✳ Extermination Camps

the Jews were forced to jump over. Those who were not imprisoned were put to work at forced labor. Those Jews who still had dwellings were herded into several buildings where many died of disease, undernourishment and brutalization. The survivors were sent in sealed cars to the "Lublin Reservation." Thus was Kalisz dejudaized.[6]

In Wloclawek, in addition to the usual torments and tortures, hallowed religious observances were degraded. As synagogues were closed by German authorities, Jews were forced to hold services in private homes. The Germans went hunting for worshipers on the eve of the Day of Atonement and dragged many in their prayer shawls to army barracks. There Jews were forced to sweep the floors of the barracks with their shawls while soldiers jeeringly took photographs. On the same night, men and women were dragged out of their beds for a forced march. Those who could not walk as fast as the Germans wanted them to were shot on the spot; some were buried by their horrified fellow Jews while still suffering their last death agonies.

In Mielec, near Krakow, thirty-five Jews were driven naked from the community baths to a nearby slaughterhouse. The Germans poured gasoline over the building and set fire to it. The shrieks of the imprisoned Jews left them unmoved and all of the victims perished.

The chronicle of senseless cruelty and slaughter moves horrifyingly from Wieruszow to Zgierz, from Aleksandrow to Piotrkow, from Lukow to Warsaw. Nor were these actions confined to the S.S. and police troops; Wehrmacht units, which at first merely stood by and allowed the slaughters to take place, soon became involved in them. When complaints of the atrocities reached the High Command, it did little more than take routine action. On the night of September 10, 1939, when Hitler was at Southern Army headquarters in an old castle near Lodz, his favorite actress, Leni Riefenstahl, rushed into the office of the chief intelligence officer, protesting that she had just seen twenty-two Jews shot and could not continue working with her film unit. The intelligence officer reported the incident to the commander of the Southern Army; he ordered an investigation and disciplinary action, but the incidents continued. The generals were to be overwhelmed by similar reports of excesses, and although some were discomfited, they put aside their scruples or limited their protests to their diaries.

The German generals were bent on a rapid, ruthless conquest of a country and people they held in low esteem, but they had not prepared for campaigns of mass liquidation. After the war, many of them pleaded initial ignorance of such plans and, then, efforts to stop them. But the documents do not bear out their protestations. Leaders of the officers' corps knew of Hitler's plans for Poland at a very early stage and made no substantial effort to stop them.

On September 10, with the Polish plan in full swing, Halder noted in his diary an episode which reveals the Army's tacit connivance. Some S.S. toughs had worked fifty Jews all day on a job of repairing a bridge, then flung them into a synagogue and shot them. At first, light sentences were imposed on the killers but these were quashed after Himmler intervened with the excuse that they came under a "general amnesty." For one of the gunners, the Judge Advocate had pleaded that "as an S.S. man, he was particularly sensitive to the sight of Jews. He had therefore acted quite thoughtlessly in a spirit of adventure." On October 19, the former Ambassador to Italy, Ulrich von Hassell, in his diary reported hearing of "the shocking bestialities of the S.S., especially toward the Jews" and implicating Army officers.

Hitler had in fact intimidated the military professionals into impotence, according to Field Marshal Keitel, by threatening them with S.S. and Gestapo overseers. Hitler had warned the generals "to restrict themselves to their military duties." The Army would either accept the distasteful "occurrences" or accept S.S. commissars in each military unit "to carry out the exterminations." For professional soldiers, the prospect of having an S.S. agent at the elbow of each military commander was insupportable.

Himmler and Heydrich, however, wanted the generals involved. To ensure the Army's acquiescence, Heydrich paid a visit on September 19 to General Eduard Wagner, the Quartermaster General, and told him of S.S. plans for the "housecleaning of Jews, intelligentsia, clergy and the nobility." Wagner then promptly reported back to Halder that "housecleaning" missions must be made known to the Army in order to ensure their accomplishment. The Army's response was merely a request that "housecleaning" be deferred until the Army withdrew and turned the country over to the civil administration. The generals also warned that "nothing must occur which would afford foreign countries an opportunity to launch any sort of atrocity campaign based on such incidents." They did not, apparently, oppose the wiping out of Jews and certain classes of Poles, but wanted to avoid blame.

Hitler's plan for Europe was conquest for exploitation. For him, the continent was a huge storehouse of human and material resources to be devoured by Germany. His directive to Hans Frank, the administrator of occupied Poland, was to turn Poland's "economic, cultural, and political structure into a heap of rubble." On October 3, Frank spoke to Army staff officers at Posen and outlined his plans for the occupation of Poland. "Poland," he said, "can be administered by utilizing the country through ruthless exploitation, removal of all supplies, raw materials, machines, factory installations, etc., which are important for the German war economy . . . [and] reduction of the entire Polish economy to absolute minimum necessity for bare existence of the population. . . . The Poles shall be the slaves of the Greater German World Empire."

If, after this, the Army leaders still had doubts as to the deadly serious-ness of Hitler's plans, they were dissolved after Wagner himself reported to Halder the results of a conference with Hitler. Frank's words were mild compared with those of the master planner. As Hitler's self-styled "devil-ish plan" was executed, men returned to Germany with shocking stories. On Christmas Day, von Hassell recorded in his diary:

"Nostitz [a German diplomat] very depressed, told about absolutely shameless actions in Poland, particularly by S.S. Conditions there as re-gards sanitation defied description, especially in the Jewish district and in the resettlement areas. The shooting of hundreds of innocent Jews was the order of the day. . . . Frank carrying on like a megalomaniacal pasha. . . . Perhaps we may hope that the behavior of the S.S. will be the quick-est way to enlighten the Army."

But the Army, it seems, was past enlightenment. Since 1934, the gen-erals had been shown the nature of the Hitler-state; yet they continued to think of it in nineteenth-century terms; their outlook was archaic as well as muddled. Because they wanted to reestablish German military supremacy in Europe, they anchored their hopes to the terrible genius of Hitler, who was bold where they were narrow and cautious. At first his unwilling, then willing, collaborators, they eventually became his benumbed followers, and although their caste-conscious traditions were violated by the Austrian upstart, they were incapable or unwilling to mount the kind of opposition that was necessary to stop him.

After Hindenburg's death, all officers and men in the armed forces were required to take an oath, not to the state or nation as had been customary in the past, but of personal fealty to Hitler. It was this oath that created ambiguous rationalizations and alleged problems of conscience for gen-erals at Nuremberg: "I swear by God this sacred oath, that I will render unconditional obedience to Adolf Hitler, the Führer of the German Reich and people, Supreme Commander of the Armed Forces, and will be ready as a brave soldier to risk my life at any time for this oath."

The impotence of the Army, even in the face of the predicted spread of unrestrained violence to Germany itself, was clearly discerned toward the end of 1939 by General Johannes Blaskowitz, head of Oberost, High Command East. His words are a microcosm of the inner decay of Europe at this time: an overwrought sensibility paralyzed by an inability to act. Blaskowitz wrote:

> . . . There is reason to foresee that the outcry from foreign countries can only increase, resulting in serious political damage—all the more since the atrocities really have taken place and cannot be denied by any manner or means. . . . We need not mention again the unhappy role played by the Wehrmacht, forced to be a passive witness to these crimes. . . . But the

worse effect that the present situation will have on the German people is the unlimited brutalization and moral depravity which will spread like an epidemic through the most valuable German human material. If the high officials and the S.S. continue to call for violence and brutality, brutal men will soon reign supreme. With disconcerting speed depraved birds of a feather find one another out and band together in order to satisfy their pathological and bestial instincts—as they are now doing in Poland. They can be barely kept in hand; for they have good reason to feel that they have official sanction and justification to commit the most horrible of acts.[7]

The Wehrmacht need not have been a "passive witness." From 1938 until the end of the war, there was a long, tortuous and broken-backed history of "plots" against Hitler—plans to arrest or assassinate him, at times to prevent him from declaring war, at other times plans to substitute another regime to negotiate peace with the Allies. But such occasions coincided with fears that Hitler was leading them to disaster. When Hitler was winning, the generals remembered their oath of allegiance to him. They also remembered this oath at Nuremberg when they claimed they had to uphold it or be dishonored, even while disapproving many of Hitler's orders. But the idea of disobeying an order was obviously not inconceivable during the frequent occasions when plots were hatched against Hitler.[8] Nor is there any evidence in the few instances recorded that any soldier or officer was punished for refusing to carry out executions against Jews.

For Heinrich Himmler, the outbreak of the war was the dawn of a new era. Now, at last, the fearful architecture of the S.S. state, the foundations of which he had been quietly laying for several years, began to take shape. Hitler was increasingly preoccupied with military affairs, and soon allowed the internal management of the Reich to slip into the hands of Himmler and Bormann. The generals were busy at the front. Himmler filled the power vacuum.

Poland had long been marked out by Himmler as an area perfectly suited for the practical application of S.S. ideology and racial experiments. However, the division of authority between the Wehrmacht and the civil authorities after the occupation had not been worked out in advance. Himmler fully exploited this situation. His police forces and special S.S. units, the *Einsatzgruppen*, aggressively forged into prime positions with destructive power. They were given the mission to destroy Polish culture and prepare Polish Jewry for the "final solution."

The S.S. and Security Police came into positions of control in Poland almost immediately. By contrast, in the Reich-Protektorat area, the rise of Himmler's forces was almost imperceptible.[9] As the destructive process swept into more drastic phases, it increasingly took on the characteristics of a police operation. Movement controls, round-ups, concentration camps, arbitrary killings were all quite natural functions of Himmler's police machine. The destructive plan was first outlined by Heydrich in a directive on September 21, 1939. His orders were issued before the civil administration had a chance to organize itself. This sequence, however, does not mean that Jews were destroyed who may have been otherwise saved. Both the civil and police authorities were bent on destroying Jews; the difference was simply one of pace. The competition between them, which was often very fierce, did not benefit Jews, but made their destruction swifter. Had the civilian authorities acted alone, however, the pace would have been slower; more use would have been made of Jewish man-power; more would have survived.

The "little terror" of September–November 1939 was terrible enough, but was not comparable to the methodical exterminations of 1941 during the invasion of Russia. By June 1941, the independence of the police units in the rear areas of the Army was defined, after lengthy conferences, with great care and precision. By then, the killing machinery was more smoothly coordinated.

The fighting in Poland had hardly stopped when Himmler began hounding Jews and Poles from homes where they had lived for generations in order to bring "racial" Germans together. Under Himmler's colorless, clerkish exterior stormed romantic visions of a regenerated, "pure" Germanic people. The demographic convulsion of Europe was not too rash a process to undertake, if only he could succeed in bringing under an enlarged Reich all "racial" Germans and *Volksdeutsche* living under foreign governments. Danzig, West Prussia, Poznan, and eastern Upper Silesia—all within the area annexed by Germany after the Polish conquest —were to be completely cleared of Poles and Jews and then filled with Germans.

The beginning of the population upheavals in eastern Europe coincided with the formation of a new Nazi agency. On October 6, Himmler added yet another title to his bulging portfolio and became Reich Commissioner for Strengthening German Folkdom (*Reichskommisar für die Festigung Deutschen Volktums*—RKFDV). He could now officially repatriate all Germans who lived under foreign rule. That part of Poland into which Jews and Poles were driven was called the Government-General (map, p. 151). It included the districts of Krakow, Radom, Lublin, Warsaw, and, later, eastern Galicia. While Heydrich whipped Poles and Jews east-ward into the camps and ghettos of the Government-General, Himmler drove Germans westward into the enlarged Reich which now included the annexed or incorporated areas of western Poland.

The Germans never reached a clear decision about the nature of the Government-General and what vague ideas they may have had were made more confusing by the sudden advance of the Soviet army into Poland on

September 17. The Soviet Union took the eastern half of Poland. The Germans then classified and reclassified their share of the Polish population—about twenty-two million—according to fluctuating theories of race and nationality. However, they could not avoid certain alternatives: to absorb these millions, to kill them, or to retain useful elements. At times, they did all three simultaneously.

The twenty-two million Poles and Jews were originally divided about equally between two distinct administrative areas: the annexed territories and the Government-General, but the areas did not correspond to ethnic differences between the populations. The criteria of Germanness sometimes involved factors of language, cultural interests, "loyalty" to Germany and membership in German organizations. Active fighters in the "battle of nationality" had to be salvaged, removed from Polish surroundings and re-Germanized. No Jew, theoretically, was permitted to remain in the German-pure sector, but many thousands did.

On October 9, just three days after taking over his new post, Himmler decreed that 550,000 of the 650,000 Jews living in the annexed Polish provinces plus all Poles not fit for "assimilation" be moved into the territory of the Government-General. Within a year, 1,200,000 Poles and 300,000 Jews were uprooted and driven east, but less than 500,000 *Volksdeutsche* were settled in their place. Two secret protocols to the Nazi-Soviet Pact had pledged Russian transfer of several hundred thousand "racial" Germans under their jurisdiction (including almost 150,000 living in the Russian share of Poland). But Himmler's mad fantasies were aborted. A sweeping typhus epidemic, unwelcome leakage of information to the foreign press, and the failure of Germans to settle down according to plan created unforeseen problems. Each German theoretically occupied the space of three Poles and Jews, but as late as July 1942, 120,000 Germans were still housed in camps, and a year later only 20,000 of these found permanent dwellings. These numbers were vastly enlarged after the Battle of Stalingrad when more *Volksdeutsche* streamed west and swelled the displaced Germans to millions. Himmler was not in the least affected by the human uprooting involved in this *Völkerwanderung* so long as it was inspired by dreams of remaking the world into a pure Aryan paradise. Later, his obsessive searches led him to probe the secret of Aryan origins and to collect skulls of Jewish-Bolshevik commissars while immense armies were maneuvering over the frozen plains of Russia, smashing each other to pieces; and yet later, with the Reich crashing down on him, he interrupted his conversations with Count Bernadotte in order to hold forth on the hidden secrets of Nordic runes and their relation to the characters of the Japanese alphabet.[10]

The evacuation of Jews from the annexed part of Poland was sudden and chaotic. Invariably, they were ordered to leave their homes without warning or preparation. They were allowed to carry with them only small supplies of food and few personal belongings. They scattered en route, taking shelter and aid in communities not yet expelled. In March 1940, dispossessed Jews were to be found in 250 localities of occupied Poland. They were housed in barracks, schools, synagogues and in private homes. All movement surged eastward into the Government-General. Once a million and a half Jews were concentrated here with no possibility, as yet, of pushing farther east, bureaucratic tensions mounted. Governor General Frank had looked forward to a "colossal unburdening" of his Jews by transporting them to Madagascar, but his hopes never materialized. Instead, trains of Jews continued to roll into his preserve and evacuations from the Reich itself continued to swell the population of the Government-General. Meanwhile, hundreds of thousands of ethnic Germans from Polish Volhynia and eastern Galicia, Baltic Germans and "Germanizable" Czechs and Poles poured into camps of the enlarged Reich—western Poland.

Jews were concentrated into forced labor troops under Higher S.S. and Police Leaders by a decree of October 26, 1939, but the unplanned evacuations precluded a rational census of occupations or any systematic use of Jewish labor. A half-million Jews (of the million and a half at the end of 1940) in the Government-General were technically eligible for the heaviest labor, but the Germans made little productive use of them. It is estimated that only 80,000 of them were used as late as the summer of 1941. This is, at first glance, an astonishing fact. Whatever asset value the Jews of Poland had for the Germans, it clearly did not lie in their property. The Polish Jews as a whole were poor. But their potential labor productivity was substantial: the Jews of Poland constituted an unusually high percentage of the available skilled labor.

At first, during the early weeks of the occupation, military and civilian officers seized Jews in the streets and forced them to clear rubble, fill antitank ditches and shovel snow. Then, following the October decree, whenever Jews were needed by a particular agency, they were picked up in the street, organized into labor columns and put to work. In an attempt to mitigate the terror aroused by the press gangs which took people at random, the Jewish councils offered to provide labor battalions according to German specifications. But the arbitrary seizures continued. The Higher S.S. and Police Leader in the Government-General, Friedrich Krüger, proposed the compilation of a central register including occupation, age, sex, and other data for each Jew. This was, of course, a police bid for the control of Jewish labor. But Frank conceded nothing. In his diary he noted that a large card-index system was necessary for satisfactory use of Jewish labor, but decided it was too big a project: "To do this, sweeping planning is necessary. For the time being, Jews had to be gathered in columns and

Nazi officials ride through Berlin to enforce the anti-Jewish boycott of April 1, 1933. The sign on the truck reads, "Germans, beware. Do not buy from Jews." YIVO.

German woman wears sign, "I am a swine." She is guilty of *Rassenschande*, "racial shame." The 1935 Nuremberg Laws and later regulations made Germans having any contact with Jews impure. "Race defilement is worse than murder," the Nazis said. YIVO.

An issue of Julius Streicher's notorious Jew-baiting *Der Stürmer*. This weekly, which ran to several hundred thousand copies, was directed particularly to children. The line at the bottom reads: "The Jews are our misfortune." FRANKENHUIS.

Dr. Leo Baeck, leader of German Jewry during the Holocaust, was Rabbi of Berlin and head of the *Reichsvertretung der Juden in Deutschland*. Arrested several times by the Gestapo, he was sent to Theresienstadt in Czechoslovakia when he was almost seventy. Eichmann was surprised to find him still alive in 1945. BAECK.

According to these two signs in the Netherlands, Jews were forbidden to travel the road at left, while only limited movement was permitted on the road at right. FRANKENHUIS.

A Polish Jew packs his bundles. Forced expulsions of Jews began as soon as the Nazis invaded Poland in September 1939. YIVO.

The marketplace in Lublin, Poland, during the early thirties. The Nazis created a ghetto in Lublin in March 1941 and began mass exterminations in the spring of 1942. YIVO.

German Jews crowd a consulate office in an effort to leave Germany. By 1937 one-fourth of the Jewish population had emigrated. After the war started, emigration became all but impossible. YIVO.

In November 1938 the Nazis began closing and absorbing Jewish-owned stores as part of their Aryanization policy. The Brünn department store in Berlin was painted with signs, stars and caricatures before it was Aryanized. YIVO.

On May 15, 1940, the day the Netherlands surrendered, many Jews chose to take their own lives rather than be killed by the Nazis. This row of tombstones in The Hague is called "suicide row." FRANKENHUIS.

Joel Schaap (whose grave is in the front row above) had owned a jewelry store next to the Queen's palace in The Hague. His family saw the Queen fleeing by the back door and knew that the Netherlands was lost. Mrs. Schaap's suicide note to her mother is shown here. It ends, "We are very calm and intend to go to sleep quietly." FRANKENHUIS.

"V = Vampire. Therefore, death to the Jews," was painted alongside swastikas on a synagogue wall in The Hague during the Nazi occupation. This synagogue was the only building in this part of the city that was not destroyed by American and British bombing. FRANKENHUIS.

Jews in the Netherlands await deportation to camps at Westerbork or Vught. To deceive deportees, the Nazis at first allowed families to leave together and passed out questionnaires asking if they preferred kosher food. NETHERLANDS.

Dutch women working in the fields at Camp Westerbork. First established by Holland as a camp for Jewish refugees, Westerbork became a Nazi assembly point for Jews destined for Auschwitz and Sobibor. More than 100,000 Dutch Jews were killed between 1942 and 1944. NETHERLANDS.

Joop Westerweel, a non-Jewish school principal in Lundsrecht, Holland, helped Jewish children escape through France and over the Pyrenees into Spain. He was caught and executed by the Gestapo. NETHERLANDS.

All identity papers of Jews in German-occupied countries were stamped with "J." This one was used in the Netherlands. FRANKENHUIS.

Some Dutch Jews obtained papers certifying that they had been baptized. Papers such as this one saved the lives of a few Jews. FRANKENHUIS.

Bekanntmachung

Der Höhere SS- und Polizeiführer Nordwest gibt bekannt:

Vom Polizeistandgericht Assen wurden am 20.9.1943 wegen der Überfälle auf das Gemeindehaus Stadskanaal und das Gemeindehaus Exloo und wegen des Mordes an dem Altmitglied der NSB Reilingh, die nachbenannten Niederländer zum Tode verurteilt:

1. **Händler Johannes Vis,**
   geb. 24.5.1913 in Baaradeel, wohnh. Stadskanaal.
2. **Reisender Anne Rutgers,**
   geb. 19.1.1911 in Groningen, wohnh. Stadskanaal.
3. **Buchhalter Jan Toet,**
   geb. 23.6.1918 in Staphorst, wohnh. Staphorst.
4. **Krankenwärter Geert Por,**
   geb. 7.10.1917 in Peize, wohnh. Zuidlaren.
5. **Maschinist Pieter van Laarhoven,**
   geb. 1.7.1919 in Hasselt, wohnh. Hasselt.
6. **Gemeindebeamter Wessel Knot,**
   geb. 16.3.1915 in Zuidlaren, wohnh. Exloo.
7. **Arbeitsamtleiter Rendert Poel,**
   geb. 24.4.1908 in Grijpskerk, wohnh. Borger.
8. **HBS-Schüler Jans Diemer,**
   geb. 22.9.1922 in Borger, wohnh. in Borger.
9. **Landwirt Roelof Tuin,**
   geb. 27.4.1906 in Onstwedde, wohnh. Valthermond.
10. **Gemeindebeamter Andries Diepenbrug,**
    geb. 10.4.1902 in Hengelo, wohnh. Odoorn.

Das Urteil wurde 2 Stunden nach Verkündung vollstreckt.

Der Höhere SS- und Polizeiführer für die besetzten Niederländischen Gebiete

RAUTER,
SS-Obergruppenführer u. General d. Pol.

ASSEN, den 21. Sept. 1943.

Bekendmaking

Der Höhere SS- und Polizeiführer Nordwest maakt bekend:

Door het Polizeistandgericht Assen werden op den 20.9.1943 ter dood veroordeeld, wegens overvallen op het gemeentehuis in Stadskanaal en het gemeentehuis in Exloo en wegens moord op den N.S.B.-'er Reilingh, de volgende personen:

1. **Koopman Johannes Vis,**
   geb. 24.5.1913 in Baaradeel, woonachtig Stadskanaal.
2. **Reiziger Anne Rutgers,**
   geb. 19.1.1911 in Groningen, woonachtig Stadskanaal.
3. **Boekhouder Jan Toet,**
   geb. 23.6.1918 in Staphorst, woonachtig Staphorst.
4. **Ziekenverpleger Geert Por,**
   geb. 7.10.1917 in Peize, woonachtig in Zuidlaren.
5. **Machinist Pieter van Laarhoven,**
   geb. 1.7.1919 in Hasselt, woonachtig Hasselt.
6. **Gemeenteambtenaar Wessel Knot,**
   geb. 16.3.1915 in Zuidlaren, woonachtig Exloo.
7. **Directeur Arbeidsbureau Rendert Poel,**
   geb. 24.4.1908 te Grijpskerk, woonachtig Borger.
8. **H.B.S.-leerling Jans Diemer,**
   geb. 22.9.1922 in Borger, woonachtig Borger.
9. **Landbouwer Roelof Tuin,**
   geb. 27.4.1906 in Onstwedde, woonachtig Valthermond.
10. **Gemeenteambtenaar Andries Diepenbrug,**
    geb. 10.4.1902 in Hengelo, woonachtig Odoorn.

Twee uren na de uitspraak werd het vonnis voltrokken.

Der Höhere SS- und Polizeiführer für die besetzten Niederländischen Gebiete

RAUTER,
SS-Obergruppenführer u. General d. Pol.

ASSEN, 21 Sept. 1943.

During the occupation of the Netherlands, the Nazis publicized acts of local resistance and Nazi reprisals to suppress opposition. This list of ten people shot was signed by Hans Rauter, Higher S.S. and Police Leader for Holland. FRANKENHUIS.

Although they saved most of their native-born Jews, the French did not or could not save Jewish immigrants from deportation. The refugees were interned at camps, such as Beaune-la-Rolande (above). During the Nazi occupation, 80,000 Jews were sent "to the East" in cattle trains. CENTRE.

Jews await deportation in the Vélodrôme d'Hiver, a converted sports stadium in Paris, July 1942. Almost 7,000 Jews, including 4,000 children, were rounded up, kept there for five days, sent to deportation camps, and then to Auschwitz. CENTRE.

With luggage in hand, stateless Jewish refugees in France prepare to board a train that will take them to Auschwitz. CENTRE.

Deportees gather at common washtrough at Drancy, Paris, a way station to Auschwitz. CENTRE.

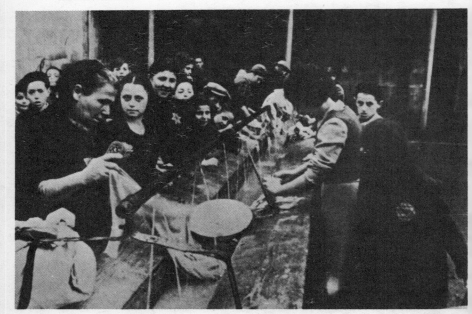

Inmates receiving soup rations at Theresienstadt, Czechoslovakia. Although it was described as a "model" ghetto, Theresienstadt was a transit stop on the way to Auschwitz. Of the 140,000 Jews sent to Theresienstadt, only 17,000 survived. YIVO.

Women's workshop at Theresienstadt. Up to 58,000 Jews at one time were crowded into the town which had numbered 8,000 before the war. YIVO.

Artwork done by eight- to fourteen-year-old children at Theresienstadt. The drawings on this page show the freedom and happiness they remembered before the war. Above, a playground, with jump ropes, trees and flowers. Below, a family gathered for a Passover seder. STATE.

These drawings show the stark realities of life in the Ghetto. Above, bunk beds stacked three high. Below, the hanging of a man wearing a Jewish star. Of the estimated 15,000 children at Theresienstadt, only 100 survived. STATE.

Jews wait in line at Bohušovice, near Theresienstadt. Trains from here took the deportees to Auschwitz. YIVO.

had to be employed wherever there was a pressing need. It is the task of the chief of the district to determine these needs."[11]

Out of the labor columns, which were used for day-to-day emergency work, there developed a more permanent type of forced labor, the labor camps. The first proposal for a large-scale project came, significantly, from Police Chief Himmler. In February 1940, he suggested to von Brauchitsch, Commander in Chief of the Army, the construction of an enormous anti-tank ditch along the newly formed frontiers of the East, facing the Red Army. For the building of this line, Himmler dreamed of using all Polish Jews. In the course of further planning, the project became less grandiose. The ditch was confined to the gap between the Bug and San rivers and required not millions of Jews but only 30,000. Labor camps were set up at Belzec and Plazow and in other localities along the Bug and San rivers, and until October 1940, Jews worked on the so-called Otto line. This assignment was considered one of the worst, with a very high death rate.

A canalization project in the Lublin district used 45,000 Jews in over 40 camps and a land-restoration project in the Warsaw district, 25,000 Jews. In the incorporated territories, despite the "cleansing" operations, there were also many labor camps, particularly in Upper Silesia, which used Jewish labor.

While Himmler was creating gigantic work projects for Jews, one of his aides found a site, of ominous portent, for a new camp. On February 21, 1940, S.S. *Oberführer* Richard Glücks, head of the Concentration Camp Inspectorate, looking around near Krakow, informed Himmler that he had found a "suitable site" for a new "quarantine camp" at Auschwitz, a dreary and marshy town of 12,000 people, where there stood a former Austrian cavalry barracks and some factories. Work was started immediately and on June 14, Auschwitz was officially opened as a concentration camp for certain Polish political prisoners. Meanwhile, the directors of I. G. Farben, the giant German chemical trust, found Auschwitz to be a "suitable" site for a new synthetic coal-oil and rubber plant which could be worked by cheap slave labor. To superintend the new camp and supply of slave labor, there arrived at Auschwitz in the spring of 1940 a gang of notorious S.S. men, among them Josef Kramer, who would later be known as the "beast of Belsen," and Rudolf Franz Höss, a convicted murderer who had spent most of his life in prison, first as convict, then as jailer, and who, at the age of forty-six, would calmly admit to superintending the extermination of two and a half million people, not counting another half million who had been allowed to "succumb to starvation."

At first the camp inmates in the Government-General were used only in outdoor projects, but later, industrial plants moved into some of the camps, and camps were built near major plants. Cheap camp labor thus became a permanent institution. The survival of the hardiest under condi-

tions that defy description gave the Germans the basis on which the weak
and sick Jews could be classed as "unproductive" and then sent off to be
killed. This process of progressive decimation of workers by starvation and
disease began at once in the labor camps. On some projects, the Army
agreed to pay two zlotys to each man per day, about forty cents. Most
other German agencies paid nothing but insisted that the Jewish councils
pay the workers. In the economic withering that occurred in the ghettos
within two years, these wages became less than a pittance. Food was supplied in some camps by the nearest Jewish council, and in others by the
civil administration. The chief ingredients of the workers' diet were bread,
watery soup, potatoes, margarine and meat leftovers. Working from dawn
to dusk, seven days a week, the Jews were driven to collapse. A survivor
reports that even small camps, with 400 to 500 inmates, had approximately
twelve dead every day.[12]

The Jews in the labor camps were hired out to civilian contractors by
the Security Police, the civil government or the municipal authorities.
Everywhere there was gross embezzlement. The Higher S.S. and Police
Leaders were not subordinated to an economic office of the S.S. until
March 1942. Meanwhile, they grew rich. The Police Leader in the Lublin
district, the notorious Odilo Globocnik, founded Jewish "cooperative"
workshops and then turned them into labor camps for his own benefit.
Official Reich agencies were not required to pay any wages and were free
not only to exploit their workers without limit but to pocket as much as
they wanted for the "upkeep" of the camps.

It was only in certain ghettos that private employers tried to maintain
their Jewish working force alive and productive. But this was a losing battle against the destructive tide of the rest of the Nazi empire. The Army,
likewise, had little influence. Very early in the Nazi occupation of the
East the generals protested the waste of Jewish labor and continued to
register objections throughout the war with Russia, without avail. In a
report, "The War Economy in Poland, 1939–40," the generals wrote:
"These unplanned evacuations have prevented any census being taken and
any systematic use of Jewish labor, while filling the ghettos (Warsaw,
especially) with a miserable proletariat. . . . The continuation of these
population transfers menaces the social and economic future of the region
and is an immediate danger to the health of the economy."[13]

Hans Frank, the administrator of the Government-General, has been
called a typical example of Nazi intellectual gangster—nimble-minded,
energetic, well read not only in the law but in general literature, and devoted to the arts, especially music. But behind this civilized veneer lay an
icy, ambitious, bloodthirsty man. Frank's job, besides squeezing food,
supplies and forced labor out of Poland, was to eliminate the Polish intelli-

gentsia (the code name for this operation was "Extraordinary Pacification Action") and make short shrift of the Jews who were herded into his area against his will. On the first anniversary of his regime, he spoke to a Nazi assembly in Poland: "My dear comrades!" he shouted, "I could not eliminate all lice and Jews in only one year. But in the course of time, and if you will help me, this end will be attained." A little later, he confessed that it was difficult "to shoot or poison the three and a half million Jews in the Government-General, but we shall be able to take measures which will lead, somehow, to their annihilation."

Frank fumed at Himmler's dumping of Jews into his province because of the subsequent disorder and upheaval of economic life which damaged his prestige; as a result, he and Himmler (and Heydrich) were in continuous broiling feuds. Frank was so desperate—there was such pandemonium in the Government-General—that he claimed he needed 40,000 German civil servants to govern his domain. On March 8, 1940, he tried to assert his sole authority publicly: "There exists in the Government-General no power that is higher, stronger in influence and with greater authority than the Governor General. . . . This includes the S.S."

But Himmler had already won. Even Göring's order on March 23 to halt deportations into the Government-General did not stop him. The S.S. covertly continued them until the summer of 1940. After that time, deportations to the East were publicly described as "resettlement."

At Nuremberg, although Frank placed the blame for subsequent massacres of the Jews of Poland on the police chiefs Globocnik and Krüger, he admitted to a share in the collective responsibility for the extermination of Polish Jewry: "My conscience will not allow me to throw the responsibility on these small people. . . . A thousand years will pass and the guilt of Germany will not be erased." And yet, his vanity, split off from his seeming contrition, prevented him, as late as May 1945, from destroying forty-two volumes detailing his acts and speeches. These journals were found by Americans in his hotel room at Heuhaus, Bavaria, and were so incriminating that when he heard about them, he tried to slit his wrists.[14]

The economic chaos that Frank dreaded cast doubt on his administration, yet he agreed with the police bosses that Jews must be expelled from private trade and industry and put to manual labor. Those who could not be put to work need not be kept alive. But other German agencies, more directly concerned with wartime production, argued that the maximum value of the lowliest worker was impossible to extract if his family were killed off, or if he were deprived of incentives offered to others. These objections, however, never got very far.

Every German involved in the control of Poland, from Himmler down, was more concerned with racial experiments, eliminating "undesirables" and maintaining an impressive facade of order than with the creation of a productive labor force to strengthen the German war effort. The destruction of the Jews was not a gainful operation. It not only placed a great strain on administrative bureaucracies, which were often understaffed, but it was a very costly operation to carry out after the killing phase was inaugurated. The economic loss to Germany was staggering. Estimates of the total value of Jewish war production lost are put at three billion reichsmarks, a figure which swamps the entire income derived from the destruction process after the "final solution" had started.[15] Even by 1944, when the labor shortage reached four million, military arguments could not prevail over racial fantasies. But winning the war was, in fact, secondary to killing Jews. Himmler never pretended otherwise. When plied with arguments in favor of the war effort, he replied: "The argument of war production, which nowadays in Germany is the favorite reason for opposing anything at all, I do not recognize in the first place." It is very possible that German military victory was sacrificed to the dreams of racist cranks intoxicated by the idea that many human beings deserved less regard than the lowliest animal.

National economic self-interest did not govern the Nazi solution of the Jewish problem. Ideology got the better of survival. Individual profiteering, however, was rampant in the Third Reich. One of the most notorious of Nazi looters was S.S. Brigade Chief Odilo Globocnik. Globocnik was an old crony of Frank who was in charge of all population transfers in the Lublin district of the Government-General. Globocnik had helped to organize the Nazi terror in Austria before the Anschluss and played an important role in the Nazi seizure of Austria. As a reward, he was made Nazi Gauleiter of Vienna, but his peculations there were too much even for the Nazis, and he was downgraded. But his brutality and ruthlessness were the right combination for Poland. At Heydrich's suggestion, Hitler pardoned him and in November 1939 he was appointed chief of the S.S. and police in Lublin. He was entrusted with "the systematic organization of all matters pertaining to the Jews of the district of Lublin," and immediately set up a special Division for Jewish Affairs which prepared forced labor projects. Like other police leaders, Globocnik constantly feuded with the governor, Zörner, and other civil authorities, and, as always, won out. It was Globocnik who decided to set up Lublin as a reception center for "destructive elements." His plan was submitted to Frank, but before Frank officially approved it, transports of Jews from the Reich, from Austria and from incorporated Poland began streaming into Lublin. At the other end, Adolf Eichmann was eagerly cooperating with Globocnik.

Zörner's own officer on Jewish affairs fought with Globocnik over these sudden, unplanned deportations, but Globocnik said there was no thought of allowing Jews or Gypsies to settle permanently or semipermanently.

They would soon be shipped off to various labor camps.[16] It is clear that from the very beginning of their control of Jews, the police had no plans for solving the Jewish problem by emigration, or territorially. The talk about "colonization" was simply a device to fool the Jews and keep them calm during the transportation process. The transfers, beginning with Jews from Vienna in October 1939, also included Jews from Czechoslovakia, Germany and annexed parts of Poland, and continued through July 1940. Besides these chaotic deportations, Globocnik brought thousands of Jewish war prisoners from the Polish army to Lublin and set them up in a special camp, first at 7 Lipowa Street in Lublin and later in Maidanek.

At a conference in Heydrich's office on January 30, 1940, it was already reported that 78,000 Jews had been transported to the Lublin district and that an additional 400,000 were expected during the following months.

Globocnik's labor camps became halfway houses to extermination centers. In 1941, he became head of all of the extermination camps in the Government-General—Treblinka and the three camps in the Lublin district which he had founded: Belzec, Maidanek and Sobibor—and he was assigned to annihilate all of the Jews in the Government-General. This assignment was coded "Einsatz Reinhard," to memorialize the death of Heydrich in June 1942.

Globocnik rammed through his own ideas about camps for Jews in vehement sessions with the civil governor and his agents—with the knowledge and consent of the highest authorities in Berlin. He set up the first camps in the early summer of 1940. By July there were more than 30 camps containing 10,000 Jews, the largest of which was Belzec. He assigned a Major Dolf, one of Hitler's oldest friends, as the commandant of the camp at Belzec, where he became known as one of the worst of the Nazi sadists. In the labor camps, Jews were slowly tortured or starved to death or were wasted by disease. However, this death rate was too slow for the Nazis. It was soon accelerated by faster techniques for mass killing.

Besides his vision of a world cleansed of Jews, Himmler foresaw the "disappearance of Poles from the world." He expressly formulated the mission of the German people as "the destruction of all Poles," but fortunately this vision did not materialize. Many civilian Poles were killed and enslaved and the Polish intelligentsia were virtually destroyed, but the brunt of destruction in Poland was borne by Jews. The total civilian dead in Poland during the war and German occupation was estimated by Polish authorities at 5,384,000 in 1945. Of these, 3,200,000 were Jews.[17] Preparations for this huge industry of death had been made soon after the invasion of Poland.

10 Heydrich's Order of September 21, 1939

The period from 1939 to 1941 marked the transition from forced emigration of Jews to their annihilation. Poland, the historic center and nourisher of European Jewry, was to be the Nazi laboratory for this process. This was the very heartland of Jewry. Here were concentrated the great masses of Jews and the intellectual and spiritual roots of Jewish life everywhere. Here evolved the most populous, most cohesive and, culturally, the most homogeneous communities in Europe. The little town or village, the *shtetl*, was the stronghold of this culture. The *shtetl* often existed in the midst of Polish or Russian life physically and geographically, but psychologically and spiritually, it was a world unto itself, a community that seemed to telescope centuries of Jewish history into the living moment. Its life was full of extremes: at once ignominious and exalted, squalid and formless by Western standards, but strangely irradiated and vividly alive.

The *shtetl* was a forlorn impoverished settlement in a vast and hostile non-Jewish world, yet it disdained that world and felt superior to it. The *shtetl* Jew lived in the timeless world of the Bible. He experienced the landscape, the drama and festivals of biblical Palestine more vividly than the events of twentieth-century Poland. He regularly celebrated a harvest that his ancestors had not celebrated for sixty generations. He knew little about the Polish kings or contemporary rulers but was much more at home with stories about the King of Bashan, David, the King of the Amorites and Nebuchadnezzar. He knew little about oaks or pines, or fields of rye or wheat where his bread came from, but he could talk freely about vineyards, date palms and pomegranates. His life was completely enwrapped in traditional religious precepts and practices and he could talk and pray unabashedly to God. Reflecting the split world he inhabited, the *shtetl* Jew spoke Yiddish, wrote and read in Hebrew, and talked to his Polish neighbors in Polish.

In the large Jewish centers in Poland—Warsaw, Vilna, Bialystok, Krakow—there was a rapid assimilation of Western life, but Jewish institutions, political activity, Jewish scholarship, the theater and press were still vigorous and expressive at the time of the Nazi occupation. This Jewry—*shtetl* and urban—of three and a quarter million people was the *Untermenschentum* in the German scale of human value—not simply the dregs of humanity, but subhumanity. The careful hairsplitting decisions that the German bureaucracy applied to the definition of the Jew in the Reich were unnecessary in the East where the most drastic measures could be taken with impunity. A despised people living in thickly populated areas that were already segregated from the surrounding population could be shut off entirely from the rest of the world by resurrecting the medieval ghetto and adding certain new Nazi devices. The Nazis were well aware that Jews in Poland lived precariously in the midst of widespread popular anti-Semitism. Their laboratory of Jewish destruction could not have succeeded anywhere in Europe as successfully as in Poland. Here began the experiments in ghettoization; here were established hundreds of forced labor camps; and here were established all of the extermination camps.

When the Crusaders began to kill local "infidels" on their way to the Holy Land, the Jews of Western Europe began to look to the East for a haven. Poland became their refuge.

These two peoples, Jews and Poles, have in the past experienced great tragedy both in their separate and common destinies, making the tragedy of the war years a terrible climax to a double inheritance of deformities. Two thirds of the three million Jews of the new Polish Republic created in 1919 experienced the segregated and depressed life of the Russian Pale. The Poles also had been deformed by Russian partitions of their country and by generations of Russian domination. But this common disability did nothing to create common bonds. The loyalty of ex-Russian Jews to the new Polish state was widely doubted, particularly since they became part of Poland after the overthrow of the tsarist regime in Russia. The Jews were grateful to the Bolshevik regime whereas the first act of free Poland was to engage in a bitter and aggressive war against it.

The new Russian Constitution of 1917 abolished all laws which laid disabilities upon any citizens based on race or religion. It granted freedom of residence, freedom of movement, access to work, property and education. Overnight, Jews were granted equality. Their life was fundamentally changed and they strained every effort to support the new government. The Poles, however, hated the Russians for having helped to extinguish their state in 1772, 1793, and 1795, and yearned for freedom from any Russian regime, whether tsarist or Bolshevik.

Like the other states formed after the First World War, Poland wanted to carve the largest possible slices out of the German and Austro-Hungarian empires and confront the peace conference with a *fait accompli*. In this drive, the Poles aimed to suppress or destroy everything that was not Polish and persecuted Jews in the process. In eastern Galicia, for example, they fought the Ukrainians. When they stormed Lemberg in November 1918, they promised their troops that, as a reward, they could plunder the Jews for forty-eight hours in the Cossack manner. Sixty-four Jews were killed and thirty-eight houses and the synagogue were burned. A pogrom also broke out in Kielce. On April 5, 1919, 75 Jews in Pinsk, attending a meeting, were attacked by soldiers and denounced as Bolsheviks. Thirty-five were marched to the marketplace, lined up against the wall of the cathedral and shot. (An American commission investigating the pogroms later stated officially that there was absolutely no Bolshevik connection.) A number of women who had been arrested were stripped and flogged and taken through a gauntlet of Polish soldiers.

Later, in the spring of 1919, similar episodes occurred in Lida and Vilna and sparked a general outbreak of anti-Jewish violence. Thirty-nine Jews were killed in Lida; sixty-five in Vilna. Pogroms also broke out in Kolbussowa and Czestochowa. It became common for Jews throughout Poland to be attacked and robbed on the streets, for Jewish men to have their beards cut off forcibly, for Jewish homes to be burned. Conditions became so intolerable that American and British official missions were sent to Poland to make studies. But it was already too late for goodwill efforts. Jews were now represented as the enemies of the new Polish state and, for the Polish people as a whole, Jews were outside the limits of the law. Neither the civil nor military authorities protested the lawlessness.

In May 1920, Poland chose to launch a new war against the Ukraine and Lithuania, both large Jewish centers. This time, the Jews were the prey of both sides. In retreat, the Polish Army was particularly vicious, and only the presence of representatives of the JDC, wearing American uniforms, had any restraining influence.

Two million Jews from the Russian Empire came under the jurisdiction of the new Polish Republic in 1919. These masses were depressed physically and politically and were despised by their neighbors who were ex-Russians, ex-Austrians and ex-Germans. The Polish Government lacked both stability and authority during the early years of its existence and a vague state of war continued for many months between Poles and Bolsheviks and between Poles and Ukrainians. The Jews never benefited from these clashes.

Whether the Jews and Poles alone could have worked out a way of living together is a moot question, but the formulation worked out in the Minorities Treaty bore no relationship to the existing economic or political realities in Poland and had the built-in defects of most solutions imposed by outsiders. For example, the grant of full individual political equality though praiseworthy was not realistic in the context of a still largely feudal system and widespread political illiteracy. But that the Poles would have been less anti-Semitic if the Jews had not claimed minority rights is unlikely. So far as Jews and Poles were concerned, improvements in their relationship could come only within the framework of a sound Polish economy and reformed social system, neither of which developed. Both politically and socially, the country remained undeveloped and the Jewish problem assumed acute proportions.

Cut off from employment in most occupational fields, the more than three million Jews of Poland clung to cities and towns where they engaged in trade, crafts and small family workshops. They constituted 10 percent of the population of Poland—the largest in Europe—and their distribution made them seem even more numerous to the Poles. In Warsaw, for example, Jews formed one third of the population, while in several smaller towns including Pinsk, Grodno and Bialystok, they outnumbered non-Jews. The urban and small-town Pole was constantly aware of the presence of Jews, not only in statistical terms, but because Jews in Poland were, for the most part, noticeably different from other groups. They spoke Yiddish, wrote using the Hebrew alphabet and dressed differently. Orthodox Jews were conspicuously different. They observed dietary laws and a Saturday Sabbath. In subtle as well as obvious ways, Jews constituted a separate community distinguished from the Polish population as Ukrainians, White Russians and Lithuanians were not. Many Jews, moreover, struggled to achieve political equality and economic opportunity, and every stir they made registered strong anti-Semitic reactions. Government ministers themselves sought solutions of national economic problems at the expense of Jews.

The stark economic fact of life in Poland during the interwar period was that there was never enough to go round. The population growth (from 27 million in 1921 to 34 million in 1931) was always ahead of national income. There was always unemployment, and the government was chronically faced with insufficient credit, an unstable currency and inexperienced administrators. Revenue came largely from urban taxation and a large proportion of taxes was laid on the towns where Jews lived. As a result, Jews perpetually paid a disproportionate share of the tax bill. Often overlooked was the fact that hundreds of thousands of unskilled Jewish workers and petty artisans in the towns barely maintained themselves above starvation. It has been said that at least 50 percent of Polish Jews were near destitution, saved from starvation largely by the JDC.

National income flagged in Poland largely because the country failed to find new markets to replace the Russian market which had absorbed 90 percent of all Polish exports before 1914. The war had ravaged the country and most of the population had been kept from starvation by foreign relief.

To Polish officials and political leaders, it seemed natural that, as there was not enough to go round, the persons skipped should not be Poles. The extreme nationalist parties continually exposed officials who, they said, "favored Jews at the expense of Poles." After 1924, when new American immigration restrictions drastically reduced immigration quotas, Polish Jews who could not emigrate and were mainly dependent on occupations in industry and commerce required a thorough overhauling of their backward conditions. There were too many tiny shops whose whole stock of goods could have been bought for a few zlotys. Many workshops were poorly equipped and unhygienic. Children toiled in them. Too many Jews staved off hunger by vague *luft-mensch* (insubstantial) occupations. However, when Jewish shopkeepers tried to get credit to make needed changes, they were denied. When the government imposed regulations and tests of efficiency, they were pressed most strictly against the Jews. As a result, Jewish economic life declined during the life of the Polish Republic. The crushing tax burden, the government's refusal to grant credit, their exclusion from public employment and from the land forced countless Jews to rely on American Jews for help.

Politically, the Jews likewise had to retreat. Equality under the law for the Jews was opposed by almost all Polish political parties and by the Catholic Church. Despite Poland's pledge to uphold the principle of equality for all minorities, a whole series of tsarist ordinances on Jews and other groups remained in force until 1931. After 1931, the economic depression gave anti-Semitic forces in the country new slogans. Jews suffered both from government measures and the rising unrest in the country. As the crisis deepened, nationalist groups became more violent and outbreaks against Jews in the universities became more frequent. Riots were instigated by the *Endeks* (National Democrats) and the *Naras* (National Radicals). Medical schools admitted Jews to courses in anatomy only if they could supply a proportionate number of Jewish cadavers for dissection. "Ghetto benches" were introduced in November 1937, segregating Jews and Christians at lectures. Jewish economic freedom through education was now a blasted hope.

The government did not so much inflame popular anti-Semitism as appease it by neglecting to punish instigators of violence. From 1929 on, the government failed to suppress the *Endek* and *Nara* agitators and bullies. Clerical anti-Semitism meanwhile followed well-worn lines in denouncing the Talmud and "harmful" Jewish influences on Christian civilization. The Catholic hierarchy had the support of the *Endeks* and church pressure was often used to advance *Endek* economic and political ends. The Church, likewise, did nothing to restrain anti-Semitic outbreaks.

In its economic policy, the government not only hastened the decline of Jewish economic life, but destroyed the one realistic possibility of developing the nation's economy, for Jews, however backward they might be, carried on one fourth of the industry and two thirds of the commerce of the whole country. Their skill and experience would have formed a valuable base for modernizing Poland. Instead of utilizing this pool of experience, the Poles chose to diminish Jewish enterprise by boycotts, discriminatory taxes and pogroms. They also excluded Jews from some two hundred industrial and commercial state monopolies, including mining and forestry, printing works, chemical plants, tobacco, salt, matches, and alcohol enterprises, some of which the Jews themselves had built up. Thus large sectors of industry, commerce and finance were actually closed to Jews.

In 1934, new regulations for artisans threw hundreds of Jews out of work. In the same year, Poland unilaterally repudiated League supervision of the Polish Minorities Treaty. By the summer of 1936, anti-Jewish disorders had become daily occurrences. Poles were demanding that Jews leave the country. In September 1936, Colonel Józef Beck, the Polish Foreign Minister, raised the question of the emigration of masses of Jews before a League of Nations commission. Prefiguring Hitler by several years, Beck demanded facilities for the annual emigration of 100,000 Jews, but admitted that Poland could neither finance the emigration nor allow Jews to take their wealth out of the country.

All through 1937 the question of emigration was kept alive as a sop to the general distress. The possibility of sending Jews to Madagascar, a project also examined by Nazi Germany, was specifically investigated in agreement with the French Colonial Minister, but was abandoned in 1938.

In the entire interwar period, the most important economic questions facing the country were evaded. Not only were trade and industry neglected but millions of Polish peasants remained landless while estates of the landed gentry remained intact. Hungry peasants were incited to seize the small shops and stalls of town Jews. Economically depressed, split by nationality quarrels, and politically fragmented, Poland was not prepared to withstand the Nazi assault.[1]

Only one group in Poland seemed able to look at Polish problems without needing the lens of the Jewish question. This was the Polish Socialist Party with whom collaboration with Jews, particularly the great Jewish Bund (General Jewish Workers' Union), was continuous. The Socialists regarded the raising of the Jewish question as a danger, a diversion from looking at basic economic issues. Socialists often stood by Jews, but after 1920, there was never the slightest possibility of their securing political power. They were not, however, at their side when they were desperately needed—in the last struggles of the ghettos in 1942 and 1943.

When the Germans invaded Poland on September 1, 1939, Jews rallied to the defense of the Republic. It seemed that the common danger would create, at last, a common front. But discriminations persisted. The Army

at first refused to mobilize Jewish officers and physicians. Not until Warsaw itself was under siege were Jews allowed to defend the capital. Briefly,
Jews and Poles fought together against the Nazi invader, but within a few
days of the invasion, under the crushing might and speed of the Nazi blitz,
Poland collapsed. The government fled from Warsaw to Lublin on September 6 and within a few more days the Polish Army was overwhelmed.
In the last days of the Polish state, Jewish soldiers in Warsaw were removed from regular Polish military units and placed in unarmed special
Jewish battalions building fortifications. When the Polish Government
abandoned Warsaw, Jews threw themselves into the work of digging
trenches and building barricades together with the rest of Warsaw. But
the entry of the German Army into the city set off a wave of anti-Jewish
actions. Poles fought Jews standing with them in the endless queues
formed for food and water and helped Nazis pogromize towns and cities.
Jewish prisoners of war returning from German military camps later reported that they suffered more from Polish fellow soldiers than from the
Germans.

Before the end of the year, the Polish General Staff announced that
31,216 Jews had fallen in defense of the country, and that 61,000 had been
taken prisoner. In a strange, perhaps inexplicable way, the Jews had attachments to their life in Poland, despite the quiet desperation of many.
Their attachments were apparently stronger than their fears. In September 1939, when all of eastern Poland was occupied by Russia, over a million
Polish Jews passed under Soviet rule. They could choose Soviet citizenship
or Siberian exile. Several hundred thousand Jews chose exile rather than
renounce Polish citizenship.

Poland submitted to the stupendous power of the German Army and
Air Force on September 18, 1939. Thus two million Jews—the largest
Jewish mass by far up to that time—passed into Nazi hands. Three days
later, on September 21, Heydrich outlined his plans for their future. On
that date, he reported the results of a conference, held in Berlin the same
day. This report was sent to Einsatzgruppen chiefs, to the High Command
of the Army, officials of several Reich ministries, and the chief of the civil
administration of the occupied territories.

The full sinister implications of the plan would not evolve for several
years, but the blueprint was sketched. In the outline, Heydrich addressed
himself solely to "the Jewish problem in the occupied zone." Planned
joint measures for the ultimate goal, he warned, must be kept strictly
secret. Distinction must be made between the "ultimate goal" (eventually
this came to mean extermination) which required a prolonged period of
time, and short-term measures "leading to the fulfillment of the ultimate
goal." The first condition for attaining the final goal was the concentration

of rural Jews in the cities. Country districts were to be emptied of Jews and concentration points were to be chosen in cities with railroad connections or cities along railroad lines. All Jewish communities with fewer than five hundred Jews were to be dissolved and incorporated into the nearest concentration point. Danzig, West Prussia, Poznan and eastern Upper Silesia were to be completely cleared of Jews.

Heydrich then outlined the setting up of Jewish Councils to administer the segregated communities:

> In each Jewish community, a Council of Jewish Elders is to be set up which, as far as possible, is to be composed of the remaining influential personalities and rabbis. The Council is to be composed of 24 male Jews (depending on the size of the Jewish community). It is to be made *fully responsible* (in the literal sense of the word) for the exact execution according to terms of all instructions released or yet to be released. . . . In case of sabotage of such instructions, the Councils are to be warned of severest measures.
>
> The Jewish Councils are to take an improvised census of the Jews of their area, possibly divided into generations . . . and also according to the principal vocations, and they are to report the results in the shortest possible time. . . . The Councils of Elders are to be made acquainted with the time and date of the evacuation, the evacuation possibilities, and finally the evacuation routes. They are, then, to be made personally responsible for the evacuation of the Jews from the country. . . . The reason to be given for the concentration of the Jews to the cities is that Jews have most decidedly participated in sniper attacks and plundering. . . .
>
> The Councils of Elders . . . are to be made responsible for the proper housing of the Jews to be brought in from the country. The concentration of Jews in the cities for general reasons of security will probably bring about orders to forbid Jews to enter certain wards of the city altogether, and to forbid them, for reasons of economic necessity, for instance, to leave the ghetto, to go out after a designated evening hour, etc. . . .[2]

Immediate Aryanization of Jewish property was also ordered. Heydrich's instructions urged these measures to be taken "in closest agreement and collaboration with the German civil administration and the competent local authorities." Finally, he ordered the *Einsatzgruppen* chiefs to make surveys of Jews in their respective territories by age and occupation and to report to him the names of the concentration points and the evacuation schedules.

These instructions were the beginning of the road to extermination. The Jews in Poland would now be ghettoized and given a pseudo-autonomy through the Jewish Councils. Later, the ghettos would become death traps or way stations to the death camps and the Councils would be perverted into Nazi controls. This process took two years. Even then, not all of the Jews of the incorporated territory had been expelled and not all had been moved to towns on railway lines. There would also be incessant warfare between the police and civilians for control of the Jews. But ultimately, Heydrich would win out. Others in the Nazi hierarchy might still be uncertain about what to do with Jews, but Heydrich undoubtedly was already thinking about their destruction as early as September 1939.

Under Frank's edict of November 28, every Jewish community in the Government-General with a population of 500 to 10,000 had to elect a *Judenrat* (Jewish Council) of 12 members; every community with a population of more than 10,000 elected a *Judenrat* of 24. Jews over twelve were required to wear arm bands marked with a blue Jewish star. Numerous restrictions were imposed on their movements, but the ghettoization process was slow. The first major ghetto—created in Lodz—was not completed until 1940; Warsaw was ghettoized in October 1940, Lublin in April 1941.

The idea of using Jews to administer the segregated Jewish communities had already been tried out before the war by Eichmann in Vienna, Berlin and Prague. The principle was officially sanctioned on September 21, 1939, at Heydrich's meeting in Berlin. However, it is not yet clear where in the Nazi power structure the idea of installing Jewish Councils in Poland or elsewhere originated. Possibly it was suggested by the Nazi brand of *Judenwissenschaft*, Judaic "science," over which many Nazi pseudo scholars pored, and then given concrete form by the Nazi political and police apparatus. In any case, the basis of their scheme was their knowledge that many Jews venerated the idea of Jewish autonomy. Although apprehensive, some Jews believed that the opportunities the Nazis at first gave them for autonomy would continue an old tradition. Very soon, however, the Nazi formulation became a total disfigurement of Jewish self-government. By then, Jews had been caught in a trap from which they could not extricate themselves.

The Nazi caricature of the Councils also changed, reflecting the sudden economic and social changes that struck the Jewish communities and caused social declassment, degradation and physical depletion. The Councils also changed with the changing purposes of Nazi policy. From agencies administering religious, educational and welfare services to the Jewish communities, the Councils were transformed, step by step, into servants of Nazi policy. They announced Nazi regulations and were made responsible for their enforcement. They drew up lists of employable Jews for the labor columns, then lists for "resettlement" purposes. This was the Nazi neologism for extermination. The plan for the annihilation of Europe's Jews was officially made known to certain individual Nazis in the summer of 1941, at the time of the invasion of Russia. For a full year after this time, Jews were completely unaware of Nazi intentions. After the summer of 1942, despite the rumors and reports of exterminations, most Jews did not know what was in store or refused to believe the reports. The extent to which members of the Councils knew of Nazi intentions varied. In the communities of eastern Poland, overrun by the Nazi armies at the time of the invasion of Russia, and then wiped out by the *Einsatzgruppen*, the Councils were destroyed together with the communities. In many communities that were destroyed, there were no Councils at all. In the communities that lingered on for a year or two, the Councils that functioned became involved in the deportations. They selected those Jews who were "fit" for labor in the ghettos and those "unfit." The "unfit" were "resettled in the East," that is, they were transported to death camps.

In a serious and thorough study of this problem of "involvement," one scholar has found that Jewish losses in areas where Councils had some role in compiling lists of deportees were 403,000. He has concluded that the role played by these Councils in the deportations was negligible and could not have been decisive in the final outcome.[3] The involvement of some Councils in this process must be investigated not, as has been done, as a wholesale betrayal or collaboration, but on an individual community basis—for each community had its own peculiar characteristics—and as part of a process of gradual, unwitting enmeshment in the Nazi coil. There was a radical difference in the role and composition of the Councils in September 1939, in September 1940, in September 1941, and again in September 1942. Each date brought varying possibilities for emigration, escape, survival and hope. Each date cast up new Nazi deceptions and promises. Each date represented a new configuration in Nazi military victories or setbacks. And each date represented for Jews diminishing thresholds of the capacity to endure fear, hunger and isolation.

The Councils differed from country to country and from locality to locality.[4] They differed from time to time within the same place. They differed in name, structure and function. There was no uniform pattern. In some countries such as Norway, Bulgaria, Croatia, there were no Councils at all. In some places the organ of Jewish "self-government" was called the *Ältestenrat* (Council of the Elders); in Germany it was the *Reichsvereinigung der Juden in Deutschland* (Association of Jews in Germany); in France, it was the *Union Générale des Israélites de France*, in Romania it was the Jewish Central Organization; in Hungary, it was the Union of Communities. In Poland, there was no national body at all. The reasons for these differences are not yet clear. Elsewhere, the Nazis preferred a unified policy, an enforced *Gleichschaltung*. In the case of the Jewish Councils, they did not. Perhaps, at an earlier date than is generally believed, they knew that the Councils were only temporary expedients. It is clear at least that Heydrich as early as September 1939 planned to use them as instruments of control for the "final solution," and it is very likely that at that time he already knew this would mean extermination.

The Councils also differed in structure. Sometimes there was continuity in the composition of the Councils from the prewar period to the period under Nazi control. At times there was no connection at all. In Warsaw, for example, the original *Ältestenrat* was made up mostly of members of the prewar Advisory Council appointed by the Polish Government—leaders of the Jewish community. But the Commissioner, Maurycy Majzel, disappeared soon after the outbreak of the war, and many of the original members of the Council dropped out within the first few months or escaped from Poland. The Mayor of Warsaw then appointed Adam Czerniakow to replace Majzel, although he was not a community leader, and Czerniakow made replacements within the Council. In Romania, the traditional Jewish leadership was continued under Dr. Wilhelm Filderman, the chief rabbi and Zionist leaders.

In some areas, there was a second authority alongside the *Judenrat* which the Nazis had to reckon with, such as the Jewish Rescue Committee in Hungary and the Working Committee in Slovakia. Elsewhere, as popular hostility toward the Councils grew, parallel Jewish organizations developed. In Warsaw, besides the Council there was the Jewish Self-Help Organization and the popularly elected House Committees with overlapping as well as special activities. In the last phase of the Ghetto's struggle, the Jewish Fighting Organization became the prime ghetto force.

However, there are certain features common to all the Nazi-inspired Councils: first, the Nazi distaste for any kind of free or popular election of the Jewish representatives. The German *Reichsvertretung* (a representative body) was changed in July 1939 to the *Reichsvereinigung*, emphasizing that it was no longer a representative but an appointed body. In other communities, the head at least was always appointed by the Nazis. Thus the Nazi principle of leadership (the *Führer-prinzip*) was applied to the Jewish Councils. Second, in every case, the Jewish dream of full autonomy was cruelly exploited by the Nazis for their own purposes. The so-called Madagascar colonization project abused the ideas of Jewish settlement and pioneering—Nazis even used Zionist terminology and the experience of settlement in Palestine in their promotion of this fraud. The same approach was used in the ghetto of Theresienstadt to which German, Czech, Austrian and other western Jews were sent. The first to go there were Zionist idealists who undertook their tasks in a spirit of enthusiasm, fervently believing that they could help save the Jews of Bohemia and Moravia. Theresienstadt was viewed initially as a training and educational center for Jews who would ultimately go to Palestine. It was proclaimed the "city which the Führer has given the Jews" as promoted by the Nazi propaganda film of that name: *Der Führer schenkt den Juden eine Stadt*.

Sudden and drastic population changes in the ghettos caused upheavals in Council positions. If there was originally a measure of continuity, the Germans destroyed it, usually operating on the principle of negative selection,[5] replacing people of standing with newcomers who had no ties with the community. These men were sometimes excessively ambitious or naïve. Conditions in the ghettos were often intentionally complicated by the Nazis. Often they deliberately created conflicts by sending into the ghettos converted Jews and Gypsies, and by appointing converts (considered by the Nazis as "racial Jews") to high administrative posts, as in the case of the hated Warsaw Ghetto police chief, Jozef Szerynski. The Nazi intent throughout was to deceive Jews as to the ultimate purpose of ghettoization and "resettlement." It became impossible for Jews either to know with certainty what policy the Nazis were pursuing in a nearby community because of the forced isolation, or to know what to expect from day to day in their own. In Riga, for example, the local population was suddenly augmented by Jews from Germany. Two Councils were established—one made up of Riga Jews, the other of Jews from Germany. One day the Nazis declared that the Riga Jews were murderers who had killed Germans; the Latvian members of the Riga *Judenrat* were executed and the ghetto fell under the "authority" of the German-Jewish Council.

National loyalties and conflicts were further strained by the mean struggle to live and the stubborn Nazi-fanned hope that some Jews would be permitted to survive. The continuous search for a rational explanation of the Nazi methodology became a labyrinth of maddening circles without pattern. The Nazis supplied just enough bait to feed the Jewish need to find reasons and explanations for sudden changes. In the small Polish town of Izbica, for example, where both Polish Jews and refugees from Germany were huddled together in the ghetto, the Nazis appointed a Jewish refugee from Stettin as head of the *Judenrat*. He did not know the people of the town at all, but the Nazis said that since none of the local Jews understood the German language well enough to receive their orders, the Stettin Jew was appointed.

Population upheavals and forced expulsions form a main thread in Jewish history, but the Nazis contracted into one or two years processes that have required generations of time. Prior to the fated exterminations, severe psychological convulsions shook the communities. After a deportation, one could walk through a ghetto and not recognize anyone or be able to speak the language of the survivors. Whole groups would suddenly lose jobs, housing, families. Drastic economic and social changes were reflected in the Councils. At times, new groups were sent into a ghetto endowed with special privileges, as were the German Jews in Riga and the Danish Jews in Theresienstadt; or, in reverse, certain expellees were not only uprooted from their homes and livelihood, but were forced to live in the most degraded conditions in the ghettos to which they were deported. The Nazis deliberately aggravated social and economic cleavages, and pitted one group against another in order to create utter anarchy. They brought "divide and rule" to new summits of cunning. This premeditated technique made concerted resistance impossible and estranged the *Judenrat* from larger and larger segments of the ghettos.

In the early phase of ghettoization, many Council members with the greatest sense of social responsibility were killed by the Nazis on the pretext of some petty infraction or trumped-up "crime." The Nazis then sought out weak and corrupt characters, continuing this process of negative selection until they found the men who would be their instruments.

Ultimately, with rare exceptions, all of the members of the Councils were deported. In the process of ghetto depletion, many leaders, unable to face the mounting German pressures and filled with a sense of impotence and guilt, committed suicide (at least forty suicides have been reported). One generalization that has substantial support in the available literature may be made: in the early period of Nazi control, most Jews who were called upon to serve in the Councils felt a moral obligation to do so. They sincerely believed that they could best serve the interests of the Jewish community in this way and remain identified with its fate. They hoped to mediate the needs of the Jewish community and the demands of the Nazis in the historic way: by procrastination, bribery, appeasement, by "holding off the wild beast," by trading favors. As the Nazi demands became more brutal, protracted arguments raged over the moral problems created by membership in the Councils. Again, no generalization is possible: some members worked clandestinely with the Jewish underground while maintaining a formal front to the Nazis; others could not endure the ordeal and committed suicide or passively joined the deportations; still others collaborated shamelessly with the Germans. Some admitted that they surrendered some Jews in order to enable a remnant to survive. Rezsö Kastner, who participated in the Hungarian Jewish rescue operations, has analyzed the acute moral dilemma faced by thousands of Jews:

> If it [the *Judenrat*] functions, if it is docile, it may accelerate the process of liquidation. If it refuses to obey, it brings about sanctions against the community without being certain of delaying the process of liquidation. Between these extreme poles, there are a number of intermediate possibilities depending on the flexibility of the persons involved and on the strength of the temptation to which they are exposed. Nearly everywhere in Europe, the Judenrat followed the same road. Step by step, they were made tractable. In the beginning relatively unimportant things were asked of them, replaceable things of value like personal possessions, money and apartments. Later, however, the personal freedom of human beings was demanded. Finally, the Nazis asked for life itself. For this, it was the task of the Judenrat to decide who would go first, who later. In sacrificing to Moloch,

cruel criteria came into being, including age, merit and achievements. Personal considerations pressed to the foreground: degree of kinship, personal sympathies and even self-interest. The road the Judenrat took was tortuous, and led nearly always to the abyss. Everywhere the Jew was confronted with the same problem: Shall I—whoever I am—be the traitor in order to help or even rescue others now and then, or shall I forsake the community, surrender the dreaded responsibility to others? Is not flight from responsibility also something like betrayal? If I accept the burden, where must I draw the line that will release me from the unbearable responsibility for national suicide, for the execution of my people? How can one draw the boundary between self-sacrifice and betrayal? It is small wonder that wherever a Jewish *yishuv* [community] was left, these questions came up again and again. That demagoguery played its part in this is almost a natural phenomenon. To judge the Judenräte in restrospect, on the evidence of testimony of witnesses, files and documents, exceeds in difficulty nearly everything earthly justice has ever had to deal with.[6]

The rabbis and sages of many communities discussed these agonizing questions; some found nothing in Jewish traditional law to justify delivering Jews up to the authorities; instead, they proposed that all should be killed rather than a single Jewish soul be given up. Others counseled that it was more merciful to have fellow Jews rather than Nazis make the selections.

Undoubtedly some of the members hoped to save their own skins in their dealings with the Germans, but others honorably believed that by organizing the ghettos under German direction they would serve as a buffer between Jews and Germans and improve the lot of the ghettos. It was only after a long history of making themselves economically indispensable to hostile officials that Jews had been able to survive at all. To parley, compromise and, when necessary, bribe had become built-in Jewish reflexes in the diaspora. What no Jew in the Councils could possibly have known at the outset—even as late as the summer of 1942—was that eventually to transmit the German will would mean the deliverance of Jewish lives to the German enemy under threat of death, nor even that every step in their submission to German wishes, though it may have saved some, brought other Jews closer to their doom.

The Jews were in no position to oppose the Nazi demand for the establishment of Councils; this was made at gun point or under severe pressure and threats. Even so, individual Jews appointed to the *Judenrat* were faced from the very start with the question of whether or not they should accept appointment. Before the invasion of Russia, the consensus was that they should serve, to blunt the Nazi demands and serve the community in every possible way. They felt that Jews should organize themselves internally for basic needs: work, housing, health, education, food, law and order and, externally, to "conduct relations" with the Germans. The alternative would be chaos. The situation changed when the Germans invaded the

Soviet Union. After the invasion, Jews in the newly occupied areas that were not immediately annihilated by the *Einsatzgruppen* were reluctant to accept membership—some because they had had no experience with Councils under Soviet rule, others because they had heard something of the trials of the Councils in the German-occupied parts of Poland.[7]

In general, the Councils offered no open defiance to the Nazis. In cases where they resisted Nazi orders or cooperated with underground movements, drastic reprisals and collective punishment followed. This sequence of events led many Councils to repudiate resistance movements. At times, in the case of Lodz, for example, the absence of resistance saved the ghetto for two full years, and was considered strong reason for opposing resistance. In other cases, there was no correlation at all. The ghettos that did not resist perished with those that did.

It was Heydrich who saw enormous possibilities for exploiting the Councils and putting them to fiendish uses. He also devised the ghettos and a no-man's-land called the Lublin district. His report of September 21 had contained a curious, vague reference to the "zone of detail group I . . . located east of Krakow and bounded by Bolanico, Jaroskaw, the new demarcation line and the previous Polish-Slovakian border." Heydrich's ghettoization decree did not apply to this area, called the district of Lublin. This was the area to which Jews were pushed when the population pressure elsewhere in the Government-General became heavy. The minutes of a conference called by Heydrich in January 1940 reported that 78,000 Jews had already been transferred to Lublin; the evacuation of 400,000 more was forecast for the following months. Jews, it was said, were to engage in colonization work in a territory bounded by the Vistula, the San, and the Russian border.[8] The convoys were organized by the police without the knowledge of the civil or military authorities and soon involved Jews from Stettin, Vienna and Prague. Thus began the myth of the "Lublin Reserve."

From the very beginning of their occupation of Poland, the Nazis favored the district of Lublin, in the southeastern part of the Government-General, in experimenting with population transfers. It was first set up as a "reservation" for Jews. Then 30,000 Germans who had lived in Lublin for generations were transplanted to Warthegau in western Poland, and the Poles of that region were moved to Lublin. Just before the German invasion of Russia, a complete reversal of this plan was announced and a "purely German community" of Germans from Bulgaria, Yugoslavia and Bessarabia was projected for the Lublin district.

Similar forced population schemes had already been carried out in the Tyrol and in the occupied zones of Poland. Hitler also had more ambitious plans, such as the expulsion of the Czechs from the Protectorate, the French from Alsace, and the movement of millions of east Europeans to

Siberia. In the midst of these projects and visions, the deportation of Jews could have passed as part of a general plan. There was therefore, no suspicion, at first, that behind the mask of "resettlement" quite a different plan was being prepared.[9]

The Lublin Reservation, or as it is sometimes called, Nisko, seems to have been the brainchild of Alfred Rosenberg, head of a somewhat vague Foreign Political Office, a man who was one of Hitler's chief influences in the early years of the Nazi movement and the prophet of a new racist *Weltanschauung*.[10] Rosenberg's idea was to settle a million Jews in a 400-square-mile area in the region of Lublin, near the Russian border in occupied Poland. Himmler was given complete power to deal with the matter and he turned the project over to Heydrich.

Rosenberg's plan for a reservation where Jews could be concentrated, put under German police and exploited was sketched out even before the war began. On February 7, 1939, in Berlin in an address to foreign diplomats and representatives of the foreign press, he dealt at length with the Jewish problem. "Only one question remains to be solved," he said in the course of his speech. "What territories are the democracies willing to provide for the purpose of the settlement of some fifteen million Jews? . . . If millions of Jews are to be settled, elementary humanity towards the Jews would demand that they should not be left to themselves, but that the colony be placed under administrators trained in police work. There is no question of establishing a Jewish state, but only a Jewish reservation."[11]

An expert in Rosenberg's department, Dr. Alfred Wetzel later explained that the task of the German administration "will be to set Poles and Jews against each other. . . . It is unnecessary to add that a sanitary state for the Jews does not interest us; it is still a valid principle for us that their multiplication must be checked by every means."[12] But Rosenberg's laboratories were soon swallowed up by Adolf Eichmann's interpretation of Heydrich's letter of September 21.

Shortly after the German invasion of Poland, Eichmann called to his office a group of Jewish representatives from Berlin, Vienna and Prague and announced that Germany was about to create an autonomous Jewish territory in Lublin. He ordered them to prepare lists of Jews for voluntary deportation. The Prague and Berlin representatives refused; only the Vienna representatives agreed to comply. Eichmann then coerced the other communities to "cooperate."

The German propaganda machine, meanwhile, publicized the idea of Lublin as a Jewish reservation. Articles appeared in the foreign press linking Lublin with Hitler's address to the Reichstag on October 6, 1939, in which he spoke of the need for "adapting and regulating the Jewish problem." At the same time, the Germans launched a propaganda campaign for the plan among Polish Jews. Shmuel Zygelboim noted in his diary that on the very day they invaded Warsaw, the Germans began spreading rumors about the Lublin reservation. In Czestochowa, the officer for Jewish Affairs in the Gestapo said to a Jewish delegation which appeared before him on September 16, 1939: "All of the Lublin district will be cleared of non-Jews and Jews will be transferred there from all occupied countries. A Jewish state will be set up there." The well-known political commentator Hermann Erich Seifert wrote that Lublin would tackle the Jewish question "not with the 'humanitarian' nonsense you find in the democracies, or with soulful appeals, but according to new methods, with order and work."[13] German publicity then suddenly stopped.

In October, transports of Jews from the Reich, Austria, and Warthegau began to arrive in Lublin. Nothing at all had been done to receive the thousands of refugees. They were placed in old dilapidated schools, empty barracks, warehouses, and stables, and when there was no more room in enclosed buildings, they were simply left in open fields fenced off by barbed wire. News of the sufferings of the deportees soon reached the outside world and the foreign press published alarming reports.

The *Luxemburger Wort* for November 21, 1939, reported the following:

> The haste with which the reservation has been established out of nothing is leading to desperate situations. Sometimes trains drive on for 40 kilometers beyond Lublin and halt in the open country, where the Jews alight and have to find themselves primitive accommodations in the surrounding villages. Up to November 10, about 45,000 Jewish men, women and children from Cieszyn, Bogumin, Moravska, Ostrava, Prague, Pilzno, other towns of the Protectorate and from Vienna and the new Reich provinces, Danzig-Westpreussen and Posen-Warthegau, have been sent to the reservation. Under the supervision of the men of the SS-Death's-head Corps, the Jews are compelled to work at road-building, draining marshes and rebuilding the damaged villages. There is compulsory labor service for men up to 70 years and for women up to 55.[14]

Many trains were jammed so tightly that during the three-day journey across the Reich neither children nor old people and invalids could sit down. Many compartments were windowless. Bread and weak soup were doled out once a day. Many occupants died before the trip was over. So bad were conditions that, despite Nazi efforts to seal the deportations in secrecy, reports leaked out. Outraged neutrals complained to the German Foreign Office. Eichmann was asked to investigate, but nothing changed. One report, later published officially, was made by a sickened Dutch national who saw two trainloads of Eichmann's captives pass through Breslau on their way east:

> The sick, the aged and babies in arms were crushed into barred cattle-trucks. From my train compartment I could see that the occupants were in a terrible state. The train was in a siding, and while we were held up by railway signals, I heard scores crying for help. One Jewish mother said she

had been driven from her home in Vienna a week before and was kept with hundreds of others in a stockade outside the town until trucks took them to the railway yard for shipment. They had been aboard the train for two days and had only once received food. She said that some babies had suffocated in the crush and that the SS guards had even then forced in more people and then bolted the door. One or two children were still left over so they threw them in over the heads of those already there. The day was bitterly cold and what those poor people must have suffered at night is beyond comprehension. An old man told me the train stopped in open country once a day for twenty minutes and the doors opened for the captives to relieve themselves in the open fields. The stench was appalling, and many of the occupants had been bilious. People were standing with their arms limply hanging through the slats of the wagons as if they were dead or half dead.

When my train drew into the station, I went to the station master and told him about the conditions on the train. He replied that there was nothing he could do. The train had been booked by the SS. He had strict instructions that it should not be allowed to pull into any station, but be shunted into a siding if it could not proceed because it was best that the public did not see the trains. He seemed a humane man in many ways, and told me that many people who had passed through had clearly died during the journey from exhaustion or frostbite. He said that many of the carriages on the return journey were seen to have splashes of blood upon them and that on one occasion the bodies of tiny dead children were still in the carriages as if no one could be bothered to clear them out, or because the carriages had had to be turned around urgently for the next trip.[15]

In December 1939, the Commander in Chief of the East, Field Marshal Blaskowitz, reported that children arrived in the deportation trains frozen to death and that people were dying of hunger in the reception villages. The death rate among Jewish deportees to Lublin province was 30 percent. Here one has the lining of reality to Eichmann's verbose double-talk about "putting firm ground under the feet of the Jews."

Behind the silence of German propaganda lay the truth that large numbers of Jews deported to Lublin from western Poland, Bohemia and Austria were perishing. Non-German sources provided clues to the truth.

Among the firsthand accounts of Lublin was a report by a journalist who escaped to Palestine:

Lublin is a vale of sorrow. No human beings are they who walk its streets; all are phantoms, shadows, haunting a world that is no longer in existence. Nobody speaks in Lublin; nobody exchanges greetings. They have even ceased to weep. . . . In normal times, Lublin has a population of 72,000 Gentiles and 40,000 Jews. Today [November 1939] the number of Jews cannot be computed, but it must run into at least 200,000, perhaps a quarter of a million. The congestion, the stench, the poverty, the disease and the chaos which reign in Lublin cannot be paralleled anywhere on earth. Men live in the streets, in cattle-stalls, in cellars, in carts and in the debris of devastated houses.

Men die like flies in the thoroughfares, their bodies strewn on the roadway like old cinders. Shrouds are no longer used for the dead because none can be bought. . . . The whole city is girt with barbed wire fences, and the Nazis allow no traffic to pass through it. The water has turned foul and cannot be drunk. All the wells have become polluted. Cholera and typhus were already rampant when we reached Lublin. . . . The communal soup-kitchen can actually serve nothing but potato broth and stale, black bread. . . . Hundreds have not slept for weeks, cramped and confined in noisy freight cars. They wander about sad-eyed and distraught, like mourners at funerals. . . . One thing only is as clear as the day: the devil himself could not have devised such hell.[16]

It is doubtful that Lublin was ever more than a convenient exchange scheme for 40,000 Baltic Germans who were to go to Bohemia but Eichmann went much further. Without authorization, he took it upon himself to expel Jews from Austria and Bohemia and shoved and dumped them at will. At his trial in Jerusalem, ever ready to believe that by calling Lublin a "resettlement project," it became one, Eichmann claimed that he and his superior in Vienna and Prague, Franz Stahlecker, found Nisko on their own initiative and were convinced that it was exactly what was needed: "an area as large as possible in Poland, to be carved off for the erection of an autonomous Jewish state in the form of a protectorate." He complained bitterly about Frank's lack of cooperation and blamed the "failure" of the project on him. The reality of Nisko was described to the thousands of Jews who were deported by an S.S. officer as a place which "the Führer has promised the Jews as a new homeland. There are no dwellings; there are no houses. If you build, there will be a roof over your heads. There is no water; the wells all around carry disease. There is cholera, dysentery and typhoid. If you bore and find water, you will have water."

During this period, Polish Jews still felt that it was possible to appeal to the conscience of the Nazis. The following letter, dated March 14, 1940, was sent from the Joint Polish-Jewish Aid Commission to the Chancellery of the Reich and then forwarded to Himmler:

Despite the protests of the Government-General against the hasty and chaotic deportation of German Jews to eastern Poland, these evacuations have continued by order of the S.S. Reichsführer.

On March 12, 1940, the 160 Jews of Schneidemühl were deported in boxcars to the region of Lublin. Other convoys are expected there. The deportees had to abandon all their possessions. They were not even allowed to take suitcases. The women had to leave their purses. Some deportees had their coats taken away, especially those who had tried to protect themselves the better against the cold. They were not able to take any money, not even the twenty zlotys granted to the Stettin deportees. Nor were they able to take either food, bedding or dishes. They arrived in Lublin owning only what they were wearing on their backs.

The deportees have been sent to the villages of Piaski, Glusk and Belcyca, twenty-five to thirty kilometers from Lublin. There they found the deportees from Stettin, or those who were still alive. Men, women and children have had to walk to these villages on roads covered with deep snow in a temperature of −22° (centigrade). Of the 1,200 deportees from Stettin, 72 died during a march that lasted more than 14 hours. The majority died from exposure. Among others, a mother who was carrying a three-year-old child in her arms, trying to protect him from the cold with her own clothes, was found dead, frozen in this position. The half-frozen body of a five-year-old girl was found wearing around her neck a cardboard sign with the words, "Renate Alexander, from Hemmerstein, Pomerania." This child was visiting relatives in Stettin and was included in the deportation; her mother and father stayed in Germany. Her hands and feet had to be amputated at the Lublin Hospital. The bodies of the deportees who had died of exposure were piled on sleds and buried in the Jewish cemeteries at Piaski and Lublin.

The Government-General (district governor Zörner) has refused all responsibility for these occurrences, and for these consequences. Marshal Göring has been informed of the situation.[17]

This appeal, of course, was ignored. Nor did foreign public opinion seem to have any effect on the Nazis by this time. However, suddenly, on March 23, 1940, Göring issued an order discontinuing further transports to Lublin. In April, the Higher S.S. and Police Leader in the Government-General, Friedrich Krüger, issued a directive announcing that the plan to set up a Jewish reservation in Lublin was no longer being considered. It was easy enough to give up something that never existed. Typhus was raging in Lublin and threatening the Nazis themselves; the police were feuding with civil authorities. Zörner and Frank battled against Globocnik's massive dumping of Poles as well as Jews. For the moment, Globocnik was checked. Above all, Hitler was preparing the invasion of Norway and western Europe. "Plan Barbarossa" for the invasion of Russia had already been sketched out. Neither plan could afford the release of rolling stock for the mass transport of Jews at this time.

Those Jews who survived the freezing marches made their way to the still unenclosed Lublin ghetto or to towns along the Russian border which later were to become transfer stations for the extermination camp at Belzec. In March 1942, all Jews were driven from the entire district around Lublin. The sick and disabled were killed on the spot and the remaining Jews were removed to Belzec and Trawniki. The liquidation of Lublin was reported by the Polish Government-in-Exile in London.

For the Nazis, Lublin became a mere footnote to the vast population upheavals that convulsed the entire Government-General. But the end of Lublin did not destroy the legend of the "Lublin Reservation." In 1942 and 1943, when deportation meant deportation to extermination centers, many Jews in Poland still believed that the Germans were seeking to create a Jewish reservation in eastern Poland. Late in 1942, the German Foreign Office requested the Hungarian Government to deport a number of Jews from Hungary to Poland with the assurance that Jews would be employed building roads, after which they would be settled in a "Jewish reservation."[18]

These rumored plans did not fail to have some effect on Allied statesmen. In the spring of 1942, Zygmunt Kaczynski, a highly-placed Polish cleric in the Polish Government-in-Exile in London, came to the United States with a plan for settling the Jews in some reservation in eastern Poland or in Bessarabia after the war. Apparently the plan had the support of the Polish underground in Warsaw.

Himmler, meanwhile, was absorbed by a new project involving the Lublin district. He had uncovered a new Teutonic legend connected with Nisko, renamed the city of Lublin "Himmlerstadt" and planned to remake the whole area into the center of a German ethnic corridor from the Baltic to the Carpathians. But neither this plan nor the end of the "Lublin Reservation" stopped the deportations into the Government-General.

When the great German offensive began in western Europe in the spring of 1940, the deportations were masked by the official pretense that another reserve was being planned for European Jews in Madagascar. On July 12, Frank told his cabinet chiefs that he had persuaded Hitler to include the Jews in the Government-General in the Madagascar scheme. Yet Hitler had just told Baldur von Schirach, Gauleiter of Vienna, quite the opposite, namely, that the 50,000 surviving Jews in Vienna were to go to a "closed settlement" in the Government-General.

By the summer of 1940, half of the Jews and about 10 percent of the Poles had been expelled from western Poland into the Government-General. For Globocnik, this was a mere beginning.

Under Globocnik's brutal leadership, Lublin underwent a complete transformation. Out of the "reservation" grew labor camps where Jews were slowly worked to death, and out of the labor camps evolved the death camps with their experiments in swift killing. These plans were officially authorized by Berlin. On April 22, 1940—precisely when the "Lublin Reservation" was being shelved—Globocnik proposed his plan for creating labor camps for Jews in the Government-General. The first camps were set up early in the summer of 1940 and by July there were more than thirty camps containing 10,000 Jews.[19]

In the meantime, Jews in the Greater Reich were undergoing an ordeal of their own.

11 Dwindling Communities: 1939-1941

THE WAR SITUATION after the invasion of Poland created a certain ambivalence in the Nazi attitude toward Jews. Consistency and Party doctrine demanded that the catastrophe be blamed on them, that the war be represented as a crusade against them. But in the Greater Reich which included Austria, expediency dictated that Jewish manpower be used in the war effort during the early period. As frequently happened, the Nazis did not attempt to resolve this paradox, but followed a policy of opportunism, both recruiting and persecuting Jews at the same time. In the East, the persecution surpassed the recruiting by far; in the Greater Reich, the process was slower and more insidious.

Some 78,000 Jews had emigrated from Germany in 1939, reducing the community to 213,000, less than half of its size in 1933. After the pogroms of November 1938, there was a drastic change in the life of the community and in the status of the *Reichsvertretung*. Meetings were closely watched by Gestapo officials and Jewish leaders had to constantly justify everything they undertook—large or small—to the Gestapo. The shrinking autonomy of the *Reichsvertretung* ended completely on July 4, 1939. Under the "Tenth Degree Supplementing the Reich Law on Citizenship" of July 4, 1939, a *Reichsvereinigung der Juden in Deutschland* (Reich Association of Jews in Germany), replaced the old *Reichsvertretung*. This new body was neither representative nor voluntary. Membership for all "racial" Jews—including converts, agnostics and alienated Jews—was compulsory. Congregations and other Jewish institutions now existed only as sections or business offices of the new organization. The *Reichsvereinigung* was the administrative equivalent of a Nazi-controlled ghetto forced to preside over its own liquidation. It was charged first with getting rid of Jews as quickly as possible, and secondarily with providing schools and relief. This charge coincided with Göring's commission to Heydrich to bring about "the final solution of the Jewish problem in the European territories under German influence." Heydrich moved swiftly to handcuff the Jewish communal agencies.

In 1939 the Jewish communities were already impoverished. They were

185

also less able to sustain themselves with hard labor than those who had emigrated and had less capacity for survival. In the Old Reich, in 1939, 74 percent of the Jews remaining were over forty. German Jews were now imprisoned in a country that was preparing their step-by-step destruction, and their leaders were reduced to providing food, shelter, defense against the cold, disease and brutality. The Jews appointed to these tasks were Dr. Leo Baeck, Otto Hirsch, Heinrich Stahl, Dr. Arthur Lilienthal, Hanna Karminski and Cora Berliner. At the beginning of 1940, they supervised 142 schools, 90 homes for the aged, 26 children's homes, 14 Jewish hospitals and numerous soup kitchens. But they were in a lockstep. Eichmann's centers for emigration in Berlin, as well as in Vienna and Prague, were not dismantled with the outbreak of the war. They moved physically into the Jewish community offices. Frantic new efforts were made to find emigration outlets, but the outbreak of the war, deliberately provoked by Hitler, blocked these attempts and gave the Nazis a new propaganda weapon: the Jews could now be blamed for starting the war. The Emigration Department of the Reichsvereinigung was quickly wiped out. In August 1941, a Nazi order banned emigration for Jews between eighteen and forty-five. This age limit was soon extended to sixty. In September 1941, the government blocked sixty million marks which had been amassed by the Reichsvereinigung through emigration taxes—funds that had been earmarked for emigration assistance. Finally, on October 1, 1941, all Jewish emigration was stopped by a Gestapo order.

Jewish community activity was drastically curtailed. The Reichsvereinigung reduced its staff and services. Local communities also suffered. Prior to July 1941, they had raised and administered their own funds although they were strictly accountable to local Gesapo agents. In July, the situation changed drastically. Their funds were sent to the Reichsvereinigung, which, in turn, was forced to cut its allocations.

The economic and psychological attrition of German Jewry collided with German national self-interest and created inevitable contradictions in Nazi policy. The German need for labor was urgent. Those Jews considered "valuable" were restored to certain jobs in factories and wore badges bearing the words: Wirtschaftlich wertvoller Jude (economically valuable Jew). Unemployed Jews were put to work on construction and reclamation projects, segregated from non-Jewish workers. Destitute Jews, ineligible for public relief, were pushed into hard labor. In August 1940, 1,250 Jewish doctors and 940 dentists were conscripted for service in military hospitals. By November 1940, more than 50,000 German and Austrian Jews (as well as 200,000 shipped to Germany from the occupied territories) had been conscripted into the German labor service where they worked at bridgebuilding, railroads, hewing wood in the forests and laboring in vital industries. With the expansion of the war in 1941, the demand for labor became more acute. By June, when the *Einsatzgruppen* were beginning their killing sweep of the Jews in the Soviet Union, a decree in Germany closed Jewish schools for boys over twelve, who were ordered to work in munitions factories. Jewish professional men and scientists were also drafted to aid in the war.[1]

In August 1941, the Gestapo raided kitchens in Jewish homes and looked into pots to detect violations of food regulations. Heavy penalties were imposed on mothers whose children were given a few pieces of candy by non-Jewish neighbors. By October, six thousand Berlin Jews were arrested on charges such as these. The raids were usually carried out at night and served two purposes: to check on violations and see whether or not Jews were performing compulsory labor service. As late as the fall of 1941, the Germans were desperate for manpower of any kind, and Jews had to be used—temporarily. The *Reichsvereinigung*, during this period, had to give up a large number of its staff for forced labor. Artists from the *Kulturbund* were sent to munitions factories. In November, expulsions to Poland had left such a gap in the German labor market that industrialists demanded that Jewish laborers be released from concentration camps to work at former jobs. Some were. Physicians and nurses were also released.

At the same time, the unfavorable turn in the war imposed new deprivations. In January 1942, when the German campaign in Russia ran afoul, Jews were compelled to give up their winter coats, boots, furs, woolen articles and blankets for shipment to the Eastern front. Families were evicted from their homes in Hanover, Cologne, Bonn and Berlin, and their apartments were turned over to non-Jews who had been bombed out of their homes.

Since Jews had already lost their positions, their property and their wealth, all that was left was their earnings. Between 1939 and 1941, a series of measures eroded wage payments and fringe benefits and imposed a punitive income tax on the ground that Jews did not make contributions to Nazi "charitable organizations." The tax was a "Social Equalization Tax" of 15 percent levied on top of the regular income tax. These measures now left Jews with little more than income for the bare necessities. The Nazi bureaucrats next tackled food rationing. In their characteristic step-by-step procedure, they started with restrictions on special allotments, proceeded to supplementary rations, and finally cut basic rations and unrationed foods. Determined to close every loophole, the Agriculture Ministry also restricted shipments of food parcels from foreign countries early in 1941. The value of the contents of such parcels was deducted from the food rations. By June 1942, special rations for pregnant women, nursing mothers and children were eliminated. By this time there were so many foods on the prohibited list that food packages were simply transferred by the customs administration to German hospitals. Toward the end of the year, a circular order of the Land Ministry in the Protectorate listed the following foods barred to Jews: meats, eggs, white bread, milk, all fruits and vegetables, cheese, marmalade, fish and poultry. The deportations were depleting the Jewish communities of the Greater Reich and the Protectorate. No less was starvation.

The technical intricacies of food rationing, labor utilization and punitive taxation absorbed the time and energy of many Nazi deskmen and created a superstructure of order, but they were merely transient busywork. The end goal was the deportations.

Without authorization, Eichmann had been experimenting with drastic expulsions of German Jews as early as February 1940. This expulsion involved 1,300 Jews of Stettin and was carried out in a single night, February 13, 1940. Forced out of their homes, Jews waived all property rights and were refused permission to take any food with them. Those who could not walk to the railway station were carried on stretchers. After twenty-four hours, the first corpses were taken off the train. The deportees were taken to Lublin and from there were marched in subzero temperatures to villages fifteen miles away. The Stettin transport was so brutal that it was widely commented on in the foreign press. By March 12, 230 people had died. When questioned at his trial on the details of this transport, Eichmann said, "Yes. There is indeed a grain of truth in these reports. The reason is the excessive speed with which this deportation was ordered to be carried out: the total time from the moment the order was given to its execution was fifteen days." He did not make clear what difference it would have made to the deportees if the order had been given a month in advance, or more. The pattern for deportations had been struck.

Meanwhile, helplessly trapped, the remaining Jews in Germany watched themselves diminish under physical and emotional battering. Nazi offices kept grinding out decrees under the mystifying German compulsion to legislate against an already written off community. Jews were forbidden to use public conveyances, to stop in the streets, to own domestic animals. They could be evicted by German landlords if proper certificates were completed. No less than five learned societies were laboring to deepen the Nazi case against them.[2] However, not until the fall of 1941 were large numbers of German Jews deported to Lodz, Warsaw, Riga, Minsk, to the notorious concentration camp at Gurs, France, and the ghetto of Theresienstadt in Czechoslovakia. This upheaval coincided with the decree making it obligatory for all Jews in the Reich to wear a yellow star. The official reason for the badge decree was that the political situation had completely changed—Germany was now at war with Russia. German Jews were now identified with a new enemy.

In Austria, the decline of the community was much swifter than in Germany. By the end of 1939, only 55,000 Jews were left of a community that had numbered 185,000 in March 1938. The degree of Jewishness was carefully ascertained in the census of March 17, 1939.[3] For the first time in Austrian census taking, the question was put whether one or more of an individual's grandparents was a full Jew "by race." The declarations were made on the "Supplementary Card for Data on Descent and Education." Everyone who reported that three or four of his grandparents were full Jews was counted as a full Jew; everyone with two Jewish grandparents was counted as a "part Jew, Grade I"; and everyone with one Jewish grandparent, as a "part Jew, Grade II."[4] As a result of this census, the Nazis had their targets clearly defined and Eichmann's center exercised coercive pressure on Jews through the *Kultusgemeinde*. The Statistical Office for the Austrian District, in its December 1939 report, was noticeably pleased with Eichmann's results, except for two items: there were still too many full Jews in Vienna and too many part-Jews in the provinces. Nevertheless, four thousand Jews were leaving monthly.

The emigration of Austrian Jews overlapped deportations to the "Lublin Reserve," which started in October 1939. Eichmann told the Austrian Jewish leaders to submit lists of volunteers for emigration to Lublin. There, he said, a Jewish autonomous territory was about to be created. In October, the *Kultusgemeinde* sent out a number of mimeographed announcements with the caption: "Memorandum on Resettlement in the Polish Province." Recipients were requested to report for "colonization" work. The credulous Jews responded.

The deception as to the real nature of Lublin—one of hundreds perpetrated later—can be seen from the letter sent by the *Kultusgemeinde* to those Jews chosen:

> By order of the authorities, a large transport of Jews fit to work, up to 50 years of age, will go to Poland on October 18, 1939, to start colonizing work. You have been chosen by the authorities to go with this transport. . . . Every person in this transport is permitted to take with him clothes and equipment up to 50 kilograms in weight. Every person is allowed to take money up to 300 marks. It is of the greatest importance that all concerned should take builders' tools with them, such as mallets, saws, planes, hammers and nails, and when reporting, an exact statement must be made as to which of these tools you can provide. Should you disobey this summons which has been issued by the State authorities, you will have to face the consequences.[5]

On October 20, the first shipment of Austrian Jews from Vienna left for Poland. In the course of the month, 1,672 arrived in Lublin.[6] Meanwhile several thousand Jews had been herded in Austrian school buildings and stripped of all their possessions. Nazis destroyed their documents and identification papers. Hoping to procure much-needed foreign exchange, officials told the prospective victims that any whose relatives in the United

States purchased transportation tickets from German travel agencies in New York would be spared.[7] This was merely a snare, however; none of the deportees was spared. They were packed in cattle trucks and driven for several weeks over the countryside. Another forced expulsion of Viennese Jews to Lublin took place in February 1940, involving almost 10,000 Jews. Many died of exposure.

By the middle of 1940, the once sparkling and prosperous Viennese Jewish community was reduced to 45,000 persons, half-starving, fearful, bereft of hope. The Kultusgemeinde carried on primitive functions for these Jews until December 1942 when it was dissolved and its functions were transferred to an Ältestenrat, the Council of Elders. Typical of the technique used by the Gestapo to wear down community leaders was the experience of Dr. Paul Eppstein, a Council officer. In the spring of 1941, Eppstein was confined to a tiny cell, hardly large enough to hold him. Eichmann had a direct phone line to his cell and for several weeks tormented the man with alternating threats and promises.

Those Jews who remained in Vienna were sentenced to a life of grinding poverty and persecution. They were restricted to buying one pound of potatoes a week. In November 1941 Nazi food authorities suddenly recalled all old ration cards. For two weeks, not even the Jewish soup kitchens, which daily fed several thousands, received any food. The Kultusgemeinde carried on its feeding program aided by funds from the American Joint Distribution Committee. Its offices were housed in the only synagogue still open and the soup kitchens, when reopened, operated from one of the two Jewish schools not yet evacuated for wounded soldiers.[8] In 1942, transports of Austrian Jews were sent to Theresienstadt, another "permanent Jewish settlement," eventually swallowing up most of the already derelict community and the Jewish community leaders.

In the Protectorate there was also a vast transformation of the Jewish communities. The destruction of Jewish life here has a special poignancy because the Jews in Czechoslovakia—in Prague especially—were in the vanguard of German cultural expression and pride. The leading poets in the German milieu of Prague at the end of the nineteenth century, with the exception of Rilke, were Jews. There was a remarkable German theater in Prague in which Jews were very active. Jews had moved so rapidly into the world of German culture in Czechoslovakia that their consciousness of Jewishness was scant. The extent of assimilation very possibly exceeded even that of Germany. But like German Jews, Czech Jews very swiftly had to come to grips with their Jewish identity.

Under Eichmann's forced emigration policy, many Czech Jews were expelled to Lublin. The first transport, made up of 600 Jews from various towns and cities, left on October 26, 1939. According to Czech sources,[9]

10,000 to 20,000 were subsequently expelled from Moravska-Ostrava alone. The journey was long and cruel. Transports which left at the end of October did not arrive in the Lublin district until the end of November. Some of these deportees fell into the Soviet zone and were then caught in the war. A few straggled back to Czechoslovakia. Eichmann is reported to have camouflaged the status of these refugees as "returning from vocational training."

The expulsions were intensified under Gestapo leader Klein, reputedly a cousin of Himmler, who was brought to Prague to take charge of emigration in January 1940. Within a few weeks, however, the deportations were temporarily halted. Göring ordered Klein arrested on a charge of embezzling money taken from Jews.[10] This scandal was deflected by a campaign of vilification. The Gestapo revived the investigation of 258 unsolved murders of women and children to work up the age-old charge of ritual murder. Three million books of Jewish authorship or character were burned. The historic statue of Moses opposite the Altneu Synagogue in Prague was melted down for munitions.[11] The Czechs, however, resisted Nazi propaganda. Peasants demonstrated their sympathy for Jews at Iglava. Cafés disobeyed Nazi orders to bar Jews. Czech audiences watching Elmer Rice's *Street Scene* applauded the line, "After all, Jews are human beings."

At the beginning of 1940, the Jewish population stood at 90,000, more than half of whom were over forty. But this rate of "emigration" was still too slow. By a decree of March 5, 1940, Eichmann's Central Emigration Office was given complete control over all Jews in the Protectorate. This Nazi seizure brought radical changes in the structure and activities of Jewish community organizations. All of the provincial communities were centralized under the Prague Council and all registration services were consolidated in one office.

A somber expression of community responsibility can be sensed in a statement published by the Jewish Council in the Nazi-censored *Jüdisches Nachrichtenblatt*. The statement was published on July 26, 1940, when the noose was already quite tightly drawn:

> By decree, the Prague Jewish Community is now headed by a governing body to whose jurisdiction all communities in the country are subordinated as well. The authority [to be] exercised by this body derives from the competence of the [German] Central Agency (*Zentralstelle*) [for Jewish Emigration]. The very existence of such an authority is new in the history of the Jewish Diaspora. It is the fervent wish and the firm hope of the governing body that this authority shall operate only for the benefit of the community.[12]

Specific towns were suddenly ordered to expel their Jews. On September 5, 1940, the entire Jewish population from Klatov was expelled. On November 19, Jews were ordered to evacuate Kremzir, Geding and

Ungarisch-Ralitsh within twenty-four hours. By May 1941, Jews in eighty-three towns were expelled to the Government-General.[12a]

The Prague Council had "jurisdiction" over the whole of Czech Jewry, but it had no freedom at all and was under the constant pressure of German police terror. The slightest "lack of discipline" was severely punished. For example, in the fall of 1941, 1,000 Jews were ordered to report for "emigration to the East," but only 500 reported. The deputy of Hans Günther, Eichmann's assistant, regarded this as an act of sabotage by the Jewish leadership. He arrested the chiefs of the Emigration Department and sent them to Mauthausen where they died two weeks later.[13] The remaining leaders then tried delaying tactics. What could they do, confronted by such an overpowering enemy? Their choice was to postpone, drag on, soften, wring concessions whenever possible, and protect whatever they could. Ultimately the fate of Czech Jews was no different from the general Jewish fate, but the results of the Prague Council's policy during the first two years of the German occupation seemed to justify their approach. There were no massive deportations to Lublin. The leaders also persuaded the Germans of the practical value of using Jewish forced labor squads within the borders of the Protectorate. Historical relics and museums were saved. These were considered worthwhile holding actions. Possibly they were more a reflection of the regime of the Czech General Alois Elias than Nazi response to a Jewish Council. Within two years, Jews had been eliminated from the economic and social life of the country and were being forced to emigrate, but Elias tried to mitigate the effect of the anti-Jewish measures.[14] After September 1941, however, a regime of terror began, with the appointment of Heydrich as Acting Protector of Bohemia-Moravia. Elias was arrested and later executed. Hundreds of Czechs were shot or put in concentration camps. New blows then fell on the Jews.

The Hácha Government adopted the Nuremberg Laws, and on September 17, all Jews were ordered to wear the Jewish star. Non-Jews were forbidden to have any contact with Jews, and severe penalties were imposed on non-Jews who helped Jews in any way. All synagogues were closed. Seizures for forced labor and expulsions became brutal. By early 1942, Heydrich had selected Theresienstadt as a transit camp for Czech, German, and Austrian Jews. Theresienstadt was disguised as a "model ghetto," and admission to it was sought and bought dearly by Jews. Once in Theresienstadt, however, the Jews of Czechoslovakia were in the Gestapo trap, beyond recall. The "model ghetto" was a way station to Auschwitz —a "funnel with only one hole," as it came to be called. In Prague, it was played up as a privileged place for Jews and thousands of Czech Jews hopefully went to Theresienstadt. Many bribed Gestapo agents for this "privilege."

There is some evidence that as Protector of Bohemia and Moravia Heydrich also planned a "final solution" for the Czechs. On October 2, 1941, he delivered a secret speech to Nazi provincial governors of the Protectorate in the Czech Foreign Office. The speech has been revealed by Czech authorities and exists in Heydrich's own writing. At the time Heydrich divulged the German master plan to divide Europe into Germans and rejects. Hitler regarded the Czech lands as belonging to the historic German Reich; he claimed that "dangerous dagger blows against the Reich" had come from Czechoslovakia. Himmler had already told the S.S. generals that thirty million Slavs would have to be killed, but Heydrich doubted that he would carry out this threat. The Czechs, however, could be managed, Heydrich believed. To salvage the German parts, a vast screening process was planned. "Whether this is done," he said, "by the X-ray unit of the S.S., by investigations in the schools, or by racially examining the youths while pretending to set up a labor service, the essence of the operation is that I must have a complete picture of the Czech people. For those of good race and well intentioned, the matter will be very simple—they will be Germanized. For the others—those of inferior racial origin with hostile intentions—these people I must get rid of."[15]

The Czechs were saved from Heydrich's destructive intentions, although they had endured his regime of terror for eight months. On May 29, 1942, he was fatally injured by a bomb thrown into his car by two Czechs who had been parachuted into the country by an R.A.F. plane. He died a few days later. The Germans exacted savage revenge not only upon Lidice but upon Jews in Poland. "Einsatz Reinhard," a massive spoliation and wave of massacres visited upon them in the summer of 1942, was a memorial of mass murder for the prime mass murderer in the Third Reich.

The Jewish communities in the Greater Reich and the Protectorate had fallen away in the years of Hitler's first military conquests, 1939–41. It was during this period that the Jews of western Europe were also entrapped.

12 The Attack on the West

WHILE THE NAZIS were clawing at the Poles and Jews in western Poland, in September 1939, the Russians were taking payment for giving Hitler the opportunity to attack Poland. At first both Hitler and Stalin considered setting up a rump Polish state on the order of Napoleon's Duchy of Warsaw to mollify world opinion. But this turned out to be a fleeting idea, and by the end of September, both sides had agreed to partition the state out of existence. The initiative for this proposal actually came from Stalin but the Germans did not need much urging. The final Soviet bill was high, although a tentative division of spoils had been outlined in the secret protocol of August 23, 1939. Hitler had to give Stalin Estonia, Latvia, Lithuania and eastern Poland, almost half the country. Germany also had to pull back to the Narew-Vistula-San line, although German troops had gone far beyond it. Early in September, the German Foreign Office, anticipating a Polish collapse in a few weeks, had exhorted the Russians to invade and occupy Poland up to this line, but Stalin did not move until the seventeenth. Clearly, the Kremlin wanted Germany to bear the blame for the destruction of Poland and then to appear on the scene at the last moment as the "protector" of the Ukrainians and White Russians of eastern Poland.[1] For the fourth time, Germany and Russia had combined to partition Poland.

The Army was frankly annoyed with Hitler for submitting to such harsh terms. Russia now blocked Germany more solidly than ever from Ukrainian wheat and Romanian oil, two of Hitler's long-term objectives. Why did Hitler pay such a high price to the Russians whose troops had scarcely fired a shot? He apparently wanted to be able to deal freely now with Britain and France and for this new front had to keep Germany's rear free. However, as he turned his attention to the West, he would not forget Stalin's hard bargain.

Chamberlain had solemnly declared on March 31, 1939, that Britain and France would go to war if Germany attacked Poland. The seizure of all of Czechoslovakia had peeled away his illusions. His eyes open at last, Chamberlain now realized that Germany's domination of Europe was not simply a question of small or weak nations bowing to force. The British Empire was threatened. Hitler paused briefly. Late in August, he postponed the planned invasion of Poland and tried to buy British nonintervention by making a grandiose effort to "guarantee" the British Empire. But the British will to resist stiffened. Nonetheless, Hitler was determined to have his way, regardless of the consequences and went to war. However, the subsequent declaration of war by England and France, over which the whole world trembled, stalled into a *Sitzkrieg*, a sit-down war.

In retrospect, the German generals at Nuremberg agreed that by failing to attack in the West during the Polish campaign, the western Allies had missed a golden opportunity. "If the French," said Halder, "had seen the logic of the situation and had used the engagement of the German forces in Poland, they would have been able to cross the Rhine without our being able to prevent it and would have threatened the Ruhr area, which was the most decisive factor of the German conduct of the war." Though possessing the strongest army in the world, France was suffering from a pervasive national defeatism that affected the High Command, the government and the people. The memory of the slaughter of World War I was still vivid, and the fear of German reprisal bombing was very great. Moreover, French generals were telling their government they could not mount an offensive for two years.

Hitler inaugurated a "peace offensive" in September and was joined by the Soviet Union, but before the end of the month, he called together the commanders in chief of the Wehrmacht and told them of his decision to attack the West as soon as possible. Once again the Army objected, sent analytical memoranda detailing their objections and then withered away in the face of Hitler's iron will and wrath. Another putsch against him was halfheartedly planned and scratched. Hitler's first date on his timetable for the West was November 12. He postponed this, however, after getting unfavorable reports on the weather and railway transport situation. This was the first of no fewer than fourteen postponements throughout the fall and winter of 1939–40.

While Hitler's plan for an attack on the West was ripening, a diversionary aggression was planned against Norway and Denmark. This time the aggression was planned not by Hitler, but by the Germany Navy and a Nazi Party hack, Vidkun Quisling. The German Navy had long had its eyes on the North. With no direct access to the ocean, Germany could be crippled by a British blockade of the North Sea. In October 1939, German Navy officers urged Hitler to secure naval bases in Norway. Hitler was preoccupied with the coming attack on the West, but several considerations forced the Navy report upon his attention. First, the icing of the waters from Sweden to Germany prevented vital Swedish iron ore from coming to Germany through these shipping lanes. During the cold months, the ore had to be shipped by rail to the Norwegian port of Narvik and down the Norwegian coast by ship to Germany. Thus, a neutralized Norway would have great advantages for Germany. Second, Russia's attack on Finland in November 1939 made all of Scandinavia strategically important both to Germany and the Allies. If the Allied troops had transit across the top of Norway and Sweden, they could cut off Germany's supply of Swedish iron ore. By early March, the courageous but outnumbered Finnish Army was facing disaster. There were reports that an Anglo-French expeditionary force was about to embark from bases in Scotland and march across Norway and Sweden to Finland to try to save the Finns. A sudden armistice in that war embarrassed Hitler, but not for long. *Weseruebung*, Weser Exercise, was set for April 9.

Fantastic trickery was devised to hoodwink the Norwegians. All German warships and transports were to be camouflaged as British craft. All challenges in Morse were to be answered in English; British war flags were to be flown. Before dawn, on April 9, the Danish and Norwegian governments were presented with a German ultimatum demanding that they immediately accept the "protection of the Reich" against an Anglo-French occupation. The Norwegians resisted but were overwhelmed by the German assault. Quisling proclaimed himself the head of a new government once Oslo was firmly in German hands. This treason rallied the stunned Norwegians to a redoubled but doomed resistance. By early May the whole southern half of the country was irretrievably lost, and by early June Norway had to capitulate. Denmark offered no resistance at all—at first.

The quick conquest of Norway and Denmark gave the Germans their winter iron ore route; it also protected the entrance to the Baltic and allowed the German Navy to break into the Atlantic. For Hitler, it was another stunning military victory; for Britain, a very discouraging defeat. Nazi Germany now seemed invincible.[2]

Hitler was now ready for the West. On May 10, 1940, Holland and Belgium were attacked. Since November of the previous year, the Belgians had been warned about the coming German onslaught by the Dutch military attaché in Berlin, Colonel G. J. Sas, but they were stubbornly insistent on neutrality—which the Germans had pledged to honor—and had kept the French and British at arm's length instead of combining with them for a common defense. Meanwhile, toward the end of March, Mussolini had met with Hitler, their first meeting since Munich, and Hitler had again stirred Mussolini's old fears of being left out of the division of the spoils. Fascinated by Hitler's glittering military triumphs and longing to reassert his own flagging militancy, Mussolini drew Italy into the war three months later.

The original German plan of attack on the West had fallen into the hands of the Belgians—and thereafter the French and British—and had to

NAZI-OCCUPIED EUROPE—1942

Occupied, annexed, or controlled by Germany

Controlled by Italy

be drastically changed. A bold substitute, conceived by General Erich von Manstein, provided the ingenious strategic conception Hitler seemed to be waiting for through many months of postponement. The Manstein plan was daring, unorthodox and full of risk as well as surprise. Within five days, this plan sealed the fate of the French and British armies.

A great Anglo-French army had rushed from the French-Belgian border toward the main Belgian defense line east of Brussels—a move that exactly suited Hitler's purpose. Manstein's plan, in turn, was to launch the main German assault in the center, through the Ardennes, to be aimed at Sedan and the Channel coast. Such a move would, and did, stun the Allies. The hilly, wooded terrain was considered impractical for tanks. But German tanks slashed through. An army of them, unprecedented for size, concentration, mobility and power, struck from the Ardennes Forest, three columns wide and a hundred miles long. They advanced so fast that Hitler was sure that a French counterattack was coming from the south. In a frenzy of anxiety, he ordered the advance to stop. His hesitancy made possible the miraculous retreat of Dunkirk—hardly the specter of a second Marne—but the subsequent German military victory could scarcely have been swifter. For the Dutch, it was a five-day war, and on the fifth day the die was cast for the Belgian, French and British forces. Seven mighty German armored units rolled toward the Channel. Handicapped by a demoralized leadership, the remaining French armies were routed. On June 14, the swastika was hoisted on the Eiffel Tower and within two days, a new French government under Marshal Henri Pétain asked Germany for an armistice.

By May 1940, just before the great offensive in the West, about half the Jews and 10 percent of the Poles had been expelled from the incorporated territory of Poland. After the offensive and the display of the fantastic new power of the Nazis, the problem of public opinion was submerged and late in May the vain and garrulous Frank could say: "From May 10, 1940, the German advance in the West had made such progress that there was no longer any necessity to respect the opinion of the world."

Between that date and June 25, 1940, 350,000 Jews of western Europe passed under German rule, and an additional 130,000 came indirectly under German orders in Vichy territory. These Jews were to prove more difficult to handle than those of Eastern Europe who were pogrom-haunted and ghetto-minded even before the Nazis added new dimensions to their customary suffering. Western Jews were not enumerated in separate civil registers and could not be readily encircled; even physical identification was difficult for the Germans. Moreover, native anti-Semitic organizations were not readily at hand to aid the invader. But extermination was planned for them as for eastern Jews. The difference lay in tempo and approach.

To smokescreen the ultimate Nazi solution for western Jews, a so-called Madagascar Plan was promoted. In November 1938, Göring had mentioned Hitler's interest in the French colony of Madagascar as a place to which Jews could be sent. Himmler told his personal physician Dr. Felix Kersten that he had suggested the island off the coast of Africa as a place for Jewish settlement as far back as 1934. Poland had also considered using Madagascar as a place for getting rid of "surplus" Jews, and a government commission was sent to the island in 1937 to investigate possibilities. The local population and the influential press voiced strong opposition to the whole idea, but the Polish Government, Foreign Minister Józef Beck especially, persisted, and the French Colonial Office is known to have made studies of settlement possibilities.[3] The Nazis later made use of some of this material.

Madagascar also became the subject of international discussion after 1938. In Schacht's negotiations with the Intergovernmental Committee for Refugees calling for an international loan to finance Jewish emigration and bolster German exports, Madagascar was discussed. According to some sources, Hitler took up the matter personally with the French Ambassador in Berlin, André François-Poncet. Oswald Pirow, South African Defense Minister, played an active role in some of these negotiations. An admirer of Hitler and a self-confessed "outspoken anti-Semite," Pirow discussed the matter with Chamberlain and Hitler and intended to carry on further discussions with France, but the outbreak of a general strike there and a cabinet crisis forced him to cancel his visit. The Italian government also supported the Madagascar Plan. Italy was preparing to displace Great Britain in the Middle East and was interested in winning the friendship of the Arabs and hampering the development of Jewish Palestine. At a press conference on February 7, 1939, Alfred Rosenberg discussed the possibility of settling fifteen million Jews in Guiana or Madagascar.

The international discussion of Madagascar subsided after the announcement of Rosenberg's fantastic project not because, as Rosenberg claimed, Churchill and British Labor Party leaders attacked Hitler and made friendly negotiations impossible, but because by March 1939, after the liquidation of Czechoslovakia, Western leaders at last realized that no negotiations with Hitler were possible. There was only one side in any talks with him; every pledge or promise was thrown into the wastebasket of his mind. He understood only the language of force. But the Nazis persisted in using Madagascar in a new diplomatic game.

At first, in December 1939, they submitted peace proposals to Pope Pius XII, which included, among other items, a plan for the emigration of all German Jews to Palestine, Ethiopia and Madagascar.[4] The subsequent Nazi military victory over western Europe gave the Nazis complete power over the Jews within their control; by June 1940, this was most of Europe. Hitler could now run the whole gamut of possibilities: forced emigration, Madagascar, or annihilation. He had the freedom of choice that he craved, and toyed with one, then the other. Between the conquest of Europe and the invasion of Russia, intoxicated with his own invincibility, he played with these alternatives, throwing out one, then another flash-thought. In this diabolical freewheeling, he evidently fooled some of his own associates.

On May 14, 1940, after the myth of the "Lublin Reservation" was officially discarded, Himmler prepared a detailed memorandum entitled "Some Thoughts on the Treatment of Non-Germans in the East," in which he devoted one sentence to the Jews: "I hope that, thanks to the possibility of a large emigration of all Jews to Africa or some other colony, I shall live to see the day when the concept of Jew will have completely disappeared from Europe."[5] Himmler wrote this report in his capacity as RKFDV Commissar. Hitler wrote "very good and correct" over the memorandum and distributed copies among his Reichsleiters in eastern Europe, including Frank.

Seeing this apparent decision, Frank was overjoyed. He would finally be rid of his unbearable burden in the Government-General. On July 12, 1940, he discussed the whole plan at a meeting of his department and district chiefs in Krakow. He said:

> The Führer's decision, which came at my suggestion, is of the utmost importance. No more transports of Jews to the Government-General are to take place. It is now planned to transfer the whole Jewish tribe from the Reich, the Government-General, and the Protectorate within the shortest possible time after the conclusion of peace to some African or American colony. There is talk about the island of Madagascar, which France will have to yield for this purpose.

For a time, even the highest authorities in Germany seem to have taken the Madagascar plan quite seriously. On June 18, 1940, when Hitler and Mussolini talked about the disposition of French colonies, Hitler tried a trial balloon: "A Jewish state could be created in Madagascar," he said slyly. Italian Foreign Minister Galeazzo Ciano, in his diary entries for June 18 and 19, reported that the German Madagascar project was communicated to him by Ribbentrop. He, in turn, charged the chief of the Jewish Division in the Foreign Office, Dr. Franz Rademacher, an ambitious young jurist, with the preparation of a detailed plan from the point of view of international law.

Under the plan outlined by Rademacher,[6] France was to cede Madagascar to Germany for the purpose of solving the Jewish question. Presumably, Pétain would be accommodating. The 25,000 Frenchmen living on the island would have to leave so that the Jews would be cut off from any contact with white Europeans. Those parts of the island not occupied by German naval and air bases or by the native population would be set aside for Jewish "colonization." Farmers would leave first, but all Jews would be forced to go; there was no question of making a voluntary decision. The Jews in Madagascar were to serve as hostages in German hands for the "good behavior" of American Jews toward Germany. They would enjoy local "autonomy," according to Rademacher, and would have their own mayors, postal service, railways and so on, but the island would be administered by a German police governor who would take his orders from the central German police authorities. The project would be financed by residual Jewish funds in Europe.

Rademacher's plan was endorsed by Ribbentrop and was reportedly received by Heydrich with enthusiasm. Responsibility for details of the operation was turned over to Eichmann, who apparently was completely engrossed by his assignment for the next year. He surrounded himself with maritime experts and prepared plans for a special fleet of ships of the North German Lloyd and the Hamburg-American lines to carry the emigrants. Four million Jews were to be transported; all were required to pay for their transportation. Agents of Eichmann were sent to occupied or controlled parts of Europe to gather detailed statistics on Jews. The transports, however, were not to begin until the end of the war. This, indeed, was a big contingency.

Rademacher's office, "Deutschland III" was in constant touch with Eichmann in the Kurfürstenstrasse. Meanwhile, Eichmann's assistant, Theodor Dannecker, the future organizer of transports to Auschwitz, was busily engaged in research on Madagascar at the French Ministry for Colonies. Rademacher had merely used material from a popular German encyclopedia. A huge propaganda campaign was launched in March 1941 at the Institute of Studies on Jewish Questions at Frankfurt where Alfred Rosenberg and his assistants were broadcasting the news that Jews would soon be leaving the Continent. In the meanwhile, Hitler made sure the war would be prolonged.

In the summer of 1940, Stalin grabbed more territory and Hitler's insatiable war lust was once more aroused. On September 20, Hitler ordered his General Staff to prepare a plan of action for "Operation Barbarossa"— the code for the invasion of Russia. This meant prolongation of the war. Hitler had found his true streak; once more it would be war, but this time there would be no alternatives to the Jewish fate. The Jewish question was no longer susceptible to a territorial solution. Like other emigration schemes, Madagascar was finished business. But the myth of Madagascar, like the myth of Lublin, was purposefully kept alive to befuddle Jews and public opinion generally. Some of the Nazi bureaucrats, who at first shrank from the idea of extermination, may have used Madagascar as a sop to uncomfortable thoughts. It also is possible that some of them kept the Madagascar scheme alive hoping to stop Hitler from the extermination plan. Dr. Felix Kersten, Himmler's masseur, claims that Himmler told him that he, Himmler, was summoned to Hitler's field headquarters after the capitulation of France and informed that he would have to undertake the progressive extermination of European Jewry. Himmler alleged that he had personally urged the Madagascar project and had protested Hitler's decision, but in vain.

Hitler, however, continued to toy with the Madagascar idea at odd moments. As late as 1942 and 1943, he, Goebbels, Rosenberg and others discussed Madagascar. On May 29, 1942, several months after the Nazis officially decided upon extermination of Jews as the "final solution" at the Grossen-Wannsee Conference, Hitler declared that "Jews must not be exiled to Siberia, where the rigorous climate might toughen them and endow them with new vitality. They must be sent to Africa where climatic conditions have a debilitating effect on the human organism and lower its resistance." The original conception of Madagascar as a superghetto designed for slow death can also be discerned here. On July 24, 1942, Hitler talked with several close associates and remarked that if the Jews did not emigrate to Madagascar or some other Jewish national state after the war, he would round them up, "town by town."[7] This threat was made on the third day of the massive deportations from Warsaw to the death camp at Treblinka. Goebbels used the Madagascar plan for propaganda purposes as late as 1943. When the British occupied the island in May 1942, the Nazi and collaborationist press in France wrote that the perfidious British had been scheming since 1937 to hand over to the Jews this island "with its ideal climate" and "with all its numerous natives to slave for them" (85 percent of the natives suffered from malaria and the death rate from disease was high). The Madagascar project also was allowed to keep bubbling in order to give the Foreign Office an excuse to block Jewish emigration from Axis countries after October 1, 1941.

Not the least astonishing feature of this cynical scheme was the absorption of so many men in a project that was obviously not feasible. Eichmann's paper plans meant nothing so long as the British Navy controlled the Atlantic and the Mediterranean. Furthermore, Madagascar was French, and Pétain had no intention of permitting a large Jewish settlement there or of displacing 25,000 Frenchmen. It is significant that the French Governor General of Madagascar, Armand Annet, appointed by Vichy in December 1940, knew nothing about Nazi plans for Madagascar. Moreover, by March 1941, according to Viktor Brack of the Führer's Chancellery, it was no secret in higher party circles, that Jews were to be exterminated. At that time there was a revival of deportations into the Government-General and the enclosure of the large Polish ghettos. In France and the Low Countries, the much-postponed registration of Jews was begun, and Dutch Jewish hostages were rounded up and sent to German concentration camps.[8] These steps were taken on Himmler's orders and must certainly have been known by Eichmann.

At his trial, however, Eichmann persisted in blaming the failure of the Madagascar project on rivalries, quarrels and competition among the diverse bureaucracies. Everyone vied for supremacy, he said. Yet when confronted with Heydrich's letter of September 21, 1939, containing directives to the *Einsatzgruppen* and distinguishing between a top secret "final goal" and "stages for achieving the final aim," he admitted that "final aim" could mean only physical extermination, a basic idea "that was already rooted in the minds of the higher leaders, or the men at the very top."

The fiction died hard. It was not until February 10, 1942, that Rademacher sent the Foreign Office divisions a new ruling: "The war with the Soviet Union has in the meantime created the possibility of disposing of other territories for the Final Solution. In consequence, the Führer has decided that the Jews should be evacuated not to Madagascar but to the East. Madagascar need no longer therefore be considered in connection with the Final Solution." A new legend was thus hatched: "resettlement" in the "East." The war with Russia would provide vast new Lublins for both slow death and systematic extermination camouflaged as "deportation to the East." First, the Jews would have to be confined to ghettos.

13 The Nazi Ghetto: Warsaw

ON SEPTEMBER 19, 1939, Heydrich had met with General Wagner of the Army High Command and agreed on a "cleanup, once and for all, of Jews, intelligentsia, clergy and nobility" in Poland. On the following day, word came from Halder, the Commander in Chief of the Army, that "the ghetto idea exists in broad outline; details are not yet ready." Within another twenty-four hours, Heydrich sent his detailed plan for concentrating Jews to his mobile units throughout Poland, the *Einsatzgruppen*. Since the Army had insisted that the "cleanup" be postponed until jurisdiction was transferred from military to civil authority, there was a delay not only in the mass resettlement but in the ghettoization process. Finally, on November 15, 1939, the entire railway network of the Government-General with its 40,000 railway employees was placed at the disposal of the mass resettlement forces. By December 1, the packed trains began to roll into the Government-General. They would come at the rate of 10,000 a day, Frank had nonchalantly predicted, but this pace was too fast. Nevertheless, within the first two months of the resettlement, 200,000 Poles and Jews had been shoved into the Government-General, including 6,000 from the Greater Reich and Protectorate. Frank, meanwhile, started an evacuation program of his own in his capital, Krakow, which was *inside* the Government-General. It was intolerable, he said, to permit the representatives of the Greater German Reich to be established in a city that was "crawling" with Jews to such a degree that no "decent person" could step out into the street. The Krakow expulsions (completed in November 1940), he warned, were meant as a signal: the Jews of all Europe would have to disappear.

The campaign of terror and destruction of Jews and their property in the early months of the Polish invasion was carried on largely by the Armed S.S. (*Waffen-SS*), the Party military formations which fought as integral units of the armed forces. By the beginning of December, their activity was quelled and Heydrich's "professionals" in the S.S. began to take the center of the power stage in Poland. As the expulsions were regarded merely as temporary measures toward a "final solution," so ghettoization was intended as a makeshift process preparatory to the unnamed final solution. During the first six months of the German occupation, there was much confusion, little planning and fierce in-fighting. The first ghettos appeared, moreover, not in the Government-General, but in the incorporated territories in the winter of 1939–40. The first one was established in Tuliszkow in Wartheland, in western Poland. Once the process started, however, it moved with inexorable finality.

The marking of Jews with the Jewish star, restrictions on their movement, confiscation of their property, conscription into forced labor, and the establishment of Jewish Councils were completed within the first few months of civil rule. The formation of closed ghettos took somewhat longer. In the region of Lodz, the first large ghetto to be enclosed, the provincial governor decided on December 10, 1939, that "since the immediate evacuation of 320,000 Jews is impossible [Lodz was in incorporated Poland] they will be concentrated in an exactly delimited section." The preparations were secret, and the population shift sudden, to ensure easy confiscation of property. Freidrich Übelhör, the governor, did not look upon the ghetto as permanent. "The creation of the ghetto," he said in his December 10 order, "is, of course, only a transition measure. I shall determine at what time and with what means the ghetto—and thereby also the city of Lodz—will be cleansed of Jews. In the end, at any rate, we must burn out this bubonic plague."

Übelhör's staff selected a slum quarter in the city, the Baluty area, as the ghetto site. This district already contained 62,000 Jews; more than 100,000 Jews who lived in other parts of the city had to be rounded up and moved in. On February 8, 1940, the police president of Lodz issued his first order compelling Jews to move into the Baluty district. Every few days thereafter a schedule was posted affecting a part of the city. By February 29, all Poles and ethnic Germans had to leave. On May 10, the ghetto was closed off from the rest of the world. Germans and Poles were not to enter. Within the ghetto, from 7 P.M. to 7 A.M., Jews were not permitted to be on the streets. A unit of Order Police guarded the ghetto from the outside and for a short time a detachment of Criminal Police (*Kripo*) was attached to prevent smuggling. But this did not satisfy the *Kripo*. In their view, all Jews inside the ghetto had "more or less criminal tendencies"; a *Kripo* detachment, consequently, moved inside. The Gestapo, too, concerned itself with enemies of the state, and since Jews were prime enemies of the state, the Gestapo immediately established itself inside the ghetto. Within such an armed prison, the ghetto struggled to live.

By the end of 1941, the ghetto-formation process in the Government-General was completed. By then, Jews were entrapped in Poland.

The Warsaw Ghetto—the largest in European history—can be seen as a prototype of all the Jewish ghettos established by the Nazis in Poland.

Its life is amply documented, and its end, terrible as the others, has been memorialized by the Ghetto rising of April 1943.

A ghetto for Warsaw was proposed as early as November 4, 1939, but administrative conflicts beset the Germans and the ghetto was deferred. The conflict at the time was between Gestapo agents and the military authorities. The Gestapo at first ordered the *Judenrat* in Warsaw to carry out an ultimatum setting up a ghetto. When the Council demurred, the twenty-four members were detained as hostages, whipped and imprisoned. An appeal was made to General Neumann, the German Military Commander of Warsaw, and the difficulties of the ghetto plan were described. It was pointed out that the Jewish hospital and cemetery were excluded from the proposed ghetto, and that an already congested area, raging with typhoid, could not contain new arrivals. Neumann was astonished to hear that the ghetto order had been given and retracted it. Furious at this rebuff, the Gestapo threatened to execute the twenty-four Council members. Crowds of women besieged the community building clamoring for the release of the men. Leaders tried to calm them down, urging that no one go into a ghetto voluntarily. For five days the Jewish community waited in dread. It then tried a bribe. 300,000 zlotys (about $60,000) were raised and the Gestapo was temporarily bought off. On the sixth day the men were freed.

Ghettoization was delayed for the time being, but hung menacingly over Warsaw's Jews. In the meantime, the Jewish star had to be worn and placed on all Jewish shops, offices and apartments. A Jew could not leave the place of his registration or visit certain streets. He could be arrested without warrant and carried off for any sort of work.

Economic measures were swiftly imposed after the German occupation of Warsaw. Jewish property was registered and all assets exceeding 2,000 zlotys (a pound of bread was worth 40 zlotys) were confiscated; Jewish bank accounts were frozen and Jews were forbidden to earn more than 500 zlotys a month.

Doubtless, in November 1939, many wearers of the badge already longed for the things that were meant to go with it, the walled and sequestered ghetto and the autonomous rule of the Jewish elders.

In the summer of 1940, before the Ghetto was officially established, the Germans built walls, eight feet high, which separated the section where the Jews were concentrated from the rest of the city. This area included the old medieval ghetto and many of the important streets in the industrial section, some a mile and a half long. 80,000 Aryan Poles still lived in the Jewish quarter. This cutting out of the heart of Warsaw was at first disguised as a quarantine measure to prevent the spread of typhus which was already raging in the Jewish sector, but it had a more sinister purpose. The wall measured eleven miles and the cost of building it had to be paid by the *Judenrat* (Jewish Council). The Germans officially called the enclosed area the "district of Jewish residence," one of their more outrageous euphemisms. The word "ghetto" was to be avoided.

At this time, the summer of 1940, no Jew in Poland could have known what lay ahead. Many Nazi officials themselves believed that mass emigration of Jews was still official policy. Jews winced at ghettoization but saw it mainly as sharpened persecution. Many of them were at first relieved to have their ghettos. The shock and fear of the previous months and the dread of sudden new moves melted into the old atavistic need to be with one's own, sheltered from harm's way. At the beginning, there were no S.S. police or storm troops inside the Warsaw Ghetto. A police force of the *Judenrat* kept law and order. Jewish children could still be educated. Men and women could work outside the wall. The Ghetto, it was said, would make survival possible. The Nazis would let Jews there alone and they would survive as they had survived in the ghettos through the centuries. The Germans were to rely on this old reflex even after the death camps had been functioning for two years. They would empty a town by massacre and declare it cleansed. Fugitive Jews would still return. A remnant, they knew, had always remained.

In September 1940, the 80,000 Aryan Poles living within the "infected" area of Warsaw were ordered to move out. On October 3—Rosh Hashanah —the Nazis proclaimed the establishment of the Ghetto. By October 16, 1940, 140,000 still-dispersed Jews were ordered to move in with the 240,000 Jews already inside the Ghetto. This move concentrated almost 400,000 people within one hundred square city blocks. A third of Warsaw's population was crammed into 2.4 percent of the total area of the city. The new migrants carried all of their worldly goods into the Ghetto by hand or cart.

Tosha Bialer, who managed to escape from the Ghetto with her husband and son, has described the last days before the October 16 deadline:

Try to picture one-third of a large city's population moving through the streets in an endless stream, pushing, wheeling, dragging all their belongings from every part of the city to one small section, crowding one another more and more as they converged. No cars, no horses, no help of any sort was available to us by order of the occupying authorities. Pushcarts were about the only method of conveyance we had, and these were piled high with household goods, furnishing much amusement to the German onlookers who delighted in overturning the carts and seeing us scrambling for our effects. Many of the goods were confiscated arbitrarily without any explanation. . . . In the ghetto, as some of us had begun to call it half ironically and in jest, there was appalling chaos. Thousands of people were rushing around at the last minute trying to find a place to stay. Everything was already filled up but still they kept coming and somehow more room was found. The narrow, crooked streets of the most dilapidated section of Warsaw were crowded with pushcarts, their owners going from house to house asking the inevitable question: Have you room? The sidewalks were covered with their belongings. Children wandered, lost and crying, parents ran hither and yon seeking them, their cries drowned in the tremendous hubbub of half a million uprooted people.[1]

In setting up the Ghetto, the Germans intended to block access to the city proper and to isolate Warsaw's Jews from the Christian population. They continued the process, already well advanced, of removing Jews from Poland's economic and cultural life. All Jews in state, community and public enterprises were fired. Aryan firms were forbidden to employ Jewish workers and Jews were forbidden to use libraries, theaters, movies, railroads and streetcars. Jewish-owned factories and shops outside the Ghetto boundaries were confiscated by the Germans or looted.

Until November 15, 1940, it was still technically possible for Jews to work outside and permissible for Jews to leave the Ghetto. Then, suddenly, without warning, on November 15, the Ghetto was sealed up. All twenty-two entrances were closed and no Jews were permitted to leave. Police confiscated food carried into the Ghetto by Poles or transported in tramcars passing through the Ghetto. Mrs. Bialer describes this day:

> In the morning, as on every other, men and women go out on their way to work. . . . As they came to the various points where thoroughfares and streets crossed from the Jewish section into the non-Jewish districts, they ran against barbed wire strung across and guarded by German police who were stopping all traffic out of the Jewish section. Hastily they tried other streets, avenues, alleys, only to find in every case barbed wire or a solid brick wall well guarded. There was no way out any more. Quickly the news spread through the section. Other people came out of their houses and stared at the barricades, pathetically silent, stunned by the frightful suspicion that was creeping into their minds. Then, suddenly, the realization struck us. What had been, up till now, seemingly unrelated parts— a piece of wall here, a blocked-up house there, another piece of wall somewhere else—had overnight been joined to form an enclosure from which there was no escape. The barbed wire was the missing piece in the puzzle. Like cattle we had been herded into the corral, and the gate had been barred behind us.[1a]

Adding to the panic, sudden changes in street boundaries were ordered. On October 23, 1940, the famous Warsaw Ghetto archivist, Dr. Emmanuel Ringelblum, wrote: "Walicow and Ceglana Streets have been excluded from the Ghetto. . . . People are walking around crazy with anxiety because they don't know where to move to. Not a single street is sure of being assigned to the Ghetto but every street has something that puts it in jeopardy." The most fantistic enclaves were made. The market halls, the Law Courts in Leszno Street and many works under German direction were not included in the Ghetto although they had been in the heart of the old Jewish district. On the other hand, the Czyste Jewish Hospital was ordered to move into the Ghetto although it lacked suitable buildings for a hospital. In one of the buildings in Stawki Street, improvised for contagious diseases, there was no gas installation and the water was shut off because the pipes had frozen. In October 1941, the Ghetto lost its northeast sector, including the Tlomaczek Synagogue and in December the Jewish cemetery was walled off on grounds that coffins had been used for smuggling.[2]

The life and death of the Ghetto is described in the remarkable journal kept by Emmanuel Ringelblum and in the archives of the *Oneg Shabbat* (coded O.S. in the journal) or Sabbath celebrants, the name of a secret society created by Ringelblum to preserve for posterity the record of the destruction of Polish Jewry. There was no need for Ringelblum to be in Poland to take up this heavy task, for when the war began, he was safely in Geneva as a delegate to the World Zionist Congress. But he felt impelled to return to Poland and carry on his work in the Warsaw office of the Joint Distribution Committee. He fought in the Ghetto revolt, escaped to the Aryan section of Warsaw after the Ghetto was destroyed, but was eventually caught by the Germans and together with his wife and 12-year-old son was executed in March 1944. His diary and notes which he had carefully hidden were found in the ruins of the Warsaw Ghetto, one part in 1946, another in 1950. Ringelblum himself served as the prototype of Noach Levinson in John Hersey's *The Wall*. The journal is unique, filled with immediate impressions but keyed to history. It was composed by a trained historian who wanted above all to ascertain and record the facts of the destruction of Polish Jewry.

In September 1939, Ringelblum was thirty-nine years old. He had spent his youth in the little town of Nowy Sacsz, a historic center of Polish Chasidism, in the foothills of western Galicia where he was born. Educated at the University of Warsaw, he followed the classic pattern of the poor university student precariously earning his way. He was a young man with a strong social conscience and set up courses, meetings and lectures for workers in evening classes, work for which he received very little pay. He was also active in the General Academic Federation of Jewish Students, particularly in its self-help programs, and in the Labor Zionist Movement. He supplemented his earnings by tutoring and eventually completed work for his doctorate with a dissertation on the history of the Jews of Warsaw up to the expulsion of 1527. He taught history in a Warsaw gymnasium and again developed evening classes for adults in many towns throughout Poland. A strong drift toward communal work led him quite naturally to the JDC office in Warsaw.

Physically, Ringelblum was tall, almost a six-footer, slim and lively in temperament. He was a gregarious man, full of jokes and possessed of a wonderful sense of balance. Surviving pictures show him to be a man of very pleasant, relaxed features and inner equilibrium. He had an abiding—perhaps too naïve—faith in the masses. Much passion and anguish are compressed into his *Notes from the Warsaw Ghetto*, but such a work could have been written only by a man extraordinarily disciplined and mindful that history, too, is a kind of resistance against engulfing death, that it storms the future when the present can no longer be avenged.

Ringelblum's *Notes* are literally notes toward a history of the catastrophe, not a personal diary. At the outset (the author began his entries in November 1939), he does not know the end of the story but perceives the fatal design only gropingly as he moves along from day to day. The scope of the entries is very wide, encompassing all of life within the Ghetto and much of what was happening in the rest of Poland. Ringelblum's aim was to record the whole truth, however bitter, with as much objectivity as possible, and he steeled himself, as he similarly enjoined his colleagues in the O.S., to avoid preconceptions even about the abominable enemy.

In August 1939, a week before the German invasion of Poland, Ringelblum was a delegate to the Twenty-first World Zionist Congress in Geneva. Some of his colleagues in the Polish delegation decided to go to Palestine after the Congress; others flew to Paris or London. But Ringelblum decided to return to Warsaw. The journey was perilous. He and his friends traveled through Italy in sealed trains, then through Yugoslavia and Hungary under police protection, and finally across the Polish border. The trip to Warsaw was made in a blacked-out train under strafing by German planes. A day after his arrival in Warsaw, Ringelblum was at his desk in the JDC office.

After six days of war, Warsaw was encircled by German forces and a mass evacuation of the city began. The JDC office was badly damaged and Ringelblum, presaging a later role as archivist of the Ghetto, rescued important documents from the agency files. Thousands of Jewish refugees who had fled the captured provinces seeking the safety of the capital now found themselves trapped, hungry, with no resources. Ringelblum called an urgent meeting of community leaders. Public kitchens were set up and shelter and clothing were provided for the needy. After the fall of the city, the plight of the Jews became progressively worse.

In the midst of crucial relief activities, Ringelblum found himself in a key position. "I had daily lively contact with everything that was happening," he wrote. "News came to me of every event affecting Jews in Warsaw and its suburbs. Almost every day I saw delegations from the Polish provinces. . . . At night, when my work with the committee was done, I made notes of what I had heard during the day. In time these notes accumulated into a large volume of 100 closely written pages mirroring that period. Later, I worked the daily notes over, at first into weekly and then into monthly summaries. This I did when the Oneg Sabbath staff was quite large."[3]

Trained as a social historian as well as a teacher, he knew what the world should be told and what it had to know about the catastrophe. At first the O.S. notes were written in an atmosphere of hope and expectation of deliverance. Later, as the war dragged on, and it became starkly clear that only a miracle could save the Jews of Poland from physical extermination, the record-keeping became a pure historical act, a gesture against oblivion.

The material was accumulated methodically and professionally by a trained group carefully selected on the basis of representative occupations, social status and geographic distribution. The data they gathered had to be assembled, checked and interpreted. Community histories and monographs on health, currency and production were prepared. From the first, Ringelblum tried to persuade people to collaborate with him, but not until May 1940 did he find the nucleus of an archives staff. After the establishment of the Ghetto in November 1940, the O.S. work expanded. Ironically, the enclosure of Jews behind ghetto walls enabled them to settle down in their imprisonment and feel "safe." At first they believed that the Germans could not possibly be interested in what they did behind the walls. In this "free society of slaves" the O.S. staff increased. Dozens of new people joined and the material grew. But soon the work became conspiratorial. The O.S. could take no chances on Gestapo agents finding out about the archives.

Material was also gathered by temporary assistants—individuals who had been leaders of Jewish community life in many Polish cities and towns they had been forced to leave. These men toiled at writing the histories of the places they had left and described their experiences up to the time of their expulsion. Monographs were written on the entry of the German Army, atrocities, Jewish communal and economic life, religious life, relations with Poles, the Jewish Councils, the labor camps.

After November 15, when the Ghetto was sealed, more than 100,000 people had to find work or the means of subsistence within an economy that was no longer viable. The Germans permitted the Ghetto no contact with the outside world except through their agency, the *Transferstelle*. The products of Nazi-tolerated factories and workshops such as shoemakers, brushmakers, carpenters and hatmakers, plus the estimated output of the labor battalions were exchanged for whatever rations the authorities made available. Food allocations were made in bulk for weekly or monthly periods. Inside the Ghetto, the *Judenrat* which had officially purchased the rations, distributed them. The transfers took place at a large checkpoint, the *Umschlagplatz*, which later became the dread site of deportations. By decreasing and then choking off the food supply, the Germans were able to turn the ghettos into death traps. As the German food policy in Poland was to loot as much as possible and send it back to Germany, to keep Poles barely alive and the Jews suspended between life and death, life in the Ghetto soon became a primitive struggle to stay alive.

For a time, those workers who could find jobs in the textile factories and tanneries operated by the German manufacturer Walter Toebbens were assured a fixed income, extra food and exemption from forced labor. After the November 15 action, however, and the continuous swelling of the Ghetto population with refugees from Lodz and Krakow, there was an intensified struggle for factory jobs. The overcrowded population then began to jostle for jobs inside the Ghetto: in the bureaucracy of the Jewish Council, which operated twenty-three departments, in the tolerated workshops, as managers of apartment houses, as garbage collectors. Every sort of work was sought and until reports of the inhuman conditions in the labor camps came in, men were eager to join the labor battalions. While phone and mail contacts were still permitted, enterprising traders developed canned fish, horse meat, preserves and other products for export. Clandestine flour mills were set up in cellars and attics. Those who could not find work tried feverishly to sell jewels, utensils and clothing in order to be able to buy food. People were seen covered with feathers—this usually meant they had been reduced to selling their pillows and sheets. For a while, food packages were permitted but were soon forbidden under the pretext of "danger of contamination."

Ghettoization destroyed Jewish productivity. Not only Jews but the German Wehrmacht found this waste incomprehensible. A Wehrmacht report entitled "The War Economy in Poland, 1939–40" was bluntly critical of this waste:

> These different ordinances . . . have destroyed the economic bases of Jewish life. . . . The creation of a Jewish quarter right in the center of the city Warsaw ruthlessly split up important economic units. Prohibiting the crossing of this quarter caused losses in time and material. Two thousand Aryan businesses were moved out and 4,000 Jewish concerns were moved in. . . . Despite such complications and difficulties . . . the policy of the total expulsion of the Jews from economic life has been continued. . . . This, despite the fact that the civil administration could not deny that the Jew was practically irreplaceable in certain areas of economic life."[4]

The Army protested, but in vain.

The German control-mechanism for the ghetto, the *Judenrat*, was created in Warsaw, as in all of the other Polish ghettos. Its function was defined in the following decree: "The Judenrat is obliged, through its president or his deputy, to accept the commands of the German authorities. It is responsible for the conscientious carrying out of those commands. The orders which it issues for the carrying out of those German commands must be obeyed by all Jews."[5] Adam Czerniakow was named chairman.

The last Jewish Council before the outbreak of the war had been appointed by the Polish Government. The head, Maurycy Majzel, and some members had fled Warsaw immediately after the war started and the Council ceased functioning. A Jewish Citizens Committee was then formed, composed of representative Jewish groups in Poland. Czerniakow, who was considered an outsider in Jewish affairs, and several others, who had been members of the prewar Council, were asked to join. Czerniakow had been an official of the Polish Government; for a time he considered himself an assimilationist. He served for a while as chairman of the Craftsmen's Association and then became interested in various projects in Poland sponsored by the JDC. In the last days of the Warsaw defense, the mayor appointed him chairman of the Jewish Citizens Committee. During this period, the committee tried to provide help to the wounded and displaced Jews who had lost their apartments during the shelling or had been expelled from other towns to Warsaw by the Germans.

The Germans burst into meeting halls of the old Council on October 14 and demanded the keys to the locked doors and the safe. They took 90,000 zlotys from the safe and ordered Czerniakow to establish a Council of Elders (*Rada Starszych*) composed of twenty-four members and twenty-four alternates. The Jewish Citizens Committee began to prepare a list which was due on the following day at noon, but many members present refused to participate. Some used adopted names to mask past anti-Hitler activity. The list was at last completed and given to Sturmführer Batz. He gave each person named a letter of appointment and said that each was to carry out his, Batz', orders. The following day, Czerniakow showed several members a small bottle that he had placed in the drawer of his office table. It contained twenty-four cyanide tablets, one for each member should the need arise.[6]

Shmuel Zygelboim, a member of the Council, and later a member of the Polish National Council in London, recorded the first meeting of the Nazi-approved Council:

> The first meeting of the Judenrat took place in the middle of October. A Gestapo officer by the name of Mende came to the meeting and delivered a speech as if he were speaking to criminals. He ordered the Judenrat to stand while listening. He said that the fate of the Jews and of the Judenrat was in the hands of the Gestapo. The Judenrat is not to approach any other Nazi officer. No discussions. "The *Führer* law reigns here." What the Gestapo orders has to be executed promptly and meticulously, "not in the Jewish manner. . . ."

Three weeks after the appointment of the Judenrat in Warsaw, its members were suddenly called to an urgent meeting. It was on a Sabbath. At 12 o'clock Gestapo men came to the chairman and ordered him to call a meeting for 4 o'clock the same day. Out of the 24 members of the Judenrat only 16 could be located. With heavy hearts and grave thoughts we waited in the conference room of the Jewish community building. It was not the first time that the Gestapo had suddenly summoned us. Each time we had been faced with some new persecution order or with some obnoxious assignment which we refused to carry out. . . . At quarter past four the doors were abruptly forced open. Gestapo men entered, rifles, pistols, and whips in their hands. They took up places in half-circle around us and looked at us with angry, evil eyes without saying a word. They appeared so unexpectedly, with such force and in such a terrifying manner that all sixteen people seated around the table jumped up. For a long time there was an agonizing, stifling stillness in the room. The Gestapo men, standing around, saying nothing, looked at each one of us, some artfully smiling, until one of them barked out in barracks-like tone: "All present?"

The chairman handed him the attendance list and the Gestapo man called out each member. . . . The roll call finished, the Gestapo men, taking along the chairman, went into the latter's office. After fifteen minutes, a Gestapo officer came out and said: "You listen and be careful! The Judenrat consists of 24 members and 24 alternates. Only 16 are present. I give you half an hour to fetch the others. Forty-eight Jews must be present. No discussion. . . ." After some deliberation it was decided that in order to produce the full contingent of the membership, we will enlist Jews from outside the Judenrat wherever we may find them. We called in all clerks of the Judenrat who were present in the building at the time, and a few Jews who happened to pass by the building and a few Jews from the Jewish funeral parlors which were located close by. A list of all those present, of whom more than half were included by sheer accident, was then submitted to the Gestapo officer. He then ordered that all assemble in the meeting hall and form two lines—one of the members of the Judenrat and the other of alternates.

Thus we stood for a long time, waiting until the door was thrust open once again and about 50 Gestapo men under the command of an officer entered the hall. All carried pistols or whips. . . . Finally, in a threatening, harsh voice the officer uttered: "Jews, you listen to me, and listen carefully! The commandant has ordered that all Jews of Warsaw must leave their present homes and move to the streets that have been designated for the ghetto, not later than Tuesday. To assure that the order is strictly carried out, all 24 alternates will be taken hostages. With their heads they are responsible for the exact execution of the order. You, the members of the Judenrat, are also responsible with your heads. We are not taking you away now simply because somebody must remain here to take care of the execution of the order." The 24 Jews, present only by accident, were then surrounded by the Gestapo men. Orders were shouted:

"About face, forward march" and they marched out. Outside, in the street, trucks were waiting and the Jews were carried away.[7]

The *Judenrat* tried to alleviate hunger and disease, to provide shelter and work, and to organize a chaotic society. But it worked against impossible odds. All of the projects undertaken in good faith by the *Judenrat* were perverted by the Nazis into mechanisms of gross suffering and eventual destruction.

The evolution of the *Judenrat* "control" over manpower in the Warsaw Ghetto shows the German perversion of its intention. On October 26, 1939, the Government-General had decreed that Jews were liable to labor in "forced labor troops." In an effort to mitigate the terror aroused by the press gangs that seized people at random in the streets, the *Judenrat* offered to provide labor battalions at specified times and in specified numbers for the use of the German authorities. The Germans agreed. Although some agencies continued their seizure of Jews in the streets, many offices now made their labor quotas known to the *Judenrat*. These labor columns became a cheap source of manpower but soon the burden of paying the men fell on the *Judenrat* itself. Faced with this new problem, the *Judenrat* in Warsaw sent notices to report to work to all Jews on a rotation basis. Rich and influential Jews could generally buy their way out. The *Judenrat* then used some of this money to pay forced laborers and their families.[8] At first, this type of labor was useful only for day-to-day emergency work. Later, labor camps developed. The effort to reduce the shock of arbitrary seizure by supplying workers became a snare, however. Men at first lured by the hope of food rations for themselves and their families were soon faced by starvation. When reports of the dreadful conditions in the camps leaked back to the Ghetto, and corpses were brought back showing evidences of torture, labor quotas could not be met. Those Jews who could, paid anything to avoid conscription. The failure to meet labor quotas then brought the usual train of retaliatory measures: the already meager food supply was suspended, Council members were threatened (in some Councils they were executed), penal camps were threatened in place of work camps, families of workers were held as hostages.

Again, the *Judenrat* tried to meet the new crisis. To encourage service in the labor battalions, Jewish "supervisors," "group leaders" and police were recruited. The situation was temporarily improved. Ringelblum reports such an instance: "In the work camp at Dobrowice, the camp guard was abolished and a Jewish Law and Order Service established instead. As a result, production rose 50%. The German firm consequently raised the rations. 25% of the campers returned."[9] But a new vicious circle of compliance followed by more drastic demands was thus started. Also, in this new development, Germans were saved the police manpower that would normally have to be diverted to guard camps and forced labor columns. Again, Jewish personnel was drawn for a well-meaning purpose and twisted into a destructive one. In the very economic and administrative collaboration, in which lay the Ghetto's main chance for survival, lay the seeds of its ultimate dissolution. "The history of man," wrote Ringelblum in May 1942, "knows no similar tragedy. A nation that hates the Germans with all its soul can ransom itself from death only at the price of its contribution to the enemy's victory, a victory which means its complete extermination in Europe and perhaps in the whole world."[10] A vehement critic of the *Judenrat*, Ringelblum was acutely aware of the impasse the Nazis had so cleverly created for it, as for all Jews who had to carry out decisions affecting other Jews.

The fear of German punitive measures was stark and the measures were severe. On April 26, 1941, the head of the Department of Internal Administration for the Warsaw district sent a letter to the Jewish Council threatening to suspend the food supply for the Ghetto and turn work camps into penal camps, and threatening a retaliatory S.S. raid if the Council did not meet its labor quota. On May 11, in Otwock, 100 Jewish Council officials were taken away to work camps because the Council did not meet its quota. In Rzeszow, the Council provided only 110 instead of 120 workers. The Germans seized all of the Jewish elders and shot them down in the middle of the marketplace.

Starvation and disease quickly took their toll in the Ghetto. From 300 to 400 died daily, not counting those who were killed by the Germans in their sporadic executions. Over 43,000 Jews starved to death during the first year of the Ghetto; 15,000 died of typhus in 1941, the principal victims being the refugees from the provinces, many of whom had subsisted for weeks on boiled potato skins and water. During the winter of 1941–42, sewage pipes froze. Toilets could no longer be used and human excrement was dumped with garbage into the streets. The *Judenrat* was technically responsible for maintaining sanitary and medical facilities, but medical supplies were virtually nonexistent. A single tube of antityphus serum cost several thousand zlotys. As no medicines could be bought on the open market, the *Judenrat* had to wrangle with the German authorities for every ounce of medicine or serum; the Jews in the Ghetto then had to buy or beg from the *Judenrat*. Disinfection brigades and quarantine stations were set up, and house blockades were instituted to check the spread of epidemics. Thus both the sick and healthy alike were imprisoned in their homes. Even fresh air, a free commodity of nature, had been denied the Ghetto; boundaries had been drawn to exclude all parks and playgrounds. Hunger drove some to madness, others to slow death. The bodies of the dead were hidden so that their precious ration cards could be used.

Within the Jewish community, some would live and some would die under famine conditions. Even the sternly moral Ringelblum, who frequently critized the Jewish Council, was forced to admit that there simply was not enough food to go round even had it been distributed with scrupulous equality:

> The well-established fact is that the people who are fed in the public kitchens are all dying out, subsisting as they do only on soup and dry rationed bread. So the question arises whether it might not be more rational to set aside the money that is available for the sole use of certain select individuals, those who are socially productive, the intellectual élite and the like. However, the situation is that, in the first place, the élite themselves constitute a considerable group and there wouldn't be enough to go around even for them; and, in the second place, why should laborers and artisans, perfectly deserving people who were productive in their home towns, and whom only the war and the Ghetto existence have deprived of their productive capacity—why should they be judged worthless, the dregs of society, candidates for mass graves? One is left with the tragic dilemma: What are we to do? Are we to dole out spoonfuls to everyone, the result being that no one will survive? Or are we to give full measure to a few, with only a handful having enough to survive?[11]

The Jewish Council did not distribute with evenhanded justice. It was criticized for not doing more to alleviate the suffering of the most wretched people in the Ghetto and for not taxing fairly those who could afford to pay. The Council imposed indirect taxes on necessities and applied direct taxes universally on food cards and medicines.

In December 1941, all mail and phone contacts were suddenly broken off. By a series of decrees, Jews were specifically barred from meat, poultry, fish, eggs, vegetables, white flour and fruit. Official food rations were reduced to 800 calories a day—half of those given the Poles—and meant no more than bread, potatoes and ersatz fat. Often the potatoes were rotten or frozen. The fight against omnipotent hunger raged. "Snatchers" increased—these were people who were forced to steal in order to survive. They jumped at people carrying packages and snatched them, hoping to find some food. "Catchers" were yet another group. They snatched packages and while still running, devoured the contents, sometimes stuffing themselves full of straw and soap.

Smuggling became an absolute necessity and smugglers of all ages, sizes, and kinds, including very small children, crawled through sewers and chinks in the walls. Jews even smuggled openly in carts when the guards could be bribed. Hunger-crazed children who were able to slip through to the Polish Aryan section were often given food; more often they were shot down by Nazi guards. Children reached the Aryan side of Warsaw by digging holes under walls or by hiding near the Ghetto gates and trying to sneak through when the guards turned the other way. Parents would sit at home all day nervously awaiting the return of their only breadwinner. So desperate was the need for food that not even the death penalty for smuggling (decreed in October 1941) could stop it, for strict obedience meant a lingering death by starvation.

The stronger and luckier Jews carried on an illicit trade with Aryan Warsaw. In the teeth of Nazi threats, they established branches of production which served the Polish population. They fought the diminishing food supply not with arms—which they lacked—but with their trading skills. This trade was carried on outside the office channels of the *Transferstelle*.

Officially the Ghetto produced goods for the German Army, but it also managed to produce for Polish consumption, working with raw materials already in the Ghetto or smuggled into it. The smuggled materials were obtained from the commissariats of Czestochowa, Lodz and other cities from German allotments. Lodz manufacturers who had been expelled to Warsaw manufactured woolen socks and cotton gloves. Old ledgers were compressed and converted into cardboard valises. The brush industry was also improvised not only out of bristles, but from goose feathers, old brushes, and scrap diligently collected in the Ghetto. Several thousand Jews worked in this industry. Ersatz materials were converted into mattresses. Lithographers bought up bed linens, dyed them, printed them colorfully and sold them as kerchiefs in Polish villages. Illegal tanneries processed hides. Children fashioned toys in private homes, attics, and cellars. Airplane fragments that were smuggled into the Ghetto provided the basis for the manufacture of pots and spoons and door hinges. Wooden-soled slippers were produced with cardboard uppers. Fats, oils, and soaps were made and the Ghetto had its saw mills and rubber factories.[12] After the Ghetto had been in existence a year, even the most outspoken pessimists who had predicted death for all by starvation had to admit that their prophecies had not come true. They had feared that all funds would flow to the Aryan side to cover the cost of survival. But the Ghetto continued to trade with the other side "illegally" through smugglers or Christian workers in the Ghetto.

Old clothes were an important source of income for Christian workers employed in various shops in the Ghetto—at Brauer's, Roerich's and Shultz's. These Polish workers returned to the Aryan side each night laden with purchases which drew good prices. Jews first sold goods that could be salvaged from the Nazi plunderings. Then followed personal possessions—linens, clothing, furniture, housefurnishings and family mementos. The sale of secondhand household goods to smugglers gave the Ghetto its chief income, staved off starvation and came to be its most powerful asset. Virtually to the last hour of the Ghetto's existence, thousands of Jews were still selling old clothes. After July 1942, these were the last and only trade item. Jews carried them in rucksacks and bags or on their backs and established contact with smugglers who stole daily into the Ghetto through holes in the walls or by bribing the Ghetto guards.

According to Ringelblum, Polish smugglers sometimes spread false rumors to depress the old-clothes market, once going so far as to say that the whole ghetto would be liquidated by a certain date. Frequently heard were comments such as: "They'll turn your skin into leather sooner or later anyway. Sell your coat and buy something to eat." Police agents and informers had to be paid off continually; they preyed on the Ghetto like vultures, but the illegal shops, some of which paid as much as 30,000 zlotys ($6,000) monthly, felt that it was worth exorbitant payoffs to continue producing.

In many cases, Jews entered into partnership arrangements with Christians, giving their enterprises over to them, meanwhile remaining silent partners. According to Ringelblum, most of these transactions proved unhappy: Jewish property was simply appropriated and Jewish owners often informed on. The Jews were considered to be dead men on reprieve. In the distorted morality of the time, the Polish smuggler often seemed the most humane Christian of all and created possibly the strongest kind of Jewish-Christian bond in Poland. The Polish underground urged all Poles to support smuggling as an economic necessity and the underground press declared that, without it, the Polish city population would perish.

The Germans officially waged a fierce battle against the smugglers, both Jewish and non-Jewish. They fenced in every possible entrance to the Ghetto, commanded the Jewish Council to make the walls higher and guarded them with six rings of patrols. But in spite of the patrols and cordons of police and the many executions of smugglers, smuggling never stopped. Economic necessity became an iron master. For the Pole, it was stronger than German punitive power and stronger than the prewar propaganda which had raised the anti-Jewish boycott to the level of a noble civic duty. For the Jew, it literally kept him alive.

According to the Warsaw *Judenrat* figures, the economic structure of the Jews in the Ghetto on June 30, 1941, shows the following profile:[13]

Proprietors of business enterprises	5,115
Proprietors of industrial enterprises	3,105
Independent artisans	8,185
Employed in business enterprises	1,276
Employed in workshops and factories	2,814
Employed in the Judenrat and communal institutions	3,788
Laborers in German installations	2,000
Total:	26,283

Possibly 10,000 more were still able to live off their capital, while another 2,000 to 3,000 lived by smuggling. Thus, about 40,000 Jews were economically self-sustaining. With their families they made up about 120,000 persons, approximately 28 percent of the Ghetto. The rest were dependent on community help or starved.

By June 1942, this picture changed greatly. The number of recorded wage earners was nearly 85,000. Some of these represented fictitious workers registered in the shops and communal institutions in order to avoid deportation through the possession of a worker's card. But what is especially significant is that virtually all Jewish factories and workshops were liquidated by this time. The economy was melting away.

Smuggling prolonged life in the Ghetto but could not save it. On quite a different level, a gallant effort to ease the famine was made at Grochow, on the outskirts of Warsaw, where about sixty Zionist youth were allowed to plow tiny farms and gardens. Some of this food was smuggled in. Kitchen gardens were planted on the sites of bombed houses in the Ghetto; vegetables were grown on balconies, vacant lots, and even roofs, wherever earth could be scratched. The House Committees supplied the campers with clothing, linen and shoes. But the puny results were a mere trickle in the Ghetto's food needs. Community soup kitchens were started by the Jewish Council and operated by the Jewish Self-Help, the amalgamated Jewish welfare societies. In the summer of 1941 these kitchens served 120,000 daily "meals" of soup (often made of hay and sawdust) and bread. Some 20 percent of the Ghetto were fed in this way, less than half the number needing help. A black market inevitably developed for those well off, but was seldom available to workshop workers whose average earnings were twenty to thirty zlotys a day, just enough for a few pounds of potatoes, but not enough for a pound of fat. The poor begged in the streets.

Hunger raged through the Ghetto, more acutely felt than physical pain or the two bitter winters the Ghetto lived through. In May 1940, Ringelblum heard an eight-year-old boy scream madly: "I want to steal, I want to rob, I want to eat. I want to be a German!" Three months later, he wrote: "At a funeral for the small children from the Wolska Street orphanage, the children from the home placed a wreath at the graves with the inscription: 'To the Children Who Have Died from Hunger—From the Children Who Are Hungry.'" There was a day and night obsession with food; women tore at each other for a crust of bread.

Smuggling helped to sustain life and keep wits alive, but it aggravated social problems and created glaring inequities. By October 1941, more than one third of the Ghetto was so poor that it could not afford to pay the two-zloty tax on ration cards imposed by the Judenrat. Almost 140,000 cards had to be exempted from this payment. Holders of these cards, however, not able to buy the meager rations on the coupons, sold the coupons and depended on food from the public kitchens. Another one third of the Ghetto depended partly on the public kitchens and partly on the social agencies.

Aside from certain devious purchases on the black market, smuggling, and food growing in the Ghetto, the only food supply officially permitted was that purchased by the *Judenrat*. The food came in at the very place where manufactured products went out, at the checkpoint or *Umschlagplatz*. In 1941, no food besides bread was officially supplied. The total ration per person in that year averaged 2,500 grams per month, or a little more than 3 ounces per day.

To avoid starvation, a family of four had to spend about 1,120 zlotys a month on the black market in addition to paying for food on ration coupons, a total of 1,150 to 1,200 zlotys per month. Even for the gainfully employed in the Ghetto—a small group—the problem was almost insurmountable, for food prices on the black market were forty times the prewar level, while wages had merely doubled. In 1941 the average wage in the leading branches of production in the Ghetto, such as carpentry and brushmaking, ranged between 2.5 and 3 zlotys per hour. A skilled carpenter or brushmaker, working ten to eleven hours per day would make from 750 to 1,000 zlotys a month. Thus even a "good" income could not cover food plus other household expenses.

Moreover, only a very thin layer of the population was gainfully employed. The earning opportunities in the Ghetto were poor and became worse with each passing week. The bulk of the Ghetto population had to resort to community soup kitchens and search for ever more items to sell. In the fall of 1941, the sale of clothing and furniture averaged 20 million zlotys per month.[14] But the reserve of old things to sell was bound to dry up.

In their campaign of annihilation against the Jews of Poland, the Nazis used not only the technique of death by starvation, but also deliberately created conditions in the ghettos which made the outbreak of epidemics inevitable. Once an epidemic broke out, the authorities proceeded to "combat" it in a way that was sure to aggravate it and spread it still farther. The epidemics were blamed on the Jews and the Polish population was frightened away from the ghettos by the fear of Jews as germ-carriers. Moreover, the Nazis justified the subsequent mass murder of Polish Jews on the ground of safeguarding the health and lives of the general population. On July 11, 1943, Governor-General Frank, in a statement to a delegation of German physicians in Krakow, said that the extermination of three million Polish Jews was unavoidable for reasons of public health.

The efforts of Jews to check the epidemics were always blocked. Antityphus serum had to be smuggled into the ghettos clandestinely. In Warsaw, the Czyste Jewish Hospital was forced by Nazi officials to use uliron for the treatment of spotted typhus. This drug had a toxic effect on the patient, causing the body to become blue and cold. Many deaths resulted. Photographs were taken of every patient after the treatment and the hospital personnel were threatened if the recommended "cure" was not applied.[15]

A large part of the hospital equipment was lost or stolen when the hospital was moved to the Ghetto. More hospital patients starved and died of hunger than from disease. The *Judenrat* gave food priority to the working section of the Ghetto and relegated the sick to third place. As for the German authorities, far from allowing supplementary food for the hospitals, they sometimes confiscated the food sent out by the central depot. The hospital director said the hospital was "not even a poorhouse. . . . The food supply . . . is simply a fiction. The daily rations of about 700 calories cannot sustain the organism." Patients dreaded to go to the hospital—they often had to lie two in one bed, on wet mattresses, without sheets, in wards infested with lice.

The situation at the Baumann and Berson Children's Hospital was no better. A diary entry by a nurse dated March 20, 1941, records the hopelessness of the staff:

> I am on duty from 3 to 11. I come to my ward. It is a real hell. Children sick with the measles, two or three in one bed. . . . Shaven heads covered with sores swarming with lice. . . . I have no beds, no linens, no covers, no bedclothes. I telephone the superintendent. . . . The answer is terse: where there are two children in one bed, put a third one in and that is the end of it. . . . There is no coal. The rooms are terribly cold. They huddle under the covers, shaking with fever. . . . In the corridor lies a child of five swollen with hunger. . . . The child moves its lips begging for a piece of bread. I try to feed him . . . but his throat is locked and nothing goes down. Too late. After a few minutes he utters for the last time the words, 'a piece of bread' and falls asleep with the plea for bread on his lips.[16]

In an entry in his diary dated September 9, 1941, Frank admitted the real causes behind the outbreaks of spotted typhus: "The danger of spotted typhus has increased because of the lowered resistance of the population, especially of the youth. The nourishment of the ghetto inhabitants is insufficient. On top of that came the shortage of soap and the over crowding. The number of reported cases of spotted typhus today amounts to 2,405. The actual number must be much greater. . . . The confinement of the Jews to the ghetto is in itself a boon. It is now important to entirely isolate the ghetto."

The Nazis blockaded not only the house in which spotted typhus occurred, but the two adjacent houses. This was a severe blow to the blocked-off dwellings because it kept wage earners from working and their families from eating. The *Judenrat* pleaded for the abolition of these regulations but the Germans were deaf to all arguments. The Jews sought redress through bribes. The German commissar in charge of this department, Edward Koblinski, made a large fortune out of the Ghetto epidemics. Jewish policemen had to enforce the blockade and some are known to have been deported for allowing persons to leave blockaded houses.

The Nazis found new torments for Warsaw's diminishing inferno. Drastic and brutal population changes were made in a few hours or a few days, upheaving the momentary accommodation to an earlier upheaval. Not only were the street boundaries changed to squeeze the Ghetto ever tighter, but new groups were pushed in, increasing the density and making living conditions unbearable. The mortality rate was very high, but the overcrowding was not reduced. At the end of 1940, there were 78,625 refugees from 73 localities registered in Warsaw. By April 1941, this figure had risen to 150,000.

In September 1941, over 50,000 Jews had been put out of their dwellings and were assigned to Ghetto quarters which could accommodate only 17,000. Jews in mixed marriages with their Polish spouses and *Mischlinge* of all degrees were forced into the Ghetto. Six thousand converts were also pushed into the shrinking area. For a while they fared better than the Jews: they were cared for by Caritas, an influential Catholic welfare organization. They were also given favored positions in the Jewish police—but these proved to be only temporary privileges because when the exterminations began, they shared the doom of the rest of the Ghetto population.

The Polish police also brought to the Ghetto thousands of people who had been driven out from provincial towns. First they were taken to the parowka (steaming), the steam baths, where they were brutalized and robbed of everything. Afterward, they were driven to the Ghetto through the gate on Gesia Street. The parowkas actually became breeding nests of epidemics; clean and lice-ridden people were thrown together.

Warsaw was flooded with refugee Jews after the western part of Poland was incorporated into Germany. Not allotted housing, homeless and exhausted, they loitered in the streets and camped in courtyards and deserted factories. In cold weather they lived in ruined buildings, unheated depots, and synagogues. Made destitute overnight, they became totally dependent on charity, and older residents, already stunned by their experiences, resented them.

The Germans spared no effort to undermine Jewish fellow feeling in the Ghetto and exacerbate friction between social classes. Sudden inundations of provincial Jews and irrational changes in Ghetto boundaries were only the more obvious measures. Rumors were deliberately circulated leading strong workers to believe they were immune to the worst, while the very young, old, and ailing were made to believe they were unworthy to live in the universe of insane values devised by the Nazis. The Germans also contrived other provocations. A group of German Jews from Hanover and Berlin were deported to the Ghetto where they lived in special quarantined quarters, receiving somewhat larger rations than the Polish Jews. This was cause enough for resentment, but they further rubbed the Polish Jews the wrong way by insisting that they would ultimately return to Germany. Thousands of Jewish prisoners of war also poured into Warsaw. For them, almost as great as the problem of hunger, was the problem of clothing. They were forbidden to wear military clothing but had no civilian clothes. The Nazi-despised Gypsies also were driven into Warsaw, adding to the overcrowding, the hunger and group conflict.

These were not quixotic improvisations, but one aspect of a premeditated Nazi plan to create anarchy. The Jews were never permitted to achieve any equilibrium. Hitler's system of psychological warfare was based on the foundations of unlimited terror, utter confusion and indecisiveness of the victim. In the Ghetto, the Nazis created grave social problems and baffling inconsistencies which paralyzed the will and reason. No rational pattern was ever in evidence; this would have exposed the Nazi plan. Once the Nazis had decided on the physical destruction of every Jew, they realized the danger of Jews perceiving this. An immediate understanding of their hopeless position would have aroused large-scale resistance and the sheer weight of their numbers acting in unison would have complicated Nazi plans. Jews had to be isolated from the outside world, cut off from other ghettos, and then subdivided among themselves within the ghettos and thrust into conflict with each other to make Nazi preparations easy.

There was no end to Nazi cunning. When the Russian armies retreated from Poland, Nazis feared that the Jewish population of Russian-occupied Poland might seek to flee in the wake of the Red Army. Some Jews went voluntarily to Warsaw and other Nazi-occupied cities. They had heard that an "autonomous" Jewish community had been established in Warsaw where Jews could live safely. Such rumors had been carefully circulated. Germans also showed motion pictures of life in the alleged work camps. Old people were shown reclining comfortably in armchairs; young people were cheerfully working in factories and fields. The gullible would respond. Rumors were also spread that conditions were better in one ghetto than another. The Jews in Warsaw were said to be safer than those shut up in Lodz or Bialystock, and some Jews bribed their way into the Warsaw Ghetto. The Nazis would then plant new rumors.

Baffling Nazi concessions alternated with senseless brutality and further jolted the population. On February 18, 1941, the Nazis unaccountably allowed the Jewish Council to raise a loan from German banks on the security of certain blocked Jewish deposits. Three synagogues including the main synagogue on Tlomaczek Street were opened. In April, schools were licensed for 5,000 of the 50,000 Ghetto children. Several relief agencies, including the Joint Distribution Committee, were allowed to open offices. Suddenly, these concessions were wiped out. No one could explain why.

This perpetual upheaval also undermined morale and unity in the Ghetto. The struggle for shelter and bread left little energy for anything else, and yet some Jews managed to find miraculous reserves. The Germans expected the ghettos to disintegrate into dens of depraved criminals. There was, of course, moral corruption, swilling by robber barons and German lackeys and the eruption of savage self-interest. The Jewish police, as a whole, acted against the masses and were hated. But as in the concentration camps, there were also expressions of utter selflessness. Under unimaginable pressures, human values did not dissolve completely. Outside the control of the Jewish Council and beyond the tainted reach of the Gestapo were the House Committees organized in each building soon after the creation of the Ghetto. Each committee was composed of from five to twelve members, elected by the inhabitants of the house. A great diversity of men and women were drawn into the work of the committees, preventing evictions and aiding the poorest tenants to secure food and clothing. The House Committees also supplied work camps with clothing, shoes, and medicine when it could be procured. They set up shelters, feeding stations, clandestine kindergartens for children. When the Jewish hospital had to be evacuated and small hospital units had to be established in houses of the Ghetto, members of the committees, themselves often hungry and cold, risked contagion to serve infected houses. To a great extent, these committees helped to remedy the social injustices of the Ghetto.

An extraordinary and intense intellectual life, much of it clandestine because of German restrictions, was carried on. School classes were held for children. Several theaters performed until the end. There were classes, even laboratory work, for medical students; all Jewish holidays were celebrated. The great Yiddish and Hebrew writers were studied in reading circles. A secret organization called the Jewish Cultural Organization (*Yikor*) organized lectures and arranged literary and dramatic programs. A children's library functioned. A diverse underground press hectographed essays and militant proclamations. There were serious articles and discussions of sober themes: vengeance morality, the roots of Jewish optimism, the importance of raising the cultural level of Ghetto life, the war, events in Palestine. There were debates on the use of Polish versus Yiddish ("Do Jews continue to use Polish as a psychological protest against the ghetto, or is it a symptom of linguistic assimilation?"), and poems by little children on the essential goodness of man. There was a rage to study English, for many Jews hoped they would live to see a brighter day. In June 1942, a month before the Ghetto destruction was begun, Ringelblum wrote a long entry on the kinds of books people were reading. "We did not lose our human characteristics," he wrote; "our minds are as busy as they were before the war." Unable to avenge themselves upon the enemy directly, Jews avenged themselves imaginatively, in literature. The great novels of World War I and Lloyd George's memoirs were popular because they dealt with Germany's defeat; Tolstoy's *War and Peace* was read and reread to "see that an invincible dictator's star falls." People particularly enjoyed reading about the Russian campaign that ended in Napoleon's defeat and was the beginning of the end. "One hopes," wrote Ringelblum, "that history will repeat itself."

Hunger was also made to serve intellectual activity and science. An unusual project was started by a group of Jewish doctors in the Ghetto in February 1942, five months before the first experiments at Treblinka. Starvation was endemic. The doctors set to work examining the effects of hunger on their own diminishing bodies and on the corpses piling up in Warsaw. They pushed the work hard because they knew that they would die very soon; moreover, the Nazis seized their researches and destroyed documents. But their work pressed on and was completed a few weeks after the chief of the team was killed. Their findings were published after the war under the title *Maladie de famine: recherches cliniques sur la famine executées dans le ghetto de Varsovie en 1942.* The publication was made possible by David Guzik, an officer of the Joint Distribution Committee, who miraculously survived the Ghetto.

In the midst of a perpetually shifting population, courses were given in engraving, watchmaking, leatherwork and architectural drawing. The significance of some of these activities has been described by Mary Berg, who was imprisoned in the Ghetto at the age of sixteen. In 1941, the Germans had permitted the opening of a school of graphic arts. The typhus epidemic was already raging. Mary's entry for September 23, 1941, describes a pogrom in the Ghetto streets, but only five days later, on September 28, she describes an exhibition held in her school. Most popular were pictures of fruits and flowers, designs for powder compacts, book covers, theater posters, café signs, designs for modern homes with many windows and greenery. "The visitors at the exhibition," she wrote, "look with pride at these housing projects for the Jewish population of the free Poland of the future which will abolish the crowded houses of Krochmalna and Smocza Street, where the darkest cellars of the ghetto are situated. But when will this come about, and which of us will live to see it?"

On May 6, 1942, an instructor took his students in the graphic arts class to one of the gardens planted by Toporal (Society for the Promotion of Agriculture Among Jews) on the site of a bombed-out house. Mary recorded the event. "Today it is green there. Jewish workmen have constructed swings and benches. The pupils of our school went to paint a fresco of animal cartoons on one of the walls of the ruined house. All this is done to give the ghetto children a feeling of freedom."

Child mortality was as high as the Germans could wish, but as long as they could, the children went to classes and studied. Teachers were determined to pretend that there was a future. Children felt that it was still possible to move on to some kinder life. In the *Gazeta Zydowska* (Jewish Journal), a strictly censored paper published in Krakow, appeared the following poem by a little girl named Martha:

> I must be saving these days
> (I have no money to save),
> I must save health and strength,
> Enough to last me for a long while.
> I must save my nerves,
> And my thoughts, and my mind,
> And the fire of my spirit;
> I must be saving of tears that flow—
> I shall need them for a long, long while.
> I must save endurance these stormy days.
>
> There is so much I need in my life:
> Warmth of feeling and a kind heart—
> These things I lack; of these I must be saving!
> All these, the gifts of God,
> I wish to keep.
> How sad I should be
> If I lost them quickly.[17]

Jews in the Ghetto also "debated" problems of war strategy. They predicted the date when Kiev would fall; they figured out what would have happened had Turkey declared war on Germany; they also probed England's inactivity during the "phony war" and rose to a high pitch of hope after Russia and the United States were drawn into the war. They were tormented by growing fear of being abandoned but seemed, at no time, to have succumbed to the belief that Germany would win the war. The Allies would win and they would be rescued. Sometimes their fantasy-weaving nebulously connected them to a faraway future; sometimes it snapped. Despair was laced with hope or wry humor. A story was told that Churchill consulted a miracle-working Chasidic rabbi about the way to defeat the Nazis. "There are two possible ways," the rabbi told him, "a natural way—a million angels armed with flaming swords can fall upon Germany and destroy it; or a supernatural way—a million British soldiers can descend on Germany and destroy it."

A German demand for civilian fur coats for troops on the Russian front was interpreted as a hopeful sign that things weren't going very well for

Hitler. The Ghetto rushed to hide fur coats in cellars, attics and the houses of Aryan friends. Some were smuggled out and sold; many were burned to prevent the Germans from getting them. (One survivor estimates that, as a result, the Ghetto became poorer by several million zlotys.) This sabotage action had tangible results, but similar opportunities were lacking because of the abnormal situation in the Ghetto. Moreover, the Ghetto was not united. One of the astonishing—but also divisive—aspects of Ghetto life was the continued activity of all of the Jewish political parties and ideological trends which had existed in prewar Poland. For a while these groups worked under cover of central Jewish welfare organizations, but after the Ghetto was enclosed, their activity went underground and took on deep significance. They did not begin to coalesce until the end of 1942.

The underground press was especially important, for all of the papers, regardless of their ideological bent, strengthened the stamina of the Ghetto through its ordeal. When despair and apathy began to eat away at the Ghetto, the clandestine papers momentarily lifted flagging spirits.

The illegal youth publications were particularly active in this struggle against spiritual collapse. Issues were published in Hebrew, Yiddish and Polish and were addressed to the general reading public as well as the youth movements. There were several dozen—dailies, weeklies, and monthlies—most of them crudely hectographed. Political issues were analyzed and educational "tasks" outlined. Passive resistance to the Nazis was urged. Special bulletins covered news from the war fronts gathered from a radio concealed in the lodging of Mordecai Anilewicz at 8 Leszno Street. Anthologies of literary and historical material were also issued. The struggle in Palestine was covered with great concern and astonishingly detailed reports appeared on the growth of industry, Jewish National Fund projects, immigration, land problems and the state of the labor movement.

In spite of the progressive misery in the Ghetto, the Zionist youth groups decided to carry out a fund-raising campaign for the Jewish National Fund in 1940–41. The project was to ensure that "the covenant between the people and the land will not be broken. . . . It brings the greeting of the Jewish community in the ghetto to the free community in the Land of Israel." Every morsel of news about Palestine was eagerly read and helped to overcome the physical isolation and despair of the Ghetto.

The papers also dealt with life in the Nazi labor camps, news from the provinces, reports of acts of sabotage and resistance against the Germans. There were also accounts of the internal life of the Ghetto under conditions of terror. Brave and resolute words were addressed to faltering comrades: "The very expression of apathy," wrote the Bundist *Yugend*

Shtimme (Voice of Youth), "indicates submission to the enemy, which can cause our collapse morally and root out of our hearts our hatred for the invader. It can destroy within us the will to fight; it can undermine our resolution. . . . And because our position is so bitterly desperate our will to give up our lives for a purpose more sublime than our daily existence must be reinforced. . . . Our young people must walk with heads erect."[18]

Largely socialistic in character, the underground press also railed against the social injustices in the Ghetto and the prevalence of luxury in the midst of hunger. Sharp attacks were made against smugglers, swindlers and speculators who rose to the surface of Ghetto life under the German policy of encouraging informers and extortionists. The papers tried to strengthen morale by upholding traditional Jewish morality and treading the delicate line between countering rumors of new calamities and yet not letting Jews be deluded by false hopes. Ultimately they transmuted suffering into a stubborn will to resist. An episode toward the end of 1941 aroused the youthful writers.

The public execution of eight Jews who had been found in the Aryan side of the city on November 17, 1941, left a powerful impression. These were the first "legal" murders carried out in the Ghetto. Six of the eight were mothers who had tried to find bread for their starving children. The Ghetto press demanded vengeance. On July 3, 1942, 110 Jews were shot dead as a reprisal for the "growing disobedience" and "active resistance" to German authority. The press vowed that there would be a reckoning. This was to come.

Against these accents of life rose a numbness to death from hunger and disease. As early as February 1941, Ringelblum noted that the sight of people falling dead in the middle of the street no longer stirred people. Naked corpses were laid in mass graves separated by boards. Children began to lose their fear of dead bodies and were seen tickling them to see if they moved. Women who squatted in the streets with their children told Ringelblum they would rather die in the street than at home.

There was also the slow, pitiless decline of human feelings: the sight of frozen children could no longer evoke sorrow, only resignation; corpses were not covered; kinship ties were beginning to crumble. Ringelblum sadly commented:

A very interesting question is that of the passivity of the Jewish masses, who expire with no more than a slight sigh. Why are they all so quiet? Why does the father die, and the mother, and each of the children, without a single protest. Why haven't we done the things we threatened the world with a year ago—robbery and theft—those things whose threat forced the House Committees to buy up food for the poorer tenants? There are a great many possible answers to these questions. One is that the [German] occupation forces have so terrorized the Jewish populace that people are afraid to raise their heads. The fear that mass reprisals would be the reply to any outbreak from the hungry masses has forced the more sensitive elements into a passivity designed not to provoke any commotion in the Ghetto.[19]

Starvation and typhus quickly destroyed life in the Ghetto. Over 43,000 Jews in 1941, and over 37,000 in the first nine months of 1942 starved to death. The mortality in 1941 was nearly five times that of 1940 and in the first half of 1942, up to the deportations, nearly six times. Among the refugees, about 150,000 in April, 1941, the number of deaths from starvation was 66 percent in May–June, 1942. At the 1942 rate (26,000 deaths for the first half of the year for the entire population), the Jews of the Ghetto would have died out in eight years.[19a]

But the Nazis had no intention of waiting that long.

The first news of massacres of Jews in the Polish provinces reached the Ghetto in April 1942. Ringelblum, on April 12, recorded rumors of the arrival of an extermination brigade. News of the massacre of 40,000 Jews in the Lublin Ghetto was learned a few days later. The Jews in Warsaw simply did not believe it. Later when eyewitness reports of exterminations elsewhere in Poland filtered into the Ghetto, there still was disbelief. The war would soon end, they told themselves, and Jews would be delivered. It was easier to blame an individual storm trooper, or a particular official, than to face the fact that no act of savagery was an accident, that no German official was more or less barbaric, and that, whether he was a gentleman or a sadist, a cultivated man or an illiterate, the result would be the same. As late as June 1942, when a few Jews in the Ghetto began to grasp the nature of the German plan of systematic extermination, it was widely believed that if the alarm could be given, if only the outside world would hear, salvation would come. Grandiose but false radio communiqués as well as the intractable optimism of the Jews encouraged this state of mind. Ringelblum himself, after the news of the Lublin massacres had reached the Ghetto, expressed what must have been a universal disbelief that the nation of Goethe and Beethoven could think of methodically exterminating human beings. "It is most important," he wrote, "for the Germans to know about the exterminations. The Nazis take pains to see that the killings are secret. They use Jews to bury their murdered brethren—in the end the grave-diggers themselves are murdered. If the outside world contents itself with speeches and threats perhaps the fear of German public opinion will save us."

The Germans picked this time—the late spring of 1942—to send a special movie team from their Propaganda Section into the Ghetto to take pictures. Ringelblum has the following entry for May 19, 1942:

> Besides technical workers from the film industry, experts on "Jewish life" also participate; they are staging and directing the various scenes. It is rather difficult, on the basis of these individual scenes, to find out exactly what the picture in its entirety may represent. But what we have already seen speaks for itself. This film seems to be designed to represent all the bad features of the Jews as "subhumans." In order to give prominence to these features, the directors are resorting to experiments which are revolting and repulsive to any unbiased observer.
>
> After photographing scenes of misery in the streets, begging, etc., special scenes are set up in which German actors, made up like Jews, play their parts. Moreover, Jewish people, seized at random in the streets, are forced to participate. Thus, when a picture of a ritual bathing-establishment, the so-called *mikva*, was to be taken, fifty people were seized in Gesia Street and transported to a real *mikva* located in Zamenhofa Street. There all these people were ordered to undress completely and they were driven, both men and women, into a pool, so that pictures might be taken. (As I learned later from persons versed in these matters Jews are allowed to bathe in such ritual bathing establishments, i.e. pools with running water, but only men and women separately.)
>
> A few days later the same film team arrived in the so-called "refugee" centers, which accommodate Jews driven out from the towns in which the ghettos had been liquidated. There unimaginably pornographic pictures were taken. Old bearded Jews were ordered at pistol point to commit lascivious acts with children, with young girls, etc.
>
> On Sunday, the 17th of this month, the movie people filmed the ceremony of circumcision of a Jewish infant.

While the large trucks with motion-picture equipment were grinding cameras to film the Ghetto, an enthusiastic article appeared in the official German *Warschauer Zeitung* describing how 100,000 Jews in Warsaw who had previously been social parasites were "now productively working for the Germans." This appeared one month before the deportations to Treblinka.

In May 1942, there appeared a big sign in German in the cemetery ordering Germans not to visit the Jewish graveyard. Supposedly the reason for this ban was sanitation but, in fact, it was quite different. Crowds of Germans used to visit the cemetery to stare at the shed where daily the skeletons of the corpses of poor people who had starved in the street were heaped—candidates for mass graves. Standing there, the Germans used to discuss the Jewish question among themselves, according to Ringelblum. Some of them enjoyed the sight of the victims of Hitler's extermination policy; others expressed their revulsion at the consequences of "German culture." Apparently, these graveyard excursions left a strong imprint on the excursionists; consequently they were halted.

They were also halted because what the Nazis next planned was not for public consumption.

The cyclone of death tore through the Government-General beginning in March 1942. Heydrich and Eichmann diverted gassing vans from the Lodz area to the transit camp at Pabianice and Chelmno and then to the towns of the Lublin province and eventually Belzec. "Einsatz Reinhard" then swept up 250,000 Jews from Lvov, Krakow, Tarnow, Sosnowiece and Lublin and deported them to Belzec, Maidanek, Sobibor, Treblinka and Auschwitz before decimating Warsaw. The failure to complete the Treblinka gassing installation in April had delayed the start of the Warsaw "resettlement," and there were the invariable transport difficulties, but the 400,000 Jews in Warsaw had already been alive too long for Globocnik, Himmler and Frank.

As the hour for Warsaw struck, reports of the galloping destruction of Polish Jewry reached the outside world.

Ringelblum permitted himself a moment of rejoicing: "Friday, June 26, has been a great day for O.S.," he wrote. "This morning, the English radio broadcast about the fate of Polish Jewry. The O.S. has fulfilled a great historical mission. It has alarmed the world to our fate, and perhaps saved hundreds of thousands of Polish Jews from extermination. . . . I do not know who of our group will survive, who will be deemed worthy to work through our collected material. But one thing is clear to all of us. Our toils and tribulations . . . have not been in vain."

But no help came. The tempo of the deportations from Poland increased. The swath of death neared the Warsaw Ghetto. By June 30, Ringelblum began to surmise the reason for the world's silence:

> During the last days the Jewish population has been living under the impact of news from London. The news that the world has been stirred by the reports of the slaughter in Poland has aroused the deepest emotions in all of us. For many, many months we endured the most terrible sufferings and we kept asking ourselves: Does the world know about our sufferings, and if it knows, why is it silent? Why was the world not outraged by the fact that tens of thousands of Jews were shot to death at Ponary [near Vilna]. Why was the world silent when tens of thousands of Jews were poisoned in Chelmno? . . . Only now have we come to understand the cause of this silence: London just did not know anything about all that was happening here, and that was the reason for this silence. . . . Now we ask: if London knew, the next day, that one hundred people [Poles] were shot in the Pawiak prison, why then did it take many months before they learned in London of the hundreds of thousands murdered Jews?[20]

The absence of response by London has been explained by Stefan Korbanski, the last chief of the Polish wartime underground:

> It began with my sending to London several messages, one after the other, with the information that on July 22, 1942, the Germans had begun to

liquidate the Ghetto. In Stawki Street, 7,000 people were loaded into freight wagons and transported to Maidanek [read Treblinka], where they were all killed in gas chambers. I was extremely astonished when the BBC made no use of my messages and ignored them completely. I dispatched a special telegram, demanding to know the reasons for this silence. My astonishment grew when this urgent inquiry received no reply either. . . . I ordered the radio operators to demand a reply to all my messages. . . . They did so for several days, and apparently the daily bombardment caused the Government in London to reply at last. But the reply did not clear up the mystery; for it simply said: "Not all your radiograms lend themselves to publication."[21]

A month later, however, the BBC broadcast the news. Many months later, a Polish emissary was parachuted into Poland and told Korbanski, "Your messages were disbelieved. Neither our Government nor the British would believe them. They said you were exaggerating for the sake of anti-German propaganda. But after the British received confirmation of it through their own channels, they were filled with dismay, and the BBC broadcast your information."[22]

Several months later, the British threatened to punish the exterminators. Nothing was suggested for the rescue of those about to be exterminated.

14 The *Einsatzgruppen*

Two DAYS before the German invasion of Russia in 1941 a young Jewish student from Losice, a small town in Poland, rejoiced in his graduation from the gymnasium in Bialystok, the only boy in Losice so honored. "I was the happiest man on earth," he wrote. "In Moscow, the Medical School had accepted me; I even counted on getting there on the old goat. On the last Saturday there was a graduation ball with our own orchestra. We danced, we drank. There were Russians, Jews, Kalmuks. . . . I don't know how long it lasted, or when it ended, I only remember finding myself alone in the city park. I swear I talked to the stars."[1]

But the next day was Sunday, June 22; the young man's happiness was short-lived. He made his way to Slonim where his sister lived, barely missing death a dozen times on the way, and miraculously avoiding the round-ups of young men in Slonim. He worked for several months as a carpenter for the Wehrmacht. Then the front shifted beyond Smolensk. The young man describes his new life:

> About that time the Germans with their Lithuanian troops began to go off on mysterious expeditions into the country, taking with them trucks and plenty of ammunition, and vanishing for whole days. At first we did not pay any attention to it because they often went out against Soviet partisans, but after a while these expeditions began to intrigue me. Against partisans the soldiers went grudgingly; here they departed in jolly spirits, singing and joking. Besides, from partisan fights they returned the same day; here they would be away several days, and they never brought back any prisoners for the customary hangings. I asked the soldiers where they were going, but the answer was always the same: partisans. I could perhaps have learned something from the less disciplined and illiterate Lithuanians, but soon after the start of these expeditions they were isolated from us. Once, after an unusually long trip, we noticed blood on the trucks. We stood there and watched with frozen eyes, until the Germans landed on us with yells and kicks ordering us to wash the blood quickly off. . . .
>
> It was the night of November 12, a quiet winter night. When I came to work the next day the soldiers told us to go home. Bewildered, we stood and looked at them. All troops were out of the barracks, the trucks were warming up. The soldiers carried ammunition and hand grenades; it looked as if they were going away on another expedition. When we did not move

and merely stood there surprised by the order to go home, the soldiers began to yell, "*Heute gibt es keine Arbeit. . . . Los. . . . Nach Hause!*" Some soldiers laughed at us, others shook their heads, but most of them just looked at us through cold, half-closed eyes. When, despite the yells and the threats we still remained in place wondering what had happened, the Germans dispersed us with kicks and rifle butts.

I walked slowly home where I found Matla. She, too had been told to go home. Then as we stood talking about what might have happened, the troops were let loose upon the city.

Dragging Matla with me, I ran out of the house. I did not know where to run, but I knew we must get out of the city; we headed for the woods. Suddenly a gun fired, then another and another. Still we ran over the open fields, but the firing drove us back into the city. There we heard the roaring trucks and the crack of gunfire. We hid in a loft. Trembling women and crying children were lumped in all corners. We were soon in a panic again and crawled down. There was a latrine in the yard, and I and Matla and another girl got inside. But it was a cold day; our ears and our fingers were freezing. We tore open the boards of the latrine seat and crouched there with only our heads sticking out. They would come and have a hearty laugh. . . .

They were nearing our street. We heard them milling around the walls of the house. "*Raus,*" they roared. "*Alle Juden raus.*" We could see them through the cracks. Children showed up in doorframes and then they were gone. People revolved in place, lifting their hands, jumping into the air, covering their faces; then they lay quietly, like collapsed bags. Trucks drove off loaded to the brim, dripping blood as they moved on. New trucks arrived. Morning passed, noon passed while the slaughter progressed. They came to the loft where we were first hidden and threw them all down onto the cobblestones. I was watching them fall when they appeared in front of us. "*Raus,*" they yelled and I saw the buckles of their belts through the wooden planks. They stuck in the gun muzzles and fired. The latrine was full of fire and smoke. The rifles disappeared leaving two small holes in the rear wall. The Germans were gone. The roars subsided. . . . Dusk was settling. . . .

The houses stood empty; nobody closed the open doors. The corpses lay where they had fallen. Nobody moved, nothing stirred.[2]

This was the first of a wave of massacres to strike Slonim, a city in eastern Europe which disappeared into unquiet silence with its thousands of terrified Jews and their unuttered terrors. Slonim vanished together with Vinnitsa, Baranovice, Kovno, Mogilev, Vilna, Biala, Losice, Konstantynow, Lvov, Taropol, Chortkov, Minsk and hundreds of other little and big Jewish communities in eastern Europe. They were annihilated by *Einsatzgruppen*, mobile killing squads, which swept through the plains and forests of Poland and Russia into obscure, sleepy Jewish villages and townlets and throbbing cities, cutting down in an instant of time a million and a half lives. Their killing power derived from an agreement between Heydrich and the Wehrmacht, an agreement which drew the German Army into mass murder.

At Nuremberg, the defense tried hard to dissociate the Gestapo and the S.D. from the *Einsatzgruppen*, and to show that these groups were special-purpose units under Army command. But the S.D. and Gestapo had conceived the formation of such units as early as 1938 in case of complications arising from the invasion of Czechoslovakia. Scattered forces of *Einsatzgruppen* were active in the Sudetenland. Their tasks were more fully crystallized by the time of the invasion of Poland, but only after the invasion of Russia did they have limitless scope for their destructiveness.

The Nazi Party, the civil service and business interests all played an important role in the preliminary phases of the destruction process; the armed forces, however, had been peripheral. It was only in the crucial year of 1941—the year of the Nazi invasion of Russia—when every segment of German society was drawn into the destruction that the armed forces too became deeply involved. They were, in fact, at the very center of the Holocaust. This involvement originated in an agreement between Heydrich and the Wehrmacht in May 1941 to allow *Sonderkommandos* (Special Detachments) of the S.D. in the forward areas during the Russian campaign to "carry out certain special Security Police tasks which are not within the province of the Army." The machinery in the invaded areas was the *Einsatzgruppen*, special operations units, formed to murder Jews, Gypsies and political commissars and, incidentally, to watch the conduct of the military.

In the preliminary drafts outlining the "special tasks" of the *Einsatzgruppen*, the Army High Command forbade their employment in those parts of the Army area which might adversely affect operations. The Army acknowledged Heydrich's right to install one of his representatives in each Army area to direct the *Einsatzgruppen* "to take executive measures affecting the civilian population"—their special province. But the Wehrmacht still preserved for itself independence of action regarding the conduct of military operations and subordination of the actions of the *Einsatzgruppen* to military priorities. These old-fashioned notions were quickly smashed and the Wehrmacht very soon lent itself to unparalleled criminal actions against civilians.

Hitler openly demanded such unlawful action from the Wehrmacht on March 30, 1941, when he made a long speech to over 200 senior officers, a speech which gave rise to the so-called "Commissar Order." However, notes made on March 3 by Colonel General Alfred Jodl, chief of the operations section of the High Command, form a true starting point for the chain of events that enmeshed the German Army in mass murder. Jodl summarized Hitler's directions as follows:

> The forthcoming campaign is more than a mere armed conflict; it is a collision between two different ideologies. In view of the size of the area involved, this war will not be ended merely by the defeat of the enemy armed forces. The entire area must be split up into different states each with their own government with which we can then conclude peace. . . .

Any large-scale revolution gives rise to events which cannot subsequently be expunged. The socialist ideal can no longer be wiped out in the Russia of today. From the internal point of view, the formation of new states and governments must inevitably be based on this principle. The Bolshevist-Jewish intelligentsia must be eliminated as having been the "oppressor" of the people up to now. . . .

Furthermore, we must under all circumstances avoid allowing a nationalist Russia to appear in place of Bolshevist Russia, for history shows that this will once more become anti-German. Our object is to construct as soon as possible and using the minimum of military force, socialist states which will be dependent upon us.

This is a task so difficult that it cannot be entrusted to the Army.[3]

The exclusion of the Army from Hitler's hazy political plans for Russia was thus registered. Jodl then dutifully outlined Hitler's further directives: The Army must have an operational area, but this should be "no deeper than necessary." Instead of a military government in the conquered areas, Reich commissars were to be appointed for large, defined regions, based on "ethnographical lines" and it would be the task of the commissars to build up the machinery of the new states. The Army, once again, was specifically excluded from a traditional area of responsibility. Hitler's central function for Himmler's S.S. machinery was then unambiguously recorded by Jodl:

Frontiers will be closed where they abut on the zone of operations. If it proves necessary to employ organizations responsible to the Reichsführer S.S. in this area as well as the Secret Field Security police, the approval of the Reichsführer S.S. must be obtained. This may be necessary since all Bolshevist leaders or commissars must be liquidated forthwith. There is no question of courts martial having anything to do with these matters; they should not deal with any legal matters other than those internal to the armed forces."[4]

Jodl was then told to prepare a final draft of instructions as soon as possible and have it typed "in double spacing to allow the Führer to make further alterations."

The Wehrmacht had ceased to be its own master; its traditional independence in military matters was already circumscribed. If it did not explicitly know that under cover of the division of tasks between itself and the S.S. apparatus, the *Einsatzgruppen* would mass murder Jews in the rear areas of the Eastern front as soon as the campaign began, it did not remain in the dark long.

Hitler's meeting with the senior officers on March 30 involved the commanders in chief of the three services and the senior Army, Navy and Air Force commanders selected for the Eastern campaign together with their senior staff officers. The meeting took place in a large conference room at the Ebertstrasse end of the Great Hall of the new Reich Chancellery in Berlin. The hall was packed with officers seated in long rows of chairs according to rank and seniority. Hitler spoke forcefully for two and a half hours on the special nature of the forthcoming campaign —a "struggle between two opposing ideologies," not merely another routine military operation. Soviet commissars and officials, he said, were to be treated as criminals, whether they belonged to the armed forces or civilian ranks. They were therefore not to be regarded as soldiers nor to be treated as pisoners of war. When captured, they were to be handed over to the Field Sections of the S.D. or shot on the spot by the troops. In his dealings with the "hostile inhabitants," the German soldier need not be bound by the letter of the laws of war or military discipline, but, on the contrary, "any type of attack by the inhabitants against the Wehrmacht" should be handled with the utmost severity, including summary execution without court-martial procedure. He continued:

> The war against Russia will be such that it cannot be conducted in a knightly fashion. This struggle is one of ideologies and racial differences and will have to be conducted with unprecedented, merciless and unrelenting harshness. All officers will have to rid themselves of obsolete ideologies. I know that the necessity for such means of waging war is beyond the comprehension of you generals but . . . I insist absolutely that my orders be executed without contradiction. The commissars are the bearers of ideologies directly opposed to National Socialism. Therefore the commissars will be liquidated. German soldiers guilty of breaking international law . . . will be excused.[5]

Hitler justified these instructions on the ground that Bolshevism was a "sociological crime." When fighting the Soviets, there was no place for soldierly chivalry or "out-of-date notions" of military comradeship. Not only must the Red Army be beaten; communism must be exterminated for all time.

The officers sat in stony silence as Hitler delivered his rasping fulminations, a silence broken only twice—when the assemblage rose as Hitler entered the room through a door in the rear and went up to the rostrum, and later after he concluded his speech and left through the same door. Otherwise, not a hand moved nor a voice spoke. Franz Halder, Chief of the General Staff, made full notes of the speech and ended his comments with the words: "One of the sacrifices which commanders have to make is to overcome any scruples they may have." As he later remembered the event, the generals were outraged by the order and protested to their Commander in Chief, Brauchitsch, who informed the High Command that the officers of the Army "could never execute such orders," but Brauchitsch, in his testimony at Nuremberg, admitted that he took no such action with Hitler "because nothing in the world could change his attitude." Field Marshal von Manstein declared on the stand that "it was the first time I found myself involved in a conflict between my soldierly conceptions and my duty to obey," but as a matter of record, the order was carried out on a large scale. General Walter Warlimont, Deputy Chief of the Operations Staff under Jodl, has recorded a "conspiracy of silence" among the officers lasting more than five weeks following the March 30 conference.[6] When the silence was broken, it was to proceed with Hitler's instructions, not to repudiate them.

On May 6, a draft of an order entitled "General instructions for dealing with political leaders and for the coordinated execution of the task allotted on 31 [read 30] March 1941" by the Wehrmacht High Command was framed and followed Hitler's general orders. In the final form, the order carried no signature, an omission which meant that the Army commanders did not have to report compliance to Hitler or the High Command. Conceivably, then, the order could be circumvented or even sabotaged, but this did not happen often. In various operational orders that subsequently followed, eleven categories were enumerated and marked "for execution." Category Number 10 refers to "All Jews." Ten specific categories of the non-Jewish population are also listed, such as "all important officials of the State and Party," and "agitators and fanatical Communists." But even Heydrich, who instructed his screening teams to seek out and execute persons in these eleven categories, excluded certain "trustworthy" groups of Russians and all non-Russians in the Soviet Union unless they were "fanatical Bolsheviks, political commissars, or otherwise dangerous elements." There was to be no exception in the category "Jews."

In the spring of 1941, while certain Army generals wrestled with their consciences, one of them, Quartermaster General Wagner sent the draft of a proposed RSHA-Army agreement to Heydrich, outlining the terms under which the *Einsatzgruppen* could operate in Russia. By the end of May, the final agreement was prepared, giving the killing units complete independence to carry out measures against the civilian population in Russia. Administratively, they were to be subordinated to the military command but the RSHA was to retain functional control over their movements. The military was to furnish them with quarters, gasoline, food rations and radio communications and, in the final agreement, yielded on an important issue: not only could they operate in the Army rear areas; they could operate right on the front line. This meant that Jews would be trapped suddenly, without warning and without any chance of escaping. In keeping with the Nazi reticence to call a spade a spade, all reference to killing—which was the purpose of the *Einsatzgruppen*—was omitted. This final agreement was signed by Wagner and Heydrich late in May 1941. It had been drafted by S.S. General Walter Schellenberg, head of Gestapo counterintelligence and frequently liaison between the military and S.S. In a sworn affidavit signed on November 26, 1945, Schellenberg said that he himself had witnessed the signing of the agreement by Wagner and Heydrich, after which he was asked to leave the two men alone.

Just while leaving, I heard how they both wanted to discuss in complete privacy the Führer's command, which was apparently known in advance by each of them personally, and its far-reaching implications. . . . I must today express my firm conviction that during the secret oral discussion between Wagner and Heydrich the extensive future activity of the Combat Groups and Combat Commandos within the combat elements of the Field Army was obviously discussed and delineated so as to include even planned mass executions. The close cooperation . . . even in the first weeks of the Russian campaign makes me today give expression to my firm conviction that the *Oberbefehlshaber* [Commanders in chief] of the Army groups and armies which were to take part in the Russian campaign were accurately informed through the normal OKH [Army High Command] channels of communication about the extensive future mission of the Combat Groups . . . of the SIPO [Security Police] and S.D. as including planned mass executions of Jews, Communists, and all other elements of resistance.[7]

Within a month of the German invasion, mass killings of Jews and "Bolsheviks" was justified by Nazi claims that they had instigated an all-out partisan war behind the German lines. This line, which had not the slightest shred of truth—the Russian partisans did not organize effectively until the spring and summer of 1942—was taken up wholeheartedly by certain Army commanders, and the first consequence of army "security" policy was the practice of handing over Jews to the *Einsatzgruppen* for shooting. In Minsk, the army commander established a civilian internment camp for most of the men in the city. Secret Field Police units and personnel of *Einsatzgruppe* B combed out the camp for "Jews, criminals, functionaries, and Asiatics." In numerous operational reports, *Einsatzgruppen* refer to Army requests to *Kommandos* (squads) to execute Jews for acts of sabotage, as "precautionary" measures and to protect the security of the troops. The German Army eased itself quickly into cooperation with the killing squads.

Altogether, four *Einsatzgruppen* of battalion strength were set up. Group A was to operate in the Baltic States, Group B in White Russia, Group C in the Ukraine, and Group D in the Crimea-Caucasus (map, p. 271). Armed with unlimited authority, each of the four group commanders had between 500 and 900 men serving under him, many coming from the ranks of the Security Police and S.D., but substantial numbers from the Waffen S.S., from pools of mortorcycle riders, teletype and radio operators and clerks. Indigenous units of Ukrainians, Latvians, Lithuanians and Estonians were added as auxiliary police when numbers had to be filled out. At their training center at Pretsch in Saxony, and in the neighboring village of Düben, the men in the units were told where they were going and what they were expected to do. The training consisted largely of rifle practice and listening to lectures and exhortatory speeches on the necessity to exterminate subhumans threatening the life of the Reich.

A few days after the invasion of Russia, the squads sped away in fast cars and trucks, armed with rifles, pistols and submachine guns. They needed no cavalry, cannon, or airplanes; there would be no reconnoitering, no surprise attacks, no armed enemy. They had merely to cover vast distances quickly for their prey.

The commanders and lesser officers of the extermination squads were not military men or professional killers, but a peculiar assortment of intellectual riffraff from the old legion of German unemployed youth and professionals. In no sense were they hoodlums, delinquents or common criminals. Otto Ohlendorf, who commanded *Einsatzgruppe* D, was quite typical. In 1941, Ohlendorf was thirty-four. He had studied at three universities and held a doctor's degree in jurisprudence. He had joined the Nazi Party in 1925, the S.S. in 1926, and the S.D. in 1936, but regarded his Party activities as a sideline to his main career as research economist. By the time he joined the Security Service, he had become research director of the Institute for Applied Economic Science in Kiel. Actually, he devoted only four years, from 1939 to 1943, to full-time work for the RSHA, but during that period he commanded an extermination unit behind the Eastern front. Ohlendorf had suddenly interrupted a bureaucratic career in June 1941—he was then head of Amt III of the RSHA—to command *Einsatzgruppe* D with the rank of major general. From that murderous assignment, he slipped quietly in June 1942 into the Ministry of Economics, where he became manager of a committee on export trade. Even his chief, Walter Funk, the Minister of Economics, was unaware that he had commanded the mass execution of 90,000 people. In the last months of the war, the horrors of the bloodied Crimea had dimmed even for Ohlendorf. By then, he was in Himmler's entourage, looking not unfavorably on the July plotters and chosen by Walter Schellenberg to be included in a cabinet which was supposed to make a Himmler Government presentable to the Allies.

Next to Göring, Ohlendorf was probably the most compelling personality of all of the defendants at the Nuremberg trials. He was handsome, suave and exceedingly well poised. His voice was carefully modulated, his hands groomed and his movements, graceful and self-confident.[8] When he was on trial for his life in 1947, women spectators sent flowers to his cell. They did not know that two years before, when he appeared as a witness in the prosecution of the S.D., he had admitted to the murder of 90,000 people.

The Nuremberg judgment compared Ohlendorf to Dr. Jekyll and Mr. Hyde, a fairly common phenomenon in the Third Reich, but how and where Ohlendorf's dual nature arose cannot be fathomed. Indeed, he himself was not aware of any split at all in his personality. It may have happened soon after September 1939 when Heydrich transformed the S.D.

By then Ohlendorf's Bureau III was no longer a Citizens' Advisory Bureau but a secret police inquisition peering into the lives of everyone in the Reich. The enormity of the destructiveness of the *Einsatzgruppen* was casually let out, as if by accident, in January 1946, while Ohlendorf was being interrogated about his wartime activities by a young American naval officer, Lieutenant Commander Whitney R. Harris.

When Harris asked Ohlendorf what he had done during the war, he explained that except for one year he had been on official duty in Berlin as a foreign trade expert in the Ministry of Economics. Asked what he had done during the year away from Berlin, Ohlendorf replied, "I was chief of *Einsatzgruppe* D."

Harris knew something about the *Einsatzgruppen* and pursued the questioning: "During the year you were chief of *Einsatzgruppe* D, how many men, women and children did your group kill?"

Ohlendorf shrugged his shoulders and with only the slightest hesitation replied, "Ninety thousand."[9]

On the stand later, Judge I. T. Nikitchenko, asked: "For what reason were the children massacred?"

"The order," Ohlendorf said evenly, "was that the Jewish population should be totally exterminated." He admitted that there is "nothing worse for people spiritually than to have to shoot defenseless populations," but that it was a matter of self-defense. The Jews posed a continuous danger for the German occupation troops, Ohlendorf said, and might someday attack Germany proper. "I think I can add from my own knowledge of European history," he continued, "that the Jews during wars regularly carried on espionage service on both sides."

When the prosecutor tried to fathom the massacre of children, Ohlendorf was imperturbable. "According to orders, they were to be killed just like their parents."

The prosecutor thundered: "Will you explain to the tribunal what conceivable threat to the security of the Wehrmacht a child constituted, in your judgment?"

Ohlendorf seemed astonished that the prosecutor should linger on the question. "I believe I cannot add anything to your previous question. I did not have to determine the danger but the order said that all Jews including the children were considered to constitute a danger for the security of this area."

The prosecutor, James Heath, did not relent. "Will you agree that there was absolutely no basis for killing children except genocide and the killing of races?"

Ohlendorf did not lose his self-control. "I believe that it is very simple to explain if one starts from the fact that this order did not only try to achieve a temporary security but also a permanent security, for the children were people who would grow up and, surely, being the children of parents who had been killed, would constitute a danger no smaller than that of the parents."[9a]

Ohlendorf then explained how a typical killing took place:

In the implementation of this extermination program, the special commitment groups were subdivided into special commitment detachments, and the *Einsatzkommandos* into still smaller groups, the so-called Special Purpose Detachments [*Sonderkommandos*] and Unit Detachments [*Teilkommandos*]. Usually, the smaller units were led by a member of the S.D., the Gestapo or the criminal police. The unit selected for this task would enter a village or city and order the prominent Jewish citizens to call together all Jews for the purpose of resettlement. They were requested to hand over their valuables to the leaders of the unit, and shortly before the execution, to surrender their outer clothing. The men, women and children were led to a place of execution which in most cases was located next to a more deeply excavated antitank ditch. Then they were shot, kneeling or standing, and the corpses thrown into the ditch. I never permitted the shooting by individuals in the group D, but ordered that several of the men should shoot at the same time in order to avoid direct personal responsibility. The leaders of the unit or specially designated persons, however, had to fire the last bullet against those victims that were not dead immediately. I learned from conversations with other group leaders that some of them demanded that the victims lie down flat on the ground to be shot through the nape of the neck. I did not approve of these methods.[10]

When asked why he did not approve, Ohlendorf replied that "both for the victims and for those who carried out the executions, it was, psychologically, an immense burden to bear."

In the spring of 1942, Ohlendorf continued, an order came from Himmler to change the method of executing women and children. Henceforth they were killed in gas vans specially constructed for this purpose by two Berlin firms. "The actual purpose of these vans," Ohlendorf explained, "could not be seen from the outside. They looked like closed trucks and were so constructed that at the start of the motor, the gas [exhaust] was conducted into the van causing death in ten to fifteen minutes." The victims were induced to enter the vans by being told they were to be transported to another locality. This method, too, represented a "great ordeal" for the *Einsatzgruppen*, according to Ohlendorf, because of the distorted faces and excretions of the victims who had to be buried. Furthermore, the gas vans could kill only fifteen to twenty-five persons at one time, a rate entirely inadequate for the scale Himmler had ordered.

Ohlendorf was willing to kill Jews because of their offenses in history, he claimed, and the killings were done within the framework of an order which was "absolutely necessary militarily." But he intimated that he felt some misgivings about seeing defenseless civilians killed and admitted that he bore no personal hatred toward the Jews. This subtle complex of feelings prompted Judge Heath to ask Ohlendorf if he could not have evaded the order by illness, or by transfer to another assignment. Ohlendorf scorned these suggestions with a withering look and answer: "Despite everything, I considered this my duty and I shall consider it today as much more valuable than the cheap applause which I could have won if I had at that time betrayed my men."

Einsatzgruppe B, which operated mainly in White Russia and the area of the Moscow front, was commanded by Artur Nebe. Nebe had been a police detective in the Weimar Republic and a member of the Gestapo since 1933. During the reorganization of the security and police organizations in 1939, he became chief of Amt V, the criminal police or *Kripo*, to which he returned after spending five months in Russia. Nebe's friends tried hard to link him with the "resistance circle" in the July 1944 plot against Hitler, yet only three weeks before the assassination attempt, Nebe wrote to the S.S. Medical Service offering "asocial Gypsy half-breeds" from Auschwitz for experiments in drinking seawater.[11] His *Einsatzgruppe* executed over 45,000 Jews during the five months of his command. When Himmler visited Minsk soon after the invasion of Russia, it was Nebe who shot a hundred people in order to let Himmler see what a "liquidation" really looked like. But Himmler sickened at the sight. In the group of the condemned was a Jewish youth of about twenty with blue eyes and blond hair. Himmler questioned him, hardly believing that he could be Jewish, deploring the fact that he could not help him. The S.S. Führer was extremely nervous during the firing, especially so when the executioners failed to kill two women in the group outright. He shouted to the police sergeant not to torture them. Later he made a speech to the men in the squad admitting that theirs was a repulsive duty, but as soldiers who had to carry out orders unconditionally, they were not to feel conscience-stricken. The operations against Jews were a necessity; as in nature, the bad and verminous must be destroyed.

After this speech, Himmler and Nebe visited an insane asylum and Himmler ordered Nebe to end the suffering of the inmates as soon as possible. He also asked Nebe "to turn over in his mind" various other killing methods more humane than shooting. Nebe asked for permission to try out dynamite on mentally sick people and Himmler consented. After the war, the only film showing the working of a gas chamber was found in Nebe's Berlin flat. Gas-chamber plans were discussed at daily luncheons at RSHA headquarters in which Ohlendorf, Schellenberg, and Nebe participated. The extreme cynicism of these meetings apparently exhausted Nebe so much that he had to go on sick leave twice. In July 1943, he became a "human wreck suffering from a persecution mania," but less than a year later, he felt sufficiently recovered to offer his "Gypsy half-breeds" for seawater experiments.

Nebe returned to his office in Berlin after five months in Russia but he was not punished for changing his field of action. Otto Rasch, a former Security Police inspector who commanded *Einsatzgruppe* C for a time, overstayed his leave in Germany and later in the war refused the post of Higher S.S. and Police Leader for France-North Italy in favor of a more peaceful life as Mayor of Wurttemburg. Nor was Rasch punished. In fact, there is no record of any punitive action being taken against any *Einsatzgruppen* commanders or lesser officers who left because they could not sustain the "ruthless toughness" and "idealism" which Himmler had exhorted them to work up in moments of weakness. Not many of the men in the units left their duties, however, for less demanding ones.

The commanders of the *Einsatzgruppen* were men drawn from the police-security field. But the lesser officers were mainly professional men— lawyers, teachers, artists; there was also a physician and a clergyman. They were, by and large, in their thirties; undoubtedly they wanted power, fame and success. However, there is no indication that any of them sought an assignment to a *Kommando*. Once in the daily routine of murder, however, they brought skill and zeal to their job. They became efficient killers. One of the most mystifying transformations was that of Ernst Biberstein, a Protestant pastor for eleven years before he entered the Church Ministry, a state agency, in 1935. He joined the S.S. in 1936 and was transferred to the RSHA in 1940. On showing some misgivings about his surroundings, he was sent to the Gestapo office in Oppeln where he was involved in the deportation of Jews to the East. After Heydrich's assassination in the spring of 1942, Biberstein was sent to the field to conduct killing operations as *Einsatzkommando* 6 in Group C.

Biberstein was one of twenty-two *Einsatzgruppen* leaders tried and accused at Nuremberg. All pleaded not guilty. Not one expressed the least regret over what he had done. At most, they dwelt on the harsh necessities of war and their obedience to orders. When the president of the tribunal asked Biberstein whether, as a former churchman, he did not deem it necessary to speak words of comfort as well as to hear the last words of the Jews about to be slain, Biberstein replied, "Mr. President, one does not cast pearls before swine."

When the *Einsatzgruppen* rolled over the border into the Soviet Union, five million Jews (including two million from 1939–40 annexations) were living there, largely concentrated in the western areas, which were quickly overrun by the German Army. The mobile units moved closely behind the army, and trapped large Jewish centers in the first stages; as they moved east, they encountered fewer Jews. Possibly as many as a million and a half Jews were able to escape the first sweep of the *Einsatzgruppen* and fled deeper into Russia. Support waves of Gestapo men, units from the Government-General, Higher S.S. and Police Leaders as well as Wehrmacht soldiers helped in the massacres. Within five months, a half-million Jews were slaughtered.[12]

The Soviet-German Pact of 1939 and the combined Russian and German assault on Poland had given to Russia a string of buffer states from the Baltic to the Black Sea. By June 1941, they had endured more than a year of Soviet rule. In the Baltic States the change to Soviet rule after twenty-two years of national freedom had been a violent one and served to give the German invader a receptive territory. The Jews there were caught in a triple vise of native, Russian and German hatred. The native populations were hostile; the Russians had identified Jews with the middle class and large numbers of them were deported after the plebiscite of 1940. Those who remained lived a very restricted Jewish life. When the Germans came, they accused the Jews of having cooperated with the Russians and were soon wiped out while the native populations looked on indifferently or were incited to raise pogroms of their own.

Had more Jews in the buffer areas been guilty of the German propaganda line—that they had been agents or even collaborators of the Bolshevist regime—more of them might have lived. Tragically, many of them still expected more of Germany than Russia, for Germany, not Russia, had been their traditional refuge. As late as October 1939, thousands of Jews from Russian-occupied Poland fled to German-occupied Poland. Moreover, the mass deportations of Jews from the Baltic States in 1940 had created fear and distrust of the Soviet Union. Remembering that in World War I the Germans had come as quasi-liberators, many Jews waited hopefully for the German Army. This self-deception was not merely a product of memory. The Soviet Government, pursuing a policy of appeasement, had kept silent about Nazi measures of destruction in Europe. The Soviet press and radio ignored reports of the catastrophe that had assaulted the Jews of Europe and only at the last minute did Jews flee. The younger and more active ones went first; those who remained were the most vulnerable: women, children, old people and the physically disabled.

A German intelligence report of July 12, 1941, reveals a German officer's astonishment at this unawareness:

> The Jews are remarkably ill-informed about our attitude toward them. They do not know how Jews are treated in Germany, or for that matter in Warsaw, which after all is not so far away. Otherwise, their questions as to whether we in Germany make any distinctions between Jews and other citizens would be superfluous. Even if they do not think that under German administration they will have equal rights with the Russians, they believe, nevertheless, that we shall leave them in peace if they mind their own business and work diligently.[13]

Thus unprepared, they were physically and psychologically immobilized and vulnerable to German reassurances, ruses and traps. Unarmed and bewildered, they followed orders. The *Einsatzgruppen* quickly grasped the Jewish weaknesses and exploited them. The procedure was to order a prominent rabbi in a town to gather together the most educated Jews for "registration work"; wall posters were also used to assemble Jews for "resettlement." Those Jews who had fled the cities in anticipation of danger were allowed to return by the temporary inactivity of the Security Police, and as the native populations would not shelter them, they had no place to go other than "home." They were then easily rounded up and killed.

In the first sweep of the *Einsatzgruppen*, there was generally no need for councils; the squads simply shot up the Jewish towns. Later, the formality of a council was used to make sure no Jew had been missed. In the areas well within the old Sovietized Russia, there were no councils at all. None had existed for more than twenty years.

Ohlendorf testified that in the territory of his unit, the Jewish elders were in no position to find out what was in store for them and their communities, since "no executions took place until the Council of Jewish Elders had completed their work of making up the list." When the lists were compiled by the unsuspecting councils, "the Jews were then assembled all at once, at one time, for example, in barracks or in a large school or in a factory site." They were then taken to the place of execution.

Pogroms generally came off most effectively in those areas where anti-Jewish feeling was strongest and where return of Soviet rule was doubted. The *Einsatzgruppen* wanted local populations to share in the responsibility for murder and welcomed such help as would bring them closer to the "cleanup goal." Franz Stahlecker, Commander of Group A, wrote: "It was not less important for future purposes to establish as an unquestionable fact that the liberated population had resorted to the most severe measures against the Bolshevist and Jewish enemy, on its own initiative and without instructions from German authorities." The "spontaneous" outbreaks were most successful in the Ukraine and Baltic States, particularly in Lithuania, where the anti-Communist leaders were persuaded to turn their forces on the Jews; over 10,000 were killed in the native Baltic pogroms. These were buffer areas that had been under Soviet control for less than two years, and in which submerged anti-Semitism was still explosive.

So much had the Russians identified the Jews with the capitalistic pre-Soviet life of the country, that the Germans had to find their pogrom-raisers among the class they had the least reason to trust—the extreme anti-Soviet nationalists. Stahlecker reported:

> To our astonishment, it was at first difficult to start a vast pogrom against the Jews. It was Klimatis, leader of a group of partisans, who, at our urging, launched a pogrom that showed no signs of a German order or suggestion. He had taken his directives from a small forward detachment engaged at Kovno. During the first pogrom on the night of June 25th, the

Lithuanian partisans got rid of more than 1,500 Jews. . . . Nearly 2,300 Jews were made harmless during the following nights. The Kovno example was followed in other parts of Lithuania though on a smaller scale.[14]

Stahlecker was particularly pleased with "the understanding attitude of the Wehrmacht" during these "self-cleansing actions," but the Lithuanian partisans soon had to be disarmed and help for the Germans sought elsewhere. Three hundred Lithuanians were found to serve on *Einsatzgruppe* A. At the climax of the mass shootings of Jews there were eight Lithuanians to every German in Stahlecker's firing squads. By January 1942, Stahlecker boasted that "the prisons and then, systematically, district by district, the Lithuanian sector was cleansed of Jews of both sexes. Altogether, 136,421 people were liquidated in a great number of single actions."

A few days after the massacre in Kovno, Stahlecker summoned a few leading Jews to see him. He told them that the Germans "had no reason to intervene in their differences with the Lithuanians" and recommended to them the advantages of moving into a ghetto to prevent further pogroms. Reluctantly, they accepted the idea. Jews were then shoved into the Viriampole district, but the area could not contain the 24,000 still alive, so Stahlecker ordered a "cleansing action." All Jews not wanted by the labor office were committed to prison and executed daily in groups of fifty to a hundred.

The first step toward ghettos and "resettlements" had already been taken: on July 8, 180,000 Jews in the Baltic States were ordered to wear the Jewish badge. By the end of August 1941, ghettos had been established in Libau, Dvinsk, Kovno and Vilna. In Vilna, the German civil commissar took up the killing pace from Stahlecker and sent thousands of Jews off to prison and then to infamous Ponary where the Russians had dug pits for oil storage tanks. For the rest of Vilna Jewry, a particularly tormenting ordeal remained. The Nazi town commissar Hingst set up two separately enclosed ghettos. In Number 1 were the temporarily lucky Jews who had *Ausweise* (employment certificates); in Number 2 were herded all of the Vilna Jews who possessed no *Ausweise*. Periodically, the Gestapo recalled the work certificates or reissued them in varying colors, creating a continuous form of blackmail and torture. No Jew possessing an *Ausweis* could ever feel secure. In this way, the Number 2 Ghetto became a death pen for the very young, the old, or the unlucky who waited their turn for the execution pits. There were seven nights of slaughter in Vilna between September 5 and October 28. On September 12, Field Marshal Wilhelm Keitel destroyed the fragile lease of the inmates of Ghetto Number 1 by forbidding Wehrmacht agencies to issue further *Ausweise* to the Vilna Jews who worked for the Transport Command and the Armament Office. By the end of December 1941, 30,000 Jews in Vilna had been killed.

On October 28, a new storm broke out at Kovno. Half the Ghetto population—about 10,000 people—were carried off in a single day to the death pits at Fort Number 9. Waves of massacres followed.

The nine fortresses built by the Russian czars to protect the city of Kovno were used by the Nazis for the torture and massacre of 100,000 persons, 70,000 of them Jews. There is hardly a statement made by the survivors of the Kovno Ghetto which does not mention the Sixth, Seventh, and especially the Ninth Fortress. The German name of the Ninth Fortress was *Schlachtfeld* (slaughter ground); to the Gestapo, it was known officially as *Vernichtungstelle Kauen* (Kovno extermination site). This area served as the slaughterhouse not only of the Jewish population of Kovno, but for some Jews from France, Austria, Holland and Belgium as well. These western Jews were persuaded or forced to write home saying they had arrived safely to work in Kovno. The Lithuanian representative of the Kovno municipal government, M. Kaminskas, played a role in deceiving these Jews. Sixty-six prisoners survived until the end of 1943 and were made to exhume the bodies of the slain for cremation. They were told that the victims had been shot by the Russians in 1941, a fabrication which no one believed. With the help of the Kovno Jewish Council, the surviving prisoners made a miraculous escape to a partisan base in the Rudnitsky Forest.

A survivor of the Kovno Ghetto, Dr. Aaron Peretz, has described the effect of the executions on the children and the games they played:

> The children in the ghetto would play and laugh, and in their games the entire tragedy was reflected. They would play grave-digging: they would dig a pit and would put a child inside and call him Hitler. And they would play at being gatekeepers of the ghetto. Some of the children played the parts of Germans, some of Jews, and the Germans were angry and would beat the other children who were Jews. And they used to play funerals. . . .
>
> The Jewish child was prematurely grown up. We were amazed to observe how children three or four years old understood the tragedy of the situation, how they clammed up when it was necessary, how they knew when to hide. We ourselves could not trust our ears when we heard small children, offered a sedative, say: "Doctor, this is not necessary, I shall be quiet, I shall not scream."[15]

In Riga, the double-ghetto was not prepared until the middle of October, 1941. Here, in contrast with Vilna, the civil authorities were opposed to mass killings, but the *Einsatzgruppen* quickly moved into control. At the end of November, the ghettos were cordoned and Jewish working commandos were marched out under guard, while rows of modern blue busses pulled up alongside the ghetto gates. Some miles away, deep in the forest, execution pits had been dug by Russian prisoners of war. In three mass shootings within ten days, 27,000 Jews were murdered in Riga. Only 4,500 men and 300 women remained alive when the first of the

Reich Jews arrived and occupied the corpse-filled rooms of the "little ghetto."

On January 31, 1942, Stahlecker completed a long report to Heydrich, accompanied by a map marked with coffins in the appropriate places. "The systematic mopping-up of the Eastern Territories," wrote Stahlecker, "embraced, in accordance with the basic orders, the complete removal, if possible, of Jewry. This goal has been substantially attained—with the exception of White Russia—as a result of the execution up to the present time of 229,052 Jews. The remainder still left in the Baltic provinces is urgently required as labor and housed in ghettos." In Estonia, Latvia and Lithuania, the liquidation was almost complete, Stahlecker reported. However, the elimination of Jews in the White Russian sector (formerly the Byelorussian Soviet) was not completed because "the Jews form an extremely high percentage of the specialized workers who are indispensable because of the shortage in other reserves in this area." Besides, Stahlecker continued: "Einsatzgruppe A did not take over the area until the heavy frost had set in, which made mass executions much more difficult. A further difficulty is that the Jews live widely scattered over the whole country. In view of the enormous distances, the bad conditions of the roads, the shortage of vehicles and petrol and the small forces of Security Police and SD, it needs the utmost effort in order to be able to carry out shootings in the country. Nevertheless 41,000 Jews have been shot up to now. This number does not include those shot in operations by the former Einsatzkommandos. From estimated figures, about 19,000 partisans and criminals, that is in the majority Jews, were shot by the Armed Forces up to December 1941."[16]

In two months, Stahlecker estimated, the Commander in White Russia would be able to kill off the remaining 126,000.

In the area covered by Einsatzgruppe B there had lived in 1939 about 850,000 Jews, nearly half of them in former Polish territory. In the large formerly Polish cities such as Pinsk, Slonim and Baranovice, the large Jewish communities seem to have remained completely inert during the few days that preceded the German occupation. No news regarding the fate of the ghettos across the German demarcation line was permitted in the Russian press during the days of the German-Russian Pact. The violently anti-Jewish peasant population in this area—generally known as White Russia—also contributed to the defenselessness of the Jews. Nor did the substantial pro-Soviet resistance here during the German occupation change the popular attitudes. East of the Berezina River, however, the chances for escape were good because of the large distances between towns and the lack of all-weather roads. Einsatzgruppe B, which covered an area half of the size of western Europe, counted 45,000 Jews shot and killed five months after the German invasion, a slower killing rate than that of *Einsatzgruppe* A, but the Jews who had fled[17]—possibly as many as half a million—were caught by later sweeps as the German advance drove more deeply into Russia. For a short time, tanneries and tailoring workshops in the smaller towns and sledge-wagon workshops in Minsk and Lida were protected by the economic agencies of the Wehrmacht. White Russia also provided Jews the best if dubious hope for survival in partisan territory.

After a few months, *Einsatzgruppe* A took over this area and by the end of 1942, there was scarcely any longer a Jewish problem in White Russia. On November 23, 1942, the *Generalkommissar* of White Russia, Wilhelm Kube, wrote to Alfred Rosenberg's Ministry for the Occupied Eastern Territory and reported that the area had been reduced to 30,000 Jews, most of them still needed by the armament industries and railroads, but half of whom Kube intended to execute very soon. Fifty thousand had been killed in the Minsk area alone. In the letter, Kube also complained about the "excessive physical strain on the physical strength of the men in the S.D." necessitated by the "grave task to transfer continually new contingents of Jews from the Reich to their destiny." Kube claimed that he had his hands full coping with the partisans and Polish resistance as well as with the periodic executions of Jews. Would the Reich Commissioner please stop all further deportations of Jews into White Ruthenia?

Kube's pace of liquidation was not zealous enough, however. He was suspected of having misgivings about very drastic actions against Jews, and was known to particularly favor Reich Jews. Stahlecker had sent one of the toughest of his executioners, Dr. Juris Eduard Strauch, to keep an eye on Kube in Minsk. So far as the Russian Jews were concerned, according to Strauch, Kube could quiet his conscience because most of them were "partisan helpers." But he could not distinguish between Germans and German Jews. However, Kube's efforts to protect the "better Jews" was, at best, a delaying action. In the summer of 1943, a few months before Kube was killed by a woman employed in his household, Himmler had decided to liquidate the entire ghetto system. Ghettos were to be turned into concentration camps and their jurisdiction turned over to the S.S. and Police. Thus, by the end of 1943, the Jews in the East who had shrunk to some tens of thousands faced almost certain death.

Nevertheless, remnants in Minsk, Lida, Slonim, Baranovice and a few other White Russian ghettos survived for another year. In the fall of 1943, in the face of the overwhelming Russian advance, Himmler decreed the liquidation of any telltale traces. Grenades were thrown into cellars and bunkers where Jews had sought to hide. The dead in the streets and the living in the bunkers were included in the last conflagration of the Slonim Ghetto. At Baranovice, dogs rooted out the too hastily buried corpses.

At Novogorodek, a *kommando* killed Jews under the notorious Alfred Metzner, a civilian who first drove truckloads of Jews to the execution pits and then became a speed-killer, able to shoot victims for hours at a time, pausing only to load his carbine. Two hundred-odd Jews tunneled their way out of the completely enclosed ghetto on September 23 and had to be rounded up in the neighboring forest. A few survived the hunt.

When the civil administration took over part of the occupied territory in the Soviet Union in the summer of 1941, the *Einsatzgruppen* had already completed a large part of the ghettoization process. Moreover, as far as the Jews were concerned, there was not much difference between the agents of the RSHA and the civil commissars under Rosenberg's Ministry for the Occupied Eastern Countries. At Nuremberg, Rosenberg contended that his ministry had no hand in police measures in occupied Russia but this was a semantic nicety. On the eve of the German invasion of Russia he issued a "Brown Folder" which actually encouraged pogroms by the native populations (except where military security was involved) and "draconian measures" against Jews. Kube's superior, *Reichskommissar* of the Baltic States and White Russia, Hinrich Lohse, delivered an address to his staff on July 27, 1941, in which he said that the ghettos would receive only as much food as the rest of the population could do without, and that nothing was to interefere with his own oral instructions to the Security Police.[18] These instructions were carried out so zealously that Lohse's officials were known in Kovno as the "head-hunters." Lohse made sporadic efforts to intercede for essential Jewish workers, but the survival of some of the *Ostland* ghettos for a short time owed little to him. Rather, they owed most to General Georg Thomas in charge of the Armament Office. Rosenberg's ministry regulated general economic matters such as finance, labor and agriculture, but it had no control over war contracts. The continuous supervision of war production for the German Army, Navy and Air Force belonged to General Thomas.

Occasionally, there were bitter struggles between some of the civil officers, who tried to win over native populations and create viable communities by utilizing skilled labor, and the police forces who wanted to wipe out all Jews. Late in October 1941, a regional commissar of Sluzk in White Russia who served under *Generalkommissar* Kube, wrote him about a sadistic action carried out without his knowledge and "seriously impairing the prestige of the German nation."

> The town itself offered a picture of horror during the action. With indescribable brutality on the part of both the German police officers and particularly the Lithuanian partisans, the Jewish people, but also among them White Ruthenians, were taken out of their dwellings and herded together.
> Everywhere in the town shots were to be heard and in different streets the corpses of shot Jews accumulated. The White Ruthenians were in

greatest distress to free themselves from the encirclement. Regardless of the fact that the Jewish people, among whom were also tradesmen, were mistreated in a terribly barbarous way in the face of the White Ruthenian people, the White Ruthenians themselves were also worked over with rubber clubs and rifle butts. There was no question of an action against the Jews any more. It rather looked like a revolution. . . .

In several instances I literally had to expel with drawn pistol the German police officials as well as the Lithuanian partisans from the shops. . . . I was not present at the shooting before the town. But it should suffice, if I point out that persons shot have worked themselves out of their graves some time after they had been covered.[19]

The regional commissar had pleaded with the local battalion commander for a postponement of the killings, pointing out that Jews were working as skilled laborers and specialists, that White Russian mechanics were nonexistent. The commander did not contradict him but proceeded to encircle the Jewish quarter and start the massacre.

Kube was incensed by the regional commissar's report and sent a copy to Lohse and Rosenberg, adding a personal comment that the burial of seriously wounded people who could work themselves out of their graves was such a disgusting business that it ought to be reported to Hitler. Kube, apparently, still had his illusions. Meanwhile, vehicles loaded with ammunition for the armed forces were left standing in the streets of Sluzk. The Jewish drivers had been executed. Jewish specialists in the cannery were also killed and their work stood unattended. When questions were raised whether all Jews were to be killed regardless of the effect on the economy, Rosenberg's directive of December 18 swallowed them up; economic questions should not be considered in the solution of the Jewish problem, the directive stated. The armament industry gradually collapsed. Thousands of workers were "withdrawn"; ghettos were burned to the ground. Workshops that had once produced wooden carts, soap, candles, rope, leather and lumber for the German Army stood abandoned. There were no replacements for these thousands of Jews who toiled for the Army at a time when the lives of German soldiers were being dissolved by massive Soviet force, when they froze for lack of shoes and clothing, while Germans at home were wearing shoes with cardboard bottoms.

The greatest murder assignment of all in invaded Russia was given to *Einsatzgruppen* C and D. In their areas, the Soviet Ukraine Republic and eastern Galicia, annexed from Poland in 1939, lived the "reservoirs of Eastern Jewry" that had played such an important part in Nazi propaganda. There were two million Jews in this region. Many had fled the first drive, but before the end of 1941 between 150,000 and 200,000 had been killed in the Ukraine alone. The Nazi stampede across eastern Galicia was accompanied by pogroms in Lvov, Tarnopol, Zborow, Zloczow, and Drohobicz, with 7,000 killed in Lvov alone. By the beginning of July, *Einsatz-gruppe* C had already advanced well beyond Galicia. Four detachments were deployed across the width of the Ukraine from the Pripet Marshes to the Dniester. In the center of the line was Commando 4a, under the leadership of a Dusseldorf architect, Paul Blobel, who was to achieve a record for Jewish mass executions. Blobel was attached to the Sixth Army, commanded by Walter von Reichenau. Blobel first met Reichenau on June 26 at Sokal, where he had established his headquarters on a splendid Polish estate on the banks of the Bug River. He was walking about in a bathing suit, giving meticulous instructions to his aides. One included an order to Blobel to reduce the customary five rifle shots per victim to two in the case of Jews. While strutting about, he commented to Blobel on the "Führer Order" and the necessity for total ruthlessness.

Blobel's unit shot 2,531 Jews in Zhitomir in the last week in July and enclosed the survivors in a ghetto. Then his unit went into the main towns of the western Ukraine—Korosten, Berdichev, Uman, and Vinnitsa—and conducted further massacres. Back once more at Zhitomir within a few weeks, Blobel spoke to the garrison commander who agreed with him that the creation of the ghetto had "not stopped the gossiping and mischief of the Jews." Accordingly, he supplied Blobel with twelve army trucks and sixty Ukrainian helpers and had graves dug by Russian prisoners of war. Then 3,145 more Jews were executed. But it is with the mass killings of the Jews of Kiev that Blobel is chiefly associated.

On September 19, the day of the second massacre at Zhitomir, the Germans entered Kiev. The defense of Kiev had lasted forty-five days. It had cost the Russians an entire army group but was a dearly won victory for the Germans who, according to some military strategists, should not have fought the battle at all, but concentrated on the Moscow front.[20] A few days after the Germans entered the city, a big explosion rocked the Continental Hotel, headquarters of one of the commands. The fires spread rapidly and in fighting them hundreds of German soldiers were killed. The Kiev Jews were made reprisal victims. Notices were posted ordering Jews to report for "resettlement." They were marched in small groups, with their "resettlement" bundles, past the Jewish cemetery at the outer limits of the city to the Babi Yar ravine coiling in the sand dunes and there executed. The killing rate, almost 35,000 in two days, was unequaled even by the death factories of Treblinka and Auschwitz.

On October 22, 1944, W. H. Lawrence of the *New York Times* was shown over the Babi Yar ravine by M. Aloshin, the Kiev city architect, who told him that "a German architect" had boasted to him of the slaughter. After the war, Blobel admitted to killing only 16,000 Jews; to a Gestapo expert on church affairs, Albert Hartel, he seemed more proprietary. While the two men were driving together near Kiev early in

machine-gunned in groups of two and three hundred during the winter of 1941–42.

In the Ukraine, the Armament Inspectorate viewed the massacres with misgiving, but did not fight about the issue. On December 2, 1941, the Armament Inspector sent a letter to General Thomas enclosing a report from an economics expert, Professor Peter Seraphim of Göttingen University. The inspector pointed out that Seraphim's report was personal, not official, but that he, the inspector, agreed with the statements "in all respects." Seraphim wrote that "the kind of solution of the Jewish problem applied in the Ukraine" was based on "ideological theories," not on economic considerations, with the result that the elimination of Jews "had far-reaching economic consequences and even direct consequences for the armament industry." These Jews, Seraphim continued, represented industrial and commercial manpower badly needed and even indispensable to the armed forces. He wrote:

> The attitude of the Jewish population was anxious—obliging from the beginning. They tried to avoid everything that might displease the German administration. That they hated the German administration and army inwardly goes without saying and cannot be surprising. However, there is no proof that Jewry as a whole or even to a greater extent was implicated in acts of sabotage. Surely, there were some terrorists or saboteurs among them just as among the Ukrainians. But it cannot be said that the Jews as such represented a danger to the German armed forces. The output produced by Jews who, of course, were prompted by nothing but the feeling of fear was satisfactory to the troops and the German administration. . . .
>
> It [the planned shooting] was done entirely in public with the use of the Ukrainian militia and unfortunately in many instances also with members of the armed forces taking part voluntarily. The way these actions . . . were carried out was horrible. The great masses executed make this action more gigantic than any similar measure taken so far in the Soviet Union. So far about 150,000 to 200,000 Jews may have been executed in the part of the Ukraine belonging to the *Reichskommissariat*; no consideration was given to the interests of economy.[24]

Professor Seraphim then raised the overriding question in a rueful, rhetorical aside: "If we shoot the Jews, let the prisoners of war perish, condemn considerable parts of the urban population by hunger during the next year, the question remains unanswered: Who in all the world is then supposed to produce economic values here? In view of the manpower bottleneck in the German Reich, there is no doubt that the necessary number of Germans will not be available either now or in the near future."

But the killers had first and last claim.

In the Crimea, the area of *Einsatzgruppe D*, the Romanian share in the massacres was very substantial. On October 22, 1941, a delayed-action land mine destroyed the former Russian NKVD building in Odessa, which had become the headquarters of the Romanian 10th Division and the town commandant's office. Some German and Romanian officers were killed.

The Romanians then applied the formula adopted by the Germans in Kiev—retaliation against the Jews. Between October 23 and 25, 26,000 Odessa Jews were massacred. German reports on October 26 accused Jews of resistance activity directed from the Great Synagogue, suggesting that the Germans may have been behind the massacre. The executions, however, were carried out by Romanian soldiers. Since early October, two of Ohlendorf's detachments had stood waiting vainly to enter the city. The Romanians wanted to deal with the Odessa Jews without German interference. (The Germans had blocked them from a too-premature dumping of deported Jews from newly acquired Bukovina and Bessarabia.)

Ohlendorf finally had to give up the area between the Dniester and Bug, complaining as he quit his headquarters at Ananiev in August, that some of the German colonists in the area "considered Jews quite innocent people" and even appointed Jewish political leaders. His large-scale killings had begun in September in Nikolaiev, Kherson, and Melitopol. In November, he moved his headquarters again, this time from Nikolaiev to Simferopol in the Crimea, which was also the headquarters of Field Marshal Manstein's 11th Army. Ohlendorf claimed that Manstein wanted the shooting completed before Christmas. Accordingly, *Einsatzgruppe* D, with the assistance of Army personnel, Army trucks and gasoline, completed the shooting of 9,600 in time to permit Christmas celebrations in a city without Jews.[25] Ohlendorf's adjutant Heinz Schubert supervised the executions, making sure that the non-Jewish population was not disturbed. He also checked to see that the victims were shot "humanely," since in "the event of other killing methods, the psychic burden would have been too great for the execution *kommando*."

The entire area of the Crimea was declared free of Jews by April 16, 1942, and in June, Ohlendorf returned to Germany, having directed the killing of 90,000 Jews.

In the drives early in 1942, the Army gave extensive cooperation not only in the Crimea but in all of the military areas. General Manstein's order is particularly instructive, for he was a severely professional soldier who disliked many features of National Socialism. Like many other German military commanders, however, he subscribed to the line taken early in the war by the German High Command that Jews instigated partisan warfare and constituted destructive political and cultural influences. Elaborating on von Reichenau's order on "subhuman Jewry," which was copied for distribution to the 11th (Manstein's) and 18th Armies, Manstein explained that the Jew was the middleman between the Red Army on the front and the enemy in the rear. He said:

> The Jewish-Bolshevist system must be exterminated. The German soldier comes as the bearer of a racial concept. [He] must appreciate the necessity for the harsh punishment of Jewry. . . . The food situation at home makes

it essential that the troops should be fed off the land, and that the largest possible stocks should be placed at the disposal of the homeland. In enemy cities, a large part of the population will have to go hungry. Nothing, out of a misguided sense of humanity, may be given to prisoners of war or to the population, unless they are in the service of the Wehrmacht.[26]

The extent of Army cooperation in the executions surpassed the wildest expectations of the Einsatzgruppen and exceeded by far the minimum support functions guaranteed in the Heydrich-Wagner agreement. There are numerous testimonials to Army help—and more—by the killing kommandos. In midsummer 1941, a unit in Einsatzgruppe C reported: "Armed forces surprisingly welcome hostility against Jews." On September 8, Einsatzgruppe D reported that relations with the military were "excellent." The Army went out of its way to turn Jews over to the shooting squads, to join in killing operations, and to shoot Jewish hostages in "reprisal" for "attacks" on German forces. In some towns, commanders did not even wait for the pretext of sabotage, but requested anti-Jewish actions as "precautionary" measures. The 17th Army ordered reprisal shooting of Jews whenever sabotage could not be traced to the Ukrainian population. "We must convey the impression that we are just," explained the commander. "Whenever the perpetrator of an act of sabotage cannot be found, Ukrainians are not to be blamed. In such cases, reprisals are therefore to be carried out only against Jews and Russians."[27]

After a time, the growing callousness to death made some of the military impatient to keep up the killings when the Einsatzgruppen begged off for lack of personnel.

The erosion of the traditional military respect for prisoners of war completed the Wehrmacht surrender to the Nazi state. On July 16, 1941, Heydrich concluded an agreement with the chief of the General Armed Forces Office, General Hermann Reinecke. The text of the agreement provided that the Wehrmacht was to "free itself" from all Soviet prisoners of war who were carriers of Bolshevism.[28] The RSHA and the Army agreed that "special measures" would be carried out free from bureaucratic controls. Within a day of the signing of the agreement, Heydrich alerted his regional machinery to prepare for the selection of all "professional revolutionaries, Red Army political officers, fanatical Communists and all Jews" among the prisoners of war pouring into the Government-General and the Reich. The screening teams consisted of Einsatzgruppen who entered the prisoner-of-war camps where the Army had already done some preparatory screening and had sifted out "given appropriate elements." By December 1941, 22,000 Soviet prisoners had been thus selected, out of which 16,000 (both Jewish and non-Jewish) were killed. Later figures on such screenings are not available. Altogether more than four million Soviet prisoners perished in German camps.

Another marked change in Army mentality is revealed in discussions and conferences on the handling of prisoners suffering from some "incurable" disease such as tuberculosis or syphilis. The prisoner-of-war chief, Hans von Graevenitz, and a number of other Army officers, including physicians, suggested that Department IV-A of the RSHA take over such prisoners and kill them. This time, the Gestapo men demurred, pointing out that they could not be expected to act as hangmen for the Wehrmacht.[29]

In the war crimes trials, most of the Army generals pleaded that their hands had been tied by agreements between the High Command and the RSHA, while Himmler's police generals hid behind his comprehensive sin-canceling orders. Over a million and a half murders were thus blown about and dissipated like an anonymous vapor, uncaused and inconsequential. Yet the carefully, even exaggeratedly, written daily bulletins reporting the swelling lists of Jewish dead were feverishly compiled. The *Einsatzgruppen* were meticulous recorders. Each *kommando* sent regular reports to its respective *Einsatz* group where they were processed and relayed by radio, teletype and in written summary form to headquarters in Berlin, Section IV A-1 of the RSHA (War Crimes and Enemy Propaganda Question). From July 1941 to March 1942, reports streamed in and were assembled in the form of daily bulletins.

There were occasional military protests against the barbarous executions, but among these the main criticism is on the method of killing—the brutal open-air shootings—which did not conform to "German conceptions." The fact that Jews had to be killed in order to "solve" the Jewish problem was widely accepted. One of the very few adverse reactions was registered by a Major Rösler, a regimental commander in Zhitomir, who was an eyewitness to the exterminations of the Jews of that city at the end of July 1941. One day while sitting at headquarters, he heard rifle volleys and pistol shots. Two other officers accompanied him in the direction of the gunfire. From all directions, soldiers and civilians were running toward a railroad embankment. What he saw there, he wrote, was "so brutally base that those who approached unprepared were shaken and nauseated." Rösler stood over a ditch splattered with blood. Policemen were standing around with bloodstained uniforms. Soldiers congregated in groups, some of them in bathing shorts. Civilians were watching with their wives and children. Rösler looked into the grave. Among the corpses he saw an old man with a white beard and a cane on his arm. The man was still breathing. Rösler wrote:

> I saw nothing like it either in the First World War or during the Civil War in Russia, or in the Western campaign. I have seen many unpleasant things, having been a member of the Free Corps in 1919, but I never saw anything like this. I cannot begin to conceive the legal decisions on whose basis these executions were carried out. Everything that is happening here

seems to be absolutely incompatible with our views on education and morality. Right out in the open, as if on a stage, men murder other men. I must add that according to the accounts of the soldiers, who often see spectacles of this kind, hundreds of people are thus killed daily.[30]

Rösler's horrified reaction is unusual for the time, and yet, in his words, too, there is something still repressed. Not once does he mention the fact that the people being killed are Jews.

Among the troops, as Rösler intimated, the shootings had become sensational experiences. The soldiers not only killed and watched but took pictures, wrote letters and talked about the shootings until the news spread in the occupied territory and in Germany. Foreign journalists began to ask embarrassing questions. Not only were soldiers glued to the spectacles—it became impossible to conceal the killing sites from involuntary as well as voluntary observers.

Having unleashed the murderous impulses of the soldiers and goaded them to hate and kill without letup, certain Army officials then tried to moderate the blood lust. They urged the *Einsatzgruppen* to do their killing by night. They scolded soldiers for watching the executions and tried to make them feel ashamed of gazing at "disgusting excesses." They forbade them from taking photographs. A strenuous effort was made to stop arbitrary shootings by the soldiers themselves. At the same time, the troops had to accept the historical necessity that Jews had to be killed and stand ready to obey orders to help the S.S. and Police kill them. But —and this was crucial—a soldier must not kill for the sake of killing, or because he wanted to, but because he "overcame" himself to kill and killed with self-control, in keeping with the disciplinary traditions of the German Army. With such tortured refinements, the Army tried to cope with the problem of "excesses." Eventually, of course, the fear that the world would know what was happening even deep within Russia and the need for swift annihilation led the Nazis to contrive the technical improvements at the gassing camps where the secrecy of mass exterminations could be guarded more easily.

For the individual men in the *Einsatzgruppen*, there was no problem of "excesses." They lived in a world perforated by acts of killing and the sight of bleeding, quivering corpses—a world in which murder was a civic duty. Many of the men had enlisted in the Army but had drifted into the killing units because they were unfit for front-line duty. They got used to their work with the help of ever larger doses of alcohol. Their commanders, however, had to find justifications for the killings not only for the men but for themselves. They also had to overcome weaknesses of their own, including the possible charge of cowardice. They did not do the shooting; they supervised and reported the executions. But they could not be mere spectators or reporters. They had to share fully in the work of their men. One staff officer of *Einsatzgruppe* C has explained this compulsion: "I myself attended executions only as a witness, in order not to lay myself open to charges of cowardice. . . . Dr. Rasch [commander] insisted on principle that all officers and noncommissioned officers of the *Kommando* participate in the executions. It was impossible to stay away from them, lest one be called to account."[31]

The fiction of the Jewish danger was used in every possible variation in speeches of the commanders to their men. The Jews were held responsible for acts of sabotage, for spreading rumors, for starting fires and attacking German troops, for spreading disease, for unhygienic living conditions, for threatening ethnic German colonies, for the dangerous Jewish "influence." The supply of rationalizations never ran out, and only occasionally did the *Einsatzgruppen* balk at taking on a killing. This happened not because the men were squeamish but because they objected to doing the Army's work.

Together with the justifications was an elaborate language screen to avoid the blunt fact of murder. "Killing" and "murder" were never used in the *Einsatzgruppen* reports. Rather, words were devised to repress the deed of murder, obscure it, or justify it. The German language gave great scope for this kind of evasiveness. The *Einsatzgruppen* reports refer to actions (*Aktionen*), resettlement (*Aussiedlung*), cleansing (*Säuberung*), special treatment (*Sonderbehandlung*), elimination (*Ausschaltung*), and executive measure (*Exekutivmassnahme*)—never to killing. This enabled the killers to convey the impression that they were engaged in casual bureaucratic processes.

The *Einsatzgruppen* had rolled forward six hundred miles into Russian territory in their first sweep. Five hundred thousand Jews had been killed but at least two million were still alive in this area—a crushing burden for the killing units to contemplate. The sheer immensity of the numbers seemed unconquerable.

The demands of the killing operations had to temporarily give way under the immensity of the numbers, and the problem of a labor shortage. An intermediate period followed, during which the *Einsatzgruppen* wedged Jews into closed districts, marked them, appointed Jewish Councils, and put labor columns at the disposal of the Army and *Organization Todt*, the Reich agency in charge of construction. The Polish-type ghetto was introduced into occupied Russia as a preliminary to death.

The ghettos in Russia were formed to facilitate the second sweep of the *Einsatzgruppen*, which aimed at total obliteration of Jewish life in the East. Himmler's police forces were increased and engulfed the *Einsatzgruppen* themselves during the frenzied second round to kill off every trace of Jewish life, in woods and swamps and underground earthen bunkers as well as in towns and villages not yet made dead. Isolated Jews fleeing alone or in small groups were hunted down relentlessly, and whatever restraints may have checked the Army before were now gone. The killers, by now drunk most of the time, became intoxicated by days and nights of slaughter. The ghettos tremulously waited for their end.

The systematic concentration of Jews was left to the military and civilian authorities which had overall governmental functions in the occupied territories. The primary task of the military administration and Rosenberg's commissariats was to prepare for the second sweep of the *Einsatzgruppen* chiefly through the creation of ghettos. This is made clear in the order of *Reichskommissar* Lohse of the *Ostland:* * ". . . these provisional directives are designed only to assure minimum measures by the general and district commissars in those areas where—and so long as—further measures in the sense of the final solution of the Jewish question are not possible."³²

In the directives for Lithuania, there were quite detailed orders prefiguring the future. In addition to the marking of Jews, registrations and the formation of Councils, there were instructions to have telephones and telephone lines ripped out of the ghettos. All postal services were to be cut off. Whenever bridges had to be built over ghetto thoroughfares, the bridges were to be enclosed with barbed wire. Jews were forbidden to tear down doors, window frames or floors for fuel.³³ However, none of these details was to be published. In an extraordinary attempt at secrecy, Lohse ordered his subordinates to "get by with oral instructions to the Jewish councils."

The pacing of the "Final Solution" became a matter of some controversy and the economic indispensability of Jews was argued heatedly by certain Nazis. Even among the *Einsatzgruppen* commanders, there is on record one view that killing Jews might not, after all, solve all of Germany's problems—certainly not those of the Ukraine. In a report of *Einsatzgruppe* C, dated September 17, 1941, there is a strange note of discouragement: the vast Communist apparatus will still remain after the elimination of all Jews:

> Even if it were possible to shut out Jewry 100 per cent, we would not eliminate the center of political danger.
> The Bolshevist work is done by Jews, Russians, Georgians, Armenians, Poles, Latvians, Ukrainians; the Bolshevist apparatus is by no means identical with the Jewish population. Under such conditions we would miss the goal of political security if we replaced the main task of destroying the Communist machine with the relatively easier one of eliminating the Jews. . . .
> In the western and central Ukraine almost all urban workers, skilled mechanics and traders are Jews. If we renounce the Jewish labor potential in full, we cannot build up the urban administrative centers.³⁴

* *Reichskommissariat Ostland* comprised Lithuania, Latvia, Estonia, and part of White Russia (see map, p. 271).

The conclusion drawn is that the Germans must utilize Jewish labor, yes—but in the way that has been "utilized" in the Government-General —labor utilization leading to a "gradual liquidation." The Jews, in the last analysis, were at the disposal of the civil and military authorities only at the pleasure of the S.S. and Police.

The killers had first claim, but some Jews kept working during the winter and spring of 1942. They tried desperately to make themselves indispensable and became terrified at the thought of losing their Ausweise, working cards. A survivor has described the fever to work in the midst of a perishing Jewish world:

> The priceless Ausweise were too provocative a weapon for the police to let alone. Originally they were issued by the civil government commissars to guarantee Jewish labor against "resettlement," but the police periodically recalled the Ausweise and issued new ones in their place, creating an ongoing torment and blackmail. The certificates were cancelled from day to day and the colors were changed so that no Jew could ever feel secure with his quicksilver certificate.

While the first Einsatzgruppen sweep churned through the Crimea and Caucasus toward the end of 1941, a second had already begun in the Baltic. Himmler now aimed to destroy all remaining Soviet Jews. The killing machinery was larger and their operations were better coordinated. The forces of the Einsatzgruppen were now swamped by those of the greatly expanded S.S. and Police throughout Russia. By the late summer of 1942, Hitler had centralized antipartisan fighting and had given over to Himmler's forces all antipartisan operations in civilian areas. The antipartisan chief, Erich von dem Bach-Zalewski, could draw on Army personnel, S.S. units, police regiments and Einsatzgruppen for any operation and for any length of time. Under this guise, all of these units killed thousands of Jews in woods and swamps. The Ostland and Ukraine were bloodied by waves of massacres. A frenzy of killing possessed civil commissars as well as soldiers and S.S. units. Between August and November 1942, 363,211 Jews were killed in the districts of Bialystok, the Caucasus and the Ukraine.[35] Ghetto after ghetto was wiped out. On October 5, 1942, a German civilian construction engineer employed by a Solingen building firm under contract by the Army to erect grain storage buildings in Dubno watched the annihilation of the Dubno Ghetto in the Ukraine. Hermann Friedrich Graebe's affidavit froze the Nuremberg Court with pity and horror. It is a document which must stand as one of the most terrifying in the literature of the Holocaust:

> On 5 October 1942, when I visited the building office at Dubno, my foreman Hubert Moennikes . . . told me that in the vicinity of the site, Jews from Dubno had been shot in three large pits, each about 30 meters long and 3 meters deep. About 1,500 persons had been killed daily. All of the

5,000 Jews who had still been living in Dubno before the pogrom were to be liquidated. As the shootings had taken place in his presence he was still much upset.

Thereupon I drove to the site, accompanied by Moennikes and saw near it great mounds of earth, about 30 meters long and 2 meters high. Several trucks stood in front of the mounds. Armed Ukrainian militia drove the people off the trucks under the supervision of an S.S. man. The militia men acted as guards on the trucks and drove them to and from the pit. All these people had the regulation yellow patches on the front and back of their clothes, and thus could be recognized as Jews.

Moennikes and I went directly to the pits. Nobody bothered us. Now I heard rifle shots in quick succession, from behind one of the earth mounds. The people who had got off the trucks—men, women and children of all ages—had to undress upon the order of an S.S. man who carried a riding or dog whip. They had to put down their clothes in fixed places, sorted according to shoes, top clothing, and underclothing. I saw a heap of shoes of about 800 to 1,000 pairs, great piles of under-linen and clothing. Without screaming or weeping these people undressed, stood around in family groups, kissed each other, said farewells and waited for a sign from another S.S. man, who stood near the pit, also with a whip in his hand.

During the fifteen minutes that I stood near the pit, I heard no complaint or plea for mercy. I watched a family of about 8 persons, a man and woman, both about 50, with their children of about 1, 8 and 10, and two grown-up daughters of about 20 to 24. An old woman with snow-white hair was holding the one-year old child in her arms and singing to it and tickling it. The child was cooing with delight. The couple were looking on with tears in their eyes. The father was holding the hand of a boy of about 10 years old and speaking to him softly; the boy was fighting his tears. The father pointed toward the sky, stroked his head, and seemed to explain something to him. At that moment the S.S. man at the pit shouted something to his comrade. The later counted off about 20 persons and instructed them to go behind the earth mound. Among them was the family which I have mentioned.

I well remember a girl, slim and with black hair, who, as she passed close to me, pointed to herself and said, "Twenty-three!" I walked around the mound, and found myself confronted by a tremendous grave. People were closely wedged together and lying on top of each other so that only their heads were visible. Nearly all had blood running over their shoulders from their heads. Some of the people shot were still moving. Some were lifting their arms and turning their heads to show that they were still alive. The pit was already two-thirds full. I estimated that it already contained about a thousand people.

I looked for the man who did the shooting. He was an S.S. man, who sat at the edge of the narrow end of the pit, his feet dangling into the pit. He had a tommy gun on his knees and he was smoking a cigarette. The people, completely naked, went down some steps which were cut in the clay wall of the pit and clambered over the heads of the people lying there, to the place where the S.S. man directed them. They lay down in front of the dead or injured people; some caressed those who were still alive and spoke to them in a low voice. Then I heard a series of shots.

I looked into the pit and saw that the bodies were twitching or the heads lying already motionless on top of the bodies that lay before them. Blood was running from their necks. I was surprised that I was not ordered away, but I saw that there were two or three postmen in uniform nearby. The next batch was approaching already. They went down into the pit, lined themselves up against the previous victims and were shot.

When I walked back, around the mound, I noticed another truckload of people which had just arrived. This time it included sick and infirm people. An old, very thin woman with terribly thin legs was undressed by others who were already naked, while two people held her up. The woman appeared to be paralyzed. The naked people carried the woman around the mound. I left with Moennikes and drove in my car back to Dubno.

On the morning of the next day when I again visited the site, I saw about 30 naked people lying near the pit—about 30 to 50 meters away from it. Some of them were still alive; they looked straight in front of them with a fixed stare and seemed to notice neither the chilliness of the morning nor the workers of my firm who stood around. A girl of about 20 spoke to me and asked me to give her clothes and help her escape. At that moment we heard a fast car approach and I noticed that it was an S.S. detail. I moved away to my site. Ten minutes later we heard shots from the vicinity of the pit. The Jews still alive had been ordered to throw the corpses into the pit— then they themselves had to lie down in this to be shot in the neck.[36]

Thus were erased from history hundreds of thousands of such Jews, buried in nameless pits.

The extreme closeness of living family ties among eastern European Jews condemned many to await the fatal shot in the neck with resignation. To take flight meant abandoning parents, children, and wives, living like a hunted animal in the forests with no hiding place anywhere and haunted always by the guilt of flight. Those who did escape from the edge of the killing-pits were often denounced by local peasants and rejected or killed by anti-Semitic partisan units. Many were driven to return to the old ghetto or seek out a new one when life in the wilderness became unbearable; either meant certain death. The hardiest could sometimes survive in underground pits, with walls of seeping manure, sunless and airless, where all being and becoming were dissolved in the pit and all life the gasping for breath and the scurrying of rats, where time streamed back and forth, incessant and meaningless.

In the last days of the second sweep of the *Einsatzgruppen* in midsummer 1942, the problem of exposure of the massacres to the world concerned Himmler. Photographs had leaked out and were thought to have reached the United States. A special unit under Blobel, who organized the Kiev massacre, was ordered to erase the traces of *Einsatzgruppen* executions in the East. Blobel formed a special *Kommando*, called 1005, to dig up graves and burn the bodies. He began his operations in Chelmno, where he tried to eliminate mass graves by using dynamite. Himmler had said that even the ashes must disappear. But this method was unsuccessful and Blobel then tried constructing vast pyres of iron rails and wooden sleepers. One of the pits he had to dig up was in the Babi Yar ravine; it measured sixty yards long and more than eight feet deep.

It has been estimated that by the end of 1942 more than a million Jews had been killed as a result of the *Einsatzgruppen* operations.

By the end of 1942, the focus of attention shifted to the *Ostland*, where 100,000 or more Jews still survived, most of them in ghettos or concentration camps and several thousand roaming the forests and marshes. As Kube had already indicated, the reduction of the ghettos in that area was a "slow" process because remnants of Jewish skilled labor still survived. In this region, Jewish resistance also flared in the ghettos of Vilna, Riga and Kovno.

Distances in the *Ostland* were vast, particularly in White Russia, and some escapes into untracked wastelands could be organized by ghetto fugitives. Some survived illicitly in the partisan-controlled areas; some worked themselves into Red Army partisan units. The most dogged survived in the family camps, in which Jews refused to give up their family ties, camps in which a strange, almost eerie, human existence echoed out of the duff of the forest floor.

15 Nazi-Occupied Russia

THE JEWS IN THE SOVIET UNION were the first to be marked for extermination, and their losses, next to those of Polish Jewry, constitute the greatest of the Holocaust. It has been estimated that a total of 1,400,000 Jews perished during the Nazi invasion of the Soviet Union, most of them executed in the *Einsatzgruppen* killing sweeps.[1] Many thousands were also killed by German and Romanian soldiers, S.S. and Police units and so-called anti-partisan forces in the area of the *Einsatzgruppen* operations. About one million Jews successfully eluded the German advance. Possibly another million were saved in the general evacuation of civilians by the Soviet Government, by migrations to Central Asia and by random flight.

About 3,000,000 Jews were officially counted in the Soviet census of 1939. However, an additional two million Jews came under the jurisdiction of the Soviet Union between September 1939 and June 1940. Their losses were staggering. Official Soviet policy toward its Jews has been variable, elusive and enigmatic. At times it has fostered Jewish cultural expression; more often it has obliterated it. As it has frequently been suggested that government policy during the war made the Nazi decimations easier, an examination of the life of the Jews in the annexed areas sheds some light on later events. Much, however, still remains to be known of this pre-war period. Soviet unpreparedness for the war and the Nazi occupation of the country also profoundly affected the fate of Soviet Jews.

In September 1939, the eastern part of Poland was annexed to the Soviet Union and resident Jews in this area, in addition to numerous Polish-Jewish refugees who had fled from Nazi-occupied territories, came under Soviet rule. In June and July 1940, the three Baltic republics of Lithuania, Latvia and Estonia, in which 255,000 Jews lived, were annexed. In June 1940, Romania "returned" Bessarabia and northern Bukovina to the Soviet Union. Approximately 330,000 additional Jews came under Soviet rule. These new provinces were incorporated into the Ukrainian and White Russian Soviet republics of the USSR.

When the Red Army entered these annexed territories, the Soviet authorities began to integrate the new citizens within the administrative, economic, cultural and social frameworks that had crystallized in the USSR during the 1930's. Life in the new areas took on a definite Soviet pattern and all vestiges of the former regimes were wiped out. For Jews, this meant the extinction of a traditional religious and cultural life. A policy of Ukrainization and White-Russification was followed, bringing into political and social prominence Ukrainian and White Russian anti-Semitic nationalists. Jewish cultural and economic life was suppressed while the presence of many Jewish refugees from western, Nazi-occupied Poland who tried to maintain contact with their families on the Nazi side of the border increased the suspicions of the already suspicious Soviet NKVD (secret police) officials. Jews were accused of spying for the Nazis, and mass arrests, investigations and deportations occurred.[2] In the eastern Polish provinces occupied by the Soviets, over a million Jews had greeted the Red Army in 1939 as their savior from the Nazis. The Jews seemed to believe that the Russians would live and let live. They were not unduly concerned at first with the elimination of private enterprise and believed that they could adapt themselves to changed conditions. But this initial feeling of sympathy toward Soviet Russia passed quickly.

In the first stage of the Russian occupation, there had been evidence of Soviet concern for the welfare of the refugees, but this attitude was based largely on political considerations and did not last long. Desiring to win over the native as well as the refugee populations, the Soviet Government realized that their liberation from former Polish *pans* (masters) required proof of a better regime. However, this attitude soon gave way to a much harsher one dictated by Soviet ideological concerns and possibly influenced by the negative reactions of the refugees to life under a Soviet regime. Many of them were openly critical of Soviet regimentation and outspoken in their preference for the western way of life. They tended to concentrate in large already crowded cities such as Bialystok, Lvov, Pinsk and Rovno, and aggravated existing housing and food problems. Meanwhile, the refugees themselves suffered under the drastic new economic and social changes.

Many young Jews registered for work in the Ural coal mines. Some moved to Byelorussia and the Ukraine and even to Russia proper, finding work in industrial plants and collectives. The Jewish middle class was rapidly pauperized under the forced Soviet nationalization measures; small shopkeepers were ruined. Unable to obtain employment in the government because of their middle-class past, many had to live by the sale of personal belongings or support of relatives. The greater part of the Jewish intelligentsia, with the exception of teachers, also lost the means of earning a living. Political measures were likewise harsh. Jewish youths were forced to join the *Komsomol*, the Communist youth organization. Bundists and Zionists were arrested and many Jewish organizations and institutions were closed down as a matter of policy. Jews were thereafter exposed to conditions of a police regime, forced to live by government orders and suspected of conspiratorial activities because of the traffic across the border into Nazi-occupied Poland where many of the families of the refugees still lived. These connections and interests created a flow of activity which Soviet officials considered dangerous, and toward the end of 1939 the frontier was closed. No new refugees were permitted to enter or leave the Soviet zone.

By this time possibly as many as 200,000 refugee Jews had crossed into Soviet territory. Soviet authorities assumed that they would all become Soviet citizens and would immediately take out citizenship papers.

In March 1940, a "Repatriation Census" was carried out among the refugees. Those who objected to Soviet citizenship—a status which entailed restricted movement forbidding them to reside in border areas and large cities—were expelled in June to remote camps and villages in the Autonomous Republic of Komi and to Eastern Siberia. (This exile lasted until the amnesty of August 1941 when most of the refugees left the frigid Siberian zones and trekked to warmer regions in Central Asia.)

But many Jews hesitated or balked altogether at the idea of becoming Soviet citizens. Many were still separated from their families and hoped ultimately to rejoin them and go to Palestine or the United States. Soviet citizenship seemed a very dubious blessing. Some hoped that from Nazi-occupied Poland they would be able to smuggle themselves over the frontier to Slovakia or Italy. Other reasons prompted Jews to register for repatriation to Poland. Several thousand of these registrants were arrested by Soviet officials, and in a few cities, hunts were conducted for Jews who refused to take out Soviet papers. Registration to return to Poland provided Soviet officials with one reason for deporting Jewish refugees to Siberia.

Mass Soviet deportations started early in 1940 and continued in several waves until the outbreak of war in June 1941. Estimates of the number of Jews involved in the deportations range from 50,000 to half a million. A semi-official source puts the figure at 250,000, which is considered fairly reliable. The deportees—among whom were many non-Jewish Poles—were treated brutally. In the available fragmentary reports, the details are reminiscent of the Nazi deportations. Many died of hunger, disease and overwork at the camps in northern Russia and Siberia. However, there were no exterminations. With the outbreak of war, another 150,000 Jews from eastern Poland escaped the first German onslaught and fled east deep into Russia.

Although exceptions can be cited, a generally negative attitude toward the Jewish refugees was to become a fairly consistent feature of later Soviet policy.[3] In the period following the German invasion, the question

Baltic Sea

ESTONIA

Riga

LATVIA

LITHUANIA

GERMANY

Warsaw

BIALYSTOK DISTRICT

WHITE RUSSIAN S.S.R.

Slonim

GOVERNMENT-

Lvov

GENERAL

HUNGARY

Arad

Cluj

Jassy

Leningrad

REICHSKOMMISSARIAT OSTLAND

Einsatzgruppe A

U.S.S.R.

Smolensk

Moscow

Einsatzgruppe B

Minsk

Volhynia – Podolia

Rovno

Einsatzgruppe C

Kiev

Kursk

M I L I T A R Y   A R E A

Stalingrad

REICHSKOMMISSARIAT UKRAINE

TRANSNISTRIA

BESSARABIA

Einsatzgruppe D

Odessa

Rostov

Sea of
Azov

ROMANIA

Bucharest

Black Sea

Constanza

CRIMEA

Simferopol

Caucasus Mts.

BULGARIA

Istanbul

T U R K E Y

GERMAN OCCUPATION OF U.S.S.R., 1941–42

—I—I—I— Extent of German advance

— — — — Western boundary, U.S.S.R., June 22, 1941

of Polish-Jewish refugees also became an important counter in the political relations between the Soviet Union and the Polish Government-in-Exile. The fate of the refugees was discussed during the war, but could be determined only after the Nazi armies were flung back.

In planning the war against Russia, Hitler felt certain that Britain would quickly give up the struggle after the French defeat. Not for a moment dreaming that the British would fight on, Hitler was convinced that he could take a completely free hand in the east—the chief reason for the Western Campaign—and set about offering a moderate peace to Great Britain. Peace feelers were sent out to Churchill from Sweden, the United States and the Vatican but they were rebuffed. The British doggedly held firm. Only the restoration of the national independence of Czechoslovakia, Poland, Norway, Denmark, Holland, Belgium and France —the undoing of all of Hitler's phenomenal triumphs—would satisfy Churchill. This stand of the British completely baffled Hitler, but when it hardened, he shifted his emphasis and cunningly maneuvered to rally the German people to fight against a country that disdained peace, thereby, as he had so often done, making the enemy responsible for subsequent events.

Neither Hitler, the High Command, nor the General Staff, however, had a clear plan for prosecuting a war with Great Britain[4]—it simply was never blueprinted. This fateful neglect proved to be one of the great turning points of the war and indeed of the short life of the Third Reich and of the meteoric career of Adolf Hitler.

Operation "Sea Lion," the invasion of England, frequently postponed and mulled over, finally had to be completely given up. Göring's Luftwaffe, instead of driving British planes from the skies, suffered blows from which it never recovered. Britain could not be bombed into submission and a landing could not be effectively organized.

Meanwhile, Hitler's plan for an attack on Russia, which was never far from his mind, began to ripen. Stalin took advantage of Germany's preoccupation with England in the summer of 1940 and took the three Baltic provinces of Lithuania, Latvia and Estonia and the Romanian provinces of Bessarabia and northern Bukovina, which Germany depended on for oil and foodstuffs. These territorial grabs were not part of the Nazi-Soviet Pact and kindled Hitler's resentment.

In the middle of November, Molotov, the stubborn and wily Soviet Foreign Minister, went to Berlin to discuss a four-power pact among Germany, Italy, Japan and Russia and legitimate spheres of interest for all. Hitler talked in a vague, grandiose way about the end of the British Empire and the New Order in Europe. He implied that Russia could have the Bosporus and Dardanelles while Germany would take the rest of the

Balkans. But Molotov was tough and relentless. He made counter-demands for precise demarcations instead of "world-wide perspectives." Questions hailed down upon Hitler, but he became increasingly evasive. "There are issues," Molotov persisted, "to be clarified regarding Russia's Balkan and Black Sea interests with respect to Bulgaria, Rumania and Turkey." The discussion became heated and acrimonious; Hitler detected blackmail in the Russian bear hug. Within two weeks of this exchange, Molotov told the German Ambassador in Moscow that Russia would join the four-power pact only on condition that Russia be given a free hand in Finland, Bulgaria, the Dardanelles and the Arabian and Persian oil fields.

"Stalin is clever and cunning," Hitler told his military chiefs. "He demands more and more. He's a cold-blooded blackmailer. A German victory has become unbearable for Russia. Therefore, she must be brought to her knees as soon as possible." Infuriated by Stalin's apparently intractable stand, early in December, Hitler asked Halder to bring him the Army General Staff plan for the war against the Soviet Union.

Stalin was completely unprepared for the German attack. The two years' grace that the Soviet Union had ostensibly gained by the 1939 pact were not exploited wisely. The Russian Army followed the new western frontiers of 1939–40, leaving empty its supply dumps and emplacements on the Stalin line and creating large vulnerable spaces between fortified positions.[5] Stalin's purges in the 1930's also deprived the army of some of its most vigorous and competent officers. Moreover, Soviet leaders did not realistically translate the creeping evidence of Hitler's intentions. The buildup of German forces in western Poland, the presence of a million Nazi troops in the Balkans, the pressure thrusts east and south—all were ignored. Despite growing differences, the allegedly stark realists in the Kremlin went out of their way to appease the Nazis as late as the spring of 1941. "We will remain friends with you—through thick and thin," Stalin told German officials in Moscow. Meanwhile, Soviet deliveries of vitally needed grains, petroleum, manganese and rubber were shipped to Germany punctually. The Russian bear hug was all friendliness and conciliation.

The German invasion on the the morning of June 22, 1941, found the Russians completely bewildered and unprepared. From gun positions in the line, the Germans again and again intercepted the same message: "We are being fired on; what shall we do?" Back came the answer from headquarters: "You must be insane!" Roads were raked with machine-gun fire, tank parks were blasted; fuel stores were set afire. Thousands of horses were scattered in terror across the countryside. The invasion was the classic stencil of *Blitzkrieg* imprinted on the largest front in history.[6]

Not only were the Russians stunned militarily. There was no plan whatever for the evacuation of Soviet offices or the civilian population, nor were there any orders governing the eventuality of an invasion. Like all others, then, Jews who were not trapped by the *Einsatzgruppen*, had no recourse but unorganized flight. For the Russian people this would be the most terrible war in their history, a struggle for national survival. The Soviet Air Force was wiped out in the western areas on the first day of the invasion. Within five days, the Germans had already captured Minsk, the capital of Byelorussia, well within the Soviet Union's 1938 borders, and in a few more days they occupied all of the areas incorporated by the Soviet Union after 1939: western Byelorussia, the western Ukraine, Lithuania, Latvia and Estonia.

During the first few weeks of the invasion the mass of the Red Army in the south was battered to pieces in a colossal "annihilation battle" which cost the Russians nearly a million casualties. Certain that the war was virtually over, Hitler, on July 14, told his military leaders that the strength of the Army would be "considerably reduced in the near future." At the end of September he instructed the High Command to disband forty infantry divisions. By this time, nearly one third of the original Soviet Army had been eliminated.

Jews were thus caught during the most potent and self-confident phase of the German attack—at a time when the Russians were reeling under the incredible German advance. There is no evidence in the available literature that the scattering of the Jewish population was the result of any official evacuation. On the contrary, there is substantial evidence that Stalin forbade any public announcement of the mass killing of Jews.

The later evacuations, carried out by the Soviet Government after it recovered from the shock of the invasion, involved purely economic and administrative considerations. The most vital industrial centers—besides Riga and Minsk, which were lost during the first few days—were in central and eastern Ukraine and in Moscow and Leningrad. The transplantation of Soviet industrial might to the east—to the Urals, the Volga country, western Siberia and Central Asia—must rank among the most stupendous organizational and human achievements of the Soviet Union during the war.[7] This gigantic transplantation started in midsummer 1941 and continued into 1942 and was accompanied by a parallel migration of men.

On October 12 and 13, 1941, the capital was evacuated to Kuibyshev. Many Russians doubted that Moscow could be saved and for several days after the official evacuation there was mass panic in the city as crowds stampeded to leave. A state of siege was proclaimed in Moscow, and Stalin declared that it would be defended to the last man. The Germans were less than fifty miles away. Only toward the end of October did Russian counterattacks begin to slow down the German advance. By this time, the *Einsatzgruppen* had completed their first killing cycle.

In a war on such a scale, it is perhaps futile to discuss rescue efforts or warnings, at least in the first phases of the invasion. However, it is significant that the early Soviet suppression of facts regarding the Nazi destruction of Europe's Jews became a pattern for later Soviet policy, even after the tide of battle had turned.

At the same time, Jewish losses, immense and shattering though they were, must be seen not only within the context of official Soviet silence but as part of the most destructive war in Russia's history, a holocaust of its own which took twenty million lives. No other nation in Europe endured such great human losses during the war.

The war provided the landscape for the Nazi mass killing of Jews in the Soviet Union. Whole villages and cities were turned into infernos of death. The war also forced a huge uprooting and flight of Jews. This process was partly dictated by the urgency of sheer survival, partly by hard Soviet political demands. One of the first of these involved the Polish Government-in-Exile with which Stalin resumed relations after the German invasion. Both governments agreed to help each other in the common fight against Nazi Germany. Both were concerned with the question of the future Polish frontier, and this question involved Jews.

General Wladyslaw Sikorski, the Supreme Commander of the Polish Army, though himself willing to take a realistic view of the situation, had never officially abandoned Poland's claims to its 1939 frontiers; he had his own diehards to placate.[8] Stalin, however, insisted on Russia's right to eastern Poland. Both sides sought to validate their territorial claims through control of the local populations. This conflict was to enmesh the lives of thousands of Polish Jews in Russia.

The resumption of diplomatic relations between the Russians and the Poles was followed on August 12, 1941, by a pact providing for general amnesty for all former Polish subjects. In areas where there was a concentration of non-Polish ethnic groups, local Soviet military authorities began to draft people, including many Jews, into the Red Army. The Polish Government-in-Exile immediately demanded an explanation. The Soviet answer of December 12 was typically devious and veiled. The Soviet Government argued that no injustice had been committed against Polish citizens; in fact, it was said, they had been given preferential treatment: they had not been forced to accept a Russian passport. As to the others, the Soviet note continued, all residents of the western districts of the Ukrainian and Byelorussian republics who had lived there between November 1 and 2, 1939, were Soviet citizens.

The Polish mission to the Soviet Union, headed by Stanislaw Kot, tried to obtain a reversal of this decision. Kot believed that the question of Jewish refugees could have considerable influence on Jewish opinion in the United States and tried to use this argument against Soviet conduct.

When it became apparent that the Soviet Union would not reverse itself, Kot then urged an appeal to "world public opinion" against Soviet policy toward the Jewish refugees who were suffering because of unsolved political questions. In these Polish-Soviet discussions Stalin, playing on General Sikorski's pride, asked him: "What good to you are Byelorussians, Ukrainians and Jews? What you need are Poles; they are the best soldiers." The Poles were thus placed in the position of defending Polish Jewish refugees from the arbitrary actions of the Soviet Government because of their anxiety about the future Russian-Polish border. The question of admitting Jews into the projected Polish Army, however, was another matter.

Not only did Russians and Poles differ sharply about its composition, but Poles themselves disagreed with each other. By the fall of 1941, a Polish Army was already being formed with Soviet aid. Jews tried to join. The commander in chief was General Wladyslaw Anders, who himself had been released from a Soviet jail in the summer of 1941. In an "Order of the Day on the Question of the Jews," issued on November 11, Anders explained to his soldiers that, while he "fully understood" their anti-Semitic feelings, ". . . our present policy, which is closely connected with English policy, must nevertheless adopt a positive attitude on the Jewish problem, which exerts a considerable influence on the Anglo-Saxon world. . . . When we are again at home, after victory is won, we will deal with the Jewish problem in accordance with the size and independence of our homeland."[9] Kot tried to persuade the Polish Government-in-Exile and Anders to regard the Jewish soldiers as an integral part of the Polish Army. He believed that the proposal to establish separate Jewish units would weaken Polish demands regarding borders. He also repeatedly warned the Poles in London about the damage caused by the anti-Semitism of Army officers. At the same time, he and other Polish leaders pressed the Russians to eliminate their regulation compelling Jews to accept Soviet citizenship. The Jews, once again, were caught between two millstones.

The Soviet-Polish amnesty of August 1941 technically covered all Poles —Jewish and non-Jewish—who were in Russian prisons, camps or places of compulsory exile. This order, however, was never carried out in full because, from the very beginning, the Soviet Union intended to keep hold of as much of eastern Poland as possible. Some inmates were released gradually, but liberation was still incomplete in April 1943 when Russian-Polish relations were ruptured.

After the amnesty the great majority of released Jews streamed south to Uzbekistan, Turkmenistan and other parts of Soviet Central Asia where the climate was milder than in frigid Siberia and where there was some hope of escaping over the Iranian border nearby. The *Mossad* tracked these movements and established a post in the holy city of Meshed in northeast Iran, close to the Soviet Union. Here were organized a reception center and an escape route through Kermanshah to Iraq.[10] But few refugees trickled through. Other Jews succeeded in joining the Polish Army which also offered some hope of leaving the country. The vast majority of the estimated 300,000 Jewish refugees in Soviet Asia remained there exposed to a strange civilization and a difficult life. Many thousands died of hunger.

Parallel with this rise and fall of Jewish hopes was the sudden change in welfare policy which also affected Polish Jews in Russia. In December 1941, there had been agreements between Sikorski and the Soviet Government permitting the appointment of Polish Embassy delegates and a Soviet loan for relief purposes. The delegates were to register Polish citizens and organize relief activities. The work began in February 1942 and involved the setting up of schools, feeding centers and orphanages and the distribution of food and clothing. Several of the members of the Polish delegation were Jews and, according to the Polish Embassy, over 100,000 Jews were assisted by this agency. However, as Russian-Polish relations deteriorated, this work encountered obstacles. The Soviet Government charged Polish relief officials with "espionage" and they were ordered to stop intervening in behalf of Polish citizens. Many were arrested and their offices were closed in July 1942. The Joint Distribution Committee picked up calls for help that began reaching the United States in early 1942, but once more, the Russians threw up obstacles.

The refugees first asked for food, and food parcels were sent. But the Soviet Government collected a high and arbitrary duty on all food parcels, and letters came back to the Joint Distribution Committee saying, "Don't send parcels. We can't afford them."[11] A JDC representative went to Teheran and then to Moscow to try to work out an arrangement with the Russians but found that direct relief was impossible. Seemingly, the Russians were "too proud." However, they made one concession: parcels up to twelve pounds could be sent to individuals if the addresses were correct and if the duty was paid in advance.

It was soon found that a twelve-pound package of food sent occasionally was not an answer for people on the verge of starvation, so another approach was tried. Goods in short supply in Central Asia were sent—tea, tobacco, needles and razor blades—and these goods the Jews could barter for food. A quarter of a million parcels were sent costing five million dollars, of which almost two million went to the Russian customs.[12] Tens of thousands of Jews were undoubtedly saved by this aid.

Russian "pride" in this instance very likely played some role in the Soviet attitude toward foreign aid. At the same time, it is clear that the government was also bent on preventing the refugees from leaving the Soviet Union and on converting them into Soviet citizens. The scattering of the Jews to the distant reaches of Central Asia made it difficult, if not impossible, for them to leave. At the same time, Jewish derogation of

Soviet life among native populations in backward areas of the USSR would not have the adverse effect it allegedly had had on the people of European stock in Soviet-occupied Poland.

Meanwhile, Jews were also caught in the complications that arose between the Soviet Union and the Polish Government-in-Exile over the departure of the Army. Although it had been understood that the Polish Army would fight side by side with the Russian Army, General Anders had no such intention and made one excuse after another for not letting his men fight on the Russian front. The Polish Army contained virulently anti-Russian as well as anti-Semitic soldiers and, when Churchill suggested that it leave Russia via Iran, the Russians regarded its departure as good riddance. However, when it was finally withdrawn, most enlisted Jews were not permitted to leave with it.[13] This policy was in line with the determination of the Russians to keep as many former Poles—Jews as well as non-Jews—behind, since, by keeping this claim on former Polish citizens, they were pressing their right to eastern Poland.

The Anders Army had never welcomed Jewish enlistees. At first, recruiting boards, made up of Polish and Soviet representatives, had refused to allow Jews to join. Later, some Jews had to be baptized in order to enlist; still others were attacked by Poles at recruiting stations. Some managed to join through the help of individual board members. In 1942, when the Army began to depart from Russia in stages, it readily fell in line with Soviet claims over Jewish members. As a result, few Jews escaped from Russia by this route.

The new Soviet order projected for Poland began to take form in the midst of these developments. On December 1, 1941 the People's Commissariat for Foreign Affairs had officially stated that the USSR recognized eastern Poland as part of Soviet Russia. Polish deportees of Ukrainian, White Russian and Jewish origin of military age had been ordered to enlist in the Russian Army. On January 16, 1943, a Soviet note announced that all inhabitants of the former Polish regions as of November 1, 1939, automatically became Soviet citizens. The question of citizenship also vitally influenced the fate of the Polish Jews in the Soviet Union. Once again, as in 1939, Jewish refugees were pressed into accepting Soviet citizenship. The NKVD interviewed them individually and said they were no longer Polish citizens. Those who refused to accept Soviet citizenship were arrested.[14]

Once the Anders Army left, Russia began to cultivate pro-Soviet Poles and prepared the way for a "new Poland." The Polish Government-in-Exile was denounced for preventing active resistance to the Germans in Poland. Relations between the governments were severed April 27, 1943, following Goebbels' announcement that the Germans had found several mass graves in the Katyn Forest near Smolensk containing the bodies of thousands of Polish officers. The Sikorski Government accepted German charges that the soldiers had been executed by the Russians. Stalin refused an independent inquiry by the Red Cross and, after a prolonged and abusive diplomatic exchange, relations between the two governments were completely ruptured. The Soviet Union then began to draw up plans for a new Polish government and for a Polish Army allied to the Red Army.

Jews and Poles remaining in Soviet-occupied territory worked together in the Russian-inspired Polish Patriots' Association and the Kosciusko army in which the first cadres of leaders for the future Polish Army were trained. There was no open anti-Semitism in these organizations, but Jews who went back to Poland were urged to change their names to purely Polish-sounding ones and to keep their Jewish origins a secret. After the great Soviet victory at Kursk in 1943, the prospect that these Soviet-backed forces would reenter Poland was clear. Soon both the United States and England were won over to the so-called Curzon line. The Soviet Union could now afford to relinquish its claims to the citizenship of Poles. It stopped differentiating between Jews and ethnic Poles on the question of admission to the new Polish Army. By the end of 1943, about 30 percent of this army was made up of Jews.

Events now turned full circle. By October 1944, the new Polish Committee of National Liberation in Lublin—the basis for the new Soviet oriented Poland—set up an office for repatriation. About 130,000—almost half of the Polish Jews who survived in the Soviet Union—returned to Poland by October 1946.[15] The Soviet Union had released them because they were now "Sovietized," or soon would be. Many of these returned Jews had to endure new trials and new migrations in the ongoing struggle to achieve security, for postwar Poland was, if anything, more anti-Semitic than ever. Most of the returnees eventually made their way to Palestine.

At no time before or during the war did the Soviet Government acknowledge the declared purpose of the Nazis to destroy the Jews of Europe. No political offensive was ever launched within the Soviet Union in support of its Jews and no military action was ever taken to protect the densely populated Jewish centers. Yet when the Germans attacked, they maintained that they were waging war not against the Slavic people but against Jews, whom they described as "the bearers of Communism who grabbed all the most important political and administrative posts." The Nazis said they were saving the world from Jewish domination. This propaganda fell on fertile soil in the Ukraine and Baltic countries and penetrated far into the interior of Russia. It is very possible that, in the early period of the war, when Russian defections to the Nazis were heavy, and when immense numbers of prisoners were taken, that Soviet authorities were afraid that a pro-Jewish campaign might still further undermine military and civilian morale with the myth of a "Jewish war." The official line was that Nazi atrocities were being inflicted on the "Soviet people" in general. The Nazi campaign to wipe out European Jewry was passed over in silence.

The hypothesis that the Soviet authorities did not realize the particular fate the Nazis had designed for Jews must be dismissed in view of their excellent intelligence network and occasional reference to the problem.[16] It has been suggested that the theme of anti-Semitism was deliberately omitted from official news and propaganda to avoid singling out any one national or religious group as having suffered more than others and thus feeling entitled to special consideration in the future.

To a large extent, of course, the invasion was directed against the Soviet people and hundreds of thousands of Russians in Heydrich's ten categories marked for execution were killed during the war. However, this fact should not obscure the evidence that in the prewar period, the period of the Nazi-Soviet pact, the Soviet Government completely ignored the singular Nazi actions against Jews. An attitude of neutrality was officially taken. The Soviet Government went so far as to express its disapproval of any public denunciation of Nazism. At public meetings, in the press, and on the radio, there was silence on the mass murder of Jews. At that time the brunt of Russia's attack was directed against the "ruling classes in France and England." Government neutrality not only blinded Soviet Jews to the mortal danger facing them but reduced the non-Jewish citizen's resistance to anti-Semitism. Jewish writers among the Polish refugees were also silenced.

A certain Soviet-Jewish "line" had already crystallized in the USSR over the previous years and the new Jewish refugees had to accommodate themselves to the cultural and educational framework that had been fixed. Yiddish works were allowed within Soviet formulations but no Hebrew or Zionist material was permitted. The period between 1939 and 1941 showed a general slackening of Jewish creative expression; after the war, it virtually came to an end. Most amazing was the total blackout of information about the Nazi destruction of Jewish life in the territories already conquered by the Nazis up to 1941. This was true of the writings of both the veteran Soviet Jewish writers and those in the annexed regions.[17] The official Soviet gloss during the period 1939–41 was that Jews, Ukrainians and White Russians had been rescued from an oppressive and backward Polish regime which had been unable to defend its citizens. Any criticism of Nazi Germany was absolutely suppressed. This policy was in sharp contrast with the period of the thirties, when Nazi persecutions against the Jews were widely publicized.

Among the works of the Polish Jewish refugee writers, some of whom had personally experienced the horrors of Nazi atrocities in Poland, no reference to their experience was permitted. Not even in their letters is the Nazi terror referred to. Most works by Polish Jewish writers published during the period of the Nazi-Soviet pact dwell on the political struggle of left-wing parties and their suppression by pre-war Poland. The Soviet censorship had sealed their lips and chained their pens.

Authentic information about the efforts of the Soviet civilian population to rescue Jews in Nazi-occupied areas is virtually nonexistent. The foreign Communist press gave the impression that this aid was considerable, but their reports lack confirmation.[18] At the time the war started, Soviet anti-Semitism was neither dead nor forgotten; Stalin himself hated Jews. From the fragmentary evidence, it appears that the people of Poland, where the intensity of anti-Semitism was much greater, seem, in individual cases, to have shown more compassion in their rescue efforts than did the people in Russia. The thoroughgoing hatred of Poles toward the Nazi invader contrasts rather sharply with the more ambivalent, frequently pro-German attitude of the Soviet people—particularly in the Ukraine and White Russia. One historian who has made an exhaustive study of the Jews in the Soviet Union has concluded that the stories of the rescue of Jews by the Soviet Government were "concocted for foreign consumption," that only a fraction of the survivors owe their lives to the solicitude of the government.[19]

Accounts by non-Communist Jewish survivors indicate a callous disregard for Jews and their abandonment by Soviet forces. In Vilna, for example, which was bombed early in the war and given up by the Soviet Union to Lithuania, tens of thousands of Vilna Jews were left behind, but only scattered individuals succeeded in reaching the Soviet Union. All vehicles had been seized by the Soviet armed forces and the only civilians who were evacuated and permitted on trains were those who had membership cards in the Communist Party. Countless numbers walked on foot along highways, were overtaken by German tanks or turned back by Soviet frontier guards.[20]

A Jewish agronomist from Kovno who drove to the frontier between Latvia and the Soviet Union, northeast of Dvinsk wrote:

> This is where the calamity, the great calamity starts. We are not permitted to go further. There are already hundreds of refugees from Lithuania and Latvia near the border and their number increases from one day to the next. But regardless of how much they implore the Soviet guards, this is the answer they get: "No one is to cross—these are orders. Move back twenty steps. If you don't we'll shoot. . . ."
>
> For twelve long terrible days and nights, we have stayed near the border. Meanwhile thousands of refugees have crowded together here. Droves of people, mostly Jews, but here and there non-Jews, too, lie around in nearby

ditches, woods, and fields, and beg for permission to continue their trek so that they may save their lives. They are not allowed to pass. Only Communists, party members with the proper documents, may cross.[21]

The rescue activity "concocted for foreign consumption" appeared in the newspaper *Einikeit* (Unity), which aimed to form ties with Western Jewry and acquire the material and moral support of the West behind the Russian struggle against Nazism. Otherwise, all Soviet references to Nazi atrocities dealt with the victims as "peaceful Soviet citizens." *Einikeit* was published by the Jewish Anti-Fascist Committee, which was established in 1941 together with other anti-fascist committees for the purpose of angling the war propaganda among Jews, Slavs, scientists, youth and women of the Soviet Union for counterpart groups outside. As part of its task, the Jewish Anti-Fascist Committee regularly sent out information on events in Jewish life within the Soviet Union. It also became a focal point for all Jewish literary work during the war.

Except for the accounts in *Einikeit*, there was a policy of official silence during the war regarding the destruction of whole Jewish communities in the USSR. This attitude is reflected in the first collection of documents on Nazi atrocities published by the Soviet Government Commission for the Investigation of Nazi War Crimes published in 1943. Between 1942 and 1945, the supreme political leadership of the Red Army issued fifteen pamphlets dealing with Nazi horrors at the time of the German invasion, but Jews, as such, are not mentioned as victims.[22]

Ilya Ehrenburg, the Soviet writer, occupies a unique position in the Russian literature of the Holocaust—he published over three hundred articles during the war, most of them in the military organ, *The Red Star*, and explicitly referred to the annihilation of Jews in Pinsk, Mozyr, Rostov, Stavropol and elsewhere. However, when he attempted to portray the heroic deeds of Jews who served in the Red Army, the text was disqualified as being too "boastful."

In the second collection of documents published by the Soviet Government Commission toward the end of 1945, documentary material on the destruction of Jews as Jews in certain communities of Russia is included. Ehrenburg used some of this material in a collection in Yiddish called *The Murderers of Nations*, which he edited in 1944–45. However, Soviet policy soon reversed itself. Ehrenburg touches on this change in his memoirs: "At the end of the war, I began to collect . . . human testimonials bearing upon the total destruction of the Jews in the Soviet areas which were conquered by the Germans—letters written before their authors' death, diaries of a painter from Riga, a student from Kharkov, of old men and children. We called the book then in preparation the *Black Book*, for it portrayed the fascist horrors. However, there was much light too: courage, cooperation and love. The book was ready for publication and they said it would appear at the end of 1948. . . . At the end of 1948, they closed the Jewish Anti-Fascist Committee, terminated the newspaper *Emes* [The Truth], and scattered the prepared pages of the Black Book."[23] (Part of this projected work was sent to Romania and published as *Cartea Neagrǎ*.) The Black Book has never been published in Russia.

Since the war the Russian silence has been shattered not by official documents but by belletristic writings, such as Yevtushenko's poem "Babi Yar" and a diary of life in the Vilna ghetto, *I Must Tell*, by Masha Rolnik, originally published in Lithuanian in 1963 and translated into Russian. The diary describes the experiences of a fourteen-year-old Jewish girl in the diminishing Ghetto. Yevtushenko has also used the subject of the Holocaust in two recent poems, "The Power Station of Bratskaya" and "As Long as the Murderers Trod the Earth."

A remarkable documentary-novel also appeared in 1966, a work written by Anatoly Kuznetsov, a non-Jewish resident of Kiev, who was twelve years old when the killings at Babi Yar took place. This book was published in the Soviet magazine *Yunost*. Based on eyewitness accounts and official documents, its publication in one of the official journals of the Young Communists and its enthusiastic reception by Soviet critics seem at last to acknowledge the murderous anti-Jewish intentions of the Nazis, and, most astonishingly, the admission of Russian and Ukrainian participation in the tortures and killings at Babi Yar.

It is perhaps no coincidence that accounts of Russian survivors of prisoner of war camps are also now beginning to appear in the Soviet Union.[24] The Wehrmacht has been re-established in West Germany. Germany is a potent factor in NATO, and West German demands for unification are evident. The Soviet Government may want to remind the world of German crimes. The publications describing the Jewish tragedy may be the beginning of a slow thaw in the Soviet attitude, or merely a small official concession to keep some voices appeased. Much more significant, perhaps, is the official reply of the director of Soviet Government General Archives to a request from *Yad Vashem* (the Holocaust archival authority in Israel) for material on Nazi crimes against the Jews in Russia. The director replied: "Referring to your letter of March 24, 1965, please note that the documents at the Soviet Government Archives relating to the crimes of German Fascism in World War II are not organized according to the nationality of the victims."[25]

For the Nazis, the war in Russia extinguished the thousand-year Reich in less than four years. Everlasting space and recurrent tides of Soviet soldiers engulfed the German armies. The endless, seemingly aimless counterattacks and reckless expenditure of Russian lives disquieted some German officers as early as the fall of 1941. Colonel Bernd von Kleist wrote prophetically: "The German Army in fighting Russia is like an elephant attacking a host of ants. The elephant will kill thousands, perhaps even millions, of ants, but in the end their numbers will overcome him, and he will be eaten to the bone."[26] But it was not only the Russian spaces and soldiers that defeated Germany.

The Nazi disaster in Russia was the inevitable end-product of the *Untermensch* philosophy which ultimately destroyed even the impulse of German national self-interest. Russia, the Nazis said, was a country in which "the enemy consists not of soldiers but to a large extent only of beasts." The native populations were treated by the Nazi occupiers with barbaric cruelty and contempt, and the early fissures in Russian morale mended as the Nazis became progressively destructive. Hitler's nihilism dictated the policy. "We have a duty to 'depopulate,' much as we have the duty of caring properly for the German population," he had told Hermann Rauschning in the early 1930's. "We shall have to develop a technique of 'depopulation.' You will ask what is 'depopulation'? Do I propose to exterminate whole ethnic groups? Yes, it will add up to that."

A scant three weeks after the invasion, on July 16, at a conference of civil and military leaders, Hitler outlined Nazi plans for the future of the occupied East. This region embraced Poland, the Baltic States and occupied Russia, a huge territory which the Nazis divided into four administrative units: the Warthegau, consisting of western regions of Poland annexed to the Reich; the Ostland, including Lithuania, Latvia, Estonia, and White Russia; the Government-General in central Poland and the Ukraine. (See map, p. 271.) Hitler's plans had a deadly simplicity: "While German goals and methods must be concealed from the world at large, all the necessary measures—shooting, exiling, etc.—we *shall* take and we *can* take anyway. The order of the day is

first: conquer
second: rule
third: exploit."

Later he directly threatened punitive action against humane officials: "Anyone who talks about cherishing the local inhabitant and civilizing him goes straight off into a concentration camp."

At first, the anti-Hitler generals naïvely believed that Hitler's terror orders for Russia might shock the others into joining them. But by June 16, Hassell confirmed the hard truth:

A series of conferences with Popitz, Goerdeler, Beck and Oster to consider whether certain orders which the Army commanders have received (but which they have not yet issued) might suffice to open the eyes of the military leaders as to the nature of the regime for which they are fighting. These orders concern brutal . . . measures the troops are to take against the Bolsheviks when Russia is invaded.

We came to the conclusion that nothing was to be hoped for now. They [the generals] delude themselves. . . . Brauchitsch and Halder have already agreed to Hitler's tactics. Thus the Army must bear the onus of the murders and burnings which up to now have been confined to the S.S.[27]

During the first delirious days of victory, Hitler relaxed into dreams of a Nazified colonial empire—a million square miles of Slavic helots ruled by a handful of *Herrenvolk*. The befuddled Alfred Rosenberg was appointed to organize this empire. As "Commissar for the Central Control of Questions Connected with the East-European Region," Rosenberg divided up European Russia into commissariats and blueprinted the slow starvation of millions of Slavs while Germany drained the Soviet Union of its resources. Besides the official state spoliation, the little empires of Himmler, Göring and Bormann also fed on the Soviet Union, creating multiple tentacles that plundered and killed. Yet, as compared with Poland, there was little active opposition to the Germans in the early phase of the German occupation of the Soviet Union. In Poland, from the very first, the masses as a whole hated and opposed German rule. In the Ukraine and White Russia, many welcomed the Germans as liberators from Communist oppression.

The Nazis, however, had no plans for effectively utilizing the sympathy of a conquered people. Hitler aimed to destroy Russia as a state and to acquire vast new areas for exploitation and settlement by Germans. The East, toward which the Germans had been traditionally arrogant, would simply serve the German *Herrenvolk*. There would be not merely a change in borders and masters, but a drastic reshuffling of ethnic groups. At the very bottom were Jews, Gypsies and certain groups of Slavs and Russians who would be exterminated; next were the Great Russians who would be enslaved; then followed the Ukrainians, Byelorussians, the Balts and *Volksdeutsche*. "Inferior" elements would be transferred east; some elements would be "Germanized"; in the areas vacated, millions of Germans would be brought in and settled.

The plan was not completely new. In less virulent form, without the extermination features and without the raw Darwinism of the Nazis, it had been formulated before World War I and was justified by the German mission of *Kulturträgertum*, the mission of culture-bearing. The Nazis wanted no part of this mission, however. Only people of "pure" German blood were to inhabit the East, and the German elite—the S.S.—was to provide the "racially high-grade manpower" which would move in as fresh and superior stock. This prospect, which involved grotesque eugenic manipulation—including the kidnapping of children, forced mating and large-scale abortions—had an obsessive grip on Nazi leaders even as the German armies were in headlong retreat during the last phases of the war.[28]

As the reality of a protracted war dawned, the Nazis adopted a policy of carrot and whip, which lasted until the end of the war. Concessions were prompted by German defeats, but they were fitful and always undone by subsequent terror and intensified economic exploitation. A conflict raged between dogma and utility and, as in the annihilation of the Jews, German self-interest, in the end, was defeated by fanaticism. The native populations became the plaything of competing agencies and suddenly shifting policies. Days of murder alternated with days of extra rations. In victory, Germany could afford to spurn the help of the conquered, but prolonged war demanded prudent use of that help. The Germans continued to spurn it. So inefficient was the Nazi occupation of the East that the contributions, that is, the actual deliveries of the occupied East to the Reich itself, despite much more brutal exploitation and the much greater area and resources, amounted to only one seventh of what the Reich obtained from France. Germany could have obtained more from Russia in normal peacetime trade than from Russia by conquest.[29]

Having only exploitative and destructive goals, the Nazis had no program of political or psychological warfare for a constructive utilization of the Soviet population. They came simply as conquerors. Whatever thought was given to the response of the native population relied on anti-Bolshevism and anti-Semitism to draw the people to the German side to work and fight. The Russians, however, saw no better future under the Nazis after being liberated from Stalinism. With adroit political handling, the population in many areas might very well have been split from the Soviet cause. But the Nazis could not overcome their "ideology."

Raw force was used to compel the Russians to work. Like the Jews and inmates of camps, they were called by a degrading name, Ostarbeiter, and they had to wear a degrading insignia, an embroidered square bearing the inscription OST, on their clothing. Hundreds of thousands of hungry and sullen Russians toiled grudgingly for Germany. Slowly they realized that their new masters were much worse than the old.

In the treatment of Russian prisoners of war, the Nazis were likewise stupid as well as unbelievably cruel. Next to the annihilation of six million Jews, the biggest single German crime was the death of over four million Russian prisoners of war through starvation, exposure and execution. Hardy soldiers were reduced to creatures whining and groveling for scraps of food, to tearing dead animals to pieces with their bare hands, and to cannibalism.

In 1942, after several serious military setbacks, although they had planned no alternative to defeat or failure, the Nazis had to improvise another policy in the East to meet urgent economic and military needs. In the midst of the death transports, labor had to be recruited from the starving Russian prisoners of war. Both measures were cynical expedients; both came too late.

Not all German officials, however, accepted Hitler's and Himmler's views of the eastern populations; the futile consequences of their policies were angrily debated in some circles. At the beginning of 1942, for example, Rosenberg, apparently unaware of his own contradictions, writing to Keitel, thought it scandalous that out of 3,600,000 Russian prisoners at the time, only a few hundred thousand were still fit for work, so appalling were the conditions in which they existed. There is also an interesting report of an encounter between Dr. Kersten and Ohlendorf, the former *Einsatzgruppe* commander, in August 1943, when the war was going badly for the Germans. The Nazis were, indeed, working against disaster, but their racial fantasies were uppermost. Kersten noted in his diary that Ohlendorf disagreed sharply with the harsh occupation policy of Koch (commissar in the Ukraine and Bialystok). Disgusted with the turn of affairs, Ohlendorf had made sharply critical reports to Himmler, but nothing was changed. Ohlendorf then asked Kersten who, he said, had the "proper conception of nations as entities with a life of their own," to intervene with Himmler for him. Ohlendorf complained that Himmler wanted only optimistic reports to avoid disturbing Hitler's "lofty conceptions." Himmler himself was seen as a great source of confusion and disorder. Authority was dispersed by a host of people and new posts he created overlapped old jurisdictions.[30]

Ohlendorf had come close to the truth about the crumbling Third Reich. The S.S. hierarchy refused to give up their mythology or to see the situation as it really was. Though Himmler was self-divided by many irreconcilable drives, in one region he was still intact. He destroyed any crisscrossing of jurisdictions that interfered with his racial fantasies and felt compelled to the very end to search for "Germanic blood" among the Slavs.

Under the cold light of scrutiny, the labor shortages and native discontent in Russia can be viewed as a fragment of the whole irrational phenomenon of Nazi nihilistic imperialism. The program of resettlement and population upheaval wore a scientific air, as did so many Nazi activities, but when stripped of its false front, it was a senseless barbarian invasion. Himmler's search for "pure" Germans may have been an exhilarating mission for the S.S. in the days of early military conquests but it soon began to rot away and show itself as nothing more than a sordid power contest among Nazi leaders and murder and enslavement of subject peoples.[31]

For the Jews in Europe, the invasion of Russia and the long struggle that followed marked the beginning and end of their near extermination. After June 22, 1941, the European war spread and involved the vast depths of Russia where other European conquerors had been enticed into disaster. As the German Army moved eastward, millions of Jews were trapped in Europe. Deportations took them farther and farther from communication centers and eventually they were devoured by the extermination centers far from the eyes and ears of the world. The mass killings began in June 1941 and continued with mounting ferocity for the next three years.

Through mass exterminations, Hitler meant to burn all his bridges. No possibility of retreat or compromise was left to the hesitant or weak-hearted German. All were tied to Hitler's fate and, as the prospect of victory receded, all were dragged into a quagmire of guilt. He intended that no German would escape this guilt after his own downfall.

A protracted war demanded maximum unity among the German people. To achieve this, Hitler bound them with him in an irreversible destiny, an interlocking fate that would merge Germany's destiny with his. Complicity with him in a national mission to purge Europe of its Jews would, he believed, arouse the German people to ever greater efforts and sacrifices—including the sacrifice of conscience. Retreat of any kind would be impossible, for if they hesitated or showed "degenerate humanitarian" considerations, they would be guilty of treason and betrayal of a trust. Such black-and-white alternatives had great appeal to the "great simplifier." Goebbels expressed this reasoning in his diary entry for March 2, 1943:

> Göring realizes perfectly what is in store for all of us if we show any weakness in this war. He has no illusions about that. On the Jewish question especially, we have taken a position from which there is no escape. That is a good thing. Experience teaches that a movement and a people who have burned their bridges fight with much greater determination than those who are still able to retreat.

In the vast machine of mass murder, Hitler intended to implicate a whole people. Everyone was executioner, bureaucrat, clerk, soldier, policeman, terrorist or acquiescent onlooker.

In the context of defeat, as in the context of war, Germany's magic enemy, the Jew, served to unite the German people with their leaders. When the United Nations expressed their determination to punish criminal Nazi leaders, official propagandists told the German people that "Jews would never allow such distinctions." Thus, the people who had witnessed the exterminations of Jews or were aware of them were united in the crimes with their leaders and would suffer a like fate, Hitler said, if they surrendered.

The mounting crescendo of war excited Hitler to new and more insensate orgies of killing—of Jews, of Slavs, and of internal opposition. The escalation of the slaughter of Jews paralleled the escalation of Nazi military defeats. By the end of November 1941, German losses in the East numbered 743,000, almost a quarter of the whole Eastern Army. The all-out attack on Moscow had crumbled. Panic began to sweep over the armies. Rostov, the gateway to the Caucasus, could not be held. German guns, machines, fuel and human bodies froze in the Russian winter. At the same time, vast massacres of Jews took place in Kiev, Riga, Vilna, Kovno, Dvinsk and Rovno. Experimental gassings were begun at Auschwitz.

In December 1941, the Crimean massacres were completed and the first permanent gassing camp was opened at Chelmno. Six months after the invasion, Hitler's decision to exterminate Europe's Jews was announced to all of the State ministries at the Grossen-Wannsee Conference. The formula was called the "Final Solution." By the spring of 1942, German military reverses caused a drastic shake-up in the High Command and Hitler absorbed supreme civil and military power in the Reich. By April 1942, his field of power was complete: he controlled the life and death of every German regardless of rights or laws of the past. German losses by then numbered over a million men. For Jews, there were simultaneous mass deportations from eastern and western Europe to the death camps of Belzec and Auschwitz. In 1943, the Germans suffered military disasters at Kursk, Stalingrad, and in Tunisia. The Allies invaded Sicily. The eastern ghettos were emptied of Jews. Jammed, airless transports rumbled to Treblinka and Sobibor. New crematoria were opened at Auschwitz. Deportations swelled from Greece, Thrace and Croatia. In 1944, the Germans were caught between converging Russian and American armies, but in that year, they deported almost a half-million Hungarian Jews to Auschwitz. The crematoria burned up corpses until November.

The war in Russia unleashed the innately destructive core of Hitler's will. The decision to exterminate the Jews of Europe crystallized at the same time that the invasion of Russia was being planned. The exterminations were carried out after the invasion began and the war spread and lengthened.

16 The "Final Solution"

On July 31, 1941, six weeks after the invasion of Russia and the first death sweep of the *Einsatzgruppen*, Göring, who in 1939 had given Heydrich power to evacuate Jews from the Reich, gave him absolute power to organize "the final solution." The text of Göring's order was as follows:

> Complementing the task that was assigned to you on January 24, 1939, which dealt with carrying out emigration and evacuation, a solution of the Jewish problem as advantageous as possible, I hereby charge you with making all necessary preparation with regard to organizational and financial matters for bringing about a complete solution of the Jewish question in the German sphere of influence in Europe. Wherever other governmental agencies are involved, they are to cooperate with you. I request, furthermore, that you send me an overall plan . . . for the implementation of the desired final solution of the Jewish question.[1]

Heydrich knew quite well what Göring meant by the term "Final Solution," for he had used it himself nearly two years before, on September 21, 1939, at a secret meeting in which he had outlined "the first steps in the final solution"—the concentration of all Jews in the ghettos of the cities of Poland where they would slowly die of hunger and disease. Failing that, they would be dispatched to the East for "resettlement," that is, to their death.

Heydrich had now grasped the reins of the destruction process in his hands. His *Einsatzgruppen* were conducting massacres in the East and his Gestapo machinery was preparing for deportations from the West. The power of organizing the deportations now fell to the RSHA expert on Jewish Affairs, Adolf Eichmann.

Soon after Heydrich received the letter from Göring, Eichmann was summoned to Heydrich's office in Berlin. At his trial in Jerusalem, Eichmann testified that Heydrich opened this interview with a little speech to the effect that emigration was now impossible because of the war with Russia. He then said: "The Führer has ordered the physical extermination of the Jews." After this, "very much against his habits," Eichmann recalled:

He remained silent for a long while, as though he wanted to test the impact of the words. I remember it even today. In the first moment, I was unable to grasp the significance of what he had said, because he was so careful in choosing his words, and then I understood, and didn't say anything, because there was nothing to say anymore. For I had never thought of such a thing, such a solution through violence. I now lost everything, all joy in my work, all initiative, all interest; I was, so to speak, blown out. And then he told me: "Eichmann, you go and see Globocnik in Lublin. The Reichsführer [Himmler] has already given him the necessary orders. Have a look at what he has accomplished in the meantime. I think he uses the Russian tank trenches for the liquidation of the Jews."[2]

Eichmann was by no means among the first to be informed of Hitler's intention. Viktor Brack testified at Nuremberg that by March 1941 "it was no secret in higher Party circles that the Jews were to be exterminated." Eichmann did not belong to these circles, but he was among the first men in the lower echelons to be informed. He went to Maidanek near Lublin to see Globocnik and used the phrase "Final Solution" as a kind of password by which to identify himself. Globocnik was very obliging and showed him around with a subordinate. Eichmann recalled:

A German police captain there showed me how they had managed to build airtight chambers disguised as ordinary Polish farmers' huts, seal them hermetically, then inject the exhaust gas from a Russian U-boat motor. I remember it all very exactly because I never thought that anything like that would be possible, technically speaking. Not long afterward Heydrich had me carry an order to Major General Odilo Globocnik, S.S. commander of the Lublin district. I cannot remember whether Heydrich gave me the actual message or whether I had to draw it up. It ordered Globocnik to start liquidating a quarter million Polish Jews.

Later that year, I watched my first Jewish execution. It was at Minsk, then recently come under German occupation. I was sent by my immediate superior, General Müller. . . . He liked to send me around on his behalf. I was in effect a traveling salesman for the Gestapo, just as I once had been a traveling salesman for an oil company in Austria.

Müller had heard that Jews were being shot near Minsk and wanted a report. . . . They had already started, so I could see only the finish. Although I was wearing a leather coat which reached almost to my ankles, it was very cold. I watched the last group of Jews undress, down to their shirts. They walked the last 100 or 200 yards—they were not driven—then they jumped into the pit. It was impressive to see them all jumping into the pit without offering any resistance whatsoever. Then the men of the squad banged away into the pit with their rifles and machine pistols.

Why did that scene linger so long in my memory? Perhaps because I had children myself. And there were children in that pit. I saw a woman hold a child of a year or two into the air, pleading. At that moment all I wanted to say was, "Don't shoot, hand over the child." Then the child was hit. I was so close that later I found bits of brains splattered on my long leather coat. My driver helped me remove them. Then we returned to Berlin.[3]

Later that same winter, Müller sent Eichmann to Lodz to watch Jews being gassed. At Lodz a thousand Jews boarded buses with closed windows. As they were driven off, carbon monoxide from the exhaust pipe was conducted into the buses. A doctor suggested that Eichmann look into the bus through a peephole in the driver's seat, but he could not bear to, he said; he "simply couldn't look at any suffering." He further describes this experience: "We reached our destination and hell opened up for me for the first time. The bus in which I was riding turned and backed up before a pit about two meters deep. The doors opened. Some Poles who stood there jumped into the buses and threw the corpses into the pit. Another Pole with a pair of pliers in his hand jumped into the pit. He went through the corpses, opening their mouths. Whenever he saw a gold tooth, he pulled it out and dumped it into a small bag he was carrying."

When Eichmann reported back to Müller, he was chided for not having timed the gassing procedure in the bus. Obviously, a speedup in the production of deaths had already become an essential objective. Within a few months, German technical proficiency established an efficient industry of death.

Meanwhile, in the summer of 1941, Rudolf Höss, who had been commandant of the concentration camp at Auschwitz for a year, was summoned to report to Himmler for personal orders. Himmler told Höss that Hitler had given the order for the "Final Solution of the Jewish question," and that he, Himmler, had chosen Auschwitz as an important death camp because of its easy access by rail and because it "offered space for measures ensuring isolation." Because of its distance from Western centers, the selection of Auschwitz eventually put a heavy strain on German transport. The site, however, had other more immediate advantages in Nazi eyes: the Jewish population surrounding it was large and dense and, because it stood in what was originally Poland, in accordance with "blood-and-soil" theory, corpses of millions of Jews could be deposited there without contaminating primary German soil. According to Höss, who testified at his own trial, Himmler had said, "We, the S.S., must carry out that order. If it is not carried out now, then the Jews will later destroy the German people." During the following weeks, Eichmann came to Auschwitz and discussed necessary "details" with Höss. Höss moved slowly but methodically and, bit by bit, he built his camp into the largest death center the world has ever had.

Heydrich wanted to act as quickly as possible after receiving Göring's order, but various technical and economic matters had to be discussed first. The cooperation of many officials had to be assured. Problems of intermarriage, foreign Jews, Jews in the armament industry and other matters required special preparation. Nor could Heydrich yet act in the occupied areas or in Axis satellite states. Further, if the Final Solution was to be applied to all of Europe, the active and reliable support of all the ministries and the civil service had to be guaranteed.

To gain this support and coordinate all preparations, Heydrich called a conference of Undersecretaries of State and five key Police and S.S. officials on January 20, 1942, in a suburb of Berlin at Am Grossen Wannsee 56-58. In addition to Heydrich, fourteen men were present. Heydrich informed the conference of his appointment as executive in charge of preparing the "definitive solution of the Jewish problem." He then reviewed the emigration and economic measures already taken. By October 1941, however, Heydrich continued, Jewish emigration in a time of war presented a "danger." Now the war with Russia opened up new possibilities for the evacuation of the Jews to the East.

Eleven million Jews throughout Europe (Heydrich's figures for France and the Soviet Union were exaggerated) were to be involved in this definitive solution. Included in this sweeping program were Ireland with its 4,000 Jews and England with its 330,000—according to Heydrich's statistics. Heydrich spoke openly of a "Final Solution," but he did not define it, nor does a definition of the phrase appear anywhere in the minutes of the conference. But by this time, many Nazi bureaucrats already knew what the words meant. A month before in Krakow, on December 16, 1941, in a speech to the division chiefs of the Government-General, Frank had said that the Jews must be eliminated in one way or another, that the war would only be a partial success for Germany if Jewry survived it. Wherever they are found, and whenever possible, he said, Jews must be annihilated.

> The Jews represent for us also extraordinarily malignant gluttons. We have now approximately 2,500,000 of them in the Government-General, perhaps with the Jewish mixtures and everything that goes with it, 3,500,000 Jews. We cannot shoot or poison those 3,500,000 Jews, but we shall nevertheless be able to take measures which will lead, somehow, to their annihilation, and this is in connection with the gigantic measures to be determined in discussions from the Reich.[4]

Interoffice correspondence within Rosenberg's Ministry for Occupied Eastern Territories also proves conclusively that by December 1941, the annihilation of the Jews in the East had become a matter of official state policy. In one letter, for example, the Reich Commissioner at Riga had asked for instructions on the liquidation of Jews; he had not been able to find any directive in any regulation or decree. The reply, dated December 16, 1941, read: "Clarification of the Jewish question has most likely been achieved by now through verbal discussions. . . . Economic factors should fundamentally not be considered in the settlement of the problem. Moreover, it is requested that questions arising be settled directly with the senior S.S. and Police leaders."[4a] These leaders were then murdering Jews in the East by the hundreds of thousands.

There is not much reason to suppose that the nine civilians at Wannsee could have been shocked by anything that Heydrich said. According to Eichmann, who was among those present, Heydrich had "expected the greatest difficulties" but instead was greeted by "extraordinary enthusiasm" as he outlined his plans. A chart was shown indicating the Jewish communities to be "evacuated." Then Heydrich explained what was to happen to the "evacuees." "The Jews should now in the course of the Final Solution be brought to the East . . . for use as labor. In big labor gangs, with the sexes separated, the Jews who are capable of work are to be brought to these areas to build roads, in the course of which a large part will undoubtedly fall away through natural decline. The final residue will have to be treated accordingly. This residue will represent a natural selection, a hard core, which if freed, could rebuild Jewish life."[4b]

Characteristically, camouflage words are still used, but the meaning of the phrase "treated accordingly" had already been defined in the Einsatzgruppen actions and the gassings at Chelmno, Poland. The meaning was comprehended by the conferees at Wannsee; none demurred. The blueprint was quite simple: the Jews of Europe would first be transported to the conquered East, and there worked to death. Any survivors would then be put to death. There were none of the "difficulties" that Eichmann said Heydrich anticipated. All concurred.

Heydrich then differentiated the special classes of Jews: Jews sixty-five and over and Jews with serious disabilities—or decorations—from World War I would go to a special ghetto in Theresienstadt in Bohemia which he had just requisitioned. There followed a very involved discussion of the Mischlinge and of Jews in mixed marriages. The conference tentatively recommended that half-Jews be sterilized, but not deported.

Under pressure from Göring, Heydrich temporarily acquiesced in the exemption of certain Jewish war workers. This exemption did not extend, however, to Jews in the Government-General. Josef Bühler, who represented General Frank at the conference, denounced all of the Jews in Poland as carriers of disease and unfit for work. Since there was no transport problem in the Government-General, he urged that the "Final Solution" be organized there immediately.

The Grossen-Wannsee luncheon-meeting lasted a few hours and then formed into what Eichmann called an intimate social gathering, a very important occasion for Eichmann, who had never before met so many "high personages." He had prepared some material for the conference and after the other dignitaries had left, he sat near a fireplace with Müller, his chief, and Heydrich. He wrote:

> After the conference, Heydrich, Müller and your humble servant sat cozily around a fireplace. I noticed for the first time that Heydrich was smoking. Not only that, but he had cognac. Normally he touched nothing alcoholic. The only other time I had seen him drinking was at an office party years before. We all had drinks then. We sang songs. After a while we got up on the chairs and drank a toast, then on the table and then round and round—on the chairs and on the table again. Heydrich taught it to us. It was an old North German custom. But we sat around peacefully after our Wannsee Conference, not just talking shop but giving ourselves a rest after so many taxing hours.[5]

The irreversible decision to kill a whole people had been made.

In such impressive company, Eichmann's doubts about "such a bloody solution through violence" were now dispelled. "Here now, during this conference," he said, "the most prominent people had spoken, the Popes of the Third Reich. Not only Hitler, not only Heydrich, or Müller, or the S.S., or the Party, but the elite of the Civil Service had registered their support." At his trial, Eichmann explained at great length that he had no pricks of conscience about his work. He repeatedly told the police and the court in Jerusalem that he had done his duty, and had not only obeyed orders but obeyed the law of the land, based on the Führer's order. In recalling the conference he testified, "At that moment, I sensed a kind of Pontius Pilate feeling, for I was free of all guilt. . . . Who was I to judge? Who was I to have my own thoughts in this matter?"

After the Wannsee meeting was concluded, thirty copies of the conference record were circulated in the ministries and main offices of the S.S. Gradually the news of the Final Solution seeped into the ranks of the bureaucracy, but the knowledge did not come to all officials at once. How much a man knew depended on his proximity to the killing operations and on his insight into the nature of the destructive process. Often he repressed the knowledge. During the early months of 1942, one thing was not yet clear: the character of the "appropriate treatment"—the details, in other words, of the killing methods. This problem was not solved until spring, when gas-chamber camps were established in Poland. There was consequently a gap in time between the beginning of the deportations and the actual construction of facilities for killing the Jews. This lag is significant. Administratively, it resulted in the overcrowding of some of the eastern ghettos. Psychologically, it lent itself to the creation of the myth that Jews would merely be deported, not killed.[6]

As chief of the deportation system, Eichmann went to work immediately. He quickly became an expert in "forced evacuation," as he had been an expert in "forced emigration," and set up a network of stations all over Europe. He had Captain Gustav Richter in Bucharest, Theodor Dannecker in Paris, Ferdinand Aus der Fünten in Amsterdam, Wisliceny in Bratislava, all of them "Jewish advisers" who rounded up Jews and delivered them to the transports. Eichmann carefully set up his timetables for the transports with the Ministry of Transportation and conveyed millions of Jews to their deaths. Occasionally, he encountered difficulties —in France, Holland and Denmark. "Italy and Belgium," he also admitted, "were by and large failures. . . . It was not for nothing that I made so many trips to Paris and The Hague. My interest here was only in the number of transport trains I had to provide. Whether they were bank directors or mental cases, the people who were loaded on these trains meant nothing to me. It was really none of my business."[7]

In one country after another, Jews had to register, wear the yellow badge, and assemble for deportation to one of the extermination centers in the East. The German Foreign Office and the decree-drafting agencies worked for several years on certain assignments sketched at Wannsee. Some of the problem categories such as foreign Jews, Jews in mixed marriages, and half-Jews were never solved at all and defeated the Nazi craving for systematic thoroughness.

Like other industries, the industry of death had its departments of research, improvement, administrative services, a business office, and archives. Some aspects of these operations remain obscure because they were cloaked in great secrecy and because many of the technicians perished or disappeared after destroying their records. Moreover, after June 1942, a special unit began carefully to destroy all traces of Nazi exterminations. In April 1943, in reference to a statistical report ordered by Hitler, Himmler's secretary wrote: "The Reichsführer desires that no mention be made of the 'special treatment of the Jews.' It must be called 'transportation of the Jews toward the Russian East.'"[8] Himmler also referred to the secrecy surrounding the exterminations in a talk to a small group of followers in October 1943: "We have written a glorious page of our history," he said, "but it shall never appear on paper."

The voluminous archives of the Third Reich and the depositions and accounts of its leaders document in great detail the origin and development of Nazi plans for aggression, military campaigns and grandiose projects for a new world order, but the conception of the idea to exterminate Jews is impossible to document. If there ever were documents—and this is unlikely—explicitly outlining the plans, they are gone. The decision was unquestionably Hitler's, but the Führer Order is shrouded in secrecy; in fact, those to whom it was communicated were "bearers of secrets," and they, in turn, masked their orders and operations with camouflage words. Code names such as evacuation (*Aussiedlung*), special treatment (*Sonderbehandlung*), and resettlement (*Umsiedlung*) were devised to cover stark words like killing and extermination. "Radical solution" and "Final Solution" were also used, but whatever the language disguise, the meaning spread throughout Party and State offices, the officers' corps of the armed forces and all businesses connected with slave labor.

The extermination of millions posed no problems for Hitler. He had once told Rauschning, the former National Socialist president of the Danzig Senate: "Nature is cruel, therefore we, too, may be cruel. If I don't mind sending the pick of the German people into the hell of war without regret for the shedding of valuable German blood, then I have naturally the right to destroy millions of men of inferior races who increase like vermin." His plan for the subjugation of Eastern European peoples was no hasty improvisation but the expression of a mind that thought of political relations only in terms of master and slave. Likewise, his plans for the destruction of Jews uncoiled out of ideas he had had since his twenties. The threat to annihilate European Jewry in the event of a war was carried out when it became clear that the war would be protracted, that the Soviet Union would not crumble in a few weeks. The global extension of the war stimulated Hitler's fantasies of a vast empire of the dead and enslaved. The power to kill more life was irresistible.

A direct line runs from the early Nazi shrieks of the 1920's to kill Jews to the crematoria of 1942, with a terrifying consistency. And yet, Hitler might have altered his course on the Jewish question had strong enough opposition developed. He may have been a prisoner of his hate, but he was no prisoner of consistency as such. As the terms of the political struggle shifted, he was forced to beat his passion over contradictory "truths" and transpose his policies when it became expedient. He could work up a righteous fury over the Germans in the Tyrol, but he sacrificed them to the needs of an Italian alliance. So long as good relations with Poland were necessary to his foreign policy, he showed little concern for Poland's German minority, but when he decided to go to war against Poland, he worked himself into a frenzy of indignation over intolerable wrongs inflicted upon Germans in Poland. Next to "international Jewry," Bolshevism was the greatest menace of the world, but a Russian-German pact was drawn up and lasted for two years: the Slavs were not as "subhuman" as they were to become in 1941. It is not at all unlikely that Hitler could have found—or would have been forced to arrive at—some rationalization for a change in his anti-Jewish policy under different circumstances. If "international Jewry" had really been strong enough to affect international diplomacy when nations were toying with emigration possibilities, if it had had some genuine leverage and could have forced an emigration solution either in Palestine or elsewhere, Hitler would have backed away from his drastic policy. He could have "rid the Reich of Jews" had there been somewhere for them to go. He would also have been forced to change his policy if solid opposition to the exterminations had appeared: popular resistance at home of the kind that developed against his "euthanasia" program; a massive effort by Western Christian churches; early reprisal actions by the Allies as soon as deportations started; more widespread obstruction of the deportations—such as occurred in a few countries. Tragically, none of these countering forces developed with sufficient unity and wholeheartedness and the Nazis could self-righteously say there were no alternatives to the exterminations.

In making his decision to carry out the ultimate steps, Hitler undoubtedly acted alone. However, some leading Nazis are said to have pressed their views on him. Dr. Felix Kersten, Himmler's physiotherapist and confidant, has written in his memoirs that the order to begin systematic extermination of the Jews was given to Himmler by Hitler in the fall of 1940, and that this decision was urged upon him by Goebbels. In November 1942, Himmler confided to Kersten that he personally had proposed that Jews be settled in Madagascar, but that Goebbels prevailed:

> For months and years [Himmler said], Goebbels kept exciting the Führer to exterminate the Jews by radical means. Once the war had begun, he finally gained the upper hand. In the summer of 1940, the Führer ordered that the Jews be exterminated by degrees. [This type of exchange refers to those secret talks "unter vier Augen" (under four eyes) between Hitler and Himmler at which no one else except occasionally Bormann was allowed to be present. No records of these talks have survived.] He gave this task to the S.S. and to me. I told him, "The S.S. is ready to fight and die, from myself down to the last man, but don't give us a mission like this." The Führer became furious and said, "Himmler, you are being disobedient! . . . This is an order; I take the responsibility for it."[9]

For Himmler, Hitler's word was law, supreme over anything else. When Hitler spoke, Himmler's own convictions were at once laid aside. He regarded Hitler's orders as binding decisions, pronouncements from a world transcending this one. The phrase "The Führer is always right" had a mystical significance for him. According to Kersten, Himmler applied the extermination policy despite his own opposition to it because he was completely subservient to Hitler and because he had to prove that he was not afraid to carry out instructions to the letter. He also needed to show both Goebbels and Bormann, who kept a close watch on him, that he was a loyal executant of Hitler's orders.

It was also suggested by Viktor Brack that Martin Bormann, the Party Chancellor and something of a mystery man in the Nazi hierarchy, may have had a decisive role in reaching the "Final Solution." There can be no doubt, however, that the final decision was Hitler's.

The expression "Final Solution" (*Endlösung*) was used as early as September 1938 by Franz Stuckart who drafted the Nuremberg Laws. He wrote that the aim of racial legislation had been achieved, but that many of the decisions reached through the Nuremberg Laws would "lose their importance as the 'Final Solution' of the Jewish problem is approached." The phrase did not yet mean mass murder but shows clearly that the laws were intended only as a stopgap. The Jews would ultimately have to leave the Reich. But suppose war broke out before the Reich were free of Jews? The S.S. newspaper *Das Schwarze Korps* in November 1938 provided a possible answer: "The fate of such Jews as the outbreak of war should still find in Germany would be their final end, their annihilation." But prior to annihilation there were several intermediate steps; the expression "Final Solution" underwent progressive changes. At first prisoners of the Nuremberg Laws, the Jews then became future hostages for political demands Hitler might make on other countries. Then followed various emigration schemes, some of which, like the Madagascar Plan were taken seriously in some quarters, and perhaps fitfully by Hitler himself. The forced emigration of certain Jews into Poland in 1938 and 1939 followed —a rehearsal for the mass deportations to death camps later on. For a time, a possible "solution" lay in shoving the Jews out of Europe to some other continent, but there were no serious efforts and the Nazis themselves sabotaged many plans. Slow death in the ghettos was also a "solution." Systematic thoroughgoing destruction, however, was first applied to *Endlösung* early in 1941 when two of Hitler's fateful decisions were made. One concerned an order he gave in the spring of 1941 before the invasion of the Soviet Union. This order dispatched *Einsatzgruppen* to Soviet territory, where they moved from town to town killing Jewish inhabitants on the spot. Shortly after these "actions" had begun, Hitler handed down his second order to key Nazis dooming the rest of European Jewry.[10]

Evidence that a written order once existed was given in testimony at Nuremberg by Dieter Wisliceny, Eichmann's assistant in Slovakia and Greece and later in Hungary. Wisliceny recalled the following:

> I was sent to Berlin in July or August 1942 in connection with the status of Jews from Slovakia. . . . I was talking to Eichmann in his office in Berlin when he said that on written order of Himmler all Jews were to be exterminated. I requested to be shown the order. He took a file from the safe and showed me a top-secret document with a red border, indicating immediate action. It was addressed jointly to the Chief of the Security Police and S.D. and to the Inspector of Concentration Camps. The letter read substantially as follows: "The Führer has decided that the final solution of

the Jewish question is to start immediately. I designate the Chief of the Security Police and S.D. and the Inspector of Concentration Camps as responsible for the execution of this order. The particulars of the program are to be agreed upon by the Chief of the Security Police and S.D. and the Inspector of Concentration Camps. I am to be informed currently as to the execution of this order."

The order was signed by Himmler and was dated some time in April 1942. Eichmann told me that the words "final solution" meant the biological extermination of the Jewish race, but that for the time being able-bodied Jews were to be spared and employed in industry to meet current requirements. I was so much impressed with this document which gave Eichmann authority to kill millions of people that I said at the time, "May God forbid that our enemies should ever do anything similar to the German people." He replied, "Don't be sentimental—this is a Führer order."

I realized at the time that the order was a death warrant for millions of people and that the power to execute this order was in Eichmann's hands subject to approval of Heydrich and later Kaltenbrunner. The program of extermination was already under way and continued until late 1944. . . .[11]

What became known in Nazi higher circles as the "Führer Order on the Final Solution" was most probably given verbally to Göring, Himmler and Heydrich, who passed it down in the summer and fall of 1941 in stages. At a conference at Hitler's headquarters early in March 1941, when the invasion of Russia was imminent, Himmler was given extensive powers covering police actions in Russia. This period coincided with noticeable changes in conditions affecting Jews in every part of German-occupied territory; all of these changes were taken on orders from Himmler: the large Polish ghettos were enclosed; deportations to the Government-General were resumed; registration of Jews in France and the Low Countries took place; Dutch Jewish hostages were deported to German concentration camps. On March 25, 1941, Frank revealed to his close associates that Hitler had promised him that "the Government-General, in recognition of its accomplishments, would become the first territory to be free of Jews." By June 1941, the legal complexities involved in declaring Reich Jews stateless were waived. Hitler decided that no regulation was necessary since "after the war there would not be any Jews left in Germany anyhow."

The message was spreading. On May 20, 1941, Eichmann's office had warned all German consulates that Jewish emigration from France and Belgium was banned because "the final solution of the Jewish question" was in sight.

The mishaps caused by the public massacres in Russia led the Nazis to devise new techniques of death. There were many individual or local methods such as the use of quicklime and the injection of carbolic acid into the heart. But the officially sanctioned method, systematically carried out and responsible for the destruction of the greatest number of victims was death by asphyxiation: by carbon monoxide in the four large Polish camps (Chelmno, Belzec, Sobibor, and Treblinka) and by prussic acid fumes at Maidanek and Auschwitz. The use of carbon monoxide originated not, as one might expect, in the RSHA but in the Führer's Chancellery, Hitler's personal office, and had nothing to do with war or with the Jews, for that matter. It grew out of Hitler's "euthanasia" program of 1939 for the "suppression of lives unworthy to be lived."

An American correspondent in Berlin has recorded his first knowledge of the "mercy deaths" on September 21, 1940:

> X came up to my room in the Adlon today, and after we had disconnected my telephone and made sure that no one was listening through the crack of the door to the next room, he told me a weird story. He says the Gestapo is now systematically bumping off the mentally deficient people of the Reich. The Nazis call them "mercy deaths." He relates that Pastor Bodelschwingh, who runs a large hospital for various kinds of feeble-minded children at Bethel, was ordered arrested a few days ago because he refused to deliver up some of his more serious mental cases to the secret police. Shortly after this, his hospital is bombed. By the "British."[12]

Later, on November 25, 1940, a fuller story evolved: Pastor Friedrich Bodelschwingh had gone to Berlin to protest to a well-known surgeon. The surgeon had gone to the Chancellery, but Hitler said that nothing could be done. The surgeon and pastor then went to the Minister of Justice who seemed much more concerned over the fact that the killings were being carried out without benefit of written law, than that they were being carried out.

The correspondent's attention was called to certain death notices that appeared in several provincial newspapers. The notices were very peculiar. Only three places of death were mentioned: Grafeneck, a lonely castle near Münzingen, sixty miles from Stuttgart; Hartheim, near Linz; and Pirna, near Dresden. A typical notice appearing in the *Leipziger Neueste Nachrichten* for October 26, 1940, read as follows: "After weeks of anxious uncertainty, we received the shocking news on September 18 that our beloved Marianne died of grippe on September 15 at Pirna. The cremation took place there. Now that the urn has been received, the burial will take place privately on home soil." The form letter sent to the family explained that "because of the danger of contagion, we were forced by order of the police to have the deceased cremated at once."

The lethal chamber as a means of killing criminals or unwanted animals is an old idea, but as a method, first, to exterminate "useless mouths" —the feebleminded and mentally ill—and then, as the most efficient way to exterminate European Jews, it was used for the first time in history by the Nazis. The euthanasia program in Germany was not undertaken for the express purpose of using the mentally ill as guinea pigs for exterminating Jews; it had an independent origin. However, the men who were employed in the euthanasia program were sent East to build the installations for extermination and these men, who had come from Hitler's Chancellery or from the Health Department, were put under the authority of Himmler. This method of gassing was considered the "humane" way by certain Nazis; murder was now called "to grant a mercy death."

Hitler hesitated a long time before carrying euthanasia into practice, but his interest in gassing went back quite far. In *Mein Kampf* in 1924, he wrote that from 12,000 to 15,000 Jews should have been killed by poison gas at the beginning of World War I. (Hitler himself had been gassed in 1917.) It is significant that the euthanasia program went into effect on September 1, 1939, the day on which war was declared. Nazis could argue that the wartime need for hospital space and medical personnel justified reducing "useless mouths." Even so, the decree was never officially promulgated. Full power to implement the order was given to Philip Bouhler, head of Hitler's personal Chancellery, and Dr. Kurt Brandt, Hitler's personal physician. The organization created to administer the program was camouflaged as the "National Coordinating Agency for Therapeutic and Medical Establishments," and was given the code name "T-4," referring to its address at 4 Tiergartenstrasse in Berlin. Several well-known German psychiatrists and physicians gave T-4 their active and enthusiastic cooperation.[13]

The men who were actually in charge of the operation were Viktor Brack, who served under Bouhler, and Christian Wirth, chief of the Criminal Police in Stuttgart. A chemist, Dr. Kallmeyer, was assigned to assist them. Patients diagnosed as incurably insane were sent to stations set up throughout Germany—there may have been as many as twelve—in abandoned prisons or asylums. Because euthanasia was considered a "state" matter, decisions were made without consulting either the victims or their families. Their successive transfers from one place to another, conducted by the so-called "Charitable Foundation for Institutional Care" blotted out all traces of the patients and facilitated their quiet disappearance. During the functioning of the death camps in Poland, Wirth and his assistants continued to call themselves a "foundation" (*Stiftung*).

In the two years that the euthanasia stations functioned 50,000 or more ill persons were killed by gassing or lethal injections. Families were advised of the deaths by a form letter which stated that the patient had died of heart failure or pneumonia. Bouhler is credited with the idea of disguising the gas room as a shower bath with seats and douches, a sealed room containing pipes that canalized the exhaust of internal-combustion engines —basically the same procedure used at Auschwitz. In the case of the euthanasia program, however, there were outcries from the German people. In the case of the Jews, there were none. Secrecy surrounded both kinds of operations, but public protests to which Hitler yielded were registered only against the euthanasia program.

The existence of the euthanasia program soon became known. Families grew suspicious when they received death notices and the collective transfers of patients were noticed. There was even uneasiness in Party ranks. Families refused to send their ailing relatives to asylums. One might already be reading about the processes at Auschwitz or Treblinka in the protest sent in May 1941 to the Minister for Justice by the Frankfurt Court (*Landgericht*). This protest records the children of Hadamar (where a euthanasia station was located) shouting after the blacked-out buses, "Here are some more people being gassed," and describes the patients being taken to the gas room in paper skirts, and the corpses entering the furnace on a conveyer belt, while the smoke from the crematorium chimney is visible for miles. At night Wirth's experts drank themselves to oblivion in the little Hadamar *Gasthof* where the regular customers avoided them.[14]

The planned and rationalized aspect of euthanasia appealed to the Nazi mind. How "logical" for the state to eliminate a sick person whose unproductive existence is a terrible burden on his family and society. How "logical" to eliminate asocials and other undesirables. Such logic, combined with their fantastic faith in the state and its institutions, enabled the Nazis to make the leap that other nations have not dared to make, and to give the state the power to decide who was a mental defective, who a carrier of incurable disease, and who an asocial type. In its morbid preoccupation with youth and health, National Socialism had made illness a crime.

In the extermination of the Jews, these ideas were fused to anti-Semitism. The fear of disease among Nazis was often identified with hatred of the Jews. Jews were frequently shot because they were said to be carriers of contagious diseases or because they were "useless mouths" or vermin. The national welfare thus justified the massacres as it justified the elimination of incurables.

It was the churches, as might be expected, which protested openly against the euthanasia program and raised the moral questions that had to be asked. Pastor P. Braune of Hoffnungsthal, a leader of the Lutheran Church, sent the following memorandum to the Reich Chancellery, on July 9, 1940:

> How far can one go in destroying unworthy lives? The wholesale actions taken so far have shown that many persons clearly of sound mind have been included. . . . Are they directed only at the hopeless cases? . . . The questionnaire also lists the diseases of senility. The newest regulation calls for the elimination of children with illnesses resulting from birth trauma as well. What serious misapprehensions must come to mind! Will they stop

at the tubercular? The euthanasia program has already begun to be applied to prisoners.

Where is the limit? Who is abnormal, asocial, hopelessly sick? How will soldiers fare who acquire incurable ailments fighting for their country? Such questions have already been raised in the army circles.[15]

Pastor Braune was arrested for "irresponsible sabotage of government measures." But church protests continued and popular opposition mounted until Hitler had to discontinue the program. Although he had to retreat before spontaneous popular feeling, he assured Bouhler and Brandt that this was only a temporary suspension and that the program would be resumed after the war. The T-4 machinery was kept intact and questionnaires continued to go out. Not until the winter of 1944–45 did Brack give orders to destroy the euthanasia installations. However, T-4 personnel were used for "sanitary" missions on the Russian front during the winter of 1941–42 and their technical skill was employed in the secret extermination of Polish Jewry.

In its operations, the euthanasia program had come under the Führer's personal Chancellery; it had nothing to do with the RSHA, and yet many of the euthanasia stations were established near large concentration camps. Actually, from the summer of 1940 on, the camp administrators kept in touch with T-4, and "experts" began making periodic selections for "euthanasia" from among camp prisoners; the victims, however, were not incurables but Jews. Thus there was no real break in the activities of the "Charitable Foundations." A new code, "14f. 13," was devised for this operation and these symbols were put on falsified lunacy certificates and files of Jewish prisoners. On November 25, 1941, Dr. Fritz Mennecke, one of the "experts," wrote to his wife and described his second visit to Buchenwald: "Our second batch consisted of 1,200 Jews who do not have to be 'examined'; for them it was enough to pull from their files the reasons for their arrest and write them down on the questionnaires."[16] In the camp at Dachau, "14f. 13" was started in the fall of 1941 by a Professor Heyde, a psychiatrist, according to the testimony of the camp doctor:

> We four doctors sat at four tables placed between two huts, and several hundred prisoners had to file in front of us. The prisoners were divided according to their fitness for work and their political record. Since this commission stayed at Dachau only a few days, it was impossible for it to examine so many prisoners in so short a time. The examinations consisted solely of a rapid study of the documents in the prisoner's presence.[17]

In this way hundreds of prisoners—Aryans as well as Jews—were examined purely on their political records and were gassed at Schloss Hartheim in January 1942.

By the end of 1941, it was decided to start a widespread application of

"14f. 13." The Inspector of Concentration Camps of Office Group D of the S.S. Economic and Administrative Main Office sent the following letter to the camp commandants of several camps:

> As the camp commandants of Dachau, Sachsenhausen, Buchenwald, Mauthausen and Auschwitz have already been advised by letter, a medical commission is about to visit the above-named concentration camps shortly in order to select prisoners. A visit to the concentration camps Flossenburg, Gross-Rosen, Nuengamme and Neiderhagen is scheduled for the first half of January, 1942, for the same purpose. . . . At the conclusion of the check, a report to the Inspector of Concentration Camps is to be made, giving the number of prisoners assigned to special treatment "14f. 13."[18]

According to the original RSHA plan, among the first Jews of Europe to be exterminated were those in the occupied territories of the USSR, the *Reichskommissariat Ostland*, to which the first convoys of German Jews were sent at the end of 1941. One of the earliest documents linking the projected gassing camps with T-4 personnel is a letter from the Ministry for Occupied Regions of the East to the *Reichskommissariat* administration in Riga. In this letter, dated October 25, 1941, preliminary contacts were made between Eichmann and high officials of the ministry, after which the cooperation of the euthanasia experts was solicited:

> Herr Viktor Brack . . . is ready to collaborate in the installation of the necessary buildings and gas plants. He thinks it easier to construct the latter, of which we are short, on the spot. He would like to send his chemist, Kallmeyer, to Riga. . . . I should like to point out that S.S. Major Eichmann is in agreement with this procedure. He informs us that the camps are intended for Riga and Minsk where even Jews from the Old Reich may be sent. . . . To judge from the actual situation one need have no scruple in using Brack's method to liquidate Jews who are unsuitable for work. In this way, incidents will no longer be possible or tolerated such as occurred during the shootings at Vilna—and these shootings were public, according to the report that I have before me.[19]

The problem of finding sites, however, was not so simple. In October and November 1941, transports from the Reich began rolling into Lodz, where 60,000 Jews were to be quartered in the ghetto for the winter, and transported farther east in the spring; 5,000 were to be housed in barracks near Riga and in the ruins of the ghetto of Minsk—all movements which stirred strong objections among local officials. The plan was abandoned before the winter started and the location of the killing centers was shifted to the Government-General. In the spring of 1942, Brack ordered Wirth to report to Globocnik in Lublin. As Wirth's group prepared to leave for their new post, the men were put under an oath of silence by Himmler personally and told they must be "superhumanly inhuman." Under primitive conditions, Wirth and his crew began to construct chambers into which they piped carbon monoxide from diesel motors.

One by one, the killing centers were set up that spring. All were established in Poland. In the Lublin district, Belzec, Sobibor and Maidanek received transports from Lublin, Krakow, Radom, Galicia, the Reichsprotektorat, Slovakia and Holland. Treblinka on the Bug River was a death center for Jews from the Warsaw and Bialystok districts in the Government-General. Chelmno (Kulmhof) and Auschwitz (Oswiecim) were in the incorporated territories. (See map p. 151.)

The first installations were set up in Chelmno, near Lodz, in the form of mobile gassing vans already used in the Ukraine in September 1941. This was the place chosen for the reduction of the Lodz Ghetto, but the method was inefficient and slow: the Chelmno operation could handle only 1,000 deaths a day and the method of eliminating mass graves by dynamite proved ineffective until *Einsatzkommando* leader Blobel introduced the method he had instituted at Treblinka—constructing vast pyres of iron rails and wooden sleepers to consume the bodies so that, as Himmler had ordered, even the ashes would disappear.

As the gas pressure was irregular, the gassing trucks sometimes failed to kill quickly, and some victims died in a lingering agony. A few were able to escape during the early phase of the exterminations. One such survivor sounded the first cry of alarm to a rabbi of Grabow who wrote of Chelmno to his friends in Lodz on January 19, 1942:

> My very dear friends,
> I did not answer you until now, because I knew nothing very definite about all the things I've been told. Alas, to our great misfortune, we now know everything! I had here at my home an eyewitness who was saved by the grace of heaven. . . . I found out everything from him. The place where they are exterminated is called Chelmno, near Dabia, and they are buried in the neighboring forest of Lachow. The men are killed in two ways: shooting or gas. . . . For several days they have been taking thousands of Jews from Lodz and have done the same to them. Don't imagine that all this is written by a madman. Alas, it is the terrible tragic truth. . . . "Man, rend thy clothing, put on sackcloth with ashes, and go out into the midst of the city, and cry out with a loud and bitter cry." I am so tired that my pen can write no more. Creator of the universe, help us![20]

The Ghetto, however, refused to believe the worst until the news of the fate of the Warsaw Ghetto shocked them into reality. The Chelmno camp functioned continuously until October 1944. Between 250,000 and 300,000 Jews perished there.

Meanwhile, the euthanasia technicians, directed by Wirth, went on with their installations at Belzec, Sobibor and Treblinka. Globocnik, who was in charge of all of these camps, knew that these men had merely been loaned to him by Bouhler and Brack and would be returned when the euthanasia campaign was resumed in the Reich. Belzec, the first of the extermination camps, was opened on March 16, 1942. Here were gassed the Jews of the Lublin province who were being pushed eastward to make room for the 50,000 Austrian, German, Bohemian and Slovak Jews who had been sent east. Goebbels commented on this movement in his diary entry for March 27:

> Beginning with Lublin, the Jews in the General Government are now being evacuated eastward. The procedure is pretty barbaric and is not to be described here more definitely. Not much will remain of the Jews. About 60% of them will have to be liquidated. . . . The former *Gauleiter* of Vienna [Globocnik] who is to carry out this measure, is doing it with considerable circumspection and in a way that does not attract much attention. . . . The ghettoes that will be emptied in the cities of the General Government will now be refilled with Jews thrown out of the Reich. The process is to be repeated from time to time.

Later in 1942, there were large-scale "actions" in the Government-General, Polish annexed territory, and in former Polish White Russia.

Belzec at first involved the injection of engine-exhaust gas into a group of permanent chambers, each holding hundreds of people at a time. The installation at Belzec broke down constantly and the deportees were left in the "transfer station" for days at a time, where they crouched in the open, naked and without food or water. Sometimes they were left in railway boxcars to suffocate on sidings. At other times, victims were locked in the gas chambers for hours while efforts were made to start the diesel engines. But despite the breakdowns, Belzec claimed over a half-million persons after nine months of operation. It was closed in November 1942.

It was at Belzec in August 1942 that the superiority of hydrogen-cyanide or "Zyklon B" gassing (prussic acid fumes) over gassing by engine-exhaust fumes was demonstrated. The results of the demonstration were to involve Höss and Wirth, exponents of two different methods of killing, in a fierce professional rivalry. In each of the four death camps within the Government-General, gassing by engine-exhaust fumes was practiced, and although Zyklon B crystals were assumed to be more humane (that is, more efficient), Wirth resisted any change in the methods that had been evolved in the sinister euthanasia institutes. He was scornful of Höss, the advocate and successful practitioner of Zyklon B at Auschwitz. Höss had impressed Globocnik (who had visited Auschwitz earlier) with the superiority of Zyklon B, but it is another man, Kurt Gerstein, the protagonist in Rolf Hochhuth's play, *The Deputy*, who was present at Belzec in August, who will always be associated with the manufacture and distribution of Zyklon B gas. The story of Kurt Gerstein is one of the most enigmatic of the war, and yet in the seeming paradoxes of his life, he illuminates the way in which a "good" man in Hitler Europe gave himself to the industry of death.

Gerstein was born in 1905 in Westphalia,[21] the son of a Prussian magistrate. His family had a reputation for its high sense of duty and piety.

While still a student, Gerstein ran the local branch of the YMCA, and by 1932, he was an official of the national organization, in charge of its advanced program of biblical studies. He was a slender, blond young man whose physical features undoubtedly eased his way into the S.S. For a short time, Gerstein was enthusiastically swept up in the young Nazi movement that gripped Germans of all classes in the early years, but he soon became aware of the struggle the Nazis were waging against the Christian churches and turned against the movement with great revulsion. He began distributing anti-Nazi leaflets and spoke out against Goebbels' propaganda. In 1935, he was a victim of a public beating and in 1936, he was interned in a concentration camp, having meanwhile lost his government job as a mining engineer.

Among the first victims of Hitler's euthanasia campaign was Gerstein's sister-in-law. After learning of her death, Gerstein decided to join the S.S. in order "to see, to see clearly into its workings and then to proclaim them to the world!" He has written of this decision in his autobiography:

> Even if my life were in danger, I had no scruples about it; I had been caught out twice myself by Gestapo agents who had infiltrated into the church's most exclusive circles and who had prayed at my very side. I thought to myself: "Anything you can do, I can do better," so I volunteered for the S.S. The fact that my sister-in-law Berthe Eberling, had been put to death at Hadamar was an added incentive. I was introduced by the two Gestapo agents who had dealt with my case and I was accepted without any difficulty. One S.S. man said to me: "An idealist like you should make a fanatical party member."[22]

Gerstein was attached to the hygiene service of the S.S. and soon gained a reputation as something of a technical genius by perfecting a system for disinfecting and delousing troops and prisoners of war. One day, in the summer of 1942, he received top-secret orders to deliver a cargo of gas called Zyklon B to a "prisoner-of-war camp" in Poland. The camp was Belzec. It was there that Gerstein witnessed the mass annihilation of Polish Jews. As soon as he returned to Germany, he tried to let the world know what he had seen, but his efforts were fruitless.

His first attempt was a visit to the legation of Papal Nuncio Cesare Orsenigo in Berlin. He arrived there in civilian dress rather than in uniform and presented his credentials but was turned away. He wrote:

> My attempt to report all this to the Holy Father's chief delegate was without success. They asked me if I were a soldier. Then they refused me audience and asked me to leave the legation of his Holiness right away. I tell this to show how extremely difficult it was even for a German who was desperately hostile to the Nazis to expose the criminality of their leaders. What could be expected of an ordinary citizen if Christ's deputy on earth himself refused to hear me, even though tens of thousands of people were being slaughtered each day and a delay of mere hours seemed

to me criminal? Even the nuncio in Germany refused to be informed of this monstrous violation of Jesus' commandment: "Love thy brother as thyself."[23]

He then handed a report to the legal adviser of Cardinal Count Preysing, Archbishop of Berlin, with the request that it be forwarded to the Holy See.

Baron Gorran von Otter, attached to the Swedish Embassy in Berlin, met Gerstein on the train from Warsaw to Berlin as Gerstein was returning from his macabre mission to Belzec. The men talked all night. Von Otter sent a report of Gerstein's experience to Sweden. Gerstein was convinced that as soon as the German people learned about the exterminations they would turn against the Nazi regime. But the Swedish Government did not make public Gerstein's report or pass the information on to the Allies until August 1945. The resistance movement in Holland also knew about Gerstein's experience but withheld the information because of its incredibility: "They should not tell things to the world that nobody could believe."

Gerstein's efforts remained fruitless until the end. He tried sabotaging exterminations by pretending that certain deliveries of Zyklon B entrusted to him had been lost or spoiled. To carry out this deception, he had the contractors make out the invoices to him so that when he destroyed the shipments he could also destroy any incriminating evidence. It is not likely, however, that the chief supplier of the gas, Degesch in Frankfort, ever suffered a serious shortage of basic materials. The most Gerstein succeeded in doing seems to have been to modify the formula for the gas to eliminate an ingredient that made the deaths particularly painful.

Gerstein confided his activities and anguish to Lutheran pastors, to his wife and father, but it is impossible to know the real nature of his life in the last few years of the war. As late as March 1944, he still apparently felt free of what would seem to be inescapable complicity in a situation that he had freely chosen. At that time, he wrote to his father, the old Prussian magistrate:

> I'm still horrified at the words you shouted or rather wrote to me at a very desperate moment in my life when I was struggling with all the vital issues: "Hard times require hard methods!"—No. Phrases like that don't make what is happening acceptable to me. I can't believe, confronted with all the indescribable things I have to see, that this is my father's final comment. You should not depart for another world with these words and these thoughts. It seems to me that all of us who still have some time to live, still have the chance to reflect upon the practical possibilities and limits as well as the consequences of this total absence of moral restraint. . . . I'm aware of ideas and values we can't transgress against, except with the most drastic results. However powerless the isolated individual, and however much he honors prudence as the crowning virtue, he should never give up

those ideas and values he cherishes. He can never make excuses to his conscience by saying: "that doesn't concern me; I can't do anything about it."[24]

We do not have his father's reply, but six months later Kurt wrote again:

. . . you are wrong on one point. I never lent a hand in any of this. Whenever I received orders, I not only didn't carry them out but saw to it that they were disobeyed. For my part I come out of it all with clean hands and a clear conscience. It's very comforting to me. And I didn't act in this way out of cleverness. What does death matter, after all? I did it from principle and a sense of decency.

On May 5, 1945, the eve of the German surrender, two American Army officers were approached in the small Black Forest town of Rothweil by Gerstein. He introduced himself as the former head of the disinfection service of the Waffen S.S. and a onetime mining assessor and director of a Dusseldorf firm. He assured them that he had important information for them and handed them a seven-page memorandum in French. To lend more weight to his statements, he also gave them a set of bills for the purchase of Zyklon B gas by the RSHA; these bills were in his name. But the Americans did not detain him. He returned to Tübingen where his wife and two children were living. There he turned himself over to the French occupation authorities and gave them his autobiography.

Gerstein was taken to Cherche-Midi, the military prison in Paris. On July 25, 1945, according to the official report, he was found hanged in his cell. The inquest concluded that he had committed suicide. Possibly he had been too broken by his experiences to withstand life. And yet there is a letter from Gerstein to a member of the Dutch resistance movement, written from prison during the month in which he died, a letter so full of optimism that one questions whether, in fact, he did commit suicide. It is possible that he was killed by fellow S.S. prisoners. Caught in the S.S. machinery, having underestimated its power, Gerstein succumbed to it and served the extermination actions which he had wanted to fight. It is likely that he tried, as he had intended, to mitigate the sufferings of the prisoners. It is impossible to know to what extent he succeeded.

In 1956, the West German Information Service distributed tens of thousands of copies of Gerstein's description of the camp at Belzec. Since that time, the name of Gerstein has become synonymous with false witness and betrayal to surviving unrepentant S.S. members who are still to be found in Europe and South America. In 1949, there was a posthumous hearing for Gerstein before the de-Nazification Council of Tübingen, but the Council refused to rehabilitate him; instead, it classified him as a "petty Nazi," a man who became an instrument of the exterminations that he wanted to resist. The tribunal found that although he begged the

Vatican and Evangelical Church and the Dutch resistance to let the world know of the exterminations, he could not be absolved of responsibility for being enmeshed in them. Since he was powerless to stop the exterminations alone, the court concluded, he should have quit the S.S., whatever the cost.

This decision dramatically reveals the distance which separates those who were inside Planet Auschwitz and tried to overcome it and those who simply surrendered. Throughout the war, none of the Tübingen judges showed any opposition to the mass exterminations. Gerstein, although he failed to change events, dared to try. Had he not meddled and simply carried out orders, he would not have been guilty of daring and, thus, of failing. The court found him guilty not only for his failure but also for his initiative. Quite a different view was expressed by Pastor Martin Niemöller, who himself was inside the inferno. Niemöller testified to Gerstein's anti-Nazi convictions and described him as "a rather special kind of saint." The response to Hochhuth's play and a recent decision in Württemberg to rehabilitate Gerstein's reputation may be an indication of the influence of a new generation of Germans who agree with Niemöller.

In the account which he gave to the Americans, Gerstein described his assignment in January 1942 as chief of the *Waffen S.S.* technical disinfection services, including a section for extremely toxic gases. On August 17, 1942, Eichmann's deputy in Prague, Hans Günther, ordered him to get 100 kilos of prussic acid and accompany him and a Dr. Pfannenstiel, Professor of Hygiene at the University of Marburg, to Lublin. On the way Günther said: "This is one of the most secret matters there are, even the most secret. Anybody who talks about it will be shot immediately." At Lublin, Gerstein met Globocnik who said: "You will have to disinfect large piles of clothing coming from Jews, Poles, Czechs, etc. Your other duty will be to improve the workings of our gas chambers, which operate on the exhaust from a Diesel engine. We need a more toxic and faster working gas, something like prussic acid." Hitler had ordered more speed. Globocnick expressed the importance of carrying out such a "gigantic task" and described it as good and necessary.

On August 18, the men left for Belzec. Gerstein was introduced to Wirth, who took him around the plant. Gerstein observed everything:

> We saw no dead bodies that day, but a pestilential odor hung over the whole area. Alongside the station there was a "dressing" hut with a window for "valuables." Farther on, a room designated as "the barber." Then a corridor 150 meters long in the open air, barbed wire on both sides, with signs: "To the baths and inhalants." In front of us a building like a bath house; to the left and right, large concrete pots of geraniums or other flowers. On the roof, the Star of David. On the building, a sign: "Heckenholt Foundation."

The following morning, a little before seven, there was an announcement: "The first train will arrive in ten minutes!" A few minutes later a train arrives from Lemberg: 45 cars arrive with more than 6,000 people; 200 Ukrainians assigned to this work flung open the doors and drove the Jews out of the cars with leather whips. A loudspeaker gave instructions: "Strip, even artificial limbs and glasses. Hand all money and valuables in at the 'Valuables' window. Women and young girls are to have their hair cut in the 'barber's hut.' " (An SS Unterführer told me: "From that they make something special for submarine crews.")

Then the march began. Barbed wire on both sides, in the rear two dozen Ukrainians with rifles. They drew near. Wirth and I found ourselves in front of the death chambers. Stark naked men, women, children and cripples passed by. A tall SS man in the corner called to the unfortunates in a loud minister's voice: "Nothing is going to hurt you! Just breathe deep and it will strengthen your lungs. It's a way to prevent contagious diseases. It's a good disinfectant!" They asked him what was going to happen and he answered: "The men will have to work, build houses and streets. The women won't have to do that. They will be busy with the housework and the kitchen."

This was the last hope for some of these poor people, enough to make them march toward the death chambers without resistance. The majority knew everything; the smell betrayed it! They climbed a little wooden stairs and entered the death chambers, most of them silently, pushed by those behind them. A Jewess of about 40 with eyes like fire cursed the murderers; she disappeared into the gas chambers after being struck several times by Captain Wirth's whip. Many prayed; others asked: "Who will give us the water before we die?"

SS men pushed the men into the chambers. "Fill it up," Wirth ordered; 700–800 people in 93 square meters. The doors closed. Then I understood the reason for the "Heckenholt" sign. Heckenholt was the driver of the diesel, whose exhaust was to kill these poor unfortunates. Heckenholt tried to start the motor. It wouldn't start! Captain Wirth came up. You could see he was afraid because I was there to see the disaster. Yes, I saw everything and waited. My stopwatch clocked it all: 50 minutes, 70 minutes, and the diesel still would not start! The men were waiting in the gas chambers. You could hear them weeping, "as though in a synagogue," said Professor Pfannenstiel, his eyes glued to the window in the wooden door. Captain Wirth, furious, struck with his whip the Ukrainian who helped Heckenholt. The diesel engine started up after two hours and 49 minutes by my stopwatch. Twenty-five minutes passed. You could see through the window that many were already dead, for an electric light illuminated the interior of the room. All were dead after thirty-two minutes.

Jewish workers on the other side opened the wooden doors. They had been promised their lives in return for doing this horrible work, plus a small percentage of the money and valuables collected. The men were still standing like columns of stone, with no room to fall or lean. Even in death you could tell the families, all holding hands. It was difficult to separate them while emptying the room for the next batch. The bodies were tossed out, blue, wet with sweat and urine, the legs smeared with excrement and menstrual blood. Two dozen workers were busy checking mouths which they opened with iron hooks. . . . Dentists knocked out gold teeth, bridges and crowns with hammers.

Captain Wirth stood in the middle of them. He was in his element and, showing me a big jam box filled with teeth said, "See the weight of the gold! Just from yesterday and the day before! You can't imagine what we find every day, dollars, diamonds, gold! You'll see!" He took me over to a jeweler who was responsible for all the valuables. They also pointed out to me one of the heads of the big Berlin store Kaufhaus des Westens, and a little man whom they forced to play the violin, the chiefs of the Jewish workers' commandos. "He is a captain of the Imperial Austrian Army, Chevalier of the German Iron Cross," Wirth told me.

Then the bodies were thrown into big ditches near the gas chambers, about 100 by 20 by 12 meters. After a few days, the bodies swelled. . . . When the swelling went down again, the bodies matted down again. They told me that later they poured diesel oil over the bodies and burned them on railroad ties to make them disappear.[25]

What happened at Belzec for hundreds of thousands of Jews happened also at Treblinka and Sobibor and Maidanek. There is little to add to Gerstein's report. At Treblinka, the method was somewhat different: the gas chambers were charged with the engines of captured Russian tanks and lorries. Construction was not started until June 1942 and the camp was not ready for the planned liquidation of the Warsaw Ghetto. But in two months, 300,000 Jews were deported. There were days when as many as 10,000 people left the assembly point in Warsaw, bound for Treblinka. It is impossible to know how many perished on the trains.

For the Nazi technicians of death, production was a matter of personal prestige. For Wirth, the experience of Gerstein at Belzec was a source of mortification. His carbon monoxide technique had made a bad impression. Facing the greatest crisis of his career, he dropped his pride and begged Gerstein "not to propose any other type of gas chamber in Berlin." Gerstein obliged and ordered the Zyklon B buried, on the pretext that it had spoiled in transit. Later, he was placed in charge of production of Zyklon B which was used at Maidanek and Auschwitz. Höss and Wirth were henceforth bitter enemies, but it was Höss, who used Zyklon B at Auschwitz and proved that it was much more efficient than carbon monoxide. Even after the war, he spoke proudly of his "improvements" in creating the dense world of death that we know by the name of "Planet Auschwitz."

Treblinka, Sobibor, Chelmno and Belzec were almost exclusively death centers and had no non-Jewish inmates. Except for very minor industrial activity in Treblinka and Sobibor, they were not linked with war production. Jews sent to these camps were doomed to immediate extermination. There is only one known survivor of Belzec, Rudolf Reder, and a mere handful of survivors of the other camps. Even those Jews called *Sonderkommandos* who worked in Dante's ninth circle of hell—pulling bodies from the gas chambers, searching them and burying them—were themselves exterminated at regular intervals and replaced with new teams. Not more than a few dozen survived the *Sonderkommando* rebellions of 1943 in Treblinka and Sobibor and the one in Chelmno in January 1944.

While these four camps were in operation there was another technical development in the incorporated territory of Upper Silesia, a project built by a man who had come up in the concentration camp world, Rudolf Höss. Höss became a prime figure in the exterminations. At Nuremberg, he testified freely—even exaggeratedly—and complacently enumerated the improvements in the killing process introduced at Auschwitz, for which he took credit. In Himmler's talk with him in June 1941, Himmler had made it clear that he would be in complete charge of the death center at Auschwitz; he was ordered to make his preparations immediately. However, characteristically, Himmler tried to stimulate the zeal of his subordinates by getting them to compete with each other. Not only were Höss and Wirth (who called Höss an "awkward disciple") professional rivals; other chiefs were also assigned to work at mass-murder methods. Höss became most proficient at it, creating an industry of death by using Zyklon B and by utilizing techniques of mass production and the assembly line.

Höss' basic idea was simple enough and had a typical Nazi touch. All kinds of vermin and insects infested the Auschwitz barracks and the usual methods of disinfection were used to fight them. The Testa Company, which worked for the Wehrmacht, supplied a gas with a prussic acid base patented as Zyklon B, which served as one of the products used. Not only was it used for large-scale fumigations of buildings, but for disinfecting clothes in specially constructed gas chambers and for delousing human beings, protected by gas masks. The gas was powerful. That it should have become involved in an operation to kill Jews by the hundreds of thousands is not a mere accident. In German propaganda, Jews had frequently been portrayed as insects. Frank, Goebbels, and Himmler had repeatedly stated that the Jews were parasites who had to be exterminated like vermin. Himmler, for example, had said:

> Anti-Semitism is exactly the same as delousing. Getting rid of lice is not a question of ideology; it is a matter of cleanliness. In just this same way anti-Semitism for us has not been a question of ideology but a matter of cleanliness.

The first gassings at Auschwitz were probably conducted on September 15, 1941, as a result of Eichmann's visit to Auschwitz. Some 600 invalid Russian prisoners of war, together with 250 inmates of the Auschwitz infirmary, were locked in the cellar of Block 11, the notorious penal block in the main camp. The windows were covered with dirt and Zyklon B crystals were thrown on the floor. The next afternoon, an S.S. man, wearing a mask, opened the door and found many prisoners still alive. More crystals were thrown in and by evening all of the men were asphyxiated. Later in the year, according to Höss, the first permanent installations consisted of two farm buildings near Birkenau which were made airtight and equipped with solid wooden doors. Their capacity was small and, as there was no crematory, bodies were burned in the open. Nevertheless, these installations were used to the end. During this early phase, the victims were Russian prisoners of war, whose number Höss estimated at 70,000. Later, Aryan prisoners were generally assassinated individually by injections of potassium cyanide in the heart.

The mass extermination of Jews at Auschwitz began in the summer of 1942. The camp was now densely populated; there were at least 150,000 prisoners and laborers, guarded by more than 3,000 S.S. men. There were periodic selections at Auschwitz, but the first and most important took place when the convoy arrived. The vast majority in the transport were sent to death. The survivors, who had a life expectancy of about three months, joined the enslaved workers toiling in the vast underground of branch camps and factories attached to Auschwitz. Here, tens of thousands were worked to death in I. G. Farben factories making artificial rubber and synthetic gasoline, in the Krupp armament works, coal mines and farms, and S.S. experimental stations.

From the summer of 1942 on, a continuous stream of convoys, often at the rate of four trains daily, brought to Auschwitz victims rounded up by IVB4 and transported by Eichmann. When the two original gas chambers proved inadequate, four new installations were built by Topf and Son of Erfurt, specialists in the construction of cremation furnaces.

By adjoining the crematorium to the gas chamber, Höss could dispose of bodies quickly—his chief contribution to the process of mass murder. His other was to demonstrate the clear advantage of Zyklon B over carbon monoxide. Höss had been to Treblinka, where only 80,000 could be exterminated in half a year. Treblinka used carbon monoxide and had relatively small gas chambers; besides, at Treblinka, the victims often knew what was in store for them and created "riots and other difficulties." In these respects Höss improved on the Treblinka techniques. At Auschwitz, asphyxiation was quick—it took about fifteen minutes—and was combined with incineration under one roof, the gas chambers were large, and victims were fooled into thinking they were going through a delousing process. Some groups were taken to the "baths" to the accompaniment of light operatic music played by girls dressed in blue and white. The buildings at Auschwitz also conspired to delude the victims. The ground over the gassing cellar was converted into a well-kept lawn with flower borders; the signs at entrances merely said "Baths." On the lawn, at regular intervals, stood mushroomlike concrete forms, and these, though they might not arouse the curiosity of newcomers very much, were the shafts down which, after unscrewing the lids, the orderly was to scatter the amethyst-blue Zyklon B crystals. Surviving prisoners in nearby blocks recall the grisly signal to the orderly from a Sergeant Moll: "Na, gib ihnen schon zu fressen" ("All right, give them something to chew on").

Slowly the gas escaped from the perforations in the sheet-metal columns. Generally the victims were too tightly packed to notice this at first, but at other times they could sit comfortably gazing up at the douches, from which no water came, or at the floor which had no drainage runnels. Then they would feel the gas and crowd together away from the menacing columns and stampede toward the huge metal door where they piled up in one blue clammy blood-spattered pyramid. Twenty or thirty minutes later, electric pumps removed the poisonous air and the Sonderkommandos, wearing gas masks and gum boots and carrying hoses, went into their ghastly search for gold, teeth, and hair. Then followed the journey by lift or rail wagon to the furnaces, the mill that ground the clinker to fine ash, and the truck that scattered the ashes in the stream of the Sola.[26]

The construction of such elaborate installations required much more time than the building of the killing centers in the Government-General. Not until early 1943 were the first crematoria completed. They were solemnly dedicated in the presence of important dignitaries from Berlin. Some 8,000 Jews from Krakow, the capital of the Government-General, were the first and symbolic victims. Two more crematoria were ready six months later. The four crematoria contained 46 ovens with a total capacity of almost 12,000 bodies every 24 hours. During certain periods, entire convoys were gassed without any selections because of lack of space. The maximum of 12,000 to 15,000 per day was reached in May–June 1944, during the massive deportation of Hungarian Jews. By this time, the ovens were no longer adequate, so enormous funeral pyres were made to consume the surplus bodies. Himmler's order to stop the exterminations and dismantle the crematoria arrived in Auschwitz on November 2, 1944. There were no new transports after November.

Although the figure can never be known exactly, it is estimated that almost 2 million Jews perished at Auschwitz through immediate extermination, while another 300,000 registered prisoners (many of whom were Jews) died—some of them in the gas chambers, others from hunger, disease, inhuman labor, beatings and so-called medical experiments.

Thus, Hitler's New Order.

17 The Warsaw Ghetto Uprising

THE HUNGER that raged through the Polish ghettos was the theme not only of scientific experiments but of poetry. In this body of literature, the "testament of lost men," is a poem called "Hunger" written by Joseph Bau during the summer deportations:

> Flour, curdled into a loaf of concrete—
> a condensed payment for a day of torment,
> here is bread.
>
> Eight stomachs creeping out through the eyes
> divide it into eight equal parts,
> to the last little crumb;
> here is the idol
> to which the mind is praying.[1]

Such hunger, the Nazi highest circles believed, would extinguish Jewish life. Before the accelerated exterminations began, it was assumed that hunger would do the killing in the ghettos. Hunger was a big killer— though not as big as the Nazis wished—as was typhus. In the Warsaw Ghetto of a half-million Jews, starvation and typhus caused the deaths of 43,000 Jews in 1941 and 37,000 in the first nine months of 1942. During their short period of existence, the ghettos accounted for the death of one fifth of Polish Jewry. This was a very high mortality rate but it was not fast enough for the Nazis. They could not count on starvation, nor would they "entrust" the task of "solving the Jewish problem" to a future generation. Frank's threat, "if the Jews do not die of hunger, the measures will be intensified," was swiftly carried out.

For Warsaw, "intensified" measures began on July 22, 1942. As a fitting memorial to Heydrich, who had been assassinated near Prague on May 29, Himmler, on July 19, ordered all Jews except those in concentration camps to be deported by the end of the year. The ghettos and labor camps were to be wiped out.

The failure to complete the Treblinka gassing installation in April had delayed the Warsaw "resettlement." The war had also interfered and slowed down the transfers. The German summer offensive began on the Kharkov front on June 10 and nonmilitary transport had been temporarily suspended. But Himmler had more power over the Ministry of Transport than did the Wehrmacht High Command. On July 22, his field adjutant, General Karl Wolff, was assured, "One train a day with 5,000 Jews goes from Warsaw to Treblinka via Malkinia as well as two trains a week with 5,000 Jews each from Przemysl to Belzec."

The mass expulsions from Warsaw began on July 22, 1942, the day before the Ninth of Ab. On the following day, *Tishah b'Ab*, a day of fasting and prayer to commemorate the destruction of the Second Commonwealth by Titus in A.D. 70, the gas chambers of Treblinka began to operate. The organization of these actions on a somber Jewish holiday was no coincidence. The Nazis studied the Jewish calendar and frequently scheduled the most destructive actions while Jews were preoccupied. Within two months, 300,000 Jews were sent to their death.

On July 20, Dr. Adam Czerniakow, president of the *Judenrat*, had been summoned by the Ghetto administrator Auerswald and ordered to prepare for the *Aussiedlung* (resettlement) of "nonproductive" elements beginning on July 22. On July 21, 60 Jews, including some *Judenrat* officials, were arrested and kept as hostages at Pawiak prison while the German police companies, mainly old soldiers who guarded the Ghetto, were replaced by Ukrainian and Lithuanian militia. Captain Hermann Hoefle, of the extermination division of *Einsatz* Reinhard, took over the German *Transferstelle* under orders from Globocnik. Jews involved in the order were to report voluntarily to an evacuated hospital at the *Umschlagplatz*, the transfer station on Stawki Street near the railway. There, freight cars would take them "to the East." Hoefle said that the "resettlement" would be limited to 60,000 nonproductive workers, 6,000 a day.

The German order resulted in the assembling of inmates of Jewish prisons, old men and women and dependents living in charitable institutions. Members of the *Judenrat* and other hostages were to answer for strict fulfillment of the order.[2]

While arrested Jews sat locked up in the Pawiak, flying squads of *Einsatz* Reinhard ranged through streets of the Ghetto and broke into apartments at random, shot some Jews and then hurried away. About 100 upper-class Jews were killed this way. Suddenly, the *Judenrat* officers were released from prison without explanation. The Ghetto was in wild confusion. What did the new German measures mean? What was the reason behind the sudden order? A sense of impending doom underlay the questions. A Gestapo man was heard to say: *"Es wird schon was kommen!"* ("Something is going to happen.")

The Germans did not hand out typed orders; Auerswald dictated regulations in the *Judenrat* office. The heart of the order was Instruction No. 2 which read: "The Judenrat is responsible for producing the Jews designated daily for settlement. To accomplish this task, it is to use the Jewish Order Service. The Judenrat is to see to it that 6,000 Jews are delivered daily, not later than 4 P.M. to the *Umschlagplatz* beginning July 22." The order further stated that later, the *Judenrat* would receive definite instructions regarding the specific houses and streets to be emptied. A list of exempted categories was added in a special protocol. The *Judenrat* posted the order on notice boards amid expressions of fear, shock, anger and pleading. Black and white posters appeared all over the Ghetto. There was a mad rush for working cards at 80 Lezno Street, the German Labor Bureau. Crowds besieged the Toebbens, Hallman and Schultz factories, begging for work or trying to find friends with influence. "Shops" were improvised overnight around a few sewing machines and bolts of cloth.

The list of exempt categories was quite large and included not only Jews with valid work certificates but those fit for work, their wives and children, Jewish Council members, Jewish police and their families, and hospital and sanitary personnel and their families. All employees in institutions such as the Board of Supplies, the Jewish Social Self-Help, the Supply-Delivery Society, the Cooperative Bank, the Health Chamber, the Artisans' Association, and the Waste Removal Enterprise were made subordinate to the *Judenrat* and treated like employees of the *Judenrat*. The extent of the exemptions numbed the will to believe the worst as well as the will to resist, and even aroused wild hopes of salvation in some.

Each deportee was permitted to take along 15 kilograms of luggage (33 pounds) and precious objects such as jewels, gold, and money. Food for three days was also permitted. These allowances lulled suspicions of those who still had any material possessions. The "resettlement" would take the weak and nonproductive, but it was a resettlement, the Ghetto believed.

On July 22, at nine o'clock in the morning, several trucks with Ukrainian guards drove up before the *Judenrat* office. Lithuanian, Latvian and German guards had cordoned the entire Ghetto. Hoefle addressed Czerniakow and the other members of the Council: "Today begins the evacuation of the Jews from Warsaw. You know that there are too many Jews. To you, the *Judenrat*, I entrust the carrying out of this task. Should you neglect to acquit yourself satisfactorily, you will all hang from the same rope."[2a]

The house blockades began with the encirclement of an area by a Ghetto militia unit of 15 to 25 men under the command of a Security Police officer. All entrances and exits were closed. All tenants were then ordered to come out of their houses and present their documents. Jewish police inspected the apartments to make sure that all inhabitants had complied with the order. The commandant of the group examined the

Ausweise, released *Ausweis* holders and directed the rest to horse-drawn carts waiting to take them to the *Umschlagplatz*. No Germans were involved in the house searches.

The first day's quota was easily filled, made up of the half-dead inmates of the notorious "Death Points"—the charity refuges for the homeless, poverty-stricken Jews from the provinces, prisoners, incurables, beggars, ragpickers and corpse-gatherers. In their first actions, the Germans took their sick and helpless victims straight to the Jewish cemetery, where they were killed. These the Germans called "Transportunfähig"—"unfit for transport." This was done purposely to foster the idea that only the physically "useless" were being killed while all others would be actually resettled.

In the next few days, from eight to six the Ghetto streets were deserted, but early in the morning, from dawn to eight, and in the evenings, they were abnormally crowded. People were looking to see who had been "resettled." The typical greeting was "Are you covered?" No one ventured near the *Umschlagplatz* to see what was happening, although people were aware that trains were being shunted back and forth. To confuse the already bewildered Jews even further, the Germans extended the curfew from nine to ten. There were rumors that the German unit carrying out the action was the dread *Vernichtungskommando* (Annihilation Squad) of Lublin and Tarnow, billeted at Zelazno 103. But the Germans planted counterrumors: the resettlement would be over by July 31. Czerniakow had received daily assurances from Gestapo agents.

Meanwhile, there was no response to the Ghetto's sound of alarm sent through the Polish underground. The BBC maintained a complete radio silence.

On July 23, the second day of the deportations, the Ghetto was stunned to hear that Czerniakow, the head of the *Judenrat*, had committed suicide. On his desk stood a vial of potassium cyanide and a glass half filled with water. There were also two letters, one to his wife, asking her to forgive him but also explaining that to act in any other way had become impossible for him. On the other slip of paper was written: "Ten thousand are demanded for tomorrow, and then seven thousand each time . . ." The Germans had raised the daily quota of deportees and Czerniakow refused to comply. His body was taken away on a handcart; the Germans forbade any mourners to follow it. At half past five the following morning, he was buried in strictest secrecy, scarcely more than ten people attending. The day after his suicide, a group of S.S. officers called on the *Judenrat* to express their condolences and to repeat their assurances that Jews were in fact being resettled.

Although the masses in the Ghetto did not yet know what their fate would be, Czerniakow knew beyond any doubt that the deportations meant death for them. His suicide was criticized by some Jews in the Ghetto as unworthy of a leader, and fruitless, besides. Later, they said that he should have explicitly warned the Ghetto that compromise was no longer possible. But others believed that he hoped his act would bestir Jews to see their predicament as it really was. Cznerniakow had suffered great indignities from the Germans but stayed at his post with the most strenuous exertion of will. He was not "popular"—very few *Judenrat* leaders were—but he worked as long as he could in a distasteful job out of a sense of bitter duty. There are some survivors who believe that he could have lived without the "Jewish patch," on the Aryan side, but he refused. He also refused to resign, although he felt that his role as president of the Council was a crime against himself, a humiliation. He held on, believing he could serve Jews in a small way. When that margin evaporated, he took his life.

Meanwhile, through the rest of July and most of August, the deportees were tagged and thrust into columns and then shoved into trains. Many continued to leave voluntarily, believing that nothing could be worse than the Ghetto.

Like others, Ringelblum himself believed that the main reason for the passivity of the Jews in July was the cunning tactics of the Germans, their deception regarding the true purpose of the expulsion. The Gestapo had brought agents from Lublin to spread the fabrication of a "transfer of population to the East." Thousands of starving Jews voluntarily presented themselves at the *Umschlagplatz* in order to go east "for work." Faked letters allegedly written by deportees and brought back by Polish railwaymen were circulated. A special *Ausweis*, stamped *Einsatz* Reinhard, bearing the Nazi eagle and swastika with the inscription, "Not subject to resettlement" aroused new hopes.

After July 29, the crescendo of violence escalated. The Germans began a new phase of destruction. Up to that date, Jewish police had gone from house to house managing the selections. After July 29, this was done mainly by Germans, Ukrainians, Lithuanians and Latvians. The Jewish police thereafter acted chiefly as sentinels, messengers and searchers. During this phase, moreover, Germans began entering factories, seizing perfectly sound workers. Some of the smaller shops were entirely evacuated. Deportations became increasingly haphazard and unpredictable. *Ausweise* were torn up; entire blocks of streets were cut off by barbed wire and human cordons. The previous allowance of 15 kilograms of luggage was no longer respected. People were dragged away without any belongings. There seemed to be no pattern to the new German measures. The very senselessness of the new deportations created new anguish for Jews.

After July 29, almost no Jews reported voluntarily for deportation. On that date, the Socialist broadside *Storm* warned the Ghetto that deportations might mean death. Sensing the growing passive resistance, the Germans used their bread and marmalade ruse on July 29, 30 and 31, and again on August 2, 3 and 4. For those broken by hunger, a big loaf of bread and tin of marmalade offered as a travel ration by the German Resettlement Office were enough to break down their resistance. The enticement read: "I hereby announce to the inhabitants subject to deportation, in accordance with the orders of the Authorities, that each person who reports voluntarily for deportation on the days of July 29, 30, and 31, will be supplied with food, i.e., 3 kg. of bread and 5 kg. of marmalade. The gathering point and the place for the food distribution is Stawki Square, corner of Dzika Street." This was signed by the Chief of the Militia, July 29, 1942.

The Germans had again found "voluntary" deportees who surrendered of their own will, individually or in small groups. A young woman observed:

> They are loaded with sacks, baskets, suitcases, they drag with them the last remnants of their poor belongings, and they are all marching in the same direction—towards the Umschlagplatz. . . . Some of them are walking slowly, with drooping heads; others move nervously ahead, with unsteady, frightened eyes, seemingly in a hurry, as if they were afraid of being forced to go back. Nobody holds them back, nobody hinders them from moving forward. . . . Scarcely anyone in the ghetto is surprised at this quiet, resigned marching. From the hiding places and the shops people look at them with deep sorrow, sometimes mixed with a feeling of admiration. . . . "They have found the strength to take a decision." . . . Crushed under the burden of ghetto life, shriveled or swollen from starvation, haunted by the constant fear of being seized, these Jews could no longer go on with their fight. . . . How enticing were these three brown loaves![3]

By the end of July, 59,000 Jews from the Ghetto had been deported. The German guards surrounded the marked streets and walls of the Ghetto, the Ukrainians encircled the houses, and the Jewish police walked into the courtyards and houses to summon the inhabitants. They either came down or they were shot. A survivor wrote:

> People run from all staircases. Nervously, on the run, they clothe themselves in whatever is handy. Some descend as they are, sometimes straight from bed, others are carrying everything they can possibly take along, knapsacks, packages, pots and pans. . . . Trembling, they form groups in front of the house. They are not allowed to talk but they still try to gain the policemen's pity. From nearby houses similar groups of trembling, completely desperate people arrive and form into one long column. . . . Two, three shots signify the death of those who did not heed the call and remained in their homes. The "blockade" is finished.[4]

The deportees were herded into the *Umschlagplatz*, a large yard that measured 30 by 50 meters, surrounded by a high brick wall and the back of a hospital that the Germans had evacuated in July. A gap of several meters at the southwest corner was cut by a wire fence. Within the yard were some Jews huddled together, dejected and silent, sitting on bags and suitcases. Some cooked potatoes over a wood fire. Others were bartering rings and watches for slices of bread from guards. Still others were frantically waving credentials before indifferent police. Porters, rickshaw-pullers, cartmen and hospital aides were moving stretcher cases and equipment. When a trainload was to be taken away, cries of "Cars!" swept over the yard. Many Jews fled to the hospital building, crowding the corridors and rooms in panic. Some fainted. Some were shot by pursuing guards. As the hospital toilets were locked, people relieved themselves wherever they could. The frightened Jews cowered in dark shadows, doorways or attic rooms, wherever there was a possible escape from the police. The guards raced through the corridors, their guns crackling in the oppressive air. Some Jews flexed their muscles to show the guards how strong they were; some became crazed with fear.

A journalist has recorded the horror of the *Umschlagplatz:*

> With a surprisingly clear awareness, I feel, or rather understand, that I will cease to live before long. Maybe it will happen in the next quarter of an hour. It is strange that I am by no means stunned. My brain is functioning normally. Following my "professional" habit, I note in my memory the literary aspects of the tragedy of which I am one of the objects. I am becoming aware of the wildly widened pupils of the eyes of the girl who is standing near me. I hear her halting breath. And then I see the dull face of the Latvian, who is biting his dirty nails while watching us. . . . The air is dreadfully sticky, the stench, unbearable. I am leaning against the wall in a state of numbness. For twenty-four hours I haven't eaten, but I don't feel hungry. I am plagued by thirst. There is no water. I press my cheek against the wall. On the dirty, gray wall the design of a heart pierced by the cupid's arrow has been carved awkwardly with a pocket-knife. The inscription says: "Blima and Chilek, August, 1942." . . . Night is falling. The glare of the fire flashes from the ghetto. One hears rifle shots. The halls of the Umschlagplatz are not lighted. We are sitting in darkness. Somewhere nearby a child is crying. The whining gets on our nerves. The mother rises from the floor and walks towards the door. She passes a window. At the same moment a shot cracks from behind the window. The woman slowly slips down onto the filthy, spittle-covered floor. She is dead. . . .
>
> At night, some of the boldest take their chance. They sneak through the halls. At the height of the fifth floor there is a gang plank leading to the roof of the neighboring house on Niska Street. . . . Below, there is a guard watching in the courtyard. The first of the fugitives puts his foot on the plank. Now he is walking. But the eye of the guard already caught him. The guard fires. The man, pierced by bullets, falls down. The rest of them scuttle down into the halls. On their way they run into the guards. Violent beating starts now, hitting with rifle-butts, the crushing of bones. The wounded, lacerated people, blood-spattered, choking and spitting, return now to the halls of the Umschlagplatz. . . .

Somebody is reaching for poison. He swallows it, washing it down with a little water carefully prepared in a cruet. It was well hidden. It was not discovered during the examination. The man takes poison in front of all the people. Nobody interferes. He is passing away. Now he is delivered. . . .

An eighteen-year-old girl, separated from her mother, clutches the henchman, drops on her knees, kisses his boots. . . . Bewildered and crazed by despair, the girl runs after her mother. She grasps her skirt. The mother is unconsciously stroking the head of her daughter. Handtke [a guard] is watching the scene with the smile of an expert. Presently he apparently decides that it has attained its highest point. He raises his revolver, aims it and fires the shot. It did not miss its target. The girl falls down. On the lips of the mother a strange smile appears, already coming from beyond this world while the S.S. man pushes her ahead, lashing her with a long whip.

The selection is over. We are marching towards the cars.[5]

The hospital was generally emptied and the quota of victims rounded up by four or five in the afternoon. Gun butts and clubs drove people into the square where two S.S. men made the "final selection."

Although the Germans had evacuated the hospital, they devised a small medical aid station at the *Umschlagplatz* to further mislead Jews about the purpose of the deportations. A few daring Jews managed to use this station for rescue efforts. Two men, Nahum Remba, the secretary of the *Judenrat*, and Ala Golomb-Grinberg, were particularly active. On one side of the *Umschlagplatz*, near the barbed-wire fence, they created a clinic of two small rooms. In these rooms stood several rows of small beds covered with fresh linen, ready to receive "patients," who, in fact, became persons rescued from the *Umschlagplatz*. Daily, Remba could be seen walking around the moiling square, searching for certain faces and pulling them out of the *Umschlagplatz*. These people were then kept in the "clinic" until it was safe for them to return to the Ghetto, generally in an "ambulance" made available to Remba. Their "rescue," of course, was generally only momentary.

Remba's activities represented one form of the battle against annihilation. The activities of the Oneg Shabbat were another. With a foreboding of imminent catastrophe, the leaders of Oneg Shabbat decided to take steps to protect their archives. During the massive exterminations in July, preparations were made to seal the materials in crates and bury them. On August 3, they were buried at 68 Nowolipki and 34 Swietojerska. In the midst of the preparations, one of the workers, eighteen-year-old Naum Grzywacz wrote: "We have decided to describe the present time. Yesterday we sat up till late in the night, since we did not know whether we would survive till today. Now I am in the midst of writing, while in the streets the terrible shooting is going on. . . . Of one thing I am proud: that in these grave and fateful days, I was one of those who buried the treasure . . . in order that you should know of the tortures and murders of the Nazi tyranny." His colleague, nineteen-year-old David Grober added: "We must hurry, because we are not sure of the next hour. . . . I want the coming generations to remember our times. . . . With what ardor we dug the holes for the boxes . . . with what joy we received every bit of material. . . . How I would like to live to the moment when the treasure is dug out and the whole truth proclaimed. . . . But we certainly will not live to see it."[6]

The archives survived the youths who buried them.

The German bread-and-marmalade bait was effective while it lasted. Typically it was followed by brutal measures. Shops were pillaged on a large scale and shopworkers were murdered. Roundups became street massacres. On August 7, the Germans instituted a blockade of every street and house. Doors were smashed in; Jews in hiding were killed outright. Thousands were forcibly rounded up and marched off under guard. Two days later, the so-called Small Ghetto was liquidated.

All Jews living in this area, the southern part of the Ghetto, south of Chlodna Street, were ordered to vacate their homes by August 10. Anyone found in the banned area after six o'clock that evening would be shot. Jewish police were ordered to get five victims each day or subject their own families to deportation. The contraction and isolation process pressed on. Only certain workers in factories were permitted to remain in the Small Ghetto.[7] The *Judenrat* office was moved to Zamenhof 19, the site, ironically, of the palace of the last Polish king. Jews by the thousands were seen carrying and dragging bundles over the Chlodna Street bridge. Islands of diminishing human warmth were snatched in the compression. "Families" of Zionists, Bundists, friends of bakers, attic dwellers, tunnel builders, all clung together as the Germans contracted the life space in the Ghetto. People began to think in terms of shrinking orbits of loyalty. Whom would one wish to help in the last extremity and to whom could one turn for help? The tempo of the manhunts, meanwhile, reached a new fury.

A few children were smuggled at night to the Aryan side, their feet wrapped in burlap and their faces blackened with charred cork. They were walked to Hungary or Slovakia by Aryan-looking Jews or trusted Poles. On August 12, an underground courier was sent to Berne and Istanbul with the message: "Cousin Israel is sick and is going to live with Uncle Mavetski [*Mavet* in Hebrew means death]. Any help you can send must hurry." New hiding places had to be found in the truncated Ghetto.

On August 12, the orphanage of Janusz Korczak was "evacuated." Dr. Korczak was a Polish neurologist but was better known as a writer and educator. He had devoted his life to an orphanage for Jewish children which he had founded and directed. As a physician he could have temporarily remained in the Ghetto, exempt from deportation. But he refused to abandon his children. "He will go with them," a witness observed:

> And so a long line is formed in the front of the orphanage on Slisks Street. A long procession, children, small, tiny, rather precocious, emaciated, weak, shriveled and shrunk. They carry shabby packages, some have schoolbooks, notebooks under their arms. No one is crying.
>
> Slowly they go down the steps, line up in rows, in perfect order and discipline, as usual. Their little eyes are turned towards the doctor. They are strangely calm; they feel almost well. The doctor is going with them, so what do they have to be afraid of? They are not alone, they are not abandoned.
>
> Dr. Korczak busies himself with the children with a sober earnestness. He buttons the coat of one child, ties up a package of another, or straightens the cap of a third. Then he wipes off a tear which is rolling down the thin little face of a child. . . .
>
> Then the procession starts out. It is starting out for a trip from which— everybody feels it—one never comes back. All these young, budding lives. . . . And all this is marching quietly and orderly to the place of their untimely doom.
>
> The children are calm, but inwardly they must feel it, they must sense it intuitively. Otherwise how could you explain the deadly seriousness on their pale little faces? But they are marching quietly in orderly rows, calm and earnest, and at the head of them is Janusz Korczak.[8]

At the *Umschlagplatz*, terrible scenes were recorded: A child's eyes are gouged out by a German who desires to "make two rings out of them." The child's shrill screaming pierces the laughter of the guards. Another child's tongue is cut out with a pocketknife for making a face at a guard. A little boy asks his mother why Hitler hates him since he does not know him at all. A little girl swings a rattle and babbles, "Din, din, din. Blockade, everybody go down, quick, quick, quick, blockade."

Wholesale random selections were made at the *Umschlagplatz* in August. The victims were driven through the "kettle," or cauldron of streets swarming with masses of Jews, to a wooden gate which blocked the entire pavement. Through the gate, pale, frightened people with bloodshot eyes were driven, whiplashed by Ukrainian and Latvian guards. Families clung together trying to squeeze through the gate as one body; those who had work cards clutched them tightly. To the left was the way toward Stawki, toward the railroad siding, toward Malkinia and "the East." Women, children, the old and crippled and many young workers were pushed to the left. To the right was the road to Leszno, Karmelicka, Nowolipie, to sweat and toil and a little more life.

Sometime in August, a Jewish policeman at the *Umschlagplatz* who had memorized serial numbers on a few cars, noticed that the same cars that left in the morning returned in the afternoon. The trip took about six hours, three each way, but the policeman knew that it took a through train at least twenty hours to reach the Russian border on the Bialystok-Minsk line. "Resettlement," then, was taking place, not "in the East" but somewhere close to Warsaw.

For the difficult task of getting more exact information, the Bund sent a handsome young Jew, Zalman Friedrych, who looked like the German propagandist's dream of the blond Aryan. A Polish Socialist who worked on the railroad and knew the direction of the deportation trains advised Friedrych which route to investigate. Friedrych reached Sokolow after many trials and learned that the Germans had constructed a small branch railroad from Malkinia-Sokolow to the village of Treblinka. Each day trains packed with Jews were switched onto the new spur. At Treblinka there was a large camp divided into two sections, one for Jews, one for Poles. The residents of Sokolow had heard that terrible things were happening in Treblinka, but they had no details. While in Sokolow, Friedrych stumbled upon Azriel Wallach, Maxim Litvinov's nephew, who was badly bruised and bleeding. His clothes were in shreds. From Wallach, Friedrych learned that all the Jews brought to Treblinka were immediately put to death. They were unloaded from the trains and told they were to be bathed and cleaned before being taken to their quarters and assigned to work. Classification signs marked "Tailors," "Hatmakers," "Carpenters," and "Roadbuilders" led many Jews to the very end to believe they were being sorted for labor. Instead, they were led into hermetically sealed chambers and gassed. Wallach had been spared from immediate death to work at cleaning up the freight cars and had managed to escape.[9]

The Bund published Friedrych's gruesome report in a special edition of their paper, *Storm*. A later confirmation of the horror of Treblinka came from Yankel Wiernik, a carpenter from Warsaw. Wiernik was deported to Treblinka on August 23, 1942, and was there assigned to dispose of the corpses of the gassed Jews. He participated in the revolt of the camp prisoners, escaped, and then got in touch with some friends, the Jewish-Polish underground organization called Zegota, whose members asked him to write out all that he had experienced. During the autumn of 1943, Wiernik worked feverishly recording his ghastly memoir. A Polish underground press printed two thousand copies and a microfilm was sent to the Polish Government-in-Exile in London, and from there to the United States and Palestine.

Slowly the Jews of the Ghetto were forced to face the horrible truth. Yet many would not or could not. "Treblinka is terrifying," they said, "but Warsaw is Warsaw. The Nazis would not dare do in Warsaw what they have done in the provinces." The *Storm* report was debated: some argued that it was exaggerated. There was also still the anodyne of the working certificate. The Germans could not deport all workers, it was said.

A survivor has recorded the faith in the strawlike *Ausweise* in the midst of a perishing world.

> That summer, beginning with Lublin, the entire country was swept with deportations. Of these, the liquidation of the Warsaw ghetto in July was the most ominous; its 600,000 Jews had been the backbone of the nation. . . . Then when the people of Radom were deported, some of us saw them stop in Siedlce where a hundred smothered corpses were thrown on the ramp, the very train shuddering with the collective howl of thousands dying inside the locked boxcars. We watched and listened but did not know what it all meant. The normal processes of thinking and reacting, the horror of the truth, and the deliberate confusion planted by the Germans, all these combined to produce a frightful weariness, a wish to get it over with— whatever that entailed: deportation, resettlement, concentration camp. . . . When we heard the rushing trains we cried instinctively, "Heavens, we are all perishing." But then, once assumed, that knowledge became impossible to accept. We then went back to our daily routines. . . .
>
> In the wake of these deportations a new craze swept the town. Everybody wanted to work for the Germans. This passion started with a postcard from somewhere which informed us that "something" was going on there, and only those who worked were left untouched. . . . We worked everywhere, and did everything: fixed roads, lugged provisions, raised and erased buildings, cleaned the Germans' latrines and polished their shoes. If we all worked and obeyed orders, we would be safe, we were told; so all of Losice plunged into work. We worked where we were needed and where we were not; the young and the old and the crippled worked. Everyone hugged and cherished his working card like life insurance.[10]

Worried proprietors of the German Ghetto firms (Toebbens, Schultz, Döring, and Transavia) which manufactured goods for the war effort, and had taken over chemical, electrical and woodworking factories, together with officials of the Warsaw Armament Command and *Transferstelle*, moved to save their working force. Bearing placards, the factory agents hunted for their men in Stawki Square that now had become the cattle pen of a human abattoir. Sometimes they could extricate a victim from the clutches of a guard; the man thus "saved" would then have to decide if he could bear to leave his family. On August 16, a new type of employment certificate was issued, one of the last of the German devices in the divide-and-rule strategy. This certificate was restricted to 30,000 workers but did not cover their dependents.

Toebbens and Schultz arranged to get 8,000 workers each in a deal with the S.S. and police. The Ghetto had now been reduced to islands of inhabited tenements around the factories. The truncated Ghetto was a forced labor camp, organized according to trades. Each compound, covering a block, was surrounded by a high fence of wood or barbed wire. Workers were imprisoned within the factory area and were marched to and from work.

The attrition of the Ghetto was now complete. The master plan of playing one group against another, of alternating lulls with sudden actions, of dangling hope in every guise and then destroying it—all of the cunning German strategies had virtually wiped out the human fabric of Ghetto life. From the myth of "resettlement," based on historic Jewish traditions of autonomy, to the "bath houses" of Treblinka, the Germans had successfully deluded most Jews. In spite of eyewitness reports of the gas chambers, they would not believe that death could be the end for all. The sealing of the ghettos and the deliberately instituted regime of *Hungertod* (hunger-death) undermined the prisoners. Once physically and psychologically penned up, they struggled for a crumb of life. Orders explicitly defining categories of exemption created the illusion of a world of rules in the midst of hopeless misery. Jews believed in it. The Germans said an "action" was finished; Jews believed it. The promise of safety to one group or another left them with the belief that some would be permitted to stay alive.

In the middle of August there was a short lull. The dreaded *Umsiedlung* staff left the Ghetto. Again Jewish hopes rose. The Germans needed workers, it was said. It was senseless to kill them off. One day an announcement appeared urging all Jews who wished to go to Palestine to register. Again the horrible reality was pushed aside even after it was impossible to dismiss actual eyewitness accounts of extermination centers. The doomed sought consolation. The very evils endured appeared as guarantees of eventual salvation. In Warsaw, people took comfort in the raging typhus epidemic. The Germans were known to dread the spread of the disease. Surely, it was said, they would hesitate to transport Jews from Warsaw into other parts of the country and contaminate the country. The Ghetto walls were also viewed as a reason for confidence. Why should the Germans have built these walls, why should they have gone to the trouble of creating a special Jewish quarter, if within two years they proposed to murder all the inhabitants? Would it not have been cheaper and easier to kill all the Jews at the outset without bothering to set up the elaborate inferno of the Ghetto with its special council, its decrees, its factories? Webs of wishful thinking were spun, destroyed, and then spun again.

Within the Ghetto, however, some Jews had faced the stark truth. They knew that the Germans intended to annihilate every Jew in Poland. They urged Jews to resist physically, to make Germans pay for the Jewish dead. But their pleas fell on deaf ears. The majority could not accept what they had only dimly grasped. The handbills of the underground were first considered a German provocation to excite the Jews to resist and then give the Germans a pretext to destroy the Ghetto. While hundreds of thousands of workers, intellectuals, community figures, the flower of Jewish youth, women and children were being led away to the shambles, the realists— most of them from Zionist youth movements—looked on helplessly.

Not only in Warsaw, but in Vilna and Bialystok and in other ghettos, when armed resistance was debated, many felt that a revolt should be launched only after it had become clear that all Jews were about to be liquidated, with no hope for survival of any of them. It was universally felt that an uprising spelled death for all. Jews who considered resistance also understood that they had no prospect whatsoever of winning with their meager forces. A document recording a meeting of leaders of the *Hechalutz* movement in Bialystok, held February 27, 1943, poignantly conveys this fatalism: "The few people sitting here are the last *chalutzim* in Poland. We are entirely surrounded by the dead. You know what has happened in Warsaw: no one is left. The same is true of Bendin and Czestochowa, and probably everywhere else. We are the last. . . . There is no point in sitting together in the warmth of our memories, and there is no point in waiting for death together, collectively. . . . What we're really debating is two different kinds of death. Attack means certain death. The other way means death two or three days later. . . . I have lost everything, all those near to me; still, there persists the desire to live. But there is no choice. If I thought that not only individuals could save themselves, but fifty or sixty percent of the ghetto Jews, I would say that our decision should be to remain alive at any cost. But we are condemned to death. . . . No illusions! We have nothing to expect but a choice of two kinds of death. . . . Bialystok will be liquidated completely, like all the other cities. . . . This will be for keeps, not for fun. When we fight, it will have to be to the last. And to fight means to be killed. . . . In the face of death you can become weak and powerless, or you can become very strong, since there is nothing to lose."[11]

In Warsaw, before the decision to resist was made, there was a long period—as in the other ghettos—in which political and religious movements sharply diverged from one another in coping with the Nazi occupation and in assessing their future. These differences existed in pre-Hitler Poland and prevailed in the Ghetto. The Bund, the largest and most influential force, at first regarded the Nazis as they had regarded the prewar semi-Fascist, highly nationalistic Polish Governments. They carried on anti-Fascist activity in the Ghetto through their illegal press and contacts with the Polish trade union movement and set up groups to feed and house the homeless refugees in the Ghetto. The Zionists, although divided by factional differences, were united in their hopes for a Jewish state in Palestine. They, too, had relief committees and propaganda sections and believed that the internationalism of the Bundists was completely unrealistic for the times. The Jewish Communists, a small group, insisted that Jews were an integral part of general Polish society and refused to recognize the existence of a separate Jewish community as such. They, too, had their publications and urged the Ghetto to resort to acts of sabotage against the Germans. Their interpretation of ghettoization was that the Nazis feared a united front between the Jews and Poles against themselves and therefore separated them. The masses of Jews were unaffiliated politically and relied on religious traditions for comfort.

There were as many publications as there were parties and factions, and although ideologies differed, the publications had common aims: to combat apathy, to keep hope alive, to fight the cooperation of the Jewish police and the *Judenrat* in carrying out German orders, and to urge passive resistance. The decision to resort to arms involved agonizing dilemmas for the Ghetto and a struggle against the *Judenrat*.

The young Zionists mobilized first. Pioneer youths training to go to Palestine (*Hechalutz*) set up fighting units soon after Germany invaded the Soviet Union. They expected the Russians to repel the Germans swiftly and the retreating Germans to start pogroms. The news of the Russian defeats was first taken as Nazi bluff. After the news of the exterminations in Vilna, more Jews in the Ghetto favored active resistance, but not enough for an organized revolt. Individual attacks on the police broke out in the fall of 1941; during the first week of October, there were 194 cases. Sabotage increased. Carpenters, for example, added half a centimeter to outside dimensions of window-sash measurements. Every worker was expected to be exact in his miscalculations so that the sashes would be unsuitable for German Army barracks. Pressers scorched uniforms and sewing-machine operators sewed up pockets and reversed trousers and sleeves. But there was no munitions industry to sabotage or steal from.

Elsewhere, certain *Judenrat* officials openly or covertly aided Jewish resistance activity. Czerniakow did not. He made his position clear early. On the night of April 17, 1942, fifty-two Jews were taken from their homes and shot in the streets of the Ghetto. Among the victims were a baker, an engineer, a lawyer, organizational leaders and typesetters. The Germans had gone after the Ghetto's illegal press. Among those killed were Jews active in formative resistance.

The executions occurred soon after the Lublin deportations. Czerniakow summoned resistance leaders and argued that underground meetings and illegal publications were dangerous to the Ghetto. He pleaded that they be halted. Czerniakow and the *Judenrat* were not the only restraining forces. There were others—idealistic and high minded—who opposed a Jewish revolt for other reasons. Some based their opposition on general political considerations, others on historical grounds. Dr. Ignatz Schipper, a respected historian, argued that resistance to the Germans would invite complete destruction of the Ghetto. Still others were opposed to violence for religious reasons. The Bund, one of the most vital of Jewish movements in Poland, a party of Jewish trade unionists, Socialist in leaning, both anti-Communist and anti-Zionist, had yet another reason for opposition—at first. The Bund believed in a meaningful Jewish existence and survival in the Diaspora. It could not acknowledge catastrophe. Some Bundists urged Jews to fight, but only in a common front with the Poles in the common war against Nazi oppression. Still others believed the Ghetto could hold out until the Allies won. The long history of Jewish survival through saving what could be saved without bloodshed was also a deterrent to early physical rebellion. Most difficult for the leaders to resolve was the question of Jewish collective responsibility. In Warsaw the Nazis might destroy the lives of half a million Jews to avenge any Jewish violence against Germans. Did any Jew have the right to risk the lives of thousands in such an unequal struggle?

Arguments seesawed back and forth for months. The genesis of a Ghetto fighters' organization can be dated as early as June, 1941, when the Soviet-German war broke out. Some Jews then hoped to join the Red Army and share in the war against Fascism. But the front was hundreds of miles from the Warsaw Ghetto; there was no Red Army to latch on to. At that time there was not a ray of hope for help, not the slightest prospect of victory. And there were no arms.

In the spring of 1942, a new force appeared: the Polish Workers Party (P.P.R.) which replaced the former Communist Party and was expanded to include left-wing Socialists and Constitutionalists. Its program was to make war on the Germans in every possible place and at every possible opportunity. It favored the creation of an independent Socialist Poland, aid to the Soviet Union in its war against Germany, and aid to the Jews. In the summer of 1942, a P.P.R. representative, Andrzej Schmidt, bribed his way into the Ghetto and organized the loosely functioning left-wing groups. Sabotage actions were planned and slowdowns encouraged. A collection of German uniforms was made and hidden.

The Socialist Zionist groups agreed that the destiny of Poland depended on the combined might of the Allies; all anti-Nazis had to resist. They formed a Jewish Anti-Fascist Bloc, in collaboration with the P.P.R. in March 1942, drilled Jewish youths in groups of five and prepared them for the idea of battle. This movement proposed a united Jewish fighting force and coordination with the Polish underground. It issued a publication, Der Ruf (The Call) and tried to maintain morale in an atmosphere of despair. It was not able to hold its ground, however, and split up during the July deportations. For ideological reasons the Bund had not joined. The Bund opposed the idea of an all-Jewish force. Its spokesman said: "We shall fight when the Poles are ready to fight—not now." The Poles, however, were afraid to start a premature revolt and planned, instead, to wait until the Allies were close enough to extend aid.

The Zionist youth groups remained in the Anti-Fascist Bloc in their "Fighting Fives." Without weapons, they learned how to shoot, and without dynamite, they "made" mines. *Zukunft* (The Future), the Bundist youth, against the orders of its parent body, joined the Anti-Fascist Bloc, but the German executions of April 18 and the massive deportations in the summer of 1942 shattered its ranks. No more was heard thereafter of the Anti-Fascist Bloc, but it formed a bridge to the Jewish Fighting Organization (JFO) which succeeded it.

Zionist elements among Jewish activists had no faith in a combined Polish-Jewish front under the circumstances prevailing. Who would defend the Ghetto, they asked themselves, if all of the Jewish fighters sought out the enemy outside the Ghetto and joined the general Polish underground? These groups, during the spring and summer of 1942, decided to constitute themselves a separate, independent Jewish fighting force, fighting in and for the Ghetto. Arms were crucial.

For months before the summer deportations, these groups had sent out desperate appeals for arms to the *Armia Krajowa*,[12] the Home Army of the Polish underground representing the Polish Government-in-Exile. Their efforts were in vain. The military leaders of the *Armia Krajowa* met with General Stefan Rowecki, their commander, to plan a response to the Jewish appeal for arms and help. Rowecki expanded his view that the Germans intended to kill the Jews first, then the Poles. Thus, he argued, the Poles should aid the Jews. But the other commanders opposed any direct help. The Jewish request for arms was passed over. The Polish authorities protracted negotiations as one frantic appeal after another issued from the Ghetto. One appeal was also directed to the Allies, demanding that the German people be threatened with reprisals for the Jewish slaughter. The Home Army transmitted this request to London, but the message was never broadcast. As to arms aid, although the *Armia Krajowa* counted half a million members and was well armed, it was holding itself in readiness for a "major action" and refused to help the Ghetto fighters when help was needed. After prolonged effort, ten revolvers of poor quality were delivered at the end of December 1942. Except for sporadic acts of sabotage and propaganda, the *Armia Krajowa* did not make any effort at organized resistance against the Nazis until August 1, 1944.

Individual Jews met clandestinely and tried to pierce the fog of Nazi intent. In retrospect, many of them appear to have been naïve or credulous, but their isolation from the "real world" was unimaginably great. Physically and psychologically diminished and severed from information that could be validated, they could draw only on their own minds, their subjective readings of history, their wishful thinking, the emotional support they could mobilize for and from each other. So removed from actuality were they that intelligent men among them thought seriously about sending a courier to Switzerland to prevail upon England to recognize the Jews in Poland as citizens of Palestine!

The Jewish Fighting Organization was formed on July 28, 1942 and grew out of a meeting of all of the major movements and organizations in the Ghetto. The majority still opposed armed resistance; a minority of left-wing Zionists and *Hechalutz* groups decided on defense and resistance and organized the JFO. Before it had acquired a single revolver, it set up a structure of operations including a command staff headed by the twenty-four-year-old Mordecai Anielewicz and committees on finance, propaganda and supplies. Assisting Anielewicz as a "general staff" were Zivia Lubetkin, Samuel Breslau, Isaac Zuckerman and the twenty-seven-year-old Mordecai Tenenbaum (a gifted youth who had lived through the Soviet and Nazi occupation of Vilna and fled from ghetto to ghetto warning Jews of their fate. In August 1943, he organized the defense of the Bialystok Ghetto.). They sent a delegation of Aryan-looking Jews to the Aryan side of Warsaw to make personal contact with the Polish underground for arms. JFO handbills were distributed; the Ghetto was told that resettlement really meant death. But, uncomprehending, the masses turned away from the truth and denounced the young men and women in the JFO as *agents provocateurs*. Nevertheless, *Der Ruf* was continued and the network of "Fives" was maintained.

The P.P.R., with its own orientation, favored an immediate attack on the Jewish police. They reasoned thus: the Jewish police would be forced to call on the Polish police for help. Then the Germans would be forced to attack the Jews en masse. This attack would then serve as a signal for a general uprising of the Polish population and the initial sacrifices would serve to save the remainder of the Ghetto.[13] A handful of youths left the Ghetto to join a small Polish guerrilla band called the People's Guards; most of them were killed in the woods. The Bund persisted in its efforts to get weapons from its Socialist contacts on the Aryan side but with no results. Meanwhile, the deportations slashed at the Ghetto. The JFO struggled to maintain itself.

Soon after the JFO was formed, *Hashomer Hatzair*, Socialist Zionist youth, offered its whole arsenal as a symbol of its intention to pool all of its resources. It gave the organization one German Army Luger. Occasionally, the People's Guards bartered grenades for German uniforms. But the cache of weapons was meager.

The youths in the JFO gathered in closets and talked with burning eyes and dry lips about revenge. They stripped away their fear of death once they had determined to die only after killing Germans rather than postpone death by hiding. They stored up bread rusks, mimeographed instructions on guerrilla fighting, oiled their few revolvers, and created bunkers to "last." Next to the security of the bunkers, their prime need was weapons. As there was no munitions industry in the Ghetto, weapons had to be smuggled.

Some fighters disguised themselves as members of the Masonry Labor Battalion, which worked outside the old Ghetto to demolish the old walls along Zelazna Street. This battalion of *Platzufkazhes* was constantly under guard but if someone could slip through the Smocza-Gesia Gate, he had a chance to reach contacts outside the Ghetto. The battalion formed into columns of four at the *Judenrat* courtyard and was marched to the gate. There the sentries checked the bricklayers' papers. Under the cover of an "accident" or a diversion to distract the sentry, a JFO agent could slip out of the Ghetto, beyond the wall. A few Italian Beretta pistols were bought at seven thousand zlotys each. Complicated arrangements were then made for the delivery of the first "big" shipment of ten revolvers, coded as "four cartons of chromium-plated bolts."

The Jewish couriers who made these arrangements lived in quarters set up by Jewish girls who posed as Aryans. Behind secret walls and in obscure caches the girls hid underground papers, cash and false documents, and concealed Jews. The collection of arms, some bullets here, a Czech revolver there, was painfully slow, discouraging and acutely frustrating. Outside the city of Warsaw resounded with marching German soldiers, crunching tanks and howitzers.

Sometime in August, the shipment of ten revolvers was smuggled into the Ghetto over the wall at a point called Parysowski Place. Here the guards could be bribed. A brisk business in smuggling was carried on by Poles. Traders of the Kerzeliac market would crawl over to buy clothes and shoes and to dismantle furniture. The long-awaited revolvers, the "cartons of chromium-plated bolts," came in small covered boxes loaded on a wheelbarrow like ordinary supplies. A Pole, Stefan Mahai, pushed the wheelbarrow, followed by two youths of the underground. A policeman stopped Mahai near the smuggling point and asked to see his permit to move goods. Mahai gave him some money and was allowed to go on. A password was sounded over the wall and a member of the JFO climbed up and took the precious boxes. The weapons were put to use for the first time on August 21, not against Germans, however, but against the hated chief of the Jewish police, Jozef Szerynski, a converted Jew. Another Jewish police officer, Mieczyslaw Szmerling, was wounded. These actions marked the beginning of the end of the power of the Jewish police and foreshadowed the JFO bid for popular support against the power of the *Judenrat*. The shift in authority was to come soon.

Meanwhile, the small resistance groups had to bestir their own fellow

Jews. They posted placards explaining what Treblinka signified and called for resistance; they distributed leaflets. The masses remained inert. A Soviet bombardment the night of August 21 was interpreted as an Allied effort to stop the deportations. Late in August the young fighters acted. They set fire to a number of German factories and warehouses. Small, scattered acts of sabotage took place. The people slowly began to understand that there was no longer anything to salvage; neither was there anything to lose.

On September 5, one of the last of the *Judenrat* announcements wiped out the breath of hope for 120,000 Jews left in the Ghetto. All Jews, without exceptions, were now called for a giant selection. The announcement read:

> Upon the order of the Delegate for Resettlement Matters, the Jewish Council in Warsaw announces the following:
> 1. By Sunday, September 6, 1942, all Jews, without exceptions, remaining within the limits of the large ghetto are to gather for registration purposes in the section bounded by the streets, Smocza, Gesia, Zamenhof, Szcesliwa, and Parysow Square.
> 2. Jews are also permitted to move at night from September 5 to 6, 1942.
> 3. Food for two days and drinking utensils are to be taken along.
> 4. It is forbidden to lock the apartments.
> 5. Whosoever does not comply with this order and remains in the ghetto (outside of the above limited district) beyond 10 A.M. Sunday, September 6, 1942, will be shot.[14]

The "kettle" action followed at Mila Street and vicinity, where those selected for the transports were herded together. This time the "kettle" squeezed 120,000 Jews into an area of twelve square city blocks. The Germans had a new scheme. Each enterprise or institution was issued a certain series of numbers. As many Jews could be "legitimized" to live as the organization had numbers—no more.

As protection certificates were no longer adequate, the factory work-slaves were marked by their proprietors on different parts of the body with a distinctive stamp so that the S.S. would not make any mistakes in their manhunts. The task of selecting which Jews were to live was now left to the Jews themselves. The *Judenrat* was forced to undergo its own selection. Its numbers were reduced from 5,000 to 2,800. S.D. men set up a portable desk in the courtyard of the *Judenrat* office and the chairman had to decide "left" or "right." For each Jew, a sentence of immediate death or a short reprieve.

Selections took place at scattered points a dozen times a day. Everyone knew about Treblinka now. Life was being measured out in terms of a few hours, a few days or weeks. Babies were stuffed into suitcases of strangers as mothers tried to guess which stranger might have a reprieve.

Yet floating over the milling human skeletons there hovered the irrepressible rumor: registration *this time* could mean a change in status. Germans were to regard the Jews in the Ghetto as prisoners of war to be exchanged for German soldier prisoners via Istanbul. Some Jews still clung to such fantasies but most now knew the worst and determined not to give themselves up. "Why should we go to them?" they asked. "Let them come and get us!"

Those who could fled to hiding places in lofts, above beams, in cellars, on sloping roofs, and in alleys. They lived animal-like, prowling, seeking lairs, digging tunnels behind and below bakery ovens, while above, next door and afar could be heard gunshots and shouting. *"Alle Juden 'raus. 'Raus! 'Raus! Hinunter! Alle Juden hinunter!"* ("All Jews out! All Jews down!")

These last massive roundups caught many of the Jewish Council employees and over 1,000 Jewish policemen. Only a fragment of the old Ghetto now remained in the northeast corner. By the end of September, only 65,000 Jews were still alive, half of them without official writ to exist. Some 300,000 had been deported since July. The last raids took place on September 21, the Day of Atonement, as pious Jews mingled their prayers to God with the taste of death at the *Umschlagplatz*. On that day, 2,196 more Jews were combed out of locked rooms and cellars; 33,400 were "legally" working in factories for German firms and 2,800 of the *Judenrat* staff remained. All were billeted at their working posts. New walls were built within the Ghetto shell, dividing one group of workers from another. Between the isolated compounds there were large, desolated areas of deadly quiet streets. All communication between the walled-in sections was forbidden.

Early in October in 1942, during the lull that followed the September raids, a Polish liaison officer between the Government-in-Exile in London and the Polish underground had several talks with Zionist and Bundist leaders in the coalescing Jewish underground. The representatives of the two most ideologically disparate movements in modern Polish Jewish life would soon take the last steps to unite their organizations in a common resistance effort. Now they were meeting to tell the Pole, Jan Karski, that the Jews of Poland were doomed. This was the message he was to carry to the silent world. The representative of the Bund was Dr. Leon Feiner; the Zionist representative has not been established with certainty but was probably Menahem Kirshenbaum. Karski recalled this meeting:

> We met at twilight in a huge, empty, and half-ruined house in the suburbs. . .

The two men were unforgettable, less like men than incarnations of mass suffering and nerves strained in hopeless effort. Both lived outside the ghetto but were able, by secret means, to enter and leave it as they pleased and carry on their work there. Inside the ghetto they looked, talked and acted like the other inhabitants. To carry on their tasks outside they succeeded in changing their appearance so completely as to go absolutely undetected by the keenest scrutiny. The Bund leader, in particular, with his distinguished gray hair and whiskers, ruddy complexion, erect carriage, and general air of good health and refinement, passed easily as a Polish nobleman.

Before the war he had been a well-known lawyer with an excellent reputation as an expert in criminal law. Now he appeared before the German authorities as the owner of a large store, prosperous, dignified and unruffled. How great an effort of will this pose must have necessitated I realized later when he accompanied me to the ghetto. The air of well-being and savoir-faire seemed to vanish instantly. The well-groomed Polish merchant underwent a sudden transformation and became a Jew, one of the thousands of wretched, exhausted starving Jews that the pitiless Nazis tormented and hunted with inhuman vindictiveness.

The first thing that became clear to me as I sat there talking to them in the silence of the darkening Warsaw suburbs was the complete hopelessness of their predicament. For them, for the suffering Polish Jews, this was the end of the world. There was no possible escape for them or their fellows. This, too, was only part of the tragedy. . . . They were not afraid of death itself, and, indeed, accepted it as something inevitable. Added to this realization was the bitter knowledge that in this war, for them, there could be no hope of any victory whatsoever, none of the satisfaction which sometimes softens the prospect of death. The Zionist leader made this clear to me at once.

"You other Poles are fortunate," he began. "You are suffering, too. Many of you will die, but at least your nation goes on living. After the war Poland will be resurrected. . . . From this ocean of tears, pain, rage and humiliation your country will emerge again, but the Polish Jews will no longer exist. We will be dead. . . ."

It was an evening of nightmare, but with a painful, oppressive kind of reality that no nightmare ever had. I sat in an old rickety armchair as if I had been pinned there, barely able to utter a word while the torrents of their emotion broke over me. They paced the floor violently, their shadows dancing weirdly in the dim light cast by the single candle we could allow ourselves. It was as though they were unable even to think of their dying people and remain seated.[15]

The Jewish leaders tried to convey to Karski the monstrous things that were happening. Then they became despondent. "It's no use telling you all this. No one in the outside world can possibly understand. You don't understand."

Karski answered, "I am here to help if I can. I will be in London soon and in a position to obtain audiences with the Allied authorities. . . . I am going on an official mission on behalf of the Polish Underground. I will be accredited by the Polish Government in London. My status will be official and you must give me your official message to the outside world. You are the leaders of the Jewish underground. What do you want me to say?"

> They hesitated for a moment. . . . The Bund leader spoke first, "We want you to tell the Polish and Allied governments . . . that we are helpless in the face of the German criminals. We cannot defend ourselves and no one in Poland can defend us. The Polish underground authorities can save some of us but they cannot save masses. The Germans are not trying to enslave us as they have other people; we are being systematically murdered. . . . Our entire people will be destroyed . . . three million Polish Jews are doomed. . . . Place this responsibility on the shoulders of the Allies. Let not a single leader of the United Nations be able to say that they did not know that we were being murdered in Poland and could not be helped except from the outside."[15a]

This was the solemn message Karski was to carry to the world. By this time almost two million Jews had been killed. The truth might not be believed. It might be said that this figure was exaggerated, not authentic. Karski was to argue, convince, do anything, shout the truth until it could not be denied. The two leaders implored him to make the truth known. Their helplessness and desperation exhausted Karski. Their voices were pitched very low and yet he had the feeling that he was listening to an earthquake. "The democracies cannot calmly put up with the assertion that the Jewish people in Europe cannot be saved. If American and British citizens can be saved, why can't evacuation of even the Jewish children be arranged on a large scale, of Jewish women, of the sick, of the old?"

From the Jewish leaders in England and America, the men demanded drastic steps to arouse the world. "Tell them not to leave until they have obtained guarantees that a way has been decided upon to save the Jews. Let them accept no food or drink, let them die a slow death while the world is looking on. Let them die. This may shake the conscience of the world."

Before Karski left, the men told him that the Ghetto would go up in flames, that the remaining Jews would not die in slow torment but fighting. "We will declare war on Germans, the most hopeless declaration of war that has ever been made. . . . We are even now negotiating with your commander for the arms we need. If we get them, then, one of these days the deportation squad is going to get a bloody surprise."

Two days after this visit, Karski went to the Ghetto, wearing an old shabby suit and a cap pulled down over his eyes, accompanied by two men dressed in rags. They had reached the Ghetto through a secret passage. Karski describes what he saw:

> To pass that wall was to enter a new world utterly unlike anything that had ever been imagined. A cemetery? No, for these bodies were still moving, were indeed often violently agitated. These were still living people, if

you could call them such. For apart from their skin, eyes and voice, there was nothing human left in these palpitating figures. Everywhere there was hunger, the atrocious stench of decomposing bodies, the pitiful moans of dying children. . . . The entire population of the ghetto seemed to be living in the street. There was hardly a square yard of empty space. As we picked our way across the mud and rubble, the shadows of what had once been men or women flitted by us in pursuit of something, their eyes blazing with some insane hunger or greed.

Everyone and everything seemed to vibrate with unnatural intensity, to be in constant motion, enveloped in a haze of disease and death thru which their bodies appeared to be throbbing in disintegration. . . . Frequently we passed by corpses lying naked in the streets.

"What does it mean?" I asked my guide. "Why are they lying there naked?"

"When a Jew dies," he answered, "his family removes his clothing and throws his body in the street. If not, they have to pay the Germans to have the body buried. They have instituted a burial tax which practically no one here can afford. Besides, this saves clothing. Here, every rag counts."[15b]

Karski then was pulled into a building. His companions had heard a shot. A "hunt" was on. Two boys dressed in the uniform of the Hitler-jugend were chattering and pushing each other in spasms of merriment. They wore no caps and their light hair shone in the sun. The younger boy had a gun in his hand; his eyes roamed around looking for a target with the casual absorption of a boy at a carnival. He finally found something. Karski noticed that all of the pavements within his vision were completely deserted. Suddenly a shot rang out, followed by the noise of breaking glass and the terrible cry of a man in pain. The boy who had fired the shot shouted with joy; the other clapped him on the shoulder. They smiled at each other.

Karski stood glued to the window, afraid to change the position of his body, seized with such panic that he could not take a step or force a word out of his throat. A woman tapped him on the shoulder. "You came to see us? It won't do any good. Go back; run away. Don't torture yourself any more."

Karski broke into a run, careful to avoid touching anything or anyone. Everything seemed polluted by death and decay. He held his breath as long as he could to avoid breathing the air of the Ghetto. But two days later he repeated his visit and tried to memorize more vividly his impressions. With his same guides, he walked for three hours through the streets. Five weeks later he reported his experiences to outstanding members of the British and American governments and to Jewish leaders of both continents. He told the story to English writers and to members of the P.E.N. Club. He also told the story to Shmuel Zygelboim, a representative of the Bund in the Polish National Council in London. Finding no way to crack the world's silence, Zygelboim committed suicide.[15c]

The "illegal" survivors meanwhile, burrowing in bunkers and attics in the Ghetto, now had time to dwell on the appalling losses. They felt deep remorse and shame. On October 15 Ringelblum wrote in his notebook:

Why didn't we resist when they began to resettle 300,000 Jews from Warsaw? Why did we allow ourselves to be led like sheep to the slaughter? Why did everything come so easy to the enemy? Why didn't the hangmen suffer a single casualty? Why could 50 SS men . . . with the help of a division of some 200 Ukrainian guards and an equal number of Letts, carry out the operation so smoothly?[16]

And again, early in November:

The Jews seem to have caught their breath a little, after the heavy blows they have sustained. They have become more sober after the experiences gone through. . . . No matter to whom you talk now, you always hear the same—that we should not have agreed to the resettlement. We should have come out into the streets, set everything afire, blasted the walls and forced our way to the other side. To be sure the Germans would have taken vengeance, it would have cost tens of thousands of victims, but still not three hundred thousand.[17]

There is no answer to such tormenting questions now; there could have been none at the time when Ringelblum wrote. No one in the Ghetto had the power to lead it to a rational assessment of the meaninglessness of Hitler's policy or to an early defense against the Ghetto's imminent extinction. A half million people cannot simultaneously face the reality of its imminent extinction. After the September deportations, however, the survivors knew. The next liquidation would be the last. The remnant of leadership in the Ghetto now joined the young Zionist activists and all separate forces became part of a united Jewish National Coordinating Committee. A new revivified JFO was organized on October 20, 1942.

Ringelblum and others now knew the worst, but did they know that more important to the Nazis than winning the war against the Allies was winning the war to destroy the Jews of Europe? In the large sense, no conceivable organization of resistance by the Jews, within the terms of their imprisonment in the ghettos and camps, could have made any difference to their fate. They were starved, abandoned, isolated. They lacked arms. They were confused. Many (as Ringelblum recalled in 1944) had believed in the resettlement myth and reported voluntarily to the *Umschlagplatz*. Collective resistance by the whole Ghetto at any time would have been impossible. However, the question how they would die took on new meaning.

Jews did resist physically, not only in the Warsaw Ghetto, but in many parts of Europe. But wherever and whenever they fought back, they were doomed and they knew it. They had immeasurably less to fight with than any other resistance movement in Europe. And their efforts, like other resistance efforts in World War II, were not a determining factor in the ultimate reckoning of an Allied victory.[18] Only the titanic military might of the Allies could overcome the Nazi war machine.

What Ringelblum and the others suffered was and is common to all Jewish survivors: guilt at being alive after the storm of death, measureless as it was senseless. Why, they asked themselves, were they alive? Today, a whole generation away from the exterminations, Jewish survivors still feel the guilt.

With Ringelblum, the Ghetto survivors of the September seizures decried their inaction and resolved to fight back before they died. Even so, they could not act immediately. Three more months were needed before the first military action against the Nazis could be organized. ·

The seizures in September disrupted the underground network that had been painstakingly built and created geographic dislocations. Systems of communication between groups were broken; sections of the Ghetto that had been linked were torn apart. All of the units had to reform and seek new members to replace those who had been deported. The store of weapons was small. Renewed frantic appeals had gone out to the *Armia Krajowa* for arms. The Polish Home Army praised the Jewish Coordinating Committee for preparing a defense against the Germans but did not send any aid. This time fear was expressed that arms would be used by the Communists for their own ends. This lack of response helped to clear the mist from the eyes of the Bundists. They now realized that Poles were not going to make a common front with them against the Germans.

After the first shipment of arms was successfully smuggled, the fighters used Parysowski Point again. Disguised as poor peddlers, they approached Parysow Square and paid off the Polish smugglers who controlled the point. The traffic was soon discovered, however, and the smugglers were shot. When the patrols were strengthened, the fighters had to find a new point. They began to use Feiffer's leather factory on Okopova Street near Gliniana, bordering on the Ghetto. The factory watchman was bribed with whiskey and slipped a JFO fighter into the factory in the semidarkness while the German guard was busy checking the other side of Okopova Street. The fighter was then led into a small room packed with boxes and packages. Lights were switched off, a password was whispered through a small window, and packages of dynamite were delivered in the guise of nails and paints.[19]

There were many disappointments and betrayals in the search for weapons. Presumed friends became informers; costly revolvers proved defective; prices soared; underground agents were caught. But the work went on with feverish desperation and under great tension. The JFO also began to buy explosives and incendiaries and set up a workroom inside the Ghetto for the production of Molotov cocktails and hand grenades. The process was primitive but the results added to the firepower of the Ghetto. Polish contacts secured textbooks on chemistry and in clandestine meetings drilled the uninitiated youths into the mysteries of making hand grenades, bombs and incendiary bottles. In addition to gasoline, potassium, benzine and hydrochloric acid had to be bought, transported and then concealed. This phase of preparation was under the direction of Michael Klepfisz of the Bund.

Meanwhile, the power of the *Judenrat* under Czerniakow's successor, Marek Lichtenbaum, had atrophied. The JFO was becoming the new force in the Ghetto. It levied taxes on Jews that still had any wealth and determined the contributions of the community agencies. The *Judenrat* contributed 250,000 zlotys; the Office of Economic Requirements, 700,000. The money was used to buy weapons and explosives. Popular support now gravitated to the young fighters. Bakers and merchants delivered food for them.

By January, when the fighters had their first baptism of fire, they had a store of 143 revolvers, one machine pistol and seven rounds of ammunition per weapon. The Ghetto called them "the people's avengers." In December 1942, they overcame the guards in the prison on Nowolipie Street and freed 100 "illegal" Jews held for transport to Treblinka.

Meanwhile, the Germans made plans of their own. Early in January, Himmler visited Warsaw and was told that 40,000 Jews still remained in the Ghetto. The actual number was closer to 70,000, but even 40,000 were too many for him. He ordered the immediate deportation of 8,000. The fighters, unaware of this order, planned to attack the Nazis on January 22. On January 16, the Germans made extensive searches on the Aryan side and seized many Poles. Then on January 18, the Ghetto was suddenly surrounded and workers were ordered to the *Umschlagplatz* for deportation. The Ghetto fighters, believing that the Germans would be busy on the other side for several weeks, were taken completely by surprise. They put out a hastily mimeographed leaflet: "Jews! The enemy has moved on to the second phase of your extermination! Do not resign yourselves to death! Defend yourselves! Grab an axe, an iron bar, a knife! Let them take you this way, if they can!"

They were organized into fifty groups; all had planned to fight, but most of them could not reach ammunition stores in time. Only four barricaded battle groups were ready to offer the first armed resistance in the Ghetto. A fifth group fought in the street, at the corner of Mila and Zamenhof streets, but was pulled into a column of deportees. The entire group except Mordecai Anielewicz was killed, and all of the group's arms were lost.

The other four groups adopted guerrilla tactics. They fought from rooftops, cellars and attics, and moved from street to street through underground passages without leaving the protection of the houses. One Zionist group, D'ror (freedom, in Hebrew), had headquarters at 58 Zamenhof Street. There, forty youths waited with four hand grenades and four revolvers, clubs, metal sticks and cups of acid with which to meet the Germans. All but two youths hid. In the distance could be heard the cries of Jews being led to the Umschlagplatz and the shouts of the police, "Laufen, schneller, Laufen!" ("Run faster! Run!") The sound of boots was finally heard in the entrance hall. One middle-aged man found himself in the midst of the young fighters. He was the famous poet and teacher, Izhak Katzenelson, who had come to visit his youthful friends and then insisted on staying to help them. While the boots thudded on the steps, Katzenelson spoke briefly, with great emotion, as if he were saying farewell. "We must be happy for we are about to meet the enemy with ammunition, though it be to die; we will fight with arms, but we will fight not for ourselves but for the future generation. Let us have courage. . . . The Germans could kill a million Jews but they would not overpower us; the Jewish nation lives and it will always live."[20]

As he finished speaking, German soldiers broke down the door. The two young men in the front room were reading to divert attention from the rest hiding in the back. As the soldiers passed through, the readers opened fire and killed several Germans; the rest of D'ror fought with whatever they had. Soon the Germans turned to run, with Jewish boys and girls chasing after them. They had killed some Germans, forced others to run and had captured ammunition. Continued fighting in the streets was out of the question, so the D'ror group left the house through the attic, over the rooftops to the fourth floor of 44 Muranovska Street. Again they met Germans with fire and killed two. Again the Germans turned back.

The fighters then moved to 34 Mila Street and to the Schultz shops, raining more fire upon Germans. The soldiers came back with reinforcements but now made their searches quietly and kept close to walls. They were astounded by the sudden change in the mood of the Ghetto and realized that its final liquidation would not be easy. Jews also fought German guards at the Umschlagplatz. The January action lasted four days. The fighters killed twenty Germans and wounded fifty, but their own losses were very heavy. Altogether about a thousand Jews were killed during the brief resistance while another 6,500 were transported to death camps. But the action electrified the Ghetto. The myth of Nazi invincibility crumbled. Where the Jews killed, the Germans retreated or were forced to give up their deportation plans. These first shots of revolt showed Jews that they could kill Germans. For the thousands who could not bear arms, the thought that other Jews were avenging German crimes made death more bearable. The insurrection also had important repercussions outside the Ghetto.

The attitude of the Poles changed. The skepticism of the Polish underground toward the Ghetto fighters was replaced by respect and admiration. The Home Army, which had been unsuccessfully courted, now delivered fifty revolvers, fifty grenades and a supply of dynamite. Poles on the Aryan side were now eager to sell firepower. Legends about "hundreds" of dead Germans and the "power" of the JFO began circulating through Warsaw.

To arm five hundred fighters, millions of zlotys were needed. Jews now gave up what they had left to the new force in the Ghetto or submitted willingly to new taxes. The hesitant or rich were arbitrarily taxed. All now fully realized that next to their underground shelters, arms for defense was their greatest need, but prices for arms soared. Guns cost 12,000 zlotys each; bullets, 100 zlotys; and grenades, 10,000 zlotys each. In the first three months of 1943, about 10,000,000 zlotys were collected and sent to the Aryan side for the purchase of arms. Most important, the fighters and the Ghetto as a whole had crossed over a big psychological block: a Jewish fighting arm was now permitted to place Jewish lives in the balance, to go to war knowing that it had the full support of the Ghetto. The uses of sovereignty to which Jews had been unaccustomed for two millennia were now restored by Jewish boys and girls in Warsaw who recognized what the young Palestinian Jews had already learned four years earlier: the Jews of Europe had been abandoned to their fate and could count on no one but themselves.

During the breathing spell between the January action and April 19, when the large revolt flamed, the JFO took stock of its weaknesses, regrouped its forces and divided its military command with a commander in charge of each of the segmented ghettos. Each group adopted a communal way of living so that at all times they would be ready to fight. Their numbers increased to six hundred and fifty fighters, divided into 22 groups. Meanwhile, Jews throughout the Ghetto worked in a frenzy digging underground caves and stocking them with whatever food they could secure. Day after day, they searched for planks, bricks and other building materials. Bunkers had to be dug deep and made livable and the entrances and exits camouflaged. Whole families had to be sheltered under the earth with disguised shafts and vents for air. The burrows were vital for defense as well as hiding. The Ghetto fighters constructed an intricate network of underground cellars and tunnels, linking the various commands and defense posts and the Ghetto side of certain streets to the Aryan side. Tunnels also led from the bunkers to the Catholic and Jewish cemeteries outside the Ghetto. Concealed retreats and passages for shifting and distributing the defense forces were also devised. A staff of engineers, architects and sappers, trained under necessity, handled complex digging and building operations. Trenches and ditches were dug under pavements, behind walls and through the sewers. Attics also became vital passageways, since Jews were not permitted to appear on streets. One heavily-used route was sardonically referred to as the "Jewish Auto Strada." Holes were cut in attic walls, making it possible for people to move from house to house and street to street. Gradually the honeycomb of attic routes replaced streets as arteries of traffic. In the dark corners of the attics, food, candles and arms were bought and sold. Couriers met agents in deserted houses and exchanged zlotys for dynamite. The attics were crucially important during the April Ghetto uprising, forming the only routes through which fighting groups were moved from one position to another.

The Germans now had to adopt a new strategy. The shock of the January uprising led them to overestimate the numbers and arms of the Ghetto fighters. They also feared the spread of revolt to the Polish quarter. Their objective remained the liquidation of the Ghetto, but through different methods. In February, Himmler ordered the complete destruction of the Ghetto. But the Germans did not want an open war with the Jews. Instead of violent selections and seizures, they proposed a quiet "evacuation." They tried their last ruse, using the German industrialist Walter Toebbens to set the trap.

Early in February, Toebbens and his staff members appeared before the assembled workers in the factories and spoke glowingly of the plan to evacuate all workers and workshops to Trawniki and Poniatov, near Lublin. Here, Toebbens said, Jewish workers could work peacefully in the lap of nature, with fresh air and good food, instead of the poisoned Ghetto. He urged the workers to ignore the "malicious" rumors that deported Jews were killed. A dramatic public battle between Toebbens and the JFO followed. The Ghetto fighters posted appeals calling on all Jews to ignore German orders.

The new "resettlement" was denounced as another deathtrap. Toebbens answered: "Jewish war workers! Do not believe those who want to mislead you. They only wish to provoke you in order to bring about results that will be disastrous to you. . . . It is with the fullest conviction that I urge you to do the following: Go to Trawniki, to Poniatov, because there you will have an opportunity to live and be able to witness the end of the war. The leaders of the Jewish Fighting Organization cannot help you. They feed you with false promises."[21]

Toebbens' appeal fell on deaf ears. Instead of reporting for evacuation, Jewish workers set fire to trucks and shop machinery. The Germans then tried to revive the flickering *Judenrat* and ordered it to carry out this last action. The chairman, Marek Lichtenbaum, replied: "I have no power

The sign, "Jewish residential district; entrance forbidden," was posted at the entrance of the Lodz Ghetto in Poland. Because its textile factories were so valuable to the Germans, Lodz lasted four years—longer than any Nazi ghetto. In August 1944, however, 70,000 remaining Jews were deported to Auschwitz and gassed. SEMINARY.

Jews in Poland during the German occupation were forced to play "horsie" and other humiliating games for the entertainment of the Nazis. FRANKENHUIS.

A street in the Warsaw Ghetto soon after the wall was built in the summer of 1940. The wall, eight feet tall by eleven miles long, was first justified by the Nazis as a quarantine measure to prevent the spread of typhus. In fact, it imprisoned the Jews and made them easy victims of Nazi measures. GHETTO.

(Opposite page, top) A food ration card for the Warsaw Ghetto, April 1942, entitled the holder to 300 calories a day. In the summer of 1942, Governor-General Hans Frank wrote, "We have condemned 1,200,000 Jews to death by starvation." SEMINARY.

(Opposite page, bottom) Children and refugees suffered the most from hunger. During their short period of existence, the ghettos accounted for one fifth of the deaths of Polish Jewry—mostly from disease and starvation. SEMINARY.

Beginning in July 1942, 6,000 Jews a day
from the Warsaw Ghetto were "resettled"
in the East. The actual destination of
these railroad cars was Treblinka, where
the deportees were gassed. GHETTO.

Zalman Friedrych, a young member of
the Jewish Fighting Organization in the
Warsaw Ghetto, helped smuggle arms
from the Aryan side of Warsaw. He was
the first Jew who followed the tracks from
Warsaw to Treblinka, fifty miles away,
and thus confirmed the rumors about the
fate of the deportees. GHETTO.

Dr. Janusz Korczak, a well-known neurologist, writer and educator, headed a children's orphanage in the Warsaw Ghetto. On August 12, 1942, he accompanied the children to the gas chambers, although he himself did not have to go. YAD VASHEM.

Dr. Emmanuel Ringelblum was safe in Geneva when the war broke out. He returned to Warsaw, where he wrote the famous "Notes from the Warsaw Ghetto." He survived the uprising, but was killed by the Germans in March 1944. YAD VASHEM.

Mordecai Anilewicz, commander of the Jewish Fighting Organization in the Warsaw Ghetto uprising. He died (he took poison to avoid capture) on May 8, 1943. GHETTO.

Mordecai Tenenbaum, Zionist Youth leader, carried early reports of the exterminations from ghetto to ghetto. He helped organize the defense of the Warsaw Ghetto. GHETTO.

Resistance leader Zivia Lubetkin escaped through the sewers during the destruction of the Warsaw Ghetto. She and other survivors escaped to the Aryan zone and later fought in the Polish defense of Warsaw in August 1944. GHETTO.

German guards stand outside the gates at the beginning of the Warsaw Ghetto uprising, April 19, 1943. Despite the use of tanks, planes and heavy artillery, the first attempts to break into the ghetto were successfully repulsed by the Jewish fighters. SEMINARY.

Since the ghetto was impenetrable in a frontal attack, General Stroop's forces set fire to the buildings with incendiary bombs and flame throwers. In five weeks the Warsaw Ghetto was reduced to rubble. SEMINARY.

Routed by the fire, a Jew jumps from a window of a burning building. YIVO.

Jews lie amid the rubble of the Warsaw Ghetto after being forced out of their homes by smoke grenades. YIVO.

Although the Germans planned to annihilate the Warsaw Ghetto in three days, the rebellion continued for five weeks. Deportations continued, accompanied by mass executions on the spot. SEMINARY.

This Jewish family was killed in front of a demolished house. YIVO.

Those who were not killed during the uprising faced deportation. Above, women and children are forced into a deportation column. Below, Jews are marched to the Umschlagplatz. YIVO.

Above, Jews at the Umschlagplatz, Warsaw Ghetto, wait for cars that will take them to Treblinka. GHETTO. Below, the Auschwitz death camp. YIVO.

Fumes from Zyklon B, or prussic acid, were used at Auschwitz. After the "selections" on the station platforms, Jews were told they were to be disinfected. Gassing rooms were disguised as shower baths, sometimes equipped with seats and douches. FRANKENHUIS. Bottom, a warning to the German guards: "Be careful, gas." YIVO.

An estimated two million Jews were exterminated at Auschwitz. Shown here are a group of emaciated, dead children and a furnace, probably from Auschwitz, for burning the bodies. YIVO.

Jewish women being led through the woods to the gassing vans. The vans were used in Poland, Serbia, and White Russia for killing women and children. YIVO.

Men and children stripped naked at the execution pits. Others stand by with shovels to bury them. YIVO.

Over one million of the six million Jews destroyed were children. FRANKENHUIS.

Hannah Senesch, a young Palestinian from Hungary, parachuted into Yugoslavia on a spying mission for the British. She crossed the border into Hungary to carry on rescue activities among surviving Jews, but was captured and executed on November 6, 1944. YAD VASHEM.

After the war, British troops force women S.S. guards to bury the bodies at Belsen. YIVO.

Jewish refugees board a ship at Marseilles for Palestine, May 1946. Most of the passengers were orphans whose parents had been killed by the Nazis. WIDE WORLD.

in the Ghetto; another government rules here!" The German plan for quiet liquidation failed and both sides now made preparations for war. The fighters killed off or intimidated remnants of the Jewish police and cleansed the Ghetto of informers. Even the Gestapo shunned the Ghetto. The fighting groups trained and tried to mend shortages. Groups went out on missions day and night, collecting food, smuggling arms, freeing Jewish prisoners, hunting down robber bands and suspected collaborators. On March 6, in a major act of sabotage, JFO set fire to S.S. warehouses.

Withal, a feeling of ominous doom overhung the days before the Germans struck; Jews felt they would all die. They were still poorly armed. A letter from Anielewicz to the Warsaw representative of the Polish Government-in-Exile, dated March 18, expresses the desperation of the fighters: "The situation becomes daily more critical. . . . In the next few days, the end may come for Warsaw Jewry. . . . Our arms situation worsens continually as a result of our activities in recent weeks. . . . Now we have only ten rounds per weapon. This is catastrophic. . . . Giving weapons without ammunition creates an impression of cynical mocking about our fate."

The hoped-for aid from the Poles faded. The Government-in-Exile warned against any armed attacks as a means of helping Jews: "Reprisals would be inevitable. Such attacks are forbidden by London," was the response to Anielewicz. And yet preparations for a Jewish attack went on with intensive thoroughness.

The Ghetto also went through the motions of preparing for Passover, the holiday celebrating Jewish liberation from the Egyptians. The bakers had baked matzo out of dark flour; some wine had been hoarded for the festival; bunkers were given a spring housecleaning. Would the Germans allow the Ghetto to enjoy its last Passover? Rumors swept the Ghetto on April 18, the day before Passover eve; it was said that an action would start the following day. Many Jews packed up their bundles to move into deeper bunkers or join friends. At 2 A.M. on April 19, the outermost observation posts of the resistance received their first messages that German police and Polish "navy-blues" were encircling the outer Ghetto at 30-yard intervals. Fifteen minutes later all groups were at their battle stations. The Ghetto population was instructed to go to prepared shelters and hideouts. Every group of bunkers had its detachment of armed defenders. Couriers and scouts were disposed. The operational base was a bunker in the shop district at Leszno 74, equipped with water, electricity, two radios and a tunnel exit to the Aryan side. The headquarters bunker of the JFO was at 18 Mila Street.

At four in the morning, in small patrols, the Germans infiltrated the "interghetto" area. Here they formed into platoons and companies. At seven o'clock, armed trucks loaded with soldiers rolled toward the center of the Ghetto. Tanks and armored cars followed. Artillery pieces were placed outside the walls. In closed formations, the soldiers marched through the dead streets of the Ghetto. At the intersection of Mila and Zamenhof streets, the Ghetto fighters, barricaded at the four corners, opened fire. A hail of bullets, grenades and bombs poured down on the Germans. Their columns wavered and scattered in confusion. Tanks were brought in to force the barricades but the fighters aimed a barrage of gasoline-filled bottles, knocked one tank out and turned back two others. Twelve Germans were killed and many wounded in this ambush; one Jewish fighter was killed. Later in the morning the Germans came back with a flamethrower, setting fire to buildings on the corner and burning to death several Jewish youths.

Two other important actions took place that morning. One was at Gesia and Nalewki, where two fighter groups had been stationed to prevent German troops from entering the Ghetto from the southeast. The German assault here lasted for seven hours and forced the Jewish units to give up their base position. Again the Germans used a flamethrower and set fire to several buildings. The fighters inflicted some casualties by sniping and made their escape through a maze of attics and roof openings. On their way, they passed many refugees who had abandoned their shelters because of the fires. In 4 Kuza Street, where they set up a new position, they found themselves in a rabbi's apartment. It was Passover, the night of the first Seder.

> The apartment was in a state of chaos [a youth observed]. Bed linens were spread all around, chairs were turned upside down, various household items were strewn on the floor, and all the window panes were smashed into little bits. During the daytime, while the members of the family had sought shelter in the bunker, the house had become a mess; only the table in the middle of the room stood: festive, as if a thing apart from the other furniture.
>
> The redness of the wine in the glasses which were on the table was a reminder of the blood of the Jews who had perished on the eve of the holiday. The Hagada was recited while in the background incessant bursts of bombing and shooting, one after the other, pounded throughout the night. The scarlet reflection from the burning houses nearby illuminated the faces of those around the table in the darkened room.
>
> When the rabbi reached the passage, "Shofoch Chamatcha" ["Pour out Your wrath on the nations who have not wished to know You"], he and his family broke down and cried bitterly. I had the feeling that it was the weeping of people condemned to death, people who, outwardly, had resigned themselves to the idea of their deaths, yet were terrified when the moment neared. The rabbi lamented those who had not lived to celebrate this Seder.[22]

The third armed encounter took place at Muranowski Square, where the greatest resistance was concentrated. This was the area around the brushmakers' factory. The Germans had apparently planned to cut this section from the rest of the Ghetto and evacuate the workers. In one skirmish, a squad of Ghetto fighters appeared in the street in German uniforms and snatched two machine pistols. On the roof of one of the houses fluttered a Jewish flag alongside a Polish flag; nearby, a machine gun was mounted. Again a German tank was set on fire. The Germans were forced to retire without flushing out the factory workers. But they exacted revenge: the Ghetto hospital was attacked and the patients shot down.

At noon the Germans dammed up the sewers and flooded them, thereby hoping to wreck important communication lines and hideouts. But the fighters temporarily shut off the water by turning the valves of an auxiliary system. The remainder of the day was relatively quiet for the fighter groups. The Germans, however, carried out blockades, searches and round-ups in undefended or ruined shelters and captured several hundred Jews. Nevertheless, the fighters felt that the day was theirs; they had taken on heavily armed and trained German units and inflicted losses. They could not win or even hold out, but they would die avenging the silenced dead.

The Germans quickly realized that the Ghetto could not be cleared in one burst of action. On the second day, new tactics were used. A force of 1,293 men was used organized in assault groups of 50 to 60 men in each and scattered in all directions to clear out areas, one house at a time. The Ghetto communications system now proved invaluable. It enabled groups to retire from an assaulted house to neighboring attics and cellars and then, after the Germans completed their search, to return to their original position. The main German force still remained outside the Ghetto. The most important battle of the day occurred in the brushmakers' section again. Two German storm columns fought their way into the area under the cover of tanks, but the attack was repulsed. A detachment of several hundred followed. An electrical mine strategically planted was detonated and eight Germans were wounded. The rest were driven away by a volley of rifle shots. After they withdrew, something extraordinary happened. Three German officers carrying machine pistols and Dr. Laus, the German director of the brushmakers' factory, walked across the courtyard of the area. With gestures, they made signs of their peaceful intentions. Dr. Laus asked to speak to the local commander. When he appeared, Laus petitioned for a fifteen-minute truce for the removal of the dead and wounded. The Germans were asking Jews to agree on rules! They also promised all inhabitants an orderly evacuation to labor camps in Poniatov and Trawniki. More firing was the reply.

After the rejection of the truce, the Germans brought up to point-blank range three light howitzers and a large field gun and pounded the buildings of the area. But the brushmakers' area could not be taken. At five in the afternoon, an order was issued for all Jews residing in the workshop area to appear at certain concentration points by six the following morning for deportation to the Lublin region. Whoever refused to come would be shot.

Outside the Ghetto, JFO agents vainly tried to get help from the *Armia Krajowa* and requested an urgent meeting. The Warsaw commander wrote, "The Warsaw military salute the heroes of the Warsaw Ghetto who have shown that they can fight. I believe that a meeting is not expedient now." No response came from the Polish Government-in-Exile.

Noncombatants in the Ghetto, meanwhile began a desperate search for new shelters. Many pleaded for refuge in prepared bunkers of neighbors. Crowds swarmed in Leszno and Novolipie streets looking for an escape; some sought the Ghetto gates and tried to bribe the guards to let them pass to the Aryan section.[23] But the fighting units stood intact and began preparations for the next day. They postponed a new round of battles until the noncombatants had time to hide.

General Jürgen Stroop, who commanded the overall Ghetto action and ordered the evacuation of the workers from the shops, later commented on the Jewish resistance in the factories:

> The conditions discovered there are indescribable. I cannot imagine a greater chaos than in the Ghetto of Warsaw. The Jews had control of everything, from the chemical substances used in manufacturing explosives to clothing and equipment for the armed forces. The managers knew so little of their own shops that the Jews were in a position to produce inside these shops arms of every kind, especially hand grenades, Molotov cocktails and the like. Moreover, the Jews had succeeded in fortifying some of these factories as centers of resistance.[24]

The Ghetto defenders were elated. "What we have lived through," wrote Commander Mordecai Anielewicz to his second in command, Isaac Zuckerman, "after the two days of defense, defies description in words. We must realize that what has happened exceeds our most audacious dreams. Germans twice fled the Ghetto. One of our sectors held out for forty minutes; another six hours. . . . Our losses in men are very small. . . . I have the feeling that what we have dared is of great significance."

The Ghetto in April 1943 measured 1,000 by 300 yards. Stroop had 2,090 men, about half of them regular army or *Waffen S.S.* troops, and the rest S.S. police, reinforced by 335 Lithuanian militia and Polish police. Stroop called for tanks, armored cars, artillery, flamethrowers and aerial support. Superior German firepower could easily crush the poorly armed fighters. Stroop's main problem, however, was the tens of thousands of Jews holed up in their bunkers. The fighters were tenaciously defending these hideouts. They would all have to be dug out and burnt out, block by block and house to house. Only fire could destroy the Ghetto.

On the third day of the rebellion, Stroop continued the unceasing bombardment of the brushmakers' district, but the resistance was still stubborn and in the afternoon the Germans resorted to fire. They set simultaneous fires to the entire outer border of the brushmakers' block and within minutes flames raged wildly. Before nightfall, walls, roofs and floors were consumed by fire. Marek Edelman, the commander of the sector and one of the few survivors, has described the inferno:

> Flames cling to our smouldering clothes. The pavement melts to a sticky, black tar beneath our feet. Broken glass, littering the streets, cuts into our shoes. Our soles burn from the heat of the pavement. One by one, we stagger through the conflagration. From house to house, courtyard to court-yard, half-choked, a hundred hammers beating in our skulls, burning rafters falling over us, we finally pass the area under fire. We feel lucky just to be out of the inferno.
>
> The most difficult part of our trek remains. There is only one way to the Central Ghetto—through a small breach in the wall, closely guarded by the enemy. Five battle units will have to make their way, under the eyes of German gendarmes, "navy blue" police, and Ukrainian detachments. Tense to the breaking point, their feet wrapped in rags to stifle the sound of steps, Gutman's, Berlinski's and Grynbaum's groups get through under heavy fire. Success! Yurek Blone's group covers from behind. While the first of this group emerge on the street, however, a German searchlight illuminates the entire section. No one else, it seems, will be able to save himself. Suddenly fighter Romanowicz's single, well-aimed shot shatters the searchlight. Before the Germans collect their wits, our entire group manages to cross over. . . .
>
> What the Germans could not do, the omnipotent flames now accomplished. Thousands perished in the conflagration; the stench of burning bodies was everywhere. Charred corpses lay on balconies, in window recesses, on unburned steps. Flames drove people from their shelters, forced them from their hiding places in cellars and attics. Thousands staggered about the yards, easy prey for the Germans. . . . Weary beyond endurance, they fell asleep in driveways, beside doors, standing still, lying, and were caught asleep by German bullets. No one as much as noticed that an old man sleeping in a corner would never awaken; that a mother nursing her baby had been dead for three days; that a baby's cries and suckling were unavailing, for its mother's arms were cold, her breasts dead. Hundreds committed suicide by leaping from fourth- and fifth-story windows.[25]

The embattled detachment soon made contact with the main head-quarters at Mila 18. The first attempts by German units to disrupt the occupation of the Central Ghetto were made in the Toebbens and Schultz area. Grenades and gunfire showered on the moving truckloads of S.S. men from balconies, windows and rooftops. Many noncombatants re-mained in the workshops after the deportation deadline. Several Germans leading Jews to the *Umschlagplatz* were shot. Once again, the Germans laid siege to isolated houses, but they could not avoid battle; each house became a battleground. Light, water and gas were cut off from the Ghetto streets. Packs of police hounds were introduced to hunt down Jews in bunkers. Several sections of the Ghetto were now afire. Incendiary bombs were dropped from planes; sewers were raked with fire to prevent escape and to destroy communications. The ever-spreading fires threw a red glare over the sky in the Ghetto. The streets were saturated with thick, acrid smoke. In windows, people were enwrapped in flames.

The Germans had planned to annihilate the Ghetto in three days but the Jewish resistance was too dogged. Stroop reported that it became increasingly difficult to capture Jews. "Over and over again," he wrote, "new battle groups consisting of twenty to thirty or more Jewish fellows, eighteen to twenty-five years of age, accompanied by a corresponding number of women kindled new resistance." These battle groups were under orders to put up armed resistance to the last and, if necessary, to escape arrest by committing suicide. The women, Stroop observed, belonged to the *Chalutzim* movement. They fired pistols with both hands and used hand grenades concealed in their bloomers.[26]

A few isolated actions by Poles lifted the spirits of the fighters. A small party mined the Bonifraterska wall of the Ghetto; a saboteur band destroyed a bridge in the Eastern Railway Station and set fire to freight cars; another group attacked guards near Muranowska Square and about a hundred Jews escaped through holes in a wall to the Aryan side. The P.P.R. Youth Division pasted posters all over Warsaw with the legend; "Help the Jews!" and circulated leaflets carrying the words: "Poles! . . . The bestial slaughter of the Jewish population demonstrates the true nature of Hitlerism. This is the fate which awaits you under Hitler's rule. By fighting the enemy, we will spoil his plans. Long live the armed struggle of the whole Polish people!" There was no official aid, however.

On April 23, Himmler issued orders "to complete the combing out of the Warsaw ghetto with the greatest severity and relentless tenacity." Stroop then decided to destroy the entire residential area by setting every block on fire. "Not infrequently", he reported, "the Jews stayed in the burning buildings until, because of the heat and the fear of being burned alive, they preferred to jump down from the upper stories after having thrown mattresses and other upholstered articles into the street from the burning buildings. With their bones broken they still tried to crawl across the street into blocks of buildings which had not yet been set on fire."

Bunkers were dynamited and smoke candles lowered into sewer entrance holes. On April 25, Stroop sent a teletype to S.S. headquarters reporting that 27,464 Jews had been captured. He had generous words of commendation for the *Waffen S.S.*, the Police, and Wehrmacht engineers who "courageously climbed down the shafts to bring out the Jews," and whose "duty hours often lasted from early morning until late at night." Stroop asked the Polish population to assist in the fight against Communist agents and Jews and explicitly forbade Poles from giving refuge to Jews. He also gave Polish police permission to arrest any Jews in the Aryan part of Warsaw, promising one third of any cash in a Jew's possession. This measure added another hazard to the already very risky tenure of the Jewish couriers still darting from cover to cover on the Aryan side of the city seeking arms and help.

On Good Friday, April 23, the fifth day of battle, the JFO published a manifesto addressed to the Polish underground and to the Poles in the capital. It was a message of solidarity. "We, as well as you," the fighters wrote, "are burning with the desire to punish the enemy for all his crimes. . . . It is a fight for our freedom, as well as yours; for our human dignity and national honor, as well as yours. . . . We must continue our mutual struggle against the occupier until the very end!" Various sectors of the Polish underground and labor movements responded with messages of admiration and fraternity but no impulse to join the struggle. "An open fight at this time," they said, "would mean complete extermination for all of us." They likewise refused to organize street demonstrations and turned down a request for a protest strike as a gesture of sympathy.[27] The anti-Semitic *Endek* (National Democrats) publication *Walka* (*Struggle*) wrote: "The misery of the Jews has been earned a hundred times over."

Meanwhile, Dr. Isaac I. Schwarzbart, a Jewish representative in the Polish National Council in London received reports from Poland and sent back messages and financial aid through underground channels. A dispatch from the Ghetto fighters dated April 28 described the now hopeless struggle and appealed for Allied aid:

> The Jewish Fighting Organization addressed a proclamation to the people of Warsaw, and the Polish Workers' Parties paid tribute to the fighters of the Ghetto. Only the power of the allied nations can offer immediate and active help now. On behalf of the millions of Jews burnt and murdered and burned alive, on behalf of those fighting back and all of us condemned to die, we call the whole world: it is imperative that the powerful retaliation of the allies shall fall upon the bloodthirsty enemy immediately and not in some distant future.

This message was conveyed to the Polish Minister of Interior in London, who had virtually daily secret cable contacts with Warsaw, but was not given to Dr. Schwarzbart until May 21. Dr. Schwarzbart never received an explanation for this long delay. His diary entry for May 21, 1943, reads as follows: "Siudak gave me two telegrams from the Jewish National Committee and the Jewish Labor Organization in Warsaw. One of them is dated April 28. I can't understand why it was held back so long. Siudak blames the forwarding system. I have my doubts. I immediately forwarded both messages to Tel Aviv and to America."[28]

One result of the frantic and futile efforts of the Jewish representatives in London to stir the Allies to rush help to the vanishing Polish Jews was the suicide of Shmuel Zygelboim, a member of the Polish National Council, on May 11, 1943. Jan Karski, the Polish writer and liaison officer had visited Zygelboim in the winter of 1942 to bring shattering reports directly from the Warsaw Ghetto and pleas to shake the conscience of the world. Zygelboim felt that as he had failed to help his fellow Jews in Poland, he could express his solidarity with them only in death. In his letter of farewell addressed to the Polish President and Prime Minister he wrote:

> Behind the walls of the ghetto is now going on the last act of a tragedy unequalled in all history. The murderers themselves bear the primary responsibility for the crime of extermination of the whole population of Poland but, indirectly, this responsibility also weighs on all humanity, on the peoples and governments of the allied nations, because they have not made any attempt to do something drastic to stall the criminal deeds. By looking on indifferently while helpless millions of tortured children, women and men were murdered, those nations have associated themselves with the criminals. . . . I cannot be silent. . . . By my death I wish to make my final protest against the passivity with which the world is looking on and permitting the extermination of the Jewish people. I know how little human life is worth today, but as I was unable to do anything during my lifetime, perhaps by my death I shall contribute to breaking down the indifference of those who may now at the last moment rescue the few Polish Jews still alive.[29]

Dr. Schwarzbart sent the two telegrams from Warsaw to Anthony Eden, British Minister of Foreign Affairs. The following terse reply came from Eden's secretary: "I write on Mr. Eden's behalf to thank you for your letter of the 24th of May in which you enclosed two messages addressed to the late Mr. S. Zygelboim and yourself by the Central Committee in Poland describing Jewish resistance to the Germans in the ghetto of Warsaw."[30]

No help came from the Allies. Moreover, the persistent efforts to induce the Polish Government-in-Exile to urge the Polish people and the underground army inside Poland to help Jews did not bear any fruit until May 18, after five months of prodding. By that time, however, assistance from any source was meaningless, for most of the Jewish fighters were already dead.

By the end of April, Jewish centers of resistance in the Ghetto became sporadic and independent of one another. Fires were engulfing the whole Ghetto. Stroop had divided the city into twenty-four districts with a reinforced searching party detailed to each district. He had expected to complete combing-out operations by April 23, but pockets of resistance flared from a few of the workshops and garrison bunkers. Stroop attached pneumatic boring machines to flamethrowers, bombing planes and artillery. These were brought into action to pierce tunnels and bunkers; flamethrowers, gasoline and poison gas were then thrust into the openings. Scattered remnants of the fighting forces tried to escape to the forests and Aryan part of the city but most of them were killed or captured, some in German uniforms, wearing German decorations to disguise their identity. Flame-seared fugitives lay dead or wounded in the polluted sewers. The toughest of the fighters fought on defiantly, from buried ruins and the maze of dugouts, but it was now only a question of time before all resistance flickered out.

And yet, before the final hour, the youthful labor-conscious fighters "celebrated" May Day. The JFO command decided to commemorate the holiday of labor solidarity. At their headquarters at 18 Mila Street, there was hollow oratory and song. The echo of voices singing the "Internationale" reverberated far outside the walls of the Ghetto, but no voices responded. A broadcast was heard from Radio Moscow on the hidden radio. As a special "feature," a detachment of fighters from Nalewki 47 left in broad daylight to raid German patrols. They were dressed in German uniforms and helmets and goosestepped along the Ghetto streets. The Germans did not suspect the disguise until the fighters opened fire. Some Germans were killed; others fled for reinforcements. The Jewish fighters fought a rearguard action, eventually returning to Mila 18.[31]

In the evening, a May Day roll call was held. There were brief addresses and more songs. Words and music floated weirdly over the charred ruins of the Ghetto while Stroop analyzed the day's results from a German vantage point.

> In today's operation, a total of 1,026 Jews were killed, either in battle or while resisting. . . . All the Jews caught today were forcibly pulled out of dug-outs. Not a single one gave himself up voluntarily. A considerable part of the Jews caught were pulled out of sewers. We continued systematically blowing up or blocking up the sewer entrances. . . . In general, it has to be stated that our men need extraordinary diligence and energy to discover Jews who are still in so-called dug-outs, caves, and in the sewerage system. . . . The sum total of Jews caught so far has risen to 38,385.[32]

Five Aryan-looking youths had been sent meanwhile to reconnoiter a possible escape route through the sewers to the Aryan side of Warsaw. (Several Polish Communists and Socialists arranged temporary hideouts.) When they reached the sewer exit after several hours, they raised the manhole cover and two girls and a boy tiptoed across the silent street. A few minutes later Germans opened fire. A mass exodus through this route had to be given up. Submerged underground, clusters of unarmed Jews clung to the remaining fighter units. At night, freed from the dark and suffocating bunkers, they roamed the streets, searching for friends and families and food. Each night their numbers grew smaller. The Ghetto was vanishing.

One hundred and twenty fighters, including the command, lived in the bunker at Mila 18. Two hundred noncombatants also shared the bunker constructed on the ruins of three houses which had originally been built by Jews of the Warsaw underworld—thieves, gamblers and professional smugglers. The fighters called them the "Chumps." They generously shared their spacious and astonishingly well-equipped bunker with the others and were especially tender with the children. The Chumps also proved to be very helpful: they guided the fighters at night to spy out the German positions and foraged for food with great cunning, even after most of the landmarks of the ghetto had been obliterated by the rubble.

On May 8, the Germans raided 18 Mila. Sixty fighters were taken after two hours of fierce fighting; when the Germans realized that they could not take the bunker by direct attack, they threw a smoke bomb and explosives along the entrance shaft. Twenty-one escaped through an unguarded emergency exit. Some, including the commander, Mordecai Anielewicz, committed suicide; others suffocated from the smoke. Blueprints of the Warsaw sewer system were carried to the bunker by a P.P.R. member, but they came a day too late. Weary, trembling, and smeared with mud, the survivors stumbled to 20 Francis Kanska Street where survivors of another bunker still held on. Here, two men appeared from the Aryan side to evacuate the remnant. One of the survivors, Zivia Lubetkin, has recorded their escape through the sewers:

> With heavy hearts we descended into the sewer. The sewer was an abyss of darkness. I felt the water splash around me as I jumped and then resume its flow. I was overcome by a dreadful nausea there in the cold, filthy water. I felt that nothing—not even freedom—was worth this.
>
> Very few could come with us. The aged and the children would only die on such a trip. They did not even ask to go along. Sixty people crawled through the narrow sewer, bent almost in half, the filthy water reaching up to their knees. Each held a candle. We half-walked, half-crawled like this for twenty hours, one behind the other, without stopping, without food or drink, in that terrible cavern. Hunger and thirst weakened us. Part of our group were the eighteen who had survived the catastrophe at Mila 18 and who had not yet recovered from the effects of the gas. Some of them were unable to walk and we dragged them through the water by their hands and feet.
>
> One crawls through the sewer, and always there is the agonizing thought: how shall we explain, when we meet our comrades again, why we did not remain, why we are alive at all? All of us were poisoned by the thought of those we had left behind, and this robbed us of all possible joy in our good

fortune. More than once, one of us would fall and beg to be left lying there. But no one in all that journey was abandoned.[33]

On the morning of May 10, they reached the manhole at the Prosta-Twarda intersection on the Aryan side. A Jewish youth and a Polish comrade lifted the sewer lid and vanished. The others waited in the sewer all day. Two left before evening to try to rescue others left in the Ghetto. At midnight, Poles in the People's Guard lifted the manhole lid and handed down some soup and loaves of bread. They said they would return the following morning with trucks. Zivia Lubetkin has recalled that day:

Above us, the life of the street went on as usual. We listened to street noises, heard the gay sounds of Polish children playing in the street. One of the children in the game was called Monik, a derogatory equivalent of Moishe. We felt the world nearby. Underneath it, we lay in the filthy water.

In the morning, our messengers, Shlamek and Yorek, returned, their faces distorted with suffering. All the sewer passages to the Ghetto had been blocked. Shlamek acted like a man insane with grief.

In our sorrow we prayed that everything would come to an end. Physical and spiritual strength were ebbing. Then at ten o'clock we heard a noise and soon the tunnel was flooded with such bright light as we had not seen for many days. All of us were sure the Germans had discovered our hiding place and we rushed further into the depths of the sewer. But it was our comrades, who had come to take us out. . . .

Now when we saw each other by daylight—dirty, wrapped in rags, smeared with the filth of the sewers, faces thin and drawn, knees shaking with weariness—we were overcome with horror. Only our feverish eyes showed that we were still living human beings. All of us stretched out on the floor of the truck. . . . We did not know where we were going, nor through what streets we were passing. We did not speak. All about us was the noise of the life of Warsaw, sounds of passing automobiles and crowds of people. . . . We traveled for only one hour, but the minutes dragged. Thus we reached the Mlochini forest, seven kilometers from Warsaw.

Our escape had been organized by our comrades on the Aryan side. . . . The action was carried out by only three Jews and one Pole. . . . One of our comrades had phoned a transport company to send two trucks to Prosta Street to transport some wooden shoes. When the trucks arrived everything was ready for the rescue. Our comrades, armed, came up to the drivers and said, "There are no wooden shoes here. We have a group of Jewish fighters. You must take them to the forests outside Warsaw. Otherwise we shall kill you." They obeyed, and the first of the trucks took us outside the city. . . .

Everything was strange. About us was the green forest and a beautiful spring day. It had been a long time since we had known a forest, spring, and the sun. All that had been buried and restrained in our frozen hearts for years now stirred. I burst into tears. . . . Our future was veiled in darkness and we who had been rescued felt superfluous and alone, abandoned by God and man. What more could be done that we had not done?

We lay down on the ground, but we could not fall asleep. We thought of the mystery of the world and man, we remembered the murder of our people, the beloved dead comrades who were part of the ashes of our burned souls. The heart wondered and asked, wondered and asked—but there was no answer.[34]

Stroop, meanwhile, in the derisively beautiful May days, combed out the remaining underground hiding places in the Ghetto. A vast desert of rubble covered the once vibrant life of Jewish Warsaw and a desert of silence wiped out every human voice. Among the last of the Ghetto Jews to be hounded out was a group of Chasidim who were photographed by Stroop after their capture in May 1943 and then shot. These Chasidim were clad in their traditional garb and wore long beards and side curls, whereas most of the leading rabbis and Chasidim in Poland had shaved off their beards. The Nazis took particular delight in subjecting religious leaders to their most ferocious abuse and torture.

The group that Stroop photographed was one cell of a movement of Gur Chasidim whose members refused to submit to Nazi threats and went underground, where they lived for several years, preserving their peculiar way of life and refusing in any way to alter their physical appearance. Convinced that the paramount object of the Nazis was to destroy every vestige of Jewish religious faith, deeply religious themselves, they made their own faith the meaning of the struggle they waged against the Nazis. The main occupation of the Chasidic underground was the study of the Torah, prayer and preparation for a martyr's death which they accepted with unshakable religious ardor. The members did not enlist the aid of secret circulars, illegal bulletins or a fighting press. Nor were they sustained by the news from the fronts. Rather, they drew support from accounts of trials of faith, mystical allusions to the coming of the Messiah and the end of days, and from dreams of self-redemption.

A survivor, Mordecai Shklarchik, has left a vignette of his encounter with this group:

> They remain engraven in my memory as martyrs and heroes. They did not know the meaning of fear and nothing could quench the ardor of their faith. I first made their acquaintance in the ghetto of Slomnik. After conditions in Crakow Ghetto, where a number of underground Chassidic groups existed, had become worse, they scattered, one group reaching us in Slomnik. They occupied a garret in the attic, near my parents' home and began to study Torah. The Jewish Police insisted that they adapt themselves to existing conditions, that they shave their beards and sidecurls and discard their Chassidic garb. . . . But the young Chassidim were undeterred . . . and persisted in their own peculiar way of life. . . . I undertook all sorts of dangerous missions for them. I bombarded them with questions to which they replied briefly, "It is the will of the Creator. Blessed be He. That is all!" Upon one occasion they were arrested by German soldiers and sent to a labor camp. That same night they organized a mass-escape and, uncon-

cerned about the terrible dangers surrounding them, went back to their study of Torah elsewhere. . . . I met them again two years later in the Crakow Ghetto. . . . I found them in a cellar in the crowded ghetto.[35]

Some Jews who had escaped to the Aryan sector were advised by friendly Poles to hurry to the Hotel Polski, where Jews could live "legally." There, a strange traffic ensued. Jews bought their lives through the acquisition of foreign papers. These rescue documents had been procured through the efforts of Dr. Abraham Silberschein in Geneva who received contributions from Jews all over the world for rescue activities, including the purchase of foreign passports. Gestapo agents possessed thousands of them—for sale at high prices. Two transports of almost 3,000 Jews holding such papers left Warsaw for a new camp in Bergen-Belsen in May 1943. Here they were to be exchanged for Germans living in non-German territory. In August, a meticulous examination of the documents and the inmates was conducted, and in October, 1,800 detainees were transferred to another camp at Bergau, near Dresden. Additional transports of this type were prepared but they were destined not for Bergau, but for Auschwitz.

The Polish Council for Aid to Jews, called *Zegota*, has been credited with saving 20,000 Jews on the Aryan side of Warsaw up to the time of the final destruction of the Ghetto.[36] This group arranged for hiding places, manufactured forged documents, placed Jewish children in convents and with foster parents and helped the Jewish fighters obtain arms. At first, the P.P.R. and left-wing Socialists were mainly involved in Zegota; later, the work involved Polish humanitarians of all political and social strata.

Ringelblum was among those who had escaped to the Aryan side after the destruction of the Ghetto. He, his wife, and thirteen-year-old son and 35 other Jews were sheltered in the cellar of a Polish worker, Mieczyslaw Wolski. On March 6, 1944, a Polish informer led the Gestapo to this cellar and all 38 Jews, as well as Wolski, were executed. During his last days in hiding, Ringelblum reflected on the catastrophe and wrote bitterly of the failure of the Poles to help in the last extremity of the Ghetto. "In the course of the forty-four days of the *akzia* [actions]," he wrote, "nothing was heard from the Aryan sector. There was complete silence there as the drama unfolded before the eyes of hundreds of thousands of Poles."

The Polish Government-in-Exile issued no call to arms, no words of encouragement, no promise of aid. The Polish Socialist Party issued a proclamation to the Jews, exhorting the Ghetto not to submit. The *Armia Krajowa* held itself in readiness for some future major action. Its chief command remained in London through most of the war. A few isolated Polish groups joined the Jewish fighters but as one of their number remarked, "They were of moral significance only."

The struggle to defend the Warsaw Ghetto occurred at the same time the Soviet Union was breaking relations with the Polish Government-in-Exile. The Russians were already grooming another Polish Army—the Kosciusko Army—and the authority of the *Armia Krajowa* was threatened. The Russians had criticized the London Poles for being anti-Semitic as well as hesitant in asserting their armed strength against Germany. Their participation in the Warsaw Ghetto uprising would have refuted both charges, but they did not use this opportunity.

On May 15, 1943, the Polish Directorate of Civil Resistance, which had sent reports to England of the death transports from the Balkans, Holland and Poland, reported that the Ghetto fighters had killed more than 300 Germans and wounded about 1,000 in defense of the Ghetto.

Stroop, for his part, climaxed his elaborate, daily teletyped reports to Higher S.S. and Police Leader Krüger on May 16. "The former Jewish quarter in Warsaw," Stroop wrote, "is no longer in existence . . . [The] total number of Jews dealt with [is] 56,065, including both Jews caught and Jews whose extermination can be proved. . . . Beyond the number of 56,065 Jews, an estimated number of 5,000 to 6,000 were killed by explosions or in fires. . . . Apart from 8 buildings (Police Barracks, hospital and accommodations for housing working-parties) the former Ghetto is completely destroyed."[36]

After the destruction of the Ghetto, some Jews who had escaped to the Aryan side of Warsaw cast their lot with the guerrilla fighters in the People's Guards and fought in the countryside around the city. Some of the surviving Jewish fighters joined the *Armia Ludowa* (the People's Army) and fought in the general Warsaw uprising in August 1944. A document calling for fellow Jews to help in this revolt has survived. It was written on August 3 by Isaac Zuckerman (known as "Antek" by the Ghetto fighters), who commanded the organized Jews in the Aryan section of Warsaw. His appeal read:

To the Defenders of the Warsaw Ghetto!
To the Jews who Remain Alive!
   The population of Warsaw has been conducting an armed struggle against the German invaders for the last three days. This is our struggle, too. A year has passed since we raised the flag of the famous revolt in the Ghettos and labor camps, since we began the battle for our lives and honor, and we again join the entire Polish nation in the fight for freedom. Hundreds of Jewish youths and members of the Jewish Fighting Organization stand shoulder to shoulder with their Polish comrades at the barricades. We send our greetings to the fighters.
   Together with the rest of the Polish nation we are, today, struggling for

freedom. All of the members of the Jewish Fighting Organization who have survived and all Jewish youths capable of fighting are hereby called on to continue the struggle. No one should stay behind. Join the ranks of the rebels. Through war, we shall achieve victory, and a free, sovereign, strong and just Poland!

The Jewish Fighting Organization
(Signed) Antek, Commander[37]

This call drew the last of the Ghetto fighters into combat. The failure of the revolt marked the end of the Jewish Fighting Organization of the Warsaw Ghetto, but not of Jewish resistance. From the ghettos, the struggle moved to the forests and swamps.

18 Resistance in the Forests

AT A MEETING of the Provincial Governors of the Government-General held in Krakow December 7, 1942, Dr. Zörner, the Provincial Governor of Lublin, made the following statement: "Operations against the Jews, which generally speaking were being conducted smoothly, have recently been accelerated, causing panic and alarm, with the result that the major part of the Jews of the Ghettos have fled to the forests to join the bandits." The following month at a similar meeting in Warsaw, Zörner spoke on the same subject. "The evacuation of the Jews has been accepted by most Germans as an inescapable necessity," he said. "Regrettably, however, hasty action undertaken recently has set in motion a flight of Jews to the forests where they have joined the bandits. Thus it has been established that one band operating in Pulawy consisted of three Russians and 24 Jews."[1]

Zörner exaggerated. There was never an exodus of a "major part of the Jews of the Ghettos," but in 1942–43 as the eastern ghettos were being wiped out, small groups of Jews escaped to the woods in a desperate bid for survival and vengeance. The full story of these Jews who took to the woods against fantastic odds remains to be written. Soviet sources dealing with Jewish partisan activity are ambiguous, guarded or inaccessible; German sources can scarcely be trusted because the Nazis generally justified their most murderous actions against Jews on the ground that Jewish Räuberbanden—Himmler issued a special order forbidding the use of the word "partisan"—engaged in acts of sabotage. Jewish works still lack a cohesive unified treatment.

One Jewish writer has described the difficulties:

We are troubled by the feeling that the canvas is so large that gaps and obscurities are inevitable. In many cases even when firsthand evidence was deposed shortly after the events, there remains much that is unclear. It is only natural, of course, that certain events should stand out boldly in human memory, while others should become more vague with the passage of time. . . . And, then, how much could the individual fighter see, how deeply

could he comprehend what he saw? And even if he were unusually perceptive, his field of vision, naturally limited, was further restricted by other
factors . . . making it difficult to place the events he witnessed in their
proper perspective.[2]

The decision to resist at all, against fantastic odds, may be viewed as a
great movement against extermination, but in no sense was it united or
coordinated. Each group of Jews acted on its own responsibility, until
or unless it merged with a larger group. But even when it did, it was isolated from other Jewish units. The pulls of ghetto loyalty and dread of
reprisals no longer stifled action in the forests; the guerrillas in the woods
were free. But they were also alone.

The wide territory of Jewish partisan activities stretching over almost
the entire area of eastern Europe (in thousands of units of different character and structure and connected to different headquarters and political
centers), also makes generalization hazardous.

However, a great deal is known about scattered episodes and movements. One of the worst fears of the Jewish partisans seems to have
been the fear that all traces of their activity would be wiped out. Thousands of documents—diaries, poems, simple reports and more comprehensive accounts of individual bands—have come to light and reveal the
fact that a Jewish resistance did exist in the woods and swamps of eastern
Europe. Jews fought and killed the German enemy. But as there was
never the possibility of bringing the scattered resistance efforts under a
single command or strategy, the record may always bear the sporadic quality of the events themselves.

The Jewish partisan did not merely resort to "illegal" activities such as
disseminating newspapers or meeting clandestinely to make weapons; he
used physical force to oppose the Nazis. He attacked police stations, fired
on Nazi guards, exploded trains, disarmed enemy peasants and threw hand
grenades at tanks. Jews of all ages and stations in life participated—lads
from fifteen up, representing many different occupations; there were carpenters, fishermen, factory owners, doctors, wagoners and shopkeepers.
The mortality rate was very high and included some particularly hideous
forms of death. Some were killed by the blows of axes; some had their
hands and feet cut off, and their torsos were thrown into deep water. Others
had their eyes pierced out, or were crushed by tanks or burned alive. One
young girl, Miriam Golowieńczyc, was chopped to pieces. Jewish partisans
were killed not only by Nazis, but also by Ukrainian, Polish and Lithuanian extremists and by fellow partisans.[3] Statistics are virtually nonexistent,
but one writer estimates that the number of Jewish partisans in White
Russia and western Ukraine alone were 10,000–11,000;[4] 653 incidents of
resistance in the western areas of the Soviet Union have been recorded.[5]

Although the mortality was great, the Jewish guerrillas accomplished most in the White Russian forests where, by the end of 1942, the Russian partisan movement had become an important strategic factor. By that time, the General Staff in Moscow had extended its field of operations to the partisans and molded disciplined cadres out of individual commands and stray details.[6] The vast forests, marshes and wastelands extended for hundreds of miles and created good retreats for fugitive war prisoners, escaped soldiers and civilian escapees. The 1941 scorched earth policy ordered by Stalin did not apply to the Polish-Russian border territories which had been struck in the surprise Nazi attack, and a broad belt of villages was left from which the partisans supplied themselves. Hundreds of Jewish bands struggled to survive in these regions under immense difficulties and carried out important guerrilla missions.

It should be remembered, moreover, that many Jews within the Soviet Union fought in the Red Army and later in the Polish People's Army. Of the two and a half to three million Jews left within Soviet frontiers after the Nazi occupation, about a half million—70 percent of Jewish males fit for work—were drafted into these armies. In the early part of the war, Jewish soldiers fought to defend their land; as yet, there was no knowledge of the Nazi slaughter of Jews elsewhere in Europe. Up to the time of the German invasion, Soviet information was aligned with the rationalizations of the German-Soviet Pact of 1939. Then, for some time after the outbreak of war, the Soviet Union soft-pedaled Nazi atrocities against Jews so as not to lend support to the Nazi line that the Soviet Union was fighting the war for Jews. Gradually, however, the national feelings of the diverse ethnic groups in the Soviet Union were aroused and Jewish solidarity behind the war effort was officially rallied by the formation of the Jewish Anti-Fascist Committee. In its turn this policy likewise twisted off its original course.

The status of the "Western" Jews—the Zapadniki—was dubious. These were the Jews who had come from the territories annexed to the Soviet Union in 1939–40. Many had been removed from the front to the hinterland. By 1943, this shift reversed itself and assumed mass proportions in 1944. By that time, the defeat of Germany was certain; there was little fear that disloyal "Western" elements would desert to the enemy. After the liberation of the western regions of the USSR, many Jews who had survived the exterminations were drafted into the Red Army. By then, the Jewish identity of the Russian Jewish fighter—soldier as well as partisan— had been blurred out.

Everything in the Jewish experience during the war gave great emotional force to the creation of a separate Jewish partisan movement, but many factors—some external, some internal—made this impossible.

In the prewar period, the Jews of eastern Europe had only the most tenuous contacts with most of the villages and forests of the rural areas of Poland and Russia. In the best of times, these regions had no appeal at all for Jews. During the war, the prospect of living in the gloomy thickness of unfamiliar forests over the long bitter winters, exposed to beasts of prey and to Nazi and peasant enemies, was so terrifying that most Jews chose to accept their fate in the ghettos. Thousands consciously preferred certain death with their wives, children and parents in the doomed ghettos or "in the East."

The strong family ties of most Jews also tied them to the ghettos. Even young people, who had the best chance to survive, refused to leave their parents or their fellow Jews in the ghetto. An overpowering sense of isolation—more fearful, it seems, than death—gripped many Jews who clung to the ghettos in order not to be alone. The more robust ones could not or would not desert the ghetto. The dilemma, whether to escape or share the fate of the ghetto, was debated passionately in all of the ghettos where resistance was organized, and, in almost every case, the decision ultimately was to remain with the ghetto—to try to organize the ghetto for resistance in the final struggle, but to remain in the ghetto. This was the decision of the young fighters in Warsaw, Bialystok, Lodz, Krakow, Bendin and Vilna.

For those who made the decision to leave the ghetto, the act of escape itself—without arms or contacts—was fraught with danger. The ghettos were surrounded with barbed wire and guarded by sentries. There were also garrisons in the villages, pickets on the bridges and roads leading to the forests and unexpected ambushes. For those who got past these hazards, there was the likelihood of being turned in by peasants who were paid, or frightened, or just hated Jews. There were also Polish, Lithuanian or Ukrainian guerrilla bands who were generally as hostile as the Nazis themselves and freely killed Jews in the forests.

A few Jews fled to the forests as soon as the Nazis occupied Poland, but the main movement took place late in the ghettoization process—actually as the ghettos were being liquidated. Groups based themselves in the forests and swamplands of eastern Poland, in Volhynia, Polesie and the area around Vilna, in the Ukraine and Byelorussia (White Russia).

The destruction of Russian Jews by the murderous *Einsatzgruppen* in the occupied zone gave Soviet Jewry little time to organize channels of escape. Minsk was exceptional. Only in a few towns—Vitebsk, Bobroisk, Mogilev, Zhitomer and Borissov—were temporary ghettos created. Some groups fled unarmed, organized a Jewish fighting unit in the forests and then merged, if they survived, with larger non-Jewish guerrilla units. Others were part of a ghetto underground with some experience in camouflage, infiltration and the manufacture of weapons and carried on alone before the Soviet partisan movement developed into a strong force. In

Minsk, for example, the first mass murders occurred in August 1941; the ghetto was completely destroyed in July 1943. The exodus of fighting Jews from Minsk into the forest assumed significant proportions between November 1941 and the autumn of 1942. Thousands escaped, most of them armed with weapons and ammunition sufficient to supply two companies of Jewish partisans in the forests of Slutsk and Koydanov.[7]

Extreme danger surrounded attempts to buy weapons. Published accounts of Jewish partisan bands relate not only many cases of death to would-be purchasers of arms but large-scale actions against the ghettos because of Jewish acts of sabotage in the woods. The ghettos themselves often opposed Jewish resistance from the outside. After the first wave of massacres, the thinning and weakening survivors pleaded with the partisans to stop their actions so as not to give the Nazis another pretext for further slaughter.

Very little value attached to the Jew fighting in the forest; this denigration further reduced chances of surviving. Jews without arms or leaders are known to have escaped the ghettos and execution pits even as they were digging graves—from Radun, Vohlin, Slonim, Zhetel, Derechin, Minsk, Kletsk, Stolpce—and to have tried to form or join resistance groups. They had to be exceptionally hardy. Some took women and children with them, conscious that their abandoned ghetto had become a death trap. No supplies descended to them by plane or parachute. They were often prey for greedy and hostile villagers as well as the hounding Nazis. Such conditions attached many disabilities to Jewish partisan activity and had an adverse effect on the value of the Jew who wanted to fight. Survivors have reported how rationalizations developed which deprecated the ability of such men.[8] These Jews had to fight to the last gasp because they had no other way out. Even their heroism was considered not a heroism of choice but one of sheer necessity. On the other hand, because their lives were held so cheaply, Jewish fighters were expendable. They were often chosen—when they were admitted to a partisan group—for the most dangerous missions. They were suspected if they were successful and damned if they failed. Yet the illusion of power could impress itself upon the imagination of the peasant, and exaggerated reports of the prowess of a Jewish group are known to have been spread simply because a single broken-down Russian cannon was moved through the towns by a few Jewish guerrillas, who themselves had learned how to spread such rumors in order to earn the respect of the peasants.

The Soviet partisan movement to which most Jews in the forests were drawn by accident or luck or absence of any other alternative was probably inspired by theories of guerrilla warfare developed by the Chinese leader Mao Tse-tung. This theory of tactics requires the creation of small unconnected groups of fighters deployed over a large country for hit-and-run attacks. High value is placed on local support for the partisans. The policy of the Soviet partisan command and field officers—sometimes equivocal, sometimes hostile, occasionally friendly—may have been influenced not only by Stalin's well-known anti-Semitism, but by the requirements of Mao's kind of partisan warfare. The Jewish fighters, with their strong family ties, family-type camps and uncertain relations with the local populations clearly did not fit into the doctrines taught at the partisan officers' schools.[9]

Good relations with the local population were considered crucial by the Soviet partisans. Peasants were needed for food and weapons—it was they who had collected large supplies of weapons left by the retreating Polish and Soviet armies in 1939 and 1941–42—for intelligence information and reconnaissance. However, they were not always prepared to give aid to non-Jewish partisans; toward Jewish fighters they were, with few exceptions, hostile and sometimes murderous. Many of them had themselves taken part in the butchery of Jews and in plundering their property. They were generally ready to hate the Jewish partisan, to abuse him and complain about him to the partisan commander. If the local partisan commander himself was anti-Semitic, he could accept the allegations literally and destroy the Jew. If not, he might need to prove to the peasant that partisans were not robbers and that any irregular behavior toward the peasants would be punished. He might also want to strengthen the discipline of his unit by several death sentences.

Russian guerrillas were often ex-prisoners of war or inmates of slave-labor camps where they had been exposed to Nazi propaganda. "To get admitted into the ranks of a Soviet fighting detachment was no easy job," an ex-partisan and historian has observed. "There were some Russian units that did not admit Jews as a matter of policy. They justified this by saying that Jews neither knew how nor wanted to fight. The first requirement a Jew had to meet to get accepted was to have a weapon. Many young Jews had no way of obtaining arms and thus had no choice but to join family camps or family combat units accepting any Jew who managed to escape. . . . A Jew had no way out. He could not turn back."[10] Yet, sooner or later, with few exceptions, Jewish groups realized that their chances of survival were almost nil if they did not secure aid from the Russian bands.

The Soviet partisan movement was the largest in Europe, numbering about a million and a half fighters at its strongest. It held strategic positions behind enemy lines and operated close to the Eastern front where some of the most decisive battles of World War II were fought. Moreover, it was most active in those areas where large Jewish communities had existed for many generations—the Ukraine, White Russia, Lithuania and eastern Poland. Their units were trained to be mobile, to strike swiftly and to exploit the elements of secrecy and surprise.

In the early phases of the war, in 1941–42, Soviet units were formed spontaneously under conditions of great urgency. No attention was paid to specific principles of structure, internal organization or lines of authority. Later, the movement was brought under the control of the Communist Party and Russian domination—paralleling the supremacy of the Russians in the life of the Soviet Union as a whole.

At first, the population appears to have given little support to the partisan groups even after they had been organized by the Soviet authorities.[11] Initially detachments often dispersed and surrendered. Their subsequent growth came with fuller knowledge of German policy toward Russian prisoners of war. Many stragglers threw their lot with the partisans rather than risk being taken prisoners. The ruthless Nazi policy toward civilians also contributed many volunteers.

Unquestionably, those Jews who joined Soviet partisan units were inferior to non-Jews in combat fitness. They were mainly city dwellers, handicapped by the habits of city life and constrained from killing by the Jewish aversion to blood sports and physical violence. Many were also physically and mentally debilitated by the life in the ghettos. Nevertheless, certain characteristically Jewish skills were valuable to the partisans. There were Jewish cobblers, carpenters, locksmiths, and, perhaps most important, Jewish doctors. Among the prisoners and Soviet soldiers who reached the woods, there were few if any doctors. Much of the burden of medical service in the forest fell on the shoulders of Jewish physicians and medical workers.[12] Moreover, among these Jews who took to the forests were men of energy, nerve and leadership. They consolidated small groups of other Jews and acquired weapons. Jewish commanders of such groups—92 of medium and high rank have been identified—led purely Jewish units or units containing a Jewish majority. There were evidently many more of lower rank—the equivalent of section and platoon commanders—but their numbers are not definitely known.

One leader, Dr. Ezekiel Atlas, whose exploits are well documented, was both physician and military organizer of unusual ability.[13] Polish-born, he studied medicine in France and Italy and interned in Lodz. When the war broke out, he fled with his parents and a younger sister to Lvov, then occupied by the Russians, and later to Slonim, where he worked as a doctor. He also worked in the hospital of the neighboring town of Kozlowszczyzna. In the spring of 1942, the Germans massacred the Jews here and Atlas' parents and sister were killed. The Germans spared Atlas only because they needed doctors; he was immediately transferred to the village of Wielka-Wolia in an area of dense forests. Peasants from the entire district came to Atlas to be treated. From them, the young physician learned that some Russian soldiers who refused to surrender were still hiding in the forests. Atlas contacted them and provided them with arms, which he secured from the peasants, as well as medical care.

The soldiers asked Atlas to join them but he had resolved to go into the woods only if he could take Jews with him. On July 24, 1942, the ghetto of the little town of Dereczyn in the area was wiped out. About 300 men, women and children succeeded in escaping, some of them reaching Atlas in Wielka-Wolia. Atlas provided them with shelter and arms, and led them into the forest—a Jewish unit of 120 men. This detail became part of a mixed division later known as Brigade *Pobieda* (Victory). Atlas then prevailed on the Russian chief Boris Bullat to allow his group to spearhead an attack on the German garrison in Dereczyn to avenge the liquidation of the ghetto. One night in August, the Jewish partisans marched on the town.

The attack lasted for several hours. Atlas' men took 44 Germans, mostly police, and executed them in the same square in front of the mill where the Germans had slaughtered the Jews in the ghetto three weeks before.

Besides appeasing the need for vengeance, this action helped to change the accepted image of the Jew as a coward or worthless fighter. After the Dereczyn attack, Atlas began turning over in his mind possibilities of sabotaging German communications and made his first attempt in the middle of August. He extracted the explosives from two large artillery shells and with several of his men walked to the railway station of Rozhanka and blew up a German train—the first such sabotage action in the area. Several days later, Atlas and four others bombed and destroyed a long bridge over the Niemen River—a bridge of strategic importance—and killed three German soldiers.

Atlas himself could be seen in a tattered army uniform, wearing oversized boots, armed with a submachine gun and pistol, with several hand grenades bulging from his pockets. Survivors have testified that he was enormously popular with his men and with the Dereczyn refugees whom he protected. He frequently repeated these words: "Our private lives finished on the day our fellow Jews were massacred. Every day of life that is given to us belongs not to ourselves but to our slaughtered families!" Not many days were given to Atlas for avenging these murders—he was killed in a German raid on the Ruda Forest in December 1942—but he and his group made the most of this time. His men became demolition experts. They rebuilt abandoned cannons, unearthed boxes of ammunition and repaired old German trucks. They roamed the countryside for arms not only for themselves but for Jews who had fled the massacre of Zetl and had found refuge in the forests of Lipczany. On September 28, they rushed a grounded German plane and destroyed it as well as the pilot. On

October 5, combined partisan bands, including Atlas' unit, attacked the German garrison in Ruda-Yovarska. In this action 127 Germans and collaborators were killed, 20 were taken prisoner and 25 wagonloads of arms were captured.

The Soviet staff orders of the day frequently cited Atlas and his group for distinction; they also received Soviet decorations. However, in the citations in this case, as in all others, there was no recognition of the Jewish identity of the fighters. The Soviet press never noted the Jewish identity of Jewish partisans or underground fighters. Their exploits were attributed in the Soviet press to the general resistance movements in the USSR, Byelorussia, Lithuania, the Ukraine or Crimea. Only the names of the men or some other indication of the fighters' Jewish identity are usable as guides. Thus limited, searchers nevertheless have found numerous Jewish partisans, both officers and men in the ranks, who fought in the units of Linkov (East Byelorussia), Fiodorov (eastern Ukraine), Kovpak (Ukraine) and Inatiev (Crimea). Some of this information has been obtained from *Einikeit,* which devoted considerable attention to individual acts of Jewish heroism in battle, but there are no comprehensive statistics of Jewish participation in the war—either in the Regular Army or in partisan groups. In December 1947, the Russian Jewish writer Ilya Ehrenburg, spoke of a forthcoming "Red Book" which, he said, would reveal "the measure of Jewish resistance in the ghettos and in the partisan units. Abundant material has been collected describing the heroism of the Jewish combatants. Stress is also laid on instances of assistance on the part of non-Jews in the rescue of our brethren."[14] However, the years 1948–49 tolled the end of Jewish culture in the Soviet Union and plans for the publication of the book were shelved.

As the partisan movement expanded, the Soviet policy officially rejected all recruiting on ethnic lines, and, with few exceptions, exclusively Jewish units were merged into others. The impact of this policy was felt in 1943 when whole details of Soviet-trained guerrillas were put into partisan cadres. Autonomous Jewish groups struggled unsuccessfully to maintain their identity. In this respect, as in many others throughout the Holocaust, the Jews lost their identity when a stronger force had no use for it and when the Jews themselves needed it. Jews melted into national armies and were thereby deprived of military recognition; they also melted into the general problem of European refugees and were thus denied any special consideration as unique victims. For as yet unclarified reasons, the Soviet Union did not want all-Jewish partisan bands operating, although it fostered the formation of anti-Fascist Lithuanian, Ukrainian, White Russian and other largely "nationalistic" units.

It is difficult to weigh the factors involved. Stalin's anti-Semitism has been acknowledged. There was also anti-Semitism among certain partisan leaders who applied a very severe code of partisan "justice" against Jewish fighters. Many acts of deliberate murder and savage assault upon Jewish fighters by Soviet partisans have been recorded. Other considerations involved the general requirements of partisan tactics. All-Jewish bands were vulnerable; they had no land of their own and no base of support among the peasants. Soviet authorities could parachute White Russian, Ukrainian and Lithuanian partisans among their own people behind enemy lines. The Jews had no one. Nor could they contribute much in the way of arms. Small bands of Jews were often a military and psychological liability. These bands, however, had to seek out a Soviet partisan unit and join it or perish. For example, the independent band of Jewish fighters operating under the name "Kadima" in the forests near Bialystok declined rapidly. They could not undertake large-scale sabotage and many of their members were killed in Nazi manhunts. The group was supplied by the underground organization of the Bialystok Ghetto, and after the destruction of the ghetto in the summer of 1943, by a group of young Jewish girls who had managed to infiltrate into the Aryan section of the city. Contrary to the partisan rule of living off the country, they were compelled to purchase their supplies. Their situation became somewhat easier when the Russian partisan brigade called "Kalinovsky" entered the forests.

The Jews of the Minsk Ghetto were among the organizers of seven different partisan regiments in the forests of Naliboki, Dzershinsk and Volozhin, but these groups also lost their Jewish character eventually. A large band of Jews who succeeded in fleeing from the ghetto of Serniki found that it could not maintain itself independently in the forest and linked up with the Voroshilov Regiment. The entire band of Moshe Goldenman, who fled with sixteen Jews from the Ghetto of Korets (Volhynia) had only one revolver in their possession. In this area there were no Russian partisans, but gangs of Ukrainian Fascists called Banderas, who fought Germans and Russians as well as Jews. Goldenman's group marched to Polesia and then to the forests of Zhitomir in search of Russian partisans.[15] However, by the time the Russian partisan movement fully developed—toward the second half of 1942—many of the ghettos and labor camps were already decimated in White Russia and in the Ukraine.

While opposing the formation of separate Jewish partisan units, official Soviet policy was equally opposed to any hostile actions against Jewish fighters. This attitude was particularly evident after a central partisan command was established and discipline throughout the ranks was tightened. Thousands of Jews who were unfit for combat found shelter in Soviet partisan zones and lived there with their wives and children until the arrival of the Russian Army.

In western Byelorussia (Polesia, Baranovice and Grodno), the Jewish fighters were close to the dynamic center of the Soviet partisan organization. This was not only large in numbers and exceptionally well organized, but also commanded extensive areas over which the Germans had no control and from which there was a firm air link with Moscow. Many of the Soviet units were made up of escapees from German prisoner-of-war camps. Here, as in Lithuania and in Poland, to some extent, the ghettos of Minsk, Vilna, Brest, Pinsk and Bialystok served as important centers of the Soviet partisan movement.[16] In the Bialystok Ghetto, for example, an illegal hospital for Soviet partisans was set up. The rural population of Byelorussia was generally hostile to Jews, however, and the Polish right-wing underground, the A.K., wanted nothing less than to clear the forests of Jews. In 1944, Soviet partisan leaders in Lithuania began negotiations with the A.K. Polish "Legionnaires" to plan combined operations against the German Army. The A.K. leaders made one of their conditions the expulsion of Jewish partisan units from the forests. This proposal was rejected.[17]

Byelorussia and Lithuania were important areas of activity for the special Jewish fighting and "family" units, such as those of Zorin, Wertheim, Gilczyk, the Bielski Brothers, the units from the Vilna Ghetto, the "Forward" (Kadima) unit from the Bialystok Ghetto, the camp of the "white furs" in East Bialystok and others. The Bielski family camp was one of the few that survived.

When the Russian Army began its retreat after the German invasion in June 1941, the Poles staged anti-Jewish riots in scattered villages and cities, Vilna among them. Tobias Bielski, a Vilna Jew who had served in the Polish Army in 1927 and 1928, fled to the home of his parents in a little village near Novogrodek. When German units swept in, the family moved to Novogrodek itself. The Germans came there, too, and surrounded the house where Bielski was living. At the last moment, he managed to escape in a cart driven by a peasant girl and hid in the forest. His two brothers joined him and they decided to try to buy arms. When the Jews of Novogrodek were pushed into a ghetto, the brothers made plans to move their parents into the forest with them, but in December 1941, before they could act, their parents were massacred, together with 5,000 other Jews. Still, they managed to round up fifteen Jews, friends and relatives from the neighboring villages. The Bielski group now numbered eighteen, including a nine-month-old infant and six men of fighting age. They had no arms as yet, but after much prodding coaxed a peasant into selling them six rifles. The day of the successful purchase, they shot a German guard and took his rifle and ammunition.[18] These were the very modest beginnings of the famous "Tobias Bielski Division" of Jewish forest fighters, a protected family camp and successful guerrilla unit.

Bielski was a big man and boldly decisive. He did not weigh arguments over the question to resist or not to resist; he took to the woods after a simple decision to fight and try to kill Germans rather than be killed by them. When news of stepped-up atrocities reached him, he sent the following message to a White Russian friend in Novogrodek: "Organize as many friends and acquaintances as possible. Come to me in the woods. I wait for you. You must know the slaughter is not the first nor the last. The German had [has] decided to destroy the Jews and he will do it. So come to the woods. I wait."[19] Eight young men responded and Bielski became "commander" of a unit whose tasks were to organize, make war on the Germans and rescue other Jews. Bielski himself went to Lida and recruited five more men. Meanwhile, others began to stream in, women and children as well as men. The winter months passed in acquiring arms and training. No acts of any kind were undertaken until the spring of 1942. By the end of 1942, there were 500 fighting men in his unit and they came to be dreaded by the police in the area of Novogrodek, Lida and Zelwa. They destroyed telephone connections, dynamited railroads and laid ambushes.

Bielski's operations were encumbered by many old men, women and children who sought his protection, but he flatly refused to forsake them. Food had to be bought, foraged or requisitioned. The "family partisan camp" was protected by armed sentries and a small militia, but the noncombatants had important functions themselves: they worked, cooked, built barracks and lived as a community in the woods. The skills and previous training of all "civilians" were put to use in the organization of a school for children and a modest infirmary. The camp also boasted its own bakery and soap factory. So complete was this center in the forest that the Russian partisans named it "Jerusalem." Children occasionally gave plays to which the partisans in the region were invited. But this was possible only after Bielski had come to terms with the peasants and partisans, who were opposed to a Jewish guerrilla unit in their midst.

The villagers at first complained to the Russian partisans and accused Bielski's men of pillaging; the partisans decided to shoot it out and get rid of the Jews. Bielski tried a last-minute meeting to argue things out. He spoke to the head of the local Soviet partisan group, Victor Pancenko. "If you didn't know it before," Bielski said, "you know it now; we are not bandits or robbers. And if you are a Soviet citizen you should know that the U.S.S.R. is ready to fight the German fascists, whom we are fighting; and your motherland does not discriminate between Jews and non-Jews, but only between loyal citizens who obey orders and bandits who destroy and rob."[20] Pancenko was taken to some local farmers and shown that the accusations against Bielski were false. A local pacification was agreed on and zones of supply divided between the groups. The local farmers were told that all partisans, Jewish or not, were to be helped with food, boots and even furs. Bielski assured them that the Germans would eventually be destroyed, like Napoleon. He also warned them not to betray his men to the police.

Some peasants, however, did inform on the Jewish forest guerrillas and those who were caught were killed summarily. Stories of Bielski's exploits soon spread and his name became respected and feared. His prestige mounted in the fall of 1942. At that time, the Germans had seized the local harvest and made preparations to thresh the wheat and send bread to the front. But Bielski's men planned to wreck the huge German granaries and burn the estates and *kolkhoz* farms that the Germans had taken over. The skies above the forest and fields blazed red. Russian planes returning from bombing enemy lines saw the burning fields and dropped their remaining bombs. Panic spread among the Germans who believed that Bielski's fighters must be coordinated with the Russian command. Rumors that he had a large army concealed in the forest filled the countryside, and a reward of 10,000 marks was put on his head. These Jewish partisans finally had become part of the war against Hitler and were avenging the hundreds of thousands who had no avengers.

In March 1943, Bielski's independent career ended. A Soviet detachment was sent by the High Command of the Red Army on a special mission to unite all partisans in a fighting force. Bielski met with one hundred other unit commanders in the Gluboki forest. The meetings lasted over a week. Bielski was asked to eliminate all noncombatants—he had acquired almost a thousand by now—but he refused. He did agree, however, to incorporate his unit into the Vladimir-Lenin Brigade and to operate under a unified command. The brigade was to construct airfields for Russian planes by the autumn of 1943, but the forest base which the Jewish fighters had established was besieged. The first German attack was thrown back but a second quickly followed. There seemed to be no way to escape the enemy even in the huge forests and deep swamps. Informers multiplied. The camp in the Naliboki forest had to be abandoned. The cattle and horses were let loose and the whole camp began walking single file carrying only food and ammunition on their shoulders. At times, the mud in the swamp was waist-deep. The cannon fire roared and the rifle-shots crackled. The food supply dwindled and for fourteen days guerrillas and campers ate berries and kernels of grain. The Germans destroyed seventeen villages and hundreds of farmhouses skirting the forest to keep them out of reach of the partisans, but the Bielski unit eventually recovered its own base and again began their work of laying ambushes and killing treacherous peasants.

By the summer of 1944, the Russians broke through the Nazi lines and the Soviet commander ordered all partisan units to round up German soldiers in the forest and send them to the Soviet Union as prisoners of war. Some of the bloodiest fighting was waged during these preliberation days with the retreating Wehrmacht in battalion and even divisional strength carrying heavy equipment and making their last desperate stand. Fierce battles raged beneath the trees. On September 16 the first units of the Soviet Army met Bielski's unit. Their arms were turned over to the military authorities; the men were given testimonials and sent "home" and the unit was officially disbanded. Of the Jews in Novogrodek, only those in Bielski's unit had survived. He led 1,200 Jewish men, women and children safely out of the shelter of the forest. Bielski himself went to Palestine after the war, carrying with him carefully treasured maps of "Jerusalem," the hidden city of the Jewish partisans.

Several other family-type camps and many bands of Jewish partisans fought in White Russia. Most, however, did not experience the good fortune of the Bielski unit. Among these, the tragic dilemmas of Nekomah and the doomed end of the Vilna Ghetto form one of the most tragic chapters of the Holocaust.

The Jewish unit called Nekomah (vengeance, in Hebrew) grew out of a decision of youth groups from the great Jewish center of Vilna to escape the Ghetto and join the partisans in the woods. The story of the resistance movement in Vilna falls into two phases, the first lasting from December 1941 to September 1943, when bold preparations were made to arm the Ghetto itself for resistance; the second, from the end of 1943 through 1944, when the depleted groups took to the forests and guerrilla fighting. Both stories are touched by the courage and idealism of youth and the poignancy of a tragedy that was almost a triumph but failed.

The beginnings of the Vilna resistance are to be found in a Benedictine nunnery near Vilna, where several of the leaders of the underground were sheltered and where the first call for resistance was drafted. The Mother Superior, a thirty-five-year-old graduate of Krakow University, together with several nuns had gone into the Ghetto and slipped out with several young Jews, including Abba Kovner, Jewish poet and resistance leader. These women roamed the countryside for knives, pistols and grenades. The Mother Superior not only gave the Ghetto fighters their first weapons but instructed them in their proper use. Late in January 1942, Kovner left the nunnery to attend a secret meeting in an attic in the Ghetto where the first steps were taken to form a resistance movement.

The group called itself the United Partisan Organization (UPO). It drew up a proclamation aimed at defending the lives of the remaining Ghetto population, of sabotaging German factories and contacting the partisan movement in the nearby forest. A teacher, Tema Katz, who had escaped from the death pit of Ponary and returned to the Ghetto wounded, was present at the meeting to document the rumors about Ponary. The password of the UPO became "Lisa calls," in memory of a young girl who had gone to another ghetto to organize resistance but who had been caught and killed.

When the Mother Superior heard that a full-fledged resistance movement was forming inside the Ghetto, she sewed a yellow patch on a dress and tried to enter the Ghetto for good but barely escaped arrest. Later she tried to obtain arms for the Ghetto from a Polish underground group but was refused. "I want to join you in the ghetto," she told the young fighters, "to fight and fall with you. Yours is a holy war. You are noble men and women. And although you reject religion [some of the youths were Socialists] you have a God, a great God, and now you're closer to Him than I am. May He help you."

Jews who worked in forced-labor gangs in a nearby arsenal smuggled weapons into the Ghetto and within a few months the UPO arms supply consisted of five machine guns, fifty grenades, thirty revolvers, several rifles and thousands of bullets.[21] They were brought in under the false bottoms of tool baskets, in secret pockets, in loaves of bread, under bandages and in coffins. A bag of gunpowder was also brought in, disguised as a bag of salt, and was used in preparing eight hundred grenades made out of electric-light bulbs. Military tactics and the use of arms were taught in cellars by young instructors who kept just one step ahead of their students. The arms were hidden in sewage canals, and, most improbably, in the YIVO (Yiddish Scientific Institute) building. YIVO was one of the great treasure houses of Jewish history and literature. Under Nazi occupation, it became a victim of Rosenberg's confiscatory squads. Rosenberg accumulated in the YIVO building the Jewish libraries, museum pieces and paintings from all parts of Vilna and then systematically destroyed them.

UPO kept two printing presses working and two illegal newspapers going, one in Polish, the other in Lithuanian. A secret receiving set was installed and the news of the winter 1942 Russian offensive was received with great joy. In the midst of their own feverish activity and intense discussions of the burning question, when should they issue the call for a defense of the Ghetto, the members of UPO collected food and clothing, even false papers for Russian prisoners of war. A letter of gratitude was received from the hostages and has been recorded: "We shall remember, and when the time comes, we shall tell the people in our native land, that in Vilna, in 1942, the enslaved and tortured Jews of the ghetto did not lose their humanity. At a time when even talking to us was punishable by death, they placed their lives in jeopardy and saved other human beings from hunger and cold—victims of the same regime."[22]

In May 1942, UPO executed their first important act of sabotage, the mining of a trainload of troops at Nai-Vilaika, near Vilna. They killed two hundred German soldiers and wounded many more. The peasants picked up most of the guns and ammunition but some were retrieved later when the fighters escaped into the woods.

In describing the occasional satisfaction at being able to witness the results of their sabotage, Kovner has expressed the pent-up vengefulness of the young fighters:

> It was really hard for us to leave our work at a time when we were most eager to see the results. Though our fingers were frozen, we itched for more revenge and wanted to lie down near the tracks and see what we had accomplished. . . . Our faces might be buried in grass and mud, but in our hands was a string—thin and long, stretching from the edge of the forest to the mine under the tracks. The wire was in the clear, and in the wintertime, in the dark of night, we would stay on till the end. . . . The Jewish partisan not only wanted to sabotage the enemy, but was willing to endanger himself till the bitter end, just to see the final blast. For that brief moment, he could feel in every drop of his blood the satisfaction, the glory, the retribution: yes, a year's revenge![23]

In February 1942, UPO had made contact with the great ghettos in Bialystok and Warsaw and reported the systematic destruction of Jews in Lithuania and White Russia. The ghettos, however, refused to believe these reports. The UPO then decided to draw up a special proclamation addressed to all the Jews in German-occupied territory and distribute it as widely as possible. "The German officials prolong the existence of the ghettos for a short time," they warned. "But annihilation is a systematic process which will sooner or later reach every one of us. The political program surmounts every economic factor. Wherever there is a Jewish settlement under Hitler, there will be a Ponary. Jews! Organize yourselves! Take up arms!"

Two sisters, Sara and Reizel Silber, carried the proclamation to Bialystok and Warsaw where it was distributed among members of various parties and groups. On their return, the two sisters were caught by the Gestapo and killed. Meanwhile, a few groups had left the Ghetto determined to fight in the forests. They were armed and well drilled but were cut down and killed before they reached their destination.

The UPO then set about organizing the Ghetto for the final struggle. Bunkers were built; underground passages were dug for contact with the outside world; broadsides were issued to rally the morale of the people. Periodic acts of sabotage were carried out. Clandestine classes were held for children.

In July 1943, the Vilna Ghetto faced its most fateful decision, involving the life of a beloved leader, Itzik Vitenberg, and the whole question of the defense of the Ghetto. Vitenberg was a shoemaker by trade, the organizer and inspiration of the resistance movement and its military commander. His plan was to defend the Ghetto within its walls. To desert the unarmed population would mean to leave them to die. Vitenberg and the other leaders had no illusions about the survival ability of the Jews once exposed to the raw life of the forest. However, they planned to set fire to every military object in the city and to organize an exodus into the forest as soon as the Germans began the destruction of the Ghetto. By midsummer 1943 there were several hundred armed Jews in the Vilna Ghetto.

On July 15, 1943, Vitenberg was arrested by the Germans with the connivance of Salek Dessler, the Jewish police chief of the Ghetto. However, he was rescued by his friends and returned to resistance headquarters. After this act of defiance, a showdown was inevitable. Partisan mobilization of the Ghetto was ordered. The following morning, the Nazis delivered an ultimatum: Jews either had to give up Vitenberg or face a fire attack upon the entire Ghetto. The head of the *Judenrat*, Jacob Gens, played on the fears of the people and warned them not to let one man's safety jeopardize the safety of all. The masses, frightened by Nazi threats and grateful for having had one and a half years of "peace," for which they credited Gens, surged toward the defense headquarters and demanded that Vitenberg be given up.[24] For the young fighters this posed the tragic question whether to fight against fellow Jews. In a decision which they later regretted, they decided to yield. Vitenberg took leave of his comrades and left Abba Kovner in charge. He was taken to the Gestapo cellars and tortured. His mutilated body was later found.

In the ordeal of having to weigh painful alternatives, the resistance had given up their main chance. Vitenberg's death was a shattering blow to their morale and conscience. A terror attack then descended upon other partisan leaders and the UPO decided to take up positions in the forest.

On July 22, a group of twenty-five armed and trained members left and marched like a forced-labor column, with yellow patches on their breasts, to Nai-Vilaika. Here they picked up other Jews at work and entered the forest about five miles from Vilna. In a surprise attack they were machinegunned by Germans and only fourteen of the group reached the safety of the forest. This was the nucleus of *Nekomah*. Five German police were killed in the clash.

The Nazis were infuriated by this escape and applied their customary treatment of collective reprisal. The families of all who had fled and the foremen in the workshops where the men had worked were sent to Ponary. The workers left at the labor camp at Nai-Vilaika were killed. More destructive measures were threatened and the Ghetto was gripped by a terrible fear. Parents, in desperation, tied their children to beds to prevent them from escaping to the forests. Jewish workers were removed from all shops and put to work on railroads and the airfield, but at the end of the first day's work they were surrounded by police and pushed into prepared boxcars. Three hundred were killed after fighting broke out between the workers and the police. The rest were sent to camps in Estonia. Several dozen managed to escape by cutting through the floors of the cars. The UPO set up several barricades and distributed guns, but the Germans called in reserves and began dynamiting every building from which shots were fired. They blasted bunkers and cellars where Jews were hiding and rounded them up for new transports. The destruction of the Ghetto was imminent.

In September more escape units left the Ghetto and headed for a rendezvous in the Narocz forest, guided by an extraordinary young girl, Zelda Tregar, who moved about the city without the yellow patch and helped groups leave through secret exits. On eighteen different occasions she slipped through the German guard to bring important documents to Vilna as courier for the partisans. She brought dozens of guns from the city to the forest bases and smuggled herself into several concentration camps to lead out some of the inmates. She fell into enemy hands no less than four times but miraculously escaped each time.[25]

The last of the UPO group, 200 fighters, by now without weapons, left the Ghetto through sewers, entering under the smokestack of a vast limekiln attached to a factory. At places the sewers narrowed to eighteen inches and the fugitives had to crawl on their knees through the bilge. They struggled through the pipes for four hours. One group lost its way and disappeared; some fainted; some went mad; one youth committed suicide. The survivors finally reached the sewer opening in the courtyard of the headquarters of the Lithuanian criminal police. There, another young woman, Sonia Madeisker, who was living on the Aryan side of the city under a false name, was waiting for them. Wet and filthy, they crawled out of the hole and made their way to a cellar to dry themselves. They then paired off and reached a cemetery where some of their machine guns had been buried. At a crossing in front of a movie, three were stopped by a German patrol. In the shooting that followed several Germans were killed and the three fighters were seized, one a young girl of twenty-two. They were taken to the public square, where the last of the Jews of Vilna were being sorted for deportation, and were hanged.

The little band of Ghetto fighters, so gallant in its hopes and plans for the defense of the Ghetto and the destruction of German installations, had by now thinned into a diminished and shattered remnant. Once in the forest, however, they recovered their spirit and replenished their arms. In the first three months of their new life they carried out three train explosions in which several hundred German soldiers were killed and dynamited three bridges. Vitka Kempner, one of the girls who participated in the first action, carried a suitcase full of mines for twenty miles to Vilna, where she blew up an electrical generating station. Afterward, she slipped into the concentration camp at Kailis and guided sixty people to partisan bases. With five others, she set fire to the turpentine reserve in Olkenik and personally captured two Gestapo agents.[26]

Nekomah no longer had to worry about reprisal action for the whole Ghetto—they were on their own, but the Ghetto was no more.

The survivors of Nekomah lived to be among the first to reenter Vilna and merge their gunfire with that of the Red Army which had come to liberate the city. In the midst of the corpses of 15,000 Germans and the ghosts of a once-throbbing Jewish life, they had come home to the Ghetto to witness a bitter victory. In this "Jerusalem of Lithuania," which had been home for 60,000 Jews, the Russians found 600 Jews left hiding in the sewers. Kovner has written of that return in July 1944:

> The first things I and my friends wanted to do was to go straight to the spot we had hurriedly left nearly a year before. And so, we reached the ghetto quarter. How can I describe what we saw? A wilderness of ruins. Streets silent and deserted. And suddenly, as we entered one street, a woman ran toward us, carrying a child in her arms. At first sight she screamed and tried to hide, for some of us were dressed in German uniforms. . . . But when she recognized us, still hysterical, she poured out her story. She and her child had been hiding for eleven months in a small cave. . . . In the midst of her tale, she broke into bitter sobbing. At this point, the four-year-old child in her arms, whom we had thought a deaf mute, opened her mouth and said, "Mommy, is it all right to cry now?"[27]

Ilya Ehrenburg, who was with the young Jewish fighters when they returned to Vilna, recalled:

> About 500 Jews—young men and women—left the ghetto of Vilna. They joined the partisan groups "For Victory," "Vengeance" and "Death to Fascism." During the fighting for Vilna, they assisted our army; they caught Germans trying to break through our siege. I saw Jewish women and students of the University of Vilna . . . with grenades in hand. These young women who had a deep knowledge of literature and who, at one time, pored over their books, had now found their mission in life in this struggle. . . . I saw them while the fighting continued in the streets of Vilna.[28]

In the western Ukraine, Jewish fighters faced two main enemies: the Germans and the Ukrainian nationalists. The bands of Bulba, Melinikov and Bandera, apart from the Ukrainians who openly collaborated with the Nazis—the Ukrainian police and the S.S. Galicia unit—were murderously anti-Semitic. The Soviet partisan movement was correspondingly weak in these areas, consisting mostly of espionage and sabotage units rather than forest fighting groups.

Before the outbreak of the Russian-German war, the Nazis had made overtures to the nationalistic Ukrainian leaders. When the German armies swept through Galicia, many Ukrainians were led to believe that their hour of liberation had come. Instead, it was merely the hour of another German conquest. Eastern Galicia was incorporated into the Government-General, and the former Polish provinces of Polesia and Volhynia were joined to the Russian part of the Ukraine and absorbed into the *Reichs-kommissariat* of the Ukraine. A Ukrainian partisan movement sprang up which fought off German rule and also warred against the Jews. The masses linked their grievances to the Jews and were easily stirred up to murder them while Nazi-hired auxiliary police and fascist bands also massacred Jews under German instigation. Within these crossfires, aid to Jews in the Ukraine was rare.

The most shining exception was Metropolitan Andreas Szeptycki, Archbishop of Lvov and head of the Ukrainian Greek Catholic Church in Galicia. He was already an old man of seventy-seven, half-paralyzed and confined to a wheelchair when the Nazis overran Galicia. However, he stormed against collaborators who "shed innocent blood and make of themselves outcasts of human society by disregarding the sanctity of man." He refused any religious service to Ukrainians who murdered Jews. He wrote ringing pastoral letters and personally hid Jewish children and adults in his own church in Lvov while persuading, sometimes ordering, nuns to do the same in convents. None of these fell into Nazi hands.

There is also the exceptional record of a unit of Ukrainian partisans led by Major-General Sidor Kovpak. There are varying, even conflicting accounts of Kovpak's liberation of some Jews from the German labor camp of Skalat in eastern Galicia. Some reports indicate that when the camp was liberated, the partisans forcibly drove back those Jews who followed the soldiers and asked to join their ranks. Kovpak's actions in the labor camp are still ambiguous, and the fate of the Jews left there after his raid is still obscure. However, it is generally agreed that he allowed some Jews —the numbers vary from 30 to 100—to join his unit.[29] Those who were capable of bearing arms were formed into a separate Jewish detail and given intensive training. They were known as "Group Seven." The aged, sick and very young were placed in the homes of local peasants before Kovpak left on his fantastic 700-mile trek to the Carpathians to destroy the oil refineries in the region—a full year before the Red Army penetrated the area.

In central Poland and Galicia, the struggle of Jewish partisans was virtually hopeless. The area was thickly populated and, in the Government-General, strictly policed. The Poles and Ukrainians who lived there were, with few exceptions, savagely hostile, making it difficult for Jews to hide. Geography and demography also conspired against the Jews in this part of Poland. In sharp contrast to the border regions east of the Bug River, which had marshes, dense forests and a scattered population, the area west of the Bug was densely populated; its forests were few and small. Plains extending for hundreds of miles separated one forest from another, making the terrain easy to comb and surround.

Jews were likewise unsuccessful in their attempts to link up with Polish forces. The sharply split Polish underground required Jews to try to make contact with both main sectors: the A.K. (*Armia Krajowa*) and the A.L. (*Armia Ludowa*). The larger group, the A.K., was itself a vast movement of many forces and points of view, most of them bent on destroying Jews as eagerly as Germans. One group, the N.S.Z.—National Armed Forces— was openly murderous. The fighting unit of the P.P.S.—the Polish Social- ist Party—which belonged to the A.K., accepted Jews in the Krakow area for a time, but almost all of its other units helped the Nazis kill Jewish partisans. One historian has reported that in the regions where the A.K. operated, not a single Jewish fugitive from the ghettos remained alive.[30] In the Lublin region, where dozens of Jewish partisan camps were set up, the area became a slaughterhouse. The A.L. generally accepted Jews, but its field of operations was very restricted and the number of its units was very small.

In eastern Galicia, Jewish underground groups were associated with the P.P.R., the Polish Workers [Communist] Party, which was particularly active in Lvov. This area, too, came under the jurisdiction of the Govern- ment-General. At the head of the short-lived Jewish resistance movement in this region were Moshe Horowitz, the poet Ya'acov Szudrych and leaders of the so-called Brody Group. According to information from German, Polish and Soviet sources, Jewish resistance in this vast region was substantial but extremely scattered.[31]

In Krakow, the very heart of Frank's capital of the Government-General, daring if doomed acts of resistance were led by Zionist youths inspired by a young couple, Gusta and Shimon Drenger. For several weeks toward the end of 1942, the group threw bombs into cafes that German officers frequented, set fire to military garages and sabotaged patrol boats of the S.S. on the Vistula. In cooperation with the Polish members of the P.P.R., they attacked a workshop where German uniforms were made and de- railed a crack Krakow-Bochnia train reserved exclusively for Germans, burying several dozen officers under it. This type of collaboration was quite rare anywhere in Poland.

Gestapo agents were infiltrated into the Jewish movement and in February 1943, many were arrested, including the Drengers. Both husband and wife, each independent of the other, escaped from prison and began to organize Jewish resistance from outside the city. Through their paper *Hechalutz Halohem* (*The Fighting Pioneer*), they called on Jews as well as Poles to join the ranks of the partisans and urged Poles not to take any action against Jews. In what was possibly the last issue of the Jewish underground press in Poland, the October 1, 1943, issue of *Hechalutz*

Halohem urged surviving Jews in the Ghetto to flee to the forest, through every crack, fence and wall, to "fill the forests and the mountains" and "inform the nearest patrol of the Jewish Organization of Halutz Youth of every incident." Not a single fighter in these patrols has survived.³¹ᵃ The motto of the group—"For those who seek life—we are not the address"— proved all too prophetic.

The rugged youth organization from Brody, near Lvov, sent squads of fighters into the forest, fought off Ukrainian bands and engaged in sabotage. They also organized the last-ditch resistance in the Ghetto, fighting all the way to the deportation cars.

Resistance also flared in the neighborhood of Tarnopol, where Jewish gangs trained and drilled. Clad in S.S. uniforms, they "raided" the Ghetto allegedly to arrest and deport Jews and then released them as soon as they reached the woods.³² There was also a movement of carters and village Jews in the area who worked with the support of nonparty Poles to rescue children. Scattered units were also led by Michael Pomeranz in the vicinity of Kovel, and by a Jewish tailor, Krakowski, from Radom. Near Dolina, Jews joined groups that included cavalrymen who had left the Vlassov army (Vlassov was a Soviet general who had deserted to the Germans). For several months in 1943, they shot up German garrisons, blasted bridges and destroyed factories and farms. However, the Nazis came back in fierce counterattacks and, as happened to most Jewish units in Galicia, the one near Dolina was wiped out.

In this sector of Poland, every rifle, pistol and bullet had to be won at terrible cost. Often the only salvation for organized groups of Jews who were mercilessly routed by Polish nationalists was dispersion. The remnants of the Warsaw Ghetto, for example, who still sought an opportunity to fight against the Germans, divided into four groups of 15 to 20 men each. A group of 60 that had escaped the deportations of 1942 was destroyed by the Gestapo; another group of 30 which reached Meserich in the Lublin district made contact with a Soviet partisan group but, poorly equipped, every youth fell in battle.

The urge to live was so strong among some Jews that they fled in desperation into the woods alone. The chances of survival in such cases were about one to a hundred. People were caught in raids or were betrayed and then massacred. Many were overcome by loneliness, despair and the memory of the dead and made their way back to the doomed ghettos. Quite aware of what they were facing, men returned, because strange and puzzling though it seems, it was much safer to be in the ghettos while they lasted. There would be a burst of terror and death, then a lull into day-by-day existence. Many Jews returned to the ghettos determined not to live any longer, but when the time came to face death, they scurried through the old cycle yet again and ran into the woods or waited dumbly for the transports, retreating into a shell of solitude and watching the days tick away like a huge inexorable pendulum.

There are some accounts of town-bound Jews who became crafty woodsmen under the guidance of escaped Russian prisoners and who were initiated into the secrets of survival in the forests. They learned when and how to gather food, how to cook safely, how to distinguish between the steps of humans and those of animals, between the light of a flashlight and phosphorescent wood. They learned how to dispose of dirt dug out of a new pit, how to steal food and cover their tracks, and how to store sacks of potatoes. If they were lucky, they could have meat by slaughtering a pig or sheep in an accessible stall, but this skill too had to be learned.

Those few who survived alone or in small isolated groups in underground bunkers were exceptional. In the hands and hearts of anonymous peasants lay their fate. The compassionate as well as the moneygrubbing peasant was faced every day with the dilemma whether to yield up his charges to the Germans, who killed people sheltering Jews, or yield to his sense of pity or power.

If he agreed to a bargain, he had to be cautious so that his neighbors would not see or hear strange men digging under his barn or shed or under an orchard. Frequently his wife and children were frightened and would implore him to take stock of the terrible risk he was taking, while helpless Jews listened, trying to drown out their pain and humiliation. Many pits were so small that a man could never stand upright in them. No daylight ever penetrated—in fact, light became a mortal enemy, and darkness an ally which occasionally permitted the dwellers in the pits to see the sky, hear the rustle of trees and hoard up fresh air. At night the foul and nauseating air of the pit could be refreshed. But, after a while, the very natural sounds of breathing animals and barking dogs became cruelly hostile and dangerous.

Such prisoners were completely dependent upon the peasant for food and waited once or twice a day, liked caged animals, to be fed. Frequently the water ration was too small for both drinking and bathing. The severest problem was how to endure mentally. In the deluxe pits, a small kerosene light would permit reading or card playing; more often the oxygen was insufficient to maintain a light.

In the first stage of life in an underground bunker there was mainly thanksgiving from which to create endurance. A young boy in one family which miraculously survived in the bowels of the earth, sixty miles from Treblinka, has described this first phase:

> . . . through difficulties, dangers and discomforts, there started and flowed the life of the shelter. Each movement crystallized, each function settled, the tracks of our existence were cut with microscopic precision. We en-

dured everything at the beginning with stoic patience. Nobody complained, no one sagged. We cared for the safety of the shelter and only its good concerned us. We were in a daze that eliminated memories and dulled reactions, two powerful elements which later began to rip the shelter apart. We rejoiced at passing time, confident that we were being brought closer to the final day which was surely waiting for us somewhere on this nightmarish road. We rejoiced at the security of the shelter, and the success of our undertaking. We did everything to maintain this state and we prayed every day for patience and endurance to carry on. We grew roots; we became a part of the pit. It was all we had left.[33]

It was not long, however, before complications arose. First, there were physical eruptions: the odious and bloody presence of bedbugs, racing rats, seeping manure in the pit, and the increasing oppressiveness of the almost airless trench. Then came the frequent, unpredictable visits from the police, first to the farmhouse, then to the shed above the thin layer of a wooden cover—a few feet from seven entombed Jews. Memories of past sweet times began to flood in. In the unending tedium of the days small chores became all-consuming. Someone would rub a pair of boots for a whole day, or trim the lamp. Quarrels inside the pit became more frequent, erupting over trifles and small hurts, and a dark gloomy pessimism began to pervade the bunker. The family could hear talk overhead about the stalemate on the front and German victories, and about the seizure of Jews in hiding nearby and the execution of peasants who had helped them. A worn map of Russia was studied longingly; then hopelessly, it was folded after the Germans recaptured Kharkov. The sheltering peasant had to be given more money. A desperate mission was organized to find some money that had been hidden near the family house in Losice.

One night the young Oscar could no longer stand the suffocating pit and left it to see what had happened to his sister. Those who remained behind became hysterical at his leaving or were already mourning him. Over the moon-flooded fields, Oscar met a middle-aged man and his boy and two small girls, pathetically stranded in a huge space in which there was no shelter. Their mother had just been murdered in the ghetto of Miedzyrzec. The man's eyes bulged, his mouth was distorted. He caught the sleeves of Oscar's jacket. "You are young; you were there. Please," he implored, "where shall I go? Tell me for God's sake. To the Bialowieza forest? No, I know! To a farmer. A farmer will take me in. I know! I have cousins in America. They will pay. Where? Tell me where? Oh, don't you have any pity?"

The young man wrote:

Thus he went on. He was leaving the ghetto for the first time and had no inkling what it meant. He did not know that although the Polish forests and fields were vast and open, yet for him, each bush, each inch of earth, each human heart, would be closed. He did not know that he was going to a death which would take so miserably long that he would pray for it ten times each day. He did not know that he would envy the dead and pound his breast in guilt that all this suffering was justly inflicted for his crime in remaining alive.[34]

When Oscar saw Miedzyrzec, it was a gash of rubble in the fertile, swaying grasses of the steppes. This had been the fifth onslaught against the Ghetto. Fifty thousand Jews had been led to their death over layer after layer of ruins, now reduced to two narrow alleys surrounded by barbed wire. Feathers from torn bedding still floated in the air. Pots and furniture and photographs and books lay strewn among the rubble and cinders. Along the barbed wire wafted the perfume of the lilac trees. The young man wandered about the ruins, even clung to them, and then, after a few days, he left.

A few strays left with him, each to go in a direction unknown to the others, but where? A young girl sank to her knees when told to leave. She was afraid of the night, of the howling dogs, the gloomy forests. "Where will I go?" she cried. "What did I do? Take me back to Miedzyrzec. Take me back to the ghetto." She was lifted to her feet and told that it was impossible to go back. With a small basket in her hand, she stood at the edge of the woods looking into the infinite darkness. Suddenly she whispered "Good-bye" and walked slowly away.

The summer of 1943 was the most fertile that Poles remembered. The wheat grew sumptuously and the grain fell ahead of harvest. The meadows flamed with color while the ashes of Jews were poured into the earth. The inmates of the pit became half-mad. What were they waiting for? The war would never end, the peasant kept telling them. It made no sense to go on. To force them to leave, he stopped giving them food, forcing them to steal milk from the cow. The men in the pit stared at space with empty eyes, the women listlessly walked the corners of the pit where they could stand up. The images of massacre in the Ghetto now began to swell like a growing nightmare.

For the prisoners in the pits who could hold on through that summer, there was hopeful news that inspired the wildest dreams of freedom. Russians had reached the Dnieper and had already touched on Polish soil. In this web of fantasy, the Allies were marching on Berlin and liberation was near. Then, swiftly, brutal facts reeled them back to despair, hunger shriveled them to scarecrows, and they sat in their pestilential holes suspended in time and space, bitterly remembering the Polish song:

"Ours is the night; we have nothing else."

Part II The Deportations

19 Scandinavia

BEFORE HITLER CAME TO POWER in 1933, the Jews in Scandinavia,[1] on the rim of the European Jewish world, lived in peace and tranquillity. Their numbers were not large: about 8,000 Jews, including 1,500 refugees, lived in Sweden; 8,000 lived in Denmark; and 1,700 in Norway. The largest numbers were concentrated in the capitals. This was especially true of Denmark, where the Jewish population outside Copenhagen was exceedingly small—a significant fact in 1943 when Danish Jews were saved by flight to Sweden.

Until November 9, 1939, public opinion and government policy in all three countries on the question of absorbing Jewish refugees from the Reich were affected mainly by the economic depression of the 1930's and the usual fears that Jewish immigrants would increase unemployment or become public charges. There was, in addition, the constant fear of provoking Hitler by expressions of sympathy. Considerable pro-Nazi sentiment also prevailed among the upper social classes, and traditional respect for German culture was widespread. Many Scandinavians simply refused to believe that German Jews had actually been deprived of their rights in the Third Reich. Thus Jewish refugees fleeing from Germany were often turned away at the border.

In February 1939, for example, students of Sweden's largest university voted to oppose admission of ten Jewish physicians into Sweden, and over a thousand Swedish physicians protested against the request of a world-famous gynecologist to settle and practice in Sweden. Others feared the creation of a "Jewish question." Immigration regulations, moreover, remained quite stringent.

Under these circumstances, both Jewish and non-Jewish relief committees had to induce official agencies to adopt a more flexible attitude in interpreting the immigration laws. The Jewish community also had to collect large sums of money and tax itself heavily in order to provide necessary financial guarantees. The main effort at first was directed at influencing the governments to grant transit visas to refugees who needed a temporary asylum en route to Palestine.

In Denmark, the refugee committee obtained 1,400 Palestine permits for Jewish boys and girls from Germany and eastern Europe enabling them to train on Danish farms. As there were no problems involved in securing work permits for agricultural workers, these were easy to obtain. About 1,000 of these youngsters reached Palestine before the German occupation. More difficult were permits for 3,000 additional Jewish transit-emigrants who passed through Denmark after the German occupation, and 1,000 who remained in Denmark.

In Sweden, entry permits were obtained for 500 children, 150 transit-emigrants and 300 youths bound for Palestine. About 500 refugees arrived in Norway and more than half of these managed to leave the country before the occupation. Jewish relief committees were organized in Oslo and Trondheim, while one important non-Jewish committee led by Odd Nansen, the son of the famous explorer, took as its special province the care of the so-called "stateless" refugees, whose plight became acute after the Nazi conquest of Austria, Czechoslovakia and Poland.

Denmark and Norway were invaded on April 9, 1940. Thereafter, neutral Sweden began to take a more liberal attitude toward the refugees. Entry permits were issued to individuals with close relatives in Sweden who could guarantee their support. But by now it was too late. The exits from Europe were sealed. Through their Stockholm embassy, the Swedish Zionist Organization tried in vain to obtain from the British, Palestine certificates for 400 young farm trainees in Denmark who were in grave danger. A few Latin-American passports were secured through the efforts of a Swedish consul. These protected a small number of Dutch Jews who were interned in Bergen-Belsen until 1944. The immediate problem facing Swedish relief leaders was the situation in Norway. Subsequently, official Swedish efforts were bent toward bringing Norwegian and Danish Jews to Sweden and attempting to rescue Hungarian Jews in 1944.

A few Jews had tried to save themselves during the two-month Norwegian resistance against the Nazis by crossing the border into Sweden. But the flight was full of peril; moreover, there was general expectation that neutral Sweden too would soon be occupied. If so, the position of Jewish refugees might be worse than in their own home. Some Jews who had escaped to Sweden are known to have returned to Norway in the summer of 1940.

Indeed, the situation of the Jews of Norway during the early months of the occupation was not unbearable and certain measures taken by *Reichs-kommisar* Josef Terboven were interpreted as indirect evidence that they would not be molested. Vidkun Quisling, leader of a small pro-Nazi anti-Semitic party, became the head of the government under Terboven, but quislings were not popular among Norwegians and Jews felt comparatively safe among their anti-Nazi fellow citizens. Little by little, however, things grew worse.

In June 1941, soon after the German invasion of Russia, the Nazis rounded up all of the Jews of Tromsö and several other towns in the north of Norway and deported them to Germany. In Trondheim, stateless Jews were arrested, then soon released. Three weeks later, however, they were arrested again and some were executed. The Jews in Oslo remained unharmed, but there was an ominous portent in the decree of February 2, 1942, requiring that all documents of Jews be stamped with a "J."

On October 22, a member of the Norwegian border police was shot and killed by a non-Jew on a train near the Swedish border. On the train were ten Jews who were probably planning to escape to Sweden. They were immediately placed under arrest and on the following day their families in Oslo were imprisoned. A deadly blow then followed. On the night of October 25, all male Jews over sixteen throughout Norway were arrested and their property confiscated. This was a trick used elsewhere to disguise a deportation roundup as a forced-labor drive, but it was not entirely successful in Norway. Some Jews who had heard rumors of the Nazi plans fled to Sweden. Others were warned in time by Norwegian police who were technically involved in the roundup.

A month later, several hundred women and children were seized. They and the arrested men, numbering 531 altogether, were placed on a ship in Oslo and taken to Stettin. From there they were transported to Auschwitz. Later, several more deportations took place, claiming 770 Jews, including 100 from central Europe.

After the first sailing of the *Donau*, the ship that carried the deportees, Dr. Arvid G. Richert, the Swedish Minister in Berlin, proposed that his country receive all Jews remaining in Norway. But the German Foreign Ministry refused to discuss the matter. Nevertheless, the Swedish Consulate General in Oslo made strenuous attempts to renaturalize Jews who had formerly been Swedish citizens.[2] To the great surprise and anger of the Germans, these efforts were carried to the point of inviting some of the arrested Jews to apply for Swedish nationality. When the Germans protested, a Swedish consular official admitted having an official directive to extend his helping hand to the "poor Jews who, after all, are only human beings."

Of the Jews that escaped the *Donau* shipment, fully 900 managed to cross the Swedish border to safety. A small number survived in hiding, and 64 Jews in mixed marriages were quartered in a camp and released in March 1945.

Escape to Sweden for the 900 was perilous but heart-warming. The fugitives had to walk for days through thick forests and wild country, but

Norwegian families in the sparsely settled districts of eastern Norway provided them with food and shelter until guides came to take them past the German border patrols. Once in Sweden, they were looked after by the office for refugees under the Norwegian Embassy and by Jewish refugee committees. Almost two thirds of the Norwegian Jewish community succeeded in escaping the Nazi net.

It is the story of the Danish Jews, however, which is truly unique in the annals of the Holocaust. From the old King Christian to the lowliest fisherman, the entire Danish people resisted the destruction of its Jews and succeeded in saving most of them. Unusual, also, was the fact that Denmark retained a large measure of autonomy under German occupation, its monarchy and constitution both remaining unimpaired for nearly four years.

Denmark became known as the "model protectorate," and the government and the courts and even the press were allowed a surprising amount of freedom, a situation which led Winston Churchill to call Denmark the "sadistic murderer's canary." At the beginning of the German occupation, Denmark was indeed a well-fed and spoiled canary, willing to be compliant. The Danes had not prepared to defend themselves against a possible German invasion; their armed force strength in 1940 was only one fourth of what it had been at the outbreak of World War I and the country capitulated to Hitler almost immediately. This lack of resistance and the German view of the Danes as ethnic cousins resulted initially in an indulgent German policy, including unusual freedom for Danish Jews. The general apathy to the occupation was mistakenly interpreted by the Nazis as indifference toward measures against Danish Jews. But it soon became clear that the Danes vehemently opposed any suggestion of anti-Jewish measures, and because Germany needed not only Denmark's foodstuffs, but its marine diesel engines and parts for airplanes and armored vehicles, the Germans were held off.

In January 1942, when Himmler and Heydrich put pressure on the German Foreign Office to have the Nuremberg Laws applied to the occupied western European countries, it was reported in the American press that King Christian threatened to abdicate if the laws were imposed on Denmark. When the Germans approached the Danes rather cautiously about introducing the yellow badge, they were told that the King said: "The Jews are a part of the Danish nation. We have no Jewish problem in our country because we never had an inferiority complex in relation to the Jew. If the Jews are forced to wear the yellow star, I and my whole family shall wear it as a badge of honor." This story is probably apocryphal, but it serves to indicate how implacably the King opposed anti-Semitic legislation.[3]

Himmler then tried to proceed against the Danish Jews in the guise of security measures. In September 1942, he ordered Heinrich Müller, head of the Gestapo, to insert the names of Jews in a list of Danish Communist and resistance leaders whom he intended to arrest. No doubt Himmler believed that he could rely on the cooperation of Karl Werner Best, the Reich Minister to Denmark, who was a former legal adviser to the Gestapo. But Best had left the Gestapo to get out of the clutches of Heydrich. Enjoying the relative quiet of life in a quasi-free country, Best wrote to Ribbentrop that the proposed anti-Jewish measures would create a constitutional crisis in Denmark and suggested, instead, that the Danes remove their Jews from the civil service and from business contracts with the Germans.[4] In surveying the condition of Danish Jewry, however, Best found that their public and economic influence was very slight, hardly worth the effort if the Danish Government were to react by resigning. He then suggested the possibility of taking some action against the 1,350 Jewish refugees in the country who had fled from Germany. These Jews had been deprived of their German nationality and were thus stateless. If somehow these Jews could be given back their nationality, Best reasoned, the Reich could assume control of them without stepping on Danish sovereignty. This proposal, however, would upset the whole "legal" fabric of deportation from Germany and Berlin dropped it.

Statelessness, which left so many other Jews of western Europe exposed and expendable, was not a curse to the refugee Jews in Denmark. The Danish Government, in a rare gesture for the times, decided to protect them and not make any distinction between foreign and native Jews. Through 1942 and most of 1943, the Jews of Denmark were still unharmed. Late in 1942, an attempt was made to set fire to the Copenhagen Synagogue, but it was stopped by the Danish police. In January 1943, at a student festival in Gjørslev, Danish students announced that they wished everyone in the audience to participate in the singing of two songs —both national anthems dear to the hearts of the Danes. The Germans present were not at all surprised when the first one sung was the Danish national anthem, but they were stunned when the second was not "Deutschland über Alles" but the Zionist national anthem "Hatikvah."[5] The comparative safety of the Danish Jews, however, changed radically in the summer of 1943.

By that time, the war was going badly for the Germans. The offensive in Russia had failed, the Allies had invaded Italy and the Afrika Korps had surrendered. Restlessness stirred among the Danes. The Germans were draining the country's food supply and acts of sabotage against German installations erupted frequently. In August, the situation exploded.

The Swedish Government canceled its 1940 agreement which permitted German troops stationed in Norway to use Swedish railways. At the same time, riots broke out in Danish shipyards and Danish workers and soldiers were arrested. Danish dock workers refused to repair German ships and went on strike. The good-natured, civilized and peace-loving Danes finally reached their moment of truth. Cooperation with the Germans was no longer possible. Nazi brutality had increased with the worsening fortunes of war. The Danish Premier Erik Scavenius threatened to resign if Danish courts were required to try the arrested dock workers. Best was ordered to Berlin; Hitler personally rebuked him and ordered a state of martial law in Denmark. When Best returned to Copenhagen, he found chaos. The Danish Army was dissolving, the Scavenius government had already resigned, and the ministries were in the hands of civil servants. The German machine had struck an extraordinary obstacle: an uncooperative government and people.

Best decided to take advantage of this new situation to deport the Jews and get back into Hitler's favor. He wired Berlin that he needed police, soldiers and ships. On September 18, Rolf Günther arrived in Copenhagen with a special commando from Eichmann's office. Himmler was now sure the moment had come to enforce the Final Solution for Denmark's Jews, but he had not reckoned on a local population resolved to save its Jews nor on German officials whose stay in Denmark had apparently worn away some of the "ruthless toughness" so necessary for Nazi zeal. General Hermann von Hannecken, the German military commander whose troops were needed to help the police with the seizures, refused to transfer any of his men. He also refused to order the Danish Jews to report to the Wehrmacht offices for "work," and wrote to Berlin that Jewish deportations during the military emergency would "impair the prestige of the Wehrmacht in foreign countries" and cause the loss of Danish meat and fats. He promised only a small cordon in the harbor area to maintain law and order. Under no circumstances, he maintained, would he involve the Army in arrests.

Best had scheduled the deportations for the night of October 1. A few days earlier, a shipping expert in Copenhagen, Georg Duckwitz, who was employed as attaché of the German merchant marine, revealed Best's plan to a prominent Danish acquaintance, Hans Hedtoft (later Prime Minister of Denmark). Hedtoft, in turn, spread the news to his friends and personally warned the president of the Jewish community of the impending action.[6] On the morning of Friday, September 29, 1943, Rabbi Marcus Melchior stood before the holy ark of the 110-year-old Copenhagen Synagogue. It was the day before Rosh Hashanah. About 150 members of the congregation were present, all of them puzzled by seeing Rabbi Melchior without his rabbinical robes. Rabbi Melchior began:

> There will be no service this morning. Instead, I have very important news to tell you. Last night I received word that tomorrow the Germans plan to

raid Jewish homes throughout Copenhagen to arrest all the Danish Jews for shipment to concentration camps. They know that tomorrow is Rosh Hashanah and our families will be home. The situation is very serious. We must take action immediately. You must leave the synagogue now and contact all relatives, friends and neighbors you know are Jewish and tell them to warn the Jews. You must do this immediately, within the next few minutes, so that two or three hours from now, everyone will know what is happening. By nightfall tonight we must all be in hiding.

Rabbi Melchior's warning spread quickly. Throughout the day, Christian policemen, mail carriers, taxi drivers, shopkeepers and students passed the word on. An ambulance driver who could not think of a single acquaintance with a Jewish name entered a telephone booth, ripped out the directory and with a pencil circled what seemed to be Jewish names. He called on many of these people, total strangers, and spread the alarm. Some Jews who became frantic because they had no place to go were piled into his ambulance and taken to the Bispebjerg Hospital where they were sheltered.

On Rosh Hashanah, Gestapo squads roamed the streets, broke into synagogues and homes and made arrests on the spot. Lists of Jews were seized from Jewish community offices and property and bank deposits were confiscated. On the following day, October 1, the Swedish government offered refuge to all Danish Jews. Some Jews sought desperately to cross from Öresund in any vessel they could obtain; others tried to swim. Some 1,600 Jews were captured and interned at a camp in Horsens. Later in the month it was reported that 600 were deported to Poland: one of the transports in Copenhagen harbor was known to have sailed on October 3.

The Germans declared that Jews had been eliminated from Danish public life so as not to "poison the atmosphere." A deluge of protests poured in to the German authorities from students, clergy, political parties and officials. Street fighting broke out between Nazis and civilians. Danes sabotaged German vessels, power stations, barracks and war factories. On October 3, Copenhagen University closed for a week "in view of the disasters which have overtaken our fellow citizens." Einar Mellerup, Copenhagen police chief, was arrested on October 10 for declaring that the police dissociate themselves completely from the brutal treatment of the Jews.[7] In answer to the announcement that interned Danish soldiers would be released when all Danish Jews would be arrested, the commander-in-chief of the armed forces said, "The personnel of the Danish Army will not accept favors at the expense of other citizens."

Sweden's neutrality had benefited Germany economically; now it was to serve Danish Jews as it had Norwegian Jews before them. Sweden offered to intern all Danish Jews, but the Germans ignored the offer.

Sweden's second proposal, to accept all Danish Jewish children, also was rejected. Momentarily, it appeared that refugees might be barred from sanctuary by Sweden's adherence to the legal formalities of neutrality. The impasse was broken by a great scientist: Niels Bohr.

The Allies wanted the Nobel prize-winning Danish physicist in the United States to work on the atom bomb. On September 30, Bohr was smuggled across the sound from Denmark to Sweden in a small boat. Upon landing, he was greeted by Professor Frederick Lindemann, Churchill's personal consultant on scientific matters. The Allied plan was to have Bohr depart by plane for London, and then for the United States. But Bohr refused to budge until an appointment was arranged for him with the Swedish Foreign Minister. The appointment was set for October 1.

At the meeting, Bohr announced that he had no intention of leaving Sweden until the foreign minister promised refuge to all Danish Jews who could reach Swedish shores. The foreign minister was not very responsive, but King Gustav was. Not altogether satisfied by the king's assurance that Sweden would accept the Danish Jews, Bohr further insisted that the news be published in Swedish newspapers and broadcast by radio to Denmark. Only after the Swedish press carried the offer of refuge on its front pages and the government-owned Swedish radio beamed the message to Denmark did Bohr agree to leave.[8] Project "Little Dunkirk" quickly followed.

The escape route of course was the sea, and the only boats available were fishing craft. The Germans had ordered all other Danish vessels brought inland. Most of the refugees who made their way to the coast tried to reach Snekkersten or Elsinore, where the sound separating Denmark from Sweden is only two and a half miles wide. Residents in this area put them up in private homes, farms, inns, hotels and garages. However, the flight to the coastal towns in early October was chaotic and hasty; most of the 472 Danish Jews captured by the Germans were seized during this period. What was needed was an organized method of getting the refugees from their places of hiding to various collection points, later turning them over to fishermen who would take them across the sound.

The pivotal point was established at Mogens Staffeldt's bookshop in Copenhagen, brazenly located across the street from Gestapo headquarters in Dagmarhus. A signal was decided upon: if the store was free of Germans, a copy of Kaj Munk's poems would appear in the store window, and Jews could enter safely. Otherwise, it would be dangerous.

The first experience—involving a group of Jewish refugees in the bookshop—was a grim one. In this group were ten frightened children who had been hidden in a cellar. At one o'clock in the morning one of the children became hysterical. Soon all were screaming uncontrollably. A nearby physician was roused out of bed and told that there was an emergency. When he arrived at the back room of the store and saw the screaming children, he decided to inject them all with a sedative and make them unconscious. Later, injections became a valuable and regularly employed procedure on the sea crossings to Sweden. If the trip was particularly long, physicians also gagged and taped the mouths of children so that they would remain quiet after the injections wore off.

After passing through the bookshop, the refugees needed another station. The Bispebjerg Hospital in Copenhagen was selected. Here the whole staff eagerly mobilized itself for the rescue effort. This began on October 7, when a medical student attached to the hospital discovered forty Jews hiding in the woods south of Copenhagen. Germans were in the area; a safe place for a pickup by truck was needed. The student received permission to house the Jews temporarily at the hospital and decided to get them there by staging a mock funeral. The refugees were dressed in black and carried flowers while following a hearse through Copenhagen to the cemetery on the hospital grounds. But instead of 40 persons, there were 140 lined up in front of the hospital gate after the procession passed through the city. The "funeral" entourage slowly made its way up the tree-lined path to the chapel on the hospital grounds. A few hours later, a canvas-covered lorry drove up to the chapel and picked up forty refugees. The others could not remain in the chapel; it would take at least a day to make arrangements for them. The doctors decided to house them in the psychiatric building, one of the places the Germans would least likely search. In small groups, at five-minute intervals, the refugees were led away from the chapel to the psychiatric building.

The following morning the gatekeeper admitted two hundred additional "mourners," but the psychiatric building could not accommodate them. Dr. Karl Henry Køster, who had organized the earlier accommodations, asked Head Nurse Signe Jansen if room could be found in the nurses' quarters. Keys to thirty apartments in the nurses' section were quickly turned over. The nurses doubled up or shared their quarters with the refugees.

A continuous stream of "mourners" came to Bispebjerg Hospital and eventually the nurses put 130 apartments at their disposal. They looked after the refugees, fed, clothed, and reassured them. Within a few days, they were driven away in hospital ambulances to a rendezvous with fishermen at points along the coast. Despite the risks of raids and reprisals, the hospital staff carried on this organized rescue with aplomb. There were no heroics. During October, over two thousand Jews passed through Bispebjerg Hospital on their way to freedom. Dr. Køster himself, when the German net tightened around the hospital, was sheltered by a friend and then smuggled to Sweden. The British Embassy there arranged for him to go to London, and for the next three years he served as a medical officer with the British armed services.

Meanwhile, Von Hannecken's refusal to cooperate with the German police, coupled with orders to the German police to avoid clashes with the Danish police, meant that instead of rounding up Jews and ordering them to assembly points, the police would have to conduct door-to-door searches. Arrests during the first few days of October were under 500—mostly people who were too old to hide. These Jews were deported not to Auschwitz, but to Theresienstadt, and most of them survived the war. Their survival was due mainly to the continual interest and intervention of Danish officials and the King.

Besides the unusual rescue system of the Bispebjerg Hospital, rescue groups all over the country sprang up. Schoolteachers, clergymen, taxi drivers, shopkeepers, housewives and fishermen helped to escort Jews out of towns to small villages near the sea. Here they were again hidden until they could be smuggled across to Sweden along a seaway blockaded by Germans. The Danish fishing fleet was mobilized; organizers arranged to pay the fishermen and see that the escapees moved undetected to the beaches and vessels. Not the least of their problems was that of sheltering pious and Orthodox Jews who persisted in rigorously observing strict religious practices during their ordeal.

When it became evident that Jews were escaping to Sweden by boat, Germans used police dogs to try to sniff out the human cargo aboard the ships. To overcome this hazard, a Danish scientist concocted a powder made of dried human blood and cocaine which, when dusted on the decks of the ships, completely deadened the dogs' sense of smell. Small amounts of it were also placed in carefully folded handkerchiefs which were distributed to Danish seamen. When the Germans came aboard with their dogs, the seamen, pretending to blow their noses, would let the gray powder fall to the decks near the dogs.

As many of the Jews involved were people of modest means, the Danes themselves financed the cost of transportation, which averaged about 500 kroner ($100) per person. For example, one of the rescue organizers, Aage Bertelsen, schoolmaster of the Aarhus Cathedral College, sent a pastor to a lumber merchant, Johannes Fog, to borrow money. "Mr. Bertelsen? Who is he?" asked the merchant while he handed over 2,000 kroner, with a promise of 10,000 more. Within ten days, Johannes Fog had lent almost 150,000 kroner to the rescue project. As Bertelsen himself wrote, "Assistance to the Jews could be based on nothing but a personal relationship of trust. Money was paid and received without the giving of any receipts at all, to say nothing of any kind of account keeping."[9]

During the first week of October, Bertelsen's semidetached house at 33A Buddinge Lane in Lyngby became known in underground circles as "the house with the blue curtains." There was a continual coming and going of cars and bicycles, and the telephone rang day and night. Bertelsen's work expanded into a rescue group of sixty people, called the Lyngby

Group, which eventually smuggled over 1,000 Jews safely to the shores of Sweden. Bertelsen himself was ultimately forced to escape to Sweden, and his wife was arrested by the Gestapo. The danger of capture and black-mail were constant, but the work went on and help came from many directions. The Danish police warned of German soldiers; pastors handed out blank baptismal certificates; druggists supplied free medicines; Jewish property, religious articles, and books were carefully preserved; children rang doorbells to collect funds. Nowhere in Europe did any people re-spond to the Jewish disaster as did the Danes, and after the war their spirit of simple human decency did not flag. Every Danish Jew who returned was granted 4,505 kroner with which to start anew, and the greeting was not what it was in Poland and Romania, "What, you're still alive!" but a welcome home accompanied by flowers and keys to former homes.

The asylum granted by Sweden was also unique. Many nations pro-tested the destruction of Europe's Jews, but Sweden alone gave refuge to all Jews who could escape. When the exodus from Denmark was over, almost 6,000 full Jews, 1,310 half-Jews and 686 non-Jews married to Jews were safe in Sweden. The operation had taken less than a month. When it was completed, it was the considered opinion of Eichmann that "for various reasons the action against the Jews in Denmark has been a failure."

The case of Finland is also exceptional, in yet another way.[10] Finland was Germany's ally in the war against Russia and wholly dependent on the Germans for arms and food. In 1939, Hitler had supported Russian aggression in Finland—an extremely unpopular policy in Germany— be-cause Russia supplied Germany with needed raw materials and freed Germany to wage a one-front war. When Hitler decided to attack Russia in 1941, however, Finland became Germany's ally and was soon forced to rely on her powerful partner for necessities. The north of Finland was occupied by German troops and Nazi ideological pressure soon made it-self felt. The first move to introduce anti-Jewish legislation was made in April 1942 by three pro-Nazi members of the City Council in Helsinki, but this action was overruled. A similar effort was made in the Finnish Parliament but without success. A wave of protests swept over the country and the strong Social Democratic Party held impressive demonstrations. Temporarily frustrated, the Nazis tried a new tack.

The Gestapo, after a long campaign, had gained a foothold among the pro-Nazi elements in the Finnish police. Bluntly they demanded the sur-render of 300 Jewish refugees who had fled from Germany and Austria. The refugees, however, were hastily packed off to neutral Sweden. In July 1942, the Germans began to press for a "final solution" of the Jewish problem in Finland. To stress the importance of the matter, Himmler himself went to Finland. Included in his party on the journey was his personal physician and therapist, Dr. Felix Kersten, who was to play an important role as a middleman between Himmler and the Finnish Government in discussions of the future of Finland's 2,000 Jews.

Dr. Kersten was himself a Finnish citizen and became personal physician to Himmler largely to look after the interests of Finland. He was born in Estonia and educated in Riga. During the civil war in Russia, he enrolled as a volunteer in the Finnish Independence Army under General Mannerheim. After the war, he became a Finnish citizen and went to Germany to study chiropractic. He gained recognition in this field and in 1939 received an urgent invitation to treat Himmler for a neurogastric condition. He spent a great deal of time with the hypochondriacal Himmler and often accompanied him on trips.

Kersten, of course, knew Himmler's intentions regarding Finnish Jews and contacted the Foreign Affairs Minister Rolf Witting soon after his arrival in Helsinki. Witting listened intently to Kersten's report and then explained that the Finns would not yield to Himmler's demands despite the country's precarious military and economic position. Kersten then skillfully prevailed on Himmler to let him conduct preliminary talks with the Finnish Prime Minister and to present the German note later. Himmler gave his reluctant consent.

Finnish bread stocks were already low and Himmler several times said that the Finns would have to choose between hunger and giving up their Jews. On July 30, he personally talked with Witting in the garden of the German Embassy. In the midst of their discussion of the exploration of ocean depths, Himmler said suddenly, "I think perhaps the moment has come for Germany and Finland to reach an understanding about Sweden." Finland, he said, would receive the northern half, while Germany would annex central and southern Sweden. Witting observed that Finland had no ambitions in this direction. The talk then swung to a discussion of Finland's Jews. Witting stated firmly that the Finnish people had no sympathy with German policy, and that handing Jews over to Germany would lead to a deterioration of relations. The situation, he pointed out, would be very much aggravated by the fact that a number of Jews had heroically sacrificed their lives in the war against Russia and in the present campaign. No Finn would understand how anyone could surrender the wives and children of such men. Even the dangerous food situation would not force them to yield.

Kersten continued to put Himmler off. He said that the ministers shared his (Himmler's) views in principle, but still had doubts about immediate technical procedures. The delaying actions continued. Meanwhile, Finnish intelligence agents penetrated Himmler's apartment and photographed papers detailing plans for the final destruction of Finland's

Jews. The Finnish Cabinet, meeting in emergency session, decided unanimously to reject Himmler's demands. They refused to surrender a single Jew. The course to be taken, however, would have to be dilatory, an endless delaying action. After this session, Kersten lunched with Witting and noted in his diary, "I had lunch with Foreign Minister Witting for two hours. He told me in regard to Himmler's demands, 'Finland is a decent nation. We would rather perish together with the Jews. . . . We will not surrender the Jews!' "

Finland had a few levers to pull in holding Himmler off. Germany needed her nickel and timber as well as military positions. Finland was needed for the advance on Leningrad and occupation of Russia's ice-free ports on the Arctic Ocean. In reporting back to Himmler, Kersten cautiously pointed out the consequences of hasty action on the Jewish question. Furthermore, Kersten explained, Finland was a republic and was bound by certain laws. For example, if the Jews were to be turned over to the Germans, authorization from Parliament would be necessary. But Parliament, he added, was in summer recess and would not reconvene until November.

In the meantime, news of the delicate negotiations leaked out. Newspapers assailed Nazi racial theories and appealed for aid for Finnish Jews. The Finnish Government placed three vessels at the disposal of the Jewish community for eventual escape to Sweden. November passed without any untoward incidents. Himmler held his fire until December and then demanded action from the Finns. "The Finns will have to choose between hunger and delivering up their Jews," he said.[11] Kersten then reported to him that Parliament had sat only briefly in November because of the deteriorating military situation and had hesitated to bring up the Jewish decree, "fearing complications." Himmler flew into a rage and threatened to solve the Jewish problem in his own way. Police action was instituted. Four Jews were seized, charged with trumped-up crimes and deported. After this news spread, however, there was no further cooperation from the Finnish police. In the end, not another Jew was surrendered by the Finns.

Scandinavia, admittedly, had few Jews for the Nazi death mills. In Holland, Belgium and France, their numbers were much greater and the Nazi attack on them was commensurately ruthless.

20 Holland and Belgium

IN THE SIX WEEKS between May 10 and June 25, 1940, a half-million Jews of western Europe came under German control. With the exception of the so-called stateless Jews who had come from Germany and Poland between the two wars and the more recent refugees, the western Jews were from old, established and largely integrated communities where Jews had lived for centuries. They posed a much more difficult problem for the Germans than the two million Jews of German-occupied Poland where the Nazis had ready-made advantages such as separate civil registers, fairly compact ghettos, organized anti-Semitic forces and a long history of state-inspired pogroms. In western Europe there were no language barriers or cultural antagonisms. The western Jew had no visible characteristics different from his non-Jewish neighbor—he had long ago discarded the capote and beard of the eastern European Jew. In some assimilated communities neither he nor his neighbor was aware of any differences at all. Moreover, the western Jews were dispersed among the non-Jewish population and constituted only a small percentage of the whole. Amsterdam was the only city in western Europe with a relatively high Jewish population density; 10 percent of its population was Jewish. There was one further difference in the West: Jews considered themselves and were considered by their non-Jewish fellow citizens as nationals having all of the rights and obligations of first-class citizens. The ghettos were dissolved in the early nineteenth century. Declassment was a thing of the past.

The German occupiers were, of course, aware of these differences and hesitated before taking anti-Jewish measures. The *Statut des Juifs* was not passed in France until October 1940, and not until April 1941 was a special French Commissariat for Jewish Questions established. At no time were the Germans able to get a completely reliable Jewish census in western Europe. Moreover, native resistance movements, in keeping with the western trend toward assimilation, encouraged the involvement of fellow Jews. Consequently, there was much more solidarity between western Jews and non-Jews in their feeling and action against the Germans than was true in eastern Europe.

However, once the Nazi machinery of death began to operate, it drove on as relentlessly in the West as in the East. There were no massed executions, no layering of thousands of Jews in open pits, no horrifying shooting expeditions by *Einsatzgruppen*. The Germans in western Europe simply didn't have enough open space and Jews were not massed in concentrated target zones. But, as the meaning of the phrase "final solution of the Jewish problem" contracted into extermination, the German pauses and uncertainties in the West disappeared. The Foreign Office took care of the legal formalities, the Army kept the native population suppressed and the S.S. came in for the final roundups for the transports.

Jews salvaged more of their numbers in the West than in the East, but this was not because the Germans remained more conscious of western sensibilities. Their plans for western Jews were identical with those for eastern Jews. They were balked in some places only by the limitations of control. The remorselessly efficient apparatus of destruction was most powerful in Holland, where German control was absolute; it was less successful in France and Belgium because German control in those countries was incomplete. In Holland, Jewish losses were proportionately as great as any in the East: at least 105,000 Dutch Jews perished; fewer than 20,000 survived. In France, of 300,000, at least 65,000 were killed—some estimates are as high as 90,000. In Belgium, 25,000 Jews were murdered out of a total of 90,000.

These figures are not only a reflection of variations in German control. They also show the danger of making generalizations about certain aspects of the Holocaust, such as the role of Jewish resistance, the extent of general popular resistance, and the presence of unassimilated refugees in the midst of integrated communities. In each of the countries of western Europe—Holland, Belgium and France—these factors can be isolated and observed, but no conclusions as to their interplay can be drawn. In Holland, for example, the Jewish community was well settled and integrated and enjoyed the wholehearted support of the population in facing the Nazi crisis. Dutch resistance developed early and persisted through the Nazi occupation. Jews participated in the resistance as Dutch nationals, in the same way that they had participated in Dutch life generally. And yet, Jewish losses in Holland were shattering. In Belgium, on the other hand, the losses were much lighter, despite a less active Belgium resistance and the presence of many Jewish refugees, estranged and cut off from Belgium Jewry as well as the general community. In France, the proportion of refugees was very great—possibly as much as half the Jewish population in France during the Nazi occupation was made up of non-French Jews —and French resistance, particularly after 1942, became increasingly active. However, the resistance did not deter the deportations; in fact, the deportations were stepped up at the time that acts of resistance increased, during the winter of 1942. But the overall losses, notwithstanding the very large component of very vulnerable refugees, are considered moderate in the scale of German destruction.[1]

The potency of German control was a determining factor in the extermination program. In the West, from the outset, the German grip was strongest in the Netherlands and Jews lived there in greatest jeopardy. The Germans swept into control in a few days.

During the night of May 9–10, 1940, there were widespread German air attacks against Dutch airfields, communications and ammunition magazines, followed by massed formations of German troops suddenly coming out of the night. Before daybreak a hundred and fifty miles of front were aflame. German troops marched across the Dutch and Belgian frontiers, but the worst terror fell from the skies. Parachutists and troops, landed by air transport, seized the bridges south of Rotterdam. The German plan was to hold the bridges for German forces waiting at the border until the water-protected country submitted. German tanks crossed several of the bridges but the Dutch sealed off those across Rotterdam and wrecked the German plan. The Germans then demanded immediate surrender and threatened to bomb the city. The Dutch were forced to yield. But while surrender negotiations were under way, Nazi bombers swept over Rotterdam and wiped out most of the city. The Dutch long remembered this calculated treachery.

A German civil administration was immediately installed in Holland. At the top stood the *Reichskommissar*, an office invested with absolute power and used with ruthless efficiency by Artur von Seyss-Inquart, the man who had arranged the Anschluss by telephone and who, for a brief time, was Chancellor of Austria. Goebbels regarded this Austrian apprenticeship as particularly valuable training for the handling of subject peoples. Under Seyss-Inquart, native administrative organs were used, as they were throughout Nazi-occupied Europe. In the Netherlands, four German "General Commissariats" were set up to direct the work of the Dutch Secretaries-General, and these Commissariats in turn were responsible to Seyss-Inquart.

As *Reichskommissar*, Seyss-Inquart lost little time in beginning the destruction process in Holland, acting not only upon instructions from Berlin but on his own. The terms of the armistice with Holland, he decided, did not apply to the Jews. They were eternal enemies, "Enemies with whom we can neither come to an armistice nor to peace. . . . The Führer declared that the Jews have played their final act in Europe, and therefore they [have] played their final act."[2]

Seyss-Inquart began with economic measures. On October 22, 1940, he ordered the registration of all Jewish-owned enterprises. Economic destruction followed the Nazi pattern: Jews were dismissed from public office, jobs and professions. In the Aryanization process, the Germans in Holland, as in Bohemia-Moravia, were interested in Jewish property not only for its own sake but also as a lever against native industry. Nearly 21,000 enterprises in Holland were classed as Jewish. There was very little Jewish capital investment in Holland's major industrial concerns or financial institutions, but the Germans were interested in any toehold, however small, and within a few months of the occupation, scores of German business-men came to Holland searching for opportunities.[3] German banks also established branches in the country. After a few months of "voluntary" Aryanizations, Seyss-Inquart required official approval for all transactions and was able to eliminate interested Dutch concerns. He then had to mediate the interests of German businessmen and those of the state, for the less the Jews received, the less could be confiscated from them in the end.

For the Jews involved, half of the 21,000 firms were liquidated: the shops simply went out of existence. Another 800, involving partial Jewish management or ownership, became "self-Aryanized"—the Jews left or sold out their interest. What remained was what particularly interested the Germans: about 300 firms whose productive capacity was suitable for German acquisition.[4] The economic spoliation continued in 1941. In August, all Jewish assets, including bank deposits, cash, securities and valuables were blocked and ultimately confiscated. (These and art objects were valued at 400,000,000 guilders or $212,000,000.) A maximum of only 250 guilders (about $125) per month was permitted to Jews holding such accounts, including the Jews who had sold their businesses.

There are some accounts of Jews who were able to buy their way out of the country by selling their businesses very cheaply and buying exit permits very dearly, but these cases were few. In the summer of 1941, there were also discussions of a project that one bank official called the "ransoming of Dutch Jews against payment of a penance in Swiss francs." It involved Jews with foreign accounts. Initially, the amount of "penance" was fixed at 20,000 Swiss francs per family; later it was raised to 50,000 francs, and, by the time of the deportations, to 100,000 francs. By 1941, Jews were lucky if they could emigrate at all, having given up everything. It is estimated that only 4,000 Jews emigrated or fled from Holland in that year.

The Aryanization process affected the entire Jewish community. The rich were made poor and the middle classes were reduced to subsistence level. Thousands of Jewish workers who had lost their jobs were taken over by the Dutch Welfare Ministry to work in industrial plants or out-door projects in segregated units.

Meanwhile, the S.S. and police were preparing for more drastic measures. The first step was a registration decree signed by Seyss-Inquart on January 10, 1941. There were 140,000 Jews in Holland, including 30,000 to 40,000 refugees from Germany and Austria, concentrated in three large cities. There were also 20,000 *Mischlinge*, Jews in mixed marriages, having varying degrees of "Jewish blood" and involving the racial experts in fantastic efforts, all cast in elaborate scientific language, to determine whether they were Jewish or not. Following the registration, Jews were placed under the direction of a Jewish Council (*Joodse Raad*). This Council came into being in February 1941 under unusual circumstances.

Here, as elsewhere, the Germans counted on the customary stage-managed pogroms to be carried out by their local agents. On February 9, 1941 they provoked the first of the anti-Jewish riots in the city of Amsterdam, where 70,000 Jews lived. Early in the morning a mob of Dutch Nazis marched noisily through the streets of Amsterdam toward the old Jewish quarter. As soon as they arrived, they smashed windows, dragged Jews from moving trolleys, attacked pedestrians, and set fire to several synagogues. It took some hours for the victims to recover from the shock of the attack, but when they did they fought back. With crude weapons and with the aid of Christian neighbors they forced the mob to retreat after a savage battle. In the evening the Nazis came back with reinforcements. The Jews, meanwhile, had gathered up all the iron ware and weapons they could and distributed them among the fighters, many of them factory workers and longshoremen. Patrols of Jewish and non-Jewish workers stood ready to defend Jewish shops. Christian women appeared to take care of Jewish children. The hoodlums struck again and were repulsed, but now the Germans were no longer amused. Armed with automatic weapons and tanks, three battalions of police rolled in and attacked the outnumbered Jews and their friends who were equipped mostly with iron pipes. The Germans inflicted heavy casualties and cordoned off the Jewish section. On the same day, several prominent Jews were summoned to appear before the German commander of Amsterdam and instructed to form a Jewish Council. The Council's first task was to order the surrender of all "weapons" without delay. But the Jews of Amsterdam refused.[5]

A new outbreak of violence occurred a few days later. A German Security Police detachment entered the apartment of a Dutch Jew and was attacked by bullets and acid. In reprisal, 425 young Jews were seized from the streets of the isolated Jewish quarter and deported to Buchenwald. The Dutch were outraged and answered back. Several thousand workers in Amsterdam went out on strike. Soon the strike movement spread and created breakdowns of trolley service and other utilities in Amsterdam. Shipyards were deserted and thousands of workers walked out of armament industries. In Hilversum, where the Germans had arrested ten prominent physicians as hostages, 2,000 workers struck at the Philips plant. Almost 20,000 workers walked out of armaments industries alone. This wave of strikes, the only one in Europe in reaction to the first deportation of Jews, stunned the Germans. But it was soon crushed. Workers were arrested indiscriminately, martial law was declared and sixty Dutch workmen were sent to concentration camps. The strike was broken in two days and heavy fines were imposed on the three guilty cities, Amsterdam, Hilversum and Zaandam. However, other expressions of Dutch solidarity continued.

At first the functions of the *Joodse Raad* in Amsterdam were not quite clear. Following the bloody riots, the deputy of the *Reichskommissar* for Amsterdam called upon two rabbis and Ahen Asscher, a Dutch political figure and owner of a large diamond polishing plant. They were asked to establish an "Advisory Jewish Council" to maintain contact with the Germans. The rabbis pleaded that they had other pressing responsibilities and Asscher suggested Professor David Cohen, who was then chairman of the Committee for Jewish Refugees. The German official then warned that in the future all signs of disobedience would be severely punished and the death penalty imposed on all saboteurs. He advised the establishment of a central Jewish organization to conduct negotiations with the Germans and pledged that no further acts of retaliation would take place once an organization of this kind was established.

Asscher and Cohen immediately called a meeting of certain Jewish leaders and a *Joodse Raad* was established. This development marked a sharp change from a previous decision of other Jewish leaders. Immediately after the outbreak of the war, an organization called the Coordinating Committee had been set up, representing all Dutch Jewish communities and the major national Jewish organizations. This was a genuinely representative Jewish body. However, its chairman, L. E. Visser, rejected on principle any kind of dealing with the Germans, and when the *Joodse Raad* was established, the Coordinating Committee disintegrated. Visser was President of the Supreme Court of Holland and a man highly esteemed by both Jewish and non-Jewish Dutch. An exchange of letters between Visser and Cohen toward the end of 1941 shows that already by then Visser recognized that the *Joodse Raad* would become a tool of the Germans.

Asscher, however, was unable to grasp the enormity of the situation facing the *Joodse Raad*. Neither he nor Cohen could comprehend the depth of Nazi treachery. Asscher, who presided, was at first respected— together with Cohen, he had engaged in extensive rescue activities after 1933, and helped many "illegal" refugees reach Holland—but as the situation worsened, his authority diminished. The Germans used him, occasionally making concessions which imprisoned him further.

For a time, the local communities and national agencies continued their work, but, bit by bit, supervision of their work was absorbed by the *Joodse Raad* and the original modest staff of 25 burgeoned. Asscher and Cohen began to shape the life of Dutch Jews. The *Raad* created an ever-wider organizational network, dealt with many technical details and began to centralize activities affecting Jews throughout the country. At first, very few Jews understood that this trend would benefit only the Germans.[6]

Meanwhile the Nazi S.S. and police machinery was preparing for the total removal of Jews "to the East." The first step had been the decree of January 10, 1941. The letter "J" was added to identification cards in July 1941; travel restrictions were imposed in September and October. The provinces were then partially cleared of Jews and within Amsterdam, where more than half of Holland's Jews were concentrated, three ghetto sections were cordoned off. After May 1942, Jews had to wear the yellow Jewish star.

One of the major Nazi figures in the deportations from Holland was Higher S.S. and Police Leader Hanns Rauter. Like Seyss-Inquart, Rauter was an Austrian and served under him as head of one of the General Commissariats. He had been a *Freikorps* leader in the days following the collapse of the Hapsburg monarchy and a violent racist. It was Rauter and his *Schutzpolizei* who had plucked at random in the streets 425 young Jews and forced them to kneel for hours before being taken to Buchenwald. Rauter's assistant was Dr. Wilhelm Harster, Commander of the Security Police forces in Holland. It was to Harster's staff that Eichmann's IVB4 was attached; Eichmann's agent was Wilhelm Zöpf. One other layer of control existed: since most Dutch Jews lived in or near Amsterdam, a special office was established there, the "Central Office for Jewish Emigration," headed by Ferdinand Aus der Fünten.[7] This office was a complete fraud since virtually no Dutch Jews could emigrate after the German invasion. Orders were passed from Eichmann directly to Zöpf to Aus der Fünten.

The Nazi decrees against the Dutch Jews aroused deep resentment among the Dutch and opposition to them became a badge of patriotism. Not only had their workers led the bold strikes of February 1941, but students went on strike to protest the dismissal of Jewish teachers. To express their sympathy with the wearers of yellow stars, many Dutch citizens wore yellow flowers on their coat lapels. In Rotterdam, signs were plastered on walls throughout the city reminding the Dutch to show respect to Jews on the streets. Non-Jews often shopped for their Jewish neighbors. Intellectuals were outspoken. Both the Protestant and Catholic churches urged resistance to the anti-Jewish decrees. One typical pastoral letter read:

We know what conflicts of conscience result for those concerned. In order, therefore, to eliminate all doubts and uncertainties that you may have in this respect, we hereby declare most explicitly that no compromise in this domain of conscience is allowed; and should refusal of collaboration cause sacrifice to you, then remain steadfast in the certainty that you are fulfilling your duty towards God and man.[8]

But the enemy was too powerful, and 20,000 Dutch Christians were deported to concentration camps because they opposed Nazi racial decrees, many of them first to Buchenwald, where they were slowly tortured, then to Mauthausen in Austria.

Not only did the crushing power of the Nazis in Holland destroy Jews; the geography of the country also conspired against them. Holland is flat, and apart from marshlands in the coastal regions, there are no woods or hiding places. It is also a very small country, making it hard for anyone to submerge. Moreover, there were no exits during the Nazi occupation. On the east was the Reich; to the south was occupied Belgium; and on the west and north, the open sea. The Dutch virtues themselves obstructed the possibilities of sabotage and concealment. Records were meticulously kept and files well ordered, making it easy for Nazis to check on suspects. The small, trim Dutch homes and gardens did not easily lend themselves to underground bunker or tunnel projects. But in the teeth of these immense difficulties, Dutch Christians made thousands of heroic efforts to save Jews and hide them in attics, ceiling spaces and cellars, in private homes, cloisters and orphanges. The concealment of Anne Frank and her family described in the young girl's diary and published in Holland as *Het Achterhuis* (*The Attic*), is only one of many similar experiences.

The Jews of Holland began to hear by postcard from relatives who had been taken hostage during the February demonstrations. However, in the summer of 1941, notices began to arrive from "Standesamt II," Mauthausen, naming certain Jews who had "died of pneumonia" and informing families that their ashes could be collected from the Gestapo for a fee of 75 guilders. When the notices began coming in large numbers, they were passed on to the *Joodse Raad*, which turned them over to Swedish representatives. According to the customs of war, neutral Sweden was entrusted with the protection of Dutch citizens in the Reich and with German nationals in Dutch territory. The Swedish officials tried several times to visit Mauthausen but were held off. After this leakage to Swedish officials, German police in Holland were advised to confine arrested Dutch citizens to Holland where no curious potentially protective power could intervene. Thereafter, the Nazis did not disclose the whereabouts of the inmates and dispensed with sending death certificates to relatives.

In addition to the 425 young Jews who had been sent to Buchenwald, 390 additional hostages were seized during the strike to join them; 59 had died by May 22, 1941. The remainder were then moved to Mauthausen.

Only one has survived to tell the terrible story of Mauthausen and its quarry. The youths seized by Rauter were forced up and down 148 steps in the side of the quarry while carrying heavy boulders. One day some tried to jump over the rock escarpment. They were seen and driven on to a high-voltage wire. Others were forced to jump to their deaths. The lone survivor, Max Nebig, saved his life by volunteering for a human guinea pig operation, after which he was hidden in the TB ward at Buchenwald until the end of the war.[9]

Captain Aus der Fünten's "Central Office for Jewish Emigration," which became responsible for deportations, was created in September 1941 in Amsterdam. However, the mass deportation of Jews from Holland did not start until July 1942. The pace of the destruction of Dutch Jewry was timed to coincide with the preparations at Auschwitz.

On June 23, 1942, Eichmann informed Franz Rademacher, his contact man at the Foreign Office, that from the middle of July on, the Jewish deportation trains from the West would run daily and include 40,000 Dutch Jews in addition to 40,000 French Jews and 10,000 Belgian Jews. For "psychological reasons," the Foreign Office wanted the 25,000 "stateless" refugees in Holland deported first. Nevertheless, naturalized and even native-born Dutch Jews were included among the first arrests made by S.S. Captain Zöpf, Eichmann's agent in Holland, and Aus der Fünten. To stop Swedish intervention, the Reich Main Security Office wanted these Jews deprived of their Dutch nationality as soon as they crossed the frontier, but the Foreign Office feared that if this were done, Sweden would not protect German nationals in Dutch Guiana and elsewhere. However, since the destination of the deportees was not made known, there was no need for a denaturalizing decree. Sweden could not intervene.

Jews were first called to serve in "guarded communal work camps" in Germany. On July 4, 1942, *Sturmführer* Lages instructed Asscher and Cohen of the *Joodse Raad* to provide 4,000 Jews between sixteen and forty for "labor battalions in Germany." The *Joodse Raad* wrote to 4,000 Jews (all refugees) asking them to equip themselves with an eight-day food supply, work clothes and a knapsack and to appear at an appointed assembly point. Fear seized these Jews, as well as anger and indignation. The Germans, fearing that their call-up would fail, organized an extensive manhunt and placed 700 Jews under "protective police detention." These were threatened with deportation to Mauthausen unless the 4,000 appeared. The refugee Jews yielded under this threat and were taken to a camp known as Westerbork, at Assen, among the peat bogs near the German border. Before long, individuals were asked to come to "participate in the reconstruction of the devastated east." Then, each Tuesday morning, 1,500 to 2,000 Jews were forced to leave Westerbork "for the East."

The Germans deliberately used the threat of the concentration camp at Mauthausen as a means of intimidation. In the *Jewish Weekly* for August 7, 1942, published by the *Joodse Raad*, there was an announcement that "all Jews who do not instantly obey the order to go to Germany to ease the labor situation there, will be . . . sent to Mauthausen." The same threat was held over all Jews who refused to wear the Jewish star, and Jews who moved out of restricted areas. Westerbork had once been a camp for Jewish refugees; it was there that some of the passengers of the German liner *St. Louis* were sent in 1939 after a fruitless voyage to Havana. It was now a collecting station for the gas chambers of Auschwitz. For a time, the belief was widespread that deportations were a true "resettlement," but by August 1942 only 400 of the 2,000 Jews summoned reported; rumors were spreading that "resettlement" meant slave-labor camps or worse. On August 13, the German Foreign office representative in Holland, Otto Bene, wrote Berlin that the Jews "understood quickly what was involved from the moment deportations to the East began." By the end of the month, the Nazis had rounded up only 12,000 deportees. Soon, Amsterdam knew the worst. On October 9, Anne Frank, hidden with her family in an Amsterdam warehouse, wrote in her diary: "The British radio speaks of their being gassed."

By September 10, about 15,000 Jews had been deported but Nazi officials complained. Rauter told Himmler that the concentration of Jews was his "greatest headache"; the cooperation of the Dutch police was almost nonexistent. More drastic measures were then taken to ferret Jews out of hiding and reduce the exemptions. After October 15, Dutch Jews could be arrested not only by police, but by members of the armed forces and by Nazi Party members. Inroads were made upon the exempted family dependents of the peat-cutters in the labor camps and exempted employees of the *Joodse Raad*. Aryans who helped Jews across the border or hid them were taken to concentration camps; their property was seized. Informers were spurred by rewards of from 5 to 75 guilders per head. Early in January 1943, a descent was made on the Jewish home for mental defectives, *Apeldoornse Bos*. Nine hundred adults and children were seized and loaded on the cattle-truck train. Stretcher cases could not be reached by attendants locked in a passenger coach. The vans lumbered for four days through Germany to Auschwitz. Still, the desired quotas were not reached.

In April 1943, inspired by the action of Police Major-General Stroop in the Warsaw Ghetto, Rauter decided that Amsterdam must be emptied of its Jews, quarter by quarter, that the exempts must go to the new camp at Vught, and half-Jews, to the provinces. To placate the clergy, Jews in mixed marriages had been temporarily exempted, but as the pressure for more transports built up, degrees of "Jewishness" had to be determined.

At first, marriages between "one-quarter" and "one-half" Jews needed special authorization; later they were denied completely and new marriages between Aryans and "one-half" Jews were forbidden. Involved formulations of "Jewish" characteristics led Jews to make desperate appeals to "experts," often with grotesque results. If a Jew in a modern city did not declare himself, how could he be identified? Circumcision itself was no longer accepted as a valid criterion, inasmuch as "race," not religion, was crucial. An anthropologist in Paris, a Professor Montandon, gravely offered his professional opinion on a typical case: "Blood AB. Feet poorly arched. Septum slightly depressed at extremity. Lips very prominent. Something Jewish about total facial cast. Gestures not Jewish. Circumcision: presents character of Mohammedan operation rather than that of Jewish ritual."[10] The above-described person was declared "more than 80% Jewish." Surveys such as these were paid for and, although it is impossible to know the extent of the deals made, it is likely that the arch of the foot, the prominence of lips and "Jewish facial cast" were made to vary with the financial means of the applicant. Himmler himself is known to have sanctioned such deals involving "important" Jews and large sums of money. A memorandum written by him in December 1942 reveals his strong cash sense layered under mounds of racist preachment and self-intoxication. Considerations of hard currency could bend even Himmler's fanaticism. "I have asked the Führer," he wrote, "about the absolving of Jews against hard currency. He has authorized me to approve such cases, provided they bring in genuinely substantial sums from abroad."

One of the most astonishing decisions of the Nazis involved the 370 Sephardic Jews of Amsterdam who were allowed to ride streetcars without special permission even as the greatest of all Spanish Sephardic communities, that of Salonika, was being destroyed at Auschwitz. It was at first believed that their fortuitous survival resulted from a mere idiosyncrasy of Dr. H. G. Calmeyer, the Commissariat-General for Administration and Justice, who said that the Amsterdam Sephardim "had no affinities with Eastern Jewry." More recently it has been found that in 1942, a move was started by members of certain Dutch resistance groups to save the Sephardic Jews by "proving" that they were "racially" non-Jews. Historical and anthropological quasi-scientific memoranda were prepared and apparently accepted for a time. Dr. Calmeyer (who knew the fate of deported Jews) granted exemptions to the Sephardic Jews based on these "findings." However, as generally happened, Eichmann, with whom Calmeyer struggled, won in the end. The Sephardim were exempted until February 1944 when they, too, were deported to Auschwitz by way of Theresienstadt.[11]

Other exotic exceptions were made: picture experts, a German Olympic champion of 1896, the son-in-law of a former Dutch royal librarian. Official agencies also insisted on exempting certain categories. The armaments office of the Wehrmacht needed diamond cutters and fur dressers, and during 1942, several thousand of these escaped deportation. There was a shifting category called "exchange Jews" who could sometimes be bartered for interned German nationals, but who were often used to bring other Jews in hiding to the surface. Employees of the *Joodse Raad*, which in 1942 numbered 17,000, and converted Jews were exempted for a time, but these exemptions were soon dissolved. In November 1942, the armament industry lost hundreds of its fur and textile workers; in December 1942, Himmler ordered the diamond cutters to be brought to Vught to work for the S.S. Earth and Stone Works. From there they were deported en masse in March 1944.

Through the last few months of 1942, Rauter summarized for Himmler the situation in Holland: 8,000 workers in the Dutch labor service and their 22,000 dependents would be seized in a "lightning blow," arrested and taken to Westerbork and Vught. Of the 20,000 Jews in mixed marriages, he planned to "shove off all Jewish parts . . . insofar as these marriages have produced no children." There were 6,000 in this category. Some 20,000 had already been sent to Auschwitz. The remaining victims, he believed, could be uprooted in a vast manhunt. The Rauter machine operated relentlessly, but his operation fell behind his timetable. By the end of 1942, 38,500 Jews had been deported from Holland. More drastic measures were adopted, but almost two more years were required to complete the deportations from Holland.

The spring and summer months of 1943 were marked by the last large-scale roundups in Holland. From March to May the Germans attempted to clear the small towns and the countryside. By the end of July, 82,000 Jews had been deported from Holland, at the rate of 2,000 a week. The summer transports were allegedly "needed for the new Bunawerk factory at Auschwitz," but the Jews in these transports had gone neither to the factory nor to Auschwitz. During March, April and May, the crematoria ovens were busy with the transports from Berlin and Salonika and in June and July they were immobilized by a typhoid epidemic. Instead of Auschwitz, the 35,000 Dutch Jews transported during this period were shipped to Sobibor, a killing center in the Lublin area of Poland where no selections of any sort ever took place. Among these transports were two consisting of women and children under sixteen from the Vught camp. Their deferment as wives and children of essential workers proved short-lived.

Jews in mixed marriages were also unable to retain their immunity. The Jewish partners in these marriages were forced to choose between sterilization and deportation. Those certified barren by a Gestapo doctor received a special identity card; they also were freed from wearing the Jewish badge and could pursue a limited range of work. Many hundreds submitted to operations; others were able to buy the precious certificates from Gestapo agents. By February 1944, however, more than half of Holland's 20,000 intermarried Jews had also been deported.

The hour for members of the Jewish Council came inevitably, for some in June 1943, and for others the following year. The vise was closing. In March 1944, Rauter wrote to Himmler: "In ten days' time, the last pure Jew will be sent East from Westerbork." Actually, the last deportations from Holland continued until September 1944 when Allied patrols had already reached the Dutch border.

The Germans had tried their best to camouflage the deportations. At first only men in good physical condition were sent to the labor service. They were assured through an official promise given to the Jewish Council that they would work under the same conditions as other Dutch citizens. For a time this was true. Jews worked in Dutch-supervised labor camps under fairly normal conditions while their families received wage payments, though they were somewhat lower than those paid to non-Jews.[12] However, on October 2, 1942, Rauter's "lightning blow" struck. All Jewish workers from the thirty-six labor camps, which had been run until then by the Dutch authorities, were transferred to Westerbork, the deportation assembly depot. The persistent watchword of the *Joodse Raad* at this time was: continue to work as usual in order to avoid the worst.

The *Raad* itself meanwhile had enlarged its operations and employed 380 people (in Amsterdam alone), including Jews who were estranged from Jewish life. A large bureaucracy had developed embracing twenty-five departments responsible for synagogues, hospitals, education, finance, aid to evacuees, Jewish shops, a labor section, a department for youth and pioneer training. Both Jews and non-Jews frequently debated the justification for the existence of a *Raad* as such. Some vehemently denied its right to exist, arguing that it facilitated the devil's work; others claimed that it was able to mitigate hostile decrees and achieve a temporary respite for many Jews. The situation was a cruel centrifuge. Some Jews were not swept into the churning center for several weeks or months. Once, when Professor Cohen was asked, "In your negotiations with the Germans, do you sometimes say 'No,' or is it always 'Yes'?" Cohen replied, "Every time I make a decision, I have Mauthausen before my eyes—weeping mothers, crying children, trembling men and Jewish youngsters killed."[13]

Typical of the rapid escalation of hope and despair experienced by the Dutch Jews was the notice which appeared in the *Jewish Weekly* in October 1942. The *Joodse Raad* was permitted to register Jews who had parents, children or a spouse in Palestine. It was believed that an exchange was to be made with Germans resident in enemy countries. The *Raad* feverishly made the technical preparations, although it had nothing at all to say over the selection of those to be exchanged. The fact that it conducted the registration enhanced temporarily its esteem. However, the first group sent on this exchange basis involved Dutch Jews already in Bergen-Belsen. This was indeed the first and last Dutch Jewish contingent to be saved.

The "privileged" Jew who could hold out a little longer generally held a specially numbered and stamped certificate—the so-called "Sperr" stamp which delayed deportation. The certificate read: "The bearer of this identity card has been released from compulsory labor until further notice." A code number was entered next to this inscription indicating the category of the bearer.

Jews living in mixed marriages with children were included in the series 10,000 to 20,000. Those who had converted to Protestantism before May 9, 1940, were assigned numbers from 20,000 to 30,000. Numbers 30,000 to 40,000 included those Jews who had applied for determination of their family status. Jews who had applied for emigration and whose relatives abroad had deposited a ransom for their release, were given numbers 40,000 to 50,000. Others who were impressed by the Wehrmacht for arms and munitions factories, such as Philips and Unilever, were placed in the series from 60,000 to 70,000. Employees of the *Joodse Raad* were classified in the 80,000 to 100,000 category. Jews who could prove they had commercial relations with England and the United States received the number 120,000. This was said to be the best of the lot, because it was likely to provide security until the end of the war. The Germans, it was thought, intended to use these Jews after the war in order to reestablish commercial ties with foreign countries.[14] This was the life-death roulette. Each time the Germans required another contingent for deportation, the number of "stamp" holders diminished.

This system of "rubber stamps" was the cause of much group dissension, hatred and envy. Some groups were temporarily saved while others were deported quickly. When the *Raad* members and officers obtained a Sperr stamp, the organization became an end in itself. Jews pleaded for jobs on the *Raad*. Eventually, it assumed a grotesque shape: in Leeuwarden alone, for example, over 25 percent of the entire population had posts in the *Raad*. By October 1942, throughout Holland, the *Raad* employed over 17,000 Jews. But the German timetable churned on inexorably. The *Joodse Raad* classification schemes simply delayed the inevitable. The last large-scale actions occurred in May and June 1943 when all exempt categories dissolved and members of the *Raad* were included among the deportees. Rauter then began to hound the hidden Jews.

The Jewish resistance to the Nazi occupation assumed several forms. The eastern European Jews in Holland, who numbered several thousand, tried to organize themselves. From the beginning, they were skeptical of German promises. They had suffered many bitter experiences in the past and many had languished in prison and survived hostile anti-Semitic regimes. They tried, with only limited success, to persuade the more credulous Dutch Jews that the promises of the Germans meant nothing. In 1938 they had organized an extensive relief action to help the first Polish Jews evacuated from Germany and cast into the no-man's-land near the Polish frontier town of Szbonzyn. They also had sent aid to the beleaguered Warsaw Jews up to the time of the German invasion of Holland. When the deportations began, they sent food and other supplies into Westerbork. In the end, they too were deported.

Clandestinely, the Raad tried to blunt the Nazi terror. Some of its principal leaders gave aid to police suspects and maintained contact with the underground movement and the Zionist training farms in Gouda, Werkdorp, Elden and Lundsrecht, which continued to operate until mid-1941. At Lundsrecht, a youth underground had been formed. At the head of this small resistance group were two young teachers, Joachim "Shushu" Simon and his wife Adina. With the aid of friends, and the JDC Rescue Office in Geneva, they had succeeded in smuggling some children into Switzerland. They had cut trails across the mountains from France into temporarily safe zones, but the work was going at a snail's pace while Jewish youth was being snatched to death. A bolder plan was needed. Shushu decided to strike out across the Pyrenees to Spain. Spain was neutral, it was on the Mediterranean and might be a way out to Palestine.

Shushu was a youth in his early twenties. He had fled to Holland from Germany in 1938 and soon became a leader of the Zionist youth movement. He made contacts with the Dutch underground and their leaders were impressed by his striking intellectual gifts and natural leadership quality. The force of his personality and a curious blend of asceticism and physical energy aroused their respect. He could go without food or sleep for long periods at a time. To save a few florins of the scant funds of his group, he would walk for miles in all weather. Despite his coloring and features, which could easily arouse suspicions in Holland, he secured false Aryan papers, went to France to establish contacts and organized a route to the Spanish border and across the Pyrenees.

Shushu personally led groups three times along this perilous route. On the homeward lap of the third expedition, as he crossed the Belgian border back to Holland, he was seized by the Gestapo and imprisoned. The Nazis demanded the names of his accomplices and subjected him to torture. Shushu remained silent for a time, but in January 1943, fearful that he might weaken, he slashed his wrists.

Associated with Shushu's rescue activity was a Christian anarchist and pacifist, Joop Westerweel, a principal of the Lundsrecht high school. In his youth, he had gone as a teacher to the Dutch East Indies where he agitated against the exploitation of the natives. He returned to Holland after six years and established his school along Montessori principles. When anti-Jewish measures were introduced in Holland, Joop made the cause of the Jews his own. Although past forty, with four children, he carried on Shushu's work, leading his young charges to the foot of the Pyrenees and returning to Holland by train, horse cart, or, mostly, by foot, and then preparing for another expedition. One survivor of these journeys recalls Joop's words as he said farewell: "Cross this difficult road successfully and build your homeland, a homeland for the whole Jewish people. But do not forget that you are bound to all humanity, something which you perhaps learned in Holland. Do not forget us, your non-Jewish comrades."

In the summer of 1944, Joop too was captured, flogged, and sent to Vught. After many futile attempts, the Dutch underground established contact with him through a camp physician and attempted a rescue. In a note to the doctor, Joop described his ordeal:

> I was forced to remain on my feet from Thursday noon until Saturday noon without a break, my hands fettered and bound behind my back. I am in a tiny cell in a dark cellar. . . . My daily ration is four slices of bread and a bottle of tea. . . . They interrogate me, bind and beat me. . . . Each question is accompanied by blows and kicks. This morning I was advised that I would be court-martialed. They asked me if I cared to write a letter to my wife. I started eagerly to write but they stopped me and resumed the questioning. . . . I have a moment of respite. But on Monday it will start all over again. . . . I will not reveal any names to them I am certain of this. I still feel strong. At night when there is a respite from the torture, my wounds have a chance to heal. Mornings when question resumes, I am rested and alert. I will remain silent. I am confident of this.[15]

But the plans to rescue Joop, so painstakingly prepared, were never carried out. The doctor was caught and executed and Joop was shot to death in the woods near Vught. A letter from his wife, which reached Palestine in June 1945, was sent to those whom Joop had led.

> How good to get your letter, to know that so many of you reached Palestine. Joop would have found it wonderful if he had known it. He was shot in August. He was the mainstay of the nine others who had worked with him. You did not know him so well, but you can imagine what his loss means to me. . . . On September 6, I was sent to Ravensbrück. I shall not write about the tortures. Of one transport of 750 women, only 250 survived. We were freed by the Red Cross and are now in Sweden.
>
> In September I shall be back in Holland; but what is my house to me? I have heard nothing of my children since August 1944. Write me about Palestine; I am interested in your experiences.[16]

A number of young Dutch Jews managed to get into France by securing certificates as Dutch workers. They were light-haired and pink-cheeked and qualified to work with the German occupation forces; some were even able to secure jobs with the Gestapo. Valuable information was forwarded to the French underground and blank forms and official stamps were delivered to underground printing presses. Most of these "Aryan" workers were ultimately captured.

An expression of Dutch-Jewish solidarity appeared in Palestine in the late months of the war. An appeal was published in *Davar*, the labor daily, signed by a number of Dutch Jews who had escaped to Palestine, urging young Palestinians who had received their agricultural training in Holland to return now that large-scale resistance in Holland had become possible.

There were some attempts to lead a bunker existence in Holland and clandestine organizations rose all over the country to help Jews submerge. Endless ingenuity and stamina were required to make it possible for those who had "disappeared" to exist in the *Verschwindungsplätzer*. Jewish children were sheltered in Christian homes and most of them survived. A group of Utrecht students specialized in finding shelters for them. There was a Dutch Center for Identity Documents, which supplied many Jews with Aryan documents. The Dutch Resistance Movement rallied the Dutch to press on with this work:

> Fellow countrymen: the deportation of all Jewish citizens . . . is the final link in the long chain of inhuman measures. . . . It means the complete annihilation of the Jews. . . . The Netherlands has been deeply humiliated. . . . We must prove our honor is not lost and our conscience not silenced. . . . We ask our fellow Netherlanders to sabotage all preparations and executions of mass deportations. Remember the February strikes when an aroused people proved what it could do! We call upon burgomasters and high officials to risk their positions, if necessary, by refusing to cooperate with the Germans. We expect everyone in the position to do so to sabotage. . . .[16a]

The number of Jews reported in hiding at various periods shows not only Jewish efforts to avoid deportation calls after the summer of 1942, but also the valiant Dutch efforts to save them:[17]

September 11, 1942:	25,000
March 20, 1943:	10,000–15,000
June 25, 1943:	20,000
February 11, 1944:	11,000
At liberation:	7,000

The figures also attest to the last relentless drives of the S.S. to bag their quarry. Often those who had given Jews shelter were also murdered. These figures become heroic when it is recalled that in the last winter of the war, the Dutch also suffered a *Hungertod*. Four hundred people starved to death each day.

It has been estimated that 115,000 Jews were deported from Holland; approximately 100,000 were sent to the killing centers of Auschwitz and

Sobibor, and 15,000 more to Theresienstadt. At least 105,000 perished. In addition to the 7,000 who survived in hiding, there were 8,000 Jews in mixed marriages who survived and a few thousand miscellaneous survivors (those still working for the Germans, Bergen-Belsen survivors and some Sephardic Jews). In Holland, the Germans almost achieved their goal in entirety.

Belgium, like occupied France, was ruled exclusively by German military authorities. However, unlike Holland, which for some Nazis was considered "Germanic" and therefore intended to be a permanent protectorate, Belgium and France were "Romanic" regions to be temporarily occupied and destined for some subordinate position after the war, but not incorporation into a Greater Reich.

The German generals in both Belgium and France were chiefly interested in strengthening German military security and exploiting the economy of the occupied countries. The military authorities in both areas also wanted to avoid being entangled in the Jewish question altogether—not for humanitarian reasons, for they could and did operate with the zeal of the Gestapo often enough—but because they were fully burdened with the basic functions of a military government. In the case of Belgium, there was yet another factor: the Military Commander, General Alexander von Falkenhausen, opposed the Nazi excesses and until his own arrest—he was implicated in the July 20, 1944, conspiracy against Hitler—he more than held his own against the pressure of the Security Police except in the Antwerp area where the Gestapo was strong.

Although, at the highest level, German control in Belgium was complete, the actual day-by-day administration of the country was carried out by the old machinery of the Belgian state, that is, the civil service acting under the secretaries-general of the various government departments. (In all of Belgium in the summer of 1942, there were only 830 German civilians.) From being permanent heads of departments under a minister, many assumed the status of ministers with wide powers which they frequently exercised in the German interest.[18] Some Belgian officials, however, used their knowledge and power to circumvent German edicts and Jews were helped immensely by their interventions.

On the eve of the German invasion, the Jewish population in Belgium was about 90,000, heavily concentrated in Antwerp and Brussels and comprising large numbers of refugees. About 30,000 were refugees from Germany. As German forces began to cross the border, there was a mass flight to France and almost half the total Jewish population in Belgium fled. On October 28, 1940, when all Jews were ordered to register with the police, 42,000 reported. The Germans added 10,000 to this figure to account for the estimated number of Jewish children who were being sheltered but had not registered. There were also several thousand adults who did not register, most of them from the well-assimilated native-born Jewish population. Within the following year, the Germans tried to form a Jewish Council, but most of the prominent Belgian Jews, except two well-known rabbis, had fled the country. One of them, Dr. Salomon Ullmann, formed a committee of Jews which was transformed into the *Association des Juifs en Belgique* (Association of Jews in Belgium) on November 25, 1941. This group, however, did not yield to the demands of the S.S. deportation agents except in Brussels where, according to a Belgian government report submitted at the Eichmann trial, "the German authorities pushed their machiavellianism to the limit of forcing the Jewish Association to distribute the summonses [for deportation]." The roundups were made by German police.

Within a few months following the German occupation, preliminary anti-Jewish measures were enacted. The definition of "Jew" was formulated; Jewish lawyers and civil servants were ousted from their positions; Jewish-owned enterprises were Aryanized or liquidated, a process which took about a year to complete. To the great disappointment of the Germans, the Belgian Jews did not have much wealth to plunder. The Military Commander's report for October 1940 admitted that "the influence of Jewry upon economic life in Belgium has been rather slight. Apart from the diamond industry in the Antwerp area, Jewish participation in the Belgian economy is hardly worth mentioning."[19]

By the end of 1942, 6,388 Jewish-owned business were liquidated, and 588 were *entjudet*, that is, transferred to Aryan owners. Other confiscated assets, including bank deposits, stocks and bonds and real estate parcels, were valued at 126,800,000 reichsmarks. The resale of some of this wealth posed special problems for the military command. Belgians were averse to buying former Jewish property and the president of the Brussels Stock Exchange refused to accept securities in the absence of the Jewish owners. The shares were finally stamped "property of the German Reich," to be sold on the exchange or auctioned off to the highest bidder by the three German banks in the country.[20]

In October 1941, a curfew was established for Jews, and Jewish residence was restricted to Antwerp, Brussels, Liège and Charleroi. In May 1942, Jews were required to wear the Jewish star and men between sixteen and sixty and women between sixteen and forty were taken for forced-labor projects at Audinghem. The badge decree was opposed not only by the Belgians but by Brigadier General Eggert Reeder, the German Military Administrator under von Faulkenhausen, who apparently hoped to placate Belgian opinion. Reeder consistently refused to implement the decree and the Belgians made the wearing of the star a national cause. Teachers told their students that the star was a mark of distinction. Shopkeepers in

Antwerp sold Jewish stars in the Belgian national colors. In Brussels, on the first Sunday after the decree was issued, the streets were filled with throngs of Belgians wearing Jewish stars.[21] A conference of Belgian mayors met in Brussels and denounced the order.

In the discussions in 1942 on the projected deportations from Belgium, German officials expressed misgivings about the situation in Belgium. Werner von Bargen, the Foreign Office representative, complained that the Belgians had no "understanding" of the Jewish question. The Jews themselves, he added, were restless and the Germans had inadequate police forces. The first seizures, therefore, would be directed against Polish, Czech, Russian and other foreign Jews.[22] The first Belgian deportation quota was set at 10,000. In June, a transit camp was established at Malines, from which the trains were to run to Auschwitz. The first group of Jews, all foreign-born, left on August 4.

At first, Jews reported on the basis of a "report-for-work" order, but within a few months no Jews voluntarily reported. Subsequently, they had to be forcibly seized by German police. Eichmann complained to von Bargen via the Foreign Office about the composition of the transports. There were no native-born Jews, he wrote, and his instructions were not being carried out properly. By the middle of September the initial quota had been filled but von Bargen himself had observed large-scale evasions. Jews were hiding with Belgian families. Many had Belgian identification cards and still others were fleeing to France.[23]

The Belgian police were deftly noncooperative, losing and misplacing files on Jews and forging and manufacturing documents for them. Several Belgian officials in the Ministry of Justice saved some Jews by intervening directly. They also made substantial sums of money available for the Jewish Defense Committee which supplied thousands of Jews with false documents and supported Jews in hiding. Major E. Calberg, an official in the Food and Supply Ministry, persuaded the Red Cross to surrender to him a thousand food parcels which he distributed to Jews in hiding.[24] The Department of Registry helped Jews evade deportation by facilitating mixed marriages.

Belgian clergymen were among the most active in Europe in aiding and rescuing Jews, particularly Jewish children. Abbé Joseph André and Father Edouard Froidure saved hundreds of children with the help of generous neighbors, merchants and Belgian officials, while the people as a whole were strengthened in their resistance by the strong denunciation of the Nazi occupation by the Primate of Belgium, Joseph-Ernest Cardinal van Roey. Belgian railway workers left doors of deportation trains open to facilitate escapes. Other Belgians helped postal officials intercept exposures of Jews addressed to German authorities and warned the Jews threatened by informers. The Nazi deportation experts were effectively hamstrung.

In mid-September, Eichmann's agent in Belgium, Asche, called the members of the Jewish Association into his office and threatened the evacuation of all Jews from Belgium as punishment for their brazen passive resistance. Rabbi Ullmann and four associates were sent to the concentration camp at Breendonck. But the Germans still had their problems. By November 11, von Bargen reported to the Foreign Office that 15,000 Jews had been successfully deported, but that the roundups were increasingly difficult. Rumors of the "butchering of Jews" had spread. The Foreign Office then began to exert new pressure on the Military Administration to make a redoubled effort to hunt down Belgian nationals. A June 1943 report of the German Military Administration acknowledged that after having eliminated the Jews from the social and economic life of the country, the next stage was deportation. This, however, belonged to the "competent service of the Reich"—Eichmann's department.

After October 1942, strong young men from the conscript labor camps were included in the Auschwitz transports but attempted escapes became more frequent. On January 15, 1943, several dozen men cut their way out of a train with smuggled saws. On April 22 Belgian railwaymen left doors open in a transport containing over 1,500 Jews. Other railway workers held up a train between Tirlement and Visé, where the Committee for Jewish Defense had planned an ambush. Although 150 Jews escaped, 20 were killed in the cross fire, and over 100 were wounded. The recaptured Jews, including the wounded, were taken back to Malines and put on the July 31 transport. From this, 39 Jews escaped.

In 1943, transports of 1,500 to 1,600 Jews were filled every few months and by September 1944, when Belgium was liberated, in spite of the diminishing flow, 25,000 Jews had been delivered to Auschwitz. Some native-born Jews were first noticed in the August 3 transport and over 700 were deported on September 19, after the Gestapo invaded the homes of Jews in Antwerp and shipped them in furniture vans to Malines and then to Auschwitz. This Gestapo raid occurred contrary to the pledge Reeder had made to the Dowager Queen Elisabeth and Cardinal van Roey not to permit the deportation of native Belgian Jews, and attests to the about-face the Foreign Office made in finally yielding to Eichmann's demands to deport native Belgian Jews.[25]

In France, the Germans were balked at this line.

21 France

FRANCE, on the eve of the German invasion, was a sorely divided nation. As in England, there were many conservative and right-wing forces in the country which secretly and often openly were in sympathy with Hitler and rooted for a Fascist victory. The Left, on the other hand, had no heart for the war. They were fighting a diseased capitalism at home and only dimly saw the danger of Hitlerism. Their lodestar, the Soviet Union, was neutralized by the Nazi-Russian Pact and their leaders scored the French and British ruling classes for Russia's isolation. Innumerable political crises exhausted and embittered all parties and class hatreds all but erupted in civil war. Moreover, Frenchmen had no satisfactory answer to the question: What is Europe fighting for? The Left felt no sympathy for the reactionary Polish government which, after Munich and the acquisition of Teschen, became Hitler's lackey, while the French masses felt no call to "die for Danzig," or back the government that had undermined the French security system in eastern Europe. The propertied classes, trembling lest their interests be shattered by socialist revolution, peaceful or bloody, tried desperately to hang on to whatever promised to preserve the status quo. In this reflex of fear, the liberal bourgeoisie, the class that had supplied the Republic with so many good servants in the past, became sterile. Even worse, it betrayed the national interest and was ready to barter French independence for crumbs of security. It was this class that provided the gravediggers of France.

Only one emotion united the nation: all classes painfully remembered the horrible losses of World War I and shrank from the threat of a general war.

After the invasion of Poland, many Frenchmen believed that the Polish Army would offer long and stubborn resistance. Instead, it collapsed in three weeks. But in that critical interval, the French Army did nothing to threaten Germany on the west. This wasted opportunity to win a quick victory over the Germans was France's last. There followed the dreary *drôle de guerre*, the phony war, during which the Allies kept insisting that time was working for them, whereas the reverse was true. Nothing had been learned from the German blitzkrieg in Poland. The French generals did nothing to modernize material or tactics. Instead of building tanks, planes and antiaircraft artillery, they elaborated the movements of an outmoded foot-slogging army supported by horse-drawn artillery. Their biggest fear seems to have been the dread of traffic jams caused by motorized equipment. Added to this incapacity to coldly analyze the new German techniques of making and winning wars was political indecision. Premier Edouard Daladier exasperated his General Staff with his indecisiveness and resigned in March 1940, still uncertain whether to send expeditionary forces to Finland or Norway. The mood of the country, inevitably, was one of deep frustration.

Daladier was succeeded by Paul Reynaud,[1] a much sharper and bolder man, equipped not only with a brilliant intellect but armed with faith in the Allied cause. Reynaud was also among the very few men in France at the time who understood the character of modern warfare as well as the benighted economic orthodoxy of the Third Republic. But he recruited his associates too casually, overspent his energies in verbal pyrotechnics and lost his footing in a whirl of superficial social episodes. He had—and justifiably so—a poor opinion of the French High Command, which still thought in terms of the strategies of 1914, and discarded the archaic Commander in Chief Maurice Gamelin, but then replaced him with Maxime Weygand, a man already in his seventies, recalled to duty after long years of retirement. As fatefully, he summoned the aged Marshal Henri Pétain from his post as Ambassador to Spain to become Vice-Premier. Pétain, the hero of Verdun, was already eighty-three. Momentarily, the recall of these patriotic veterans, whose names were linked to the memories of 1916 and 1918, gave comfort to the French people and lifted them from the depths of their first despair over the French defeat in Norway. Public morale was lifted. But in both men, there lay the instinct to submit. Already by May 17, Weygand was quoted as saying that the war was lost and that reasonable conditions for an armistice should be accepted. Philosophically, he saw the European struggle not so much as a battle for national survival as a struggle between Teutonic and Anglo-Saxon civilizations, between which he felt there was little to choose. The British complained that his plans were nebulous; they and he were constantly at cross purposes. The vision of a stampeding Nazi victory seems constantly to have been before him, while the great untapped strengths—an untouched French Navy, the French Empire, a fighting England—were never drawn into his thinking. Corroding doubt about the Battle of France gripped Reynaud and left him inert in both political and military matters. He could have had de Gaulle at his side, but chose not to, until it was too late. He kept the government in Paris too long and fragmented all government power in hasty disorganized flight to Tours and neighboring areas. In the end, his proclaimed faith in an Allied victory, his promise never to make a separate peace without England and his belief that it was impossible as well as intolerable to make an accommodation with Hitler —all were whittled away. He concluded separate armistices with Germany and Italy.

On June 9, meanwhile, Pierre Laval, a former Premier and arch collaborationist, assured Rome and Berlin that he "and others" could force the resignation of the government and ground French arms. Laval had already discussed tentative armistice terms leading to a "soldier's peace" and a possible declaration of war against Britain. On June 11, Weygand told Reynaud that the Battle of France was irreversibly lost and that the government must now concern itself with maintaining order "to avoid the danger of Communism which so often follows in the wake of a military defeat."

For a few brief days, Reynaud considered shifting the base of French independence and military power to North Africa. De Gaulle, in London, was to arrange for the transport of men, weapons and supplies. But Reynaud weakened. His Cabinet was drifting away from him and Pétain threatened to resign unless an armistice was immediately requested. In this hour when the French Parliament was dispersed, Reynaud refused to assert his leadership and bowed to the Cabinet.

A compromise was finally reached, it was said, "to spare public opinion," but, in fact, it tied France hand and foot and made a further struggle impossible. Instead of crossing the Mediterranean and then asking for armistice terms, the Cabinet decided not to leave French soil until the armistice terms were made known and found clearly unacceptable. This proviso was added allegedly to prove to the French public that the government was leaving only when it became impossible to negotiate honorably with Hitler. Thus, the advantage of enjoying the freedom to parley from Africa was deliberately given up. Reynaud yielded.

On June 16, Pétain became head of the Cabinet. With great relief over the turn of events, he asked for an immediate armistice. His offer of surrender came eight full days before the firing actually stopped. In those eight days, over a million French prisoners were rounded up by the Germans without having had any chance to strike back, and Hitler crossed the Loire, securing a large chunk of French territory.

On July 11, 1940, an authoritarian regime was installed in France with Marshal Pétain as head of state. Laval was named Vice-President of the Council of Ministers. Political and civil liberties were suppressed. The ailing Third French Republic was dead, as Laval himself had declared three days before its demise: "Since parliamentary democracy wished to enter the ring against Nazism and Fascism," he cried out to the deputies, "and since it has lost the fight, it must disappear from the face of the earth."

Shocked by the sudden turn in their lives, the French now began a long and bitter trial—the Nazi occupation. The country was divided into two zones, the northern one under German military control, and the southern, so-called Free Zone, enjoying the fiction but not the reality of independence under Pétain, with its capital at Vichy. (In November 1942, the Germans and their Italian allies occupied the Free Zone and the line of demarcation collapsed.) Two thirds of the country was held by Germany. This area included the plains and broad uplands and verdant valleys of France which produce two thirds of the nation's foodstuffs. To maintain the huge garrison of three million German troops, France had to print four hundred million francs daily and pay a daily indemnity of twenty million francs. Under the armistice, the French fleet was "demobilized and disarmed" under German supervision. The collaborators serenely awaited a German victory and softer peace terms. Meanwhile, they boasted, forty whole departments in France had been spared the German heel.

Pétain was granted plenary powers, both executive and legislative; the National Assembly became a cipher. Moreover, all Vichy decrees were ineffective unless approved by the Nazi military authority. This reservation enabled Germany to exert pressure on the French Government in the Free Zone and affected the fate of Jews in France. Pétain quickly realized that he would need Laval to bolster his shaky regime and be a match for all—opponents, intriguers and hangers-on—who caballed at the Vichy court. The aged Pétain could work only two or three hours a day and Laval became the real power at Vichy.

More than Nazism, Pétain despised and feared democracy. He feared social upheaval even more. He was backed—and maneuvered—by Laval, and although Laval's treachery went too far for the old Marshal in December 1940 (Laval was forced to resign from the Cabinet because of secret negotiations with the Germans) he was restored to grace in April 1942. The names of the two men are linked with the tragic downfall of France in 1940. Although out of power during 1935–40, Laval's plotting and systematic lying and deceit during this period paved the way for the French mood of surrender. His skill lay in exploiting the crisis in French life to enlist supporters and create the atmosphere of submission to a New Order. Through shrewd manipulation of the press he created substantial support for a policy of appeasement. To the propertied class he promised confirmed possession of their wealth; to many of the Socialists, everlasting peace. Cleverly, he united all of the counterrevolutionary forces against the image of Léon Blum, Socialist Premier of France in 1937, architect of the Popular Front, and Jew. When Pétain became Head of State in 1940, he deliberately associated the name of Blum with the decline and defeat of France, although Blum had been out of office for over two years before the war started. Blum, Pétainists said, was the man of Stalin and Stalin justified Hitler. As with all such glib syllogisms, the man's real ideas were of no account.

As Minister of Foreign Affairs in 1934–35, Laval had given Mussolini the blank check to take Abyssinia. He received Ribbentrop cordially while Hitler was manifestly planning to remilitarize the Rhineland, and saw fit to rescue the Polish Foreign Minister Józef Beck when certain Polish leaders were doing their best to remove him in the interests of closer French-Polish ties. In his buying off of editors and publishers to take a pro-German line, Laval was helped in the middle thirties by a young German in Paris named Otto Abetz. Abetz was then a representative of the Nazi Party's Foreign Affairs Bureau, and Ribbentrop's unofficial delegate when he became German Foreign Minister in 1938. Abetz was also the fountainhead of German subsidies to numerous French groups. Laval and Abetz shared in common many French acquaintances—among them some of the most pro-Hitlerite men in the country, including Fernand de Brinon and Jean Luchaire. These men had staked everything on a German victory and their press campaigns scattered in papers of every coloration assiduously took a pro-Nazi line. Later, during the German occupation, these three men, Laval, Abetz and de Brinon, were escalated to power in a wholly new set of relationships.

Abetz became Ambassador of the Reich, with the full power of Ribbentrop's Foreign Office behind him; de Brinon was installed in Paris with the title of French Ambassador. He handled the political relations between Vichy and Berlin with his old German companion of an earlier day, Abetz. Laval, in the central seat of power again, though at first in a somewhat restricted framework, finally gave full scope to his scheming nature. He schemed to declare war on England; he pilfered shamelessly from public funds; he schemed to give Germany use of overseas military bases and the French fleet. And yet this traitor whose name has become synonymous with French national dishonor may have saved thousands of lives of Jews in Vichy France by holding on to some irreducible core of principle. He willingly enough gave up the refugee Jews to the Germans but refused to turn over French Jewish nationals, either native-born or naturalized.

In 1939, there were approximately 270,000 Jews in France, 200,000 of whom lived in Paris. Possibly as many as 30,000 had fled from Germany. In the wake of the German invasion of western Europe in May 1940, more than 40,000 additional Jews from Holland and Belgium streamed into France seeking refuge. Out of this new total of 310,000, about 150,000 were foreign-born, and of these, more than half were "stateless," that is, they were refugees and émigrés from Germany, Austria, Poland, Romania and Hungary—countries that were either under German domination or that had passed anti-Jewish laws depriving Jews of nationality. These "stateless" and immigrant Jews in France perished during the Nazi occupation. These Jews were sacrificed by Vichy. The native and naturalized French Jews were saved.

Hitler did not expect to conquer France and the Low Countries in six short weeks and had to improvise a conqueror's policy in the early months following the stunning German victory. There were no demographical plans for the massive shifting of populations, as in Poland. Nor was France considered as a possible laboratory for working out the "Jewish problem" in the light of Nazi race theories. In the Nazi racial schema the French had a very dubious position. During the first few months after the military victory, the Germans did not seem to care how many Jews lived in the Vichy Zone. For a time, it was even used as a dumping ground for unwanted German Jews. In no sense was it thought of as a privileged part of Europe to be purged of Jews.

To the French authorities in Vichy, the German victory was not only welcome but decisive, and German demands were not opposed, particularly in the early phase of the occupation. However, when demands for the destruction of Jews were intensified, and drastic action against French Jews was planned, Vichy resisted. The collaborators recoiled from sending their own nationals to their death. This reaction had at least two aspects: the first was Vichy's bargaining power—the Germans had to have French help under the conditions of their rule in France; the second was the French brand of anti-Semitism which expressed itself in a strongly nationalistic xenophobia. The foreign Jews were considered good riddance by many French.

For the Germans, it was vital that the Jews appear to have been tagged, arrested and deported by the French themselves. Moreover, they realized that anti-Jewish measures would have to proceed at a slower rate than in the East. Too shocking a show of brutality at first might provoke anti-German resistance. In addition, the Germans lacked sufficient police to cover the entire country and had to rely ultimately on French forces. If local French police were used, they could then assert that France was acting on her own to purge the country of its Jews. Eichmann's men at first remained in the background and acted through the German Embassy and the military administration. Some officials slyly suggested that the French be allowed to abrogate certain German measures to stimulate their own initiative on the Jewish question, but Theodor Dannecker, Eichmann's representative, soon found reason to intervene directly and the German military administration could not stem his demands.

The Vichy Government attitude toward the Jewish question was defined in an official statement made October 17, 1940. The focus is sharply on the foreign Jews:

> In its task of national reconstruction, the government has had, from the very first, to study the problem of Jews and of certain other foreigners who, abusing our hospitality, have contributed not a little to our defeat. . . . With certain quite honorable exceptions . . . the dominating influence of the Jews has made itself everywhere felt, especially in public services, leading finally to decomposition. All observers agree in affirming the evil effect of their activity in recent years. . . . Our disaster imposes on us the task of regrouping French forces whose characteristics have been fixed by long heredity.[2]

Administratively, each ministry at Vichy had a special delegate in Paris through whom it controlled its regional machinery in the Occupied Zone. The delegates of all ministries in Paris (in the Occupied Zone) were subordinated to a general delegate, Ambassador de Brinon. Furthermore, Vichy legislation covered occupied as well as unoccupied territory. Thus, the Jews in the Occupied Zone suffered a double oppression: French and German. In November 1942, when the demarcation line collapsed, German measures were enforced in all of France.

The early Vichy collaboration exceeded the hopes of the Nazis. The French adopted strong anti-Jewish measures without any prodding. They showed a truly amazing "understanding" of the Jewish problem, the Germans said. Under the *Statut des Juifs* of October 4, 1940, Jews were ousted from all public and administrative functions and from military positions; they were forbidden to teach in schools and colleges. In the liberal professions they were subject to a *numerus clausus*. They were also defined in accordance with the Nuremberg principle and were required to register. All refugee Jews forfeited all French civil rights, were not permitted to work, and were subject to internment. The French also set up a large administrative machinery to enforce these and subsequent regulations. The main components were a Jewish card-index system in the Paris prefecture of police, a special Police for Jewish Affairs, and an Aryanization agency (*Service du Controle*). Temporarily, the French resisted setting up a special Department for Jewish Affairs but, under pressure from Dannecker, yielded in April 1941. Xavier Vallat, a notorious French anti-Semite, was the first head of the *Commissariat Général aux Questions Juives*. In June 1942, he was succeeded by Louis Darquier de Pellepoix.

The Pétain regime, representing strongly nationalistic, clerical and military elements was reminiscent of the anti-Dreyfus coalition of the previous century and drew substantial popular support. Pétain was hailed as a savior by many French. Long-repressed quislings sprouted. A Nazified press declared itself the true voice of the French people. The official collaboration and the splitting of the country into two zones along a line of demarcation (which Pétain himself called "a halter around the throat of France") enabled the Germans to rule with a minimum of opposition. More than three million Germans stood menacingly on French soil. Vichy theoretically had very substantial bargaining power—it could threaten to release the French fleet to the British and order French colonial troops in North Africa to go over to the British—but these threats were never used. Laval eagerly hoped and worked for a British defeat and Pétain plainly expected a German victory. The Germans had only to worry about their dependence on native French administrators. A large French bureaucracy was needed to do Nazi tasks. In the later phases of the German occupation, this dependence gave Vichy the only measure of bargaining power it did use.

In the German power structure in France, the military administration was at first supreme in all matters. At the head of the military command from October 1940 to February 1942 was General Otto von Stülpnagel. From February 1942 to July 1944, the military commander was Heinrich von Stülpnagel, one of the generals in the Halder "conspiracy" against Hitler and subsequently involved in the July 20 attempt to kill Hitler and overthrow the Nazi regime. This Stülpnagel came to hate the brutality and terror of the Heydrich-Himmler organization and refused to lend his troops to their roundups of Jews. Just before the assassination attempt in July 1944, he arrested and locked up all 1,200 S.S. and S.D. men in Paris. However, he did his share in making the lot of the French—both Jewish and non-Jewish—fearful enough. He was a great believer in the deterrent power of shooting hostages and executed thousands in France.

Before long, two other forces were to crowd the military power over Jewish matters and then take complete control. One was Otto Abetz, once again in Paris as the Foreign Office designate, this time attached to the staff of the military commander.

By August 1940, Abetz had already been elevated to the rank of ambassador, responsible for all political matters in both occupied and unoccupied France. The enforcement of his policy depended upon military cooperation, and in matters affecting Jews, he received it. The second force, of course, was the S.S. and police. Himmler's men came on the scene more slowly and first attached themselves to Abetz. By 1942, they dominated both Abetz and the military.

The S.S. frequently clashed with the military in France, as elsewhere. Impatient to start the German occupation with swift anti-Jewish actions, Heydrich briefly experimented with drastic expulsions within France in the Polish manner in the summer and fall of 1940. He began by expelling French Jews from Colmar in Alsace, in occupied France. To the Germans, of course, Alsace was German. The expulsion started on July 16, 1940, and continued until October. Within these three months, 22,000 French Jews from Alsace-Lorraine were piled on trucks, driven across the demarcation line into Vichy France and dumped on country roads. These expulsions also included "asocials," criminals, Gypsies and insane people. By November 1940, an additional 47,000 Jews were deported from Lorraine—also claimed as German territory—to Lyon.[3]

The Alsace-Lorraine deportations had a by-product, the so-called "Aktion Bürckel." With the connivance of the local German administrators, Josef Bürckel and Robert Wagner, and on the basis of secret instructions from Heydrich, the S.S. seized 7,450 Jews from the Baden-Saar area in Germany and dumped them in Vichy France. Heydrich instigated this move without first checking with his technical superior, Minister of Interior Wilhelm Frick. Already short of dumping ground in the Government-General in Poland, Heydrich may have momentarily been thinking of using Vichy territory as a "first stage" for expelled German Jews, pending the final stage. But his actions drew strong protests. Hitler intervened personally and stopped all further deportations into the Free Zone. Evidently he did not want to antagonize Vichy unduly and may still have wanted to use Jews as potential hostages. Madagascar was still being dangled on the international scene; Vichy was not yet softened up.

Under the law of October 4, 1940, foreign and stateless Jews were subject to internment. The Jews of Baden and the Saarland were removed swiftly—some at twenty minutes' notice—and pushed into goods trains and taken across France to the camp of Les Milles near Aix-en-Provence and to camps at Gurs and Rivesaltes in the Pyrenees. Many of the deportees were ill and bedridden. Some were very old and there were numerous deaths on the journey. Eichmann boasted that "this operation was scarcely noticed by the public." Jews and other prisoners in the camps lived in crowded barracks where they slept on the ground, suffered from hunger and cold and were devoured by vermin. In the winter of 1940–41, eight hundred of the Baden-Saar group died.

The French camps could at first provide neither food nor shelter for the deportees. On October 29, General Otto von Stülpnagel transmitted a protest to the German Foreign Office from the French Armistice Commission. On November 19 Marshal Pétain requested that the deportees be returned to Germany, but the Foreign Office decided to treat this note "in a dilatory manner." A week later, von Stülpnagel was told that no action would be taken. The Saar-Baden Jews were not set at liberty. Those who survived until November 1942, when Vichy camps fell into German hands, were sent to Auschwitz.[4]

The concentration camps in France, operated by French personnel, represented a victory for Nazi doctrines. The victims were systematically dehumanized by officials using methods starkly described in Arthur Koestler's book *Scum of the Earth*. French camp commandants robbed the internees of their meager supplies; sadistic guards brutalized them; physicians prescribed violent death-dealing exercises for them. By the end of 1942, officials of these camps had sent 42,000 Jews to the East—to death —in cattle trains.

The camps, euphemistically called "shelter camps," had been originally established before the war to accommodate Loyalist refugees from Spain. Subsequently, the same wretched buildings were used to house thousands of "enemy" aliens and stateless persons, most of them Jews. When Pétain assumed power, he had at his disposal in unoccupied (Vichy) France alone twenty-six camps with a total capacity of 100,000 internees. Starvation and inhuman physical conditions killed off many of the prisoners before they were sent to the death camps; many thousands were temporarily saved by the heroic efforts of unsung Jewish and non-Jewish relief organizations which worked diligently to improve camp life and help some of the inmates escape. A nonsectarian organization known as the Nîmes Committee gained the gratitude of many a prisoner.

After Hitler's action against dumping Jews in the Vichy Zone, Heydrich's hand was stayed for the moment. However, his driving ruthlessness while others were still cautious, had already found other outlets. The refugee Jews were to be his first large kill. There were 40-50,000 refugee Jews in France who had recently fled from Holland, Belgium and Luxembourg. Abetz wanted Vichy to take responsibility for their arrests and internment under the *Statut des Juifs*. Heydrich, however, insisted that the arrests be made by his Security Police, not the French. Their nationality already forfeited, approximately 20,000 refugees were imprisoned from the summer of 1940 on through 1941 in the Vichy Zone. The camps were at Gurs, Les Milles, Rivesaltes, Noé, Récébédon and La Vernet.

In Paris, the Germans watched these developments with approval. They saw in the Vichy measures a basis for similar action in the Occupied Zone. Heydrich now stood ready to inflict the most drastic measures. But first, the military administration played its role in the economic spoliation of French Jews.

On October 18, 1940, General Otto von Stülpnagel signed a decree which defined Jewish enterprise and required that it be registered. The Aryanization process was to be handled by French officials because of the shortage of German personnel. In principle, the French were to appoint their own trustees and let the French benefit from the liquidation of Jewish economic life in the Occupied Zone. Exceptions, however, were made in all cases "where important German interests" were at stake. These interests concentrated on Jewish-owned industry. The Germans wanted speedy results, but the process was slow. The French started a campaign to deter potential buyers and undermine the trustees. The Germans countered with all sorts of legal arguments and finally urged that Jews sell their businesses themselves to "ease the mind of the French purchaser," but the program crept along very slowly. After almost two years of Aryanization in the Occupied Zone and a year in the Vichy Zone, only 21 percent of Jewish-owned enterprise was Aryanized.[5]

Heydrich now stepped into the slow French operation and reset the machinery. In December 1940, S.S. Lieutenant Theodor Dannecker, Eichmann's S.D. subordinate in Section IV B4 installed himself in Paris at 72 Avenue Foch with his staff. Their purpose was to bring Vichy into line on the Jewish question and accelerate the tempo of anti-Jewish measures. Each week both Stülpnagel and Abetz sent representatives to Dannecker's office to consult with this ex-lawyer transformed by Nazism into a feared Gestapo power. Within six months, he felt he had done enough to merit a 96-page inventory of his activities. In that time, he had turned on a barrage of propaganda aimed at segregating the French Jews from the rest of the population. He had created an Anti-Jewish Institute in Paris to give a "French twist to anti-Jewish propaganda." In April 1941, he had pressed the Vichy Government to establish the Commissariat for Jewish Questions to oversee the work of the trustees and Jewish organizations. Still dissatisfied, Dannecker kept prodding Vichy to adopt more severe measures.

Meanwhile, roundups of Jews were started in the Occupied Zone. Dannecker put to use for the first time the card index kept at the Paris prefecture of police. On May 14, 1941, 3,649 naturalized Polish Jews were rounded up and sent to concentration camps. This represented some progress for the Gestapo, but Dannecker was forced to admit that these arrests had "created more stir in Vichy circles than the arrest of 30,000 unwanted Jews from the Reich at the end of 1940." The French were not responding as he had hoped.

In August, there was another seizure of 3,429 Jews involved in "Communist de Gaullist misdeeds and assassination attempts against members of the Wehrmacht." These victims were interned in three camps in the Occupied Zone: Drancy near Paris, Pithiviers and Beaune-la-Rolande.

Dannecker had just begun to sink his teeth into his job, but for the Jews of France the persecutions were a nightmare. Letters of bewilderment, humiliation and protest were sent to Marshal Pétain and Xavier Vallat. They invoked the French Jews' traditional love of country and the honorable service of French Jews in its defense. The Acting Grand Rabbi of France, Jacob Kaplan, wrote to Vallat on July 31, 1941, asking how a Christian could possibly defame Judaism, the mother of Christianity, the foundation of the religious morality of the West, the religion of Christ. Rabbi Kaplan then quoted Pascal, Montesquieu, Chateaubriand and other

Christian writers to support his argument. He recalled to Vallat the military record of French Jews. Vallat replied though his *Chef de Cabinet*, Jarnieu:

> Dear Rabbi:
> I have the honor to acknowledge receipt of your letter of July 31, in which you quoted to me a certain number of texts which are of course well known. They would not have been refuted in any French legislation if there had not been, during the last few years, an invasion of our territory by a host of Jews having no ties with our civilization.
> I do not intend to refute in detail a certain number of your arguments, in particular the statistics you give of the Jews who have entered the armed forces and died for France. This is a matter which deserves too much respect to become the object of a controversy.
> Let me simply point out that in the government's attitude there is no anti-Semitism, simply the application of reasons of state.[6]

Jarnieu's letter reveals a certain uneasy defensiveness that was shared by other French officials. How far could they, as Christians, proceed against the Jews? On August 7, two days after Jarnieu replied to the rabbi, Marshal Pétain himself sent an inquiry to the French Ambassador at the Vatican, Léon Bérard, to ascertain the Vatican's attitude toward the anti-Jewish measures. Bérard replied at great length in a reassuring vein: "Nothing had ever been said to me at the Vatican which suggested criticism and disapproval of the legislation and regulations in question on the part of the Holy See. I can now state in addition that the pontifical authority would not seem to have been ever concerned or preoccupied with that side of French policy and that no complaint or request from France has so far given him occasion to be."[7] The Ambassador then expanded on the writings of St. Thomas Aquinas, who had long ago recommended restrictions on Jewish activity but had forbidden a policy of oppression of Jews. In the light of that tradition, Bérard continued, "an authorized person at the Vatican" had assured him that "they have no intention of quarreling with us over the Jewish statute" so long as provisions do not include prohibitions on intermarriage and so long as justice and charity are observed in the application of the law, particularly in the matter of the "liquidation of businesses in which Jews have an interest."

There were many letters to Vallat and Pétain from Jewish veterans of the French Army. Unlike the Jewish soldiers of Axis states who enjoyed a certain privileged status, the French veterans declared their solidarity with other French Jews and renounced exceptional benefits. A leader of the Jewish scouts, Marc Haguenau, wrote the following letter:

> I submit this personal protest, along with that of so many of my Jewish and non-Jewish countrymen, to tell you of my sadness at the fact that an exceptional law should be passed for one category of Frenchmen. I count in my family too many generations of French Israelites who have lived

under all regimes—monarchies, empires, republics—not to be capable of judging in a completely French spirit what a backward step this is for our country, as regards the respect for all spiritual values in which I was raised, and to which I remain attached.

I would have considered it contrary to my dignity not to make this brief and useless declaration.[8]

A moving letter was also written by General André Boris, former Inspector General of the Artillery, and oldest ranking officer among the Jews who were expelled from the French Army: "I believe," he wrote, "I have the right and duty to protest, because I neither recognize the right nor the power of anyone to set limits to the love I have for my fatherland, a love which is part of the patrimony of my heart and mind, a personal sanctuary which no one can violate."[9]

Such letters generally went unanswered; occasionally they would be answered in cautious and ambiguous terms, or the replies would refer to "present times which are too troubled and too confused to permit a sure judgment." However, for Vichy officials, the day of reckoning was approaching. The limits of permissible action were being reached.

The Vichy authorities also faced considerable opposition from the Christian clergy. Strong and moving letters of protest were addressed to them; urgent messages were read to congregations, and French Catholics were enjoined to give Jewish victims help. The Archbishop of Toulouse inveighed against the Nazi terror: "Alas, it has been destined for us to witness the dreadful spectacle of children, women and old men being treated like vile beasts; of families being torn apart and deported to unknown destinations. . . . In our diocese frightful things take place. . . . The Jews are our brethren. They belong to mankind. No Christian dare forget that!"

The Primate of France and Archbishop of Lyon, Pierre Cardinal Gerlier, defied the authorities with his letter of sympathy to the Grand Rabbi of France, after a crude Nazi attempt to burn the synagogues of Paris in October 1941. Subsequently, in pastoral letters to the Catholics of France, Cardinal Gerlier called upon them to refuse to surrender the hidden children of deported Jews. It was Cardinal Gerlier who also sponsored *L'Amitié Chretienne* (*Christian Friendship*), an organization of Protestants and Catholics which placed Jewish children in Christian institutions, and promised not to attempt to convert them. Dozens of nuns, priests, and humble monks were arrested and even gave their lives in the efforts to rescue Jews, although Laval was determined not to have clerical interference "in the internal affairs of the state of France."[10]

The network of Jewish organizations in France, meanwhile, had increasingly heavy burdens to carry. Many Jews—especially the refugees—

were now impoverished or in hiding. During the winter of 1940–41, the diverse organizations consolidated their resources and created a coordinating committee. On July 1, 1941, Dannecker reported that he had persuaded the military governor to deal only with this committee. The S.S. was obviously pressing for a French *Judenrat*. Dannecker also reached an agreement with the French welfare agency to deprive all Jews of French relief aid. Clandestinely, however, some aid continued to be given. On November 29, 1941, under German prodding, the Vichy regime ordered all Jewish organizations to dissolve and turn their property over to a new council, the *Union Générale des Israélites de France*. The new council, popularly known as UGIF, was designed to be the French counterpart of the Polish *Judenrat*. Heydrich now aimed to control the Jews of France by controlling UGIF, bringing out of hiding the Jews who had failed to register. In this he only partially succeeded.

UGIF began its operation under a series of blows. American entry in the war in December cut off French Jewry from its major source of outside help, the JDC, although some money was later funneled through Geneva. Moreover, an intensive UGIF fund-raising drive collapsed in the wake of an immense fine which the military governor suddenly imposed. On December 14, French Jews were fined a billion francs ($20 million) because of the assassination of a German officer. Jews were penalized and UGIF had to collect the money. Jewish leaders now had to dip into the fund of Jewish blocked accounts (proceeds of sales of Jewish businesses) to help poor and needy Jews. Later these funds had to be supplemented by a head tax on every Jewish adult.

UGIF[11] was a complex administrative structure, consisting of two quite separate administrations, one for occupied France and one for the Vichy Zone. Complete sections of UGIF were simply Jewish organizations that had existed before the war but were compelled to join UGIF as intact units. In the Occupied (northern) Zone there were 84 separate departments, employing many hundreds of employees. When the leaders of this zone accepted their posts, they made their reservations quite clear in a letter to Marshal Pétain, dated January 20, 1942: "We accept—willingly and insofar as we shall not have to forego our twofold dignity as Frenchmen and as adherents of the Jewish faith—to serve as mediators between you and our coreligionists, French and foreign. Nevertheless, as Frenchmen of an ancient race, whose families have clearly demonstrated it, we take the liberty to point out that it is impossible for us to accept the principle which excludes Frenchmen of the Jewish faith from the national community."

This letter was written before any deportations from France had taken place; no one, at the time, suspected any of the sinister measures that were soon to come. But even later, the leaders of UGIF were spared the tormenting trials of Jewish leaders elsewhere; in neither zone did Jews have to decide on the deportation of other Jews.

UGIF in the northern zone carried on many positive services. It maintained a number of Jewish social agencies that provided aid to thousands of Jews, particularly refugees, whose situation became increasingly difficult. It also gave relief to the Jews interned in the camps. Behind a "legal" facade, it created a network of underground assistance for Jews hounded by the police. It found asylum in non-Jewish homes for hundreds of threatened Jewish children. Special needs were coded in UGIF files. For example, "Difficult situation" on a dossier meant "I am being sought for deportation." "Food requirements" meant that a forged food card was needed for people in hiding. With the help of funds from abroad, self-defense functions were secretly carried on disguised as old organizations which had been officially closed down. A "mother-and-child clinic" effectively operated as a factory for forged documents for Jews who wanted to escape from the Occupied Zone and a special fund provided them with supplies for travel.

In the Vichy Zone, UGIF came into being only after long and arduous discussions. One group of leaders who were approached, among them Réné Mayer (later Prime Minister of France), refused to cooperate. Others demanded guarantees that UGIF would engage solely in relief activities without any political coloration whatever. This Vallat promised. UGIF in Vichy, like the one in the north, had no autonomous existence but was an amalgamation of seven organizations which had to dissolve. These became *Directoires*, or sections, such as ORT, which dealt with vocational training; CAR, which assisted refugees from Central Europe, and the Jewish Scout movement, *Les Eclaireurs Israélites de France* (EIF). Particular problems for this wing of UGIF began in November 1942, when the Germans erased the line of demarcation and occupied the Vichy Zone, subjecting all of France to their power.

Dissatisfied with the French lack of zeal in persecuting Jews, the Nazis took things into their own hands and began seizing Jews on trains and in railway stations in the former Vichy Zone. Raymond Lambert, UGIF deputy administrator, attacked these actions and went to Vichy to protest to Laval personally, but Laval refused to receive him. On his return he was denounced to the Germans by an official in the General Commissariat for Jewish Affairs and was immediately arrested and deported to Auschwitz together with his wife and four children.

After Lambert's deportation, a group in UGIF argued for scuttling the organization, but a majority feared that their resignations would harm their colleagues in the north. They remained at their posts and the constituent organizations of UGIF maintained a semblance of activity up to liberation. The heaviest blow came on January 5, 1943, when the Commissariat for Jewish Affairs ordered the Fourth *Directoire*, the Jewish Scouts, to dissolve.

Before the war, the EIF differed very little from the general scout movement in the country. When the war broke out, together with other scouts, EIF helped to evacuate children from the cities to children's homes in the provinces and to find homes for refugees. However, the German occupation confronted the Jewish Scouts with new tasks and imbued the movement with a heightened Jewish national spirit. Moreover, when the Vichy laws ousted many professional and technically trained Jews from their fields of work, these groups brought valuable new skills to the scout movement. An amateur movement was suddenly transformed.

The children's homes created in 1939 as temporary shelters became schools, centers for professional training and workshops in plumbing, carpentry, electrical work and mechanical trades. These changes were practical necessities. But EIF also wanted to develop strong youths who would become useful pioneers in Palestine. It set up agricultural training farms for boys and girls which functioned successfully for two years until the violent outbreak of persecution in the summer of 1942. The children were then dispersed among rural shops and boarded out to foster homes. Once again, EIF was forced to change its activities radically.

The brunt of the persecution now fell on foreign Jews in France. Estranged from familiar ties, without knowledge of the French language or local customs, these Jews were particularly exposed to danger and were hounded mercilessly by the Nazis. Orthodox Jews presented a special difficulty as they refused to shave off their beards. They tended to gravitate toward the big cities—Marseille, Lyon and Nice primarily—and had to be evacuated and dispersed in country homes or smuggled out of the country. The young boys and girls of "The Sixth,"[12] the most daring section of the EIF, spent their days and nights on trains and buses, going to and from the exposed centers and the evacuation zones in the Alps. They established contacts with Catholic and Protestant clergy, religious orders, friendly police officials, municipal authorities and professional smugglers. The leaders of The Sixth showed great resourcefulness and ingenuity in their rescue schemes. One member, Maurice Lobenberg, in Nice, set up a laboratory for forged documents which produced several hundred identity cards each day. (At the beginning of 1944, Lobenberg became chief of the section for forged documents in the *Mouvement de Libération Nationale*, one of the principal groups in the French Resistance. He died in the cellars of the Gestapo just a few weeks before liberation.)

Of the original 88 boys and girls of The Sixth, four were shot to death and 26 were deported, never to be heard from again. This little band saved more than 3,000 adults and over 1,000 children. It was also the nucleus out of which evolved the Jewish Fighting Organization in France (*Organisation Juive de Combat*).

The French non-Jewish population also aided these subversive Jewish rescue schemes and by 1942 were beginning to wear out the patience of the Germans. Officials doubted that Nazi propaganda was having much effect. In March 1942, the chief of the Police for Jewish Affairs reported that his men met with "incomprehension and even hostility. . . . The French population," he complained, "considers the anti-Jewish acts as something foreign, imposed on us by German authorities." Another report admitted that police control of the movement of Jews was nonexistent. "They change their dwellings constantly and camouflage themselves with the complicity of almost the total Aryan population."[12a]

Some Jews were warned of imminent arrest, house searches and raids and were able to escape from precincts and offices of prefects, even from central offices in Vichy. A story is told of a Jew with forged Aryan papers caught in the streets of Lyon and brought to the police station. There he was abandoned by the arresting officer, who left abruptly without making any charges. The head of the police precinct, instead of imprisoning the man, inquired: "Why didn't you come directly to me with your problem? I would have helped you."[13]

Numerous clandestine organizations helped supply funds to the *camouflés*. Veritable factories for the manufacture of false identification papers operated in the large cities. An elaborate procedure for securing such papers was developed. One method was called *doublage* or *synthesization*. The identity of a Frenchman known to be out of the country would be chosen. Through the reports of sympathetic acquaintants, his life would be reconstructed and his age and place of birth ascertained. Then a request for a copy of his birth certificate would be sent to the town, presumably to replace a lost original. French officials generally issued these transcripts without too much fuss. A set of additional documents, such as identity and ration cards, were also required, but the important thing was to get one genuine document to start the series. Schoolchildren collaborated in securing these precious first papers by finding out the dates of birth and birthplaces of students born in distant parts of France. Copies of these certificates were obtained and then forwarded to towns where they were needed. Often there were long delays before the *département* replied, and the danger of exposure was constant. But the work went on. Sometimes French presses, which printed official papers for the Germans, cooperated in printing forms that Jews could use.[14]

Many documents were prepared by David Rappaport, together with a faithful band of the Health Committee for Children and Mothers, at 36 Rue Amelot, Paris, which later became an important center of the French

Jewish underground. After he had been killed by the Germans, Jews used to say that he must have been one of the "Thirty-six Righteous Men," the saintly men in Jewish tradition who live in obscurity. Many children owe their lives to him.

It was also possible for Jews planted as Aryans to secure blank forms from German offices. However, the possession of skillfully forged documents did not invariably throw the Nazis or Vichy officials off the track. If *doublage* was suspected, there was terrific grilling and, in the case of men, medical examinations. Moreover, despite the moral disorder created in Europe by the Nazis, a world in which collaborators or Nazi henchmen were "law-abiding," there was still a strongly felt resistance against falsifying papers because of the taboo against illegality.

Toward the end of 1941, the Heydrich-Eichmann apparatus made their final drive against the military command and then thrust forward to control the Jews in France. A head-on collision between General Keitel and Heydrich precipitated this action, the background of which involved a quite typical Nazi feud. On the night of October 2, 1941, an attempt was made to blow up two Paris synagogues. The Security Police Commander Helmuth Knochen reported to von Stülpnagel that the French police suspected a Fascist journalist, Eugène Deloncle. Knochen, however, neglected to say that one of his own commandos, a Lieutenant Sommer, was under open arrest and that Sommer's case had been referred to the Main Security Office in Berlin. When von Stülpnagel learned unofficially from the French court of inquiry that Sommer had pleaded acting under Knochen's orders, he complained to Keitel, as head of the High Command of the Armed Forces. The S.S., he said, were increasing his difficulties with the French, which were already serious enough. He charged Knochen with forging a report and demanded his recall.[15] On November 6, Heydrich issued his blast against the military. He replied to Keitel through Quartermaster General Wagner:

> It is important to demonstrate to the world that the French nation has the necessary strength to fight the Jews and Communists. Deloncle seemed to me the best instrument in spite of his ambiguous political record. My Director of Services in Paris [Knochen] did not think it necessary to tell Stülpnagel because our experience gave little hope of his comprehension. I was fully conscious of the political consequences of these measures, the more so since I have been entrusted for years with the task of preparing the final solution of the Jewish problem.[16]

Knochen remained to direct "Action-Group France," although Stülpnagel continued to demand his recall. Quartermaster General Wagner reminded Heydrich of the agreement binding commandos of the Main Security Office to accept the orders of the Military Commander in France.

Heydrich's reply cannot be traced, but by February 5, von Stülpnagel withdrew his complaint against Knochen "because he had expressed his willingness to cooperate." The Army, as usual, was submitting to the police.

Much later, in July 1943, von Stülpnagel felt strong enough to refuse Knochen military personnel for rounding up Jews, but immediately after the Deloncle affair, von Stülpnagel seems to have caught some of the police technique from Knochen's S.S. In December 1941, he wanted a hundred hostages shot in reprisal for an assassination attempt against a Luftwaffe major. He also imposed a billion-franc fine on French Jews. In addition, he requested the deportation of a thousand Jews and five hundred Communists to the East for forced labor. Hitler approved all three recommendations.

Abetz, the German Ambassador, made sure that the hostages were described not as Frenchmen but as "Soviet and Secret Service agents of Judeo-Communist and De Gaullist origin." In Paris, 750 Jews were arrested on December 12 and taken with 300 others from the camp at Drancy to Compiègne; 97 died in Compiègne; 15 were released. In March, when transport was available, the rest boarded trains bound for Auschwitz. These Jews were the first to be deported to the East from France. Heydrich had won his victory over von Stülpnagel, but von Stülpnagel was directly responsible for the first French transports to Auschwitz.

By March 1942, the German transport problem was solved—large numbers of Russian civilian workers had already been moved to the Reich—and Eichmann informed the Foreign Office that 6,000 Jews were scheduled for immediate deportation. The Foreign Office had no objection—the Jews could be French or stateless. They washed their hands of the problem by calling it a "police matter."

Dannecker claimed the credit for being the first to propose continuous deportations from France. Things were still going too slowly, he believed. He visited Eichmann in Berlin on March 4 and said that it would be necessary to propose to the French "something really positive, like the deportation of several thousand Jews." He complained of the "corruption" of some of the French personnel in the internment camps, the granting of passes and the smuggling of food to prisoners. Women related to the male prisoners were still at large arousing the sympathy of "unknowing Frenchmen," he said.

By the spring of 1942, the Pétain regime had lost much of its early support. The hoped for New Order was, instead, a police state. In March, the dramatic Riom trials exposed the treachery of Vichy collaborators; Hitler, anticipating an Allied invasion, was impatient to grab all of France; French resistance was rumbling. Toward the end of the month, when an

English commando was hurled against the port of St. Nazaire, many local Frenchmen joined the raiders. Pétain called back Laval.

Laval re-entered the government on April 14, 1942, assuming all of the power still remaining to the faltering Pétain. His government had to keep the confidence of the Germans and bolster the shaky absolutism of the Vichy regime. This delicate balance was rendered impossible by an episode that sent Hitler into a characteristic rage. On April 17, French General Henri Giraud, who had been imprisoned by the Germans at Königstein Fortress on the Elbe, made a daring escape by lowering himself 150 feet down the side of the ancient walls and disappearing into the underbrush. He escaped to Switzerland, promising to return to Germany if Germany agreed to release 500,000 French prisoners. Four days after Giraud's arrival in Switzerland, Hitler informed Pétain that he was setting up an S.S. headquarters in Paris under the command of Karl Oberg. Gauleiter Bürckel also announced that more Frenchmen would be expelled from Lorraine. Again, the S.S. had won.

On May 5, 1942, Heydrich himself went to Paris. In talks with the French police chief, René Bousquet, he said there was now sufficient transport to remove the stateless Jews interned at Drancy in the Occupied Zone. Bousquet then casually asked if he could also remove the stateless Jews who had already been interned for over a year in the Vichy Zone. Heydrich replied that it was all a matter of transport.[17] Meanwhile, Jews in the camps of the Occupied Zone would have to be moved. At Drancy, in the four ugly skyscrapers near Le Bourget, 5,138 victims were selected. These deportees, also, were destined for Auschwitz. To deceive the deportees, Nazis exchanged French francs for Polish zlotys. Dannecker himself saw the transports off. He was described as exhibiting a "nervous twitch and ill-coordinated movements which at a distance resembled those of a drunken man."

The deportations from Drancy took place in April and June 1942. By this time preparations were also being made for large-scale marking and deportations to include French-born Jews, regardless of their hostage value or the outcries of the West. This was the meaning of the decision to compel every Jew in occupied Europe to wear a Jewish star, as the Jews of Poland had done since 1939 and the Jews of the Greater Reich, since September 1941. Eichmann had suggested the badge in March. The decree went into effect in both zones in France on June 7. When the decree was published, several textile firms were instructed to prepare 400,000 badges for the Occupied Zone for the 100,000 Jews who were expected to register. (Ten thousand Jews who were citizens of neutral countries were exempted from wearing the badge.) The Nazis counted on each of these Jews to need four badges apiece. However, only 83,000 registered. These Jews were now seriously circumscribed as well as exposed. But the Nazis were abashed as well as disappointed by the results of the decree.

Unexpected resistance developed. Some Jews decided not to wear the star; others wore it the wrong way; still others wore several stars instead of one. On the day the decree was announced, Jewish war veterans pinned on their stars next to their military decorations and paraded along Paris boulevards to the applause and cheers of large crowds. Frenchmen exchanged affectionate greetings with wearers of the star; many wore yellow stars themselves or carried yellow handkerchiefs; priests and nuns of Jewish descent, who were exempted from wearing the badge in France, publicly displayed the yellow star; students devised mischievous ways of ridiculing the order. French teachers militantly resisted the idea of tagging Jews, and children who wore the star were often treated with special tenderness.

Most astonishing was the opposition of Xavier Vallat, the Commissar for Jewish Questions, who refused to accept the decree in the Vichy Zone when it was first proposed in March. Vallat, who had told Dannecker, "I am an older anti-Semite than you," balked at this new menacing thrust against French Jews and was described by the Germans as "the Commissar for the protection of the Jews." They demanded his replacement, but the new Commissar, Darquier de Pellepoix, was no more cooperative on the matter of the Jewish badge. The Vichy regime had finally exposed the line beyond which the Germans could not trespass.

The Jewish badge decree could never be wholly enforced in the unoccupied area even after November 11, 1942, when Vichy ceased to be a free zone. The implication of the badge—to facilitate a general deportation—had been grasped. There is little doubt that Vichy officials knew the fate of the deportees. Laval, in a conversation on September 2, 1942, with the Higher S.S. and Police Leader Karl Oberg, told Oberg of rumors in diplomatic circles about the meaning of the deportations. Laval asked how to answer these inquiries. Both men finally agreed on a formulation: Laval was to say that Jews from the Occupied Zone of France were being delivered to the occupying power and were being shipped to work in the Government-General in Poland. The official French distinction, however, between French Jews and foreign Jews, puzzled the Germans. It took the Gestapo a long time to absorb the bewildering reality that even the most collaborationist French officials—including Laval—persisted in regarding French-born Jews and naturalized Jews as Frenchmen first, and Jews secondarily. Vichy contracted its own anti-Semitic ideology at the point of murder of French Jews.

Meanwhile, Dannecker pressed on with his plans as the deportation mania gripped the German police forces in Paris. Eichmann, on June 11, 1942, had called together his agents in France, Belgium and Holland to discuss deportation schedules for these countries, and a quota of 100,000 Jews was established for France for the next three months. On June 26,

Dannecker drew up a set of rules for his territory. He fixed the age limits from sixteen to forty-five and included French nationals as well as stateless Jews. Fifty thousand were to come from each zone; all were to be sent to Auschwitz. These goals were somewhat steep, however, as events were to reveal.

The possibility that France might not produce so many Jews for Auschwitz apparently did not worry Eichmann or Dannecker. But transport problems did. The buildup of the German spring offensive required the sudden transfer of 37,000 freight cars and 1,000 locomotives from the Occupied Zone of France to Germany. So urgent was the need that the cars were rushed out empty. Cars were also needed for the transfer of 350,000 French laborers to the Reich. Nevertheless, Eichmann was undeterred. He wangled transport from the Wehrmacht, sufficient for a trainload every other day. This supply would enable him to transport 15,000 Jews per month from France. The operation was to start in the provincial cities; the first trainload on the projected schedule was to leave Bordeaux on July 13. Meanwhile, the question of French aid had to be thrashed out.

Eichmann's deportation schedule called for a quota of 22,000 Jews from Paris and 10,000 in the Vichy Zone. The S.S. were now confronted with the problem of a police shortage. In all of occupied France, the German police numbered only 3,000. This was 2,000 less than was available for a much smaller Holland. For making the seizures, the S.S. men had to draw on the French police, particularly in Paris where there were now about 140,000 Jews. According to the Vichy police, 28,000 of these were stateless, possessing registered addresses in Paris. Convinced that with the help of the French police he could arrest 22,000 of the 28,000, Dannecker chose the Vélodrôme d'Hiver, a sports stadium on the Boulevard de Grenelle, as a collection center. The French police agreed to make the arrests and station themselves on the deportation trains.

The decision to give Dannecker French police aid was Laval's. Bousquet had refused to have anything to do with deportations and Jean Leguay, who represented the Vichy Ministry of Police in Paris, hedged—it might take weeks, he said, to round up thousands of "undesirables" and it would require at least 2,500 police. Knochen then applied pressure to Laval. He told him that the German Government had decided to deport every Jew from France. No distinction would be made between French nationals and others. The Paris prefect of police had already been notified of this decision. Laval then decided to speak to Oberg and salvage what he could.

Dannecker, meanwhile, learned that Bousquet's real attitude would not be known until after Laval's visit to Oberg. At that time, presumably, Laval would be persuaded to give Darquier full power over the Vichy police chief.

On June 27, Laval met with Oberg, the Higher S.S. and Police Leader.

Oberg made a compromise proposal: if the French police would co-operate in the operation, the seizures, for the time, would be confined to stateless Jews. "The trains are ready," Oberg said. "The Jewish problem has no frontiers for us. The police must help us or we shall do the arresting without any distinction between French Jews and others." Oberg then told Laval that the Jews were being sent to Poland where a "Jewish state" would be set up for them. Laval agreed to the compromise. He decided to save the French nationals and involve the police in the roundups. "I did all I could," he wrote later, "considering the fact that my first duty was to my fellow countrymen of Jewish extraction whose interests I could not sacrifice. The right of asylum was not respected in this case. How could it have been otherwise in a country which was occupied by the German Army?"[17a]

This compromise gave immunity to French Jews but was bought at the price of the lives of non-French Jews. Both French and German police could now seize stateless Jews, children as well as adults, in both zones. Laval did express the wish that children in the Vichy Zone not be separated from their parents. The question of the Jewish children in the Occupied Zone, he is reported to have said, did not "interest" him.

Even after Laval's talk with Oberg, Eichmann complained that Vichy made "ever-increasing obstacles." The Gestapo, however, still believed the French police could be made to round up French Jews. On July 1, Eichmann briefed Dannecker and Knochen to demand the "indispensable legal basis whereby the French Jews become stateless the moment they crossed the border." The cautious bureaucrat wanted to take no chances. Ambitious plans were drawn up for deportation trains to leave from many points, but Bousquet now tried a delaying tactic. He told Dannecker that he thought a new registration of Jews would be needed. Barring that, the quota of 10,000 Jews from the Vichy Zone could be obtained from the internment camps.

Dannecker himself inspected the camps and said the reports of the Vichy arrests of 1940 were grossly exaggerated. The three main camps of Les Milles, Gurs and Rivesaltes, he said, contained less than 6,000 Jews, including the survivors of "Aktion Bürckel." Dannecker decided that since the camps could not provide enough Jews, a general roundup was needed, concentrated in Paris. July 16 was set as the date. July 14 had to be avoided —the French national holiday had to be respected.

Meanwhile Nazi plans for the Bordeaux trainload were curtailed because of the compromise with Laval. In all of Bordeaux, only 150 stateless Jews could be found, and the transport was canceled. Eichmann was both furious and disgusted, and demanded an explanation for the fiasco. The RSHA had conducted lengthy negotiations with the Reich Transport Ministry to obtain cars and now the transport had to be canceled. He protested to his subordinate Heinz Röthke that this sort of thing had never happened before. He could not even report it to the Gestapo Chief, Müller. In a strange reflex of helplessness—or possibly to humiliate Röthke —he threatened to drop France altogether from German deportation plans. Röthke urged him to reconsider: "I request," he said, "that this should not be done. It was not the fault of our office if this train had to be canceled . . . the subsequent trains will leave according to plan." Röthke proved to be right—for the time being. There were no further Bordeaux incidents, but there were to be other difficulties. The focus then shifted to Paris.

Beginning at 4 A.M. on July 16, the stateless Jews in the capital were seized. Arrests were made by ordinary French police. In two days of roundups, 12,884 Jews were captured, including 4,051 children. Men without families were sent directly to Drancy. Families and all women and children were taken to the Vélodrôme d'Hiver. The herding of several thousand children and adults into the bleak spaces of the Vélodrôme d'Hiver was to recreate in the City of Light the ordeal of the Polish ghettos. For five days the prisoners were penned up without any food. A single street hydrant supplied the water, and ten latrines, the lavatory facilities. Several women gave birth to children during those five days. Thirty people died and a number lost their sanity. A triple epidemic of scarlet fever, measles and diphtheria broke out. On the fifth day, the mothers and fathers were separated from the children, never to see them again. The parents were sent to Drancy, the children to the camps at Pithiviers and Beaune-la-Rolande.

Darquier de Pellepoix, the newly appointed Commissioner for Jewish Affairs, asked that the children be sent to orphanages, but Eichmann, on the phone from Berlin, gave other instructions. There would be enough trains at the end of August, he said, to take the children to the Government-General in Poland. The children were subsequently taken to Drancy, the French railhead for Auschwitz. For several weeks, women internees there cared for them in vermin-infested rooms. When the time came to take them to the trains, the children struggled. Dr. George Wellers, a survivor of Drancy and Auschwitz, has described this scene: "It happened sometimes that a whole roomful of a hundred children, as if seized with ungovernable panic and frenzy, no longer listened to the cajoling of the grown-ups who could not get them downstairs. It was then that they called the gendarmes, who carried the children in their arms, screaming with terror."[18]

In Röthke's deportation file, a memorandum was found, dated November 11, 1942. It reported that in the boxcars returning empty from Auschwitz, Belgian railwaymen had found twenty-five bodies of children from two to four years old.

Some children had been arrested in the Vichy Zone but were released through the intervention of the Oeuvre de Secours aux Enfants (Children's Aid Society—OSE), a unit within UGIF. The Gestapo believed that Laval had tricked them. The children seized in the Occupied Zone, however, were doomed. UGIF and individuals—Jews and non-Jews—made frantic efforts to have them released but failed. The Nazis, on their side, tried to deceive onlookers into thinking that whole families were going "to the East." They rigged a synthetically mixed transport. On August 13, Leguay, representing the French police in the Occupied Zone, declared in conference with Dannecker that the first transport from the Occupied Zone would cross the demarcation line on August 17. Transports from southern France, meanwhile, were to be routed to Drancy where they would be "mixed" with Jewish children from Pithiviers and Beaune-la-Rolande "in the proportion of 500–700 adults per 300–500 children." These trains left at the end of August when, as Eichmann promised, "children's trains can roll."

By the middle of August 1942, 25,000 Jews had been deported from France, but all had come from the Occupied Zone. None had yet been deported from the Vichy Zone. German diplomats and S.S. police now began to apply additional pressure to Laval. Not very much was needed. Laval declared himself ready to hand over the foreign Jews from the Vichy Zone and again proposed that the Germans also take along children under sixteen so as to "reunite families." The Germans were elated if somewhat taken aback by this offer. One of the German negotiators, Rudolph Rahn, remarked to Laval that the whole business was a little unsavory. To which Laval made an irritated reply: "Well, what am I to do? I offered these foreign Jews to the Allies, but they didn't take them off my hands." By September 1, 9,000 stateless Jews in Vichy had been turned over to the Germans. While this transfer was being made, the Nazis planned one of their clumsier subterfuges, a denaturalization scheme.

With the actions of the summer of 1942, a low point had been reached in the power or willingness of the Laval-Pétain regime to withstand German pressures. But counterpressures were building up. The clergy began to protest strongly against the deportations. The delegate of the American Friends Service Committee entered a protest. (To this, Laval made a stinging rejoinder: ". . . these foreign Jews had always been a problem in France and . . . the French Government was glad that a change in the German attitude toward them gave France an opportunity to get rid of them." Laval then asked the Quaker delegate why the United States did not take these Jews.) Another protest was lodged by the Swiss Minister to Vichy, Walter Stucki (although his country was at that very moment tightening its frontiers against fleeing refugees). Stucki was also serving as the acting delegate of the International Red Cross Committee for France and made his protest directly to Pétain. He complained that children were being seized from institutions where they had been cared for by Swiss charity. Pétain is said to have "deplored" the situation, but added that it was a matter of "internal concern."

Laval warned the French clergy and the Papal Nuncio not to interfere in French policy on Jewish matters; "anti-Jewish matters were not exactly new to the Church," he added sharply. His threats were implemented, and in the Lyon diocese, a number of priests were arrested for reading protest declarations to congregations and for harboring Jewish children. But Laval himself was approaching the limit of his anti-Jewish collaboration. The Germans were still not wholly satisfied with the pace of deportations from France. Other countries were far ahead of France. The Jewish experts in the RSHA determined to break down the French resistance. As a start, the French would have to revoke the naturalizations granted to French Jews after 1933. This circuitous device was supposed to relieve the French of handing over French Jews.

The Germans attacked on all sides: Laval, Pétain, the French Police Chief, the Vichy bureaucracy. But there was no yielding. The Germans then began to bargain. They promised immunity to all French-born Jews in the Occupied Zone. But for almost a year the French procrastinated. Laval threw up one obstruction after another. When the terms of the decree were drawn up, Laval casually reported that he had lost his copy. Then he insisted that three months elapse to enable Jews to study the matter and lodge their objections. He stressed Pétain's strong objections. In the end, the denaturalization of French Jews was never effected. The Germans then switched their attack to the foreign Jews in France who were under the protection of Axis states—Hungary, Romania, and Italy. But again the Germans were stymied.[19] The Romanians at first agreed to relinquish their Jews but then withdrew their consent. The Hungarians insisted that the Romanians act first. Both Hungary and Romania actually waited to see what Italy would do. But Germany's principal Axis partner refused to do anything at all. The Italian Consul General insisted on an agreement from Röthke that no Italian subject in France would be touched by the Germans without Italian consent. As a result of these difficulties, fewer and fewer transports of Jews left France. Instead of catching up, the French sector was falling farther and farther behind other countries. Then, in November, the Germans thought they had fresh opportunities.

Early in November 1942, the Allies made landings in Morocco and Algiers. In a lightning countermove, the Germans occupied Vichy France, giving them a large new area of control. Yet, this very control and the new military situation created problems.

Just when the Germans needed more police, in heavier concentrations, their forces were stretched very thin over both zones. German armies had been driven out of Sicily and most of southern Russia. Vichy realized that Germany was losing the war. Outside France, German military might was caving in. But now the biggest factor mitigating the threat against the Jews in the Vichy Zone was Italy.

As Germany's ally, Italy shared the occupation of the old Vichy Zone of France. Italian soldiers occupied the coastal area and the towns and villages of eight departments: Alpes Maritimes, Var, Hautes Alpes, Basses Alpes, Isère, Drôme, Savoie and Haute Savoie. The French population received the Italians with suppressed hatred or quiet resignation. The Italians welcomed the soldiers as their own. The Jews looked on the marching troops with anxiety and fear but also with hopefulness.

The German military defeats of the period aggravated the fury of the Germans and their Vichy collaborators and intensified anti-Semitic actions. At the same time they gave heart to the French resistance. The Maquis in the hills of Haute Savoie and the Vosges gained new recruits. Acts of sabotage against the Nazi invader increased. The frozen silence of the people in the first months of the occupation was beginning to thaw. The Vichy regime was criticized for the French defeat. A spirit of resistance was coming to life. More and more of France's national treasure and resources were being poured into the German war machine. Thousands of French workers were being trucked into the Reich. When the Germans swept into the Vichy Zone, the country was turned into a fortress but not of France's making. Her coasts bristled with guns emplaced by foreign soldiers.

At first the Italians were too busy fortifying coastal defenses entrusted to them to pay any attention to the problem of the Jews. Then, on December 20, 1942, an official action precipitated an Italian move. The French Prefect of Alpes Maritimes had issued a decree ordering all foreign Jews in his department to go to the Drôme and Ardèche departments, now under German jurisdiction. There was no doubt that these Jews would be deported. An influential half-Jew, Angelo Donati, immediately appealed to the Italian Consul General in Nice and urged a reconsideration. He pointed out that all Italian Jews in the district would be affected by the decree and that Italy would have to bear the responsibility for the deportation of any Jews. The Consul General was sympathetic and wrote to Rome for instructions.

The Italian Government protested the French decree and gradually Italian authorities set aside Vichy measures affecting Jews. By the thousands, Jews came streaming into the Italian zone to place themselves under Italian protection. Vichy protested to the Italian commander against this infringement of its national sovereignty. Ribbentrop then intervened through diplomatic channels and Himmler sent emissaries to Rome. All of these efforts failed. An appeal was made at last to Mussolini, who promised to rouse his generals out of their "stupid sentimental notions." But the Italian zone remained a sanctuary for Jews up to the Italian surrender in September 1943. A Jew could breathe freely by making a one-hour trip from Lyon to Grenoble or from Marseille to Nice without having to cross a frontier. Possibly as many as 30,000 Jews, most of them stateless, fled to this safe zone.

These refugees were particularly exposed. They were not permitted to work and had to depend on charity. Many were Orthodox Jews and could be identified as Jews, physically. French Jews could more easily camouflage their identity and improvise ways of making a living. Many could rely on helpful non-Jewish friends. Moreover, the badge decree of June 1942 for the Occupied Zone further exposed the foreign Jews. The Gestapo published a list of public places out-of-bounds for badge-wearers, and the list was so long there was little a Jew could do except walk the streets. Shops were available to Jews from three to four in the afternoon. A refugee Jew could easily be picked up at 4:05 and put on an Auschwitz transport via Drancy. As the pressure against émigré Jews mounted, the victims sought new hiding places. A strange refuge was found, temporarily, in the Riviera.

The luxury-loving French Riviera—Nice particularly—had become a Jewish refuge before the Italian occupation.[20] Soon after the German invasion of France, there was a large exodus from Paris to the south and a center for refugees along the Riviera sprang up spontaneously. All along the Côte d'Azur, from Fréjus to Cannes, Nice and Menton, in the great villas and hotels, were encamped thousands of refugee Jews, finding bizarre shelter in one of the playgrounds of the world. During the war, the large hotels and amusement centers were left vacant. Landlords had plenty of room and found no trouble evading Vichy's anti-Jewish housing restrictions. If the refugee could prove to the police that he had enough money to maintain himself without working, he was generally not molested. Word quickly spread that a Jewish refugee could live in comparative safety on the Riviera and thousands of Jews streamed there.

First came wealthy Jews, then moderately prosperous ones and finally, Jews without any means. Jewish charities developed and helped the destitute Jews gain quasi-legal status with the police. Rabbis and Orthodox Jews also found comfort in this incongruous haven. Under the "forced residence" regulations in Vichy France, Orthodox Jews were often assigned to non-Jewish villages where they had no synagogue and no access to kosher food. They could not appear in streets in their traditional garb. For others whose savings were exhausted, the problems of simple existence became immense. For these Jews, too, Nice was a refuge. Local committees provided housing for them in the large Hotel Roosevelt and rented a large hall which served as a synagogue and study room. The comparative serenity of their life in Nice, in the very center of French anti-Semitic and Fascist organizations and propaganda machinery, is one of the strangest paradoxes of this era. In Nice one could see rabbis in their traditional garb walking through the streets or listen to Talmudic discussions and old Hebrew prayers at the same time that the most fanatical Jew-haters were working off their froth.

The serenity was temporary, of course. As the pressure on Vichy grew stronger, anti-Semitic agitation in the press and radio became more violent. Demonstrations and attacks became more frequent. Jews were called criminals, black marketeers and agitators. It was said that they were eating the bread of the French people. Then came the welcome balm of the Italian period.

The Vichy government had forbidden Jews to travel to the expanded area of Italian control and ordered identity and food-ration cards stamped with a "J" to trap them more easily. Himmler reported that the French police were willing to help collect the wandering Jews but that east of the Rhone River, Italian troops of the Fourth Italian Army balked. The Italian Armistice Commission and the Italian Foreign Office were also "uncooperative," he said. Early in February 1943, a French police officer at Lyon attempted to implement a Vichy order for the arrest of 300 Jews in the area, but the Italian general in Grenoble protested and demanded the release of the imprisoned Jews. The police officer was forced to comply. Early in March, after two German officers in Paris were attacked, the French police were ordered to round up 2,000 Jews for a "penance" transport to the East. Jews were arrested in Grenoble and Annecy in the Italian zone. In the Grenoble area, Italian soldiers surrounded the imprisoned Jews to prevent their departure, while at Annecy, Italian troops encircled the French police barracks and forced the release of the arrested Jews.[21]

The German Ambassador to Italy complained to Italian Foreign Minister Count Ciano but was put off, and both Ribbentrop and the Ambassador laid their troubles before Mussolini. Very possibly, Mussolini said, the French were deliberately trying to create dissension between Germany and Italy. He quite agreed with Ribbentrop that the military mentality did not grasp the Jewish problem fully—their mode of thinking was different. He then took what seemed like a drastic step. On March 20, 1943, he transferred jurisdiction over Jewish matters from the Italian Army to the Interior Ministry in Rome. This ministry established a Commissariat for Jewish Questions in Nice and appointed as commissar a police inspector, Guido Lospinoso. Italian police detailed to his command were set up into a *Polizia Raziale*—a racial police. But the Italian police were a breed apart.

Lospinoso was instructed to transfer all Jews from the coastal area to the interior where the Jews were assigned to "forced residence." When the German Ambassador queried the Italian Foreign Office about the fate of these Jews after they were confined, he asked if they would be "shipped off." The Italian official replied that "this was not being considered at present." A cat-and-mouse game ensued.

Lospinoso successfully evaded the Germans by sending lesser officials to confer with them; they, in turn, pleaded insufficient authority to deal with Jewish policy matters. To further confound and infuriate the Germans, Lospinoso's chief aide was Angelo Donati—the same man who had protested a French order in December 1942.

Meanwhile, the Italian Chief of Staff had persuaded Mussolini that the French police were not to be trusted. The registration of the Jews in the Italian zone was subsequently handled by the Italian police. This last maneuver provoked Himmler to send Gestapo Chief Müller himself on a visit to Rome to waylay Lospinoso. But Lospinoso was a step ahead of him, appearing and disappearing elusively. Not until May 26 was he definitely located in Marseille. By then, with the aid of Donati, he had safely put Jews up in Megève, St. Gervain and Vence—well within the Italian zone. On July 10, the Marseille Gestapo reported to Röthke that Lospinoso had moved 22,000 Jews under these humane conditions. Röthke himself believed the figure was close to 50,000. The Italians, the Germans concluded, were not really serious about the Jewish problem.

The man apparently responsible for Lospinoso's active sympathy in behalf of Jews was a French Capuchin, Father Marie-Benoit.[22] While still a young man, Father Marie-Benoit won recognition as a scholar in Judaica, but his academic interest became abruptly practical when Hitler invaded France. Gifted with exceptional ability as an organizer and possessing great energy, the black-bearded Capuchin transformed the monastery at 51 Rue Croix-de-Regnier in Marseille into a rescue agency. A busy passport mill in the cellar fabricated and distributed hundreds of identification cards, certificates of baptism and other documents. Smuggling routes into Spain and Switzerland were set up for Jews and anti-Nazi refugees. The Gestapo became suspicious of the priest's activity, particularly after the German occupation of the Vichy Zone which included the rescue center of Marseilles. Smuggling forays into Spain and Switzerland were soon out of the question, but one avenue of escape remained—the Riviera and Haute-Savoie which were occupied by Italy.

Father Marie-Benoit went to Nice for help. He met with representatives of UGIF and several important Italian officials and laid before them his plan to move Jews across the demarcation line. When Lospinoso was appointed Commissioner of Jewish Affairs, the rescue workers feared a change in Italian policy. Through the intercession of an aged Jesuit, Father

Bremont of Nice, Father Marie-Benoit met Donati. After a long talk together, they decided to see General Lospinoso. There is no record of their conversation, but it is generally believed that Father Marie-Benoit's eloquence and compassion influenced Lospinoso to resist the German pressures.

But the game of twisting the Gestapo's tail was nearing its end. By late July, Mussolini had already agreed to hand over to the Germans the whole of the Italian Zone except Nice. On July 25, he was deposed. The new Badoglio government had liberal instructions for the sheltering of the Jews, but these were not published until September 1. During this critical interval, the forces working in behalf of the Jews were lost in the confusion of the Italian surrender.

Father Marie-Benoit requested an audience with Pope Pius XII to plead for Vatican support of a plan to admit all of the refugee Jews in the south of France to Italy. The Pope seemed favorably disposed. A letter from Nice, dated August 8, to Judge Léon Meiss (who later became President of the French Central Jewish Consistory) and signed "J.F." (unidentified) touches on this visit:

> During his stay in Italy, D. [Donati] . . . took certain steps to obtain permission for the Jews of the Italian zone to enter Italy. From all he told me on this subject, I received the impression that the attitude is not too favorable. Italy may become the theatre of military operations, and in such a state of affairs, it is more than natural to see her hesitate before admitting about twenty thousand aliens. However, the problem may find an affirmative solution as regards the Jews who are now in a place of residence assigned to them—this concerns approximately three thousand persons. On the other hand, D. has seen Father Marie-Benoit who had called the Vatican's attention to the situation of the Jews. He had been received by the Pope himself, and succeeded in arousing his interest in the fate of the Jews in France. It seems that the Pope is quite in favor of permitting the Jews—if and when the case arises—to enter Italy, and he will support all the efforts made for this purpose.[23]

The Badoglio government had decided not to oppose the flight of Jews to Italy. Donati had actually secured an agreement whereby Italy agreed to admit 30,000. The Allied powers, after the armistice with Italy, were to transfer the Jews to North Africa.

As an alternate plan, Father Marie-Benoit and Donati also tried to influence British and American officials to allow these Jews to go to Morocco, Algiers and Tunisia, which the Allies already occupied. They consented and Badoglio agreed to supply four ships. The American Joint Distribution Committee agreed to finance the project. On September 3, Badoglio secretly concluded the armistice with the Allies but it was agreed that the news not be made public for four weeks. During those four weeks Donati and Father Marie-Benoit hoped to arrange the evacuation from Nice. But for diplomatic and strategic reasons, the Allies did not keep the news a secret and made the announcement of Italy's surrender on September 8. This doomed the Jews in southern France. Hastily, the Italians began to evacuate their positions in Nice and the Jews were left adrift. Within a few days, the Security Police swept through the entire zone vacated by the Italians. They raided hotels, homes and rooms day and night. Suspects were taken for physical examinations. Thousands of Jews were dragged to an assembly center and taken off. Thousands of others fled in panic, to their undoing, across the Alps, attempting to reach the frontiers of Switzerland or Italy.

The Gestapo had waited for this moment. Alois Brunner, one of Eichmann's deportation experts, had gone to Marseille to direct a seizure of Jews for shipment to Drancy. Now it was the French police who refused to help. They became increasingly reluctant to cooperate in arrests or seizures and the Germans were forced to rely on their own forces. The Italians had left no effective Jewish registration system and in places where they kept lists of a sort, they were destroyed by the French police. Brunner was reduced to street manhunts.

Eichmann followed Brunner into Nice soon after the German Army entered. He had heard that 15,000 Jews were hiding in the mountain areas near the Principality of Monaco, technically a sovereign state. The German Consul at Monaco was instructed by the German Foreign Office to arrange for the entry of the Security Police, but the Consul could locate only a thousand Jews, all of them old residents. Eichmann persisted in hunting down these Jews for almost a year. By July 1944, in response to his inquiries, the Consul reported that most of these thousand had found their way to Switzerland or Spain or into the Maquis. Only forty-five remained, all of them adequately protected. Only a few had been taken to Drancy.

Elsewhere in France, the Jews were submerging. They went into hiding by the tens of thousands. Röthke, through most of 1943, continued hoping that Laval would yield up the French Jews naturalized after 1933 and make 50,000 Jews immediately available for deportation, but Laval consistently refused. Knochen told Müller that the Americans were offering France the Italian colonies and the Rhine and that Laval would certainly hand over more Jews if the Germans bid higher. Röthke then tried to get the help of the German Army in France, but von Stülpnagel absolutely refused to permit German soldiers to assist in the arrests. Brunner then tried to create a kind of Jewish police. A number of Jews were allowed out of Drancy to collect friends and relatives by various appeals to sentiment or blackmail threats, but they were not successful and were withdrawn after a few weeks.

By the time the Italians surrendered to the Allies, 52,000 Jews had been deported from France, 6,000 of whom were French nationals, and 13,000 of whom came from the Vichy Zone. This was only half the prey the Nazis had wanted in France. They were forced to conclude that the French "no longer wished to follow them" on the Jewish question.

In the last months before liberation, the German juggernaut of destruction was very considerably slowed down. There was no catching up with the fast tempo of deportations from Holland. Massed roundups were now impossible, and the Germans were forced to make episodic raids on arbitrary targets. They raided children's homes, labor camps, prisons, homes for the aged and other institutions run by UGIF. Brunner was told to remove Jews from all French camps and prisons without advance notice and prevent the French authorities from taking them elsewhere. In the early morning hours of April 6, 1944, Security Police in the Lyon sector forced their way into the Colonie des Enfants at Eyzieux and moved out fifty-one persons, including five women and forty-one children between three and thirteen. To reach Jews in hiding, rewards were announced to lure informers. Payments would be made, after seizures, from the effects of the victims. Orders were given to guard transports with special care; some Jews were known to have escaped. To prevent further escapes, Knochen and Brunner recommended that Jews be tied to each other with a long rope. The Gestapo made renewed efforts to cut into protected groups of Jews.

Two transports left for Auschwitz in April and another in May. The Allied invasion of the Continent in June created new dangers for Jews as well as salvation. The Gestapo ran amuck in Lyon. Jews were picked up and murdered at random and in mass executions—a pattern of killing-in-retreat that the Germans were to use in every country they occupied. In July, the Paris orphanages and the Rothschild Home for the Aged were attacked. But the tide had turned. The transports had to be stopped.

French railways were being bombed to a standstill. The evacuation of Drancy, which the Nazis planned for August 10, had to be canceled and 700 Jews remained in the camp when the Allies arrived. Reports reached Geneva describing guerrilla activities by French Jews who had escaped from labor camps in Poland and were raiding camps in France. The Vichy radio announced the assassination of François de la Rocque, head of the anti-Semitic Fascist *Croix de Feu*. Moreover, the Normandy invasion sent a new surge of life into the French underground movements and multiplied the problems of the German forces.

Jews were active in the French resistance, constituting 15 to 20 percent of the active membership of the resistance organizations.[24] Among these were *Libération*, which gathered military information for representatives of Free France in London from 1941 to 1943, when the Germans discovered the organization and put an end to it. Other important groups in which they fought were *Combat, Franc-Tireur, Liberté,* and *France Combattante.* A Jew, Jaques Bingen, represented General de Gaulle among the resistance organizations in occupied France. Bingen was arrested in 1944 by the Vichy police and, fearful of betraying his comrades, took poison. Maurice Schumann was the radio voice of Free France. A Moroccan Jew, Max Guedj, is credited with having shot down the greatest number of German planes of any French flyer.

During the first phase of the Nazi occupation, the French resistance movement had been weak. The Pétain regime was widely accepted while extreme left-wing and Communist groups opposed any underground activity during the life of the Hitler-Stalin Pact. When the general French resistance movement gathered strength in 1942, most French Jews threw their lot with it. There was also a Jewish separatist movement, however, formed by those who felt that since Jews had been singled out for specific and unique attack, there should be autonomous Jewish fighting units.

In the summer of 1940, under the initiative of the poet David Knout,[25] a small group gathered to draw up plans for a secret organization to fight the Germans. At first this handful of Jewish fighters met with almost general skepticism. But two years later, when the large-scale deportations began, their appeal found a response. With the financial aid of the Zionist Organization of France, a Jewish military organization was formed. Its most active forces were recruited from the ranks of the EIF. The Maquis, who at first opposed having separate Jewish detachments, at length yielded and assisted them with arms and military directives. These units, which became part of the FFI (French Forces of the Interior), were organized into two divisions: *Combattants Zionistes* and *Combattants Juifs* (non-Zionist). Though their chief emphasis was on military skills, their formal program included all aspects of Jewish resistance: the rescue of children, the organization of youth convoys to Palestine, smuggling of Jews across borders, the punishment of traitors, the manufacture of documents, and Jewish studies. Their secret printing presses turned out excerpts from Herzl and Isaiah and Hebrew grammars as well as militant proclamations. An attempt was made to issue a journal, *Quand Même (In Spite of Everything),* but the printer was arrested after the publication of two numbers and the experiment was not renewed.

A vivid impression of the Jewish Maquis is conveyed in a reminiscence by a member of the French resistance, Hubert Beuve-Mery, the editor of *Le Monde,* who fought side by side with them:

> It chanced that I had Jewish fellow fighters. These were not two or three Jews, lost in the mass of the Maquis, but a company of two divisions, consisting almost exclusively of Jews, with its Jewish group leaders, Jewish

section officers and a Jewish captain. The nucleus of this group came from the Jewish scouts. . . .

The suspicious tolerance which they enjoyed during the first few months of the Vichy regime did not last long. Placed outside the pale of the nation and constantly harassed, they tried to cope with their calamity collectively. Secretly, they undertook a task which was exhausting and terribly dangerous. But it was necessary to live, preferably with the consolation and fragile protection of a common shelter.

The group settled on a farm and took to agriculture. . . . Suddenly came the landings [in Normandy]. The group constituted itself into a military formation and joined the Maquis in a body. . . . The Germans launched an attack on one of the cantonments of the Jewish company. The struggle was violent but short. . . . The Germans made short work of the wounded and the camp was burned down.

A few days later, the American breakthrough in Brittany led to a new disposition of forces. . . . Certain types of offensive operations now became possible for this daring group. The most stirring and most successful was the attack on a very heavily armed German train, carrying, among other things, five 20-millimeter rapid-fire cannon. It was a young Jewish sublieutenant, a recent graduate of the Ecole Polytechnique, who set off the charge, despite the risk of being buried or torn to pieces by the imminent explosion. A machine gun manned entirely by Jews engaged in a very unequal duel with German guns. After the cannonade ceased, Jewish patrols from time to time would remind the Germans that they were not forgotten. In the morning . . . the Germans lost courage. From their improvised shelters, the attacking Jews were able to see the German commanding officer come down toward the road, symbolically and picturesquely enveloped in a sheet. While a young Jewish soldier made the Germans explain to him how the cannon was operated so that he would be sure he could operate it, a rabbinical student counted the terrified prisoners who thus fell into hands of the E.I.F. "*Ich bin Jude,*" he kept repeating as he went from one to another. It was the sole act of proud vengeance by these soldiers who suddenly became masters over their executioners.

Today, accompanied by these precious cannon . . . these Jews are fighting somewhere on the eastern front.[26]

This group also distinguished itself in the fighting near Castres on August 19, 1944. It vanquished and captured the German garrison in the city, numbering about 3,500 men.

Oblique evidence of the role of the Jews in the French resistance was provided by the Germans themselves. They tried constantly to discredit it by labeling it "Jewish" and "foreign." Occasionally, as in the Radio Paris broadcast of February 13, 1944, they would editorialize on a disclosure, aiming to shock "true Frenchmen." On that date, the German-controlled broadcast reproached the French Committee of Liberation in Brazzaville for acclaiming ten saboteurs in Paris as "liberators and true Frenchmen": "Is Grieswachs, the perpetrator of two outrages, a Frenchman? No, he is a Jew, a Polish Jew. Is Elek, who was responsible for eight derailments and the deaths of dozens of people, a Frenchman? No, he is a Hungarian Jew. Is Weissbrod, who derailed three trains, a Frenchman? No, he is a Polish Jew. The other terrorists are also Jews: Lifshitz, Fingerweiss, Stockwerk and Reiman."[27] The Free French were apparently not embarrassed by these disclosures.

The deportations from France reached their climax in the summer of 1943. By that time, 52,000 Jews had been deported. However, Eichmann's forces succeeded in filling eighteen more transports between July 1943 and liberation—some of them carrying 1,000 Jews each to Auschwitz. The estimated total of murdered Jews from France is 80,000.

For Jews, these were irreplaceable losses. For Himmler, however, the record in France was a source of embarrassment. When a Nazi town official in Saxony wrote to the S.S. Reichsführer on July 25, 1944, expressing astonishment that Jews, according to the press, were still turning up in Normandy, Himmler could only make a fumbling reply. The total removal of Jews from France, he said, was "extremely difficult" because of the "very strained relations" with the Military Administration.[28]

In Italy, the Nazis encountered strains and difficulties of a different kind.

22 Italy

MUSSOLINI'S ACCESSION TO POWER in 1922 did not affect the affairs of the Jews of Italy. From the time of the abolition of the papal ghetto in Rome in 1870, Jews had rapidly and quite thoroughly been absorbed into the life of the country and Mussolini had no intention of arousing anti-Semitism where none had existed. Frequently between 1922 and 1936 he and other Fascist leaders repeated the same phrase, "The Jewish problem does not exist in Italy." In contrast with Germany, anti-Semitism possessed no value as an instrument of propaganda in Italy, even under Mussolini's fiercely chauvinistic dictatorship.

Privately, however, Mussolini's attitude was more ambivalent and more complicated. After Italian Fascism finished with its brief leftist, anti-capitalist program, Mussolini underlined the "Jewish character" of Bolshevism. But this idea lasted scarcely a year. Already by 1920 he was saying, "Bolshevism is not, as people believe, a Jewish phenomenon. What is true, on the contrary, is that Bolshevism is leading to the utter ruin of the Jews of Eastern Europe." In the period that followed, during which Italian Fascism sought a rapprochement with the Vatican, Mussolini opposed the expressions of Jewish "separatism" in general and of Zionism in particular.[1] The Lateran pacts of 1929 gave new impetus to the anti-Zionist tendencies, inasmuch as the Vatican too was opposed to Zionism. Occasionally, Mussolini also spoke out against "Jewish power" in the Western world, but this resentment, very different from Hitler's, also involved respect. In June 1932, he said, "I have no love for the Jews, but they have great influence everywhere. It is better to leave them alone. His anti-Semitism has already brought Hitler more enemies than is necessary."[2] This attitude, in turn, was sometimes displaced by an exaggerated philo-Semitism which he struck in public.

His attitude toward mixed marriages also reveals an inner contradiction in his feelings about Jews. When his daughter Edda wanted to marry the son of a Jewish colonel in 1929—the year of the concordat with the Vatican—Mussolini inveighed against the idea and said that the marriage would not and could not be carried out. But when the editors of an Italian-

Jewish journal protested against the ever-growing number of mixed marriages, Mussolini was furious.

It seems doubtful that in the early period, Mussolini was at all influenced by the anti-Semitic theories of his German admirers. When he visited Berlin in 1922, he was not favorably impressed by the extreme anti-Semitism of the Nazis, and after the attempted Hitler putsch of November 9, 1923, he expressed violent distaste for the "Nazi buffoons." As late as April 22, 1937, by which time Mussolini had come to admire many other features of German Nazism, he told the Austrian Chancellor Schuschnigg: "It is clear that there are substantial differences between Fascism and Nazism. We are Catholics, proud of our religion and respectful to it. We do not accept the Nazi racial theories, still less their juridical consequences."

Nevertheless, Mussolini's suspicions about Jews persisted and inevitably found expression. There were very few Jews either in important government positions or in the higher Fascist Party hierarchy. Only one Jew, Aldo Finzi, was a member of the first Grand Council and he was baptized and married to the niece of a cardinal. No Jew was admitted to the Italian Academy. It can perhaps be argued that a large percentage of Italian Jews were opposed to Mussolini and did not want to serve in his regime, but their political attitudes were not linked to any Jewish or anti-Jewish aspects of Italian Fascism, but rather to more general political principles.

The first deterioration in the Jewish position in Italy occurred in 1933 when Hitler became Chancellor of Germany. The triumph of German Fascism was officially approved in Italy,[3] but quite naturally deplored by Italian Jews. While Mussolini aimed at strengthening Germany to weaken France, Italian Jews identified with German Jews in the Nazi persecutions. The Italian Government began a double-track policy. On the one hand, it condemned Hitler's racialism; on the other, it unleashed a veritable anti-Semitic campaign in the press—the first in the history of modern Italy. This campaign culminated in the Turin trial of March 30, 1934, in which seventeen anti-Fascists, mostly Jews, were convicted. By Mussolini's order, the Jewish origin of the accused was thrown into bold relief. The Italian dictator continued his uncertain weaving.

At the International Fascist Congress in Montreux in December 1934, a strong anti-Semitic resolution was adopted. Jews were accused of furnishing elements "useful to international revolutions destructive to the ideas of country and Christian civilization." And yet Italian Jews were permitted to send help to German Jews. This view, however, did not prevent Mussolini from advising Dollfuss to add a dash of anti-Semitism to his program to take the wind out of the sails of the Austrian Nazis. Then in the autumn of 1935, on the eve of the attack on Ethiopia, Mussolini made an extravagantly philo-Semitic declaration. "Wherever," he said, "I have detected the faintest trace of anti-Semitic discrimination in the life of the State, I have at once suppressed it. . . . Neither I nor any exponent of the régime, has ever put forward a view hostile to the Jews. In these great days for the Italian nation, I declare that Italian and Jewish ideals are fully merged into one."[3a]

Later, Mussolini and other Italian notables, including the King, believed that "international Jewry" was hostile to the Ethiopian campaign and had initiated sanctions against Italy. From this time on, Mussolini's imperialist adventurism dominated Italian policy.

Beginning in 1936, the aims of Italian foreign policy dictated the line. Italian-German collaboration began in Spain, and it is not a coincidence that in September 1936, a month before Ciano's visit to Hitler, another anti-Semitic campaign was launched in the press. Immediately after Ciano's journey, Mussolini began to remove Jews from Italian journalism. Giorgio Pini, the editor in chief of *Il Popolo d'Italia*, remonstrated with Mussolini when the removal of a brilliant Jewish columnist was being discussed. "You must understand," Mussolini argued, "what impression it would make abroad if political polemics in Mussolini's own paper were entrusted to a Jew."[4]

Gradually, Mussolini also changed his mind about "Jewish power." Anti-Semitism obviously had not hindered Hitler from going from one diplomatic triumph to another. Quite the reverse: racialism was proving to be a useful weapon in Hitler's triumphs. Once Mussolini had decided to march with Hitler "to the end," a complete revamping of former Italian attitudes was necessary. Many problems stood in the way. What should be done with the Jewish generals in the Italian Army, the Jewish professors in the universities, the Jewish officials in the Fascist diplomatic service and administration—Italians whose loyalty to Italy was undeniable? How could the Italian people be led to accept anti-Semitism in a society where Jews were quite fully accepted? And yet, Mussolini's burning ambitions for glory and empire which he could win only in alliance with Hitler made a new ideology urgent. The impression is often conveyed that Italian racial legislation was merely an example of "scandalous German interference" or Nazi pressure. Indeed, when Italy became the weak member of the Axis, the Nazis prodded her on to adopt harsh anti-Jewish measures, but in the early period of the partnership, Mussolini acted independently. On her side, Germany, at least Hitler (in contrast with other Nazi leaders) always overestimated Italy and considered her a great power in whose internal affairs it was not permissible to intervene. According to Goebbels, Hitler did not really face the truth about Mussolini's regime until after the debacle of July 25, 1943, when the Duce was overthrown. As late as March 1943, the Germans hesitated to intervene in the Italian Jewish problem. S.S. Major Carltheo Zeitschel, attached to the German Embassy in Paris as an expert on the Jewish question, made the following observation on March 24, 1943: "The German Embassy in Rome has for years had the strictest orders from Berlin not to do anything which could in any way disturb the friendly relations between Italy and Germany. It seems, therefore, that it would be inconceivable for the German Embassy in Rome even to raise so delicate a question as that of the Jews of Italy. My cautious inquiries produced similar replies from the political directors of the Embassy."[5]

But if the Nazis did not intervene in Italian Jewish policy, they surely served as models for Mussolini when he finally decided to adopt racist legislation. He began working himself up in 1938. Ciano's diary entries during the year record the following pertinent items: On July 10: "[The Duce] intends to introduce the concentration camp with more severe methods than those used in the present form of police detention. A first hint of the turn of the screw will be given by a bonfire of Jewish, Masonic and pro-French literature." On July 30: ". . . following the Pope's speech [Pope Pius XI], violently critical of racialism, I summoned the Nuncio and gave him a warning—if the Vatican continues on this path, a clash is inevitable because since the conquest of the Empire the Duce regards the racial question as fundamental." On August 8: "He has ordered that all Jews are to be struck off the diplomatic list. I am to begin by recalling them to Rome."[5a]

Beginning in September 1938, the Interior Ministry started work on an anti-Jewish charter under Mussolini's direction, and yet, when the General Secretary of the Fascist Party suggested the unconditional expulsion of all Jews from the Party, Mussolini rejected the idea out of hand. He was still far from adopting a "total" program against Jews.

By the middle of November, the Italian anti-Jewish laws were ready. They included a definition of Jew, which included everyone having two Jewish parents; or one parent, if the other was a foreigner; if the mother was Jewish and the father unknown; or if one parent was Jewish and the other non-Jewish, provided that the offspring (as of October 1, 1938) were considered Jewish. Jews were excluded from the armed forces, the civil service and the Fascist Party, and from businesses employing a hundred or more Italians, but exceptions were made for war veterans and old-time Fascists. Jews were also forbidden to own real estate in excess of 20,000 lira and farm property valued over 5,000 lira. A later decree of June 29, 1939 restricted Jewish professionals to serving Jews only, except in cases of proved necessity. Marriages between Jews and non-Jews were forbidden. Jewish children were expelled from Italian schools. Finally, the basic law of November 17, 1938, nullified all naturalizations of Jews obtained after January 1, 1919. All denaturalized Jews and all foreign Jews were forced to leave Italy and its possessions by March 12, 1939.[6]

When the drafting of the November laws was completed, Mussolini had talks with King Victor Emmanuel, the man who had to sign them. "Three times in the course of their conversation this morning," Ciano observed, "the King said to him that he feels an 'infinite pity for the Jews.' He cited cases of persecution, among them that of General Pugliese, an old man of 80, loaded with medals and wounds, who had been deprived of his housekeeper. The Duce said that there are 20,000 spineless people in Italy who are moved by the fate of the Jews. The King replied that he is one of them."

This code was not mild; many Jews suffered—particularly those who worked in government offices and on farms. By October 1941, 7,000 of Italy's 50,000 Jews had left Italy, including 6,000 citizens. But there is a vast difference between the Italian and the German commitment to anti-Semitism. In Italy, Mussolini used anti-Semitism as an opportunistic tactic for imperialistic strategy; in Germany, Hitler's anti-Semitism had captured and possessed the whole of the man and the nation. In Italy, there was no anti-Semitic tradition; in Germany, anti-Semitism had put down deep roots. In Italy, the enforcement of the laws was slow and lax; in Germany, it was swift and literal. It is impossible to imagine Hitler saying, even in private, what Mussolini told his sister about the country's racial laws:

> In Italy, racialism and anti-Semitism were being made to appear as politically important as they are unimportant in their substance. The racial purity of this nation, over which have passed so many invasions and which has absorbed so many peoples from the four points of the compass and the Semitic peril in a nation like ours . . . are clearly absurd fables which should be left for certain fanatics to write [about].
>
> But if circumstances had brought me to a Rome-Moscow Axis, I would perhaps have dressed up the Italian workers, who are so taken up with their jobs, just as promptly and with a detachment which the racialists might call Mediterranean, with the corresponding fable of Stakhanovite ethics and the happiness they bring. And in this case, too, it would have been a question of a showy but cheap token payment.[7]

As Mussolini's anti-Semitism was supposed to be a sly, tongue-in-cheek maneuver, he even encouraged evasions. For example, in the talk with his sister, he said, "I know, by the way, that you and other members of your family are helping the Jews, and I am not displeased, but think that thereby you can show the utter elasticity of our racial laws." These elasticities notwithstanding, many Italian Jews suffered. It has been reliably estimated that the total number of exemptions from the racial laws did not exceed 3,000,[8] and many of these were only partial exemptions. The bulk of Italian Jews felt painful changes in their lives. Nevertheless, as compared with Germany or most of the German-occupied countries, the plight of the Italian Jews was bearable. They had not been totally deprived of their property; many could still work; socially, they were not ostracized and, most significantly, they were not ghettoized.

However, the foreign Jews who had not left the country were interned. By May 1942, a thousand were confined to camps at Salerno, Cosenza and Chieti. In the late summer of 1942, some Italian Jews were called up for labor in Rome, Bologna, Milan and Tripoli, but the Italians made no preparations for deporting any Jews. The Germans at this time were getting all of their stations ready for massive deportations, but they did not interfere in Italy. On September 24, 1942, Ribbentrop called Martin Luther, head of a special division in the Foreign Office devoted to the Jewish question, and issued instructions on deportation strategy for various countries of Europe. With respect to Italy, Luther was instructed to do nothing. The question would be reserved for a personal discussion between Hitler and Mussolini, or between Ribbentrop and Count Ciano. Meanwhile outside Italy, in Italian-occupied Europe—in parts of France, Croatia and Yugoslavia—a generous policy toward Jews was pursued by Italian Army officers and members of the Italian Foreign Office, often without Mussolini's knowledge or in opposition to his explicit instructions.

By January 1943, the S.S. was growing impatient. Italian Jews in German-controlled areas were conspicuously immune from the waves of deportations. Ribbentrop instructed the German Ambassador to tell Ciano that in German eyes, Jews of Italian nationality were also Jews. In February, before Ribbentrop left for a visit to Rome, Himmler asked him to ask the Italians to stop sabotaging the RSHA measures in German-controlled areas. He also wanted the Italians to bring their measures up to the German level in Italy, but the Italians hedged and the Germans did not press too hard. But by now Mussolini was ill, disillusioned and frightened and the Italians were sick of the war.

The Allied landings in Sicily early in July led to a quick collapse of Italian Fascism. On July 25, Mussolini was overthrown and three days later the Fascist Party was dissolved. The new government of Marshal Badoglio did not repeal the anti-Jewish laws, but in September it surrendered to the Allies. The Germans acted quickly. They set to work disarming the Italian Army and occupying the country. For several days, the German forces in central and south Italy were critically exposed. Two German divisions in the vicinity of Rome faced five Italian divisions. Had the powerful Allied invasion fleet moved north to the capital, as the Germans had expected, the war in Italy might have taken a very different turn and the Third Reich might have been defeated a year earlier than it was.[9] But the Allies did not press their advantage by sea or air; nor did they utilize the large Italian forces at their disposal. The Germans could well breathe a sigh of relief when the American Fifth Army landed not near Rome but at Salerno, south of Naples. No Allied parachutists appeared over the Rome airfields as they had feared. The Italian divisions surrendered almost without firing a shot and were disarmed. Now, the Germans could easily hold Rome and, for the time being, even Naples. This gave them possession of two thirds of Italy, including the industrial north, whose factories were immediately put to work turning out arms for Germany. The Duce was rescued and a new "Fascist Republic" organized. Miraculously, Hitler now had a new base of power; tragically, Europe would be convulsed by more bloody warfare. For the Jews of Italy, their time of trial had come.

On September 25, the RSHA sent a circular to all of its branches at home and afield specifying that "in agreement with the Foreign Office" all Jews of listed nationalities could now be included in deportation measures. Italy headed the list; measures there were to be carried out at once.[10] The deportations started in Rome and then shifted to the north.

There were 8,000 Jews in Rome at this time, some of whom on their way south after the Allied landings had stopped en route. When the Germans entered the city, many of them went into hiding, including Chief Rabbi Israel Zolli, who was convinced that the monasteries and convents of the Church would offer refuge. In the Rome police station, Maresciallo Mario di Marco began preparing false identity cards for Jews while his superior Angelo de Fiore resisted German efforts to take over Jewish registration lists. Before the roundups began, Herbert Kappler, the German Security Police commander, demanded 50 kilograms of gold (about $50,000) from the Jewish community and threatened to take 300 hostages if the money was not delivered. Since so many Jews had already dispersed throughout the city, the money could not be raised. Rabbi Zolli then went to the Vatican and arranged a loan of 15 kilograms (about $17,000) with the head of the Vatican Treasury, Bernardino Nogana. The money was then delivered to the German Embassy. The crisis came in October.

Early in the month, a consul at the German Embassy wrote to Ribbentrop to tell him that Kappler had been ordered by Berlin to arrest 8,000 Jews in Rome and transport them to northern Italy, "where they are supposed to be liquidated." The German commander in Rome, General Stahel intended to implement this order only if agreed to by Ribbentrop. "Personally," the consul concluded, "I am of the opinion that it would be better business to mobilize Jews for defense construction."[11] The answer from Berlin was that Hitler had ordered the Jews of Rome to be brought to Mauthausen as hostages. Under no circumstances was the consul to interfere in the matter.

Notwithstanding this information, it was generally known in embassy and Vatican circles that Himmler intended to send the Jews of Rome to Auschwitz. On October 16, Bishop Ludwig Hudal, rector of the German church in Rome, made a last-minute appeal to the German Military Commander, General Stahel:

> I have just been informed by a high Vatican office in the immediate circle of the Holy Circle that the arrests of Jews of Italian nationality have begun this morning. In the interest of the good relations which have existed until now between the Vatican and the high German military command . . . I would be very grateful if you would give an order to stop these arrests in Rome and its vicinity right away. I fear that otherwise the Pope will have to make an open stand, which will serve the anti-German propaganda as a weapon against us.[12]

The appeal, however, was fruitless. The arrests were not stopped. Nor did the Pope make an open stand—much to the relief of the Germans, and much to the disappointment of others. The action against the Jews began during the night of October 15–16 and continued for twenty-four hours. But the Nazis seized a scant 1,000 for Auschwitz; the remaining 7,000 Jews had been warned in time and went into hiding. Many were sheltered in monasteries and convents and others—the estimates vary from several dozen to several thousand—in the Vatican itself.

One day after the completion of the roundups, the German Ambassador at the Vatican, Ernst von Weizsäcker, reported to Berlin that the College of Cardinals was particularly shocked because the seizures were made, so to speak, under the windows of the Pope. The reaction, observed Weizsäcker, might have been muted if the Jews had been kept in Italy for forced labor. Now, anti-German circles in Rome were urging the Pope to speak out. "It is said," he reported, "that bishops in French cities where similar things happened, had taken a clear stand." The Pope, thought Weizsäcker, as head of the Church and Bishop of Rome, could not very well do less. Already comparisons were being made between the present pontiff and the "much more temperamental Pius XI."[13]

The Pope, however, did not express the views of the Curia. He remained silent. Whatever pressure may have been exerted was unsuccessful. On October 28 Weizsäcker wrote to the Foreign Office that the whole affair now appeared to be liquidated: "The Pope," he said, "although pressed on many sides, has not allowed himself to be drawn into any expression of disapproval against the deportations of the Jews of Rome. Even though this attitude may be held against him by our opponents and used by Protestant circles in Anglo-Saxon countries for propagandistic purposes against Catholicism, he has done everything in this touchy matter to avoid burdening relations with the German Government and German agencies in Rome."[14]

From October until June 4, 1944, when the Allies entered Rome, the

Jews of the city led haunted lives, constantly subject to roundups and arrest. However, the chief German target was northern Italy where 35,000 Jews were concentrated. Most of them began to disperse as soon as the German Army poured across the northern Italian passes in the late summer of 1943. Sporadic arrests were made after the German occupation in September, but a more systematic plan was worked out early in October when Martin Sandberger, a former *Einsatzgruppe* commander in Russia, took charge of the Gestapo in Mussolini's new capital, Verona, and Theodor Dannecker, fresh from France, became Jewish Commissioner for Italy.

The Jews were dispersed in the north, but the Gestapo found plenty of empty prisoner-of-war camps north of the Apennines for those who could be caught as well as for Italian opponents of the new "Fascist Republic" and Yugoslav partisans. The catch, however, was meager for the first few months and the RSHA complained that Italian delays had allowed most of the Jews to find hiding places in small villages which the S.S. could not comb. Mussolini then gave the S.S. a legal handle. On December 1, the radio broadcast the announcement of a new Italian law which Mussolini obligingly provided for the S.S. The law branded the Jews as "enemy foreigners" and ordered the transfer of all Jews to concentration camps. The RSHA was smugly pleased. It could supply Italy with "experienced advisers" and lull both Jews and Italians into thinking that the camps constituted a "final solution" rather than a preparatory step to death. This tactical maneuver was spelled out in a letter from the German Foreign Office to Gestapo chief Heinrich Müller on December 14, 1943: "The Foreign Office considers as not feasible the plan . . . that the Jews collected in concentration camps be made available for deportations to the Eastern Territories. For tactical and political reasons, such a request should be put off until the seizure of the Jews by the Italian organs has been concluded. . . . The Foreign Office, on the basis of its experience, feels that if the request to hand over these Jews is made now, the seizing operation will be greatly impaired or perhaps fail altogether."[15]

While the Security Police and Fascist helpers concentrated their victims in camps, Italian bureaucrats busied themselves with the confiscation of abandoned Jewish property. In March 1944, the Germans sprang their trap: the main camp at Fossoli di Carpi, near Modena, which had been relatively mild under Italian administration, was turned over to the Germans and deportations to Auschwitz began. Transports to Mauthausen from another camp, Gries, near Bolzano, also left. The Italian Search Committee for Deported Jews estimates that 10,271 Jews were deported from Italy during the twenty months of the "Fascist Republic." Approximately 4,500 left Fossoli and Gries in known Auschwitz transports; a further 600 have been traced to Mauthausen. As many as 5,000 are listed as having been sent to Germany or Poland from centers other than Rome, Fossoli and Bolzano, of which there are no train records. The Jewish losses in Italy have been placed at from 8,500 to 9,500,[16] one of the least successful of the Nazi deportations.

In the Reich, however, the S.S. more than made up for their poor Italian record.

23 The Greater Reich

THE FIRST TRANSPORTS "to the East" were made from the Old Reich itself in the fall of 1941. However, the careful preparatory work which is often found at the beginning of many of the most destructive actions of the Nazis was conspicuously missing from these first deportations. Chaotic, hastily organized, and brutally enforced, they began before procedures for the "Final Solution" had been settled by the RSHA, and even before the technical plans for extermination had been completed. Between October 15 and 31, 20,000 Jews—mostly old persons—were sent notices, assembled and deported to Lodz. The destination of Lodz was an afterthought. Originally, the first transports from Germany were scheduled to go to the Russian ghettos, but these had not yet been cleared and the Transport Command of the Wehrmacht had banned the use of the Russian railway system. Furthermore, the German authorities in Lodz had strongly protested the influx of new arrivals in that overcrowded ghetto, but Heydrich and Eichmann were impatient to have the Jews disappear from the Third Reich. Later, in November, 50,000 German and Czech Jews were deported to occupied Russia, principally to Riga and Minsk. These transports also violated Wehrmacht orders to stop the trains and clear the railways so that needed supplies could be dispatched to the front. Skilled men and armament workers exempted from deportation by the Ministry of Justice were also pulled into Heydrich's violent police sweep. Not until the Wannsee Conference of January 1942 did the RSHA chief acknowledge the various gradations of privilege and exemption—and then only fitfully.

The deportees to Lodz were killed within a few weeks. The transports to Riga and Minsk survived for several months. The plan to fill the emptied Russian ghettos with Reich Jews was supposed to be a carefully guarded secret known only to the most restricted circles in Germany, but it was commonly known in the occupied Russian territory that the houses of the dead Jews would soon be filled by Jews from the Reich. Besides the disorder and breakdown of official secrecy, there was sudden death.

The Reich Jews began to arrive in November. Some were sent to the Salaspils camp near Riga to be worked to death in icy temperatures.

469

Others were sent to the Riga ghetto. The new arrivals had a foreboding of what was to befall them. The apartments they found were wrecked and some of the furnishings were bloodied. Mrs. Jeanette Wolff, a leading Socialist figure in pre-Hitler Germany, and Deputy Mayor of Berlin in the postwar period, has recorded her experience in the trip to Riga from Dortmund early in 1942:

On the morning of January 25, a long and dismal march brought us to a train standing near the railroad station. Rumors spread that it was going to Riga in Latvia. We rode five days in the cold train without warm food and tortured by thirst. A few people at a time were permitted to leave each car to get water; and a few minutes were allowed for cleaning ourselves in the snow. Men and women had to perform their toilet on the rail embankment in each other's presence. In the terrible cold, hundreds of people froze parts of their bodies and developed gangrenous fingers and toes, and many died after reaching the camp. The Jewish community of Dortmund had collected three carloads of food to tide us over the first days of deportation. The cars were detached from the train in Königsberg. Such baggage as sewing machines, mattresses and stoves, which we had been permitted to take along, we never saw again.

At the Shirotowa station in Riga, German and Latvian SS welcomed us with sticks and rifle butts. Our hand baggage was taken away. It was a beautiful day and a glorious winter sun shone on the untracked snow. The contrast of nature with human brutality hit me hard. The snow covered ground where thousands had been murdered.

The SS drove us to the ghetto. The houses looked as if vandals had visited them. Floors and stairs were littered with broken furniture and china, torn clothing and shoes, plaster and damaged household articles. Toilets and pipes had been smashed. It was obvious that the previous residents had left in great haste just before we came, but we did not at once understand why. We soon heard rumors that they had been killed. Eleven transports of perhaps two thousand people each had been sent to take their place. The older people and some children in our transport who could not walk from the Riga station were put on sleds, and we never saw them again. . . .

New transports arrived. There was no space; three and more families were already living in one room. The commandant of the ghetto, Karl Wilhelm Krause, developed a method of finding space which was called *Aktion*: liquidation of a portion of the inhabitants. Sometimes whole transports were taken directly from the station to the Bikernik Forest and shot there. Groups of young men were sent to a place called Salaspils, where they were given a hunger ration and were literally worked to death, burying thousands of Jews and Russian prisoners of war who been shot or had died of hunger. A transport of about 1300 people from Berlin, among them 750 children from the orphan asylum, was sent there, and only 80 sturdy men were kept apart and sent to work in a cement plant. All that arrived in the ghetto was the clothing and the shoes of 750 children and 450 men and women, sometimes smeared with blood.

During the first two weeks we received no food. We looked in the garbage for frozen potato peelings, vegetable refuse, and so forth, and cleaned, cooked, and ate the stuff. We mixed potato peelings with flour and baked them without fat. The stoves were broken and smoked heavily. If an army bread truck driving through the ghetto stopped long enough, we stole bread. When food came, it was a starvation ration: 220 grams of mouldy bread—equivalent to four slices a day—and later fish and herring scraps from the smokehouses. Three slices of bread were the only present we could give my husband on his birthday. Juliane and Edith [Mrs. Wolff's daughters] brought food from other parts of town, although that was punishable by death. Friends who had come with us died of hunger and exposure. Most people had lost their will to live.[1]

Those who did not perish from physical attrition were marched to the execution pits deep in the forest and killed. Mrs. Wolff, one of the few survivors, made her way back to life through sheer will, luck and skill as a seamstress. She brushed death daily but in spite of her harrowing ordeal, including the loss of her husband and two daughters, she felt the need to continue the struggle for life and freedom where she had begun it, in Germany.

The deportees to Minsk were also annihilated, but several thousand Jews won a temporary reprieve there through the unexpected intercession of the Generalkommissar of White Russia, Gauleiter Wilhelm Kube. In December 1941, he wrote to his chief, Hinrich Lohse:

> The Jews within the next few weeks will probably die of cold or hunger. They constitute a tremendous danger of epidemics for us, because, naturally, they are exposed to the 22 epidemics which rage over White Ruthenia. . . . On my own responsibility, I am not going to give the S.D. instructions on "handling" these people, although some formations of the Wehrmacht and the police are already eager to get possession of the Jews from the Reich. The S.D. have already—without asking—taken away 400 mattresses from them and also confiscated all sorts of things. I beg you to send me instructions. These Jews include war veterans, holders of the Iron Cross, those wounded in war, half-Aryans, and even three-quarter Aryans. . . . I do not lack hardness and I am ready to contribute to the solution of the Jewish problem, but people who come from the same cultural circles as ourselves are different from the bestial, aboriginal hordes. . . . I ask you to consider the honor of our Reich and our party, and give clear instructions to take care of what is necessary in a form which is humane.[2]

Kube managed to protect over 6,000 Jews until the following July. Not only did some belong to his "cultural circle," but others formed the remnants of a Jewish skilled labor force including mechanics, clerks, interpreters and builders of sledge wagons for the Wehrmacht. A tough Nazi, S.S. Lieutenant Colonel Eduard Strauch, was sent to Minsk to keep an eye on Kube, and the S.D. of White Russia submitted a long report listing the many failings of this old Gauleiter: he had shaken hands with a Jew who had rescued his car from a burning garage, he had confessed to enjoying the music of Mendelssohn and Offenbach, and he had been seen giving sweets to Jewish children. Strauch complained of Kube's sympathy for German Jews, which, he said, bordered on treason.

By July 1942, a very different Kube wrote Lohse to applaud the liquidation of 55,000 Jews in White Russia within ten weeks. By that time the intensified slaughter in Russia had blunted his sensitivities. Jews in White Russia had become "the main bearer of the partisan movement in the East" and Kube insisted on killing them. In September 1943, he was killed by a bomb thrown into his billet by his chambermaid, a partisan. By then the "Jewish problem" in Russia had been solved for almost a year and the last handful of Reich Jews there had just been killed by gassing vans. None survived the war.

The first deportations "to the East" were scheduled in the Reich-Protectorate area. The German people were intended to be the first to "benefit" from a society purged of Jews. But the deportations were not merely a matter of seizures and transport. A manual of procedure was required. The victims had to be defined, their movements restricted, their property disposed of, essential and special categories classified, and areas cleared for destruction. These problems increased beyond Germany's boundaries. Foreign personnel had to be used, native populations had to be subdued, and gaps left by Jews had to be filled. Within Germany itself, there were certain difficulties. At times, the Heydrich machine was balked. Conflicts with other jurisdictions developed. The very damage dealt to the national interest in certain kinds of deportations created obstructions. There was also the German propensity for covering all possible situations with legal devices, a baffling but compulsive need for officially appropriate cover—perhaps to muffle the ghastly impact of the deed of murder—which created innumerable delays and obstacles. As a consequence, the Reich could not be made *Judenrein* with all speed, and the first deportations to Auschwitz came, not from Germany, but from the countries of western Europe.

Two trial deportations had taken place in 1940, the first consisting of 1,300 Jews from Stettin who were sent, under inhuman conditions, to Poland in February 1940; and the second, 7,500 Jews from Baden and the Saar, who were sent to camps in Vichy France in October 1940. These, however, lacked the elaborate "legal" preparations of later deportations. The expulsions to Lodz and to the ghettos of occupied Russia were chaotic. Himmler apparently hesitated to exterminate German Jews on German territory before having some kind of official authorization. Legal rationalization was needed. Late in 1941, one step was taken in this direction—the nationality of German Jews deported outside the borders of the Reich was removed: they could be summarily executed anywhere in occupied territory, although not on German soil. To extend the Auschwitz plan to Reich Jews, a blanket cover of outlawry was needed. Early in

1942, a newly appointed Reichskommissar for Justice, Dr. Otto Thierack, was happy to oblige.

Thierack's action grew out of Hitler's order to the Reichstag in April 1942 to abrogate all statutory law for the duration of the war. The first use of this sweeping order had affected Karl Lasch who was a friend of Hans Frank. At this time Frank was not only Governor-General in Poland but Reichskommissar for Justice. Lasch was executed without trial on a charge of peculation. This execution triggered off the vast murderous power of the Reichstag action. Frank made a tour of the law schools that summer, advocating the return of constitutional law, but was stopped in his tracks by Hitler, who not only removed him from his post as Reichskommissar of Justice, but stripped him of all party honors. His successor, Thierack, was a strong party man who "was authorized to deviate from the existing law in order to establish a truly National Socialist administration of justice." Seeking to ingratiate himself, Thierack invited Goebbels to lecture to the members of the People's Court. Goebbels accepted the invitation and thundered against the continued access to the courts by some Jews. In September, Thierack saw Himmler and they agreed that all Jews, as well as Poles, Russians and Gypsies, could be committed to concentration camps without the formality of charges. These groups, Thierack said, could be surrendered to the police who then "can take the necessary measures unhampered by the laws of criminal evidence." Later, on October 13, Thierack wrote to Martin Bormann saying that "the administration of justice can only make a small contribution to the extermination of members of these peoples."[3] The last vestige of protection for the Reich Jews—the criminal code—was thus withdrawn. No legal obstacles now blocked Himmler's extermination plans. The wearing of the Jewish badge had already become obligatory on September 1, 1941, and by March 1942, all deported Jews were declared "hostile to the nation and State"; their property could now be readily confiscated.

Finding a general legal basis for the concept of Jewish "subhuman" also preoccupied the German rule drafters[4] and resulted in involuted argumentation as well as bizarre dilemmas. Thus, one proposed law forbade Jews from testifying under oath—the oath of a Jew was considered quite worthless. However, this inability to take an oath must not work to his advantage. On the other hand, the testimony was to be treated "like a deposition under oath." The Wehrmacht Command saw through this fuzz and commented pointedly: "This regulation would lead to an unjustified overvaluation of unsworn Jewish testimony as against the unsworn testimony of witnesses who could take an oath." By the time this decree was fit to print, in July 1943, there were virtually no full Jews at liberty in Germany except those married to Aryans.

The half-Jews and Jews in mixed marriages provided the legalistic hairsplitters with their most exasperating, and in the end insoluble, problem. Countless meetings and involved pieces of correspondence discuss these groups at great length. Hitler's "Final Solution" formula oversimplified the problem. An insight into the strange realms of thought which these vexing questions provoked can be seen in the following opinion of the State Secretary in the Ministry of the Interior, Wilhelm Stuckart, who had helped draft the Nuremberg Laws:

> The fact is that in deporting half-Jews, German blood is being sacrificed. I have always considered it biologically very dangerous to introduce German blood into the enemy camp. This blood will only produce personalities who will place at the service of the enemy those precious qualities inherited with their German blood. The half-Jews' intelligence and excellent education, linked to their ancestral Germanic heritage, make them natural leaders outside of Germany and consequently, dangerous enemies. . . . Therefore, I prefer to see half-Jews die a natural death inside Germany, although from three to four decades may be necessary to achieve this purpose.[5]

These half-Jews and quarter-Jews were the *Mischlinge*, 150,000 souls in the Reich-Protectorate area who were living proof of a task unfinished, of a solution that could not be "final," and a predicament that the most painstaking bureaucrat could not escape. The *Mischlinge* of the first degree were defined by the Nuremberg Laws as half-Jews (descended from two Jewish grandparents) who did not adhere to the Jewish religion and were not married to Jews. *Mischlinge* of the second degree, or quarter-Jews, were descended from one Jewish grandparent. The *Mischlinge*, generally speaking, were not subjected to the destruction process and were distinguished from "Jews." Whether a half-Jew was to be classified as a Jew or *Mischling* depended ultimately, if religious affiliation was not formal, on how he regarded himself. The attitude and intention of the individual had to be weighed as well as his conduct.

The German courts were deeply involved in determining the status of individuals who really constituted a third "race," a group that was neither German nor Jewish. The court interpretations had to balance off the protection of the German community against the destruction of the Jews. Nothing illustrates more clearly the fallacy of the Nazi definition of race than their decisions. In some cases, for example, a person with four German grandparents was classified as Jewish![6]

For the courts, the cases involved tortuous windings of language; for the individual involved, it was a literal matter of life or death. At first, procedures for reclassification from a Jew to a *Mischling*, known as *Befreiung* ("liberation"), meant release from the massive battery of anti-Jewish measures. Later such a reclassification meant freedom from deportation and the death centers, for the *Mischlinge* suffered only small disabilities: they were excluded from the civil service and Nazi Party; they could serve in the Army only as common soldiers; they could not marry Germans without official consent. Applications for "liberation" increased in volume in 1942 as the destruction process accelerated, while pressure from Party leaders and the police to transform the *Mischlinge* into Jews became correspondingly strong.

Toward the end of 1941, when the "Final Solution" was at hand, the problem of the *Mischlinge* still stood in the way. They were unfinished business.

Drastic reclassifications were suggested at the Wannsee Conference in January 1942. *Mischlinge* of the first degree were to be classified as Jews, unless "liberation" was granted for "services rendered to the German people" or other "merits." *Mischlinge* of the second degree were to be treated as Germans but if they were not married to Germans they could be classed as Jews on the basis of appearance, police reports or "Jewish behavior." Sterilization was proposed for those who wanted to avoid deportation. However, it was pointed out, sterilization would not change things. *Mischlinge* would still be *Mischlinge*. They would be abroad in the community, in sports, in the Army, at work—carriers of "Jewish blood." The difficulties of the bureaucrats were compounded when it was admitted that sterilization techniques had not been perfected. Until the end of 1944, doctors continued to experiment on girls in Block 10 of the main camp at Auschwitz and performed ghastly operations.

This issue could not be resolved at the Wannsee Conference or in subsequent meetings; discussions continued in voluminous correspondence. The interests of the German nation were subjected to careful analysis. How could workers and fighters already "liberated" be branded as Jews? It would be most illogical to deport "real" *Mischlinge*. Also, there was the matter of German relatives to consider: the psychological repercussions at home in the event of deportations would be incalculable. Finally, there was the decisive consideration raised by Stuckart—deporting half-Jews would mean abandoning that half of their blood which was German.

The arguments seesawed back and forth for months, but in the end, the *Mischlinge* were neither deported nor sterilized. They were extremely vulnerable at all times because their behavior could be interpreted as that of a "full Jew," and such a charge meant death. But their status defied the best efforts of many conscientious Nazis, and most of them survived the war.

Closely linked to the *Mischling* problem was the question of Jews in mixed marriages. Most Jews in mixed marriages were parents of *Mischlinge* and their fate often hinged on whether or not their children were classified as *Mischlinge*. If the couple were lucky, they received a "privileged" status and could avoid deportation. Until the extermination phase of

Nazi action against the Jews, Jews in mixed marriages were generally exempt from anti-Jewish measures.[7] Heydrich, of course, opposed this line, and at the Wannsee Conference it was decided that all Jews in mixed marriages would be deported. A later conference in March 1942 further decided that all "racially mixed marriages" had to be dissolved. The Jewish partner would then be deported. If the Aryan partner failed to apply for a divorce within a given time, the public prosecutor would file a petition and the courts were to grant a divorce in all such cases. The Justice Ministry fought this assault on the courts and on the Catholic Church.

Meanwhile, the deadlock over the planned divorce procedure had been submitted to Hitler for a final decision, but he refused to consider it. The Jews in "privileged" marriages thereafter led the life of hostages of the Gestapo, and any trumped-up complaint meant deportation, but most of them (about 28,000) survived the war. The sheer fortuitousness of their life in the Greater Reich is appalling to consider: a *Mischling*, perhaps genuinely thinking and feeling himself to be a Jew, had to alter everything in his makeup in order to prove himself worthy to be a German in order to live. A Jew in a mixed marriage walked on eggshells day and night—if he failed to add "Israel" when signing a postal order, or if he smoked a cigarette in the street, or if he received a food parcel—he could be sent to his death. A Christian non-Aryan (of whom several thousand had been seized and deported) who had converted after 1935 and was officially baptized, nonetheless had to wear the Jewish star, had to avoid contact with Aryans at church services and bear other humiliations, at the same time suffering the contempt of other Jews. The spiritual anguish of these men and women was extreme.

Other special problems that could not be smothered by Heydrich's plans involved yet other categories. What should be done, for example, about old people who could not conceivably be considered dangerous to the Reich? Or war veterans, particularly disabled and decorated ones who had fought for Germany, a distinction every German, even the most Nazified, could understand? Or the problem of so-called prominent Jews whose disappearance in a death camp might provoke inquiries from abroad? For these groups Heydrich himself created a special ghetto in Theresienstadt, Czechoslovakia, about 35 miles from Prague.

At first Theresienstadt was designed for old people, sixty-five and over, who were expected to die soon. Since the standard explanation for deportations was that Jews were a danger to the Reich and had to be "evacuated," the deportation of old people required a somewhat different explanation. They were no danger; many of them lived in old-age homes. By setting up Theresienstadt for old Jews who, as Heydrich said, "could not stand the strain of resettlement," Heydrich actually strengthened the myth of resettlement. In other promotional propaganda, Theresienstadt was described as a "model ghetto" and a "Jewish reservation." A second group, the war veterans, was added to avoid interventions or at least sympathetic interest on the part of the German Army itself. Later came Jews married to Aryans who had lost their exemption, senior civil servants, members of the *Reichsvereinigung* of German Jews and ultimately "privileged" Jews who had bought their way into what was called the "model ghetto," the town "governed" by Jews, but whose exit, it turned out, was Auschwitz.

By May 1945 only 17,000 had survived the overall transfer of 130,000 Jews from the Reich-Protectorate area. This became the meaning of "favored transport." In the "transfers of residence" to Theresienstadt, as the deportations were euphemistically called, the *Reichsvereinigung* of German Jews was directed to draw up an agreement for the purchase of a place in the ghetto. The deportee transferred all of his property to the *Reichsvereinigung* and in return, he was supposed to be guaranteed food, clothing, housing and medical care for life. When the last officials of the *Reichsvereinigung* were themselves sent to Theresienstadt, the Reich confiscated the funds in the Association's treasury.

Theresienstadt had once been a fortress town of 7,000 or 8,000 soldiers and peasants, but a rather sleepy one for a garrison. Heydrich ordered the evacuation of the German Army in November 1941. By January 1942, streams of Jews began arriving through the huge moss-covered fortress walls into the old brick barracks. By the end of 1942, over 85,000 Jews were crowded into ugly quarters, wasting away or being readied for Auschwitz.

Theresienstadt lay on the Ohre River in a gentle plain among meadows and low, sloping hills. In the distance were the blue-tinged mountains of Bohemia. But the town itself was grim. Its chief features were high scarps and deep moats, fortress walls and huge gray barracks. Streets intersected each other at right angles and the old, dark and dismal homes were indistinguishable from the barracks. The S.S. camp command overflowed into the town and took up numerous houses as well as barracks. Streets leading from the outside to these buildings were lined with barbed wire and wooden fences.

Systematic paperwork in Nazi Europe very possibly celebrated its greatest triumph in Theresienstadt and provided countless jobs for S.S. men who preferred fighting the internal enemy to fighting at the front. Detailed statistics, charts, surveys and reports created a huge supply of useless and often fraudulent records. It has been estimated that every prioner in the Ghetto was entered in at least seventeen different files and registers.

The creation of Theresienstadt was the last major anti-Jewish measure ordered by Heydrich—he was assassinated shortly afterward. The ghetto had its own S.S. command, headed first by Dr. Siegfried Seidl, then Anton Burger, and finally Karl Rahm—all Eichmann's men. Under S.S. control was a Council of Elders, whose first head was Jakub Edelstein. The Council was made up of heterogeneous elements—Czech, German and Austrian—which in time created certain clashes and strains, and which involved S.S. men themselves in actions based on their national preferences. But in the early period, among the Czech leaders particularly, Theresienstadt was looked upon as a way of rescuing Jews from the dreadful conditions in Poland.

For Czech Jews, the Nazi deception played on the Jewish desire for autonomy. When the Nazis announced that an "autonomous ghetto" for Jews would be set up in the territory of the Protectorate, Jewish community leaders in Prague received the news with a certain feeling of relief. They not only looked upon Theresienstadt as a way of saving Jews from Poland, but also believed that it was essential to remain in contact with fellow Czechs. Before the first departures for Theresienstadt, a special department, "Department G," was established within the Jewish community organization to serve as a contact point and intermediary for legal and underground supplies for Theresienstadt. Energetic and diligent men worked with Otto Zucker, the first head of "Department G" and made possible subsequent improvements in living conditions of the Ghetto. A great deal of construction material, for example, was ordered for the Nazis and then disappeared into the recesses of the Ghetto to form the basis for making chimneys, stoves, beds, children's carriages and for building rooms in attics. Czech Jewish leaders also managed to get S.D. approval for the purchase of straw directly from the countryside. Theresienstadt was soon flooded with straw—cars of it containing smuggled medicine, supplies and no fewer than twenty-six crates of books.

Proposals for the organization of the Ghetto were speedily drawn up and plans were worked out for making Theresienstadt self-sufficient. Seidl, installed at the Prague *Zentralstelle* in the summer of 1941, had already been appointed future commander of Theresienstadt. On his orders, the Prague Jewish community set up a work team of technicians to prepare the Ghetto. Among these experts were thirty-five city administrators, a transport specialist, the foreman of an automobile repair shop, two telephone operators, a postal authority and forty-one economists. Volunteers also joined the work team, the *Aufbaukommando*. Prague Jews were ready, hopeful, credulous.

They had expended much energy, enthusiasm, and travail in rebuilding the decrepit and dilapidated houses and barracks of Terezin. The Nazis, for their part, continued to play on the Jewish desire for autonomy and permitted the Ghetto its own guard, currency, technical and legal section and finance department. The currency bore the effigy of Moses holding the Tablets of the Law.

The first transport arrived in Theresienstadt on November 24, 1941, and consisted of 342 young men in the *Aufbaukommando* who hoped to rebuild the camp. On November 30 and December 2, another transport of 2,000 Jews from Prague (including old people) arrived, and on December 4, another contingent of 1,000 young men came to help the *Aufbaukommando*. The first *Judenältester*, Edelstein, and his assistant Otto Zucker, arrived with this group which had been screened by Seidl. A survivor of these early transports has recalled his first impressions of the Ghetto:

> The men leave for work every day in groups. They are always accompanied by sentries. At the end of the first week in December, they are separated from the women and children and the staff also move into a special building.
>
> The hopes for life in the work camp gradually disappear with the wave of prohibitions and orders issued daily: men are forbidden to meet together with women; it is forbidden to write home; contact with the Gentile population is prohibited; smoking is punished; nobody is allowed to walk on the pavement and every uniformed person must be saluted. It is forbidden to separate from the work group, to leave one's lodging after curfew, to use the shops, to sing or whistle in the streets, to collect horse chestnuts, to pick field flowers, to touch a chimney-sweep "for luck." The prisoners have to hand in money, stamps and writing paper, cigarettes and tobacco, tinned foods and many other things. They are punished by 10 to 50 blows with a cane for small offenses, for larger ones by several months' imprisonment as well. Punishment by beating is frequent and must be carried out by the prisoners themselves. S.S.-man Bergel supervises the beating and takes a hand in it himself with great pleasure . . .
>
> Orders of the self-governing body are issued daily, passing on the orders of the Nazi Command. There S.S. *Obersturmführer* Dr. Siegfried Seidl is in charge with his henchmen. The basic organization takes shape: every room has its commander, several rooms together form a group . . . The food commissariat is established, the technical commissariat, the sick bay, kitchen, central labour office and disciplinary service. But there are no vehicles for transport, no equipment for the clinic, not enough boilers for the kitchen, there is not enough water, there is no fuel, there is nothing at all.[7a]

Life in the "model ghetto" swiftly destroyed the old life. On January 10, 1942, nine prisoners were hanged for engaging in prohibited, furtive conversations and for sending illegal messages. Seven others were hanged on February 2. Children, segregated in separate buildings, were often not allowed on the streets. On Sundays, they were marched two abreast under police escort to see their mothers in the women's quarters. Decrepit funeral hearses that once belonged to the Jewish community became the sole form of transport. Old people—living and dead—as well as supplies, were transported in worn-out carriages that had to be pulled by Jews harnessed to them like beasts of burden.

In June 1942, basic changes took place in the camp. The average age rose suddenly as a result of new transports of old people. The Nazis ordered a speedy evacuation of the non-Jewish population of Theresienstadt, thus robbing the prisoners of contact with the outside world. The Council of Elders had to administer over 200 dilapidated old houses and prepare them for new arrivals. For the first time, transports began to arrive from Germany and Austria, most of them men and women over sixty-five. Many had traveled for 20 hours in sealed trains. These included invalids, holders of war medals, and others who were led to believe that their departure meant "privileged resettlement." They had signed fraudulent contracts for accommodation in the ghetto for old persons and had paid tens of thousands of marks for the privilege of going to Theresienstadt. Old German Jews brought with them their top hats, tails, lace dresses and parasols. But their old world quickly vanished. In Theresienstadt they were forced to live in dirty attics or underground cells; many quickly succumbed to pneumonia, diarrhea, hunger.

Because of the sudden overcrowding of the camp, rations were reduced; workers received the largest rations at the expense of the old and sick. It became common to see old, bent, underfed figures wandering around the camp begging for watery soup and poking about the piles of rotten potatoes. In July, 32 died daily; in August, 75; in September, 131. When an official of the Council of Elders reported this to Seidl, he answered laconically, "The clock is going right."

Of the 88,000 Jews in the Protectorate in 1942, 73,608 were transported to Theresienstadt; of these, over 60,000 were sent to various extermination camps, including 30,000 to Auschwitz. But the legends about the Ghetto persisted. It was Himmler's idea to exhibit Theresienstadt as a "model ghetto." Heydrich's successor, Ernst Kaltenbrunner, who did not understand the necessity for such laborious mythmaking, simply looked upon Theresienstadt as a nuisance. In February 1943, over half of the 47,000 inmates, most of them over sixty, could not work. Kaltenbrunner urged Himmler to permit a lossening up of the group over sixty. He explained that they were not only useless but carriers of epidemics. He then assured Himmler that he would seize only those Jews who "enjoy no special relations or connections with anybody and who possess no high decorations of any sort." But Himmler demurred, replying: "The Reichsführer-S.S. does not wish the transport of Jews from Theresienstadt because such transport would disturb the tendency to permit the Jews in the old people's ghetto of Theresienstadt to live and die there in peace."

Various diplomatic tours were conducted through this "model ghetto." Himmler believed that through these visits the gas-chamber rumors had been discounted abroad. As late as April 1945, he even used Theresienstadt as his passport to respectability, telling Dr. Norbert Masur of the World Jewish Congress the following: "Theresienstadt is not a camp in

a farmyard; others were hidden behind walls in the work room and have survived.

The most poignant of all, however, are the sketches and the paintings of children under sixteen. These youngsters never saw butterflies or poplars or white chestnut blossoms, but nevertheless painted them. The drawings of the children were found in cardboard folders wrapped in rough paper clearly marked with the numbers of the houses (L417, B7, S3) in which the children lived. The collection, which consists of four thousand drawings, has been preserved by the State Jewish Museum in Prague.

A collection of children's poetry also exists. Characteristically, in the Theresienstadt prison where there was so much abnormal deprivation, the children wrote about what was gone, what they could no longer have. "The Butterfly" by Pavel Friedman was written on April 6, 1942:

> He was the last, truly the last.
> Such yellowness was bitter and blinding
> Like the sun's tear shattered on stone.
> That was his true color.
> And how easily he climbed, and how high.
> Certainly, climbing, he wanted
> To kiss the last of my world.
>
> I have been here for seven weeks,
> "Ghettoized."
> Who loved me have found me,
> Daisies call to me,
> And the branches also of the white chestnut in the yard.
> But I haven't seen a butterfly here.
> The last one was the last one.
> There are no butterflies, here, in the ghetto.[10]

A fifteen-year-old boy, Peter Fischel, who died in Auschwitz in 1944 has recorded in prose the dreary file of days at Theresienstadt:

> We have got used to getting up at 7 o'clock in the morning, standing in a long line at midday, and at 7 o'clock in the evening, holding a plate into which they pour some hot water tasting a trifle salty, or perhaps with a suggestion of coffee, or to get a small portion of potatoes. We have got used to sleeping without beds, to greeting any person wearing a uniform, to keeping off the footpaths. We have got used to having our faces slapped for no reason whatsoever, to getting hit, and to killings. We have got used to seeing people wallowing in their own excrement, to seeing coffins full of dead bodies, to seeing the sick lying in filth and stench and to seeing the doctors powerless.[11]

Of the 15,000 children in Theresienstadt, 100 survived.

A rich supply of talent worked creatively in the very jaws of death. Scholars discussed metaphysical problems; physicians and nurses tended the sick and dying; craftsmen repaired watches, shoes and clothing; gardeners toiled over plots of land and beautified them. Musical and dramatic activities engaged and even consumed highly gifted artists. There were master performances of Smetana's *Bartered Bride* and Verdi's *Requiem*; a delightful opera especially written for children, *Brundibar*, was presented. Actors played *Liliom*, read *Faust*, and recited Villon's poetry. The great plays of the European repertoire were presented to avid audiences. In the Zwangsgemeinschaft—the compulsory community—of Theresienstadt, feverish intellectual and artistic effort wrestled with dread of the pink slips —the signal for transport call-ups.

A so-called family camp was established at Auschwitz, and many volunteers from Theresienstadt signed up hoping to rejoin family members who had left on earlier transports. This camp was called "Arbeitslager Birkenau" and was set up to refute rumors about gassings in the world press and keep the transports running. Birkenau was the only one of the thirty-nine camps in Auschwitz where families could live together. The Jews from Theresienstadt were strictly isolated from other inmates at Auschwitz and enjoyed certain temporary privileges, such as food parcels and mail. By the end of 1943, 10,000 Jews lived in the Theresienstadt "family camp." The Nazis continued this deception and volunteer deportees from Theresienstadt were available for later transports.

There has recently come to light evidence of a resistance movement in Theresienstadt as early as 1942. This group called "Maffia" was made up mainly of former officers and men in the Czech Army. Their aim was to disrupt the production of war materials (ammunition boxes and mica) and delay their delivery. In 1944, when the truth about Auschwitz was known, efforts were made to warn the Ghetto. On April 5, 1944, Vitezslav Lederer escaped from Auschwitz dressed in an S.S. uniform, and with the aid of Václav Veselák, who went regularly to the Theresienstadt barracks to shave Czech policemen in the Ghetto, made his way back to the Ghetto and tried to warn the prisoners about the gas chambers. But most refused to believe him, finding more comfort and credibility in the postcards being sent from Auschwitz. Lederer brought letters, arms and radio parts into the Ghetto and helped a small group prepare for resistance during the expected liquidation of the Ghetto. However, any possible action by the prisoners was thwarted by the crafty camouflage of the Nazis: the beautification campaign, the visit of the Red Cross delegation, the film production and the luring of prisoners into the so-called labor and family transports. The news of Nazi retreats on the fighting fronts also led many Jews to believe that they would be needed by the Nazis as an alibi after the war.

The chief forms of resistance in the Ghetto were in terms of creative expression through drama, satirical cabaret, poetry and music. Many survivors have written of the extraordinary vividness and rare artistic quality of performances at Theresienstadt. Much activity was clandestine, or at best, semi-legal, and performances were held in wretched attics. Although the public use of the Czech language was forbidden, some of the most memorable programs were in Czech. The Chaplin-like Karel Schwenk created topical and sardonic cabaret that lifted the morale of the prisoners of Theresienstadt and enabled them to face another day of their miserable life. One of his most unforgettable productions was "The Last Cyclist," based on the old saying that "Jews and cyclists are responsible for all misfortunes." The plot is an allegory of Hitler-Europe, but with a happy ending. All cyclists and those who cannot prove that their ancestors had been pedestrians for six generations are deported to a horrible island by lunatic rulers of a mythical country. One cyclist—the last—escapes deportation and is first exhibited in a zoo. Everything can be blamed on him. In the end, however, he prevails, and the rule of the lunatics is defeated, at least on the stage.

Some shred of human dignity could be salvaged through this kind of bitter humor and an illusion of triumph created. In the popular children's opera "Brundibar," all of the children of Theresienstadt were swept up in their collective hatred of a wicked organ grinder who refuses to let needy children sing for money in the district he considers his own beat. Animals finally advise the children to get together and fight the wicked man. The evil Brundibar is finally defeated. Again, the gay marching song that expresses their victory became a substitute defiance of the evil Jews were helpless to fight in the Ghetto: "Beat your drum, we have won . . . We did not give in! We were not afraid . . . !" The character of Brundibar, however, was so skillfully humanized by the fourteen-year-old orphan Honza Treichlinger that Honza became a camp celebrity despite his role. Like most other children at Theresienstadt, he was swallowed up by the transports.

In the spring of 1942, the first transports of Jewish officials and employees of the *Reichsvereinigung* were sent to Theresienstadt. Gradually by the spring of 1943 the whole *Reichsvereinigung* was engulfed in deportations. Only Rabbi Baeck and Moritz Henschel survived the war. Among the Jewish leaders, apparently only one man knew the destiny of the deportees. This was Rabbi Baeck, who had learned the truth about "resettlement in the East" in the summer of 1941:

The first news from the east that I saw was post cards from Lublin and Warsaw. From them we gathered that the deportees were wretched, that hunger and disease were widespread, and that the Polish Jews were trying to help in such contacts as they had with the deported and while they themselves still could.

I got the first indication of the scope of Nazi bestiality in the summer of 1941. A Gentile woman told me that she had voluntarily gone along with her Jewish husband when he was deported. In Poland they were separated. She saw hundreds of Jews crowded into busses which were driven off and came back empty. The rumor that the busses had a gassing mechanism was confirmed by the apparatus attached to all but one of them. This one carried a group to bury those who were gassed; afterward the gravediggers were shot. Similar stories were told by soldiers who came back on furlough. Thus I learned that the lot of Jews shipped east was either slave labor or death. It was still later that I first heard the name Auschwitz mentioned in connection with atrocities.[12]

Auschwitz was described to him in 1943 in Theresienstadt. In grappling with both experiences, Dr. Baeck had to decide what to do with the terrible burden of these accounts. Would any good purpose be served in allowing such ghastly news to be known? He decided finally that nothing would be gained by sharing it. He told no one.

In August 1943, a fellow inmate, A Czech engineer named Grünberg, told Baeck about Auschwitz. Grünberg, in turn, had received the story at firsthand from a Jewish friend who had escaped from the Polish death camp. Grünberg spoke to Rabbi Baeck alone and bound him to silence.

"I have to tell someone," he said agitatedly. "I was waked last night by my best friend whom I have not seen for a long time. I knew that he had not been sent to Theresienstadt, so I asked how he got here. He cut me short, and told me to listen carefully. He had to tell me. I had to know. But first I must promise not to tell anyone else. He was half Jewish and had been sent east. He ended up in the huge camp of Auschwitz. Like everyone else there he went through a process of selection and was assigned to do slave labor. The others were led away and gassed to death. He knows that definitely; everyone at Auschwitz knows it. He was sent to a labor camp from which he escaped and made his way back to Prague." How had he [Grünberg] gotten into Theresienstadt? A Czech policeman outside took a bribe. We talked for a short while and then he left. He was much excited and said he wanted to warn me and save me.[13]

Rabbi Baeck struggled with this information, just as he had two years previously with the knowledge that deportation to the East could mean only slave labor or death. Should he convince Grünberg to repeat what he had heard before the Council of Elders? If they knew, the whole camp would know within a few hours. "Living in the expectation of death by gassing would only be the harder," he decided. There was also the possible alternative of labor, he believed. Extermination was not inevitable. No one was told.

In the same spirit of wanting to cushion a horror, Dr. Baeck had made a similar decision when in December 1942, the Gestapo demanded Jewish orderlies to help in the seizures. In Germany, the Gestapo was on home territory and tens of thousands of Gestapo men were available for the roundups of several hundred thousand Jews, but in the large cities their forces were thinned out. Rabbi Baeck decided not to oppose the demand. "I made it a principle," he explained, "to accept no appointments from the Nazis and to do nothing which might help them. But later, when the question arose whether Jewish orderlies should help pick up Jews for deportation, I took the position that it would be better for them to do it, because they could at least be more gentle and helpful than the Gestapo and make the ordeal easier. It was scarcely in our power to oppose the order effectively."[14]

This is a reference to the protection against the brutal treatment of the Jews by S.S. men under Major Alois Brunner. Brunner came to Berlin in December 1942 as Eichmann's deportation expert and introduced the Ordnungsdienst, the Order Service, in Germany. These orderlies were frequently well-bred and well-educated persons who assisted panic-stricken Jews being served their deportation notices. These notices were generally mailed by the Gestapo a week or two before the deportations. A typical letter was the following: "You and your family are to report at 8 A.M. January 20 [1941] at the Bourse Hall in Dortmund to go on labor assignment to the east." The letter included details as to how much money and baggage could be taken along. The Ordnungsdienst helped to organize the transports and occasionally accompanied the deportees to assembly points. At times, if quotas were not met, they had to select deportees. In Germany, the Order Service, had no uniforms and did not carry out any police functions. They wore red armbands which temporarily exempted them from deportation. In due course, they, too, were deported. There is a reminiscence of a young Jewish woman, a social worker in Berlin, who worked in the Jewish Order Service, that conveys the anguish and bewilderment of the searchers themselves:

At 8 o'clock in the evening we were summoned to the headquarters of the community. The Gestapo told us that a convoy of orphans was to leave, and that since the necessary quota would not be supplied by children's homes, we had to find orphans living with private families and bring them to the transit camp. We young Jewish girls were to go out and look for Jewish children. Even today, I do not understand how I found the courage and strength to do it. I was 20 at the time. We received a pass for the night and a list of four or five addresses. They gave us until 4 in the morning.

We set out in pairs, looking for the houses in the dark. Since doors were locked at 9 in Berlin, we had to wake up the porter and show our pass. The Jewish apartments opened only after we rang the bell a great many times, for this was a frightening hour of the night, when arrests were made, when a family turned pale at every ringing of the doorbell and the wife went to look for bags while the husband opened the door.

Seeing us with our stars, the people began to breathe again, but what terrible scenes we witnessed after they learned the reason for our coming.[15]

Dr. Baeck faced the constant prospect of arrest stoically. He had been imprisoned five times before the signing of the Munich Pact and was sent to Theresienstadt in January of 1943, when he was almost seventy. In the hothouse prison of Theresienstadt, where life had to be lived for the moment, for one never knew when it might be the last, in a world pitching between excitement and despair, a great German social psychologist, H. G. Adler, himself a prisoner in Theresienstadt, tried to fathom the answer to the profound question: How can Judaism thrive in slavery, in the antechamber to death? Adler was blackly pessimistic and severe in his judgments. But in his terms, he found only one man, Rabbi Baeck, who exemplified what he considered the authentic Jewish response. Baeck, with his bent figure and snow-white beard, could be seen ministering daily to the inmates, lecturing on Plato and Kant, pulling garbage wagons or deeply involved in the *Jugendfürsorge* (Youth Care Services). The Nazis were sure that he would wither away. In April 1945, he was confronted by Eichmann, who was visibly shocked at seeing him. "Herr Baeck, are you still alive?" he asked, then adding coldly, "I thought you were dead."

"You are apparently announcing a future occurrence," the rabbi answered evenly.

After the liberation of Theresienstadt by the Russians on May 12, 1945, Rabbi Baeck helped in the evacuation of the camp. Early in June, the Russian commandant of the camp told him that an American officer in Prague, Major Patrick Dolan, had some medicine for him for the camp. In Prague, Dolan gave Baeck the supplies and said that he had a special permit to go to England. Rabbi Baeck waited for another month, however, and joined his daughter in London early in July. He died in 1956.

The public visits to the "model ghetto" began in 1943. A German Red Cross delegation visited Theresienstadt in August. During the next month, to keep up appearances, Eichmann permitted 4,000 Czech Jews leaving Theresienstadt to travel in family groups and take their luggage. At Auschwitz, they were given six months' quarantine in the isolation section of the Birkenau camp. Here they were reasonably well treated and encouraged to send letters. This ruse deceived the Jews of Theresienstadt, as elsewhere. Even after having been in Auschwitz for some time as workers on a temporary lease, they did not know the whole truth although they were only several hundred meters from the gas chambers.

But they learned all too soon. A Slovak Jewish doctor in charge of the

Birkenau infirmary records warned Freddi Hirsch, their camp leader, that his people had been marked for SB (*Sonderbehandlung*), or "special treatment." Moreover, the Jewish unit working at the crematoria was believed ready to mutiny if the Czech Jews could get arms. However, on March 7, 1944, the day the quarantine expired, Hirsch, fearing that a revolt would lead to an inhuman massacre of children, killed himself with veronal and the Czech Jews were gassed.[16] At the last moment they were told to send off postdated letters to their friends and relatives reporting how well they were and requesting parcels. In the basement dressing rooms of the crematorium, some fought armed guards with their bare hands and entered the gas chambers with bleeding wounds and broken bones. Philip Müller, a survivor of the *Sonderkommando*, has testified that they died singing the Czech national anthem and "Hatikvah."

There was to be another transport to the "family camp" in late 1943, but the Nazi plan did not come off. On October 2, 1943, the Gestapo started to deport the Jews of Denmark. This attempt turned out to be one of Germany's big failures: most of the Danish Jews were saved; only 360 were deported. Moreover, the deportees were not sent to Auschwitz, but to Theresienstadt, where the Danish king was assured of their safety. These deportees never left Theresienstadt, and their treatment as a whole was better than that accorded the other prisoners, but the mendacity of the Nazis in first receiving them into the ghetto-camp was characteristic.

Danish prisoners were given cigarettes and led into the camp mess hall for their first meal. They ate heartily on a white tablecloth and when dessert was served, they were given stationery and told to write home and describe the conditions at Theresienstadt. Those were the last tablecloths they were to see, and the last decent meal they were to have for a long time. A few days later, they were shown what would happen to them if they protested their rations: they were made to witness the hanging of fifteen young Czech Jews who had complained. On November 11, as punishment for the shame Germany suffered in defeat after World War I, the Danish Jews joined the rest of the prisoners who were forced to stand in an open field all day. They also had to participate in a census and an old men's free-for-all. About a hundred of the camp's oldest prisoners, many of them ill and feeble, were collected in an open field and ordered to beat each other up. When at first they refused, the S.S. men went among them and began to punch them so hard that some of them fell unconscious. The Danish Jews, too, became work slaves, half-people who momentarily expected to be shipped away. But they never left Theresienstadt, nor did they die of starvation as other prisoners did. The attitude of the home country made the difference. The Danish government kept up a steady barrage of inquiries to the Germans to see how Danish Jews were being treated. Moreover, a regular delivery of food parcels was organized which maintained the relative well-being of Danish Jews and buoyed up their morale. Attached to the parcels was a two-way mailing piece, which required the signature of the receiver and which had to be returned to the sender. The Germans, apt to be impressed by this kind of efficiency, passed the Danish parcels on. As social status in the camps revolved around the possession of food, clothing and cigarettes, the Danish Jews were sought after and envied. They became an elite in Theresienstadt.

In addition to sending food to their citizens, the Danish government also sent medical supplies and finally, after tireless pressure upon the Germans, succeeded in sending a Danish Red Cross commission to Theresienstadt in the summer of 1944.

Meanwhile, a new brutality shook Theresienstadt. Anton Burger had replaced Seidl at the end of July 1943. Burger had a fanatical hatred of Czechs and soon put to an end Edelstein's tenure in the Council of Elders. On November 9, Edelstein was taken to a prison bunker and accused of falsifying daily reports and aiding in the escape of 55 persons from the Ghetto. He and his family were killed in Auschwitz. This episode had harsh consequences for the Ghetto. The S.S. command ordered the counting of prisoners for November 11. Forty thousand people were driven outside in the early morning and were left to stand in a cold, drizzling rain all day without food or water until the census was carried out. The entire valley was surrounded by gendarmes armed with machine guns while a plane circled the prison. Panic broke out at night. Mothers tried to protect their children from being crushed, old people sank to the ground from weariness and hunger. The plain was finally cleared at midnight. Three hundred people died in the senseless census.

Burger was recalled in February and replaced by Karl Rahm, a choleric brute who was sent to Theresienstadt to play a "beautifying comedy" to the end in preparation for the visit of the Danish Red Cross Commission.

The commission, headed by Dr. Frantz Hvass of the Danish Foreign Ministry, arrived on June 23, after the camp had been completely refurbished and prettied up. For the commission's benefit, tablecloths, new silverware and flowers were put on all tables in the mess hall, and the waiters wore clean uniforms and spotless white gloves. New barracks were constructed, and new beds, furniture and clothing were given to the prisoners. Those prisoners who bore signs of torture or who had been crippled were shipped out of the camp. The streets running through Theresienstadt were cleaned. Concerts, lectures, and sporting events were organized at the camp and a special children's pavilion was built and stocked with play equipment. A sham self-government was created and its head, Dr. Paul Eppstein, was given his own apartment on the campgrounds and a limousine with an S.S. officer posing as a chauffeur. Worthless money was printed to show that the prisoners at Theresienstadt were paid for their labor. Rahm canceled the order requiring saluting of uniformed men and prohibited the use of "Achtung." All fences and barriers were removed. All S.S. men were dressed in mufti. The Czech police temporarily disappeared.

However, the population of the ghetto, then 34,000, was much too big for an impressive picture of a "model ghetto," so between May 15 and May 18, while flower beds were busily being dug and house fronts painted, 3,000 Jews were sent to Auschwitz to reduce the numbers. In this transport were the young and healthy Jews, chosen so that the visitors could see that Theresienstadt was a home for the aged and privileged, not a transit camp for the East. It was calculated—rightly, as it turned out—that the delegation would not go upstairs, but since the ground floors of the barracks could be seen from the street, occupants were moved to the upper floors and the lower floors were redecorated.

The visit of June 23 was a Nazi success. There were parcels for the Danish Jews, and a message from the Danish King. The Potemkin village was believed. The delegation seems to have been particularly impressed by the hospital and the Jewish theater. Addressing the prisoners, Dr. Hvass said, "The King sends his best regards to you, and I also have best greetings from Bishop Fuglsang-Damgaard, who asked me to tell you that he prays for you."

As Dr. Hvass and the others passed among the Danish Jews to shake their hands, a fellow prisoner remarked to the rabbi: "It is now that I feel redeemed as a human being in my own eyes. Once again I have a certain value as a man. These Danes have given it back to me."[17]

For most prisoners, however, the commission's visit had a crushing effect. Rabbi Baeck wrote: "Perhaps they knew the real conditions—but it looked as if they did not want to know the truth. The effect on our morale was devastating. We felt forgotten and forsaken."

Were the visitors really impressed by conditions at Theresienstadt? They seem to have been, judging from the glowing report they delivered a month later to the International Red Cross in Stockholm. They described Theresienstadt more as an ideal suburban community than a ghetto-camp. But after the war, Dr. Hvass claimed that he had purposely exaggerated so that the Germans would allow the Danes to continue sending food and medical supplies to the camp.

Following the stage-managed "Verschönerungsaktion" a Nazi propaganda film was made in Theresienstadt, aimed at proving that it was indeed a model Ghetto. Kurt Gerron, a well-known UFA actor and director was ordered to produce the film during the summer of 1944. An S.S. director told him what to shoot and S.S. forces menacingly guarded the camera crew. Thousands of Ghetto inmates were forced to join in this last Nazi fraud. Some were taken to S.S. swimming pools; 2,000 were taken to a meadow outside the Ghetto to be entertained at an open-air cabaret; others had to attend an obligatory five o'clock tea in an improvised coffee house to the tune of a twelve-piece jazz band. A transport of children from Holland was photographed, with Rahm tenderly lifting each child out of the cars. Shops were opened. A genuine Bechstein piano appeared. The Council of Elders were shown meeting, not in the gloomy Magdeburg barracks, but in a brightly lighted and elegantly equipped office. There were scenes showing Jews standing before a savings bank window and closeups of swirling banknotes. Jews were also shown talking to prominent Czech officials and military officers.[17a] Then, suddenly, this farce stopped as abruptly as it had started. The Gestapo had lost too much time.

All possible resistance was crushed. According to Rahm's testimony after the war, no repetition of the Warsaw Ghetto revolt could be tolerated. Sudden searches were conducted. Former army officers were called up for deportation. The Ghetto painters were tortured and killed during this period.

For the summer slowdown Müller and Eichmann exacted a terrible vengeance. At a time when the German frontiers on both east and west had been breached, they ordered a huge new deportation from Theresienstadt. One transport, which left for Auschwitz on September 28, 1944, consisted of 2,300 volunteers, the working elite of the camp who thought they were going to German factories. To make the illusion complete, the Nazis did not permit the inclusion of previously punished prisoners or "anti-social" elements. Some 900 perished immediately, including Dr. Otto Zucker, who left as manager of the work camp. After postcards had arrived from some of the deportees, a transport of wives and children was organized by the unknowing widow of Dr. Zucker. The whole transport was gassed. Crematorium No. 1 was found strewn with the permits that had been given the deportees to join their husbands and fathers at their place of work—one of Eichmann's ghoulish flashes.[18]

A report on the liquidation of the Czech "family camp" in Birkenau was filed at the British Embassy in Switzerland by a Dr. Kopecky who represented the Czech Government-in-Exile in Geneva. On June 25, 1944, the report was forwarded to London and Washington with requests for bombing the gas chambers and threatening Germans and Hungarians with reprisals.

Another transport was ordered for September 29 and October 6, and after that there seemed no end to them. The Nazis were so sure that the prisoners were unaware of their destination that they threatened any who did not leave willingly with a concentration camp! One labor transport was actually returned to Theresienstadt and the members reported on their "hard work" in Germany.

And so the deception continued. Even when other leaders, including Dr. Paul Eppstein, were arrested, it was thought that their fate would not be shared by the rank and file. Eppstein was shot in the police prison, the *Kleine Festung* near Theresienstadt, for plotting the defense of the ghetto.

Early in 1945, 5,000 Czech and German Jews married to Aryans were sent to Theresienstadt and in the last few weeks of the war it became a terminal for Jewish survivors from Poland and Hungary, pushed west and then south by the retreat of the Wehrmacht.

On April 6, 1945, Eichmann showed Paul Dunand of the Swiss Red Cross through Theresienstadt. It was a very formal occasion and in the evening General Karl Frank, Protector for Bohemia and Moravia, gave the Red Cross delegation a reception in the Hradschin Palace in Prague. Himmler was already trying to find a bridge of respectability to the Allies. Eichmann, as well, now tried. He took Monsieur Dunand into a corner of the great salon and told him that the Jews of Theresienstadt were actually better off than many Germans. Himmler, he said, "wanted the Jews to acquire a sense of racial community through the exercise of almost complete autonomy." Afterward, they were to be transported to some region where they could live separated from the German population. He added, however, that he did not approve all the humane measures which Himmler intended to introduce.

Eichmann had promised Dunand that not a single Jew would be deported from Theresienstadt, but on April 12, Dunand learned that the S.S. had destroyed all of the records kept in the Magdeburg barracks in the Ghetto. This he regarded as a sign that a last-minute execution was intended. According to Wisliceny, Eichmann had proposed the liquidation of Theresienstadt in February, and according to Kurt Gerstein, Eichmann's subordinate Hans Günther asked him how much Zyklon B was needed to gas the entire remnant of the Ghetto in the open moat of the fortress. These threats were averted, however, and on May 11, Theresienstadt, with 32,000 inmates, more than a third of whom were non-Jews was delivered to the Russians. Over 12,000 recent arrivals from German camps had to be isolated in two barrack blocks because of typhus. The "model ghetto" and Auschwitz, its outlet, had claimed 110,000 lives.

From 1941 to 1944, the victims had undergone preliminary trials in their "homes."

The dwindling communities of the Protectorate had been ravaged by the deportations. And Jews were racked by doubt and fear. Was Theresienstadt the real end?

Following a hailstorm of orders, decrees, prohibitions and injunctions issued by the Ministry of the Interior, the *Reichsprotektor* and the Gestapo, the Nazis registered a thousand Jews daily in preparation for the deportations. Long questionnaires had to be filled out; whole families had to go personally to the *Zentralstelle* with files of papers. The transports were dispatched from collection centers, the largest of which was in Prague on the site of the former radio section of the Prague Sample Fair. People sat or lay on the ground according to assigned numbers and were called to various tables to turn in keys to flats, ration books, remaining money and valuables, personal documents and to fill out more question-naires—all accompanied by shouting, running insults, blows.

The first five transports left Prague for Lodz on October 16, 21, and 31 and on November 3, 1941. On November 26, a transport of 1,000 Jews left Brno for Minsk. The next transports left for Terezín.

On March 6, 1942, Eichmann met with Section IV B 4 in Düsseldorf to plan the deportation of 55,000 Jews in the Greater Reich (Germany, Austria, the annexed provinces in Poland and the Protectorate). He was particularly concerned with the evacuation of 20,000 Jews from Prague and 18,000 from Vienna. There was a discussion of the legal aspects of property liquidation and transport. The trains, he explained, had a capacity of 700, but 1,000 Jews must be loaded onto them. Above all, the element of secrecy must be kept. "For reasons of urgency and secrecy," he said, "the State police stations shall be informed of the date of departure by telephone, six days in advance, under code name DA. . . . Under no cir-cumstances must the Jews know of the preparations made for their evacu-ation. Complete secrecy is therefore necessary."[19]

By 1942, the deportations from Germany had become methodically or-ganized. The transport experts had hit their stride but despair and resigna-tion had overtaken German Jewry. A high proportion scheduled for de-portation committed suicide. For a time such suicides caused the Ministry of Finance problems: Jewish property owned by persons who had taken their lives could not be confiscated. But a legalism was found. Suicides were counted as persons who had already been deported. The Gestapo then confiscated their property as property belonging to "persons hostile to the People and State."

The Jews who remained on reprieve were physically and spiritually spent. They had no contacts with anti-Fascist movements which, in other countries, gave Jews some comfort and hope. Moreover, they had endured their ordeal longest—since 1933. They had been pauperized, humiliated, and half-starved longer than any other Jews in Europe. They were weary to death.

The utter futility of physical resistance was dramatized for them in the summer of 1942 on the occasion of an exhibit in Berlin called "The Soviet Paradise"—a scathing satire of Soviet Russia. Sabotage of the exhibit was organized by a group of Jewish Communists under the leadership of Her-bert Baum. Five Germans were killed; 250 Jews were promptly arrested as hostages and shot and another 250 were deported. Gestapo chief Müller told the *Reichsvereinigung* that if something similar happened again 250 Jews would be taken for every German killed. This act of resistance, although it was not rooted in defense of Jews, was regarded by German Jews at the time—as would be any kind of physical effort by a weak group—as pointless and harmful. It was the only episode of its kind.

Over 100,000 Jews had been deported from the Reich and more than 200,000 from the Reich Protectorate area in the deportations of 1942. Economic considerations were not permitted to stand in the way of the "Final Solution." In the fall of 1942, Hitler himself ordered that all Jews be removed from the armament industry. The deportation of the war veterans ran its inevitable course, and the temporarily deferred workers in essential industry were swept up in the deportations to the killing centers in 1943. The war veterans were originally "immune" from the first "resettlement" actions, but after the establishment of the Theresienstadt Ghetto, they were deported rather quickly, the "worthy" and decorated veterans to Theresienstadt, the "less qualified," having less than 50 percent disability, or lacking an Iron Cross, directly to the death centers. Neither the vague appeals to German honor nor the intervention of the Wehrmacht materialized.

Not the least of the many incomprehensible aspects of the Holocaust was the deliberate annihilation of tens of thousands of skilled Jewish workers who toiled arduously for the Reich war effort. Plant managers and owners begged the Army not to permit the deportation of productive workers. The Army High Command made its own requests of the Labor Ministry. Early in 1942, Göring himself, in charge of the Four-Year Plan ordered *all* Jews in war industries exempted from deportation. The labor shortages grew and industrialists clamored for more labor, specifically for more Jewish workers who were admittedly industrious and able. In September 1942, when many Reich Jews were being deported for forced labor, the Speer Ministry, in charge of armaments, proposed importing foreign Jews for munitions factories. The Gestapo crushed all rational plans and proposals. And yet, a few agencies that did not ask too many questions went ahead on their own and brought Jewish workers into the Reich. Nearly 20,000 Soviet Jews were imported for various work projects in East Prussia, another 50,000 worked in Silesian camps and several thousand survived in a Krupp naval artillery factory near Breslau. The consuming destructiveness of the death machinery could not completely destroy self-interest.

In the letters[20] of the period there is often a concealed description of what is really happening. "Going on a journey" means "being deported," but the deportees did not know what kind of journey they were going on. There is great restraint and a quiet resignation in the writers; their language is vague and faraway, conveying the ghostly atmosphere in which

Jews lived. Dr. Cora Berliner, German staff member in the Emigration Department of the *Reichsvereinigung* was deported from Berlin in June 1942, never to return. Among her last letters was one written to Dr. Hans Schäffer, a Weimar official in the German Ministry of Finance, who left Germany to live in Sweden. The letter is dated June 21, 1942:

> Dear Herr Schäffer:
> . . . These are days of remembrance; it was a year ago that Otto [Dr. Otto Hirsch, Director of the *Reichsvereinigung*] left us. Tomorrow I and a number of my friends . . . will start on our journey. It was a very sudden decision and there are many preparations to be made. . . .
> I doubt whether I shall meet Tulla [a cousin] although I shall probably be going in the same direction. . . . I don't know when I shall write you again. Hannah will give you news. . . . There have been times lately when I felt that I kept too much outside reality. Now there will be new impressions and new possibilities to prove one's mettle,
>
> > With all my heart,
> > Yours,
> > Cora

The "Hannah" of this letter was Dr. Berliner's closest friend, Hannah Karminski, who was also in the *Reichsvereinigung*, in the Welfare Department. A few days after Dr. Berliner was deported, Mrs. Karminski wrote the following brief note to Dr. Schäffer:

> . . . I feel that a letter to you will help me get over this sense of infinite loneliness. . . . They went off on Tuesday night, a group of the best of our people. And not to be one of them was very painful. . . . It is hard to be here now, and the morphine of work will have to help sustain us. . . . "Usually it always worked out," she said. And she wants me to assure you that she believes with all her heart in a reunion.

A month later she sent another letter to Dr. Schäffer. In a few words one feels the slipping away of an individual life and a whole culture:

> . . . There is hardly anyone left with whom I could talk about Cora and who would understand how anxious one is, and this longing. . . . You mention former journeys. Haven't you been to Minsk once? It is not certain but I did want to ask you about it. I see Mrs. Ollendorff once a week when I make my farewell visits at the home for the aged. Each time we are glad to be able to look forward to another week. . . .
> Alas—no, there is no longer any satisfaction in this work: it has not much to do with social work as we knew it, and where it is a question of human beings, not of real estate or monies, liquidation is particularly difficult. Since we are, however, dealing with human beings, there are still moments when "still-being-here" appears meaningful and makes sense—and that must suffice as "satisfaction."
> C. and the other friends took books along. . . . As far as I know, C. took *Faust*, Part I. When I went to see them on the last day before the departure, they were sitting in the courtyard in the sun reading Goethe. . . .

Mrs. Karminski went on her "journey" in November 1942.

In 1943, new groups were cut into. The Church had protested the compulsory divorce decree, but the Gestapo was growing impatient. Before the decree was announced, police in Berlin seized a number of Jews married to Aryans and several thousand Christian non-Aryans. The roundups took place in February and March 1943. On February 27, something startling and unparalleled happened: the Aryan wives of the arrested Christian non-Aryans followed them to their detention site and stood for several hours screaming and howling for their men. This was the Factory-Action (*Fabrik-Aktion*).

While most of the previous deportations had been conducted on the basis of name lists and advance notices, this deportation was carried out suddenly. Jewish workers in the factories were seized by S.S. men the morning of the 27th, loaded onto trucks, and transported to six different concentration points. Men in mixed marriages were separated from the others and transferred to the Rosenstrasse Camp. It was here that the wives demonstrated. About 100 men were kept at Rosenstrasse for a week, being prepared for deportation, but the Aryan wives stirred up such a row that the men were released.

A newspaper reported:

> The demonstrators, who numbered about 6,000, returned again and again, pushing forward and calling for their husbands, and demanded their release. The headquarters of the Gestapo was at the Burgstrasse, not far from the scene of unrest. A few machine guns would have sufficed to sweep away the protesting women, but the S.S. men did not shoot, not this time. Thoroughly alarmed by the event, the like of which had never occurred in the history of the Third Reich, the Burgstrasse was drawn into negotiations in which they pacified, made promises and finally released the prisoners.[21]

The secrecy of the destruction process had been endangered.

The potential power of public protest, so very little used in Nazi Germany, is alluded to by Goebbels. On March 2, he wrote that the weekend roundup had not quite succeeded. "Our better circles, especially intellectuals," had warned the Jews. A few days later he wrote, "The seizure of Jewish men and women of privileged mixed marriages had a sensational effect especially in Bohemian circles, for among actors, in particular, such marriages are still quite common." Finally, he commented on a crowd protesting the evacuation of a home for the aged: "To our regret, some unpleasant events have occurred in front of a Jewish home for the aged, where the populace assembled in great masses and some of them even protested in favor of the Jews. I instructed the S.D. to discontinue the evacuation at the present time of crisis. We had better postpone it for some weeks and then we shall be able to carry out the action much more thoroughly."

The subsequent action was, in fact, quite thorough. Despite Goebbels' order, over 12,000 Jews were deported throughout the whole of March, diminishing the number of German Jews to 31,910. Of these, only half were "full" Jews. Goebbels was approaching his heart's desire: the purging of Berlin of all its Jews.

In these last hours of German Jewry, one last flicker of Jewish spiritual pride lived briefly in the remnants of the Zionist agricultural training camps. Their last recorded moments, so different from those of the Jewish youths in the Polish ghettos, bear traces of a German-like romanticization of danger and a blindness to reality. These youths were strangely entwined in a culture that now sought their destruction. Their training camps had been transformed into labor camps but were still suffused with a characteristically strong group spirit which insulated the youths against despair. They had refused to go underground individually or to attempt border crossings. Had they lived in Poland, they would have been leaders of the ghetto revolts. In Germany, their final affirmation was of a different quality.

The last of the camps had been at Forst, Paderborn and Neuendorf. Bit by bit their ranks were thinned out by deportations. The last group was brought to Berlin to the concentration point at Grosse/Hamburg Street to join the transport of April 19. A survivor of Auschwitz, Anneliese Borinsky, has described those last days at Grosse/Hamburg on the eve of Passover.

We are walking on the outskirts of town, escorted by guards in front of us, on both sides and behind us. It seems that the Berliners are used to such sights. We go into Grosse/Hamburg Street, and then into the building, whose large gates open before us and shut again behind the last one of us— we are to know and keep in mind: now we are imprisoned.

We walk up stairs, go through corridors lined with barred doors, and behind the bars crowd people's faces, curiously peering at us. A slight shiver runs down our spines. We take possession of our rooms. The group occupies four adjoining rooms in the same corridor. We came in the afternoon of Sabbath eve; in the evening we sing *Shir Ha-ma'alot* [Psalms, A Song of Ascent].

A strange atmosphere reigns in this house. A mixture of despair and sharp-witted mockery, of a last glow of will-to-live and desire to drain once more all that life has for giving. A kind of Magic Mountain. And we stand here now, amongst all this, with strength and assurance—perhaps a bit too demonstrative—and preparedness. In the morning we have our muster in the corridor. The orders echo in the building's vacuum. We do our morning exercises, after obtaining permission from the S.S. officer in charge, in the small garden . . . beside which lies the small ancient cemetery where Moses Mendelssohn is buried. All this brings into our hearts a feeling of tragic irony. Down here we hold our official singing-club, we sing our songs, and the Gestapo listens to them, and if they understand their contents, then maybe they smile on those fools who sing in this situation: We form a new generation, a strong generation! Our demand—honor for the Jew! We are fighting for liberty, equality, the reign of law! And every evening we sit close up in the corridor and sing. A few of the others join us and listen to us; others dance and have fun down there, a floor below us. . . . On Monday, at reveille, one last muster. Last words of belief in benevolent fate, of belief in one's companion, of parting—pray that it not be final. Handshakes all around. And again everything happens very fast. . . . Outside, once more, stand trucks. One after the other they are loaded and drive off. The direction—North.

At one of the freight stations we get off. A train is waiting already. Closed cattle-cars with tiny vents. A little bit of hay on the floor. We settle down hurriedly . . . tonight in every car, one of us manages the *Seder*— we tell that today we are living the *Haggada*. We spent that night without sleeping a wink. . . . From time to time we see people working on the tracks. Amongst them—star-bearers. Many of them in P.O.W. uniforms. We ask them where, what is the probable target of our trip. They shrug their shoulders. One of them points to the sky. We fail to understand the hint.[22]

On June 10, 1943, a Gestapo agent appeared in the main building of the community building on Oranienburgstrasse in Berlin and announced that the Jewish community of Berlin had ceased to exist. He also announced that all employees who had no Aryan blood were under arrest. The same announcement was made at the *Reichsvereinigung* office at 158 Kantstrasse. On June 16 the last handful of workers were taken by furniture van to the Putlitzstrasse railway station where hospital patients were being loaded. At dusk the train left Berlin under the designation "Transport 1 (Berlin) 96."

The Greater Reich had been declared technically free of Jews by May 1943, but besides the 33,000 part-Jews and Jews in mixed marriages, there were also several thousand underground Jews who roamed the streets without ration or identity cards and who were precariously sheltered at night by Aryan friends.

Thereafter, the skeleton community of half-Jews and Jews in mixed marriages lived the life of hostages of the Gestapo. In Frankfurt, the Gauleiter ordered the monthly arrest of at least 100 Jews in mixed marriages. "Partial" Jews caught smoking in the street, receiving a food parcel, or using a trolley car were subject to deportation. In Vienna in 1943, a small staff of Jewish Council members remained to look after the interests of 6,000 Jews in mixed marriages and their children. In February 1944, 40 Council members were deported to Auschwitz. Some Jews were killed in an Allied bombing of March 1945 of the Gestapo building where Council members worked. When Georges Dunand of the International Red Cross visited Vienna soon afterward, the Jewish community hospital was reduced to concentration camp conditions by the stream of half-humans from camps along the "South-East Wall" on the Austro-Hungarian border. This was the institutional residue of a once-flourishing community. The last Jewish synagogue in the Greater Reich was in this hospital.

The German people observed these periodic enforced departures of their neighbors impassively. There was no resistance movement in Germany from which Jews could draw comfort and support as in other countries. Germans could have effectively resisted Hitler during the first few years of his regime, but no resistance movement emerged during the war years. The plots of the generals sprouted periodically and then withered away. Once terror had been incorporated into the law, or had replaced it, it took extraordinary courage to oppose Nazism. An incessant barrage of propaganda blunted the consciences of many and repressed the awareness of criminal actions. Others felt too weak to struggle against the evils of the regime. The few small groups that opposed Hitler had a much more difficult time than resistance fighters in Holland, France, Yugoslavia, and other countries where people fought against tyranny as well as a foreign oppressor. In Germany, the regime had widespread support and opponents were identified as traitors.

Another difficulty was the absence of a revolutionary tradition in Germany. One of the few outspoken opponents of the regime, Pastor Dietrich Bonhoeffer expressed this deficiency with great clarity:

> Who would deny that the German, again and again, has done his utmost in bravery, and has risked his life while obeying orders, following his calling or doing his work. . . . But in doing so, he has not understood the world; he has not anticipated that his willingness to subordinate his ego and to risk his life for his calling can be abused for evil. . . . Thus, the German never grasped a decisive and fundamental idea: the necessity to act freely and responsibly even if it impaired his work and his calling.[23]

The clergy in Germany faced this question; some made courageous stands in the early period of the Nazi assault on Christian teachings and protested the new religion of blood and race. A proclamation expressing this protest was read in Confessional churches in March 1935 and led to the arrest of 700 pastors. There were other more isolated episodes of rare moral heroism: the handful of young students in Munich, led by Sophie and Hans Scholl, who tried to battle the Nazi terror with their purity of spirit and "White Rose" leaflets. There were the searing words of Pastor Bonhoeffer in Geneva, "I pray for the defeat of my country. Only in defeat can we atone for the terrible crimes we have committed." But these were indeed exceptional responses, and except for the Confessional Church under Pastor Martin Niemoeller, the major churches of Germany were passive throughout the extermination of German Jewry. There was no outcry about the "evacuation of the Jews" as there had been about the "mercy killings" and church intervention, when it occurred, was limited to the *Mischlinge* or partners in mixed marriages.

The churches, like other institutions in Germany, succumbed to Hitler. They had yielded early in the regime.

In Hitler's speech of March 23, 1933, to the Reichstag, he paid tribute to the Christian faiths as "essential elements for safeguarding the soul of the German people" and promised to respect their rights. Four months later, he concluded a pact with the Vatican in which the Catholic Church was guaranteed the right to regulate its own affairs. The Concordat undoubtedly gave the Nazi Government the prestige it greatly needed at the time, but it was an agreement which Hitler never kept. In 1937, Pope Pius XI issued the famous encyclical, *Mit brennender Sorge* ("With Burning Sorrow"), charging the government with evasion and violation of the Concordat.

The encyclical also rejected the myths of race and blood as contrary to revealed Christian truth, but it did not criticize anti-Semitism as such. Among others, the philosopher Dr. Edith Stein, a Jewish convert to Catholicism, who was ultimately gassed at Auschwitz, had earlier requested the Pope to issue an encyclical on the Jewish question, but this was never done.

After Hitler consolidated his power in the middle thirties, he imposed upon all churches the so-called Aryan paragraph, eliminating from church employment all "racial Jews" and Aryans married to Jews. In 1933, the number of Jewish converts was approximately 50,000, and half-Jews and quarter-Jews, 100,000. After the incorporation of Austria, there were an additional 100,000 converted Jews and half- and quarter-Jews. (In January 1942, when extermination of Jews became official state policy, there were over 150,000 *Mischlinge* and intermarried Jews in the Reich-Protectorate area.) Alarmed by Nazi plans, the Catholic and Protestant churches formed organizations for the protection of these non-Aryans. Subsequently, the concern of the churches was limited to Christian non-Aryans.

The intervention of Church officials in behalf of converted Jews was intensified with the onset of mass deportations to the East beginning in October 1941. Rumors began to spread about the fate of the Jews who had been deported. By the end of 1941, the first news had trickled back about the German Jews who had been shot by *Einsatzgruppen* near Minsk and Riga. In August 1942, Kurt Gerstein, who had joined the S.S. to investigate the exterminations for himself, tried to tell the Papal Nuncio in Berlin about a gassing he had witnessed near Lublin. He urged other church officials to forward his report to the Pope and protest the exterminations. These efforts were fruitless. During the same period, further reports about the exterminations reached the Catholic hierarchy through Catholic offices serving in

Poland and in Russia. One such officer, Dr. Alfons Hildenbrand, took special leave from his unit stationed near Minsk to report the massacres he had witnessed to Michael Cardinal Faulhaber in Germany. There is also reliable evidence that Dr. Hans Globke, a Catholic and high official in the Ministry of the Interior, was another source of information. For a long time, Dr. Joseph Müller, an officer in military intelligence and also a confidant of Cardinal Faulhaber, had kept church officials well informed about the systematic atrocities in Poland. By the end of 1942, at the latest, the German episcopate had quite full knowledge of the destruction of Jews in the East.[23a]

The silence of the Catholic Church in Germany was not simply a reaction to the wave of persecution and death that struck German Jewry during the Hitler period, but was a product of a long tradition of German hostility to Jews and Judaism. By the same token, the antagonistic attitude of the church hierarchy to Jews before and after Hitler influenced popular attitudes. German Catholicism clashed frequently with National Socialism both before and after Hitler's advent to power. But anti-Semitism was not a major issue at conflict. During the period of the Weimar Republic, as Nazi activity rose, the German bishops spoke out against Hitler's glorification of race and blood but very rarely against the virulent anti-Semitic propaganda or violence of the growing Nazi movement. On April 26, 1933, shortly after coming to power, Hitler had a talk with Catholic Church dignitaries and reminded them that for 1,500 years the Church had regarded the Jews as parasites and had banished them to ghettos. He was merely going to continue what the Church had started, he added. The reaction of the Church representatives is not known, but from this period on, German bishops began to declare their appreciation of the important natural values of race and racial purity so long as there was no offense to the "moral law."

The article on "Race" in the authoritative *Handbook on Current Religious Problems* published in 1937 expressed this position in the following words:

> Every people bears itself the responsibility for its successful existence, and the intake of entirely foreign blood will always represent a risk for a nationality that has proven its historical worth. Hence, no people may be denied the right to maintain undisturbed their previous racial stock and to enact safeguards for this purpose. The Christian religion merely demands that the means used do not offend against moral law and natural justice.[24]

This book, edited by Archbishop Konrad Gröber, contained numerous anti-Semitic sections. Lesser Church dignitaries took their cue from their Archbishop and most of them swam with the prevailing anti-Jewish tide. Typical are the following phrases: The Jews had had a "demoralizing influence on religiosity and national character"; the Jews, as a spiritual community, had brought the German people "more damage than benefit"; most of the unhealthy and un-German developments in art since the nineteenth century had been the work of "the uprooted and aesthetically perverted Jew"; the "greatest miracle of the Bible is that the true religion could hold its own and maintain itself against the voice of the Semitic blood."[25]

The embarrassing fact that Jesus had been a Jew was explained by conceding that although he could not be made into an Aryan, he had been fundamentally different from the Jews of his time. "The Christian religion," said Bishop Hilfrich of Limburg in his pastoral letter for Lent 1939, "has not grown out of the nature of this people, that is, is not influenced by their racial characteristics. Rather, it has had to make its way against this people."

These opinions were published in the period between 1933 and 1939 and prepared the way for later attitudes. The Church also bowed to the Nuremberg Laws of September 15, 1935, although they infringed on its spiritual jurisdiction. The Nuremberg Laws made it illegal for two Catholics to marry if one was considered "non-Aryan" (a converted Jew). Yet the Church entitled every Catholic, whether baptized as a child or adult, to the sacraments. The Church conformed to Nazi laws; some elements welcomed them as "indispensable safeguards for the qualitative makeup of the German people."

The cooperation of the Church with the Nazi state was also freely given when Church records had to be checked to determine proof of Aryan descent. Under Nazi law, this depended on the religious status of parents and grandparents. The question whether the Church should lend its help to the Nazi state in sorting out people of Jewish descent was never debated. This cooperation of the Church continued until the end of the war, through the period when the price of being Jewish was not merely dismissal from a government job, but death. By the end of 1942, more than 100,000 German Jews had been sent to their death in the East, and the earlier vague rumors about their fate had been replaced by details of mass gassings. The Church stood by silently. In the past, the episcopate had denied sacraments to Catholics who engaged in dueling; no such penalty was suggested for the Catholic gas-chamber technicians.

A distinguished German sociologist who has made a study of the role of the Catholic Church in Germany during the Hitler period has concluded that "the Catholic press and Catholic organizations gave their total commitment to the nation's cause," while the German Catholic "supported Hitler's war not only because such support was required by the Nazi rulers, but also because his religious leaders formally called upon him to do so." In reflecting on the possible moral dilemma facing German Catholics, this writer comments:

> Certainly it is an indisputable fact that at no time was the Catholic population released from its moral obligation to obey the legitimate authority of the National Socialist rulers under which those Catholics were placed by

the 1933 directives of their spiritual leaders; at no time was the German Catholic led to believe that the regime was an evil unworthy of his support.[25a]

A few Catholic churchmen stand out boldly from this picture, among them, sixty-five-year-old Provost Bernard Lichtenberg of St. Hedwig's Cathedral in Berlin. On the morning after the *Kristallnacht* pogrom, Provost Lichtenberg prayed for the persecuted non-Aryan Christians and Jews and added: "What took place yesterday, we know; what will be tomorrow, we do not know; but what happens today, that we have witnessed; outside, the synagogue is burning, and that, also, is a house of God."

Ignoring the Gestapo spies in his church, Father Lichtenberg spoke out in words that were like a pure flame in the Nazi night: "In a number of Berlin homes, an anonymous inflammatory rag against the Jews is being distributed. It says that any German who, from allegedly false sentimentality, helps the Jews, commits treason against his own people. Do not let yourself be led astray by such un-Christian thoughts, but act according to the clear command of Christ: Thou shalt love thy neighbor as thyself." Provost Lichtenberg continued to say daily prayers for all Jews, baptized and "pure." He was denounced by two women university students and arrested in October 1941, after the first mass deportation. While searching his apartment, police found notes for an undelivered sermon, urging his congregants to reject the Nazi myth that Jews wanted to destroy Germany. During questioning by the police, the Provost declared that deportation of Jews was irreconcilable with Christian moral law. He asked that he be allowed to accompany them to the East and pray for them. He was placed on trial before a special court and sentenced to two years' imprisonment for abuse of the pulpit. On his release in October 1943, he was seized by the Gestapo and sent to Dachau. Too ill to travel, he died on the way in a hospital at Hof.[26]

Cardinal Faulhaber of Munich, after some early ambiguous statements, also spoke out: "History teaches us," he said, "that God always punished tormentors of . . . the Jews. No Roman Catholic approves of the persecutions of Jews in Germany. . . . Racial hatred is a poisonous weed in our life." In October 1938, when the Chief Rabbi of Munich became convinced that his synagogue was in danger, Cardinal Faulhaber provided a truck for the removal of Torah scrolls and other devotional objects. Nazi mobs, infuriated by the Cardinal's action, demonstrated before his home, shouting, "Away with Faulhaber, the Jew friend!"

In the western German provinces, the Bishop of Münster (later Cardinal) Clemens August Count von Galen, delivered trenchant sermons against the antireligious character of the regime. Bishop Theophil Wurm in Württemberg, who had been arrested in 1933 for his protests against the Nazi "Nordic hybrid religion," sent the following memorandum to the authorities in the spring of 1943: "There must be an end to putting to death members of other nations and races who are not even accorded trial by either civil or military courts. What is happening weighs heavily on the conscience of all Christians. . . . A day will come when we will pay for this." He saw as "just retribution" the screaming Allied bombs that gutted homes and churches and put to flight thousands of Germans.

One of the very bold organizations of the time was *Büro Grüber*, established by Pastor Heinrich Grüber of Berlin-Kaulsdorf. While mainly helping Protestants of Jewish descent, this group also helped a number of Jews emigrate during the years 1936–40. When the Nazis banned emigration the bureau was closed down and Grüber was flung into a concentration camp. Pastor Werner Sylten and Pastor Martin Albert continued the work until they too were imprisoned and the Berlin office smashed. One surviving branch office remained in charge of Dr. Herman Maas in Heidelberg. But his obduracy resulted in a death sentence—later commuted—and he was sent to a concentration camp. After liberation, Maas wrote extensively about German guilt and hope for Jewish revival in Palestine. He was the first German to be invited to visit Israel.[26a]

Close to half the population of the Greater Reich was Catholic, but the old Reich was predominantly a Protestant nation. Most German Protestants had been deeply conditioned not only by Martin Luther's vehement and often coarse anti-Semitism but by his insistence on absolute obedience to political authority. In no country, with the exception of czarist Russia, had the clergy been so completely servile to the authority of the state as the Protestant clergy of Germany. In the past they had stood solidly behind the King, the Junkers, and the Army, and opposed the rising democratic and liberal movements of the nineteenth century. They had also opposed the Weimar Republic. Quite openly they supported the Nationalist and Nazi opponents of the Republic and welcomed the advent of Hitler. However, there was some early resistance to Hitler's plan to bring the Protestant churches (there were over twenty-five independent regional organizations) under his direction through a Reich Bishop. Dr. Martin Niemoeller, an early admirer and supporter of Hitler, led this movement to resist the political and religious pressures of Nazism. A schism resulted and led to the formation of a separate Confessional Church which protested the anti-Christian tendencies of the regime and its anti-Semitic measures. Several hundred pastors of the Confessional Church were imprisoned during the early years of the Third Reich, and Dr. Niemoeller himself was imprisoned at Sachsenhausen and Dachau until liberation. The majority of Protestant clergymen, however, submitted to the regime and by 1938 they swore an oath of allegiance to Hitler, binding themselves legally and morally to obey him.

There had been a few exceptional acts and protests in Germany, but the churches—both Protestant and Catholic—permitted themselves to become stifled and absorbed, as had all other institutions in Germany, by the Nazi machine. In 1945, after the war, there were a number of Lutheran churchmen who met at Stuttgart and declared themselves to be bound to the German people "in a community of suffering, but also in a solidarity of guilt."

"We let God wait ten years," Pastor Niemoeller had said.

24 Yugoslavia

OVER A MILLION AND A HALF JEWS lived within the German sphere of influence in the Balkans. The deportations in this area achieved varying results ranging from almost total annihilation in Serbia and Greece to the sheltering of most Jews against Nazi transfers in Bulgaria. In Bulgaria as well as Romania, two countries that had joined the Nazi camp for opportunistic reasons, the changing tide of war slowed down the destructive process. Ultimately, Romania and Bulgaria joined the Allies as cobelligerents against Germany. Hungary also attempted to make the switch but failed and over half of Hungarian Jewry was destroyed.

The Balkans were a seething cauldron of internal and external pressures and the continuous boiling up of old envies and hatreds that Wilsonian formulas for national self-determination could scarcely resolve. Migrations, conquests and reconquests had caused an intermixture of nationalities which could not be straightened out by any ethnic frontier. Foreign rule in many regions caused a bristling nationalism which was taught virtually as a state religion. In the midst of these mutual hostilities, Jews were the targets, first of persecution and then destruction.

Mussolini's ambitions in the Balkans were as rabid as Hitler's, aimed sharply at Yugoslavia and Greece, but not limited to them, while Russia's thrust to the Mediterranean was as old as her history. Hitler aimed to stop both Russian and Italian drives and exploit long-smoldering ethnic fires and territorial ambitions. He created Croatia out of Yugoslavia, and Slovakia out of Czechoslovakia. Bessarabia and Bukovina, after a brief takeover by Russia, were ceded to Romania when Germany invaded the USSR. Hungary was allowed to expand north, east and south. Bulgaria was given Thrace. In every case, however, Hitler exacted payment: military concessions and the destruction of Jews. Yugoslavia was the first country in southeastern Europe to suffer the Nazi onslaught, and its Jews were the first to experience Nazi mass murder.

Hitler's move into Yugoslavia was prompted by his Axis partner's adventurism in Greece and his own decision to invade Russia. Chafing under Germany's glittering, unshared victories, Mussolini tried a solo venture in

Greece in the fall of 1940, but failed miserably. The Italian defeat threatened Germany's position in the Balkans; conversely, it strengthened Britain's strategic position in the Mediterranean. Early in 1941 British desert forces had driven Italian armies out of North Africa in audacious campaigns. Admiral Erich Raeder had warned Hitler that the fight for this region was of decisive importance to Germany and must be a major strategic objective. But Hitler was not convinced.[1] He had never been able to envisage the war in the Mediterranean and North Africa as a main theater of operations. More and more he was becoming obsessed with Russia and the necessity for a showdown. The fateful directive for the invasion of the USSR, coded "Operation Barbarossa," was dated December 18, 1940, and the target date for the opening of the assault was May 15, 1941. However, before Barbarossa could get under way, the Balkans had to be secured.

A German Army was massed in Romania in February 1941. By this time, the Greeks had caused the Italians to retreat. British troops were expected momentarily. Once the British came, Hitler figured, they would bomb the Romanian oil fields and Barbarossa would be delayed. To avert this, Germany had to move troops from Romania into Greece through Bulgaria. Bulgaria had gambled on the wrong side in World War I. She made a similar miscalculation in February 1941, when she accepted Hitler's assurance that the war was already won. Even more, she was tempted by the promise of gaining territory in Greece. On the night of February 28, German units crossed the Danube from Romania and took up strategic positions in Bulgaria. In the following month, after the Greeks were defeated, Bulgaria annexed Thrace from Greece and Macedonia from Yugoslavia.

Yugoslavia, however, was not as accommodating as Bulgaria. The existing collaborationist government was overthrown in a popular uprising which suddenly upset Yugoslavia's puppet status and Hitler's plans.

The independence of Yugoslavia had been steadily deteriorating since 1934 when King Alexander was murdered. Italy's political hostility and Germany's advance into southeast Europe quickened the process while, internally, the antagonism between the Serbs and Croats aggravated the situation. The Soviet-Nazi Pact of 1939 seemed to deliver the Balkans at a stroke to the Axis. When Russia occupied Bessarabia and Bukovina, and Hungary, Transylvania, the net around Yugoslavia closed.

The Yugoslav regent, Prince Paul, had carried the policy of neutrality to the limit for fear of provoking Germany; ministers and leading politicians were afraid to speak. There was one exception, however—an Air Force general, named Dušan Simović, who represented nationalist elements among the officers' corps. Simović's office at Zemun became a center of of Yugoslav opposition to German penetration into the Balkans and Yugoslavian inertia. Meanwhile, on March 1, 1941, Bulgaria had joined the Tripartite Pact, and Yugoslavia was pressured into following suit. By that date, German motorized forces were already at the Yugoslavian frontiers. On March 18, Prince Paul left Yugoslavia on a secret visit to Berchtesgaden. Under great pressure, he verbally committed his country to Bulgaria's course. Prime Minister Cvetković left Belgrade March 24 from a suburban railway station on a Vienna-bound train and, unknown to the public and press, signed a pact with Hitler the following day. The conspirators then began to act.

The small circle around Simović had been preparing for action in case of capitulation. The leader of the planned rising was General Bora Mirković, commander of the Yugoslav Air Force. When news of the pact began to circulate in Belgrade, the conspirators took over the government in a bloodless coup in the name of the young King Peter II. Prince Paul then signed the act of abdication and was allowed to leave for Greece.

The overthrow of the collaborationist government set loose an outburst of popular enthusiasm. The streets of Belgrade were thronged with Serbs chanting "Rather war than the pact; rather death than slavery." There was dancing in the squares and English and French flags were draped everywhere. The young King who, by climbing down a rain-pipe had made his own escape from Regency tutelage, took the oath in Belgrade Cathedral amid great acclaim. The military coup aroused a surge of national vitality. The Serbs had flung their defiance at Hitler at the moment of his greatest power.[2]

These events threw Hitler into an uncontrollable rage and in a characteristically impulsive reaction, he decided to crush Yugoslavia. Eroded by vanity and fury, he took the coup as a personal affront. He called for the immediate invasion of Yugoslavia and instructed Ribbentrop to advise Hungary, Romania and Italy that they would get spoils for their efforts in the conquest. Germany meanwhile planned to take important copper and coal-mining districts for herself. As the support for the coup had come principally from the work of Serbs, the Axis powers regarded them as their main enemy and favored the Croats who were later rewarded with "independence."

The gallant little country that had dared to defy Hitler was pitilessly smashed in a few days. On April 6, the Nazis bombed Belgrade, reducing much of the city to rubble and killing 50,000 persons. Hitler achieved his revenge, but at a very high price. The German diversion against Yugoslavia (and reinforcements for Greece) forced the postponement of the attack against Russia by five full weeks, a delay that would prove crucial.[3] The interval between May 15, when the attack was originally scheduled, and June 22, when it finally came, represented the additional time the German generals on the Russian front needed for certain victory. Later these were to be five weeks of deep snow and subzero temperatures that blocked the movement of the German Armies. The Balkan campaign set back the timetable for Barbarossa. German generals ever afterward would lament the loss of those five weeks.

Moreover, Hitler's preoccupation with the destruction of Russia blinded him to the desperation of Britain's situation. A successful German offensive against Egypt and the Suez at this time would have been a deadly blow against the British Empire.

After the German conquest, Yugoslavia ceased to exist as a nation and its prewar Jewish population of about 75,000 was distributed to new masters: 12,000 remained in Serbia, largely concentrated in Belgrade; about 30,000 fell under the jurisdiction of Croatia, a German satellite; 20,000 from the Bachka region and 8,000 from the former Macedonian towns of Skopje, Bitolj and Pirot came under Hungarian rule. The remainder were distributed to Montenegro (under Italian control), Slovenia (divided between Italy and Germany)and Bosnia-Herzegovina (disputed between Serbia and Croatia. See map, p. 550.) Yugoslavia was expunged from the map.

The pro-German regime of Cvetković-Maček in 1935 had already destroyed the peaceful life of Yugoslav Jews by progressively harsh legislation; the German conquest destroyed Jewish life altogether. Eighty percent of Yugoslavia's Jews were wiped out. The worst massacres occurred in Serbia.

Serbia together with Greece fell within the jurisdiction of the German Military Organization *Südost* (Southeast). After the military occupation zone in Russia and the military governments in the West, *Südost* constituted the third largest German Army stronghold in Axis Europe. The keystone of the German administration was the military commander in Serbia, Franz Böhme. Under him and preparing for a crucial role in the destruction of Serbian Jews, was Dr. Harald Turner, chief of the administrative staff. Economic matters, including Aryanizations, were handled by a special office outside the military command under Dr. Franz Neuhausen. "Political security" was handled by an *Einsatzgruppe* followed by S.S. and police forces. A Serbian puppet government was installed in August, 1941.

The destruction of Serbian Jews was swift. On May 31, 1941, the military administration issued a definition of Jews, ordered the removal of Jews from public service and the professions, required the registration of Jewish property, introduced forced labor and the compulsory wearing of the Jewish star. Compulsory Aryanization was decreed on July 22. However, long before the clerical details involved in these procedures were elaborated, Serbian Jews were destroyed.

Serbia was densely occupied by German troops. Hitler personally felt a violent hatred for the Serbs, possibly deriving from his Austrian childhood and undoubtedly inflamed by the March coup. A powerful partisan movement rose up in Serbia in the summer of 1941 and drew horrifying reprisals. The most vulnerable and immediate target, however, were the Jews. The first killings took place on July 29, 1941, when a young member of *Hashomer Hatzair*, Almoslino by name, set fire to a German military truck in Belgrade. All Jewish adult men were ordered to assemble in a city square. They were divided according to their occupation and every tenth man was ordered to fall out. The Jews believed that the Germans were organizing a transport for forced labor, a common occurrence at the time. When one hundred men had been selected, the Germans declared that they were hostages and would be shot if Almoslino was not surrendered within forty-eight hours. He was not found and the Jews were killed. This was only the beginning.

As partisan warfare spread, the Nazis decided on straight revenge on the Jews and Serbians. For every dead German soldier or civilian, a hundred Jews and Serbians were killed; for every wounded German; fifty were killed. The operations soon resembled the killings in Russia by the *Einsatzgruppen*, except that in Serbia roles were reversed. The *Einsatzgruppen* screened the victims, while the shooting was done by Army troops. The preliminaries in this process involved ghettoization.

In the late summer of 1941, all male Jews in Belgrade were placed in two concentration camps within the city—Topovske Supe and Banjica— and in Šabac, about forty miles west of Belgrade. At the same time, Jewish men throughout Serbia were systematically rounded up. At the beginning of August, 16,000 Jews from Bachka and Banat were put across the Danube by the Hungarians and interned in the miserable huts in the Belgrade Ghetto. The German Minister Plenipotentiary to Serbia, Felix Benzler, was afraid of saboteurs in the Ghetto. On September 12, he wrote to Ribbentrop and requested that the Jews be sent to one of the islands in the Danube, or to the Government-General, or to occupied USSR. The Belgrade Ghetto was being swelled by additional Jews and according to Benzler, 8,000 were males of fighting age, "potential saboteurs," who could not be accommodated in the existing camps of Serbia. Unless Jews were sent to Russia or Poland, he said, he would not be able to carry out Ribbentrop's order to clear the able-bodied Jews out of the Ghetto. In the margin of Benzler's message, Franz Rademacher, the Foreign Office advisor on Jewish Affairs, had made the following notation: "According to information from . . . Eichmann . . . reception in Russia and in the Government-General is impossible. Even Jews from Germany cannot be received there. Eichmann proposes killing by shooting [*Eichmann schlägt Erschiessen vor*]." Rademacher had turned to Eichmann as a matter of course for instructions in dealing with the Jews.

The military, however, preferred deportations. Franz Böhme, the commanding general, knew that deportations had been carried out successfully elsewhere. He suggested dumping them on Romanian soil, but Ribbentrop objected. On October 2, a conference with Heydrich was scheduled to clear up the matter, but events of the same day overtook discussions. In Topola, a German truck convoy was ambushed by partisans and 22 Germans were killed. Two days later, General Franz Böhme instructed an army contingent to shoot 2,100 inmates of the Šabac and Belgrade camps—Jews and Gypsies. Then on October 10, Böhme ordered the sudden arrest of all Communists, all Jews and "nationalistically and democratically inclined inhabitants." A detachment of the Einsatzgruppe screened the inmates and prepared them for killing. Special instructions were issued to the troops for carrying out the shootings. The executions were to be carried out with rifles from a distance of eight to ten yards. The men were to aim at the head or chest "to avoid unnecessary touching of corpses." The victims were to stand at the edge of the grave, then, in mass shootings, they were to kneel facing the grave. Each Kommando was to be accompanied by a military doctor who was to give the order for any "mercy shots." The shootings were to be confined to men.

The contradiction that Jews were paying for the resistance of Serbs out of all proportion to Jewish resistance did not escape certain Nazis. Nor did it deter them. The military administrator, Turner, wrote to the Higher S.S. and Police Leader in Danzig:

> Actually, it is false if one has to be accurate about it, that for murdered Germans—on whose account the ratio 1:100 should really be borne by Serbs—100 Jews are shot instead; but the Jews we already had in the camps—after all, they, too, are Serb nationals—and besides, they have to disappear. At any rate, I don't have to accuse myself that on my part there has been any lack of necessary ruthless action for the preservation of German prestige and the protection of members of the German Wehrmacht.[4]

Heydrich, meanwhile, sent a "specialist" to Belgrade to finish up matters. Rademacher arrived in Belgrade on October 18 and reported back to Luther, his chief, within a week, informing him that the adult male Jews in Belgrade numbered not 8,000, but only 4,000. Moreover, Böhme had already shot half of them. Of the remainder, 500 were exempted workers constructing the new Zemun Ghetto camp, and the other 1,500 would be shot before the end of the week. This disposal still left Belgrade with 20,000 Jewish women, children and old people. Rademacher recommended that they be concentrated in a ghetto in the Gypsy sector of Belgrade. There he said, "a minimum of food would be provided for the winter, and as soon as the final solution of the Jewish question was reached and the technical means were available, the Jews would be deported by water to the reception camps in the East."[5] Turner, in the meantime, urged the quick removal of these Jews to the prison town of Mitrovica, near Belgrade, on the Danube.

On December 8, Benzler came to Berlin, complaining that the island was under water. The situation in the Belgrade Ghetto had become desperate. Rademacher refused to see him but sent word that the Belgrade Jews could not be moved even in the spring. Ribbentrop, meanwhile, had asked Heydrich to deport the Belgrade Jews to eastern Poland. The Nazi leaders in Belgrade soon found their own solution.

Outside Yugoslavia, the shootings of hostages were evoking protests. The Foreign Office was deluged with complaints, but they were fobbed off by the clever Ernst von Weizsäcker of the Foreign Office. Weizsäcker also succeeded in deflecting an imminent protest from the papal representative. "The nuncio today [December 5, 1941] groped around to the well-known subject of hostages," Weizsäcker observed,

> in order to determine whether a discussion between him and me about the question of shooting hostages—of late in Serbia—would be fruitful. I replied to the nuncio that, among all foreign governments which have concerned themselves with this question, the Vatican had conducted itself most cleverly, in that it took the hint I had furtively extended to Papal Counselor Colli upon a social occasion. If the Vatican should, nevertheless, feel constrained to return to this subject, I would be obliged to give to the nuncio the same answer that Mexico, Haiti and other governments had received already. The nuncio saw this point completely and pointed out that he had not really touched this topic and that he had no desire to touch it.[6]

The removal of Jewish women and children in Belgrade was finally resolved. Turner insisted that it was against the principles of German military honor to take women as hostages. As he disliked ghettos, and as Mitrovica was unusable, his choice for "resettlement" fell upon Semlin (Zemun) near Belgrade, which was under Croat jurisdiction. The Croat Government had generously given its permission to construct a camp there. On November 3, Turner ordered a count of all women and children in Serbia. After this was done, troop units began to move the families of the dead hostages to Semlin, once the site of a world's fair. Semlin, however, was no transit to Poland; it was the end of the road.

From time to time, a group of women and children were loaded onto gas vans and driven out to the woods. During the spring and summer of 1942, at least 6,000 Jewish women and children from Semlin were gassed in vans. A few women were able to bribe guards and escaped. Not until October 1952, however, when several Gestapo officers in Serbia were brought to trial, was the use of gassing vans revealed.

Soon after the war, the Yugoslav State Commission reported that these Jews had been deported to the death camps in Poland. In 1948, the International Red Cross laconically reported that "three camps were known to be situated in Serbia. The detainees who had been quartered there temporarily were afterwards taken to an unknown destination and nothing further was heard of them."⁷ No Serbian Jews were deported to Poland, however. The "unknown destination" was the gassing van.

In May 1942—a little prematurely—the RSHA was informed that Serbia was free of Jews. By the end of July, Belgrade was completely *Judenrein* and in the following October the Belgrade Jewish Bureau of the Gestapo was closed down "because there were no longer any Jews living in its operational area." Even earlier, toward the end of August, Turner made some notes for a new chief and wrote with obvious satisfaction: "Serbia only country in which Jewish question and Gypsy question solved."

In Croatia, the Nazis also achieved their "solution."

The puppet state of Croatia was created in great haste on April 10, 1941, after Yugoslavia was crushed. On April 11, the day after the German Army occupied the Croat city of Zagreb, the German Foreign Office trouble shooter Edmund Veesenmayer was in the city discussing with Croat leaders plans for a Croat Government. By April 16, the most important offices had been filled and Ante Pavelić, founder of the terrorist Ustasha movement and instigator of the assassination of the former Yugoslav King Alexander, became the head of state. Fascist Croatia had been created and guaranteed not only by Germany but by Italy as well. However, the two occupying powers never completely controlled Pavelić. He played Italian ambitions in Yugoslavia—particularly the desire for Dalmatia—against the Germans. The Duke of Spoleto, a nephew of the King of Italy, became the King of Croatia, and, adding to Germany's future problems, Italian military units occupied the southeast of the country.

The precise boundaries dividing Italian and German spheres of influence in Croatia were never clearly drawn. The Italian occupation zone included almost half of Croatia proper, Dalmatia and Montenegro; part of this area was officially annexed by Italy. German troops occupied the rest of the country. This division of spheres and zones was to have an important role in the struggle of Croatian Jewry for survival.

The Ustashi were fanatics bent on the destruction of both Serbia and Jews. The movement had formed at the end of World War I to protest the union of Serbia and Croatia. During the interwar period of exile in Italy and Hungary, the Ustashi perpetrated acts of sabotage and political assassination while awaiting the day of reckoning. When unleashed after April 1941, the Ustashi murdered and tortured Jews and Serbs in indescribably bestial fashion. One of the most notorious camps in Hitler Europe, Jasenovac, was in Croatia. Here the Ustashi used primitive implements in putting their victims to death—knives, axes, hammers and other iron tools. A characteristic method was binding pairs of prisoners, back to back, and then throwing them into the Sava River. One source estimates that 770,000 Serbs, 40,000 Gypsies and 20,000 Jews were done to death in the Jasenovac camp.[8]

The new Croat Government lost no time in introducing anti-Jewish measures. On April 30, a definition of the term "Jew" was framed and within a short time the government enacted all of the measures which German experts had toiled over for eight years. Possibly reflecting a crack in the anti-Jewish monolith caused by the marriage of some of the Ustashi leaders (including Pavelić) to Jewish women, non-Aryans who had made "worthwhile contributions to the Croat cause" before April 10, 1941, were granted the full rights of Aryans. These "honorary Aryans" were the subject of German complaints but the exact number of exempted Jews has not been determined.

The economic destitution of the 30,000 Croat Jews came swiftly within the first few months. A wave of massacres then struck the Jews in the summer of 1941. Survivors were sent to the three labor-extermination camps of Jasenovac, Laborgrad and Pag Island, north of Zadar, and to the salt mines at Karlovac and Yudovo. By the summer of 1942, the Croatian Government seemed ready for deportations. The German Foreign Office made its characteristic gesture: did the Croat Government plan to recall its Jews from the Reich, or agree to their deportation? Predictably, Pavelić agreed to deport them and the remaining Jews in Croatia.

There remained only one problem: about 5,000 Jews lived in the Italian-occupied zone of Croatia where none of the anti-Jewish laws had yet been applied. There, as in southern France and Greece, the Germans tried to goad the Italians into action against the Jews but failed. General Mario Roatta, the commanding general in the Italian Military Zone II, centered around Dubrovnik and Mostar, was especially obdurate. He had promised equal treatment to all inhabitants under his jurisdiction, refusing even to evict Jewish tenants from their apartments to make room for the German Todt Organization. His explanation was simply that anti-Jewish measures were "incompatible with the honor of the Italian Army." The German Foreign Minister in Croatia, Siegfried Kasche, reported his difficulties with the Italians to Ribbentrop and the matter was referred to Mussolini. Mussolini offered no opposition to German plans, but a ruse engineered by the Italian Foreign Office further sidetracked the deportations.

Mussolini's son-in-law, Count Galeazzo Ciano, head of the Italian Foreign Office, ordered General Roatta to conduct an elaborate and prolonged registration of the Jews in the Italian zone based on various categories of citizenship. This procedure took so long that Ribbentrop urged Hitler to send two German divisions and an S.S. battalion to the Italian zone to assist in the deportations. Nothing came of this plan. Negotiations between Italians and Croatians on the fate of the Jews were then begun. The

German interest in bauxite deposits in Mostar played some role in the course of these talks. At first the Italians offered to take the Jews to Italy. The Croat negotiators insisted that if this happened, all Jewish property in the Italian zone would revert to the Croat Government. When the Germans heard of these proposals, the German Ambassador in Italy rushed to the Italian Foreign Office to demand an explanation. He was reassured that "Italy was not Palestine," that Croatian Jews would be interned after the registration was completed. (None were, however.) Meanwhile, the Italians had actually taken some Jews to Italy—1,161 to Porto Re in Istria and some to the Dalmatian island of Lopud. About 2,000 Jews were also sent to the island of Arbe in the Gulf of Kvarner away from the continental area of the Italian zone where frequent changes in the demarcation lines put them in jeopardy.

Mussolini meanwhile had a stormy interview with General Roatta and insisted that the Jews be interned in Trieste—which had a direct rail connection with Auschwitz—as had been promised Ribbentrop. Roatta successfully argued him out of this idea and when later it was discussed with the Croatians, the Italians said that they could not spare the necessary shipping. They also refused requests for "labor battalions" of Jews. As the year 1942 drew to a close, it became clear that the Italians would not cooperate in the deportations.

In the German zone, deportations began in August 1942. Statistics on the full account of these transports are still incomplete. By the end of 1942, 4,927 Jews had been deported; additional small groups were transported during 1943 and 1944. In March 1943, a representative of the *Reichsbahn* in Zagreb agreed to furnish cars to be hooked up to regularly scheduled trains for the deportation of 2,000 Jews to Auschwitz via Austria. Subsequent pressure was put on the Italians but in vain. The Italians flatly refused to surrender any Jews. After the fall of Mussolini, a representative in the Foreign Ministry of the Badoglio Government urged General Roatta not to surrender the Croatian Jews under any circumstances. In September 1943, however, after the Italian armistice, the Italian zone disappeared altogether. Some Jews went into hiding; others joined Tito's partisans (a detachment in the fourth Partisan Brigade won special distinction), while still others found sanctuary in Fiume (Rijeka).

In April 1944, Kasche made a final report to Berlin, in which he declared that the Jewish question in Croatia had been solved except for three categories: honorary Aryans, Jews in mixed marriages and *Mischlinge*, the same groups that could not be completely erased in the Reich itself. In the meantime, Pavelic had had his hands full dealing with partisans who raged throughout Croatia from Zemun to Zagreb. The Ustashi fought them with savage inhumanity, making a common practice of gouging out their eyes and collecting them in wicker baskets.[9] But Pavelic's power shrank as the partisan movement swelled and German victory receded. By the spring of 1944, when he visited Hitler at Klessheim, his power had become so restricted that he was known derisively as "the Mayor of Zagreb." Thereafter, he kept an eye on the Western Allies and recognized the negotiable value of Jews. He accepted the Red Cross conventions regarding civilian internees and allowed the Red Cross to inspect Jewish labor camps. He also granted the American Joint Distribution Committee the right to send food and money to the skeleton Jewish community still left in Zagreb.

Kasche complained that German agencies had brought in Jews from outside Croatia "to conduct official and economic transactions" and that in certain public positions no substitutes for Jews could be found.[10] Kaltenbrunner ordered an investigation of this situation and in October 1944 the rest of the Zagreb Jewish community were sent to camps. A little over one tenth of Zagreb's prewar Jewish population—1,647—survived the war.

In Greece, the Nazis waited until 1942 to start their campaign of mass murder. The annihilation of Greek Jewry, too, was almost total.

25 Greece

THE GERMAN MILITARY ORGANIZATION *Südost* controlled part of Greece as well as Serbia after the German sweep of the Balkans in April 1941. In Greece, the Germans occupied eastern Thrace, Salonika and the island of Crete. The Italians, meanwhile, occupied "old Greece," with the capital at Athens. The Ionian islands, western Thrace and Macedonia were annexed by Bulgaria.

Of the 70,000 Jews in prewar Greece, more than 50,000 lived in Salonika alone. The bulk of Greek Jewry was thus concentrated within the German grasp. About 13,000 lived under Italian jurisdiction and 6,000 in the new Bulgarian territories.

The Jews of Salonika were marked for destruction first, but the Germans delayed their blows until the summer of 1942—a full nine months after the deportations from Serbia had ended.

On April 9, 1941, German armored columns had entered Salonika. Two days later, the *Messagero*, a Jewish-Spanish daily, was suppressed and many houses and public buildings—Jewish and non-Jewish—were requisitioned for military needs. On April 15, the members of the Jewish Community Council were arrested and the Council offices raided. The Chief Rabbi of Salonika, Dr. Zevi Koretz, who was in Athens when the Germans entered the city, was arrested upon his return in May and sent to Vienna where he was imprisoned for eight months.

During the first few weeks of the Nazi occupation, placards went up forbidding Jews to enter cafés; orders were given requiring them to give up their radios. Meanwhile, a quisling newspaper appeared, called the *New Europe*, which devoted a great deal of space to anti-Semitic propaganda.[1] There were occasional cases of assault, and some Jews were arrested and executed as Communists. For over a year, however, no specific anti-Jewish regulations were introduced. Jews had shared the fortunes of war with Greeks during the Italian-Greek conflict and likewise shared life under the widely hated Nazi occupation. The Jews of Greece were thus unaware of any possible fate separate from the fate of the rest of Greece.

This delay in time caused by the problem of transporting Greek Jews great distances to Auschwitz and by the shortage of S.S. and police forces, did not benefit the Jews in Greece in any way. During the winter of 1941–42, they were scarcely better off than the Jews in the hunger-haunted ghettos of Poland. Some 20,000 were near starvation and several thousand more were ill with spotted typhus. Nevertheless, in July 1942, the administration office of the Salonika-Aegean Military Command decreed heavy labor conscription for Jewish men. This marked the beginning of specifically Jewish persecution. On July 11, 1942, orders were issued by the Salonika-Aegean Military Command requiring all male Jews between eighteen and forty-five to report to Liberty Square in Salonika and register for forced labor. So debilitated was the Jewish population that the German Todt Organization could not find three or four thousand workers fit for railway construction. Some men labeled "fit" were sent to work and soon perished in malarial swamps.[2] The military found it more profitable to sell exemptions to those Jews who could afford to buy their way out, and in October, Dr. Alfred Merten, counselor to the Military Administration, stopped conscription temporarily upon payment of a community fine of two and a half billion drachmas (about $40,000).[3]

It seemed that Salonika Jews would now be let alone. A false sense of security lulled the community. However, seizures and expropriations of Jewish property soon followed, culminating in the spoliation of the ancient Salonika cemetery. On December 6, tombstones were plundered and used to line latrines and pave streets. On the same day, Major Wulff of Eichmann's office made a preliminary visit to Salonika and shortly afterward, Eichmann himself paid a brief visit with his adjutant Rolf Günther. On February 6, 1943, the RSHA deportation specialists Dieter Wisliceny and Alois Brunner arrived in Salonika to carry out the deportations in the German zone.

By this time, the Germans realized that their Italian partners, who had refused to collaborate in anti-Jewish measures elsewhere were following the same policy in Greece. While the forced-labor system was still in effect in the German-controlled area, some Salonika Jews began to move into the Italian zone. In order to check this flow, the Germans had asked the Italian administration to cooperate in jointly introducing a Jewish badge decree. But the Italians refused. The Italian commander, General Carlo Geloso, said he lacked necessary instructions from his government. The Germans then moved with great speed in their own zone. Within five months, the Salonika Jewish community—the greatest center of Sephardic Jewry in the world—was wiped out.

All Jews five years or older were required to wear a Jewish star. By the end of February, a Jewish ghetto in Salonika was decreed—a ghetto divided into three noncontiguous parts. The poorest Jews of Salonika were concentrated in the Baron de Hirsch quarter. This was a camp of huts near the railway station—an area that had once been used as a refuge for Jews fleeing the pogroms of Mogilev and Kishinev in the 1890's. The Nazis made of it a funnel leading to the death transports. The Jews in the de Hirsch quarter were the first to be transported to the "East." When this ghetto was emptied, Jews from the other two ghetto sections filled it up again. Within three months, this process of filling, emptying and refilling the de Hirsch quarter carried off 43,000 Jews to Auschwitz.

The presence of Wisliceny and Brunner in Salonika was not understood by the Jews of the city, but they were there for only one purpose: to deport Greek Jews as quickly as possible. A few who survived Auschwitz have testified that documents of grants of land in the Ukraine were brought into the de Hirsch camp and shown to the credulous inmates. There were also picture postcards of a fictitious place called Waldsee, sent by the first transports to relatives still in Salonika. Rabbi Koretz, meanwhile, had been returned from Vienna to Salonika and on December 11, 1942, was appointed by the Nazis to head the Jewish Community Council. His knowledge of German undoubtedly influenced his appointment. When Merten summoned him after the ghettoization order was given, he tried to reassure the rabbi. The Jewish population had no cause for concern, he explained, but the de Hirsch quarter would have to be emptied because Communists there threatened the security of the occupation army. Jews, he maintained, would not be harmed. They would be sent to the Polish city of Krakow and there could take up a "new life."[4]

On March 14, the day before the first transport left, Rabbi Koretz was ordered to call a meeting in the synagogue of the de Hirsch camp and announce that all detainees were to leave for Krakow the following day. He told the assembled Jews that the large Jewish community in Krakow would look after their needs and that they would be able to find work there. "There is no way out," he said, "but to gird our loins and go out into exile. The times are difficult, tragic; we must arm ourselves with patience and courage."[5] The stunned congregation shouted him down, protesting his words. But they made their preparations. For the labor conscripts, deportation seemed preferable to their miserable life. Young couples made hasty marriages to face life together in the "East." To complete the deception, the Nazis distributed Polish paper money and allowed certain possessions to be carried. Bread, dried fruit and olives were supplied by the Transport Command of the Wehrmacht.

Although some Jews in the Greek resistance had warned the Jews of Salonika to flee[6] the country, only 3,400 had done so. No one in Salonika or in Athens at the time knew exactly what the deportations meant. There had been no news from France—some Greek Jews had gone there—where transports had gone to the death camps a full year before. Nor was there any news of Polish Jewry. Another deterrent to flight was the public execution of a few Jews who were caught trying to escape.

The death camps were virtually unknown in Greece even after the war was over. In March 1945, several months after the liberation of Greece, Leon Beatty of Ioannina, who had survived a transport from Athens to Auschwitz, returned to Salonika and told the remaining handful of Salonika Jews about his experiences. They refused to believe him and thought his mind had become deranged.[7]

Rabbi Koretz, however, knew about the ghettos in Poland and knew that Greek Jews would have to face oppression and hunger. He was so mindful of conditions in Poland that when the Military Administration announced that they needed 3,000 Jews of the deportees for military work in Greece, he appealed to the Germans to take 15,000.[8] He also urged Jews to volunteer for such work, believing that forced labor in Greece was still preferable to deportations to Poland. But there were few volunteers. Jews took their chances and went to Poland instead.

Political means were then tried. Rabbi Koretz proposed that half the possessions of Salonika Jews be turned over to the Germans in return for the privilege of remaining in Greece. This proposal was transmitted to Berlin but was quickly rejected. At the beginning of 1943, when John Rhallis, the Greek puppet Prime Minister, arrived in Salonika, the Jews in Athens petitioned him to stop the deportations. Rabbi Koretz urged him to send the Jews to the Greek islands. On April 10, following this appeal, Rabbi Koretz was dismissed and arrested. He was held in the de Hirsch ghetto for a short time and in June was sent to Bergen-Belsen where he died of typhoid fever.

Eichmann, meanwhile, had ordered Brunner to transport the Salonika Jews to Auschwitz without further delay. No exceptions were to be made. The 1,000-mile trip to Auschwitz took from seven to nine days. Sixty people of all ages and physical states were packed into each boxcar; many perished on the way. On March 15, 2,800 were deported and by the end of the month the figure rose to 13,435. By the middle of May, the last of the labor conscripts were moved, swelling the total of deportees to 42,830. Virtually all perished.

Höss later told Wisliceny that the Salonika Jews were "all of such poor quality" that they had to be exterminated quickly. (A few women were spared for the sterilization experiments in Block 10 of the Auschwitz main camp.) For three weeks the Salonika Jews stopped the crematoria at Auschwitz: they had brought ravaging spotted typhus to the camp and transports were suspended during the subsequent quarantine. Thereafter, the extermination of Greek Jews was carried out with great speed.

Swift as this action was, however, there were a few problems created by two foreign representatives, the Italian Consul General in Salonika and the

Spanish chargé d'affaires in Athens.[9] Their efforts affected the lives of almost 1,000 Jews in Greece.

Early in the deportations, the RSHA had complained that Italian Consul General Castrucci was handing out naturalization papers to Greek Jews in Salonika. Castrucci had saved 550 Jews this way, most of them women, who had been plucked out of the de Hirsch camp at the last moment and were then put on the troop train to Athens in the Italian zone. The German Foreign Office interceded with the Italian Government to have the naturalizations stopped, but Castrucci persisted, reminding the Germans of "special Italian rights in the Greek sphere." Several hundred more were saved by Spanish intervention: 367 reached Spain after the war and were transported to Palestine by the Joint Distribution Committee.

Spain's interest in eastern Sephardic Jews dated from the period of the Russian pogroms of the late nineteenth century when Spain offered refuge to Jews who had fled Russia. A decree had also permitted Jews of "proved Spanish descent" in the former Ottoman Empire to become Spanish citizens. In practice, however, there was a great deal of confusion and delay in carrying out these regulations and the number of Jews in former Ottoman areas who obtained Spanish passports was small.[10] In dealing with the 600 Spanish Jews in Greece, the Franco Government carried on a tradition of procrastination, and through the spring and summer of 1943 the Germans and Spaniards continued to haggle about the Spanish Jews.

At first the Germans suggested that they be sent to Spain, but Eduard Gasset, the Spanish chargé d'affaires, was instructed to accept only 50 of the 600. At the same time, Spain wanted to make sure they would not be killed if they remained under German jurisdiction. The German Foreign Office, meanwhile, had to treat neutral Spain circumspectly. Eichmann was told to treat the Spanish Jews in such a way that if they emigrated later there would be no "undesired atrocity propaganda." Finally, in August 1943, the German Foreign Office decided to treat them as "exchange Jews" and they became the first inmates of Bergen-Belsen in Germany, the so-called residence camp. On August 2, 367 left Salonika.

The German Foreign Office continued its painstaking efforts simultaneously to camouflage and promote the "Final Solution." Several months after the decision on Bergen-Belsen, a representative of the Spanish Embassy in Berlin declared that his government was now prepared to repatriate all Spanish Jews in occupied territories. The German Foreign Office, however, said that it was too late. Only those Jews who had not been "sent East" could be returned to Spain. Eberhard von Thadden of the Foreign Office explained that the papers identifying the deportees had been destroyed in the last air raid on Berlin. Besides, the deportees were engaged in "the East" on work so secret that it could not be revealed to enemy intelligence.

Until their surrender in September 1943, the Italians adroitly side-stepped German blandishments and pressure. They refused to collaborate in the destruction of Greek Jews. Eichmann had good reason for concluding that the Italians lacked "sincerity of implementation" to cooperate with the Germans on the Jewish question. After September 1943, however, the 13,000 Jews under Italian protection lost their short reprieve. They, as well as the Jews in Albania, Montenegro and the Dodecanese islands, were fully exposed thereafter. All fell under the German Military Organization *Südost*. The first blows fell on Athens, where about 3,500 Jews—many of them having found sanctuary in the city—were living.

The Nazis now put into effect the anti-Jewish laws which the Italian regime had substantially ignored. The German authorities carried out searches day and night, and offered rewards to Greeks who denounced Jews. On September 27, General Jürgen Stroop, the Nazi general who organized the destruction of the Warsaw Ghetto, took charge in Athens and began a ruthless roundup. On October 3, he ordered all Jews to register with German authorities within five days or be killed. The Jewish resistance groups tried to organize an evacuation of all 3,500 Jews from the city, but the task was hopeless. Only a few hundred Athenian Jews were removed to remote mountain villages.[11] The Germans expected to trap 8,000 Jews in the registration but only 1,200 reported. As punishment for such "disobedience," the German Military Commander ordered the confiscation of Jewish property. Immediately after the Italian capitulation, the Jewish community leaders had destroyed all official Jewish records, enabling some Jews to remain in hiding, but the Nazis did not have to rely entirely on records. Athenian Jews were seized in the synagogues at Friday night services, and 900 perished.[12] An additional 500 were dragged from their hiding places and taken to a temporary camp at Heidar. Some Jews in Athens managed to stay alive with the help of the Red Cross and their non-Jewish neighbors, who brought them food and money, but half of the Jewish population in Athens perished in the deportations of April and June 1944. The Germans also took over Kastoria, Ioannia, Arta, Corfu, Preveza and Kana.

In March 1944, the Germans mobilized trucks and guards to make the roundups of all Jews left on the mainland outside Athens. Over 5,000 were deported in these seizures. The islands of Corfu, Rhodes and Crete, where another 5,000 Jews lived, were more difficult for the Germans to manage. The original plan scheduled the deportations for July 1944, but the last transport did not reach Birkenau until August 17. It contained the entire Jewish population of the island of Rhodes, 1,200 people. They had fallen into German hands the previous September following an abortive British attempt to induce the Italians to surrender the island.

On July 17, the first day of the deportation, a German soldier who went to the city of Rhodes to see a dentist, noticed hundreds of men, women and children standing and facing a wall in the blistering heat. Greek and Turkish civilians who offered them something to drink were kept away. The soldier also noticed that the Jews had very little baggage. He began talking to other German soldiers standing guard and was told that the Jews did not need any baggage since they would not live very long.[13] The Military Commander in the Aegean, Lieutenant General Ulrich Kleemann, when informed that the deportation had aroused doubts and gossip among the soldiers, ordered all such discussions to stop. These were matters, he said, that soldiers, "from their narrow point of view," could not judge.

Local German officials elsewhere commented on dangers involved in rounding up Jews on the Aegean Islands. Demobilized Italians on Corfu, for example, had warned the Jews there to hide in the mountains. Under an Allied-Nazi arrangement, Red Cross ships were permitted to enter Greek harbors with food in order to combat widespread hunger. In May there was such a ship in the harbor of Corfu, where visitors could see everything and spread "atrocity propaganda." It was also pointed out that Greek police and sailors might be bribed. Nevertheless, the deportations ground on. On June 17, 1,800 Corfu Jews were seized and 260 were deported from Crete.

Almost 2,000 miles from Auschwitz, the tentacles of the "Final Solution" stretched their murderous reach to the faraway Greek islands. At a time when the Germans were abandoning great quantities of their stores to the Greek partisans, and when the cluttering up of their evacuation routes with deportation trains violated every military consideration, the transports rolled blindly on. When the final count of losses in Greece was made, it was estimated that 60,000 Greek Jews had been deported to Auschwitz. Of these, only 1,475 survived the war.

The attitude of the non-Jewish population to the deportations varied. In Salonika it was somewhat equivocal. While under Turkish rule (until 1912), the Jews of Salonika had enjoyed a tolerant and hospitable atmosphere. They worked at the same occupations that Paul of Tarsus noted when he visited the city: crafts, trade and waterfront activity. Most of the stevedores and harbor workers in Salonika were Jewish. The end of Turkish rule brought marked changes but no threat to organic community life.[14] Population exchanges between Greece and Turkey in 1923–24 brought about a rapid increase in the Greek population, while economic instability and anti-Semitic agitation in the years after World War I caused a substantial migration of Jews to France and Palestine. Between 1900 and 1941, the Jewish population of Salonika declined from 80,000 to 46,000. However, Jews there still lived tolerably well.

Nevertheless, the former residents of Turkey who were transferred to

Greece on an exchange basis lived more competitively among the Jews than had the older Turks. Contact between the Jewish and non-Jewish population was spotty. One of the few survivors, Rabbi Michael Molho, has speculated that "local factors were active in the implementation of the deportations in order to get rid of competitors who proved a burden to them in their common life."[15] Only 70 Jews—most married to non-Jews —found hiding places among non-Jews in Salonika.

There was, however, some intervention in behalf of Jews by Greek officials and agencies. Within a few days after the first deportation, the Salonika Bar presented a petition to the Prime Minister urging that Greek Jews be interned on a Greek island. This plan was also supported by the Metropolitan Theophilos Damaskinos, who later became Regent for the throne. Damaskinos suggested using Jewish assets for a communal maintenance fund, but this idea was rejected. The Greek civil governor in the German zone wanted to use these assets for the Greek refugees whom the Bulgarians had expelled from Thrace. (According to Wisliceny, it was through this Greek civil governor that the German Military Administration gained control of Jewish houses, and through the Security Police, the cash which the deportees had to surrender.) In Athens and the Aegean Islands, the local population seems to have been more protective. The Jewish communities there were small and the local attitude undoubtedly was influenced by the humane policy of the Italian forces.

Jewish resistance efforts in Greece grew out of the national defense against the Italian invasion of 1940 in which 13,000 Jews fought. After the German intervention in the Greek-Italian war and the conclusion of the armistice, most of the Greek Army was demobilized. A few battalions, however, fled to the southern part of the country, mainly to Athens. Over 1,500 Salonikan Jews joined them to carry on the struggle against Germany. After the German Army occupied Athens, however, the war on the mainland officially came to an end. The Greek Government fled to Crete, where some Greeks and remnants of the British Army continued fighting. On the mainland, the war was carried on by guerrillas and partisan fighters in the mountains and cities of Greece.[16]

At the end of 1941, the 54 Greek underground resistance organizations were consolidated into two main bodies, the National Organization under General Napoleon Zervas, centered in Epirus, and the National Liberation Front, centered in Athens. Young Jews, especially college and university students in Athens, enrolled in the National Liberation Front and carried out sabotage against German installations, communications and ships carrying German munitions.

Early in 1942, the British High Command in Cairo learned that Rommel's *Afrika Korps* was being reinforced by new military units arriving from Greece. The only rail line available to the Germans passed over the

Gorgopotamos Bridge which connected northern and southern Greece. General Zervas was requested to blow up this bridge. In the commando raid which carried out this operation, there were over 40 Jews.[17]

All-Jewish or predominantly Jewish resistance groups were formed in Salonika, Athens and in Thessaly early in 1943. The Jewish resistance unit in Salonika was led by the well-known journalist Elie Veissi. Veissi knew German well and was able to gain the confidence of certain German officers who were billeted in his house. Through these contacts he was able to gather valuable information which he then transmitted to the British in Cairo. But Veissi's group was not strong enough to influence Salonika Jews to flee. Warnings were sounded and a few thousand fled to Athens; the rest either did not hear the warnings or refused to heed them. Veissi himself was arrested by the Germans on April 29, 1943—toward the end of the Salonika deportations—and deported to Auschwitz.

In the town of Volo in Thessaly, the local Metropolitan Joachim warned Rabbi Moshe Pesah of the imminent seizure of all Jews by the Germans. Contacts were made with nearby partisans and most of the 822 Jews living in Volo were spirited out of town. All but 130 survived.[18]

In Athens, the chief task was to find hiding places for Jews and secure false identity papers. Police Chief Ebert authorized his subordinates to grant new papers to all who applied for them. Flight to Turkey across the Aegean was also organized and some of the Jewish youth who escaped this way enrolled in the Palestine Brigade and Free Hellenic Forces.

A small group of Jewish partisans, passing as Greek Orthodox communicants, succeeded in infiltrating German shipping installations in Piraeus and carried out sabotage with their Greek comrades. But the crowning act of Greek-Jewish resistance was the blowing up of two crematoria in Auschwitz. There were 135 Greek Jews in the unit that consigned Jews to the crematoria. At the head of this unit were three former officers of the Greek Army, Lieutenant Colonel Joseph Baruch, and two lieutenants, José Levy and Maurice Aron.[19] These men decided to dynamite the crematoria and end the Auschwitz exterminations. Detailed plans were made to carry out the action at noon on September 6, 1944. Bit by bit, they managed to collect stores of dynamite and weapons from German warehouses. On the morning of September 6, the Greek Jews, with the help of two units of French Jews and one of Hungarian Jews, blew up two of the four crematoria at Auschwitz. They fought off the Germans for over an hour and killed four German officers and twelve German soldiers, but all were shot down in the struggle.

An estimated 60,000 Greek Jews perished during the Nazi occupation, almost totally destroying Jewish life there. A similar fate struck the Jews of Slovakia.

26 Slovakia

GERMAN POWER in Slovakia was much weaker than in Greece, where it was decisive in the scale and intensity of Jewish destruction, but the lack of power in Slovakia was compensated by local support of Nazi aims on the "Jewish question."

Jews in Czechoslovakia had enjoyed economic, cultural and religious equality during the twenty-year life of the Republic, but their situation began to deteriorate after Munich, when the Sudetenland was annexed to the Reich and Teschen, to Poland. After Hitler's Vienna Award of November 1938, which gave certain parts of Slovakia and Ruthenia to Hungary, their situation became worse. The remainder of Slovakia was granted autonomy within the federal state renamed Czecho-Slovakia. Slovak nationalist and extremist clerical elements guided the new regime to a one-party, pro-German state and began immediately to take measures against Jews.

Sharply contrasted with the liberal and secularist traditions in Bohemia and Moravia, stood Slovakia, which had become a recalcitrant part of the Czech state in 1919. In Slovakia the traditions were antiliberal, clerical and strongly nationalist. The centuries-old domination by Hungary had left its mark. The chief political party, the Slovak People's Party, drew most of its support from the peasants and its leaders largely from the priesthood. It clamored from the beginning for more autonomy within the Czech state, and when both Hitler and Mussolini held out the promise of independence, not only the natural bent of the party but external influences inclined Slovakia toward Fascism.

The Slovak People's Party, a strongly Catholic Party, had been organized in 1918 by a priest, Andrej Hlinka. From the beginning, it was hostile toward the liberal Czechoslovak regime. Hlinka died during the Munich crisis and was succeeded by Dr. Josef Tiso, also a Catholic priest. Like the Sudetenland German Party, the Slovak People's Party served as a fifth column during the partition of Czechoslovakia and, once in power, announced its intention of solving the "Jewish problem" in Slovakia in the German manner. Germany, for its part, welcomed these views and praised

Slovakia for its quick acceptance of the spirit of a "New Europe." Strategic considerations formed no small part of Germany's attitude, for Slovakian roads, railways and airfields were used in the Reich's war against Poland.

The Slovaks undoubtedly had legitimate grievances against the Czech Republic, but they were not insoluble and very likely would have been settled in less turbulent times. When the Republic was established, the Slovaks had been promised a Swiss-type cantonal system, but had not received it. They also deeply resented the imprisonment of Dr. Vojtech Tuka, a respected professor, who had been sentenced to fifteen years' imprisonment for treason, although it is doubtful that he was guilty of more than advocating Slovak autonomy. But whatever the grievances, they were serious enough to fit perfectly into Hitler's plan to dismember Czechoslovakia. Before the end of 1938, Slovakia and Ruthenia were granted autonomy. After Munich, Slovakian leaders eagerly looked to Germany for "guidance." On February 12, 1939, Hitler received Dr. Tuka in Berlin. "My Führer," Tuka began, "I lay the destiny of my people in your hands. From you my people await their complete liberation."

Hitler's reply was at first hesitant; Tuka's request had not been expected. Hitler admitted that he had not understood the Slovak problem. Had he known the Slovaks wanted to be independent, it would have been arranged at Munich. But, he added reassuringly, he could guarantee an independent Slovakia at any time. Tuka was thrilled. He said later, "This was the greatest day of my life."

For the Czech Government, however, the separatist agitation threatened to crack the integrity of the state. The Slovakian and Ruthenian Governments were dismissed and their leaders were arrested. This was unexpectedly decisive action for the tottering regime of President Emil Hácha and angered Hitler. He quickly decided that the time had come to take Bohemia and Moravia by ultimatum and, incidentally, to "liberate" Slovakia. Tiso, supposedly under house arrest, escaped from a monastery and was packed into a plane by the Germans and flown to Berlin. Hungarian troop movements were reported on the Slovak frontier. Did Slovakia want independence or not? Hitler asked. On Tiso's return, the "independence" of Slovakia was proclaimed in Bratislava on March 14, 1939. Dr. Tiso was appointed Prime Minister of the new state and Professor Tuka his deputy. On the following day, Tiso appealed to Hitler, asking him for the "protection" of the Reich. This was given officially on March 23. The Slovak state was now a satellite of the Reich.

During the first few months of Slovak independence, sporadic measures were taken against Jews, limiting their economic activity. In the second half of 1939, more stringent steps were taken. Aryan trustees were appointed to operate the large Jewish enterprises. Jews were expelled from government offices and the army; many were obliged to do forced labor. However, the drastic measures came after Hitler and the Slovak leaders met in Salzburg on July 28, 1940, and agreed to introduce into Slovakia a "National Socialist" regime. Tuka was now elevated to the position of Prime Minister and Minister of Foreign Affairs, and Sano Mach, the commander of the Hlinka Guards, became the Minister of Interior. A heavy barrage of anti-Jewish propaganda ushered in the Tuka regime. The films *Jud Süss* and *The Rothschild House* were sent to Slovakia from Germany. Dieter Wisliceny from the Reich Security Main Office arrived in Slovakia as "adviser for Jewish affairs," accompanied by a score of other "advisers" attached to various ministries. A German expert, Viktor Nageler, was assigned to organize the Hlinka Guards on the model of the Nazi storm troops.

During this early period, there was already a sharp decline in the Jewish population as well as a deterioration in its position. Of Slovakia's 135,000 Jews in 1938, about 42,000 came under Hungarian rule in November 1938. They were later deported, mostly to Auschwitz. A few thousand more emigrated, leaving about 89,000 in the country at the end of 1940, a little over 3 percent of the population.

Issues were soon found to arouse popular anti-Semitism. The Jews, not the Germans, were blamed for the loss of rich, fertile areas (Kosice Province) of Slovakia to Hungary. They were accused of assimilating and spreading Hungarian culture, thereby causing the loss of part of Slovakia. Anti-Jewish propaganda, previously disguised in nationalist and demagogic slogans, now openly demanded the "return" of Slovak property "stolen" by the Jews. The troops of the Hlinka Guards began organizing street attacks and arrests of Jews; the looting of their property became commonplace. Jews born in regions of Slovakia annexed by Hungary were forcibly taken from their homes at night, placed on trucks and transported to these territories. During this period, Adolf Eichmann made his first visit to Slovakia to organize the "transfer." The Hungarian Government, however, refused to accept them, and they were sent back to Slovakia.

As a result of the Salzburg Conference, two state agencies were established to deal with the Jewish problem. One was the Central Office for Economy, which ousted Jews from the economic and social life of the country and transferred their property to Aryans. The powers of this agency, however, were not confined to economic matters. Under the direction of Augustin Morávek, who had gone to Germany and Hungary to study their anti-Jewish techniques, orders were issued depriving Jews of civil rights and freedom of movement. They were denied access to public places and contact with non-Jews. Step by step they were forced to hand in their stocks, jewels, furs and blankets. Through Morávek's drive, the Aryanization process was carried out quickly. By the end of 1941, 10,025

Jewish enterprises were liquidated and 2,223 were transferred to Aryan owners. The Aryanized property was valued at more than 3 billion crowns (about $8,000,000).

This transfer of wealth gave government and party leaders and their friends and families sudden wealth. Morávek himself was later removed from office because of his peculations, but not before he had laid the groundwork for the deportation of Jews from Slovakia. As early as 1941, he proposed transferring Jews to the labor camps in the Government-General of Poland. "The Jewish question in Slovakia," he said, "will find its solution when the last Jew will leave the borders of the State."

The second agency, the Ministry of the Interior, was even more power-ful than the Economy Office. It concerned itself with defining Jews, con-centrating them and, finally, deporting them. This was Sano Mach's province. In the autumn of 1941, Mach set up "Department 14" within his Ministry and charged it with carrying out the deportation of Jews.

In September 1940, a Jewish Council had been established—Ústredňa Židov—the sole Jewish agency authorized to organize Jewish life and carry out the state's orders. No fewer than 175 Jewish organizations and socie-ties were liquidated in this process. Morávek appointed a Jewish elder, Heinrich Schwartz, to head the Council, together with ten members of a presidium reflecting the varied trends in Jewish life—Orthodox, Zionist and non-Zionist. Up to 1941, the tasks imposed on the Council were dic-tated by the so-called Madagascar Plan and emigration from Slovakia was encouraged. The emigration department was directed by Gisi Fleischmann, who later became the center of a daring ransom scheme.

In April 1941, Schwartz was arrested and replaced by a man who obeyed Morávek's orders literally. The Jewish Council for a time became Morá-vek's tool and created distrust among Slovakian Jews. To give greater expression to Jewish needs, a clandestine splinter movement sprang up called the "Working Group." This included some members of the Council but was devoted wholly to rescuing Jews. In April 1942, the Council was dissolved. Its officers were arrested and sentenced to forced labor for having warned Jews of deportations.

Mach chafed impatiently under "moderate" measures and finally suc-ceeded in September 1941 in pushing through a Jewish Code. Among its 270 articles was a severe "racial" definition of Jews which embraced about 15,000 converted Jews. The new regulations also obliged Jews to wear the yellow badge and serve in forced labor. By the end of the year, labor camps were functioning in Sered, Vyhne, Nováky, Ilava, Žilina and Zohor. On the pretext of providing additional housing for the population of Bratislava, 10,000 Jews of the capital were evicted to certain district towns and labor camps. This step, of course, was a willful preparation for the herding of

Jews at assembly points. In his report to the German Foreign Ministry, the German Minister to Slovakia, Hans Ludin, described this action as an application of the ghettoization principle used in Poland.

Other stringent measures followed: large-scale dismissals from government employment, restrictions on professionals, confiscation of Jewish-owned real estate; prohibition against intermarriage and taxation of remaining movable property and other assets. These measures left Slovakian Jews impoverished and dispensable. The government required no prodding by Germany.

Slovakian officials began to negotiate with the Germans for the removal of their Jews in the fall of 1941, when both Tiso and Tuka asked Himmler for German assistance. At that time, they learned about the German plan to concentrate the Jews of Europe "in the East" and agreed to allow Slovak Jews in Germany to be deported as long as Slovakia's claims to Jewish property there were not prejudiced. They then found a golden opportunity to get rid of their own Jews. Early in 1942, when the Germans demanded 20,000 additional workers from Slovakia, 20,000 young Slovak Jews from sixteen to thirty-five were supplied.

This arrangement, however, did not satisfy the Slovak authorities, for while they were being rid of the young, they were still saddled with old people and children. Arguing that "in the spirit of Christianity" families should not be separated, they proposed sending off entire families. This meant the deportation of all Jews in Slovakia.

At first, Eichmann refused to accept this proposal, citing "technical" problems, but by the end of March 1942, he had agreed on condition that Jews lose their Slovak citizenship and that 500 reichsmarks be paid by the Slovak Government for every deported Jew. His explanation, a typical falsification, was that the deportation of Jews entailed additional expenses for the training of unskilled workers. The Slovak Government finally consented. Tuka, however, demanded a guarantee that the Jews would not be returned to Slovakia and that the Reich would not present future claims on their property. Curiously, this arrangement was not very profitable for the Slovak Government: the state tax on Jewish property yielded 56 million marks; the cost of transporting Jews was 45 million. The added loss in Jewish productivity created an absolute economic loss, but the deportations were nonetheless rushed.

The organization of the first transports was entrusted to Department 14 in collaboration with Hlinka Guards and regular police. At the beginning of March, five concentration points were set up at Poprad, Patronka, Sered, Žilina and Nováky. Pleas to cancel the deportations were made by Jews, public figures and certain church leaders. A protest note had also been sent by the Vatican on March 14, but was left unanswered. On March 26, the first transport left carrying 1,000 girls from Poprad to Auschwitz. This was the first transport sent to Auschwitz by Section IV B 4. After this, transports left in quick succession for Auschwitz or Lublin. By the end of May, 40,000 Slovakian Jews had been deported.[1]

It is not clear how much the Slovak Government knew about the destiny of the Jews before the deportations started, but soon after they had begun, two notes were handed Tuka from the Vatican. In them, the Vatican explained that the Jews were being sent not to the Government-General for labor, but to the East to be murdered.[2] At the end of April, information arrived in Slovakia about the fate of the first deportations to Poland from the first escapees. This information was immediately sent by the Jewish Council to Switzerland, England and Palestine. Rabbi Armin Frieder, a member of the Council, gave this report to President Tiso but it did not change his course. The news quickly spread among the Jews of Slovakia and thousands fled to Hungary to seek refuge. It has been estimated that by the end of the year, 7,000 had escaped and more trickled across the border in the following year. Thereafter, church pressures also began to affect the numbers deported.

In the spring of 1942, thousands of Jews sought protection by converting to Christianity. Although Slovakia was a staunchly Catholic country, many of the conversions were made by the Protestant and Greek Orthodox churches, which seem to have been less stringent than Catholics in their requirements. But church denomination aside, another question persists: Why did Jews bother to convert at all, since the controlling factor in the law was the religion of one grandparent, not baptism? Clutching at straws in their predicament, they grasped at anything that promised hope, even dim hope, and the churches symbolized that hope. The very willingness of the clergy to grant conversions seemed a great omen. Government officials railed at the clergy for what was termed their casual and irresponsible behavior, but the conversions did not stop. The churches also made themselves felt in the drafting of a new law which was passed by the Slovak Parliament on May 15, 1942.

This law did not exempt all converted Jews from the definition of Jew, but it did exempt those who had been converted before the establishment of the Slovak state on March 14, 1939. This was a much milder definition than the one of 1941. Exemptions were also conferred on family members of the baptized Jews—husbands, wives, children and parents. Exceptions were also made of certain essential categories: professionals, work certificate holders, and the remaining entrepreneurs together with their families. In addition, the law exempted all Jews in mixed marriages.

By June the deportations had slowed down. Tuka, however, was eager for them to continue. Looking for a way to blame the Germans for their "coercion" (he seemed particularly anxious to prove to the Vatican that the Germans had coerced Slovakia), he applied to Berlin for support, even suggesting that they use "diplomatic pressure" on him.[3] On June 26, Tuka met with the German envoy Ludin and Dieter Wisliceny, his Jewish adviser. Wisliceny critically summarized the deportations to date: A total of 52,000 Jews had been deported. Thirty-five thousand remained, many with protective certificates. Those certificates, Wisliceny emphasized, would have to be reviewed and every Slovak employer would have to prove the need to keep Jewish workers. Thirty-five thousand undeported Jews were creating a bad impression, he said. Great praise was heaped on Morávek for being "clean and uncompromising," but none for Dr. Anton Vašek, head of Department 14. Wisliceny said Vašek made agreements with everybody and tied his own hands.[4]

On the day of the conference, Ludin wrote to the German Foreign Office reporting that the deportations were becoming unpopular but that Tuka wanted to press on with them. However, by the end of the summer, the deportations ground to a halt as a number of disparate threads wove themselves around the fate of the Slovakian Jews.

For one, Wisliceny told Eichmann that Tuka kept plaguing him to arrange an official Slovak inspection of the "settlements" in Poland. This pressure arose in the Vatican. The Vatican letter of March 14 protesting the deportations was answered belatedly by Slovak officials, at the Vatican. They depicted resettlement conditions as "humane." It is likely that Tuka met with Heydrich sometime in April and drew up such a reply. The "meddling of the Vatican in the Slovak Jewish policy" is also mentioned in a letter sent at this time from Ludin to the German Foreign Ministry. Ludin advised the Slovak envoy to the Holy See to explain to Rome that the Jews left for the Reich as laborers, in the same capacity as the 120,000 Slovak laborers who were mobilized. Ludin's letter continues, ". . . the fallacy of this comparison is understood here [by the Slovaks] but is considered to be a most convincing argument for the Vatican. In fact the Slovak note will suffice to answer the protest of the Pope."

In June, nevertheless, the Papal Nuncio appealed to the Slovak Government for an inspection, and Tuka, in turn, began to pressure Wisliceny, who spoke to Eichmann. Eichmann was at first evasive. In August, Wisliceny visited him in Berlin and raised the question again. This time Eichmann declared flatly that inspection was out of the question; the Jews were no longer alive. He then showed Wisliceny the secret order, signed by Himmler the previous April, decreeing the progressive extermination of all Jews. The request for inspections, however, continued through 1944.

Rumors about the death camps had also leaked out among the people. In July 1942, a group of 700 ethnic German "asocials" from Germany were to be "resettled." As they were about to leave, a rumor began to circulate that they would be "boiled into soap" (*zur Seife verkocht* werden).⁵ The uneasiness surrounding the deportations was met by counterpropaganda which the Germans had prepared. Articles were planted in newspapers presenting in great detail a pleasant life for Slovakian Jews in exile. Jews were said to have everything they needed: work, sufficient food and shelter, rabbis, doctors, self-government and other attractive features. The postcard ruse was also used. Cards were written by deportees when they first arrived at Auschwitz describing tolerable conditions. The cards were stockpiled and long after the deportees were dead, the cards were sent as addressed, in small batches, to relatives and friends. In this way the impression was created that Jews in the "resettlement" were alive and well. As the requests for on-the-spot inspections built up—in 1943 several were made by Slovakian bishops—Eichmann referred to these post-cards and news articles in a letter to the Jewish expert in the Foreign Office. Eichmann had finally permitted someone to visit the camps to refute rumors and "calm public opinion," and this visit, too, is mentioned in the letter. The visitor was the editor of a German ethnic magazine, Fritz Fiala, who was accompanied by Wisliceny. Fiala's report was censored by Himmler himself before it was published. The Slovak papers carried his article, illustrated with photographs, and it was reprinted in the Romanian press and in the Pariser Zeitung. Eichmann's letter to the Foreign Office is dated June 2, 1943:

> With reference to the proposal put forward by Prime Minister Dr. Tuka to the German Minister in Bratislava to send a mixed Slovakian commission to one of the Jewish camps in the occupied territories, I wish to state that an inspection of this kind has already been undertaken recently . . . by Faila, the chief editor of the periodical Der Grenzbote.
>
> With regard to the description of conditions in Jewish camps . . . attention should be drawn to the comprehensive series of articles by this editor which have appeared with numerous photographs, etc., in the periodicals Der Grenzbote, Slovak, Slovenska, Politika, Gardiste, Magyar Hirlap and the Pariser Zeitung. . . .
>
> For the rest, to counteract the fantastic rumors circulating in Slovakia about the fate of the evacuated Jews, attention should be drawn to the postal communications of these Jews with Slovakia, which are forwarded directly through the adviser on Jewish affairs with the German Legation in Bratislava [Wisliceny] and which amounted, by the way, to more than 1,000 letters and postcards for February–March this year. Concerning the information apparently desired by Prime Minister Dr. Tuka about the conditions in the camps, no objections would be raised by this office against any possible scrutinizing of the correspondence before it is forwarded to the addressees.⁶

As usual, Eichmann had heaped up another mountain of words to muffle murder.

The Germans, meanwhile, continued to prod the Slovaks to continue the deportations. They tried making them more profitable by dropping the cost per deported Jew from 500 reichsmarks to 300. This, however, was not enough of an inducement. Tuka's enthusiasm for deportation seems to have dried up toward the end of 1942 as the prospects of a German victory grew dimmer by the day. There were 35,000 Jews still precariously safe in Slovakia and they were to remain so while a strange ransom proposal slowly wound its way beginning in Slovakia in the mind of a rabbi. It was then conveyed to the Nazis by a dauntless young woman and eventually fanned out to embrace all of Europe's surviving Jews, Allied leaders and Eichmann himself in tense and desperate negotiations. This was the Europa Plan.

Both the Europa Plan and the more limited ransom scheme from which it developed—a proposal for rescuing the Jews of Slovakia—were originally conceived by Rabbi Michael Dov Ber Weissmandel, a member of the *Pracovná Skupina* (Working Group), which tried to save the remnants of Slovakian Jewry after the transports of midsummer 1942 had stopped. The leader of the group was 30-year-old Gisi Fleischmann, former head of WIZO in Slovakia, a women's Zionist organization devoted chiefly to child welfare. She had married a prosperous coffee importer and was the mother of two children, whom she had sent to Palestine before the outbreak of war. She herself stayed behind to help organize the rescue of Jewish children from Poland into Slovakia and, when the situation in Slovakia deteriorated, from Slovakia into Hungary. A network of smugglers had brought the children to her; when it became unsafe for the children to stay in Slovakia, she sent them over the border into Hungary, mostly on foot, sometimes on freight cars. She bribed frontier police and locomotive engineers and hired smugglers. Ingenious schemes were devised to conceal the identity of the children. Not all could be trusted to cross the frontier secretly at night with strange men, nor could their safety be guaranteed. Smaller children were not able to make the arduous walk across mountain passes; many were hidden in coal carts and hay wagons. They were assembled in Budapest and eventually some were taken to Palestine. Funds from the Joint Distribution Committee (JDC) in Geneva financed much of this activity. But important as this work was, irreplaceable as each child was, it was a trifle beside the immense need. The food that was sent to Poland prolonged life for a few days or weeks; for every child saved, thousands more perished. The Working Group then decided to gamble for bigger stakes. Why not try to ransom all Slovakian Jews at a single stroke?

At first they tried to prevent new transports from leaving by bribing Vašek and Wisliceny, who promised *"désintéressement"*—not to persist with the deportations. Small sums were received monthly for this purpose from the JDC. Valuable support was given the group by Slovak Minister of Education and Culture Dr. Jozef Sivák, who kept them informed of official discussions concerning Jews. Gisi decided to speak boldly to Wisliceny. Sometime in August a meeting was arranged by Andrej Steiner, a member of the Working Group. Under what specific conditions, she asked, would the deportations be entirely stopped? Wisliceny did not mince words. For fifty thousand pounds sterling in cash, he replied, they would stop. Jews would have to live in labor camps, but they would be safe. Gisi asked for time to get in touch with the necessary Jewish organizations. She was given four weeks. Hastily she wrote to Saly Mayer, in charge of the Swiss office of the JDC, and explained Wisliceny's proposition. Mayer, however, was a cautious administrator of funds and would not consider a risky transaction with Nazis. The whole idea was beyond his reach. He would readily send food and money to needy Jews but would not risk losing precious funds on such a farfetched gamble. Furthermore, he reminded her, he would need the permission of the American Government to release funds.[7]

Wisliceny, meanwhile, had given the order to stop deportations and was now waiting for the cash. Through a courier, Gisi bombarded the Jewish Agency office in Istanbul and the fifty thousand pounds finally arrived after the grace period had expired. All of this took valuable time during which Wisliceny made it quite plain that he was not to be put off. From September 18 to October 20 he dispatched three more transports of 1,000 Jews increasing to 58,000 the number of Jews from Slovakia who had already perished.

From this date, however, until the suppression of the Slovak uprising in October 1944, not a single transport left Slovakia. Wisliceny, it seems, kept his word.

Wisliceny was apparently eager for the negotiations to succeed. He was something of a bon vivant and wanted to make money out of living Jews. Not an ideological killer, by the end of 1942 he may already have wanted an alibi for the Allies.[8] According to him, Eichmann opposed the Slovak ransom scheme (and, later, the Europa Plan) from the beginning, but did not reject it outright and forwarded both propositions to Himmler. In November 1942, Himmler agreed to the transfer of $20,000 as advance payment from the Working Group to the S.S. Chief Office for Economy and Administration (WVHA) and permitted Wisliceny to continue talks with the Jewish group. According to Wisliceny, he was influenced by the fact that such negotiations would be good enemy counterpropaganda. It was precisely at this time that the BBC broadcast information on the mass exterminations. RSHA chief, Ernst Kaltenbrunner, also began thinking in terms of ransom: there exists a letter from him to Himmler, dated November 24, 1942, in which he suggests selling emigration certificates to rich Slovak Jews so as to raise money for the S.S. in Hungary.

Although Himmler is generally described as one of the least corruptible of the Nazi leaders, he was not averse to bribes with an ideological twist. Quite early in the war, he had permitted certain S.S. bureaus to arrange for the emigration of rich Jews in exchange of payment in hard currency —dollars or Swiss francs—which ostensibly were earmarked for equipping the *Waffen S.S.*[9] This had also been done in the Netherlands where about 50 Dutch Jews had been able to ransom themselves for $10,000 per person.

As early as May 1941, Ulrich von Hassell, German Ambassador to Italy in the early Hitler regime, and a seasoned diplomat who has been described as "the diplomatic adviser of the secret opposition to Hitler," noted in his diary the first stirrings of a rumor that Himmler might be in favor of a separate peace with Britain. The following September, he wrote, "It was apparent that in Himmler's outfit they were seriously worried [over the frustration following the invasion of Russia] and looking for a way out." He also makes reference to payments of large sums of money to the S.S. for the release of prisoners in the concentration camps.

In March 1944, Himmler dispatched Kurt Becher on a special mission to Hungary to lay his hands on one of the richest prizes there—the Jewish-owned Manfred Weiss Works, the largest munitions enterprise in Hungary. The Weiss family had intermarried extensively with Christians and the "Aryan" members of the family owned about 55 percent of the stock. These stocks were turned over to the S.S. and forty-eight members of the family, including thirty-eight Jews, were permitted to go to Portugal. Nine others remained in Hungary as hostages. In justifying this seizure to the Hungarians, Himmler explained that the Weiss Works would assure his S.S. a dependable supply of the finest weapons for the remainder of the war and would equip the *Waffen S.S.* during the peaceful reconstruction effort to follow. In plain terms, Himmler wanted a self-sufficient S.S. army with which he could bludgeon the Wehrmacht. However, this was only one aspect of his split-level designs.

The Reichsführer S.S. himself also wanted a track kept open to the Allies and endorsed the biggest ransom scheme of the period in Hungary in the summer of 1944. For a time, in 1943 when the Europa Plan was proposed, he was not averse to deals which would save Jews in return for money. But in 1943 he was more divided than later about what he wanted most—dead Jews or live Jews in exchange for money. By August 1943, that part of him that wanted dead Jews won out and the Europa Plan was annulled. Whether the decisive factor was the destructive element in Himmler or the inability of the Working Group to raise the necessary funds is still not clear—there are no official German documents on the negotiations. According to the letters and notes of the Working Group, Wisliceny insisted that they failed only because the money was not provided in time.[9a]

The Europa Plan, also inspired by Rabbi Weissmandel, sought to rescue all of Europe's remaining Jews for a price. Again Wisliceny was the negotiator. (In 1946, in a Bratislava prison, he claimed credit for the plan.) He, too, was operating on a double track. By February 1943, he had been transferred to Greece, where he did as he was ordered and conducted swift and merciless deportations, but this assignment went on simultaneously with his conciliatory talks with the Working Group in Bratislava. Again, Gisi Fleischmann represented the Working Group. Wisliceny told her:

> We have already done business, and I am now in a position to make more extensive proposals. If you can bring us two million dollars, we will stop the deportations throughout all Europe [except in Poland and Germany]. . . . The Jewish question in those lands must be settled once and for all. I cannot help you there. The result of my efforts in Berlin is a "Plan for Europe," which will apply to all the countries of Europe other than Germany and Poland. . . . If you bring us two million dollars, you may be certain that the Jews in Bulgaria, Rumania, France, Belgium, Holland, Greece and Scandinavia will survive this war.[10]

The lives of a million Jews were now being sold at two dollars per head. On the basis of Wisliceny's offer, within three months, a fund was put aside by the World Jewish Congress, but a full year passed before legal obstacles were cleared and before any part of it could be transferred. Special couriers were again dispatched to Geneva and Istanbul. The representatives of the Jewish Agency were ready to accept the offer immediately. The Jews in Palestine were also willing to raise the necessary money, although it would mean stopping all other rescue activities in Europe financed through Istanbul. They were prepared to send $100,000 at once. Could not the JDC make up the rest?

Geneva had become a second Lisbon; refugees trickled in from every part of Europe and were assisted by the JDC office which served as a lifeline for the Jews of occupied Europe. It had important contacts in the Swiss and Swedish embassies, who were in touch with surviving Jewish communities, and agents—Jewish and non-Jewish—who learned where money and medicine were needed. The guardian of this office, Saly Mayer, dispensed huge sums (in the form of Swiss francs)—he even put money into Swiss diplomatic pouches—but before he moved any funds at all, he had to have the permission of the United States Treasury to buy Swiss francs.[11] The JDC reported to the Treasury on all of its activities and within "reasonable limits" was allowed to do what it could. Those limits were reached when private charitable aid was believed to help the German economy or war effort. Straitjacketed by these restrictions and by his own cautious temperament, Mayer declared that the JDC was ready to guarantee the payment of $2 million to an account in Wisliceny's name in the United States, but that the money could not be given to him until after the war—scarcely a realistic proposal from Wisliceny's standpoint.

Gisi Fleischmann hardly dared pass on this offer to the S.S. leader; when she did, she pleaded the excuse of currency restrictions. Wisliceny became impatient, but Gisi played for time. Wisliceny finally made a counterproposition. He asked for $200,000 for every month that passed without deportations. Mayer was prepared to deposit this amount in a Swiss bank in Wisliceny's name, but again insisted that the account be blocked until the end of the war. Gisi, stunned by this new blow, did not take the reply to Wisliceny. Instead, she asked if she could go to Budapest to raise the money. She was given the necessary travel permits, but this mission also failed. Finally, some money came from Istanbul and Gisi went to Wisliceny with $57,000 as an advance payment.[12] She begged for a further delay.

Wisliceny gave her two more weeks—the last extension, he said. A few days later, he intercepted a letter containing Mayer's proposal that the money be put into a blocked account in a Swiss bank. Wisliceny was furious and sent for Gisi. "The money must be put here, on my desk, in proper bank notes and not in the form of a check postdated to the end of the war. After the war, you people won't treat me and my kind as business associates. You know very well how you'll act just as soon as you can lay your hands on us."[13]

The new time limit expired. The JDC did not receive official American clearance to send $2 million to Gisi Fleischmann—a sum that would have financed the German war effort for one day. Nor was the JDC bold enough to bypass government regulations in a period when old-fashioned niceties were obsolete. Wisliceny returned the initial payment to Gisi, showing that he at least had really meant business. In May 1944, after the machinery of the "Final Solution" had spread to Hungary, it was this same Wisliceny who picked up the threads of negotiation with the Budapest Relief Committee which led to Eichmann's "blood-for-goods" deal with Joel Brand.

The breakdown in negotiations with Wisliceny caused bitter disappointment among the Working Group. They could not understand how Jewish organizations had been stopped from acting independently. Britain's official observance of a two-minute silence in Parliament in December 1942, in reaction to the reports of the exterminations, seemed a mockery. To add to their bitterness, the May 1943 Anglo-American Conference on Refugees in Bermuda came and went without achieving any practical results. The Working Group had anxiously awaited its outcome, hoping that it might influence the German response to the Europa Plan. The Germans, of course, were also watching the conference with interest and cynicism. At the very time that the conference was in session, Goebbels, in a speech, sarcastically remarked that the same countries in which public sympathy for Jews was growing were the very ones not prepared to receive them.

Himmler's bluff was never called. Ultimately it was the British who refused to break the strict currency regulations for the sake of rescue purposes and frankly admitted their "deep concern" over managing large numbers of Jews should they be released from enemy territory.[14] (The U.S. Treasury Department awaited British clearance.)

While the Working Group was trying to obtain money for the Europa Plan, extremists in the Slovak Government again proposed deportations. Minister of the Interior Mach, in a radio speech on February 7, 1943, openly declared that within two months Jews would be deported. "March will come," he said, "April will come and the transports will roll again." But they did not—at least for a time. During this lull, and as an adjunct to the negotiations with Wisliceny, the Working Group made strenuous efforts to make Jews in labor camps economically valuable to the state. With some of the funds coming in from the JDC in Geneva, efforts were concentrated on developing industries in the camps. About thirty workshops were set up producing textiles, furniture, toys and chemical products, all of which were delivered to the state and public institutions. The productivity of these camps was mentioned by Ludin in a report in which he underscored the number of highly skilled workers who enjoyed "far-reaching freedom." In his view, they were not labor camps at all, but production centers.

This situation caused mixed reactions among Slovak officials. The total income of the camps and labor centers for 1943 was almost 50 million Slovak crowns. Government agencies obviously benefited. Jews also benefited, a situation which some officials deplored. (Mach also believed that Jews should be punished for their "overconfidence" as a result of the Red Army victories on the Eastern Front in the last half of 1943.) Other officials, however, whose offices benefited were pleased with the results and wanted the workshops to continue. Ludin was inclined to blame this "backward step" on Vašek, who, instead of attending to his job, was busy writing a book while his staff merely made routine inspections of the camps. Hoping to distract him, the Working Group diligently encouraged Vašek in his aspirations to become the historian of the era, and lawyers on the Jewish Council assisted him in the actual compilation of a book called The Anti-Jewish Legislation in Slovakia.[14a]

The German Foreign Office did not resume its serious pressure on Slovakia until December 1943, when it sent a special emissary, Edmund Veesenmayer, to Bratislava to speed the "cleanup" of the Jewish question.

When he arrived, he told Wisliceny that he had a directive from Hitler to talk bluntly with Tiso. In January 1944, Eichmann called for more transports "so that there should be someone to inspect in Jewish camps." Tiso promised Veesenmayer more intensive action. By April 1, 1944, he said, 16,000 to 18,000 unconverted Jews would be placed in concentration camps, with no exemptions granted. Later, Tuka promised to intern 10,000 converted Jews as well. Slowly, the preparations were made. All Bratislava Jews were ordered to register with the police. Some fled to Hungary. But by April 1, the Slovakian Government had not yet acted.

The summer months passed and the Red Army pushed closer to Slovakia's eastern frontier. Anti-Nazi demonstrations and acts of sabotage broke out and at the end of August, a revolt erupted, led by left-wing elements. The Slovak Army became completely demoralized and soldiers deserted en masse. Martial law was declared and on August 25, President Tiso appealed to Hitler for help. This came quickly and by October the revolt was crushed. With the Germans in control of the country, the deportations were resumed.

Meanwhile, in the spring of 1944, the flow of Jewish refugees from Slovakia into Hungary reversed itself as massive deportations from Hungary began. Thousands—possibly as many as 10,000—streamed back to seek shelter in their old homes. The first eyewitness accounts of Auschwitz were also reported in Slovakia at this time. Two escapees, Alfred Wetzler and Rudolf Vrba, who had been deported from Slovakia in 1942, made a miraculous escape from Auschwitz in the spring of 1944. They possessed exact data on the structure of the camp, the transports and the method of killing. In Žilina, where they arrived, a member of the Working Group recorded their account. The escapees also drew a plan of the camp, of the crematoria and the roads leading to them—material which was sent to Jewish agencies throughout the world, and to Allied governments.

The account was also sent to the head of the Orthodox community, Philip Freudiger, in Hungary, to warn Hungarian Jews of what lay in store, together with a letter from Rabbi Weissmandel. This information was sent to Switzerland in June through the Apostolic Delegate and was soon publicized throughout the entire free world. In the United States, the techniques of death at Auschwitz were published by the War Refugee Board in November 1944.

Rabbi Weissmandel's letter urgently appealed for the immediate bombing of railroad centers leading to the death camps and the gassing installations to save the Jews of Hungary from death. Jewish agencies made appeals to all of the Allied governments. The answer was "No." It came in the form of a letter from Richard Law of the British Foreign Office to Dr. Chaim Weizmann: the matter had received "the most careful consideration" of the air staff, Law wrote, but was refused "in view of the very great technical difficulties involved." This statement surely could not refer to bombing technicalities, or air strength calculations, for by this time American and British air power was supreme.

Not a single weapon was dropped, however, on any of the ghettos or extermination camps—either to aid the inmates resist, or to damage or destroy the Nazi controls. At the very minimum, such drops would have buoyed up the morale of the imprisoned Jews and given them a sense of being linked to the Allied cause and of existing as an object of their concern. Such morale-lifting drops would have been technically possible toward the end of 1943, after the penetration of the Ploesti oil fields in Romania in August by the Allied Combined Bomber Offensive. In the autumn these were followed by deep penetration missions to targets in Poland and East Prussia. Industrial targets in Germany had been hit with destructive results even earlier. By the spring of 1944, the Allied strategic air offensive soared into high gear and decisive Allied air superiority was achieved over Europe. Oil targets in Austria, Hungary, the Balkans, southern Poland and Romania were assigned to the Fifteenth Air Force based in Italy. This unit aided the Russians by striking targets against the Eastern Front and by running "shuttle" missions to bases in the Soviet Union. Much of the Fifteenth's activity involved dropping supplies to anti-German partisan movements in Yugoslavia, to attacking Axis ports in France and Greece and to pounding the Brenner Pass through which German armies in Italy were supplied.[15]

Special super-secret air missions also took place in the Balkans in the autumn of 1944 involving the parachuting of agents, radios, ammunition, weapons, food, medicine and money to partisan groups in enemy territory and delivery of supplies to resistance movements. The evacuation of downed Allied flyers was part of this work and in September 1944, nearly 1,150 Americans were evacuated from Romania alone. In the last four months of 1944, 830 clandestine Allied landings were made in Greece and Yugoslavia. Billions of leaflets were dropped into this area urging civilians to resist and German soldiers to give up.[16] However, except for the incidental activity of the Palestinian parachutists, which was permitted only after their military orders were carried out, none of this help was directed toward the Jews trapped in death camps or death transports that ran on schedule from the ghettos of eastern Europe to the gas chambers.

The "technical difficulties" referred to by the British Foreign Office, one must assume, revolved around the alarm expressed by Eden in May 1943, when the exterminations in Bulgaria were discussed with the American Secretary of State, Cordell Hull. Rescue operations, Eden said, would arouse the Jews in Germany and Poland to appeal for refuge, but there was no place to put them. "Technical difficulties" were also involved in the British refusal to break the strict currency regulations which prevented the transfer of funds for rescue purposes.

The Slovak uprising of 1944[17] doomed those Jews still alive in Slovakia. The Germans found a ready excuse for these murders by blaming the revolt on the Jews—although 90 percent of the Jewish youth had already been deported. Some Jews of course were involved. In the labor camp of Nováky, all Jews were liberated and given arms as the result of a contact between Akiva Neufeld, a young Jewish prisoner in the camp at Sered, and the Slovak rebels in Banská-Bystrica, the center of resistance. It is also known that many of the Jews who fought concealed their identity and used Aryan papers, fearing exposure by the Germans and Fascist sympathizers among the Slovakians. The partisan struggle in Slovakia involved at least 60,000 Slovak soldiers and 15,000 irregulars of no fewer than 27 nationalities. No more than a few thousand Jewish youths are believed to have participated. After the revolt was put down, Slovak Fascist leaders tended to exaggerate the number of Jews who had participated. One minister, for example, said that most of the Russian, Czech and French insurgents were Jews. On the basis of this sort of information and his own "evidence," Gottlob Berger, commanding general of the S.S. forces in Slovakia, reported to Himmler that the Jews had participated decisively in the uprising. This report fatefully affected subsequent deportations.

Though the exact number of Jews in the uprising cannot be established with certainty, a courageous effort of a small band of Jewish parachutists to rally Jews is known.

In the middle of September 1944, four Palestinian parachutists from a British unit reached the areas of Slovakia held by the rebels. Two were assigned to contact the Working Group in Bratislava—Chaviva Reik and Zvi Ben Ya'acov—and two others to Hungary. Those Jews who had reached the liberated areas congregated mainly in Banská-Bystrica and roamed the streets looking for food and shelter. They were hardly potential fighters. For weeks the young parachutists tried to bolster these refugees and find living essentials for them. Contact with the Working Group could not be made. On October 28, Banská-Bystrica fell and the parachutists, together with a group of local Jewish fighters, retreated to the mountains to join a partisan band. A week later they were attacked by a German unit and virtually wiped out. The young parachutists were captured and taken to a prison in Kremnicka where they were executed on November 20.

The failure of the revolt is generally attributed to a lack of coordination between the Czechoslovakian Government-in-Exile, which was directing some of the units from London, and the Red Army, which was directing others. Each party was guided by different objectives: The Czech Government-in-Exile wanted to liberate part of the country and set up a government that would restore the old Czech Republic, while the Red Army wanted to liberate the country as a whole. All forces had relied on the quick advance of the Russians, a scant hundred miles away, but they had not counted on the difficult, heavy fighting in the Carpathian Mountains. The battle for the Dukla Pass, for example, lasted a full month, until October 6, and losses on both sides were severe. Not until April 1945 did the Red Army occupy and liberate Slovakia.

German Wehrmacht troops and S.S. units had begun rounding up Jews as soon as the uprising started. *Einsatzgruppe H* had set up five *kommandos* and 24 support points throughout Slovakia. As of December 9, out of 19,000 captured prisoners, 4,653 were Jews; 2,257 were immediately killed. The others were sent to concentration camps. The notorious Alois Brunner had arrived in Slovakia at the end of September to direct the final roundups and deportations. From October 1944 to March 1945, 13,500 more Jews were deported to Auschwitz, Ravensbrück, Bergen-Belsen, Sachsenhausen—and the last transports—to Theresienstadt. An S.S. general in Slovakia, Hermann Hoefle, testified in March 1948 that Himmler himself came to Bratislava sometime in September, and in the presence of Hoefle, Father Tiso and Ludin, had insisted on the total deportation of the Jews for "military reasons." The internees of Marienthal (a camp under the Slovak Ministry of Foreign Affairs) who possessed American citizenship were sent to Germany as exchange prisoners. There remained in the whole of Slovakia in March 1945 not more than 5,000 Jews forced to live clandestinely with "Aryan" papers or in bunkers.

The new Slovak Government which had been formed on September 5 (without Tuka and Mach) was headed by Dr. Stefan Tiso, a nephew of the former President. It had to step gingerly between two forces: the Germans with whom officials now had to ingratiate themselves, and pressures against continuing the deportations on the part of the Vatican and important diplomatic missions. On the one hand, the new leaders had to blot out the bad effects of the uprising; on the other hand, they could not disguise their uneasiness over the many protests and interventions which were developing. The Germans, however, were entirely willing to accept full responsibility. As the Allies threatened no reprisal action, the Germans had nothing to fear. Ludin told the young Tiso to explain that the Reich demanded from Slovakia a radical solution,[18] and Tiso complied. To the Vatican protest of September 20, which derived largely from an urgent appeal by a compassionate Nuncio in Istanbul—Monsignor Angelo Roncalli (later Pope John XXIII)—Tiso replied, "In spite of all protests, the German Security Forces continue the transfer of Jews to

Germany, explaining this action by the uprising and as necessary security measures." When the delegate of the International Red Cross, Georges Dunand, arrived in Slovakia late in October 1944, with funds from the JDC to try to salvage what he could, he was referred to the German Legation. His request to establish a shelter for Jewish children was rejected on the ground that any shelter of this type could turn into a center of resistance. Appeals from Sweden and the International Red Cross President were also turned aside. The Jews had become fomenters of uprisings.

The atmosphere of the time is vividly conveyed in a sketch[19] of an encounter between Dunand and a young Jew, Arnold Bumi, who escaped from Sered at the time of the uprising and hid out in one shelter after another, feigned a story about a marriage to an Aryan woman, found a temporary job with a tailor and was seized, finally, by the Gestapo. He then escaped from their lorry and was able to pick up his old job. When he read about Dunand's visit to Slovakia, he sent an emissary to arrange a talk. Dunand himself has recorded their meeting:

> I met Bumi in the darkness of night, during the days of the blackout. An anonymous messenger first asked me whether I would be ready to step outside my house in the evening to meet someone who wanted to talk to me. Upstairs, in my small flat, I left my pocketbook, my passport and the keys of my writing-desk. I went down worried and anxious, remembering the horrible meeting with the father of Marianka, who was arrested. In front of the gate, I discovered a shadow, and slowly discerned the face of a very young man, revealing a mixture of enthusiasm, fanaticism and zeal. . . . And again the same question: is he a spy, a common thief, or a true underground fighter?
>
> And I still remember the conversation, which was conducted in German as was the custom here. . . . Bumi was one of the remnants of the Jewish youth movement, now dwindled to some dozen of young men and women, meeting night in, night out, as long as they were not arrested. They distributed food, clothing and money, prepared additional "bunkers" and hid away furniture—or children—with Christian families. At night they secretly passed on parcels or banknotes to children, women or men in disguise, in order to provide supplies to those who were in hiding. They made it their business to follow policemen, traitors and double agents. Their numbers were shrinking from week to week.[20]

This encounter led Bumi and a few of his friends into more involved rescue work. They were to distribute money which Dunand had brought from the Geneva JDC office. Bumi met people and distributed money, clothes and papers; he turned his workshop into a refugee station and helped hunted people find new quarters. A German proprietor of a printer's shop, Julius Natali, often helped him with printed documents and remained his contact with Rabbi Weissmandel to the end. To escape arrest, people jumped out of windows and hid behind stoves. Farm families and a few police officers gave their help. A police inspector gave Bumi the necessary rubber stamps and, more important, the right color ink, for forging personal documents.

In March 1945, Bumi was finally caught and taken to a room with a table and two armchairs. From a clothes hanger hung a leather whip. His arms were lifted to a horizontal position and an armchair was placed on his outstretched palms. When it dropped after a few minutes, he was kicked and slashed with the whip until he lost consciousness. When he recovered, it was Brunner himself who was grilling him. Brunner wanted all of the details of his contact with Dunand, the amount of money he received from him and the names of the people whom he had helped. Hoping to escape somehow if he got to the street, Bumi agreed to point out the houses where Jews were in hiding. A rope was tied around his hands and a hole cut in one of his coat pockets. He was forced to put his hands into one pocket and the rope was pulled into the hole and between his legs. One of the Gestapo men tied the other end of the rope around his hands. In this truss, Bumi was walked through the streets in broad daylight. He was taken back to the camp at Sered and put into solitary confinement for two days. Then, surrounded by ten S.S. men, he was marched to the railway station and put on a car to Theresienstadt, the last convoy to go there. In keeping with the insane rhythm of a Hitlerized continent, he was assigned to the *Freizeitgestaltung*, the leisure-time programming committee, at Theresienstadt.

When he arrived, a concert was being rehearsed but was canceled when news came that thousands of prisoners were expected from various camps. Soon the trains started coming in. When the doors of the wagons were opened, barely living skeletons toppled out, the remnant from the camps in Germany.

Gisi Fleischmann and others in the Working Group made a desperate last-hour effort to stop the deportations of 1944. This time, ransom negotiations were carried on by Colonel Kurt Becher, who had already had some experience of this kind in Hungary. Becher flew from Bratislava to Berlin and tried to prevail upon Himmler to stop the deportations, but Himmler was adamant. "Military reasons" were compelling, he said. When Becher returned to Bratislava on September 25, the Jews were already in the hands of Brunner.

The leaders of the Working Group, including Gisi Fleischmann and Rabbi Weissmandel, were among those taken to the camp at Sered. Rezsö Kastner, of the Budapest Rescue Committee, asked Becher to have Eichmann telegraph Brunner to return Gisi. Eichmann sent such a telegram in Becher's presence but, as soon as Becher left, he dispatched another canceling the first.

A Swedish file was found on Gisi's person, a file she intended to use on the train if she were deported. This information was reported to Brunner, who ordered her to be handcuffed and placed in a special railway car, separated from her comrades. Early in October 1944, she was sent to Auschwitz with a special directive to the camp—"RU" (*Rückkehr unerwunscht*; Return undesirable)—and was gassed, possibly only days before Himmler gave the order to stop the exterminations. Rabbi Weissmandel escaped by jumping off his deportation car. He made his way to Switzerland and, after the war, to the United States.

By the spring of 1945, when the Red Army occupied Slovakia, the Jewish community had been annihilated. The deaths that resulted from deportations of 1942 and 1944 numbered 68,000–71,000; the survivors, including returnees, numbered 20,000–25,000. In the Czechoslovakian provinces annexed by Hungary, the losses were 30,000 in Kosice (originally 42,000) and 85,000 in Ruthenia (originally 102,000). This chapter of the Holocaust constitutes one of the most shattering destructions of any Jewish community in Europe.

27 Bulgaria

THE CASE OF BULGARIA is unique among the satellite governments in Hitler's Europe, for no Jews from Old Bulgaria were deported in spite of strong German pressures. This resistance was partly a reflection of the weight of public opinion and partly the measure of Bulgaria's limited enthusiasm for a role as Germany's ally. Bulgaria joined the Axis in March 1941, but unlike Slovakia or Croatia, Bulgaria did not owe its existence to Germany; it was in the German camp for opportunistic reasons. As a result of two lost contests—the Second Balkan War and World War I— Bulgaria had territorial grievances against all of her neighbors and hoped for redress under German patronage. She was not disappointed: Romania gave her southern Dobrudja, Yugoslavia ceded Macedonia, and Greece, Thrace.

Thus enlarged by these immense gains, Bulgaria waged war, but only in a restricted sense. Her military contribution consisted mainly in garrisoning the territories acquired for her by Germany. At no time was the country occupied, nor were any Bulgarian forces dispatched to fight on fronts outside the country. When Germany opened its eastern campaign, Bulgaria did not even declare war on the "Bolshevik enemy." Bulgarians had strong ties with the Russian people and a war against them was unthinkable. In the West, too, Bulgaria was not eager to acquire new foes and declarations of war against the Western powers were postponed as long as possible. Above all, Bulgaria did not want to commit herself irrevocably to the Axis cause and thus close off a possible escape route if one should be needed. This same reluctance to go the whole Nazi way is seen in Bulgaria's Jewish policy. It was only in the occupied territories of Macedonia and Thrace that Jews were delivered into German hands for destruction. The Jews of Old Bulgaria were protected.

In its treatment of Jews, Bulgaria was largely influenced by the Turkish tradition. Both public opinion and the government were favorably disposed toward Jewish communal activity. A "live-and-let-live" atmosphere prevailed. Compared with other central or southeastern European countries, the Jews in Bulgaria did not play a significant role in the political or cultural life of the nation. Economically, there were no direct clashes of interest.

The first ripples of Nazism reached Bulgaria in 1934. There were, at that time, 48,000 Jews in Bulgaria, over half of them in Sofia, the capital. Their numbers already declining, there was a noticeable concentration in the larger cities. The changed atmosphere can be traced partly to the exposure of Bulgarian students to Hitlerism while attending German and Austrian universities. Returning home, these students joined a movement corresponding to the National Socialist Party in Germany, under the leadership of Khristo Kunchev. Their program included demands for a boycott of Jewish business, the closing of Jewish banks and the removal of Jews from influential positions—altogether meaningless slogans in Bulgaria. German economic and political pressures added to the anti-Jewish agitation but the press and public did not succumb. Nevertheless, the pressures continued.

Political developments in the 1930's also contributed to Bulgaria's slowly changing orientation. A bloodless coup had been attempted in 1935, one which had republican leanings, but King Boris acted quickly and consolidated his position by creating a system of personal rule through the appointment of a prime minister who would be his own man—Georgi Kiosseivanov. From the start, the King's program fell under the shadow of Germany's increasing interest in southeastern Europe. The Munich Pact seriously undermined Bulgaria's confidence in the Western democracies and the Nazi-Soviet agreement left her no further room for exploring political choices.

These developments yoked to Bulgaria's territorial ambitions made her alliance of convenience with Germany inevitable as well as expedient. During the interwar period, Bulgaria's relations with Greece and Yugoslavia had often been tense. Bulgaria wanted an Aegean outlet at the expense of Greece and the restoration of territory in Macedonia that she had lost to Yugoslavia. When Bulgaria signed the Tripartite Pact in March 1941, these revisionist claims were uppermost. German troops were permitted to enter the country, and from bases in Bulgaria, German troops launched their attack on Yugoslavia and Greece. Yet, in spite of these concessions, the Soviet Minister remained in Sofia and substantially assisted underground resistance forces supporting the Russian cause. Bulgaria was Germany's least solid ally and, although King Boris never favored the alliance with Germany, he was unable to resist the pressure of Bulgarian nationalists to annex Macedonia and Thrace—territorial aspirations which, in fact, he shared.

Persecution of Bulgarian Jews began in 1941. In July 1940, the government announced that it intended to introduce anti-Jewish measures, and in August, Jewish community representatives were officially forewarned. In the beginning, the purpose of the laws was the economic impoverishment of Bulgarian Jews. The first important measure, called "The Law for the Protection of the Nation," was passed by the Bulgarian Parliament on January 24, 1941; regulations for its implementation were passed by the Ministerial Council on February 13. The purpose of the law was to "protect" the nation from the Jews who were proclaimed enemies of the state. Jews were forbidden to be owners or investors in cultural institutions, theaters, cinemas, publishing houses, record and film companies. They could work in agriculture, but only on other people's property and were denied the right to own farmland. The law was particularly severe on Jews in public administration and the civil service—virtually all such

TERRITORIAL ENLARGEMENT OF

HUNGARY, BULGARIA, AND ROMANIA

DURING WORLD WAR II

Enlarged Hungary

Enlarged Bulgaria

Enlarged Romania

positions had to be resigned. Moreover, Jews could not hold positions in private or public credit or banking houses. They could not be employed as agents, bookkeepers, accountants or clerks and were forbidden to own pharmacies.[1]

All moneys received by Jews in the course of this rapid economic liquidation had to be deposited with the Bulgarian Credit Bank, where they were frozen. All Jewish assets, movable and immovable, likewise had to be reported to this bank.

Jewish organizational life was also banned. The legal definition of the Jew conformed to racist standards: anyone with one Jewish parent was declared a Jew. Citizenship, religious affiliation and all other "legal and formalistic circumstances" were considered irrelevant. Except for Jews converted before September 1, 1940, and a few exempt groups, the rest had to register as Jews and use Jewish first names. Jews were even prohibited from having Bulgarian-sounding surnames ending in -ov, -ev and -ich. If they were aliens, they could not become Bulgarian citizens. If they were citizens, they could not vote or be elected to public office. They were forbidden to marry non-Jews and could move about only with special police permission. They could be expelled from towns and confined to specific areas.

This last provision was potentially very dangerous, for over 26,000 Jews lived in Sofia. Such a concentration could easily serve the deportation process. However, the Bulgarians ultimately used this measure as a weapon of delay and an excuse for thwarting deportations altogether.

The January law also provided for a category of privileged Jews of a few thousand including war volunteers, decorated veterans and war orphans. A *numerus clausus* was applied to Jewish professionals and businessmen, based on the percentage of Jews in the cities. (Privileged Jews were excluded from this count.) The subsequent reduction of Jewish activity was based on the proportion of Jews in the total population—about 1 percent. The number of professionals was reduced from 521 to 149; 4,272 business enterprises were reduced to 761.[2] Those unable to continue their functions were subjected to forced sale and the money—about $7 million —was confiscated by the government.

The Bulgarian Government and court were Fascist in sympathy and readily joined the Tripartite Pact on March 1, 1941. After Germany attacked Yugoslavia, anti-Jewish propaganda and legislation were intensified. Bulgarian Jews were compelled to work in labor squads set up by the military. At first they wore Bulgarian uniforms, but the German Minister Adolf Beckerle protested, and Jews were segregated, divested of their uniforms and given heavy labor assignments. In August 1941, they were forced to wear a Jewish star, the first instance of marking in Bulgaria. In Ruse and Dupnitsa, local officials forbade Jews to walk in certain streets, to leave their homes during air-raid alarms and to buy food at certain hours. By the spring of 1943, about 10,000 Jews between twenty-one and forty-seven were in forced labor for the Axis, building roads and railroads. The Germans were encouraged by these signs, and assumed that Bulgaria would readily cooperate in the deportation measures—particularly after the Bulgarian Foreign Minister Ivan Popov had suggested that a common policy for all of Europe be adopted in handling the Jewish question.[3]

Popov made this suggestion in a discussion with von Ribbentrop during a reception given the German Foreign Minister on November 26, 1941. Popov spoke of the difficulties the Bulgarian Government was having in enforcing its anti-Jewish laws. Hungary, Romania and Spain had protested against having their nationals in Bulgaria included in the application of these laws. Ribbentrop himself assured Popov that, "at the end of the war, all Jews would have to leave Europe"; hence there was no need to heed foreign protests. Ribbentrop took Popov's remarks to mean that Bulgaria was looking to Germany for guidance in taking a free hand with foreign Jews. The myth of resettlement in Poland was being assiduously cultivated by Germany at this time—on the eve of the Grossen-Wannsee Conference—and the Bulgarians were expected to turn over their Jews for "resettlement." Ribbentrop anticipated no difficulties at all from them. Meanwhile, Bulgarian measures had to be stepped up to deportation level.

Berlin sent instructions to Beckerle in June 1942, asking him to sound out the Bulgarians on deportations. He replied that they were agreeable. Whether the Bulgarians knew the implications of deportation is not known, but in the late summer of 1942, anti-Jewish measures were intensified. German pressure may have been pointedly effective at this time because Russian victories in southern Russia put Bulgaria's acquisitions from Greece, Yugoslavia and Romania in jeopardy. The definition of Jew was sharpened. The Office of the Commissar for Jewish Questions was formed. The wearing of the Jewish star was introduced for the entire Jewish population on September 23. Apartment restrictions for Jews in Sofia were announced, and unemployed Jews were ordered to leave the city. Emigration from Bulgaria was barred except for a few Italians and Spanish citizens who had first to liquidate all of their property.

On August 26, 1942, the Ministerial Council of Fascist Bulgaria set up the Commissariat for the Jewish Problem within the Bulgarian Ministry of the Interior, and Alexander Belev was appointed Commissar. Belev's apparatus, which was designed to eliminate Bulgarian Jewry, was financed by funds taken from frozen Jewish bank accounts and put into a fund called the "Jewish Community." All of the property of Jewish religious communities and cultural and educational institutions was likewise "legally" plundered.

The RSHA told the Foreign Office to go into action and to offer the services of Germany in subsequent resettlement actions. Bulgaria seemed ripe.

Meanwhile, the Bulgarian measures were being snagged both by deliberate procrastination and public opposition. For example, Interior Minister Peter Gabrowski directed the press to cease its discussions of the "Jewish question" and hinted repeatedly to Belev that King Boris and the Cabinet wanted a letup in anti-Jewish measures.[4] On September 27, a crowd of 350 Jews assembled in the courtyard of the Interior Ministry and petitioned for an extension of the expulsion deadline. To the amazement of employees watching from the windows, Gabrowski delivered a half-hour speech which served to calm the Jews. He assured them that "the worst was already over."

The developments surrounding the wearing of the badge also displeased the Germans. Not only was the star a very small one, but most Jews refused to wear it in the early period. Those who did, wore it arrogantly, and often pinned it next to a picture of the King. The protest against the Jewish badge swelled after Metropolitan Stephan of Sofia delivered a sermon in which he declared that God had determined the fate of Jews and that men had no right to persecute them. He personally intervened to free all converted Jews from wearing the star and hid the Chief Rabbi of Sofia in his home. Within a few days of his sermon, the Minister of Justice demanded that the compulsory wearing of the star be abolished. By the beginning of October 1942, the Bulgarian Government halted the production of badges by cutting off the electricity from the factory manufacturing them.[5] This step was justified on the ground of the wartime power shortage. Later, however, during 1943–44, there was more stringent enforcement of the badge decree and it was not revoked until August 1944.

Church leaders, moreover, had acquiesced to conversions through "mercy baptisms." To bypass the September 1, 1940 deadline, many priests testified that Jewish applicants for formal baptism after that date had actually been converted to Christianity some time earlier. It was tacitly agreed that such converts, if they wanted to, could renounce their vows after the war.[6] Several priests were censured by the government for being too generous with their dispensations, but the Bulgarian people seem to have wholeheartedly supported the clergy in this and other lifesaving deceits.

The RSHA experts now looked for a vulnerable spot in the stiffening Bulgarian resistance. They found it in the Bulgarian-occupied territories of Macedonia and Thrace. The local populations were not anti-Semitic— quite the reverse—but the Bulgarian Government took no note of public opinion. The 14,000 Jews there had not been allowed to acquire Bulgarian citizenship, and under prodding by the ubiquitous Theodore Dannecker, who arrived in Bulgaria in January 1943 from his mission in France, the

Bulgarian Government consented to their deportation. The agreement with Dannecker also provided for the deportation of 6,000 "prominent" Jews from Old Bulgaria. His quota was 20,000, but the Bulgarian King ordered all planned deportations from Old Bulgaria stopped.

In March 1943, the Jews from the annexed provinces left "for the East": 7,132 Macedonian Jews left by rail and 4,221 Thracian Jews by ship. From quiet, remote mountain valleys and little towns that were scarcely more than villages came Jewish peasants in lambskin caps and brightly colored shawls to board boxcars and barges for their long journey to the bathhouses of Auschwitz and Treblinka.

The annihilation of Macedonian Jewry in 1943 destroyed Yugoslavia's oldest Jewish community, one which can be traced back to the twelfth century and probably earlier. Jewish settlement here swelled after the expulsion from Spain in 1492. Until the middle of the nineteenth century, most Jews in Macedonia were merchants and Jews and Greeks dominated the commercial life of the country, but in the second half of the century both Jews and Greeks lost their position to Macedonian non-Jews. However, until 1941, Macedonian Jews still actively engaged in commerce.

The three chief Jewish communities were in Skoplje, Bitolj and Štip. On April 6, 1941, the Germans attacked Yugoslavia and bombed Skoplje on the same day. The massive looting that followed destroyed Jewish economic life. After the German conquest of Macedonia, Bulgaria was invited to occupy the country. When most of the German units left, Macedonian Jews were relieved: they felt sure they would have an easier fate under the Bulgarians. But they were deceived.

On October 4, 1941, Macedonian Jews were forbidden to engage in any industry or commerce. Jewish craftsmen survived for some time longer. In 1942, every Macedonian Jew had to hand over one fifth of any remaining property, movable as well as immovable. Jews were no longer allowed to rent or live in state-owned buildings. By February 1943, the speedy liquidation of craftsmen's shops was also decreed. Proceeds had to be deposited in frozen accounts of the Bulgarian National Bank. Shops which were not liquidated by March 1 were confiscated.[7]

After Belev's appointment, the German Minister Plenipotentiary Beckerle discussed the "solution" of the Jewish problem with Gabrowski, Bulgarian Minister of the Interior. Both men agreed that Bulgaria hand over a first installment of 20,000 Jews, most of them to come from the newly annexed territories. Deportations to the Reich were to start in March. An oral agreement was also worked out between Dannecker and Belev on February 2, 1943. Belev suggested subsequently that cooperation between the police and army authorities would be necessary and that the Jews in camps be told that they were being moved from one district in

Bulgaria to another—not to Germany. After their departure, there would be total property confiscation by the state.

On February 3, Belev issued telegraphic instructions to all representatives in his Commissariat throughout the country instructing them to make up lists of all Jews in their areas by sex, age and occupation. On February 22, a written agreement was signed by Dannecker and Belev for the deportation of 20,000 Jews of any age or sex to the "Eastern German Provinces." "The Reich is ready to receive the Jews into its Eastern provinces" the agreement read. "The Bulgarian Ministry of the Interior will take care that the transports shall consist of Jews only. . . . The Bulgarian Government can under no circumstances demand the return of the Jews thus deported. . . ." On March 2, the Bulgarian Ministerial Council confirmed the agreement and preparations for the deportations were begun immediately.[8]

The morning of March 11 were the last hours of freedom for the Jews of Macedonia. At two o'clock that morning several hundred men mobilized as police were assembled in the police headquarters of Skoplje, Bitolj and Štip to carry out the deportations. They were instructed to collect Jews from their houses according to lists prepared in advance and to hand them over to the camp command. Each group of men was given a number of square punched pasteboard cards. Each card was inscribed with the name of the head of the family, the street address and apartment number. Each group was also given string with which to attach house and apartment keys. The policemen were instructed to try to convince the Jews that they were being temporarily moved to other parts of Bulgaria and that they would return to their homes as soon as the war was over. They were also to tell the Jews to take along all of their cash and jewelry. Outside the police buildings, several hundred cart drivers and their carts waited to transport sick Jews and luggage.

To prevent escape across the border to Albania, border guards were increased. This was done because Bulgarian officials had learned that some Jews had already heard of what might await them. At 3 A.M. on March 11, Bulgarian Army units blockaded Skoplje. All along the streets of the town, armed soldiers were stationed to prevent Jews from leaving their flats. A survivor has described the scene:

As if we had foreseen the calamity, we went to bed in our clothes. At about 5 A.M. we heard that the entire town was blockaded. Nothing was audible except the dull thuds of police boots. A dog kept whining. . . . Two armed policemen accompanied by three police detectives violently threw open the door and started calling our names from a list.

"Take with you gold, jewelry, cash and your valuables," one of the detectives said, "so that it may come in handy when in need." In the street a freight cart was waiting, and a few families were assembled. . . . We were shivering, partly with cold and partly with terror. Everyone kept looking at his mother, sister or brother, as if he would not see them again.

In the courtyard of the [State Tobacco] Monopoly a few tables were arranged and these were flanked by policemen and detectives. On the tables were spread out jewelry, gold articles and watches, and the pockets of the detectives were bulging. We took out of our pockets all we had taken with us. . . . "Take out all your money, the money and the gold," an agent kept shouting, "for if I search you and find a thing on you, I will shoot you like dogs." I cast a glance into the neighboring room and saw a detective pulling the jewelry off my wife and my grandmother. They went over every part of the body. What humiliation![9]

The Skoplje Jews were taken to a temporary concentration camp on the premises of the State Tobacco Monopoly in the town. Four children are known to have been saved, three by a Catholic priest and one by a Macedonian electrician. Eleven Jews escaped to Albania.

On the same day, at Bitolj, the Jewish quarter was divided into twenty sections and an army blockade was established. Between five and six in the morning, Jews were told to be ready in an hour's time. At seven, they left their homes under police escort and were taken to the railway station where they were searched and all of their valuables seized. A witness has recalled:

They loaded us into cattle wagons, fifty to sixty people in one wagon together with the luggage. There was not enough room and many had to stand. There was no water. The children kept on crying. . . . In one wagon a woman was in labor . . . and there was no doctor at hand. We reached Skoplje at midnight. . . . They opened the wagons and in the darkness pushed us into two big buildings. Our train had had the wagons carrying the Jews from Stip coupled to it. We kept stumbling over each other in the darkness, dragging along our luggage, the children, the aged and the sick. Squeezed in the mass and continuously beaten by the Bulgarian soldiers, we tried to get into the building. At dawn we learned that we were in Skoplje, in the Monopoly building, and that all the Jews of the whole of Macedonia had been rounded up that day.[10]

In the Monopoly, 8,000 Macedonian Jews were confined to 30 rooms in four buildings. A doctor from Bitolj has described conditions there:

In one room there were over 500 persons. . . . We and the Jews from Stip were kept locked in during the whole of the day because the plundering search of the Jews from Skoplje was still in progress. . . . When some of us tried to peep through the windows, a policeman fired in the air. . . .

On March 13, they opened the door for the first time and allowed us to go to the latrines. . . . They let out the 500 that were in our room and gave us half an hour, whereupon they locked us up again so that more than half the people never managed to relieve themselves or to get water. . . . The food was distributed once daily and it consisted of 250 grams of bread and usually a watery dish of beans or rice. . . . They gave us smoked meat from time to time, but it was so foul that we could not eat it in spite of our hunger. . . .

Under the pretext of searching us for hidden money, gold or foreign currency, they forced us sadistically to undress completely. . . . Sometimes they would even take away baby diapers. . . .[11]

Some inmates have recorded the generosity of the people of Skoplje who stood on railway wagons and threw bread over the walls of the camp, but their simple humanity was not to be enjoyed for long. On March 22, the first transport of Jews left Skoplje for Treblinka, the second left on March 25, and the third, on March 29. The Commissariat for Jewish Problems in Sofia had issued instructions on the organization of the deportations. Bulgarian police escorted the first train as far as the Lapovo Station where a 35-man German military unit was waiting. A Gestapo unit took over the second and third trains from the start. Within a few days, 7,132 Jews[11a] were delivered to the Treblinka crematoria. The rest had died in camp or on the trains or had been released because they were foreign citizens.

The complete liquidation of the property of Macedonia's Jews started the day after the roundups. German authorities received the finest cupboards, couches, carpets, mirrors and pianos with which to fit out apartments for their officers. Local police broke into Jewish apartments and looted at will. Because of large-scale thefts, the public auction did not yield as much as had been expected: the Bulgarians had anticipated 50 million leva, but the yield was only 33 million, about $400,000.

At the same time that the Macedonian Jews were being transported to death houses, 4,221 Jews from Thrace were being deported from the port of Lom by ship. A non-Jewish nurse, Nadejda Vasileva, has recorded the scenes of anguish at the Lom railway station and the shouts of the Jews in Bulgarian and Ladino from the cars: "Aren't there any humane people who will give us at least some water?" When she tried to distribute water, she was threatened by police. She wrote:

A big crowd was gathering at Vidinska Street, Bulgarians, local Jews and Turks. All were crying. They started filling all kinds of utensils with water and passing them to me. I went on distributing, falling down, stumbling on excrement, and a few gypsies sent by the crowd, came nearer and helped me carry the water from carriage to carriage. All of a sudden, from the other side of the Customs, came a group of people in plain clothes and uniforms—Bulgarian and German uniforms. There were shouts: "Get back! Who gave permission to this woman to come and distribute?" Nobody answered as the rifles were aimed at the crowd. Slavi Pantov (President of the Merchants' Association) came ahead and asked me: "Who asked you to do these crazy things? Go back! I am going to have you arrested."[12]

New transports came the following day and special permission was given Mrs. Vasileva to distribute food at the Southern Station. Only Gypsies were allowed to carry the food to the trains; Jews and Bulgarians could not come near them. The parcels accumulated but nothing could be touched until the arrival of the Commissar for Jewish Affairs. When he came, he inspected the food, picked up a home-baked loaf of bread and shouted: "Nothing can stop these Jews! You see that they made signs on that loaf!" He broke it into pieces and threw it away. Several Gypsies helped Mrs. Vasileva distribute the rest through holes and windows in the cars. A railroad worker came through with a hose and dribbled in some water. From a rear car, there were shouts that there was no water or air. An old man had died and a woman had given birth to a child. A nurse appeared in a foreign uniform and begged to be allowed to treat the sick people inside, but was refused. Mrs. Vasileva followed the cars on foot along the railroad to the Port Station. On the ground at the harbor were scraps of salted fish for those who were going to their death.[13] From Lom, the deportees were taken by barges to Vienna on the first stage of their journey to the railroad siding at Auschwitz.

While the Macedonian and Thracian exterminations were being completed in March 1943, British Foreign Secretary Anthony Eden arrived in Washington for conferences with American leaders. During one of these, the American Secretary of State Cordell Hull brought up the problem of rescuing European Jews. Harry Hopkins, President Roosevelt's adviser, summarized the exchange:

> Hull raised the question of the 60 or 70 thousand Jews that are in Bulgaria and are threatened with extermination unless we could get them out and, very urgently, pressed Eden for an answer to the problem. Eden replied that the whole problem of the Jews in Europe is very difficult and that we should move very cautiously about offering to take all Jews out of a country like Bulgaria. If we do that, then the Jews of the world will be wanting us to make similar offers in Poland and Germany. Hitler might well take us up on any such offer and there simply are not enough ships and means of transportation in the world to handle them.[14]

The Germans pushed on. After the Jews of Thrace were sent to Treblinka, Belov ordered the internment of "prominent" Jews in Plovdiv, Kustendil, Russe and Varna. But opposition was growing. Forty members of Parliament (Sobranje) protested this action and the King ordered all planned deportations from Old Bulgaria stopped.

The deportation of 11,353 Jews was a little more than half of Dannecker's quota. Ribbentrop was far from pleased and expressed his dissatisfaction to King Boris who visited Berlin in April. In the past, the King had not been afraid to lecture Hitler in fluent German from time to time; to Ribbentrop, he said that he had ordered the evacuations confined to Macedonia and Thrace. "Only a small number of Bolshevik-Communist elements" from Old Bulgaria would be deported; the rest of the Jews were needed for road construction, he said, and would be kept in labor camps. Ribbentrop observed that this was "unacceptable," that the only correct solution of the Jewish problem was "the most radical solution." The Bulgarian King did not agree.

King Boris' plan, however, was held up for lack of camps and barracks. Belev, the Commissar for Jewish Affairs, under fresh pressure from the German Legation, proposed the expulsion of Jews from the capital. Even this the King tried to prevent by proposing a total civilian evacuation of Sofia because of imminent air attacks—the Allies were raiding the oil fields. of Romania at this time. The German countermove followed on May 20. The Berlin radio announced the expulsion of Jews from Sofia within three days. The King submitted.

In the expulsion, all but 2,000 exempted Jews from Sofia were quartered with Jewish families in the countryside or in schoolhouses. To the disappointment of the Germans, however, the evacuation from the capital had been accompanied by protests. Crowds of Bulgarians tried to stop the Jews at the railway station. A large demonstration converged on the Royal Palace. Police were called to break it up and 400 people were arrested. The Reich Main Security Office continued its pressure on the Foreign Office, but Beckerle had to admit that direct pressure on the Bulgarian Government just did not work. "Having lived all their lives with Armenians, Greeks and Gypsies," he concluded, "the Bulgarians see no harm in the Jew to justify special measures against him." Beckerle still hoped, however, that the Jews would make such a nuisance of themselves in the countryside that a "final solution operation" would soon be possible.

While Jews were being expelled from Sofia, Dannecker made plans to ship them by sea from the provinces to the East. In June, six Danube ships were set aside for this purpose.

Food shortages and rent inflation did indeed follow the release of 20,000 Jews into rural villages, but these results caused the Bulgarian Government to regret rather than gloat over its action. Instead of anti-Semitism, the expelled Jews had aroused the sympathy of the peasants. Moreover, the Bulgarian underground distributed leaflets instructing partisans to enter Jewish camps and punish guards who maltreated Jews. Unions of Bulgarian workers, lawyers, town meetings, and certain army officers sent protests against anti-Jewish measures to Parliament, the Cabinet and the King. Protesting deputations arrived in Sofia from Plovdiv, Iambol and Kustendil. By 1943, a German victory seemed dubious.

On August 28, 1943, King Boris died under mysterious circumstances. The Germans thereupon tightened their grip and a new Cabinet was formed, entirely subservient to Germany. However, acts of sabotage and armed clashes with the police became more frequent and serious. A general revolutionary rising was plotted for September 2. After Italy's surrender on September 8, opposition to the government and disaffection in the armed forces grew deeper.

In November, a new Cabinet under Dobri Boshilov began to modify anti-Jewish measures. The Jews expelled from Sofia were allowed to return temporarily in order to settle their affairs. The first deadline of November 30 was postponed to December 20 and then dissolved completely. By January 1944, mass bombing of Bulgaria began and a capitulatory mood spread. Plans to deport the Jews were completely shelved and emigration to Palestine was officially permitted. Horst Wagner in the German Foreign Office explained the Bulgarian refusal to deport the Jews in terms of Bulgaria's fear of the Allies. He reported that the Bulgarians had an "insane fear of air raids." The Bulgarians never published the fact that their pursuit planes had participated in the shooting down of American bombers. Wagner concluded that only one factor could change the Bulgarian decision —German military successes. But these were not forthcoming. The Germans had exhausted their pressure points. They had no military victories to rattle and no military force in Bulgaria to threaten. Beckerle finally concluded that the situation was hopeless. Nothing more could be done.

Confronted with civil war, the Bulgarian Government resigned on May 22, 1944, and was replaced by another which hesitantly tried to cut itself adrift from Germany. Under Ivan Bagrianov, the new government had to concede Macedonia to Yugoslavia and in August 1944, it approached the Allies for an armistice. The Cabinet then began a full retreat on anti-Jewish measures. Throughout July and August, secret negotiations were conducted in Istanbul between Ira Hirschmann, President Roosevelt's special representative from the War Refugee Board, and Bulgarian Minister Nikola Balabanov. In August, Balabanov wrote to Hirschmann expressing regret for Bulgarian anti-Jewish measures and pledging to abolish them "at an opportune moment." On August 26, Bulgaria withdrew from the war and within a few days declared her neutrality. The Russians, however, found this role "absolutely insufficient" and Bulgaria declared war on Germany on September 5.

For a full year following the King's death, Bulgaria's Jews lived in a twilit world, half-persecuted, half-protected. But they were not deported. In August 1944, just before the Soviet invasion of Bulgaria, the morning papers in Sofia, in dramatic headlines, announced the Cabinet's decision to revoke all anti-Jewish laws.

Hitler's annihilation program destroyed 11,353 Jews in Bulgaria—all of them from the annexed territories. In Romania, the pattern was similar —the greatest losses were in the annexed areas. However, the losses there were immense, not "moderate," and the threats facing the Jews of Old Romania were much more menacing than they were in Old Bulgaria. Furthermore, the Romanians themselves did much of the killing.

28 Romania

WHILE GERMANY WAS BUSY during the summer of 1940 conquering western Europe, Stalin took advantage of Hitler's preoccupation and moved into the Balkans. On the night of June 26, Russia, which already controlled half of prewar Poland, delivered an ultimatum to Romania demanding Bessarabia and Bukovina. On Germany's advice, Romania yielded. Hungary and Bulgaria, too, then demanded slices of Romanian territory. Hungary, in fact, was prepared to go to war to win back Transylvania, which Romania had gained after World War I. This contingency worried Germany—it would cut off her main source of crude oil and probably bring the Russians in to occupy all of Romania. Because of these considerations Romania was browbeaten into accepting a German-dictated settlement. On July 1, King Carol proclaimed a "reorientation" of Romania's foreign policy. Berlin and Rome now moved to satisfy Hungary's territorial demands. Romania gave up half of Transylvania to Hungary. When this territorial loss was announced, the Romanian Foreign Minister looked at the redrawn map of his country and fainted. In September, Romania also had to give up Dobrudja to Bulgaria. Ostensibly for her reasonableness, but primarily to give Hitler a legal excuse for subsequent aggressions, Romania received a guarantee of the rest of her territory from Germany and Italy. Later, German military missions were sent into Romania to protect the oil districts and the southern flank of a new eastern front that Hitler was envisioning.[1] By early 1941, a formidable German Army of 680,000 troops was massed in Romania which bordered the Ukraine for 300 miles and put German troops within easy striking distance of the Soviet Union.

Romania's cooperation was soon rewarded. She joined the Axis and recovered Bukovina and Bessarabia from Russia. Later, however, when the tide of war turned, these provinces were lost again. Romania then joined the Russians and recovered Transylvania. The opportunism of this switch and the vehement drive of the Romanians—first against the Russians and then against the Germans—were also evident in Romania's handling of the "Jewish problem." The fate of Romania's Jews oscillated between Romanian opportunism and destructiveness. Each political change and each territorial loss or gain was a pretext for massacres of Jews.

Probably no country has had a darker record in the treatment of its Jews than Romania. It was the most virulently anti-Semitic country in pre-war Europe. Notwithstanding the intervention of the great powers several times prior to World War I, the Romanian Government had consistently refused to recognize its Jews as Romanian nationals, and except for a few hundred families, all Romanian Jews remained resident aliens suffering gross disabilities and enduring great persecution.

A famine in 1899 further aggravated their wretched conditions. Many fled the country, but, curiously, the government sought to stem the tide of emigration. This large exodus of Jews drew Western statesmen to survey the conditions under which Romanian Jews were living. Negotiations regarding immigration to the United States led the American Secretary of State John Hay to compose the now-famous note to the Romanian Government. In it Hay wrote:

> . . . by the cumulative effects of successive restrictions, the Jews of Rumania have become reduced to a state of wretched misery. Shut out from nearly every avenue of self-support which is open to the poor of other lands, and ground down by poverty as the natural result of their discriminatory treatment, they are rendered incapable of lifting themselves from the enforced degradation they endure. . . . Human beings so circumscribed have virtually no alternative but submissive suffering or flight to some land less unfavorable to them.[2]

These were strong words for an outside power.

In 1900, the American Commissioner of Immigration summarized the special legislation affecting Romanian Jews:

> A Jew may not secure, hold or work land in a rural district; he may not reside in a rural district; he may reside only in one of 71 towns designated as abiding places for Jews. He may not follow the occupation of an apothecary, a lawyer, stockbroker, member of the . . . Stock Exchange, a peddlar or regular dealer. These are only a few of the callings denied him. . . . A still further impediment is found in the regulation which forbids employers of labor to employ Jews until they have first employed two Christians.[3]

Romanian officials were afraid of exposing the real situation besetting Jews and tried to minimize the effects of state policy. Romania required a large public loan at the time, and the mass flight of Jews had shaken the credit of the state. This fear of world opinion at the turn of the century was very similar to the situation confronting Romania in 1944 when the nation's self-interest was again jeopardized by its anti-Jewish policy. There was also the same deception as to what the state had actually inflicted upon the Jews.

After World War I, the Jews remaining in Romania continued to suffer from economic oppression and the new struggle to obtain political equality. Moreover, the large exodus of Jews had been more than offset by the large new Jewish populations acquired by Romania in 1919. These Jews had come from Bukovina, Bessarabia and Transylvania and increased the total Jewish population to 800,000. Virtually the only economic fields open to them were trade and artisan crafts, and Jewish activity in these fields created deep resentment. The country as a whole was poor, and centuries of poverty, disorder and corruption made reform efforts almost hopeless. The buoyant capitalist development in central Europe was slow to affect Romania. Jewish commercial enterprise constituted virtually the only middle-class activity in the country and aroused the envy of peasants and landlords.

Moreover, there was very little assimilation in the Western sense. Neither Romanian nor Jew was attracted to the other; the two lived apart. Jews were considered foreigners—even those who served in the Romanian Army. An ominous anti-Semitic movement flared in the two universities at Bucharest and Jassy and in secondary schools. In the mid-thirties, the attack on the citizenship of Jews, which was a constant feature of Romanian political life, sharpened.

At Versailles, the Romanian Government had finally accepted a minority treaty granting Jews citizenship, but the minorities statute, incorporated in the peace treaty of 1919, was never fully honored in the newly acquired territories of Romania. In 1937, during the pro-Nazi regime of Octavian Goga, 225,000 Jews in the annexed territories were stripped of their citizenship and an additional 91,000 were classed as foreigners. The decree in these cases was modeled after German laws. Thus, when the Jews of Bessarabia and Bukovina passed under Soviet rule in June 1940, they became enemies as well as foreigners in the eyes of the Romanian Government.

In the economic sphere, between 1938 and 1940, under German tutelage, the Romanian Government took further measures against Jews. The quota system was introduced for industrial workers. All Jews were dismissed from civil service and the Army, and many were discharged from government service. Jews were also prohibited from acquiring property and restricted in practicing professions. In July 1940, the Romanian head of government met Hitler and told him that the solution of the "Jewish question" in Romania would come about after Hitler had solved this question in Europe as a whole. Romania would willingly assist. More drastic anti-Jewish measures followed.

Romania's position became increasingly precarious as the war progressed. Poland, with whom she was allied, was conquered while the collapse of France in May 1940 brought further demoralization to a nation whose foreign policy for over a generation had been principally based on French strength. A few months later, Romania lost Bessarabia and Bukovina to the Soviet Union and Transylvania to Hungary and Bulgaria. Hoping to recover these losses, Romania became Germany's most ardent satellite.

Meanwhile, the Romanian ruler, King Carol II, was forced to abdicate because of Romania's heavy territorial losses—one third of her territory and three million Romanians within two months. The government that formed in September 1940 was a combination of the old ruling class and the Fascist semirevolutionary Iron Guard movement. At the head was a general of the regular Army, Ion Antonescu, and immediately under him as Vice-Premier was the Iron Guard leader, Horia Sima. However, relations between the two men and between the elements they represented were never good. The Iron Guard did not trust Antonescu, nor he, them. The Fascists in the Iron Guard really wanted to make a social revolution; they also wanted to eliminate Jews. Criminal groups among them wanted loot and easy wealth. In November 1940, the Guardists massacred political prisoners and some university professors. Throughout that winter, there were outrages and massacres of Jews reaching a climax of excess in January 1941. The Guardists also struck against the Antonescu government, but their coup was crushed with the connivance of Germany in a complete reversal of Nazi policy.[4] The Germans, on their side, were trying to lay their hands on as much Romanian wealth as possible, and the Iron Guard had plundered to excess. Besides, Hitler needed a stable disciplined regime in Romania and Antonescu's dictatorship provided it—at least for a time.

It lasted for four years. The ultimate fate of Romanian Jewry under this regime hung on several factors: the changing tide of war, the nature of the Romanian bureaucratic apparatus, geography, the access of certain Jewish leaders to government officials, the Romanian-German relationship and the perennial force of nationalism. The 350,000 Jews in Old Romania, in the main, survived. In Transylvania, 150,000 were engulfed in the Hungarian deportations, while the 300,000 Jews in Bessarabia and Bukovina bore the brunt of Romanian destructive frenzy and the German *Einsatzgruppen*. The Romanian bureaucracy was not only corrupt, which made it inefficient and unpredictable, but it followed an extremely uneven course against Romanian Jewry. At times it moved with great violence and speed against Jews, even surpassing the German pace; at other times, it balked at Nazi pressure or suddenly stopped the killing process generated by its own leaders.

From the very first contacts with Jewish leaders in September 1940, Antonescu showed a hypocritical courtesy that characterized his approach to Jewish problems throughout his regime. He assured the Jewish leader, Dr. Wilhelm Filderman, that no harm would come to the Jews as long as they did not boycott his government or take economic measures that would harm the state. (Filderman had successfully led Romanian Jews to stop all economic activity during the reactionary Goga-Cuza regime of 1937–38.) He justified the early excesses of the Iron Guard as the "romanticism of long-suffering youth" but promised to check their illegal persecutions.

However, these promises proved empty.[5] Though he may have objected to the Iron Guard's crude methods, he was known to be an avowed anti-Semite himself. Nevertheless, he feared the very thing Filderman kept reminding him of: the ruin of Romanian trade and industry following anti-Semitic persecutions. Even the Nazis in Germany, Filderman pointed out, had not acted so hastily as Romania in economic matters. Mindful of the dangers of swift unplanned expropriation of Jewish property, Antonescu, on October 16, 1940, wrote to Sima:

> Both the Fascist and the National-Socialist Revolutions not only did not destroy the bourgeois economy but even supported it. I myself cannot destroy both the Jewish economy and the liberal economy simultaneously because this economy is a bourgeois Rumanian one. . . . The means being used to oust the Jews from economic affairs [are] causing a serious economic crisis—not by destruction, daily beatings or embargoes . . . can we improve the economic situation.[6]

During the brief period of legionnaire participation in the government, two important anti-Jewish measures were passed: on October 5, 1940, the state expropriated land owned by Jews, and on November 16, a decree was passed gradually dismissing Jews employed in private commerce and industry. Both measures were implemented by the creation of a Central Office of "Romanianization" in the Labor Ministry. The activities of this office were directed against Armenian and Greek businessmen as well as Jews. The new Romanian property owners, however, had neither capital nor business acumen to satisfactorily replace the old. The Germans watched these transfers skeptically, for the distribution of Jewish property did not include them. Between September 6, 1940, and January 23, 1941, real property valued at 1 billion lei was sold for 216 million, of which only 52 million lei actually were paid.

The zigzag course of Romanian-Jewish experience now began.

A partial explanation for the special character of the Romanian persecution of its Jews lies in the political-military relationship between Romania and Germany. Germany needed Romania for its oil, grains, fats and meat. However, Romania was a military ally, not a conquered country. As early as the beginning of 1942, Germany's demand for increased Romanian military aid encountered opposition, and after Stalingrad—which was not only a German defeat but a military catastrophe for Romania—the opposition increased. By the spring of 1943, Hitler wrote personally to Antonescu urging him to counteract the panic in the Romanian Army during its retreat. By then, Hitler knew that on the initiative of Mihai Antonescu, the Romanian Vice-Premier, certain Romanian politicians were negotiating with the British.

Moreover, the struggle of the Jewish leadership in Romania against the destructive process also contributed to saving part of Romanian Jewry. At the very beginning of the persecutions, a Jewish Council was secretly set up, led by Filderman, a former member of the Romanian Parliament and Chairman of the Union of Jewish Communities. This Council was a merger of all of the main forces in Romanian Jewish life. Its leaders kept an alert eye on events, weighed the changes which took place in the course of the war, and exploited the growing tensions between Germany and Romania. They also took advantage of the squabbles between various anti-Semitic groups, the opposition of the defunct political parties to Antonescu, and changing public opinion as the fortunes of the war changed. They brought into action certain outside pressures—the Papal Delegate, the representatives of Switzerland, Sweden, and Turkey, the Queen Mother, heads of the Orthodox Church and leaders of outlawed political parties. They succeeded in having annulled many ordinances affecting Jews in Old Romania, such as those setting up ghettos, requiring the wearing of the yellow badge and the mobilization of the deportation machinery.

Filderman had gone to school with Antonescu and was able to make certain appeals to him personally. He also maintained contacts with the Ministry of Interior, the Ministry of the National Economy, the Treasury, the Security Police and the Romanian Red Cross. There was scarcely a single decree that escaped Filderman's scrutiny and referral to some Romanian authority. His persistence and pride, his use of legal evidence, the appeals to conscience and national economic interest often resulted in mitigating severe decrees and annulling others. In probing the tangled political web in Romania, Filderman had to gauge the full measure of Antonescu's anti-Semitism.

During the Iron Guard revolt, Antonescu had tried to pacify the legionnaires with the following words: "Do not fight because the loss of any legionnaire will make it all the easier for the Jews and Free Masons to seize power." When the legionnaire revolt was finally subdued, however, he admitted that "the revolutionaries staged a terrible blood-bath. They did not pay the least heed to the most elementary rules of humanity and their lust for blood knew no limits. . . . I am in possession of conclusive proofs of the way in which the legionnaires tortured and robbed wealthy Jews."[7] But this revulsion did not prevent Antonescu from indulging his own form of anti-Semitism.

The Jews suffered both from the civil war which raged in the country during this period and from direct actions perpetrated by the state. This violence has been described by eyewitnesses as an unspeakable butchery. Iron Guardists stormed into the Jewish quarter of Bucharest, burning synagogues and demolishing homes and stores. For miles around the city, bodies of slain Jews were found, without clothes and without teeth. In the morgue, bodies were so cut up they were no longer recognizably human. In the municipal slaughterhouse bodies were observed hanging like carcasses of cattle. In a week of bloody fighting, over a thousand Jews were killed, with both sides freely murdering Jews. Two weeks later, after the Iron Guard was suppressed, Sima blamed the Jews for his defeat. He complained to Himmler that Antonescu was really a friend of the British and was "simply used as an instrument by the Jews and Masons." Himmler, however, had only to wait for Antonescu's regime to reorganize itself; it was becoming an ideal ally—a respectable, military dictatorship. Meanwhile, a German apparatus of power was forming in the background. Its principal figures were Minister Manfred von Killinger, chief of the German Army mission; Major General Hauffe, the liaison officer to the Romanian Army and Gustav Richter, Jewish adviser in the legation. Richter's mission was to secure Romanian anti-Jewish laws on the German model.

The government's anti-Semitic policy did not change after Antonescu expelled the Legion. As the sole power left, Antonescu had to prove that he could carry on the struggle against the Jews without the help of the Legion. Besides, von Killinger, who arrived in Romania a few days after the revolt was put down, insisted that the Legion's program be carried out. Antonescu was thus virtually a prisoner in the hands of the Germans who had supported him against the Legion.

Two important measures were passed after the Iron Guard was ousted from the government. On March 21, 1941, Jews were forbidden to change their religion. The Nuncio Andreia Cassulo protested this as contrary to the Concordat with the Catholic Church guaranteeing its freedom of action, but the regulation was not changed. Then on March 27, the state was permitted to expropriate Jewish homes. This law was announced on the very day that Rosenberg's *Institut für Erforschung der Judenfrage* in Frankfurt was opened. Romania's Vice-Premier Mihai Antonescu declared that this law was a token of esteem for Herr Rosenberg. Like landed property, Jewish-owned real estate was now entrusted to the Romanianization Office. A much more sinister move then was threatened: ghettoization in a number of Romanians towns and in Bucharest.

Dr. Filderman learned of this plan, and on April 8, 1941, he sent a memorandum to the Minister of the Interior, first protesting the inhumanity of the measure and then exposing its economic harm: "As a result of the implementation of the Urban Confiscation Law [depriving Jews of their homes], the value of all real estate will fall and the value of 'Urban Loan' shares will decrease. The establishment of the ghettoes will cause a general collapse in the shares," Filderman added. The order was canceled.

This development coincided with—and may have been influenced by—Dr. Filderman's negotiations to free Romanian funds frozen by the United

States Treasury Department. One hundred thousand dollars were thereby released, enabling American Romanians to return to Romania in exchange for the emigration of Romanian Jews to the United States.

The official rate of exchange at the time was 200 lei to the dollar (the black-market rate was 1,000 lei to the dollar) but the Romanian Government set the rate at 1,200 to the dollar, and called the difference a "special tax." Thus $100,000 of Romanian money in the United States became available immediately and the Romanian Government began to plan the return of American Romanians to Romania in exchange for Romanian Jews. The government was to provide all purchasers of the dollars with passports for emigration.[8] Payment for the dollars was to be in lei. A Jew who bought dollars would be obliged to leave Romania within a year.

On June 20, 1941, circulars were sent to all the Jewish communities in the country informing them of the exchange plan—an agreement which suggested untold possibilities to the Romanian Government for tapping new wealth. But there was scarcely any time for officials to relish this suddenly promising cash value of Jews. Nor could Filderman enjoy the prospect of saving Romanian Jews. On June 22 Germany invaded Russia and a reign of terror descended upon the Jews.

On the eve of the war against the Soviet Union, the German High Command instructed Romania to remove all suspicious persons from the area of military operations to prevent sabotage and espionage. The Romanian Minister of Interior applied this order to Jews and issued immediate evacuation orders. Jews in the towns and villages between the Pruth and Sereth rivers and throughout Moldavia were evacuated. Those in Constanza, Poliesti, Galati and Dorohoi were confined to camps or arrested. Leaders of Jewish communities were held as hostages. A rumor circulated through Jassy, the capital of Moldavia and German Military Headquarters, that Soviet parachutists had landed near the city. The Army ordered an immediate search of Jewish homes. Army deserters who feared that this search would lead to their arrest, fired on the troops and spread a rumor that Jews were firing on the soldiers. A massacre followed. An Italian journalist, Curzio Malaparte, witnessed the pogrom:

> The town was ablaze. Thick clouds of smoke hung over the lower sections along the banks of the river. The houses and trees close to the burning buildings stood out clearly and looked bigger than they were, like enlarged photographs. . . . There was something dead about the scene, and at the same time, something too precise, as in a photograph. . . . Up and down the narrow twisting streets leading towards the centre of town, I heard all about me desperate barking, banging of doors, shattering of glass and of china, smothered screams, imploring voices calling mama! mama!, horrible beseeching cries . . . and the sharp retort of a shot, the whizzing of a bullet and the strident, frightful German voices. In Unirii Square, a group of S.S. men kneeling by the Prince Gutsa Voda monument fired their tommy-

guns towards the little square where the statue of Prince Ghiha in Moldavian costume stands. . . . By the light of the fires a black, gesticulating throng, mostly women, could be seen huddled at the foot of the monument. . . . Hordes of Jews pursued by soldiers and maddened civilians armed with knives and crowbars fled along the streets; groups of policemen smashed in house doors with their rifle butts; windows opened suddenly and screaming dishevelled women in nightgowns appeared with their arms raised in the air; some threw themselves from windows and their faces hit the asphalt with a dull thud. . . . Where the slaughter had been heaviest the feet slipped in blood; everywhere the hysterical and ferocious toil of the pogrom filled the houses and streets with shots, with weeping, with terrible screams and cruel laughter.[9]

The Jassy pogrom dwarfed the Bucharest action—an estimated 14,000 Jews were murdered.

On June 24, there was a heavy Russian air attack on the city and Iron Guardists, once again under government protection, denounced Jews for signaling to Russian planes. Jews had to give up their field glasses, electric torches and cameras. On June 28, the Guardists faked a Jewish machine-gun attack on Romanian soldiers from the Salchana Synagogue. That night, the Iron Guard broke into Jewish homes and began a roundup under the cover of an air-raid alarm. In the early morning, all the Jews of Jassy were assembled in the Prefecture square. The Romanian police allowed women and children to leave but some women followed their husbands. The men were taken into the courtyard to be deported. Some, who had exemption certificates, tried to flee but were shot as fugitives. Five hundred were executed for allegedly signaling to the enemy and firing on troops. Cattle cars awaited the rest. The destination was Poduloea.

Into a single train, five thousand Jews were packed, 200 to each sealed boxcar. Three days later, but only 20 miles from Jassy, part of the train was detached and the Jewish elders of Poduloea awaited the passengers. When the train doors were opened, 2,000 bodies rolled out, dead from suffocation.

Poduloea is a Romanian village on the Bessarabian frontier. On June 28, Malaparte motored to Poduloea with the Italian Consul in Jassy who was looking for one of the deported Jews. The train was made up of ten cattle cars and for three days 200 Jews piled into each car had been sealed in airless pens. Malaparte ordered soldiers at the station to open the cars. They refused. The Consul then insisted that the stationmaster order the soldiers to open the doors. Malaparte watched: "A throng of prisoners hurled itself at Sartori [Italian Consul], knocking him down and falling on top of him. The dead were fleeing from the train. They dropped in masses —with dull thuds, like concrete statues. Buried under the corpses, crushed by their huge, cold weight, Sartori struggled and wriggled trying to free himself from under that dead burden, from under that frozen mountain;

finally he disappeared beneath the pile of corpses, as if it were an avalanche of stones."[10]

Out of two thousand corpses, one baby, a few months old, was still alive. It had fainted, but it still breathed. One arm was broken. The mother had held him with his mouth glued to the door jamb, sucking a thin thread of air with his lips while his mother had been crushed by the immense pressure of packed bodies in the car. The baby was found clutched between the knees of his dead mother. Another 800 bodies were dropped off at Tergu Frumos, where the Jewish Council was asked "if it would like some Jewish Communists." Some victims had stripped off their clothes in the suffocating heat and used them to hang themselves. These events foreshadowed worse things to come.

In midsummer 1941, in an atmosphere of widespread pogroms, Romanian officials began to put into effect the yellow badge measure. The press openly acknowledged the purpose of the decree. One paper said: "The Jews will thus be despised everywhere. . . . The nation should know that the yellow badge means treason, espionage, murder, communism and the destruction of the Holy Cross." Another paper declared: "The Jews are a people of haters, traitors and spies who never liked the Rumanians." Mass arrests of Jews were also carried out in many places. Dr. Filderman, in a memorandum to the Ministry of the Interior, asked how Jews could logically be made answerable for acts of terror if they were not free to commit such acts. He also asked how Jews whom the government called "Judeo-Capitalists" could also be regarded as Bolshevist agents. Ironically, he argued that in Germany the Jewish community leaders "are considered an official institution, in constant contact with the government," whereas in Romania the leaders are imprisoned and killed, leaving the community unable to fill the public duties imposed upon it by law. He told Mihai Antonescu that the yellow badge order was plainly illegal.[11] Filderman also reminded officials that the badge was not used in Germany, Italy or Hungary, that it would cause social conflict and depress economic activity because Jews would be afraid to leave their homes. He also threatened to resign his own position as leader of the Jewish community. Quite boldly he hinted that the decree was passed against the will of the Minister of the Interior, thus suggesting that the Germans were behind the order. He prepared a special memorandum for the head of the Orthodox Church, Patriarch Nikodemus, identifying the Star of David as a symbol sacred to Christianity as well as to Judaism and showing that by accepting the decree, Christians would be mocking a valued religious symbol and hating their fellowmen. The man was tireless in his labors. Finally, on September 8 he was summoned to the Bucharest Police Prefect and told that the order had not been annulled.

That same evening he had an interview with Antonescu and repeated all of the arguments he had used before. Antonescu made a sarcastic remark about Filderman's "library of memoranda" but after a brief discussion, turned to Vice-Premier Mihai Antonescu, and said, "I want you to give an order that the wearing of the identification badge be abolished throughout the country."[12]

There can be no doubt that this cancellation saved the lives of many thousands of Jews. The press continued its anti-Semitic agitation and the Germans their pressure, but the annulment of the badge decree showed that the Romanian Government did not plan the wholesale destruction of Romanian Jews. Mihai Antonescu, however, found it necessary to warn Dr. Filderman about using "provocative" language. "I have taken a series of steps for the benefit of the Jewish population," he wrote to the Federation of Jewish Communities, "but I will not tolerate provocative language. If Dr. Filderman wishes us to receive him and hear his complaints, he need no longer use provocative language."[12a]

But Filderman maintained a steady flow of memoranda. He prevailed on the government to permit aid to be sent to the Jews in Transnistria, a region between the Dniester and Bug rivers (map, p. 550); he petitioned to have the deportations from Bessarabia and Bukovina stopped; he interceded for threatened groups. Finally, his activities became so troublesome that on December 16, 1941, the government disbanded the Federation of Jewish Communities, of which he was the head. The Center for Romanian Jews (*Centrala Evreilor din Romania*), which replaced it, was managed by two men who were handpicked by the Romanian government. But Filderman continued his petitions and applications. In the fall of 1941 his concern was chiefly over the Jews of Bukovina and Bessarabia.

It was in the "lost provinces" of Bukovina and Bessarabia (which Romania recaptured from the Soviet Union), with a Jewish population of 300,000, that Jews suffered the brunt of the Romanian destructive frenzy. This area had already been preempted by *Einsatzgruppe D*, a force of 600 Germans charged with the staggering assignment of killing all southern Ukrainian Jews.

In Bukovina, as in Ruthenia and the Protectorate, the Germans set about killing people who were proud of their German heritage. In Bukovina, Jews, together with the ethnic German settlers, were fervent supporters of "Germanism" and it was partly because of the Jews that Bukovina, with its preponderantly Romanian and Ruthenian population, became a stronghold of German culture prior to the Hitler period. The Romanian Army helped in these killings and, on occasion, did not respect the Nazi schedule. In August 1941, the Romanians, on their own, decided to shove the Bessarabian Jews across the Dniester River into what was still a German military area. Their object was to utilize the killing services of

Einsatzgruppe D. After some 15,000 Jews had been driven across the river, the German 11th Army gave orders to block traffic over the Dniester bridgehead at Mogilev-Podolsk but the Romanians, on their side, blocked the way back. Again and again the *Einsatz* squads turned back Jews; repeatedly, more Jews came across. In the process of being shoved back and forth, thousands of Jews died on roadsides from exhaustion, hunger and gunfire. When Antonescu was reported considering the transporting of 60,000 Jews from Old Romania into Bessarabia, the Germans had to act quickly; the *Einsatzgruppe* could not cope with so many Jews.

The *Einsatzgruppen* leaders were still apparently making strenuous efforts to distinguish between "ideological" killing under discipline and mere killing. The Romanians, they complained, were disorderly. An *Einsatzgruppe* report of July 25, 1941, reads: "There would be nothing to say against numerous executions of Jews if it were not that the technical preparation and the method of execution is defective. The Romanians leave the executed people where they have fallen without burying them." The Romanian "lack of discipline" drew frequent criticism from the Germans.

In Bessarabia, there were locally instigated massacres in most of the towns, and when Otto Ohlendorf's *Einsatz* killers entered the region early in July to execute Jews they also complained of too much Romanian zeal, lack of planning and too much looting to achieve systematic killing. His squads eventually overcame this "disorder" and systematically killed 90,000 Jews.

The German Legation advised the Romanian Government "to proceed with the elimination of the Jewish element in a systematic and slow manner," suggesting that Romania was "ahead" of Germany in destroying Jews. Hitler, too, in conversations with Goebbels in August, had slyly suggested that Antonescu had proceeded against the Jews in a "far more radical fashion" than the Germans. The Nazi police commanders smugly talked of restraining the Romanians from "uncontrolled" actions, but the Romanians, of course, were only following the Germans. Antonescu knew that in the wake of the German armies in Russia, killing squads murdered Jews wherever they found them. By pushing Jews from Bessarabia and Bukovina into German rear areas, he knew very well what their end would be. Meanwhile, the Romanians added to the Jewish dead. In Odessa alone, without any help from the *Einsatzgruppe*, they were responsible for the slaughter of 60,000 Jews.

On October 16, 1941, after a long siege, the 4th Romanian Army captured Odessa. A German military intelligence agent reported that for four days, over 11,000 Jews were imprisoned in the Central Prison of Odessa without food or water. On October 22, partisans blew up Romanian headquarters on Engel Street and several dozen Romanian soldiers were killed.

Antonescu ordered 2,000 civilians shot for every dead officer; 100 for every ordinary soldier. The quotas were exceeded out of all bounds. During the night of October 22–23, 19,000 Jews were driven into the harbor area and shot. Another 40,000 were transported to Dalnic outside the city and shot down in antitank ditches.[13]

While the Axis prospects for winning the war seemed good, the Romanians were planning to turn Odessa into a sort of brighter and better Bucharest. Not only were there restaurants, shops, gambling dens, cabarets, brothels and European-style opera and ballet, but there was a serious attempt to convince the people that they were going to remain part of Greater Romania. Romanians distributed a geography book which demonstrated that practically the whole of southern Russia was "geopolitically" part of Romania, largely inhabited by descendants of the ancient Dacians. Those who could prove any Moldavian blood were promised various privileges. To have a Jewish grandmother was dangerous, but to have a Moldavian grandparent was like a title of nobility.

Odessa became another city in Europe without Jews. When a visitor to the city in 1944 asked, "What happened to the Jews?" a man answered:

> Oh, they bumped off an awful lot. . . . Some were allowed to escape—with a little money you could buy *anything* from the Rumanians, even a passport in the name of Richelieu. We had a family of Jews living in our cellar and we took them food once a week. The Rumanian cops knew about them but didn't bother. They said that if so many Jews were bumped off, it was because the Germans had demanded it. "No dead Jews, no Odessa," they said. Anyway, that's what the Rumanians told us.[14]

But Odessa was only part of Bessarabia. Thousands of other Jews had to be disposed of, and a division of operations acknowledged.

An agreement (the so-called Tighina Agreement) was finally worked out on August 30, 1941, between the German and Romanian military staffs. They created Transnistria, between the Bug and Dniester rivers, as a temporary dumping ground for Jews from Bessarabia and Bukovina. With certain qualifications, the Romanians were to administer camps in Transnistria where Jews would be assigned to forced labor until military operations were concluded. Afterward, they were to be transported "to the East." The deportations of Jews from Bukovina and Bessarabia were carried out as part of Hitler's all-embracing plan for destroying the Jews of the East and formed part of Hitler's instructions (*Richtlinien*) to Antonescu on the handling of the "Jewish question" in Romania.

Eichmann's representative in Bucharest, Gustav Richter, reported on October 17 that Antonescu planned to push these Jews beyond the Bug where the Germans would dispose of them: "According to information received today from Generaldirektor Lecca," Richter reported, "11,000 Jews are being evacuated from Bukovina and Bessarabia into two forests in the Bug River area. So far as he could learn, this action is based upon an order issued by Marshal Antonescu. The purpose of the action is the liquidation of these Jews."¹⁵ However, this report apparently represented Lecca's wishful thinking rather than Antonescu's actual intentions. This plan was never executed along Nazi lines, although the Romanian destruction of Jews west of the Bug was horrible enough. For the time being Jews remained between the Dniester and the Bug, mainly in camps at Pechora, Tulchin, Balta, Bershad and Trostyanets. Gradually they were sorted out. Those accused of collaborating with the Russians were sent to prison camps; the rest were sent to Golta, Yampol, Mogilev-Podolsk, Rimnitsa and Tiraspol, already overcrowded and destitute. Moreover, as the starvation policy in Transnistria created acute problems, there was renewed Romanian pressure to force the Jews eastward into *Reichskommissariat* Ukraine east of the Bug River.

Antonescu had had some vague plans to convert Transnistria into a model Romanian settlement through large-scale Romanian colonization but the project never materialized. On November 11, 1941, Gheorghe Alexianu, the Governor of Transnistria, ordered this area converted into a gigantic penal colony for Jews, including 100,000 Soviet Jews and thousands of new deportees. In each community assigned to Jews, they were to form a "colony." All work was to be paid in the form of produce, worth two marks per day for skilled workers, one for nonskilled. Like the refugees who were transported to the Polish ghettos, the Romanian newcomers to Transnistria suffered even more than the local population. Messages and letters from the deportees, though heavily censored, contained pleas for money to save the writers from starvation, but the authorities were quite ready to let hunger and disease kill them off. The relief action which the Jewish Central Office was finally authorized to take came late and was completely inadequate. Until January 30, 1942, the Jews in Transnistria were completely isolated from the rest of the world. After that date, messages were frequently sent through friendly couriers, generally soldiers, although such contacts were officially forbidden. Money was also transmitted through the couriers, at charges of 30 to 50 percent of the sums transmitted.

Besides money, Jews from Old Romania sent used clothing, scrap iron, lumber and building materials into the camps. Often the transports of these materials were held up for months by government officials, particularly so in Tiraspol, which was notorious for its inhuman treatment of Jews. About 40 million lei were transmitted through official channels during the first six months. This amount averaged 150 lei per person, just enough to buy one third of a loaf of bread.

In July 1942, the Jewish Central Office urged that an International

Red Cross commission be sent to Transnistria to see if the Jews there were accorded minimum human rights and adequate food and medical supplies. However, this request to Antonescu went unanswered. Instead, a government-appointed Jewish commission was sent. This group was permitted to visit only four of the hundred places in Transnistria to which Jews had been deported—Mogilev, Odessa, Shmerinka and Crasna—and could not be independent in its investigation or in its conclusions. Nevertheless, even in the guarded language of its report, conditions were described as deplorable. In some places, as many as 40 and 50 people were crowded together in one room; the commission registered 8,000 orphans in the communities visited, 5,000 of whom had lost both parents. In Mogilev's three orphanages, most of the 900 children had to remain in bed because they had no clothes and slept four to six in a single bed.[16]

The camps in Transnistria were among the most appalling in Europe, located in a barren stretch of the Ukraine laid waste by the retreating Russians. The camps were under the command of Romanian Army officers who were in turn responsible to the local prefects—also Army personnel. Those in charge made no pretense of distributing food, and starvation was rampant. Some inmates, reduced to selling all of their clothes for food, were seen running around naked, eating grass and potato peelings. In the Vertujen camp, the arrivals were told, "You have come in on two feet, and if you do not end your lives here, you will be allowed to leave on four only." The Jews in that camp were fed on a diet of cattle food that resulted in paralysis. One survivor has written that, at the Bucharest war crimes trial after the war, a number of Jewish witnesses including a ballerina were able to walk only on all fours. Starvation and typhus killed off 23,000 Jews in the Vertujen camp.

Bogdanovka, in the Golta prefecture, was Romania's greatest death center. In the camp at Bogdanovka, bread was sold at the rate of one loaf for five gold rubles. When the gold gave out, the camp commander ordered mass shootings. In December 1941, Jews were driven into stables and shot, and when the stables were filled with corpses, they were destroyed by fire. Those who could not be squeezed into stables were marched to a precipice above the Bug River. There they were stripped of all of their belongings; gold teeth were forcibly extracted and if rings could not be easily removed, fingers were chopped off. Forced to stand naked in temperatures 40 degrees below zero, they were shot and the corpses dropped into the river. Within a week, 48,000 Jews were massacred. The shootings were extended to two other camps in the prefecture, bringing the total to 70,000.[17]

When the deportations to Transnistria neared their climax in October

1941, Dr. Filderman addressed a second petition to Marshal Antonescu appealing to have the deportations stopped. He wrote:

> I have today (October 11) received a heartrending call from the management of the ghetto at Kishinev. On the morning of the 8th of this month 1500 persons left, most of them by foot, taking only what they could carry with them. Nearly all of them will die since it was cold and they were almost naked, without food and without the slightest possibility of getting supplies—they set out on a journey that will last at least eight days, in rain, cold and snow. Only the sick, the aged and the children traveled in carts, but no account was taken of the women who also went by foot. This is death, death without indictment, without any charge other than that of being Jews. I beseech you, once again, Marshal, not to permit such an atrocious tragedy to happen.[18]

Antonescu's letter of reply was published in all of the newspapers and served as an incitement for further pogroms. The Romanians, said Antonescu, had paid with their blood for the hatred of Filderman's Jews. In Odessa, he charged, the Jews had "goaded" the Soviet troops into unnecessarily prolonged resistance "merely in order to inflict casualties upon us." In Bukovina and Bessarabia, the Jews had received the Red Army with flowers, they set their houses on fire before abandoning them, they put hand grenades in children's pockets. "Do not grieve," he concluded, "for things not worth grieving about. Grieve for things worth while. Weep with the mothers whose sons died in such torment and not with those who brought upon themselves and are now bringing on you so much suffering."[19]

The deportations were not stopped. Two short years later, Antonescu could not remember that he had designed Transnistria as a death trap for Jews.

In Bessarabia, on the eve of deportations at the beginning of September 1941, a military census counted only 126,434 Jews. Thus, more than 150,000 had left Bessarabia by the time the Romanians had reoccupied it in June. Some of these had been deported by the Russians earlier and some had fled before the Romanian occupation. It is impossible to know how many survived. Many died of hunger and typhus and at the hands of *Einsatzgruppen*. It is estimated that 30,000–40,000 bought baptism certificates and saved themselves. The rest were caught by the forced expulsion to Transnistria. In Bukovina, in the smaller towns, the Jews were killed by Ukrainian bands from Galicia even before the Germans arrived. Ohlendorf's killing squads murdered Jews in the larger cities. Possibly 30,000 were considered essential to the economy, and exempted. The Romanians forced the remainder across the Dniester. By 1942, 185,000 Jews were in Transnistria.

A new wave of Romanian deportations early in 1942 went straight across the Bug River into German-held territory, *Reichskommissariat* Ukraine. These actions spread consternation among the Germans, and all levels of jurisdiction complained: the Army commanders, Rosenberg's Ministry for Occupied Eastern territories, the Foreign Office in Berlin, and Eichmann himself. The Germans were not yet ready for new batches of Jews and needed more time to plan the operations. They said they feared the spread of typhus. Besides, Eichmann's timetable called for giving the Reich Jews "priority." The deportation expert could not very well condemn the Romanians for their zeal, but he pointed out that deportations from Romania were "planless and premature" at the time. Antonescu was warned, but deportations across the Bug continued. The Germans retaliated by forcing back 28,000 Jews into the numerous ethnic German colonies in Transnistria where they were killed. As late as June 28, there were reports of Romanian officials shoving Jews on the unready Germans in the Ukraine. By then, two thirds of the Jews in Transnistria were dead or perishing. The survival of the remaining third revolved around developments in Old Romania, and a sudden reversal of Romanian policy. The enthusiastic ally was beginning to show signs of cooling.

Many forces influenced Antonescu to change his course by midsummer 1942—some rather trivial, others of greater weight, among which the most important was the changing tide of war. Goebbels, in a diary entry for May 21, noted the sudden assertion of Romanian independence:

In Rumania measures are being taken against German elements there—of all people. They have been forbidden to wear uniforms and have had to suffer all sorts of other humiliations. The situation has become so bad that Killinger for a while thought of resigning. . . . Antonescu further promised, as a result of a protest by von Ribbentrop, to call the Deputy Premier, Mihai Antonescu, to order, for constantly interfering with Axis policies in the Balkans. I don't suppose much will come of it, however.[19a]

Goebbels was referring to Transylvania, half of which Romania had recently annexed, an area heavily populated with ethnic Germans. In May 1942, Antonescu forbade Germans there to wear Nazi Party uniforms. Meanwhile, he continued to try to put Jews across the Bug River against German orders. By August, Himmler chose to schedule the deportation of Jews in Transylvania, Jews who up to this time had been spared. Germany exerted pressure on Romania for more Jews of her choice but her denial of Jews of Romania's choice may have been one factor in turning the scales in Antonescu's mind against deportations. On August 17, came Himmler's order to deport Jews from Arad, Timisoara and Turda, all of which were in Transylvania. On August 19, S.S. men penetrated Romanian-administered Transnistria and abducted thousands of Jews and transported them "to the East" to be killed.

Meanwhile, on July 26, Eichmann appeared confident that Richter had scored a complete breakthrough on deportations from Old Romania. "Political and technical preparations," he wrote, "have been completed . . . to such an extent that the evacuation transports will be able to roll in a short time. It is planned to remove the Jews of Rumania in a series of transports beginning approximately September 10, 1942, to the district of Lublin, where the employable segment will be allocated for labor utilization, while the remainder will be subjected to special treatment." Eichmann now requested permission "to carry out the shoving-out work in the planned manner."

But Antonescu was playing a double game. He sedulously cultivated Eichmann's belief that Romania, by midsummer 1942, was preparing technically and politically for the final drastic actions against its remaining Jews. Eichmann's timetable scheduled the first transports from Old Romania to begin September 10, 1942. Arrangements were made for Radu Lecca, Commissar for Jewish Affairs, to go to Berlin to discuss details of the operation with the German Foreign Office and the RSHA.

Lecca's visit during the week of August 20 was apparently regarded in Berlin as a mere formality. Antonescu had, after all, given his consent to deportations, and Lecca was not considered a very important figure. No one bothered to give him much attention. When he returned to Romania, he complained of having received severe insults in Berlin. Killinger complained that the S.S. representative Richter, who had handled the matter without him, was responsible for the diplomatic brush-off. The German Foreign Office tried to salvage the situation when it realized that the Romanian Government apparently took this slight seriously, but their efforts failed. Antonescu's decision not to turn Romanian Jews over to the Germans for deportation hardened during the autumn of 1942. German officials continued the pressures and appeals, but in vain. Antonescu held fast. The Germans were completely taken aback by the switch in Romanian policy.

The Romanians turned their backs on the German-dictated course because national self-interest demanded a new line. The Romanian war effort had become too costly and too bloody. In November 1942, Romania's Third and Fourth Army Corps were wiped out. Romanian leaders began to doubt that Germany could win. There were staggering Romanian losses at Stalingrad; the country's wealth was being drained by Germany. "Civilized" world opinion also began to tip the balance as German victory dimmed. Romania now wanted a bridge to the Allies. Berlin's brush-off of Lecca added insult to Germany's unwarranted interference of Romanian sovereignty in Transylvania, where Antonescu was touchy. The Germans had been uncooperative in Transnistria. It was time to woo the West and Mihai Antonescu was wasting no time. While leading the Nazis on, he was also giving audiences to the Transylvanian Metropolitan Balan, and to

Papal Nuncio Cassulo. He was also meeting with Swiss and Swedish ministers and representatives of the International Red Cross. He had even ordered an inquiry into the German massacres of Jews who had been deported beyond the Bug River.[20] The Nazi-projected September transports from Old Romania did not leave. The Jews in these areas survived the war.

The anti-Jewish policies of Old Romania had been outlined in a manual called *Instructions for the Treatment of the Jewish Question,* personally handed to Antonescu by Hitler before the German invasion of Russia. In addition, Richter had been sent to Bucharest on April 1, 1941, to bring Romanian anti-Jewish legislation to the German level and to remain in Romania until the "Final Solution" of the Jewish question had been achieved.

In the 89 anti-Jewish laws and decrees passed by the Romanian Government between 1938 and May 1, 1942, the Romanians sometimes outdid their German model, but the effect of these measures was not uniformly drastic. The most heavily persecuted Jews were immigrants and those in the annexed provinces. The Jews in Old Romania were treated less harshly and did not feel all of the state's blows.

The most privileged were those Jews who had been Romanian citizens before December 30, 1918, and descendants of front-line soldiers in the Romanian Army. Resident Jews, but noncitizens, who had lived in Romania before December 30, 1918, were more vulnerable. Many lost their jobs and property, but as a whole, Jews were not eliminated from the Romanian economy. A somewhat novel and characteristically Romanian regulation enabled those who were "indispensable" to the economy to buy exemptions by making payments to the state. Side by side with the massacres, there had sprung up a flourishing business in the sale of exemptions. All officials engaged in this traffic. Moreover, there was no compulsory transfer of commercial and industrial enterprises—something the Germans had deplored—because Jewish manufacturers and businessmen filled an essential role in the Romanian economy and could not be replaced.[21] A forced-labor system was also introduced but did not apply to essential workers. At the end of 1941, more than half of the total of Jewish workers were considered essential. As Dr. Filderman had warned, the Romanians could not afford to cleanse the Romanian economy of Jews.

The Romanian Government extracted large sums from Jews who were safe as long as they could keep paying and levied heavy taxes on Jewish businessmen. In the fall of 1941, a forced loan amounting to $14 million was also imposed on the Jewish community. Alive, the Jews in Old Romania were more profitable than they were dead.

Although a Jewish Central Office replaced the Federation of Jewish Community Organizations, the ghettoization process was not a thoroughgoing one. All persons who had at least one Jewish grandparent had to register with the Jewish Central Office, but the elaborate system of movement restrictions and badge identification was never applied in Old Romania. Jews were required to have travel permits but they could be procured at six dollars per travel day—another revenue source for the money-hungry Romanian officials, and another loophole for Jews.

German pressure to deport the Jews of Old Romania to Poland became strong at the height of Romanian operations in Transnistria, at the end of 1941. At this time the Romanian Government was asked to allow Germany to deal freely with the Romanian Jews in the Reich. When the Romanian Government agreed, the Germans assumed that this consent also covered Romanian Jews elsewhere in occupied countries, for example, in France and the Protectorate, and that Old Romania itself was now ready to be rid of all of its Jews. Instead, most unexpectedly, Romania balked. The Romanians, the Germans were to learn, were not ideological killers; they killed Jews for economic reasons, and they refused to kill them for the same reasons. By the middle of the summer of 1942, the Romanians had become fervent supporters of Jewish emigration to Palestine at $1,330 per person.

Palestine had been discussed in diplomatic circles from time to time. In the fall of 1941 the Turkish Minister in Bucharest suggested to the American Minister there that 300,000 Romanian Jews be transported to Palestine via Turkey. But the American State Department raised strong objections. On November 12, 1941, Cavendish W. Cannon of the European Division wrote to the acting chief of the division (Ray Atherton) and the adviser on political relations (James C. Dunn) that no formal note should be sent to the British. The arguments against tackling the problem were ships, the "Arab question," the possibility of Jewish pressure for an asylum in the western hemisphere, "and a possible request for similar treatment of Jews in all countries where there has been intense persecution."[22] These objections to rescue schemes were to serve for the duration of the war.

Only one perilous route of escape was possible for Romanian Jews— the port of Constanza on the Black Sea. For Antonescu, selling Jewish lives and ships might be highly profitable. For the Jews themselves, however hopeful some might be, the project already had a tragic past and bleak future.

When Antonescu came to power in 1940, many Jews had been extremely apprehensive about the new regime and thousands left Black Sea ports of Romania bound for Palestine. They traveled on unseaworthy vessels which became known as "coffin ships," many of which sank with hundreds aboard. Thousands of others died trying to evade British pursuit. Those who survived the crossing were threatened with deportation when they arrived in British-mandated Palestine.

On November 20, 1940, the Palestine Government announced its new policy for combating the "illegal" boats. From that date, all refugees attempting to enter Palestine "illegally" would be deported to a British colony, the island of Mauritius in the Indian Ocean. The British also refused to give Palestine certificates to Jews in enemy-occupied nations on the ground that German agents might worm their way into Palestine on the refugee boats. For the desperate refugees, however, Istanbul, in neutral territorial waters, where no German ship had the right to search, remained a beacon of hope. Once in Istanbul, they could try to contrive an escape.

On December 16, 1941, the tragedy of the *S.S. Struma* exposed this illusion.

The *Struma* disaster[23] actually began in the fall of 1941 when the plight of Romanian Jewry was growing increasingly severe. News of a possible chance to sail to Palestine on the *Struma* spread among Jews. The ship flew the Panamanian flag. It had been bought in Bulgaria where the ship's agents had given their word that a new diesel engine and other features made the ship seaworthy. They also promised that their representative would obtain immigration certificates in Istanbul, where unused certificates from the official schedule were said to be available. However, when the ship arrived in Constanza, it turned out to be nothing but a ramshackle cattle boat, originally built as a riverboat for the Danube. On December 16, packed with 769 refugees, the vessel broke down. A company agent admitted that he lacked the means to repair the defective engine or supply the passengers with food. The Bulgarian captain informed the Turkish port authorities that since his country was an enemy of Britain, he could not take the ship through the Dardanelles. The passengers, fearing that he might take them to islands in the Aegean, then occupied by German and Italian troops, tried to get a Turkish captain. Some of the passengers had obtained certificates before Romania was declared an enemy state, but most had not. Meanwhile, under Arab pressure, the Turkish authorities refused to grant the passengers permission to land. The Joint Distribution Committee and the Jewish community in Istanbul provided food and medicine for the *Struma*.

There were still thousands of unused certificates under the White Paper policy, and efforts were made to have the British relax their immigration policy. Jewish Agency officials tried vainly to get British permission for the refugees to enter Palestine. They were not even allowed to allot certificates in their possession, on the ground that the refugee Jews were enemy subjects.

The helpless ship lay in the Bosphorus for ten weeks until Turkish officials insisted that it leave. On February 16, the British Consulate in Istanbul was informed that immigration certificates had been authorized for the seventy children aboard. However, one week later, when the Turkish authorities were asked to take the children ashore, they replied that they had not yet received British instructions to do so. The International Red Cross asked Turkish authorities to postpone the ship's departure; they promised that the vessel would not be forced to leave until February 26. But three days earlier, on February 23, eighty Turkish policemen forced their way onto the ship against the resistance of the passengers and tied it by cable to a tug. Without adequate water, food or fuel, and with a crippled engine, the *Struma* was tugged into the Black Sea. At 10 P.M. on February 23, the vessel was thirty miles out at sea, and the tug detached itself. The following morning the *Struma* sank. One man saved his life; the rest were drowned. The lone passenger survivor, David Stolier, recalled:

> The sea was very calm. The ship did not move from its location. Then, suddenly, shortly before nine in the morning a violent explosion shook the ship, and within minutes it sank into the sea.
> I was swept overboard by the force of the blast. When I surfaced, I saw scores of people struggling in the waves. Screams of terror rose from the sinking ship. Pieces of wood were floating around in the water, and some, including myself, managed to grab hold of them in an attempt to save themselves. But the water was icy cold and the people grew weaker and weaker. One by one, their grips relaxed and they sank beneath the waves. By the time it was noon, I was alone. . . . My thick leather jacket warmed me a bit. That saved me.

Late in the afternoon Stolier spied a bench floating nearby. He got hold of it, dragged it onto the platform he was clinging to and sat on it. There he sat in the vastness of the icy sea, broken only by birds that flew overhead and lighted on the floating corpses and scattered debris. He passed the night trying not to fall asleep or to freeze. The following morning, a small Turkish boat picked him up. Seven hundred and sixty-eight refugees, including 70 children, had perished.

The direct cause of the disaster is unknown. Turkish authorities maintain that the *Struma* had either hit a mine or had been attacked by a Russian submarine, but these explanations satisfied few people. The British were consistently unyielding about Palestine; the Nazis undoubtedly brought diplomatic pressure to bear on Turkey to expel the *Struma* from Istanbul. Escape through Constanza was now hopeless.

Eichmann meanwhile, was in relentless pursuit of Romanian Jews. He was determined that none should escape his grasp. The German Foreign Office, at the same time, wanted to prove to the Grand Mufti of Jerusalem that Jewish emigration to Palestine was being blocked. On March 3, 1942, a week after the explosion of the *Struma*, Eichmann wrote to Counselor von Hahn of the Foreign Office:

> According to reliable information which must be kept secret, negotiations, which might prove successful, are being conducted by Jewish officials in Rumania with Turkey, through their offices in Istanbul, for the grant of Turkish transit visas to a group of 1000 Jewish children and 100 Jewish adults from Rumania who should be brought by land in cooperation with Wagons-Lits, via Bulgaria and Turkey to Palestine.
>
> It is requested to do whatever possible in order to prevent the planned emigration.[24]

The disaster of the *Struma*, occurring just as reports of actual exterminations were being heard for the first time, was burned into the memory of all Jews in Europe and Palestine. The British public, too, was outraged that their government should be treating Jewish refugees from the Balkans as though they were enemies. Questions involving the Government's White Paper policy were raised in the House of Commons. But the Government stood fast. Harold Macmillan, Under-Secretary for the Colonies, explained on March 17: "It is not in our power to give guarantees nor to take measures of a nature that may compromise the present policy regarding illegal measures."

The World Jewish Congress, meanwhile, had urged the American State Department to allow Jewish organizations to deposit money for rescue purposes to the credit of Axis officials in blocked accounts in Switzerland. After eight months, a license was finally issued. This was done over the opposition of the British Foreign Office, which was concerned with the "difficulties of disposing of any considerable number of Jews" in the event of their release from Axis Europe. Antonescu knew of the World Jewish Congress plan.

On December 12, 1942, he had told the Jewish Central Office to find 75,000 applicants for Palestine visas. In return for the right to emigrate, each Jew would pay the Romanian state $1,330; the overall figure was $100 million for all 75,000. The German Ambassador, Killinger, learned from Lecca, the Romanian Commissar on Jewish Affairs, that Antonescu "wanted to kill two birds with one stone and get rid of a large number of Jews in a comfortable manner." But the results were meager. Only a small trickle of Romanian and Hungarian Jewish children were guided to Palestine through Istanbul, and some overland across Bulgaria.

At the end of May 1943, Killinger reported to the German Foreign Office that Antonescu had seen Hitler on April 12–13 to discuss Romania's continued role in the war and, that, in the course of the conversations, Hitler had allegedly agreed to allow 70,000 Romanian Jewish children to go to Palestine. Whether Hitler actually made this promise to Antonescu cannot be known with certainty. If he did, he certainly did not mean to honor it. According to a Foreign Office interpreter, Dr. Paul Schmidt, Antonescu suggested a separate peace with the Allies during this visit (which followed Stalingrad) and Hitler may have made several promises of this kind to appease him. But all of the plans to rescue Jews were obstructed in every possible way and Antonescu's greed was frustrated. The German Foreign Office torpedoed every proposal.

When Killinger reported that a representative of the International Red Cross had asked Antonescu to permit Jews to leave Romania in Red Cross ships, the German Foreign Office refused safe conduct and repeated the Grand Mufti's argument that Palestine was an Arab country. Killinger then denied that Hitler had made any promise to release Jews; he said that his talk with Antonescu was "merely intended to investigate if the emigration of Jewish children could be approved."

The British, meanwhile, offered to accept nothing approximating Antonescu's figure of 75,000 Jews into Palestine, but a fraction of this number. They agreed to allow 5,000 above the 15,000 annual quota of immigrants to enter Palestine. Eichmann countered. He insisted that these 20,000 Jews be exchanged for 20,000 Germans interned in England and worked out elaborate arrangements for the exchange. The German Foreign Office then demanded that the Jews be sent not to Palestine but to England, in order to create anti-Semitism there. Eichmann advised the Foreign Office experts to negotiate with dispatch; the only place where 5,000 Jewish children could be found was the Lodz Ghetto, "which," he said, "would soon be liquidated under Himmler's direction."

The British offer was argued and dissected by rival Foreign Office experts until May 2, 1944. It was a trivial offer in the midst of a Jewish catastrophe. But it was not only the maze of German obstructions that doomed it. There were no ships to be had—at least from Allied sources—and new disappointments flowed from Allied rebuffs. A grotesque irony attaches to these rejections. While Jewish refugees were being trapped for death by an alleged lack of ships, the United States was using precious shipping space to carry to American shores German prisoners of war. Between 1942 and 1945, 371,683 Germans (and 50,273 Italians) were conveyed to the United States.[25]

A thousand thorns barred the way to Palestine and yet more Jews escaped through the Danube-Constanza-Istanbul-Palestine route than through any other at this time. But this was accomplished not through the efforts of the British or the Romanians or the Allies but of Palestine Jews, and their achievements were very modest.

With British permission, two Jewish parachutists in a British detachment had been dropped in Romania in the spring of 1944. Their parachutes were discovered and a large reward for their whereabouts led to a widespread search. The youths hid for many hours in a religious ritual bath, and then in a railroad car filled with crates of chickens. Finally they made their way to Bucharest and began clandestinely to search for boats. The Zionist leadership in the city helped to secure the *Mefkura* and organize a boatload of refugees. However, a German warship sank the boat and survivors were machine-gunned as they swam away from the blazing ship. Included among the victims were both parents of one of the parachutists. But the youths did not stop. They bribed Romanian officials, arranged effective interventions and worked doggedly to organize new boatloads. Possibly as many as 4,000 Jews were brought out of Romania this way.

Palestine did not provide Antonescu with a way out, but for the record, he had shown the world that Romania was not barring the way for Jews who could afford to leave the country. Later, in 1944, when military events required that he ingratiate himself with the Allies, he distorted the past record of Romanian persecution beyond recognition.

The Germans, meanwhile, had given up Romania as a copartner in the Nazi program for the "Final Solution." By January 1943, Himmler himself decided that the situation in Romania was hopeless; nothing could be done there anymore, he concluded. The S.S. and Police left the country. The former Romanian zealots and collaborators in the work of destroying Jews were now not only willing to sell them but most anxious to blot out all previous record of Jewish slaughter. Antonescu tried particularly to obliterate the past reality of the camps in Transnistria.

By late 1943, Jews in Transnistria who had survived earlier killings numbered about 70,000. They were still camp prisoners. A hint of a change in policy was presaged by government action in the summer of 1943, possibly influenced by Filderman's own deportation to Transnistria and his activity there.

Filderman had kept up a constant barrage of memoranda on Romanian officials until May 26, 1943, when he and his wife were themselves deported to Transnistria. His last memorandum protested the four-billion lei tax on the Jewish community. In a report to Antonescu, Lecca, the Commissar for Jewish Affairs, had demanded that Filderman be punished for sabotaging government decisions, and Antonescu had apparently yielded. A well-known Romanian journalist, B. Branisteanu, made the following entry in his diary after hearing about Filderman's deportation:

Dr. Filderman merely recorded, one after the other, a series of true statements. In fact his memorandum is a description of all the severe material suffering which has been inflicted on the Jews. The spiritual suffering can be seen behind the material suffering, even though Dr. Filderman does not stress it at all. But every man with a heart can understand it and feel it. Behind the confiscation of property, the taking over of enterprises . . . and behind the change-over of owners, clerks and workers can be glimpsed not only the material suffering but also the spiritual torment, the humiliation and the penury. . . . It is clear that one who reads the lines and between the lines of the memorandum, must account to himself for all these things, and if he caused them, he cannot feel at ease. In vain he may recall the arguments used to justify these things. . . . It is not Dr. Filderman's memorandum but man's conscience itself which is awakened . . . and evokes the thought—for what purpose?[26]

In Transnistria, Dr. Filderman did not cease his work. He personally carried out many social welfare projects, including a cooperative and a hospital, and sent many reports of actual conditions in the camps to the government. In the summer of 1943, Antonescu finally approved the return of disabled persons, widows, war orphans, soldiers, government pensioners, converted Jews and persons over seventy from Transnistria. Antonescu's decision was not only influenced by Filderman's appeals and second thoughts about his reputation, but many interventions especially those of the Papal Nuncio Cassulo. The Romanian Chief Rabbi Alexander Shafran, on March 1, 1943, had given the Nuncio a memorandum and photographic evidence concerning the terrible plight of orphans in Transnistria. Time and time again, the Nuncio had requested permission to visit the camps there; finally, in the spring of 1943, he was permitted to go. After his visit, he met with Lecca and received a promise from him to grant numerous improvements and changes, including the removal of all deportees from German-governed territory. Lecca informed Richter of this intervention and violated most of his promises. Large-scale rescue efforts were frustrated, but some Jews were returned.[26a]

Then in November 1943, Antonescu called a conference to discuss the evacuation of Transnistria and save the remaining Jews from destruction at the hands of the Germans. The Red Army had swept across the Dnieper and was making a rapid advance toward the Bug; Antonescu undoubtedly wanted some leverage for the coming trial with a victorious Soviet Union.

The extraordinary thing about the conference deliberations[27] was Antonescu's inability to recall why so many Jews had died in Transnistria. How was it, he asked, that he had so many dead Jews on his hands? Who was to blame? What measures could be taken quickly to save the remaining Jews? Antonescu suggested that a big sanitorium be established in Vijnita, a major Jewish center that had been dissolved. "Regarding the Jews who are in danger of being murdered by the Germans," he continued, "you have to take measures and warn the Germans that I don't tolerate this matter, because in the last analysis I will have a bad reputation for these terrible murders. Instead of letting this happen, we will take them away from there and bring them into this area [Vijnita]."

Antonescu feared for his reputation; he did not want to be thought of as a mass murderer. On the other hand, he had no intention of using any

Romanian resources to rehabilitate the Jews of Transnistria. They would have to be helped by other Jews and interested foreign countries. Another massive tax netting over a million dollars was collected from the Jews in Old Romania for food and clothing, and shipments from abroad were solicited. "We contribute nothing," Antonescu warned.

By December 1943, when the Russian advance had reached the Bug River, Mihai Antonescu saw Charles Kolb of the Swiss Red Cross and told him that the Romanian Government would repatriate all of the Jews in Transnistria who had survived. Kolb visited the reservation during the middle of the month, accompanied by a government mission. On his return, 1,800 Jewish orphans were received in Jassy and Kolb's report was published in Bucharest. He strongly recommended that fraudulent conversion of the Jewish charitable funds stop and that relief in kind be sent. However, funds contributed by Romanian Jews remained a lucrative source of revenue to Romanian officials until the Russian reconquest of Transnistria. Kolb also reported that there were about 7,000 Jewish orphans in Transnistria. The Romanian Government became interested in the possibility of a new Palestine project. It was possible to operate a small daily steamer from Constanza to Istanbul carrying a modest number of Jews within the White Paper quota. But the belligerents again refused the necessary safe conducts.

Vijnita could not accommodate all of the Jews in Transnistria, and the rather hazy evacuation plans of the November conference cannot be traced definitely, but by early February 1944, Antonescu permitted Jews to be withdrawn to southern Transnistria away from the front lines. Sometime in February or March 1944, the Romanian Minister to Turkey, Alexander Cretsianu, assured Ira Hirschmann, a representative of the United States War Refugee Board, that the Transnistria camps would be disbanded. President Roosevelt had sent Hirschmann on a mission to Turkey to negotiate on all possible levels for the rescue of Jews still left in Europe.

At his post in Ankara, Hirschmann had been receiving direct reports of the horrors of Transnistria. To be so close to a deathtrap and unable to do anything was unbearably frustrating. A hostile frontier, barbed wire, armed guards and airplane patrols blocked access to the camps. While the Allies bombarded the Ploesti oil fields and Bucharest, Hirschmann decided to bypass normal diplomatic procedure and try to make some sort of deal with the enemy.[28] Armed with a letter to Cretsianu from the prewar Romanian Minister to the United States, Hirschmann asked Gilbert Simond, a representative of the International Red Cross in Ankara, to arrange a meeting with the Romanian Minister. Such a meeting, of course, was risky. Hirschmann knew that he was under the surveillance of German and Japanese agents in Turkey and that he was being shadowed by the British as well. He had been given special official sanction to deal with the enemy but was warned that if these dealings were revealed, his usefulness would be over and he would have to be recalled. He himself had heard a propaganda broadcast from Berlin ask, "What is Jew Hirschmann doing in Ankara? Certainly, he can be up to no good."

But Cretsianu agreed to a secret rendezvous at Simond's house on the outskirts of Ankara. Despite his experience as a diplomat, Cretsianu was nervous. For an hour they spoke in generalities and Hirschmann searched for some clue, some reaction in Cretsianu that might shift the talk to Transnistria. It came finally after a casual mention of the Russians. Cretsianu said quite simply, "It's the Russians we fear, not the Americans."

Hirschmann answered with brutal directness: "Mr. Minister, you, Antonescu, and your families are going to be killed. The Russians will do it. I will offer you a visa for every member of your family in exchange for one simple act which will cost you nothing."

"And what is that?" he asked.

"Open the doors of the camps in Transnistria. These are your citizens, but if you don't want them, we will take them."

Cretsianu seemed genuinely surprised that an American President would send a personal representative to negotiate over some Jews. Hirschmann now felt more relaxed. He commented on Cretsianu's father's fine record as a diplomat in Washington and suggested that the son, too, might serve in the United States. "Why not get out of the war?" Hirschmann continued. "We will offer you an honorable peace and you will have the distinction of being the first Balkan country to break away from Hitler."

When Cretsianu asked Hirschmann precisely what he wanted, Hirschmann was ready with specific proposals: the disbanding of the camps in Transnistria, the immediate release of 5,000 children for debarkation to Palestine from Constanza and the end of all persecution of Jews in Romania. In return, Hirschmann promised the goodwill of the United States Government if Romania broke with the Nazis and four visas for Cretsianu and his family.

Within a week of the conference, Hirschmann again met Cretsianu who excitedly read him snatches of a telegram from Antonescu. All of Hirschmann's requests had been granted. As Hirschmann had promised, visas were made available for the Cretsianus at the American Embassy in Ankara. However, the overture for peace talks between Romania and the Allies never materialized. The rapid advance of the Red Army overtook these efforts of Romania to escape the Soviet grasp.

Aside from Hirschmann's visit, there were other developments that had aroused Jewish hopes in Romania. The Swedish press in January 1944 reported that the Antonescu government had concluded a "compensation agreement" with the Jewish Central Office in Bucharest. But the government proposals were actually only halfhearted and completely inadequate for the rescue of even a small portion of the Transnistria deportees. On January 20, the International Red Cross reported that Romania was prepared to permit 6,500 Jews originally from Bukovina and now in Transnistria to return to Romania. In February 1944, a London dispatch disclosed that the Romanian Government had informed Allied officials that it was prepared to release all Jews in Transnistria, to bring them to Bucharest, and then cooperate in transferring them on Romanian ships to any refuge selected by the Allies. However, the Allies were not willing to receive tens of thousands of refugees and the British Government clearly refused to permit their entry into Palestine.

In April, the War Refugee Board, in the wake of Hirschmann's talk, confidently announced that "more than 40,000 Jews interned by the Rumanians in Transnistria have been removed to comparative safety out of the way of retreating Nazi armies because of the pressure exerted by the War Refugee Board." It further reported that the deportees were being transferred to "an undisclosed port in Rumania" and that "as many as possible will be sent to Turkey and then to Palestine."

But this confidence proved to be unfounded. Only 300 refugees entered Palestine in March and an additional 99 in April. Many of the so-called repatriated Jews were redrafted for forced labor. The figure of 40,000 seems too high. When the Antonescu regime collapsed, the total number of Jewish repatriates in Romania was reliably estimated at from 15,000 to 17,000.[29]

These results owe nothing to Antonescu's misgivings about the deportations because of guilt. Events had forced his hand. A letter to a Jewish architect named Clejan, dated February 4, 1944, shows Antonescu as he really felt about the Jews of Transnistria: ". . . Despite the fact that I had decided on the expulsion of the Jews from Bessarabia and Bukovina, I was prevented from carrying this out by all sorts of interventions. I now regret that I did not adhere to my original intention, for it has been conclusively proved to me that among those who remain are the greatest number of enemies of the State."[29a] Had he had his way, all of the Jews of Transnistria would have disappeared.

Between March 15 and April 15, the Russian Army overran all of Transnistria and a curtain of silence was lowered. The number of Jewish survivors mentioned in the Hirschmann-Cretsianu talks was 48,000, but Meir Teich, a survivor of Transnistria, has estimated that 60,000 Jews in Transnistria survived the war—"a great miracle due partly to the cowardice and weakness of Rumanians who could be easily influenced and bought with bribes, and partly," according to Teich, "to the innate vitality of the Jewish communal organization and the tenacity of its leaders who organized resistance and knew how to exploit the weaknesses of the murderers."[30] Primitive and improvised means were used to create rudimentary communities out of uprooted, panic-ridden and destitute masses of Jews.

Teich was president of the Jewish community of Suceava in Bukovina at the time of the Romanian deportations into Transnistria. Suceava was the first of the Jewish communities in Bukovina to be deported. Teich was called to the Prefect on October 9, 1941, at six in the morning and told that half of the Jewish population had to leave within three hours for "resettlement" in the district of Mogilev-Podolski; the rest would follow the next day. Hand luggage, warm clothing and food were allowed to be taken along. At first, the seriously ill and the aged were permitted to remain behind, but this reprieve was soon annulled and these groups left on a third transport. At Ataki, Teich succeeded in buying some trucks at exorbitant prices from a sympathetic official he knew. In the former Jewish quarter of Ataki not a single house had been left whole. Decomposed corpses were scattered over the slushy streets in the crumbling ruins. Among the living there was great resentment each time a new transport arrived, for each new transport meant that more groups would be forcibly shipped across the Dniester, and crossing the Dniester meant certain death.

The Jews from Suceava soon saw for themselves what this crossing meant. They watched the Jews from Yedinets being chased "like a pack of wild dogs" to the ferry. They were emaciated skeletons, clad in rags, driven on by whips, and by gunshot. A few of the Jewish leaders in Ataki recommended active resistance since there seemed no alternative to death, but without arms and with utterly demoralized people, very few would have followed their lead. Instead, they made a stubborn and tenacious struggle for survival by older methods: interventions with officials, bribes and self-organization. Teich's assistant, an energetic physician, Dr. Abraham Reicher, made a trip to Mogilev alone and succeeded in obtaining access to two blocks of houses. Luggage, money and other valuables were smuggled across the river in order to be able to buy protection and barter for food. By judicious bribes, Dr. Reicher had succeeded in having the town of Shargorod, about 40 miles north of Mogilev, allocated for 900 Bukovinian Jews, including 500 from Suceava. While they made a brief stay in Mogilev, the Suceava group established a home for the aged and sick. They then made an orderly trek to Shargorod, just barely averting the rage of a Romanian official who was incensed at the "special" treatment of Teich's group.

At Shargorod, there were already about 2,500 Jews, 1,800 of whom were native. The rest had come from Bessarabia. The Bessarabians could have escaped to safety, but in order to avoid persecution as "Communists," they pretended to be native Jews. Their knowledge of the Ukrainian language helped them in this deception. The local Jews had already undergone occupation by Germans, Hungarians, Italians, and, most recently,

Germans again. Now, the Germans had appointed a Ukrainian-nationalist administration and the terror of the current Ukrainian militia was the most frightful regime of all. There were no Romanian military forces or gendarmerie in Shargorod, merely a few guards who protected deliveries of food and a Romanian praetor who had arrived recently. Friction between the Romanians and Ukrainians had already developed and the arrival of a new group of Jews created new conflicts. The Ukrainian praetor showed open hostility toward the Jews but the Romanian praetor, impressed by official Romanian signatures on papers, told Teich to put his group in Jewish houses and "wait and see." The local Jews had no room to spare, but they were helpful and generous. The death convoys had been cheated. The main problems were the vehemence of the Ukrainian militia and the procurement of food.

By day, the militiamen beat up Jews; by night, they robbed them. After much discussion, the Shargorod Ghetto decided to establish its own self-defense, a police force. Dr. Reicher won the Romanian praetor over to the idea and a Jewish police force eventually took over the complete security service of the town. The group was selected very carefully and served Jewish community interests completely. As to the food problem, the exorbitant prices of the most basic foods meant that only a very few could afford them; the others were in dire need. The Ghetto therefore decided to establish communal services: They set up their own bakery, a canteen for the poor which served soup to several hundred people, and a cooperative shop. Soon, however, new problems replaced the old.

By mid-November, a group of 900 new deportees arrived from Dorohoi, with orders to leave within a day. Nearly all of them were children and women, who were deported while their husbands were at work in Braila. The weather was bitter cold but no amount of pleading or pressure could prevail on the praetor to permit them to remain. When they set out for their forced march, many Ukrainian women who had come to the market crowded around the deportees and gave them food for the journey. In front of the praetor's office, they knelt down and blocked the road, raising their fists and crying out: "You Burjui, how can you be so hard against human beings!" The transport was returned and eventually all of the deportees remained. But the praetor warned Teich that there was now a great danger of epidemics.

It was true. This large influx of people resulted in unhygienic overcrowding everywhere. There was widespread lice infestation; water had to be drawn from contaminated wells; there were no toilets. Over 7,000 people lived in 337 houses and a few public buildings. Within three months almost the entire Ghetto, including the doctors, was struck down with typhus. The community was still unorganized and helpless.

This situation was duplicated in the whole Mogilev district. The communities then began to master their situation. A Grand Council of 25 was convened, made up of representatives of regional and urban communities; the ghettos did not maintain separate existences but joined together administratively. All available funds were pooled and the Council applied itself first to the problem of combating hunger and disease. The canteen raised the number of meals served to 1,500 and both the bakery and cooperative were expanded. Provisional hospitals were set up and disinfection stations established. A soap factory was built which covered local needs and also sold the surplus to the Ukrainian population. The power station and waterworks were repaired and the wells were cleaned. Streets were cleared daily and public toilets were built. Medical supplies eventually came from Jews in Bucharest and were centralized. A human community was forming.

Ukrainian Jews from Vinnitsa and Nemerov, fleeing from the Germans beyond the Bug River, were clandestinely absorbed into Shargorod and the Council later won the privilege of issuing their own identity cards.

One of the most serious problems facing the community was labor service. Officially, all of the Jews in Transnistria between twelve and sixty were required to work. The remuneration was to be paid in food coupons. But the Romanian Government never paid the coupons. At first, the workers tried to evade the call-ups, but police made house-to-house roundups and people were picked off the streets. Finally, deportation across the Bug was threatened. The community decided to consider the labor service a collectively imposed burden, to be shared by all. There was to be no favoritism. An impartial recruiting commission was appointed and three doctors established a comprehensive work classification scheme. No one qualified to do heavy work could buy himself off or offer substitutes. For light work, however, people could pay their way out. The money collected created a fund which provided well-paid jobs for volunteers. There was initial resistance to this rigorous plan, but the community eventually accepted it and was grateful for its success.

The most extensive work project in 1942 was the construction of a road from Murafa to the Jaroshinska railway station, a project which eventually benefited the Russians. About 1,500 Jewish workers completed the road in five months. They did not receive the full equivalent of wages to which they were entitled but between the government ration and the community canteen, they ate adequately and suffered no deaths or serious illnesses.

For 1943, plans were drawn up for other projects and approved by the Odessa Central Labor Office. But a menacing new official threatened the hard-won stability of Shargorod. He was the new Prefect, a Colonel Loghin, who had previously terrorized Jews in Tulchin and driven them across the Bug. Now he was in the Mogilev district. Loghin rescinded the new work plans of the community and together with Alexianu schemed to annihilate the Jews of the whole Mogilev district. Work brigades were sent outside the known territory and were subjected to brutal conditions and low food rations. Fortunately, other jobs in factories and farms in and near Shargorod were available and most of the community remained intact.

The child welfare department was one of the most important within the Council. During the first winter, there were many children who had lost their parents and had to beg their way from place to place, learning to hide during the murderous pogroms that swept the Ukraine, then picking themselves up and wandering again. Many of these children reached Shargorod wretched and derelict, physically wracked by hunger and fear. When they found Teich, they would often say, "*Ir must zain mein tate*" (You must be my father). By 1942 Shargorod had established an orphanage which sheltered, fed and educated several hundred children, many of whom eventually went to Palestine.

The Shargorod communal treasury was exhausted within the first few months of Ghetto existence and new sources of income had to be found. The small monthly subsidies from the Bucharest Assistance Committee, which began in January 1942, constituted less than one tenth of the community budget. Voluntary donations helped somewhat, but were not adequate. The Council imposed direct and indirect taxes and also took advantage of the then existing currency variations. For example, at the official rate of exchange of one mark to 60 lei, a wagonload of salt in Shargorod cost 1,500,000 lei (25,000 marks). But in Bucharest, it could be bought, transport included, for 30,000 lei (500 marks). The Bucharest Aid Committee was permitted to send to Shargorod shipments of salt, cloth and other goods which it could buy cheaply. The community was legally required to distribute all such shipments to the deportees, but it kept only the barest minimum and sold the rest to the Ukrainian population at prevailing market prices, thus obtaining badly needed cash. When the first wagonload of salt arrived, it was sold to a Ukrainian cooperative for 25,000 marks. This money was used to set up the orphanage and cover the community budget for one month.

In November 1943, by which time the Romanian Government was anxious to convince civilized world opinion that the deportees to Transnistria were not being maltreated, a large official commission visited the reservation in preparation for the projected Red Cross inspection. Teich was asked to work out a statute for all of the ghettos in Transnistria. He and several other Jewish leaders were taken to Odessa; for three days the men were confined in an insect-ridden cellar. It was explained later that since there was no longer a ghetto in Odessa, the Romanian police did not know where else Jews could be accommodated.

Charles Kolb of the Red Cross visited Shargorod on December 16. The Romanian officials at first tried to monitor his talks with Teich but Kolb protested and the two men were left alone. In his report to the Geneva committee, Kolb made special reference to the unusually good impression the community at Shargorod had made on him. He also credited the Romanian authorities with "help and understanding," later explaining to Teich that he was in the midst of a bitter fight for their consent to numerous relaxations and did not want to arouse their anger. The Danish inspection of Theresienstadt in the summer of 1943 similarly blunted its report of actual conditions in the "model ghetto."

As early as 1942, the Shargorod Ghetto had learned of the existence of a partisan organization nearby and the social welfare budget was disguised to enable small supportive funds to be diverted. In January 1943, the Romanian police discovered a secret partisan group operating in Zhmerinka; a list of its members included some of the leaders of the Ghetto. The men named were arrested and scheduled for court-martial and the Romanian military command began to check for new suspects. The leaders of the nearby Berschad Ghetto were denounced by an informer and subsequently tortured and shot, but the Shargorod leaders escaped from prison and returned to the Ghetto. They remained in hiding for some time, then joined a partisan unit, and maintained contact with the Ghetto.

The experience of the Shargorod Ghetto with the Russians was a mixture of contrary elements: at first there was a pervasive sense of solidarity and comfort; later this dissolved into shocking disappointment and disbelief. In January 1944, a man in the Romanian Secret Service called Teich on the phone and instructed him to send two Jewish policemen to the village of Ivashkowzi, a few miles away. He said that his gendarmes had run away from partisans there and that he wanted to know what was going on. Teich was hesitant; the whole thing could be a trap. But he wanted to make contact with an important partisan command post which he had heard was near Ivashkowzi. He agreed to go, saying that he would use the opportunity to visit an orphanage in the village.

Teich was given a pass for himself and two other men who, it turned out, were disguised partisans, and provided with a car which he filled with supplies. The trio easily passed the Ukrainian militia patrols, went on to the orphanage where the supplies were delivered, and then went to the partisan headquarters. There they were received by a Russian divisional general who had parachuted into the area shortly before. He assured Teich that he would defend the Ghetto in any crisis. Relieved to have this assurance, Teich returned to Shargorod and reported to the Romanian authorities that he had not seen any partisans or found anything suspicious. Swift changes in the life of the Ghetto now began.

In March 1944, after the disorderly German retreat from Uman, the Ghetto prepared for its own withdrawal. German troops and Hiwis (Ukrainian nationalist auxiliaries) passed through the town and the Ghetto experienced its most critical days. In retreat, the German Army was often most wantonly murderous. Jews hid in caves and cellars, and were able to save themselves. But a new crisis loomed. A sergeant in a special Romanian unit that followed the Germans was disarmed by the Jewish police and given some food. He admitted his intention to surrender to the Russians but warned that his unit had drenched the roads with Jewish blood and would surely finish off Shargorod too. Teich immediately notified the partisan command and by nightfall a Russian cavalry troop rode in and occupied the area. At a big meeting celebrating liberation, Teich was invited to attend and make a speech. Profuse thanks were conveyed to the Ghetto for its help to the partisans.

On March 21, Russian Army and partisan officers carried on investigations of the ghetto period and protocols were signed by the Ghetto administration, "turning over" the Ghetto to the Russians. On the following day, however, the officers left and were succeeded by Russian NKVD agents and counter-espionage personnel. The supplies of all of the Jewish institutions were immediately requisitioned and a shipment of clothing from Bucharest was confiscated. Teich was threatened with arrest unless he surrendered all property. He gave up everything except community records and funds, whereupon he was arrested and terrorized for four days. Everything finally had to be yielded up.

The Russian security forces then conducted house searches, arrests, deportations and recruitment into the Army and forced labor. A Russian police-instigated reign of terror left the community once more abandoned. The promises and assurances of the partisans evaporated. Some Jews fled during the following weeks, but most were cut off at Brichany, Balti and Cernauti and were repatriated a year later, in April 1945. Teich himself was imprisoned by the Russians at Vinnitsa for six months. He then went to Brichany, where he organized the repatriation of 3,000 Jews to Jassy.

Southeast of Mogilev, the Transnistria deportees faced even more severe trials and Teich estimates that only from 20 to 30 percent were saved as compared with 70 to 80 percent in the Mogilev district.

As the Russians drew closer, Jews were haunted by the fear that the Germans would murder them on the spot or transport them to death camps. But the danger passed. On March 30, the retreating German Army passed through Czernowitz, a scant 20 miles from Galicia, where Polish Jewry had been annihilated. Czernowitz contained 15,000 Jews; all miraculously survived the German retreat.

However, in May, the badge decree was introduced in Moldavia and a few months later, a forced-labor system was started. The German Commander in the area was unable to understand why so many Jews were still alive. By August, the situation for Romanian Jews became much more dangerous. The example of Hungary had just shown what might happen to almost half a million Jews when a satellite government thought of surrender. On August 23, Eichmann had already arrived from Budapest to deal with the Jews of the border towns, Arad and Timisoara—the Jews he had expected to deport in September 1942.

However, he had to return to Budapest quickly. The Soviet Army had broken through the German-Romanian lines in Bessarabia and Moldavia. On August 23, King Michael, who commanded the loyalty of the Romanian Army, invited both Antonescus to the palace and had them arrested. He announced that Romania was no longer at war with the Allies and ordered the Germans to remove their Army within three days. An hour after receiving this ultimatum, the Germans sent bombers over Bucharest. The consequences for Germany were disastrous. Romania, hoping to reconquer northern Transylvania, formally declared war on Germany on August 25.

Within a few weeks, twenty-six German divisions were destroyed by Soviet forces and their new Romanian allies. These events were decisive for now all of southeastern Europe was opened up to the Red Army.

Palestinian Jews, still struggling to organize boatloads of refugees, now had a new factor to reckon with. How would the Russians treat the remaining Jews in Romania? What would be their attitude toward emigration to Palestine?

Moshe Auerbach, no longer the unsophisticated farmer from Galil, arrived in Bucharest in October. He was armed with a press card from the Hebrew newspaper *Davar*, but he needed something more impressive. He also needed a device to test Communist intentions.

The Red Cross organization had practically collapsed in Romania; its pro-German sponsors had disappeared, its treasury was empty, and its staff was unpaid. Auerbach saw his opportunity. He went to the Red Cross offices, coolly announced that he was the new head, liberally paid off the old staff and moved in. The cover of the Red Cross was now to be used for the rescue of Jews. Auerbach applied to Russian officials for a collective passport for a new group of passengers and obtained it. The port authorities created no difficulties. He bought the *Taurus* and 900 Jews got through the straits without Turkish or British intervention.[31]

Romanian Jewish losses are considered "moderate" by the grotesque standards of the Holocaust. In 1947, the Jewish population living within the borders of prewar Romania was 428,000—the largest Jewish population of any country in Europe outside the Soviet Union. This total included 300,000 survivors of Old Romania and 128,000 from Transnistrian, Hungarian and German camps, as well as refugees from Bukovina and Bessarabia. Estimates of the number of Jews killed in enlarged Romania range from 200,000 to 530,000. At the very least figure, the losses are very heavy. Adjoining Romania, in Hungary, they were heavier still.

29 Hungary

In 1944, only one country in Europe—Hungary—stood intact against the cataclysmic destruction of Jews that had swept the rest of the continent. The 750,000 Jews of Hungary lived in an enclave of time and space, vaguely aware of the destruction of great communities of Jews elsewhere, protected merely by a fragile political boundary. The knowledge of the Holocaust—such as it was—proved of little use to Hungarian Jews, and the political boundary, a frail shelter, for once the German Army crossed the frontier and overran the country, disaster overtook them as well. Though the last to be attacked, Hungarian Jewry suffered the most concentrated and methodical deportation and extermination of any in Europe. For forty-six straight days, beginning May 15, with the end of the war in sight, and in full view of the whole world, the Nazi machine of death worked ceaselessly and wiped out almost 400,000 Jews.

Like Bulgaria and Romania, Hungary had joined the Axis to gain territory. With Germany's help a threefold expansion was accomplished in less than three years and the territory that Hungary had lost in 1919 was recovered from Yugoslavia, Slovakia and Romania. The fatal moment for Hungary was April 1941, when the Germans insisted on the passage of their troops through Hungary for the attack on Yugoslavia and on Hungarian help in the attack. The newly annexed areas (see map, p. 550) of southern Slovakia, Bachka, Carpatho-Ukraine and northern Transylvania contained 324,000 Jews. They were not considered Hungarian nationals and were thus subject to the first despoilments and deportations.

Hungary had neither the conviction nor the force of arms to oppose German demands, but neither did she always yield to them. Hungarian prime ministers during the six-year period, 1938–1944, ranged from men who served Germany first to those who collaborated reluctantly and tried to pull Hungary out of the German entanglement and out of the quicksand of a losing war. As prime ministers changed, the fate of Hungarian Jews changed also. The moderates slowed down the Holocaust; extremists hastened it.[1] As a consequence, Hungarian Jews experienced sharply defined cycles of hope and despair. Periods of calm alternated with outbursts of destruction. Undoubtedly, these sudden changes robbed the Jews of Hungary of any chance to realistically evaluate their predicament and depleted their psychological and physical energies. In the end, German pressure triumphed, even as German armies on every front were being cut to pieces.

After World War I, Hungary smarted under the loss of large territories and population blocs. Chaotic economic conditions were aggravated by the influx of hundreds of thousands of Hungarian refugees from the lost territories. Since Jews had been the staunchest partisans of the West that had dismembered the great Austro-Hungarian Empire and had inflicted harsh peace terms, resentment was immediately directed against them. Moreover, much of the odium of the abortive Communist dictatorship of Béla Kun attached to Jews as a group because of their large representation in the short-lived Kun regime (most of these were agents recruited from Hungarian prisoners of war and sent back to Hungary by the Soviet Government). A counterrevolution soon swept Kun out of power and London and Paris backed Admiral Miklós Horthy as Regent for a country without either a navy or a king. The Horthy regime started out with a blaze of pogroms that lasted for two years. Most of the leading Communists escaped to the Soviet Union leaving middle-class Jews, who had overwhelmingly opposed Kun, and Galician refugees as the chief targets of the persecution.

Conditions gradually settled down but below the surface of seeming stability lay the misery of the landless masses and the dangerous irredentism of many Hungarians. There was frequent defamation of Hungarian Jews in the press, platform and pulpit.

In the early 1930's there was a noticeable German infiltration into Hungary and the growth of Nazi groups. These strengthened the half-million German minority already resident in the country and revived the postwar anti-Semitic movement.

After Hitler's triumph in 1933, anti-Jewish movements gained ground in Hungary, as elsewhere in Europe. Leaders went to Germany, were subsidized, returned to Hungary and agitated. Budapest became the scene of anti-Jewish shouting and menacing crowds. Typically, the disorders spread to the universities. Jews were alarmed, but attributed the agitation to the territorial losses suffered by Hungary in 1919. Their first encounter with the swastika was to mark the beginning of an ordeal which, in its last horrifying stages, took them very far from discussions over the grave injustices of the Treaty of Trianon.

On Easter Sunday in 1933, a number of German students touring the Balkans attended a performance of the Passion Play in the village of

Budaörs, near Budapest. They wore brown shirts and the swastika emblem, and their faces were disfigured by livid dueling scars. After the play, they laid a huge wreath with a black swastika in the center and adorned with a large white flag. Crowds came to stare. The wreath was the first of its kind in Hungary. The German students swarmed into Hungarian villages, seeking fresh adherents to the Nazi Party. A colony of Nazi newspaper correspondents arrived soon afterward and settled in Budapest, followed by German "economic experts" and government representatives. Welt-dienst, a racist propaganda organization directed by Alfred Rosenberg, installed a well-known Hungarian professor of science in a committee called the Hungarian Committee for the Extermination of Noxious In-sects, from which he published a weekly and thundered Nazi broadsides.[2]

Within the next few years, German authorities issued veiled threats connecting realization of Hungary's territorial aims with the "Jewish ques-tion." The Germans strongly hinted that Hungary's inconsequential man-ner of handling this question was responsible for her failure to obtain a revision of the 1919 treaties. Blackmail against government officials was added to other forms of pressure. On March 11, 1938, the Anschluss brought Nazi Germany to the very doors of Hungary. Still serving as Re-gent, Horthy felt the smoking presence of the Nazi fire. The strongly pro-German prime minister, Béla Imrédy, decided to catch some of the Nazi heat to recharge Hungary's smoldering ambitions. Early in March he complained of the concentration of Jews in Budapest, their influence over national culture, their "undue part in the economic life of the country." They are, he concluded, "a continual source of irritation in the communal life of the nation."

Two months later, Hungary passed the first of three sets of anti-Jewish measures, each of them used as bargaining counters in discussions with Germany. The May 1938 measure, called a Bill for the More Effective Protection of Social and Economic Life, aimed at reducing Jewish eco-nomic activity and—much more significantly—at drastically defining a Jew. Under the terms of the bill, all Jews who had converted after July 31, 1919, were to be henceforth considered as Jews. Liberal and Socialist deputies spoke eloquently against the bill but failed to defeat it. The Catholic spokesman, Justin Cardinal Seredi, Prince Primate of Hungary, urged more protection for the baptized Jews but otherwise favored the bill. His reasoning was that, if the bill passed, "It would be possible to avoid emphasis being laid on the Jewish question and thus to allay anti-Semitism." Of this view, one historian of the period wrote: "This attitude turned out to be a fatal mistake. It was the stone that started the land-slide."[3]

The bill passed with the following preamble: "The expansion of the

Jews is as detrimental to the nation as it is dangerous; we must take steps to defend ourselves against their propagation; their relegation to the background is a national duty."

Hungary was to receive her territorial reward from a truncated Czechoslovakia in just six months.

Hitler began making stiffer demands on the Czechs during the summer of 1938. At the same time, he coaxed Hungary, Italy and Poland to agree to carve up the future spoils with him. On August 23, Hitler entertained Admiral Horthy and other members of the Hungarian Government aboard the liner *Patria* in Kiel Bay. If they wanted to get in on the Czech feast, he told them, they must hurry. "He who wants to sit at the table," he said, "must at least help in the kitchen."

For a time Hungary hesitated. Yugoslavia and Romania threatened to move against her if she attacked Czechoslovakia. The Hungarians, still hesitant, did not attack but threatened force and made demands for plebiscites in the territories claimed. After Munich, no longer uncertain, the Hungarians swooped down on the Czech province of Kosice. The population of Kosice included 42,000 Jews. Ribbentrop made the take-over official on November 2, 1938.

This territorial acquisition was followed by a second Hungarian anti-Jewish measure. This new bill, introduced on December 23, 1938, was designed to pinch back even further the definition of a converted Jew. Entitled a Bill to Restrict Jewish Penetration in the Public Affairs and Economic Life of the Country, the measure was acclaimed by pro-Nazi deputies as "the most beautiful Christmas present they could hope for." Jews struggled to defeat it. They invoked the principles of equality in the Hungarian Constitution and urged fundamental remedies for social and economic grievances so as not to make one group a target for abuse.

The appeal of the Jews, however, could not counterbalance the lure of new territorial gains, and was ignored. In March, Hungary received the eastern tip of Czechoslovakia, called Ruthenia, and the Magyar districts in Romania (northern Transylvania) and Yugoslavia, and in May the new bill was enacted into law.

The independence of the "Republic of Carpatho-Ukraine," created out of Ruthenia, was proclaimed on March 14 and lasted just twenty-four hours. Its appeal to Hitler for "protection" was in vain, for Hitler had already awarded this territory to Hungary. Horthy's excitement over this gift is expressed in a handwritten letter he addressed to Hitler on March 13:

Your Excellency:
    Heartfelt thanks! I cannot express how happy I am, for this headwater region Ruthenia is, for Hungary—I dislike using big words—a vital question. . . . We are tackling the matter with enthusiasm. The plans are

already laid. On Thursday, the 16th, a frontier incident will take place, to be followed Saturday by the big thrust.[4]

As things turned out, there was no need for an incident. Hungarian troops simply moved into Ruthenia, timing their entry with that of the Germans to the west. Well over 100,000 Jews lived among the Magyars in this newly acquired territory. In light of the terrors in store for them, their life as Hungarian loyalists in the former Czech Republic is grimly ironic: these Jews had actually suffered in Czechoslovakia for their pro-Magyar sentiments and their struggle to retain the Hungarian language in the face of Czech demands for assimilation into the new nation.

The first and second Hungarian anti-Jewish measures were the product of the Imrédy regime. At the end of March 1939, Imrédy was succeeded by Count Paul Teleki. A prime minister of moderate views, Teleki tried during the next two years to stave off German pressures. At first Hitler wanted his cooperation in the attack on Poland. However, in July 1939, Teleki wrote Hitler that "Hungary could not, on moral grounds, be in a position to take armed action against Poland." This letter threw Hitler into one of his customary rages. He reminded the Hungarian Foreign Minister that it had been through Germany's generosity that Czech territory was gained for Hungary. Poland, of course, presented no military problem for Hitler; no help from Hungary—or any other country—was needed, but passage through Hungary was expedient. When the war started, Teleki stood his ground and refused to grant German troops passage through Hungary to Poland. In December 1940, still trying to avoid being dragged into the Nazi military camp, Teleki framed a treaty of friendship with Yugoslavia. By this action, both governments hoped to support each other's neutrality even though both had joined the Tripartite Pact. The Yugoslav *coup d'état* of March 27, 1941, and a new Yugoslavian treaty with Russia inflamed Hitler to attack Yugoslavia. Again Teleki opposed German passage through Hungary, but this time Regent Horthy consented and the Hungarian General Staff, in which German influence was very strong, insisted. Foreign Minister László Bardossy pledged Hungary's participation in the German move and, unable to change the course of events, the overwrought Teleki committed suicide. In his farewell note to Horthy, Teleki wrote: "We have committed perjury. . . . We signed a pact of perpetual friendship with the South Slavs and yet, out of cowardice, we have now allied ourselves with criminals. . . . I accuse myself and consider myself guilty of not having been able to prevent the decisions taken by Your Excellency. It may well be that I shall render the nation à service by my death."[5]

But Teleki's suicide was fruitless. On the night that he took his life,

German motorized columns crossed the Hungarian frontier and pushed on to Yugoslavia. The following day, Horthy called on Bardossy to form a cabinet. Bardossy was a somewhat colorless career diplomat who at first opposed Hungary's entry into the war against Russia. But the pro-German inclinations of the General Command and the prospect of picking up the still "unredeemed" province of Bachka, which Hungary had lost to Yugoslavia following World War I, influenced the Government to take this momentous step.[6] There was another territorial morsel that tempted Hungary: southern Transylvania. Having already annexed northern Transylvania in 1940 at Romania's expense, the Hungarians were enticed into the war against Russia by the prospect of obtaining southern Transylvania.

For the Germans, Hungary's entry was crucial. Although her military contribution to the war effort was smaller than Romania's, Hungary's network of railways was vital for supplying German forces in Russia and the Balkans. Moreover, until the summer of 1944, Hungary was free from Allied bombing; she also produced valuable foodstuffs and equipment. Most important was Germany's need to hold the open Hungarian plain.

The Bardossy regime lasted just one year, from March 1941 to March 1942. Bardossy was anxious to win German approval through radical anti-Jewish measures. It was his government that was responsible for the first mass killings of Jews in Hungarian territory. In the late summer of 1941, as soon as Bardossy heard that the Germans intended deporting Jews to Russia, a Hungarian police decree ordered the expulsion of 22,000 "stateless" Jews from the Carpatho-Ukraine to Podolia into the teeth of the German *Einsatzgruppen*. The Germans at first were unprepared for the Hungarian action and protested that such a large movement would menace their communications, but the Hungarians would not allow the Jews to return, and by September 1, some 11,000 were killed by *Einsatzgruppen* assisted by Hungarian units. The massacre took place near Kamenetz-Podolsk on the banks of the Dniester. A second major killing took place in January 1942, when the Hungarian commanding officer in occupied Yugoslavia shot 4,000 Jews and 6,000 Serbs in the town of Novi Sad in Bachka. The general and his accomplices were later indicted but found sanctuary in Germany at Hitler's personal invitation. Massacres, however, did not represent "official" Hungarian policy and the massacre at Novi Sad was finally stopped by Horthy.

The Hungarian occupation of northern Transylvania was also oppressive. Jewish property was confiscated and Jews in government and public employment were dismissed from their jobs; 20,000 Jews from eighteen to forty-eight were conscripted into forced labor and sent to the Russian-German front. Like every other satellite government, Hungary saw in the German deportation plans an opportunity to despoil newly acquired Jewish populations. In 1944, the deportations from Transylvania were almost total. Out of 150,000 Jews, all but 30,000 perished.

Besides permitting the Kamenetz-Podolsk and Novi Sad massacres, Bardossy sponsored, in 1941, a new bill—the third—defining once again who was a Jew. The 1941 definition, the most severe of all, was adopted after an open controversy in the Upper House of the Hungarian Parliament and adversely affected almost 100,000 Hungarians who, even in Germany, would not have been considered "racial Jews." This definition surpassed the Nuremberg principle and was probably the most far-reaching of any of the definitions in Hitler-occupied Europe. In Germany, for example, a half-Jew who was not affiliated with the Jewish religion and who was married to a quarter-Jew, was considered a non-Jew; in Hungary, however, such a person was considered a Jew. In Germany, a person with a single Jewish grandparent was not considered a "racial Jew"; in Hungary, he was so considered if the half-Jewish parent was Jewish by definition and if the offspring was born after the law went into effect. In the eyes of the Church (Catholic, mainly; Calvinist and Lutheran, to a lesser extent), the chief victims of the law were converts, whose conversion the state was rejecting. This was a great blow to the churches, for they had already waged a battle for the converted Jews. For "full" Jews, the implications of the 1941 law were harsh: it appeared that the churches had cast them aside and would not fight to save them.[7]

Hungarian expropriation of Jewish property and restrictions on economic activity followed the first anti-Jewish measures in 1938, but officials took a long time to apply them. They had to move slowly in this field because the Jews of Hungary were not merely a middle class, but, to a large extent, the middle class in a country of abnormal economic features. In the Hungarian non-Jewish economy, at one extreme, there were poverty-stricken landless peasants, and, at the other, an elite landowning aristocracy. The somewhat faded upper class in Hungary had its typical class aversion to business activity, although they bought up Jewish land eagerly enough. At the same time, there were few non-Jewish Hungarians who had the capital or ability to operate enterprises which the Jews were forced to give up. So indispensable had Jews become to a viable Hungarian economy that the Germans themselves, at first displeased, had to resign themselves to the spread of "questionable Aryan firms" and a floundering group of new entrepreneurs. German firms had no enthusiasm for trading with them. Jews were slowly eased out of the professions, commerce, journalism, the schools and universities and public employment by quota regulations. Jewish participation in various fields was not to exceed certain percentages fixed by law—for example, 6 percent in trade, 6 percent in professions,

12 percent of the labor force in individual firms.[8] Such a statistical approach toward establishing the relative influence of Jews in various fields had already developed in the early years of the Horthy regime.

By the end of 1942, Jews had been ousted completely from certain fields and over 200,000 Jews lost their customary work. And yet in this process of economic attrition, a wedge of German self-interest lodged itself: the Germans needed Hungarian currency and could not afford to stop shipments to Jews who remained in business; nor could they boycott supplies to Jewish firms in armaments. For many thousands of Jews, however, the attrition brought hardships and in some cases there were last-ditch efforts to shift to allowable trades. In the large-scale displacement, however, there were too many applicants for the available jobs. The Hungarian Government closed this gap by resorting to forced-labor projects.

The basis for the Hungarian forced-labor system was a law under which Jews were liable for "auxiliary service" in the Hungarian Army as distinguished from "armed service." Soon after Hungary declared war against Russia, Jews were conscripted into labor gangs and were exposed to fearful atrocities. Of the 130,000 Jewish men up to the age of sixty who were ultimately drafted into these projects, 50,000 died from hunger, typhus and murder.[9]

Jews in the Hungarian labor gangs worked with army engineers building roads and bridges and clearing mines under penal conditions often as inhuman as those in the German concentration camps. When the war broke out, tens of thousands of conscripts, insufficiently clothed, were sent to frontier districts occupied by the Hungarian troops. Most of these early contingents perished. Among the "Jewish troops" were the lame, half-blind and mentally disturbed. Hangings, shootings and cruel beatings were commonplace. Sometimes there were mass killings, as in the military hospital near Korasten where 500 conscripts lay ill with typhoid fever. One night the hospital was ringed with machine guns and set on fire. Those who attempted to flee were shot down. There are also reports of so-called shooting parties in which Jews would be forced to climb trees and jump like monkeys from branch to branch. If they fell, they were pierced with bayonets; if they jumped too slowly they were driven by guards wielding whips and sticks. Sometimes they were suspended from the trees by their tied wrists. If they fainted they would be drenched with cold water and left to freeze in the Russian cold. Other conscripts were chained and thrown bodily into campfires.

At first the worst excesses occurred in the frontier areas where the influence of the German S.S. was strongest. Hungarian territory proper was spared these horrors for a while. Indeed, the accounts of forced-labor conditions in Russia were scarcely believed. However, the pogrom of January 6, 1942, carried out in Novi Sad showed that Hungarian troops as well as

German could slaughter Jews. The sadism of some Hungarian commanders was frightful: Jews were buried alive or were forced to parade naked in frigid weather. The Germans, for their part, seeing Jews on the front lines in Hungarian uniforms—the uniforms of an ally—but identified by yellow arm bands, shot them by the thousands. Some units, however, survived Russian capture.

In the winter of 1942–43, there were 40,000 Jews working near the Don and in other parts of the Ukraine laying and clearing mines and digging tanktraps. They had been robbed of their winter clothing and had to work in summer shirts and trousers. In the first breakthrough by the Russians near the Don on January 13, 1943, thousands were taken prisoner by the Russians; some Jews probably survived.[10] Moreover, the very real labor shortages of both the Germans and Hungarians forced both to forgo completely destructive solutions in Hungary. The Second Hungarian Army in Russia, for example, maintained a technical company for repair and demolition of public utilities. Its personnel was 75 percent Jewish. In Germany, Albert Speer, Reich Minister of Armaments and head of *Organization Todt*, the German military construction agency, tried to integrate the Hungarian Jewish Labor Service into his industrial machine. Early in 1943, he asked the Foreign Office for 10,000 Hungarian Jews to work the Serbian copper mines at Bor. All Jews had been killed in Serbia the previous year and no other labor was available in the territory. This time, a request for Jewish labor was allowed by Himmler. The Hungarians were partially cooperative: they agreed to deliver 3,000 Jews in exchange for 100 tons of copper per month. By September 1944, there were 6,000 Jews working in the mines. Only part of the group survived, however. When the camp was liquidated, 2,000 of the workers were marched for miles without food or water to Cservenka, under Hungarian jurisdiction, and shot by S.S. forces. One survivor, Zalman Teichman crawled out of the death pit and recorded the last days of the 2,000 men.[11]

The Hungarian Minister of Defense, Vilmos Nagy, was sympathetic to the plight of the Jews in forced-labor gangs and went to the front personally in the winter of 1942 to investigate conditions. His recommendations, however, were sabotaged by local commanders and he was soon removed from office.

The organization of the Jewish labor companies and the early massacres had taken place under the Bardossy regime. In March 1942 Horthy dismissed Bardossy because of a disagreement regarding the succession of his son Stephen as Regent. The new premier was Count Nicholas Kállay, a member of a very old Hungarian family, a strong nationalist who disliked the Germans and a political moderate. Politically, Hungary still possessed parliamentary institutions, though of a very limited character. The largest party, the government "Life Party" (M.E.P.) had a left, center and right, and was sharply divided on both home and foreign policy. Its extreme right was strongly pro-Axis and wished to suppress the parties of the left, especially the social democrats. The left wing of M.E.P., though definitely conservative in outlook, wished to preserve the existing degree of political freedom and favored resistance to German demands. On the whole, it was pro-British and aimed to bring Hungary out of the war.[12]

Kállay's regime coincided with the period of the most drastic measures against Europe's Jews. Virtually every country in Europe during this time, whether occupied or controlled by the Nazis, had delivered several million Jews to the transports and gas chambers. But not Hungary. Kállay yielded in small ways: he intensified expropriations and enlarged the labor companies, but he refused to deport a single Hungarian Jew. When finally he was deposed, Hungary's resistance crumbled.

Soon after Kállay took office in March 1942, Jews from Austria, Slovakia and Poland streamed into Hungary, and in subsequent months Hungary was the goal of many refugees fleeing roundups and deportations. These Jews were not welcomed or assisted by the government, but they were not turned over to the Germans. To a large extent, this attitude stemmed not from humanitarian considerations so much as jealously guarded sovereignty. The Kállay government was also extremely touchy about threats against Hungarian Jews elsewhere in Europe especially if other Jews seemed less vulnerable. For example, in the summer of 1942, when Hungarian Jews in France were required to wear the Jewish star, Hungary wanted to make sure that Italian and Romanian Jews would also be affected. At the same time, Hungary also wanted to share in the confiscations of Hungarian Jewish property in Europe. German officials reassured the Hungarian Minister to Berlin, Döme Sztójay, that all Jews in occupied countries were getting the same treatment. What was of overriding importance to the Germans, however, was the evacuation of these Jews to the East; in this process, the Germans naturally wanted to include Hungary. Soon the pressure was on.

In subsequent talks between Sztójay and Martin Luther, head of the German Foreign Office department Deutschland, Sztójay, who prided himself on his anti-Semitism, and who later became a vigorously pro-German Prime Minister, conveyed some of Kállay's misgivings about proposed evacuation measures. Kállay probably knew that during this period the Slovak Government had failed to obtain permission to send an inspector to the "Jewish reserve" in Poland. Sztójay reported that Kállay was disturbed by certain rumors regarding the treatment of Jews in the East and did not want to be "accused of having exposed the Hungarian Jews to misery or worse after their evacuation." Was a continuous existence in the East possible for them, he asked, after their evacuation? Luther assured Sztójay that the Hungarian Jews would at first be employed on road building and then settled in a Jewish reserve. There was no need for any un-easiness, he observed, but the German Government was insistent about evacuating all Hungarian Jews from occupied Europe and from Hungary itself by December 31, 1942. This satisfied Sztójay, but not Kállay.

A number of informal meetings with Hungarians who were critical of their country's "insufficient" anti-Jewish measures had led German officials to anticipate early compliance with their demands. One discussion of this type involved Kállay's personal secretary and Dieter Wisliceny, the S.S. adviser in Bratislava. But the expected reply from Kállay himself after the Luther-Sztójay talks never came. The true position of the government was revealed by the Prime Minister's reply to a demand from a deputy in the Hungarian Parliament that Jews be incarcerated in labor camps and ghet-tos. To this, Kállay simply said: such incarceration "cannot be carried out within the existing framework of legal norms."

The Germans did not give up; their pressures continued. But Kállay held firm. Finally, on December 14, he ordered Sztójay not only to reject Luther's "Jewish reserve" proposal, but to ask for an extension of the time limit for repatriating Hungarian Jews from German-held territory. In Janu-ary 1943, he abolished an Office for Jewish Affairs that had been created. Luther sternly took Sztójay to task. Hungary was becoming a rebellious satellite state, but Germany could not afford to take countermeasures at this time. Early in February the Germans suffered a disaster at Stalingrad. Clearly, however, a high-level understanding between Hungary and Ger-many was needed.

On April 17, 1943, the whole question of German demands against Hungary's Jews was reopened by Hitler and Ribbentrop in talks with the Hungarian Regent, Admiral Horthy. The three men conferred alone, at-tended only by the official interpreter, Dr. Paul Schmidt, in Klessheim Castle, near Salzburg. Hitler began the discussion by claiming that the English were suffering greater losses than the Germans during the air raids. Furthermore, he boasted, severe German measures had put a stop to all crimes during the blackouts. He then described to Horthy German rationing measures, which allegedly stopped the black market. When Horthy remarked that Hungary could not master these problems, Hitler answered that the Jews were at fault. When Horthy countered by asking what he should do with Hungary's Jews, now that the base of their eco-nomic existence had been removed—he could not kill them off—Ribben-trop declared that the Jews either had to be annihilated or taken to concentration camps. There was no other possibility. Thereupon, Hitler delivered a monologue, recorded in the minutes of Dr. Schmidt:

> Where the Jews were left to themselves, as for instance, in Poland, the most terrible misery and decay prevailed. They are just pure parasites. In Poland this state of affairs has been fundamentally cleared up. If the Jews

there did not want to work, they were shot. If they could not work, they had to succumb. They had to be treated like tuberculosis bacilli, with which a healthy body may become infected. This was not cruel, if one remembers that even innocent creatures of nature, such as hares and deer, have to be killed, so that no harm is caused by them. Why should the beasts who wanted to bring us Bolshevism be spared more. Nations that did not rid themselves of Jews perished. One of the most famous examples is the downfall of that people who were once so proud, the Persians, who today lead a pitiful existence as Armenians.[13]

These minutes, Hitler's only recorded admission of the exterminations in Poland, were an expression of his extreme frustration with Hungary's uncertain loyalty. Hitler hid nothing in this outburst. He had apparently overrated the anti-Semitism of Hungarian leaders and had counted on their going the limit, whereas the Kállay government stood at the brink. Kállay also began to look cautiously for an escape from the declining Axis fortunes. Nor was he alone. By the summer of 1943, most members of the Hungarian Government longed for an opportunity to get out of the war. The surrender of Italy at first raised their hopes, but the German occupation of Italy dashed them. Their depression was further compounded by the Russian advance. Kállay was willing to surrender to the Western powers, but not to the Red Army. The Hungarian dislike of Russia was reinforced by memories of the 1918 revolution, the Communist regime of Béla Kun and fears for the fundamentally weak and outdated Hungarian social system. During the summer of 1943, Kállay made contact with the representatives of the Western Allies in several neutral capitals. At this time he wanted to withdraw all Hungarian forces to the 1941 frontiers—with Germany's consent—and to withdraw from the war, hoping that the Russians would advance against Germany through Poland and bypass Hungary. Above all, he wanted to remain neutral until the Western powers were in a position to defend Hungary from German vengeance. In his talks with the West, he persistently opposed the presence of Russian troops on Hungarian soil.

But the Western powers were firm. They refused to shut out their ally and make a separate peace with Hungary. This led Kállay to hesitate. The ghost of Galeazzo Ciano and other "traitors to the Axis" who had been executed loomed before him. Meanwhile, German mistrust of him grew. Gloomy reports had been filed in Berlin by observers of the Hungarian scene following the Klessheim conference. Dr. Edmund Veesenmayer, the Foreign Office troubleshooter who later became Minister to Hungary, wrote to Himmler that Horthy's only attachment to Germany was his mortal fear of Bolshevism, and that the Hungarian Government welcomed Jewish refugees in the belief that they would protect the country from Allied air attacks. S.S. agents reported that the Hungarians would not consent to the liquidation of the Jews during the war, and in ingratiating themselves with the "Anglo-Americans" would give the Jews "the best possible treatment." The Germans viewed the Kállay regime as the great stumbling block to closer German-Hungarian relations.

Kállay, meanwhile, was under great pressure from Sztójay to dissolve the Jewish obstacle and avoid further German intervention. Simultaneous with Hitler's stormy interview with Horthy, Ribbentrop raised the Jewish question with Sztójay. Ribbentrop reviewed all of the reasons that had led Germany to decide on a radical solution of the Jewish problem while the war continued. Hitler, he said, was bitterly disappointed over Hungary's lack of cooperation. On April 23, 1943, Sztójay wrote to Kállay and warned him of an expected intervention: "National Socialism abhors and despises the Jews and considers them to be its greatest and most inveterate enemy with whom it is engaged in a life and death struggle." It had been established, Sztójay added, that the Jews were actively serving the enemy, acting as spies, committing acts of sabotage, undermining the people's morale and jeopardizing to the utmost the prosecution of the war. Hitler therefore decreed that by the summer of 1943, all Jews of Germany and German-occupied countries were to be moved to the Eastern, i.e., Russian territories. "Sooner or later," Sztójay continued, "a positive German intervention in Hungary in this matter must be expected."[14]

Meanwhile, right-wing movements in Hungary continued their agitation. As German armies suffered defeats, they accused Hungarian Jews of engaging in activities "detrimental to the interests of the country." But Kállay did not yield. He removed the last vestige of doubt about his position in a public speech at the end of May. Kállay said:

> In Hungary live more Jews than in all of western Europe. . . . It is self-explanatory that we must attempt to solve this problem; hence the necessity for temporary measures and an appropriate regulation. The final solution, however, can be none other than the complete resettlement of Jewry. But I cannot bring myself to keep this problem on the agenda so long as the basic prerequisite of the solution, namely, the answer to the question—where the Jews are to be resettled—is not given. Hungary will never deviate from those precepts of humanity which, in the course of its history, it has always maintained in racial and religious questions.[15]

The Germans were now convinced that Kállay would have to go. Once again he had resisted their pressure and turned away from the extreme course of destroying Hungary's Jews. The Nazis needed something more drastic than diplomatic pressure in Hungary.

Moreover, the Hungarian Government was easing out of the war by the end of the summer of 1943. Hungarian troops were used very sparingly on the Eastern Front and war production lagged. Feelers to the Allies were repeated. On August 19, Kállay broadcast another speech—this time on Hungary's need for peace—which threatened Germany with exposure to a direct Allied advance across the Hungarian plain. The Kállay government was also beginning to make important contacts with the Budapest Zionist Relief Committee, the Vaadah, which was regarded as a bridge for negotiating with the Allies—the same type of bridge that Himmler himself was to use later.[16]

The retreating Germans had to exploit two forces against Hungary's dwindling interest in the Axis cause: the enfeeblement and near senility of Regent Horthy, who had a dread fear of Russia, and the existence of an anti-Kállay movement, the small native *Nyilas*, or Arrow Cross Fascists. Contact with anti-Kállay forces was made by Veesenmayer during his second trip to Budapest, in December 1943. The following month, an S.D. report notified Berlin that Horthy was about to demand the return of the Hungarian troops from the Eastern Front. German Security Police quickly drew up lists of "acceptable" Hungarian Cabinet members and planned alternative methods of wrecking the Kállay government.

On March 15, 1944, just three weeks before the first Russian patrols reached the Hungarian plain, Horthy was again called to Klessheim Castle on the pretext of discussing with Hitler the withdrawal of Hungarian forces from Russia. Once there, however, he was faced with an ultimatum from Hitler under conditions of virtual arrest. While he was detained, the Nazis staged a fake air raid and cut the telephone line to Budapest. The old man had to face another Hitler barrage. Kállay had been in touch with the British, Hitler shouted, and would have to be dismissed. Hungary would have to choose between a German military occupation and a German-approved government, and definite steps would have to be taken to liquidate the Jewish problem once and for all.

Horthy weakly submitted to a German-approved government, but this was mere window dressing, for by the time Horthy returned to Budapest on March 19, an army of German officials representing the Foreign Office, the S.S. and Police, the Army and private industry had swarmed into Hungary and taken up positions in numerous offices throughout the country. Prominent liberals and left-wing politicians had been arrested. On his return, Horthy also learned that during his twenty-four-hour detention, a German military task force had seized the airports of Budapest. German motorized divisions had entered from all sides. Another shock awaited Horthy in Budapest: a special sleeping car had been attached to his train carrying the new German Minister and General Plentipotentiary, Veesenmayer, who was now in Hungary to give orders to the Hungarian Government.

Horthy gave a report of his visit to the Crown Council, adding bitterly that he was accused of the crime of not having carried out Hitler's wishes on the Jewish question and of "not having permitted the Jews to be massacred." Kállay fled to Turkey. Horthy then began to negotiate with

Veesenmayer about the appointment of a new Prime Minister. Veesenmayer proposed Béla Imrédy, the pro-Fascist Prime Minister in 1938–39; Horthy nominated the Hungarian Minister to Berlin, Sztójay, and to him fell the appointment. Sztójay was like putty in the hands of the Nazis and his chief Cabinet officers, most of them from the Arrow Cross movement, took up their new tasks eagerly.

Veesenmayer had extensive powers to supervise and expedite a change of government and "keep the old man [Horthy] properly isolated." He was an S.S. colonel and had successfully performed several missions as Himmler's liaison with other ministries. In Hungary, he claimed to be the supreme coordinator of all German agencies within the country. His view was that the liquidation of the Jewish problem was "a prerequisite for involving Hungary in the war." But it was Adolf Eichmann, together with a heavy battery of deportation specialists that had converged on Budapest, who was to dominate events in Hungary in the subsequent months.

In the middle of March, while Horthy was being numbed by Hitler's verbal lashing, Eichmann was assembling at the Mauthausen camp in Austria the most devastating unit of Jewish killing specialists in the history of the Holocaust. He had called together Dieter Wisliceny from Slovakia and Greece, Theodor Dannecker from France and Bulgaria, Alois Brunner from Paris, Hermann Krumey from Vienna and Siegfried Seidl from Theresienstadt and Bergen-Belsen. These men and their assistants came to Budapest at the end of March and formed the *Sondereinsatzkommando* Eichmann, the Eichmann Special Operation Unit. Their work elsewhere in Europe was finished; now all of their experience could be concentrated on Hungary.

The visible physical move to Hungary of what had once been a highly secret department exposes the immense importance of the destruction of Hungarian Jewry in Hitler's mind and the single-mindedness of his purpose. Nothing was now to be concealed from the world; the camouflage was unmasked. Eichmann himself, for the first time in his career, was to work in the open and become a public personality. The once obscure and cautious deskman had now become a cynical, hard-drinking, luxury-loving Nazi satrap operating out of the Majestic Hotel, one of the best in Budapest. His ostentatious standard of living, however, had not changed his function. While hunting down the last Jewish prey left in Europe, he was, in his own words, a "bloodhound." After hoodwinking the Jewish leadership into thinking Hungarian Jews would be safe from deportations, with lightning speed, he set in motion the destruction machinery that had been perfected over the past four years. Eichmann's presence in Hungary exposed Hitler's real motive in blackmailing Horthy: it was not so much to keep Hungary in the war that he had threatened Horthy, for the fast

Russian advance was making Hungary's participation wholly academic. It was to eliminate the Jews of Hungary. Had Horthy been younger and firmer, he might have staved off Hitler's blackmail and Eichmann's pursuit of every living Hungarian Jew, and thus saved hundred of thousands of lives.

Eichmann's first thrust was toward the leadership of the Jewish community. On Sunday morning, March 19, the leaders of Budapest Jewry met in the Sip Street premises of the Jewish Council. Tension and anxiety were in the air. The members already knew that German troops had crossed the frontier at many points and had occupied the capital. In the middle of the meeting, three small yellow cars bearing the letters "Pol" on their license plates drew up before the building. A message was given to the committee saying that the German police would return the following day at 10 A.M. to meet with the Council. When the Council reported this episode to the Hungarian Government its advice was blunt: "Carry out any orders you may receive from the Germans."

The Jewish leaders knew about the fate of the rest of Europe in greater or lesser detail. They knew what had been happening "in the East" and what they themselves might be exposed to. Eichmann now had to dispel these fears and create the impression that Hungarian Jews would be treated differently. He accomplished this with great cunning and deception, and without losing any time.

The Jewish leaders came to the Council office as instructed and waited apprehensively for several hours. Some, fearing they would be arrested, brought small suitcases; others brought their families. Finally, a small delegation from the Eichmann commando appeared, headed by Krumey, a lean dyspeptic Berlin merchant whose charming manner concealed savage destructive power. Krumey addressed the president of the Budapest Jewish Council, Dr. Samuel Stern respectfully. When he noticed the luggage, he politely reassured the members that no one would be arrested and that any Jews who had been arrested the previous night would be released. Certain restrictions would be imposed, he added, but there would be no deportations. Krumey then told the Jewish representatives that a new Judenrat would have to be formed and two lists drawn up: one listing all Jewish institutions and their heads, and the other itemizing the real estate still owned by the Jews in Budapest. The leaders were reminded to stay in town and not to change their addresses. They were then dismissed.

The following day, Krumey and Wisliceny again met with the Jewish representatives and ordered them to evacuate schools, synagogues and other buildings of the Jewish community. They were also ordered to provide 600 blankets and 300 mattresses. "If our demand is not met," they were told, "we will have the responsible leaders shot. . . . If it is possible to execute some 10,000 Jews within ten minutes, a demand of this nature can be met within an hour and a half."[17] By 5 P.M., 600 blankets were taken from Jews conscripted into labor service and 300 mattresses were removed from Jewish hospitals. Wisliceny then assured them that "everything goes on as usual."

Shocked by the German tactics, Jews again protested to the Hungarian authorities. The official answer this time came from the Minister of Justice who said: "The armed power maintaining the sovereignty of the Hungarian State has collapsed. The Regent is a prisoner and two armed German grenadiers are standing outside his door."[18]

During the next few days, the Nazis mixed their brutality with just enough politeness to fool the frightened, credulous Jewish leaders. There were requests for more blankets, typewriters, women's lingerie, kitchen equipment, brooms, autos, radios, glassware, original Watteaus and cologne. Eichmann was heard expressing an interest in Jewish culture and visited the Jewish Museum and the Jewish Library. On March 31, he invited the Council to attend a conference at his hotel. At that meeting, Eichmann gave one of the most successful performances of his career, virtually hypnotizing the leaders, and through them, most of Hungarian Jewry.

First, he said, there was some bad news. Jewish labor battalions would have to be enlarged to increase the output of Hungary's war industries, but the workers would be treated well and would probably be allowed to go home each night. Then he announced that the new Central Council would have jurisdiction over all of the Jews in Hungary, including the converted Jews, (who were "more wealthy and should be made to pay more") and would channel all German orders. It would centralize all information and act as a financial and taxing agency. The Jews of Hungary had nothing to fear from the Germans, Eichmann concluded, unless they refused to cooperate. But no one was to attempt to mislead him, he warned, for in these matters he had had a great deal of experience. However, all regulations were to remain in force for the duration of the war only. The measures against the Jews were only "temporary," and after the war, the Germans would again become *gemütlich* ("nice"), he said. Furthermore, he wished to safeguard Jews from any individual atrocity and asked that any incidents of this nature be reported to him at once— even if the person involved was a German soldier. Immediate and drastic action was promised.[18a]

An erratic pattern of German activity followed which the Jewish leaders could not realistically appraise. The Orthodox Synagogue on Kazincsy Street was converted into a stable. Well-known Jews were arrested and interned at the College for Rabbis, which became a Gestapo prison. Then, unexpectedly, the Gestapo intervened and released some of the prisoners. Some Nazi promises were kept. There were runs on banks but German officials reassured Jews that they would suffer no loss and urged them to keep their deposits intact. Moreover, the provinces were not threatened for the time being and the absence of calls for help from that quarter seems to have lulled the Jewish leadership in Budapest. Meanwhile, valuable time was being lost as the specious German promises were half-believed. Council leaders began to think in terms of dangerous illusions: if they obeyed Eichmann's orders, the Hungarian Jews would be safe. The disappearance of European Jewry would stop at Hungary's borders. Above all, the imminence of a German defeat nourished these illusions.

A new Eichman-approved Central Council of Hungarian Jews was formed. Again, Samuel Stern was at the head. This new organization, called the Association of Jewish Communities, urged all Jewish groups throughout Hungary to obey its instructions. Once the Association was secured as a German tool, Veesenmayer drove the Hungarian Government to intensify anti-Jewish measures and continue where the Bardossy regime had stopped. Hungarian cooperation was obtained through an agreement between Veesenmayer and Sztójay, concluded in Eichmann's presence. The star decree, for which the Germans had waited so long, was passed on March 29. This was followed by restrictions on the movement of Jews and by extreme economic measures. Jewish stores and offices were closed down, the Minister of Justice justifying this as a protective measure against looting. Automobiles, radios, books, art objects and articles of clothing owned by Jews were confiscated. Telephones were removed. The Food Ministry issued orders which deprived Jews of all butter, eggs, rice, and restricted the purchase of sugar, fat, milk and meat. Jewish deposits were then frozen and Jews were not permitted to possess more than 3,000 pengö ($720) in ready cash. The possession of arms was forbidden. Jewish libraries and archives were confiscated. The publication of works by Jewish authors was banned.

Protests against these measures poured in. László Baky, State Secretary in the Hungarian Ministry of the Interior in charge of the Hungarian police, and one of the most fanatical of the Arrow Cross members, made official answer to them: "It is the patriotic duty," he declared, "of every Hungarian who knows or learns of any member of the Jewish population attempting to disregard or disobey or contravene these regulations, to report the fact immediately to the nearest police station." After the war, it was revealed that Baky was Himmler's confidential agent in Hungary and had played a leading role in preparing the way for the events of March 19. He also compiled vital data which enabled the Germans to destroy the left-wing political front immediately after the German entry into Hungary.

The decree ordering all Jews to wear the Jewish star drew the churches into the Nazi-Hungarian events of 1944. In contrast with other countries where there were several exempted groups, Hungarian anti-Jewish legislation exempted only Jewish World War veterans. Tens of thousands of Christianized Jews, including some clergymen, were forced to wear the star. Cardinal Seredi reacted immediately. He wrote to Sztójay declaring that he would forbid his clergymen to wear the star. Within a few days, the Prime Minister backed down and clergymen, wives and children of exempted veterans, widows and orphans of World War II soldiers, and Jews in mixed marriages were put in the exempt category. But Cardinal Seredi demanded more, which, for full Jews, was equivalent to abandonment.

He wanted all converted Jews protected. "It is not right," he wrote to Sztójay, "that Jews should have a particular power over Christian priests or monks, or over Christians in general. . . . Christians should no longer be obliged to wear the Star of David, for this is not the emblem of the Christians but of the Jewish faith. The exhibition of this sign by Christians is tantamount to apostasy." He said further that the Jewish decrees filled him with "deep sorrow and grave anguish" and urged that they be amended.[19] This letter, however, was not published. Sztójay rejected the Cardinal's request to exempt all converts from wearing the star and this refusal exposed at least 100,000 converted Jews to deportation. Jews appealed to the Directorate of the Reformed Church to oppose the star decree, but like Cardinal Seredi, the religious leader of the Reformed Church, Bishop László Ravasz, mainly protested the stigmatization of converted Jews. Sztójay finally conceded that converted Jews could wear the cross as well as the Star of David, a fitting irony for the times.

A hint of future ghettoization measures came after a heavy air raid by American planes on April 3, 1944. Eichmann ordered the Jewish Council to evacuate 500 apartments of Jews for "homeless air-raid victims." The evacuation was to take place within twenty-four hours and furniture, clothing and other essentials were to be left in the apartments. When the evacuation was completed, keys to 2,500 apartments were turned over, 80 percent of which were never used. This episode caused the first popular outcry against the Council, with hundreds of Jews demonstrating outside the Council building.[20] Throughout the rest of April there was a massive wave of arrests of Jews who had moved without permission. By the end of the month over 8,000 had been arrested, most of them charged with moving in and out of Budapest without permission. The arrests were made by the Eichmann commando and the Hungarian police. Those arrested were among the first Jewish deportees from Hungary.

Meanwhile, the whole of Ruthenia, upper Hungary and northern Transylvania were declared operational territory at the request of the German

General Staff and by early April, military authorities began the rounding up of Jews in these annexed provinces into ghettos.[21] A coordinated plan for the swift disposal of the Jews of Hungary was then mapped out by Eichmann's unit and László Endre who was State Secretary in charge of Jewish affairs in the Hungarian Department of the Interior.

Endre had formed a close friendship with Eichmann, with whom he shared three traits: a passion for horses, a love for liquor, and an intense hatred of Jews. Eichmann was often a guest at Endre's estate outside Budapest, and wild orgies there were widely gossiped about.

The strategy of this team was to fool the Jews as long as possible by starting the deportations from the outer perimeter of the country and working toward the center. Hungary was divided into six basic areas—five zones and the city of Budapest. The order of the deportations from the zones was determined by three considerations: first, the approach of the Red Army which threatened to enter Hungary through the Carpathian Mountains; second, the belief that Hungarian cooperation could be most easily secured if the first deportees came from the recently annexed territories; third, reassurance of the well-established Jews in Old Hungary. While the Jews from the Carpathio-Ukraine and Transylvania were being removed, the Jews in Old Hungary would be told that drastic measures affected only non-Magyarized Jews.[22]

The Nazi-inspired operation was to transfer all Jews living in towns of less than 10,000 to larger cities and camps. The impending ghettoization had been outlined by Baky at a meeting early in April, when Hungarian officials were given confidential instructions. "The Royal Hungarian Government intends to rid the country of the Jews," Baky said. They "will be taken to prearranged assembly centers regardless of age and sex," and then be transferred to ghettos. The operation would be handled by the police and gendarmerie of each district, with the German Security Police acting in an "advisory capacity." After the conference, Lieutenant Colonel László Ferenczy, liaison between the gendarmerie and the German police, set up a Hungarian extermination squad with the cover name of "The International Storage and Transportation Company."

On the first day of Passover, the roundup of Jews in Carpatho-Ukraine began. In planning the ghettoization, the *Sondereinsatzkommando* demanded a sociographic map from the Jewish Council. By April 23, it had not yet been produced. Wisliceny summoned the Jewish leaders to a meeting at which they were forced to stand while he berated them for being so slow. He also threatened to deport them to Dachau. The Council had clung to straws; members had hoped unrealistically that the Jews of Hungary would be spared. Now they were forced to watch the inexorable Nazi machine go to work with unparalleled speed on their own Jews.

On the same day that Wisliceny railed at the Jewish leaders, Veesenmayer reported to Ribbentrop that in the Carpathian area the work of putting Jews in the ghettos had begun; 150,000 had already been evacuated. By the end of the week he expected the number to reach 300,000. "The same procedure," he added, "is already in preparation in Transylvania and in a number of counties bordering on Romania. An additional 250,000 to 300,000 are to be dealt with. Subsequently, it will be the turn of the other counties bordering on Serbia and Croatia, with the final ghetto work to be done in the interior of the country, and, in conclusion, in Budapest."[23] The Ministry of the Interior, now taking its orders from the Eichmann commando—Horthy had told Sztójay that he would not sign any new anti-Jewish decrees—confined the Jews in such wretched quarters that they became an impossible burden on the civil administration. This was Heydrich's classical method in which Eichmann had been carefully trained.[24] Before the end of April, Hungarian officials were "begging" Eichmann to take the Jews off their hands. Thousands of Jews were huddled in brick factories behind barbed wire and in the open country near railway branch lines. Typhus and hunger quickly took their toll. Daily food rations had been set at one fifth of a pound of bread and two cups of soup. Living conditions in the improvised camps soon became so intolerable that the imprisoned Jews were only too glad to leave them. They felt relief when the trains arrived—the trains, they told themselves, that would take them to the interior of Hungary where better conditions awaited them. The trains, instead, were destined for Auschwitz.

Although Ferenczy was technically in charge of deportations, Eichmann's special assistants actually controlled the organization of the transports. Particularly during the first stage of the deportations, when most Jews did not realize that the concentrations were merely a first step to deportation, Eichmann kept in the background. He wanted to keep Nazi uniforms out of sight until the ghettoization process was completed. Later his *Sondereinsatzkommando* was clearly in evidence. The roundups were conducted by Hungarian police and gendarmerie. Gendarmes accompanied the trains of deportees to Kosice (Kassa), where S.S. men took over for the remainder of the distance to Auschwitz.

The first transport left on April 28, 1944. Fifteen hundred Jews suitable for labor were taken from the internment camp at Kistarcsa and sent to Auschwitz. There they were compelled to write encouraging notes to their relatives with datelines from "Waldsee." The notes were brought by an S.S. courier to Budapest and were distributed by the Jewish Council. Between April 24 and May 2, Endre accompanied Eichmann and Wisliceny on an inspection of the provincial ghettos at Kosice, Ungvar and other towns in Carpatho-Ukraine. Wisliceny proposed moving them to the center of the country but Endre protested that there was nowhere to put them. Eichmann then persuaded Endre to deport them to Germany.

A report of the camp inspections was then made to Horthy, who subsequently reported: "Endre has found everything in perfect order. The provincial ghettoes have the character of sanitoria. At last the Jews have taken up an open-air life and exchanged their former mode of life with a healthier one."[25] Horthy, too, was unable to face reality.

The ghettos were now virtually sealed off from Budapest. Some money was smuggled through by well-meaning Christians and Jewish couriers, but trains and railway stations were constantly subject to lightning raids for document checks. Moreover, it was almost impossible for Jews to hide in the provinces—they were too easily identified. Nor could they flee to the capital. For a time, the Jewish Council had issued its own travel permits enabling hundreds of Jews to reach Budapest and escape deportation. But the Gestapo soon took this power away. Protests to the government were futile. When the Council addressed appeals to Eichmann detailing reports of wretched conditions in the northeastern region of the country, he said: "Not a single word of the report is true, for as I have just inspected the provincial ghettos, I really ought to know. The accommodation of the Jews is no worse than that of the German soldiers during maneuvers and fresh air will only do their health the world of good." If there were any outrages, he added, it was the fault of the Hungarians: "Endre wants to devour the Jews with sweetpaper!"

On May 4–5, a conference on the deportations was held in Vienna. Representatives from Eichmann's unit, the Hungarian and Slovak railways and Hungarian police attended. They agreed to begin the large Hungarian transports to Auschwitz by the middle of May. Four transports would leave daily, each containing 3,000 Jews. The first deportations were to empty Zone I, which included the Carpatho-Ukraine and some contiguous areas stretching into former Romanian territory. While the conference was in session, 200,000 Jews in Zone I were being concentrated in ten ghettos and camps.

Punctually, on May 15, the massive deportations began.

30 The Brand Mission

THE MEMBERS of the Jewish Council in Hungary could not bring themselves to believe that the Nazis planned their extermination until it was too late for them to escape. Another Jewish movement, however, fully understood Nazi intentions from the beginning and attempted to thwart them. This was the Vaadah Ezra va Hazalah, the Council for Assistance and Rescue. For several years the Vaadah had been in touch with the Working Group in Bratislava and in the spring of 1944, before the Hungarian deportations began, the Vaadah had received two messages from Slovakia. One said that the Germans were working feverishly at Auschwitz to restore the gas chambers and crematoria "which had not been in operation for months." Included in this message was a remark quoted by an NCO of the S.S. that "soon we will get fine Hungarian sausages." The second message reported that an agreement had been reached among German, Hungarian and Slovakian railway interests to direct 120 trains via Presov toward Auschwitz. This information had been passed on to Bratislava by an anti-Nazi Slovakian railway official. It was obvious that it concerned deportation trains.

The Vaadah had sent some of its young members to the camps in the provinces to warn Jews that deportations meant death, but their warnings were ignored. In one camp at Mukachevo, the Vaadah emissary met Jews who would listen to him and who resisted deportation. But this was an exceptional case; most Jews refused to contemplate their own annihilation. Moreover, although Auschwitz had been alerted and the preparatory machinery set in motion, the situation in Hungary was not altogether hopeless. A crucial period followed in which the death trains could have been stopped. Parallel with the destructive preparations, Eichmann was busy on quite another front negotiating with the founder of the Vaadah, Joel Brand, over the lives of Hungary's Jews. The members of the Vaadah were themselves hopeful, even after the deportations began, of rescuing Hungarian Jewry. Their hopes were pinned on a ransom proposal which Eichmann discussed with Brand.

By 1944, the Vaadah was a force to be reckoned with: it had a network of couriers, important contacts in diplomatic circles and agents in the Abwehr, the German Army Intelligence Service. It smuggled Jewish refugees from Poland, Slovakia, Romania and Yugoslavia and successfully forged certificates of baptism and certificates for Palestine. It was linked to the American Jewish Joint Distribution Committee, which helped to finance it, and to the Jewish Agency office in Istanbul. The Vaadah was a genuine underground movement, illegal and conspiratorial; in contrast with the Jewish Council, it had no illusions about Nazi plans and no second thoughts about their innocent-sounding phrases. The Nazi officials who negotiated with the Vaadah knew that these Jews were not deluding themselves. In their talks together there was no fogging up; the facts were stripped of all vague wordage. The Jews of the Vaadah knew that they were dealing with mass murderers of great cunning; the Nazis knew that the Vaadah knew.

The beginnings of the movement, however, were accidental; both the movement and the man who founded it stumbled into history. This occurred soon after the expulsions of "foreign" Jews to east Galicia and the Ukraine in September 1941—into areas given to Hungary after the successful invasion of Russia. Among those deported were relatives of Brand's wife who urged Brand to try to save them. But where to begin? Then, one evening, while sitting in a coffeehouse, he saw a man fond of the easy life but always short of cash. It was rumored that he worked for the Hungarian Secret Service. On an impulse, Brand offered to pay him well if he could bring back his relatives from Kaminetz-Podolsk. After four trips, the man ransomed not only these Jews but several others as well. They told the Brands that the Germans were preparing for the physical extermination of European Jewry. From this small private effort the Vaadah was born. Brand's apartment in Buljovsky Street in Budapest became a clandestine headquarters. Gradually, the scope of the rescue work and the composition of the organization broadened.

The nucleus of the Vaadah consisted of Brand, Dr. Rezsö Kastner and Samuel Springmann—all Labor Zionists. Brand's special task was the actual rescue work—to get refugees across the frontier from the Ukraine, Poland and Slovakia and to prepare false documents for them. Kastner negotiated with the other Zionist parties, with the official Jewish community and with Hungarian politicians. Springmann, a jeweler by trade, had good connections with the diplomatic corps in Budapest. He soon acquired the services of Hungarian and German secret agents and managed to infiltrate Vaadah agents into the ranks of the Hungarian police. He also established contacts with foreign countries and sent couriers to the ghettos of Poland. The men who served in the Vaadah had to overcome not only natural fears, for the risks were great, but the taboo against illegality. The organized Jewish community in Hungary, unable to understand that the

Hitler terror was a wholly new order of life that made conventional diplomacy obsolete, opposed the methods of the Vaadah. Hungarian Jewry had been comparatively safe until March 1944. Illegal methods were deplored. After the deportations started, however, the Council, which had stood apart from the Vaadah, came to its support. The Council president Stern, who was a member of the Hungarian Upper House and a man of aristocratic birth, later admitted to Kastner: "You and your friends, alone among us, were right. I must confess that I deeply regret not having supported you from the beginning. Much misfortune might have been avoided if I had done so."

Poland was the first great battlefield and it became essential for the Vaadah to establish contacts there. The police in Kosice were bribed by Slovakian friends of the Vaadah and reported which stretches of frontier were unguarded and safe for refugee crossings. After receiving detailed instructions, most of the refugees made their way across the frontier by themselves. They would arrive in Kosice at dark, go to the synagogue to meet the Vaadah representative who then took them to Budapest. Sometimes the refugees were swathed in bandages to appear ill so that their ignorance of the Hungarian language would pass unnoticed.

The Vaadah set up a regular intelligence center in Budapest and refugees were closely questioned: what was the situation in the ghettos? which officials ran the extermination apparatus? how were the Jewish Councils reacting? what were the possibilities of escape? All of this information was recorded, studied and sent in the form of memoranda by way of Istanbul and Switzerland to Jewish Agency officials. They, in turn, kept the Allies fully informed. Professional smugglers and bandits were also employed to dispatch Hungarian police friends to the Polish border, bring refugees out of Poland and "arrest" them as Hungarian deserters. The smugglers then collected their payment and turned the refugees over to the Vaadah contact. Blackmail and infiltration of enemy agents became routine problems. Once, when some of the Vaadah were arrested through the work of an informer, Raffi Friedel (who later became the Israeli Consul in Prague) led a group of Jewish youths, dressed in the uniform of the Hungarian Arrow Cross Party, and conducted a mock seizure of the prisoners.

Brand soon became so preoccupied with the Vaadah that he turned over his business, a weaving factory, to one of his workers, a non-Jewish woman. A plump, elderly, countrified woman, no one would have guessed that she hid an arsenal of guns for the Vaadah or that her office and workshop were frequently used by refugees. Other non-Jews were extremely helpful. A young bank clerk and his wife hid money as well as arms, took care of illegal printing machines and found lodgings for the refugees. A Budapest policeman often warned the Vaadah of impending raids; janitors in illegal offices remained mute about their occupants.

The forging of papers—birth certificates, baptismal certificates, residence and ration cards and registration forms—was at first very primitive, but arrangements were soon made with printers and the work became more professional. Documents were made available within twenty-four hours. The forging of Palestine certificates was another crucial activity. Under the British White Paper of 1939, immigration to Palestine for the five subsequent years was limited to 15,000 persons a year. In the assignment of quotas for 1944, Hungary was allocated 50 certificates per month, valid only for children. But Hungarian police, and later the German police, ignored this British restriction to children. The Vaadah soon realized that the mere possession of a certificate could save a Jew from deportation; these documents saved Jews in prisons and camps. They had the effect of safe-conducts and the Vaadah began to forge them in wholesale lots.

Passports from neutral countries were also lifesaving documents. George Mandel, who worked in the Geneva Consulate of the Republic of San Salvador, was particularly generous with passports from his country. If anyone wrote to him, sending a short biographical sketch and photograph, Mandel would send him a San Salvador passport. The recipient would become, in effect, a neutral alien. The Vaadah sent a courier to Mandel and was given hundreds of official passports, all duly stamped and signed; the courier had only to supply the names.

The members of the Vaadah often discussed among themselves and with the Hungarian Social Democrats the possibility of sabotage and diversionary action behind German lines, but had to give up the idea. There was virtually no resistance movement in Hungary. The people seem to have had no desire at all to carry on an underground struggle against the Germans either before or after Hungary lost its nominal independence in March 1944. Some of the young *chalutzim*, pioneering Zionist youths, who had prepared to go to Palestine, were armed, but only for the purposes of defense. Many able-bodied Jewish men would normally have been available but they had been conscripted for forced labor. Because of their limited numbers and resources, the Vaadah decided to forego active resistance and give rescue activity first priority.

The Vaadah grew stronger and more confident and daring, but it was haunted by its own inadequacy. The gap between its efforts and the scale of destruction in eastern Europe was widening day by day. Tens of thousands were being saved, but hundreds of thousands were being killed. The possibility of accomplishing more by direct negotiations with the Germans had already been probed by Gisi Fleischmann. So long as she could produce cash on demand from Wisliceny, the Jews of Slovakia had been safe. She failed in the end because others in a position to help refused to operate "illegally" or make deals with the Germans. The money that Wisliceny demanded was not raised. The Vaadah decided to go on with Gisi Fleischmann's unrealized plan. Possibilities were suggested in March 1944, four months after negotiations with Wisliceny in Slovaka had broken down. Wisliceny again was the negotiator, at first.

At the same time, Brand was asked to meet an Abwehr agent, a Dr. Schmidt. Brand was taken to an excellent riverside restaurant on the Danube and Schmidt cheerfully told him that the perpetual struggle between the S.S. and the German Army was at last over:[2] the Jewish problem was now being handed over to the Army, he said. Jews would now be regarded as an important asset to the German war economy; they would be put in work camps with their families and conditions would be vastly improved. Arbitrary executions and deportations were to cease immediately. All countries except Hungary were to be affected. When Brand asked what would happen to Hungary, Schmidt replied, "There are some special regulations that are about to be applied to Hungary, but we don't want to discuss that today."

Schmidt surprised Brand by not demanding money in exchange for the proposed concessions. He did require one thing, however: that Brand forward to the Jewish Agency a list of the Germans involved in the alleged policy change. The list of several dozen names, among them many high-ranking German officers and all of the Abwehr agents in Budapest, was sent to Istanbul as requested. Schmidt also gave Brand some puzzling advice. He suggested that the Vaadah ask the Jewish Agency for a large sum of money immediately; he recommended a million dollars, but refused to be drawn out beyond saying that communications were becoming more difficult and that having a reserve on hand would be a good idea.

After a lengthy debate over the meaning of this episode, the Vaadah commissioned Brand and three others to sound out Josef Winniger, another Abwehr agent whom they knew quite well. Winniger was at first very cagey and mystifying, but at last told what he knew. "Listen, Brand," he said, "I'll tell you something that would cost me my neck if you gave me away. Next week, Budapest is to be occupied by German troops. The decision has been taken. Hungary will cease to be an independent country."[3] The Vaadah representatives stood frozen when they heard this news. What could be done in so little time?

They hurried back to the others and convened a large conference of the whole movement. All sorts of improbable schemes were proposed, but finally several decisions were made: to set up small resistance groups and collect as many weapons as possible; to inform the leading officials of the Hungarian opposition parties of Winniger's warning and contact the Hungarian secret service; to inform escaped Allied prisoners of war and to send a special courier to Istanbul to alert the Jewish Agency and the Allies.

On March 19, 1944, the day that German troops marched into Budapest, Winniger burst in on Brand while he was taking a bath and warned him to dress quickly and disappear for a few days. All liberal politicians and some Jews were already arrested and the S.S. was looking for Brand. Winniger admitted that the Army was quite powerless to stop the excesses. Brand consented to be taken into protective custody by the Abwehr agents. They, in turn, had no intention of letting him be captured by the S.S. They also moved his wife to a safe address. When Brand learned that Wisliceny, the man who had talked to Gisi Fleischmann, was in Budapest, he felt encouraged. If the Vaadah could get in touch with him, perhaps he could be bought. The Abwehr agents were offered twenty thousand dollars to arrange a personal meeting, but they agreed only to tell Wisliceny that a meeting was desired. The message alone cost Vaadah twenty thousand dollars.

Meanwhile, Kastner got in touch with Gisi Fleischmann and other underground contacts in Slovakia. They wrote to Wisliceny and urged him to contact the Vaadah. Wisliceny had already met with Jewish Council leaders in Budapest and had shown one member, Philip Freudiger, a letter from Rabbi Weissmandel of Slovakia urging that he continue dealing with Wisliceny on the Europa Plan. Wisliceny had also pressured them into accepting a Jewish Council to carry out German regulations affecting Jews. The Abwehr agents urged the Vaadah to cooperate in this matter, but the Vaadah categorically refused. They were all too familiar with the uses the Germans had made of similar councils in Poland. Finally, Schmidt was prevailed upon to meet with Wisliceny and arrange to have him meet Brand. The Vaadah was to offer $2 million in exchange for all of the Jews still alive; 10 percent would be paid when negotiations began and $200,000 a month thereafter. The Abwehr agents were to get $200,000 as their share. The meeting was arranged.

Brand repeated this proposition to Wisliceny and laid down three conditions: that the mass executions and deportations stop, that no more ghettos be established, and that Jews who had certificates be permitted to go to Palestine. Wisliceny balked only at the last point, the matter of emigration, citing Germany's relationship to the Mufti of Jerusalem as the difficulty. He intimated that more money might be needed but agreed to take the $200,000 in advance, to be presented at the next meeting. Wisliceny also agreed to release some of the Jewish prisoners who had been arrested in Budapest.

Within two weeks, with the help of Dr. Stern, the Jewish Council president, who now realized that support for the Vaadah was crucial, $200,000 was raised. The next meeting, however, was not with Wisliceny, but with Lieutenant Colonel Krumey of Eichmann's *Sondereinsatzkommando*. Brand was at first alarmed by this change but Krumey assured him that he was authorized to negotiate by Himmler himself. Krumey's presence also seemed to indicate the official, not merely private, nature of the meetings. There were several protracted discussions involving conditions in the camps, certificate-holders and, most fundamentally, the actual evacuation of a million Jews. Where could they be sent? Brand tried to stall for time on this point, the most vulnerable of all. Otherwise, Krumey seemed cooperative, going so far as to issue special permits to allow Vaadah representatives to visit the camps near Budapest. There remained the problem of establishing telephone contact with Istanbul for official authorization to go ahead. The Vaadah was hopeful and expectant. While they waited, the Germans took the initiative.

On April 25, Winniger met Brand early in the morning and told him that Eichmann wanted to see him. Brand knew that in the early period of the war, Eichmann had favored the emigration of Jews. Since that time he had deported millions to death. His power had become immense. What were his motives now? Brand would soon know. At nine o'clock, Winniger said, an S.S. car would pick him up across from the Café Opera and take him to Eichmann. Promptly at the appointed time a black Mercedes drew up and drove Brand to the Hotel Majestic. Eichmann received him immediately and got to the point quickly. He spoke in short, clipped sentences.

"I suppose you know who I am. I was in charge of the 'actions' in Germany, Poland, and Czechoslovakia. Now it is Hungary's turn. I have already investigated you and your people of the Joint and the *Sochnuth* [Jewish Agency], and I have verified your ability to make a deal. Now then, I am prepared to sell you one million Jews. Not the whole lot—you wouldn't be able to raise enough money for that. But you could manage a million. Goods for blood; blood for goods. You can take them from any country you like, wherever you can find them. From Hungary, Poland, the eastern provinces, from Terezin, from Auschwitz—wherever you want. Whom do you want to save? Men who can beget children? Women who can bear them? Old people? Children? Sit down and talk."[4]

Brand sat down. He was strangely not frightened. As Eichmann spoke, it became clear that he meant business. The man across from him, who had sent millions to the gas chambers, looked like an ordinary bank clerk except for his eyes. They were like steel—blue and hard. Brand said quite calmly that he could not choose which Jews were to live; he wanted to save all of them. As for goods, they were practically impossible to get; all Jewish property had already been seized. But Eichmann insisted on goods, not money, and although he commended Brand's "idealism," he said that he could not "sell all of the Jews of Europe." He wanted Brand to contact the Jewish Agency leaders and representatives of the Allies and come back with a concrete offer. Brand decided to go to Istanbul, where Jewish leaders had direct links with the Allies in Jerusalem and Cairo. Eichmann warned Brand that his wife and mother and children would be kept in custody pending his return. With a warning that under no circumstances was any Hungarian to know about their talk on pain of death, he was dismissed.

The Vaadah was elated; a miraculous opportunity to save tens of thousands of Jews now seemed at hand. Brand spent a few days cautiously treading his way through a thicket of competing German power groups. The Abwehr, aware that the war was lost and eager to gain credit with the Allies, wanted Brand to negotiate with them rather than the S.S.; other agents sent by the S.S. wanted him to furnish information against Abwehr men so that they could be arrested. The Vaadah stuck with Eichmann. Eichmann's boss was Himmler and it was the S.S. that controlled the death houses.

Eichmann summoned Brand again after a few days and handed him a parcel from Switzerland which the Gestapo had intercepted. Eichmann calmly told him that it contained 270 Swiss francs and over $50,000— money with which to help Jewish children. "Here is your money," Eichmann said, dispensing with preliminaries. "You must acknowledge its receipt at once." Eichmann also handed over a pile of letters which contained more money. Later, when the Vaadah counted it all, the total sum was more than $120,000. Brand was astounded. Was it a trap? Eichmann then made his bargain. He asked Brand specifically for ten thousand trucks, complete with spare parts and equipped for winter conditions. These would be used exclusively on the Eastern Front. He also offered a "decent price" for a few thousand tons of tea, coffee, soap and chocolate. What sort of guarantee could he give to show his good faith, Brand asked. Eichmann replied with words that convinced Brand that he was serious: "If you return from Istanbul and tell me that the offer has been accepted, I will close Auschwitz and bring ten percent of the promised million to the frontier. You can take one hundred thousand Jews away, and afterward bring me one thousand trucks. We'll go on like that. A thousand trucks for every hundred thousand Jews."[5]

Brand was beside himself with excitement. He doubted that the Allies would give Eichmann trucks to save Jews, but he was convinced that some alternative course could be found. He told Eichmann that he was sure his offer would be accepted and left flooded with hope. The Vaadah now telegraphed to Istanbul that Brand would soon be there. A reply came quickly: "Joel should come. Chaim awaits him." Brand assumed that this referred to Chaim Weizmann, the head of the Jewish Agency. This meant that the matter would be handled on the highest level and showed that the Agency understood the importance of the mission. As soon as he received the cable, Brand went to see Eichmann and said he was ready to go. He appealed to Eichmann to stop the roundups in

Carpathia and Transylvania, but Eichmann impatiently rejected the appeal. Brand then asked about the several hundred Jews, some holding emigration certificates for Palestine, whom Wisliceny and Krumey had promised could leave Hungary immediately. Eichmann agreed to allow them to leave but insisted that they be sent first to Vienna, and then taken down the Danube to Constanza. (Eventually this group totaled 1,709, but they left Europe via Bergen-Belsen and Switzerland; some were furnished with false certificates by the Vaadah.) Eichmann threatened to call off everything unless Brand acted quickly.

Brand was a good choice for this strange mission. Nothing in his past could have equipped him completely for it, but he had had a versatile career and possessed great practical sense and stamina. He was born in Russian Carpathia (formerly Hungarian Slovakia) and lived comfortably in middle-class circumstances. His father, a contractor, had founded the Budapest telephone company. While Brand was still a child, his family moved to Germany and Brand studied there. At nineteen, he decided to travel and tramped across the United States, working on roads, in factories and coal mines. He also went to sea and roamed the countries of Asia. After five years of this kind of experience, he returned to Germany. When Hitler seized power in 1933, Brand felt finished with Europe and planned to go to Palestine, but he had extensive family responsibilities in Budapest and gave up emigration plans for the time being.

Before Brand left, he received the formal support of organized Hungarian Jewry. Some members of the Central Council thought that he was not sufficiently clever for the mission, but Stern gave him an official letter and endorsement attesting that his journey was in the interests of the whole of Hungarian Jewry and that their fate hung on the results of his mission. On May 15, the day the massive deportations began, Brand was summoned to see Eichmann for the last time. A plane would be ready for him within a few days, Eichmann said, and he must complete his work quickly. He admitted that deportations would not stop. "Twelve thousand Jews will be transported daily, but I am prepared to send them to Austria and not to Auschwitz. I will keep part of them in Slovakia. The transports will wait there until you come back and they can then be easily rerouted to the Spanish border. If you don't return or if you aren't back in good time, these people will go to Auschwitz."[6]

Brand could not budge him on his decision to go ahead with the deportations, but Eichmann agreed "to put the brakes on" if Brand brought or cabled him a definite decision in two weeks. His last words to Brand were: "Hurry up, Herr Brand, and come back quickly. I haven't been joking."

Kastner warned Brand to be on guard against the English, to try to deal directly with Weizmann, and, above all, to keep alive the negotiations with Eichmann. The Vaadah instructed him to bring back some, indeed, any counterproposal. They were convinced that, in the last resort, Eichmann would take food or money. They urged Brand to do everything possible to break the conspiracy of silence surrounding the fate of European Jewry. On May 16, Krumey drove him to Vienna, where he was to take a plane to Istanbul, and gave him a German passport made out in the name of Eugen Brand, an engineer from Erfurt. Shortly before he took off, Krumey asked Brand not to forget him and other "honorable officers" like him in his negotiations in Turkey. Krumey, too, felt the impending collapse of the Nazi regime and needed credentials attesting to his humanity from the very people he was helping to destroy.

When Brand arrived in Istanbul, he was immediately jolted from his hopes. The Chaim he met was not the Chaim Weizmann he expected, but the Jewish Agency chief of the Istanbul office, Chaim Barlasz. There was no visa for him and therefore no permission to land. The Turkish airport officials said that he would have to return to Vienna. The secret "world power" which Eichmann thought Brand represented was not even able to get a Turkish visa for him. Quickly, the scales fell from Brand's eyes; the Jewish leaders in Istanbul did not inhabit the same world as his.

Eichmann had foisted a companion on Brand—Bandi Grosz, a counter-intelligence agent—to spy on him. Grosz was a true product of the war, a double or triple agent who at one time had been a member of the Abwehr. He had also helped the Vaadah. He frequently traveled to Istanbul on a courier's pass, and helped the Vaadah establish efficient communications with Istanbul, bringing money from the Jewish Agency and putting the Vaadah in touch with leading conspirators against Hitler. Now, while keeping watch on Brand, he also used his connections in Turkey to assist Brand's mission for the moment. Brand later found out that Grosz was also on a special mission to establish contact with the British or Americans so that Himmler could begin negotiations for a separate peace and drive a wedge between the West and the Soviet Union.

While Brand waited numbly at the airport, Grosz phoned Machmed Bey, president of the Turkish Transport Company, and asked him to certify Brand for the Minister of Interior. Within half an hour, the Turkish officials stamped Brand's pass and Grosz took him to the Hotel Palace Pera, the headquarters of the Jewish delegation. They greeted him with great displays of emotion and awaited his words with intense excitement. But Brand was burning with anger and frustration. He spoke for several hours, describing in full detail the misery and daily terror in Hungary and every twist in his negotiations with the Nazi leaders:

Comrades, I do not understand what you have done up to now. . . . With whom am I expected to deal? Have you the authority to make decisions in this matter, decisions on which the fate of millions of people will depend? It is a question of days, of hours. Eichmann will not wait. Every day twelve thousand people are being driven into cattle cars. Eichmann has promised to keep them in Austria until I come back, but what guarantee have I that they will not go straight to the gas chambers? Are you prepared to accept the responsibility for the slaughter of even a thousand more Jews, just because no one with the authority of the Executive has turned up at the right time in Constantinople? . . . You must arrange by cable for someone to come at once. . . . Tomorrow I will cable Eichmann and tell him that all goes well and that his offer is accepted in principle, provided the deportations are stopped immediately. If Eichmann does that, representatives of the Germans and of the *Sochnuth* can meet in some neutral country to work out the details. We must not give them trucks but we can propose food. If worse comes to worst, we can offer them money. . . . Do you know what is involved, comrades? Things are getting difficult for the Germans. They want to negotiate. The ground is burning under their feet. They want to strike a bargain. Eichmann has promised us an advance of a hundred thousand Jews. Do you understand what this means? . . . I insist that a man come here whom the whole world knows. The Germans are sure to keep a watch on us here, and their secret service will know at once if Weizmann or Shertok are here. Even if we cannot accomplish anything concrete with the Allies while I am here, I can then at least go back to Eichmann and tell him that the Agency has accepted his offer. Then Auschwitz can be blown up.[7]

Brand stirred his fellow Jews; many wept openly. But he had fantastically overestimated their power. They were not even sure a cable would get through to Jerusalem; no one had enough influence to arrange for a plane. The delegates were sincere enough and conscientious, Brand concluded, but they had not left the frontier of legality. They were not staring death in the face day after day as were he and his friends in Budapest. Moreover, they clung to pet projects while the new situation required a total mobilization behind Eichmann's proposal. Some still wanted to push "illegal" immigration into Palestine despite the shipping problems; others favored military resistance against the Germans. One delegate wanted to form a Jewish legion. Brand felt that these steps were now wholly unrealistic. However, he gave the men military and intelligence data to pass on to the Allies and demanded the bombing of the gas chambers and crematoria of Auschwitz, as well as diversions and air strikes against junctions on the rail lines leading to Auschwitz. He also told them where parachutists could land, what they needed to get through, and the names and addresses of people who could help them.

Brand was at the end of his mission; he felt depleted and depressed. There was only one bright spot; the Jewish Agency had contacted the American Ambassador to Turkey, Laurence Steinhardt, who asked Brand to come to Ankara as quickly as possible. Everything was made ready for this new journey.

Brand and Barlasz, who was to accompany him, had already bought their train tickets for Ankara and were waiting at the station when Brand was suddenly stopped by the Turkish police and detained. He was told that his visa was valid only for Istanbul, not Ankara. Barlasz then decided to see Steinhardt alone. For several days, Brand faced expulsion. He learned that Grosz was also being hunted. What unseen hand was pulling the strings? Were the British trying to sabotage his mission? Then he dismissed his suspicions. "It was unbelievable," he said, "that Britain, who had fought on alone after all the rest of Europe had surrendered to despotism, that Britain, whom we had praised as the stubborn champion of freedom, should now wish to sacrifice us, the weakest and the most pitiful of the oppressed." But a new frustration arose that left no further doubts.

Moshe Shertok, the chief of the Political Department of the Jewish Agency, had been expected momentarily from Jerusalem. Brand, who had succeeded in having the Turks renew his permit from day to day, waited for him by the hour. Days passed. Brand had to improvise. He sent cables to Budapest saying that a provisional agreement had been concluded and that special delegates were already on their way to Turkey. Later he learned that his wife and several leaders of the Vaadah were arrested by the Hungarian police and tortured to force them to reveal the nature of his mission. Ironically, they were finally freed by the Germans who were afraid they might talk and blurt out the Nazi complicity in Brand's mission.

Meanwhile, Barlasz returned from Ankara. In his talks with Steinhardt, the American Ambassador seemed deeply moved. He advised Barlasz not to let Brand travel to Jerusalem before receiving definite assurance from the British that he would be allowed to return. Barlasz cabled this warning to Jerusalem. Later Brand learned that Shertok was making every effort to get to Istanbul, but that he had been unable to get the necessary papers. Shertok also urged Brand to have his residence permit extended until his arrival, but, barring that, not to go to Jerusalem in the present circumstances, but to return to Hungary.

Meanwhile, Steinhardt had sent a report to the United States Government on the Brand mission. In response, Roosevelt sent Ira Hirschmann to Istanbul as a special plenipotentiary. This was Hirschmann's second mission to Turkey. His first intervention had been partly successful in saving some of the Jews in Transnistria.

By June 1, thirteen days after Brand had arrived in Turkey, the Jewish Agency delegates told him that Turkey had refused Shertok an entry visa and that they would have to meet each other in Syria or Jerusalem. Brand protested; this would delay matters further. What was the reason behind Turkey's refusal? Shertok had visited Turkey frequently during the war. Was a trap being set for him? The delegates assured Brand that both the

British and Americans had promised to give his mission first priority. It was finally decided that he meet Shertok in Aleppo, in British-occupied Syria. Brand again protested but was told that the British were expecting him there, that acceptance of the German proposals depended on the Allies. The Agency delegates had no choice; they had promised that he would go. Brand at last gave in.

Eichmann's two-week limit was up, but Brand believed that his cables pledging a provisional agreement would satisfy him for the time. Before leaving for Aleppo, he cabled Eichmann that he was en route to Syria to meet the Allies and pursue the negotiations at the highest level. On June 5, he boarded the Taurus Express for Aleppo, accompanied by Echud Avriel, a member of the delegation and a *Mossad* agent. Avriel told Brand that Turkey had sent a detective along to make sure that he would not try to jump the train.

At Ankara, the train stopped for an hour. Two men were waiting for Brand and Avriel. They took them aside; one man spoke agitatedly: "We have information that Joel Brand is being lured into a trap. Shertok was not granted a visa because the British want to entice Brand into British-controlled territory and then arrest him. I warn you both, and in particular Brand, against continuing this journey. In this matter, the British are not our friends, and they do not want Brand's mission to succeed. Unless Brand goes back at once, he will not be able to return before the end of the war, for the British will put him in prison."[8]

The conversation completely bewildered Brand. He could not bring himself to believe that the British would now refuse to help. Both men went back to the train and rode on, depressed and uncertain about their decision. They crossed the Syrian frontier early the next morning. At the British checkpoint, Brand realized at once that the officials knew who he was. Brand gave his luggage to a porter and was about to follow him to the platform when a man in civilian clothes entered his compartment and addressed him in English.

"Mr. Brand?"

"Oh, yes."

"This way, please."

Brand tried to follow the porter but the Englishman barred the way and pointed in the other direction. Before Brand could collect his wits, two plainclothesmen had forced him into a jeep; its engine was already running. He tried to resist and called for Avriel, but he was nowhere to be seen. The jeep shot off and took Brand to a large dormitory in a barracks. There were no guards and no other soldiers except a few noncommissioned men who sat around a table reading newspapers. None of them spoke. Brand selected a bed; his luggage was brought to him. A little later he was invited to join the men at the table and was served an excellent breakfast. The Englishmen spoke about the weather and addressed him very politely but made no effort to question him. Brand was unable to decide whether or not he was arrested; he was certainly not at liberty.

On the following day he was brought before an officer who politely asked him his name. Brand replied, "I am not permitted to answer any questions. I am a Jewish emissary, and I am not allowed to make any statement except in the presence of a representative of the Jewish Agency." The officer said that his request would be granted. Tomorrow he would be able to see Shertok. Brand felt reassured; he was now convinced that he was not under arrest, but merely being detained.

After breakfast the following morning, he was taken by jeep to an Arab villa and then into a room furnished in Oriental style. Several British officers and civilians were seated. As he came in, a dignified middle-aged man rose and walked toward him. It was Moshe Shertok. He greeted Brand cordially and opened the conversation. "Comrade Brand," he began, "I know your story but shall ask you now to give me exact details. You can speak quite openly. Our British friends here are most interested in your report, and we have nothing to hide from them. Can you speak English fluently?"

Brand replied that he could express himself better in German. He spoke for over ten hours, describing in great detail the catastrophe that had overtaken the Jews of Poland and the Baltic States, the history of the Vaadah, its illegal work, Gisi Fleischmann's negotiations in Bratislava, the first days of the German invasion of Hungary, and his own talks with Wisliceny and Eichmann. The Englishmen seemed deeply stirred, but they said nothing. The only sound besides his voice was the scratching of the stenographers' pencils. Occasionally Shertok would interrupt to ask a question. Several times the session broke up for refreshments. Before Brand could get to the heart of his mission—his answer for Eichmann and the British counterproposal—Shertok withdrew to a corner with the British and talked to them with great intensity. He then turned to Brand and laid a hand on his shoulder. "Dear Joel, I have something very bitter to tell you. You must now go on farther south. The British insist on it. I have done all I can to make them alter their decision, but it is an order from a higher authority and I cannot change it."

For a few seconds, Brand was unable to grasp what Shertok had said. When at last he realized that he was to be arrested, his nerves snapped. He shouted:

"Don't you understand what you're doing? This is plain murder! Mass murder! If I don't go back, our best people will be slaughtered. My wife! My mother! My children! They will be the first to go. You've got to let me return. I have come here under a flag of truce, on a special mission.

You can agree or not as you will, but you have no right to seize an emissary. I am not even an emissary from the enemy. The Germans are my enemy just as much as they are the enemies of the Allies, and far more bitter enemies, too. I am here as the delegate of a million people condemned to death. Their lives depend on my return. Who gives you the right to lay hands on me? What harm have I done England? So far as we could we have helped the Allies. . . . What do you want from us? What do you want from me?"[9]

He begged, he threatened, he wept. Shertok tried to calm him. "Joel, this is just as hard for me as it is for you. I will not rest until you are free once more. I will fly direct to London and have the matter taken up at the highest level. I am sure you will be set free and will be able to continue the negotiations. We will see that matters are put right. But now, at this moment, we are powerless and must do what we are told, you as much as I."[10]

Shertok, himself visibly shaken, offered to take Brand in his own car to the Allied officials in Jerusalem, but the English officials refused their permission. Brand was then taken to the station, accompanied by a young British officer, and put on a sleeper. Through the night on the way to Haifa, he often thought of escaping, to return illegally to German territory, to try to save whatever he could. But he felt too small—"a man thrown by chance into the boiling cauldron of history"—to take on so much responsibility. He also was a disciplined Zionist and later said he "lacked the courage to defy discipline."

In the morning he reached the soil of Palestine and sat on the carriage steps gazing into the distance, breathing the air of the land of Jewish dreams. His guard left him alone with his thoughts. In Haifa, there was a long wait and Brand was left to walk around Barclay's Bank while the officer did some business inside the building. Again he was tempted to escape and hide among his own people, but the British police would have no trouble finding him. He called to a nearby man, told him who he was, and that the British had arrested him. He urged the man to hurry to the Jewish Agency and have someone kidnap him before his train left for Cairo. The English officer came back but Brand was sure that he had seen nothing, but months later, in a Cairo prison, the same officer asked Brand who the man had been. The two men left for Cairo without delay.

In London, Shertok urged the British Foreign Office to act on Brand's proposal. He was still hopeful. On June 30, he cabled his colleagues that the matter was before the War Cabinet. On July 6, both Shertok and Weizmann carried their plea directly to Foreign Secretary Eden. They found him "maddeningly hesitant." His main argument was that "there must be no negotiation with the enemy." Weizmann admitted that the Gestapo offer probably had ulterior motives, but that in the false hope of achieving their ends, they would be prepared to free a certain number of Jews. "The whole thing," he said, "may boil down to a question of money, and the ransom should be paid."

On July 7, Weizmann urged the Foreign Office to approach the R.A.F. with the proposal to bomb the death camps at Auschwitz. This would mean, Weizmann said, that "the Allies were waging a direct war on the extermination of victims of Nazi oppression and would give the lie to the oft-repeated assertion of Nazis that the Allies were not really displeased with the action of the Nazis in ridding Europe of Jews."[11]

The reply to Weizmann from the Foreign Office came almost two months later. On September 1, 1944, he was informed that the bombing of the death camps had been rejected by the R.A.F. for "technical reasons."

In Cairo, Brand was a prisoner, although his cell was a well-furnished room. He was told that his detention was a military necessity but that he would soon return to Hungary. The Germans, his interrogator explained, would use everything in their power, including torture, to make him describe what he had seen in the British theater of war, and it was therefore for his own welfare that he was being detained. He could thus say he had seen nothing. It was still unbearable for Brand to renounce his faith in England. He found the interrogator's remark consoling and tried to drive all doubts from his mind. The English officer then explained that his duty was to obtain all possible information connected with his mission and send daily reports to London.

There now began an exhaustive interrogation that lasted for months, eight hours a day. Brand had to theorize about Eichmann's intentions and the motives of various S.S. leaders. Why did they want trucks? Could the Allies say they would deliver them, and then not honor their agreement? How could a hundred thousand Jews be transported to a neutral frontier? Patiently, hour by hour, Brand talked on, emphasizing at every opportunity the importance of keeping negotiations open, to start the ball rolling by winning time until Germany collapsed.

One hopeful sign appeared during the first week of Brand's imprisonment. Ira Hirschmann had come to Cairo to see him. Brand was taken to a private house on the Nile and introduced to Hirschmann. "President Roosevelt has sent me here to talk to you, Mr. Brand. I flew from New York to Constantinople but got there too late. So I followed you to Aleppo and missed you again, both there and in Jerusalem. Finally I came on here to see you."

Later, Brand was to learn of the obstacles the British had put in Hirschmann's way. Ambassador Steinhardt in Ankara told Hirschmann that the British had spirited Brand over the border to Syria. But Hirschmann had been instructed to interview Brand at all costs. He finally wrung from the British Minister the admission that he had been taken to Cairo and was under surveillance by British Intelligence. The entire matter was now in the hands of Lord Moyne, Deputy Minister of State in the Middle East. Hirschmann then flew to Cairo where he was given a message from Lord Moyne: Anthony Eden had invited Hirschmann to come to London at once where the matter at hand would be taken up on the "highest levels." Hirschmann, however, decided not to permit the British to change his instructions. He finally saw Lord Moyne, who also pressed him to go to London where he would find Moshe Shertok as well as Eden. Hirschmann countered: "Mr. Minister, I come from a sporting people. So do you. I will agree to take my instructions from Mr. Eden if you will agree to take yours from Mr. Hull. I will go to London if you will go to Washington."

Hirschmann reassured Brand and promised that he would soon be released to continue his mission. The American Government, he added, did not approve of the way the English were handling the matter. Again, Brand waited. The interrogations were resumed. He then went on a hunger strike for over a week until he received word from Avriel that the news from Shertok in London was good. "We believe," Avriel wrote, "that our basic demands have been as good as met." Again buoyed up, Brand broke his hunger strike. His captivity was made more pleasant, and he was invited to attend clubs, parties, and movies with English soldiers. As someone who had recently been in occupied Europe, he was viewed as an object of some curiosity; his English escorts nicknamed him "Hess Number Two." The quizzing continued, but more subtly, in a relaxed social atmosphere. One day at the British-Egyptian Club, Brand talked with a British official who did not introduce himself but whom Brand identified as Lord Moyne. The Englishman asked about the details of the Eichmann offer, the goods, and the number of Jews in the first group. "And how many will there be altogether?" he asked.

"Eichmann spoke of a million," Brand replied.

"What on earth are you thinking of, Mr. Brand?" Moyne protested. "What shall I do with those million Jews? Where shall I put them?"

"If there is no place for us on this planet," Brand said, "then there is no alternative to the gas chambers for our people."

But there were no longer a million Jews to consider. Since Brand had left Budapest, a half million had been killed, 400,000 from Hungary alone. Brand, however, did not know the full horror until July 20 when he read a Reuters report in the Cairo papers. The mass murders were acknowledged. The British policy was also now made clear; they never for a moment had taken his mission seriously. The Reuters report read:

> We learn from reliable sources that the Germans have recently made a proposal amounting to blackmail.
> They state that they are willing to spare the Hungarian Jews if the Allies will agree to a partial lifting of the blockade. It is understood that out of

the 800,000 Hungarian Jews, 400,000 have already been deported to Poland, where they have been gassed by the Nazis. The same fate now awaits the remaining 400,000 Jews.

The Germans have chosen this moment to dispatch from Hungary to Turkey two emissaries with proposals that are alleged to have been put forward by the Gestapo. These proposals consist of an offer to free the remaining Hungarian Jews and to put an end to the policy of liquidation, in exchange for certain concessions, namely, the lifting of the blockade to allow the entry of army lorries and other goods.

The two emissaries have made it known that the policy of annihilation of the Jews will be continued if these demands are not fulfilled. An examination of the proposals has shown that they have no serious or solid foundation and that they consist of a mixture of blackmail and threats and are designed to sow discord among the Allies with a view to crippling the war effort. It is quite clear that the Allies will not be deterred by any German threats or offers from making every effort to alleviate the fate of the Jews, wherever and whenever possible.[12]

The British had composed their explanations for rejecting Brand's mission. There were to be no negotiations and no bombing of the rail lines to Auschwitz or of Auschwitz itself.

The publicity given his mission shocked and embittered Brand. It convinced him that the British were his enemies as well as the Germans. Avriel was dead wrong; Shertok had been fed syrupy words. Later, Brand was to find out that the Vaadah had succeeded in resuming negotiations with Kurt Becher after Brand's interim agreement had arrived in Budapest on July 7. Himmler had authorized this renewal of negotiations. The blow of the British news release then followed.

At the beginning of September, the British decided that their business with Brand was finished. His name would be changed to Jacobsen and he would be released to an army camp with the rank and pay of a lieutenant in the British Army. He would have complete freedom except that he could not reveal his real identity and recent mission. Brand spent a month at a camp near Cairo. Bitter, worn out, and isolated from news of his comrades in Budapest, he wrote to the Jewish Agency in Jerusalem saying that he no longer felt bound by Shertok's instructions in Aleppo and would try to flee. The British intercepted the letter and on October 5, he was put on a train to Jerusalem. There he was told that the conscience of the world had at last been awakened—President Roosevelt, Pope Pius XII, and King Gustavus V of Sweden were intervening for the Jews left in Hungary—largely through his efforts, that he must not think that his mission was a failure. All around were hopeful, busy, credulous people. Only one man in Palestine seemed to understand Brand's sense of immense guilt and frustration.

The man was Moshe Shertok, who returned from London a few weeks after Brand had arrived in Jerusalem. Shertok was addressing a large audience in Haifa one evening and saw Brand in the hall. He interrupted his speech and said:

"Comrades, someone has just come into the hall who has been the cause of my making several journeys to London. This man has given us a great task to perform which, to my sorrow, I have only been able to accomplish in part. The Allies were not prepared to cooperate in the way this man requested. Had they done so, hundreds of thousands of our brothers would be alive today. They did not give us what we asked, but, instead, they gave us the Jewish Brigade of the British Army. You well know how dear to my heart was the organization of the Jewish Brigade. Nevertheless, I declare now, before the whole world, that I would have sacrificed the Jewish Brigade if I could thereby have accomplished more of what this man requested."[13]

Brand had to remain in Palestine for the duration of the war. He spent his time shuttling between Jerusalem and Tel Aviv, trying to piece together the ordeal of Hungary's Jews during his imprisonment. He also disguised himself as a latrine cleaner to gain access to the sealed camp of Atlit in Haifa, where England confined the "illegal" refugees from Hitler Europe. There he passed out fruit and cigarettes while the refugees talked about the world which they had fled but in which hundreds of thousands of others were doomed to die.

His mission, full of great hope and promise, had dribbled out.

31 The Beginning of the End

WHILE BRAND WAS ON HIS FUTILE ERRAND, Eichmann shifted to the second front of his double role, that of deportation expert. This was, after all, his specialty, the work that aroused his greatest enthusiasm. Not accustomed to negotiating for the rescue of Jewish lives, he took more naturally to destroying them. Himmler was busy with his own private negotiations, trying to make contact with the Allies, and so long as Brand was off on his mission, Eichmann was not to be diverted from his. The Hungarian zealots—the Arrow Cross leaders in the Hungarian Ministry of the Interior —now had their turn in turning loose the "bloodhound" in Eichmann.

He lost no time. On May 15, 1944, while Brand was making his last-minute preparations to leave the country, the transfers began.

The tempo of the Hungarian deportations was furious. Within the first nine days, 116,000 Jews were transported to Auschwitz, and by the end of June, 381,600 had been deported. In this *Aktion Höss*, between 250,000 and 300,000 Jews were gassed or shot to death. The 46-day blaze that consumed half of Hungarian Jewry was unequaled by the Nazis in any other country. A force of 20,000 gendarmerie and Hungarian police added their share to this mass death.

The roundup of Jews began in the Carpatho-Ukraine and adjacent areas stretching into former Romanian territory. The operation was carried out by Hungarian police, who drove the victims to embarkation points with great brutality. Small children were whipped into a fast walking pace; hospital cases were dragged to the trains; women were publicly stripped and subjected to physical examination by midwives and searched for valuables. The disabled were taken bodily and hurled into the cars. Newborn infants were flung into the trains after their mothers. The floors of the freight cars measured 215 square feet. Seventy-five people were crammed into each car, packed one on top of another as there was not enough room to stand. The police used clubs and bayonets and occasionally fired rifles to pack the cars more tightly. Each compartment was equipped with a two-gallon bucket for water and another for waste. In many of the transports, no food was supplied at all; in others, bread from half a pound to four pounds per person was issued. When the cars were packed to the satisfaction of the police, they were sealed and the windows were nailed shut.[1]

Eichmann's drinking companion and co-worker in the Hungarian Department of the Interior, Lázsló Endre, had mobilized a force of 5,000 Hungarian police to manage this operation. It was completed in such a blaze of speed that well-organized resistance would have had serious difficulties. The Jews had no resistance organization at all. The Vaadah had made some efforts to reach the provinces and warn Jews in the ghettos and camps to flee, but their numbers, small to begin with, had been further thinned out by conscriptions of able-bodied men into the Hungarian labor force. Many Jews still deluded themselves about the nature of the deportations and still believed the postcards which the earlier transportees had been forced to send, that the deportees were in "Waldsee" safe and well. Moreover, under the anti-Jewish legislation of previous years, it had become difficult for the overcrowded Jewish communities in Carpathia and Transylvania to subsist. Many Jews there suffered from undernourishment and lacked physical resistance.[2] They went quite voluntarily to the assembly points. Posters called for people to leave their homes and proceed to certain stations. This "official" call also cut at the roots of possible resistance. Orthodox Jews simply refused to accept the idea that they were to be exterminated. An exceptional case, the president of the Cluj orthodox community, Zsiga Leb, confirmed this incredulity to Brand:

> I told everyone I could reach to get away from the ghetto, and flee to Rumania, or go underground with false papers. One out of a hundred followed my advice. . . . The most difficult task is to convince the orthodox Jews of the danger that hangs over them. These people simply cannot bring themselves to contemplate the possibility of their extermination. A typical example of this is my uncle. . . . When I urged him to go underground, he assembled a number of aged Jews and, pointing at me, cried: "Don't listen to him. The president of our community is a blasphemer. He says that God will allow it to come to pass that our very devout community, which has done so much good and has helped so many of the poor, will be exterminated. Do not listen to him and his schemes. May the will of the Almighty be done. Pray to God, for He alone is our protection!"[3]

Meanwhile, Brand was undergoing his ordeal in Istanbul. At the same time, his wife Hansi and Kastner were pleading with Eichmann to stop the deportations. He refused, saying, "It's up to you and your people in Constantinople to have everything settled quickly." Kastner then wired Brand that deportations were being resumed.

Toward the end of May, several young Polish Jews in Transylvania were arrested by the Hungarian police while crossing the Romanian frontier. They were tortured until one of them betrayed the name of the printer who had supplied the false documents they carried. The arrest of the printer then led to the seizure of many of the Vaadah's papers and the arrest of Hansi Brand and Kastner. The Hungarian police had heard vague rumors about Brand's journey and wanted to know on what kind of mission the Germans had sent him.

Hansi was tortured and her feet bastinadoed so that she could not walk for weeks, but she remained silent. Eichmann, meanwhile, fearing that under constant interrogation, the prisoners would disclose his role in Brand's mission, requested custody of them. Prime Minister Sztójay intervened and the prisoners were turned over to the Gestapo who then released them within an hour. Kastner then began to press Eichmann to make good his promise to allow a specially prepared list of Jews from the provinces to be brought to Budapest. All of these held emigration certificates to Palestine.

Kastner had been negotiating over this group of Jews since April. According to Brand, the Vaadah had at first been afraid to give Eichmann any names at all but then decided to take the risk. Eichmann meanwhile, balked at any concessions, claiming that he had to "clear this Jewish filth out of the provinces" and that he had promised Endre that not a single living Jew would ever return to Hungary. Kastner, however, persisted, believing that, since the Allies and Jewish Agency leaders had no evidence whatsoever that the Germans seriously intended to keep their part of Eichmann's bargain, the gesture of saving this group of almost 2,000 Jews —the so-called Bergen-Belsen transport—would show that the Nazis could be reached, that a crack could be made in the Nazi monolith. The crack might then be widened.

Wisliceny broke the stalemate in these discussions. He told Eichmann that the Hungarians—who were jealous of Gestapo profiteering—could be put off by explaining that the Germans were on the track of a "dangerous Zionist conspiracy" that involved some of the provincial ghettos, and that the "conspirators" had to be isolated. Otherwise they would create unrest and hinder the war effort. Eichmann seems to have enjoyed this ploy and agreed to Kastner's suggestion that a group from Cluj, Kastner's home town, and other former Romanian towns, be set up in a camp in Budapest which would ultimately house the Bergen-Belsen transport.

Quickly, the Vaadah in Budapest constructed several large barracks near the Deaf-Mute Institute on Columbia Street, where 300 Jews from Cluj arrived on July 10. Here they were guarded by five S.S. men who were ordered to protect them against the Hungarian police.[4] These were the first of the "negotiable personalities" of the Bergen-Belsen transport. Each member of the transport paid Eichmann $1,000. Eichmann's original limit for this transport was 600. Literal to the ends of his fingernails when he wanted to be, he used this figure because it represented the number of Palestine certificates Britain had allotted the Hungarian office of the Jewish

Agency in March 1944 for the next year. Eichmann then budged slightly —he would allow 700 to be saved. The negotiations continued, shifting from Eichmann to the German Legation and back. Kastner eventually maneuvered the figure to 1,600, and the total number that ultimately was shipped from Bergen-Belsen to Bregenz, Switzerland, was 1,709.

Meanwhile, with sudden impatience, Eichmann was demanding Brand's return. Unaware of what was happening in Aleppo, the Vaadah momentarily expected the text of an interim agreement. But Eichmann wanted Brand in the flesh. The Vaadah then took a new tack. Kastner asked Eichmann to hold back 100,000 Jews marked for deportation for 5 million Swiss francs ($1 million) which the Vaadah was prepared to pay. He considered the deal and on June 14 said he was ready to transport up to 30,000 Hungarian Jews to Austria and "keep them on ice there." On the basis of a subsequent agreement, six trainloads comprising 18,000 Jews from Budapest and the provinces (mainly from Debrecen, Szeged, Snolnok and Balassagyarmat) were moved to Austria. They lived for the rest of the war in special camps in Strasshof and most survived the war.

The five million Swiss francs had been collected from the Budapest Jews in the form of jewels, gold and notes, and were offered as a token payment until the arrival of Brand's interim agreement. These were handed over, not to Eichmann, but to S.S. Colonel Kurt Becher, Chief of the Economic Staff of the Field S.S., Budapest. Becher, who is credited with having persuaded Himmler to bargain with Europe's surviving Jews toward the end of the war and who was Himmler's representative in the last transactions with the Jews, already had considerable experience in acquiring Jewish property. He had negotiated with the Manfred Weiss combine and bought the famous Schelderhann stud farm from the Oppenheim family in emigration deals that benefited the S.S. Becher never turned over the five million francs, as such, to Eichmann. Instead, he credited the Vaadah collection to a general account of Jewish "disbursements," out of which payments were made for the release of the Bergen-Belsen transport into Switzerland. He was not fully informed about Eichmann's transaction involving the 18,000 Jews and considered the whole amount as payment for the Bergen-Belsen transport. In his notes, however, Kastner mentions the immediate delivery to Eichmann of 15 tons of coffee and 65,000 reichsmarks.

Eichmann had no personal interest at all in the successful outcome of negotiations with Jews or Allies, whereas Becher did. And yet a strong professional jealousy existed. Eichmann's antagonism toward Becher was revealed at his trial in Jerusalem. Eichmann openly admitted:

> Becher came to see me and informed me that he was Himmler's plenipotentiary who had come to extract from Hungary equipment for the Reichsführer S.S. and for the Waffen S.S., the fighting arm of the S.S. From our discussion during our frequent visits, I soon realized that this

man was trying to do what Himmler had formerly forbidden except for special cases—to arrange for Jews to emigrate in return for foreign currency and equipment. . . . Here was a man, deciding on these matters who came to trespass on my preserves. . . . I was very angry at the idea of this man, who was not a member of the Police force, occupying himself with emigration matters while I had to help and participate in the deportations.[5]

Although Eichmann refused to stop the deportations pending Brand's return, the Vaadah continued to believe that further concessions could be wrung from him. They were heartened by the Strasshof transports. Frantic appeals for some encouraging sign were sent to Istanbul, but there was no reply, no stir. Bitterness gripped them. Help was nowhere to be found, not from the Allies, not from the Jews outside Europe, not from the churches. The Allies apparently were not going to act quickly on Brand's proposal; moreover, they were doing nothing about the urgent request sent through Switzerland to bomb the railway junctions on the Košice-Presov-Auschwitz line. Nor was there help from world Jewry. Kastner expressed the Vaadah's reproachfulness toward Jews who had not done their utmost. "They were outside," he wrote; "we were inside. They were not immediately affected; we were the victims. They moralized; we feared death. They had sympathy for us and believed themselves to be powerless. We wanted to live and believed rescue had to be possible." Brand castigated the Jews in Palestine: "You have kept on the right side of the law. You have refused to declare a general strike. If there was no other way, you should have used force to get out of prison."

Within the Catholic Church in Hungary, meanwhile, there had been some protests, concerned mainly with converted Jews. On May 15, when the deportations started in Zone I, Papal Nuncio Angelo Rotta sent the following note to the Hungarian Foreign Office:

> The Hungarian Government is prepared to deport 100,000 persons. . . . The whole world knows what deportation means in practice.
> The Apostolic Nunciature considers it to be its duty to protest against such measures. Not from a false sense of compassion, but on behalf of thousands of Christians, it once again appeals to the Hungarian Government not to continue this war against the Jews beyond the limits prescribed by the laws of nature and the commandments of God and to avoid any proceedings against which the Holy See and the conscience of the whole Christian world would be compelled to protest.[6]

Bishop László Ravasz of the Universal Reformed Assembly had called on Sztójay on May 9 to protest the atrocities and later urged joint action with the Catholics, but Cardinal Seredi did not respond. The two Protestant Churches presented a joint memorandum on June 23 urging protection for converted Jews. This document spoke clearly about the meaning of the deportations, as well as the "Jewish mentality." It stated:

> This journey is leading to final destruction. We protest against devout members of our congregations being punished only for being considered Jews from a racial point of view. They are being punished for a Jewish mentality from which they, and in many cases, their ancestors, have solemnly disconnected themselves. Their lives, as regards Christian spirit and morality, are not considered in the least.

A somewhat testy exchange between two Catholic representatives occurred during this period, each accusing the other of insufficient intervention. On June 5, the Papal Nuncio protested against the deportation of the aged and infirm. Within the next few days, complaints were made against the seeming indifference of the Primate, Cardinal Seredi. On June 8, the Nuncio called on him and asked why the bishops had failed to oppose the Government more energetically. Cardinal Seredi said that he and the bishops had done everything necessary in defense of the Jews. Then he countered: "As to the part played by the Nunciature, many people are not content with it. It is often asked why there is an Apostolic Nunciature in Budapest if it does not act. On the other hand, if it has acted, nobody knows in what manner. It is also considered perplexing that the Vatican maintains diplomatic relations with the German Government which is to blame for the atrocities."[7] The Nuncio replied by saying that his protest had been broadcast by the BBC.

Cardinal Seredi finally broke his public silence by issuing a pastoral letter, a strange document in several ways. The cleric issued the letter reluctantly, in a defeatist mood, frankly declaring that he expected "no result from this step." However, when Sztójay held up its distribution, explaining that his government was under external pressure and that the extreme Nyilas—Arrow Cross—might seize power, the Cardinal protested the delay. He finally agreed to delay publication if he could be assured that the Budapest deportations would be canceled. Sztójay promised the cancellation "for the time being." Finally on Sunday, July 1—the day after the fourth of the five zones outside the capital had been emptied of Jews —700 copies of the pastoral letter were received by pastors and read to congregations. The letter itself is a peculiar one, long and winding, dealing with workers' wages, hours, insurance and other miscellaneous matters. One passage concerned Jews, but it was hardly a ringing protest:

> We do not deny that a number of Jews have executed a wickedly destructive influence on the Hungarian economic, social and moral life. . . . Consequently, we raise no objections to steps being taken, so far as the financial system of the State is concerned. Neither do we protest against the objectionable influence being eliminated; on the contrary, we would like to see it vanish. However, we would be neglecting our moral and episcopal duties

were we not to guard against justice suffering damage and against our Hungarian fellow-citizens and our Catholic faithful being wrong merely on account of their origin.[8]

Within a few days, the Minister of Justice promised that deportations of converted Jews would cease; Cardinal Seredi then ordered his pastoral letter suppressed. During this period, the equivocal intervention of religious leaders accomplished very little. Later, toward the end of 1944, when a new wave of deportations was instigated by the Arrow Cross, the churches and Papal Nunciature sheltered some Jews, issued safe-conducts and forged certificates of various kinds.

The rest of the world was also far removed from the intense flame which the Vaadah kept burning around the mission of their comrade, Joel Brand. As all else was failing, they felt that his mission must not. The hour was late and Jews were perishing by the thousands, but some had been saved by efforts of the Vaadah. Many were still alive. The Vaadah was convinced that the Germans were vulnerable to bargains and bribes. As for the Germans, Himmler himself was now keenly interested in whatever leverage could be gained from a ransom deal. Eichmann preferred to send Jews to the death camps, except for the private arrangements that he could make, or offers made under pressure from Himmler. Still, he was taking his orders from Himmler. Other German officials are known to have optimistically awaited the outcome of Eichmann's proposition to Brand. Prematurely, some Nazi leaders, including Himmler, had lulled themselves into thinking that the Allies would welcome German support of an anti-Russian crusade and awaited with great interest the Western reaction to the proposition that 10,000 trucks be delivered for exclusive German use on the Eastern Front.

If one can believe Eichmann's story, as he told it to the Dutch journalist Wilhelm Sassen in Argentina, he considered his arrangements with Kastner regarding the Bergen-Belsen transport and the release of 18,000 Jews to Austria as a private matter, supplementing the "blood-for-goods" deal. He told Sassen:

All my own agreements with Jewish officials were more or less side transactions to the exchange of the million Jews for 10,000 winterized trucks with trailers. Becher and I were twice ordered to Himmler in Berlin to discuss it. Whether Himmler settled the actual terms of the exchange or whether he left it to me, I do not remember. . . . I do remember Himmler's specifically saying to me: "Eichmann, motorize the 8th and 22nd S.S. Cavalry Divisions." This indicated the personal concern of Himmler, who was soon to take over the Reserve Army, in receiving those trucks. They were far more important than the lives of individual Jews. What did he care about a million Jews? His concern was his divisions. He apparently did not want to motorize these two divisions, but rather to equip them for use as a sort of fast-moving task force.[9]

Himmler had also been interested in making contact with the Allies for some time. After the Russian victory at Kursk in the summer of 1943 —possibly the greatest tank battle ever fought—he had no illusions about the outcome of the war and began to toy with the idea of trying to save himself through a palace revolution.

This idea conflicted with his boundless loyalty to Hitler, of whom he had told his masseur, Dr. Kersten: "Everything that I am I owe to him." Nevertheless, after the summer of 1943, Himmler was a sorely divided man. Various ransom schemes were proposed in that year, but Himmler's intentions were never seriously tested. Kersten had urged him to stop the war at the end of 1943 and he softened toward the idea. He particularly enjoyed Kersten's suggestion that history would remember him as a great leader who had put an end to a senseless war. He would earn the gratitude of the world. The big stumbling block was his own gratitude toward Hitler. Even so, Kersten repeatedly influenced Himmler—usually when he was ill—to oppose Hitler's orders.[10]

When Himmler was well, he was so overlaid with rules and fantasies and blind obedience to his master that he became inaccessible. Evidently, no Allied strategists were interested in piercing the emotional armor plate of the second most powerful man in the Third Reich. Nor did Allied intelligence pursue his interest in conspiracy or ransom schemes.

According to Kersten, a different kind of vulnerability appeared in Himmler's armor in 1942, involving the progressive physical and mental deterioration of Hitler. In December 1942, Kersten himself saw a secret medical report on Hitler's symptoms—all associated with syphilis (the condition is now believed to have been Parkinson's disease). Himmler was determined to keep the quack Dr. Theodor Morrell, who promised to keep Hitler going until the war was won. Kersten explained that such an illness weakens a man's judgment, impairs critical faculties and produces delusions, especially megalomania. How could Himmler let such a man decide the fate of millions of people? How could his orders be respected? Himmler, paralyzed by his sense of loyalty, answered that Germany would lose the war if Hitler did not lead the country. Furthermore, there was no provision for a succession. When Kersten pressed for an honorable peace by Himmler based on this new situation, Himmler answered by saying that people would believe that his motives were selfish, that he was merely trying to seize power for himself. This fear of betraying Hitler's trust was tenacious but not omnipotent and gave way on occasion. The Reichsführer S.S., like many Nazi leaders, lived on split-levels.

Although he winced at the thought of hunters shooting defenseless animals, Himmler seems to have enjoyed the terror he could inspire in his fellow Germans. However, he never comprehended the hatred in which he was held abroad. To foreigners and neutrals, he liked to appear as an executive, a senior bureaucrat utterly opposed to Communism—one, in short, who was ideally suited by his position to preserve order in the country during any period of "difficulty" and to lead Germany back into the family of nations.[11]

In dallying with conspiracy, Himmler used Dr. Carl Langbehn, an old acquaintance and neighbor. In the past, Langbehn had approached Himmler on behalf of his old law tutor who had been thrown into a concentration camp because of his Jewish ancestry. Himmler had been obliging and ordered the man's release and permission to leave the country. Emboldened, undoubtedly, by the friendship and protection of such a powerful neighbor, Langbehn assumed prominence in one circle of resistance centered about Johannes Popitz. Once the Prussian Minister of Finance in the early Nazi period, Popitz, by 1938, had awakened to the true nature of Nazism and joined opposition groups. A brilliant Greek scholar as well as economist, he met with General Beck, Hassell and others in a Wednesday Club that became a "resistance" center.

As early as January 1943, Himmler was close on the trail of the conspirators—closer than any of them realized—but kept in friendly contact with the group. Popitz, especially, began to see in Himmler a possible replacement for Hitler, as Himmler, seemingly so fanatically loyal to Hitler, began to see himself. Yet almost to the end, he played a double game, in the course of which he ended the life of many a conspirator.

After the German defeat at Kursk, Langbehn began to raise with Himmler, as tactfully as possible, the idea of a meeting with Popitz. The purpose was twofold: to test Himmler's reaction to the notion of a palace revolution and to see if Himmler was willing to discuss in general terms an approach to the Allies for ending the war.

Both sides seem to have had the intention of double-crossing each other. The conspirators hoped to use the S.S. to get rid of Hitler, then turn on it with the full weight of the Army. On his side, Himmler simply intended to use Popitz and Langbehn as a respectable front for opening negotiations with the Allies.[12] If the West should prove receptive, there would be no difficulty over Himmler's assuming the power to implement the plan, for he had at his command the perfect machinery for a coup d'état: the apparatus of the police, the S.D. and the S.S.

The final details of the meeting between Himmler and Popitz were arranged by Himmler's personal Chief of Staff, Karl Wolff, for August 26. The four men—Himmler, Wolff, Popitz and Langbehn—met in a room at the Reich Ministry of the Interior. After some innocuous pleasantries, Popitz discreetly brought the discussion around to the possibility of Himmler's accession to power. He approached the question from the angle of the critical military and political situation facing Germany. Was it not possible that things had gotten a little beyond the Führer's control? Should he not be relieved of some of the heavy burdens he bore? Could not some of his power be transferred to some strong personality—Himmler himself perhaps?

Not surprisingly, there is no record of what Himmler said. But what is significant is that he did not clamp Popitz and Langbehn into prison or worse—for gross sedition. Popitz later told Goerdeler that Himmler was "not averse in principle" to certain suggestions. Two days after the meeting Langbehn received a travel permit for Switzerland, where he was to "feel out . . . the reactions of the Allies to a change of regime."

To give the conspirators this much slack in the line seemed to them almost too good to be true. But they had not reckoned on their cunning and ruthless partner. Himmler's vanity may have been flattered by Popitz' suggestions, but he was far too shrewd not to recognize the essential enmity between himself and the conspirators. Himmler also knew that eliminating Hitler was only a preliminary. A purge of the whole Nazi apparatus would follow. Moreover, Himmler had enemies within his own world who themselves were waiting for the right moment to succeed Hitler. The power struggle became more obsessive and foul as the military decline accelerated.

Langbehn left Berlin with his wife at the end of August and traveled to Bern. There he sought out American and British intelligence agents and spoke less guardedly than was wise. It may be that he feared for his own skin if he did not return to Himmler with some form of positive encouragement. In any case, one of the lesser contacts (probably the Free French) sent a telegram to London stating: "Himmler's lawyer confirms the hopelessness of Germany's military and political situation and has arrived to put out peace-feelers."

The telegram was sent in a cipher which the Germans had already broken and it was decoded by both the Abwehr and the S.D. Canaris, head of the Abwehr, which was already planning an anti-Hitler coup of its own, warned Popitz that there was trouble ahead, but both men were sure that Himmler could be counted on for protection. Walter Schellenberg then intervened. Schellenberg was at that time head of Gestapo counterintelligence. Later, ironically, it was this same man who tried to prod Himmler to make concessions to the Allies regarding the release of Jews from concentration camps. In 1943, although his motives are not entirely clear, he seems to have wanted to put his chief in a cast-iron frame.

When Langbehn and his wife crossed the border into Germany, they were immediately arrested on Schellenberg's orders. Thinking at first that the arrest might have been arranged purposely to cover their tracks, the Langbehns made no effort to contact Himmler. Schellenberg, meanwhile, took the decoded message to Gestapo head Müller, who himself made no secret of wanting to succeed Himmler. Müller immediately showed the message to Bormann and from Bormann it went promptly to Hitler. As had happened before and would happen again, Himmler squirmed out of an incriminating situation and the affair blew over. Langbehn was transferred to Mauthausen; Himmler managed to have his trial postponed several times. Popitz, meanwhile, tried twice to approach Himmler and secure Langbehn's release but Himmler refused to see him. Popitz was arrested after the July 20 attempted coup and executed. Langbehn also was executed but not before the S.S. tortured him in the most barbarous way, finishing by tearing off his genitals.[13]

Himmler's loyalty had again conquered. There was nothing in Himmler to counterbalance the power of Hitler's sway over him, but, by the same token, there was no Allied gesture to probe that part of him that was vulnerable to negotiations aimed at ending the war sooner or saving lives. Such external pressure may possibly have provided the counterbalance that he himself lacked.

Eichmann, meanwhile, did not see any conflict between his role as master deportation expert and negotiator for Himmler. The active participation of the Hungarians in the deportations gave him the opportunity to blame them for the cruelties of the transfers. He deplored the Hungarian barbarities in loading the transports, the lack of food and water, and thought the German methods were "much better," but he was nonetheless proud of his achievement in "shipping the Jews off in a lightning operation." Once the deportations to Auschwitz "were running smoothly," he wrote, "I turned to concentrate on negotiations with the Jewish political and community officials in Budapest. In this I was carrying out the second basic objective of Reichsführer Himmler." He waited impatiently for Brand's return.

Early in July, however, the Jewish Agency delegation in Istanbul decided that Brand could not be spared from the negotiations with the British to return to Hungary. They substituted a financial expert, Menachem Bader, and requested a visa for him. Eichmann complied; he sent one to the German Embassy in Istanbul and arranged a plane reservation. But the British refused to give Bader, a Palestine citizen, an exit permit. Nothing came of this plan. Finally, the delegates at Istanbul decided to send the interim agreement (which Brand had drafted over a month before) to Budapest in the diplomatic bag of a neutral country. Kastner hurried to the S.S. headquarters on July 7. When the document arrived, Becher declared, "Himmler will accept this. I will go to Berlin and put it through." Eichmann ordered Kastner to send a telegram to Istanbul immediately, saying: "We are ready to negotiate. Nominate your representatives." Again, the Vaadah experienced a surge of hope, but this quickly turned to despair. A long night of waiting ensued.

Negotiations were ultimately continued in Switzerland, on neutral soil, on a bridge over the Rhine at St. Margarethen, but not until August 21.

Besides indulging in peace-making fantasies, and ordering negotiations with Jews, Himmler in midsummer 1944 enjoyed power at the summit of several immense empires: he was head of the S.S., the Waffen (armed) S.S., the Secret Police and the Criminal Police, the Security Service, foreign intelligence, the concentration camps, V-weapons and the Home Army. By this time Walter Schellenberg and others in Himmler's immediate entourage were prodding Himmler to succeed Hitler as head of state and save Germany by negotiating a compromise peace. Though slavishly loyal to Hitler, the Reichsführer S.S. neither condemned nor condoned these suggestions. Within a short time, the plot of July 20 miscarried and Himmler gained new accessions of power: he became commander in chief of the Reserve Army, took over control of all prisoner-of-war camps from the Army, and was himself in command of an Army Group on the Vistula front. The Brand mission with its possibilities for fortifying his personal power and the swelling power of the S.S. must have been fully appreciated by Himmler. His grandiose visions never condescended to mere military victory but he certainly realized that the days of the Third Reich were numbered.

Meanwhile, according to Eichmann,

> the deportations had to continue in spite of our pending deal. But the Jews were, to a certain extent, "put on ice," held in a camp ready to be moved at any time. . . . If the deal had succeeded, I believe I could have arranged to ship the first 20,000 Jews in two days via Rumania to Palestine or even via France to Spain. If there had been any delay, it would have come from the side of the receivers. The plain fact was that there was no place on earth that would have been ready to accept the Jews, not even this one million.[14]

In Budapest, the Vaadah waited vainly week after week for word from the Allies. Finally, on July 19, the BBC broadcast an indignant rejection to the ransom offer, labeling it a piece of shameless blackmail. This hope was now destroyed.

During this period, an immense change in Hungary's political and moral climate was taking place. The deportation timetable had moved swiftly, and was closing in on Budapest's 200,000 Jews. By July 9, all five zones in Hungary outside the capital had been emptied of Jews. Over 437,000 had been deported. Endre had already decided to isolate the Jews in Budapest by housing them in industrial plants. Camps were set up in Csepel and Horthyliget in the buildings of the Weiss Manfred steel works and bombed out airplane factories. Raids were made on trolleys, railroad stations and in cemeteries, catching Jews in the capital for "labor service."

Regent Horthy, long inert and half-captive, was at last beginning to stir. Uneasy over the growing foreign protests against the deportations, he had a long talk with Veesenmayer on July 4, and said that he was being bombarded daily with telegrams from all sides—from the Vatican, the King of Sweden, from Switzerland and the International Red Cross. The American Secretary of State Cordell Hull was threatening reprisals against those responsible. Neutral countries were demanding that Hungarian Jews be allowed to emigrate or receive protective foreign passports.

Prime Minister Sztójay himself was ready to call a halt. On July 5, he read Veesenmayer secret messages sent by American and British missions in Bern to their governments and deciphered by Hungarian counterintelligence. They contained a detailed description of the fate of the deportees and suggested target bombing of all collaborating Hungarian agencies. Exact street and house numbers were named. One message contained the names of seventy Hungarians and Germans who were responsible for the deportations. Ironically, all of this information had been sent to Bern by the Vaadah weeks before, but no action had been taken. Now, the Hungarians had intercepted the information and were frightened by it into action. On July 6, Sztójay told Veesenmayer that Horthy had ordered the deportations stopped.

Tragically late, the British as well as the American governments were applying pressure on Horthy. On July 7, Anthony Eden and Brendan Bracken declared in the House of Commons that hundreds of thousands of Jews were being exterminated in Hungary. This announcement followed the belated action of the Swiss Government in releasing accumulated news from the censorship ban. In the United States, too, the news of the near-annihilation of Hungarian Jewry was slow to surface. It was on April 7 that the two Slovak writers of the War Refugee Board report had made their sensational escape from Auschwitz to Bratislava. Three months later, the Allied and neutral press reported the massive gassings of Hungarian Jews. By then, most of the 437,000 who had been deported had already perished.

Even so, doubts persisted.

The Russians had discovered Maidanek—two miles from Lublin—on July 23, 1944. A week later, the Soviet writer Konstantin Simonov wrote a full account in *Pravda* of the death camp in which 1,500,000 persons were gassed. The *London Illustrated News* and *Sphere* published special issues, including photographs of human bones, gas chambers and ovens in Maidanek. Other media were still skeptical. In August 1944, Alexander Werth, a British correspondent for the *Sunday Times*, who spent the entire war period covering the war in the Soviet Union, sent a detailed report on Maidanek to the BBC. The BBC refused to use it, however, suspecting that it was a "Russian propaganda stunt." American newspapers also could scarcely accept the enormous dimensions of the Nazi extermina-tions. The comment of the *New York Herald Tribune* at the time Werth filed his report was: "Maybe we should wait for further corroboration of the horror story that comes from Lublin. Even on top of all we have been taught of the maniacal Nazi ruthlessness, this example sounds inconceiv-able. . . . The picture presented by American correspondents requires no comment except that, if authentic, the regime capable of such crimes deserves annihilation."[15]

Meanwhile, Horthy's order to stop the deportations was being opposed. Andor Jarosz, the Hungarian Minister of the Interior, told Veesenmayer that he was ready and willing to disobey Horthy's orders if S.S. units could be kept out of Budapest. The Jews in the capital could be removed to the provinces; the "second lap of their journey would then be easy," he said. Veesenmayer promised his assistance. Then, in an unexpectedly swift move, Horthy dismissed State Secretaries Endre and Baky and issued warrants for their arrest. When Veesenmayer threatened punitive action, however, the Regent beat a temporary retreat and reinstated them.

Eichmann, characteristically, continued to make his own rules. Fever-ishly working against time, on July 12, he made use of the 150 S.S. men still in the *Einsatzgruppe* barracks at Kistarcsa and Csepel, near Budapest, and put 1,700 Jews on a train to Auschwitz. Jewish leaders protested to Horthy and he promptly ordered the train stopped at the frontier and sent back. The train was returned, but the joy of the deportees was short-lived. On July 19, S.S. men descended on Kistarcsa, locked up the Hungarian commandant and his assistants and shouted that Eichmann would not have his orders overruled—even by Horthy. A survivor, Dr. Alexander Brodie, who was responsible for providing the camp with food from the Central Jewish Council, rushed to the Council office to sound an alarm only to discover that all of the members were being held in Eichmann's Schwabenberg office by one of Eichmann's assistants, Otto Hunsche. At 7 P.M. Hunsche was called to the phone and ordered to release the men. By then, however, the deportation train had already reached the border, too late for Horthy's intervention.

A feverish search for key political and military controls followed. On July 14, Ribbentrop instructed Veesenmayer to deliver a blunt ultimatum to Horthy threatening a total military occupation of Hungary if the depor-tations were not resumed, but the warning was not heeded. To Horthy, the German threats were now meaningless: Russian troops were already pouring into neighboring Galicia and the entire southern front was in retreat. Endre and Baky, as well as Jarosz, were dismissed for good. On July 27, the Sztójay government, still hanging on, declared itself ready to transfer the Jews in the capital to Hungarian camps. The Germans, still confident of their power, decided to form a "more reliable government."

However, in their calculations, they had overlooked the Regent as well as the collapsing German military position. When the new government was formed in August, it was Horthy who formed it in the light of an expected Allied victory.

During July, after Horthy's order had stopped the deportations, the Germans waged a heavy press and publicity campaign. The German Legation in Bern invited foreign diplomats to see a film dealing with the deportations from Nagyvárad in Transylvania. The opening scenes were particularly harsh, showing women and children being thrashed and robbed by Hungarian gendarmes. Trains were crammed; there was no food to be had. Not a single German soldier or policeman could be seen. Dominating the scene were Hungarian gendarmes with their characteristic hats with cocks' feathers. The scene suddenly changed and Red Cross nurses were shown opening the sealed freight cars, extracting the corpses, giving fresh water and food to the sick. The Germans were then shown allowing Jews to rest and recover and later assigning them easy jobs.[16] The Hungarians also competed for foreign favor.

On July 18, Sztójay informed the foreign legations of the new Hungarian policy. Jews, he said, were no longer being sent abroad for "labor purposes." They could emigrate to Sweden, Switzerland and Palestine, and food parcels could be sent to persons in concentration camps. The situation between the Germans and Horthy, meanwhile, had become very tense. S.S. detachments encircled Budapest, but this time Horthy stuck fast. Ferenczy then began a skillful double cross. He told Horthy that he was ready to turn against the Germans if enough Hungarian forces backed him up, explaining that there were "no real German forces, only depots and hospitals."

The direction of German-Hungarian relations was finally changed by decisive military realities. By late August, the German military position in Hungary had become untenable. On August 24, the Soviet Army broke through the Romanian defenses in Bessarabia. News also came that the Allies were within reach of Paris. The Romanian King told the Germans that he would have to conclude an armistice with the Russians and that the German Army would have to be removed. The Germans replied by bombing the royal palace in Bucharest. Within a few weeks, however, twenty-six German divisions were hacked to pieces by invading Russians and their new Romanian allies.[17] On August 25, during the Romanian switch, Horthy installed a new prime minister, General Geza Lakatos. On the same day, the Eichmann *Kommando* withdrew from Hungary, and that evening Wisliceny telephoned Kastner and said, "You have won, Herr Kastner. Our staff is leaving." Eichmann himself, as it turned out, retired to an estate in the provinces, biding his time, while Veesenmayer behind the scenes plotted the overthrow of the Horthy regime.

It soon became evident to the Germans that Lakatos had been appointed to conclude an armistice with the Allies. He disarmed the Budapest gendarmerie and demanded that Hungary have a free hand in the Jewish question. When he was shown Sztójay's agreement to remove Budapest Jews to the provinces, he said quite simply that there were no guards to take care of them, no camps to put them in and no transport to remove them. Horthy, meanwhile, reassured the Jewish Council that there would be no deportations from Budapest and no labor camps. A Hungarian armistice mission left for Moscow. Token measures such as the reopening of Jewish stores and relaxation of the curfew were passed to show the goodwill of the new regime. The Germans, however, were far from ready to quit Hungary. Germany itself would be invaded if Hungary were overrun by the Russians. Besides, there were still some living Jews in Hungary.

As August 27 approached, Jews in Budapest grew uneasy. This was the date Eichmann had set for their deportation. In the midst of numerous neutral interventions and protests, the Germans made new preparations. They were concentrating troops for a new seizure of power by the Hungarian Arrow Cross leader Ferenc Szalasy. On August 27, using the date to win the confidence of both the Jews and Horthy, Ferenczy took a message to Eichmann saying that the Hungarian Government would not allow deportations to be resumed and would, if necessary, resist the Germans if they did.

The Lakatos Cabinet took office on August 30. On September 7, at a meeting of the Crown Council, Horthy said that it was time to consider an armistice. The Russians already controlled the passes of the southern Carpathians and were advancing into Transylvania. However, he insisted that Germany be informed of Hungary's intentions. The Hungarian Minister for Home Defense proposed that the Germans transfer five divisions from the Western Front to defend Transylvania. He was sure Germany would refuse and thereby give Hungary an excuse for starting negotiations with Russia. But the Hungarians were surprised by a new German thrust. Several German Army divisions were sent to garrison Budapest. Szalasy had a talk with Veesenmayer on August 31 and offered to seize power with German help. Ferenczy agreed to stay at his job until the take-over. The Lakatos Government, meanwhile, prepared to arrest Szalasy and other Arrow Cross leaders, but they enjoyed complete German protection and could not be touched. The power struggle in Hungary seesawed for another month.

The inconclusive haggling over Jewish lives continued on the bridge at St. Margarethen through the early autumn of 1944. Becher kept pressing Himmler to keep negotiations open even after the British rejection of Brand's appeal, and Himmler agreed. On the day after the British broadcast their rejection, Count von Stauffenberg's bomb exploded in Hitler's headquarters. The S.S. police tightened their controls against future internal ruptures, but privately, Himmler understood the drift of events. He acquiesced in Becher's prodding and sent Becher as his authorized representative to Switzerland to continue talks with a Jewish representative—this time Saly Mayer. This new series of talks began on August 21. Becher, accompanied by Kastner, repeated Eichmann's argument: deportations would stop if goods were delivered. But Mayer had no power to put forth any concrete proposals and was rendered helpless by American currency restrictions. He tried to appeal to the conscience of Becher and delivered humanitarian homilies, but these merely exasperated Becher. The gassings continued.

There was a second inconclusive meeting on September 1 when Mayer's lawyer explained: "We have nothing positive to say to you. We have only been authorized by the American authorities not to say no." The "Jewish power" which Eichmann and Himmler and Becher apparently believed to be invincible was no more evident in Mayer than in Brand. Nothing came of these talks.

At the beginning of October, the Red Army broke into southern Hungary; the thrust of the Soviet Second Ukraine Army was only a hundred miles from Budapest. On October 14, the Germans sent the 24th Panzer Division into Budapest with forty tanks. This unit was ordered to depose Horthy and Lakatos. Accompanying the unit was S.S. Major General Otto Skorzeny, the man who had successfully kidnapped Mussolini in July 1943 when his regime was toppled. On the morning of October 15, Skorzeny lured Horthy's son Nicholas to a German-held building by making him believe he was to meet a secret agent of Tito. The young Horthy was wrapped in blankets, thrown into a truck and taken to an airport. From there he was to be taken to Mauthausen. This kidnapping occurred a few hours before Horthy was scheduled to broadcast an armistice appeal. He had been irresolute about this decision and kept postponing action. The Germans undoubtedly had been tipped off about the broadcast and timed the abduction accordingly. Veesenmayer told the old Regent that at the least sign of "treason," his son would be shot. Horthy broke under this threat and promised to annul everything. On October 16, both he and Lakatos surrendered and were imprisoned in Germany.

The Germans no longer had a regent to legitimize their actions; consequently, they combined the offices of regent and prime minister and vested them in the Arrow Cross leader Ferenc Szalasy, a man who would do their bidding with fanatical zeal. Hungarian Jews now were to undergo a new nightmare—this time under the redoubled fanaticism of Eichmann and Szalasy.

These last drastic actions against the remaining Jews of Hungary followed the ill-starred July 20 conspiracy to assassinate Hitler and form part of the backlash fury that Hitler generated to avenge the "treason" of the conspirators and force the pace of the war. Half-mad, deteriorating in mind and body, he whipped beaten armies, demoralized generals and a bomb-dazed nation to a final effort that prolonged for almost a year the agony of a war that Germany had already lost.

The war to exterminate European Jewry was still very much part of that war. However, Himmler by 1944 could be diverted from the bloodletting. As the iron ring drew tighter around Germany, he pushed his schemes for a separate peace with England and the United States, believing that negotiations with Jews and for Jews were an important link in these plans. With Eichmann, however, there was no letup. During the short-lived Lakatos regime, he went to Romania to finish up some work he had left in September 1942—the deportation of Jews in the border towns of Arad and Timisoara. He had also kept his eye on Slovakia, where a full-fledged revolt broke out at the approach of the Red Army, and sent Brunner to catch 14,000 Jews in the chaos of a disintegrating German Army. In the fall of 1944, he planned to make his final killing in Hungary.

Eichmann returned to Budapest on October 17, two days after the Szalasy government took power, and immediately resumed his interrupted plan for Budapest's Jews. He began negotiations with Hungarian officials for the deportation of 50,000 Jews on foot, allegedly to work in Germany. Tens of thousands of laborers were needed in the large underground bunkers where pusuit planes and V-2 weapons were assembled. Romania and Bulgaria were already out of reach of the S.S. net. A desperate shortage of labor in the Reich forced the Germans to scrape at the remnants of living Jews in the still-occupied areas. Railway transportation had been disorganized as a result of Allied bombings. According to testimony at his trial, Eichmann conceived the idea of the forced march as a result of the bombings which had destroyed the railway line. Jews were to be marched to the Austrian border, 120 miles distant. Eichmann planned to move 50,000 Jews in the first roundup, and 50,000 later on. The remaining Jews in Hungary were then to be concentrated in labor camps and a ghetto—with the predictable results of Nazi ghettoization and forced labor.

On the morning of October 20, Hungarian police began knocking on doors in Budapest marked with stars, seizing all men from sixteen to sixty. By evening, 22,000 had been rounded up. During the next three days, the drive was extended to women between sixteen and forty. By the end of the week, 35,000 Jews had been drafted. On November 10, the seven-day treks began. The destination was Hegyeshalom. Columns of men and women walked through snow, rain and sleet, without food toward Austria. They slept in stables, pigsties or in the open. Those who fell from exhaustion were shot or died from exposure.

These death marches now openly exposed the conflict between Himmler, Becher and Schellenberg on one hand, and Eichmann, Müller and Kaltenbrunner, on the other. Three days before the first forced march, Becher had a talk with a representative from the War Refugee Board who told him that Cordell Hull, the American Secretary of State, had finally consented to transfer some money to Switzerland. Becher thereupon promised that nonworkers would be deported from Budapest and that Jews in camps would have the protection of international law.[18] This promise, however, was not kept. Becher protested the marches to Himmler and Eichmann was ordered to stop sending small children on death columns but Eichmann made no exceptions for the very young, the very old or infirm. Wisliceny told Kastner that 1,200 Jews died on the first march, including women of eighty. Himmler sent S.S. Lieutenant General Max Jüttner to watch a march and report back. At Nuremberg, Jüttner described what he saw:

> Two-thirds of the way to Budapest we saw columns of Jewish women up to sixty years old, escorted by Honved guards. There were many stragglers lying in the road in the intervals between the columns. . . . I was told that the responsible man was Eichmann. I was aware that I might incur disagreeable consequences in sending for him, but he was not in Budapest, so I saw a captain whose name I do not recall and told him his business. He said he was not under my orders and I threatened to inform Himmler in order that this wrong which cried to heaven should be put right. Three days later I sent Himmler a strong report—apparently without result.[19]

Jüttner's report reached Himmler at an inopportune time. It came with the news that Edward Stettinius, Hull's successor, had canceled the transfer of money to Switzerland—the money Hull had permitted for the negotiators. Stettinius also forbade all contact with the Nazis. This action pulled the last prop out of the negotiating structure Kastner was trying to fashion for the formal Saly Mayer. Again, Himmler postponed the decision to abandon deportations.

Jüttner also approached Otto Winkelmann, the Higher S.S. and Police Leader in Hungary, but Winkelmann said that he was helpless. Eichmann had jurisdiction over the deportations and was not under his command. Jüttner also complained to Eichmann's office and was told not to intervene, that Eichmann took orders from the RSHA exclusively.

Still uncurbed, Eichmann fumed against Jüttner, who, he said, "was not in any position to judge whether people who had been seven or eight days on the road would be treated as fit for work or otherwise." He had received only half of the 70,000 workers promised him by Szalasy. As for Wisliceny, who had returned some sick Jews to Budapest, Eichmann said he would bring him before a court-martial.

Accompanying Jüttner en route from Vienna to Budapest, S.S. Lieutenant Colonel Rudolf Höss, the commandant of Auschwitz—no stranger to mass death—was also shocked by the brutality of the march and complained to Becher. Höss had come straight from Himmler's headquarters, where a new policy had been laid down as a result of Becher's meeting with Roswell McClelland, an American negotiator who had replaced Saly Mayer. Eichmann ignored all protests.

Some deportees were driven into the Danube. A Red Cross report describes a midwinter scene:

> In Gönyü, we saw that a part of the deportees were driven on board the ships anchored in the Danube over night. Many—in their great distress—committed suicide. In the still of the night one scream was followed by the other; the doomed people were jumping into the Danube which was covered with drifting ice. . . . With our own eyes we saw the gendarmes driving the Jews, who arrived in pitch darkness, over the narrow gangplank covered with ice, so that scores of them slipped into the icy river.[20]

On November 21, Eichmann ordered a second forced march to Hegyeshalom. But his whip was losing its sting. The German position on all fronts was collapsing. Kastner bombarded Becher with appeals and demands that he go at once to Himmler. Having left someone else to carry on the bargaining in Switzerland, Becher went to Berlin and, according to his own account, prevailed on Himmler to stop the foot marches. Sometime late in November, Himmler gave the decisive order: the foot marches were to stop.

Credit for stopping the marches was also claimed by Jüttner and Winkelmann. About 15,000 Jews on forced marches had been rescued by agents of the neutral powers, the Red Cross, the Papal Nuncio and the Swedish emissary Raoul Wallenberg. Szalasy himself had become uneasy and on November 21 had also issued an order canceling all further foot marches because of the high death rate among Jewish women. On November 29, the German S.D. commander in Budapest demanded 17,000 workers; they were allowed to travel to the Austrian border by train.

Very few of the 35,000 to 40,000 deportees to Hegyeshalom survived the marches. Most of the women who reached Austria were distributed among the German concentration camps, and the men who remained on the Austrian border to dig and quarry along the "South East Wall" worked and died in conditions of gross inhumanity.[21]

Raoul Wallenberg, a thirty-two-year-old native of Stockholm, in his capacity as owner of an import-export firm had visited Budapest a few times and made friends as well as business contacts there. In reply to requests made by Jewish organizations, he consented to stay in Budapest in a quasi-official capacity to help Hungarian Jews. The Swedish Minister made him an envoy extraordinary with the rank of Secretary to the Swedish Legation in Budapest.

Wallenberg had arrived in Budapest on July 9, 1944, and set to work immediately establishing a new department in the embassy under his charge, a so-called Section C. Its sole function was the rescue of Jews. From the initial twenty voluntary workers, the staff of Section C grew to 660. Section C issued several hundred Swedish passports to Hungarian Jews with relatives or business contacts in Sweden. Wallenberg also devised the "protective passport," a certificate emblazoned with the Swedish colors, the embassy stamp and his signature, which placed Jews under Swedish protection. The Papal Nuncio, the Swiss, Portuguese and Spanish representatives followed suit and also issued protective passports.

Wallenberg cultivated these neutral legations as well as high-ranking Hungarian officials, some of whom were won over to his plans by bribes. He also followed the columns of Jews marched to Hegyeshalom and comforted the victims with food, warm clothing and shoes. In Budapest, he manufactured protective letters for Jews scheduled to be deported and Hungarian authorities were sometimes persuaded to remove holders of these letters from the transports. It has been estimated that 4,000 Jews were saved this way.[22] Fullhearted help was also extended by the Swiss Consul Karl Lutz.

Among the Catholic clerics who helped some Hungarian Jews survive was the benign Angelo Roncalli, who later became Pope John XXIII. During the catastrophic summer of 1944, Roncalli was Apostolic Delegate to Turkey. Ira Hirschmann, the roving one-man representative of the War Refugee Board, who was in the area at this time, had tried appealing to various Catholics to intervene during the deportations. He had tried, for example, to appeal to von Papen, the German Ambassador to Turkey, who had a sly talent for self-preservation, but this effort failed. Late in the summer of 1944, he decided to see the Pope's highest emissary.

Monsignor Roncalli at the time lived in a spacious house, high on a hill, on the island of Buyuk Ada in the Sea of Marmora, forty miles from Istanbul. It was an idyllic place, affording a stunning view of the sea, remotely distant from the Hungarian shambles. Hirschmann had come with Gilbert Simond of the Red Cross. Roncalli was warm, gracious and convivial. He urged the men to enjoy the view and some wine before they took up more serious matters. Then suddenly, after amiably chatting, he said, "*Dunque, cominciamo. . . .* Now let us begin."

Roncalli listened intently as Hirschmann outlined the desperate plight of the Budapest Jews. He pulled his chair closer to the men and asked quietly: "Do you have any contact with people in Hungary who will co-operate?" Hirschmann nodded. Then Roncalli asked, "Do you think the

Jews there would be willing to undergo baptism ceremonies?" Not prepared for this suggestion, Hirschmann at first hesitated, but then said decisively that they would be ready. Roncalli said that some baptismal certificates had already been issued by nuns. Hirschmann agreed to make certain contacts and arrange for a large-scale baptism.

When he visited Israel after the war, Hirschmann saw the Brands and asked what results Roncalli's efforts had achieved. Hansi Brand smiled and said that a number of Jews were indeed saved by these certificates, and that besides the originals, the Vaadah printing press had turned out many facsimiles.[23]

On other official fronts, however, rescue activities had bogged down. Finally, early in November, a very different kind of man replaced Saly Mayer in the negotiations with the Nazis. He was an American, a Quaker, and a man who knew how to do business without moralizing. Roswell McClelland was also an official representative of the American War Refugee Board, and this status gave him substantially more bargaining power than Mayer or Brand could command. McClelland told Becher:

> I am here to help. I am ready to agree that twenty million francs shall be deposited in Switzerland. This money can be found by Joint. You ask for goods. But you cannot expect the Joint to procure them for you. Germany herself must make those arrangements. I reserve the right to keep a check on the goods that are bought and also on what the Germans give in return. It is of course a matter for the Swiss government to decide whether or not export permits will be granted for those goods. But under the circumstances I am ready to approach the federal government on your behalf.[24]

McClelland made only one demand upon the Germans: that they protect all civilians without distinction of race or creed. This interview was the first substantial talk to take place after Brand's departure from Budapest. He had left on May 16. Becher's talk with McClelland was held on November 5. Six months had elapsed before Cordell Hull had finally authorized the transfer of five million francs to the JDC in Switzerland. During this time, hundreds of thousands of Jews had perished not only in Hungary but in the ghetto of Lodz, and in deportations from the islands of Greece, from Italy, in Theresienstadt, and the Polish labor camps. Now, at last, the prospects of some sort of deal seemed good—only to be cut down before the end of the month by Edward Stettinius, Hull's successor. Eichmann, in the meantime, threatened to deport every Jew in Budapest if the twenty million francs were not paid.

By this time—the end of November—Himmler's own self-interest required the end of the exterminations and on November 25 he ordered the gassings to stop. Becher gave up any hope of receiving any money through McClelland and was no longer interested in what the Nazis could get out of the Jews. During the last months of the war he wanted, above all, to have his name associated with the rescue of the scattered survivors and went from camp to camp trying to force the diehard Eichmann-Kaltenbrunner-Müller combine to obey Himmler's order. He did not always succeed. Indeed, he was so anxious to ingratiate himself with the Allies that he resorted to a subterfuge to secure the departure of the Bergen-Belsen transport. The transport left in three stages: in August and December 1944 and in early 1945. When, late in November, Eichmann threatened to deport every Jew in Budapest unless the 20-million-franc ransom was paid, Becher cabled Eichmann from Switzerland that the first installment of 5 million francs had been deposited in an S.S. account, but that the Allies insisted on delivery of the rest of the transport before paying the balance. The ruse worked. On December 6, a group of 1,368 Jews arrived in Bregenz, Switzerland. Himmler actually did not get the 5 million francs until February 1945 and none of the remaining 15 million.

There now remained in Budapest about 100,000 Jews who had been shoved into a huge Ghetto. Many thousands of them held "protective passports." Under the short-lived Lakatos Government, Swiss, Swedish, Spanish and Portuguese Consulates had been allowed to register prospective emigrants under their protection. Horthy had also granted extraterritoriality to the Red Cross. The Szalasy Government was not recognized by any neutral state and Szalasy himself was apparently willing to barter concessions to Jews for recognition. But he was thwarted by Arrow Cross elements that outran the S.S. murder squads in ferocity—particularly Minister for Internal Affairs Emil Kovarcz.

In the last weeks before the Russians took Budapest, as many as half of the Jews in the city clung to their papers. But they had lost their value. Arrow Cross murder gangs ranged through the streets and dragged Jews to the banks of the Danube and shot them. Each morning for weeks corpses were found heaped on the pavements of the streets or floating on the river. By now foreign diplomats competed with each other to help Jews, but Kovarcz continued to send out his killers. He respected only the power of the German weapons. Early in December, shortly after Himmler had issued his order to destroy the gas chambers and stop the annihilation of Jews, Kovarcz decided on the immediate slaughter of all the Jews in the Ghetto. Taking a page from Kaltenbrunner and Müller, who defied Himmler's order, Kovarcz was determined to destroy every single witness to the massacres. Szalasy, fearing Russian reprisals, opposed him but a majority of the Cabinet agreed. The surviving Jewish leadership now was to make the supremely ironical gesture of calling on certain Germans to save the rest of Budapest's Jews.[25]

Dr. Stern and other members of the Jewish Council met with the

Vaadah and urged them to use their connections to stop Kovarcz. Andreas Biss, Joel Brand's cousin, who had gone to Slovakia to try to save Gisi Fleischmann, and who carried on the work of the Vaadah while Kastner was in Switzerland, was delegated to see Becher. He found him in a very bad humor; the negotiations in Switzerland to which he had deeply committed himself were disintegrating and he was afraid Himmler would hold him responsible.

When Biss entered his room and asked him to intervene with the Hungarians, Becher began by shouting, "What on earth do you take me for, Herr Biss? What do you expect me to do now? I've taken everything upon myself; I've risked my neck for you a dozen times, and all you've done is to deceive me and let me down. What do you imagine Eichmann will think of me? The transport [Bergen-Belsen] has gone to Switzerland, and we've had nothing in return from Saly Mayer. No money, no goods, nothing."

Biss moved in skillfully. "Colonel," he said, "there is more to this than meets the eye. If the Hungarians are allowed to murder the remaining Jews, the Allies will hold the Germans responsible. All Germans, without exception. You know, sir, as well as I do, how the war is going. There is no longer any point in beating about the bush. You now have a real chance of doing something for us."

"But I'm not alone here," Becher replied. "Every step I take will be observed by others. If you had only delivered the thirty trucks from Slovakia, I would at least have had something to show. I have to cover myself."

The thirty trucks had actually been dug up somehow by a German wholesale merchant, Alois Steger, who had helped the Vaadah in the past, but Becher apparently knew nothing about them. Steger was a Sudeten German but he lived in Bratislava. When Hitler came to power, he did everything he could to save his Jewish friends and frequently drove to Berlin taking food for Jewish families and helping Jews cross the frontier. He owned a bonded warehouse on the Slovak-Hungarian border and undertook important contracts for the export of machines from Germany to Hungary. When the deportations started in Czechoslovakia, he spent a great deal of time between Bratislava and Budapest smuggling Jews into Hungary.

After Brand's departure, when Budapest Jews were threatened, he guaranteed to Becher the delivery of thirty trucks if he could save them. Biss told Becher that Steger had trucks and that they were at his disposal. Becher confirmed this and a chain of actions quickly followed. Becher phoned Himmler and Himmler ordered Otto Winkelmann, the Higher S.S. and Police Leader in Hungary, to order Kovarcz to stop all actions against the Jews. The police felt they now had an alibi for themselves when the Russians arrived. But the Jews living outside the Ghetto were still open game.

The camp on Columbus Street where part of the Bergen-Belsen transport had once been sheltered fell under a new attack. The Vaadah had kept the camp going as a shelter for several thousand refugees. A red-and-white flag was hoisted but Eichmann, still in hot pursuit of cleansing the earth of Jews, drove the refugees of the Columbus Street camp out into the open country. Auschwitz was dismantled but Eichmann's deportation reflex was still very much alive.

The Russians entered Pest on January 16, and Buda four weeks later. To the hunger and terror of the huddled Jews of Budapest, the siege added physical maiming, anarchy and more death. In the last hours of their stay in Budapest, the S.S. tried to destroy the Vaadah, but failed. Just before leaving, one agent phoned Brand's wife Hansi after a fruitless search and said she was needed urgently. Hansi, who had answered the phone herself, said, "I'm sorry, but I myself am looking for Frau Brand. As soon as I find her, I will send her along to you."

Although the Soviet Union considered Hungary its exclusive field of operations, it showed no interest in the fate of Hungarian Jewry. It did not protest the deportation of Jews, leaving this entirely to the Western powers.

Allied air attacks struck Budapest hard. The Ghetto was hit frequently and thousands of survivors had to look continuously for new places to live. Food supplies diminished and scarlet fever and dysentery raged. But the Szalasy Government refused to surrender. On December 23, Secretary of State Dr. Pal Vágó declared: "We will defend Budapest to the last man. Every street corner, every window must become a death-dealing fortress!" The Nyilas (Arrow Cross) terror rose to new excesses. On Christmas Eve, the Children's Homes of the International Red Cross, which sheltered several thousand Jewish children, were stormed. While bombs and mines exploded all over the city, the Nyilas drove the children across the Buda into the Radetsky barracks. Here Jewish workers in labor companies, clad in Nyilas uniforms, turned them back with forged orders. Tragically the children were placed in homes where caretakers denounced them to Nyilas members. Some of the children were shot; some were thrown into the Danube; a few managed to escape.

Eichmann's last visit to Budapest was made during Christmas week. He came to the Ghetto looking for Jewish Council members but found the Council building empty. In a rage, he hit the porter over the head with a pistol and left with a threat to execute his whole family if the Council did not show up later that day. However, Eichmann left Budapest for good that night.

During this time, Minister of the Interior Gabor Vajna issued a decree ordering all Jews in hiding to move into the Ghetto voluntarily. Any found outside the Ghetto after December 31 would be executed. The only exceptions to the decree were the patients and nursing staff of the hospitals in Wesselènyi Street and Bethlen Square. Notwithstanding these exceptions, on December 28, S.S. men and Nyilas made a raid on the Bethlen Square Hospital. All of the male patients were ordered to the courtyard late at night, while the women were assembled in the cellar. On the following morning, they were all driven to the gallery of an auditorium and locked up for twenty-four hours while their rooms were searched for valuables. Later, 28 young men were picked out and shot. Nyilas horrors drew the following report from the head of the Institute of Forensic Medicine:

> In the most brutal manner, the Nyilas made short work of their victims. A few were simply shot, but the majority were mercilessly tortured. From the distorted faces of the corpses, the conclusion could be drawn that their sufferings had been ghastly. Very few blown-out brains or heart shots were to be found; on the other hand, there was overwhelming evidence of the most brutal ill-treatment. Shooting out of eyes, scalping, deliberate breaking of bones and abdominal knife-wounds were Nyilas specialities. The naked bodies bore signs of thrashing; the heads and faces were badly bruised. The corpses of men and women of all ages together with those of children and infants were brought into the Institute of Forensic Medicine during the days preceding Christmas.[26]

There were about 10,000 Jews living outside the Ghetto. Some lived in Catholic and Calvinist institutions; others were sheltered by individual Christians. Ingenious schemes were used to safeguard the refugees. Father Jacob Raile, Prior of the Jesuit College, dressed the men in police uniforms and made a "police station" out of a porter's lodge. Ranolder Institute established a fake war industry plant employing 100 girls. Many monks and nuns were tortured by the Nyilas in their manhunts, and some were killed with their charges. Miss J. M. Haining, the gallant head of the Girls' School attached to the Scottish Mission, was herself sent to Auschwitz.

To cope with this new persecution, Wallenberg transferred his offices to Pest, on the left bank of the Danube, to be closer to the threatened Jews. He rented thirty-two large buildings, put them under the protection of the Swedish Embassy and filled them with Jews. The Swedish Red Cross and other neutral embassies cooperated and the so-called International Ghetto came into existence. It sheltered about 35,000 Jews.

Zionist youth members also engaged in daredevil rescue activities. Clad in illegal uniforms and equipped with false papers, groups patrolled the streets nightly, wearing Nyilas armlets or disguised as members of the National Guard. Sometimes they accosted real Nyilas members, ordered them to show their documents and then declared them false. The documents were then confiscated and used for further rescues. The youths also worked together with the International Red Cross, which had made contact with Ferenczy, whom they had induced to grant favors in return for food parcels.

Wallenberg reported that the Ghetto would be starving by January 5. There was very little water or food and no heat. As to the government order to force the occupants of the International Ghetto into the Central Ghetto, Wallenberg commented:

> In the Foreigners' Ghetto, in which some 35,000 persons are held, the food position is similar to that in the Central Ghetto. It would be absolutely impossible for the inhabitants of the Foreigners' Ghetto to take even the minutest quantity of food with them on such a foot march. For humane reasons, this plan must be described as utterly crazy and inhuman. The Royal Swedish Legation is not aware of any similar plan ever having been carried out by any other civilized government.[27]

On January 16, the Russians liberated the area of the International Ghetto. The Central Ghetto was liberated the following night. The first Russian patrol entered the Ghetto from Wesselènyi Street by crawling through an air-raid shelter. By telephone, they gave directions which silenced the last resistance of German batteries. Thousands of Jews stormed the planks which had imprisoned them. Crowds wearing yellow stars streamed into the streets seeking their families and food. Half-dead, they came into the sunshine and air, crying, shouting, praying, running. But the end had not yet come. The Nyilas terror moved to Buda where massacres of Jews continued until February 13 when the fighting finally ended; 550,000 Jews from the enlarged Hungarian realm had perished in nine months—seven, counting the two-month pause. The deportations ended December 8. Thousands died in the ghettos as well as in the "protected houses" of the Swedish and Swiss legations as a result of starvation, air bombardment or disease. Kastner estimated that the Hungarians themselves were responsible for the death of 80,000 during the Szalasy regime.

Capitulation to the Russians did not end the troubles of the Hungarian Jews. The foreign legation staffs and the Red Cross representatives who had offered tangible aid and comfort in the last part of 1944, were ordered to leave Hungary. The new conquerors also refused to allow the funds of the Joint Distribution Committee to be used. It was on a JDC mission that Wallenberg set off on January 17 with two officers to see Marshal Malinovsky at his headquarters at Debrecen. He was never seen again.

After some months, the Swedish Foreign Office was notified that Wallenberg "was in good health under Russian protection." Late in 1946, Stalin promised the Swedish Minister in Moscow a full investigation of his whereabouts. But in spite of earlier assurances, the Moscow magazine *New Times* declared in February 1948 that Wallenberg must have been killed either by S.S. men or by members of the Arrow Cross. Persistent requests for more precise information were not answered. In 1952, several former Axis officials released from Russian prisons claimed they had seen or spoken to Wallenberg in a Moscow prison. Then, on February 7, 1957, a news dispatch from the U.S.S.R. revealed that Wallenberg had died, allegedly of a heart attack, in the dread Lubyanka Prison in Moscow on July 17, 1947—two years after his imprisonment.

The efforts of the Nazis to camouflage the fate of Hungarian Jewry have been documented by an album of 203 photographs taken on the death platform of Birkenau and explicated at the Frankfurt trials of 1964. The photographic reporting by the Germans was meant to serve as an alibi to disprove the disclosures of the inmates who had escaped from Birkenau just before the deportations of Hungarian Jews began.

S.S. photographers were assigned to photograph what was called "the resettlement of Hungarian Jews" in their new "settled areas" in Birkenau and "Waldsee" and in so doing to create a soothing effect. They did their job while standing on the roofs of boxcars and moving vans and from watchtowers. Ostensibly there was nothing shocking in these pictures. The "settlers" who were photographed do not appear agitated because when they arrived in Birkenau they did not know what lay ahead. The S.S. men were polite and full of smiles and many of the victims smiled back—into the cameras. Not one picture portrays a sick man or a corpse. Nor were cameras trained on the S.S. guards or watchdogs. There are, moreover, no photographs of the furnace yards, stripping rooms, gas chambers, the warehouse for corpses, or of the crematoria.[28]

The Nazis succeeded beyond their expectations in destroying the substance of Hungarian Jewry. But their Hungarian aides played an indispensable role. The complicity of Endre, Sztójay, Szalasy, the Horthy gendarmerie, and Horthy himself is clear. Horthy, for instance, when he appointed Baky and Endre, said in an aside: "I hate the Jews, the Communists and the Galicians. Out of our country with them!" Veesenmayer, although on trial for his own life before the People's Court in Budapest, approached the truth about Hungarian cooperation in the following statement made November 20, 1945:

> If the Hungarians had opposed with iron consistency the demand of the Germans concerning Jewish affairs, a solution of this demand would not have been at all possible. There is no doubt that the Germans brought pressure to bear in this matter, but 1945 [read 1944] was already a year of crisis and there were not enough police forces available for the selection, capture and deportation of a million people. This was a large-scale police

action whose execution during a period of three months was only made possible by the enthusiastic participation of the entire Hungarian police apparatus. We were not able to bring the necessary troops for this from the outside inasmuch as this operation could only be carried out by troops that were familiar with the country and its population as well as the language of the land.[29]

In May 1945, in a hunting lodge near Bad Ischl, Kurt Becher waited for American troops to arrest him. There was still some unfinished business with the Vaadah. Becher possessed six strongboxes of valuables—currency, gold, and jewels—that had been collected from the Jews of Budapest as their contribution to rescue efforts. Becher had never turned these boxes over to Himmler. Hoping that a last-minute gesture of goodwill to the Jews would help save him, Becher sought out a Vaadah member, Moshe Schweiger, who was imprisoned at Mauthausen. Schweiger was given preferential treatment through Becher's intervention. Before being captured himself, Becher summoned Schweiger to his lodge and extracted two promises from him: he was to tell Kastner in Switzerland that he, Becher, was a prisoner of the Americans, and that he would return the strongboxes to him. "This is what I got for organizing the Bergen-Belsen Rescue Train that reached Switzerland," Becher said. "I promised Dr. Kastner that I would return it if at all possible. I wanted to keep the valuables to help the Jewish people."[30]

After the Americans took Becher prisoner, Schweiger gave the strongboxes to American counterespionage officers and wrote to the Jewish Agency in Palestine about this episode. In Tel Aviv, while scanning incoming documents on the Jewish catastrophe, Joel Brand saw Schweiger's report. To the bitter frustration over his own mission was added the irony of this return of jewels and baubles representing so much hope and some bartered lives among the hundreds of thousands who had perished.

32 Rescuers and Bystanders

UNTIL OR UNLESS new Allied documents become available, the evidence is clear that the Allied nations at war with Germany did not include rescue of Jews as one of their wartime objectives or security for the surviving remnant one of their postwar goals. They promised heavy retribution for the guilty, but throughout the war blurred out acknowledgment that Hitler's war involved, as one of his prime objectives, the extermination of European Jewry. Instead, they condemned, in broadly general terms, Hitler's racist policy and strictured in general his "monstrous crimes" and "atrocities." Yet Hitler left no doubt at any time that he was warring on Jews, and that he would annihilate, not the Poles or the Gypsies or the Russians, but the Jews.

It is true, of course, that many Poles and Gypsies and Russians were murdered as racial inferiors or "asocials"; Nazi atrocities tortured and bled all of Europe and Slavs and Gypsies suffered great losses. But it was the Jews alone that were marked for complete annihilation. Other peoples could save themselves by showing that they were "Germanizable." Elaborate screenings were devised in all of the occupied countries so that "worthwhile" elements would be salvaged. The general plan for the East foresaw massive population transfers and perpetual enslavement of Slav populations, but there was no blueprint for their extermination.

There was also a great difference between the Nazi treatment of Jews and Gypsies, although both have often been linked together. The Nazi attitude toward the Gypsies was ambivalent: at one extreme was a certain fascination with the supposed racial purity of Gypsies; at the other, was the view that Gypsies were subhuman and ought to be eliminated. In the case of the Jews, after June 1941, there were no alternatives. None were to stay alive. Moreover, Nazi action against Gypsies was confined to Germany and German-controlled territory, particularly Poland. No attempts were made to carry out anti-Gypsy programs for all of Europe. Romania and Hungary, for example, which contained large Gypsy populations, were not pressured to act against them.[1] The archracist fanatic Himmler had a confessed weakness for Gypsies, according to Rudolf Höss, the commandant of Auschwitz: "The Reichsfüher S.S. wanted to insure that the two main Gypsy stocks [the Sinte and Lalleri Gypsies] be preserved," Höss testified. ". . . In his view they were the direct descendants of the original Indo-Germanic race, and had preserved their ways and customs more or less pure and intact."² One cannot imagine Himmler indulging a fantasy of this kind about a "pure" stock among Jews. As it was, at least 30,000 Gypsies from the Greater Reich were gassed at Auschwitz—a large and terrible figure.

The number of Gypsies in Europe in 1900 was estimated at about one million, but there are no statistics for the period of World War II. The Nazis could not elevate the Gypsy "menace" into a myth, but the arguments for their "solution" involved the obsessive German concern with "health" and "purity." The Gypsies were said to have a foul heredity, and were described as habitual criminals and parasites imperiling German racial purity. In short, they were "asocials" and deemed unworthy to live. In the invaded areas of the Soviet Union, the Einsatzgruppen were ordered to exterminate them at the same time and in the same way as the Jews, but no definitive totals are available. In the area assigned to Einsatzgruppe D—the Crimea—after the systematic killing of the Gypsies had begun, an order exempted all "nonmigratory" Gypsies from destruction if they could prove a two-year period of residence where they were found. In Serbia, Gypsies as well as Jews were shot as hostages by the German Army. In Croatia, Pavelic's Ustashis were the principal initiators of the Gypsy massacres. The official Yugoslavian Inquiry Commission set the number of victims in Yugoslavia at 28,000. Possibly as many as 100,000 Gypsies perished during the Hitler era in Europe—a very heavy loss. Yet, in the Nazi scheme for a New Order, it was the Jews and the Jews alone who were marked for total obliteration.

However, this unparalleled destruction stirred no commensurate rescue or braking action. The world was impassive. It was also accustomed to Jewish suffering.

Reflecting the widespread unwillingness to give rescue efforts for Jews any special consideration, the Bermuda Refugee Conference, which was convened in the spring of 1943, declared that "it would be unfair to put nationals who professed the Jewish faith on a priority list for relief."

The conference was an outgrowth of a great demonstration in New York City's Madison Square Garden, called by major Jewish organizations on March 1, 1943, when American Jewry demanded negotiations with Axis Powers through neutral countries for removal of as many Jews as possible to safe places and arrangements to permit feeding of Jews in ghettos. On March 2, the State Department announced that a meeting of American and British statesmen would deal with the problem. The Bermuda Refugee Conference was the result. Admission to the conference was denied to representative Jewish bodies. The delegates rejected the idea of negotiating with the Axis and did not consider the conference authorized to recommend food shipments to ghettos.

Much earlier, in January 1942, eight governments-in-exile and the French National Committee meeting in London showed a similar diffidence. The representatives branded the German regime of terror in strong language, but when the American Jewish Congress asked the conference to condemn the specific crimes against Jews, the governments-in-exile said that such a "reference might be equivalent to an implicit recognition of the racial theories which we all reject." This line of evasion was dangerously close to the evasiveness the Nazis themselves had perfected: in their language system, any acknowledgment of the crime of murder might be equivalent to an implicit recognition of the act of murder. The Allies refused to acknowledge that Jews as Jews were being murdered.

The Allies were not only reluctant to describe the destruction of Jews in simple, blunt language. They held back official confirmation of the exterminations after they had been reported (in the summer of 1942) until December 17, 1942—a period of almost five months in which a million Jews were killed. On that date the American Department of State joined the other Allied Governments in a declaration which pledged that the responsible perpetrators of the exterminations "shall not escape retribution." No plan, however, was suggested to put an end to the exterminations, nor was any reprisal action against the Germans threatened at the time.

Secretary of Treasury Henry Morgenthau, Jr., who experienced this diplomatic inertia at firsthand has strongly castigated the American State Department:

> We knew in Washington, from August 1942 on, that the Nazis were planning to exterminate all the Jews of Europe. Yet, for nearly 18 months after the first reports of the Nazi horror plan, the State Department did practically nothing. Officials dodged their grim responsibility, procrastinated when concrete rescue schemes were placed before them, and even suppressed information about atrocities in order to prevent an outraged public opinion from forcing their hand. . . . The Treasury's responsibility for licensing monetary transactions abroad meant that we had to pass on the financial phases of refugee relief plans. This gave us a front-row view of those 18 terrible months of inefficiency, buck-passing, bureaucratic delay and sometimes what appeared to be calculated obstructionism. . . . Cautious and temporizing by nature, these officials always preferred committees to action. . . . Lacking either the administrative drive or the emotional commitment, they could not bring about prompt United States action on behalf of the desperate people.[3]

On August 1, 1942, the chief of the Geneva office of the World Jewish Congress, Dr. Gerhardt Riegner, heard through a German industrialist "that a plan had been discussed in Hitler's headquarters for the extermination of all Jews in Nazi-occupied lands." Riegner sent this information via the American and British consulates to Dr. Stephen S. Wise, president of the American Jewish Congress, who, in turn gave this report to Undersecretary of State Sumner Welles. The Undersecretary then asked him not to release the information until it could be confirmed. Three months were spent checking Riegner's report.

Welles instructed Leland Harrison, the American Minister in Switzerland, to cooperate with Riegner. Finally, in November 1942, four sworn statements arrived in Washington, backing up Riegner's report. Welles delivered the documents to Wise and told him to make them public. For weeks thereafter the State Department was bombarded with demands for urgent action. But, as Morgenthau has described it, the State Department's reaction "took the form of trying to shut off at the source the flow of information which nourished it."

On January 21, 1943, Welles received a cable from the Legation in Bern containing another message from the Geneva office of the World Jewish Congress: by now, Jews were being killed in Poland at the rate of 6,000 a day. The State Department decided that the question still had to be "explored." Some of its political experts then decided to suppress this flow of information altogether. The reply to the Legation in Bern was as follows:

> In the future we would suggest that you do not accept reports submitted to you to be transmitted to private persons in the United States unless such action is advisable because of extraordinary circumstances. Such private messages circumvent neutral countries' censorship and it is felt that by sending them we risk the possibility that steps would necessarily be taken by the neutral countries to curtail or forbid our means of communication for confidential official matter.[4]

The cable (the text of which Morgenthau vainly tried to obtain for months) was initialed by four officers in the European Division of the State Department. There is every reason to believe that in the press of work, Welles, whose concern for the victims of Nazism had been demonstrated many times, signed the cable without fully realizing its contents. On April 10, 1943, apparently unaware that he had signed a cable suppressing the flow of information, Welles asked the Bern Legation to send additional reports from Riegner on the plight of the Jews. This was the kind of information Harrison had been "instructed" not to send two months earlier. Months passed without any action. Not until December did the State Department cable the Treasury Department's clearance of the financial phases of the refugee relief plan. Harrison then replied that in accordance with standing instructions he had referred the license to the British Legation which needed specific advice from London before it could pass on the request.

The reply from London, received on December 17, 1943, typified what Morgenthau called the "satanic combination of British chill and diplomatic double-talk, cold and correct, and adding up to a sentence of death." Quoting a letter from the Ministry of Economic Warfare to the American Embassy in London, the cable said: "The Foreign Office is concerned with the difficulty of disposing of any considerable number of Jews should they be released from enemy territory. For this reason, they are reluctant even to approve of the preliminary financial arrangements, although these were now acceptable to the Ministry of Economic Warfare."[5] None of the rescue or ransom schemes, out of which Jews snatched a ray of hope, had the fullhearted support of any Allied official agency. It was only in January 1944 that an independent agency, the United States War Refugee Board, was created with the power to negotiate and spend money without being straitjacketed by the State Department. By then, millions of Jews had perished.

On the morning after the British Foreign Office letter was received, the Treasury Department had a long staff meeting. Their conclusions were unanimous. The entire matter had dragged on too long; the issue must be put directly to Hull or the President himself. On December 20, Morgenthau and John Pehle, the head of Foreign Funds Control in the Treasury Department, had a long talk with Hull and pointed out that the British position went far beyond the concrete issue under discussion. But Hull himself had already sent a strong reply to London, saying that the British message had been "read with astonishment" and that the State Department was "unable to agree with the point of view set forth." This philosophy, he continued, "is incompatible with the policy of the United States Government and with previously expressed policy as it has been understood by us."[6]

The State Department also blocked the possible rescue of Jews from Romania. In March 1943, the World Jewish Congress cabled Washington that there was a real chance of rescuing 70,000 Jews in France and Romania provided funds could be sent to Switzerland. Money had already been collected but would not be made available to Nazis. Deposits would be made in blocked accounts in Switzerland. The State Department, which, according to Morgenthau, "scoffed at economic warfare in other connections" said that this transaction would benefit the enemy.

On July 22, Dr. Wise called on the President to see what was causing the delay. Roosevelt was deeply sympathetic and forwarded a memorandum of their conversation to Morgenthau. Morgenthau then sent a summary to Hull, who again issued a vigorous demurrer: "Any view that this would make funds available to the enemy is not correct; the funds would remain blocked in Switzerland until the end of the war."[7] Again months passed without action. Not until December 18, 1943, did the State Department cable license W–2115 to Geneva authorizing the payment of francs and

lei "to evacuate persons whose lives were in danger, or to sustain them."
It was the first license of its kind issued during the war.

On January 16, 1944 Morgenthau himself prepared a highly confidential document for the President, charging that certain State Department officials:

1. Utterly failed to prevent the extermination of Jews in German-controlled Europe. . . .
2. Hid their gross procrastination behind such window dressing as "intergovernmental organizations to survey the whole refugee problem. . . ."[8]

Again, the President seemed sympathetic. He knew, according to Morgenthau, that Mrs. Roosevelt had been frustrated for months in her efforts to get entrance permits from the State Department for 5,000 refugee children.

On January 22, 1944, the President took the jurisdiction of rescue activity out of the hands of the State Department and established the War Refugee Board. At its first meeting, Hull insisted: "One thing I want is, I want this out of the State Department. I want it outside."[9]

While Allied Governments refused unequivocally to describe the special character of Hitler's war on European Jews, reports in the press during the Holocaust were remarkably clear and prompt. This was particularly true of the British press. From the beginning of the Nazi regime, newsmen filed accurate reports of violence in the streets of Germany and terror in the concentration camps. During the period from 1933 to 1938, when Jews constituted only a small part of the camp prison population, British papers stressed the fate of the Jewish prisoners. The Government, too, added detailed information on the pre-extermination period. On October 31, 1939, just five months after a Government White Paper had been issued restricting Jewish immigration to Palestine, quite another kind of White Paper was published. It was called "Papers Concerning the Treatment of German Nationals in Germany." It dealt mainly with Germany's barbarous treatment of its Jews. However, until December 1942, when another White Paper was issued describing the German plan to exterminate European Jewry, the British Government maintained an official silence. By contrast, the press in Britain continuously told the British people what was happening.

This information came partly from neutral sources, mainly Stockholm, and partly from news reaching the American Jewish Joint Distribution Committee. It also owed much to the famous "couriers"—men, women and youths, Jewish and non-Jewish, who, over and over again, succeeded in making miraculous journeys to and from the Polish ghettos. During the autumn of 1939 and the early part of 1940, the British press carried many accounts of the massacres of Jews in Poland and mass murders in many Polish towns. Before the end of 1939, the famous cartoonist David Low drew a picture for the *Evening Standard* showing a goods train being methodically loaded with Jews.

By the middle of 1942, the press was filled with one story after another detailing the slaughter of Jews. At first these reports came mainly from the Russian front; a few papers hinted that these might be Russian-inspired. But on June 27, the Polish Government-in-Exile in London, scarcely an organ of Russian propaganda, issued a White Book of German atrocities containing much information about the particular sufferings of the Jews. This publication was the subject of a broadcast of the BBC European Service by Arthur Cardinal Hinsley, Roman Catholic Archbishop of Westminster. The newspapers editorialized on the documentation of these new horrors but there appeared no suggestion as to how they could be stopped or what reprisal action might be taken if they continued. The London *Daily Telegraph* of June 27, for example, commented that "the chronicle of massacre . . . is wholly in keeping with Hitler's many times avowed policy, and there will be ample means of verification when the time comes for judgment and expiation." Reports of gassings followed. By July, a report circulated describing "a new poison gas discovered by the Nazis following experiments on Jews and political prisoners." This was Zyklon B.[10]

On December 10, 1942, the Polish Government-in-Exile in London issued a publication called *The Mass Extermination of Jews in German-Occupied Poland*. This was widely publicized in the British press and created profound shock. The worst, at last, had been officially acknowledged. On December 17, Britain, the United States and the Soviet Union made a "declaration of solemn protest" against the exterminations and members of the House of Commons rose and stood in silence for two minutes after the declaration was read by Anthony Eden. The deliberate plan to exterminate all of the Jews under Nazi rule was now widely recognized and acknowledged to be in process. But no efforts were made to stop the process.

In view of the shattering Jewish losses—even today at a generation's remove, the scale of destruction is scarcely credible—the nagging question persists: Why were no genuine large-scale rescue efforts attempted? Why were none commensurate with the dimensions of the exterminations proposed? If air threats against the camps and death centers were not yet possible in 1942, why were not reprisal actions against the Nazis or Nazi prisoners threatened? Why was the whole stress of the Allied response on postwar punishment when, at the time that many of the Allied threats were made, Germany was fully confident of military victory and had no reason to fear punishment after the war?

It is difficult to avoid the conclusion that the Allies had written the

Jews off as wartime casualties. This was true not only in the early phases of the war when the Germans had the killing power to do as they liked, but in 1943 and 1944 when the offensive passed to the Allies. One of the bitterest disappointments of all was the failure of the Allies to save almost half a million Hungarian Jews when the Germans were in head-long retreat on all fronts. The failure to bomb the rail lines to the death camps has already been noted. In reflecting on the vocabulary of "legit-imate" enemy targets, one stands aghast at the quality of a civilization that readily bombs factories that produce chemicals but assiduously avoids disrupting the operations of those that produce human corpses. If, as the British said, bombing the death camps posed "certain technical diffi-culties"—these have never been clarified—there were other alternatives. With the knowledge that Hungary in 1944 was gripped by the fear of Allied air raids, the Allies had a potent weapon. The Hungarians were con-centrating Jews in cities of 10,000 or more, preparatory to their deportation. Had the Allies promised immunity to those cities so long as Jews were not deported, Hungary might have cooperated. Such a threat had a precedent. When rumors of the creation of a ghetto in Budapest circulated at the beginning of April 1944, the BBC declared that if a ghetto was created, the Allies would bomb residential parts of the city as well as objectives of military importance. This threat was enough to deter Endre from creating a ghetto in Budapest.

In the fall of 1944, after the Hungarian deportations had run their course to the gates of Budapest—having been stopped there largely by intercepted threats of pinpoint bombings of Government offices in the capital—Churchill echoed the familiar refrain: the culprits must be pun-ished. He wrote to Eden:

> There is no doubt that this is probably the greatest and most horrible crime ever committed in the whole history of the world, and it has been done by scientific machinery by nominally civilised men in the name of a great State and one of the leading races of Europe. It is quite clear that all concerned in this crime who may fall into our hands, including the people who only obeyed orders by carrying out the butcheries should be put to death after their association with the murders has been proved. . . . There should therefore, in my opinion, be no negotiations of any kind on this subject. Declarations should be made in public, so that everyone connected with it will be hunted down and put to death.[11]

The persecutors were to be punished, the Allies promised, but the victims were not to be saved.

When various ransom schemes came to the fore, it took the American State Department eight months to permit Jewish organizations to deposit money to the credit of Axis officials in blocked accounts in Switzerland. This was done only after tremendous pressure was brought to bear and in the face of opposition from the British Foreign Office, which was concerned with the "disposing" of Jews released from Nazi-occupied Europe. When, in March 1943, in a conference with the British, Hull had brought up the possibility of rescuing seventy thousand Bulgarian Jews, Eden had expressed fears that "then the Jews of the world will be wanting us to make similar offers in Poland and Germany." Lack of shipping and "dangers" to British security were also argued.

After the war, in commenting on various ransom schemes, Hull noted the State Department's reluctance to deposit money abroad in the name of the Nazis, but at the same time made an unusually frank admission that the Nazis were susceptible to them. He wrote in his memoirs:

> The Germans permitted Jews to leave only when they were amply paid to do so. We were reluctant to deposit sums of money to the credit of the Nazis, even though the deposits were to be made in Switzerland, were to be liquidated only after the end of the war, and apparently could not be used by the Nazi leaders. Moreover, the State Department did not have the large sums of money and the personnel needed to carry out a plan of reaching and bribing the German officials in charge of the extermination program.[12]

Money, in fact, was the least of the problems. Major Jewish organizations could and did raise the necessary sums. Whether or not the Nazis would have accepted blocked payments for sizable rescue operations, such as the Europa Plan or the "blood-for-goods" plan of Eichmann, may be debated. Eichmann balked, but Wisliceny, Becher and Himmler were certainly interested. At the same time, the Allies did not aggressively pursue ransom opportunities when the Nazis appeared susceptible to such deals. The door, finally opened by Hull on November 5, 1944, was closed almost immediately when his successor, Edward Stettinius, ordered that ransom negotiations with the Nazis be broken off.

Another fundamental question is posed by Allied behavior—the British, in particular—in the face of the acknowledged war which Hitler was waging to obliterate the Jews of Europe. This concerns the effort of Jews in Palestine to take up arms, as Jews, against Hitler. The failure of England to approve the most elementary right of a people to defend itself is one of the cruelest chapters in the Holocaust. The Nazis soon enough showed that everything was permissible. The horrible reality that Hitlerism had created the twentieth-century antiman, a being devoid of conscience or guilt, was grasped by some Jews before their end. It is doubtful, however, that Jews comprehended the extent of official British complicity in their destruction. The British cruelty was masked by layers of history involving the struggle for political democracy, individual liberties and a humane community of men. But it was the British who not only hunted down defenseless refugees on the high seas and caged them like wild beasts but who denied the legally constituted Jewish community of Palestine the right to come to the aid of their fellow Jews on the Continent. Palestine Jews began their struggle before the invasion of Poland and continued it for five long years before the British relented and allowed the formation of a Jewish Brigade.

On August 29, 1939, Weizmann wrote to Chamberlain: "Jews have a contribution to make in the defense of sacred values and wish to fight side by side with Great Britain. The Jewish Agency is ready to enter into immediate arrangements for utilizing Jewish manpower, technical ability, resources, etc." On September 5, he requested a meeting on the subject with Leslie Hore-Belisha, British Secretary of State for War. On September 6, he went to see Charles Corbin, the French Ambassador in London, to offer recruitment of a Jewish Legion in France. No one responded; the Jews had no power to act outside their national allegiances. Within the next few weeks Weizmann bombarded dozens of British men of affairs of all parties and editors with his proposal. Meanwhile, in Palestine, the British had sentenced forty-three young Jews to long imprisonment terms for "indulging in military training."[13]

In May 1940, after Churchill had formed a new government, he instructed his new Colonial Secretary Lord Lloyd to place no obstacle in the way of the Jewish war effort. The arms searches in Palestine stopped, but no official action was taken to implement Churchill's directive. On June 14, after Italy had entered the war, Weizmann again pressed for the mobilization of Palestine Jewry's military strength. "If we have to go down," he appealed, "we are entitled to go down fighting, and the Mandatory Power is in duty bound to grant us this elementary human right."

On September 13, 1940, it appeared that the way had been cleared. Anthony Eden, Secretary of State for War, wrote to Weizmann and reported that "the Government had decided to proceed with the organization of a Jewish Army on the same basis as the Czech and Polish Army." But in the following months, this decision was to be eroded by delays and evasions. In February 1941, the Jewish Army project was ratified by the War Cabinet, but on March 4 the new Colonial Secretary Lord Moyne wrote to Weizmann that "the raising of the Jewish contingent has had to be postponed . . . owing to a lack of equipment." It was this same Lord Moyne who a few weeks earlier (February 14) refused Weizmann's impassioned plea for a special allocation of immigration certificates to Romanian Jews because of a critical situation there. "Rumania," wrote Lord Moyne, "is regarded as enemy occupied territory. The machinery for verification of the *bona fides* of applicants . . . has disappeared. I feel sure that this reply will come as a disappointment to you."

Later, on October 23, Moyne wrote again. This time the Brigade project was impossible, he said, because the Government had to give every aid to the Russians.

The exasperating correspondence dragged on for several years. On July 12, 1944, by which time over five million Jews had perished, Prime Minister Churchill, was still writing to his Secretary of State for War, urging the formation of a Jewish Brigade:

> I am anxious to reply promptly to Dr. Weizmann's request for the formation of a Jewish fighting force put forward in his letter of July 4, of which you have been given a copy. I understand that you wish to have the views of Generals Wilson and Paget before submitting to the Cabinet a scheme for the formation of a Jewish brigade force. As this matter has now been under consideration for some time, I should be glad if you would arrange for a report setting out your proposals to be submitted to the Cabinet early next week.[14]

Another memorandum was dispatched to the Secretary of State for War on July 26. By that time, obviously put out by the tedious objections of the War Office, Churchill sarcastically dismissed the questions raised: "I believe it is the wish of the Jews themselves to fight the Germans anywhere. It is with the Germans they have their quarrel. There is no need to put the conditions in such a form as to imply that the War Office in its infinite wisdom might wish to send the Jews to fight the Japanese and that otherwise there would be no use in having the brigade group."[15]

At the same time, Churchill wrote to Sir Edward Bridges, an aide who had reported to him that a "Jewish brigade group would be carefully examined" by the War Office. Churchill observed to Bridges that "when the War Office say they will carefully examine a thing, they mean they will do it in."

The Jewish Brigade was "done in" until September 1944.

Even Churchill, despite his opposition to the War Office's red tape and many speeches lauding Zionism, did nothing to save Jewish lives. During the war, he too ignored appeals to lift the immigration restrictions set forth in the White Paper of 1939. By the time of his death in 1965, however, the pain of this omission had receded. He was praised then for having been in sympathy with Jewish aspirations in Palestine and was even eulogized as a "Zionist."

The major rescue efforts devolved upon the Jews themselves. The uphill work of *Mossad* in Europe had been temporarily halted after the tragedy of the *Struma* in February 1942. Small boats continued to struggle to reach Palestine, but the organized efforts of *Mossad* shifted from Europe to the Middle East—to Syria, Lebanon, Iraq, North Africa and Egypt. As the doors of Europe were locked against them, they tried to force passage into Palestine elsewhere. However, another Jewish rescue effort unfolded, this one also with the grudging consent of Britain, toward the end of the war. Basically, it was not a rescue effort at all but a military action which the participants hoped would have as a by-product, rescue activity. The participants were thirty-two youthful parachutists from Palestine.

The achievements of the Jewish parachutists were on a small scale but their presence in Yugoslavia, Hungary, Romania and Slovakia electrified the surviving Jews with fresh hope. They walked miles to see them and hear their strong words of encouragement. As every rational expectation of help had proved illusory, the living presence of these Jewish youths swelled into legends and their exploits took on a spectacular character. Had Britain permitted not thirty-two but several hundred to drop down behind enemy lines, and had they been permitted to start their work early in the war, instead of late, the legends might have been less grandiose and the material rescue greater.

The volunteers were furnished by Haganah, the Jewish Defense Organization of Palestine, which had already established the nucleus of a Jewish underground rescue movement centered in Istanbul. Haganah leaders hoped to organize Jewish resistance throughout the Balkans and aid the partisan movement. For years they had urged the organization of parachutists. The Palestinian Jews, however, were caught up in the reality of a war in which the fate of Jews was discounted. For their plans to succeed, they needed arms, Allied help and, above all, permission from the British. They could obtain none of these unless they could demonstrate that their activities would advance the general war effort, not merely Jewish rescue needs.

The Allied bombing of the Ploesti oil fields in Romania in 1943 supplied a compelling military reason that finally overcame British opposition. During the bombings, many airmen were downed because of inadequate intelligence. The British began to see the value of using the Palestinian Jews as parachutists. Many of the volunteers came from the Balkan nations and knew the languages of the region. They were familiar with the terrain and could secure valuable information through contacts with underground movements. They could also assist in the escape of prisoners of war and in the rescue of downed airmen. After their purely military missions were accomplished, they could try to save Jews. This agreement as to priorities had to be scrupulously honored by the parachutists.

Two hundred and forty youths were trained. Thirty-two set out on Balkan missions.[16] Seven were killed; twenty-five returned, some after suffering imprisonment and torture. The parachutists were courageous, idealistic, quick-witted. They had to be spies as well as flyers, secret agents as well as saviors. A special aura of drama and gallantry surrounds their exploits, for they broke the vast silence and passivity of onlookers of the Holocaust in the days before liberation and cracked the trancelike helplessness that gripped the victims. Their life in Palestine seems to have prepared—even destined—them for their peculiar mission. All were members of *kibbutzim* (cooperative agricultural settlements) where they had lived the arduous, ascetic life of pioneering settlers. They were Jewish heroes in a doomed story, for they led no armies and had no homeland of their own. They struggled in a vacuum of indifference and bureaucratic inertia, stoically pitting their frail power against a Hitler-saturated continent. They have all become legends—Reuben Dafni and Joel Nussbacker in Yugoslavia and Hungary, Joshua Trachtenberg in Romania, Enzo Sereni in Italy, Hayim Hermesch in Slovakia—but none more so than one of the two girls among them, Hannah Senesch.

Hannah was born in Budapest, the daughter of a wealthy assimilated Hungarian Jewish family. A sensitive, introspective girl, she might have become a minor poet in another age, but the span of her life coincided with the rise of Nazism and its conquest of Europe. She had gone to Palestine in 1939, a confirmed Zionist, but Hitler's conquest of Europe impelled her to return home. She decided to return to Hungary to carry on rescue activity among surviving Jews early in 1944—just at the time that the British approved a plan to organize a group of parachutists and drop them behind enemy lines in the Balkans. Hannah was one of the thirty-two chosen. Her diary records this strange coincidence: "How strangely things develop! On January 8, I wrote of the idea which suddenly stirred me. . . . A few days ago, a comrade came and told me of the mission being planned . . . just what I dreamed of. . . . I feel a fatality in this, just as at the time before I went to Palestine. Then, too, I was not my own master. I was caught by an idea that did not let me rest. I knew that I would enter Palestine, no matter what difficulties were in my way. Now I again feel this tension towards an important and necessary task—as well as the inevitability of the task."

By the middle of June, her group was in training in Cairo. They were to be dropped over Yugoslavia, some to stay and others to cross over into Hungary. They all wore British uniforms and were instructed to identify themselves as "Palestinian members of the British Air Force with rights of prisoners of war," if captured.

The first lap of Hannah's mission was the flight from the training center in Cairo to Bari, in southeastern Italy on the Adriatic. From there, her group was flown to Brindisi by a Polish crew and then dropped over Yugoslavia where they were to contact Tito's partisans. On March 13, 1944, just past midnight on a clear moonlit night, the parachutists jumped. One of the men had an incendiary bomb with a complete set of false documents strapped to his leg; if the group fell into enemy hands, he merely had to strike the bomb to destroy the incriminating documents. The pilot, however, overshot his target by eight miles and Hannah was temporarily separated from the others. Finally reunited, they moved into liberated territory near the Hungarian border and encountered friendly Slovenian partisans who made a festive party for them and listened raptly to stories of Jewish communal settlement in Palestine. British and American missions to Tito were contacted and definite assignments were laid out for the parachutists when word came that Germany had invaded Hungary.

The news stunned Hannah particularly. She had originally planned to enter Hungary as a refugee but this was no longer feasible. She would now have to smuggle herself across the border. Another blow soon fell: a big German offensive dislodged the partisans from the section where the parachutists had landed. The group then decided to go on to Croatia where the 10th Corps of partisans had made some progress. For almost a month, they trudged through 200 miles of enemy territory, along the path of the main railroad line from Vienna to Belgrade, fighting off enemy patrols, finally making contact with the assigned group. Ironically, however, they were not able to announce their identity as Jews. The partisan general explained that his troops were operating in territory that had been strongly infected by Nazi propaganda. If they were to learn that the parachutists were Jews, he said, his troops would conclude that Hitler was right: Jews rule Britain and the world! The parachutists reluctantly agreed to conceal their identity and spoke Hebrew to each other. To the Yugoslav partisans, they explained that they were Welshmen, speaking Welsh.

Meanwhile, the parachutists who remained in Yugoslavia made maps which, when supplemented by radio information, served as guides for Allied airmen and organized search parties for stranded airmen and escaped prisoners. Against the advice of her companions, Hannah had insisted on crossing into Hungary. She crossed the frontier on June 9, but the smugglers who had helped her were themselves caught and her whereabouts were revealed. The Hungarian police found her radio code and grilled her about her activities. When she refused to reveal her mission, they tried physical torture. When this too failed, they found something else they believed would be persuasive.

Mrs. Catherine Senesch, Hannah's mother, was still in Budapest, completely unaware of her daughter's mission. On June 17, 1944, she was summoned to the Hadek, the Army headquarters, to be a "witness."[17] There she was closely questioned. Where was her daughter? Why had she left Hungary? What had she studied at school? "But what do you think," the examiner asked, when the mother said she believed her daughter was in Haifa, "where is she now?"

"I don't know," the mother answered. The police officer continued: "If you don't know, I'll tell you. She's here, next door. Call her, persuade her to tell you everything she knows. If she doesn't talk, this will be your last meeting with your daughter."

Within a few minutes, four people came in, Hannah among them. She was no longer in uniform. Her clothes were disordered, her hair disheveled. She had bruises under her eyes and one of her teeth was broken. Her mother deliberately controlled herself so as not to afford the officials the pleasure of a scene, but she barely recognized her daughter. The two women embraced each other and Mrs. Senesch quickly realized that she must not urge Hannah to talk. They were left alone for a few minutes, but Hannah did not confide her mission; she could only reassure her mother that she was not hurt.

Mrs. Senesch was warned not to say a word about their meeting. She burned all of Hannah's letters but within a few days she herself was arrested by the Gestapo and confined to the same prison as Hannah. The charm and valor of the young girl and the pathos of the older woman made a deep impression on some of the prison attendants and they arranged brief, stolen meetings between them. Mrs. Senesch was released after three months.

When Hungary seemed ready to capitulate to the Russians in October, Hannah was jubilant and awaited liberation momentarily. But the Arrow Cross coup of October 15 wrecked these hopes. Hannah's trial was set for October 28 and a verdict was promised within eight days. Mrs. Senesch, meanwhile, unsuccessfully tried to contact Kastner to obtain his help in getting her daughter released.[18] She continued to visit the prison but was held off by guards; the verdict on her daughter had not yet been decided, they said. She was then told that she needed a special pass from a certain judge, but he was on a trip. His chambers were empty. When he appeared at last, he said the case no longer belonged to him. Mrs. Senesch appealed to him: "At least help me. Tell me whom to apply to. Eight days have already passed." The judge was at first evasive, but finally answered. "This is war," he said. "We are under emergency law. A radio transmitter was found in her possession. The court found her guilty of treason and sentenced her to the maximum penalty. We have already carried out the verdict."

On November 6, on a cold, foggy morning, Hannah Senesch had been executed as a British spy in the prison courtyard.

British permission for the parachutists to leap into Hitler-Europe came very late in the war and made very modest contributions to Jewish resistance and rescue activities. More tangible results were achieved by the *Mossad*, which had begun its work much earlier and did not wait for Allied clearance, although it had to struggle against Allied indifference and obstruction. After the *Struma* tragedy the *Mossad* had discontinued its operations in Europe and worked from posts in North Africa and the Middle East. By the summer of 1943, however, a new chink opened up in Europe and the *Mossad* decided to establish a base in Istanbul. The immediate occasion for a shift in operation was a letter from Lord Cranborne, British Colonial Secretary, to the British Ambassador in Turkey. In the letter, Lord Cranborne stressed the main British policy with respect to the Jews of Europe: they were not to be encouraged to escape, nor were they to be organized or helped, he said. However, if, despite all British efforts, they should succeed in reaching Turkey, they should be given entry visas to Palestine. The Haganah security-intelligence section, SHAI, learned of this new twist in British policy and an emigration effort was again attempted.

Once established in Istanbul, the Mossad had to prove that Jews could be evacuated, that it was a terrible mistake to treat them as enemy citizens and that, by aiding them, the war effort was not being impeded, as was claimed, but advanced. The Mossad had to work in great secrecy and could not afford to let the Germans, British or Americans discover their plans, but unofficially, many diplomats, military observers and government officials placed great value on the resourcefulness of the Mossad. Services and favors were exchanged. Curiously, certain individuals in British Intelligence, contrary to official government policy, would have liked joint British-Mossad activity in the Black Sea area. British contacts with that part of the world had been infrequent and difficult and Mossad agents were admittedly ingenious, but official cooperation was never permitted. Besides its organization of ships, the Mossad made contact with the parachutists and with the Jewish Agency office in Istanbul, and all three tried to fashion a chain of links between the severed Jewish communities of Europe.

From Istanbul the Jewish Agency had established links to Budapest, Bucharest and Sofia. Budapest served as a relay station with couriers to Poland, Theresienstadt, Germany, Austria and Italy. Istanbul also had direct contact with Palestine and Switzerland. At first, attempts were made to contact the communities by mail. The Jewish Agency office in Istanbul had the names and addresses of Jewish leaders throughout Europe. No one knew whether they were dead or alive, but hundreds of letters were sent to the old addresses, signed by a Turkish girl and mailed from various parts of Turkey so as not to throw suspicion on any single post office. The code used was very simple, involving key words in Hebrew such as "Ezra," meaning help and "Artzi," meaning someone from the land of Palestine. The few letters that were received were at first mystifying, but gradually the messages could be deciphered and veiled replies began coming to Istanbul. When finally a postcard arrived signed "Zivia" [Lubetkin], one of the surviving heroines of the Warsaw Ghetto uprising, it meant that Poland at last had been penetrated. The news of the death of Adam Czerniakow, head of the Ghetto Judenrat, was first learned when Istanbul received a letter saying that "Czerniakow had gone to visit Dr. Ruppin."

Ruppin was a well-known Palestinian economist, by then deceased. The Gestapo censor had never heard of Dr. Ruppin, but Jewish representatives in Istanbul were all familiar with the name. The message was clear.

After mail contacts were established, money and rescue instructions were sent through paid agents or Jewish couriers, many of them young Jewish girls who could pass as Aryans. The first communication sent by messenger reached Budapest in February 1943, and the first personal contact with Poland was made on July 17. A paid German agent undertook to reach the ghetto of Bendin, in the heart of Poland, to deliver a letter to Frumka Plotinitski, an almost legendary figure in the annals of the Holocaust. He had orders to try to bring her back to Istanbul, but she refused to leave Poland, finally making her way to the Warsaw Ghetto where she was killed. It was Frumka, one of the most daring of the couriers, who was among the young messengers who brought to the Polish ghettos the news of the tragic massacres in Vilna during the German invasion of Russia. The contact with Frumka in the summer of 1943 was the first direct contact that Palestine and Istanbul had had with Poland since the beginning of the war. To the handful of survivors in the Polish ghettos, the message from the world of living Jews was a near miracle. But the reply written by Frumka was from a world of the dead and dying. "When this letter reaches you," her letter begins, "we will no longer be alive." The letter then describes the gassing of 80,000 Jews in Lodz, the exterminations in Lithuania, the Warsaw Ghetto defense and the subsequent destruction of Polish Jewry.

These fragile forces, then, the Jewish resistance efforts and the Joint Distribution Committee activity stemming from Geneva, constituted the chief rescue efforts in behalf of Jews during the Holocaust. An immense abyss lay between the instruments of death and the instruments of salvation.

The Allies did not attempt the physical rescue of Jews during a time when they might possibly have been saved, and Palestinian Jews were blocked in their rescue operations. However, assuming that the Jews of Europe could have been saved, they had no place to go. In two thousand years' experience with Christian Europe, they had reached the nadir of oppressiveness. As Brand had told Lord Moyne, there was no longer any room for them on planet earth. There were some Christian voices that fearlessly spoke out against this unchristian condition. Many were silent, however, while others made baptism the sole criterion of protestation and rescue. Baptism became the sign over which the Church thrust its shield. For the millions who lacked this sign, the shield was denied. And for the thousands who possessed the sign and committed murder, the shield was not withdrawn. Excommunication of the exterminators was never threatened.

Nearly 80 percent of the population of German-invaded Europe fell under the sway of the Church of Rome but the Mother Church did not condemn the exterminations or the exterminators, as such. The Vatican, the great institutional embodiment of Roman Catholic power, remained silent through the Holocaust. All of the documents surrounding this silence are as yet unavailable, but the fact of the silence is a matter of record. Whether this was a morally justifiable position is a question that has already generated a great deal of controversy; argumentation will undoubtedly continue after the official papers are released. The reasons for the silence will be documented, and the weighing of alternatives which led to the Vatican policy, explained. It is very doubtful that, even then, a final judgment on the Vatican's judgment will be possible. Objectively, one cannot prove or disprove the effectiveness of a strong moral protest by the Vatican against the exterminations. No one can be absolutely sure that it would have been a deterrent to further exterminations, or a stimulus; that it would have strengthened the Church, or weakened it. Besides, the fullest of explications can never recover the atmosphere of the years of the Holocaust or seize hold of the totality of forces that shook Europe to its foundations during the Nazi conquests. There were many inconstant shifting factors, Hitler's madness being not the least of them. Sometimes he gave way to a posture of strength or stubbornness; sometimes he was incited by it. The exterminators were balked by the maddening obstruction of the Italians and Bulgarians and the French. At times, braking actions occurred because of trivial legalisms that loomed oversize to Hitler or his subordinates. Most of the time, ordinary standards were smashed. But these speculations aside, there was strong criticism of the Pope's failure to act in the midst of the atrocities and expectation that he would speak out. This criticism still continues.

Those who justify the Pope's policy claim that protests against the mass murders would have made the situation facing the Jews and others facing death even worse than it was, that his silence was praiseworthy because he could better render practical aid quietly where it was needed. It is also justified on the ground that as spiritual ruler of all Christendom, the Pope could not specify incidents of violence and destructiveness, but had to condemn broadly all acts of injustice and inhumanity committed by both sides during the war. Otherwise, it is said, his words would have been exploited politically by each. Another reason may have been an unwillingness to denounce Nazi atrocities for fear that the German people, in the bitterness of their defeat, would reproach him later on for having contributed, if only indirectly, to that defeat.

The Pope undoubtedly suffered much personal anguish in having taken the path of caution, reserve and "neutrality," and he was often disappointed and surprised that his generalities lamenting suffering multitudes, or countless exiles torn from their homes by the hurricane of war, or thousands condemned to death were not plainly understood as references to Jews or Poles or other specific groups killed or tortured through no fault of their own. But it is also true that very few groups gained strength or comfort from his words. The Poles were the first to protest, indirectly, against the extreme reserve of the Pope's message of Christmas 1942, which was meant to cry out against Nazi savagery, but which withheld the identity of the persecutor.

A week after this message was proclaimed, Wladyslaw Raczkiewicz, President of the Polish Government-in-Exile, implored the Pope to speak out plainly. He wrote:

> At this tragic moment my people are fighting not merely for their lives but for everything that has been sacred in their eyes. They want justice, not vengeance. They do not ask so much for material or diplomatic help . . . but they implore that a voice be raised to show clearly and plainly where the evil lies and to condemn those in the service of evil. . . . At certain times of trial in Poland's past . . . Your Holiness' great predecessors addressed fatherly words to the Polish people. Today . . . the Apostolic See must break silence so that those who die . . . in defense of their faith and their traditions may receive the blessing of the successor of Christ.[19]

Jews also hoped for an unequivocal denunciation of the cause of their trial. Their agony, they felt, could be no worse than it already was. Appeals were made to the Vatican by Jews in the midst of the Holocaust and those distant from it. But the hoped-for protest never came. The power of threatening an interdict of Germany or excommunication of leading Catholic Nazis was never used if, indeed, it was even discussed in Vatican circles. Critics of the Vatican believe that widespread public exposure of the myth of resettlement broadcast over the Vatican radio might have saved the lives of the thousands who believed the assurances of the Nazis, or at least enabled many more than did to choose the way in which they would die. It is also believed that more Christians would have helped and sheltered Jews had the Vatican spoken out.

Quite early in the war, the Vatican expressed its interest in a German victory. In June 1940, the Wilhelmstrasse was informed that the Vatican hoped France would follow the example of Belgium and capitulate. On June 10, just before Italy declared war, Nuncio Cesare Orsenigo, Papal Nuncio in Berlin, called on Ernst Wörmann, chief of the Political Division of the German Foreign Office. "The Nuncio called on me today," Wörmann observed, "in connection with current matters. In the conversation, he gave very cordial expression to his pleasure at the German victories. It seemed as if he could not wait for Italy to enter the war and he remarked jokingly that he hoped the Germans would march into Paris by way of Versailles."[20]

Eugene Cardinal Tisserant, meanwhile, extremely worried about a Hitler-dominated Europe, wrote of his misgivings to Emmanuel Cardinal Suhard, Archbishop of Paris, on June 11:

> Since the beginning of November, I have persistently requested the Holy See to issue an encyclical on the duty of the individual to obey the dictates of conscience because this is the vital point of Christianity. . . . I fear that history may have reason to reproach the Holy See with having pursued a policy of convenience to itself and very little else. This is said in the extreme, particularly when one has lived under Pius XI. And everyone is counting on the fact that Rome, having once been declared an open city, no one in the Curia would have to suffer; this is ignominious. It is all the more ignominious because the Secretariat of State and the Nuncio have persuaded large numbers of nuns and monks [the monks in question were French] not to leave, so as to provide Italy with hostages.[21]

As to how much exact information the Vatican had regarding the exterminations, it can be inferred that it possessed a substantial amount dating from the spring of 1942. Two notes from the Vatican acknowledging that Jews were being sent east to be murdered were sent to Prime Minister Tuka of Slovakia in February 1942. On March 17, 1942, it is known that representatives of the Jewish Agency, the World Jewish Congress and Swiss Jews, after an interview with Monsignor Filippo Bernardini, the Apostolic Nuncio in Bern, forwarded to him a letter and detailed memorandum summarizing the situation facing Jews in central and eastern Europe, including the mass murder of Jews in Bukovina and Bessarabia. In August 1942, Kurt Gerstein told Dr. Winter, the legal adviser of Cardinal Count Preysing, Bishop of Berlin, about the gassings he had witnessed near Lublin and urged that his report be forwarded to the Pope. There is no reason to doubt that it was. During this period, other reports were made by Catholic officers serving in Poland and Russia. Moreover, the extent and high quality of Vatican intelligence is well known.[21a] As the news of the mass killings spread, questions began to be raised regarding the Vatican's silence.

In July 1942, Harold H. Tittmann, Jr., the assistant to President Roosevelt's personal representative at the Vatican, Myron C. Taylor, pointed out to the Vatican that its silence was "endangering its moral prestige and is undermining faith both in the Church and in the Holy Father himself."[22] In September 1942, having received proper authorization by Secretary of State Hull, Tittmann and several other diplomatic representatives at the Vatican formally requested the Pope to condemn the "incredible horrors" perpetrated by the Nazis. A few days later, Taylor forwarded to the Papal Secretary of State, Luigi Maglione, a memorandum from the Jewish Agency reporting mass executions of Jews in Poland and occupied Russia, and describing the deportations from Germany, Holland, Belgium, France and Slovakia to the death camps. Taylor inquired whether the Vatican could confirm these reports, and if so, "whether the Holy Father has any suggestions as to any practical manner in which the forces of civilized opinion could be utilized in order to prevent a continuation of these barbarities."[23] In reply to Taylor's note, on October 10 the Vatican said that up to the present time it had not been possible to verify the accuracy of reports concerning the severe measures that were being taken against the Jews, but "it is well known that the Holy See is taking advantage of every opportunity offered in order to mitigate the suffering of non-Aryans."[24]

After the Allies had denounced the exterminations in December 1942, Tittmann again asked the Papal Secretary of State whether the Holy See could not issue a similar statement. Maglione answered that in line with its policy of neutrality, the Vatican could not protest particular atrocities and had to condemn immoral actions in general. He assured Tittmann that everything possible was being done behind the scenes to help the Jews.[25]

Two days later, in the course of a long Christmas message broadcast by the Vatican radio, Pope Pius XII made another of his many pleas for a more humane conduct of hostilities. In June 1943, in an address to the Sacred College of Cardinals, the Pope spoke of his twofold duty to be impartial and to stress moral errors. This statement raises the question of Vatican adherence to neutrality as well as its interpretation of "war crimes." The Vatican was not strictly neutral during the war but had broken its silence at least twice: on the occasion of the Russian attack on Finland and upon Germany's violation of the neutrality of Holland, Belgium and Luxemburg. On the matter of "war crimes," it would appear that the Vatican accepted the gassings of Jews as merely another kind of inhumanity of which all belligerents in a war are guilty. The findings at Nuremberg were based on a similar equivalence. Yet, the gassings had not the slightest connection with German military operations and can hardly be considered a "war" aim. The destruction of the Jews did not advance German military power in a single battle.

In the June 23rd address, the Pope had given special attention, he recalled, to the plight of those who were still being harassed because of their nationality or descent. Much had been done that could not yet be described. Every public statement had to be weighed carefully "in the interest of those suffering so that their situation would not inadvertently be made still more difficult and unbearable." Unfortunately, the Pope added, the Church's pleas for compassion and for the observance of the elementary norms of humanity had encountered doors "which no key was able to open."[26]

This is a reference to the many interventions of varying success in behalf of converted Jews and "racial" Jews. The precise nature of these interventions has not yet been divulged. Some surely saved lives, but it is not clear whether the effective pressure came primarily from the local clergy, with reinforced backing by the Vatican or from the Vatican itself. In the case of Slovakia, for example, the political leaders, who themselves were clergymen, for a time ignored Vatican interventions. On the other hand, through the nine months of the Nazi occupation of Rome, Jews—the estimates vary greatly—found shelter and protection in the buildings and offices of the Vatican. In this situation the Pope functioned as the Bishop of Rome and could intervene directly. Elsewhere, the influence of the Papacy seemed to be directly correlated with the vigor, or absence of it, of the local church. Without the support of the local clergy, Vatican intervention by itself was not strong enough, or was not conveyed with sufficient force to exert the desired pressure.

The Pope himself touched on this matter of local initiative in a letter to Bishop Preysing on April 30, 1943: "So far as episcopal declarations are concerned, We leave to pastors on the spot the task of assessing whether, and to what extent, the danger of reprisals . . . counsel restraint—despite reasons that might exist for intervention—in order to avoid greater evils. This is one of the motives for the limitations which We impose on Ourself in Our declarations."

In contrast with the Pope's decision to give the bishops liberty of action, the Orthodox Church adopted a different policy. The Orthodox Patriarch of Constantinople wrote to all of his bishops in the Balkans and in central Europe, urging them to help Jews and to announce in their churches that concealing Jews was a sacred duty. This might explain the fact that in Slovakia, an essentially Catholic country, more Jews were temporarily able to escape deportation by "conversion" to the Orthodox Church than to Roman Catholicism.[27]

This reliance on the prevailing attitudes within the national church may be an expression of the limits of the real power that the Vatican can exert over its dominion, or may have been Pope Pius XII's manner of expressing that power. Had another man—Pope John XXIII or Pope Pius XI—been the incumbent Pope during the Holocaust, possibly there would have been an early and unequivocal condemnation of the exterminations. The elevation of Eugenio Cardinal Pacelli to the Papacy in the spring of 1939 brought to the chair of St. Peter a man who, in contrast to his predecessor, was unemotional and dispassionate, a master of the language of diplomatic ambiguity. "Pius XII," recalls Domenico Cardinal Tardini, "was by nature meek and almost timid. He was not born with the temperament of a fighter. In this he was different from his great predecessor." But was Vatican policy so different under Pius XI?

Pope Pius XI, had issued the celebrated *Mit Brennender Sorge* ("With Burning Concern") in 1937. This was the Pope who, underscoring the incompatibility between Christianity and racism, had exclaimed, "Spiritually, we are all Semites." It was Pius XI who, when Hitler visited Rome in 1938, dramatically left the city with a pungent farewell: "This air makes us sick." In the light of the neutralist position of Pius XII, these expressions seem very courageous. Yet, Pius XI did not condemn anti-Semitism per se, but only indirectly, in the attack on the myths of blood and race, and like Pius XII and the German episcopate, limited his interventions in Germany to Catholic non-Aryans. At the request of Cardinal Bertram, in September 1933, the Papal Secretary of State put in a word in behalf of German Catholics of Jewish descent who suffered social and economic difficulties.

Pope Pius XI, moreover, could not dissociate himself from modern Catholic anti-Semitism which emphasized the role of the Jews in liberal and anti-clerical movements. These, as seen by certain Catholic thinkers, were destroying the temporal power of the Pope. This new accretion to the old body of religious anti-Semitism gave weighty authority to the already strong twentieth-century secular anti-Semitism which viewed Jews as being responsible for the French Revolution, the doctrine of equality and dangerous economic changes. This modern Catholic anti-Semitism, indeed, overlapped the other in identifying Jews as dominating the new economy with the intention of controlling it and exploiting it for their own benefit.[28] These views found expression in the influential Jesuit magazine *Civiltà Cattolica*, published in Rome and traditionally close to Vatican thinking (the editor is appointed by the Pope). Pius XI may have taken issue generally with the Nazi glorification of race, but the fact remains that he never discussed or condemned anti-Semitism specifically. He condemned all forms of racism. The Church officially approved certain kinds of anti-Semitism. Neither Pius XI nor Pius XII resolved this fundamental dilemma facing the Church and the articles in *Civiltà Cattolica* expose the contradictions of attempting to hold two incompatible positions.

Although it was Cardinal Pacelli (later Pius XII) who was anxious for the quick conclusion of a concordat with Hitler, it was during the regime of Pope Pius XI that the concordat was pressed and completed. Moreover, in greeting von Papen, whom Hitler had sent to Rome for preliminary discussions of the concordat, Pius XI told von Papen how "pleased" he was "that the German Government now had at its head a man uncompromisingly opposed to Communism and Russian nihilism in all its forms. Indeed the atmosphere was so cordial," von Papen recalled, "that I was able to settle the details of a draft agreement at a speed quite unusual in Vatican affairs." Soon after the concordat was concluded in 1933, Pope Pius XI publicly praised Hitler as "the first statesman to join him in open disavowal of Bolshevism."[28a]

After July 1933, when the Nazi Government and the Papal Nuncio, Cardinal Pacelli, had signed a concordat defining in detail the position of the Catholic Church in Germany, the Church soon found itself struggling with the contradiction between its sympathy for anti-Semitic measures in Germany and its opposition to the anti-Catholic designs of Nazi racialism. In 1934, Civiltà Cattolica expressed disappointment at the appalling waste of the Nazi brand of anti-Semitism. This anti-Semitism, it said, "did not stem from the religious convictions nor the Christian conscience, but from . . . their [Nazi] desire to upset the order of religion and society." However, "we do not deny the fact that we could understand them, or even praise them, if their policy were restricted within acceptable bounds of defence against Jewish organizations and institutions."[29]

In Italy, meanwhile, the signing of the 1929 concordat between Mussolini and Pius XI for the mutual benefit of both church and state added yet another thrust against Jewry. In this instance, the temporarily favorable attitude of the Fascist state toward Jewish hopes in Palestine took a sudden and sharp turn for the worse. The Fascist state yielded to the Vatican on this matter. Attacks on Jews and Zionism were now redoubled, with Fascist publications adding intensity to an already old Vatican antagonism to Jewish settlement in the Holy Land. The Fascist Government switched its line again in the 1930's and became temporarily sympathetic to Zionism against the Vatican's disapproval. But the effect of this was not helpful to the Jews. The increasing isolation of the Church served to weaken it and its diminishing margin of power left no room for ringing moral protests.

Economic as well as political considerations also played no small part in shaping Vatican attitudes toward Jews in the Hitler period. In the modern shift in Italy to a capitalist economy, the Vatican suffered heavy financial losses when it tried to convert part of its agrarian-feudal economy to a commercial-capitalist one. These losses very probably strengthened the Vatican leaders in their conviction that they had an important mission to prevent Jewish competition and "domination" from interfering with their own economic interests.[30]

It is true that the Fascist state of Mussolini soon went its own way. The hopes of the Church that the concordat would enable it to increase its influence over the entire state were shattered. But this outcome made the Church more insecure and isolated—a condition which ultimately must have figured in Pius XII's silence during the exterminations. His primary consideration was to protect the dwindling power the Church still had, not to fling itself into a struggle to battle for the survival of a people about whom it was equivocal. Much more important than purely moral considerations was the Vatican's own battle for survival.

After the death of Pius XI, Catholic anti-Semitism became stronger both in Italy and outside it. Both Jesuits and other prominent Catholics tried to blur out the generally held opinion that the late Pope had found fault with racial anti-Semitism; they described these opinions as exaggerated or false.

The situation facing the Catholic Church in Germany during this period was particularly critical. Given the indifference of the German population toward the fate of the Jews and the sympathetic attitude of the German hierarchy toward Nazi anti-Semitism, a forceful stand by Pius XII on the exterminations might well have led to wide-scale desertions from the Church. When Dr. Edoardo Senatro, the Berlin correspondent of *L'Osservatore Romano*, asked him whether he would not protest the exterminations, the Pope is reported to have answered, "Dear friend, do not forget that millions of Catholics serve in the German armies. Shall I bring them into conflicts of conscience?"[31]

The Pope knew that the German Catholics were not prepared to suffer martyrdom for their Church; still less were they willing to incur the wrath of their Nazi rulers for the sake of the Jews whom their own bishops for years had castigated as a harmful influence in German life.[32] Besides, on the eve of Pius XI's death in February 1939, relations between the Vatican and the Third Reich had approached the breaking point and Pius XII set about repairing them. Before his death Pius XI had been reproached for "mobilizing the entire world against the new Germany." A whispering campaign had spread the rumor that he had Jewish blood in his veins—that his mother was a Dutch Jewess. "I see my listeners tremble with horror," Cardinal Faulhaber of Munich had said, in giving the lie to the rumor. "This lie is especially likely to expose the Pope's reputation to derision in Germany."[33]

In contrast, Pius XII maintained diplomatic relations with Berlin throughout the Hitler period. Not until June 2, 1945, did he find words strong enough to describe the "satanic specter of National Socialism." Nor did he denounce the concordat of 1933, although Hitler soon enough violated it. Moreover, there has been speculation that the Vatican's awareness of a plan to institute a Nazi papacy played a role in the Pope's caution and wariness in treating with Nazi Germany. The conception of a Nazi theocracy headed by Adolf Hitler was revealed in the memoirs of Alfred Rosenberg, published in 1949, and was probably known to the Vatican. This specter, if conjured up, must have been at least as alarming as the memory of the Avignon captivity.

Not only was the Pope's reputation endangered in Germany; the Church itself was threatened. To what extent the German Catholic bishops led their congregations and to what extent their views mirrored Catholic public opinion cannot be discerned. But that the Church in Germany felt obliged to compromise with the Nazi virus—if indeed it was not infected by it—is abundantly clear. The German Catholic Church never went as far as certain Protestant churches that proclaimed the "Aryanism" of Jesus, but it openly embraced racist formulations that permeated the Nazified world of Germany. Had the German episcopate adopted an attitude of intransigent opposition to Hitler, the Catholic masses would probably have deserted the Church altogether.[34] It fought against Nazi anti-Christian campaigns and attacks on its work and institutions but it accepted the racist and anti-Semitic dogmas of the Nazi regime.

Moreover, the Pope's undisguised appreciation of German culture and expressed warmth toward the German people may have been a personal force in his unwillingness to condemn bluntly the Nazi regime. He often referred to the twelve years that he had spent in Germany as Papal Nuncio with rarely expressed feelings of "esteem and love." These were, he said, the best years of his life.

The Vatican could not, of course, in spite of its avowed neutralism, insulate itself against the political tides that threatened it. Nor could it avoid dilemmas that placed it in a compromising position. There was religious persecution in all countries under German rule, and yet the Vatican found itself helpless to protest effectively. In January 1942, it had announced that it could not recognize any territorial changes which resulted in the absorption of new areas into Germany—Sudetenland, Bohemia and Moravia, western Poland—and which were not covered by any formal agreement between the Reich and the Vatican. This situation, of course, pleased Hitler, who observed that "as a legal consequence of the abolition of the sovereign rights of the states, relations between ourselves and the Vatican have become redundant." Similarly, the Vatican's preference for National Socialism as against Communism led it to strange political impasses. At no point did the Vatican wish to undermine or weaken Germany's "struggle" against Russian Communism. Father Robert Leiber, one of the Pope's secretaries, recalls that Pius XII had always looked upon Russian Bolshevism as more dangerous than German National Socialism.[35] From the spring of 1943 on, fear of the Bolshevization of Europe seemed to dominate the political thinking of the Vatican, but it remained silent on what was going on in Germany because of the apparent need to preserve that "bastion" against Soviet expansion. After Stalingrad, the Vatican seems to have been interested in bringing about a separate peace between the Western Allies and the Axis. Then the Allied landing in Sicily on July 10, 1943, seriously exposed Italy. A separate armistice signed by Italy would weaken Germany, but to let Italy remain at war would risk the spread of Communism throughout Italy as well as physical destruction. In the late summer of 1943, the Papal Secretary of State declared that the fate of Europe depended upon a German victory on the Eastern Front. The Pope himself spoke frankly on July 5, 1943, when the new German Ambassador to the Vatican, Ernst von Weizsäcker, presented his credentials. After the ceremony, the Pope granted Weizsäcker a private audience. In Weizsäcker's report to Berlin, the following reference was made to the war against Russia:

> . . . This topic [the general situation] afforded me an opportunity to lay proper emphasis on the German effort against Bolshevism. The Pope spoke of his own experiences with the Communists in Munich in 1919. He condemned the mindless formula of our opponents demanding "unconditional surrender." . . . The conversation which lasted about half an hour was conducted by the Pope without visible passion, but with an undertone of spiritual fervor which was transformed into a recognition of common interests only when the discussion turned to the handling of the fight against the Bolsheviks. . . .[36]

Later, on September 23, 1943, Weizsäcker sent a telegram to Ribbentrop analyzing three documents characteristic of the Pope's political attitude. The third, he wrote,

> is particularly interesting. It contains an exposition by Cardinal Secretary of State Maglione to the Italian Government of the dangers threatening the world. Maglione says that the fate of Europe depends on the victorious resistance by Germany on the Russian front. The German Army is the only possible bulwark—"baluardo"—against Bolshevism. Should this bulwark break, European culture would be finished.

The Vatican, then, through the Holocaust was not only a prisoner of its own history of anti-Semitism but was the product of a historical conditioning as strong as that of any other human institution. It needed to find arenas of power in an era of shrinking religious response and had to weigh the political consequences of impulsively acting out of moral fervor. In the years of fateful concern to European Jews, this institution was entrusted to a man who undoubtedly believed he was being scrupulously neutral in his appraisal of world-shattering events but who, admittedly, believed that National Socialism was a lesser evil than Communism. In this context alone, were no other considerations involved, how could Jews be viewed other than as unfortunate expendables? After all, it was the Nazis, not the Bolsheviks, who were destroying them.

Another great institution from which Jews hoped for aid during the Holocaust was also passive as a result of its conditioning. This was the International Committee of the Red Cross (ICRC), which was the prisoner of old international conventions in a period when these were meaningless. The ICRC, a committee of twenty-five Swiss citizens, maintains contact with Red Cross societies in fifty-seven countries. Its function has been to preserve some elements of civilized conduct in wartime and to relieve the suffering of prisoners and other victims of war. A special mandate to watch over all victims of persecution has been entrusted to the ICRC at conferences since 1921. This mandate recognizes the existence of international law and usage regarding the treatment of civilian internees, deportees and hostages of enemy as well as domestic nationality.

The national Red Cross Society of the country in which civil war or disturbances break out has the primary obligation to give necessary assistance to all victims impartially. If, however, the national society cannot undertake the relief alone, it must request the aid of the ICRC which, in turn, has to obtain the consent of the government involved to carry out relief work. If the government refuses its consent, the ICRC is required to issue a public exposé of the facts. In view of its wide mandate, what prevented the International Red Cross from extending its protection to the hundreds of thousands of Jews held in Nazi concentration camps?

In one of its official reports, the ICRC attempts to explain its predicament:

> Under National Socialism, the Jews had become in truth outcasts, condemned by rigid racial legislation to suffer tyranny, persecution and systematic extermination. No kind of protection shielded them: being neither prisoners of war nor civilian internees, they formed a separate category, without the benefit of any Convention. The supervision which the International Committee of the Red Cross was empowered to exercise in favor of prisoners and internees did not apply to them. . . . These unfortunate citizens shared the same fate as political deportees, were deprived of civil rights, were given less favored treatment than enemy nationals, who at least had the benefit of a statute. They were penned into concentration camps and ghettos, recruited for forced labor, subjected to grave brutalities and sent to death camps, without anyone being allowed to intervene in these matters. . . .
>
> The Committee could not dissociate themselves from these victims, on whose behalf it received the most insistent appeals, but for whom the means of action seemed especially limited, since in the absence of any basis in law, its activities depended to a very great extent upon the good will of the belligerent States. . . .
>
> Enquiries as a matter of principle concerning the Jews led to no result, and continued protests would have been resented by the authorities concerned and might have been detrimental to the Jews themselves and to the whole field of the Committee's activities. In consequence, the Committee, while avoiding useless protests, did its utmost to help the Jews by practical means, and its delegates abroad were instructed on these lines.[37]

The "utmost" of the ICRC is generally deplored as having been too little and too late. The ICRC yielded to the typical Nazi device of creating a new classification for a familiar category: in this instance the Nazis declared that Jews were not internees, but *detainees*.[38] This gave them a penal instead of a civil status, but at the same time, they were not con-

sidered prisoners of war, and the ICRC withheld help until 1944. Not
until October 1944 did the Committee finally send a note to the German
Ministry of Foreign Affairs requesting that all foreigners held in Germany
and German-occupied areas be recognized as civilian prisoners of war. By
that time, of course, millions of Jews had perished and the Germans were
in no position any longer to fortify themselves behind perverse nomen-
clature.

From the summer of 1942 on, when the death deportations began,
Jewish organizations had conferred with a number of agencies on the need
to feed all enslaved people in Europe as well as Jews as a distinct group.
Meetings were held with the United States Board of Economic Warfare,
the Treasury Department and the International and American Red Cross.
Jewish representatives urged that the Jews in Europe be treated as prisoners
of war. But there was no progress on this point. Not until August 1944,
did these authorities agree to trial shipments of food and medicine for a
three-month period. (The sole exception was a shipment of prunes, dried
vegetables and condensed milk to Theresienstadt in September 1943.)
This was made possible only after the War Refugee Board exerted pressure. A memorandum in the archives of the World Jewish Congress, dated
May 4, 1944, exposes the tangled skein of obstruction:

> It appears that the War Refugee Board as well as the IRCC and the Amer-
> ican Red Cross are powerless to induce the blockade authorities to change
> their policies with respect to the use of Red Cross food parcels for the Jews
> in the internment, concentration and the labor camps. There are large
> stocks of Red Cross parcels in Switzerland. Mr. Ryan of the American Red
> Cross refused to authorize their use . . . for this purpose claiming that
> "these parcels are earmarked for exclusive use of such internees as are offi-
> cially recognized as civilian internees. Should the blockade authorities learn
> that they had been distributed to people who do not fall in this category,
> the entire Red Cross parcel service for prisoners of war and civilian internees
> would be jeopardized! We have been negotiating on this matter for a year
> and a half without making the slightest progress."[39]

Had the reclassification of Jews been firmly ordered in 1942, their fate
might have been different. The Germans could not have afforded to
threaten reprisals against the Red Cross; they needed it too much to protect their own nationals, war prisoners and civilians held in Allied countries, of whom there were many more than Allied prisoners. This bargaining
power of the ICRC was never used, however, and the organization's extreme caution in the matter exposed it to much criticism both during the
war and later. The Red Cross explanation was an already familiar one:
noninterference in the internal affairs of Germany and unwillingness to
make a special case of Jews. A report reads:

> Perhaps we should have resorted to pounding tables and making a scandal.
> Maybe so! But if assistance to the Jews would have been our only task, one
> could have probably envisaged such an attitude. But this was not our only

mission. Assistance to Jews as well as other deportees was not based on a juridical principle only. To make a rumpus on account of the Jewish question would have meant to put in jeopardy everything, without saving one single Jew.[40]

The Red Cross made no "rumpus" about the Jewish question.

Suffering suffers no comparisons, but they are inescapable. The ICRC made truly heroic efforts during the wartime famine in Greece, where thanks to its energetic intervention, British consent was obtained to lift the blockade for huge shipments coming from half the world. In this case, Canada furnished grain, Sweden the ships and manpower, and Americans the money. The chain of ships, in a period of acute shipping shortage, was not severed up to the day that UNRRA took over. In comparison, it took almost a year for the World Jewish Congress to obtain a license from the United States Treasury Department to sustain Jewish lives left in Europe at the end of 1943. On December 18, 1943, a license was finally cabled to Geneva over strong British opposition. A little more than four million Swiss francs were released and distributed in France, Belgium, Holland, Bulgaria, Romania and Slovakia—a small sum, but, by then the number of Jews left was correspondingly small. Later, similar efforts to transfer funds for rescue efforts were persistently blocked.

The rigid neutrality that all parties adopted toward the Jews during the Holocaust began to slip in 1944, and the ICRC was no exception. Definitions as well as attitudes eased after the Red Cross, the Vatican and Allied authorities finally entered the shambles and saw with their own eyes what they had not believed, or had repressed, or had bypassed in silence.

One further possibility for the rescue of Jews existed but was never probed. This was to exert pressure on Germany based on her fear of retaliation. Such a course was suggested in the summer of 1943. On June 22, 1943, Jan Ciechanowski, Ambassador of the Polish Government-in-Exile to Washington, received Jan Karski, secret envoy of the anti-Communist underground in Poland. He was also received by President Roosevelt for whom he sketched a picture of the concentration camps and to whom he gave a nerve-shattering description of his own visit—disguised as a policeman—to Treblinka and Belzec. "Our underground authorities," Karski reported, "are absolutely sure that the Germans are out to exterminate the entire Jewish population of Europe . . . I was instructed by the leaders of our Underground to tell the British and American military authorities that only through direct reprisals, such as mass bombing of German cities, after dropping millions of leaflets telling the Germans that they were being bombed in reprisal for exterminating Jews, could this mass extermination be stopped or at least limited."[40a]

During the summer of 1943, Allied bombers did drop leaflets on Germany informing the German people of the exterminations and supplying many details, such as the discovery of mass graves, but no reprisals were threatened.

In considering the possibilities of Allied reprisal, it should be remembered that two categories of Jews were exempt from deportation simply because the Germans feared retaliation. These groups were Jews who were nationals of enemy nations and Jewish war prisoners of French, Belgian, Dutch and Polish nationality. The prisoners of war were protected by the Geneva convention and their camps could be inspected by the Red Cross. These prisoners could be exchanged for German prisoners held by the Allies. Liberated Jewish prisoners, of course, could be seized the day they returned to their native country and then deported. Nevertheless, the Germans were generally vulnerable to threats when their own nationals were involved. They avoided violations of existing conventions when there was reason to fear what the Allies might do to their prisoners. But the Allies did not use this leverage to stop the exterminations.

As evidence of Germany's interest in prisoner exchanges, there is a memorandum signed by Rademacher on February 20, 1943, dealing with the treatment of Jews of foreign nationality. The German Foreign Office, Rademacher noted, has decided "to refrain temporarily from the deportation of about 30,000 Dutch, Belgian, French, Norwegian and Soviet Russian Jews . . . in order to hold these people ready for an eventual exchange; those concerned are Jews with family ties or economic, political or friendly relations with the citizens of the enemy states."[41] There is no evidence that the Allies ever tried to exploit this vulnerability by threatening reprisal action against German internees in order to stop the exterminations of Jews. Not only was Germany interested in prisoner exchanges. A precedent also existed. When Japan was accused of using gas against the Chinese, there was a solemn warning by the President of the United States who threatened to retaliate against the Japanese with gas warfare. Millions of Jews were suffocated in the lethal gas chambers but no one threatened any retaliation.

Under Nazism, Germans reached out farther and more drastically in their range of destruction than any other people in history. The Allies were fully aware of this unprecedented scale of killing and denounced the monstrous crimes of the Nazis. However, they refused to acknowledge the special character of the German action against Jews and likewise refused to acknowledge the special identity of Jewish victims. In this formulation, the Jewish fate was linked with the fate of other peoples. Jews were lost among "French hostages," the "people of Poland," the "territories of the Soviet Union." By the same token, the Jews of German nationality became Germans when it suited Allied purposes and were frequently treated as "enemy aliens" after they had lost their nationality. During the war, the

British said there were "enemy agents" and "undesirable elements" among the Jews trying to get to Palestine. After the war, the immigrants were said to be "under Soviet influence." Camouflage terms to conceal rationalizations of behavior toward Jews were not a Nazi monopoly.

During the war, the rescue of Jews interfered with the principle of victory first. After the war, it conflicted with efforts of rival partners in the wartime alliance to woo occupied Germany. The liberation of Jewish survivors was a fortuitous by-product of military victory, an accidental consequence which taxed many Allied officers with sticky problems for which they had neither time nor taste. The ghostly remnant returned to the cemeteries that had been made of their old communities and had to endure the last ignominy: a new round of persecution. Hitler had been defeated, but anti-Semitism had not. Jews were once more condemned as parasites, ritual murderers, war makers, and in the Soviet Union, as cosmopolitans or spies. The arithmetic of the Holocaust died quickly. Just as there had been no Allied plan to rescue Jews during the war, there was none to give surviving Jews any security in Europe after the war.

The Jewish experience in Europe was plainly finished.

33 The Return

A BEWILDERING SURGE of conciliatory talks, orders to stop the exterminations, counterorders, sudden evacuations of camps, last-hour death house revolts and submissive surrender of certain camps to the Allied armies crisscrossed the Nazi landscape in the last year of the war. There was no coordinated Allied plan for the release or safekeeping of inmates of the camps, and thousands of Jews as well as other prisoners perished even as their liberators stampeded the Nazi empire.

In July 1944, there were two massive shifts of Jewish survivors. One involved the evacuation of labor camps and prisoners in Poland as a result of the Russian invasion of the Government-General. This usually meant either on-the-spot shooting of the prisoners or deportation to Auschwitz and gas-chamber selections. Some thousands were also shipped to Germany where they joined the second large mass, the Hungarian Jews, some of whom had been put to work in the underground aircraft factories. These movements swelled the population in the camps in Germany to oversaturation, and more were intended. An additional 100,000 Jews still survived in labor camps in upper Silesia and the Czestochowa region of Poland where a Soviet offensive threatened. Himmler had not yet decided whether to blow up the crematoria or keep their chimneys blazing. The July 20 plot against Hitler made him feel quite sure that he would be the right person to treat with the Allies, yet he was also torn by his loyalty to Hitler. The Reichsführer S.S., in the summer of 1944, was still a very self-divided man and the stomach convulsions and severe headaches which afflicted him through most of the war were becoming increasingly severe.

On July 18, British censorship had released the story of the Joel Brand mission, revealing to the world that Himmler had tried to sell the remaining Jews in Hungary. On July 24, during a period of accelerated exterminations at Auschwitz, the Russians disemboweled the extermination center at Lublin. Their discovery of the crematorium, with its five furnaces and human bones, its 535 drums of Zyklon B gas and steel retorts of carbon-monoxide gas filled the Russian and, eventually, the Allied press. Still, the Nazi machine lurched on. The ideological fire seems to have gone out of many of the Nazi exterminators but the gassings continued.

The decision to halt the exterminations had a long and twisted history. The Hungarian deportations from Budapest were stopped by Horthy early in July, but the Himmler order to stop the gassings and dismantle the crematoria was not issued until October or November 1944. According to Dr. Kastner, it was on August 24 that Kurt Becher, in his negotiations with Saly Mayer, first offered to stop the selections in the camps. At this time, there was also a rumor that the German Ministry of Propaganda wanted to conduct an international delegation through Auschwitz to repudiate the accusations made against Lublin. But the gassings continued. In August, the Lodz Jews were killed at Auschwitz, and in September and October, the Slovakian and Theresienstadt transports arrived. Germany had not yet achieved the "Final Solution."

In August 1944, Eichmann reported to Himmler that six million Jews were dead, but Himmler was dissatisfied with the estimate; he was sure the number must be greater. Accordingly, he told Eichmann that he would send a statistical expert to the RSHA who would work out the figures more exactly. While the count was being reviewed, the Auschwitz death machine ground to a halt. The exact date cannot be ascertained. Some accounts indicate that the order was received at Auschwitz on November 2; others, on November 17. On November 26, Becher showed Dr. Kastner a telegram that had just come from Himmler: "The crematoria at Auschwitz are to be dismantled," it read; "the Jews working in the Reich are to get normal Eastern workers' rations. In the absence of Jewish hospitals they may be treated with Aryan patients." However, according to Becher, Himmler actually had given this order earlier.

In Becher's version, some time before the middle of October, he had persuaded Himmler to send two copies of an order to S.S. Lieutenant General Oswald Pohl, head of the Economic Administration of the camps, and to Kaltenbrunner, Heydrich's successor, making them responsible for stopping the killing of Jews.[1] But they as well as Eichmann and Müller ignored the order and continued to gas Jews from Theresienstadt, Italy and the Krakow region. There were no further selections, however, after October 30.

As the end drew near, the crematoria slaves, the Jews who had to dispose of the bodies of exterminated fellow Jews, or forfeit their own lives, decided to rebel. In August 1944, their number had been reduced by progressive exterminations. Most of those left were Jews from the Athens and Corfu deportations, forced to live within the enclosure of the crematoria. A secret committee, led by the future Polish Minister-President Josef Cirankiewicz, smuggled some automatic pistols and grenades into the crematoria area, but the man who was to have led the revolt from the outside, a Jewish officer in the Greek Army, was killed. The plans were picked up by an informer and the men in Crematorium IV were taken and gassed. The secret committee then devised a more ambitious plan for the three remaining crematoria but a series of mishaps balked them. Arms were to be smuggled by Poles to a Jewish deportation train, but the train left ahead of schedule and without the arms. Soon realizing that they had been abandoned, the men in Crematorium III set fire to the building to warn the men in Crematorium I who were armed, but the fire was not seen in time. Overpowering a few S.S. guards, the men in Crematorium III scattered over the entire camp, but as they tried to cut through the wire they were shot down. There was one survivor, Dr. Charles Bendel, a Paris physician and medical officer of the unit. He tried to commit suicide by taking gardenal but was miraculously brought around by fellow doctors and hidden in the infirmary.[2] The camp counterintelligence system quickly traced the source of the explosives to the Krupp fuse factory within the camp. The women who had supplied them were publicly hanged.

The last act of Nazi slaughter at Auschwitz occurred late in November when the last of the crematoria *kommandos* were mysteriously disposed of in the woods. Jewish work details were then assigned to clean out the remaining crematoria and the buildings were finally blown up. Auschwitz, however, still clung to its tens of thousands of prisoners. For two more months the inmates languished or died awaiting the Soviet offensive. On December 16, the U.S. Air Force discovered the camp and dropped a few bombs. One month later, Soviet armored columns moved out of Baranow. By January 16, 1945, the Russians had reached the I. G. Farben calcium mines at Kressendorf and on the same day Soviet planes attacked the camp.

Three days later, the camp finally gave up its human skeletons. At 4 P.M. on January 19, while the rumble of Soviet artillery fire was heard in Auschwitz itself, the camp administration marched out the 58,000 inmates. For many of the emaciated prisoners, this journey—first by foot in freezing weather under the guns of the S.S. and then for days on end in open trucks —was their last. Survivors were dumped into German camps—Bergen-Belsen, Buchenwald and Mauthausen—where the food supply was shut off and typhus raged. Corpses rotted in barracks and on dung heaps. Rats attacked those still alive and the dead were eaten by the living, crazed by hunger. In this, the winter of liberation, the outside world saw for the first time a new species that had evolved in the concentration camp world, the *Mussulmen.* "It was impossible to extract from their lips their names much less their date of birth," a university professor observed. "Kindness itself had not the power to make them speak. They would only look at you with a long expressionless stare. If they tried to answer, their tongues could not reach their dried up palates to make a sound. One was aware only of a poisonous breath rising out of entrails already in a state of decomposition."[3]

At least 80,000 inmates in the charnel houses that lay between the Rhine and Oder died in the last two months of the war. The lives of the others, estimated at 250,000 by Wisliceny at the beginning of February 1945, hung on a seesaw of two wills—Himmler's and Hitler's. By this time, Himmler was ready to sell Jews alive to the Allies in exchange for his own immunity, but Hitler vowed that they would all die—Jews as well as Nazi leaders—in the last death agony of the Third Reich. Toward the end of January 1945, while the open wagons dragged the half-living and frozen dead from Silesia to western Germany, Professor Karl Burckhardt, President of the International Red Cross, finally made contact with the German Foreign Office.

Burckhardt was told that relief would be permitted to reach the camps in trucks if they were provided by the Red Cross and driven by "trusted" prisoners of war. Himmler, meanwhile, had permitted several thousand inmates to go to Switzerland and Sweden, largely through the intervention of his masseur, Dr. Felix Kersten, who had gained small concessions from Himmler from time to time, especially during severe attacks of stomach convulsions. To Himmler, Kersten was "the magic Buddha who cures everything by massage" and through his successful therapy, a curiously intimate relationship had developed between the two men. Kersten could not divert Himmler from his determination to carry out Hitler's order to exterminate the Jews, but he had frustrated his plan to kill off the Jews of Finland and foiled the plot to deport three million Dutch citizens to eastern Europe. He also successfully intervened in the release of thousands of Norwegian and Danish prisoners of war.

Himmler was also being cautiously prodded by the vice-president of the Swedish Red Cross, Count Folke Bernadotte, a seasoned diplomat who differed from Kersten in his approach to rescue efforts. Bernadotte saw no advantage in dwelling on the Jewish issue which he felt irritated Himmler, and aimed rather at getting a general agreement to release prisoners. Once such an agreement was reached, he believed, as many Jews as possible should be included in the rescue action.[4] It is a matter of some controversy as to which of the men—Kersten or Bernadotte—both of whom prodded Himmler to release Jews, had the most effect. But however one views their efforts, their interventions did bear some fruit.

The release of 2,700 Jews from Theresienstadt in February 1945 was the result of Kersten's prodding. In August 1944, Kersten was requested by a former Swiss patient to intervene with Himmler to advance a scheme of certain Swiss industrialists and the International Red Cross to get 20,000 Jews out of concentration camps into Switzerland and then to the south of France. The informant reported that Germans were negotiating in Zurich for the release of Jews for a price. Himmler began to weaken under Kersten's prodding. Then he stiffened. According to Kersten, his chief concern was that the world press might interpret these negotiations as a sign of weakness on Germany's part. However, eventually, Kersten's prodding in this instance saved the lives of 2,700 Jews in Theresienstadt. "Kersten massages a life out of me with every rub," Himmler admitted. (The World Jewish Congress credits him with the rescue of 60,000 Jews.)

On February 6, the third transport of Hungarian Jews from Bergen-Belsen arrived in Switzerland. Very possibly Becher's negotiations with Saly Mayer played some part in this transfer because Himmler finally received five million francs through the Swiss President at this time "on the understanding that it would be used to finance further emigration through the Red Cross." According to Becher, Himmler allotted this money to the Swiss Red Cross plan, but the news of the release of Jewish prisoners was published in the Swiss newspapers and reached Hitler. It elicited such an outburst of rage that Himmler thought he himself would be shot. Frightened out of his wits but relieved to be still alive, Himmler immediately sent instructions "to let no camp inmate in the southern half of Germany fall into enemy hands alive."

Count Bernadotte pursued his line, nevertheless, and saw Himmler on February 17, asking only for the release of the Danish and Norwegian captives. Kaltenbrunner, meanwhile, was playing a double game of his own. He told Bernadotte that he did not intend to assist in any way in giving him access to the camps, but at the same time resumed the Swiss negotiations in order to store up some credit for himself with the Allies. He received Professor Burckhardt on March 12, agreeing to let a Red Cross representative reside in each camp to distribute relief and to exchange French and Belgian internees for Germans. He also assured Burckhardt that all of the prisoners in Theresienstadt would be repatriated. Meanwhile, the chaos in the camps nullified all of the layers of negotiations. Eichmann contradicted orders by Himmler, and Himmler remanded his own. By the end of March, no Red Cross representative had yet entered any of the camps.

In March, the commander of Mauthausen, near Linz, received orders to receive thousands of Jews who had been at work on the *Süd-Ost* wall, the southeast defense line. These Jews were marched on foot, many without shoes, clad in rags and ravaged by hunger, while railway cars were shunted to side rails and abandoned to Allied bombers, who now, apparently, found no "technical difficulties" in their mission. In April, in the Marienbad railway station, a train containing 3,000 inmates of Rehnsdorf camp, a branch of Buchenwald, was also bombed. A thousand or so escaped into the woods but were caught by Nazi guards, brought back to the station and shot.

Meanwhile, the entire Nazi edifice was rotting away, but desperate men continued to give desperate orders. At Yalta, the Allies made it plain that, despite their great differences, they intended to preserve at least the semblance of unity of purpose. They agreed on the "unconditional surrender" of the Reich. The Nazi orders not to yield another yard of ground gave the fighting in the East a horribly bitter senselessness and in the Reich itself, German soil, which for so long had escaped retribution, was visited by scenes previsioned by Goya. Nazi blood lust now began to devour Germans. Over the Oder River, members of the Home Army could see the bodies of "malcontents," former comrades-in-arms, swinging from the twisted girders of blownup bridges where they had been hanged by special S.S. roving courts-martial, pronouncing and executing sentence at will. Every tree in the Hindenberg Alee in Danzig had been used as a gibbet, and the dangling soldiers kicked and threshed, sometimes for hours, with placards pinned to their uniforms: "I hang here because I left my unit without permission." Many of the "deserters" had been schoolboy flak gunners who had gone to visit their parents for a few hours, proud of the opportunity to display their new uniforms. Their protestations went unheard. The bitter-enders killed wantonly: "It is an act of racial duty according to Teutonic tradition," they said, "to exterminate even the kinsmen of those who surrender themselves into captivity without being wounded."[5]

The Nazi leaders, immured in a Berlin bunker, were in fantastic mental states. When word came on April 13 of Roosevelt's death, Göring said to Hitler: "My Führer, I congratulate you! Roosevelt is dead. It is written in the stars that the second half of April will be the turning point for us." In this world, completely out of touch with reality, staff conferences were held and military orders and communiqués were issued.

Himmler, meanwhile, was preoccupied with his "conscience" as well as his health, and with global matters of politics and reconciliation as well as his split feeling of loyalty to Hitler. He had been paying periodic visits to Dr. Karl Gebhardt's clinic at Hohenlychen for treatment of his inflamed state. Gebhardt, who had deliberately infected women inmates at Ravensbrück with gas gangrene, kept Himmler on a regimen of strychnine, hormone "tonic" and belladonna. For spiritual fare, the Reichsführer S.S. alternated between the Army reports brought twice daily and soul-searching exercises. When the spring thaw came, he was affected profoundly, he told Schellenberg, and became convinced of the existence of God.

Schellenberg, meanwhile, had come out openly urging Himmler to seize power and negotiate with the West. In the hospital room at Dr. Gebhardt's clinic, Himmler could be seen jack-booted, wearing an ankle-length field-gray greatcoat over his pajamas, the Knight's Grand Cross at his throat. Some time late in March, he talked with General Heinz Guderian, who suggested that they both see Hitler and urge him to conclude an armistice, a suggestion to which Himmler replied: "My dear Colonel-General, it is still too early for that." But a day later he is reported to have told another general, Colonel-General Gotthard Heinrici: "The time has come to enter into negotiations with our western neighbors. I have initiated steps. My agents have established contact."[6]

Hysterical scenes of ranting and shouting went on in Hitler's underground bunker where the Führer wildly flung accusations of cowardice and negligence at his generals and aides. When he dismissed Guderian on March 28, the last rational and independent military influence was removed from German affairs. Those who remained stuck as close to Hitler as possible, watching for a miraculous change in German fortunes and a chance to advance their own personal ambitions. Hitler himself was living the end he had foreshadowed to Rauschning in 1934: "Even if we should not conquer, we should drag half the world into destruction with us, and leave no one to triumph over Germany . . . we shall never capitulate, no never! We may be destroyed, but if we are, we shall drag a world with us—a world in flames." Eastward toward the "front" streamed Hitler Youth, apprentices, foreign "brigades," the sweepings of prisons and hospitals. Patton and Montgomery had already crossed the Rhine and the armies of Zhukov and Koniev were reinforcing bridgeheads across the Oder. Early in April the Red Cross finally pierced the Nazi fortress of Buchenwald.

On April 3, some Swiss delegates were allowed to interview the camp spokesmen at Oranienburg, but the talks were carried on in the presence of the murder staff. The prisoners scarcely dared open their mouths. During the following week, over half of Buchenwald's 50,000 inmates were evacuated to the south of Germany. When the Americans arrived a few days later, they found cartloads of unburied corpses and Ilsa Koch's human lampshades. On April 15, at Belsen, the British troops were shattered by what they found. On April 6, Eichmann had promised to conduct Georges Dunand of the Red Cross through Belsen to see how the authorities were dealing with the typhus epidemic. By the time Dunand came to Berlin, Eichmann had flown.

At Belsen, in Camp 1, in a rectangle measuring one mile by 400 yards, the British troops found 28,000 women, 12,000 men, and 13,000 unburied corpses. Within a few days, 13,000 more died. In this plague-cursed spot of earth, every rag and stick had to be burned with the unburied corpses. Two miles away in the larders of the panzer training school were stored 800 tons of food and a bakery that had the capacity to produce 60,000 loaves of bread a day. The British troops trembled at what they saw in Belsen. When questioned about this Rudolf Höss at Nuremberg explained that "rations for the detainees were again and again severely curtailed by the provincial economic administration offices. This then led to a situation where detainees in the camps no longer had sufficient powers of resistance against plagues and epidemics."

The validated horrors of Buchenwald and Belsen shocked the world. But they merely angered Himmler. His promise to stop the evacuations of camps was retracted. In a remarkable display of self-righteousness, the Reichsführer S.S. announced his new determined stand on April 19. The occasion was not a meeting with the last staunch cohorts of the S.S. but with Dr. Kersten and a Jew from the free world, Dr. Norbert Masur, who was director of the Swedish section of the World Jewish Congress. Kersten had arranged the meeting by persuading Himmler that the judgment of history would go harshly for the German people unless there was some belated gesture to reverse German policy against the Jews. The invocation of history appealed to Himmler and a meeting was arranged at Kersten's Hartzwalde house. The men met in an atmosphere of secrecy as well as wringing irony: Himmler had to steal away from a supper party in the Reich Chancellery bunker in Berlin on the eve of Hitler's birthday to meet with a Jew.

He came, he said, "to bury the hatchet" and to say, for posterity, that had he had his way, "many things would have been done differently."[7] But before long, he reverted to form, declaring:

> It was my intention to hand over the concentration camps undefended, as I had announced. I allowed Bergen-Belsen and Buchenwald to be overrun, but I got no thanks for it. In Belsen, they chained up one of the guards and photographed him among the bodies of dead prisoners, and these pictures are now published by the press throughout the world. In Buchenwald, the hospital caught fire from a burning American tank and the charred corpses were photographed throughout the world . . . the statements in hate against us concerning the concentration camps did not induce me to continue my policy of surrendering the camps undefended. Consequently, a few days ago I allowed a camp in Saxony to be evacuated as the American tanks approached. Why should I do otherwise?[8]

Dr. Masur then explained that the Allied press could not be muzzled in return for his concessions. In a democratic society, he said, even the government could not stop the printing of undesirable news. Himmler, however, insisted that the power of "world Jewry" was such that the press could be silenced at any moment.

Meanwhile, Bernadotte's negotiations had resulted in the release on April 15 of 423 surviving Danish Jews in Theresienstadt and their return home. A Red Cross delegate finally penetrated Mauthausen on April 23 and saw the forced-labor columns return to camp carrying their dead. The crematorium chimney was still smoking. At his request, 134 French internees were liberated. Another Red Cross representative learned from an S.S. lieutenant that the camp commandant had planned to collect the inmates in the underground airplane factory at Gusen and blow the place up. Kaltenbrunner was later both blamed for this plan and credited with ordering the commandant to deliver Mauthausen to the Americans intact.

The accusations and counteraccusations flew thick and fast, but the days of the Third Reich were coming to an end at last. Military realities were inescapable. After April 25, Mauthausen, Dachau and Theresienstadt were cut off from Berlin and were handed over to the Allies. However, Ravensbrück, Oranienburg and Sachsenhausen, which were in the Berlin area—where Hitler's ranting and screaming could be figuratively heard—were evacuated. The Red Cross delegates tried fruitlessly to bargain with Müller to have these camps delivered to them. The inmates of Oranienburg were marched off toward Wittstock, sixty miles to the northwest. Some food was brought to the ghostly columns and the sick were carried off to Allied lines in Swedish Red Cross trucks.

At Ravensbrück, Himmler had promised Bernadotte that 1,500 ill prisoners could have Red Cross protection, that all Scandinavians could be taken away by the Swedish Red Cross, and that all other westerners could be evacuated by train to Malchow. The "easterners," however—Polish and Hungarian Jewish women—would have to cover the forty miles on foot. (At the last moment, Swedish trucks took 7,000 of these women to Flensburg.) Most of the Jewish prisoners at Sachsenhausen had already been dumped at Belsen and the 650 non-Jews were marched off in the general direction of Lübeck. They were halted in Below Forest, where the Swedish Red Cross rescued several hundred invalids and prevented the rest from being murdered by following the convoy to the Allied lines at Schwerin. Up to the time of the Red Cross overtake, about 100 prisoners had died on the march, most of them shot by the S.S. as stragglers.

As these phantoms stumbled through the springtime countryside, whipped into pace by guards rushing toward ever-shrinking pockets of the Reich, Himmler was making his last thrust out of uncertainty. On April 24, at the Swedish Consulate in Lübeck, he offered conditional surrender to the Allies.

The electricity in the consulate had been cut and the three men present—Bernadotte, Schellenberg and Himmler—sat in candlelight. They had scarcely taken their seats when an air raid sent them to the cellar. After midnight, they returned to the consulate offices. For the first time in days of negotiation and vacillation, Himmler spoke clearly. "The Führer's great life," he said, "is drawing to its close." Possibly he was already dead, Himmler conjectured; if not, he would certainly be dead within the next few days. He had gone to Berlin to perish with its inhabitants and it would be only a matter of days before Berlin would fall. Formerly, Himmler had been unable to break his oath to Hitler; now, everything had changed. He empowered Bernadotte to communicate to the Western Allies his offer of surrender.[9] In the East, however, he would not surrender. There he said the Germans would continue to fight until the Western Allies had advanced to relieve them. This sublime certainty that the breach between the Western Allies and the Soviet Union was inevitable and that Nazi Germany would serve the Allies in April 1945 was shared by many Nazi leaders.

Himmler wrote a personal letter for Bernadotte to take to Stockholm as proof of his offer and then turned to important procedural matters: What name should he choose for the new political party which his government should represent? Should he bow or shake hands when introduced to General Eisenhower?

Bernadotte left and returned to Germany on April 27, saying that neither Himmler nor a limited surrender was acceptable to the Western powers. Fearful of Himmler's anger at this rebuff, Schellenberg secured the astrologer Wulf to accompany him to Himmler to blunt the disappointment over this news. In the meantime, a report of Himmler's negotiations with Bernadotte was brought to Hitler. The British press published a Reuters report of Himmler's offer of a conditional surrender and his indiscreet remark that Hitler was probably dying of a cerebral hemorrhage. Hitler was outraged by the news. The faithful Heinrich— der treue Heinrich—whose loyalty had always been unquestioned, had also betrayed him. There can be no doubt that to Hitler, this treachery was the signal for the end.[10] In the past, Himmler had hesitated before making his decisions. His wavering had sometimes been exasperating. Now he had made a decision about his Führer's end. On the night of April 28–29, Hitler wrote his last will and testament and he married Eva Braun. He also spoke of his suicide plans, but not before he had ordered his new Commander in Chief of the Luftwaffe to arrest Himmler and execute him.

Hitler left no retreat for Germany. His last desperate gambles for victory had failed. As Germany had lost the war, the whole nation would suffer. Deservedly so, he said. Nothing more clearly shows Hitler's utter contempt for the fate of his own people than the barbarous directives he issued in the last hours of the war. Having already sapped the conscience of the nation by abolishing law and making murder a civic duty, he ordered all military and industrial installations destroyed so that nothing would be left with which the German people could start their reconstruction. The country was to be made into a vast wasteland. As his own personal fate had been sealed, so would Germany's. "If the war is lost," he told Albert Speer, the War Production Minister, "the nation will also perish. This fate is inevitable." A destructive Götterdämmerung was his only legacy.

By the end of April, the Nazi empire, which had once stretched from the Caucasus to the Atlantic, had shrunk to a small corridor in the heart of Germany. The Russians were storming the gates of Berlin, where fifty feet beneath the ground in a concrete bunker, Hitler raged against the

Nazi hierarchs and generals who had "betrayed" him. The flawed
Himmler and Göring were expelled from the Party and all state offices.
On April 30, Hitler made elaborate ritualistic preparations for his and
Eva Braun's suicide. Their bodies were to be burned to avoid the fate of
Mussolini and his mistress at the hands of the mob.

In the end, as in the beginning, Hitler reviled the Jews. They were, he
repeated, the cause of the war and the "universal poisoner of all nations."
For the last time, he charged the German people to "uphold the laws of
race." There was no word of remorse or regret for the ruined world he had
made.

On May 7, 1945, in a little schoolhouse at Reims, where Eisenhower
had made his headquarters, Germany surrendered unconditionally. Not
Himmler, however, but General Alfred Jodl, acting for Hitler's successor,
Admiral Karl Dönitz, signed the surrender terms.

Himmler, whose name had terrorized Europe during the long Nazi
night, had fled to Flensburg on the Danish border, where Dönitz had
set up a rump government. The former S.S. Reichsführer had shaved off
his moustache, tied a black patch over his left eye and put on an Army
private's uniform. He tried to make his way back to his native Bavaria,
but at a British control point near Bremerhaven, he was questioned and
admitted his identity. He was taken to the Second Army Headquarters
at Lüneburg where he was stripped and searched and made to change
into a British uniform to make sure he had no poison on his person. But
the search was not thorough. Himmler had concealed a vial of potassium
cyanide in his gums. When his mouth was finally searched on May 23,
he bit into the vial and was dead in twelve minutes.

An eerie, infinitely welcome silence settled over the Continent for the
first time since September 1, 1939. For almost six years Europe had been
the landscape of the most heinous barbarities in history. Its ancient cities
were in ruins. Millions of its families mourned piercing human losses.
Thousands of corpses still lay unburied. But the evil of the Third Reich
had finally been destroyed. No trace of German authority remained. Down
to the smallest villages, Germany was governed by the conquering enemy
troops who furnished not only a structure of law and order but food and
fuel to keep the German people alive. In the vast desert of rubble, the
German people faced the meaning as well as the end of the Third Reich.

Amid the desolation, following the German surrender, the Allies reopened Max Reinhardt's Deutsches Theater in Berlin with a performance
of Lessing's classic, *Nathan the Wise*. The play was directed by Fritz
Wisten and the part of the dervish was taken by Alfred Balthoff, both
Jews who had stayed alive underground. It was an hour of empty, mocking
triumph for the few German Jews who had survived the war. In it, a Jew

proclaims the message of tolerance and humanity. Twelve years before, on October 1, 1933, the same play had been the opening work in the drama schedule of the *Jüdischer Kulturbund*. Alfred Balthoff had been one of the *Kulturbund* actors.

For the surviving Jews in Europe, however, the words tolerance and humanity were hollow. Europe, in the twelve years between 1933 and 1945, had become a vast cemetery of Jews whose remains were ashes in unnamed graves. There was no return possible. For most non-Jews after liberation, the existence of any Jewish survivors was a shock. "What, you still alive?" was a common greeting. In returning to their desolated communities, Jews hoped for some word of welcome, but with very few exceptions they found none. Post-Hitler Europe was plainly untenable for Jewish survivors and Heine's ticket to its civilization, so hopefully purchased, was turned in. Hitler's "Final Solution" did not physically destroy all of Europe's Jews, but it succeeded in destroying Europe as a home for those who escaped the "solution." Today in Poland, once the heartland of European Jewry, there live 35,000 Jews, half of them concentrated in Silesia. This is what is left of a prewar community of 3,300,000 and a postwar community of 350,000.

Those Jews still alive at liberation, and still possessed of will, knew they must liberate themselves. Many soon found themselves languishing in D.P. camps in place of concentration camps. The hope, as expressed by one poet, that "the Allied conquerors might be the bearers of an Ark that would deliver us from the Deluge" was soon dashed. There was only one way left: Palestine.

Emigration of Jews to Palestine started in Poland before the whole country was liberated. In the summer of 1944, in the Lublin region, Zionist youth leaders began to organize the emigration of survivors. The first steps had already been taken toward organizing the famous *bricha*, the underground routes of escape from Europe to Palestine. Frontiers were still fluid and many Jews passed as Romanians, Greeks and Italians. Some also moved with army detachments. They surged toward Romania, then through Hungary, Yugoslavia and Austria to Italy. By the fall of 1945, the camps in Italy were very crowded. Another exodus from Europe took Jews to the camps of Germany and Austria in the American zones.

On July 1, 1945, forty-one delegates from more than twenty places in Bavaria gathered at Feldafing among wooded hills to chart the course of a still tenuous movement. At this conference, the *Sheerit Hapletah*, the Saving Remnant, welded its destiny to Palestine. The Central Committee of Liberated Jews was formed and a proclamation was addressed to the Allied leaders at Potsdam demanding the immediate annulment of the British White Paper of 1939 and the establishment of a Jewish state. "We who are at the brink of a new and unknown life," the proclamation read, "have within us the firm faith and hope that those who freed us from slavery and death will also aid us in the reconstruction of a peaceful and secure home."[11]

However, indifference, legalism and British obduracy severely tested the faith of these delegates as well as those of enlarged conferences that were called later. Meanwhile, the Jews in Germany were augmented by a large stream of refugees from Poland, Romania and Hungary, driven by new bursts of maniacal persecution. In Kielce, Poland, for example, on July 4, 1946, an old-style post-Hitler pogrom erupted. A Polish boy was coached to say that he had been caught by Jews, imprisoned in a cellar, and abused. He was also told to say that in the same cellar he saw the bodies of other children. Like the old ritual-murder fabrications, this story had no basis in fact. But it was believed. A mob fell upon the Jewish community house and forty-one Jews were killed. With monotonous predictability, pogroms erupted all over Poland. Repatriation had become a meaningless slogan.

American authorities were at first startled by the influx of refugees but soon instructed camp officials to regard them as "persons displaced by enemy action." Arrivals came at the rate of several thousand weekly, bringing the starved and ragged as well as those who were still unravaged. This exodus led a British official, Lieutenant General Sir Frederick Morgan, UNRRA chief of operations in Germany, to conjure up the not-yet-dead conspiracy myth. He declared before newsmen that an unknown secret Jewish organization was behind the infiltration into Germany from the East, that European Jews were "growing into a world force." He doubted the "monotonous story about pogroms," saying that the Jews arriving from Poland were "well-dressed and fed, rosy-cheeked" and "have plenty of money." He added, "they certainly do not look like persecuted people."[12]

This "force" intended to live. The Central Committee of Liberated Jews was a government-in-being. It handled legislative, judicial and executive functions defined in a constitution. It served as liaison with military and civil authorities, organized and stimulated emigration, established synagogues, schools and workshops, a press, hospitals and sports. It prosecuted restitution claims, protected the legal rights of survivors and directed numerous cultural and economic projects. Jewish autonomy which the Nazis had cynically abused now came into full flowering.

The Committee lacked only two things: an army and a flag. In all other respects, it was a legal living reality for the *Sheerit Hapletah*, a de facto nation. The force of this reality was so strong that it was finally granted official recognition by the American Government in September 1946 as "a government without a flag."

The British, meanwhile, were guided by the sentiments expressed by

Sir Frederick Morgan. They withdrew the Jewish Brigade from Austria and tightened frontier controls. In Germany, they denied admission of displaced persons to their zone after June 30, 1946. Thus blocked by the British, Jews poured into the American zone in Germany and Austria. By the end of 1946, 183,600 Jews were in American areas—about 90 percent of all displaced Jews in the western zones of Germany and Austria.

Again, as during the war, not only was Britain cutting off living space for Jewish life; it was also choking escape. Still vainly trying to appease the Arab world and maintain pre-eminence in the Middle East, Britain was sending parachutists and infantry to Palestine to drive out Jews who were struggling to enter and imprison those who tried to remain. Refugees continued to be hounded on the seas.

The D.P. camp inmates became restive. A new Anglo-Palestine Commission conducted investigations over the same worn ground. As the first chill of the cold war fell on the wartime alliance, the United States shifted its political focus. Germany became the new battleground between the East and West, and the United States began to rebuild the German economy. Local German self-rule was initiated and German officials found themselves with unexpected power. The camp populations grew increasingly apprehensive. This time, however, Jews acted boldly. Unlike the ghetto response to the young fighters in 1942 and 1943—slow to evolve and activated in the last extremity—the Jews in the camps acted while there was time. Under the guidance of Mossad leaders and demobilized soldiers of the Palestine Brigade who appeared in Munich, Vienna, Lodz and Rome, Jews took their silent leave of Europe. Under the cover of night, they trekked over mountains and valleys—men, women and children by the thousands—toward the beaches of Marseilles, Port-de-Bouc, La Spezia and Venice, into the sea and the dogged struggle to outwit the British Navy. This time, the deportation trains did not suck them back to a death-drenched continent. The exodus came like a tidal wave. The British could no longer hold it back.

The Jews had learned yet another lesson from the catastrophe. No longer would they petition or plead for their security or rely on legal rectitude and promises to achieve it. Their right to live was neither a wartime nor postwar objective of the Allied powers. Jews had to secure it for themselves. Tenaciously they clung to that small scallop of desert which is their home by faith, by history and by honorable pledge from the League of Nations and Britain. Thrust into history were the desperate scramble for emigration certificates, carefully phrased memoranda of the Jewish Agency to the august Mandatory Government, the elaborate rigmarole of exit and entrance permits, the Jewish faith in the world's conscience.

A new breed of Jews had come out of Palestine: tough, realistic and militant. They were bringing into Palestine not refugees who ask for mercy, but *ma'apilim*, stormers of obstacles. For their new, official writ to enter the land, they chose their oldest source, the Bible. On the passengers of the *Feda*, a wooden cargo ship which the British held at gunpoint at La Spezia in April 1946, relenting only after the refugees had fasted four days, the new "passports" read: "Mr. . . . has been found qualified by the representatives of the *Yishuv* [Jewish community in Palestine] for repatriation to Palestine. By authority, *Ezekiel*, 37: 'And they shall abide in the land that I have given unto Jacob My servant wherein your fathers abode, and they shall abide therein, even they and their children, and their children's children forever.' "[13]

APPENDIX

Estimates of Jewish Losses
in Nazi-Occupied Europe, 1939–1945

1. Anglo-American Committee of Inquiry Regarding the Problems
   of European Jewry and Palestine, April 1946.

Germany (1938 frontiers)	195,000
Austria	53,000
Czechoslovakia (1938)	255,000
Denmark	1,500*
France	140,000
Belgium	57,000
Luxembourg	3,000
Norway	1,000
Holland	120,000
Italy	20,000
Yugoslavia	64,000
Greece	64,000
Bulgaria (pre-1941 frontier)	5,000
Romania (pre-1940 frontier)	530,000
Hungary (1938 frontiers)	200,000
Poland (1939 frontiers)	3,271,000
U.S.S.R. (pre-1939 frontiers plus Baltic States)	1,050,000
	6,029,500
Less dispersed refugees	308,000
Total	5,721,500

* Chiefly refugees in Sweden.

2. Estimates by Gerald Reitlinger, *The Final Solution*, 1953.

	Low	High
Germany (1938 frontiers)	160,000	180,000
Austria	58,000	60,000
Czechoslovakia (1938)	233,000	243,000
Denmark	Less than 100	

2. Estimates by Gerald Reitlinger, *The Final Solution*, 1953. (*Cont'd*)

France	60,000	65,000
Belgium	25,000	28,000
Luxembourg	3,000	3,000
Norway	700	700
Holland	104,000	104,000
Italy	8,500	9,500
Yugoslavia	55,000	58,000
Greece	57,000	60,000
Bulgaria (pre-1941 frontier)	———	———
Romania (pre-1940 frontier)	200,000*	220,000*
Hungary (1938 frontiers)	180,000	200,000
Poland (1939 frontiers)	2,350,000*	2,600,000*
U.S.S.R. (pre-1939 frontiers plus Baltic States)	700,000*	750,000*
Totals	4,194,200*	4,581,200*

* Owing to lack of reliable information at the time of writing, these figures must be regarded as conjectural (Reitlinger, p. 501). Reitlinger's considerably lower estimates are traceable largely to what he calls "highly conjectural estimates" of losses in territory presently controlled by the Soviet Union and losses in Romania. He has also pointed to the "widely differing estimates of the Jewish populations of Russia, Poland, Hungary, Romania and the Balkans" before the war. Reitlinger bases much of his statistical summary on the "Korherr Report" (Nuremberg documents No. 5192–4), which was sent to Himmler in March 1943. Dr. Korherr was an actuary, employed by Himmler to compile a balance sheet from the resettlement lists kept in Eichmann's office. For a detailed analysis of the above figures, see Appendix I, Statistical Summary of the Final Solution, in Reitlinger, pp. 489–500.

3a. Losses Estimated by Raul Hilberg, *The Destruction of the European Jews*, 1961.†

	1939	1945
Austria	60,000	7,000
Belgium	90,000	40,000
Bulgaria	50,000	47,000
Czechoslovakia	315,000	44,000

† Statistics for 1939 refer to prewar borders. Postwar frontiers have been used for 1945. The figure of 80,000 for Germany includes 60,000 displaced persons. The estimate for the U.S.S.R. comprises about 300,000 refugees, deportees and survivors from newly acquired territories (Hilberg, p. 670).

3a. Losses Estimated by Raul Hilberg, *The Destruction of the European Jews,* 1961. (*Cont'd*)

Denmark	6,500	5,500
France	270,000	200,000
Germany	240,000	80,000
Greece	74,000	12,000
Hungary	400,000	200,000
Italy	50,000	33,000
Luxembourg	3,000	1,000
Netherlands	140,000	20,000
Norway	2,000	1,000
Poland	3,350,000	50,000
Romania	800,000	430,000
U.S.S.R.	3,020,000	2,600,000
Estonia	4,500	
Latvia	95,000	
Lithuania	145,000	
Yugoslavia	75,000	12,000
	9,180,000	3,782,500

3b. Statistical Recapitulation of Jewish Dead by Territory (Borders as of August 1939).

Reich-Protektorat Area	250,000
U.S.S.R.	700,000
Baltic States	200,000
Poland	3,000,000
Low Countries	130,000
France and Italy	70,000
Yugoslavia	60,000
Greece and Rhodes	60,000
Slovakia	60,000
Romania	270,000
Hungary and Carpatho-Ukraine	300,000
Total	5,100,000

(Hilberg, p. 767.)

4. Estimates of Jewish Losses by Jacob Lestchinsky,
Balance Sheet of Extermination, American Jewish Congress, 1946.*

Country (Prewar borders)	Jewish Population September 1939	Number of Jews Lost
Poland	3,250,000	2,850,000
U.S.S.R. (Occupied Area)	2,100,000	1,500,000
Romania	850,000	425,000
Hungary	400,000	200,000
Czechoslovakia	315,000	240,000
France†	300,000	90,000
Germany	193,000	110,000‡
Austria	90,000	45,000
Lithuania	150,000	130,000
Holland	150,000	105,000
Latvia	95,000	80,000
Belgium†	90,000	40,000
Yugoslavia	75,000	55,000
Greece	75,000	60,000
Italy†	57,000	15,000
Bulgaria	50,000	7,000
Denmark, Estonia, Norway, Luxembourg, Danzig	15,000	5,000
Totals	8,255,000	5,957,000

* Revised in 1955, Yad Vashem Bulletin, No. 10, April 1961.
† Figures include refugees.
‡ Does not include Jewish victims killed between 1933 and 1939, estimated at between 30,000 and 40,000 by Lestchinsky.

NOTES

MANY OF THE DOCUMENTS marked PS, EC and L in the notes refer to documents from the original Nuremberg Trial of 1945–46, most of which are to be found in the American edition of the trial: *The Trial of the Major War Criminals*. English translations of most of this material, which was published in the original languages of the documents, are printed in *Nazi Conspiracy and Aggression* (Washington, D.C., 10 vols., 1946–48) and in mimeographed transcripts in major depository libraries. There were twelve subsequent trials at Nuremberg conducted by United States military tribunals and part of the testimony and documents presented at these trials is contained in *Trials of War Criminals Before the Nuremberg Military Tribunals* (Washington, D.C., Government Printing Office, 15 vols., 1951–52). Documents marked NG and NO are to be found in this collection. Several excerpts from documents quoted below were also taken from a compilation of Nuremberg documents collected by the American and British prosecuting staffs: *Nazi Germany's War Against the Jews* (New York, American Jewish Conference, 1947).

The classification symbols are convenient abbreviations. The letters "EC" stand for "Economic Case" and refer to those documents which were processed by the Economic Section of the Office of the United States Chief Counsel (OCC) working at Frankfurt. "L" is an abbreviation for "London" and refers to those documents processed in the London office of the OCC. "PS" is an abbreviation of "Paris-Storey" and identifies those documents which, though obtained in Germany, were processed by the OCC office in Paris and later in Nuremberg. The letter "R" refers to documents screened and translated by Lt. Walter Rothschild of the London Branch of the OSS. "D" refers to documents originally processed by the British prosecuting staff. Documents marked NO refer to those issued by Nazi organizations such as the S.S., the Gestapo, the S.D., etc., and those marked NG refer to documents of German Government agencies and ministries.

CHAPTER 1

1. Howard K. Smith, *Last Train from Berlin* (New York, Alfred A. Knopf, 1942), pp. 64–70.

2. Adolf Hitler, *Mein Kampf* (Boston, Houghton Mifflin, 1943), p. 654.

3. Thomas Mann, *Germany and the Germans*. Address delivered at the Library of Congress, May 29, 1945 (Washington, 1945), p. 5.

4. Carlton J. H. Hayes, *A Generation of Materialism* (New York, Harper & Brothers, 1941), pp. 242–85.

5. Quoted in William L. Shirer, *The Rise and Fall of the Third Reich* (Greenwich, Conn., Fawcett, 1962), p. 158.

6. Ismar Elbogen, *A Century of Jewish Life* (Philadelphia, Jewish Publication Society of America, 1944), pp. 155–56.

7. Norman Cohn, "The Myth of the Jewish World-Conspiracy: A Case Study in Collective Psychopathology," *Commentary*, June 1966, pp. 35–42. Cohn is the director of the newly created Center for Research in Collective Psychopathology at

the University of Sussex, England, where experts in psychology, social anthropology, sociology, history and politics will try to fathom the Nazi phenomenon of men carrying out mass murder without guilt.

8. Quoted in Leo Alexander, "War Crimes and Their Motivation," *Journal of Criminal Law and Criminology*, Vol. XXXIX, September–October, 1948, p. 315.

9. Hannah Vogt, *The Burden of Guilt: A Short History of Germany, 1914–1945* (New York, Oxford University Press, 1964), p. 97.

10. Shirer, *op. cit.*, pp. 93–94.

CHAPTER 2

1. These events are vividly described in Shirer, *op. cit.*, pp. 263–319, and in Alan Bullock, *Hitler: A Study in Tyranny* (New York, Harper & Brothers, 1958), pp. 109–283.

2. Despite provocation and incitement by the Nazis, there was no sign of a revolution, Communist or Socialist. But something sensational had to be invented before the March 5 election. A half-witted Dutch Communist who had committed arson, Marinus van der Lubbe, gave the Nazis the dupe they needed, but the main job was done by storm troopers. The idea for the fire almost certainly originated with Goebbels and Göring. The subsequent trial cast a great deal of suspicion on the Nazis but it came too late to have any practical effect.

3. Helmut Heiber, *Adolf Hitler* (London, Oswald Wolff Ltd., 1961), p. 97.

4. *Ibid.*, pp. 19–20, and Mordecai Lenski, "Who Inspired Hitler's Plans to Destroy the Jews?" *Yad Vashem Bulletin*, No. 14, March 1964, pp. 49–52. According to Lenski, it is doubtful that Hitler did more than leaf through Chamberlain's work which was intended primarily for intellectuals, or that he ever read Gobineau, who would have been "incomprehensible" to him. After the war, Dr. Wilfred Daim of Vienna visited Lanz, by then an old man. Lanz reported that Hitler had visited him in 1909 and had asked for copies of *Ostara* missing from his files. Moreover, in 1932, Lanz wrote to a member of his order: "Hitler is one of our pupils. We will yet be privileged to see that he, together with us, will win and will be able to establish a movement so powerful that it will shake the world." Lanz' order still exists, though its founder died in 1954. There seems to be some conflict over his name; Lenski refers to him as Lanz von Liebenfels.

5. Hitler, *op. cit.*, pp. 56–59.

6. *Ibid.*, pp. 123–24.

7. Gertrud M. Kurth, "The Complex Behind Hitler's Anti-Semitism: A Psychoanalytic Study in History," *Commentary*, Vol. 5, No. 1, January 1948, pp. 77–82.

8. Konrad Heiden, *Der Führer: Hitler's Rise to Power* (Boston, Houghton Mifflin Company, 1944), p. 36.

9. Marvin Lowenthal, *The Jews of Germany: A Story of 16 Centuries* (Philadelphia, Jewish Publication Society of America, 1939), p. 368.

10. Julius Streicher, "Beat the World Enemy," *Völkischer Beobachter*, March 31, 1933, PS-2410.

11. Joseph Tenenbaum, "The Anti-Jewish Boycott Movement in the United States," in *Yad Vashem Studies* (Jerusalem), Vol. III, 1959, p. 153.

CHAPTER 3

1. Lord Russell of Liverpool, *The Scourge of the Swastika: A Short History of Nazi Crimes* (New York, Ballantine Books, 1956), pp. 7–8.

2. Erich Kahler, *The Tower and the Abyss: An Inquiry into the Transformation of the Individual* (New York, George Braziller Inc., 1957), p. 62.

3. Hermann Rauschning, *The Voice of Destruction* (New York, G. P. Putnam's Sons, 1940), pp. 16, 83, 252.

4. Shirer, *op. cit.*, p. 258.

5. Account based on Charles Wighton, *Heydrich: Hitler's Most Evil Henchman* (Philadelphia, Chilton Co., 1962), pp. 40–44.

6. Telford Taylor, *Sword and Swastika: Generals and Nazis in the Third Reich* (New York, Simon and Schuster, 1952), pp. 129–30.

7. S.S. Oberst-Gruppenführer Daluege (Chief of the Order Police) to Wolff, Chief of Himmler's Personal Staff, Feb. 28, 1943, NO-2861.

8. Alexander Dallin, *German Rule in Russia 1941–1945: A Study of Occupation Policies* (New York, The Macmillan Co., 1957), pp. 596–97.

9. Wighton, *op. cit.*, pp. 21–30.

10. In the Germany of 1904, when Heydrich was born, a Jewish grandmother was of no particular significance one way or another if the grandchild or parents had converted. Heydrich himself was baptized by a Catholic priest and brought up as a devout Catholic child, according to Wighton. In the past, some writers (including Wighton) have suggested the possibility of Heydrich's Jewish ancestry, based largely on the authority of Himmler's doctor, Dr. Felix Kersten, but more recent works have dropped the idea. According to Jacob Robinson, *And the Crooked Shall Be Made Straight* (Philadelphia, Jewish Publication Society of America, 1965, pp. 145–46), an exhaustive search of the records of the Berlin Document Center, where the Central Archives of the Nazi Party are kept, shows that the allegation is false.

11. Shirer, *op. cit.*, pp. 1247–48.

CHAPTER 4

1. Robert Weltsch, Introduction to *Yearbook I* of the Leo Baeck Institute of Jews from Germany (London, 1956), p. xix.

2. Max Gruenewald, "The Beginning of the Reichsvertretung," in *Yearbook I* of the Leo Baeck Institute (London, 1956), p. 59.

3. *Ibid.*, pp. 66–67.

4. Ernst Simon, "Jewish Adult Education in Nazi Germany as Spiritual Resistance," in *Yearbook I* of the Leo Baeck Institute (London, 1956), pp. 68–89.

5. Martin Buber, "Die Stunde und die Erkenntnis," in *Jüdische Rundschau*, May 1933, pp. 104–10. Quoted in *ibid.*, p. 71.

6. Solomon Colodner, "Jewish Education under National Socialism," in *Yad Vashem Studies*, III, *op. cit.*, pp. 161–85.

7. Hans Gaertner, "Problems of Jewish Schools in Germany During the Hitler Regime," in *Yearbook I*, Leo Baeck Institute (London, 1956), pp. 129–30.

8. *Ibid.*, p. 132.

9. Herbert Freeden, "A Jewish Theatre Under the Swastika," in *Yearbook I*, Leo Baeck Institute (London, 1956), pp. 142–62.

10. Excerpt of affidavit of S. R. Fuller, October 18, 1945, giving account of a conversation with Schacht, Sept. 23, 1935, EC-450.

11. Raul Hilberg, *The Destruction of the European Jews* (Chicago, Quadrangle Books, 1961), p. 47.

12. *Ibid.*, p. 60.

CHAPTER 5

1. Shaul Esh, "Between Discrimination and Extermination: The Fateful Year 1938," *Yad Vashem Studies* (Jerusalem), Vol. II, 1956, p. 85.

2. Bella Fromm, *Blood and Banquets* (New York, Garden City Publishing Co., 1944), p. 274.

3. Werner Rosenstock, "Exodus 1933–1939," in Yearbook I, Leo Baeck Institute (London, 1956), p. 376.

4. Hans Habe, The Mission (New York, Coward-McCann, 1966).

5. Ernst Marcus, "The German Foreign Office and the Palestine Question in the Period 1933–39," in Yad Vashem Studies (Jerusalem), Vol. II, 1956, p. 194.

6. Moshe Pearlman, The Capture and Trial of Adolf Eichmann (New York, Simon & Schuster, 1963), pp. 234–35.

7. Three teletyped orders from Heydrich to all stations of the State Police, November 10, 1938, on measures against the Jews, PS–3051.

8. Report of Samuel W. Honaker, American Consul General, to United States Ambassador Hugh R. Wilson in Berlin, November 12, 1938, PS–2604.

9. From David H. Buffum to Ralph C. Busser in Berlin, November 21, 1938. Quoted in Henry A. Zeiger, ed., The Case Against Adolf Eichmann (New York, The New American Library, 1960), pp. 36–38.

10. K. Y. Ball-Kaduri, "The Central Jewish Organizations in Berlin During the Pogrom of November 1938," in Yad Vashem Studies (Jerusalem), Vol. III, 1959, pp. 261–67.

11. Ibid., p. 277.

12. Ibid., p. 276.

13. Arthur Prinz, "The Role of the Gestapo in Obstructing and Promoting Jewish Emigration," in Yad Vashem Studies (Jerusalem), Vol. II, 1959, p. 213.

14. K. Y. Ball-Kaduri, op. cit., pp. 274–75.

15. Herbert Freeden, op. cit., p. 162.

16. Hilberg, op. cit., p. 24.

17. Excerpt from a top secret memorandum concerning the meeting of the Reich Defense Council, November 18, 1938, PS–3575.

18. Account based on stenographic report of the meeting on "The Jewish Question" under the chairmanship of Fieldmarshal Göring, November 12, 1938, PS–1816.

19. Hilberg, op. cit., p. 82.

20. Excerpts from report of Göring's commissioners for investigation of Aryanizations carried out in Franconia between 9/11/38 and 9/2/39, PS–1757.

21. Stenographic report of the meeting, November 12, 1938, op. cit.

22. Excerpt from speech by Walter Funk, November 15, 1938, on elimination of Jews from the German economy, PS–3545.

23. Hilberg, op. cit., p. 29.

24. Schacht's fiscal methods are described in Norbert Muhlen, Schacht: Hitler's Magician (Toronto, Longmans, Green, 1939).

CHAPTER 6

1. The Austrian conspirators of March 1938, all of whom received high official appointments, included some of the major war criminals in Hitler's Reich: Odilo Globocnik became the first Gauleiter of Vienna and later the Higher S.S. and Police Leader for Lublin province; Josef Bürckel conducted the deportations from Alsace and the Saar; Seyss-Inquart became Reich Commissar for the Netherlands; Ernst Kaltenbrunner succeeded Heydrich as head of the RSHA after Heydrich's assassination.

2. Account of events leading to Anschluss based on Shirer, op. cit., pp. 440–84.

3. Ibid., p. 477.

4. G. E. R. Gedye, Betrayal in Central Europe (New York, Harper & Brothers, 1939), p. 293.

5. Ibid., pp. 294–95.

6. *Ibid.*, pp. 312–13. Göring later admitted that enforced industrialization for rearmament was made possible by exhausting the state treasury of Austria and by the Aryanization of Jewish property (PS–5375).

7. *Ibid.*, p. 315.

8. Report of Auerbach to Eliahu Dobkin, head of Jewish Agency Immigration Department, Jerusalem, dated October 25, 1938. Quoted in J. H. Rosenkranz, "The Kristallnacht in Austria in the Light of the Historical Sources," *Yad Vashem Bulletin* (Jerusalem), No. 14, March 1964, pp. 36–37.

9. "An Official Nazi Report on the November (1938) Pogroms in Vienna," in *Yad Vashem Bulletin* (Jerusalem), No. 2, December 1957, p. 28.

10. Report from S.D. commander of Styria-Graz, dated November 24, 1938. Quoted in Rosenkranz, *op. cit.*, p. 41.

11. Leon Poliakov, *Harvest of Hate: The Nazi Program for the Destruction of the Jews of Europe* (Syracuse, N.Y., Syracuse University Press, 1954), p. 25. Hilberg credits this idea to Josef Bürckel, *Reichskommissar* in charge of "reunification of Austria with the Reich" (p. 259).

12. Comer Clarke, *Eichmann: The Man and His Crimes* (New York, Ballantine Books, 1960), pp. 10–11.

13. Editors of *Life*, "Eichmann Tells His Own Damning Story," *Life*, November 28, 1960, p. 22.

14. Account of Eichmann's assignment to Palestine and text of letter in Quentin Reynolds and others, *Minister of Death* (New York, Viking Press, 1960), pp. 71–78.

15. Affidavit of Dieter Wisliceny, Bratislava, November 18, 1946, quoted in Tuviah Friedman, *The Hunter* (New York, Doubleday & Co., 1961), p. 158.

16. Quoted in Robinson, *op. cit.* (see fn. 10, Chap. 3), p. 229.

17. The testimony of Mayer is quoted in Pearlman, *op. cit.*, pp. 245–46.

18. Reynolds, *op. cit.*, pp. 81–83.

19. These episodes are described in *ibid.*, pp. 84–85.

20. Report of Statistical Office for Reich Gau Ostmark, December 15, 1939, PS–1949. During the November pogroms, Max Rothenberg, director of the Palestine Office and Dr. Josef Löwenherz, chairman of the *Kultusgemeinde*, were in London trying to finance the emigration of Austrian Jews.

21. Editors of *Life*, "Eichmann Tells His Own Damning Story," *op. cit.*, p. 24.

22. Eichmann's personal file, NO–2259.

23. German Foreign Office Circular, January 31, 1939, "The Jewish Question as a Factor in German Foreign Policy in the Year 1938," PS–3358.

24. *Ibid.*

CHAPTER 7

1. Taylor, *op. cit.*, p. 164.

2. *Ibid.*, p. 194.

3. *Ibid.*, pp. 198–99.

4. Shirer, *op. cit.*, p. 511.

5. *Ibid.*, pp. 516–16.

6. Reynolds, *op. cit.*, pp. 90–94.

7. Robinson, *op. cit.*, p. 211.

8. *Ibid.*

9. *Ibid.*, p. 212.

10. *The American Jewish Yearbook, 1940–41* (New York), p. 350.

11. *Ibid.*

12. *Ibid.*, p. 351.

CHAPTER 8

1. Prinz, op. cit., pp. 206–7.
2. Ibid., p. 208.
3. Ribbentrop to Hitler, December 8, 1938, "Documents on German Foreign Policy 1918–1945," Series D, Vol. IV, The Aftermath of Munich (Washington, D.C.: Department of State, 1951), pp. 481–82.
4. Prinz, Ibid., pp. 214–15.
5. Portion of affidavit of Raymond H. Geist, formerly American Consul and First Secretary of Embassy in Berlin, Germany, 1929–1939, dated August 28, 1945, PS–1759.
6. Agar, op. cit., p. 87.
7. Ibid., p. 88.
8. Jewish Immigration into Palestine, 1933–1945:

1933	30,327	1938	12,868	1943	8,507
1934	42,359	1939	27,561	1944	14,464
1935	61,854	1940	8,398	1945	13,121
1936	29,727	1941	5,886		
1937	10,536	1942	3,733		

9. Memorandum submitted by Reichsvertretung to Intergovernmental Conference on Refugees in Evian, July 1938. In Mark Wischnitzer, "Jewish Emigration from Germany, 1933–1938," Jewish Social Studies, January 1940, pp. 23–44.
10. Marcus, op. cit., p. 182.
11. Note on the transfer agreement (Ha'avara-Abkommen), Ministry of Foreign Affairs, March 10, 1938, NG–1889.
12. Marcus, op. cit., pp. 191–92.
13. Jon and David Kimche, The Secret Roads: The "Illegal" Migration of a People, 1938–1948 (London, Secker and Warburg, 1954), p. 404.
14. Pierre van Passen, Days of Our Years (New York, Hillman-Curl, Inc., 1940), p. 404.
15. Winston S. Churchill, Their Finest Hour (Boston, Houghton Mifflin, 1949), Vol. II of The Second World War, p. 173.
16. Ephraim Dekel, Shai: Exploits of Haganah Intelligence (New York, Thos. Yoseloff, 1959), p. 280.
17. Agar, op. cit., pp. 137–38.
18. Gerald Reitlinger, The Final Solution (New York, A.S. Barnes and Co., 1953), p. 498.
19. Ibid., p. 49. Reitlinger also records that by December 1941 there were 20,000 European Jews in Shanghai and 4,000 in Kobe, most of them having arrived after September 1939.
20. German Foreign Office Circular, January 31, 1939, PS–3358, op. cit.
21. American Jewish Yearbook, 1940–41, pp. 444–45.
22. Ibid., p. 454.
23. Account based on Aaron Zwergbaum, "Exile in Mauritius," in Yad Vashem Studies (Jerusalem, 1960), Vol. IV, pp. 191–257.

CHAPTER 9

1. Later, in August, after the military conference at Obersalzberg, where Hitler lectured the military chiefs on the plans and prospects for war, only General Georg Thomas, head of the Economic and Armaments Branch of the OKW (the High Command) challenged Hitler. And this was done not directly, but through General Keitel, OKW Chief. Thomas scoffed at the idea of a quick war and quick peace

and argued that an attack on Poland would unleash a world war. There were would-be conspirators among the *Abwehr*, the intelligence bureau of OKW, and opponents of Hitler such as Ulrich von Hassell, the anti-Nazi diplomat; Carl Goerdeler, the mayor of Leipzig; the retired General Beck; the opportunistic Schacht, who had been dismissed as Minister of Economics. These men and others wanted to get rid of Hitler for various reasons but, as Shirer observes, "they were gripped by utter confusion and a paralyzing sense of futility. Hitler's hold on Germany—on the Army, the police, the government, the people—was too complete to be loosened or undermined by anything they could think of doing."

General Halder, who had been active in an anti-Hitler group just eleven months earlier, was now busy with plans to smash Poland and apparently eager to do so.

2. Lord Russell of Liverpool, *op. cit.*, p. 115.

3. *Ibid.*, pp. 115–16.

4. *American Jewish Yearbook, 1940–41*, p. 371.

5. *Ibid.*, p. 376.

6. Jacob Apenszlak, ed., *The Black Book of Polish Jewry* (New York, Roy Publishers, 1943), pp. 4–7.

7. Quoted in Poliakov, *op. cit.*, p. 42.

8. Edward Crankshaw, *Gestapo: Instrument of Tyranny* (New York, Viking Press, 1956), p. 234.

9. Hilberg, *op. cit.*, p. 137.

10. Crankshaw, *op. cit.*, pp. 22–23.

11. Diary of Hans Frank, Governor General of Poland. Minutes of second conference of the Departmental Chiefs on December 8, 1939, PS–2233A.

12. Affidavit by Schönberg, July 21, 1946, PS–4071.

13. "The War Economy in Poland, 1939–40," EC–344.

14. Reitlinger, *op. cit.*, p. 38.

15. Hilberg, *op. cit.*, p. 646.

16. Philip Friedman, "The Lublin Reservation and the Madagascar Plan," *YIVO Annual of Jewish Social Science* (New York, 1953), Vol. VIII, p. 157. (Material gathered from Lublin Documents, Archives of the Jewish Historical Institute, Warsaw.)

17. *Statement on War Losses and Damages of Poland in 1939–45* (Warsaw, Presidium of the Council of Ministers, War Indemnities Office, 1947), p. 43. Cited by Robinson, *op. cit.*, p. 157.

CHAPTER 10

1. Historical survey based on Elbogen, *op. cit.*, pp. 532–39 and Parkes, *op. cit.*, pp. 128–64. Reports of pogroms of 1918–1919 in Maurice Samuel, *Little Did I Know* (New York, Knopf, 1963), pp. 233–38.

2. Special Delivery Letter, September 21, 1939, from Chief of the Security Police to chiefs of all detail groups of the Security Police concerning the Jewish problem in occupied zone, PS–3363.

3. Robinson, *op. cit.*, pp. 166–68.

4. Philip Friedman, "Preliminary and Methodological Problems of the Research on the Jewish Catastrophe in the Nazi Period," *Yad Vashem Studies*, Vol. II, pp. 95–113.

5. Robinson, *op. cit.*, pp. 156–57.

6. Quoted from Rezsö Kastner, *Der Bericht des jüdischen Rettungskomittees aus Budapest 1942–1945* (Geneva, 1946), pp. 67–68.

7. Robinson, *op. cit.*, p. 160.

8. Minutes of a conference called by Heydrich on January 30, 1940, NO–5322.

9. Friedman, "The Lublin Reservation and the Madagascar Plan," op. cit., pp. 152–53.

10. Rosenberg was a Russian Balt who fled to Germany after the Bolshevik Revolution. A very mediocre man, he impressed Hitler because he had been granted a diploma from a school of architecture. He joined the embryonic Nazi Party in 1919 and within a few years became editor of the *Völkischer Beobachter*. Unaccountably, for a number of years, he was considered the intellectual leader of the Nazi Party and heir to the mantle of Houston Stewart Chamberlain.

11. *Völkischer Beobachter*, February 8, 1939. Quoted in *Black Book of Polish Jewry*, p. 91.

12. Statement by Councillor Wetzel, Berlin, November 25, 1939. PS–660.

13. Friedman, "The Lublin Reservation and the Madagascar Plan," op. cit., p. 155.

14. Quoted in *Black Book of Polish Jewry*, p. 236.

15. Clarke, op. cit., pp. 46–47.

16. S. Moldawer, "The Road to Lublin," *Contemporary Jewish Record*, Vol. 3 March–April, 1940, pp. 119–33.

17. Anonymous letter to Hans Lammers, chief of Reich Chancellery, NG–2490.

18. Note from Luther on his interview with the Hungarian Ambassador Sztójay, Berlin, October 6, 1942, NG–1800.

19. Friedman, "The Lublin Reservation and the Madagascar Plan," op. cit., p. 163.

CHAPTER 11

1. *American Jewish Yearbook, 1941–42* (New York), pp. 205–6.

2. Poliakov, op. cit., p. 60.

3. Report of Statistical Office for Reich Gau Ostmark, December 15, 1939, on reduction in numbers of Jews especially in Vienna districts, PS–1949.

4. *Ibid.*

5. *Black Book of Poland* (New York, American Jewish Black Book Committee, 1945), p. 241.

6. Friedman, "The Lublin Reservation and the Madagascar Plan," op. cit., p. 158. These estimates of deported Jews vary.

7. *American Jewish Yearbook, 1941–42*, pp. 209–10.

8. *American Jewish Yearbook, 1942–43*, pp. 190–91.

9. Friedman, "The Lublin Reservation," p. 158.

10. *American Jewish Yearbook, 1940–41*, p. 351.

11. *Ibid.*, p. 352.

12. Quoted in Robinson, op. cit., p. 329.

12a. *American Jewish Yearbook, 1941–42*, p. 211.

13. Philip Friedman, "Aspects of the Jewish Communal Crisis in the Period of the Nazi Regime in Germany, Austria and Czechoslovakia," in *Essays on Jewish Life and Thought, Presented in Honor of Salo Wittmayer Baron* (New York, Columbia University Press, 1959), p. 216.

14. *American Jewish Yearbook, 1941–42*, p. 211.

15. Wighton, op. cit., pp. 246–51.

CHAPTER 12

1. Taylor, op. cit., p. 356.

2. Military and political events summarized from Shirer, op. cit., pp. 890–920.

3. Friedman, "The Lublin Reservation," op. cit., pp. 165–66.

4. Camille M. Cianfarra, *The Vatican and the War* (New York, Literary Classics Inc., 1944), pp. 145–46.

5. Friedman, "The Lublin Reservation," *op. cit.*, pp. 169–70.

6. Memorandum from Rademacher, July 3, 1940, NG 2586–B.

7. H. Picker, ed., *Hitler's Tischgespräche* (Bonn, 1951), p. 311.

8. Reitlinger, *op. cit.*, p. 80.

CHAPTER 13

1. Tosha Bialer, "Behind the Wall," *Collier's*, February 20, 1943, p. 17.

1a. *Ibid.*, February 27, 1943, p. 29.

2. On January 30, 1942, a Swiss Red Cross driver who visited the cemetery saw the immense mass burial pit and recorded the evidence that 90 percent of the corpses were dead from hunger. This information could not be published until 1945 because of the Swiss neutrality censorship. (Reitlinger, p. 62.)

3. Emmanuel Ringelblum, *Notes from the Warsaw Ghetto*, ed. and tr. by Jacob Sloan (New York, McGraw-Hill, 1958), p. xviii. Biographical sketch of Ringelblum in Introduction by Jacob Sloan.

4. Quoted in Poliakov, *op. cit.*, pp. 39–40.

5. *Black Book of Polish Jewry, op. cit.*, p. 36.

6. A. Hartglass, "How Did Cherniakow Become Head of the Warsaw Judenrat?" In *Yad Vashem Bulletin*, August 1964, No. 15, pp. 4–7.

7. Quoted in Robinson, *op. cit.*, pp. 154–56. From the *Zygelboim Book*, compiled by J. S. Herz (New York, Unser Tsait, 1947), pp. 120–21.

8. Bernard Goldstein, *The Stars Bear Witness* (New York, Viking Press, 1949), pp. 35–36.

9. Ringelblum, *op. cit.*, pp. 181–82.

10. *Ibid.*, p. 263.

11. *Ibid.*, p. 285.

12. S. L. Schneiderman, "The Last Testament of Emmanuel Ringelblum," in *Midstream*, Spring 1961, p. 43.

13. Isaiah Trunk, "Epidemics and Mortality in the Warsaw Ghetto 1939–1942," in *YIVO Annual VIII*, p. 89. Material quoted from an underground organ of the Bund, dated July 1941.

14. *Ibid.*, Quoted from *Bleter far geshichte* (Warsaw, 1948), Vol. II, p. 282.

15. *Ibid.*, pp. 82–83.

16. *Ibid.*, p. 104. Quoted from Ringelblum Archives No. 1308. The nurse was D. Wagman.

17. Quoted in Marie Syrkin, *Blessed Is the Match: The Story of Jewish Resistance* (Philadelphia, Jewish Publication Society of America, 1947), p. 182.

18. Joseph Kermish, "The Underground Press in the Warsaw Ghetto," in *Yad Vashem Studies* (Jerusalem, 1957), Vol. I, pp. 104–5.

19. Ringelblum, *op. cit.*, p. 206.

19a. Trunk, *op. cit.*, pp. 115, 120, 122.

20. *Ibid.*, pp. 240–41.

21. Stefan Korbanski, *Fighting Warsaw: the Story of the Polish Underground State, 1939–1945* (New York, The Macmillan Co., 1956), p. 253.

CHAPTER 14

1. Oscar Pinkus, *The House of Ashes* (Cleveland, World Publishing Co., 1964), p. 60.

2. *Ibid.*, p. 61.

3. Walter Warlimont, *Inside Hitler's Headquarters, 1939–1945* (New York, Frederick A. Praeger, 1964), pp. 150–51 (Quoted from Section L War Diary, March 3, 1941).

4. *Ibid.*, p. 151.

5. Halder affidavit at Nuremberg, Nov. 22, 1945. Quoted in Shirer, op. cit., pp. 1088–9.

6. Warlimont, *op. cit.*, p. 163.

7. Affidavit of Walter Schellenberg, November 26, 1945, on activities of *Einsatzgruppen* of the SIPO and S.D. in executing Jewish prisoners of war on Eastern Front and in carrying out mass executions of Jews in the East, PS–3710.

8. Michael A. Musmanno, *The Eichmann Kommandos* (Philadelphia, Macrae Smith Co., 1961), p. 106.

9. Whitney R. Harris, *Tyranny on Trial: The Evidence at Nuremberg* (Dallas, Texas, Southern Methodist University Press, 1954), pp. 349–50.

10. Affidavit of Otto Ohlendorf, November 5, 1945, PS–2620.

11. Reitlinger, *op. cit.*, pp. 186–89.

12. Hilberg, *op. cit.*, p. 196.

13. Report of Sonderführer Schröter enclosed in *Reichskommissar Ostland* to *Generalkommissar* White Russia, August 4, 1941. Quoted in Hilberg, *op. cit.*, p. 207.

14. *Einsatzgruppe* A report of activity up to October 15, 1941. Dated January 31, 1942, L-180.

15. Quoted in Robinson, *op. cit.*, pp. 122–123.

16. Excerpt from a top-secret report of *Einsatzgruppe* A, October 16, 1941, to January 31, 1942, PS-2273.

17. On the road from Smolensk to Moscow, *Einsatzgruppe* B reported that in many Soviet towns the Russians had evacuated the entire Jewish population. However, there is no evidence of an official Soviet evacuation plan for Jews.

18. Enclosure in letter from Reich Commissioner for Baltic States to Rosenberg, August 13, 1941, concerning provisional directives on treatment of Jews in area of *Reichskommissariat* Ostland, PS–1138.

19. Memorandum, November 21, 1943, enclosing copies of report concerning execution of Jews in Minsk. Kube to Reich Commissioner for Eastern Territories Lohse enclosing report of Carl (Commissioner for territory of Sluzk) to Kube, PS-1104.

20. Reitlinger, *op cit.*, p. 233.

21. "Babi Yar" by Yevgeny Yevtushenko, tr. by Marie Syrkin. Courtesy of Miss Syrkin.

22. Reitlinger, *op. cit.*, p. 233.

23. Army order, October 10, 1941, covering letter on Conduct of Troops in Eastern Territories, D-411.

24. Letter from Armament Inspector in the Ukraine to General Thomas, Chief of the Industrial Armament Department, OKW, December 2, 1941, enclosing report by Professor Seraphim on the execution of 150,000 to 200,000 Jews in the Ukraine, PS-3257.

25. Affidavit by Werner Braune, Commander *Sonderkommando* 11b, July 8, 1947, NO-4234.

26. Quoted in Alexander Werth, *Russia at War* (New York, E. P. Dutton & Co., 1964), p. 706.

27. Order by Southern Army Group Rear Area/Section VII, August 16, 1941, NOKW-1691.

28. Hilberg, *op. cit.*, p. 220.

29. Affidavit by Kurt Lindow, July 29, 1947, NO-5481.

30. Deputy Commander of Wehrkreis [Army District] IX in Kassel to Chief of

Replacement Army, enclosing Rösler report dated January 3, 1942. Quoted in Poliakov, *op. cit.*, p. 134.

31. Affidavit by Karl Hennicke, September 4, 1947, NO-4999.

32. Wetzel to Foreign Office, May 16, 1942, enclosing Lohse directive to General Commissars, August 19, 1941, NG-4815.

33. Hilberg, *op. cit.*, p. 231.

34. RSHA, IV-A-1, Operational Report USSR No. 58, September 17, 1941, NO-3151.

35. Himmler to Hitler, December 20, 1942, NO-511; December 26, 1942, NO-1128. After February 1942, *Einsatzgruppen* reports are not available and references to their shootings are fragmentary. However, these reports from Himmler to Hitler cover killing actions against Jews in the last part of 1942 and probably include the last operations of the *Einsatzgruppen*.

36. Three affidavits of Hermann Friedrich Graebe, November 10 and 13, 1945, including eyewitness accounts of slaughter of all Jews in Dubno, Ukraine, in October 1942 and slaughter of 5,000 Jews in the Rovno ghetto, Ukraine, PS-2992.

CHAPTER 15

1. Hilberg, *op. cit.*, p. 256.

2. Peter Meyer and Bernard D. Weinryb, *The Jews in the Soviet Satellites* (Syracuse, N.Y., Syracuse University Press, 1953), p. 330.

3. Meir Korzen, "Problems Arising Out of Research into the History of Jewish Refugees in the U.S.S.R. during the Second World War." *Yad Vashem Studies*, Vol. III, p. 122.

4. Bullock (p. 544) notes that Admiral Erich Raeder, the Commander in Chief of the German Navy, had set his staff to work on the problems involved in an attack across the English Channel as early as November 1939, but Hitler showed no interest in such an operation until the French surrender. Even then, he moved reluctantly, assuming that the British would be willing to come to terms.

5. Alan Clark, *Barbarossa*, p. 31.

6. *Ibid.*, p. 47.

7. Werth, *op. cit.*, pp. 213–14.

8. *Ibid.*, pp. 640–41.

9. Shimon Redlich, "Jewish Refugees from Poland as a Factor in Relations Between the Polish and Soviet Governments During World War II," *Yad Vashem Bulletin*, No. 14, March 1964, p. 34.

10. Kimche, *op. cit.*, p. 64.

11. Agar, *op. cit.*, pp. 120–121.

12. *Ibid.*, p. 122.

13. Korzen, *op. cit.*, p. 122.

14. Meyer and Weinryb, *op. cit.*, p. 360.

15. *Ibid.*, p. 362.

16. John A. Armstrong, ed. *Soviet Partisans in World War II* (Madison, Wis., Univ. of Wisconsin Press, 1964), pp. 279–280.

17. Chone Szmeruk, "Yiddish Publications in the U.S.S.R. from the Late Thirties to 1948," *Yad Vashem Studies*, Vol. IV, 1960, pp. 114–16.

18. Solomon M. Schwarz, *The Jews in the Soviet Union* (Syracuse, N.Y., Syracuse University Press, 1951), p. 314.

19. *Ibid.*, p. 197.

20. *Ibid.*, p. 222.

21. *Ibid.*, p. 223.

22. Joseph Guri, "The Jewish Holocaust in Soviet Writings," *Yad Vashem Bulletin*, No. 18, April 1966, pp. 4–5.

23. *Ibid.*, p. 7.

24. Raya Kagan, "Russians on German Concentration Camps," *Yad Vashem Bulletin*, No. 4–5, October 1959, p. 23.

25. Guri, *op. cit.*, p. 11.

26. Quoted in Sir J. W. Wheeler-Bennett, *Nemesis of Power: The German Army in Politics, 1918–45* (London, Macmillan, 1953), p. 515.

27. Ulrich Von Hassell, *The Von Hassell Diaries, 1938–1944* (New York, Doubleday, 1947), pp. 198–99.

28. Alexander Dallin, *German Rule in Russia 1941–1945: A Study of Occupation Policies* (New York, The Macmillan Co., 1957), pp. 376–77.

29. *Ibid.*, pp. 406–7.

30. Felix Kersten, *The Kersten Memoirs 1940–1945* (New York, The Macmillan Co., 1957), p. 206.

31. Robert L. Koehl, *German Resettlement and Population Policy, 1939–1945* (Cambridge, Harvard University Press, 1957), pp. 2–3.

CHAPTER 16

1. Letter from Göring to Heydrich, July 31, 1941, PS-710.

2. Pearlman, *op. cit.*, pp. 205–206.

3. *Life*, November 28, 1960, *op. cit.*, p. 102.

4. Speech of Hans Frank, December 16, 1941, PS-2233D.

4a. Letter from Main Division 2 of Ministry for the Occupied Eastern Territories, December 18, 1941, to Reich Commissioner for the East, PS-3666.

4b. "Secret Business of the Reich": Minutes of the conference held January 20, 1942, at Am Grossen Wannsee, NG-2586.

5. *Life*, November 28, 1960, *op. cit.*, pp. 24, 101.

6. Hilberg, *op. cit.*, pp. 265–66.

7. *Life*, November 28, 1960, *op. cit.*, p. 101.

8. Instructions given by R. Brandt, Himmler's secretary, to Korherr, inspector for statistics, April 10, 1942, NO-5196.

9. Kersten, *op. cit.*, p. 161.

10. Hilberg, *op. cit.*, p. 177.

11. Affidavit of Wisliceny in Bratislava prison, November 18, 1946. Quoted in Friedman, *The Hunter*, p. 158.

12. William L. Shirer, *Berlin Diary: The Journal of a Foreign Correspondent, 1934–1941* (New York, Alfred A. Knopf, 1941), p. 512.

13. Poliakov, *op. cit.*, pp. 184–85.

14. Reitlinger, *op. cit.*, p. 131. According to Brack, there were at least six euthanasia institutes: Grafeneck in Württemberg; Hartheim, near Linz; Sonnenstein, near Dresden; Bernberg, near Dessau; Hadamar in Hessen; and Brandenburg, near Berlin. There were additional gassing centers for children at Eichberg, Idstein, Kantenhof, and Görden. It is believed by some authorities that children continued to be "mercy-killed" until 1945.

15. Quoted in Poliakov, *op. cit.*, p. 190.

16. Letter from Mennecke to his wife, Mathilde, Weimar, February 25, 1947, NO-907.

17. Affidavit of Julius Muthig, April 17, 1945, NO-2799.

18. Alexander Mitscherlich and Fred Mielke, *Doctors of Infamy*, tr. Heinz Norden (New York, Henry Schuman, 1949), pp. 118ff.

19. Report by Wetzel to the *Reichskommissariat Ostland* on "The Solution of the Jewish Question," October 25, 1941, NO-365.

20. Quoted in Poliakov, *op. cit.*, pp. 153–54.

21. Account of Gerstein's life in Leon Poliakov, "The Spy of God," *Commentary*, August 1965, pp. 67–70.

22. *Ibid.*, pp. 67–68.

23. *Ibid.*, p. 68.

24. *Ibid.*, p. 69.

25. Testimony of Kurt Gerstein, PS-1553.

26. Reitlinger, *op. cit.*, p. 151.

CHAPTER 17

1. Joseph Bau, "Hunger," tr. by Adam Gillon, in *Israel Speaks*, May 9, 1952, p. 5.

2. *The Black Book of Polish Jewry*, pp. 126–27.

2a. *Ibid.*, p. 127.

3. Quoted in Philip Friedman (ed.), *Martyrs and Fighters: The Epic of the Warsaw Ghetto* (New York, Frederick A. Praeger, 1954), p. 155. The young woman, Feigele Wladka, was a Bund youth member of the resistance movement. She lived in the Ghetto and outside it on Aryan papers.

4. *Ibid.*, pp. 152–53 (excerpt from Marek Edelman, *The Ghetto Fights*).

5. *Ibid.*, pp. 157–59.

6. *Ibid.*, pp. 134–35.

7. Joseph Tenenbaum, *Underground: The Story of a People* (New York, Philosophical Library, 1952), p. 85.

8. Friedman, *Martyrs and Fighters*, *op. cit.*, p. 179 (excerpt from Hillel Seidman, *Tagbuch fun Varshever Ghetto*, Buenos Aires, 1947).

9. Goldstein, *op. cit.*, p. 118.

10. Oscar Pinkus, *op. cit.*, pp. 70–71.

11. From "On the Agenda: Death," in *Commentary*, Vol. 8, No. 2, August, 1949, pp. 105–106. The document was preserved by a Polish peasant living near Bialystok and was originally published in the appendix to *Churbn Vilne* (*The Destruction of Vilna*), by S. Z. Katsherginsky (New York, United Vilner Relief Committee, 1947).

12. J. Kermish, "The Ghetto's Two-Front Struggle," *Yad Vashem Bulletin*, No. 13, October, 1963, p. 12. In his book *The Secret Army*, General Tadeusz Bor-Komorowski states that the Home Army was ready to come to the assistance of the Jews "with supplies of arms and ammunition and to coordinate their attacks outside with Jewish resistance within," but that the Jews rejected this offer. This statement cannot be substantiated. The Polish underground did not engage in military resistance against the Nazis until August 1944.

13. Leonard Tushnet, *To Die With Honor: The Uprising of the Jews in the Warsaw Ghetto* (New York, The Citadel Press, 1965), pp. 31–32.

14. *The Black Book of Polish Jewry*, pp. 164–65.

15. Jan Karski, *Story of a Secret State* (Boston, Houghton Mifflin Company, 1944), pp. 320–33.

15a. *Ibid.*, p. 323.

15b. *Ibid.*, pp. 330–31.

15c. *Ibid.*, pp. 331–38.

16. Ringelblum, *Notes from the Warsaw Ghetto*, p. 310.

17. *Ibid.*, p. 326.

18. Henri Michel, "The Allies and the Resistance," *Yad Vashem Studies*, Vol. V, 1963, p. 317.

19. Meyer Barkai, *The Fighting Ghettos* (Philadelphia, J. B. Lippincott Company, 1962), pp. 31–36.

20. Account based on "Warsaw: the January 1943 Uprising," by Zivia Lubetkin, in *ibid.*, pp. 19–28.

21. Quoted in Friedman, *Martyrs and Fighters*, pp. 224–25.

22. Account from Barkai, *op. cit.*, pp. 49–50 (extract by Tuvia Bozikovsky).

23. *Ibid.*, pp. 57–58 (excerpt by Leizer Levine).

24. Official report of Stroop, S.S. and Police Leader of Warsaw, entitled "The Warsaw Ghetto Is No More," describing destruction of Warsaw Ghetto in April–May, 1943, PS-1061.

25. Leo W. Schwarz, ed., *The Root and the Bough* (New York, Rinehart and Company, 1949), pp. 61–62 (quoted from Marek Edelman, *The Last Stand*).

26. Official report of Stroop, *op. cit.*

27. Goldstein, *op. cit.*, p. 194.

28. Friedman, *Martyrs and Fighters*, p. 271.

29. *Ibid.*, pp. 275–76.

30. Quoted in *ibid.*, p. 272.

31. Tenenbaum, *Underground*, p. 118.

32. See note 26.

33. Zivia Lubetkin, "The Last Days of the Warsaw Ghetto," *Commentary*, May 1947, pp. 408–9.

34. *Ibid.*, pp. 409–11.

35. M. Praeger, "A Chassidic Underground in the Polish Ghettos," *Yad Vashem Bulletin*, No. 6–7, June 1960, pp. 10–12.

36. See note 26.

37. Barkai, *op. cit.*, p. 97.

CHAPTER 18

1. Quoted in Nachman Blumenthal, "The Plight of the Jewish Partisans," *Yad Vashem Bulletin*, No. 1, April 1957, p. 4.

2. Statement of S. Cholavsky, editor of *The Book of Jewish Partisans* (Merchavia, Israel, 1958), in *Yad Vashem Bulletin*, No. 4/5, October 1959, p. 17.

3. Dov Levin, "Life and Death of Jewish Partisans," *Yad Vashem Bulletin*, No. 18, April 1966, pp. 44–45.

4. Schwarz, *Jews in the Soviet Union*, p. 327.

5. Levin, *op. cit.*, p. 44.

6. Tenenbaum, *Underground*, p. 389.

7. A. Z. Braun and Dov Levin, "Factors and Motivations in Jewish Resistance," *Yad Vashem Bulletin*, No. 2, December 1957, p. 4.

8. Tenenbaum, *op. cit.*, p. 392.

9. Friedman, "Preliminary and Methodological Problems of Research on the Jewish Catastrophe in the Nazi Period," *op. cit.*, pp. 130–31.

10. Moshe Kahanovich, historian of Jewish partisan movement, quoted in Schwarz, *Jews in the Soviet Union*, p. 323

11. Dallin, *op. cit.*, p. 74.

12. Werth, *op. cit.*, p. 720, and A. Zvi Bar-On, "The Jews in the Soviet Partisan Movement," *Yad Vashem Studies*, Vol. IV, p. 176.

13. Account based on J. Granatstein and M. Kahanovich, "Dr. Ezekiel Atlas, Doctor and Partisan Leader," *Yad Vashem Bulletin*, No. 8/9, March 1961, pp. 41–43, and Barkai, *op. cit.*, p. 177.

14. Joseph Guri, "Jewish Participation in the Red Army in World War II," *Yad Vashem Bulletin*, No. 16, February 1965, p. 13.

15. Moshe Kahanovich, "Why No Separate Jewish Partisan Movement Was Established During World War II," *Yad Vashem Studies*, Vol. I, p. 164.

16. Bernard Mark, "Problems Related to the Study of the Jewish Resistance Movement in the Second World War," *Yad Vashem Studies*, Vol. III, p. 54.

17. *Ibid.*, p. 55.

18. Schwarz, *The Root and the Bough*, pp. 112–14 ("Brigade in Action," by Tobias Bielski).

19. Quoted in Syrkin, *op. cit.*, p. 256.

20. Barkai, *op. cit.*, pp. 241–42.

21. Schwarz, *The Root and the Bough*, p. 69 ("Never Say This Is the Last Road," by Abraham Sutzkever).

22. *Ibid.*, p. 75.

23. Barkai, *op. cit.*, pp. 193–94.

24. Tenenbaum, *op. cit.*, p. 353.

25. Schwarz, *The Root and the Bough*, p. 92.

26. *Ibid.*, p. 91.

27. Pearlman, *op. cit.*, pp. 324–25.

28. Joseph Guri, "Ilya Ehrenburg Among Jewish Partisans," *Yad Vashem Bulletin*, No. 16, February 1965, p. 14.

29. Barkai, *op. cit.*, p. 184, and Emmanuel Brand, "The Forest Ablaze: A Jewish Partisan Group in the Kovpak Division," *Yad Vashem Bulletin*, No. 2, December 1957, p. 16. According to Nachman Blumenthal, Kovpak's army was defeated and survivors had to retreat in small groups to their base. The partisans hid their arms and disguised themselves as peasants. Local Ukrainians helped many of them. In this situation, Jews were considered an encumbrance and many "vanished" on their way back. (Blumenthal, "The Plight of the Jewish Partisan," *op. cit.*, p. 6.)

30. Kahanovich, *op. cit.*, p. 165.

31. Mark, *op. cit.*, p. 53.

31a. Aryeh Bauminger, "The Rising in the Cracow Ghetto," *Yad Vashem Bulletin*, March 1961, pp. 22–25.

32. Tenenbaum, *op. cit.*, p. 416.

33. Pinkus, *op. cit.*, pp. 146–47.

34. *Ibid.*, p. 183.

CHAPTER 19

1. Historical sketch based on Hugo Valentin, "Rescue and Relief Activities in Behalf of Jewish Victims of Nazism in Scandinavia," *YIVO Annual*, Vol. VIII, pp. 224–34.

2. Hilberg, *op. cit.*, p. 356.

3. According to Harold Flender, *Rescue in Denmark* (New York, Simon and Schuster, 1963), p. 63, there is no evidence to substantiate stories about King Christian X and the Star of David, although it is well known that he was implacably opposed to the introduction of any anti-Semitic measures. When he learned of German plans to introduce anti-Jewish measures, he wrote the following warning to Reich Minister Karl W. Best: "I desire to stress to you—not only because of human concern for citizens of my country but also because of the fear of further consequences in future relations between Germany and Denmark—that specific measures in regard to a group of people who have enjoyed full rights of citizenship in Denmark for more than 100 years would have the most severe consequences." This letter, however, never reached Best. The King had given it to the Danish Foreign Minister to deliver to Best personally, but Best refused to see him.

4. Hilberg, *op. cit.*, p. 358.

5. Flender, op. cit., p. 33.

6. Aage Bertelsen, October '43 (New York, G. P. Putnam's Sons, 1954), pp. 17–19.

7. "Chronicles: Denmark," Contemporary Jewish Record, Vol. VI, No. 6, December 1943, p. 645.

8. Flender, op. cit., pp. 75–77.

9. Bertelsen, op. cit., pp. 66ff.

10. Philip Friedman, Their Brothers' Keepers (New York, Crown Publishing Co., 1957), pp. 143–48.

11. Kersten, op. cit., pp. 144–45.

CHAPTER 20

1. Oscar Handlin, "Jewish Resistance to the Nazis," Commentary, November 1962, pp. 398–405.

2. "Four Years in Holland," 1944, by Reichsminister Artur von Seyss-Inquart, PS-3430.

3. Hilberg, op. cit., p. 366.

4. Ibid., p. 368.

5. Friedman, Their Brothers' Keepers, pp. 61–62.

6. Genesis of Joodse Raad based on account in Israel Taubes, "The Jewish Council of Amsterdam," and Hartog Beem, "The Jewish Council of the Province of Vriesland," Yad Vashem Bulletin, No. 17, December, 1965, pp. 21–30. Also, "Supplements and Corrigenda," pp. 31–33.

7. Robinson, op. cit., p. 242.

8. Quoted in Syrkin, op. cit., p. 275.

9. Reitlinger, op. cit., pp. 331–32.

10. Quoted in Poliakov, op. cit., p. 173.

11. Robinson, op. cit., p. 241.

12. Beem, op. cit., p. 23.

13. Taubes, op. cit., p. 26.

14. Ibid., p. 29.

15. Friedman, Their Brothers' Keepers, p. 67.

16. Syrkin, op. cit., p. 286.

16a. Friedman, Their Brothers' Keepers, p. 64.

17. Reports by Otto Bene (Foreign Office Representative in Holland) to Foreign Office, NG-2631. Also, Report by Dutch Government, October 16, 1945, PS-1726.

18. Arnold and Veronica Toynbee, Hitler's Europe (London, Oxford University Press, 1954), pp. 480–81.

19. Report by Military Commander for October 1940, NG-2380.

20. Hilberg, op. cit., p. 387.

21. Friedman, Their Brothers' Keepers, p. 40.

22. Von Bargen to Foreign Office, July 9, 1942, NG-5209.

23. Von Bargen to Foreign Office, September 24, 1942, NG-5219.

24. Friedman, Their Brothers' Keepers, p. 68.

25. Robinson, op. cit., p. 239.

CHAPTER 21

1. Political and military background based on Pertinax, The Gravediggers of France (Garden City, N.Y., Doubleday, Doran and Company, 1944).

2. Quoted in Donald A. Lowrie, The Hunted Children (New York, W. W. Norton Company, 1963), pp. 58–59.

3. Excerpt from "Survey of Jews and Poles up to November 15, 1940, from Collection of Restricted Intra-office Documents," compiled by Chief of Security Police and the S.D., PS-2916.

4. Reitlinger, op. cit., p. 76.

5. Hilberg, op. cit., pp. 395–96.

6. Text of correspondence in *American Jewish Yearbook, 1945–1946*, pp. 113–17.

7. Quoted in Poliakov, *Harvest of Hate*, pp. 299–301.

8. *Ibid.*, p. 54.

9. Quoted in Syrkin, op. cit., p. 293.

10. Friedman, *Their Brothers' Keepers*, p. 50.

11. Information on Union Générale des Israélites de France based on Z. Szajkowski, "Glimpses of the History of Jews in Occupied France," *Yad Vashem Studies*, Vol. II, pp. 133–57; Z. Szajkowski, "The Organization of UGIF in Nazi-controlled France," *Jewish Social Studies*, IX, July 1947, pp. 239–56; Leon Poliakov, "Jewish Resistance in France," *YIVO Annual*, VIII, 1953, pp. 252–59.

12. The name may derive from the fact that there were six divisions in the "Youth" Directorate; the sixth was the Social Assistance Division. Poliakov suggests that the name may also have originated in derision of the German fifth column.

12a. RF 1225.

13. Friedman, *Their Brothers' Keepers*, p. 46.

14. Syrkin, op. cit., pp. 296–97.

15. Reitlinger, op. cit., p. 308.

16. Quoted in *ibid.*, pp. 308–9, from documents of French Nuremberg prosecution (printed in *Persecution des Juifs en France et dans les autres pays de l'ouest presentée a Nuremberg*, Paris, Centre de Documentation Juive Contemporaine (CDJC), 1948).

17. Schleier to Foreign Office, September 11, 1942, NG-5109.

17a. Quoted in Hilberg, op. cit., p. 407, from Pierre Laval, *Diary* (New York, 1948), p. 99.

18. George Wellers, *De Drancy à Auschwitz* (Paris, CDJC, 1946), p. 58.

19. The first registration decreed by the Germans ordered all Jews to register by October 20, 1941. A French law of June 2, 1941, provided for a census of Jews but none for the whole of France was ever completed.

20. Account based on Zanvel Diamant, "Jewish Refugees on the French Riviera," *YIVO Annual*, Vol. VIII, 1953, pp. 264–80.

21. Hilberg, op. cit., pp. 414–15.

22. Account of Father Marie-Benoit based on Friedman, *Their Brothers' Keepers*, pp. 55–59.

23. Quoted in Z. Szajkowski, "The French Central Jewish Consistory During the Second World War," *Yad Vashem Studies*, Vol. III, pp. 197–98.

24. Poliakov, "Jewish Resistance in France," op. cit., p. 261.

25. *Ibid.*, p. 260.

26. David Knout, "Contribution à l'histoire de la Résistance Juive en France, 1940–1944," *Temps présents*, October 1944, No. 7, p. 124.

27. Syrkin, op. cit., p. 306.

28. Mutschmann to Himmler, July 25, 1944, NO-2779.

CHAPTER 22

1. Meir Michaelis, "The Attitude of the Fascist Regime to the Jews in Italy," *Yad Vashem Studies*, Vol. IV, 1960, pp. 9–10.

2. Ernst Rüdiger von Starhemberg, *Between Hitler and Mussolini: Memoirs* (New York, Harper & Brothers, 1942), p. 93.

3. Michaelis, op. cit., pp. 14–15.

3a. Message to American Jewish Students, quoted in ibid., p. 18.

4. Quoted in ibid., pp. 22–23.

5. Quoted in ibid., p. 34 from Leon Poliakov and Jacques Sabille, Jews Under the Italian Occupation, 1955, p. 191.

5a. Michaelis, op. cit., pp. 36–37.

6. Hilberg, op. cit., pp. 423–24.

7. Michaelis, op. cit., pp. 38–39. Quoted from Edvidge Mussolini, Mio Fratello Benito, 1957, p. 175.

8. Robinson, op. cit., p. 247.

9. Shirer, The Rise and Fall of the Third Reich, pp. 1300–1301.

10. Von Thadden to missions abroad, October 12, 1943, enclosing RSHA circular dated September 23, 1943, NG-2652-H.

11. Consul Moellhausen (Rome) to Ribbentrop, October 6, 1943, NG-5027.

12. Gumpert to Foreign Office, enclosing message from Hudal, October 16, 1943, NG-5027.

13. Weizsäcker to Foreign Office, October 17, 1943, NG-5027.

14. Ibid., October 28, 1943, NG-5027.

15. Inland II [S.S. and Police] from Wagner to Hencke to Ribbentrop, December 4, 1943, NG-5026.

16. Reitlinger, op. cit., p. 495.

CHAPTER 23

1. Jeanette Wolff, "For Life and Freedom," in Eric H. Boehm, ed., We Survived: The Stories of the Hidden and the Hunted of Nazi Germany (New Haven, Yale University Press, 1949), pp. 256–259.

2. Kube to Lohse, December 16, 1941, PS-3665.

3. Thierack to Bormann, October 11, 1942, NG-558.

4. Poliakov, Harvest of Hate, p. 58.

5. Opinion given by Ministry of Interior on subject of the "Final Solution of the Jewish Question," Berlin, March 16, 1942, NG-2586.

6. Hilberg, op. cit., p. 52.

7. Ibid., p. 275.

7a. Josef Polák, "The Camp," in Terezín (Prague, Council of Jewish Communities in the Czech Lands, 1965), p. 24.

8. Heinrich Liebrecht, "Therefore Will I Deliver Him," in Boehm, op. cit., p. 23.

9. M. Ansbacher, "Art in the Period of the European Jewish Disaster," Yad Vashem Bulletin, June 1960, pp. 15–17.

10. Reproduced through the courtesy of the State Jewish Museum in Prague.

11. Ibid.

12. Leo Baeck, "A People Stands Before Its God," We Survived, pp. 289–90 (see note 1).

13. Ibid., p. 293.

14. Ibid., p. 288.

15. From testimony collected by Hans Klee in Switzerland, 1943. Quoted in Poliakov, op. cit., pp. 147–48.

16. Report of War Refugee Board, November 1944, L-22.

17. Account based on Flender, op. cit., pp. 214–23.

17a. Hans Hofer, "The Film about Terezín," in Terezín, pp. 181–184.

18. Reitlinger, op. cit., pp. 171–72.

19. Account of conversations held in the Central Security Office of the Reich, Section 1V B 4 on March 6, 1942, Düsseldorf, Yad Vashem Bulletin, June 1960, p. 44.

20. Letters of Cora Berliner and Hannah Karminski. Quoted in *Leo Baeck Year-book* II (London, 1957), p. 314.

21. Quoted in K. Y. Ball-Kaduri, "Berlin Is 'Purged' of Jews: The Jews of Berlin in 1943," *Yad Vashem Studies*, Vol. V (Jerusalem, 1963), pp. 279–80.

22. *Ibid.*, pp. 287–88.

23. Vogt, *op. cit.*, p. 237.

23a. Guenter Lewy, "Pius XII, the Jews and the German Catholic Church," *Commentary*, February 1964, pp. 27–28.

24. Article "Rasse," in Konrad Gröber, ed., *Handbuch der religiösen Gegenwartsfragen* (Freiburg, Herder, 1937), p. 536.

25. *Ibid.*

25a. Gordon Zahn, *German Catholics and Hitler's Wars* (New York, Sheed and Ward, 1962), pp. 56, 73.

26. Friedman, *Their Brothers' Keepers*, pp. 95–96.

26a. *Ibid.*, pp. 96–100.

CHAPTER 24

1. Shirer, *The Rise and Fall of the Third Reich*, p. 1073.

2. Churchill, *The Grand Alliance* (Vol. III of *The Second World War*), pp. 156–63.

3. Shirer, *The Rise and Fall of the Third Reich*, p. 1080.

4. Turner to Hildebrandt, October 17, 1941, NO-5810.

5. Memo by Rademacher, October 25, 1941, NG-3354.

6. Weizsäcker to Wörmann, December 5, 1941, NG-4519.

7. *Report of Activities of CIRC in Second World War* (Geneva, 1948), Vol. II, p. 251.

8. David Alkalay, "The Fate of the Jews of Yugoslavia," *Yad Vashem Bulletin*, No. 4/5, October 1959, p. 18.

9. Curzio Malaparte, *Kaputt* (New York, Avon Books, 1966), p. 257.

10. Kasche to Foreign Office, April 22, 1944, enclosing report by Helm, dated April 18, 1944, NG-2349.

CHAPTER 25

1. Cecil Roth, "The Last Days of Jewish Salonica," *Commentary*, July 1950, pp. 50–51.

2. *Ibid.*, p. 51.

3. *Ibid.*

4. Nathan Eck, "New Light on the Charges Against the Last Chief Rabbi of Salonica," *Yad Vashem Bulletin*, No. 17, December 1965, pp. 9–10.

5. *Ibid.*, p. 10.

6. Isaac Kabeli, "The Resistance of the Greek Jews," *YIVO Annual*, Vol. VIII, 1953, p. 286.

7. Michael Molho, ed., *In Memoriam: 1940–1944, Hommage aux Victimes Juives des Nazis en Grèce* (Salonika, N. Nicolaides, 1948), Vol. I, pp. 157–58.

8. *Ibid.*, p. 87.

9. Hilberg, *op. cit.*, p. 447.

10. Reitlinger, *op. cit.*, pp. 376–77.

11. Kabeli, *op. cit.*, p. 286.

12. Robinson, *op. cit.*, p. 213. Based on information from the representative of the American Joint Distribution Committee in Athens, H. Benruby.

13. Affidavit by Erwin Lenz, May 10, 1947, NOKW-1715.

14. Roth, *op. cit.*, p. 50.

15. Molho, op. cit., p. 150.
16. Kabeli, op. cit., pp. 281–82.
17. Ibid., p. 283.
18. Friedman, Their Brothers' Keepers, p. 110.
19. Kabeli, op. cit., p. 287.

CHAPTER 26

1. Livia Rotkirchen, The Destruction of Slovak Jewry: A Documentary History (Jerusalem, Yad Vashem, 1961). The English summary has been used to document events described in this chapter.
2. Affidavit by Hans Gmelin, June 15, 1948, NG-5921. Gmelin was a member of the German Legation in Bratislava.
3. Hans Ludin to Foreign Office, June 26, 1942, NG-4407.
4. Summary of Slovak deportation conference held June 26, 1942; summary dated June 30, 1942, NG-4553.
5. Karmasin (chief of ethnic Germans in Slovakia) to Himmler, July 29, 1942, NO-1660.
6. Eichmann to von Thadden, June 2, 1943. Quoted in Hilberg, op. cit., pp. 470–71.
7. Alexander Weissberg, Desperate Mission: Joel Brand's Story (New York, Criterion Books, 1958), pp. 53–61.
8. Wisliceny was the only member of Eichmann's staff to give evidence for the prosecution at Nuremberg.
9. Poliakov, Harvest of Hate, p. 254.
9a. Rotkirchen, op. cit., p. xxxv.
10. Weissberg, op. cit., p. 56.
11. Agar, op. cit., p. 148.
12. There are no official S.S. records of these negotiations. The amount of money is variously estimated. Syrkin (op. cit., p. 106), for example, estimates the figure at $80,000. This account is based on Weissberg, op. cit., pp. 57–59.
13. Weissberg, op. cit., p. 59.
14. Henry Morgenthau, Jr., "The Morgenthau Diaries VI—The Refugee Run-Around," Collier's, November 1, 1947, pp. 22–23, 62, 65.
14a. Rotkirchen, op. cit., pp. xxxix.
15. James F. Sunderman, ed., World War II in the Air (New York, Franklin Watts, Inc., 1963), p. 174.
16. Ibid., p. 237.
17. Account of uprising based on Livia Rotkirchen, "Activities of the Jewish Underground in Slovakia," Yad Vashem Bulletin, No. 8/9, March 1961, pp. 28–30.
18. Ludin to Foreign Office, October 4, 1944, NG-5100.
19. Arnold (Bumi) Lazar, "Reminiscences from Fascist Slovakia," Yad Vashem Bulletin, No. 18, April 1966, pp. 17–25.
20. Georges Dunand, Ne perdez pas leur trace (Histoire et Société d'aujourd'hui, Editions de la Bacconière, Neuchâtel, 1950), p. 224.

CHAPTER 27

1. Aleksandar Matkovski, "The Destruction of Macedonian Jewry in 1943," in Yad Vasham Studies (Jerusalem, 1959), Vol. III, pp. 211–13.
2. Hilberg, op. cit., p. 477.
3. Ibid., p. 479.
4. King Boris' personal role in saving Bulgarian Jews is questioned by some scholars

who feel that the associations of writers, lawyers, doctors, individual members of Parliament and the Greek Orthodox Church were much more influential and courageous than he.

5. Friedman, *Their Brothers' Keepers*, p. 41, and Hilberg, *op. cit.*, p. 489. Some sources disagree, citing evidence of fuller compliance with the badge decree. See Robinson, *op. cit.*, pp. 258, 361.

6. *Ibid.*, p. 105.

7. Matkovski, *op. cit.*, pp. 214–15.

8. Ibid., pp. 224–25. (Quoted from Natan Grinberg, *Dokumenti* (*Documents*), Sofia, 1945, pp. 8–9.)

9. *Ibid.*, pp. 228–29. Declaration of Heskija Pijade.

10. *Ibid.*, pp. 230–31.

11. *Ibid.*, pp. 232–33.

11a. Figure is based on statistics compiled in Matkovski's monograph. Other sources vary slightly.

12. Nadejda Slavi Vasileva, "On the Catastrophe of the Thracian Jews," in *Yad Vashem Studies* (Jerusalem, 1959), Vol. III, p. 296.

13. *Ibid.*, pp. 298–300.

14. Robert E. Sherwood, *Roosevelt and Hopkins* (New York, Harper & Brothers, 1948), p. 717.

CHAPTER 28

1. Shirer, *Rise and Fall of the Third Reich*, p. 1050.

2. Quoted in Elbogen, *op. cit.*, p. 364.

3. Quoted in *ibid.*, p. 355.

4. Hugh Seton-Watson, *The East European Revolution* (New York, Frederick Praeger, 1956), pp. 83–84.

5. Theodore Lavi, "Documents on the Struggle of Rumanian Jewry for Its Rights During the Second World War" (Part I), *Yad Vashem Studies* (Jerusalem, 1960), Vol. IV, pp. 274–75.

6. *Ibid.*

7. Jenö (Eugene) Levai, *The Black Book of the Martyrdom of Hungarian Jewry* (Zurich, Central European Times, 1948), p. 70.

8. Lavi, *op. cit.*, pp. 277–78.

9. Curzio Malaparte, *Kaputt* (New York, Avon, 1966), pp. 131–32.

10. *Ibid.*, pp. 163–64.

11. Lavi, *op. cit.*, pp. 280–81.

12. *Ibid.*, p. 288.

12a. *Ibid.*

13. Hilberg, *op. cit.*, pp. 200–201.

14. Werth, *op. cit.*, pp. 819–20.

15. Foreign Office Correspondence, August 1941 to April 1944, giving reports and notes on conferences on anti-Jewish action in foreign countries. File Memo dated October 17, 1941, PS-3319. [Signature illegible.]

16. Joseph B. Shechtman, "The Transnistria Reservation," *YIVO Annual*, VIII, 1953, pp. 178–87.

17. Levai, *op. cit.*, p. 73.

18. Lavi, *op. cit.*, p. 291.

19. *Ibid.*, p. 293.

19a. Joseph Goebbels, *Diaries, 1942–1943* (Garden City, N.Y., Doubleday, 1948), p. 223.

20. Reitlinger, *op. cit.*, pp. 404–5.

21. Hilberg, *op. cit*, p. 489.

22. Memorandum of Cavendish W. Cannon, November 12, 1941. *Foreign Relations of the United States, 1941* (Washington, D.C., Government Printing Office, 1959), Vol. II, pp. 875–76.

23. Background and account by Stolier based on Bracha Habas, *The Gate Breakers* (New York, Yoseloff, 1963), pp. 151–57.

24. Quoted in *Yad Vashem Bulletin*, No. 10, April 1961, p. 1.

25. U.S. Army, Office of Chief of Military History, *History of Prisoner of War Utilization by the U.S. Army, 1776–1945*. (Department of the Army Pamphlet 20-213, June 1955.) p. 91.

26. Lavi, *op. cit.*, p. 299.

26a. Theodore Lavi, "The Vatican's Endeavors on Behalf of Rumanian Jewry During the Second World War," *Yad Vashem Studies*, V, p. 414.

27. Excerpts are quoted in Hilberg, *op. cit.*, pp. 506–7, Memo from Barabeanu to Lecca, November 25, 1943, enclosing minutes of Transnistria Conference, held November 17, 1943. Files of Bucharest Legation, OccE5a-5. (Lecca passed the manuscript together with his comments to other German officials.)

28. Ira A. Hirschmann's meeting with Cretsianu based on *Caution to the Winds* (New York, David McKay, 1962), pp. 153–58.

29. Shechtman, *op. cit.*, p. 195.

29a. Lavi, "The Vatican's Endeavors . . . ," p. 416.

30. Account based on Meier Teich, "The Jewish Self-Administration in Ghetto Shargorod (Transnistria)," *Yad Vashem Studies* (Jerusalem, 1958), Vol. II, pp. 219–54

31. Kimche, *op. cit.*, pp. 71–72.

CHAPTER 29

1. Hilberg, *op. cit.*, p. 511.

2. Levai, *op. cit.*, pp. 6–7.

3. *Ibid.*, p. 12.

4. Documents on German Foreign Policy, 1918–1945, Series D, Vol. IV, *The Aftermath of Munich* (Washington, 1951), p. 241.

5. Levai, *op. cit.*, p. 23.

6. On June 26, 1941, German and Hungarian military authorities announced that Soviet aircraft had bombarded the Hungarian (ex-Czech) city of Kassa (Kosice). The announcement of this violation of Hungarian territory—the truth of which has never been established—was followed by a Hungarian declaration of war.

7. Hilberg, *op. cit.*, p. 514.

8. *Ibid.*, pp. 514–16, and Meyer and Weinryb, *op. cit.*, p. 384.

9. Affidavit (dated September 13, 1945) of Dr. Rudolf (Rezsö) Kastner, former president of the Hungarian Zionist Organization, describing German persecution of Hungarian Jews, PS-2605.

10. In October 1946, the National Association of Hungarian Jews reported that there were still about 25,000 former Jewish forced laborers of Hungarian nationality in the Soviet Union as prisoners of war working in factories and on farms. There were also 10,000 Hungarian Jewish women liberated from German concentration camps by Red Army units. According to Meyer and Weinryb, *op. cit.*, p. 395, repatriation efforts have failed and their fate today is unknown.

11. Nathan Eck, "The March of Death from Serbia to Hungary (September 1944)," including the memoirs of Zalman Teichman describing his journey from Bor to Cservenka-Temesvar. *Yad Vashem Studies*, Vol. II, pp. 255–94.

12. Seton-Watson, *op. cit.*, p. 100.

13. Summary of Klessheim conference, held on April 17, 1943, signed by Schmidt, April 18, 1943, D-736.

14. Levai, *op. cit.*, pp. 33–36.

15. *Donauzeitung* (Belgrade), June 1, 1943, quoted in Hilberg, *op. cit.*, pp. 525–26.

16. Reitlinger, *op. cit.*, p. 418.

17. Levai, *op. cit.*, p. 81.

18. *Ibid.*

18a. *Ibid.*, pp. 82–83.

19. *Ibid.*, p. 119. In a subsequent letter to Sztójay, Cardinal Seredi, disappointed with Sztójay's reply, wrote that he must repeat his "demand for discrimination between converted Jews and Jews adhering to the Israelite faith. This applied especially to cases in which Christians of Jewish origin are to be housed with Israelites in the same flats, ghettos, labor camps, etc. As Christians are separated from Jews in the labor battalions, so they should be separated in the above cases. This at least we owe our Christian co-religionists." (*Ibid.*, p. 121.)

20. *Ibid.*, p. 92.

21. Affidavit by Kastner, PS-2605.

22. Hilberg, *op. cit.*, pp. 535–36.

23. Veesenmayer to Foreign Office, April 23, 1944, NG-2233.

24. Reitlinger, *op. cit.*, p. 421.

25. Levai, *op. cit.*, p. 125.

CHAPTER 30

1. Much of the material for this chapter has been drawn from Weissberg, *op. cit.*

2. This was a reference to a long-standing conflict between the Army's Abwehr and Himmler's RSHA, the Central Security Office, which wanted to take over the Abwehr and depose its head, Admiral Wilhelm Canaris. In 1943 and 1944, many Abwehr agents were involved in various plots to overthrow Hitler and make contact with the Allies. Himmler kept a close watch on these activities and periodically Abwehr members were tortured and executed. On February 18, 1944, Hitler ordered the Abwehr dissolved and its functions taken over by the RSHA.

Schmidt's request for the list of Germans was tied to events of July 20, 1944, when certain Army officers tried to kill Hitler in an unsuccessful attempt at a coup. Schmidt wanted his Abwehr agents protected after the war for their involvement in the July 20 conspiracy. Vaadah leaders were thus looked upon as guarantors of Abwehr protection after the war. Brand found out after the war that all of the Abwehr agents in Budapest were implicated in the July 20 plot.

3. Weissberg, *op. cit.*, p. 65.

4. *Ibid.*, pp. 91–92.

5. *Ibid.*, p. 105.

6. *Ibid.*, pp. 119–20.

7. *Ibid.*, p. 131.

8. *Ibid.*, p. 157.

9. *Ibid.*, p. 164.

10. *Ibid.*, p. 165.

11. Meyer W. Weisgal, ed., *Chaim Weizmann: A Biography by Several Hands* (New York, Atheneum, 1963), p. 273.

12. *The Times* (London), July 20, 1944.

13. Weissberg, *op. cit.*, pp. 210–11.

CHAPTER 31

1. Notes made by Philip Freudiger, member of Central Jewish Council of Hungary, in Weissberg, *op. cit.*, pp. 219–22.

2. Reitlinger, *op. cit.*, p. 424.

3. Quoted in Weissberg, op. cit., pp. 122–23.

4. According to Kastner's report, Eichmann actually agreed to a figure of 200 from Cluj, but well-placed bribes brought this figure up to 300. The question of who to save presented the Vaadah leaders with a crucial moral dilemma. Kastner included some of his friends and relatives from Cluj—a decision for which he was later bitterly criticized by certain Hungarian survivors in Israel. Both this reaction and Kastner's behavior may be flawed, but they are humanly understandable. In the subsequent passage of time, the passions on both sides have subsided. It would seem that Kastner's ability to gain some concessions from Eichmann is the most important consideration. In this light, he and the Vaadah may be credited with substantial rescue activity: the transfer of 15,000 to 18,000 Jews to Austria (authorities differ on the precise number) and the survival of 13,500; the placement of 5,000 Jewish children in shelters of the International Red Cross in Budapest; and efforts to obtain 15,000 Swedish and Swiss protective passports. These rescues are in addition to the Bergen-Belsen transports which involved the selection of ten categories: Orthodox Jews, Zionists, orphans, refugees, "prominent Jews," etc. This summary of rescue activity is based on Robinson, op. cit., p. 333.

5. Pearlman, op. cit., p. 451.

6. Text in Levai, op. cit., p. 197.

7. Quoted in ibid., p. 202.

8. Text of complete letter in ibid., pp. 207–10.

9. "Eichmann's Own Story: Part II," Life, December 5, 1960, pp. 146–47.

10. Kersten, op. cit., p. 176.

11. Clark, Barbarossa, p. 339.

12. Ibid., p. 340.

13. Ibid., pp. 339–40, 347–50.

14. "Eichmann's Own Story: Part II," op. cit., pp. 147–48.

15. Quoted in Werth, op. cit., pp. 898–99.

16. Levai, op. cit., p. 305.

17. Hilberg, op. cit., p. 551.

18. Kastner, Bericht, op. cit., p. 115.

19. Affidavit of Jüttner, May 3, 1948, NG-5216.

20. Quoted in Levai, op. cit., pp. 372–73.

21. Reitlinger, op. cit., p. 445.

22. Friedman, Their Brothers' Keepers, pp. 160–62.

23. Hirschmann, Caution to the Winds, pp. 179–81.

24. Weissberg, op. cit., p. 265.

25. Account based on Weissberg, op. cit., pp. 281–90.

26. Quoted in Levai, op. cit., pp. 402–3.

27. Quoted in ibid., p. 406.

28. Erich Kulka, "Photographs as Evidence in the Frankfurt Court," Yad Vashem Bulletin, No. 17, December 1965, p. 56. The album of photographs was found by Mrs. Lilly Zalmonovitz who was deported from Carpatho-Russia to Auschwitz where she was selected to work in Germany. When liberated in 1945, she found the album in an abandoned attic in Nordhausen.

29. Quoted in Jenö (Eugene) Levai, "The Hungarian Deportations in the Light of the Eichmann Trial," Yad Vashem Studies, Vol. V, p. 91.

30. Quoted in Gideon Dean, "The Kastner Affair," The Reconstructionist, February 10, 1956, Vol. XXI, No. 20, p. 15. At Nuremberg, Kastner testified in Becher's behalf, citing evidence of Becher's interventions in behalf of Jews.

CHAPTER 32

1. Robinson, *op. cit.*, pp. 97–98.

2. Rudolf Höss, *Commandant of Auschwitz* (Cleveland, World Publishing Company, n.d.), p. 137.

3. Morgenthau, *op. cit.*, pp. 22–23.

4. Text of Cable 354, dated February 10, 1943, quoted in *ibid.*, p. 23.

5. Quoted in *ibid.*, p. 23.

6. *Ibid.*, p. 65.

7. *Ibid.*, p. 62.

8. *Ibid.*, p. 65.

9. *Ibid.*

10. Material on press coverage drawn from Andrew Sharf, "The British Press and the Holocaust," *Yad Vashem Studies*, Vol. V, pp. 169–91.

11. Churchill to Eden, July 11, 1944, in Churchill, *Triumph and Tragedy*, p. 693.

12. Cordell Hull, *Memoirs* (New York, The Macmillan Co., 1948), Vol. II, p. 1539.

13. Weisgal, ed., *op. cit.*, pp. 259–270.

14. Churchill, *Triumph and Tragedy*, p. 693.

15. *Ibid.*, p. 697.

16. Account based on Syrkin, *op. cit.*, pp. 13–54, and Dorothy and Pesah Bar-Adon, *The Seven Who Fell* (Tel Aviv, Palestine Pioneer Library, No. 11, n.d.).

17. Account based on Catherine Senesch, "The Death of Hannah Senesch," *Midstream*, Autumn 1958, Vol. IV, No. 4. (Testimony of Mrs. Senesch at trial of Rezsö Kastner in 1955 in Jerusalem. Translated by Jacob Sloan.)

18. It was impossible for the Vaadah to approach the Sztójay regime on the matter of the parachutists. They did intervene, however, during the Lakatos regime, and on October 14, the Minister of War promised to release the imprisoned parachutists. This pledge was shattered by the Arrow Cross coup on October 15.

19. Quoted in Saul Friedländer, *Pius XII and the Third Reich: A Documentation* (New York, Alfred A. Knopf, 1966), pp. 132–33.

20. *Ibid.*, p. 54.

21. *Ibid.*, pp. 56–57. (This letter was found by the Germans when looting the Archbishop's palace in Paris and forwarded to the Reich Chancellery on September 25, 1940.)

21a. See Bernard Wall, *Report on the Vatican* (London, Weidenfield and Nicholson, 1956).

22. *Foreign Relations of the United States*, III, p. 776.

23. Taylor to Maglione, September 26, 1942, *ibid.*

24. Tittmann's summary of the Holy See statement of October 10, 1942. *Ibid.*, p. 777. This seems to contradict the affidavit of Hans Gmelin, June 15, 1948, NG-5921. Gmelin, a member of the German Legation in Bratislava, testified that in February 1942 the Apostolic Nuncio delivered two notes to Tuka (see Chapter 26). In these notes the Vatican stated that Jews were being murdered in the Government-General.

25. Tittmann to the Department of State, December 22, 1942, *Department of State Papers*, 740,0016, European War 1939/689.

26. Pius XII to the Cardinals, June 2, 1943. Excerpts in *Amtsblatt für die Erzdiözse München und Freising*, August 12, 1943. Quoted in Lewy, "Pius XII, the Jews and the German Catholic Church," p. 31.

27. Friedländer, *op. cit.*, p. 144.

28. Carpi, *op. cit.*, p. 44.

28a. Franz von Papen, *Memoirs* (New York, Dutton, 1953), p. 279.

29. *Civiltà Cattolica*, Rome, 1934, No. 2024. Quoted in *ibid.*, p. 51.

30. Carpi, *op. cit.*, p. 45.

31. Statement of Dr. Senatro on March 11, 1963, at a public discussion in Berlin. Quoted in Lewy, *op. cit.*, p. 33.

32. Lewy, *op. cit.*, p. 33.

33. Quoted in Leon Poliakov, "Pope Pius XII and the Nazis," *Jewish Frontier*, April 1964, Vol. XXXI, No. 3, p. 10.

34. *Ibid.*

35. Lewy, *op. cit.*, p. 33.

36. Telegram from Weizsäcker to Berlin, July 5, 1943. Quoted in Friedländer, *op. cit.*, pp. 179–80.

37. *Report of the International Committee of the Red Cross on Its Activities During the Second World War* (Geneva, 1948), Vol. I, p. 641.

38. Joseph Tenenbaum, "Red Cross to the Rescue," *Yad Vashem Bulletin*, October 1959, No. 4/5, p. 7.

39. Quoted in *ibid.*, p. 8.

40. Quotation from *Inter Arma Caritas: The Work of the International Committee of the Red Cross during the Second World War* (Geneva, I.C.R.C. 1947), p. 67, in *ibid.*, p. 7.

40a. Jan Ciechanowski, *Defeat in Victory* (Garden City, Doubleday, 1947), pp. 182 ff.

41. Memorandum by Rademacher, February 20, 1943, NG-2586.

CHAPTER 33

1. Affidavit by Kurt Becher, March 8, 1946, PS-3762.

2. Reitlinger, *op. cit.*, p. 457.

3. *Témoignages Strasbourgeois, De l'Université aux Camps de Concentration* (Paris, 1947), p. 89.

4. The relative contributions of both Bernadotte and Kersten in these rescue activities caused considerable controversy after the war. In "Kersten, Himmler and Count Bernadotte," *Atlantic Monthly*, February 1953, pp. 43–45, the English historian H. R. Trevor-Roper challenged Bernadotte's alleged role and emphasized Kersten's. However, in 1956, a Swedish Foreign Office White Paper was published which was critical of Trevor-Roper's interpretation and assigned Bernadotte a more central role.

5. Clark, *Barbarossa*, pp. 440–41.

6. *Ibid.*, p. 445.

7. Kersten, *op. cit.*, p. 286.

8. Transcript of talks with Himmler supplied by Dr. Masur. Quoted in Reitlinger, *op. cit.*, pp. 470–71.

9. H. R. Trevor-Roper, *The Last Days of Hitler* (New York, Berkley-Medallion Books, 1957), pp. 115–16.

10. *Ibid.*, p. 143.

11. The story of the organization of the *Sheerit Hapletah* is told in Leo W. Schwarz, *The Redeemers* (New York, Farrar, Straus & Giroux, 1953).

12. "UNRRA Aide Scents Jews' Exodus Plot," *New York Times*, January 3, 1946, pp. 1, 3.

13. Syrkin, *op. cit.*, p. 321.

746 INDEX